Imagination and Art: Explorations in Contemporary Theory

Value Inquiry Book Series

Founding Editor
Robert Ginsberg

Executive Editor
Leonidas Donskis†

Managing Editor
J.D. Mininger

VOLUME 351

Philosophy and Religion

Editor
Rod Nicholls (*Cape Breton University*)

Founding Editor
Ken Bryson (*Cape Breton University*)

Editorial Board
Deane-Peter Baker, *University of New South Wales (UNSW)* – Ken Bryson, *Cape Breton University* – G. Elijah Dann, *Simon Fraser University* – Russ Dumke, *University of the Incarnate Word* – Carl Kalwaitis, *Marian University* – Ruby Ramji, *Cape Breton University* – Gregory MacLeod, *Cape Breton University* – Harriet E. Barber, *University of San Diego* – Stephen Clark, *University of Liverpool, and U. of Bristol* – Gwen Griffith-Dickson, *Heythrop College, University of London* – Jim Kanaris, *McGill University* – William Sweet, *Saint Francis Xavier University* – Pawel Kawalec, *John Paul II Catholic University of Lublin* – Esther McIntosh, *York St. John University* – Ludwig Nagl, *University of Vienna* – Alana M. Vincent, *University of Chester*

The titles published in this series are listed at *brill.com/vibs* and *brill.com/par*

Imagination and Art: Explorations in Contemporary Theory

Edited by

Keith Moser and Ananta Ch. Sukla

BRILL
RODOPI

LEIDEN | BOSTON

Cover illustration: 'Lightbulb', pixabay.com. Image under creative commons license.

The Library of Congress Cataloging-in-Publication Data is available online at http://catalog.loc.gov
Library of Congress Cataloging-in-Publication Data

Names: Moser, Keith A., editor. | Sukla, Ananta Charana, 1942- editor.
Title: Imagination and art : explorations in contemporary theory / edited
by Keith Moser and Ananta Ch. Sukla.
Description: Leiden ; Boston : Brill/Rodopi, [2020] | Series: Value inquiry
book, 0929-8436 ; volume 351 | Includes bibliographical references and
index.
Identifiers: LCCN 2020025227 | ISBN 9789004435162 (hardback) | ISBN
9789004436350 (ebook)
Subjects: LCSH: Imagination. | Creation (Literary, artistic, etc.)
Classification: LCC BF408 .I4545 2020 | DDC 701/.15--dc23
LC record available at https://lccn.loc.gov/2020025227

Typeface for the Latin, Greek, and Cyrillic scripts: "Brill". See and download: brill.com/brill-typeface.

ISSN 0929-8436
ISBN 978-90-04-43516-2 (hardback)
ISBN 978-90-04-43635-0 (e-book)

Copyright 2020 by Koninklijke Brill NV, Leiden, The Netherlands.
Koninklijke Brill NV incorporates the imprints Brill, Brill Hes & De Graaf, Brill Nijhoff, Brill Rodopi,
Brill Sense, Hotei Publishing, mentis Verlag, Verlag Ferdinand Schöningh and Wilhelm Fink Verlag.
All rights reserved. No part of this publication may be reproduced, translated, stored in a retrieval system,
or transmitted in any form or by any means, electronic, mechanical, photocopying, recording or otherwise,
without prior written permission from the publisher.
Authorization to photocopy items for internal or personal use is granted by Koninklijke Brill NV provided
that the appropriate fees are paid directly to The Copyright Clearance Center, 222 Rosewood Drive, Suite
910, Danvers, MA 01923, USA. Fees are subject to change.

This book is printed on acid-free paper and produced in a sustainable manner.

To Ananta Ch. Sukla

For bequeathing the invaluable gift of imagining beyond porous disciplinary boundaries to current and future scholars who humbly follow in your footsteps

∴

Contents

Acknowledgments XIII
List of Figures XIV
Notes on Contributors XVII

Introduction 1
Keith Moser

PART 1
Historical Imagination and Judgement

1 Imagination and Art in Classical Greece and Rome 35
David Konstan

2 Poetic Imagination and Cultural Memory in Greek History and Mythology 50
Claude Calame

3 History, Imagination and the Narrative of Loss: Philosophical Questions about the Task of Historical Judgment 67
Allen Speight

PART 2
Gendered Imagination

4 Imagining the Captive Amazon in Myth, Art, and History 83
Adrienne Mayor

5 Gender and Imagination: A Feminist Analysis of Shahrnush Parsipur's *Women Without Men* 111
Reshmi Mukherjee

PART 3
Imagination and Ethics

6 Psychoanalysis, Imagination, and Imaginative Resistance: A Genesis of the Post-Freudian World 139
Carol Steinberg Gould

VIII

7 Craving Sameness, Accepting Difference: Imaginative Possibilities for Solidarity and Social Justice 155
  Chandra Kavanagh

8 The Importance of Imagination/*Phantasia* for the Moral Psychology of Virtue Ethics 174
  David Collins

9 The Infanticidal Logic of Mimesis as Horizon of the Imaginable 206
  A. Samuel Kimball

10 The Relationship between Imagination and Christian Prayer 227
  Michel Dion

PART 4
Phenomenological and Epistemological Perspectives

11 The Work Texts Do: Toward a Phenomenology of Imagining Imaginatively 255
  Charles Altieri

12 Conceiving and Imagining: Examples and Lessons 281
  Jody Azzouni

13 The Dance of Perception: The Rôle of the Imagination in Simone Weil's Early Epistemology 304
  Warren Heiti

14 One Imagination or Many? Or None? 332
  Rob van Gerwen

15 Nietzsche on Theatricality and Imagination 346
  Roderick Nicholls

PART 5
Postmodern Perspectives

16 *Simulacral* Imagination and the Nexus of Power in a Post-Marxist Universe 381
  Keith Moser

CONTENTS IX

17 Jean-François Lyotard, the Radical Imagination, and the Aesthetic of the
Differend 412
Victor E. Taylor

18 The Possibility of a Productive Imagination in the Work of Deleuze and
Guattari 425
Erik Bormanis

PART 6
Imagination in Scientific Modeling and Biosemiotics

19 Of Predators and Prey: Imagination in Scientific Modeling 451
Fiora Salis

20 Geometry and the Imagination 475
Justin Humphreys

21 Art and Imagination: The Evolution of Meanings 503
Wendy Wheeler

PART 7
Aesthetic Perspectives

22 Image, Image-Making, and Imagination 535
Dominic Gregory

23 Depiction, Imagination, and Photography 559
Jiri Benovksy

24 Imagination and Identification in Photography and Film 582
David Fenner

25 Imagination in Musical Composition, Performance, and Listening: John
Cage's Blurring of Boundaries in Music and Life in *4'33"* 594
Deborah Fillerup Weagel

26 Kinesthetic Imagining and Dance Appreciation 621
Renee M. Conroy

27 Imagination in Games: Formulation, Re-actualization and Gaining a World 646
Ton Kruse

28 "'I AM not mad, most noble Festus.' No. But I Have Been": Possible Worlds Theory and the Complex, Imaginative Worlds of Sarban's *The Sound of his Horn* 669
Riyukta Raghunath

PART 8
Non-Western Perspectives

29 The Deep Frivolity of Life: An Indian Aesthetic Phenomenology of *Fun* 695
Arindam Chakrabarti

30 The Symbolic Force of Rocks in the Chinese Imagination 708
Yanping Gao

31 Magic from the Repressed: Imagination and Memories in Contemporary Japanese Literary Narratives 721
Amy Lee

32 The Metaphysics of Creativity: Imagination in Sufism, from the Qur'an into Ibn al-'Arabi 735
Ali Hussain

PART 9
Artists Reflect on Imagination: An Imaginative Epilogue

33 Free Thinking about Imagination: How Is It to Imagine What Imagination Is? 761
Marion Renauld

34 The Nativity of Images 769
Ton Kruse

CONTENTS   XI

35   Signal: Poetry and Imagination   772
     Jesse Graves

36   The Echo of Voices   774
     Umar Timol

37   Poem, Liberty   775
     Louise Dupré

38   Why to Wish for the Witch   778
     Lisa Fay Coutley

     Index   781

Acknowledgments

First of all, I would like to express my sincere gratitude to Ananta Ch. Sukla for his invitation to collaborate on this project. It is truly an honor to be a small part of your enduring legacy. Moreover, I am indebted to Lynn Holt, Wendy Wheeler, and Isaac Joslin for reading my introduction and offering constructive feedback. I would also like to take advantage of this opportunity to thank Roderick Nicholls whose assistance at the beginning of this arduous process is deeply appreciated. I must also take a moment to laud the dedication of my fellow contributors who believed in the originality and significance of this project from the onset. It is due to your tireless efforts that *Imagination and Art: Explorations in Contemporary Theory* is one of the most rewarding projects with which I have ever been involved. On a final note, I must lament the recent passing of the sailor-philosopher Michel Serres who taught me how to think and *imagine* otherwise. In the words of Ananta Ch. Sukla, whose academic publications and works of creative fiction have also created a passageway through what Serres refers to as the perilous *Northwest Passage*, I acknowledge the contributions of those for whom "writing is neither a hobby nor a profession," but the very fabric of your existence.

Keith Moser
Mississippi State University, U.S.A.

Figures

4.1 Wounded Amazon, Roman marble copy of Greek bronze statue ca 450 BC, Metropolitan Museum [Wiki Commons] 84

4.2 Captive Amazons, engraving, Robert von Spalart, *Historical Pictures of the Costumes of the Principal People of Antiquity and of the Middle Ages*, 1796 85

4.3 Theseus seizes a struggling Antiope, red-figure amphora, 490 BC, Louvre G197, drawing by W.H. Roscher, 1884 87

4.4 Theseus carrying Antiope to his chariot, Attic black-figure cup, British Museum AN473143001, London E41, © The British Museum 2003. Image reproduced with the expressed written consent of The British Museum 87

4.5 Theseus abducting Antiope in his chariot, Apulian hydria, drawing in Gerhard, *Apulische Vasenbilder*, 1845, pl. E 88

4.6 Theseus seizing Antiope, relief, west pediment of temple of Apollo, Eretria, 500–515 BC, cast [Wiki Commons] 88

4.7 Theseus and Antiope, metope, Athenian Treasury at Delphi, 510–470 BC, photo by Mathias Berlin [Wiki Commons] 89

4.8 Etruscan urn, Theseus capturing Antiope, surrounded by four mounted Amazons, ca 480 BC. AN256885001, ©Trustees of the British Museum, © The British Museum 2003. Image reproduced with the expressed written consent of The British Museum 89

4.9 Dancer or captive Amazon. Terracotta, mold-cast, 13.6 cm (5.3 in). Yale University Art Gallery, Gift of Ambassador and Mrs. William Witman II, B.A. 1935; 1993.46.49 90

4.10 Possible illustration of Herodotus's account of the Amazon captives who escaped the Greeks and battled and then allied with Scythian men in the Bosporus region. Drawing of limestone relief, Taman Peninsula, Pushkin Museum no. 143, Moscow, © The Pushkin State Museum of Fine Arts. Image reproduced with the expressed written consent of The Pushkin State Museum of Fine Arts 94

4.11 Chiomara, woodcut, Johannes Zainer, 1474, Penn Provenance Project, Wikimedia Commons 98

4.12 Silver *denarius* coin of Julius Caesar, 49–44 BC, depicting female and male captives of Gaul and other European tribes bound at the foot of his military trophies. British Museum, AN624041001, © The British Museum 2003. Image reproduced with the expressed written consent of The British Museum 100

4.13 Two pairs of female and male barbarian captives (Gauls/Celts/Germans), as Romans raise a trophy with their weapons, carved Arabian onyx cameo, the Gemma Augustea, 1st century AD, Kunsthistorisches Museum, Vienna. Photo by James Steakley, 2013 [Wiki Commons] 101

FIGURES

4.14 Roman, via collatina sarcophagus with Amazonomachy and Amazon captives, ca AD 150, Capitoline Museum, Rome, photo by Josiah Ober 101

4.15 Roman sarcophagus with three pairs of captive Amazons, AD 180–220, British Museum, © The British Museum 2003. Image reproduced with the expressed written consent of The British Museum 102

4.16 Zenobia in chains, modern sculpture by Harriet Hosmer, 1859. St Louis Art Museum. *Courtesy of the Huntington Art Collections, San Marino, California* 103

17.1 Plan de l'exposition. The exhibition floor plan is reproduced in Jean-Louis Déotte, "*Les Immateriaux* de Lyotard (1985): un programme figural," *Appareil* (2012): 10 420

20.1 The problem of mean proportionals. Given A, M, and D, find K and I such that AM:AI::AI:AK::AK:AD 476

20.2 Archytas' constructed solution to the problem of mean proportionals. Since KI is perpendicular to AD, AM=AB. Since Mθ is perpendicular to AD, AMI is a right angle. Thus, AMI, AIK, and AKD are similar angles, so AM:AI::AI:AK::AK:AD 477

20.3 Euclid I.1. The radius AB=AC and the radius BC=BA. But AB=BA. Therefore, AB=AC=BC, so the constructed triangle is equilateral 487

20.4 The internal angles of a triangle are equal to two right angles 492

20.5 The Poincaré disk model of hyperbolic geometry. Consider the construction of an equilateral triangle given a segment AB in this model. As in the Euclidean proof illustrated in Figure 3, one constructs circles around A and B, with the shared radius AB. The same proof holds, according to which the lines drawn to C are equal to the radius. The model shows that this result is independent of Euclid's fifth postulate 497

20.6 M.C. Escher's *Circle Limit IV* (*Heaven and Hell*). As one moves from the center of the circle outward, the tessellated demons and angels become progressively smaller 497

22.1 A bicycle. Photograph by Dominic Gregory 543

22.2 William H. Rau, *New Main Line at Duncannon* (*about 1890–1900*). William H. Rau (American, 1855–1920), *New Main Line at Duncannon*, about 1890–1900, Gelatin silver print 44 × 54.6 cm (17 5/16 × 21 1/2 in.), The J. Paul Getty Museum, Los Angeles. Digital image courtesy of the Getty's Open Content Program 547

22.3 Screenshot from *Paperboy* (Atari Games, 1984). This screenshot falls under the "fair use" provision of Section 107 of Title 17 of the United States code 548

22.4 Kanō Tsunenobu, *Scenes from the Tale of Genji* (1677) (Isabella Stewart Gardner Museum, Boston). This image is licensed under a Creative Commons Attribution by the Isabella Stewart Gardner Museum, Boston (https://www.gardnermuseum.org/organization/rights-reproductions) 552

22.5 *Old man (perhaps Tobit) reading to a seated woman* (17th Century), copy after Rembrandt van Rijn, © Victoria and Albert Museum, London. I originally reproduced

XVI   FIGURES

this image in *Showing, Sensing, and Seeming: Distinctively Sensory Representations and Their Contents* (2013)   554

23.1   A woman in the street I. Photograph by Jiri Benovksy   570
23.2   A woman in the street II. Photograph by Jiri Benovksy   570
23.3   Multiple-exposure photograph. Photograph by Jiri Benovksy   574
23.4   Multiple-exposure photograph. Photograph by Jiri Benovsky   574
23.5   Representation of color by a black and white photograph. This image first appeared in Benovksy, "Depiction and imagination."   576
23.6   The juggler. This image first appeared in Benovksy, "Depiction and imagination."   576
25.1   Sixty-four hexagrams from the King Wen sequence of the I Ching. File: *Wikimedia Commons*, https://commons.wikimedia.org/wiki/File:King_Wen_(I_Ching).png   605
28.1   The textual universe of *The Sound of his Horn*   674
28.2   Accessibility relations between TAW1 and the actual world   683
28.3   Accessibility relations between TAW2 and the actual world   684
28.4   Rethinking the accessibility relations between TAW2 and the actual world   685
28.5   Textual universe of *The Sound of his Horn* from the point of view of readers for whom Alan is an unreliable narrator   688
34.1   Ton Kruse, "9-7-2017"; ball-point on three note-book pages, three times A7; 2017   771

Notes on Contributors

Charles Altieri
received his PhD in English from The University of North Carolina, Chapel Hill. He taught at SUNY Buffalo and The University of Washington before ending up at Berkeley for the past 28 years. He has focused on teaching modern American Poetry, Shakespeare, classical epic, and the work of several theorists and philosophers. He has published many books and essays, the last of which are *Wallace Stevens and the Demands of Modernity* (2013) and *Reckoning with Imagination: Wittgenstein and the Aesthetics of Literary Experience.* His new book on *Constructivist Modernisms: Strategies for Resisting Materialism* will come out from The University of New Mexico Press in Spring 2021.

Jody Azzouni
is Professor of Philosophy at Tufts University. He has published books and articles in philosophy of logic, metaphysics, epistemology, philosophy of mathematics, and philosophy of science. "Attributing knowledge" is his latest book from Oxford University Press. He also writes (and publishes) short stories and poems. "Something is wrong with the food. Maybe with all it" is his latest short story, appearing in *The Literary Review.*

Jiri Benovsky
having been struck by Descartes' evil demon thought-experiment, first began to study metaphysics to try to find proof that the world really exists. He did not find that proof, but at least he found an academic way to live where he can not only go climbing and skiing in the mountains but also spend his days thinking about existence, reality, time, art, and the aesthetics of photography. He is the author of several books, including recently: *Eliminativism, Objects, and Persons. The Virtues of Non-existence* (Routledge, 2018), *Mind and Matter. Panpsychism, Dual-aspect Monism, and the Combination Problem* (2018, Springer), and *Metametaphysics* (2016, Springer). More information on Benovsky's work can be found online at www.jiribenovsky.org.

Erik Bormanis
is a Philosophy PhD candidate at Stony Brook University, interested in questions of social inclusion and exclusion, belonging, sense-making, and political affect. In addressing these problems, he draws upon the resources of 20th Century Continental Philosophy, Phenomenology, and Contemporary Political thought.

Claude Calame

is Director of studies at the École des Hautes Études en Sciences Sociales in Paris. He was a Professor of Greek language and literature at the University of Lausanne. He also taught at the Universities of Urbino and Siena in Italy in addition to Yale University in the U.S. He has published numerous books in English translation including *Masks of Authority. Fiction and Pragmatics in Ancient Greek Poetics, Poetic and Performative Memory in Ancient Greece, Greek Mythology. Poetics, Pragmatics and Fiction*; and most recently in French *La tragédie chorale. Poésie grecque et rituel musical.*

Arindam Chakrabarti

earned his DPhil at Oxford University and taught Western and Indian philosophies in Kolkata India, at University College London, The University of Washington, The University of Delhi, and The University of Hawaii for the last 36 years. In 2018, he accepted the Nirmal and Augustina Mattoo Chair of Indic Humanities in the Department of Philosophy at Stony Brook University. He has published ten books and more than a hundred papers in English, Sanskrit, and Bengali, co-edited with the late Sir Peter Strawson *Universals, Concepts and Qualities: New Essays on the Meaning of Predicates* and edited *Bloomsbury Research Handbook on Indian Aesthetics and Philosophy of Art* (2016). His monograph *Realisms Interlinked: Objects, Subjects and Other Subjects* came out with Bloomsbury Academic in 2019.

David Collins

is a doctoral candidate in philosophy at McGill University in Montreal, where he is finishing a dissertation on R.G. Collingwood's aesthetics that explores links between Collingwood's thinking and process philosophy, American pragmatism, and existential phenomenology. He comes to philosophy from a background teaching and working creatively in film and theatre. Along with aesthetics and Collingwood's philosophy more generally, he has strong interests in moral philosophy—in particular, neo-Aristotelian virtue ethics and Simone de Beauvoir's existentialist ethics—and the connections between artistic and ethical value, especially as conceived "aretaically" rather than instrumentally.

Renee M. Conroy

is Associate Professor of Philosophy at Purdue University Northwest and a Fulbright Scholar. Her published work focuses on issues in the aesthetics of nature and the philosophy of dance, with special emphasis on ways of appreciating the past and various phenomena associated with the "aesthetics of return." Her articles on these topics appear in the *Journal of Aesthetics and Art Criticism*; *Midwest Studies in Philosophy*; *Ethics, Place and Environment*; *The Continuum Companion to Aesthetics*; *Philosophical Perspectives on Ruins, Monuments, and Memorials*; and other aesthetics anthologies.

Lisa Fay Coutley

is the author of *tether* (Black Lawrence Press, April 2020), *Errata* (Southern Illinois University Press, 2015), winner of the Crab Orchard Series in Poetry Open Competition Award, and *In the Carnival of Breathing* (Black Lawrence Press, 2011), winner of the Black River Chapbook Competition. She is the recipient of a fellowship from the National Endowment for the Arts and is an Assistant Professor of Poetry and Creative Nonfiction in the Writer's Workshop at the University of Nebraska at Omaha.

Michel Dion

is Full Professor of business ethics at the École de gestion, Université de Sherbrooke (Québec, Canada). His main fields of research include: business ethics, ethical leadership and organizational culture; financial crime and corporate governance; literature and organizational life; religion/spirituality and management. He has published: *Financial Crime and Existential Philosophy* (Springer, 2014); *Texte littéraire et réflexion éthique. Rilke, Mann, Hesse, Musil, Zweig* (Liber, 2013); *L'être et le crime. Dostoïevski, Wilde, Faulkner, Capote, Auster* (Nota bene, 2013); *Littérature et organisation. Dostoïevski, Proust, Musil, Kundera* (Nota bene, 2011).

Louise Dupré

born in Québec (Canada), has published twenty books, which have received many awards. *Plus haut que les flammes* (*Beyond the flames*) and *La main hantée* (*The Haunted Hand*) both won the Governor General's Award for poetry. Many of her collections of poetry and several of her novels have been translated into English or other languages. Dupré is a member of the Academy of Letters of Quebec. In December 2014, she was appointed to the Order of Canada "for her contributions to Quebec literature as a poet, novelist, playwright, essayist and professor."

David Fenner

Professor of Philosophy and Art, has been teaching at the University of North Florida – apart from a year's post-doc at the University of St Andrews (Scotland) – since 1992. He is the author of *The Aesthetic Attitude, Introducing Aesthetics*, and *Art in Context*.

Yanping Gao

holds a PhD in Aesthetics from Chinese Academy of Social Sciences in Beijing (CASS), where she is currently an associate researcher in the Institute of Literature. She is the author of *Winckelmann's Vision of Greek Art* (2016). She has translated numerous works including "Feeling and Form" (2013), *Act and Affect* (2018), and *Chinese Way of Thinking* (2018). She is the editor of the journal *International Aesthetics* (Beijing) and an editorial board member of *Journal of Somaesthetics*. Her interests range from art history and Winckelmann studies, to somaesthetics, comparative cultural studies, and contemporary French philosophy.

Carol Steinberg Gould

PhD, is a Professor in the Department of Philosophy at Florida Atlantic University. She teaches and publishes widely in Aesthetics, Philosophy of Psychiatry, Ancient Philosophy, and, more recently, Japanese Philosophy. She is currently working on a book for Bloomsbury on the aesthetics of persons and subjectivity.

Jesse Graves

is the author of four poetry collections, including *Tennessee Landscape with Blighted Pine* and the forthcoming *Merciful Days*. His work received the James Still Award for Writing about the Appalachian South from the Fellowship of Southern Writers and the Philip H. Freund Prize for Creative Writing from Cornell University. Graves has been an editor on several collections of poetry and scholarship, including three volumes of *The Southern Poetry Anthology* and *The Complete Poems of James Agee*. He teaches at East Tennessee State University, where he is Poet-in-Residence and Professor of English.

Dominic Gregory

works at the University of Sheffield in the Department of Philosophy. He has published papers on a wide range of philosophical topics, including aesthetics, epistemology, formal and philosophical logic, metaphysics, and the philosophy of mind, and his book on imagistic representations, *Showing, Sensing, and Seeing*, was published by OUP in 2013.

Warren Heiti

is a professor in the Departments of Philosophy and Liberal Studies at Vancouver Island University. He is the author of *Hydrologos* (Pedlar Press, 2011) and co-editor of *Chamber Music: The Poetry of Jan Zwicky* (Wilfrid Laurier University Press, 2015). His work has been published in *Ethics and the Environment*, *Philosophical Investigations*, and *Philosophy and Literature*.

NOTES ON CONTRIBUTORS

Justin Humphreys

is a senior fellow and instructor in the Department of Philosophy at the University of Pennsylvania, and he was previously a lecturer in philosophy at the University of Pittsburgh. He received his PhD from the New School for Social Research, and wrote his dissertation on Aristotle's concept of imagination. His primary area of expertise is the ancient philosophy of mathematics, and he has interests in classical phenomenology and pragmatism. Humphreys' research has been published in journals including *Ancient Philosophy, Apeiron,* and *Transactions of the Charles S. Peirce Society.* He was awarded the Hans Jonas Prize and the American Philosophical Association's William James Prize.

Ali Hussain

has a PhD in Islamic Studies from the University of Michigan, Department of Middle Eastern Studies. His dissertation explores the image of Jesus Christ in the writings of Muḥyī al-Dīn Ibn al-'Arabī (d. 1240) and later Sufism. His other interests include the intersection of creativity and spirituality in Islamic thought and the contemporary cultural challenges facing the American Muslim community. He recently founded The Nostalgic Remembrance Institute, an initiative focused on investigating these questions, through research and educational events.

Chandra Kavanagh

received her PhD from McMaster University in 2019, where she studied biomedical ethics and feminist philosophy. She is currently employed as the Ethics Officer for the Newfoundland and Labrador Health Research Ethics Authority. She also serves as an instructor for the Memorial University Philosophy Department and the Memorial University School of Medicine. Chandra's presentations on political and ethical issues have received high acclaim across Canada, the United States, Europe and Australia and she has been widely published in both academic and popular media.

Amy Lee

has a background in comparative literature and cultural studies. She has published creative non-fiction as well as critical studies in the area of contemporary feminist fiction, autobiographical writing, and using literature for creative learning experiences. She recently completed an MA in Buddhist Studies and is seeking new insights into the autobiographies of Buddhist monks and how the self is presented or hidden in such writings. She is an Associate Professor in the Department of Humanities and Creative Writing at Hong Kong Baptist University where she takes advantage of narratives to create interactive and interdisciplinary learning experiences for students.

A. Samuel Kimball

is Professor of English at the University of North Florida, where he has taught since 1988. He has published on American literature (Hawthorne, Melville, Poe) and on film (*Matrix, Terminator 2, Alien Resurrection, Pulp Fiction, Twin Peaks, Chinatown, Crash, Fog of War, Tyson*). His book, *The Infanticidal Logic of Evolution and Culture* (Delaware 2007) addresses the deconstruction implications of the evolutionary economy, implications that the literary western tradition has struggled to represent. He is currently working on a book-length study, "What Is ~~My~~ Our Consciousness for?"

David Konstan

is Professor of Classics at New York University. He is the author of *The Emotions of the Ancient Greeks* (2006); *"A Life Worthy of the Gods": The Materialist Psychology of Epicurus* (2008); *Before Forgiveness: The Origins of a Moral Idea* (2010); *Beauty: The Fortunes of an Ancient Greek Idea* (2014); and *In the Orbit of Love: Affection in Ancient Greece and Rome* (2018). He is a past president of the American Philological Association, and a fellow of the American Academy of Arts and Sciences and Honorary Fellow of the Australian Academy of the Humanities.

Ton Kruse

is a contemporary artist and independent researcher. He studied Autonomous Art at the Academy for Visual Art of Enschede. He received a Master's degree at the University of the Arts in Utrecht. He graduated with honors in critical studies and philosophical hermeneutics at the Theological and Philosophical College of Fontys University Hengelo. Owing to his unique background as an academic researcher and artist, his artistry is inextricably linked to theoretical reflection regardless of the medium in question. His diverse body of art and academic production demonstrate that form and content cannot be separated. Instead, they are both at the service of understanding.

Adrienne Mayor

is a research scholar in the Classics Department and History and Philosophy of Science Program at Stanford University. She is the author of *The Amazons: Lives and Legends of Warrior Women across the Ancient World; Gods and Robots: Myths, Machines, and Ancient Dreams of Technology; The First Fossil Hunters: Dinosaurs, Mammoths and Myths in Greek and Roman Times; Greek Fire, Poison Arrows & Scorpion Bombs: Biological and Chemical Warfare in the Ancient World*; and *The Poison King* (2010 National Book Award nonfiction finalist).

NOTES ON CONTRIBUTORS XXIII

Keith Moser

is Professor of French and Francophone Studies at Mississippi State University. He is the author of seven full-length book projects. His latest monograph is entitled *The Encyclopedic Philosophy of Michel Serres: Writing the Modern World and Anticipating the Future* (2016). Moser has also contributed sixty-seven essays to peer-reviewed publications representing many divergent fields including French and Francophone studies, environmental ethics, ecocriticism, ecolinguistics, biosemiotics, social justice, popular culture, and Maghrebi/Harki literature.

Reshmi Mukherjee

is an Assistant Professor of English at Boise State University. She holds a PhD in Comparative and World Literature from the University of Illinois Urbana-Champaign, and an MPhil degree in Women's Studies from Jadavpur University, Kolkata, India. Her research and teaching focus on representations of race, gender, sexuality, and subalternity in literatures of the global South, with particular interest in diasporic, exilic, *testimonio*, and refugee narratives. Her area of specialization is postcolonial theory, transnational feminism, and culture studies. Her publications have appeared in *Boundary2, Toronto Quarterly, Journal of the African Literature Association, Assay: A Journal of Nonfiction Studies, and South Asian Review*.

Roderick Nicholls

is an Associate Professor of Philosophy at Cape Breton University, Nova Scotia, Canada. His teaching interests include philosophy and the meaning of life, Nietzsche, and contemporary continental philosophy. His publications include book chapters and articles on theater aesthetics. He is also a practitioner of theater with extensive experience directing and designing plays. *The Philosophy of Spirituality: Analytic, Continental, and Multicultural Approaches of a New Field of Philosophy* (co-edited with Heather Salazar) is his most recent publication.

Riyukta Raghunath

received her PhD from Sheffield Hallam University in 2017. Her doctoral thesis is titled *Alternative Realities: Counterfactual Historical Fiction and Possible Worlds Theory* and focuses on devising a cognitive-narratological methodology based on Possible Worlds Theory with which to analyze counterfactual historical fiction. She is active in the fields of cognitive-narratology and counterfactual historical fiction and is a current member of the Poetics and Linguistics

Association and the European Narratology Network. Riyukta's future research will explore developing Possible Worlds Theory using empirical data. She is currently a lecturer in the English department at New College of the Humanities, UK.

Marion Renauld

is an artist who works with the act of writing poetry itself, proposing performances and installations with words in the public space. Moreover, she received her PhD in Philosophy from Université de Lorraine in France. In addition to various articles about fiction, literature and the interactions between robots and humans, she published a book in 2014 entitled *Philosophie de la fiction. Vers une approche pragmatiste du roman* with the *Presses Universitaires de Rennes.*

Fiora Salis

is Associate Lecturer in Philosophy at the University of York and Research Associate at the London School of Economics. She obtained a PhD in Philosophy from the University of Barcelona and was FCT Postdoctoral Fellow at the University of Lisbon and Marie Skłodowska-Curie Fellow at the London School of Economics. Her research interests lie at the intersection of Philosophy of Mind and Language, Aesthetics and Philosophy of Science. She currently works on fiction, imagination, fictional names, desire, scientific models, and scientific discovery.

Allen Speight

(PhD, University of Chicago) is Associate Professor of Philosophy at Boston University. A recipient of Fulbright, DAAD and Berlin Prize Fellowships, he is the author of *Hegel, Literature and the Problem of Agency* (Cambridge University Press, 2001); *The Philosophy of Hegel* (McGill-Queen's University Press/ Acumen, 2008) and of numerous articles on German idealism and romanticism; he is also editor of *Philosophy, Narrative and Life* (Boston Studies in Philosophy, Religion and Public Life, 2015); co-editor/translator (with Brady Bowman) of *Hegel's Heidelberg Writings* (Cambridge University Press, 2009); and co-editor (with Sarah Vandegrift Eldridge) of *Goethe's "Wilhelm Meister's Apprenticeship" and Philosophy* (Oxford University Press, forthcoming 2020).

Victor E. Taylor

is the author most recently of *Christianity, Plasticity, and Spectral Heritages* (Palgrave Macmillan, 2017) and editor of *Divisible Derridas* (Davies Group,

Publishers, 2017). Currently, he is the executive editor of the *Journal for Cultural and Religious Theory* and working on a book manuscript tentatively entitled *Smearing in Literature and Everyday Life.*

Umar Timol

is a Mauritian poet and photographer. He is the author of four collections of poetry. He has received two grants from the National Book Center. He has participated in many poetry festivals around the world. He displayed an exhibition of photographic portraits of Mauritian writers at the Blue Penny Museum in Mauritius in 2019.

Rob van Gerwen

is senior lecturer in the Department of Philosophy at Utrecht University. He has taught at UCU and various art schools. He is co-founder of the Dutch Association of Aesthetics, and owns a company, Consilium Philosophicum. He has written or (co-)edited seven books on aesthetics: *Modern Philosophers on Art* (Dutch, 2017); *Art and Experience* (1996); *Shall We Stay in Touch. On How We Remove the Mind from Our Worldview* (Dutch, 2018); *Richard Wollheim on the Art of Painting* with Cambridge University Press; *Experiencing Music* (Dutch, 2014). He is editor-in-chief of the open access, peer-reviewed journal *Aesthetic Investigations.*

Deborah Fillerup Weagel

teaches in the English Department at the University of New Mexico. She earned a bachelor's degree in art, master's degrees in music theory/composition and in French, and a PhD in English. She coedited, with Feroza Jussawalla, *Emerging South Asian Women Writers: Essays and Interviews* (2016), and she has published *Words and Music: Camus, Beckett, Cage, Gould* (2010), *Women and Contemporary World Literature: Power, Fragmentation, and Metaphor* (2009), and *Interconnections: Essays on Music, Art, Literature, and Gender* (2004). Her articles have appeared in a variety of academic journals, and she has presented her work at professional conferences on an international level, most recently in Mulhouse, France.

Wendy Wheeler

PhD (1994) University of Sussex, is Emeritus Professor of English Literature and Cultural Inquiry at London Metropolitan University. She has been a Visiting Research Fellow and Professor at universities in the UK, USA and Australia, and is the author of five books and more than 50 articles and chapters, especially on biosemiotics, nature and culture. Her latest book is *Expecting the Earth: Life|Culture|Biosemiotics* (2016). She is currently working with biologists, biosemioticians and philosophers on a Royal Society of Edinburgh funded interdisciplinary research project – *Living Organisms and Their Choices* – at the Eidyn Research Centre, Department of Philosophy, University of Edinburgh.

Introduction

Keith Moser

Building upon the renewed interest in the Philosophy of Imagination sparked by recent seminal works including *Models as Make-Believe: Imagination, Fiction and Scientific Representation* (2012), *The Cultural Imaginary of the Internet: Virtual Utopias and Dystopias* (2014), *Art and Imagination: A Study in the Philosophy of Mind* (2015), *Imagination and the Imaginary* (2015), *The Routledge Handbook of Philosophy of Imagination* (2016), and *Handbook of Imagination and Culture* (2017),[1] this transdisciplinary project represents the most ambitious and comprehensive study of imagination to date. The eclectic group of international scholars who comprise this volume propose bold and innovative theoretical frameworks for (re-) conceptualizing imagination in all of its divergent forms. Moreover, as the title unequivocally implies, this collection explores the complex nuances, paradoxes, and aporias related to the plethora of artistic mediums in which the human imagination manifests itself.

As a fundamental attribute of our species, which other organisms also seem to possess with varying degrees of sophistication from a biosemiotic standpoint,[2] imagination is the very fabric of what it means to be human into which everything is woven. Whether we like it or not, "Human beings are imaginers, we play games of make-believe, we enter into fictional worlds of stories."[3] In simple terms, "we are fundamentally imaginative beings" with a heightened biological predilection for recounting, disseminating, and perpetuating imaginative metanarratives that influence our way of being-in-the-world in addition to how our sense of Self is constituted.[4] Given that the products of our imagination through which many of our quotidian experiences are filtered

---

1   See Adam Toon, *Models as Make-Believe: Imagination, Fiction and Scientific Representation* (New York: Palgrave Macmillan, 2012); Majid Yar, *The Cultural Imaginary of the Internet: Virtual Utopias and Dystopias* (Basingstoke, UK: Palgrave Macmillan, 2014); Roger Scruton, *Art and Imagination: A Study in the Philosophy of Mind* (South Bend, IN: St. Augustine's Press, 2015); Kathleen Lennon, *Imagination and the Imaginary* (New York and London: Routledge, 2015); Amy Kind, ed., *The Routledge Handbook of Philosophy of Imagination* (London and New York: Routledge, 2016); Tania Zittoun, and Vlad Glaveanu, eds., *Handbook of Imagination and Culture* (Oxford: Oxford University Press, 2017).

2   This point will be briefly addressed later in the introduction. Additionally, the biosemiotician Wendy Wheeler delves into this issue at great length in Chapter 21.

3   Liao, Shen-yi, Nina Strohminger, and Chandra Sekhar Sripada, "Empirically Investigating Imaginative Resistance," *British Journal of Aesthetics* 54, no. 3 (2014): 340.

4   Kevin Honeycutt, "The Musical Philosophy of Bertrand de Jouvenel," *The Review of Politics* 79, no. 3 (2017): 396.

© KONINKLIJKE BRILL NV, LEIDEN, 2020 | DOI:10.1163/9789004436350_002

affect how we relate to others and the biosphere to which we are inextricably linked, the imagination is the resin that binds human civilization together for better or worse.

As evidenced throughout the volume, one of the many unique contributions of this book is its radical transdisciplinarity that epitomizes what Sydney Lévy refers to as an "ecology of knowledge"[5] that strives to reconnect the disciplines in an effort to understand what is at stake in discussions revolving around the imagination more fully. Taking advantage of what Edgar Morin terms "ecologized thinking,"[6] which is one of the basic tenets of his larger approach to engaging in philosophical inquiry that he labels "complex thought," *Imagination and Art* weaves connections[7] between different ways of knowing that cannot be contained within the narrow confines of one specific field. In this regard, the study of imagination is a quintessential interdiscipline bifurcating in all directions that seemingly knows no bounds. For this reason, this collection unapologetically transgresses traditional disciplinary demarcations in an attempt to offer fresh new perspectives about imagination. From an interdisciplinary standpoint, a few of the novel frames of reference that stand out in comparison to the aforementioned previous investigations of imagination are reflections concerning the "gendered imagination" (a concept developed by researchers such as Belinda Leach,[8] Deanna Smid,[9] and Patricia Mohammed,[10] see Chapters 4 and 5), the biosemiotic imagination (Chapter 21), the Sufi Imagination (Chapter 32), and Carol Gould's insights into the highly charged notion of "imaginative resistance" inspired by Freud's theory of repression (Chapter 6).[11]

---

5   Sydney Lévy, "Introduction: An Ecology of Knowledge: Michel Serres," *SubStance* 26, no. 2 (1997): 3–5.

6   Edgar Morin, *La Méthode*, tome 2, *La vie de la vie* (Paris: Points, 2014), 87. All translations are my own unless otherwise indicated.

7   Michel Serres, who shares many affinities with Morin, promotes this same kind of transdisciplinary philosophical method for broaching complex phenomena. For this reason, he is often referred to as the "weaver philosopher" by numerous researchers. For instance, see Anne Baudart, "Le philosophe-tisserand: paganisme et christianisme," in *Michel Serres, Cahiers de l'Herne*, eds. François L'Yvonnet, and Christiane Frémont (Paris: Herne, 2010), 251–60.

8   Belinda Leach, "Agency and the Gendered Imagination: Women's Actions and Local Culture in Steelworker Families," *Identities: Global Studies in Culture and Power* 12, no. 1 (2005): 1–22.

9   Deanna Smid, *The Imagination in Early Modern English Literature* (Leiden: Brill, 2017).

10   Patricia Mohammed, *Gendered Realities: Essays in Caribbean Feminist Thought* (Kingston, Jamaica: The University of the West Indies Press, 2002).

11   For an overview of the controversies surrounding the concept of "imaginative resistance," including the attacks launched by "imaginative resistance doubters," see Liao, Strohminger, and Sripada, "Empirically Investigating Imaginative Resistance," 339–55.

INTRODUCTION

In addition to these theoretical strengths, *Imagination and Art* incorporates ecological considerations that are often overlooked (Chapters 5 and 21). Furthermore, this present exploration is the first academic publication that directly gives a platform to contemporary artists[12] in the final section "Artists Reflect on Imagination: An Imaginative Epilogue." Given that novelists, poets, sculptors, musicians, painters and other kinds of artists appear to be endowed with the sharpest and most powerful imaginative attributes of all, this nontheoretical portion of the book could be described as a form of "imagination in action" that allows us to catch a glimpse of true artistry conceived by those "who are widely recognized as having special powers of imagination."[13] Nonetheless, this brief section is merely a point of departure for creating a dialogic space between researchers who study the imagination and artists who possess even more of it than the so-called average person. Other scholars from varied academic backgrounds are thus encouraged to continue to fill this significant research gap in the future.

Another especially noteworthy feature of this volume, which is underrepresented in the prior studies mentioned above, is its strong postmodern-avant-garde focus (Chapters 15–18) that is a crucial component for understanding how human identity is mediated, constructed, and renegotiated through imagination. Unfortunately, many forms of the social imaginary exploit our innate penchant for generating imaginative visions of the world and our relationship to it to the alarming point of creating what intercultural theorists like Amin Maalouf and Issa Asgarally[14] term "les identités meurtrières" (deadly identities)[15] linked to an incessant cycle of violence, xenophobia, persecution, and exploitation. However, David Collins, Michel Dion, Samuel Kimball, and Chandra Kavanagh demonstrate that the products of our imagination are in a constant state of evolution. As opposed to being static, our imaginary ideological structures, which the pioneer of the interdiscipline of Ecolinguistics Arran Stibbe calls the *stories-we-live-by*,[16] can be modified over time and replaced

---

12   I am evidently employing this term in a very general sense referring to novelists, poets, photographers, painters, sculptors, etc.

13   Amy Kind, "How Imagination Gives Rise to Knowledge," in *Perceptual Imagination and Perceptual Memory*, eds. Fiona Macpherson, and Fabian Dorsch (Oxford: Oxford University Press, 2018), 229.

14   Issa Asgarally, *L'interculturel ou la guerre* (Port-Louis, Mauritius: MSM, 2005).

15   Amin Maalouf, *Les identités meurtrières* (Paris: Grasset, 1998).

16   Arran Stibbe, *Ecolinguistics: Language, Ecology, and the Stories We Live by* (London and New York: Routledge, 2015). On page 4, Stibbe offers the following operational definition for this concept: "*Stories-we-live-by* are stories in the minds of multiple individuals across a culture."

with more beneficial discourses. Whereas it was once deemed acceptable by philosophers like Aristotle to terminate the life of an "abnormal child," as Kimball highlights in "The Infanticidal Logic of Mimesis as Horizon of the Imaginable," Kavanagh underscores how the social imaginary eventually paved the way for a more humane treatment of members of society who suffer from a given disability.

Given that postmodern thought incessantly implores us to "go back to the drawing board," it represents an invaluable counter-hegemonic tool for *deconstructing* problematic discourses.[17] Postmodern philosophers like Jacques Derrida, Jean-François Lyotard, Gilles Deleuze, and Félix Guattari realize that "[s]uch imaginaries both make possible social life and are themselves social entities carried in stories, myths, practices, visual representations, and institutional structures."[18] Moreover, many postmodern thinkers also recognize that only through imagination can we explore "the manifold of other possibilities."[19] Owing to its very nature that problematizes and challenges accepted boundaries, Derrida's concept of *limitrophy* offers a concrete example of how postmodern theories can help to reshape the social imaginary. In *The Animal That Therefore I am*, Derrida proposes the following operational definition for his notion of limitrophy:

> Limitrophy is therefore my subject. Not just because it will concern what sprouts or grows at the limit, around the limit, by maintaining the limit, but also what feeds the limit generates it, raises it, and complicates it. Everything I'll say will consist, certainty not in effacing the limit, but in multiplying its figures, in complicating, thickening, delinearizing, folding, and dividing the line precisely by making it increase and multiply.[20]

In this collection of posthumous lectures, which has become a seminal text in Environmental Ethics in addition to *The Beast and Sovereign* series, Derrida provides insights into how the moral community can be expanded through the imaginative, moral exercise of limitrophy. In essence, "the imagination is a consequential steering mechanism in how humans make their own future realities. Imagining new aspects of oneself ... can lead to an expanded identity,

---

17   Jacques Derrida, *The Animal That Therefore I Am*, trans. David Wills (Fordham, NY: Fordham University Press, 2008), 76.

18   Lennon, *Imagination and the Imaginary*, 73.

19   John Sallis, *Force of Imagination: The Sense of the Elemental* (Bloomington, IN: Indiana University Press, 2000), 204.

20   Derrida, *The Animal That Therefore I Am*, 29.

INTRODUCTION

new social relations, and changed sense of self."[21] By harnessing the veritable force of imagination, which allows us to envision new borders that are more inclusive, Derrida suggests that we will be able to extend the doctrine of moral considerability to more human and other-than-human "fellows" who have traditionally been left in the shadows.[22]

Not only does the postmodern rethinking of imagination have much to contribute to the interdiscipline itself as a whole, but Baudrillard's radical reworking of symbolic exchange in contemporary consumer republics (a term coined by the historian Lizabeth Cohen)[23] is also a key source of inspiration for philosophical debates centered on what could be defined as the *simulacral imagination*. In a global landscape in which many of our imaginings are now mediated through a plethora of divergent screens, the question of how the Self is currently being reformulated and (re-) appropriated through technology is of the utmost importance. As I will more systematically outline soon in my succinct discussion of the major theories presented in the "Postmodern Perspectives" section, Baudrillard's concepts of "hyperreality" and "integral reality" provide an intriguing lens from which to view the evolution of human imagination in both society and art in general.

On a final note concerning the originality of this project, the "Non-Western Perspectives" portion is intentionally designed to highlight important cultural differences in terms of how the social imaginary manifests itself in non-occidental civilizations around the world. In *The West and the Rest: Discourse and Power*, the cultural theorist Stuart Hall reminds us that the very notion of the West is a "short-hand generalization"[24] with "no simple or single meaning."[25] For Hall, not only is the idea of Western society a social construct that reinforces hegemonic power structures, but it is also predicated upon a type of simplistic, reductionistic oppositional thinking pitting *Occidentalism* against *Orientalism*. As Edward Said theorizes in *Orientalism*, the West-Orient binary is emblematic of a "'colonial discourse'- a discourse that presents the Orient as

---

21   Alex Gillespie, Kevin Corti, Simon Evans, and Brett Heasman, "Imagining the Self Through Cultural Technologies," in *Handbook of Imagination and Culture*, eds. Tania Zittoun, and Vlad Glaveanu (Oxford: Oxford University Press, 2017), 313.

22   Jacques Derrida, *The Beast and the Sovereign*, trans. Geoffrey Bennington, vol. 1 (Chicago: Chicago University Press, 2011), 106.

23   See Lizabeth Cohen, *A Consumers' Republic: The Politics of Mass Consumption in Postwar America* (New York: Vintage Book, 2003).

24   Stuart Hall, *The West and the Rest: Discourse and Power* (Cambridge: Polity Press, 1992), 185.

25   Hall, *The West and the Rest*, 185.

Other."[26] Even if the words "West" and "Western" are inherently problematic, which is a position that is difficult to refute, I am employing this terminology in the absence of better alternatives.[27] Regardless of the imperfect phrasing that one finds to be the least flawed, Arindham Chakrabarti, Yangping Gao, Amy Lee, and Ali Hussain all note that there are legitimate differences related to how the social imaginary is constructed, shared, maintained, and renegotiated in Arabic, Indian, Chinese, and Japanese culture. Specifically, Amy Lee persuasively contends that there are unique cultural elements that are an integral part of the contemporary Japanese imagination which are usually relegated to the periphery (if mentioned at all) in academic publications with an evident Western bias. For this reason, this section is another example of how *Imagination and Art: Explorations in Contemporary Theory* deliberately broadens ongoing discussions about the imagination.

Owing to the wide-ranging nature of the theoretical frameworks presented in this volume representing many different philosophical, cultural, and artistic traditions, some of which are often ignored, these diverse viewpoints are sometimes conflicting. Nevertheless, even if exactly *how* we engage with art and what it means to inhabit the elaborate fictional (sometimes counterfactual-Chapter 28) worlds into which we breathe life remain contentious subjects that are open to debate, art does indeed appear to be a catalyst for stimulating the imagination. Hence, it could be argued that art has a major role to play for those who are in search of more beneficial *stories-to-live-by* connected to our stable sense of Self and our fragmented understanding of the world in which we live and die. According to the educational theorist Maxine Greene and the American philosopher Richard Rorty, this is precisely why Imagination (or Imagination Studies) is such an essential interdiscipline that should be a staple of numerous fields instead of being reduced to the "pariah of the philosophy of mind."[28]

In her promotion of the gradual evolution of the "social imagination"[29] through the implementation of what she calls the "theater of the oppressed" into the classroom, Greene posits that the arts serve "as a catalyst for nudging learners toward a more relationally imaginative way of being-a being that is

---

26 Shehla Burney, *Pedagogy of the Other: Edward Said, Postcolonial Theory, and Strategies for Critique* (New York: Peter Lang, 2012), 23.

27 As Martin Müller explains, the Global North and Global South binary is an equally flawed concept. See Martin Müller, "In Search of the Global East: Thinking Between North and South," *Geopolitics* (October 2018): 1–22, https://doi.org/10.1080/14650045.2018.1477757.

28 Edward Casey, *Imagining: A Phenomenological Study* (Bloomington, IN: Indiana University Press, 1979), 19.

29 Greene prefers the expression "social imagination."

INTRODUCTION 7

part *of*, not simply *in*, the world."[30] Greene also argues that "the arts have the potential to provoke, inspire, and, most of all, to move."[31] Greene's vision of the imagination places the arts at the fore of social reformation, due to their ability to transform the reader, listener, spectator, or viewer by revealing other perspectives. Likewise, Rorty "claims that literature exposes us to many different types of people with different ways of being in the world and different points of view."[32] From a Derridean angle, Greene and Rorty maintain that the power of art is linked to the ethical imperative of limitrophy.

Although many theorists would undoubtedly take issue with the veracity of the claim that the imagination should be tapped into and honed for moral purposes in a systematic fashion through art leading to an expanded identity, all of the contributors to this present investigation strive to rehabilitate imagination and art in a bleak and unreceptive intellectual landscape. In spite of the fact that "[t]hese early years of the twenty-first century have witnessed a groundswell of philosophical interest in imagination," far too many academicians still do not consider the study of imagination to be as vital as many other kinds of inquiry.[33] As Charles Altieri explains in Chapter 11, the passionate call launched by David Norton for a "renewed vigor" connected to the importance of imagination as a valid discipline in 1968 has been answered, but much work remains to be done.[34] Even when we are seemingly only "having fun" (see Chapter 29) or playing what appears to be a banal game (see Chapter 27), the products of our imagination should be taken seriously.

In addition to their staunch defense of the academic value of (re-) examining the imagination, this group of researchers is united by their non-reductionistic approach that transcends the pitfalls of binary logic. In response to the pervasive attitude that "imagination and 'reason' are adversaries,"[35] this volume lauds "the polyphony of imagination"[36] that cannot be appropriated in such a simplistic manner. As Rob van Gerwen underscores in Chapter 14, there are many different types of imagination that cannot be compartmentalized so

---

30   Kelly Guyotte, "Aesthetic Movements of a Social Imagination: Refusing Stasis and Educating Relationally/Critically/Responsibly," *Critical Questions in Education* 9, no. 1 (2018): 64.

31   Guyotte, "Aesthetic Movements of a Social Imagination," 65.

32   Maria Lara, "Richard Rorty: Becoming a Contemporary Political Philosopher," *Contemporary Pragmatism* 11, no. 1 (2014): 77.

33   Amy Kind, "Introduction," in *The Routledge Handbook of Philosophy of Imagination*, ed. Amy Kind (London and New York: Routledge, 2016), 1.

34   David Norton, "Philosophy and Imagination," *The Centennial Review* 12, no. 4 (1968): 393.

35   Norton, "Philosophy and Imagination," 406.

36   Eva Vass, "Musical Co-creativity and Learning in the Kokas Pedagogy: Polyphony of Movement and Imagination," *Thinking Skills and Creativity* 31 (2019): 190.

easily into a dichotomous thought paradigm. Even though it would be difficult to advocate in favor of the position that all forms of imagination such as "'exotic' daydreams"[37] are replete with philosophical merit, this does not mean that "imagination is (always) the mistress of falsehood and error."[38]

From a Derridean angle, the problem is the word "imagination" itself that represents a "false singular"[39] in linguistic terms. Similar to how Derrida replaces the word "animal" with the neologism "animot" in *The Animal That Therefore I am* in order to combat "a sin against rigorous thinking,"[40] the "general singular"[41] "imagination" is perhaps too misleading to the point of obfuscating the multiplicity of human imaginings that can be strikingly different depending upon the precise context in question. Derrida's justification for his new word "animot," which would be pronounced identically in both the singular and plural forms in French (animot, animots), is clearly part of his larger project to weaken dominant anthropocentric discourses. Nevertheless, the overall concept of wanting "to have the plural ... heard in the singular" is still applicable to the present discussion of the potentially deceptive nature of the word "imagination" in English and other languages.[42] In this vein, it is worth debating whether one word suffices for accurately describing the wide array of situations in which the human imagination is active. As a result of this linguistic inadequacy, philosophers and other theorists from antiquity to the present have been forced to create meaningful distinctions between *phantasia, phantasma*, "productive imagination," "reproductive imagination," "transcendental imagination," "synthetic imagination," and "creative imagination."[43] Before having a genuine conversation about the role of the imagination, knowing what sort of imaginings to which someone is referring is a precondition.

Further compounding this confusion associated with the general singular, imagining is often conflated with other mental states like believing, supposing, and conceiving. Without succumbing to reductionistic explanations that do

---

37   Anna Ichino, "Imagination and Belief in Action," *Philosophia* (2018): 9, https://doi .org/10.1007/s11406-019-00067-7.

38   Casey, *Imagining: A Phenomenological Study*, 16.

39   Lynn Turner, "Telefoam: Species on the Shores of Cixous and Derrida," *European Journal of English Studies* 18, no. 2 (2014): 163.

40   Derrida, *The Animal That Therefore I Am*, 48.

41   Derrida, *The Animal That Therefore I Am*, 47.

42   Derrida, *The Animal That Therefore I Am*, 47.

43   Evidently, this is a non-exhaustive list of the many different types of imagination identified by theorists for eons. For instance, Gaston Bachelard's reflections about the "imagination of matter" represent an important contribution to the philosophy of science. In Chapter 30, Yangping Gao highlights the significance of Bachelard's material imagination.

INTRODUCTION 9

not properly represent the complexity of the relationship between imagination and other mental states, Neil Sinhababu maintains that it is possible in many instances to delineate a clear separation between imagination and belief. Sinhababu explains that imagining one is a superhero like Spiderman or a celebrity differs greatly from the delusion of actually believing it.[44] Arguing along similar lines, Anna Ichino asserts, "imagining that you have won the lottery is not the same as believing that you have won."[45] As Jody Azzouni (Chapter 12) demonstrates in his nuanced reflection dedicated to the differences between conceiving and imagining (or the lack thereof[46]), "conceivability and imagination ... are in a messy state."[47] Consequently, Azzouni and other scholars have no choice but to confront the previously mentioned nuances, paradoxes, and aporias directly in an effort to shed light on the thorny distinction between imagining and conceiving.

In addition to embracing the Morinian ideal of ecologized thinking-complex thought by refusing to gloss over the complex quandaries that inevitably rise to the surface in these kinds of discussions, many researchers in this volume also emphasize the epistemological value of certain types of imaginings. To be more precise, several scholars in this collection promote a form of disciplined imagination that leads to important insights about ourselves, others, and the universe. This defense of the epistemological virtues of imagination closely corresponds to Amy Kind's concept of "imagination under constraints,"[48] David Norton's theory of the "'empirical' imagination,"[49] the notion of "experience projection,"[50] Lynn Holt's concept of "rational imagination,"[51] and the "gap-filling model"[52] heavily influenced by David Hume. As Warren Heiti (Chapter 13) outlines in his analysis of Simone Weil's early epistemology, many

---

44   Neil Sinhababu, "Imagination and Belief," in *The Routledge Handbook of Philosophy of Imagination*, ed. Amy Kind (London and New York: Routledge, 2016), 113.

45   Ichino, "Imagination and Belief in Action," 1.

46   As Amy Kind notes, "some philosophers take there to be no difference between imagining and conceiving," Kind, "Introduction," 3.

47   Francesco Berto, and Tom Schoonen, "Conceivability and Possibility: Some Dilemmas for Humeans," *Synthese* 195, no. 6 (2018): 2698.

48   Amy Kind, "Imagining Under Constraints," in *Knowledge Through Imagination*, eds. Amy Kind and Peter Kung (Oxford: Oxford University Press, 2016), 145–59.

49   Norton, "Philosophy and Imagination," 403.

50   Robert Mitchell, "Can Animals Imagine?," in *The Routledge Handbook of Philosophy of Imagination*, ed. Amy Kind (London and New York: Routledge, 2016), 332.

51   See especially Chapter five from Lynn Holt, *Apprehension: Reason in the Absence of Rules* (London: Ashgate, 2002).

52   Vlad Glaveanu, Maciej Karwowski, Dorota Jankowska, and Constance de Saint-Laurent. "Creative Imagination," in *Handbook of Imagination and Culture*, eds. Tania Zittoun, and Vlad Glaveanu (Oxford: Oxford University Press, 2017), 76.

thinkers including Weil reach the conclusion that imagination is an indispensable pathway for knowledge acquisition.

Far from being "epistemologically insignificant,"[53] many neuroscientists have now confirmed through empirical investigation that imagination is a "process of image making that resolves gaps arising from biological and cultural-historical constraints, and that enables ongoing time-space coordination necessary for thought and action."[54] When our imaginings are "clear and distinct" in Cartesian terms because they are supported by evidence, Hume's hypothesis that it is through our imagination that we are able to fill in the missing puzzle pieces in order to create a more global vision of world and our relationship to it is validated. As I explore throughout my aptly named monograph *The Encyclopedic Philosophy of Michel Serres: Writing the Modern World and Anticipating the Future* (2016), Michel Serres also subscribes to this view of imagination.[55] In particular, Serres affirms that honing our imagination is a philosophical exercise *par excellence*, for it enables us to envision probable outcomes based on the current trajectory of society. In fact, it is Serres's uncanny ability to imagine that has cemented his legacy as a pioneer who blazed the trail for those who followed in the field of Information Studies,[56] Sensory Studies, and Environmental Ethics.

Jordan Ryan's analysis of the role that imagination plays in historical thinking reflects this same epistemological conviction that Serres espouses beginning with his first publication *Hermès: La Communication* in 1968. Deconstructing the naïve interpretation of history as merely an objective recounting of the "facts," Ryan declares,

> What the historian infers constructively from the data is 'essentially imagined'... The imagination fills the gap between them. Imagination without evidence results not in history, but in historical fiction ... There is reciprocity here: the need for evidence places a check on the imagination, while imagination allows the historian to make inferences, discoveries and hypotheses beyond what the evidence directly provides.[57]

---

53   Amy Kind, "How Imagination Gives Rise to Knowledge," 228.

54   Etienne Pelaprat, and Michael Cole, "'Minding the Gap': Imagination, Creativity and Human Cognition," *Integrative Psychological Behavior* 45, no. 4 (2011): 397.

55   Keith Moser, *The Encyclopedic Philosophy of Michel Serres: Writing the Modern World and Anticipating the Future* (Augusta, GA: Anaphora Literary Press, 2016).

56   I address this point systematically in Chapter 16.

57   Jordan Ryan, "Jesus at the Crossroads of Inference and Imagination,"*Journal for the Study of the Historical Jesus* 13, no. 1 (2015): 85.

INTRODUCTION

In "Jesus at the Crossroads," Ryan clearly recognizes the academic value of a disciplined form of imagination that is fueled by evidence and sound logic. According to Ryan, the most objective reconstructions of past events are rendered possible by the imagination of a historian who is forced to speculate on the basis of proof in an attempt to remove as much bias as possible.

In the first section of the book, David Konstan, Claude Calame, and Allen Speight lend credence to Ryan's theories about the significance of imagination in historical thinking and judgement. Specifically, Speight and Calame pose essential historiographical and philosophical questions related to historical agency. Moreover, in Chapter 4, Mayor's interpretation of what evidence suggests concerning the courageous warrior women commonly referred to as Amazons in Greek Mythology is revealing on multiple levels. First of all, the case of the largely forgotten Amazons illustrates how the official historical master narrative, which becomes engrained in cultural myths linked to nation-building,[58] is part of a larger collective memory that shapes a given society. In the social imaginary, it is often impossible to create a clear distinction between history and art. Furthermore, it is sometimes only through art that the contributions of disenfranchised moral and ethnic minorities become visible. In the biased historical imagination of those whose version of the story is usually disseminated to the masses, minority voices are stifled by a lack of historical consideration or interest. Even if the tales of the Amazons in Greek Mythology contain appalling misogynistic elements, these stories may be the only avenue for expanding the limits of traditional historiography in the absence of adequate documentation about these women-warriors.

The problem is that history has often been written and transmitted in the service of the *gendered imagination*. Explaining that male and female roles, stereotypes, and attitudes are socially constructed in every society through the social imaginary, Patricia Mohammed reveals, "there are no originary narratives without the archetypes of masculinity and femininity, there is no culture without gender and no gender without culture."[59] As evidenced by the cult of the "founding fathers" in the United States for which there is no female equivalent whatsoever, many historical reconstructions need to be collectively (re)-imagined to include the accomplishments, exploits, and discoveries of women. In the Derridean sense, the historical metanarratives that are privileged over competing views tend to be *phallogocentric*. For this reason, Derrida champions a

---

58   In his intriguing and lyrical reflection about imagination in the final section, the Dutch artist Ton Kruse effectively makes this point as well.

59   Mohammed, *Gendered Realities*, 72.

"reorientation of discourse, history and the tradition."[60] The concept of the historical imagination is a useful theoretical tool, because it offers a viable path for multiplying the dimensions through which collective stories are recounted, shared, and preserved. Additionally, reflecting upon the importance of disciplined imagination linked to evidence opens up a dialogic space in which historians, writers, painters, dancers, sculptors, etc. can create a more inclusive version of the metanarratives that are tied to our sense of collective identity and belonging. As opposed to protecting "tooth and nail one of our (cultural) affiliations" to the exclusion of other viewpoints, Serres beckons us to expand our sense of Self by complicating and multiplying the historical and cultural limits through our imagination.[61]

All of the essays that constitute this volume, including those from the first two sections "Historical Imagination and Judgement" and "Gendered Imagination," support the point of view that the study of imagination is an interdiscipline. Instead of being just a subfield of the philosophy of mind, these thirty-two chapters beg us to ponder what does not fall within the purview of human imagination from an academic standpoint. Similar to how historians conceive reconstructions to connect the remaining dots (or fragments), it is a sense of imaginative wonder that seems to be at the heart of the thirst for knowledge in all disciplines. Although it may initially sound paradoxical, scientific explanations of the world derive inspiration from an empirical imagination that seeks possible answers to unexplained phenomena. In essence, "all scientific theories are works of the imagination"[62] that generate "new insights into the familiar natural world."[63] In the context of Adam Smith's theories about the scientific imagination, Robin Downey reiterates, "there are gaps in the scientist's observations, which cause surprise and wonder."[64] In this regard, Fiora Salis (Chapter 19) explains how the scientific imagination operates leading to monumental breakthroughs by bridging these gaps.

Given that scientists have to rely on evidence in order to make logical hypotheses and inferences, Helen de Cruz and Johan de Smedt describe scientific inquiry as "structured imagination" linked to near and distant analogies.[65] In

---

60   Carole Dely, "Jacques Derrida: The 'Perchance' of a Coming of the Otherwoman," *Sens Public* (October 2007): n. pag., http://sens-public.org/article312.html?lang=fr#.

61   Michel Serres, *Atlas* (Paris: Flammarion, 1994), 210.

62   Robin Downie, "Science and the Imagination in the Age of Reason," *Journal of Medical Ethics and Medical Humanities* 27 (2001): 59.

63   Downie, "Science and the Imagination in the Age of Reason," 60.

64   Downie, "Science and the Imagination in the Age of Reason," 59.

65   Helen De Cruz, and Johan de Smedt, "Science as Structured Imagination," *Journal of Creative Behavior* 44, no. 1 (2010): 29–44.

INTRODUCTION

his research related to the importance of imagination in scientific modelling in both physical and theoretical models, Adam Toon deconstructs "our common-sense view of science" concretized by the misperception that imagination is more of a hindrance, or even a stumbling block, than an indispensable tool for scientists.[66] In *Models as Make-Believe: Imagination, Fiction and Scientific Representation,* Toon hypothesizes that a scientist who knows how to wield the power of a disciplined form of imagination is not that dissimilar from a literary scholar, philosopher, or writer. Adopting the *indirect fiction* view, which stipulates that fictional agents are indirect representations of the world, Toon contends that "scientists sometimes conjure up imagined systems, just as novelists conjure up fictional characters."[67]

Providing numerous examples to substantiate this claim, Toon observes that "[m]ost models are inaccurate (or incorrect or unrealistic) in some way."[68] Despite the unheralded discoveries of the twentieth and twenty-first century associated with the dawn of modern medicine, as systematically outlined by the historian Roy Porter in *The Greatest Benefit to Mankind: A Medical History of Humanity,*[69] scale models, theoretical paradigms, and equations still represent the world indirectly. Even in the so-called "exact sciences," the imagination is the driver of knowledge acquisition.[70] Furthermore, Edward Grant compellingly posits that the "natural philosophers [who] began to use their imaginations in ways that had never been done before in any civilization or culture" in the late Middle Ages served as the initial impetus for the aforementioned unprecedented scientific findings that have radically altered the human condition compared to our not-so-distant human ancestors.[71] The scientific inferences about the theory of atomism made by the pre-Socratic philosophers Leucippus and Democritus in antiquity through meticulous observation and documentation further strengthen Grant's assertion. In both the humanities and hard sciences, a type of constrained imagination informed by available

---

66   Adam Toon, "Imagination in Scientific Modeling," in *The Routledge Handbook of Philosophy of Imagination,* ed. Amy Kind (London and New York: Routledge, 2016), 451.

67   Toon, *Models as Make-Believe,* 56.

68   Toon, *Models as Make-Believe,* 23.

69   Roy Porter, *The Greatest Benefit to Mankind: A Medical History of Humanity* (New York: W.W. Norton & Company, 1999).

70   Edward Grant, "How Theology, Imagination, and the Spirit of Inquiry Shaped Natural Philosophy in the Late Middle Ages," *History of Science* 49, no. 1 (2011): 89.

71   Grant, "How Theology, Imagination, and the Spirit of Inquiry Shaped Natural Philosophy," 101. See also Chapter four from Moser, *The Encyclopedic Philosophy of Michel Serres* entitled "(Re-) envisioning Technology and Science to Imagine a Better World of Tomorrow."

evidence, experience, and observation is what results in novel ideas and discoveries.

In Chapter 20, Justin Humphreys highlights the pivotal role assumed by the imagination in another field that is usually considered to be part of the hard sciences: Geometry. Humphrey's discussion related to whether geometrical propositions are analytic or synthetic, which delves into the theories of Aristotle, Syrianus, and Proclus that are later revisited by Kant and Frege in the modern era, demonstrates the significance of the mathematical imagination in both Euclidian and Non-Euclidian geometry. Not only is "the central role of visualization and hence imagination in ancient geometry"[72] overdue for more recognition, but "cultivating the power of imagination of the mathematician"[73] is how mathematical innovation is fostered. According to Daniel Campos, who builds upon the theories of Charles Sanders Peirce, it is "imaginatively creating framing hypotheses"[74] within "various systems of diagrammatic representation"[75] that separates the most brilliant mathematical minds from the mediocre ones. Many people would not immediately associate either science or mathematics with imagination. However, Salis and Humphreys illustrate that the imagination abounds in scientific and mathematical reasoning.

Another interdisciplinary perspective that is noteworthy is the connections that Michel Dion weaves between Christian prayer and the imagination. Dion elucidates that it is imagination that enables believers to create communicational links between this world and the divine realm. On a basic level, faith is predicated upon the capacity to envision "a world different from the one we experience."[76] In "Dream Hermeneutics: Bob Marley, Paul Ricœur and the Productive Imagination," Christopher J. Duncanson-Hales utilizes Ricœur's framework for understanding the "religious productive imagination" that undergirds various conceptions of the divine.[77] As Michael Paul Gallagher notes, spiritual leaders and Christian thinkers have often warned believers of the alleged perils of letting the imagination run wild based on the conviction that we can easily be misled and deceived by our senses, thereby falling into the trap of hedonistic

---

72   Andrew Arana, "Imagination in Mathematics," in *The Routledge Handbook of Philosophy of Imagination*, ed. Amy Kind (London and New York: Routledge, 2016), 464.

73   Daniel Campos, "Peirce's Philosophy of Mathematical Education: Fostering Reasoning Abilities for Mathematical Inquiry," *Studies in Philosophy and Education* 29, no. 5 (2010): 436.

74   Campos, "Peirce's Philosophy of Mathematical Education," 427.

75   Campos, "Peirce's Philosophy of Mathematical Education," 438.

76   Christopher Duncanson-Hales, "Dread Hermeneutics: Paul Ricœur and the Productive Imagination," *Black Theology* 15, no. 2 (2017): 158.

77   Duncanson-Hales, "Dread Hermeneutics," 156.

INTRODUCTION

pleasures. In spite of the complicated and sometimes conflictual relationship between Christian ideology and imagination, there would be no "religious consciousness" at all without our imagination.[78] From a Christian viewpoint, it is "a personal and prayerful encounter with Christ [that] creates a new imagination in us."[79]

In addition to the scientific imagination, the mathematical imagination, and the religious productive imagination, another vantage point that stands out compared to earlier studies is Wendy Wheeler's investigation of the biosemiotic imagination. Even if *Homo sapiens* do appear to be endowed with heightened imaginative abilities, as we have clearly established, the main biosemiotic premise that "the essence of the entire life process is semiosis" helps to nuance problematic anthropocentric thought paradigms centered on binary logic.[80] Whereas most mainstream biosemioticians agree that the human primary modeling device of language is the most sophisticated form of communication on this planet, this does not mean that other organisms are incapable of communicating at all. Deeply influenced by the founding father of Biosemiotics, the German biologist Jakob von Uexküll who he cites directly on numerous occasions, Derrida adopts the biosemiotic worldview that semiosis "is synonymous with life" in *The Animal That Therefore I am* and *The Beast and Sovereign* series.[81] As Derrida declares, "Mark, gamma, trace, and différance refer differentially to all living things."[82] Derrida further clarifies that all of the other sentient beings with whom we share this biosphere have been deemed "poor in the world" owing to their supposed lack of any semiosic faculties at all.[83]

Appealing to scientific logic and recent findings related to the surprising complexity of non-human communication, Derrida disputes the idea that other species do not have "a self, imagination, [or] a relation to the future."[84] Derrida alludes to a growing body of evidence that unequivocally suggests that other organisms take advantage of their semiosic faculties in order to communicate purposefully and meaningfully and to predict future outcomes through

---

78   Michael Paul Gallagher, "Theology and Imagination: From Theory to Practice," *Christian Higher Education* 5 (2006): 85.

79   Gallagher, "Theology and Imagination," 91.

80   Louise Weslting, *The Logos of the Living World Merleau-Ponty, Animals, and Language* (New York: Fordham University Press, 2013), 111.

81   Wendy Wheeler, "The book of Nature: Biosemiotics and the Evolution of Literature," in *The Evolution of Literature: Legacies of Darwin in European Cultures*, eds. Nicholas Saul and Simon James (Amsterdam: Rodopi, 2011), 177.

82   Derrida, *The Animal That Therefore I Am*, 104.

83   Derrida, *The Beast and the Sovereign*, 346.

84   Derrida, *The Animal That Therefore I Am*, 62.

imagination.[85] Even if the human *Umwelt* is the most complex semiosic space of all, biosemioticians contest the notion that other species are totally deprived of communication and imagination. With the notable exception of Robert Mitchell's essay "Can Animals Imagine?" from *The Routledge Handbook of Philosophy of Imagination*, this subject has rarely been broached by most scholars who explore the imagination. Since Mitchell only scratches the surface of this vast and inexhaustible subject without mentioning Biosemiotics, Wheeler's study is one of the most original contributions to an area in which research is scant.

Moreover, in a recent paper entitled "Imagination and Event in Uexküll and Bazin," Jonathan Wright appeals to the force of art arguing that it allows us to catch a glimpse of the complexity of communication and imagination in other-than-human societies.[86] First, Wright reminds the reader that von Uexküll's seminal work *A Foray Into the Worlds of Animals and Humans* begins by asking us to imagine the sophistication of the communication that transpires within other-than-human realms. Using André Bazin as an example, Wright speculates that the cinematic medium represents an ideal form of experience projection, in spite of its apparent limitations, for revisiting other-than-human imagination.[87] In her essay "Animal Life in the Cinematic Umwelt," Anat Pick also indicates that the moving image is capable of conceiving a fictional space that bridges the divide between human and animal worlds. Identifying films that "engage with interior animal worlds, rendered, as far as possible from the perspective of the creature itself,"[88] Pick maintains that the viewer is struck by the biocentric realization that "animals too are active perceivers of the world"[89] and imaginers. Wright and Pick's theories are reminiscent of Serres's experimental text *Yeux* (2014) in which he implores the reader to reflect upon what it means to *see* and to *be seen* by other sentient beings.[90] Furthermore, this view of the transformative power of cinema recalls Rorty's passion for literature that exposes us to different perspectives to the greatest extent possible. In the

---

85   For a more comprehensive discussion of Derrida's biosemiotic theories, see my forthcoming article in the special issue of *Yearbook of the Irish Philosophical Society* dedicated to "Humans and Other Animals."

86   Jonathan Wright, "Imagination and Event in Uexküll and Bazin," Unpublished manuscript, 2019, typescript, n. pag. https://www.academia.edu/38644818/Imagination_and_Event_in_Uexk%C3%BCll_and_Bazin.

87   Wright, "Imagination and Event in Uexküll and Bazin," n. pag.

88   Anat Pick, "Animal Life in the Cinematic Umwelt," in *Animal Life and the Moving Image*, eds. Michael Lawrence, and Laura McMahon (London: Bloomsbury, 2015), 222.

89   Pick, "Animal Life in the Cinematic Unwelt," 225.

90   See Michel Serres, *Yeux* (Paris: Le Pommier, 2014).

INTRODUCTION

Anthropocene epoch, it is also a reminder that anthropocentric, *ecosuicidal* identities can be reconstituted and renegotiated through the social imaginary.

In the section "Postmodern Perspectives," the aforementioned postmodern-avant-garde take on how the social imaginary is being reconstructed through technological advances is also highly relevant in the era of information. The plethora of digital tools that allow artists, marketers, politicians, and others to fabricate images that are strikingly realistic has revived classic debates related to the "tension between appearances and reality" for obvious reasons.[91] Additionally, decades before the advent of the digital age, the French *new novel* and avant-garde movements irreverently pushed back against the artistic ideal of mimesis, taking aim at the traditional view in many literary circles that the ultimate goal of an artist is to transmit an image that is a faithful representation of reality within the limitations of the artistic space. In this vein, Roderick Nicholls (Chapter 15) discusses at the end of the preceding section "Phenomenological and Epistemological Perspectives" how avant-garde dramaturgs launched a subversive revolt against theatrical conventions including *la règle* (*les règles*) *de bienséance*. In an attempt to break out of the mold and to create plays that were more innovative and original, avant-garde playwrights like Alfred Jarry, Samuel Beckett, and Eugène Ionesco conceived imaginative works that are "non-representational" in the traditional sense.[92] When plays like *Ubu roi*, *La cantratrice chauve*, and *En attendant Godot* were originally performed, they sparked outrage, disbelief, and incomprehension. For playwrights who simply refused to play the game of mimetic representation, the standard tools for literary and theatrical analysis were woefully inadequate.

A salient feature of this "shift away from representational form" in Beckett's theater is a provocative encounter with silence.[93] Far from being mundane, the poignant silence that is ubiquitous throughout Beckett's plays forces us to confront the absurdity of the human condition in the Camusian sense characterized by unavoidable anguish and death. As Dermot Moran explains in "Beckett and Philosophy," "This stark Beckettian world cries out for philosophical

---

91   Dennis Sansom, "Can Irony Enrich the Aesthetic Imagination?: Why Søren Kierkegaard's Explanation of Irony Is Better Than Richard Rorty's," *The Journal of Aesthetic Education* 51, no. 2 (2017): 18.

92   Daniel Albright, *Beckett and Aesthetics* (Cambridge: Cambridge University Press. 2003), 3.

93   John Wall, "'L'au-delà du dehors-dedans': Paradox, Space, and Movement in Beckett," in *Early Modern Beckett/Beckett Et Le Debut de L'Ere Moderne: Beckett Between/Beckett Entre Deux*, eds. Angela Moorjani, Danielle de Ruyter, and Dúnlaith Bird (Amsterdam: Rodopi, 2012), 310.

interpretation."[94] In Chapter 25, Deborah Fillerup Weagel analyzes how the avant-garde musical composer John Cage's famous "silent" piece "4'33" creates "an open space of possibility" through imagination that compels the listener to think harder about the essence of music.[95] Similar to the overtly hostile reactions triggered by avant-garde theater, "its initial reception was characterised by puzzlement and irritation."[96] Given that it is impossible to reproduce a musical composition mimetically comprised of ambient sounds like the wind, coughing, whispering, fidgeting, laughing, and sneezing that will vary during each performance, Michel Remy asserts that "4'33" is non-representational.[97] The fact that Cage was fascinated with silence to the point of spending time in an anechoic chamber at Harvard where he heard his heartbeat and the blood flowing through his veins is why his re-imagining of the omnipresent musicality of life should not be dismissed as a form of fancy.[98] In a world in which complete silence is impossible, Cage argues that music is everywhere. The controversial composer also maintains that it is not as easy as we think to distinguish between music and noise. In his essay *Musique* (2011), Serres encourages us to reattune ourselves to the "musical" sounds of the world endlessly emanating from the chaotic, indiscriminate ecological forces that thrust us into existence starting with a *big bang*.[99] Cage and Serres's musical vision is indicative of a call to imagine designed to renew our severed connection with the biosphere in an age of globalization and urbanization. For Serres, this primordial musicality is a grim reminder that our "parasitic" relationship with the remainder of the cosmos is untenable.

In the face of "increasingly mediated reality where the object is losing in the competition with its simulation,"[100] Cage tries to reduce or efface "the very gap

---

94   Dermot Moran, "Beckett and Philosophy," in *Samuel Beckett-One Hundred Years*, ed. Christopher Murray (Dublin: New Island Press, 2006), 94.

95   James Fielding, "An Aesthetics of the Ordinary: Wittgenstein and John Cage," *The Journal of Aesthetics and Art Criticism* 72, no. 2 (2014): 160.

96   Julian Dodd, "What 4'33" Is," *Australasian Journal of Philosophy 96, no. 4 (2017): 631.*

97   Michel Remy, "Le miroir du silence: Essai sur la problématique de la représentation dans 4'33" de John Cage," *Cycnos* 20, no. 2 (2003): n. pag., http://revel.unice.fr/cycnos/index .html?id=80.

98   Remy, "Le Miroir du silence," n. pag.

99   See Michel Serres, *Musique* (Paris: Le Pommier, 2011).

100   Joan Retallack, "Poethics of a Complex Realism," in *The Poethical Wager*, ed. Joan Retallack (Berkeley: University of California Press, 2004), 206.

INTRODUCTION   19

between art and everyday life"[101] in an effort to resist the "acute crisis of simulation"[102] that is on the verge of eclipsing the real in Baudrillard's radical *semiurgy*. For a few ephemeral moments, "4'33"" attempts to peel back the thick layers of hyperreal artifice that have led to the "collapse … of the real."[103] Many theorists would disagree vehemently with Baudrillard's assertion in his later texts such as *The Intelligence of Evil* and *The Transparency of Evil* that "we are entering into a final phase of this enterprise of simulation" that he refers to as "integral reality" in which commercial simulacra have now substituted themselves for the real entirely.[104] However, even if Baudrillard's main point concerning our increasing inability to discern between reality and its representation in an atmosphere in which the modern subject is continuously bombarded by an avalanche of signs is perhaps overstated, it is hard to deny that realistically rendered images often stand in for the real in the social imaginary. Dominic Gregory (Chapter 22), Jiri Benovksy (Chapter 23), and David Fenner's (Chapter 24) reflections related to image-making in photography and cinema support Baudrillard's central arguments. Even if the "perfect crime" (i.e. the utter implosion of reality) has yet to be committed, the *simulacral imagination* is alive and well.[105]

Lending credence to Baudrillard's affirmation that the real is often quite disconnected from the carefully manufactured images that transcend commonplace reality, thereby taking on a life of their own, Gregory, Benovksy, and Fenner deconstruct the naïve misperception that the camera is able to capture a moment in time in a perfectively objective manner. In defense of the alleged "neutrality of the camera,"[106] many people assert that the "camera does not lie." Given the myriad of tools that allow a contemporary artist to manipulate images to such an extent that they only bare a vague resemblance to the original, "there is no innocent eye of the photographer."[107] Unable to "conserve

---

101   Joan Retallack, "Poethics of a Complex Realism," in *John Cage: Composed in America*, eds. Marjorie Perloff, and Charles Junkerman (Chicago: University of Chicago Press, 1994), 253.
102   Jean Baudrillard, *Seduction*, trans. Brian Singer (New York: St. Martin's Press, 1990), 48.
103   Baudrillard, *Seduction*, 180.
104   Jean Baudrillard, *The Intelligence of Evil*, trans. Chris Turner (New York: Berg, 2005), 34.
105   See Jean Baudrillard, *The Perfect Crime*, trans. Chris Turner (New York: Verso, 2008).
106   Eli Friedlander, "Walter Benjamin on Photography and Fantasy," *Critical Horizons* 18, no. 4 (2017): 305.
107   Etela Farkašová, "Poly(con)textuality of the Photographic Image," *Human Affairs* 1 (2005): 12.

reality itself,"[108] Benovksy highlights all of the artistic choices that a photographer or director makes that could be more accurately described as a "realistic deception"[109] as opposed to a slice of reality.

Even when images are not distorted beyond recognition by software programs like Adobe Photoshop, the person behind the camera controls the lighting through aperture and shutter speed settings in addition to choosing her or his preferred angles. In his landmark essay *The Stars* (1957), Edgar Morin reveals, "To all of the artifices of makeup and plastic surgery are added those of photography. The cameraman must always control the angles of his shots ... must always eliminate every infraction of beauty from his field of vision. Projectors redistribute light and shadow over the stars' faces according to the same ideal requirements."[110] Baudrillard and Morin explain how the digital filters that enable photographers and filmmakers to remove perceived corporal imperfections generate an idealistic vision of human sexuality that is grounded in hyperreality corresponding to a "code of beauty" linked to the incessant acquisition of cosmetic products.[111] The endless transmission of deceptive, "seductive" simulacra denoting "perfect happiness"[112] and beauty that are within reach for all "citizen consumers"[113] debunks the supposed neutrality of the camera. In this regard, the concept of the *simulacral imagination* demonstrates that realistically rendered images are far from being a reliable representation of reality.

Even when there is no evident commercial agenda behind the deluge of simulations that concretize the human experience in the age of information, common sense reminds us that people always pose for the camera in certain ways. For instance, social conventions dictate that we smile when being photographed in most situations. Even during the most tragic periods of our lives, we usually play society's game by displaying "characteristic signs of happiness" in front of the camera.[114] Furthermore, nearly everyone knows someone who constantly projected signs of happiness through contrived photographs and videos on social media networks like Facebook before later revealing their profound malaise and anguish that were antithetical to these utopian images. These common examples support Baudrillard's position that the timeless

---

108   Farkašová, "Poly(con)textuality of the Photographic Image," 13.

109   Farkašová, "Poly(con)textuality of the Photographic Image," 16.

110   Edgar Morin, *The Stars*, trans. Richard Howard (Minneapolis, MN: University of Minnesota Press, 2005), 35.

111   Jean Baudrillard, *The Consumer Society*, trans. George Ritzer (London: Sage, 1998), 26.

112   Baudrillard, *The Consumer Society*, 25.

113   Baudrillard, *The Consumer Society*, 167.

114   Baudrillard, *The Consumer Society*, 31.

INTRODUCTION

search for happiness and fulfillment has been appropriated and commodified by the *simulacral imagination*, or the skillful imposition of image-based (hyper-) reality representing symbolic fantasies that supersede the real.

Even theorists who do not subscribe to Baudrillard's dystopian rethinking of symbolic exchange, which he maintains is the most powerful form of social control ever conceived (see Chapter 16), underscore how "new technologies are intervening in the core mechanics of identity formation."[115] In simple terms, "our material existence is being reformulated through imagination" in virtual realms that enable us to explore new ways of being in the world and relating to others.[116] In Chapter 27, Ton Kruse attempts to shed light on the importance of the all-encompassing fictional worlds in which millions of people dwell when they play video games for countless hours. Kruse's reflection also reminds us that video games are the most commercially successful art form of the twenty-first century. Specifically, he probes the complicated relationship between these virtual universes in which some individuals are immersed during nearly every waking moment and external reality.

Regardless of whether one accepts or rejects the theory of hyperreality, people all around the planet are undoubtedly renegotiating their sense of Self through cultural technologies. The force of what Alberto Romele refers to as "emagination" has expanded our identity in unprecedented ways.[117] For avid video gamers, an avatar is an extension of the human body permitting us to redefine the parameters of our inner self in a non-Euclidian space. In a recent interview with Hans Ulrich Obrist, Serres argues, "inside the space that is the Internet there exists a law that has nothing to do with the law that organizes the space we previously lived in."[118] According to Serres, living in a different space changes everything entirely. Additionally, Serres identifies virtual technology as one of the greatest forms of exo-Darwinian ingenuity that our species has ever created. As Alan Schrift notes, Serres contends that the process of exo-Darwinian evolution, which now allows us to control certain aspects of our evolutionary destiny, began with the invention of the first tools by our human ancestors.[119] An avatar is an example of a highly-sophisticated type

---

115   Gillespie, Corti, Evans, and Heasman, "Imagining the Self Through Cultural Technologies," 309.

116   Gillespie, Corti, Evans, and Heasman, "Imagining the Self Through Cultural Technologies," 310.

117   Alberto Romele, "Imaginative Machines," *Techné: Research in Philosophy and Technology* 22, no. 1 (2018): 104.

118   Hans Obrist, "Michel Serres," *032C* 25 (Winter 2013–2014): 120.

119   Alan Schrift, *Poststructuralism and Critical Theory's Second Generation* (New York: Routledge, 2004), 193.

of exo-Darwinian innovation that extends human capabilities. Millions of gamers are redefining what it means to be human in simulated worlds experienced in real time that transform "our possible selves into real selves" in another space that is governed by different laws and constraints.[120] It is once again the artistic imagination mediated through technological devices that is leading the way for this social transformation.

In Chapter 26, Renee Conroy's reflections about kinesthetic imagination and dance appreciation illustrate that art-world games of make-believe have always been a lens through which we can (re-) envision aspects of our inner selves that are often overlooked in addition to probing new possibilities well before the birth of the digital age. It is important to note that cultural artefacts like avatars are an extension of human corporality as opposed to being a replacement for it. Without the entire body and the information that our brain interprets through our senses, there would be no imagination of which to speak at all. For this reason, researchers in the fields of Theater and Performance Studies and Sensory Studies posit that "the knowing body" is a conduit for knowledge acquisition that is connected to our stable sense of Self.[121] As Ana Deligiannis theorizes, "the body and imagination operate as pathways of knowledge through the use of movement as active imagination."[122] Instead of being mistrustful of our sensorial faculties, the concept of the "somatic imagination" implores us to hone our senses to their full potential.[123]

Numerous Serres scholars including Ian Tucker, William Paulson, and Nicholas Chare[124] have observed that the *somatic imagination* takes the shape of a "sensual journey"[125] in the philosopher's diverse *œuvre* that urges us to "feel, touch, taste, and see the world."[126] For Serres, "the somatic encounter with a

---

120 Gillespie, Corti, Evans, and Heasman, "Imagining the Self Through Cultural Technologies," 316.
121 Julia Gray, and Pia Kontos, "An Aesthetic of Relationality: Embodiment, Imagination, and the Necessity of Playing the Fool in Research-Informed Theater," *Qualitative Inquiry* 24, no. 7 (2018): 441.
122 Ana Deligiannis, "Imagining with the Body in Analytical Psychology. Movement as Active Imagination: An Interdisciplinary Perspective from Philosophy and Neuroscience," *The Journal of Analytical Psychology* 63, no. 2 (2018): 166.
123 Hiie Saumaa, "Annie Payson Call's Training in Release and Somatic Imagination," *Dance Research Journal* 49, no. 1 (2017): 70–86.
124 Ian Tucker, "Sense and the Limits of Knowledge: Bodily Connections in the Work of Serres," *Theory Culture Society* 28, no. 1 (2011): 149–60; William Paulson, "Writing that Matters," *SubStance* 83 (1997): 22–36; Nicholas Chare, "Pressing the Flesh," *Parallax* 18, no. 2 (2012): 95–99.
125 Ian Tucker, "Sense and the Limits of Knowledge," 158.
126 Tucker, "Sense and The Limits of Knowledge," 150.

INTRODUCTION 23

turbulent, physical world" is a philosophical exercise linked to the process of knowledge formation.[127] In his groundbreaking essay *The Five Senses*, which has become a seminal text in Sensory Studies, Serres provocatively poses the following question: "What if philosophy came to us from the senses?"[128] In *Variations on the Body*, published seventeen years after *The Five Senses*, he further develops his theories connected to the *somatic imagination*. After thanking his physical education teachers and athletic coaches for helping him learn how to sharpen his sensorial faculties in his youth, Serres declares, "The origin of knowledge resides in the body ... We don't know anyone or anything until the body takes on its form, its appearance, its movement, its *habitus*, until the body joins in a dance with its demeanor."[129] Although Serres is evidently being lyrical, this section of the book is one of the many passages in which he pinpoints dancers, mimes, clowns, and artisans as artists who know how to train their body and mind. Rejecting mind-body dualism, Serres promotes dancing as an art form that is laden with philosophical value due to our "embodied condition."[130] Similarly, Conroy's essay encourages us to take dance seriously as a type of *somatic imagination* that warrants more attention in academic circles.

As briefly mentioned earlier, the final theoretical section of the volume reflects the kind of ecologized thinking for which Morin advocates by expanding the conversation to include non-Western perspectives regarding various kinds of imagination. Similar to how scholars have only scratched the surface of the notion of the *somatic imagination*, Arindham Chakrabarti, Yangping Gao, Amy Lee, and Ali Hussain explore fundamental differences related to how the social imaginary is (re-) created, shared, preserved, and continually reconstructed in Arabic, Indian, Chinese, and Japanese culture through art. In spite of his aforementioned efforts to nuance the dominant metanarratives linked to the *gendered imagination*, which he convincingly claims are too *phallogentric*, Derrida ignited a polemical controversy during a visit to China in 2001. Much to the bewilderment of a stunned audience, Derrida declared, "China does not have any philosophy ... only thought."[131] As a maverick philosopher who spearheaded the fight against ethnocentrism and logocentrism for decades, it is debatable exactly what Derrida meant by this surprising statement. Nonetheless, as

---

127 William Paulson, "Writing that Matters," *SubStance* 83 (1997): 24.
128 Michel Serres, *Les cinq sens* (Paris: Grasset, 1985), 211.
129 Michel Serres, *Variations on the Body*, trans. Randolph Burks (Minneapolis, MN: Univocal Publishing, 2012), 70–71.
130 Deligiannis, Ana. "Imagining with the Body in Analytical Psychology," 168.
131 Carine Defoort, and Ge Zhaoguang, "Editors' Introduction," *Contemporary Chinese Thought* 37, no. 1 (2005): 3.

Sean Meighoo highlights, it is possible that even Derrida could not rid himself of Western bias completely.[132]

In *Taking Back Philosophy: A Multicultural Manifesto*, Bryan van Norden argues that "philosophical ideas from outside this [Western] tradition are largely undervalued or overlooked, if not outright ignored."[133] Although several influential academic studies have generated a renewed interest in imagination in the twenty-first century, this eurocentrism is evident in many of these recent projects as well. Consequently, the final portion of this book is merely a starting point for highlighting the contributions of other philosophical and artistic traditions to the study of imagination. In Chapter 30, Yangping Gao explains how the deep respect that many Chinese people have for stones and rocks finds its origins in Daoist philosophy. As opposed to being indicative of a type of meaningless reverie, Gao contends that "ecological imaginings" in traditional Chinese culture, including the imagination of rocks, reflect a coherent biocentric worldview.[134] Defending the richness of Chinese spiritual and philosophical paradigms, Gao demonstrates that the reverence for rocks in Chinese society is a metonymical reflection of what Gaston Bachelard referred to as the "imagination of matter" that deserves more critical attention.

In her investigation of contemporary Japanese literary narratives written by three authors representing vastly different genres and writing styles, Amy Lee also underscores the singularity of the Japanese imagination. Lee explains that Japanese products of the imagination are epitomized by a fusion of ancient and modern customs that is unique to this island nation. Compared to other civilizations in which only a few faint traces of ancient traditions remain, Lee maintains that the artistic imagination is one of the main counter-hegemonic tools for resisting what the Indian theorist Vandana Shiva terms "monocultures of the mind."[135] Counterpointing "the distant gaze of the globalising dominant system" and the alleged universality of Western values with a hybrid mix of the ancient and modern, Japanese artists struggle to fend off the nefarious effects of cultural imperialism.[136]

In his essay examining the concept of "fun" itself in Indian aesthetics, Arindam Chakrabarti also notes the pervasive influence of American-style globalization that has been exported to all corners of the planet. As a testament to

---

132   Sean Meighoo, "Derrida's Chinese Prejudice," *Cultural Critique* 68 (2008): 163–209.

133   Jessica Logue, "Review of Bryan W. Van Norden's 'Taking Back Philosophy,'" *Essays in Philosophy* 19, no. 2 (2018): 2.

134   James Smith, "New Bachelards? Reveries, Elements and Twenty-First Century Materialism," *Altre Modernità* (2012): 164.

135   Vandana Shiva, "Monocultures of the Mind," *The Trumpeter* 10, no. 4 (1993): 1–11.

136   Shiva, "Monocultures of the Mind," 2.

INTRODUCTION

how this monolithic model has encroached upon all facets of traditional cultures, Chakrabarti laments how American forms of entertainment dominate the contemporary global landscape. Building upon the theories that Neil Postman develops in *Amusing Ourselves to Death*,[137] Chakrabarti discusses the impact of what Morin refers to as "a monoculture subjected to the hazards of the global market" characterized by the omnipresent entertainment industry.[138] This vision of what constitutes "fun" "is blind to the cultural riches of archaic societies" whose social imaginary is being withered away by hegemonic, monocultural forces.[139]

Chapter 32 represents a different kind of intellectual myopia that has traditionally prevented any sort of meaningful dialogue concerning the similarities and differences between the Christian and Muslim imagination. Given that "language and religion have been the central instrument in the emergence and identity of a culture," several researchers such as Alamghir Hashmi, James Morris, and Faisal Devji[140] have started to fill this research gap that is a byproduct of eurocentrism.[141] Just as certain core beliefs have shaped and sustained the collective imagination of the Christian community around the world, Hussain elucidates how the main tenets of Islam are closely tied to the (re-) construction of the social imaginary in Muslim societies. Additionally, Hussain's explanation of the essential role that imagination plays in Sufism reveals noteworthy distinctions between this mystical branch of Islam and other schools of Muslim thought.

In summary, the diversity of the forms of imagination outlined throughout this transdisciplinary collection suggests that the study of imagination has a very promising future within academia as a whole. Regardless of the theoretical approaches for investigating the imagination that a given scholar prefers, *Imagination and Art: Explorations in Contemporary Theory* has demonstrated that this inexhaustible field of inquiry is a serious academic venture that should

---

137   Neil Postman, *Amusing Ourselves to Death: Public Discourse in the Age of Show Business* (London: Penguin Books, 2005).

138   Edgar Morin, and Anne Brigitte Kern, *Homeland Earth*, trans. Sean M. Kelly, and Roger LaPointe (Cresskill, NJ: Hampton Press, 1999), 60.

139   Morin and Kern, *Homeland Earth*, 60.

140   Alamgir Hashmi, *The Worlds of Muslim Imagination* (Islamabad: Gulmohar, 1986); James Morris, "Imaging Islam: Intellect and Imagination in Islamic Philosophy, Poetry, and Painting," *Religion and the Arts* 12, no. 1 (2008): 294–318; Faisal Devji, "India in the Muslim Imagination: Cartography and Landscape in 19th Century Urdu Literature," *South Asia Multidisciplinary Academic Journal* (2014): n. pag., http://journals.openedition.org/samaj/3751.

141   Ananta Sukla, "Oriya Culture: Legitimacy and Identity," *Journal of Comparative Literature and Aesthetics* 30, no. 1–2 (2007): 5.

take center stage instead of hiding in the shadows. Moreover, the concept of the social imaginary reminds us that when the world in which we live becomes increasingly problematic to the point of falling prey to "deadly identities" that denigrate the Other or destroy the planet that we call home, it is time to *imagine* new possibilities. As Richard Rorty and Maxine Greene assert, the values that undergird human civilizations are not written in stone for all of eternity. In the face of far-right nationalism, xenophobia, obscurantism, and overt racism that have once again infiltrated the political imaginary in the United States and abroad, it is worth remembering that our collective sense of Self can be reconstituted in a more positive way. Furthermore, it is often through art that the *stories-we-live-by* are modified leading to an expanded identity. In the words of the iconic British singer-songwriter John Lennon, our ability to evolve as a society is largely determined by our capacity to *imagine* the world of tomorrow and to attempt to realize it. Given that we are imaginative beings, Rorty asserts that "the only source of redemption is the human imagination."[142] He concludes "that this fact should occasion pride rather than despair."[143] By virtue of our imagination, we truly hold the key to our own future. The only question is: which door will we choose to unlock in the coming years?

References

Albright, Daniel. *Beckett and Aesthetics*. Cambridge: Cambridge University Press. 2003.

Arana, Andrew. "Imagination in Mathematics." In *The Routledge Handbook of Philosophy of Imagination*, edited by Amy Kind, 463–77. London and New York: Routledge, 2016.

Asgarally, Issa. *L'interculturel ou la guerre*. Port-Louis, Mauritius: MSM. 2005.

Baudart, Anne. "Le philosophe-tisserand: paganisme et christianisme." In *Michel Serres, Cahiers de l'Herne*, edited by François L'Yvonnet, and Christiane Frémont, 251–60. Paris: Herne, 2010.

Baudrillard, Jean. *Seduction*. Translated by Brian Singer. New York: St. Martin's Press. 1990.

Baudrillard, Jean. *The Consumer Society*. Translated by George Ritzer. London: Sage, 1998.

---

142 Richard Rorty, "The Decline of Redemptive Truth and the Rise of a Literary Culture," *Studia Universitatis Babes Bolyai - Studia Europaea* 1, no. 46 (2001): 29.

143 Rorty, "The Decline of Redemptive Truth," 29.

Baudrillard, Jean. *The Intelligence of Evil*. Translated by Chris Turner. New York: Berg. 2005.

Baudrillard, Jean. *The Perfect Crime*. Translated by Chris Turner. New York: Verso. 2008.

Berto, Francesco, and Tom Schoonen, "Conceivability and Possibility: Some Dilemmas for Humeans." *Synthese* 195, no. 6 (2018): 2697–715.

Burney, Shehla. *Pedagogy of the Other: Edward Said, Postcolonial Theory, and Strategies for Critique*. New York: Peter Lang. 2012.

Campos, Daniel. "Peirce's Philosophy of Mathematical Education: Fostering Reasoning Abilities for Mathematical Inquiry." *Studies in Philosophy and Education* 29, no. 5 (2010): 421–39.

Casey, Edward. *Imagining: A Phenomenological Study*. Bloomington, IN: Indiana University Press. 1979.

Chare, Nicholas. "Pressing the Flesh." *Parallax* 18, no. 2 (2012): 95–99.

Cohen, Lizabeth. *A Consumers' Republic: The Politics of Mass Consumption in Postwar America*. New York: Vintage Books. 2003.

De Cruz, Helen, and Johan de Smedt, "Science as Structured Imagination." *Journal of Creative Behavior* 44, no. 1 (2010): 29–44.

Defoort, Carine, and Ge Zhaoguang. "Editors' Introduction." *Contemporary Chinese Thought* 37, no. 1 (2005): 3–10.

Deligiannis, Ana. "Imagining with the Body in Analytical Psychology. Movement as Active Imagination: An Interdisciplinary Perspective from Philosophy and Neuroscience." *The Journal of Analytical Psychology* 63, no. 2 (2018): 166–85.

Dely, Carole. "Jacques Derrida: The 'Perchance' of a Coming of the Otherwoman." *Sens Public* (October 2007): n. pag., http://sens-public.org/article312.html?lang=fr#.

Derrida, Jacques. *The Animal That Therefore I Am*. Translated by David Wills. Fordham, NY: Fordham University Press. 2008.

Derrida, Jacques. *The Beast and the Sovereign*. Vol. 1. Translated by Geoffrey Bennington. Chicago: Chicago University Press. 2011.

Devji, Faisal. "India in the Muslim Imagination: Cartography and Landscape in 19th Century Urdu Literature." *South Asia Multidisciplinary Academic Journal* (2014): n. pag., http://journals.openedition.org/samaj/3751.

Dodd, Julian. "What "4'33" Is." *Australasian Journal of Philosophy* 96, no. 4 (2017): 629–41.

Downie, Robin. "Science and the Imagination in the Age of Reason." *Journal of Medical Ethics and Medical Humanities* 27 (2001): 58–63.

Duncanson-Hales, Christopher. "Dread Hermeneutics: Paul Ricœur and the Productive Imagination." *Black Theology* 15, no. 2 (2017): 156–75.

Farkašová, Etela. "Poly(con)textuality of the Photographic Image." *Human Affairs* 1 (2005): 12–21.

Fielding, James. "An Aesthetics of the Ordinary: Wittgenstein and John Cage." *The Journal of Aesthetics and Art Criticism* 72, no. 2 (2014): 157–67.

Friedlander, Eli. "Walter Benjamin on Photography and Fantasy." *Critical Horizons* 18, no. 4 (2017): 295–306.

Gallagher, Michael Paul. "Theology and Imagination: From Theory to Practice." *Christian Higher Education* 5 (2006): 83–96.

Gillespie, Alex, Kevin Corti, Simon Evans, and Brett Heasman. "Imagining the Self Through Cultural Technologies." In *Handbook of Imagination and Culture*, edited by Tania Zittoun, and Vlad Glaveanu, 301–18. Oxford: Oxford University Press. 2017.

Glaveanu, Vlad, Maciej Karwowski, Dorota Jankowska, and Constance de Saint-Laurent. "Creative Imagination." In *Handbook of Imagination and Culture*, edited by Tania Zittoun, and Vlad Glaveanu, 61–86. Oxford: Oxford University Press. 2017.

Grant, Edward. "How Theology, Imagination, and the Spirit of Inquiry Shaped Natural Philosophy in the Late Middle Ages." *History of Science* 49, no. 1 (2011): 89–108.

Gray, Julia, and Pia Kontos. "An Aesthetic of Relationality: Embodiment, Imagination, and the Necessity of Playing the Fool in Research-Informed Theater." *Qualitative Inquiry* 24, no. 7 (2018): 440–52.

Guyotte, Kelly. "Aesthetic Movements of a Social Imagination: Refusing Stasis and Educating Relationally/Critically/Responsibly." *Critical Questions in Education* 9, no. 1 (2018): 62–73.

Hall, Stuart. *The West and the Rest: Discourse and Power*. Cambridge: Polity Press. 1992.

Hashmi, Alamgir. *The Worlds of Muslim Imagination*. Islamabad: Gulmohar. 1986.

Holt, Lynn. *Apprehension: Reason in the Absence of Rules*. London: Ashgate. 2002.

Honeycutt, Kevin. "The Musical Philosophy of Bertrand de Jouvenel." *The Review of Politics* 79, no. 3 (2017): 389–412.

Ichino, Anna. "Imagination and Belief in Action." *Philosophia* (2018): 1–19. https://doi .org/10.1007/s11406-019-00067-7.

Kind, Amy. "How Imagination Gives Rise to Knowledge." In *Perceptual Imagination and Perceptual Memory*, edited by Fiona Macpherson, and Fabian Dorsch, 227–46. Oxford: Oxford University Press, 2018.

Kind, Amy. "Imagining Under Constraints." In *Knowledge Through Imagination*, edited by Amy Kind and Peter Kung, 145–59. Oxford: Oxford University Press, 2016.

Kind, Amy, ed. *The Routledge Handbook of Philosophy of Imagination*. London and New York: Routledge. 2016.

Lara, Maria. "Richard Rorty: Becoming a Contemporary Political Philosopher." *Contemporary Pragmatism* 11, no. 1 (2014): 69–82.

Lévy, Sydney. "Introduction: An Ecology of Knowledge: Michel Serres." *SubStance* 26, no. 2 (1997): 3–5.

Leach, Belinda. "Agency and the Gendered Imagination: Women's Actions and Local Culture in Steelworker Families." *Identities: Global Studies in Culture and Power* 12, no. 1 (2005): 1–22.

Lennon, Kathleen. *Imagination and the Imaginary*. New York and London: Routledge. 2015.

Liao, Shen-yi, Nina Strohminger, and Chandra Sekhar Sripada. "Empirically Investigating Imaginative Resistance." *British Journal of Aesthetics* 54, no. 3 (2014): 339–55.

Logue, Jessica. "Review of Bryan W. Van Norden's 'Taking Back Philosophy.'" *Essays in Philosophy* 19, no. 2 (2018): 1–4.

Maalouf, Amin. *Les identités meurtrières*. Paris: Grasset. 1998.

Meighoo, Sean. "Derrida's Chinese Prejudice." *Cultural Critique* 68 (2008): 163–209.

Mitchell, Robert. "Can Animals Imagine?" In *The Routledge Handbook of Philosophy of Imagination*, edited by Amy Kind, 326–38. London and New York: Routledge, v2016.

Mohammed, Patricia. *Gendered Realities: Essays in Caribbean Feminist Thought*. Kingston, Jamaica: The University of the West Indies Press. 2002.

Moran, Dermot. "Beckett and Philosophy." In *Samuel Beckett-One Hundred Years*, edited by Christopher Murray, 93–110. Dublin: New Island Press, 2006.

Morin, Edgar. *La Méthode*. Tome 2, *La vie de la vie*. Paris: Points. 2014.

Morin, Edgar. *The Stars*. Translated by Richard Howard. Minneapolis, MN: University of Minnesota Press. 2005.

Morris, James. "Imaging Islam: Intellect and Imagination in Islamic Philosophy, Poetry, and Painting." *Religion and the Arts* 12, no. 1 (2008): 294–318.

Moser, Keith. *The Encyclopedic Philosophy of Michel Serres: Writing the Modern World and Anticipating the Future*. Augusta, GA: Anaphora Literary Press. 2016.

Müller, Martin. "In Search of the Global East: Thinking Between North and South." *Geopolitics* (October 2018): 1–22. https://doi.org/10.1080/14650045.2018.1477757.

Norton, David. "Philosophy and Imagination." *The Centennial Review* 12, no. 4 (1968): 392–414.

Obrist, Hans. "Michel Serres." *032C* 25 (Winter 2013–2014): 119–23.

Paulson, William. "Writing that Matters." *SubStance* 83 (1997): 22–36.

Pelaprat, Etienne, and Michael Cole. "'Minding the Gap': Imagination, Creativity and Human Cognition." *Integrative Psychological Behavior* 45, no. 4 (2011): 397–418.

Pick, Anat. "Animal Life in the Cinematic Umwelt." In *Animal Life and the Moving Image*, edited by Michael Lawrence, and Laura McMahon, 221–37. London: Bloomsbury, 2015.

Porter, Roy. *The Greatest Benefit to Mankind: A Medical History of Humanity*. New York: W.W. Norton & Company. 1999.

Postman, Neil. *Amusing Ourselves to Death: Public Discourse in the Age of Show Business*. London: Penguin Books. 2005.

Remy, Michel. "Le miroir du silence: Essai sur la problématique de la représentation dans 4'33" de John Cage." *Cycnos* 20, no. 2 (2003): n. pag., http://revel.unice.fr/cycnos/index.html?id=80.

Retallack, Joan. "Poethics of a Complex Realism." In *The Poethical Wager*, edited by Joan Retallack, 196–221. Berkeley: University of California Press, 2004.

Retallack, Joan. "Poethics of a Complex Realism." In *John Cage: Composed in America*, edited by Marjorie Perloff and Charles Junkerman, 242–73. Chicago: University of Chicago Press, 1994.

Romele, Alberto. "Imaginative Machines." *Techné: Research in Philosophy and Technology* 22, no. 1 (2018): 98–125.

Rorty, Richard. "The Decline of Redemptive Truth and the Rise of a Literary Culture." *Studia Universitatis Babes-Bolyai - Studia Europaea* 1, no. 46 (2001): 19–36.

Ryan, Jordan. "Jesus at the Crossroads of Inference and Imagination." *Journal for the Study of the Historical Jesus* 13, no. 1 (2015): 66–89.

Sallis, John. *Force of Imagination: The Sense of the Elemental*. Bloomington, IN: Indiana University Press. 2000.

Sansom, Dennis. "Can Irony Enrich the Aesthetic Imagination?: Why Søren Kierkegaard's Explanation of Irony Is Better Than Richard Rorty's." *The Journal of Aesthetic Education* 51, no. 2 (2017): 17–32.

Saumaa, Hiie. "Annie Payson Call's Training in Release and Somatic Imagination." *Dance Research Journal* 49, no. 1 (2017): 70–86.

Schrift, Alan. *Poststructuralism and Critical Theory's Second Generation*. New York: Routledge. 2004.

Scruton, Roger. *Art and Imagination: A Study in the Philosophy of Mind*. South Bend, IN: St. Augustine's Press. 2015.

Serres, Michel. *Atlas*. Paris: Flammarion. 1994.

Serres, Michel. *Les cinq sens*. Paris: Grasset. 1985.

Serres, Michel. *Musique*. Paris: Le Pommier. 2011.

Serres, Michel. *Variations on the Body*. Translated by Randolph Burks. Minneapolis, MN: Univocal Publishing. 2012.

Serres, Michel. *Yeux*. Paris: Le Pommier. 2014.

Shiva, Vandana. "Monocultures of the Mind." *The Trumpeter* 10, no. 4 (1993): 1–11.

Sinhababu, Neil. "Imagination and Belief." In *The Routledge Handbook of Philosophy of Imagination*, edited by Amy Kind, 111–23. London and New York: Routledge, 2016.

Smid, Deanna. *The Imagination in Early Modern English Literature*. Leiden: Brill. 2017.

Smith, James. "New Bachelards? Reveries, Elements and Twenty-First Century Materialism." *Altre Modernità* (2012): 156–67.

Stibbe, Arran. *Ecolinguistics: Language, Ecology, and the Stories We Live by*. London and New York: Routledge. 2015.

Sukla, Ananta. "Oriya Culture: Legitimacy and Identity." *Journal of Comparative Literature and Aesthetics* 30, no. 1–2 (2007): 9–19.

Toon, Adam. "Imagination in Scientific Modeling." In *The Routledge Handbook of Philosophy of Imagination*, edited by Amy Kind, 451–62. London and New York: Routledge, 2016.

INTRODUCTION

Toon, Adam. *Models as Make-Believe: Imagination, Fiction and Scientific Representation*. Basingstoke, UK: Palgrave Macmillan. 2012.

Tucker, Ian. "Sense and the Limits of Knowledge: Bodily Connections in the Work of Serres." *Theory Culture Society* 28, no. 1 (2011): 149–60.

Turner, Lynn. "Telefoam: Species on the Shores of Cixous and Derrida." *European Journal of English Studies* 18, no. 2 (2014): 158–71.

Vass, Eva. "Musical Co-creativity and Learning in the Kokas Pedagogy: Polyphony of Movement and Imagination." *Thinking Skills and Creativity* 31 (2019): 179–97.

Wall, John. "'L'au-delà du dehors-dedans': Paradox, Space, and Movement in Beckett." In *Early Modern Beckett/Beckett Et Le Debut de L'Ere Moderne: Beckett Between/Beckett Entre Deux*, edited by Angela Moorjani, Danielle de Ruyter, and Dúnlaith Bird, 307–20. Amsterdam: Rodopi, 2012.

Weslting, Louise. *The Logos of the Living World Merleau-Ponty, Animals, and Language*. New York: Fordham University Press. 2013.

Wheeler, Wendy. "The book of Nature: Biosemiotics and the Evolution of Literature." In *The Evolution of Literature: Legacies of Darwin in European Cultures*, edited by Nicholas Saul and Simon James, 171–84. Amsterdam: Rodopi, 2011.

Wright, Jonathan. "Imagination and Event in Uexküll and Bazin." Unpublished manuscript, 2019, typescript, https://www.academia.edu/38644818/Imagination_and_Event_in_Uexk%C3%BCll_and_Bazin.

Yar, Majid. *The Cultural Imaginary of the Internet: Virtual Utopias and Dystopias*. Basingstoke, UK: Palgrave Macmillan. 2014.

Zittoun, Tania, and Vlad Glaveanu, eds. *Handbook of Imagination and Culture*. Oxford: Oxford University Press. 2017.

PART 1

Historical Imagination and Judgement

∴

CHAPTER 1

Imagination and Art in Classical Greece and Rome

David Konstan

In the middle of the second century AD, Lucian, a sophisticated comic story-teller and satirist who hailed from Syria but wrote in excellent classical Greek, composed a short tale called *The True History*.[1] In it he narrates how he, that is, the narrator's persona, sailed with some companions through the Pillars of Hercules (the Strait of Gibraltar) and into the Western Ocean. After being driven astray by a storm, they arrive at a strange island with rivers of wine and other marvels. From here a whirlwind snatches them up and carries them to the moon, where they find themselves involved in a war between the kings of the Moon and Sun, with armies of all sorts of weird creatures. Back on Earth, the men are swallowed by an enormous whale, inside which are whole populations. After passing a sea of milk and an island made of cheese, they reach the Isle of the Blessed, where they meet the heroes of the Trojan War and Homer himself, along with Herodotus, whom Cicero dubbed the "father of history" but whom Lucian regards as a bare-faced liar or teller of tall tales in his *Histories*. On the way back they stop off at Calypso's island – the goddess who had promised Odysseus immortality in the *Odyssey*, though he refused and chose to return to his wife Penelope, even though she would age and lose her beauty. As Lucian tells it, Odysseus repented afterwards and sends Circe a note explaining that he now would like to take her up on her offer. They sail around the Ocean, which is conceived of as a river running round the entire land mass of the world, and even discover a remote continent, at which point the tale ends.

---

1 For good discussions of Lucian's art, see J. Bompaire, *Lucien écrivain: imitation et création* (Paris: E. de Boccard, 1958); Graham Anderson, *Studies in Lucian's Comic Fiction* (Leiden: E.J. Brill, 1976 = *Mnemosyne* supplement 43); Jennifer A. Hall, *Lucian's Satire* (New York: Arno Press, 1981); Bracht Branham, *Unruly Eloquence: Lucian and the Comedy of Traditions* (Cambridge, MA: Harvard University Press, 1989); Alain Billault, ed., *Lucien de Samosate* (Lyons: Centre d'Études Romaines et Gallo-Romaines, 1991); Aristoula Georgiadou and David J. Larmour, "Lucian and Historiography: *De historia conscribenda* and *Verae historiae*," in W. Haase, ed., *Aufstieg und Niedergang der römischen Welt* II.34.2 (Berlin: Walter de Gruyter, 1994), 1448–509; Massimo Fusillo, "The Mirror of the Moon: Lucian's A True Story – From Satire to Utopia," in Simon Swain, ed., *Oxford Readings in the Greek Novel* (Oxford: Oxford University Press, 1999), 351–81; Tim Whitmarsh, *Greek Literature and the Roman Empire: The Politics of Imitation* (Oxford: Oxford University Press, 2001).

The story has been called the earliest surviving example of science fiction.[2] It is certainly a tale filled with marvels, and belongs to a genre that was well known in antiquity, in which strange adventures were reported, including travels in remote places where life forms differed radically from those with which we are familiar.[3] These were recognized as paradoxical, that is, contrary to expectation and for the most part absurd, though entertaining. They were what we would unhesitatingly call works of imagination. But did the Greeks and Romans recognize imagination in this sense, and regard such impossible accounts as products of a special faculty or capacity to visualize things that have never been experienced – what we might call fictional worlds, things that exist in the mind and are communicated in language but are understood not to be real? To put it differently, did they have a clear conception of what we call fantasy?

Imagination derives from a Latin word, *imago*, which means an "image" or, more concretely, a mask, for instance the kind that noble families preserved of deceased ancestors, and were true to life since they were effectively made from wax casts of the faces of renowned forbears. Fantasy, however, derives from a Greek word, *phantasia*, which in turn is a noun formed from the verb *phainomai* (cf. "phenomenon"), meaning "seem" or "appear." The notion of seeming might appear to contrast with being or truth: what merely seems to be the case may be false, and must be confirmed if it is to be believed. When philosophers got hold of the word, they gave it a variety of senses.[4] *Phantasia* meant what we

---

2 On Lucian and science fiction, See Aristoula Georgiadou and David H.J. Larmour, *Lucian's Science Fiction Novel, True Histories: Interpretation and Commentary* (Leiden: Brill, 1998 = *Mnemosyne* supplement 179).

3 On literature featuring marvelous, incredible, and paradoxical adventures, see Kai Brodersen, *Phlegon von Tralleis, Das Buch der Wunder und Zeugnisse seiner Wirkungsgeschichte* (Darmstadt: Wissenschaftliche Buchgesellschaft, 2002); A. Giannini, "Studi sulla paradossografia greca," *Acme* 17 (1964): 99–140; William F. Hansen, *Phlegon of Tralles' Book of Marvels* (Exeter: University of Exeter Press, 1996); G. Schepens, and K. Delcroix, "Ancient Paradoxography: Origin, Evolution, Production and Reception," in O. Pecere and A. Stramaglia, eds., *La letteratura di consumo nel mondo greco-latino* (Cassino: Università degli studi di Cassino, 1996) 373–460; the genre had an influence on the miracles recounted in saints' lives.

4 See especially Anne Sheppard, *The Poetics of Phantasia: Imagination in Ancient Aesthetics* (London: Bloomsbury, 2014). Sheppard deals in successive chapters with three aspects of *phantasia* in classical philosophy. First, *phantasia* implies visualization, the idea that writers or orators "bring before their eyes" what they describe and cause the reader effectively to see the event as though they were present at it; this aspect of ancient rhetoric is discussed below. See also Mireille Armisen, "La notion d'imagination chez les Anciens: I – Les philosophes," *Pallas* 26 (1979): 11–51, and "La notion d'imagination chez les Anciens: II – La rhétorique," *Pallas* 27 (1980) : 3–37. Sheppard goes on to examine the neo-Platonic tradition, in which the mind visualizes and understands abstract phenomena such as mathematical forms and

IMAGINATION AND ART IN CLASSICAL GREECE AND ROME   37

perceive – not sensation directly so much as the mental register of what we think we see or hear. A straight stick in water looks bent: it is not, in reality, but we see it that way – that is the sense of it that we have in our minds. We can summon up that visual impression (and many others) at a later time, and so *phantasia* has something to do with memory as well. Suppose that I call up in my mind an image of something that is not true, something that I perhaps saw in a dream the night before (although the Greeks normally spoke of seeing dreams, not things in a dream).[5] Ought we, then, to say that we have found the faculty we were seeking, and that *phantasia*, as the capacity to summon up images, whether true or false, is (at least in some of its uses) just what we call imagination?

Let us consider the case more closely. When I recollect having seen a stick that looked bent, though I either guessed or knew that it was not, I am summoning up in my mind a sense impression – just the way it looked at the time. The process of recalling is active, in the sense that it is something I do voluntarily (although of course certain stimuli may have reminded me of that stick and the occasion on which I saw it, and so to this extent my recollection has an external cause). But I am not modifying the impression I received then; I am simply reproducing it. True, I have the picture in my mind even though the object itself is absent; in this respect, we can say that I am imagining it rather than actually seeing it. But that is not what we mean by creative imagination, the kind of impossible things that Lucian described in his *True History*, which he had never seen and no one could ever see. Those episodes were

---

transcendental entities. The third chapter, in turn, examines *phantasia* in connection with divine inspiration. This is an important study, but does not touch primarily on the concept of literary imagination and creativity discussed in the present chapter. See also Stijn Bussels, *The Animated Image: Roman Theory on Naturalism, Vividness and Divine Power* (Leiden: Leiden University Press, 2012). For a detailed review of Bussels and Sheppard, see Karel Thein, "The Poetics of Mind and Matter: Some Remarks on Ancient Images and Imagination," *Eirene* 51 (2015): 303–34. For vividness in ancient rhetoric generally, and in particular in connection with descriptions of works of art, see Ruth Webb, *Ekphrasis, Imagination and Persuasion in Ancient Rhetorical Theory and Practice* (Farnham: Ashgate, 2009).

5   See David Shulman and Guy Stroumsa, "Introduction," in David Shulman and Guy Stroumsa, eds., *Dream Cultures: Explorations in the Comparative History of Dreaming* (Oxford: Oxford University Press, 1999), 3–15: "Although one should be careful not to draw direct analogies between linguistic patterns and religious perceptions, variation in the ontological status of dreams is also reflected in language. *Blepo oneiron* ("I see a dream," Greek), *halamti halom* ("I dreamt a dream," Hebrew), *es träumt mir/ich traume, je rêve*: these are very different ways, chosen almost at random, of referring to the simple act of dreaming" (p. 6; I am informed that the Chinese expression is "I make a dream"). On ancient dreams generally, see William V. Harris, *Dreams and Experience in Classical Antiquity* (Cambridge, MA: Harvard University Press, 2009).

concocted, it would seem, purely out of Lucian's intellect: they were utter fantasy, or what we might call the products of pure imagination (they were certainly not visualizations of transcendental or mystical realities, in the spirit of the neo-Platonists). Let us leave the philosophers aside, for a moment, with their reflections on how we process sense impressions and what happens when we recall something or, still more mysterious, dream of something. Lucian has created a world of his own, a world that announces itself as fictional, as fantastical, as absurd.

From the time of Aristotle, and indeed before him, art, whether pictorial or literary, was valued for its ability to represent reality as accurately as possible. The term employed in this connection was *mimêsis*, that is, the imitation or representation of an object in another medium. A good painting was faithful to what the subject of the painting looked like, and a good story represented correctly or truthfully the way the subject of the painting appeared. Greek art is famously realistic or naturalistic, and indeed, as Michael Squire has argued, the Greeks bequeathed to us our idea of what the body should and inevitably does look like.[6] Reality looks to us the way the Greek artists and sculptors represented it. We may presume that they too viewed their artistic works as corresponding closely to the world as they perceived it, not only in plastic media but also in narratives and on the stage. They recognized as realistic the heroes whose adventures were recounted in epic or dramatized in the theater, even if they were conscious of a certain exaggeration or elevation in their abilities (as Homer puts it, no two men today could lift the stone that Ajax hurled at Hector; *Iliad* 5.302–04). Yes, Achilles was uncannily powerful and Odysseus preternaturally clever and even devious, but the portraits of them that they found in Homer's *Iliad* and *Odyssey* showed in a fully plausible way how such exceptional men would behave in the situations in which they found themselves. Apart from a bit of amplification, which hardly requires a great deal of imagination, the poets depicted lifelike characters who acted as we would expect and indeed might ourselves act in comparable circumstances. Epic, tragedy, and comedy were exercises in imitation, not the kind of creative freedom in which Lucian indulged.

Mimesis, as Stephen Halliwell has brilliantly shown, had a complex signification in classical Greek, and I do not wish to reduce it to mere faithful

---

6   Michael Squire, *The Art of the Body: Antiquity and its Legacy* (Oxford: Oxford University Press, 2011): "like it or not – and there have been many reasons for not liking it – antiquity has supplied the mould for all subsequent attempts to figure and figure out the human body" (p. xi).

reproduction.[7] Besides, what was imitated, even on Aristotle's own theory, was not so much the actual features of an individual or the trajectory of a person's life, but a potentially universal pattern of experience, what Aristotle in the *Poetics* called a complete action with a beginning, middle, and end. Things do not necessarily come packaged so neatly in real life; the poet selects, arranges, discovers and communicates the essential patterns that are revealed in perfectly constructed stories – perfectly constructed not by the standards of narratology but as a fully realized *praxis* or action.[8] Surely this kind of mimesis is imaginative.

Well, yes and no. It takes insight to perceive the fundamental patterns that are played out in life, and talent to capture them in their most essential outline, as Aristotle prescribed; but insight, even genius of this sort, is not pure invention. The poet sees, captures, and reduces to the purest form what is out there in the world. The very word "invention" derives from a Latin word meaning "discover" or "come upon"; it denoted in classical Roman rhetoric the ability to select the tropes, quotations, and arguments best suited to make one's case.[9] The process that Aristotle envisages in the creation of a plot or *muthos*, which he called the soul of drama, is not a matter of fantasy but a distillation of how things really are, as seen, to be sure, by the sharpest of intellects or, to use a metaphor of which Plato was fond, by the mind's own eye, and one which, in the case of great poets and artists, has excellent vision. Poets are not purveyors of falsehoods; as Aristotle provocatively put it in his *Poetics*, poetry is more philosophical than history, for history simply records what has happened, but poetry, that is, narrative art, reveals the kinds of things that happen. It is, if anything, truer than history (*Poetics* 9.1451a38-b7).[10]

Very well: this is Aristotle's view, and other critics in antiquity too maintained that mimesis or imitation was the soul of art. What is called for in a poet is not imagination but a deeper or truer kind of perception. A good orator needed to recreate a scene so vividly that his auditors actually saw it – he had to

---

7   See Stephen Halliwell, *The Aesthetics of Mimesis: Ancient Texts and Modern Problems* (Princeton: Princeton University Press, 2002); see also David Konstan, *Beauty: The Transformations of an Ancient Greek Idea* (Oxford: Oxford University Press, 2014), Chapter 6.

8   See David Konstan, "In Defense of Croesus, or Suspense as an Aesthetic Emotion," *Aisthe* 3 (2008): 1–15, http://www.ifcs.ufrj.br/~aisthe/vol%20II/KONSTAN.pdf; reprinted in Fernando Santoro, Tatiana Ribeiro, and Henrique Cairus, eds., *Pathos: A Poética das Emoções* (Rio de Janeiro: Arquimedes Editora, 2009).

9   The key text is Cicero's youthful treatise, *De inventione*.

10 Cf. John M. Armstrong, "Aristotle on the Philosophical Nature of Poetry," *The Classical Quarterly* N.S. 48 (1998): 447–55; Silvia Carli, "Poetry is More Philosophical than History: Aristotle on *Mimêsis* and Form," *The Review of Metaphysics* 64 (2010): 303–36.

bring it before their eyes, as the expression went (*pro ommatôn* in Greek). Brilliant clarity was the objective, language so controlled and contrived as to erase the difference between hearing of an event and being an eye-witness. As Quintilian puts it: "The man who is really sensitive to such impressions will have the greatest power over the emotions ... And it is a power easily acquired ... I am complaining that a man has been murdered. Shall I not bring before my eyes all the circumstances, which, it is reasonable to imagine, must have occurred in such a connection? Shall I not see the assassin burst suddenly from his hiding-place, the victim tremble, cry for help, beg for mercy, or turn to run? Shall I not see the fatal blow delivered and the body fall? Will not the blood, the deathly pallor, the groan of agony, the death-rattle, be indelibly impressed upon my mind? From such impressions arises that *enargeia* which Cicero calls illumination and actuality, which makes us seem not so much to narrate as to exhibit the actual scene, while our emotions will be no less actively stirred than if we were present at the actual occurrence" (6.29–32, trans. H.E. Butler). The advantages of such a style in the courtroom or the assembly are obvious. But again, this is not imagination in the sense of creating a fictional world, a place that is not our ordinary reality but operates by its own rules – a product of the author's or the artist's own fantasy, in which the purpose of vivid illustration is not to recreate a plausible scene but rather to make one believe, for a moment, that one is seeing or participating in a world that is not ours.

This would seem to have been Lucian's intention in composing his *True History*: no reader would ever believe that any such thing had occurred, no one was fooled or taken in; this was strictly Lucian's own fantasy and nothing more. Yet this very distance on the part of the reader – not the willing suspension of disbelief but the sophisticated awareness that the story is utter nonsense and was never intended to be anything more – is anything but a way of participating in a fictional world. Readers in antiquity will have interpreted Lucian's tale not as a creatively imaginative composition but as a parody. Precisely by naming it *The True History*, Lucian has called attention to the fact that it is anything but true, of course; but at the same time, he situated his narrative within the genre of history. He took bits and pieces from the more preposterous myths and credulous beliefs of his time, like the existence of Hades or the Isles of the Blessed, and assembled them into a sequence that exposed their absurdity. Ancient fantasy did not seek to absorb the reader into the invented world, but to keep its artificial and purely constructed nature always in view. Still, the events that Lucian depicted might be regarded as an act of imagination on his part – the creation of a universe that seems governed by different laws than our own, however implausible it may seem.

We might counter that Lucian's strategy is not simply one of free invention but rather of manipulating traditional formulas and episodes according to a

IMAGINATION AND ART IN CLASSICAL GREECE AND ROME

few elementary rules. What ancient artists and critics valued was not free composition but rather skill, what the Greeks called *tekhnê* and the Romans called *ars*. In the war between the Sun and the Moon as described in the *True History*, Lucian seems to outdo himself in the creation of the weird creatures that compose the opposing armies, that of the Sun under the command of Phaethon, the son of Apollo, whereas Endymion, who, legend had it, had been snatched up by the goddess of the moon as her lover, leads the lunar forces. In the past, as Endymion explains to his Greek visitors, Phaethon countered a colonization attempt on Endymion's part with a battalion of Horse-Ants. But now Endymion, with the assistance of the Greeks, will launch his troops mounted on 80,000 vultures along with auxiliaries riding odd birds with vegetable wings. As Lucian writes (and it is worth citing his text *in extenso*):

> Endymion had also a contingent from the North of 30,000 Flea-archers and 50,000 Wind-coursers. The former have their name from the great fleas, each of the bulk of a dozen elephants, which they ride. The Wind-coursers are infantry, moving through the air without wings; they effect this by so girding their shirts, which reach to the ankle, that they hold the wind like a sail and propel their wearers ship-fashion. These troops are usually employed as skirmishers. 70,000 Ostrich-slingers and 50,000 Horse-cranes were said to be on their way from the stars over Cappadocia. But as they failed to arrive I did not actually see them; and a description from hearsay I am not prepared to give, as the marvels related of them put some strain on belief. Such was Endymion's force ... When the time came, the array was as follows: on the right were the Horse-vultures, and the King with the *élite* of his forces, including ourselves. The Salad-wings held the left, and in the centre were the various allies. The infantry were in round numbers 60,000,000; they were enabled to fall in thus: there are in the Moon great numbers of gigantic spiders, considerably larger than an average Aegean island; these were instructed to stretch webs across from the Moon to Lucifer ... On the enemy's side, Phaethon occupied the left with his Horse-ants; they are great winged animals resembling our ants except in size; but the largest of them would measure a couple of acres ... On their right was about an equal force of Sky-gnats –archers mounted on great gnats; and next them the Sky-pirouetters, light-armed infantry only, but of some military value; they slung monstrous radishes at long range, a wound from which was almost immediately fatal, turning to gangrene at once; they were supposed to anoint their missiles with mallow juice. Next came the Stalk-fungi, 10,000 heavy-armed troops for close quarters; the explanation of their name is that their shields are mushrooms, and their spears asparagus stalks. Their neighbours were the

Dog-acorns, Phaethon's contingent from Sirius. These were 5,000 in number, dog-faced men fighting on winged acorns.

trans. FOWLER and FOWLER

Lucian's technique is evident: make some things impossibly large, for instance fleas twelve times the size of elephants, which can thus be mounted by humans, spiders as large as islands, ants an acre or two in magnitude. Other items are simply harder than they are in nature: radishes that serve as lances, shields made of mushrooms, spears of asparagus: the shapes are appropriate to their function. The forces are arranged as armies regularly were in Rome, with infantry occupying the center, lighter troops serving as auxiliaries and using various kinds of weaponry, a battle line that would have been entirely familiar to Lucian's readers. Lucian has the gall to mention "70,000 Ostrich-slingers and 50,000 Horse-cranes" that failed to arrive in time, the existence of which he refuses to vouch for since they beggar belief – as though the other creatures were perfectly credible.

What Lucian has done, then, is to exaggerate or recombine familiar elements. How did they occur to him? Is his conception of such beings a matter of imagination, as imagination is conceived today? In her introduction to *The Routledge Handbook of Philosophy of Imagination* (2016), Amy Kind identifies "four basic claims about imagination that enjoy near universal agreement." These claims are: (1) that not every use of the word imagination signifies an act of imagination; (2) "Imagination is a primitive mental state type (or group of types), irreducible to other mental state types"; (3) imagination is intentional, that is, it is about or has an object (I imagine such and such); and (4) "Imagination is not constitutively constrained by truth," that is, it is speculative and not simply descriptive.[11] As Kind observes, philosophers differ on how imagining and conceiving are related (if they are), and on many other points. And we must be clear that Kind is not discussion precisely literary imagination here. But the areas of agreement that she specifies will suffice for our purposes here. In brief: imagining (in the relevant sense) is a specific mental state concerned with objects that need not correspond to something real or true.

Epicureanism, one of the major philosophical tendencies in classical antiquity, embraced a radical materialism. The universe consists of tiny particles of matter, called atoms, and void; everything else is simply one or another compound of these atoms in different arrangements. Perception was explained by way of very thin emanations or lamina (called *eidôla* or "idols" in Greek, and

---

11   Amy Kind, "Introduction: Exploring Imagination," in Amy Kind, ed., *The Routledge Handbook of Philosophy of Imagination* (New York: Routledge, 2016), 1–11.

IMAGINATION AND ART IN CLASSICAL GREECE AND ROME   43

simulacra in Latin), continually emitted by objects, that impinged directly on the senses, from which they were transmitted to the mental organ (located in the chest rather than in the head by Epicureans and likewise by Stoics). Just what the transmission process was is debated among scholars; either the sense impressions themselves or the impressions transmitted to the mind (or that reached the mind directly, in some cases) were sometimes called *phantasmata*, that is, appearances. These appearances, it must be emphasized, simply recorded the impression that the atomic images made. This is why Epicurus famously claimed that all sense impressions are true. We may go astray by drawing unwarranted conclusions from such impressions, for example, if we suppose that the stick in the water that looks bent to us is really crooked. But that is an addition of belief, as the Epicureans called it; if we limit ourselves to the proposition that the stick looks bent, we cannot go wrong, nor can the evidence of any other sense contradict this impression.

What, then, of our thoughts of creatures such as centaurs, half horse and half human, which do not and cannot exist, according to the Epicureans (the combination is biologically impossible). What are we doing when we think of centaurs, or giants, or for that matter immense ants or radishes as tough as lances? This would seem to be a case of *phantasia*, or imagination, in the modern sense of the term, a "primitive mental state type" that is "not constitutively constrained by truth." The Epicureans, however, would not have agreed. What we see (or think of) is true, even if no such creatures are to be found, or can conceivably be found, in the real world. Here is the exposition of Lucretius, the Roman poet, contemporary with Cicero and Julius Caesar, who expounded Epicurus' philosophy in Latin verse:

> Now mark, and hear what things move the mind, and learn in a few words whence the things which come into it do come. I say first of all, that idols of things wander about many in number in many ways in all directions round, extremely thin; and these when they meet, readily unite, like a cobweb or piece of gold-leaf. For these idols are far thinner in texture than those which take possession of the eyes and provoke vision; since these enter in through the porous parts of the body and stir the fine nature of the mind within and provoke sensation. Therefore we see Centaurs and limbs of Scyllas and Cerberus-like faces of dogs and idols of those who are dead, whose bones earth holds in its embrace; since idols of every kind are everywhere borne about, partly those which are spontaneously produced within the air, partly all those which withdraw from various things and those which are formed by compounding the shapes of these. For assuredly no image of Centaur is formed out of a live one,

since no such nature of living creature ever existed; but when images of a horse and a man have by chance come together, they readily adhere at once, as we said before, on account of their fine nature and thin texture. All other things of the kind are produced in like fashion.

4.726–48, trans. MUNRO[12]

Lucretius goes on to explain that some images that are very fine can impinge directly on the mind. This is what happens in sleep, save that, when we are in that state, we cannot discriminate between impressions that, while accurate, do not correspond to real objects in the world and those that do:

when sleep has prostrated the body, for no other reason does the mind's intelligence wake, except because the very same idols provoke our minds which provoke them when we are awake, and to such a degree that we seem without a doubt to perceive him whom life has left and death and earth gotten hold of. This nature constrains to come to pass because all the senses of the body are then hampered and at rest throughout the limbs and cannot refute the unreal by real things. Moreover memory is prostrate and relaxed in sleep and protests not that he has long been in the grasp of death and destruction whom the mind believes it sees alive.

4.757–67, trans. MUNRO

A dream of someone who has died or of a monstrous creature that cannot possibly exist is not dissimilar in principle from a waking perception of a perfectly

---

12 nunc age, quae moveant animum res accipe, et unde quae veniunt veniant in mentem percipe paucis. principio hoc dico, rerum simulacra vagari multa modis multis in cunctas undique partis tenvia, quae facile inter se iunguntur in auris, obvia cum veniunt, ut aranea bratteaque auri. quippe etenim multo magis haec sunt tenvia textu quam quae percipiunt oculos visumque lacessunt, corporis haec quoniam penetrant per rara cientque tenvem animi naturam intus sensumque lacessunt. Centauros itaque et Scyllarum membra videmus Cerbereasque canum facies simulacraque eorum quorum morte obita tellus amplectitur ossa; omnigenus quoniam passim simulacra feruntur, partim sponte sua quae fiunt aëre in ipso, partim quae variis ab rebus cumque recedunt et quae confiunt ex horum facta figuris. nam certe ex vivo Centauri non fit imago, nulla fuit quoniam talis natura animata; verum ubi equi atque hominis casu convenit imago, haerescit facile extemplo, quod diximus ante, propter subtilem naturam et tenvia texta. cetera de genere hoc eadem ratione creantur.

It is not an accident, I believe, that the final word, *creantur* ("are created") is an anagram of "Centaur," and suggests that such hybrids as Centaurs result from the rearrangement of elements (*elementa* in Latin signifies both atoms and letters). On this kind of punning in Lucretius, see the seminal article by Paul Friedländer, "The Pattern of Sound and Atomistic Theory in Lucretius," *American Journal of Philology* 62 (1941): 16–34.

real object: both are caused by idols or simulacra that impress the senses or the mind. The difference is that when we are awake we check the impression by what we know from experience to be true, and so do not draw false conclusions about the nature of the source of such images. We may call to mind a Centaur, but in doing so we are attending to an accidental combination of simulacra that produces something that we could never validate by a closer look: you can readily find horses and human beings and approach as near as you like, but you will never encounter a Centaur up close. The point, however, is that neither have you exercised a faculty or "mental state type" when perceiving such a creature: you have received a sense impression (or an impression directly on the mind) caused by a perfectly real impact of those films emitted by objects in the world, save that the films got a bit messed up in transmission (after all, they have to pass through air and meet other such films along the way). The process is exactly the same as recollecting people who have passed away: their simulacra too continue to float in the air (or perhaps, are stored somewhere in the mind, which is conceived as strictly physical), and we truly saw them. The only error would be the additional assumption that they continue to be alive.[13]

The Epicureans were obliged to be very inventive in accounting for such things as vision, given how strict a set of limitations they placed on explanatory principles: there were no noumenal items, no disembodied thoughts, none of the metaphysical apparatus favored by Plato and in a different way by Aristotle. But though their materialist account of vision, and more especially of dreams, hallucinations, and the ideas we have of monstrous and impossible creature, was both strained and particular to their school, they were not exceptional in treating impressions we may have of such items as analogous to perception rather than the product of a special faculty or mental state such as we consider imagination to be. As Deborah Modrak shows in her chapter on *phantasia* in the same volume edited by Amy Kind, we cannot force the Aristotelian concept into anything like an idea of imagination.[14] To return, then, to Lucian's wonderful fantasy, all that he described about those armies of the Sun and Moon, and that his readers brought to mind and even imagined that they saw as he so vividly described them, was not the result of his imagination, perfervid

---

13 There are many studies of Epicurean epistemology and the role of simulacra in sensation in thought. For a recent study that takes account of newly edited fragments of Epicurus' treatise, *On Nature*, Giuliana Leone, *Epicuro Sulla natura libro II* (Naples: Bibliopolis, 2012). For good general introductions to Epicurus' thought, see Tim O'Keefe, *Epicureanism* (Durham: Acumen, 2010), and Francesco Verde, *Epicuro* (Rome: Carocci, 2013).

14 Deborah K.W. Modrak, "Aristotle on *Phantasia*," in Amy Kind, ed., *The Routledge Handbook of Philosophy of Imagination* (New York: Routledge, 2016), 15–26.

or otherwise. Lucian had plucked out of the continual flow of simulacra in the world (as the Epicureans would have it) some odd combinations that corresponded to no real object (though they did to a mental object, we might say), and presented them in literary form. No special faculty was required.

In this essay, I have not attempted to come to grips with the classical philosophy of mind or perception, which is a very rich subject in itself. Nor have I tried to engage with the several types of ancient literary interpretation that we can to some extent recover from our lamentably fragmentary sources on this question. Rather, I hope to have shown that the category of imagination, as this is construed in modern philosophy and literary criticism, was not a part of the ancient vocabulary of mind. There are many reasons for this absence. But one of special relevance to literature may reside in the very different notion of reading that obtained in classical antiquity, at least in comparison with modern conceptions, in which we seem to enter a separate world of fiction, a dream-like space accessible to the imagination rather than the senses. In his influential book, *The Rise of the Novel*, Ian Watt (who situated the emergence of this new genre in 18th-century Britain), saw in Samuel Richardson, the author of *Pamela* and *Clarissa*, the prophet of a new way of writing and reading:

> his readers found in his novels the same complete engrossment of their inner feelings, and the same welcome withdrawal into an imaginary world vibrant with more intimately satisfying personal relationships than ordinary life provided, that they had afforded Richardson in the writing.... [C]easing to be conscious of the printed page before our eyes we surrender ourselves entirely to the world of illusion which the printed novel describes. This effect is heightened by the fact that we are usually alone when we read, and that the book, for the time being, becomes a kind of extension of our personal life.[15]

This is not, I believe, how ancient readers approached a text. Reading alone was disapproved of; people read together, and aloud (though silent reading was a possibility if circumstances required it).[16] What is more, they read

---

15 Ian Watt, *The Rise of the Novel: Studies in Defoe, Richardson and Fielding* (London: Chatto and Windus, 1957), 198. Cf. David Konstan, "The Active Reader in Classical Antiquity," *Argos: Revista de la Asociación Argentina de Estudios Clásicos* 30 (2006): 5–16; also, David Konstan, "'The Birth of the Reader': Plutarch as Literary Critic," *Scholia* 13 (2004): 3–27, Spanish version under the title, "'El nacimiento del lector': Plutarco como crítico literario," *Praesentia* 13 (2012), http://erevistas.saber.ula.ve/index.php/praesentia/article/view/4229.

16 Synesius, in a letter (154) describing the composition of his essay, *On Dreams*, describes how he was moved to write it by a vision, and that in two or three passages, he has the impression that he has become someone other than himself and one more among the

actively, and engaged with the text as though with an interlocutor. Such a reading practice did not lend itself to the kind of immersion in an imaginative universe described by Watt. Here is how the Christian bishop Synesius, who lived at the end of the fourth century, described his reading experience:

> Often, I prefer not to wait for the outcome of a book to derive some good from it, but I lift my eyes and wrestle with the writer, letting not a moment go by but giving myself over to the occasion, and, as if reading on, I string together from my own mind what I think follows, and then I test what is said against what is written. And I am frequently aware of having chanced upon the same thought and the same wording. It has also sometimes happened that I have hit the argument, and what may stray from the wording nevertheless very much approximates the harmoniousness of the composition. And even if the thought was different, it was still something suitable, at all events, to the man who created the book, and one of which he would not have disapproved if he had argued it.[17]

Allowing for the difference in genre between what was likely the good bishops reading materials – although we ought to recall that at least two of the five ancient Greek novels were ascribed to Christian prelates by ancient sources – Synesius' words give us a fairly good picture, I suggest, of how Lucian's readers would have received his text: they would have wrestled with the author, as it were, imagining his purpose and his technique and perhaps even attempting to anticipate his words before confirming that this was indeed what he had written. They would not have expected to experience that "welcome withdrawal into an imaginary world" that Ian Watt identified as the essence of novelistic pleasure.

References

Anderson, Graham. *Studies in Lucian's Comic Fiction*, Leiden: E.J. Brill, 1976 = *Mnemosyne* supplement 43.
Armisen, Mireille. "La notion d'imagination chez les Anciens: I – Les philosophes." *Pallas* 26 (1979): 11–51.

---

audience of his work (Ἔστι δὲ οὗ τῶν λόγων δίς που καὶ τρίς, ὥσπερ τις ἕτερος ὢν ἐμαυτοῦ γέγονα μετὰ τῶν παρόντων ἀκροατής). This is a fascinating indication of the degree to which a writer imagines his text as something performed; in suggesting that his work was somehow produced through him, by way of inspiration, he perceives himself not as reading his own work but hearing it.

17 *Dio* 18.1–5, my translation.

Armisen, Mireille. "La notion d'imagination chez les Anciens: II – La rhétorique." *Pallas* 27 (1980): 3–37.

Armstrong, John M. "Aristotle on the Philosophical Nature of Poetry." *The Classical Quarterly* N.S. 48 (1998): 447–55.

Billault, Alain, ed. *Lucien de Samosate*. Lyons: Centre d'Études Romaines et Gallo-Romaines, 1991.

Bompaire, J. *Lucien écrivain: imitation et creation*. Paris: E. de Boccard, 1958.

Branham, Bracht. *Unruly Eloquence: Lucian and the Comedy of Traditions*. Cambridge, MA: Harvard University Press, 1989.

Brodersen, Kai. *Phlegon von Tralleis, Das Buch der Wunder und Zeugnisse seiner Wirkungsgeschichte*. Darmstadt: Wissenschaftliche Buchgesellschaft, 2002.

Bussels, Stijn. *The Animated Image: Roman Theory on Naturalism, Vividness and Divine Power*. Leiden: Leiden University Press, 2012.

Carli, Silvia. "Poetry is More Philosophical than History: Aristotle on *Mimêsis* and Form." *The Review of Metaphysics* 64 (2010): 303–36.

Friedländer, Paul. "The Pattern of Sound and Atomistic Theory in Lucretius." *American Journal of Philology* 62 (1941): 16–34.

Fusillo, Massimo. "The Mirror of the Moon: Lucian's A True Story – From Satire to Utopia." In *Oxford Readings in the Greek Novel*, edited by Simon Swain, 351–58. Oxford: Oxford University Press, 1999.

Georgiadou, Aristoula and David J. Larmour. "Lucian and Historiography: *De historia conscribenda* and *Verae historiae*." In *Aufstieg und Niedergang der römischen Welt* II.34.2, edited by W. Haase, 1448–509. Berlin: Walter de Gruyter, 1994.

Georgiadou, Aristoula and David H.J. Larmour. *Lucian's Science Fiction Novel, True Histories: Interpretation and Commentary*. Leiden: Brill, 1998 = *Mnemosyne* supplement 179.

Giannini, A. "Studi sulla paradossografia greca." *Acme* 17 (1964): 99–140.

Hall, Jennifer A. *Lucian's Satire*, New York: Arno Press, 1981.

Halliwell, Stephen. *The Aesthetics of Mimesis: Ancient Texts and Modern Problems*. Princeton: Princeton University Press, 2002.

Hansen, William F. *Phlegon of Tralles' Book of Marvels*. Exeter: University of Exeter Press, 1996.

Harris, William V. *Dreams and Experience in Classical Antiquity*. Cambridge MA: Harvard University Press, 2009.

Konstan, David. "'The Birth of the Reader': Plutarch as Literary Critic." *Scholia* 13 (2004): 3–27; Spanish version: "'El nacimiento del lector': Plutarco como crítico literario." *Praesentia* 13 (2012). http://erevistas.saber.ula.ve/index.php/praesentia/article/view/4229.

Konstan, David. "The Active Reader in Classical Antiquity." *Argos: Revista de la Asociación Argentina de Estudios Clásicos* 30 (2006): 5–16.

Konstan, David. "In Defense of Croesus, or Suspense as an Aesthetic Emotion." *Aisthe* 3 (2008): 1–15. http://www.ifcs.ufrj.br/~aisthe/vol%20II/KONSTAN.pdf; reprinted in *Pathos: A Poética das Emoções*, edited by Fernando Santoro, Tatiana Ribeiro, and Henrique Cairus. Rio de Janeiro: Arquimedes Editora, 2009.

Konstan, David. *Beauty: The Transformations of an Ancient Greek Idea*. Oxford: Oxford University Press, 2014.

Leone, Giuliana. *Epicuro Sulla natura libro II*. Naples: Bibliopolis, 2012.

Modrak, Deborah. "Aristotle on *Phantasia*." In *The Routledge Handbook of Philosophy of Imagination*, edited by Amy Kind, 15–26. New York: Routledge, 2016.

O'Keefe, Tim. *Epicureanism*. Durham: Acumen, 2010.

Schepens, G. and K. Delcroix. "Ancient Paradoxography: Origin, Evolution, Production and Reception." In *La letteratura di consumo nel mondo greco-latino*, edited by O. Pecere and A. Stramaglia, 373–460. Cassino: Università degli studi di Cassino, 1996.

Sheppard, Anne. *The Poetics of* Phantasia: *Imagination in Ancient Aesthetics*. London: Bloomsbury, 2014.

Shulman, David and Guy Stroumsa. "Introduction." In *Dream Cultures: Explorations in the Comparative History of Dreaming*, edited by David Shulman and Guy Stroumsa, 3–15. Oxford: Oxford University Press, 1999.

Squire, Michael. *The Art of the Body: Antiquity and its Legacy*. Oxford: Oxford University Press, 2011.

Thein, Karel. "The Poetics of Mind and Matter: Some Remarks on Ancient Images and Imagination." *Eirene* 51 (2015): 303–34.

Verde, Francesco. *Epicuro*. Rome: Carocci, 2013.

Watt, Ian. *The Rise of the Novel: Studies in Defoe, Richardson and Fielding*. London: Chatto and Windus, 1957.

Webb, Ruth. *Ekphrasis, Imagination and Persuasion in Ancient Rhetorical Theory and Practice*. Farnham: Ashgate, 2009.

Whitmarsh, Tim. *Greek Literature and the Roman Empire: The Politics of Imitation*. Oxford: Oxford University Press, 2001.

CHAPTER 2

Poetic Imagination and Cultural Memory in Greek History and Mythology

Claude Calame

In a recent book entitled *Apologies to Thucydides*,[1] the American anthropologist Marshall Sahlins wonders about the actors of history.[2] His study, which takes the form of an apology to the ancient Greek historian Thucydides, is based on the Anglo-Saxon concept of "agency." Who are the "agents" of history? Individuals, as traditional historiography has claimed for so many years? Collectivities – ethnic groups, peoples, social classes, cultural communities? Structures – whether economic or social? As sensitive as he is to the different forms of verbal creation which configure the past of a community, the Hellenist I am once again feels himself called upon by this anthropological question – a question of anthropological relevance as it refers to culture: "who are the agents of history?" Furthermore, "what kind of collective memory is attached to them and with what kind of pragmatics?"

1 Historical Configuration through Discourse: From the Peloponnesian War to the Polynesian War

Sahlins' inquiry develops along both historic and comparative lines; his goal is to defend an "anthropological historiography." Both the method and the thesis are demonstrated in his comparison, which is essential to any anthropological perspective. Here the anthropological comparison is between the Peloponnesian War and the Polynesian War, along with the analogous near-pun of the

---

1 Responding to an invitation from Professor Wei Zhang, this paper was presented in translation by Amanda L. Iacobelli for the Department of History at Fudan University on October 10, 2013. It develops along cultural memory themes a thesis already sketched out in "Mémoire poétique et pratiques historiographiques: la Grèce classique," *AWAL. Cahiers d'études berbères* 40–41 (2009–2010): 121–28. The expanded English version has been published under the title "From Cultural Memory to Poetic Memory: Ancient Greek Practices of History Beyond the 'Great Divide,'" *Fudan Journal of the Humanities and Social Sciences* 7, no. 4 (2014): 639–52.

2 Marshall Sahlins, *Apologies to Thucydides. Understanding History as Culture and Vice Versa* (Chicago-London: The University of Chicago Press, 2004), 1–11.

© KONINKLIJKE BRILL NV, LEIDEN, 2020 | DOI:10.1163/9789004436350_004

two terms in English. One took place twenty-five centuries ago in the Eastern Mediterranean, a thirty-year conflict in which the Spartan hoplites and their continental allies confronted the Athenians. Due in large part to their fleet, the Athenians had extended their economic and military might throughout the Aegean basin. The other was conducted by the island kingdom of Bau against the more continental kingdom of Reva in the Fiji archipelago between 1843 and 1855. Both were wars of territorial and economic expansion, marked by acts of blind destruction and cold cruelty.

The conclusion drawn by the anthropologist and historian is twofold: "The event was contingent, but it unfolded in the terms of a particular field, from which the actors drew their reasons and the happening found its meaning."[3] He further clarifies, "who or what is a historical actor, what is a historical act and what will be its historical consequences: these are determinations of a cultural order, and differently determined in different orders. No history, then, without culture."[4] The conclusion implicit within the comparative study by the anthropological historian is that history is formed from an intermingling of arbitrary "eventuality" (chance) and cultural considerations. Adopting the historical and anthropological perspective Sahlins employs in his study, I would add that this intermingling of arbitrary events and culturally-determined acts gives history not only a temporal depth, but also a spatial one.

Additionally, the anthropological procedure Sahlins adopts in his historiographical work, and from which he draws conclusions about the parameters of "agency" in history, is based on forms of discourse, which is to say on verbal documents: Thucydides' historiographical narrative for the Peloponnesian War, and essentially the narratives of Methodist missionaries working in Fiji in the mid-nineteenth century during the Polynesian War. This is to say that the anthropologist bases his work on two forms of historiographical and cultural memory, corresponding to very different modes of narration; they are two forms of "history" configured not just narratively, but also culturally by the historian both as witness and as writer. On the Greek side, the historiographer ascribes motives to the progression of the long confrontation between Peloponnesians and Athenians; he draws them from his own culture, and thus from the culture of the war's actors themselves: quite beyond the vagaries of mortal existence, there is for Thucydides a (Greek) human nature with its ambitions and its will to power. In the Fiji Islands, on the other hand, the Methodist ministers refer to a very different culture from that of the indigenous participants in the war between two Polynesian kingdoms: European culture of the 19th

---

3 Sahlins, *Apologies to Thucydides. Understanding History as Culture and Vice Versa*, 291.
4 Sahlins, *Apologies to Thucydides. Understanding History as Culture and Vice Versa*, 292.

Century alongside Christian theodicy and such Western concepts as cannibalism. As divergent as they are, both forms of historiography are founded upon an "anthropology" in the form of a global concept of man and his actions including his motives.

Sahlins is not particularly sensitive to the procedures of verbal configuration and of "mise en discours" ("placing into discourse") which permits the course of events to become history in the primary sense of the word: a meaningful history, a history with its own logic (temporal, but spatial as well), history as representation and as discursive configuration;[5] a useful and effective history (as Thucydides claims in 1, 22. 4, at the end of his "archaeology": a *ktêma es aeí*); in the end a history which contributes to constituting an active memory, a discursive historiography with its own pragmatics which nourishes cultural memory – I shall return to this point soon. Thus, this is a history which moves from its first meaning, as inquiry into the past and discursive configuration into a verbal form, to a second meaning, as a past whose configured image is retained in memory (often as a sequence of politico-military events). Moreover, historiography's "mise en discours" (including verbal configuration) far from making history into pure fiction, reinforces its referential and pragmatic dimension.[6]

In speaking of the insertion of a history into shared memory, a memory which functions for both identity and collective recognition, an effective cultural memory, there are two important observations to be made:
– Through verbal configuration, through its discursive form, history-historiography corresponds to the ordering of the course of past events to make of it a history in the ordinary meaning of the term: a meaningful history. This historiographical ordering with its (cultural) logic is oriented by the author of the historiographical discourse, in the name of an anthropology as already mentioned. This global concept of man ascribes motives to the past actions of men. It analyzes their logic, their meaning, and their reason. Often paired with a cosmology, this concept of man and his actions which orients any historiography is dependent upon a cultural paradigm marked in both space and time.

---

5 The idea of configuring historic time through emplotment was developed by Ricoeur in 1983. See Paul Ricoeur, *Temps et récit 1* (Paris: Seuil, 1983), 101–09. It would be preferable to widen this concept to include the act of placing into discourse, in order to take the enunciative dimension of historical discourse into account. See also Claude Calame, *Pratiques poétiques de la mémoire*. English translation: *Poetic and Performative Memory in Ancient Greece: Heroic Reference and Ritual Gestures in Time and Space* (Washington-Cambridge MA: Harvard University Press, 2009), 5–54.

6 On the discursive, provisional, and unstable nature of any "historic truth," see for example Enzo Traverso, *Le passé, modes d'emploi. Histoire, mémoire, politique* (Paris: La Fabrique. 2005), 66–79.

POETIC IMAGINATION AND CULTURAL MEMORY

53

– This narrative and discursive orientation is marked on the level of verbal creation (and imagination in the literal meaning of the word) both in the way the "narrative" is organized, as well as in the mode of its enunciation – on the level of "narrative" ("récit") and on the level of "discourse" ("discours"), to use two operational categories proposed by the French linguist Émile Benveniste.[7] Whether we are discussing simple evaluative utterances or explicit enunciative interventions by the author, these enunciative strategies are located in space and time. They relate the recounted time and the place of the historical action to the present of the enunciation; they thus refer indirectly to the historical and cultural circumstances of communication of any discourse, and especially of historiographical discourse.

Within the forms of history which constitute a collectively shared memory, this enunciative stamp can become a genuine strategy. It ensures the pragmatics of historiographical discourse through a rhetoric which also has an esthetic and affective element. Enunciative procedures not only allow one to address any form of discourse to its public, with a view to touching and convincing them; it is also this enunciative dimension which relates the anthropological ordering of the past and its spatial-temporal configuration to the present time and the present space of the enunciation, to the individual historic and cultural conjuncture from which the historiographical discourse emerged. Hence, it ensures a social and cultural effect both esthetically and affectively; generally through a ritualized publication and performance, it is inscribed into memory, an effective collective memory, a dynamic cultural memory.

2 Cultural Memory and the Great Divide

Every society in every period stockpiles its own texts and forms of discourse, images and rites whose recurrent use allows it to stabilize and to transmit an image of itself through a shared knowledge – a knowledge especially of the past, through a tradition in which the use of writing contributes to expressing it and diffusing it. It is upon this institutionalized knowledge within collective

---

7 See Émile Benveniste, *Problèmes de linguistique générale* (Paris: Gallimard, 1966), 237–50 as well as Émile Benveniste, *Problèmes de linguistique générale* II (Paris: Gallimard, 1974), 79–88 (on the "formal apparatus of enunciation.") In referring to this distinction between "history/narrative" and "discourse," the ways in which the Greeks approach a heroic past has allowed me several times to show how extensively both of these levels are intermingled with discursive reality: see especially my study from 2009 (Claude Calame, "Referential Fiction and Poetic Ritual: Towards a Pragmatics of Myth (Sappho 17 and Bacchylides 13)." *Trends in Classics* 1 (2009): 1–17).

memory and centered on meaning (*Sinn*) that the group would base the consciousness of its own unity and particularity. Such, at least, is the definition of "cultural memory" that the Egyptologist Jan Assmann provides in several comparative studies of historiographic and religious traditions in ancient societies.[8] In a theoretical contribution entitled *"Was ist 'kulturelles Gedächtnis'?,"* the German historian of ancient religions shows that this concept rests on a clear distinction between what he calls *Bindungsgedächtnis* on the one hand and *Bildungsgedächtnis* on the other; either "connective memory" on the one hand or "formative memory" on the other. Assmann first takes up Maurice Halbwachs' concept of collective memory. He draws from it that quite apart from its organic and neuronal basis within each individual, memory not only has a social dimension, but also a cultural one: not that Culture has a memory, but that the internal world of the subject depends on the affective and social frame-conditions (*Rahmenbedingungen*) of memory in general.[9]

Nonetheless, in contrast to Halbwachs' distinction between lived memory and tradition, this collective and social memory, according to Assmann, is anchored in a tradition; it thus depends on a vertical communication process (between generations), which is combined synchronously with horizontal communication in interactive exchange.[10] The basis of collective memory within a tradition begs the questions of what allows any cultural memory to be constituted and maintained. Assmann essentially identifies only two elements: ritual practices and verbal/textual expressions. *So weit, so gut.* Such is the question that I would like to take up here, from the point of view of historical anthropology and ethnopoetics; such is the question I would like to ask about cultural memory as far as it is shaped by a partly imaginative configuration of the past as transmitted by discursive forms; and thus a question relying on the anthropological conception of history developed by Sahlins and a tentative answer relying on a scenario (between "myth" and "ritual") borrowed from the classical era of ancient Greek culture.

When speaking of the role played by tradition within a cultural memory, Assmann, the historian of ancient religions, borrows from the anthorpologist Claude Lévi-Strauss the famous distinction between cold and hot societies. Whereas the former are those cultures without writing and whose traditions are entirely oral; the latter term refers to societies with access to a system of

---

8   Jan Assmann, *Das kulturelle Gedächtnis: Schrift, Erinnerung und politische Identität in frühen Hochkulturen* (München: C.H. Beck, 1992), 19–25.

9   Assmann, *Religion und Kulturelles Gedächtnis. Zehn Studien*, 11–44.

10   In his study from 2008, Assmann draws a distinction between three overlapping forms and levels of memory: inner and personal memory, social and communicative memory and memory of the remote past (i.e. cultural memory).

transcription and graphic communication of the spoken word. In other words, Assmann implicitly places the concept of cultural memory within the often-criticized "Great Divide" or "Great Dichotomy," also taken up by Jack Goody[11] on the contrast between oral/written. Societies without writing, labelled "cold" societies, have a "connective" memory; a collective memory *par excellence*, a memory of 80 to 100 years based on reiteration of the ritual which reproduces the immutable order of the cosmos. In contrast, "hot" societies, those with a graphic transcription system, "interiorize" (*verinnerlichen*) history; they maintain a historical memory through that dynamic which could extend up to thousands of years. *Bindungsgedächtnis* on the one hand, *Bildungsgedächtnis* on the other – "connective memory" on one hand, "formative memory" on the other. This structural and evolutive partition is reminiscent of the German Romantic distinction between *Zivilisation* and *Kultur*. From a religious point of view, this division reproduces the distinction between the *Stammeskulturen*, tribal cultures, and the great civilizations founded on a religion of the book (and of the normative text). In this dichotomous point of view, writing is given as an instrument of liberation, ensuring "the free life of the mind," *das freie Leben des Geistes*, under the explicit authority of Hegel...[12] In such a eurocentric perspective, there is apparently no room neither for the great Indian culture, nor for the Chinese one!

In passing from an oral culture, based on the tradition of Homeric poems, to the literate culture of the Hellenistic period, does Greece pass from a form of connective memory to a form of "formative" and historical memory? Like Assmann, Plato at the beginning of the *Timaeus* (22a-23e) is already faced with the limited temporal arc of Greek history as told by Solon, who bases it on memory within the depth of Egyptian temporality based on written record. Using a single example of a tragedy composed and transmitted in writing, but presented in ritual public performance, I would like to contest two strongly held prejudices concerning collective and cultural memory.

On the one hand, the use of writing in the composition and communication of tradition does not mean the loss of any pragmatic dimension, nor, especially for ancient Greece, does it mean any passage to a literature in the modern sense of the term.[13] On the other hand, in ancient classical Greece, the *arkhaîa*

---

11   Jack Goody, *The Domestication of the Savage Mind* (Cambridge: Cambridge University Press, 1977), 146–62.

12   Assmann, *Religion und Kulturelles Gedächtnis. Zehn Studien*, 32–34, 42–44.

13   On auxiliary uses of writing in Greek poetry from the Classical period, see Andrew Ford, "From Letters to Literature: Reading the 'Song Culture' of Classical Greece," in *Written Texts and the Rise of Literate Culture in Ancient Greece*, ed. Harvey Yunis (Cambridge: Cambridge University Press, 2003), 1–37. For references to different forms of genealogical

related to the heroic past and to the ancient history of the community which we call "myths" and which we attribute in general to traditional societies, are an integral part of their collective historical memory – with or without writing. Cultural memory bears on a configured past, regularly conceived to be a foundation for the present. This present itself is subject to history as a course of events and as lived time, with its agents who respond to a specific cultural anthropology and with its own contingencies – to take up Sahlins' idea once again. This pragmatic relationship between a configured past and an evolutive present is actualized in ritualized discursive forms. This is how the historic tradition of a local culture becomes a "mode of action," to use Mondher Kilani's phrase concerning the compositions of a traditional poet re-actualized in a contemporary festival where the memory of the Tunisian oasis of El Ksar is celebrated.[14] In ancient Greece, whether epic poetry, political discourse, religious song, or tragedy, all verbal and discursive forms deny the pertinence of any clear distinction between *Bindungs-* and *Bildungsgedächtnis*.

3   Ancient Greece: An "Anthropopoietic" Cultural Memory

In traditional societies where cultural dissemination rests on discursive oral forms, as is the case in classical Greece, the effect of practical memory is reinforced by the poetic form assumed for discourse on the past; it is carried within the rhythmic recitation of musical song which configures the community's space and time. In this regard, three points of view are especially relevant:
– On a semantic level, through poetic creation and imagination, numerous metaphors tend to give figurative images and representations of this collective past. Consequently, they contribute to the aesthetic effect of what ancient rhetoricians term *enárgeia* and *evidentia*: in terms of verisimilitude, this entails a "placing before the eyes" through verbal means, thereby transforming the listener into a spectator by calling on his imagination in the true sense of the term.[15]

---

historiography in Classical Athens, see Rosalind Thomas, *Oral tradition and written records in Classical Athens* (Cambridge: Cambridge University Press, 1989), 15–34,155–95.

14   Mondher Kilani, *La construction de la mémoire. Le lignage et la sainteté dans l'oasis d'El Ksar* (Genève: Labor & Fides, 1992), 298–306.

15   On the importance of visual witnessing in Greek historiography, see François Hartog, *Évidence de l'histoire. Ce que voient les historiens* (Paris: Éditions de l'EHESS, 2005), 45–88; on rhetorical and deictic procedures meant to "place before the eyes," see Claude Calame, "Vraisemblance référentielle, nécessité narrative, poétique de la vue. L'historiographie grecque classique entre factuel et fictive," *Annales. Histoire, Sciences sociales* 67 (2012):

- From a rhythmic point of view, the metric cadence and the musical melody render performances of these poetic forms acts of song that are part of festive collective celebrations, which are often religious. Rhythm, when attached to poetic genres conditioned by specific forms of performance, guarantees these forms of historical discourse a ritual realization as a social and religious act. The community memory it configures follows the cadence of linear time and the cyclic time of a recurring calendar; it fuses together the time of the narrative and the time of the ritual.
- Finally, physically, rhythmic and ritualized recitation inscribes the poetic historical discourse not only in the intellect, but also in the body largely through emotion. It makes collective memory into a cadenced bodily experience, an "anthropopoietic" practice of the cultural construction of man in society,[16] in both the intellectual and physical sense. Through ritualized recitation, narrative poems which evoke and configure the past of the community thus maintain a collective cultural memory. This is an active rhythmic memory which acts both in and through ritual practice, which is often religious. It occurs within and is intended for a given historical, political, social, and religious situation. This is a collective memory about an "imagined" past shared in the ritual action itself.[17]

4   Rhetorical and Political Uses of the "Mythic" Past

Especially in ancient Greece, the collective and founding past, constantly brought to life through cultural memory and through long discursive forms, corresponds to what we, as part of a long anthropological tradition, refer to using the operative concept of "myth." For the Greeks, this does not refer to *mûthos*, a word which refers to a form of efficacious discourse arguing in favor of relying readily on a narrative; but rather it refers to *arkhaîa*, *palaiá*, and *patrôia*, to the heroicized actions of the ancestors who are often protagonists

---

      81–101, and Calame, *Pratiques poétiques de la mémoire. Représentations de l'espace-temps en Grèce ancienne*, 56–64.

16   For a more comprehensive discussion of this concept of the cultural creation of the human in different ways, see Affergan, Borutti, Calame, Fabietti, Kilani, and Remotti 2003.

17   Some examples of these ritualized poetic forms of memory in Ancient Greece, from Homeric songs to tragedy, dithyramb and religious song, can be found in my study from 2006 (Claude Calame, "Récit héroïque et pratique religieuse: le passé poétique des cités grecques classiques," *Annales. Histoire, Sciences Sociales* 61 (2006): 527–51). See also Claude Calame, "Referential Fiction and Poetic Ritual: Towards a Pragmatics of Myth (Sappho 17 and Bacchylides 13)," 1–17.

in the Trojan War. Evidently, these traditions vary from one city to another.[18] The paradigmatic function, and sometimes even the founding function, of these mighty epic deeds are constantly reworked. This process occurs through the discursive poetic forms already mentioned, in such a way that the cultural and civic memory in which they are inscribed may be made to answer to the needs of the present.

In 338 B.C., just after the battle of Chaeronea which seals the victory of Philip II of Macedon over the Athenians, the citizen Leocrates flees the city and seeks refuge in Rhodes. Upon his return to Athens, he is brought before the courts by the great orator Lycurgus who accuses him of treason. In addressing the Athenians, Lycurgus invokes a series of examples of civic courage, which are all precisely the opposite of Leocrates' cowardly conduct.[19] He begins with an anonymous narrative (*légetai*) which, though it may appear relatively fictional (*muthôdésteron*), is nonetheless well-suited to even the youngest of his listeners. Utility once again takes precedence over verisimilitude in this Sicilian story; it presents a father in a desperate situation who is saved by his son with the help of the gods.

But we must leave Sicily and continue our journey to Athens to evoke *palaiá*, the heroic past which for us corresponds to myth. There, once again, it is an anonymous tale that reports (*phasi*) the incursion into Attica of Eumolpus, King of Thrace and son of Poseidon; this took place in the ancient and local time of the founding heroes of the city. In the face of this danger, Erechtheus, the King of Athens, consults the Oracle at Delphi who advises him to sacrifice his daughter to gain victory over Eumolpus. The King obeys the Oracle, sacrifices his daughter, and succeeds in chasing the invaders from his country. This exemplary tale is known to us largely through a tragedy by Euripides, which Lycurgus cites at length. The floor is given to the wife of Erechtheus, who is asked to approve the sacrifice of her daughter; the quote permits the orator to give a poetic turn to his argument. The orator evokes the tragic speech of the legendary and poetic figure Praxithea, whom he quotes as an example of greatness of soul and civic nobility. Prepared to sacrifice both her family and her house (*oîkos*) for the city, Praxithea adopts first a feminine perspective and then a masculine one, praising motherhood which allows one to beget citizens capable of defending the homeland:

---

18   For these questions having to do with an attempt at transcultural translation, please see my critical study on myth and history (Claude Calame, *Mythe et histoire dans l'Antiquité grecque. La fondation symbolique d'une colonie.* 2nd ed. (Paris: Les Belles Lettres, 2011), 19–81).

19   Lycurgus, *Against Leocrates*, 95–97.

POETIC IMAGINATION AND CULTURAL MEMORY

> This girl who is mine only by birth,
> I will give her as a sacrifice for the country.
> Indeed, if the city is taken, what will remain to me of my own children?
> Whatever I can do, I will have done it to assure its safety.
> Others will assume power; as for me, I will save this city
> ...
> Citizens, make good use of the fruit of my womb;
> Insure your safety; win the victory. It is not possible
> that for the price of one life I refuse to save your city.
> O homeland, may all who live within you love you as much as I.

Having no male descendants, and in the name of native birth which the Athenians demand, the king's wife agrees to the sacrifice of her daughter. At the end of the tragedy, she will be the sole survivor. The two sisters of the girl who died on the altar ultimately sacrifice themselves in an act of solidarity. At the end of a victorious battle, Erechtheus has been killed by Poseidon's trident. Moreover, the future patron god of the city demands revenge for the death of his son Eumolpus. The King of Attica thus returns to the bowels of the earth from which he sprang as Erichthonius; he was born from the semen of Hephaestus spread on fertile ground in his vain attempt to unite with the virgin Athena.

None of the improbabilities of this founding narrative (i.e. human sacrifice, a literal birth from native soil, death through burial in the earth by the will of a god) are mentioned by the orator. This is because "myth" presented poetically and dramatically upon the Attica stage finds its historical reality and its pragmatic impact in a dual relationship with the present. On the one hand, its protagonists are the ancestors of Athenians whose own fathers were educated in this tradition; and on the other we owe to a poet this creation of an example showing that love of country takes precedence even over love of one's own children. The orator's conclusion leaves no room for appeal: "If women are capable of such an act, then men must have an absolute preference for their homeland, and never abandon it by fleeing, nor dishonor it for the Greeks as Leocrates has done."[20] Since Erechtheus is seen as the founder of the Eleusian

---

20 Lycurgus, *Against Leocrates,* 98–101, quoting Euripides, *Erechtheus* fr. 360 Kannicht (= 14 Jouan-Van Looy). The dual role assumed by Praxithea as mother and as citizen is well defined by Violaine Sebillotte-Cuchet, "La place de la maternité dans la rhétorique patriotique de l'Athènes classique (v^e–ive siècles avant notre ère): autour de Praxithéa," in *Les mères de la patrie: Représentations et constructions d'une figure nationale* (*Cahiers de la MRSH* 45), ed. L. Fournier-Finocchiaro (Paris: *Cahiers de la MRSH* 45, 2006), 237–50. See also Giulia Sissa and Marcel Detienne, *La vie quotidienne des dieux grecs* (Paris: Hachette, 1989), 238–45.

Mysteries, not only is the founding myth staging him still historical reality in the Fourth Century, but within both tragedy and political speech, it is accorded a specific pragmatic which renews the cultural memory of the city.

5 The Dramatization of the *Arkhaîa* and Their Symbolic Effectiveness

At the end of the fifth century, Euripides' tragedy had already established for itself a particularly strong relationship between the *arkhaîon* presented on stage at the theater of Dionysus and the religious practices of its Athenian spectators. Indeed, the tragic plot ends with the singing of a threnody, a funeral song deploring the destiny of Erechtheus' family, as well as that of a city prey to the destructive madness of Poseidon in the throes of his anger. Then Athena herself intervenes, with all the brilliance of a *dea ex machina* and with the authoritative voice of the city's patron goddess. In the etiological perspective which often concludes Euripides' tragedies, the divinity grants religious honors to all the Athenian protagonists of the play just performed.[21] The three daughters of Athens' sovereign couple will be the objects of musical offerings of choral dances by girls, performed around the inaccessible tomb/sanctuary, as well as sacrificial offerings before the city engages in battles. Their father Erechtheus will be honored through sacrifices of oxen in a shrine situated on the Acropolis, conjointly with Poseidon, now appeased and having become the second tutelary divinity of the city. Finally, his spouse Praxithea becomes the first priestess of Athena, and she will be celebrated in the sacrifices offered by Athenians on the altars of the Acropolis.[22]

Athena, the tutelary goddess, concludes her performative and institutionalizing declaration in this manner:

> For your husband, I order that for him be built
> a shrine in the center of the city, within a stone wall.
> In memory of he who killed him, Erechtheus will be invoked
> Under the name of august Poseidon, his epiclesis,
> on the occasion of sacrifices of oxen which citizens will make to him.

---

21 The etiological conclusions of Euripides' tragedies are far from being the poet's own invention, and generally correspond to the religion practiced; on this controversial question, see especially Christiane Sourvinou-Inwood, *Tragedy and Athenian Religion* (Lanham-Boulder-New York-Oxford: Lexington Books, 2003), 414–22.

22 Euripides, *Erechtheus* fr. 370, 55–100 Kannicht (= fr. 22, 55–100 Jouan-Van Looy) ; the figure of Poseidon-Erechtheus is described in all his different functions by Darthou. See Sonia Darthou, "Retour à la terre: la fin de la Geste d'Érechthée," *Kernos* 18 (2005): 69–83.

POETIC IMAGINATION AND CULTURAL MEMORY

> For you (Praxithea) who set straight the foundations of this city,
> I grant that you be the first to sacrifice the offerings
> which will be consumed on my altars: you will be my priestess.
> What must be accomplished on this earth, you have just heard.

Through the intervention of Athena in her on-stage epiphany, the dramatized narrative of the fabulous and tragic death of the legendary king Erechtheus leads not only to the instituting of religious acts honoring the two tutelary divinities of the city, but especially to the exposition of religious practices done annually by the spectators gathered within the theater-shrine of Dionysus that rests against the Acropolis. The pragmatic relationship between the founding narrative presented upon the Attic stage and the *hic et nunc* of the dramatic performance with its religious and social implications is all the more marked, given that the plot performed offers a double relationship with the historical situation of the musical and religious performance, just like any performance of tragedy in the shrine-theater consecrated to the god Dionysus.

On the one hand, a reminder of the "myth" of the invasion of Attica by troops of the Thracian sovereign Eumolpus recalls the incursions of the Spartan army which marked the first phase of the Peloponnesian war concluded at the time of the tragedy's performance in 422. On the other hand, this ritualized dramatization probably coincides strongly with the construction of the Erechtheion designed to replace the old temple of Athena destroyed by the Persians before the battle of Salamis. As a "place of memory," this shrine with its heterogeneous architecture is designed to bring together all relics of the primordial and founding history of Attica and of Athens, from the trace in Acropolis rock of Poseidon's trident which caused Aegean water to flow, to Athena's olive tree, reborn immediately after the burning of the Acropolis by Xerxes.[23] Thus, through its inclusion within the confines of the city and in its religious calendar, it offers an architectural reference to the different narratives that display the economic and civic fertility of Attican soil, which are especially reactivated at the musical and religious contest dedicated to Dionysus Eleuthereus.

As the founding narrative for Athens, the staging of the death of Erechtheus and his three daughters finds its religious and social effectiveness in the power of a dramatic form. Revised by Euripides, it gets its referential and pragmatic

---

23 For details on this point, see my study from 2011. (Claude Calame, "Myth and Performance on the Athenian Stage: Praxithea, Erechtheus, Their Daughters, and the Etiology of Autochthony," *Classical Philology* 106 (2011): 1–19). On the Erechteion and its construction, see my references in earlier footnotes.

reality from the community musical performance without which it would not exist. The cultural memory of the city is thus revived and reoriented through its inscription within religious space, through ritual celebration and through a poetic discourse with a written transcription.[24] This is undoubtedly *Bindungsgedächtnis*, but also *Bildungsgedächtnis*, along with the historic and dynamic dimension Assman denies to the former in a long outmoded perspective of anthropological primitivism.

6 The Ritualized Exemplarity of Homeric Heroes

But the tragic example of an Athenian heroine who adopts the values of the citizen without rejecting motherhood and the love of children inscribed within feminine nature is apparently not sufficient in itself to convince the Athenian public of the rhetor Lycurgus. He must go back in time even farther. Just as for the melic poets, the obligatory reference in maintaining any Greek cultural memory is the Pan-Hellenic tradition represented by Homeric poetry. The founding and maintaining of the civic community's memory is done through evoking the mighty warlike deeds of masculine warriors on that fictional narrative ground which is the Trojan battlefield. In this particular case, the complementary and persuasive example of the unconditional love which the citizen-soldier owes his city is given by the hero Hector exhorting the Trojans to defend the homeland: to die in combat is to die with glory, to save not only the land of the fathers, but also one's spouse, children, and household.

> Come! Fight near the ships, in masses
> He among you who is wounded from afar or struck from nearby,
> will come to death, and, at the end of his destiny, will die, it is true!
> There is no shame for the one who dies defending his country.
> His wife and his children remain safe for the future;
> his house, his patrimony are intact,
> from the day when the Achaeans have left with their ships
> for the shores of their homeland

In choosing not the death of Hector, but rather the harangue that the great Iliadic hero addresses to his soldiers before combat, the political orator Lycurgus is able to identify his rhetorical perspective with that of the great Trojan hero.

---

24 The founding nature of the "evolutionist paradigm" and what is at stake in nineteenth-century anthropology are the subject of a critical analysis by Kilani. See Mondher Kilani, *Anthropologie. Du local au global* (Paris: Armand Colin, 2009), 211–28.

POETIC IMAGINATION AND CULTURAL MEMORY

Through this enunciative strategy, he confers in oratorical performance a certain effectiveness not only to the content of his speech, but also to the harangue itself. This is no doubt the reason why the political rhetor recalls the ancestral law according to which the epic verses of Homer and other poets were recited in the great rhapsode contest every four years which marked the celebration of the Great *Panathenaea*. These are rhapsodic recitations of the heroic acts of a Pan-Hellenic past meant to honor the tutelary goddess of the city, Athena, *hic et nunc*. Lycurgus says so explicitly: the most beautiful heroic acts of the Greeks are nothing if they are not revived in a ritual "demonstration" (*epídeixis*).[25]

For this reason, it is at the great religious and civic celebration of the tutelary goddess of Athens (the *Panathenaia*), at the conclusion of the procession in which the city gave itself to itself in a symbolic spectacle, and through ritual recitation, that the Homeric fictions receive their effectiveness. It is through the beauty of Homer's verse, through the emotions they inspire, and through their ritualized poetic performance that the high deeds of the heroes of the Trojan War are incessantly given as examples of the acts of citizens, in spite of their often hyperbolic and violent nature. Through ritualized rhapsodic recitation within a religious and political framework, these individual heroic acts are inscribed in a revived collective and civic cultural memory, with poetic oral performances and historiographic practices of a writing; a writing which is nothing more than the support for ritualized oral recitations and secondary (written) dissemination between *Bindungs-* and *Bildungsgedächtnis*.

7   Myth and History: Spatial-Temporal Configurations for the Present

Invoked by the poetic practices of classical Greece, these reflections on the pragmatics of poetic forms in the institution of a collective and active memory invite us to substitute for the concept of "regime of temporality" that of "spatial-temporal logic." Through different discursive forms, spatial-temporal logic relates to a particular historical, social, and religious situation – a "regime of truth" which would correspond to a particular "discursive formation," to extend Michel Foucault's concept.[26] It is a logic of discursive and pragmatic

---

25   Lycurgus, *Against Leocrates* 102–04, quoting Homer, *Iliad* 15, 494–99. For the model of warrior virtues furnished by "Homer" in classical Athens, see for example Aristophanes, *Frogs* 1036, and for classical rhetoric, Isocrates, *Panegyricus* 159.

26   The concept of regimes of temporality was developed especially by François Hartog, *Régimes d'historicité. Présentisme et expériences du temps* (Paris: Seuil. 2003, 11–30); On the passage from regimes of historicity to logics of temporality and regimes of (historic) truth, see Claude Calame, *Pratiques poétiques de la mémoire. Représentations de*

configuration of the space and time proper to a cultural community. Such a logic is stabilized as a regime of memory and truth. While activated in ritual song, it is through ritual that the historical past, configured as collective memory, is actualized in the present which refers to it and which gives its own orientation to its logic. Moreover, it is through ritual practice that the community of belief to which it is addressed is realized, through discursive configuration, and through the regime of historical and memorial truth activated by such a logic.[27] From this vantage point, the transitory nature of spatial-temporal logic of historical action necessarily depends upon a cultural paradigm. The paradigm itself depends on a particular historic and territorial context, within a dynamic of change and conflict, especially when in contact with other cultural ensembles.

Together with an approach to (ancient) texts inspired by a discourse analysis that pays careful attention to enunciative procedures, the pragmatics of discursive "poetic" practices upon a past oriented by the present thus requires an anthropological perspective, and more specifically an ethnopoetic one. But – as we underscored at the beginning of the chapter – talking about anthropological procedures also entails discussing the comparative method. From the Great Divide, renewed by Jan Assman writing on cultural memory, we conclude with Marshall Sahlins' hypothesis about the actors and agents of history returning to the question of the discursive forms of implicit memory on which his study in historical and comparative anthropology is based.

If one accepts that history is made from the intersection between the hazards of eventuality and the will of actors driven by cultural motives, Sahlins' comparative study on the Peloponnesian War and Polynesian War was composed in the crucial years of a third imperialist enterprise: the Persian Gulf War. This war in Iraq was motivated by a neo-colonial ideology of the supremacy of Christian civilization and through the implicit anthropology at the base of worldwide capitalism and (naturalized) market laws. This conflict was also inspired by deep economic and financial motives related to the appropriation of energy resources, conducted with an arrogance and cruelty all the more

---

l'espace-temps en Grèce ancienne (Paris: La Découverte, 2006), 64–79; on the idea of discursive formation, see Michel Foucault, *L'archéologie du savoir* (Paris: Gallimard, 1969), 149–54.

27   On the essential relationship of any discursive configuration of the past with the present where it functions as collective and active memory, see Kilani's study from 2003 (Mondher Kilani, "L'art de l'oubli. Construction de la mémoire et narration historique," in *Poétiques comparées des mythes. De l'Antiquité à la modernité*, ed. U. Heidmann (Lausanne: Payot, 2003), 213–42); on belief as an indispensable social construction in assuring the pragmatics of both native (memorial) knowledge and of anthropological knowledge, refer to Mondher Kilani's critical study *L'invention de l'autre. Essais sur le discours anthropologique* (Lausanne: Payot, 1994), 236–62.

cynical in that it is based on a technology and financial might without parallel either in the "imperialist" Athens of the fifth century, or with the Fijis in the mid-nineteenth century. Any comparative approach, particularly in historical anthropology, invites us to return to the present that must be (re-) examined from an objective, unbiased lens. This scholarly endeavor is the crucial goal of the "comparative triangle": *comparandum, comparatum* and *comparans*.[28]

References

Affergan, Francis, Borutti, Silvana, Calame, Claude, Fabietti, Ugo, Kilani, Mondher, and Francesco Remotti. *Figures de l'humain. Les représentations de l'anthropologie*. Paris: Éditions de l'EHESS. 2003.

Assmann, Jan. "Communicative and cultural memory." In *Cultural Memory Studies. An International and Interdisciplinary Handbook*, edited by A. Erll and A. Nünning, 109–18. Berlin-New York: De Gruyter, 2008.

Assmann, Jan. *Das kulturelle Gedächtnis: Schrift, Erinnerung und politische Identität in frühen Hochkulturen*. München: C.H. Beck. 1992.

Assmann, Jan. *Religion und Kulturelles Gedächtnis. Zehn Studien*. München: C.H. Beck. 2006.

Benveniste, Émile. *Problèmes de linguistique générale*. Paris: Gallimard. 1966.

Benveniste, Émile. *Problèmes de linguistique générale* II. Paris: Gallimard. 1974.

Calame, Claude. "Comparatisme en histoire des religions et regard transversal : le triangle comparatif." In *Comparer en histoire des religions antiques. Controverses et propositions*, edited by C. Calame and B. Lincoln, 35–51. Liège: Presses universitaires de Liège, 2012.

Calame, Claude. "Myth and Performance on the Athenian Stage: Praxithea, Erechtheus, Their Daughters, and the Etiology of Autochthony." *Classical Philology* 106 (2011): 1–19.

Calame, Claude. *Mythe et histoire dans l'Antiquité grecque. La fondation symbolique d'une colonie*. 2nd ed. Paris: Les Belles Lettres. 2011.

Calame, Claude. *Pratiques poétiques de la mémoire. Représentations de l'espace-temps en Grèce ancienne*. Paris: La Découverte. 2006.

Calame, Claude. *Qu'est-ce que la mythologie grecque?* Paris: Gallimard. 2015.

Calame, Claude. "Récit héroïque et pratique religieuse: le passé poétique des cités grecques classiques." *Annales. Histoire, Sciences Sociales* 61 (2006): 527–51.

---

28 On the "comparative triangle," see Claude Calame, "Comparatisme en histoire des religions et regard transversal : le triangle comparatif." In *Comparer en histoire des religions antiques. Controverses et propositions*, edited by C. Calame and B. Lincoln, 35–51. Liège: Presses universitaires de Liège, 2012.

Calame, Claude. "Referential Fiction and Poetic Ritual: Towards a Pragmatics of Myth (Sappho 17 and Bacchylides 13)." *Trends in Classics* 1 (2009): 1–17.

Calame, Claude. "Vraisemblance référentielle, nécessité narrative, poétique de la vue. L'historiographie grecque classique entre factuel et fictive." *Annales. Histoire, Sciences sociales* 67 (2012): 81–101.

Darthou, Sonia. "Retour à la terre: la fin de la Geste d'Érechthée." *Kernos* 18 (2005): 69–83.

Ford, Andrew. "From Letters to Literature: Reading the 'Song Culture' of Classical Greece." In *Written Texts and the Rise of Literate Culture in Ancient Greece*, edited by Harvey Yunis, 15–37. Cambridge: Cambridge University Press. 2003.

Foucault, Michel. *L'archéologie du savoir*. Paris: Gallimard. 1969.

Goody, Jack. *The Domestication of the Savage Mind*. Cambridge: Cambridge University Press. 1977.

Hartog, François. *Évidence de l'histoire. Ce que voient les historiens*. Paris: Éditions de l'EHESS. 2005.

Hartog, François. *Régimes d'historicité. Présentisme et expériences du temps*. Paris: Seuil. 2003.

Kilani, Mondher. *Anthropologie. Du local au global*. Paris: Armand Colin. 2009.

Kilani, Mondher. *La construction de la mémoire. Le lignage et la sainteté dans l'oasis d'El Ksar*. Genève: Labor & Fides. 1992.

Kilani, Mondher. "L'art de l'oubli. Construction de la mémoire et narration historique." In *Poétiques comparées des mythes. De l'Antiquité à la modernité*, edited by U. Heidmann, 213–42. Lausanne: Payot. 2003.

Kilani, Mondher. *L'invention de l'autre. Essais sur le discours anthropologique*. Lausanne: Payot. 1994.

Kilani, Mondher. *Guerre et sacrifice. La violence extrême*. Paris: PUF. 2006.

Ricœur, Paul. *Temps et récit I*. Paris: Seuil. 1983.

Sahlins, Marshall. *Apologies to Thucydides. Understanding History as Culture and Vice Versa*. Chicago-London: The University of Chicago Press. 2004.

Sebillotte Cuchet, Violaine. "La place de la maternité dans la rhétorique patriotique de l'Athènes classique (V^e–IVe siècles avant notre ère): autour de Praxithéa." In *Les mères de la patrie: Représentations et constructions d'une figure nationale*, edited by L. Fournier-Finocchiaro, 237–50. Paris: *Cahiers de la MRSH* 45, 2006.

Sissa, Giulia, and Marcel Detienne. *La vie quotidienne des dieux grecs*. Paris: Hachette. 1989.

Sourvinou-Inwood, Christiane. *Tragedy and Athenian Religion*. Lanham-Boulder-New York-Oxford: Lexington Books. 2003.

Thomas, Rosalind. *Oral tradition and written records in Classical Athens*. Cambridge: Cambridge University Press. 1989.

Traverso, Enzo. *Le passé, modes d'emploi. Histoire, mémoire, politique*. Paris: La Fabrique. 2006.

CHAPTER 3

History, Imagination and the Narrative of Loss: Philosophical Questions about the Task of Historical Judgment

Allen Speight

A consideration of the role of imagination in historical thinking and judgment poses significant questions, both philosophically and practically. On the one hand, there is the question of whether one *can* judge at all if there is a sense of moral or temporal distance (or both) from historical agents—especially those caught up in difficult or pressing situations. As Gershom Scholem argued about the Holocaust, those who were "compelled to make terrible decisions in circumstances that we cannot even begin to reproduce or reconstruct" are not persons about whom one can say "whether they were right or wrong. *Nor do I presume to judge.* I was not there."[1] On the other hand, philosophical consideration of the task of historical judgment has led to the sort of universalizing tendency most famously articulated perhaps by Hegel, who (supposedly following Schiller) claimed that "World history (*Weltgeschichte*) is a court of judgment (*Weltgericht*)": judgment is the privilege of the perspective of world history, precisely because "in its universality ... the particular ... is present only as ideal."[2]

One of the more sustained philosophical reflections on the problems that underlie these stances toward historical judgment—connected to an argument as to why neither of these stances can in the end be philosophically adequate—is that articulated by Hannah Arendt, who explored them in a range of contexts, from her reporting on the Eichmann trial to her final work, with a particular eye on questions raised by the searing historical events of the 20th century's experience of war and totalitarianism. Central to Arendt's view of judgment was the distinct role of the faculty of *imagination*: as she argued in an early (1953) essay "Understanding and Politics," imagination "alone enables us to *see things in their proper perspective*, to put that which is too close at

---

1 Ronald Beiner, "Interpretive Essay" in Hannah Arendt, *Lectures on Kant's Political Philosophy* (Chicago: University of Chicago Press, 1992), 99.

2 Hegel, *Elements of the Philosophy of Right*, trans. H.B. Nisbet (Cambridge: Cambridge University Press, 1991), 372.

© KONINKLIJKE BRILL NV, LEIDEN, 2020 | DOI:10.1163/9789004436350_005

a certain distance so that we can see and understand it without bias and prejudice, to bridge abysses of remoteness until we can see and understand everything that is too far away from us as though it were our own affair. This 'distancing' of some things and bridging the abysses of others is part of the dialogue of understanding."[3]

While there are a number of ways in which Arendt's thoughts on the topic of historical imagination and judgment have been explored in the past, I have chosen to frame this essay in terms of a pair of epigraphs that Arendt apparently intended to open the third and final volume of her *Life of the Mind*, which was to have been devoted to the topic of *Judging*. In what follows, I will explore the background of these two quotations and their importance for Arendt's developing thoughts about historical imagination and judgment. In the first section, I will examine the development of Arendt's long-term fascination with the first of the epigraphs, which comes from Lucan's portrayal of the Roman Cato in his poem *Pharsalia* or *On the Civil War* and which held a wider importance in Arendt's view for ancient and modern conceptions of the relation between politics and intellectual life. In the second section, I will follow the shift Arendt's account of judging undergoes—from an activity undertaken by agents within the political world to one in which poets and storytellers are prominent—by examining the context of Lucan's poetic re-imagination of Cato and, in turn, of two famous interpretations of Lucan's reading (those of Hobbes and Dante) that raise questions for Arendt. In the final section, I will link this examination of the poetic context of the Cato epigraph to Arendt's second epigraph to *Judging*, which comes from the end of Goethe's *Faust*, with three distinct aspects of her mature account of judgment and imagination that deserve attention: the *solitariness* of judging, its connection to the reciprocal relation between *action and suffering* and the demand for *narrative integrity* it requires. As will be argued, Arendt's use of *literary* works to frame the problem of *historical* judgment is a key piece of evidence for her claim that it is the *imagination* above all—and particularly the work of poets and storytellers—that holds the important key for coming to terms with the problems inherent in judging the actions of historical figures. For it is only from the poet's or storyteller's imaginative and often solitary distance that historical judgment with a proper perspective can emerge.

---

3   Quoted in Beiner, "Interpretive Essay," 96–97.

HISTORY, IMAGINATION AND THE NARRATIVE OF LOSS

1 The First Epigraph to *Judging*: Arendt on Cato and the "Vanquished Cause"

Rolled into her typewriter at her death was a single sheet of paper that was blank, except for the title of Arendt's last book and two remarkable quotations that had played a significant role over the years in her thought.[4] The first was drawn from the Latin poet Lucan, who gave these lines to the soon-to-be-defeated Cato: "*Victrix causa diis placuit sed victa Catoni* (the victorious cause is pleasing to the gods but that of the vanquished is pleasing to Cato)." The second was from the final act of Goethe's *Faust* (Part II):

> Könnt' ich Magie von meinem Pfad entfernen,
> Die Zaubersprüche ganz und gar verlernen,
> Stünd' ich Natur vor Dir, ein Mann allein,
> Da wär's der Mühe wert ein Mensch zu sein.[5]

(Could I but clear my path at every turning/ Of spells, all magic utterly unlearning, Were I but Man, with Nature for my frame, The name of human would be worth the claim).[6]

Arendt's epigraphs to "judging" offer an especially helpful framework for considering history, judgment and the role of the imagination for a number of reasons. Both quotations represent key moments of judgment about the significance of decisive action in life—one connected to the biography of a political figure at a key moment in Roman history, one to a fictional character's coming to terms with his life—but both appear within works of the *poetic* imagination. Moreover, both seem to have had long-standing significance for Arendt in differing contexts over her own work and life.

In this section, I will trace Arendt's developing appropriation of the first quotation about Cato. Its initial appearances in her published work come in early writings of hers about the politician Friedrich von Gentz, who had once played a role in the social circle surrounding Rahel Varnhagen but had become a somewhat forgotten figure in the years following his death in 1832. The first of these was in a short essay Arendt published in 1932 in German in the *Kölnische Zeitung* marking the centennial of Gentz' death; the second was in Arendt's first publication in English, a book review ("A Believer in European Unity") that Arendt published ten years later in the *Review of Politics* of a biography about Gentz

---

4 Beiner, "Interpretive Essay," 89.
5 *Faust*, Part II, Act V, lines 11404-7.
6 *Faust*, trans. Walter Arndt (New York: Norton, 1996).

(Paul R. Sweet's *Friedrich von Gentz: Defender of the Old Order*). In these writings, Arendt sketches Gentz as someone whose political beliefs changed significantly over time—from those of a seemingly enthusiastic believer in the French Revolution to the conservative defender of the "old" (and anti-Napoleonic) order appropriate for the diplomatic work he conducted on behalf of Metternich and others while serving as adviser and writer of minutes at the Congress of Vienna and the Carlsbad Congress. As Arendt reports it, the quotation about Cato had become a sort of *Sprichwort* for him, and part of her task is to understand what resonance the quotation had for Gentz.

Although Gentz was present at a number of key events shaping the structures of European power in the post-Napoleonic era, the attempts of the leading politicians for whom he worked were not successful at bolstering the "old order" of Europe. As Gentz came to realize that much of what he had taken as a political goal was a lost cause in the post-Napoleonic world, he justified himself in a way that distanced himself from that world: "As a pure observer of the world, he assigns himself a place in it. He does not seek to render an account for any cause but only for himself, or rather, for the role he played."[7] Arendt links Gentz with the Romantics—and in particular with Friedrich Schlegel, who had, like Gentz, moved from a more revolutionary earlier stance to the conservative confines of the Viennese court. "To take part in the world, though only in the form of knowledge, to be a witness to it, appears to be the greatest opportunity available to the Romantics. Gentz sacrificed to it his philosophical outlook, his status, and his fame as a writer. His success at knowing all there really was to know left him ultimately indifferent toward the destruction of everything he had sought to achieve in his political life."[8] It was from "this distancing himself from everything specific—and not from any fixed conviction or determinate point of view" that the quotation about Cato ultimately came to have importance for him. In Jerome Kohn's words it was thus *"from such a spectator's view*, his 'participatory knowledge' of his age's spirit and its secrets ... that he found his political credo."[9]

Arendt's placement of the Cato quotation within her deft character sketch of Gentz gives it an interesting historical and political resonance, one that connects to the questions of emerging freedom and social status that pervade her analysis of the salon world of Rahel Varnhagen, the daughter of a wealthy

---

7   Hannah Arendt, "Friedrich von Gentz, on the 100th Anniversary of his Death, June 9, 1932," in *Essays in Understanding 1930–1954: Formation, Exile and Totalitarianism* (New York: Schocken, 1994), 54.

8   Arendt, "Friedrich von Gentz," 56.

9   Jerome Kohn, "Introduction" to Arendt, *Essays in Understanding 1930–1954: Formation, Exile and Totalitarianism*, xxii (italicization mine).

HISTORY, IMAGINATION AND THE NARRATIVE OF LOSS

Berlin merchant about whom Arendt wrote a biography. But the quotation's significance for Arendt was clearly not limited to the distinct use Gentz made of it—as Kohn puts it, almost a preference for the defeated cause "because it was defeated"—but had a deeper political resonance. This deeper resonance clearly also went beyond the specific cultural setting of Gentz's circle, as well, as evidenced by its appearance in a letter to Karl Jaspers that Arendt wrote on July 24, 1954.[10] If Gentz' citation of the phrase had reflected a certain powerlessness of a merely intellectual sort, now Arendt appears to invoke the political power of Cato's own example, as she insists that the quotation exemplifies the "spirit of republicanism."

Moving from these earlier appeals to the Cato quotation, we can now see an important issue that will be key to interpreting the context of the quotation's use as the *Judging* epigraph. As Ronald Beiner has argued, Arendt's view on judging shifted significantly from a view that concentrated attention on agents within the political world to a later view which emphasized the spectatorial standpoint of poets and storytellers: "The emphasis shifts from the representative thought and enlarged mentality of political agents to the spectatorship and retrospective judgment of historians and storytellers. The blind poet, at a remove from the action and therefore capable of disinterested reflection, now becomes the emblem of judging."[11]

From the perspective of this shift in her account of judging, Arendt's first epigraph—although it is about a key political figure at the end of the Roman republic—should nonetheless be read as one that derives from a poet's imagination of what that figure *might* have said. In other words: the Cato who must be explored behind Arendt's invocation of him is most importantly a *poet*'s Cato.

2   The Vanquished Cause and the Poetic Imagination: from Lucan to Dante

If Arendt's own view of judgment changed over time in the way that Ronald Beiner has argued—from a view embedding the activity of judgment within political agents to one that gives pride of place to the work of poets and storytellers—we must consider not simply the role of a figure like Cato but the

---

10   Quoted by Jerome Kohn, "Introduction": "You must know that quote from Cato: *Victrix causa diis placuit sed victa Catoni*. That is the spirit of republicanism" (*Hannah Arendt/ Karl Jaspers Briefwechsel 1926–1969* (Munich: Piper, 1985), 281).

11   Beiner, "Interpretive Essay," 109.

poetic context in which this quotation about Cato has appeared. The focus shifts from how one makes sense of Cato's stance toward judgment to how Lucan as a poet represented that stance in his poem *Pharsalia* or *On the Civil War* and what significance that may have for the tradition that follows. Before turning back to Arendt, I consider two such readers—both concerned about issues of politics and historical judgment but nonetheless offering substantially different imaginative appreciations of Cato's claim: Hobbes and Dante.

Lucan's portrayal of Cato is framed particularly around the Stoic virtue for which the Roman senator was famous. Rather than give in to Caesar and submit to an imperial yoke in a world where only one man rules, Cato takes his own life. This Stoic fortitude is what shines through in Lucan's portrayal of Cato. Politically, Lucan's sympathies are clearly republican rather than imperial, and his Cato stands as a paragon of Stoic virtue in contrast to the anti-hero Caesar (as well as Caesar's opponent Pompey). Lucan praises the

> creed of austere Cato: to observe moderation, to hold the goal,
> to follow nature, to devote his life to his country,
> to believe that he was born not for himself but for all the world.
> In his eyes to conquer hunger was a feast, to ward off winter
> With a roof was a mighty palace, and to draw across
> His limbs the rough toga in the manner of the roman citizen of old
> Was a precious robe ... for Rome he is father and for Rome he is husband,
> His goodness was for the state; into none of Cato's acts
> Did self-centered pleasure creep in and take a share. [II.380–90][12]

Lucan shapes this picture of Cato's virtue in the context of an account of Rome's civil war. The poem's title refers to the battle of Pharsalus which occurred on August 9, 48 BCE between Caesar's forces and those of Pompey the Great, and Lucan makes clear how terrible such civil division is: "a mighty people attacking its own guts with victorious sword-hand." The line that Arendt quotes is itself framed in terms of the indecisiveness of civil war:

> Who more justly took up weapons
> is forbidden knowledge; each has on his side a great authority:
> the conquering gods the gods, the conquered Cato. [I. 126–28]

---

12   Translations from Lucan, *Civil War*, trans. Susan H. Braund (Oxford: Oxford University Press, 1992).

HISTORY, IMAGINATION AND THE NARRATIVE OF LOSS

Lucan seems to be particularly concerned to represent Cato as free from conventional views of the gods. Later in the poem, when Cato is before an oracle he ponders what question a man of his independent virtue could even ask:

> What question, Labienus, do you bid me ask? Whether I prefer
> to meet my death in battle, free, to witnessing a tyranny?
> Whether it makes no difference if our lives be short or long?...
> We know the answer: Ammon will not plant it deeper in me.
> We are all connected with the gods above, and even if the shrine is silent
> we do nothing without God's will; no need has deity of any
> utterances: the Creator told us at our birth once and always
> whatever we can know... Why do we seek gods any further?
> Whatever you are, whatever you experience, is Jupiter.
> Let those unsure and always dubious of future events
> require fortune-tellers; no oracles make me certain,
> certain death does. Coward and brave must fall;
> it is enough that Jupiter has said this. [IX.566–84]

Lucan's portrait in this sense correlates with other accounts of Cato in ancient literature, including Plutarch's memorable account of Cato's final moments—something we do not see in Lucan, although the suicide scene may well have been in a missing later book. Plutarch describes Cato on his last night in his camp at Utica debating with friends the Stoic notion that the good man only is free and then going off alone to read Plato's *Phaedo* and taking the sword with the words "Now I am master of myself."[13]

This portrait of Cato's virtues in life and death has inspired many readers, not all of them sympathetic with the cause of republicanism for which he advocated. Before turning back to Arendt, I'll mention two readers who shape concerns around the notion of Cato's "losing cause."

The first reader I'll consider is Thomas Hobbes, who recognized that the notion of a "losing cause" is not without difficulty for our question of historical judgment. Hobbes disliked very much the line about Cato's taking the losing side for the potential it opened up for political discord. From a Hobbesian perspective, Lucan's setting up the line about the "vanquished cause" has only emphasized the potential for civil strife ("Each has on his side a great authority"). Hobbes' worry is that the losing cause is also a *cause* and hence partitive, and as history abundantly teaches citing it can incite a resistant anger among the

---

13 "Cato the Younger," *Plutarch's Lives*, Rev. ed. (Arthur Hugh Clough). Trans. John Dryden (New York: Modern Library, 2001), 958.

vanquished, rather than simply offering an opportunity to have their side heard when history is written. (A quick example: the most famous location in the United States where one can find these lines of Lucan invoked is of course in Arlington Cemetery, at the base of the Confederate Monument, where the sculptor, the Jewish Confederate war hero Moses Ezekiel, has them linked in the original Latin with the Great Seal of the Confederacy.)

One reading of Cato's lines that shares Hobbes' concern about civil discord but that nonetheless sees him as a pivotally important figure with a positive valence on the historical imagination is that given by the poet Dante. The Latin poet Lucan has an interesting place within the poetic hierarchy of predecessors significant for Dante poet and pilgrim. In *Inferno* Canto IV, Vergil as guide for Dante pilgrim introduces him to three other poets in order to make up a sort of infernal group portrait of the six greatest poets of all time: Homer, of course, is first in this group portrait (*poeta sovrano*, consummate poet, as Vergil calls him, who holds a sword and moves before the other three as their "lord," as Vergil says), then Horace the satirist, and third Ovid and the fourth Lucan, whom Vergil calls, intriguingly, *l'ultimo*, the final or ultimate in this series (the poet at the greatest distance, as some have suggested, from Vergil or Homer).

Just as Lucan plays a surprising role in the *Commedia* so does his figure of Cato. He appears, as a grizzled and graying elder ("patriarch" in Mandelbaum's translation) suddenly and perplexingly at the base of Purgatory. Why is Cato of all figures the one who greets Dante just after his emergence from hell? Why is a first century BC Stoic Roman senator and pagan who committed suicide not only saved in the harrowing of hell (along with Old Testament figures) but in fact the crucial introductory figure to purgatory itself, who welcomes pilgrims to the mountain and in fact, as Robert Hollander has argued, watches over the realm as a whole (up to the introduction of Matelda)?

The appearance of patriarch Cato, surprising as it is, is nonetheless well-prepared-for in Dante's *Commedia*. As Kevin Brownlee has recently argued, in all of the places where we might expect to find Cato in *Inferno*, Dante has carefully noted the presence of his absence.[14] Although Cato was a virtuous pagan, he is not to be found in Canto IV among the virtuous pagans in Limbo—but his wife Marcia is. Although Cato is a suicide, he is not to be found in Canto XIII among the grove of suicides, but Dante pilgrim goes out of his way as he leaves the grove to say that the ground on which he now steps is "a sand not different in kind from that on which the feet of Cato had once tramped." Finally, although Cato was one of Caesar's prominent opponents, he is not to be found in

---

14   Kevin Brownlee, "Dante and the Classical Poets," in *The Cambridge Companion to Dante* (Cambridge: Cambridge University Press, 2007), c. 7.

the situation of Brutus and Cassius whom Dante, the great advocate of imperial Roman power, has placed unforgettably in the mouth of Satan in the scene just immediately preceding Cato's appearance at the beginning of Purgatory.

But Dante's evident carefulness in making us feel the absence of Cato in these earlier scenes prior to his appearance as the gatekeeper of purgatory only makes the question more perplexing. Why should Dante be allowed to portray Cato as saved? Why this figure and not others as the guide on the ascent of purgatory? It's here that we must start to notice how differently Dante must read even the more extravagantly Stoical moments of Lucan's Cato. Dante invites us to an act of value redescription. It is neither as a paragon of Stoic virtue nor as a suicide that Dante is considering Lucan's Cato. If Lucan has emphasized Cato's deeds in terms of a Stoic resistance or even inflexibility in the face of an alien power (be that, for Lucan's Cato, the allure of sensuality or of Caesar), Dante stresses Cato's actions as done in the name of a liberty that, like the reed Cato offers Dante, *bends* before another power. Stoic resistance has metamorphosized into Christian humility and awareness of suffering. If there is an extravagance to the resistance of Lucan's Cato, it is because Stoic value theory is being tested against the degenerate world of Neronian politics (a world in which Lucan himself was of course a victim).

In Dante's writing about Cato elsewhere, he clearly sees Cato in these terms, as an exemplar of freedom by means of willing sacrifice. In the *De Monarchia*, which Arendt carefully read, the discussion of the legitimacy of Roman rule Cato is one of a number of examples of Romans who acted for the common good, but distinguished for his "inarticulable sacrifice," one performed "to kindle the love of liberty in the world."[15]

If we now think back to Lucan's famous lines about Cato as the advocate for the losing side, this transvaluation of values from Stoic to Christian shows us a new conception of the importance of suffering. On the personal level, there is a striking intimacy about this for Dante, as there is in most of the great moments in the *Commedia*.

Dante certainly remembered Lucan's claim that Cato's "party" after the death of Caesar's only remaining opponent Pompey was "wholly that of freedom." One can hear in these lines an influence behind the advice Dante pilgrim gets from his great-great grandfather Cacciagauida in *Paradiso* XVII: that his honor would be best kept "if your party is yourself." Robert Hollander has suggested the lines from Cato's appearance giving Romans their laws as the very final moment on Aeneas' shield can be read as virtually identifying the

---

15   Dante, *On World Government or De Monarchia*, trans. Herbert W. Schneider (New York: Library of Liberal Arts, 1949), ii.v, translation amended.

two: the Latin is "his dantem iura Catonem." Perhaps that helps explain why Dante pilgrim sees his relation to Cato on first sight in terms of the relation of a son to a father: he is indeed "Dante's Cato."

Cato's Stoic sense of liberty yields to the Christian in Dante's reading because it allows the soul to refuse to be alienated in a world of suffering, allows the individual to know that there is no such thing as alien divinity or fortune behind the difficulties that can cause exile (in Dante's case) or even the disappearance of the political structures that have made one's political life possible (in Cato's case). It's an unsettling view, but Dante's notion of a "party of one" need not be politically partisan in the sense that Hobbes finds problematic. On Dante's reading, Lucan's line stresses not the division of authority between Cato and Caesar (and hence the potential nursing of a grudge on the part of the loser) but rather the advent of a new divine order implicit underneath the whole contest: it is only the pagan gods who could be said to favor victors in such contests; what Cato's Stoicism was reaching toward was, however, a divine view on which human beings can know and sympathize with suffering in the world we inhabit because they know that god does not take sides in the way that Roman religion believed. Dante is thus struck with the question we saw Lucan's Cato pose above: "the Creator told us at our birth once and always whatever we can know... Why do we seek gods any further?... Coward and brave both must fall."

3   **Life, Narration and Freedom: The Context of the Second Epigraph of** *Judging* **and Three Arendtian Desiderata for the Use of the Historical Imagination**

The exploration of Lucan's Cato and its differing interpretations in Hobbes and Dante brought us to a standpoint—that of the judging "party of one"—which gestures toward the importance of the second epigraph for *Judging*, to which I now turn. The quotation from Goethe's *Faust* likewise had an enduring importance for Arendt. The lines come from the final act of *Faust, Part II*: four allegorical figures (Want, Debt, Care and Need) have appeared before Faust at the stroke of midnight and his reflections are on the "unlearning" of the magic whose appeal had tempted him at the beginning of Part I.

These lines Goethe gives Faust, much like those Lucan gives Cato, have been read in many different ways over the years—they not only have a similarity to Prospero's lines at the end of the *Tempest* but return to the key issues of freedom and salvation that we saw as part of Dante's reading of Lucan. The key to the connection between Arendt's two epigraphs, however, comes just before

HISTORY, IMAGINATION AND THE NARRATIVE OF LOSS

the lines she quotes: as Faust points out that only three of the four allegorical figures have left, he comes to the realization that "I have not fought my way to freedom yet" (line 11403). This line—which expresses presumably the *solitary* task of both Lucan's and Dante's Cato to fight for freedom—connects obviously to Arendt's framing of the Cato quotation as the "spirit of republicanism" (with all the attendant risks both Hobbes and Dante would have seen) and with the issues of *suffering*'s connection to action and judgment.

On the question of solitariness, it's important to remember Beiner's account of the turn in Arendt's position about judging—from an activity characteristic of political actors to an activity requiring both solitariness and distance from action: "The more she reflected on the faculty of judging, the more inclined she was to regard it as the prerogative of the solitary (though public-spirited) contemplator as opposed to the actor (whose activity is necessarily nonsolitary). One acts with others; one judges by oneself (even though one does so by making present in one's imagination those who are absent). In judging, as understood by Arendt, one weighs the *possible* judgments of an imagined other, not the actual judgments of real interlocutors."[16]

On the question of the relation between solitary judgment and its connection to the reciprocal relation between action and suffering in Arendt, it's instructive to compare her use of the two epigraphs to *Judging* with two other remarkable epigraphs that have long been discussed by her readers: those of the section on "Action" in *The Human Condition*. The first epigraph comes (without specific reference to source) from Isak Dinesen: "All sorrows can be borne if you put them into a story or tell a story about them"; the second is a longish quotation in Latin from Dante's *De Monarchia*, the last sentence of which Arendt translates herself as "nothing acts unless [by acting] it makes patent its latent self."[17]

Dinesen's claim about narrative and suffering is one which Arendt further glosses in her remarkable sketch of the novelist in *Men in Dark Times*. In this short narrative of Dinesen's life, Arendt takes up Dinesen's thought about how stories can help sorrows be borne in light of some possible misunderstandings that proved difficult in the novelist's own experience. Dinesen's disastrous early marriage to the British aristocrat Denys Finch-Hatton, Arendt claims, had its genesis in her own personal narrative—became a story she "had planned to act out in her life" that somehow recapitulated her suicide father's grief over an early infatuation with a noblewoman. Arendt's take on this makes clear what I will call a notion of *narrative integrity*:

---

16 Ronald Beiner, "Interpretive Essay," 92.

17 Arendt, *The Human Condition* (Chicago: University of Chicago Press, 1958), 175.

It is true that storytelling reveals meaning without committing the error of defining it, that it brings about consent and reconciliation with things as they really are, and that we may even trust it to contain eventually by implication that last word which we expect from the "day of judgment." And yet, if we listen to Isak Dinesen's "philosophy" of storytelling and think of her life in the light of it, we cannot help becoming aware of how the slightest misunderstanding, the slightest shift of emphasis in the wrong direction, will inevitably ruin everything...

As far as I know, she never wrote a story about [her] ... sordid marriage affair, but she did write some tales about what must have been for her the obvious lesson of her youthful follies, namely, about the "sin" of making a story come true, of interfering with life according to a preconceived pattern, instead of waiting patiently for the story to emerge, of repeating in imagination as distinguished from creating a fiction and then trying to live up to it.[18]

Although the focus in our discussion has been on the question of *historical* imagination—and not that of personal narrative or literary fiction—Arendt's clarity that historical judgment is in its distance from the course of life nonetheless the distinctive and solitary task of imaginative thinkers, poets and storytellers requires a consideration of these issues of integrity pertinent to all forms of narrative. In their historical form, what we might call the "narrative of lost causes" that she links to Cato is clearly one that, like Dinesen's own autobiography, is (as Hobbes especially wanted to emphasize for the question of civil order) open to dangerous forms of misconstrual and misunderstanding. The historical Cato himself seems to have recognized the potential for that, as he takes up a serious form of the Stoic "imitation of Socrates" but nonetheless insists to a young follower that such imitation would not be right for everyone.[19]

The question of imitation and misconstrual leads to the second epigraph to "Action." Arendt's notion that action involves some inherent self-disclosure— the "making patent" of what is latent, as her peculiar translation of Dante has it. Arendt's appropriation of this passage has been well discussed by Susannah

---

18   Arendt, *Men in Dark Times* (New York: Harcourt Brace, 1983), 105–06.

19   "[T]here was one Statyllius, a young man, in the flower of his age, of a brave spirit, and very desirous to imitate the constancy of Cato. Cato entreated him to go away, as he was a noted enemy of Caesar, but without success. Then Cato looked at Apollonides, the Stoic philosopher, and Demetrius, the Peripatetic; 'It belongs to you to cool the fever of this young man's spirit and to make him know what is good for him'" ("Cato the Younger," *Plutarch's Lives*, Rev. ed. (Arthur Hugh Clough). Trans. John Dryden (New York: Modern Library, 2001), 956.).

Gottlieb for the new emphasis Arendt means to put on the inherent *plurality* involved in action—for there can be no self-disclosure without *someone* to whom one is disclosing oneself—and, with that plurality, the inherent suffering entailed.[20]

Taking these three points together allows us to see three desiderata in the use of imagination in historical judgment for Arendt: the requisite distance of *solitude*, the *narrative integrity* required for the fullest understanding of relevant historical circumstances to emerge and the *reciprocality of action and suffering* involved in a world of plural agents. As we have seen, all three of these criteria seem to be involved in Arendt's view of the appropriate consideration due history as seen from the side of its "lost causes"—a notion which, as she was clearly aware, can create its own problems of misconstrual if these three desiderata are left out of the picture.

References

Arendt, Hannah. *Between Past and Future: Eight Exercises in Political Thought.* New York: Penguin Classics. 2006.

Arendt, Hannah. *Essays in Understanding 1930–1954: Formation, Exile and Totalitarianism.* New York: Schocken. 1994.

Arendt, Hannah. *Hannah Arendt/Karl Jaspers Briefwechsel 1926–1969.* Munich: Piper. 1985.

Arendt, Hannah. *Lectures on Kant's Political Philosophy*, edited by Ronald Beiner. Chicago: University of Chicago Press. 1992.

Arendt, Hannah. *Men in Dark Times.* New York: Harcourt, Brace and World. 1968.

Arendt, Hannah. *Rahel Varnhagen: The Life of a Jewish Woman*, translated by Richard and Clara Winston. New York: Harcourt Brace. 1974.

Arendt, Hannah. *The Human Condition.* Chicago: University of Chicago Press. 1958.

Bartsch, Shadi. *Ideology in Cold Blood: A Reading of Lucan's Civil War.* Cambridge: Harvard University Press. 1997.

---

20   "Entirely absorbed with the relation of the agent to itself, the analysis of action Dante undertakes in *De Monarchia,* as might be expected from its title, fails to consider the plurality of agents and thus misses what, for Arendt, is the essential condition of action. Because of this condition, doing cannot be purified of passivity, and its delight cannot be dissociated from suffering" (Susannah Young-ah Gottlieb, *Regions of Sorrow: Anxiety and Messianism in Hannah Arendt and W.H. Auden* [Palo Alto: Stanford University Press, 2003], 161–62).

Benhabib, Seyla. "Hannah Arendt and the Redemptive Power of Narrative." In *Hannah Arendt: Critical Essays*, edited by Lewis P. Hinchman and Sandra K. Hinchman, 111–42. Albany: State University Press of New York, 1994.

Brownlee, Kevin. "Dante and the Classical Poets." In *The Cambridge Companion to Dante*, edited by Rachel Jacoff, c. 7. Cambridge: Cambridge University Press, 2007.

Curtis, Kimberly. *Our Sense of the Real: Aesthetic Experience and Arendtian Politics.* Ithaca and London: Cornell University Press. 1999.

Goethe. *Faust.* Translated by Walter Arndt. New York: Norton. 1996.

Gottlieb, Susannah Young-ah. *Regions of Sorrow: Anxiety and Messianism in Hannah Arendt and W.H. Auden.* Palo Alto: Stanford University Press. 2003.

Hegel, G.W.F. *Elements of the Philosophy of Right.* edited by Allen W. Wood and translated by H.B. Nisbet. Cambridge: Cambridge University Press. 1991.

Hegel, G.W.F. *Phenomenology of Spirit.* translated by A.V. Miller. Oxford: Oxford University Press. 1977.

Johnson, Ralph. *Momentary Monsters: Lucan and his Heroes.* Ithaca and London: Cornell University Press. 1987.

Kristeva, Julia. *Hannah Arendt: Life Is a Narrative.* Toronto: University of Toronto Press. 2001.

Leibovici, Martine. "Arendt's 'Rahel Varnhagen': A New Kind of Narration in the Impasses of German-Jewish Assimilation and *Existenzphilosophie.*" *Social Research* 74, no. 3 (Fall 2007): 903–22.

Lucan, *Civil War.* Translated by Susan H. Braund. Oxford: Oxford University Press. 1992.

Speight, Allen. "Arendt and Hegel on the Tragic Nature of Action." *Philosophy and Social Criticism* 28, no. 5 (2002): 523–36.

Speight, Allen. "Arendt on Narrative Theory and Practice." In "Arendt, Politics, and Culture," special issue, *College Literature* 38, no. 1 (Winter 2011): 115–30.

Speight, Allen. *Hegel, Literature and the Problem of Agency.* Cambridge: Cambridge University Press. 2001.

Strong, Tracy B. *Politics without Vision: Thinking Without a Banister in the Twentieth Century.* Chicago: University of Chicago Press. 2012.

Taminiaux, Jacques. *The Thracian Maid and the Professional Thinker.* Albany: SUNY Press. 1997.

Tessin, Etienne, and Jerome Melançon. "...sed victa Catoni: The Defeated Cause of Revolution." *Social Research* 74, no. 4 (2007): 1109–112.

Villa, Dana. *Arendt and Heidegger.* Princeton, NJ: Princeton University Press. 1996.

Wolin, Richard. *The Politics of Being: The Political Thought of Martin Heidegger.* New York: Columbia University Press. 1990.

PART 2

Gendered Imagination

∴

CHAPTER 4

Imagining the Captive Amazon in Myth, Art, and History

Adrienne Mayor

In Greek mythology, Amazons were fierce warrior women dwelling in exotic barbarian lands of the East. Described as archenemies of the Greeks and adamantly opposed to traditional marriage, Amazons were deemed "the equals of men" in bravery and battle skills. Unlike typical Greek women whose lives were expected to be spent indoors minding children and weaving, non-Greek Amazons of myth gloried in a vigorous outdoor life of riding, hunting, warfare, and sexual independence—in other words they behaved like free Greek males. In Classical art and literature, Amazons were consistently portrayed as beautiful, athletic, and fearless. In Amazonomachy scenes in vase paintings and sculpture, Amazons fight heroically and skillfully against Greek warriors. Unlike the iconography of Persians and other real foreign enemies on the point of death at the hands of Greeks, Amazons were not pictured fleeing danger or gesturing for mercy.[1]

Despite their noble courage and erotic appeal, however, Amazons in Greek myth and art were typically doomed to defeat and death in battles and duels with Greek warriors. Even though Amazons were presented as attractive, worthy adversaries for the greatest Greek heroes, as "Oriental" Others, the Amazons were set up to be ultimately defeated and killed by Greek champions. For the Greeks, the idea of Amazons and Amazon-like females evoked ambivalent emotions of awe, admiration, desire, and fear. The exploits of Amazons and their warrior queens were wildly popular in oral and written traditions and public and private art, at once thrilling and disturbing.

---

1 Thanks to modern archaeological excavations of hundreds of graves of nomadic horsewomen buried with weapons from the Black Sea to the Altai region, we now know that Amazons of myth were influenced by the lives of Saka-Scythian and related peoples whose women fought as well as the men. The lives of these historical women, often identified as "Amazons," were described realistically by Greco-Roman writers. See Adrienne Mayor, *The Amazons: Lives and Legends of Warrior Women Across the Ancient World* (Princeton: Princeton University Press, 2014), and Dietrich von Bothmer, *Amazons in Greek* Art (Oxford: Clarendon Press, 1957). I thank Keith Moser for invaluable editorial suggestions.

© KONINKLIJKE BRILL NV, LEIDEN, 2020 | DOI:10.1163/9789004436350_006

FIGURE 4.1   Wounded Amazon, Roman marble copy of Greek bronze statue ca 450 BC, Metropolitan Museum [Wiki Commons]

In artistic illustrations of Amazonomachies, a few suspenseful scenes on pottery show Amazons overcoming Greek male opponents, but for the most part wounded and dead Amazons abound in classical vase paintings and sculpture (fig. 4.1). The motif of the wounded, dying, and dead Amazon was favored in Roman art as well. This pervasive theme of killing Amazons in classical myth, art, and literature has received extensive theoretical attention.[2] But another category has not attracted much attention: the captive Amazon (fig. 4.2).

The rarity of Amazons imagined as prisoners of war makes the examples we find in myths, historical sources, and artistic representations all the more striking and worth discussing. The paradoxical emotions aroused by the problematic figure of the Amazon are further complicated when such formidable

---

2 See Kenneth Dowden, "The Amazons: Development and Function," *Rheinisches Museum für Philologie* 140 (1997): 97–128; Josine Blok, *The Early Amazons: Modern and Ancient Perspectives on a Persistent Myth* (Leiden: Brill, 1995), 394–407; Brunilde S. Ridgway, "A Story of Five Amazons," *American Journal of Archaeology* 78, no. 1 (1974): 1–17; Mayor, *The Amazons: Lives and Legends of Warrior Women Across the Ancient World*, 26–27; and notes.

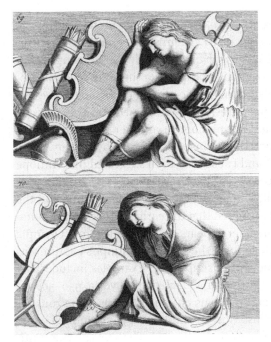

FIGURE 4.2   Captive Amazons, engraving, Robert von Spalart, *Historical Pictures of the Costumes of the Principal People of Antiquity and of the Middle Ages*, 1796

women were portrayed as captured alive, restrained and seemingly vulnerable to "domestication" by individual males and by powerful states. If the cycle of myths about Amazons reveals cultural beliefs about national origins, defenses against Others, and colonial conquest, those features are even more sharply illuminated in accounts of captive Amazons, in which we can discern paradoxical dyads, tensions between male/female roles, dominance/submission, wild/tame, freedom/restraint, and "deadly identities" neutralized by appropriation and assimilation.

Beyond the Mediterranean world, Amazon-like warrior women also figured in ancient epics, legends, and histories of Central Asia and China. The following pages consider how Amazons and warrior women were imagined as captives in myth, art, literature, and historical sources in ancient Greece and Italy with comparative examples from Islamic accounts, Central Asian oral epic poems, and Chinese chronicles.

1   Antiope, Captive Amazon Bride

Antiope is the quintessential captive Amazon of Greek myth. She figures in Athenian city foundation narratives about their national hero Theseus. In some versions, Theseus carried out his own expedition to fight the Amazons in their homeland of Pontus on the Black Sea (Themiscyra, now northeast Turkey). In alternate versions, Theseus accompanied Heracles on his Ninth Labor to obtain the war belt of the Amazon queen Hippolyta (in some accounts Antiope is sometimes called Hippolyta). In one recounting of the myth, Theseus and Antiope engaged in combat in Pontus; she was defeated and Theseus took her as his prisoner, with Heracles' permission. In another version, Theseus lured the Amazon onto his ship and thus kidnapped Antiope by trickery. Some Greek authors, such as Isocrates[3] and Pausanias[4] even suggested that Antiope fell in love with Theseus during the voyage back to Greece.[5]

Several vase paintings and reliefs depict Theseus battling Antiope and the Amazons in Pontus. Some scholars suggest that the earliest artistic representation of Theseus taking Antiope prisoner appears on a tripod leg from Olympia dating to 600 BC. By the late sixth century, the scene of Antiope's capture was illustrated in vase paintings, some with inscriptions.[6] Examples include Theseus taking Antiope away in his chariot on a black-figure hydria, 550–500 BC (Munich 302082); a krater showing Amazons chasing Theseus as he runs toward his chariot with Antiope in his arms; an amphora, 490 BC, in the Louvre with Theseus on foot carrying away Antiope (fig. 4.3); Theseus carrying Antiope to his chariot on a black figure cup in the British Museum (fig. 4.4); a black-figure hydria in the Metropolitan Museum (NY 12.198.3); a black-figure cup, Oxford 1927; an Apulian vase showing Antiope carried off in a chariot (fig. 4.5); and a black-figure vase made in Boeotia 550–500 BC. These painted scenes imagine the defeated Amazon with her weapons, struggling and gesturing as she is forcibly seized by Theseus.

Sculpted scenes of Theseus violently seizing Antiope also appear on the temple of Apollo at Eretria, dating to 515–500 BC (fig. 4.6) and on the Athenian Treasury at Delphi, dating to 510–470 BC (fig. 4.7). An elaborate Etruscan bronze cinerary urn of about 480 BC is decorated with four Amazon archers on horseback surrounding a man holding a woman (fig. 4.8). The pair has been identified by art scholars as a couple "dancing" but the presence of the hostile Amazons and the way the man is grasping the woman strongly suggests that they are Theseus and Antiope.[7]

---

3   Isocrates 12.193.

4   Pausanias, *Description of Greece* 1.21.

5   Mayor, *The Amazons: Lives and Legends of Warrior Women Across the Ancient World,* 261–66.

6   Timothy Gantz, *Early Greek Myth: A Guide to Literary and Artistic Sources*, vol. 2 (Baltimore: Johns Hopkins University Press, 1993), 282–85; von Bothmer, *Amazons in Greek* Art, 124–30.

7   Mayor, *The Amazons: Lives and Legends of Warrior Women Across the Ancient World*, 261; and figure 16.

FIGURE 4.3 Theseus seizes a struggling Antiope, red-figure amphora, 490 BC, Louvre G197
DRAWING BY W.H. ROSCHER, 1884

FIGURE 4.4 Theseus carrying Antiope to his chariot, Attic black-figure cup, British Museum AN473143001, London E41
© THE BRITISH MUSEUM 2003. IMAGE REPRODUCED WITH THE EXPRESSED WRITTEN CONSENT OF THE BRITISH MUSEUM

Ironically, the Etruscan figure of Antiope was misidentified as a dancer, while on another artifact a female figure with raised arms has been identified as either a captive Amazon or a dancer. She appears in mass-produced molded terracotta figurines from Boeotia, 330–300 BC.[8] Bending over an altar or table

---

8   Frances Middleton, and Katelyn Burgess, Figurine. *Figurine of a Dancer/Captive*. Yale University Art Gallery, New Haven, CT. 2012–2013. http://artgallery.yale.edu/collections/objects/7394.

FIGURE 4.5   Theseus abducting Antiope in his chariot, Apulian hydria
DRAWING IN GERHARD, *APULISCHE VASENBILDER*, 1845, PL. E.

FIGURE 4.6
Theseus seizing Antiope, relief, west pediment of temple of Apollo, Eretria, 515–500 BC, cast [WIKI COMMONS]

with arms held over her head, the woman wears typical Amazon garb: Phrygian cap over long hair, and boots, with one breast bared (fig. 4.9). The position of the arms leads some to think she is a bound Amazon. However, the figurine might represent a barbarian dancer (likely a slave woman, another sort of captive) performing the *oklasma*, a dance originating in Phrygia or Thrace. Other artistic images of *oklasma* dancers in "Oriental" Amazon-style costume appear in terracotta figures, gems, and vase paintings (eg, south Italian vase with

FIGURE 4.7   Theseus and Antiope, metope, Athenian Treasury at Delphi, 510–470 BC
PHOTO BY MATHIAS BERLIN [WIKI COMMONS]

FIGURE 4.8   Etruscan urn, Theseus capturing Antiope, surrounded by four mounted Amazons, ca 480 BC
AN256885001, ©TRUSTEES OF THE BRITISH MUSEUM, © THE BRITISH MUSEUM 2003. IMAGE REPRODUCED WITH THE EXPRESSED WRITTEN CONSENT OF THE BRITISH MUSEUM

FIGURE 4.9   Dancer or captive Amazon. Terracotta, mold-cast, 13.6 cm (5.3 in). Yale University Art Gallery, gift of Ambassador and Mrs. William Witman II, B.A. 1935; 1993.46.49

Amazon dancer, British Museum 1772,0320, and a kneeling *oklasma* dancer in the Boston Museum of Fine Arts, fourth century BC, 01.8103). *Oklasma* dancers sway and clasp their hands above their heads and wear Amazon-style caps and costumes.[9]

Theseus brought Antiope back to Athens as his war bride, making her the only Amazon in Hellenic myth to lose her freedom by marriage to a Greek. The story continued in Athens, where Antiope gave birth to Theseus's son Hippolytus, named after Antiope's slain sister Hippolyta. According to the myth, the enraged Amazons of Pontus vowed to avenge the death of Hippolyta and the abduction of Antiope. They dispatched a large Amazon army to invade Athens. After ferocious battles with high casualties on both sides, the Athenians finally emerged victorious. This hard-won victory was celebrated in numerous artworks in Athens, including monumental reliefs on the Parthenon and on the great shield of the colossal statue of Athena.

A number of vase paintings portray Antiope fighting on the side of Theseus and the Athenians. But at least six vases illustrate Antiope fighting alongside

---

9   Thanks to Arlechina Verdigris for information on comparative *oklasma* dancers.

the invading Amazons.[10] Artistic and literary evidence shows that there was a remarkable array of options open for Athenians to imagine Antiope's decision. In an interesting alternative story,[11] Theseus deserted Antiope and married Phaedra. During their wedding celebration, Antiope and the Amazons attacked Athens. In the main thread of the myth, however, Antiope came to view herself as an Athenian wife and mother; she took up weapons again and helped Theseus defend the city against the Amazon attack. In the fighting, Antiope was killed by a spear intended for Theseus, thrown by an Amazon named Molpadia. She was believed to be buried in a grave near the city gate: her revered tomb, beside that of Molpadia, was described by the Greek traveler Pausanias in the second century AD.

The earliest literary references to the myth of Theseus abducting Antiope appeared in the sixth and fifth centuries BC, by Pherekydes, Pindar, Simonides, and Euripides. Later accounts speculating on how Antiope became Theseus's captive wife in Athens include Apollodorus,[12] Pausanias,[13] Hyginus,[14] Plutarch[15] and Statius.[16] As we will see, the 5th-century BC historian Herodotus seems to refer indirectly to the Athenian foundation myth in his account of many Amazons taken prisoner by the Greeks during a battle in Pontus in the distant past.

Antiope was the only Amazon to suffer captivity in Greek mythology. Indeed, one can find more tales about Amazons and formidable foreign women capturing Greek males. Examples include Heracles enslaved by the Lydian queen Omphale, Odysseus held by Circe and Calypso, and the Athenian belief that Amazons maimed or killed baby boys and enslaved men for sex and reproduction.[17]

The marriage of Theseus and Antiope explored a "what if" question for the Greeks, who simultaneously feared and respected independent, headstrong women. The myth asks, What would happen if a Greek man married a strong-willed foreign woman who gloried in physical strength and warfare? She would be the opposite of proper Greek wives, mothers, sisters, and daughters, who

---

10   Mayor, *The Amazons: Lives and Legends of Warrior Women Across the Ancient World*, 275–76.
11   Apollodorus, *Epitome* 1.16–17.
12   Apollodorus, *Epitome* 1.16.
13   Pausanias, *Description of Greece* 1.2.1.
14   Hyginus, *Fabulae* 30.
15   Plutarch, *Theseus* 26.1.
16   Statius, *Thebaid*; Gantz, *Early Greek Myth: A Guide to Literary and Artistic Sources*, vol. 2., 282–85.
17   Gantz, *Early Greek Myth: A Guide to Literary and Artistic Sources*, vol. 1., 439–40; Gantz, *Early Greek Myth: A Guide to Literary and Artistic Sources*, vol. 2., 704–05, 707; Mayor, *The Amazons: Lives and Legends of Warrior Women Across the Ancient World*, 155–58.

were typically kept indoors, weaving and minding children. Because Amazons notoriously rejected traditional patriarchal marriage as it was practiced in Greece, the only way to marry an Amazon would be to capture her by violence, trickery, or seduction.

But could a "wild" Amazon ever be "tamed" or "domesticated," convinced to give up her freedom? In the great Battle for Athens, the myth evokes suspense: would Antiope be loyal to Theseus or her Amazon sisters? It is interesting here to consider the case of Medea, a powerful, independent foreign sorceress of Colchis, in the Caucasus, a land associated with Amazons. In the myth of Jason and the Argonauts' Quest for the Golden Fleece, when Jason arrived in Colchis, the king's daughter Medea fell in love with him. Using her intelligence and magic, she helped Jason overcome dangers and win the Golden Fleece. She was not a captive—she willingly abandoned her home and family and accompanied the Argonauts on their journey back to Greece. But as one of Jason's wives in Corinth, Medea began to feel like a prisoner and resented his new, younger wife Glauke. Medea committed great violence: she killed her children with Jason, murdered Glauke and Glauke's father Cleon, and then fled from Greece.[18] Notably, in Euripides' tragedy *Medea* (431 BC) her impassioned monologue expressing the wrongs she has suffered in exile has led some to see Medea as the first feminist heroine in literature. She chooses her fate and escapes, but at great cost.

The story of Antiope's submission to Theseus, her acceptance of her new role as his queen in Athens, and then her decision to defend her adoptive city could be used to justify the Greeks' patriarchal restraint of their women. But the story of Antiope's capture and appropriation also served to glorify the Athenians' resistance against the invading army of fearsome female fighters, the Amazons. Athens was able to achieve victory over the Amazons with—and perhaps even partly because of—the help of Antiope and her fighting skills. The abducted Amazon betrayed her own Amazon sisters and now took the side of the Greeks. Notably, however, the existence of alternative stories, reflected in vase paintings, in which Antiope remembers herself as an Amazon and joins their attack on Athens, testifies to the anxiety aroused by the idea of bringing a war-loving independent female into the city.

---

18   Mayor, *The Amazons: Lives and Legends of Warrior Women Across the Ancient World*, 259–70; Gantz, *Early Greek Myth: A Guide to Literary and Artistic Sources*, vol. 1., 340–41, 358–73.

2   Herodotus: Escape of the Captive Amazons

The only other captive Amazons in ancient Greek literature appear in a mytho-historical context, in a foundation legend explaining the origin of the Sarmatians, a Scythian tribe that appeared on the northern steppes in about the 7th century BC. Herodotus[19] describes a Greek expedition to Pontus on the Black Sea in the remote past, apparently alluding to the ancient myths of Heracles and Theseus. The Greeks, Herodotus says, defeated an army of Amazons on the Thermodon River and "captured as many of the women as they could." The Amazon prisoners were placed in three ships, to be taken back to Greece. But as the fleet sailed westward in the Black Sea, the Amazons rose up and overcame the Greek sailors, killing every man on board.

The Amazons had no sailing skills. The ships were swept away by storms and currents, and the Amazon captives were shipwrecked in the northern Black Sea coast. The women traveled inland on foot and stole horses from local Scythians. They resumed their former lifestyle. Ultimately, these Amazons allied with a group of young Scythians sent to track them. The young men hoped to "tame" the "wild Amazons" but the women demanded equality. The men acquiesced and the group migrated together north of the Don River to establish the new tribe known as Sarmatians, known for egalitarian sex roles.[20] In this narrative, presented as historical by Herodotus who heard the story on his travels among the Black Sea Scythians, the group of captive Amazons did not suffer the fate of the mythical Antiope. Instead, they managed to regain their weapons and were resourceful enough to slay their Greek captors at sea and escape to freedom.

According to Bulgarian classicist Ivan Marazov, a Thracian vessel may illustrate this Herodotean story of the escaped Amazon prisoners of war. Russian scholar Elena Savostina interprets a battle scene depicting Scythian men fighting Amazons carved on a limestone as an illustration of the Herodotus account.[21] Indeed, the males on the relief are not Greeks but appear to be Scythians, since they are dressed and armed like the Amazons they are fighting. Dated to 350–300 BC, the limestone relief is part of a large, artistically complex frieze discovered in the Taman Peninsula/Bosporus. This is the geographic region where the Amazon escapees in the story were shipwrecked and tangled

---

19   Herodotus 4.110–17.
20   Mayor, *The Amazons: Lives and Legends of Warrior Women Across the Ancient* World, 52–58.
21   Ivan Marazov, *Thrace and the Ancient World: Vassil Bojkov Collection* (Sofia, Bulgaria: Thrace Foundation, 2011), 168–71; Elena Savostina, Sculpture. Museum Text for Amazonomachy Limestone Relief. Pushkin Museum, Moscow. 2011. http://www.anticart.ru/data/bospor/143_amason_battle/index.php.

FIGURE 4.10   Possible illustration of Herodotus's account of the Amazon captives who escaped the Greeks and battled and then allied with Scythian men in the Bosporus region. Drawing of limestone relief, Taman Peninsula, Pushkin Museum no. 143, Moscow
© THE PUSHKIN STATE MUSEUM OF FINE ARTS. IMAGE REPRODUCED WITH THE EXPRESSED WRITTEN CONSENT OF THE PUSHKIN STATE MUSEUM OF FINE ARTS

with local Scythians (fig. 4.10). Another possibility is that the relief depicts a battle between Tirgatao, Warrior Queen of the Ixomatae, and another Scythian tribe, discussed below.

3   Enslaved Barbarian Women

Ancient vase painters' fascination with tattooed foreign females opens an intriguing question about the former status of some slave women portrayed in Athenian vase paintings. Greeks did not consider tattoos marks of beauty for themselves but were intrigued by this barbarian practice. From historical sources, we know that Thracian and other non-Greek women around the Black Sea and beyond decorated their bodies with tattoos of geometric and animal designs. Archaeological discoveries confirm that nomadic steppe women were so tattooed. The Greeks knew that these women came from relatively egalitarian tribes in which females participated in battle, and writers such as Herodotus and Plato equated them with mythic Amazons.[22] The majority of slaves in Athens originated from these groups. Several scenes on fifth century BC pottery depict heavily tattooed Thracian and foreign women wielding swords and

---

22   Mayor, *The Amazons: Lives and Legends of Warrior Women Across the Ancient World*, 95–116.

axes in violent scenes; there are also numerous images of tattooed slave women engaged in domestic work. These tattooed slave women would have been captured in warfare and/or purchased by Greeks from around the Black Sea and thus likely to have been captive women capable of fighting.

4 Xenophon's Captive "Amazons," ca 400 BC

The Greek general Xenophon led a large mercenary army from Persia north through Anatolia to the Black Sea and back to Greece, in about 400 BC. In his memoir of the "March of the 10,000,"[23] Xenophon described how his soldiers captured women from local villages to be concubines and servants on their route through Persia. On the long march through dangerous territories and rugged terrain, the soldiers and the captive women shared hardships. They came to trust and depend on each other for survival; they learned each other's languages and formed bonds of friendship beyond the sexual roles of captor and prisoner. Xenophon writes that the women helped the Greek soldiers fend off attacks from hostile tribes. We don't know whether the women had been previously trained to use weapons. But, notably, at a banquet hosted by Paphlagonian chieftains, one of the women performed a war dance with weapons. When the chiefs expressed surprise, the Greeks proudly compared their women to Amazons.[24] Like the mythic notion that Antiope would loyally defend her captor's city against enemies—even Amazons—Xenophon's historical incident suggests that despite their ambivalence about forceful women, the Greeks and other ancient cultures desired to somehow ally themselves with Amazons and their power. It also shows that over time the captive women began to consider themselves the helpmeets of their captors.

5 Tirgatao, Warrior-Queen of the Ixomatae, 430–387 BC

A historical Amazon-like warrior queen of the late 5th-early 4th century BC escaped from captivity, according to Polyaenus in his book of clever war strategies.[25] Tirgatao (Persian, "Arrow Power"), a warrior-princess of the Ixomatae, a Maeotian tribe whose horsewomen-archers participated in warfare, married

---

23 Xenophon, *Anabasis* 4.3.18–19, 6.1.11–13.

24 Mayor, *The Amazons: Lives and Legends of Warrior Women Across the Ancient World*, 140–41.

25 Polyaenus, *Stratagems* 8.55.

Hecataeus, king of the Sinds, an Adyge tribe of the Taman Peninsula and northeast coast of the Black Sea. Their marriage sealed an alliance between their peoples. At a certain point Hecataeus lost his throne, but was restored by his protector, Satyrus, king of the Bosporus. Satyrus then demanded that Hecataeus imprison Tirgatao in a tower in Sinda. But Tirgatao escaped from the tower and eluded Satyrus's men, traveling by difficult mountain trails by night and hiding in forests by day. When she reached her homeland, the Ixomatae acclaimed her as their leader. Taking up her previous life, she campaigned against hostile tribes. Tirgatao also foiled an assassination attempt by Satyrus and then led her armies to lay waste to Satyrus's kingdom.

6   Philip II of Macedon's Captive "Amazons," 339 BC

In 339 BC, Philip II of Macedon defeated a vast confederation of Scythian tribes from the Danube to the Sea of Azov, led by their ruler Ateas. The nomad-archers on horseback from this region were known to include Amazon-like women warriors, as mentioned in ancient Greek and Latin sources and as shown by archaeological discoveries of numerous ancient graves of armed women.[26] After his victory over Ateas, Philip brought back 20,000 Scythian mares for breeding and 20,000 Scythian women as captives, destined to become slaves and wives in Macedonia.[27] Among Scythian nomads, women were expert horse-riders and archers like the men, and so some of these women would have been active warriors. On the long march back to Macedonia, however, Philip's army was attacked by another Scythian tribe. In the melee, all the captured women and horse escaped back to Scythia. One can imagine that the female prisoners actively retrieved and rode the horses to freedom, possibly joining the Scythian tribe that attacked Philip's retreating army.

7   Romans and "Amazon" Captives

As the Romans expanded their reach and conquests in Europe and across the Mediterranean in Africa and Asia Minor, their soldiers encountered many peoples whose fighting forces included women. Numerous Roman-era historians described bellicose women fighting beside their men among the Celts (Gauls),

---

26   Mayor, *The Amazons: Lives and Legends of Warrior Women Across the Ancient World*, 63–71.

27   Justin 9.2–3.

IMAGINING THE CAPTIVE AMAZON IN MYTH, ART, AND HISTORY   97

Britons, Spanish, North African, and Germanic tribes. Battling the Celtic Ambrones at Aque Sextiae in 102 BC, for example, Marius's army faced female fighters as fierce as the men, charging with hideous war cries and wielding swords and axes. When the Romans fought the Germanic Marcomanni and Quadi along the Danube, AD 166–180, they discovered the bodies of women in armor on the battlefields. The Romans also observed females fighting in the troops of the Bracari of Spain.[28] As discussed below, Roman victory monuments included representations of female prisoners of war with weapons.

8   Chiomara of the Galatians, 189 BC

Modern authors of "Celtic warrior women" compilations often include a story about "Chiomaca," the wife of the Galatian chief, Ortiagon, in 186 BC. But in the original ancient accounts, this woman's name was Chiomara not Chiomaca and she was a noncombatant captured in 189 BC (not 186 BC), after the Romans led by Gnaeus Manlius Vulso defeated the Galatians (Greco-Gauls in Asia Minor). The ancient sources are Plutarch *Bravery of Women*[29] based on Polybius; Livy;[30] Valerius Maximus;[31] and Florus.[32] According to the ancient accounts, Chiomara did not fight in battle but was captured along with other Galatian women and slaves. She was raped by a centurion, who then demanded ransom. She sent her slave with the demand. When two Galatians arrived to deliver the ransom, the centurion embraced her. Behind his back, Chiomara gave the envoys a signal to kill the centurion. Chiomara then wrapped his head in her robe and delivered it to her husband Ortiagon to demonstrate her resolve and revenge on the rapist.[33]

The story of Chiomara's bravery was illustrated by medieval and later artists (FIG 4.11). It is interesting to trace the modern permutations of this story in English versions. No ancient historians described Chiomara taking part in the battle. Yet typical modern accounts, such as this one by Jones, claim that during

---

28   Plutarch, *Marius* 19.7; Dio Cassius 72.1–3; Appian *Spanish Wars* 6.72.
29   Plutarch, *Bravery of Women* 21.1.
30   Livy 38.24.2.
31   Valerius Maximus 6.1. ext2.
32   Florus 1.27.6; 2.11.6.
33   Sandra Péré-Noguez, "Chiomara, Camma et autres princesses…. Une histoire des femmes dans les societes 'celtiques' est-elle possible?," *Pallas* 90 (2013): 159–76; Stephane Ratti, "Le viol de Chiomara: Sur la signification de Tite-Live 38.24," *Dialogues d'Histoire Ancienne* 22, no. 1 (1996): 95–131.

FIGURE 4.11   Chiomara, woodcut, Johannes Zainer, 1474, Penn Provenance Project, Wikimedia Commons

the battle with the Romans the Gaulish men retreated but "Chiomaca stood her ground and killed several Roman soldiers before she was captured [and] raped by a centurion. Later she escaped, found the officer, cut his head off, and presented it to her husband."[34] Jones erroneously cites Norma Goodrich, *Medieval Myths*, for this account, but Jones actually found the story in Jessica Salmonson, who gives this version: "Chiomaca: A martial princess of the Gauls ... captured ... in 186 BC ... She refused to leave the battlefield but raged on with her few companions. When captured, she was raped by a centurion. She subsequently killed the centurion and chopped off his head which she delivered to her husband."[35] Salmonson cited Sarah Hale, who in 1855 had spelled Chiomara's name correctly

---

34   David E. Jones, *Women Warriors: A History* (Dulles, VA: Potomac Books, 1997), 148.
35   Jones, *Women Warriors: A History*, 148, cited Norma Goodrich, *Medieval Myths* (New York: Signet, 1977), 57, but took the account from Jessica Amanda Salmonson, *The Encyclopedia of Amazons* (New York: Paragon House, 1991), 57.

IMAGINING THE CAPTIVE AMAZON IN MYTH, ART, AND HISTORY   99

but said nothing about her fighting in battle.[36] In her elaborate account of the delivery of the ransom, Hale says that the two Galatians killed the centurion as he accepted the gold and that Chiomara then cut off his head and presented it to her husband. Hale's account adheres to the ancient reports. Although it is not clear that Chiomara ever participated in the actual combat, she was a brave and resourceful woman who escaped her captor by initiating violence.

9   Pompey's Captive "Amazons," 66–61 BC

In 66 BC, in the Third Mithradatic War, Pompey's Roman army pursued Mithradates VI from Pontus to the southern foothills of the Caucasus, ancient Colchis (modern Georgia). In Caucasian Albanian and Iberia, Pompey's soldiers fought battles against an aggressive coalition of tribes, numbering about 60,000, allied with Mithradates. Plutarch and Appian reported that "Amazons" joined these forces, and like Marius's men in 102 BC (above), Pompey's soldiers discovered warrior women among the dead with wounds showing they had fought courageously. Pompey even captured some of these women warriors. In his magnificent Triumph of 61 BC, Pompey paraded his most illustrious prisoners of war, including a group of Amazons from the southern Caucasus, labeled "queens of the Scythians."[37] Breaking with Roman traditions, Pompey's captives were not killed at the end of his Triumph, but the fate of his "Amazon" prisoners is unknown. They may have been married to Roman aristocrats, or Pompey may have returned them to their homeland, as he did for the other captives after his Triumph.[38]

10   Captive Amazons in Statius, *Thebaid*, AD 92

In the *Thebaid* epic, written in AD 92, the Latin poet Statius envisions an imperial Roman Triumph-like procession for the Greek hero Theseus upon his return to Athens, after fighting Scythians and Amazons in the Caucasus. Statius describes Antiope shown off as the grand prize, along with a group of other

---

36   Salmonson, *The Encyclopedia of Amazons*, 57, cited Sarah Hale, *Women's Record: or Sketches of All Distinguished Women, from Creation to A.D. 1854* (New York: Harper & Bros, 1855), 30.

37   Plutarch, *Pompey* 35 and 45; Appian, *Mithradatic Wars* 12.15–17.

38   Mayor, *The Amazons: Lives and Legends of Warrior Women Across the Ancient World*, 345–49.

unbowed, "unafraid warrior-maids" and the Amazons' war chariots, blood-stained baldrics, quivers, bows and arrows, and other weapons plundered from the defeated army of women. Statius even portrays Antiope as already pregnant, ready to bear her "enemy-lord's offspring." In the poem, Theseus "entreats" his captive bride to "dismiss thoughts of battle" and dedicate her bow and arrows to their "marriage bower."[39] Statius imagines how the captured Amazons were co-opted as wives and mothers by the victors, paralleling the realities of Greek and Roman warfare and the usual fates of defeated enemy women.

11 Roman Artistic Representations of Female Captives

Barbarian male and female prisoners of war appear in triumphal imagery celebrating Roman victories on coins, reliefs, and gems of the Republic and Empire. Not all the captive women pictured were combatants, perhaps especially those shown with children. But in view of the written histories of the Roman campaigns that mention female fighters among the Gauls and other peoples, it is safe to assume that some of the captured women shown in military contexts, seated and bound beside male warriors next to their weapons, could be understood as women who had participated in battles (FIGS 4.12 and 4.13).

As Romans became aware that many barbarian fighting forces included women, captive Amazons began to be popular features on marble sarcophagi featuring Amazonomachies and battles with barbarians. Two typical examples are in Rome's Capitoline Museum and the British Museum (FIGS 4.14 and 4.15). Some scholars suggest that the dejected captive Amazons on the coffins are

FIGURE 4.12   Silver *denarius* coin of Julius Caesar, 49–44 BC, depicting female and male captives of Gaul and other European tribes bound at the foot of his military trophies. British Museum, AN624041001
© THE BRITISH MUSEUM 2003. IMAGE REPRODUCED WITH THE EXPRESSED WRITTEN CONSENT OF THE BRITISH MUSEUM

---

39   Statius, *Thebaid* 12.519–39, 635–38.

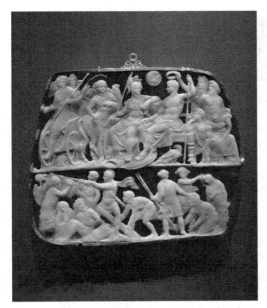

FIGURE 4.13   Two pairs of female and male barbarian captives (Gauls/Celts/Germans), as Romans raise a trophy with their weapons, carved Arabian onyx cameo, the Gemma Augustea, 1st century AD, Kunsthistorisches Museum, Vienna
PHOTO BY JAMES STEAKLEY, 2013 [WIKI COMMONS]

FIGURE 4.14   Roman, via collatina sarcophagus with Amazonomachy and Amazon captives, ca AD 150, Capitoline Museum, Rome
PHOTO BY JOSIAH OBER

only meant to represent defeated foreign peoples in general,[40] but the images could well reflect Roman encounters with genuine warrior women among the conquered peoples of Europe.

---

40   Fred S. Kleiner, *A History of Roman Art: Enhanced Edition* (Boston: Wadsworth, 2010), 224–25.

FIGURE 4.15   Roman sarcophagus with three pairs of captive Amazons, AD 180–220, British Museum,
© THE BRITISH MUSEUM 2003. IMAGE REPRODUCED WITH THE EXPRESSED WRITTEN CONSENT OF THE BRITISH MUSEUM

12   Queen Zenobia of Palmyra, Captured in AD 272

In AD 272, near Antioch and again at Emesa, Emperor Aurelian overcame the army led by Queen Bat Zabbai, of Arab-Aramaic descent, known to the Romans as Zenobia, whose conquests created the Palmyrene Empire, extending from Asia Minor to Egypt. Zenobia retreated to Palmyra (Syria) and resisted the Romans but was finally captured at the Euphrates River. Aurelian spared the life of this famous warrior queen, in order to parade her through the streets of Rome in heavy golden chains, followed by her empty golden war-chariot and members of her family.[41] Zenobia's fate is uncertain, but after the Triumph, it was reported that Aurelian and other Romans married Zenobia's daughters. Zenobia was said to live the rest of her life in Rome as a kind of celebrity conquest, married to a senator or a noble and living in a villa near Tivoli (fig. 4.16). In this plausible scenario, Zenobia and her daughters were absorbed into their captors' society.[42]

13   Emperor Aurelian's Gothic "Amazons," AD 273

During his reign (AD 270–275), Emperor Aurelian counted among his victories his defeats of the Goths and the Gauls, as well as Queen Zenobia of Palmyra and her allies. His Triumphs of AD 272–274 showed off rich booty and thousands of prisoners of war. Marching along with the exotic giraffes, elephants, tigers, and captives displayed in Rome was a group of ten women, dressed exactly like the male warriors. These warrior women "had been captured among the Goths" and they were labeled with a "placard declaring them to be of the race of the Amazons—for placards were borne before all, displaying the names

---

41   *Historia Augusta, Aurelian* 34.
42   Pat Southern, *Empress Zenobia: Palmyra's Rebel Queen* (London: Continuum, 2008).

FIGURE 4.16
Zenobia in chains, modern sculpture by Harriet Hosmer, 1859. St Louis Art Museum
COURTESY OF THE HUNTINGTON ART COLLECTIONS, SAN MARINO, CALIFORNIA

of their nations."[43] This group of Goth warrior women recalls Pompey's display of the captured "Scythian queens" from the Caucasus in 61 BC, described above. Aurelian minted copper coins (AD 274, British Museum 1962,1212.293) depicting himself on the obverse and on the reverse, Deus Sol Invictus (the Unconquered Sun God) whipping a pair of captives.

14   The Islamic-Arab Warrior Woman Khawlah, AD 636

It is interesting to compare some experiences of captive female fighters in stories of other ancient cultures to discern patterns similar to Greece and Rome. The legendary woman named Khawlah bint al-Azwar (Khaula Bint al-Kindiyyah) was described as a tall and ferocious fighter swathed in black and green garments and armed with a sword. With her female companions Oserrah, Alfra'Bint Ghifar al-Humayriah, and Wafeira, Khawlah led Arab forces commanded by Khalid ibn al-Walid against the Byzantine Empire's army, culminating at the Battle of Yarmouk (AD 636), ending Byzantine rule in Syria.

---

43   *Historia Augusta, Aurelian* 33–34.

According to the legend, Khawlah was captured by the Byzantines at the Battle of Sabhura, near Damascus (Syria). Khawlah urged her fellow female prisoners to take up tent poles and stakes to use as swords. With these makeshift weapons the women killed about 30 Byzantine soldiers and escaped.[44] This feat calls to mind the image of the Amazons who rose up against the Greek sailors in the Herodotus tale and Khawlah became an iconic Islamic heroine.

15   The Islamic Arab Warrior Woman Ayesha, AD 656

One of the most well-known women who fought in a battle in the early Islamic period was the last wife and widow of Muhammad, Ayesha (A'isha). After the Prophet's death in AD 632, wars broke out between Muslim factions. Ayesha, mounted on a war-camel, bravely led a revolt against Khalif Ali, culminating in the bloody battle in AD 656 at Basra (Iraq). In what became known as the "Battle of the Camel," Ayesha was captured by Khalif Ali. He treated her with respect and released her when she promised to spend the rest of her life tending Muhammad's grave.[45]

16   Janyl Myrza, Heroine of Kyrgyz Epic

Ancient oral traditions, epic sagas, poems, ballads, and folklore of Central Asian nomad groups have been perpetuated over the centuries by bards. Of about forty known Kyrgyz oral epics, only a few, such as the famous *Manas* saga, have been recorded in writing and most have not been translated into any other languages. One of these oral epics recounts the adventures of a Nogai warrior woman, Janyl Myrza. "Sir" Janyl is believed to have been a historical figure from the Tien Shan region (central Kyrgyzstan) whose bravery and prowess later became legendary. A daring horsewoman-archer, Janyl won great "power and respect among the Nogai people."

In the epic, Janyl kills Khan Tursun of Kashgar and many other invaders and challengers. She is captured through a ruse and forced to marry Kalmatay, the elderly chieftain of an enemy tribe. Janyl is compelled to give up her military

---

44   Jones, *Women Warriors: A History*, 19–20; and the Arab historian al-Waqidi cited by Ma'an Abul Hsun. For stories of Islamic warrior women, including captives, see Remke Kruk, *The Warrior Women of Islam* (London: Tauris, 2014).

45   Wiebke Walther, *Women in Islam, from Medieval to Modern Times* (Princeton, NJ: Markus Wiener, 1993), 106–07.

life and assume the role of a wife. But when her husband's people and land are threatened by another tribe, Janyl is urged to don her armor and take up her weapons again to defend them. She does—and after her great victory, she "returns to her own home to look after her own people."[46] There are interesting parallels between Janyl and Antiope: both are independent warrior women who lose their freedom and are forced into a patriarchal marriage. As noted earlier, some ancient Greek versions of Antiope's myth say she was kidnapped by trickery and Janyl was also tricked. The plot detail serves to emphasize the women's combat prowess, forcing foes to use underhanded ruses. Both women accepted living as traditional wives in their captors' homelands, and then in an emergency—an attack by enemy forces—each woman took up her weapons and fought for her adopted people. Similar themes appear in Chinese accounts of warrior women.

17   Fu Hao of the Shang Dynasty, China, 1250–1192 BC

China's earliest documented female general was Fu Hao, whose rich tomb was excavated in 1976 in north-central China. Fu Hao was buried with hundreds of jade objects from the Tarim Basin, including bronze weapons and inscriptions describing her military exploits. Fu Hao's father was not Chinese but a chieftain of horse people-archers of the northwest Tarim-Altai region, one of myriad nomadic tribes of the steppes whose women were trained to ride to war alongside the men. Agreements between the Chinese and these powerful tribes were often sealed by marriage exchanges: Fu Hao was sent to join the harem of Wu Ding, ruler of the Shang Dynasty (1250–1192). Because of her strong personality and experience, she became supreme commander of large armies, defending China's northwestern borders from marauding nomadic tribes like her own.

Although Fu Hao was not technically a prisoner of war but a kind of hostage-bride, this historical warrior woman shares some features with famed Amazon of Greek myth, Antiope. Like Antiope who fought for Athens against her sister Amazons, Fu Hao was assimilated into the Shang Dynasty as a concubine in the king's harem, but she recovered her people's warrior spirit and fought for the emperor's homeland defense forces.[47]

---

46   Ian Bek, "Sir Janyl," Postcard from Bishkek, Last modified July 9, 2012, http://ianbek .kg/?p=8759.

47   Mayor, *The Amazons: Lives and Legends of Warrior Women Across the Ancient* World, 414–16; notes 3 and 5; Barbara Peterson et al., *Notable Women of China: Shang Dynasty to the Early Twentieth Century* (New York: Sharpe, 2000), 13–16.

18 Liang Hongyu, Song Dynasty, China, AD 1102–1135

About 2,000 years after Fu Hao, another female general gained fame in China in the Song Dynasty (AD 1102–1135) during the wars against the Jurchen's Jin Dynasty. Liang Hongyu ("Red Jade") was the daughter of a general who fought on the western frontier. She was taught battle skills and martial arts and became an expert archer and a strong wrestler, at that time a popular sport for women as well as men. At one point, Liang Hongyu was captured and forced to entertain at banquets in wrestling matches. After a time, she had saved enough money to buy her freedom and married Han Shizhong, a general fighting the Jurchens. Liang Hongyu and Han Shizhong led armies together. Liang Hongyu was again captured, this time by rebels who demanded that Han surrender in exchange for her freedom. But Liang Hongyu devised a clever plan of escape and she and Han went on to crush the rebels and then the Jurchins. In the great naval battle of 1129 on the Yangtze River, Liang Hongyu successfully directed the charge against the Jurchins, and won the rank of "Lady Protector of the Nation."[48] In Chinese artworks, Liang Hongyu is typically shown with her sword or aboard ship directing the naval engagement by drumming.

19 Conclusion

Defeated mythic Amazons, such as Hippolyta and Penthesilea in Greek myth and Camilla in Virgil's *Aeneid* epic, were usually killed in combat by the enemy. Indeed, honorable death in battle was the destiny sought by most warrior women in myth and in reality, since, as many ancient historical accounts report, being a female prisoner of war meant rape, becoming the wife of the enemy, and bearing his children. Accordingly, most female fighters in ancient myth, legend, and history were determined to fight to the death to avoid capture and enslavement, and some civilian women committed suicide when taken prisoner.

As noted, Antiope was unique as the only Amazon in myth to become a traditional Greek wife after she was abducted. Notably, Antiope's mythic story is the most detailed ancient account of a captive warrior woman, with multiple scenarios imagined in literary and artistic accounts. Whether Antiope was defeated in combat as prisoner of war, taken as sexual booty by the victors, or kidnapped by a ruse, her captivity and co-option was not simply an assertion of Greek male dominance. Antiope's abduction was also a way of recruiting a bold

---

48   Peterson et al., *Notable Women of China: Shang Dynasty to the Early Twentieth Century*, 275.

IMAGINING THE CAPTIVE AMAZON IN MYTH, ART, AND HISTORY   107

Amazon woman into Athens' great history, as a kind of assimilated founder-mother. Theseus was the founding father of Athens. Bearing Theseus's son imported noble Amazon bloodlines into Athenian genealogy.[49] The idea of somehow tapping into the "Amazonian spirit" and controlling the power of Amazons was attractive. Notably, a great many ancient Greek cities in Anatolia claimed to have been founded by Amazons and they issued coins honoring their Amazon heroines. The city of Soloi even issued coins with an image of Antiope when they allied with Athens.[50]

The idea of appropriating females from foreign cultures known for warlike women into Greece might have been influenced by slavery practices in classical antiquity. Women from barbarian tribes dwelling in Thrace, the Black Sea area, Caucasus, and Anatolia—territories where Amazons were said to be located—were ubiquitous in Athenian households and public venues. Moreover, some leading Athenian citizens married women from those lands and brought them back to Athens. The presence of foreign slaves and wives from lands so strongly associated with Amazons parallels the mythic story of a captive Amazon queen transported from Pontus to Athens.

Abduction, seduction, rape, and forced marriage of admirable, dangerous yet desirable foreign women by Greeks and, later by Romans, is perennial pattern in myth and in history. The Romans traced their heritage back to the "heroic rape" of the women of the Sabines, a native Italian people conquered by the early Romans. The captive Sabine women were later revered as the mothers of the first Romans. In Book 11 of the *Aeneid*, his epic poem about the foundation of Rome, Virgil included a noble Amazon-like warrior, Camilla of the Volsci. Accompanied by several female warrior companions, Camilla led the Volscians against the legendary Roman hero Aeneas. Historically, the Volsci were a bellicose tribe that had been overcome and absorbed into the early Roman empire. By Virgil's time, many aristocratic Romans prided themselves on their Volscian heritage and presumably their links to the warrior woman Camilla. With this in mind, the Roman senator or noble who married Zenobia enhanced his reputation in Rome by "taming" a warrior queen.

Accommodation to the captors' culture was one option for women prisoners in antiquity. As we have seen, other historical "Amazons" replicated Antiope's experience. The Persian women captured by Xenophon's Greek soldiers became trusted companions and the men bragged that they had warlike

---

49   Gantz, *Early Greek Myth: A Guide to Literary and Artistic Sources*, vol. 1., 283.
50   Mayor, *The Amazons: Lives and Legends of Warrior Women Across the Ancient World*, 261–65.

barbarian women on their side. Janyl Myrza, the war heroine of Kyrgyz epic, was captured by a ruse and forced into matrimony, but she later took up her weapons and saved her adoptive land from attack, like Antiope. In Bronze Age China, Fu Hao, a nomadic warrior maiden sent as a bride to the Shang emperor, marshaled her battle skills and intelligence to become the supreme commander of his armies.

Some captured Amazons and historical warrior women managed to regain their freedom and resume their previous lives, like the nomadic Scythian women who escaped with their horses from Philip ii of Macedon. The Arab fighter Ayesha won her release by agreeing to peace and she lived a long life. The warrior-queen Bat Zabbai/Zenobia of Palmyra lived out the rest of her days peacefully in Rome. As we've seen, some captive warrior women formed alliances with male warriors who approved of the women's battle prowess, self-sufficiency, and courage. Examples include the shipwrecked Amazons who joined the Scythian men in Herodotus's account and Liang Hongyu, who joined her military husband to lead the Song armies to victories.

For some, violence was an option, for escape or revenge. The captive Amazons trapped in the ships in Herodotus's account slaughtered their Greek captors. The Galatian woman Chiomara escaped by having her centurion-rapist slain and then beheading him. The Islamic warrior Khawlah and her fellow prisoners attacked and killed their enemy guards. Tirgatao of the Ixomatae slipped out of her prison tower and then returned to take revenge on her captor.

Captive Amazons and warrior women could have multiple meanings depending on perspective and context. For the Greeks, Antiope was not only a sexual prize for a mythic hero known for seizing women, but, as in many of the stories of warrior women here, Antiope could also be seen as fortifying Athenian city walls and bloodlines with her "Amazon" power. In the Roman era, the image of the captive Amazon, as in Statius's *Thebaid* epic and on Roman sarcophagi, could symbolize defeated peoples as a group, but also represented real warlike barbarian women who resisted Roman rule. During the Republic and the Empire, Roman legions took prisoners of war of both sexes. Pompey was the first Roman general to display Amazon-like captives in Rome. Julius Caesar and many Roman emperors depicted pairs of captives, male and female, with their weapons and armor on their coinage, commemorative gems, and victory monuments. For the Romans, Triumphs displaying exotic women warriors such as Zenobia and the Goth "Amazons" provided public spectacles. In similar fashion, female gladiatrixes, who were often captives or slaves, provided exciting theater. In China, when Liang Hongyu was captured she was forced to wrestle as entertainment for her enemies.

IMAGINING THE CAPTIVE AMAZON IN MYTH, ART, AND HISTORY

Although the fates of the Scythian, Goth, and other anonymous foreign female fighters taken by the Romans were not reported, it is likely they were raped, sold as slaves, or married off rather than sacrificed like many male captives. For their captors, all defeated women, combatants and noncombatants alike, were booty used for sex and servitude. For the warrior women themselves, if rape and enslavement as a servant or wife were inevitable, they could try to come to terms with their new status, while planning escape or winning some form of liberty either by wits or violence.

References

Abul Hsun, Ma'an. "Khawla Bint Al-Azwar: The Islamic Heroine." *Al Shindagah* 52 (May-June 2003): n.p. http://www.alshindagah.com/mayjun2003/woman.html.

Bek, Ian. "Sir Janyl." Postcard from Bishkek. Last modified July 9, 2012. http://ianbek.kg/?p=8759.

Blok, Josine. *The Early Amazons: Modern and Ancient Perspectives on a Persistent Myth*. Leiden: Brill. 1995.

Bothmer, Dietrich von. *Amazons in Greek Art*. Oxford: Clarendon Press. 1957.

Dowden, Kenneth. "The Amazons: Development and Function." *Rheinisches Museum fur Philologie* 140 (1997): 97–128.

Gantz, Timothy. *Early Greek Myth: A Guide to Literary and Artistic Sources*, 2 vols, Baltimore: Johns Hopkins University Press. 1993.

Hale, Sarah. *Women's Record: or Sketches of All Distinguished Women, from Creation to A.D. 1854*. New York: Harper & Bros. 1855.

Jones, David E. *Women Warriors: A History*. Dulles, VA: Potomac Books. 1997.

Kleiner, Fred S. *A History of Roman Art: Enhanced Edition*. Boston: Wadsworth. 2010.

Kruk, Remke. *The Warrior Women of Islam*. London: Tauris. 2014.

Marazov, Ivan. *Thrace and the Ancient World: Vassil Bojkov Collection*. Sofia, Bulgaria: Thrace Foundation. 2011.

Mayor, Adrienne. *The Amazons: Lives and Legends of Warrior Women Across the Ancient World*. Princeton: Princeton University Press. 2014.

Middleton, Frances and Katelyn Burgess. Figurine. *Figurine of a Dancer/Captive*. Yale University Art Gallery, New Haven, CT. 2012–2013. http://artgallery.yale.edu/collections/objects/7394.

Péré-Noguez, Sandra. "Chiomara, Camma et autres princesses ... Une histoire des femmes dans les societes 'celtiques' est-elle possible?" *Pallas* 90 (2013): 159–76.

Peterson, Barbara, He Hong Fei, Wang Jiyu, Han Tie, and Zhang Guangyu, eds. *Notable Women of China: Shang Dynasty to the Early Twentieth Century*. New York: Sharpe. 2000.

Ratti, Stephane. "Le viol de Chiomara: Sur la signification de Tite-Live 38.24." *Dialogues d'Histoire Ancienne* 22, no. 1 (1996): 95–131.

Ridgway, Brunilde S. "A Story of Five Amazons." *American Journal of Archaeology* 78, no. 1 (1974): 1–17.

Salmonson, Jessica Amanda. *The Encyclopedia of Amazons.* New York: Paragon House. 1991.

Savostina, Elena. Sculpture. Museum Text for Amazonomachy Limestone Relief. Pushkin Museum, Moscow. 2011. http://www.anticart.ru/data/bospor/143_amason_battle/index.php.

Southern, Pat. *Empress Zenobia: Palmyra's Rebel Queen.* London: Continuum. 2008.

Walther, Wiebke. *Women in Islam, from Medieval to Modern Times.* Princeton, NJ: Markus Wiener. 1993.

CHAPTER 5

Gender and Imagination: A Feminist Analysis of Shahrnush Parsipur's *Women Without Men*

Reshmi Mukherjee

In *The Republic of Imagination* (2015), Iranian writer Azhar Nafisi talks about the value of imaginative knowledge as a way of perceiving the world and uniting "the community of mankind" across continents and time.[1] She links this knowledge to literary imagination as the lifeline of a democratic society, a powerful tool in the fight against totalitarianism and states: "without the writers who take us into their imagined stories, we would lose our ability to dream and crave the freedoms we so often take for granted."[2] *Women Without Men* (1989), written more than two decades earlier, speaks about something similar and much more.[3] Shahrnush Parsipur links feminism to imagining, not just thought and ideas, but how we can think about feminist imagining as a political act and, therefore, think of imagination as a radical process. By writing about the taboo subject of gender injustice during a tumulus time in Iranian history, she places politics and imagination in the same spectrum of cognition and action that Desiree Lewis explains as disrupting the normative idea that imagination is an ahistorical process and eludes the real world of politics. The novella paves bold ways of thinking by debunking the universality of enlightenment thinking as phallo-centric and mediated by patriarchal knowledge systems.[4] This chapter studies Parsipur's radical imagination through the surrealist technique of automatic writing in addition to how she weaves aesthetic experimentation, Iranian women's right issues, and resistance to the patriarchal state ideology together. Alongside, it examines the theoretical lenses of ecofeminism, necroresistance, and psychoanalysis, to conclude that Parsipur's writing is rhizomatic in nature. Parsipur embraces a multiplicity of writing

---

1 Azhar Nafisi, *The Republic of Imagination* (New York: Penguin Books, 2015).

2 Carol Memmott, "'The Republic of Imagination' of Azar Nafisi," *New York Times*, October 30, 2014, https://www.chicagotribune.com/entertainment/books/ct-prj-republic-of-imagination-azar-nafisi-20141030-story.html.

3 Shahrnush Parsipur, *Women Without Men*, trans. Kamran Talattof and Jocelyn Sharlet (Syracuse, NY: Syracuse University Press, 1998).

4 Desiree Lewis, "Feminism and the Radical Imagination," *Agenda: Empowering Women for Gender Equity* 21, no. 72 (2007): 18–31.

© KONINKLIJKE BRILL NV, LEIDEN, 2020 | DOI:10.1163/9789004436350_007

techniques that can move in many directions and are always connected to many lines of "thinking, [imagining and being] and acting."[5]

Set under the backdrop of a dictatorial state that restricts women's access to citizenship rights, *Women Without Men* (from here on WWM) is a story about the journey of five women Mahdokt, Munis, Faizeh, Zarrinkolah, and Farrokhlaqa in search of freedom. The non-linear narrative style makes it difficult to estimate the exact time frame of the story, but it spans over a period of thirty years, before and after the Islamic revolution of Iran, barring one instance (death of Munis) that directly alludes to the British and the United States led coup d'état of 1953.[6] Much of what happens in the text is related to the events that occurred after the 1979 revolution, especially the power given to the elitist religious groups who mandated the division of public and private spaces, marked by strict rules, to discipline women and constitute them as docile subjects and reduce them to mere objects for sexual gratification. The five women in the novella represent the different layers of the Iranian social fabric and their experience of gendered forms of violence, psychological, physical, and sexual, which bring them to the garden of Karaj. The garden resembles the Foucauldian idea of a "crisis heterotopia," "a socially forbidden place reserved for individuals who are alienated from the center and live at the margins and in a state of crisis vis a vis the state."[7] It, however, proves beneficial for the women and helps resolve their crisis by manifesting their repressed desire, and renegotiating their gender roles in the domineering cultural and political climate.

Parsipur's style of writing speaks about her political ideology as she breaks the stereotypical image of the Muslim woman as a docile subject and represents the characters as active agents and not passive victims of a repressive state history. She radically transforms female bodies from sites for cultural mediation to bodies with assigned meanings and subjectivity, and sites for resistance that challenge the social contours of society.[8] The characters break the taboos surrounding virginity and the sexual desire of the female body and use

---

5 Azhar Nafisi, "Imagination as Subversion: Narrative as a Tool of Civic Awareness," in *Muslim Women and the Politics of Participation*, eds. Mahnaz Afkhami and Erika Freidl (Syracuse: Syracuse University Press, 1997), 68.

6 Kamran Talatoff, "Breaking Taboos in Iranian Women's Literature," *World Literature Today* 78, no. 3–4 (2004): 45.

7 Michel Foucault, "Of Other Spaces: Utopias and Heterotopias," trans. Jay Miskowiec, *Architecture/Mouvement/Continuité* (October 1984): 4.

8 Kamran Talattof and Jocelyn Sharlet, "Afterword," in Shahrnush Parsipur, *Women Without Men*, trans. Kamran Talattof and Jocelyn Sharlet (Syracuse: Syracuse University Press, 1998), 173.

their bodies and minds as interchangeable identities and astatic spaces to resist the bio-political warfare and the control of female bodies. As such, they are represented as an eccentric group who occupy a liminal space in society and are neither alive nor dead (Munis): neither innocent nor a victim (Faizeh): nonhuman-human tree (Mahdokt): androgynous (Zarrinkolah): and neither evil nor a saint (Farrokhlaqa). They subvert the given gender and sexual identity that is constituted to uphold patriarchal values and, much like feminist philosopher Donna Haraway's definition of Cyborgs, change to "illegitimate offspring of militarism and patriarchal capitalism, not to mention [religious vanguards], often exceedingly unfaithful to their origins."[9] In other words, they detach themselves from the Oedipal project so that they "can no longer be the source for appropriation or incorporation by the Other."[10] Their temporary refuge in the garden of Karaj and a rejection of that space at the end is symbolic and indicates that they cannot be contained by rigid boundaries of "the public-private divide, organic family connection, intimacy, and or perversity."[11]

One of the most intriguing aspects of Parsipur's writing of *WWM* is how she remediates the surrealist technique of automatic writing to suit her ideological and political goals. She reconstitutes the traditional surrealist representations of women as disembodied entities (André Breton), presenting them as subversive, radical, and avant-garde agents of change instead, much like the French Surrealist artist, photographer, and writer Claude Cahun. Thus, automatic writing, which seeks to make a direct connection between latent thought and manifest thinking by bypassing repression, provides Parsipur the perfect medium for: (a) articulating the fluid thematic design of her novella, wherein women's bodies morph into unnatural and supernatural forms, and, (b) criticizing both western and state ideologies that perceive and situate Iranian women as a silent minority. In other words, Parsipur's Surrealist mode of writing bridges action with thought, and implements automatic writing as both aesthetic experimentation and a critique of ideology. This displaced and condensed critique of ideology also allowed her to evade State censure.

The use of automatic writing to articulate female voice-consciousness, however, is not unique and, western feminist Surrealists have experimented with this form as well. Western feminist surrealists Whitney Chadwick, Helaine Posner, and Katy Kline, while commenting on the exhibition "Mirror Images:

---

9   Donna Haraway, "A Cyborg Manifesto: Science, Technology, and Social Feminism in the Twentieth Century," in *Simians, Cyborgs, and Women: The Reinvention of Nature*, ed. Donna Haraway (New York: Routledge, 1991), 154.

10   Haraway, "A Cyborg Manifesto," 151.

11   Haraway, "A Cyborg Manifesto," 151.

Women, Surrealism, and Self-Representation," observe that the body of self-portraits by the women Surrealist artists of the 1920s and 1940s are unique and have few similarities with the works of their male colleagues:

> While male Surrealists rooted the disruptive and creative potential of erotic desire in the masculine libido and exalted woman as muse in fetishized images that celebrate her as "other," women artists turned to their own reality. They located the sources of Surrealism's disruption of rational boundaries within their own subjectivity, and gave it concrete form in works that explore the female body as a site of conflicting desires, and femininity as a taut web of social expectations, historical assumptions, and ideological constructions.[12]

Parsipur's style is closely aligned to western feminist experimentations with language and writing, although she alters the modalities of representing the female subjects in her novella and represents the female bodies as objects/spaces exploited for the exertion of power and, at the same time, as radical spaces from where resistance to all forms of violence is possible. Consequently, the female body is both a site *of* social, cultural, political, and religious constructions and a site *for* dismantling it as well. The female body is given double agency much like Claude Cahun's "Autoportraits," where the body is both the subject that reflects, and subject-object that is reflected.[13] In *WWM*, though, this double function of the female subject is a radical step towards disrupting the I/Other relationship and rupturing the otherness of the *woman* in a patriarchal world order. The "Other" here is the patronymic social, cultural, political, religious, and international law that constitutes the *woman* as the other of the man. An otherness that is inextricably bound with the woman's internalization of her image that reflects the male Other's desire of it.[14] It questions female subject-hood that is already fragmented because it is mediated through the Other's identity of the self. An example of this is the image of repressed Muslim women, who are a construction of the gaze of the western Other and represented as fetish objects in the socio-political, historical discourses and literary texts about the non-west.

---

12 Whitney Chadwick, "An Infinite Play of Empty Mirrors," in *Mirror Women, Surrealism, and Self Representation*, ed. Whitney Chadwick (Cambridge: MIT press, 1998), x–xii.

13 Katy Kline, "In or Out of the Picture," in *Mirror Women, Surrealism, and Images Self-Representation*, ed. Whitney Chadwick (Cambridge: MIT press, 1998), 67.

14 Chadwick, "An Infinite Play of Empty Mirrors," 9.

GENDER AND IMAGINATION

Nonetheless, it should be mentioned here that Parsipur's adaptation of automatic writing is not a blind following of the western tradition or a mere writing back to the Other. Her representation of the female body as a surrealist subject addresses a major gap in western feminist scholarship and surrealist literature/art as well. European and American feminist surrealists, to critique male surrealists' disembodied representation of white female bodies, almost always portrayed able-bodied, uncovered white women as the quintessential symbol of feminist liberation. This in turn has excised non-white and clothed bodies of "Third World" women and the linear representation of empowerment validates a hegemonic subject position via a singular discourse that celebrates "liberated" white women as the true agent of revolution. Consequently, this chapter argues that Parsipur's story, in contrast, destabilizes this hierarchical arrangement of female bodies and possibly calls for a politics of affiliation by understanding the differences between First and Third world feminisms. Again, to reiterate an earlier point, it is not a writing back to the first world feminist rhetoric about the helplessness of "third world" women either, but like a rhizome, *WWM* "resists structures of domination" and can be read as part of the global feminist call for equal partnership.[15] *WWM*, therefore, breaks the cultural assumptions about the silent women of Iran and the west's need to save [all] Muslim women from Muslim men.[16] It speaks about women's rights, freedom, and sexual desires and Parsipur erases certain preconceived notions and represents them as speaking subjects, transforming a local text into a global manifesto. In this regard, her literary work echoes with Anne Donadey, Human Ahmed-Ghosh, Perin Gurel, Minoo Moallem, Mahnaz Afkhami, Afsaneh Najmabadi, Valentine M. Moghadam, Saba Mahmood, Shirin Neshat and others, who relentlessly advocate against the othering of non-western women and constructing them "as a victim of her culture," especially post-revolutionary Iranian women.[17] These scholars have adopted various methods to represent Iranian women as complex subjects and not as generic veiled women with no consciousness. Afsaneh Najmabadi in her article "Veiled Discourse" marks the beginning of objective representation of Persian women in 19th century travel narratives, political and moral essays, plays, novels, etc. The documents portray the women as "terrains 'of political and cultural contestation and as ... important metaphor[s] for demarcating the self and the other.' [And] these

---

15   Deleuze and Guattari, *A Thousand Plateaus: Capitalism and Schizophrenia*, 8.

16   Lila Abu-Lughod, "Do Muslim Women Really Need Saving?," *American Anthropologist* 104, no. 3 (September 2002): 783–90.

17   Perin Gurel, "Transnational Feminism, Islam, and the Other Woman: How to Teach," *Radical Teacher*, no. 86 (December 2009): 66.

contestations continue to be central to contemporary politics of Iran and many other many other Islamic societies of the Middle East."[18] Nima Naghibi in *Rethinking Global Sisterhood* takes the example of the Orientalist evocation of *One Thousand and One Nights* to discuss how these representations produced "exoticized, veiled, and silent Persian women."[19] And, in turn facilitated British and American women writers to "counterpose a figural category—the subjugated female [o]ther ... to occupy a subject position of power in relation to Persian women."[20] She concludes that this image of "figural subjugation" has a direct impact on First world and third world feminist collaboration and their binary relationship based on power and agency. "Third world women" have continued to suffer othering within western feminist discourses of empowerment and, therefore, the alliance of global sisterhood has not been successful so far. Anthropologist Lila Abu-Lughod in "Do Muslim Women Need Saving," implies the danger of such representations and cites Laura Bush's speech defending the United States' military occupation of Afghanistan post 9/11 as a need for saving Afghan women from Taliban men.[21] Abu-Lughod argues that this reiterates British colonial discourse about India as "saving brown women from brown men" and installs a feeling of collective guilt, and that the "female other" has always been used as a pawn to attack the other's country, reducing women to mere victims. Her argument is important for western and transnational feminist practices because it connects this savior complex with political and economic factors that benefit such de-subjectification of Muslim women in today's global politics, especially when fighting terrorism is not only a concern for homeland security but part of global capitalist intervention.

The above-mentioned works by renowned feminists are helpful in reading Parsipur's work, not to make her more acceptable to the Anglo-American readers, but to expand the importance of her work as an example of experimental writing and historical imagination to counter *phallogocentric* narratives that silence gendered others. Just like experimental literature is about *unrepressing* questions like: "what is literature, what is its function in the 'mainstream,' and in so doing, it lays everything open to challenge and reconfiguration," Parsipur uses surrealism to rupture the constitution of *woman* as the object of the

---

18   Afsaneh Najmabadi, "Veiled Discourse-Unveiled Bodies," *Feminist Studies* 19, no. 3 (Autumn 1993): 487–518.

19   Nima Naghibi, *Rethinking Global Sisterhood* (Minneapolis: University of Minnesota Press, 2007), xv.

20   Naghibi, *Rethinking Global Sisterhood*, xv.

21   Abu-Lughod, "Do Muslim Women Really Need Saving?," 783–90.

GENDER AND IMAGINATION

western and non-western male other's desire in the first place.[22] Much like the early Surrealists, whose writing was "a radical reevaluation of society through the medium of an artistic movement," Parsipur too uses this literary method as a reawakening to oppression. Moreover, the manifesto style of writing both combines and separates politics and aesthetics in favor of a Utopian (hetero-topic) image.[23]

In surrealism, an *objet trouvé* or a found object is very important. *Objet trouvé* is in itself a creative act, Breton places an emphasis on those objects/spaces of interest that have been dismissed by critics as void of aesthetic interest.[24] Consequently, since a Surrealist object is not structured and lacks any specific dimension and/or meaning, it cannot be characterized rationally. To read and write about such an object is also to engage in automatism, whereby one has to suspend conscious thinking and privilege the unconscious mind to perceive this object in an unconventional manner. This unconventional representation of space is an automatic technique of deconstructing systems of reading, writing, and language formation that frame our cognitive abilities and imagination. For example, we are all part of an inherited system of thought and communication constituted by the words we use yet words and meanings are a priori and we have no part in the construction of that meaning making system. What we think is almost always influenced by the signs and signifiers we use in the form of words, and when we attempt to express a thought verbally or through the written words, we must again revert to an imposed system to do so.

The garden in Karaj is an *objet trouvé* and performs a similar function. It already has an established non-art function because in Iran the garden has a seemingly deep and superimposed meaning. Persians gardens were considered a sacred place and as the center of the world that binds everything together like an umbilicus. The four corners of the rectangular garden are the four parts of the world with a center (represented by a fountain or a water body) where everything comes together in a microcosmic way. Rugs are also reproductions of the garden, where the "whole world comes to enact its symbolic perfection" and it is spatially temporal in nature because it can move

---

22   Joe Bray, Alison Gibbons, and Brian McHale, "Introduction," in *The Routledge Companion to Experimental Literature*, eds. Joe Bray, Alison Gibbons, and Brian McHale (London and New York: Routledge Francis and Taylor Group, 2012), 1.

23   Laura Winkel, "Manifestos and Ars Poetica," in *The Routledge Companion to Experimental Literature*, eds. Joe Bray, Alison Gibbons, and Brian McHale (London and New York: Routledge Francis and Taylor Group, 2012), 254.

24   Clifford Browder, "Dreams and the Surrealist Object," in *André Breton: Arbiter of Surrealism*, ed. Clifford Browder (Geneva: Librarie Druz, 1967), 97.

in-between spaces, and is not restricted as such.[25] The garden then, although a small place in the world, also represents a totality and in that sense, it is the oldest utopia that has existed because it is central to the mythical literature and cultural imagination in the Persian and Islamic tradition. The presence of the garden in *WWM* serves a subversive purpose as well that challenges the happy, totalizing image of what the Persian garden originally represented. Parsipur reconstructs the sacred peaceful space as a state of crisis or, to use Michel Foucault's term, a crisis heterotopia or a heterotopia of deviation. Foucault defines heterotopias as spaces that are in a flux and lay in-between two spaces, one real and one that gives the illusion of being the real. He gives the example of a mirror, which reflects the image in its totality, only that, what it reflects on the other side is not real but a reflection of the real. Hence, heterotopias almost always exist in opposition to utopias that represent a lack and are in a constant state of crisis.

In the beginning of the novella, the garden in *WWM* was a popular spot, but the planting of Mahdokt (one of the protagonists in the novella) as a human tree leads to its sudden change from a popular to a subaltern place, alienated from the center and holds no interest to the outside world.[26] The marginalization of the garden from the mainstream transforms it into a non-functioning space as well and a perfect surreal object, much like Breton's concept of the *objet trouvé*. In this moment in the text, the presence of a human, non-human tree/nature also signifies a rupture changing the symbolic meaning of the domestic and public world at the same time, further confirming the garden's presence as useless and undesirable: "[The family] are completely besides themselves with disgrace... They said they would sell the garden cheap on condition that their name be withheld..."[27] When Farrokhlaqa, a rich and lonely widow, who murdered her arrogant and insensitive husband, comes to buy the garden and notices Mahdokt, the gardener tells her how the family has disowned the garden because planting oneself as a tree is a sign of madness, to which she reacts by saying: "If she is insane, they should put her in a mental asylum."[28] When the realtor informs her of the reason for their failure to do so because no matter "how hard they try, they can't get her out of the ground,"

---

25   Michel Foucault, "Of Other Spaces: Utopias and Heterotopias," trans. Jay Miskowiec, *Architecture /Mouvement/ Continuité* (October 1984), 6.

26   I use the word subaltern following Gayatri Spivak's use of it to mean a marginal subject/ place, a position with no identity.

27   Shahrnush Parsipur, *Women Without Men*, trans. Kamran Talattof and Jocelyn Sharlet (Syracuse, NY: Syracuse University Press, 1998), 88.

28   Parsipur, *Women Without Men*, 87.

GENDER AND IMAGINATION

Farrokhlaqa accepts it as a challenge with the hope that Mahdokt's presence as an *aporia* will attract more visitors in Karaj.[29]

In relation to Foucault's examples of heterotopias of deviation, the asylums, brothels, retirement homes, and prisons, where the dwellers of these spaces are social outcasts, Parsipur's characters are also marginalized from the *mainstream*. The garden and its inhabitants function in conflict and exist in a perpetual state of chaos and to exemplify this extraordinary setting, she uses contrasting images to describe the garden as: "sweet and sour, half village and half city, silent battle of light green with dark green, a beautiful pool contaminated with scums and frogs" to take it as far away as possible from the idea of a utopia.[30] The physical location of the garden is equally abstruse, it is not centrally located nor is it at the margin and lies somewhere between Tehran and Karaj. In other words, it occupies space and has a physical presence, but its location is unmarked on the map hence, unidentifiable as such. Parsipur's writing makes the readers think of the rupture within the theoretical concept of the signifier- signified (word and meaning) relationship that drastically alters the garden from a sacred spot to a de-sanctified space. Besides, she refrains from using words and imageries that are normally used to describe the garden as a blissful place, and on the contrary, it is shown as a kind of [inverse] utopic space [order amidst chaos] "where women live together without men," and "men" stand for the patronymic social order.[31] Accordingly, the occupants of this space, like the space itself, reside outside the heteronormative and misogynist rules of the state, however, its presence as a dead and abandoned place with reminiscence of partial objects that linger in latency poses a certain kind of threat to the mainstream. This un-restricted existence of the female dwellers is socially problematic because it is in direct collision with the state repressive policy that organize spaces in a certain way to control the female subjects that dwell in it. Therefore, Parsipur, as a rebuttal, pays special attention to the portrayal of the garden as a liminal space with a porous boundary and as a metaphor for freedom of thought and expression for the inhabitants: "[we] are going to Karaj to reap the benefits of our toil and get rid of the men who control us."[32] It is ironic, however, that the women also feel a *lack* in their identity, which like the hetereotopia is a reflection of the real, and determined by the symbolic Other, the law that structures and controls our conscious mind. Their connection with nature serves as a mirror, that deconstructs (not

---

29   Parsipur, *Women Without Men*, 87.
30   Parsipur, *Women Without Men*, 1.
31   Parsipur, *Women Without Men*, 152.
32   Parsipur, *Women Without Men*, 78.

reflects) the idea of the real and helps resolve their crisis, even if temporarily. For example, Farrokhlaqa fails to write poetry but is satisfied with her imagination, the very essence of being a human that helps create a sense of the "Self." Munis, the unintelligent woman becomes knowledgeable and the keeper of everybody's conscience; Faizeh, the realist accepts the fallacy of amorous relationships; Mahdokt, the human tree asexually reproduces more children (seeds) than any other woman in the world; and Zarrinkolah, the prostitute, gives birth to a lily, the national symbol for purity and peace.[33]

From an architectural and heterotopological point of view, this garden is very similar to one of the foremost surrealists André Breton's ideal place for automatic writing sessions.[34] In his manifesto, Breton mentions his dream castle, which, despite being in ruins, is the ideal Surrealist destination in a rustic setting not far from Paris and the inside décor is anything but comfortable, or even organized. A few of his friends including Louis Aragon, Philippe Soupault, Paul Eluard, and Robert Desnos were all permanent guests in his house. With each one busy with themselves, there is an atmosphere of self-respect, but no cordiality: "the doors are always open, and one does not begin by 'thanking' everyone, you know."[35] However, what differentiates Parsipur from Breton is that the garden of Karaj is not the ultimate space for the characters to fulfill their desires. The moment they try to attach themselves to the space, a sense of permanence is assumed and the space ruptures, and the garden ceases to be interesting. The place of liberation stops functioning as such and the friendship between the female protagonists is broken as they separate from each other and exit the garden.[36] Therefore, the relationship the women share with the garden is one of suturing objects in a derelict space that can be detached at any time with or without destroying the other. This part-object relationship adds to the temporality of a typical Surrealist subject-object that is always fragmented and clumsy. Interestingly, the garden, unlike the mythical rendition of the Persian garden, resolves conflicts without binding the women together in solidarity and it helps them realize their aspirations and choose accordingly. Not everyone dismisses the importance of men in their life, nor do they engage in a utopic vision of homo-social living arrangement. The novella ends with Faizeh marrying the hypocritical Amir and their life is "neither good nor bad. It just goes on," while Farrokhlaqa marries Mr. Marikh for his money and their

---

33 Parsipur, *Women Without Men*, 123–31.

34 Heterotopology is the study of heterotopic spaces (Foucault).

35 André Breton, "Surrealist Situation of the Object," in *Manifestos of Surrealism*, André Breton (Ann Arbor: University of Michigan Press, 1969), 53.

36 Parsipur, *Women Without Men*, 119.

GENDER AND IMAGINATION

relationship is "satisfactory, neither warm nor cold," and Munis becomes a teacher due to lack of other options.[37]

The garden of Karaj and the first female protagonist of the narrative, Mahdokt's story, are connected to each other like a labyrinth, and like the garden, she is also a surrealist *objet trouvé*. Mahdokt is found/identified by Farrokhlaqa (another protagonist in the narrative) within another found object (the garden) and therefore, she exists as a doubly dysfunctional subject-object and is in a state of permanent crisis. After planting herself as a tree, her value as a domestic woman and reproductive labor is lessened because she can neither marry nor reproduce children and, therefore, both she and the garden have a diminishing value in the market. When Farrokhlaqa found her she "was buried knee-deep in the ground clad is rags. She was standing stiffly and looking at Farokklaqa and Ostovari."[38] It is interesting to note that Mahdokt's insignificant and harmless presence to the outside world also allows for a certain kind of autonomy that it not granted to the other characters in *WWM*. Her choice of planting herself is read as a sign of her debilitating mental health by the other characters, but it is quite possible to also read it as a rebellious act against forced heteronormative sexual acts. In this context, Parsipur uses the trope of the apparent harmless yet mad presence to represent the types of ideological resistance that the Iranian women conducted during that period, sexual rights issues and ecofeminism being the two main ones.

The story of Mahdokt begins with a calm and peaceful ambience in the garden where she is sitting by the pool, enjoying the juxtaposition of light and the dark shadows of the willows, and thinking about traveling and knitting sweaters for the orphan children of Iran.

> "Such nice children," she thought.
> She wouldn't have minded having some of them as her own. What was wrong with that?[39]

This moment is disrupted by the whimpering of the gardener, mercilessly beating the maid in a moment of heightened sexual arousal. She sees the garderner seeing her and he may have "wanted to escape," but continued with his business.[40] This act of the gardener is an insult to Mahdokt, both as a woman and his employer; the difference in their class status, not gender, demanded that

---

37   Parsipur, *Women Without Men*, 128–30.
38   Parsipur, *Women Without Men*, 89.
39   Parsipur, *Women Without Men*, 1998, 1–2.
40   Parsipur, *Women Without Men*, 7.

the gardener should have stopped. Instead, his sexual urges overpower him, nullifying Mahdokt's social privilege. While it is not the focus of this essay to advocate for higher-class position as an empowering agent, this moment is a rupture in Mahdokt's identity and her understanding of male dominance as well. This is the moment of recognition of the power inbuilt in a heteronormative sexual relationship where the man has an a priori privileged position, irrespective of one's class. The merciless beating of the maid and the maid's extending of her hand towards Mahdokt depict an inherent violence in a sexual relationship that is sadistic in nature and normalized within the discourse of male sexual pleasure and gratification. This raw expression of carnal desire, which is abhorrent to Mahdokt, validates her decision to escape this cycle of abuse and plant herself as a tree and mark her stance against female sexual violence: "[her] heart stopped ... the world around her went dark, and her legs began to tremble."[41]

Before becoming a human-tree, Mahdokt was a simple unmarried schoolteacher. Like the other women of her class, she too preserved her virginity as the most important thing in a woman's life and misunderstood it to be a permanent *thing*. She embodies the idea of virginity to a point that she is repulsed by the very thought of sexual intercourse that will lead to losing it and the gesture of planting herself and her virgin identity also marks her refusal to become the docile subject of the state and to subvert this temporary identity into a permanent one. Yet, at the same time, she reproduces naturally without disrupting her bodily integrity and Mahdokt's becoming of the tree can be read as Parsipur's way of advocating for women's right to their body and reclaiming its ownership.

Mahdokt's planting of herself yields two other results as well: first, the ability to produce seeds/children through an asexual reproduction, a process of reproduction from a single organism whereby the offspring inherits the genes of one parent only. And, this process of reproduction disavows the name of the father, challenging patriarchy directly and stopping the formation of the Oedipal complex.[42] She takes great pride in thinking about the seeds as her children, who will plant themselves in different parts of the world and be called by different variations of her name, "[she] would cover the entire world ... Gradually they would pronounce her name so many times until it would become Maduk in some places and Maaduk in others."[43] Thus, at the end of the novella, when, with the help of the gardener and Zarrinkolah, she becomes fertile and

---

41   Parsipur, *Women Without Men*, 7.

42   Haraway, "A Cyborg Manifesto."

43   Parsipur, *Women Without Men*, 11.

GENDER AND IMAGINATION

produces seeds, she transitions from a dysfunctional found object to a reproductive nonhuman human and along the way, anthropomorphizing the natural world as well. The seeds that she produces are blown away to different parts of the world, fulfilling her dreams of traveling the world and becoming a global citizen, a symbolic gesture about liberation from all forms of bondage:

> In an eternal metamorphosis the parts of Mahdokt separated from each other ... Finally it was finished. The tree had turned completely into seeds. A strong wind blew the seeds ... she traveled all over the world.[44]

The second reason for Mahdokt's planting of herself in the family garden, which she and her brother inherited, stems from the fear of it being confiscated by the locals, and/or the government, and also to preserve nature. After the former gardener quit his job and her brother, Hoshang, expressed concern about leaving the garden without a caretaker: "anyone can put four benches by the river and rent them out for forty tomans a day to groups of men who wanted to hang out," Mahdokt decides to plant herself.[45] Her decision is automatic and there is no apparent connection other than the fact that the yellowish green color of her face with shadows under her eyes resembled the bark of a tree which was strong like her virginity.[46] It can be argued that Parsipur, via Mahdokt, re-imagines women's relationship with nature and writes a narrative using her body as a text."[47] Making *WWM* relevant to the history of its time because the *coup d'état* of 1953 that restored the Shah as the ultimate despotic ruler and Iranian oil to joint US-British ownership, forced the country to negotiate between modernity and traditional values of the nation. While the woman's body becomes a site for control and maintenance of traditional gender roles, nature and natural resources were exploited for the development of the nation and making profit in the global market economy. Parsipur captures this moment of crisis through Mahdokt's asexual reproduction and makes an ecofeminist statement. She also perhaps stands in solidarity with the modernist Persian poet Forugh Farrokhzad (1935–1967) who connected ecopolitics to the state of women in Iran after the coup of 1953.[48]

---

44   Parsipur, *Women Without Men*, 121–22.

45   Parsipur, *Women Without Men*, 9.

46   Parsipur, *Women Without Men*, 10.

47   Gretchen T. Legler, "Ecofeminist Literary Criticism," in *Ecofeminism*, ed. Karen J. Warren (Bloomington: Indiana University Press, 1997), 230.

48   Zolfagharkahni Moslem, "Ecological Analysis of the Poetry of Forough Farrokhzad based on the Theory of Ecocriticism," *Journal on Studies of Literary Theory and Genres* 1, no. 2 (March 2016): 115–42.

The use the ecofeminist lens to compare the oppression of women and children with the exploitation of nonhuman nature is important because the children, like women and elements of non-human nature, were also subject to social oppression during this time and anyone who did not fit into the labor force, were socially alienated. One of the reasons given by Mahdokt for planting herself was out of her concern for the orphan children of Iran who were uncared for and, even if the government "sometimes announced on the radio or on television that something must be done about the children," no one really cared about them.[49] Therefore, when Mahdokt imagines knitting a thousand sweaters for the children to shield them from the bitter cold weather, it is a shared empathy that stems from the need to guard innocent lives from being exploited. Moreover, nature does play a big role in the narrative because the women, after settling in the garden of Karaj, invest productive labor power in Mahdokt for her to bloom into a full-fledged tree. Nature also serves as a metaphor whereby the sprouting of leaves in Mahdokt is symbolic of a certain kind of liberation for these women as well and their connection to the nonhuman-human nature becomes embedded in their ability to destabilize the utopia myth and construct the garden as a heterotopic space. It is only after Mahdokt explodes into seeds and is blown away that everyone else is able to resolve their conflict and break free.

The second story in the novella is about the two friends Munis and Faizeh, and their resistance and/or submission to the idea of virginity is in stark contrast with Mahdokt's complete submission. Parsipur places particular importance on being a virgin for women in Iran and she has mentioned elsewhere that this emphasis was necessary in the narrative to break the taboo that exists in Iranian societies.[50] Hence, virginity, as represented in the story, is a critical construct that can be understood through a different analytical lens and is in contradiction to the other character's understanding of it.[51]

The story of the thirty-eight-year-old virgin Munis starts with a scene depicting her limited access to the outside world and a subject of constant surveillance by her elder brother, Amir. She is confined within the house at all times and is forced into a submissive position that has reduced her to a naïve, docile subject: "[a]s they drank it Munis glanced at the radio. Although she was older, she didn't dare turn it back on ... whenever somebody cried Munis cried too, without understanding why."[52] Nonetheless, Munis does not lack

---

49   Parsipur, *Women Without Men*, 5.

50   Parsipur, *Women Without Men*, 135.

51   Parsipur, *Women Without Men*, 135.

52   Parsipur, *Women Without Men*, 19–21.

GENDER AND IMAGINATION

consciousness, but has to perform gender assigned roles to compensate for being single and a burden to the family. She is interested in the politics of the outside world but cannot participate because she has no access to the public space, given that much of her knowledge about the self and the other is secondary. Therefore, when Faizeh, her friend who is ten years younger, corrects her knowledge of virginity "as a hole and not a curtain," the embarrassment of not knowing forces Munis to commit suicide.[53] After jumping off the terrace, when she falls into the streets of the riot-infested Tehran of 1953, she touches the dead body of a man and experiences both death and the body of a man for the first time. Adopting a typical surrealist technique, Parsipur creates a sudden break in the narrative and death is fictionalized via a cinematic reference and some graphic images. Furthermore, Munis' reaction to her fall is one of relief and she is only aware of her own death through the death of the other when the dead man explains to her "[t]here is a French movie called 'It's too late.' I am now at that stage—it's too late."[54] On hearing this satirical description of death and trivializing of life, Munis goes into a celebratory trance and roams around Tehran as a free subject.

Munis' celebration of death/freedom is an act of "necroresistance" where she kills herself to stop the violence of the Other (Amir) and to defend a woman's right to knowledge about her own body and self. This form of resistance is self-destructive, but argues against the valorization of life as the only way to read resistance. Banu Bagru coined this term as an essential contribution to conceptualizing both the possibilities and limitations of the rebellion on the terrain of biopolitics and to biopolitical theory more broadly.[55] Following Bagru's line of argument, it is possible to imagine death in the novella as bearing a symbolic meaning for Munis and it is in death that she finally escapes the cycle of oppression and is set free to pursue her desire for knowledge as well. In fact, Munis dies twice in the story; the second time is when she returns home after a month and her brother, suspecting that she ran away with another man, kills her as part of the "family honor restoring" ritual. The second time too, death is used as a metaphor for release and to criticize practices that deprive women of the right to live and access to knowledge but grant men the sovereign power to kill. Therefore, as part of the automatic writing style and to depict feminist resistance, Munis' fear of death is transformed into a powerful state of empowerment as she clearly states that her dying was voluntary because "[she] decided

---

53   Parsipur, *Women Without Men*, 30.
54   Parsipur, *Women Without Men*, 31.
55   Banu Bargu, *Starve and Immolate: The Politics of Human Weapons* (New York: Columbia University Press, 2016), 1–37.

to escape the prison of family life."[56] In fact, her presence in the story is purposely intertwined with death to make it ambiguous and question women's freedom from the clutches of repressive patriarchal laws and whether Munis can only attain freedom in death.

In the process and in a classic surrealist way, Parsipur, by posing the question of life and death, take the readers' attention towards the unconscious mind. She portrays Munis' journey from the domestic to the outside world as a reversal of life and death story whereby her life begins in death. Her journey echoes Breton's fictional character Nadja, who roams aimlessly in the streets of Paris to reinvent it in a new light. Munis too reinvents Tehran, however, there is one difference: Nadja's actions are guided and inescapable from Breton's imagination, she is his creation, his muse, a child-woman, a *femme-enfant*, "a medium that ultimately enables [Breton's] surreal vision."[57] Munis is not Nadja rather, she is an automatic subject in the true sense of the term. Parsipur is different from Breton and her surreal vision is practiced via the autonomy of the characters' imaginative power and not as mediators of their actions. Munis' liberation comes with knowledge that is arbitrary and not structured within an institutional pattern:

> ...the title of a book caught her eye *The Secret of Sexual Satisfaction or How to Know Our Bodies* ... She read from cover to cover ... On the third day she looked up. The trees and sunshine and streets all had new meanings for her. She had grown up.[58]

Munis goes through a rigorous process of unlearning (un-constituting her subjectivity) to learn about a taboo subject, until she is drenched in knowledge and consumed by it. In this particular moment, Parsipur's portrayal of Munis' process of un-constituting involves the de-objectifying of the self that imagines itself "as if from outside of her body ... implicating [herself] in a masculine dynamic that projects the woman as the 'other.'"[59] This perspective echoes western feminist surrealists like Chadwick. Especially the moment in the narrative when she finishes reading the book and looks around the city, and everything has changed. This newly acquired knowledge gives Munis a magical power with which she can enter the reality of both the corporeal and the

---

56   Parsipur, *Women Without Men*, 95.

57   Ileana Alexandra Orlich, "Surrealism and The Feminine Element: André Breton's Nadja and Gellu Naum's Zenobia," *Philologica Jassyensia* 2, no. 3 (2006): 213.

58   Parsipur, *Women Without Men*, 33.

59   Chadwick, "An Infinite Play of Empty Mirrors," 8.

GENDER AND IMAGINATION

metaphysical world and she can read minds and has access to the past, present, and the future. It is in this state of half dead and half alive that Munis takes the journey in the direction of freedom towards the garden in Karaj.

In this journey though, Munis is accompanied by her friend Faizeh, who is disappointed after Amir refuses to marry her and she leaves for the garden to resolve her crisis. Like Mahdokt, twenty-eight-year-old feisty and competitive Faizeh is also heavily invested in preserving her identity as a virgin except that she does not think it to be permanent and/or an abstract *thing*. She thinks of it as a capital that will raise her price in the marriage market, therefore, she represses her sexual desire for the retention of virginity because there is a demand for it and the ability to supply it will yield high profit. She is in love with Munis' brother Amir and wants to gift her virginity to him, fulfilling her role as the model Iranian woman. Faizeh, accordingly, is also the most practical character in the novella and her presence signals a sense of corporeality in a surreal text. She is so invested in fulfilling her dream that when Amir accidentally kills Munis (her friend), she helps him bury the body and promises to keep it a secret. She even takes advantage of the situation and makes an elaborate plan for her future thinking that by helping Amir they have become confidantes and in exchange for keeping his secret he would marry her. Along with being intelligent, shrewd, and extremely manipulative, she uses her body to lure Amir into falling in love with her and she breaks a social code of conduct and openly expresses her sexual desire by "[taking] off her chador and ... [swatting] down in front of Amir ... pulling a handkerchief from between her breasts ... while she was sitting like that her underwear showed."[60] However, Amir ironically reads this action as unbecoming of a woman and confesses that, "if she were his sister, he would kill her too."[61] When Faizeh comes to know of Amir's intentions, it breaks her perception of the reality, dismantling her disillusionment of the virgin identity altogether. This rupture in identity formation is a typical surrealist technique of automatic writing that functions through disruption. Faizeh had done everything to become the perfect female subject that she is expected to be but Amir's response represents societal hypocrisy and the inbuilt misogyny of the Iranian society of the time. Therefore, when Munis rises from the grave on the day of Amir's marriage to leave for Karaj, Faizeh asks for forgiveness and accompanies her to the garden.

Faizeh's loss of faith in human relationships and her friend Munis' permanent liberation from domestic confinement are simultaneous events in the story. Munis' journey from Tehran to Karaj is marked by her desire that the

---

60   Parsipur, *Women Without Men*, 37.
61   Parsipur, *Women Without Men*, 37.

garden will give her the space to nurture herself and be recognized as a knowledgeable person and not just a "good" woman. Unfortunately, though, both women get raped on their way to the garden, and this moment of violence is important in the story because Parsipur, through Munis and Faizeh's experience of sexual assault, represents the female body as a radical and subversive space:

> He pulled off her chador ... Faizeh shouted for help ... Munis, silently endured everything The assistant driver did not seem satisfied. He said, 'Ismail, this one [Munis] was like a rag doll. 'You get what you get. That one [Faizeh]was a slut.'[62]

Faizeh's loss of virginity marks a symbolic death and loss of identity, but Munis' reaction marks a radical shift in the discourse on female sexuality. Parsipur does not undermine rape as a trivial matter but Munis' comment implies two things: first, as a form of resistance against the construction of female subjectivity through her body parts, therefore, she does not place too much importance on the loss of virginity, and second, Munis is not alive, hence cannot feel anything. Moreover, virginity for Munis is like femininity, a masquerade to perform gender roles that endorses patriarchy. Therefore, while she recognizes the act of rape as violence, she does not believe that it reduces women to nothingness or a lacking subject. On the contrary, Munis uses this experience as a mandatory hurdle that has to be crossed to reach her goal. When Farrokhlaqa asks about it, she explains it as a "dangerous ... walk along the road. Either you are strong enough to face the danger, or you're not, and you return like a lamb to the flock."[63]

Faizeh, on the other hand, is devastated because virginity is her asset and she too, like Mahdokt, idealized it as a *phallic organ* privileged in the symbolic order, albeit in a different way. A psychoanalytic reading is the most apt for understanding Faizeh and the other women's idealization of virginity. In the beginning, Mahdokt, Faizeh, and Munis, for different reasons, had understood virginity as a powerful female characteristic, therefore, having or being "it" is really important for retaining their position in society. But the realization that this powerful position, or the myth of virginity is not real helps the women dissociate from the Other's image of the self, both in the literal and in the metaphorical sense. For Faizeh, this experience creates a permanent void but Munis realizes that virginity ("it") is a discourse, a reflection of socio-cultural laws

---

62   Parsipur, *Women Without Men*, 79.
63   Parsipur, *Women Without Men*, 96.

GENDER AND IMAGINATION 129

that construct women's subjectivity and being in the name of the Other (patriarchal social law): "To hell with it. We were virgins, now we are not. It's nothing to cry over ... I died and was reborn twice ... By God, believe me, virginity is not important."[64] To put it differently, we can imagine "it" or any other discourse for that matter as a signifier standing in for the Other's (male) desire. The disciplining of subjects is achieved at this level of positioning discourse as the signifier of the Other's desire, hence as that to which the subject must necessarily submit. If the retention of virginity promises and connotes purity, innocence, and social dignity, it is a check against subversive promiscuous behavior, and the basis for monogamous patronymic social relationships. It is a state of being desired by the symbolic Other to which all individual subjects must conform. Therefore, virginity is a signifier representing the law of the symbolic order, which demarcates the parameters of civilized and sexual behaviors.

The other function of this discourse on virginity is about the privileging of the phallic jouissance, the enjoyment desired by men for whom women must always keep themselves prepared. In other words, the whole metaphor of virginity is organized around the fetishization of phallic jouissance and it is created in order to bring out the importance of phallic jouissance over and above everything else. In this context, Mahdokt's refusal to give that pleasure (retain her virginity and reproduce asexually) can also be seen as a marker of a rebellion against privileging the Other's desire. Hence, she remains a virgin and denies men the pleasure of breaking a social convention, or fulfilling a rite of passage. Likewise, Munis also realizes that laws related to virginity are geared towards men, endowing them with the ephemeral feeling of being in control of breaking the taboo. In this regard, remaining a virgin is not about being powerful, but making the other powerful, hence, the desire for purity (virginity) is changed to a desire for liberation from oppression.

Parsipur reiterates the myth surrounding sexual identity and the purity of the female body with the young prostitute, Zarrinkolah's story. Zarrin, as is required of her, serves twenty-six to thirty customers daily, and she is also the youngest of the five women to come to Karaj. She is a public woman and her sexual and class identity is very different from Mahdokt, Munis, and Faizeh, who come from respectable backgrounds and belong to the realm of the domestic, hence private. Yet, Zarrin's transformation from a sexual object to an asexual subject into a symbol of peace makes her one of the most innocent characters in the novella.

As a prostitute, Zarrin's position, much like a pre-established function of the *objet trouvé*, is already marked by her status of a fallen woman. She acquires

---

64   Parsipur, *Women Without Men*, 100.

this identity by giving pleasure to her male customers at the cost of dehumanizing herself. In other words, the customers serve as a mirror through which her position in society is acquired; hence they also occupy the position of the Other (law) and she performs her role accordingly. When, in the course of the narrative, the customers become headless and eyeless, that Other cannot show his position in this dialectic of desire, leaving Zarin in a state of crisis. She misrecognizes this emptiness as her new identity and embodies it as such. Unlike Faizeh, her loss of identity is not a result of forceful sexual intercourse leading to the loss of virginity. Instead, Zarin's inability to feel sexual intercourse is what marks her change. She performs a rigorous cleansing of her body, scrubbing every little mark and contour until her body starts changing:

> The bath worker scrubbed until Zarrinkolah's skin was raw ... she did it fifty times. Her entire body was burning from the chafing of the sponge ... her body felt like a piece of straw. She became a small woman of twenty-six with a heart as big as a sea.[65]

With the cleansing ritual, she tries to resurrect her non-virgin body as the only capital that can be marketed for profit. Before undergoing this change, she held a precarious position in the mode of production narrative, whereby her body is both the capital and the labor while her pimp and the customers enjoy the profit. After her vision of headless male customers, Zarin is unable to negotiate this new female subject that cannot profit the male other. The cleansing ritual leaves her body unrecognizable and she becomes androgynous with an ambiguous gender identity. This particular image is reminiscent of the feminist surrealist Claude Cahun's subjects whose image presents the possibility of a third sex, "uniting masculine and feminine traits, but existing as neither one nor the other."[66] Like Cahun, Parsipur also marks this moment to represent "a surrealist dialogue between the self and a reality that are unknowable ... and disrupt the integrity of the body."[67] Zarin's androgynous appearance very soon becomes a transparent surface and her body loses its corporeality altogether, "she changed color. She was becoming transparent. Little by little it became possible to see right through her."[68] When she arrives at the garden, her asexual female body is regarded as auspicious by the other characters, and Zarin the prostitute is elevated to a divine pedestal as a symbol of purity and peace

---

65 Parsipur, *Women Without Men*, 75–77.
66 Kline, "In or Out of the Picture," 71.
67 Kline, "In or Out of the Picture," 71.
68 Parsipur, *Women Without Men*, 109.

GENDER AND IMAGINATION 131

whose milk alone can make Mahdokt fertile and help the garden/nature bloom again. In due course, Zarrin gives birth to a lily and is flown away along with the petals, symbolizing a journey towards peace and harmony and her transformation marks a purposeful contradiction in the narration:

> At dawn a lily was born. The gardener took the lily to the river ... He gave her the container, and she filled it with her milk ... He said, "its frozen. That's good ... it's hibernating. By spring it will be unlike any tree you've ever seen." The gardener dripped the milk into the ground at the foot of the tree until sunrise.[69]

Parsipur uses Zarrin's body like Claude Cahun, Meret Oppenheim, and Frida Kahlo, who used "their own bodies to destabilize the boundaries of gender and sexual identity."[70] For example, Zarin turns into a symbol of purity whereas, Faizeh, the vanguard of virginity, is labeled as a slut by her rapist.[71] Zarin's transformation to the most important woman in the group, who saves the garden and the world, is symbolic of the image of the Iranian woman that Parsipur wants to prioritize by disrupting normative discourses on women and virtue. She keeps the essential meaning of the lily in Persian culture intact (peace, serenity, and spirituality) but reconstitutes the image of the woman who embodies those characteristics. It is a bold step in literary representation because it challenges the normative image of the Iranian woman. In post revolution Iran, writing was highly censored and women could only be represented in a linear fashion, either as religious and kind or as foolish and mad creatures. Parsipur is one of the first women writers to break away from the female model of Islamic tales, a religious, dogmatic, passive, and docile subject, and after the publication of the novella, she received imprisonment for her open discussion of female sexual desire and for placing the prostitute on a higher pedestal instead of ostracizing her. She uses both art and literature to link it with social reformation.

In fact, all the characters in the novella are portrayed in a manner that questions stereotypical and linear representations of the Iranian woman. The fifth character in WWM is Farrokhlaqa, the owner of the garden who gives refuge to the women but maintains a hierarchy that puts her in a privileged position in comparison to Mahdokt, Munis, Faizeh, and Zarrinkolah. She represents aristocracy in Iranian society, where freedom has a different meaning altogether.

---

69   Parsipur, *Women Without Men*, 116–17.
70   Chadwick, "An Infinite Play of Empty Mirrors," 14.
71   Parsipur, *Women Without Men*, 79.

Unlike the other characters, Farrokhlaqa's resistance to dominance is trivial and she does not confront patriarchy. Rather, she is focused on attaining a superior position within the patriarchal social order and becoming one of them. There is an obsession to be recognized as an important person in society or, to be validated by the "Other's" world. She inhabits a fantasy world and thrives on borrowed identity imitating Vivian Leigh from the Hollywood movie *Gone With the Wind* and, therefore, her actions, words, demeanor- everything- is a caricature of a fictional character that is nonexistent.[72] When her husband Golchehreh challenged her that she could never enjoy the life of her dreams since she had reached menopause, Farrokhlaqa snaps and kills him in cold blood.[73] Her final action of killing is a reaction to years of abuse by her husband, who was a sadist and a representative of the oppressive and toxic masculine culture of Iran during that time and by killing him she frees herself from his bondage forever:

> whenever he was in the house, she would lose her ability to move, and she would hide in a corner ... she knew only this, and she knew instinctively, that Golchehreh went out, mobility and happiness would come to her.[74]

It cannot be denied though that Farrokhlaqa's character is in opposition with the other characters, especially Mahdokt, Munis, and Zarin. She is enmeshed in the capitalist form of economic practices and is always looking for an opportunity to turn everything, including human relationships, into a profitable venture. She invites the women to live with her in the garden with the hope that each one of them, with their unique qualities, will benefit her in some form or the other. She gives refuge to Munis for her farsightedness, Mahdokt, she thinks, can bring good luck, Faizeh can cook, and Zarin becomes a soothing presence who can entertain the guests with her enigma. But when Farroklaqa fails to become successful (writing poetry, becoming a politician), these same people become a burden to her and as soon she is able to get rid of them, she marries someone to climb the social ladder and attain the fame that she craved.[75] Farrokhlaqa is also an example of Iranian women's unfulfilled dreams and repressed desire that can lead to extreme violence. It also poses the question about women's agency and what are the options left when, even

---

72 Parsipur, *Women Without Men*, 64.

73 Parsipur, *Women Without Men*, 70.

74 Parsipur, *Women Without Men*, 56.

75 Parsipur, *Women Without Men*, 130.

GENDER AND IMAGINATION

if there is economic stability, the society does not allow women the freedom for personal growth. Interestingly, her characterization in the narrative liberates Iranian women from a linear representation of victimhood, and her ability to kill to fulfill her dreams portrays a violent picture of Iranian women that are a threat to society as a whole.

In a typical automatic style, *Women Without Men* ends with a sudden break in rhythm and a complete fragmentation of the characters' *raison d'être*. They leave the garden of Karaj and adopt new roles, like Munis, Mahdokht, and Zarin disappear in search of new adventures, and Faizeh and Farrokhlaqa return to Tehran and become part of the mainstream. The narrative ends with the confirmation that neither one of them are happy nor sad, pointing to a state of being that it is once again far from ideal.

The translator of *wwm* from Persian to English, Persis M Karim, at the end of the novella adds: "[f]or while these characters end up leaving the garden ... the readers are left not with a simplistic argument ... that the world or women would be better off without men. They should not simply exist or act in reaction against that society. They must find their own inner voices guided by psychological visions of what is possible."[76] In that sense, the characters, like the text, are connected to the larger socio-cultural and political issues and Parsipur's choice of the automatic writing technique creates a rhizomatic text/ space wherein aesthetic or stylistic experimentation approximates the thematic and ideological cursives of the novella. This technique is just like Gilles Deleuze and Félix Guattari in the introduction to the second volume of *Capitalism and Schizophrenia* who re-appropriate the word rhizome, a botanical reference, to construct a model for explaining the process of constitution and reception of a book. According to Deleuze, just like a rhizome is not structured by hierarchies or guided by linear lines, a book should also serve similar purposes. Hence, rhizomatic thought is about multiplicity, it can move in many directions, and is always connected to many other lines of thinking, acting, and being. The rhizomatic process of writing, then, "creates smooth space, and cut across boundaries imposed by vertical lines of hierarchies and order."[77] Of the four rhizomatic principles, connection, heterogeneity, multiplicity, and asignifying rupture, *Women Without Men* follows all of them. Specifically, it asignifies rupture and "establishes connections between semiotic chains, organizations of power, and circumstances relative to the arts, sciences, and social struggles."[78] The novella's conclusion indicates a regeneration of the characters and their

---

76   Parsipur, *Women Without Men*, 167.
77   Deleuze and Guattari, *A Thousand Plateaus: Capitalism and Schizophrenia*, 7.
78   Deleuze and Guattari, *A Thousand Plateaus: Capitalism and Schizophrenia*, 7.

continued growth, forming new lines and pathways. It makes a direct suggestion, via Munis, Mahdokt, and Zarin to read Iranian women as active agents and not passive victims of history waiting to be saved.

Women Without Men can also be read as the manifesto of Third world feminist voices that speak against marginalization of Iranian women in national and international history. In adopting the surrealist technique of automatic writing, Parsipur challenges gendered representational politics by drawing from feminist surrealist writers, artists, and photographers alike. But Parsipur's surrealism is transnational in nature and crosses racial, linguistic, and gender binaries. She writes against the distortion of the female body, mind, and subjectivity without alluding to a particular body type; her subjects are neither veiled nor unveiled, they are neither white nor black, nor brown, nor yellow and their politics is based on gender and sexual rights and not on binary oppositions based on race, culture, and religion. The characters, especially Mahdokt who speaks about global citizenship, cross boundaries and grow outside of Iran. Mahdokt spreads her seeds across the world, implying a multiplicity of the self. The characters fill the gap in mainstream surrealism as well as feminist discourses and the story can also be read as the radical imagination of herstory that breaks the silence imposed by history.

Unlike Parsipur, the call for global alliance through feminist methodologies is not present in the works of western surrealists like Dorothea Tanning, Claude Kahun, Freida Kahlo, Gisele Prassinos, Leonara Carrington, and Meret Oppenheim, to name a few. All these artists have resisted male surrealist representations of the female other by concentrating on representations that are ideologically specific (naked and white) to disrupt the voyeuristic gaze of the western male. Therefore, most representations are absorbed in countering the mutable, eroticized, dismembered images with female subjects who are self-possessed and capable of producing new narratives of the self. This counter representation, however, is not counterproductive to feminist ideology, but it definitely narrows the path for feminist intervention. It contests western representations of the white woman's body as a fetish object, but does not question the representation of the non-white women. One can question why western feminist surrealists should be concerned about third world politics? The answer is embedded in the history of the surrealist movement that was initiated to transgress borders and question hierarchies. In that sense, surrealism is closely aligned with feminist ideology, which adheres closely to this notion and is committed to eradicating hierarchies, gender or otherwise, and "is non-monolithic, contentious, and in flux."[79] Therefore, when feminist surrealists

---

79   Perin, "Transnational Feminism, Islam, and the Other Woman: How to Teach," 3.

GENDER AND IMAGINATION   135

adopt this movement it is not only to critique male surrealists, but also to counter gender and sexual inequality across borders.

Parsipur's novella, while calling for a global alliance of feminist issues, does not conform to the myth that the mere fact of being a woman can unite us. But at the same time, it leaves scope for a space that can accommodate first, second, third, and fourth world feminisms along with a "cathartic crisis ... that strives to organize around issues, encourage complex analyses of how gender and sexuality intersect with other sites of power, and support local and global actors."[80] It calls for solidarity of global sisterhood and unity via a radical imagination that promises to eradicate all forms of inequality and listen to the *other* instead of silencing her.

References

Abu-Lughod, Lila. "Do Muslim Women Really Need Saving?" *American Anthropologist* 104, no. 3 (September 2002): 783–90.

Bargu, Banu. *Starve and Immolate: The Politics of Human Weapons*. New York: Columbia University Press. 2016.

Bray, Joe, Alison Gibbons, and Brian McHale, eds., *The Routledge Companion to Experimental Literature*. London and New York: Routledge. 2012.

Breton, André. *Manifestoes of Surrealism*. Minneapolis: The University of Michigan Press. 1969.

Browder, Clifford. "Dreams and the Surrealist Object." In *André Breton: Arbiter of Surrealism*, edited by Clifford Browder, 89–100. Geneva: Librarie Druz. 1967.

Chadwick, Whitney. ed., *Mirror Women, Surrealism, and Self Representation*. Minneapolis: MIT press. 1998.

Deleuze, Gilles and Félix Guattari. *A Thousand Plateaus: Capitalism and Schizophrenia*. Translated by Brian Massumi. Minneapolis: University of Minnesota Press. 1997.

Foucault, Michel. "Of Other Spaces: Utopias and Heterotopias." Translated by Jay Miskowiec. *Architecture /Mouvement/ Continuité* (October 1984): 1–9.

Gurel, Perin. "Transnational Feminism, Islam, and the Other Woman: How to Teach." *The Radical Teacher* no. 86 (Winter 2009): 66–70.

Haraway, Donna. *Simians, Cyborgs, and Women: The Reinvention of Nature*. New York: Routledge. 1991.

Kline, Katy. "In or Out of the Picture." In *Mirror Women, Surrealism, and Self-Representation*, edited by Whitney Chadwick, 66–81. Cambridge: MIT press, 1998.

---

80   Perin, "Transnational Feminism, Islam, and the Other Woman: How to Teach," 3.

Kurth-Schai, Ruthanne. "Ecofeminism and Children." In *Ecofeminism*, edited by Karen J. Warren, 193–211. Bloomington: Indiana University Press, 1997.

Lewis, Desiree. "Feminism and the Radical Imagination." *Agenda: Empowering Women for Gender Equity* 2e1, no. 72 (2007): 18–31.

Legler, Gretchen T. "Ecofeminist Literary Criticism." In *Ecofeminism*, edited by Karen J. Warren, 227–38. Bloomington: Indiana University Press, 1997.

Memmott, Carol. "'The Republic of Imagination' of Azar Nafisi." *New York Times*, October 30, 2014, https://www.chicagotribune.com/entertainment/books/ct-prj-republic-of-imagination-azar-nafisi-20141030-story.html.

Moslem, Zolfagharkahni. "Ecological Analysis of the Poetry of Forough Farrokhzad Based on the Theory of Ecocriticism." *Journal on Studies of Literary Theory and Genres* 1, no. 2 (March 2016): 115–42.

Nafisi, Azhar. "Imagination as Subversion: Narrative as a Tool of Civic Awareness." In *Muslim Women and the Politics of Participation,* edited by Mahnaz Afkhami and Erika Freidl, 58–71. Syracuse: Syracuse University Press, 1997.

Nafisi, Azhar. *The Republic of Imagination.* New York: Penguin Books. 2015.

Naghibi, Nima. *Rethinking Global Sisterhood.* Minneapolis: University of Minnesota Press. 2007.

Najmabadi, Afsaneh. "Veiled Discourse-Unveiled Bodies." *Feminist Studies* 19, no. 3 (Autumn 1993): 487–518.

Orlich, Ileana Alexandra. "Surrealism and The Feminine Element: André Breton's Nadja and Gellu Naum's Zenobia." *Philologica Jassyensia* 2, no. 3 (2006): 213–24.

Parsipur, Shahrnush. *Women Without Men.* Translated by Kamran Talattof and Jocelyn Sharlet. Syracuse, NY: Syracuse University Press. 1998.

Talatoff, Kamran. "Breaking Taboos in Iranian Women's Literature." *World Literature Today* 78, no. 3–4 (2004): 43–46.

Whyte, Jessica. Review of *Starve and Immolate: The Politics of Human Weapons*, by Banu Bargu. *Political Theory* 45, no. 5 (October 2016): 1–4.

Winkel, Laura. "Manifestos and Ars Poetica." In *The Routledge Companion to Experimental Literature*, edited by Joe Bray, Alison Gibbons, and Brian McHale, 253–66. London and New York: Routledge, 2012.

PART 3

Imagination and Ethics

∵

CHAPTER 6

Psychoanalysis, Imagination, and Imaginative Resistance: A Genesis of the Post-Freudian World

Carol Steinberg Gould

[Creative writers] are valuable allies, and their testimony is to be rated high, for they usually know many things between heaven and earth that our academic wisdom does not even dream of. In psychic knowledge ... they are far ahead of us ordinary people, because they draw from sources that we have not yet made accessible for science... Our interest [is] for the way in which story-tellers make use of dreams...[1]

My general topic is "Psychoanalysis and Imagination," each notion in itself is quite complex, the conjunction even more so. From its birth, psychoanalysis has appreciated the vital role of imagination in such psychic tasks as fantasies, dreamwork, and transference. The two meet at yet another, perhaps surprising, point: the problem contemporary philosophers term "Imaginative Resistance." Over the last thirty years, as philosophers have offered competing solutions, Imaginative Resistance has moved beyond Philosophy of Literature. In this chapter, I offer a two-step solution to the problem: First, I remove the aesthetic blame from the reader for the reader's imaginative disruption. Then, to explain the phenomenon, I mine the Freudian notions of repression and the unconscious in order to argue for another solution to it. Repression, we shall see, gives us a model for understanding Imaginative Resistance and thus a new way to approach this problem bedeviling contemporary philosophers. I cannot defend here the *existence* of the unconscious or the mechanism of repression, which have long been the subject of philosophical and neurobiological contention;[2] rather, I am using them as a heuristic device to cast light on Imaginative Resistance. Let us now turn to the philosophical debate.

---

1 Sigmund Freud, *Delusion and Dream in the Light of Psychoanalysis of Gradiva and Selected Papers on Hysteria and other Psychoneuroses*, trans. Helen M. Downey (New York: publisher unavailable, 1921), Part II, Section I.

2 To put my cards on the table, I am sympathetic to these ideas and find them scientifically defensible. For an excellent defense of the Freudian scheme against Grünbaum's well-known attack, see Michael T. Michael, "The Case for the Freud-Beuer Theory of Hysteria: A Response

1   What Imaginative Resistance Is

Imaginative Resistance is part of current debates in Philosophy of Literature, Philosophy of Mind, Epistemology, and Philosophy of Emotions. Despite the admirable technical sophistication of many of the discussions, philosophers could fruitfully treat the concept with more nuance were they to consider the role of the unconscious and psychoanalysis, more broadly. One might speculate that philosophers overlook the unconscious because the problem of Imaginative Resistance is traced back to Hume, the radical empiricist who surely would be inimical to any hint of the unconscious, particularly the part inaccessible to perception or introspection.[3] Thus, the issue(s) have been framed in terms of his outlook.

Kendall Walton[4] and Richard Moran[5] initiated the contemporary dialogue in 1990 and 1994, respectively. As Moran puts it:

> The problem of emotions and emotion in fictions that occupies the attention of contemporary philosophers, however, poses the prior question of how it is so much possible for a person to get emotionally worked up over what she knows to be unreal, merely fictional.[6]

The current focus of the debate has been specifically about getting so "emotionally worked up" about some *moral* abomination in the fiction that our imagination fails us—or as Tamar Szabó Gendler formulates it, in "The Puzzle of Imaginative Resistance,"[7] it is "the puzzle of explaining our comparative difficulty in imagining fictional worlds that we take to be morally deviant."[8] Miyazono and Liao describe it as, "the phenomenon in which we, who are otherwise competent imaginers, experience a constraint in taking part in an imaginative

---

   to Grünbaum's foundational Objection to Psychoanalysis," *The International Journal of Psychoanalysis* 100, no. 1 (2019): 32–51.

3   The Unconscious consists of the preconscious—which contains things that can be brought to consciousness and the Unconscious proper, the repository of urges and desires "censored" from awareness.

4   Kendall Walton, *Mimesis as Make-Believe* (Cambridge, MA: Harvard University Press, 1990).

5   Richard Moran, "The Expression of Feeling in Imagination," *The Philosophical Review* 103, no. 1 (1994): 75–106.

6   Moran, "The Expression of Feeling in Imagination," 75.

7   Tamar Szabó Gendler, "The Puzzle of Imaginative Resistance," *Journal of Philosophy*, 97, no. 2 (2000): 55–81.

8   Here (p. 56) she cites Richard Moran's terminology in his "The Expression of Feeling in Imagination," 75–106.

activity."[9] Gendler's formulation may seem confusing, because we have no problem in imaginatively experiencing many works of literature, either reading them or watching them on stage, even when the protagonist is utterly nefarious. Many start with the following as a paradigm sentence that triggers Imaginative Resistance: "In killing her baby, Giselda did the right thing; after all, it was a girl."[10] Clearly infanticide violates the moral norms of modern Western culture. Consider this sentence embedded in a story in which infanticide occurs, as it does in so many works of literature. As a reader, I do not find the sentence as powerful as many other discussants apparently do.

Stuart Brock offers a far more effective sample trigger: Using Thomas Hardy's *Jude the Obscure*, he asks us to imagine that Jude feels unambivalent relief, when he sees the bodies of his children who had apparently died violently; after all, he muses, "there were too many children anyway."[11] Let us suppose that a reader finds this so cold and inappropriate a response to the sight of one's own dead babies that these readers cannot continue their sincere imaginative engagement. They no longer empathize with such a callous man. Thus, this hypothetical author did not succeed in holding their attention.

So, why is Imaginative Resistance puzzling? One reason is that it is more than one puzzle. Kendall Walton,[12] in an important article rightly points out that philosophers conflate several puzzles of Imaginative Resistance. The burgeoning philosophical literature is vast and goes beyond the bounds of this article. Miyazono and Liao offer the following fourfold taxonomy of puzzles:[13] (1) The Imaginative (2) the Fictionality (3) the Phenomenological and (4) the Aesthetic Value puzzles. The puzzle of (4) is "Why does the reader think or judge that the [work] would be *aesthetically* superior" if the moral abomination (sentence, plot, etc.) "were omitted?"

Puzzle (4) applies only to certain types of Imaginative Resistance (and it presumes a certain aesthetic moralism not universally accepted). It is worth noting that Imaginative Resistance is precisely what Plato fears does *not*

---

9   Kengo Miyazono, and Shen-yi Liao, "The Cognitive Architecture of Imaginative Resistance," in *The Routledge Handbook of Philosophy of Imagination,* ed. Amy Kind (London and New York: Routledge, 2016), 233.

10 Kendall Walton, "On the (So-Called) Puzzle of Imaginative Resistance," in *The Architecture of the Imagination: New Essays on Pretence, Possibility, and Fiction,* ed. Shaun Nichols (Oxford: Oxford University Press, 2006), 137–48.

11 Stuart Brock, "The Puzzle of Imaginative Failure," *The Philosophical Quarterly* 62, no. 248 (2012): 444.

12 Walton, "On the (So-Called) Puzzle of Imaginative Resistance," 137–48.

13 See, too, Walton, "On the (So-Called) Puzzle of Imaginative Resistance," 137–48; Brian Weatherson, "Morality, Fiction, and Possibility," *Philosophers' Imprint* 4, no. 3 (2004): 1–27.

happen, at least not in compelling works.[14] If a fiction gets us emotionally "worked up," then it is aesthetically successful. On the contrary, he claims that we do not believe it is false; we suspend disbelief and, worse, sympathize with characters who, for example feel untainted relief at the death of their children, who succumb to wanton passion, who commit incest, or who gratify other primal taboos. That is, we have no trouble resisting imaginatively. The problem, for Plato, is that we all too easily slip into the protagonist's point of view and feel sympathy. We can occupy the protagonist's point of view if, and only if, according to him, we believe that what the protagonist experiences is real. Plato objects to literary narratives on the grounds that only a select few people have the rational sophistication to feel moral repugnance and thus be jolted out of their epistemic immersion in the fiction. (Plato holds the premise that moral defects of various sorts improve a work aesthetically by giving us additional complexity.) Thus, if we do experience Imaginative Resistance, then the work is not aesthetically good. It is an artistic failure. Plato, then, would see Puzzle (4) as a pseudo-problem.

Yet Imaginative Resistance does occur in our experience of some artworks; in fact, according to some ancient sources, a prominent case, indeed an interesting case, did so in the time of Socrates, fifth century (B.C.E.) Athens with Euripides's *Hippolytus*. Euripides, according to some, wrote two versions of the play, the first depicting Phaedra as explicitly propositioning her stepson, Hippolytus, with the next (the surviving one) representing her teeming with passion in anguished silence. Some scholars point to evidence from antiquity that Euripides reworked the myth again because the first version was so scandalous and irreverent that the Athenians could not watch it. The audience was so horrified at the idea of a sexually aggressive Phaedra (virtuous, legitimate wife of none other than Theseus, heroic monster slayer and legendary king of Athens)

---

14   For Gendler, we resist morally approving of acts in a fiction that we believe to be wrong in the actual world we inhabit. This, however, cannot be right. If it were right, we could not become immersed in many canonical fictional narratives, some of which I discuss in this chapter (think of *Hamlet*, *Lolita*, *The Merchant of Venice*, *Rigoletto*, *Medea*, and so on). For her, we hold fictions to the same values that we do actuality, because we have a higher-order desire not to hold these values. Getting into a fiction in which the world or the protagonist is morally repugnant, would violate our sense of ourselves as praiseworthy moral agents. Note that this view would preclude our imaginative engagement with works from other cultures, for example, *The Tale of Genji*. Yet we do engage with works from other cultures and historical periods, in which the embedded values are ethically foreign or repulsive to us. Plato advocates censorship precisely because he believes that such works *change* our values; the values of most, he would argue, are not so firmly anchored that a meritocratic state can risk allowing citizens access to literature with ethically deviant values.

that most present could not bring themselves to *imagine* sympathizing with such a Phaedra.[15] Their moral disgust would not allow them to suspend disbelief. Plato would see this as an artistic failure on Euripides's part. Had Euripides been successful, he would have kept the audience enthralled, just as he did in two other great plays whose plots include the evil of infanticide: the second *Hippolytus* and *Medea*, the latter, a story of infanticide for the questionable motive of a wife's revenge for being jilted (the Athenians allowed for infanticide in some cases, but not erotic vengeance and not after early infancy).[16]

Some philosophers[17] insightfully discuss an equivocation in the various treatments of the Imaginative Resistance puzzle. One, some claim, can easily trade on three different meanings of "Resistance," with the following contrived names: Wontianism, Cantianism, and Hardianism. What is the difference between (1) "Wontianism" (2) "Cantianism," and (3) "Hardianism?"[18] Brock describes the distinction among these stances as follows:

(1)   Wontianism: The reader does not want to imagine x, refuses to imagine x (x being the fictional world or some constituent of it) and is therefore unwilling to do so.

(2)   Cantianism: The reader cannot believe x, even if she is willing, or wants, to do so.

(3)   Hardianism: The reader is willing and able to imagine x but finds it difficult to do so.

In the first *Hippolytus*, the audience will not accept the character of Phaedra as an overt, uncontrollable seductress. It is not a logical or physical impossibility; rather it is too revolting and shocking to them. This would be a case of Wontianism, for they are unwilling to inhabit the possible world in which the virtuous queen cannot control her lust. This, according to the Wontian, represents an artistic flaw. The moral evil detracts from the work aesthetically. The Cantian and Hardian would probably agree on this last point. I, on the contrary, argue below that a moral evil does *not* detract from the work aesthetically;

---

15   For a contrarian view, see John C. Gilbert, "Euripides' Hippolytus Plays: Which Came First?," *The Classical Quarterly* 47, no. 1 (1997): 85–97. Gilbert argues that this is just ancient gossip, at best, hypothesis.

16   All of the three great tragedians (Aeschylus, Sophocles, and Euripides) depict taboos that do not, and did not, interfere with the audience's imaginative experience: they depict matricide, patricide, infanticide, incest, cooking one's own children, bestiality ... and so it goes.

17   For example, see Brock "The Puzzle of Imaginative Failure," 443–63; Gendler, "The Puzzle of Imaginative Resistance," 55–81; Tyler Doggett, and Andy Egan, "Wanting Things You Don't Want: The Case for an Imaginative Analogue of Desire," *Philosophers' Imprint* 7, no. 9 (2007): 1–17.

18   (1) and (2) are from Gendler, (3) from Tyler Doggett and Andy Egan.

rather, an aesthetic flaw makes us focus on the morality and prevents us from aesthetic immersion.

We can, however, observe another type of "wontianism" that Brock (and, to the best of my knowledge, others) do not mention, a type that is compatible with, even necessitates, artistic success: Let us call this type "Imaginative Refusal." A reader or spectator might find a narrative so abhorrent that she stops reading or, if she is at a performance, walks out of a theatre. Brock, making a different point, quotes a passage in *American Psycho* that I simply stopped reading halfway through the second sentence. So vividly and convincingly does the author portray the rapist's affectless account of the extreme violence of his act that I refused to read another word, just as I might have plugged my ears or walked out had the rapist been testifying in a courtroom. Imaginative Refusal is a different sort of experiential response to immorality in fiction than is Imaginative Resistance.

To return to these matters, we must ask: were Imaginative Resistance grounded in our phenomenological dissonance or moral aversion, why does a reader of, say, Kafka's stunning *The Metamorphosis* not experience a jarring pull from the fiction? This question asks *not* why a reader experiences Imaginative Resistance, but rather why a reader *does not* experience Imaginative Resistance.

2   Reader vs. Author

Brock offers what he considers "a novel solution to the [traditional] puzzle," which he terms "Imaginative Failure," instead of "Imaginative Resistance." Although Brock focuses on cases in fiction that "conflict with the reader's moral judgments and are not backed up by reasons,"[19] he avers that philosophers disagree as to whether "deviant aesthetic evaluations or conceptual possibilities" also lead to Imaginative Failure or Resistance. First, we should note a point about Brock's formulation of the trigger conditions as those that (a) "conflict with the reader's moral judgments" and (b) "are not backed up by reasons." Contrary to Brock's assessment, literary authors not only do *not*, but *should not*, have to defend rationally (that is, overtly, explicitly, logically) any moral universe they design. This will be relevant later both to one of my theses and Brock's own solution. This may be what Brock means when he says later that the puzzle is "explaining why readers don't imagine what actions are right or

---

19   Brock "The Puzzle of Imaginative Failure," 445.

PSYCHOANALYSIS, IMAGINATION, AND IMAGINATIVE RESISTANCE   145

wrong *for the reasons outlined in the* fiction."[20] Like Brock, I ascribe Imaginative Failure to an author's artistic failure or lapse. To establish his thesis, Brock examines and rejects Searle's claim that while literary authors make assertions with declarative sentences in narrating a fiction, they perform a different sort of illocutionary act than when they make assertions outside of a fictional text. Brock instead concludes that authors need to give the readers extra-textual cues if the reader is to experience the work with imaginative success. Without going into the details of Brock's arguments, and particularly his rebuttal of Searle, suffice it to say, that a good literary artwork need not and does not extend outside the world of the fiction.

Artistically successful authors draw a world, by using elegant, precise, preferably originally arranged, language and syntax (be their style lush, spare, poetic, etc.), by creating a persuasive narrator, psychologically complex characters, compelling imagistic description, and an inventive narrative line. Whatever moral universe the author depicts the characters or protagonist(s) as inhabiting is one which we readers enter willingly; we do so precisely because of the consistency and vivacity of the authorial imagination, as well as the author's skill at fashioning it with words and images. It is misleading, therefore, to expect authors to defend "with reasons" the moral environment in their fictions.[21] Many great, even though morally appalling, works come to mind in which the moral universe is indefensible. Consider Aeschylus's *Oresteia,* Nabokov's *Lolita,* Shakespeare's *Hamlet,* Euripides's *Medea,* and Delia Owens' *Where the Crawdads Sing.* Note that in reading any one of these specimen works, the reader's imaginative immersion does not pause even at the reprehensible moral content, such as, racist stereotypes, infanticide, pedophilia, patriarchal dominance, or wanton, unmotivated murder. Great literature is replete with moral abominations, including infanticide, patricide, racism, cannibalism, regicide, gratuitous psychological cruelty and so the list goes on.

The real puzzle of Imaginative Resistance is why in these cases we do not experience Imaginative Resistance or Failure, but why we do in others. Brock's solution is arguably on the right track but stops short of its destination. He rightly points out that he brings something new to the debate. As he puts it, our failure as readers is really "a failure on the author's part to make clear that she is inviting the reader to imagine what she is saying..."[22] Given Brock's

---

20   Brock "The Puzzle of Imaginative Failure," 446–47.
21   Brock recognizes that an author does not defend a moral viewpoint in the way that a philosopher does. The aim of this chapter, however, is neither an analysis nor critique of his article, which would lead us away from the role of repression in Imaginative Resistance. I give more attention to his article than others because I am sympathetic to some, only some, of his points.
22   Brock "The Puzzle of Imaginative Failure," 445.

analysis, his renaming the puzzle "Imaginative Failure" rather than "Imaginative Resistance" is apt. The word "Failure" makes us consider where does the responsibility for the failure lie—in the reader, the author, or the interaction between them?

Brock points out that some blame rests on the author. Most other analyses do not address who or what is responsible. Is it the author, who has lapsed artistically, the reader, or an interaction between them?[23] Imaginative Resistance (or "Imaginative Failure") goes beyond the moral realm and also the literary. But let us stay with literature for now. Consider Kafka's nonpareil opening of *The Metamorphosis*. If written by a lesser author, the Phenomenological Puzzle would arise from our experiencing "jarring confusion." Gregor Samsa awakens one day to find himself a member of another species, a large, vile insect—"vermin." This is, of course, physically impossible, highly implausible; even so, we do not refuse or resist imagining it.

Gregor himself does not evince astonishment, bewilderment, or even disbelief at his change. Nor does anyone in his family. Why do we not experience Imaginative Resistance or, in Brock's terms, Imaginative Failure, in reading *The Metamorphosis*? It is assuredly because Kafka achieves a literary *tour de force* by designing a coherent world, with a wild, internal logic of its own. As the events unfold and we learn about the family's dynamics and his father's brutality and laziness, each ensuing event is inevitable, even his father's ultimate act of violence. Kafka gives us a preposterous, crazy world, albeit a possible world, in which we find yet *another* case of infanticide. No sympathetic reader of the work,[24] I suspect, experiences Imaginative Resistance, because Kafka has drawn a psychologically consistent world. Why do we not resist imagining the morally unimaginable in *The Metamorphosis?* Gregor's father throws an apple at Gregor in his new incarnation, which ultimately causes Gregor's death. Because of the way Kafka has drawn the nuances of his father's base, authoritarian character, it seems utterly believable, and it breaks the reader's heart.

---

23 Some readers experience imaginative resistance or failure in reading certain aesthetically fine works. For example, many feminist readers cannot get past the first few pages of certain Philip Roth novels.

24 There must be some readers who could not get past the first page or two, because they find the story so preposterous. Such a reader would be a literary equivalent of Arthur Danto's hypothetical Testadura, who does not realize that s/he has entered the artworld. Testadura cannot see that Duchamp's *Fountain* is not a urinal that belongs in a men's restroom rather than on display, nor that Duchamp's *Bicycle Wheel* does not belong on someone's bicycle. To use one of Danto's favorite examples Testadura does not understand that Rauschenberg's bed actually belongs in an art exhibition, rather than a bedroom.

Gregor is a good soul, generous and loving. We are on his side, although none of us would want to be vermin. We feel dejected, disappointed, but we do not refuse to imagine it. Nor do we fail or resist imagining that Gregor, once a human, has become an insect. One might say that in this case, we have no problem resisting, or failing, to believe that his father kills him as if he were in fact a bug. Gregor, of course, is, profoundly human, as we know from our access to his interior. His father happily commits infanticide, and still our imaginative experience is unbroken. It remains intact because our identification with Gregor remains unbroken. He does not fight back, as one might think a giant bug could do, and a human being morally *should* do: Gregor's self-effacement is arguably an ethical flaw in his character. According to most ethical systems, it is imperative that one treat every person with respect, and Gregor himself is a person—even in a non-human form. Gregor's acceptance (submission to the despotic father) is a neurotic manifestation of his masochistic, infantile desire to mythologize his father, the father who never allowed him to individuate. We feel the self-disgust and resignation that Gregor feels, which is painful and morally abhorrent.[25]

As for Imaginative Resistance, philosophers dispute whether it occurs and, if so, whether the correct account is cognitive, conative, attitudinal, or emotive; each of these analyses rests on the assumption that a person's moral beliefs play the leading role.[26] We should note, then, that the various treatments of Imaginative Resistance rest on our identities as moral agents, with a set of moral beliefs that guide our actions and push the limits of what we are willing or able to imagine. Is it the case that Imaginative Resistance arises from moral repugnance?

Why will the reader resist something morally deviant? We do not avoid reports in our everyday lives, for instance, when we listen to analyses of legal cases, hear news, gossip, read tabloids, deliberate about moral dilemmas, and more abstractly, speculate on hypothetical cases in discussions of moral principles. Why can we imagine cannibalism, terrorism, or drug dealing as a moral wrong, but "resist imagining" it in our phenomenological experience of literature? One reason is that hearing about a case of a drug runner or speculating about it in an abstract moral discussion allows us to remain phenomenologically distant; we experience it in the third person. To imagine it in aesthetically fine literature draws us phenomenologically so close that we imaginatively

---

25 Many readers do interpret Gregor's transformation as representing a common neurotic dynamic.

26 For an account of this taxonomy, see Miyazono and Liao, "The Cognitive Architecture of Imaginative Resistance," 233–46.

experience it in the first person. This occurs only if the literary work has sufficient aesthetic value so that we identify with a character and view the world from their perspective. We can imagine it, say, in a hypothetical case in moral philosophy, for example: Someone offers you a vast sum of money to deliver some drugs to a gang leader. If you were reading a novel in which the protagonist did so, you could well find it too disgraceful to imagine. This would, of course, break our imaginative engagement, our "making-believe." If the feeling of disgrace were to jolt readers out of their immersion in the work, then either the work is an artistic failure or the reader's imagination is limited. In some works, the moral dilemma the protagonist faces is extreme and the protagonist's choice may seem wrong. Some good examples include *The Sopranos*, Euripides's *Medea*, Shakespeare's *Hamlet*, Verdi's *Rigoletto*, Aeschylus's *Agamemnon*, and Vittoria de Secca's 1948 film, *The Bicycle Thief* (*Ladri di Biciclette*). In *Agamemnon*, the protagonist chooses to sacrifice his daughter ("the flower of her father's house") for the sake of military victory. In *Medea*, the eponymous protagonist kills her two young sons. The enormity of violating so primal a social taboo could easily induce self-loathing. Yet the reader or spectator sustains imaginative engagement. Hamlet kills his girlfriend's father in cold blood (for starters) and, in various ways, drives her to suicide. The audience is willing to sustain identification with these protagonists. As noted above, we do not engage in Imaginative Resistance, when a work is so good that it will not allow us to do so. We do not even realize that a writer is pulling us away from our moral universe.

When we experience Imaginative Resistance, it is not because we are Philistines. As we have seen, the models offered have been misleading or incomplete. Freud's psychoanalytic concept of repression and its attendant notion of resistance offers us insight into the phenomenon and what an apt model of Imaginative Resistance should include.

3   A Psychoanalytical Solution

The nineteenth century saw a vigorous debate about the relation between scientific thought and imagination. Although Freud saw himself as a scientist, we find science, philosophy, and art plaited together within his work. Freud, in fact, anticipated the contemporary philosophical concept of Imaginative Resistance, although he did so in a different domain than the literary and moral. Let us briefly consider his foundational principles and the sense in which he could be said to have dethroned the Cartesian model.

Freud took his most important intellectual contribution to culture to be a philosophical one, namely, having overturned the Cartesian concept of mind as essentially consciousness to which the subject alone had access. Others had acknowledged that people have unconscious mental activity.

Freud, in his *An Autobiographical Study*, explicitly argues against what philosophers would later call "privileged access," an implication of the Cartesian view of the mind as subjectivity. Freud does not address the issue of whether our sense data are private to the individual; rather he argues vigorously against the privacy or privileged status of emotions, desires, and feelings. Freud takes philosophy seriously, as he demonstrates by the depth of his arguments against the Cartesian tradition. He had studied philosophy with the philosopher and psychologist Franz Brentano, one of the seminal figures in philosophy of mind with his notion of intentionality. As he tells us, Freud mapped out the terrain of the unconscious as his work evolved.[27] He divides the unconscious into the preconscious, the storehouse of mental content that can be brought to consciousness, and the unconscious, *tout court*.[28] He prided himself, too, on his insight about the phenomenon of repression. His pioneering idea of a complex subterranean mental life is one reason we think of ourselves as living in a "post-Freudian" era. It changed our understanding of the human condition and the fields of inquiry that study it.

Freudian psychoanalysis begins from the premise that we each have a unique history and interior life. Our fears and desires are part of our individuality; but for Freud, none of us has privileged access to our own feelings, values, and desires. For Descartes, we do have privileged access. Descartes maintains that our subjectivity is what each of us knows best. Our subjective awareness is the foundation of all of our other beliefs. I cannot know another's subjective experiences, although I can, and do, know my own. In fact, my subjective awareness is the only certainty I can have. Thus, for Descartes, the mind, the self, is essentially subjective consciousness. Descartes defines the mental as conscious awareness, while Freud defines it quite differently. Thus, Freud takes his theory as repudiating Descartes and doing so in a new idiom. For Freud, our various and variegated intentional states can be better known by someone else, in particular someone, that is, an analyst, who has hermeneutic expertise

---

27   This section of the *Study*, which shows his esteem for philosophy, is included in Peter Gay, *The Freud Reader* (New York and London: Norton & Company, 1989), 18–19.

28   See Billig's remark on this in Michael Billig, *Conversation Creating the Unconscious* (Cambridge: Cambridge University Press, 1999), 40–42. It is crucial to keep in mind that as Freud develops intellectually, he refines his notion of the Preconscious.

at observing the nuances of a person's words, gestures, activities, and even reports of their dreams. Far from being an authority on our own states, we are least-equipped to understand them or even acknowledge them. Like everyone else, each of us has an unconscious interior world that we unwittingly disclose to others; ironically, Freud tells us, we ourselves resist acknowledging this picture of our interiors as a faithful mirror. How is this possible? The psychoanalytic model reveals that the unconscious is the repository of our impulses, desires, etc.; our patterns and behavior in general are the result of our aims to keep these desires and drives from emerging into consciousness. Just as the *cogitio* and the primacy of subjective consciousness form the basis of Cartesian philosophy, so the unconscious with its mechanisms of repression, censorship, and resistance form the foundation of psychoanalysis.

At the foundation of psychoanalytic theory is a commitment to there being an unconscious element exerting force over human behavior. Freud's formulation of it and its various mechanisms of course transformed as he developed as an intellectual and clinician. The philosophical and neurobiological objections to it (and details based on his intellectual culture) notwithstanding, it raises important philosophical questions not only about mental pathology, but also about human agency, human development, human nature, social relations, artistic creativity, artistic experience, and the possibility for our achieving *eudaimonia.*

Broadly speaking, Freud began his odyssey with the goal of understanding apparently irrational behavior. Such irrationality, he came to insist, was governed by a logic of its own. In his early creative development, Freud became particularly fascinated by the phenomena of hysteria,[29] dreams, and in our self-sabotaging efforts to gratify unconscious impulses and desires. In the analytic space, the clinical dyad of analyst and analysand explores the vast terrain of the unconscious, the place of repressed desires and impulses that we gratify through dreams, fantasies, and other seemingly inexplicable acts (compulsions, parapraxes, fetishes, hysterical conversions, etc.).

According to Freud, we push to our unconscious what we feel is wrong or dangerous. It is because the ego fears the consequences of certain desires that it represses the urges towards doing them. Because of our unconscious desire to maintain the integrity of our ego identity and our healthy narcissism, we feel

---

29   "Hysteria" is broader than "hysterical conversion" in that the latter is a bodily manifestation of an unconscious trauma, while the former may refer to bodily or more general behavioral manifestations (for example, Anna O's apparent inability to speak in her mother tongue).

anxious expressing certain desires and beliefs, even in—or especially in—imagination, because we would risk losing our love and security from significant others, or, depending on our stage of development, ourselves. Repression is a defense mechanism. For Freud, as Madison reminds us:

> Repression shows itself in two forms, first the process responsible for symptom formation, and in therapy as the same process responsible, now, for resistance: [quoting Freud] "In what way can we now account for this fact ... that the patient struggles so energetically against the relief of his symptoms ... We can say that we have come upon the traces of powerful forces at work here opposing any change in the condition; they must [i.e., one 'must' infer] be the same forces that originally induced the condition ... A vehement effort must have been exercised to prevent the mental process in question from penetrating into consciousness and as a result it has remained unconscious..."[30]

Resistance, that energetic struggle, works in tandem with repression. A small boy might repress his desire to kill his brother, and this may manifest itself later as a compulsion to wash his hands, for example, and/or have an unhealthy dependence on his brother. In therapy, he resists any insinuation that he ever desired to harm his brother. To acknowledge it would evoke that early fear of punishment, rejection, and loss of love.

Freud never abandoned his exceedingly complex notion of Resistance, nor that of avoidance, although both gain complexity as his theories develop. Essentially, however, they are connected to repression. Freud wants us to keep in mind that resistance of some of our repressed impulses is adaptive, even necessary for social relations and for society itself.[31] Many others are maladaptive in that they generate neurotic symptoms, which create unhappiness in everyday adult life. In the analytic dynamic, the closer the analyst brings the analysand to the repressed feelings, memories, interpretations, or attachments, the more powerfully the analysand resists and then expresses even more so the neurotic symptom. If a repressed desire is so threatening as to be repressed, the ego repeats releasing the repressed desire, *except now* the desire is encoded in symbolic form. That is what explains the repetition of seemingly irrational

---

30 Peter Madison, *Freud's Concept of Repression and Defence: Its Theoretical and Observational Language* (Oxford: University of Minnesota Press, 1961), 32; Billig also mentions variously the positive function of repression.

31 In his later period, Freud explores human drives, impulses, and desires on the macrolevel. He famously argues for our need to resist many desires and urges in *Civilization and its Discontents*, which is partly about the tension between the individual and the polis.

acts: They are soothing; they do important work within the psyche. This is why Freud maintains that irrational acts are actually rationally motivated; we have reasons for them. The ego avoids a desire, emotion, or instinct by repressing it. What the analysand resists most is what the "censor" allows out only in symbolic form (dreams, neurotic compulsions, fantasies, paraphilias, patterns of embarrassing parapraxes, even works of art, etc.). We express or release what is horrifying or shameful in ways we feel are safe.

What is the connection between resistance in the psychoanalytic clinic and in the literary space? As indicated earlier, Imaginative Resistance occurs when the author fails to create a seamless, complex, compelling fictional world. Returning for a moment to *The Metamorphosis* or *Medea*, we do not experience Imaginative Resistance because the fictional world designed is irresistible.

The author is an illusionist who conceals the moral flaws of the protagonist. If the author loses control of the material, we become aware of the moral ambiguity in a fiction and thus resist inhabiting it imaginatively.

One might ask how it is possible for us ever to recognize the evil in a character we had initially found sympathetic. When a work fascinates us and we later probe it critically, we appreciate the work intellectually. At a temporal distance, we have an intellectual experience, rather than an aesthetic one. In *Hamlet*, for example, we may see upon reflecting, that Hamlet was nonchalant about killing Polonius and had no remorse about it. His murderous intentions towards Claudius were understandable and drive the plot of the play. We could adduce other examples from this tragedy. When we later reflect on how Shakespeare made us sympathetic towards Hamlet from the start, we still like the character, but now see his moral complexity. We do not find our sympathetic feelings towards him in any way threatening to our own sense of moral integrity.

A talented psychoanalyst will discover the analysand's repressed traumatic memory or desire by insightful observation of the verbal and nonverbal behavior. The analysand's anxiety makes the resistance more apparent, the closer the analyst gets to the source of the neurotic symptom. The reader who experiences Imaginative Resistance is structurally like the neurotic who is becoming uncomfortable as the analyst probes more deeply. In both cases, the story is eroding—neither fiction can continue to do its work. In the case of the literary narrative, the writer's task is to keep the reader enchanted so that the reader will *not* resist or refuse imaginatively; in the case of the analysand, the censor's task is to keep the trauma repressed so that the ego *will* resist or refuse to remember. The censor that stands at the gateway of the unconscious is like the author in that it creates a fiction. It allows the unconscious, repressed desire to express itself only metaphorically. When we experience Imaginative Resistance in fiction, we are avoiding identifying with the character. Because the fiction is ill-designed, we cannot imaginatively enact the character's deeds and judgments. The successful analytic process leads one to exert resistance in the clinical space, in order to avoid the impending epiphany.

We find here a promising model for the phenomenological dynamic of Imaginative Resistance: Both the unconscious censor and the successful author create narratives or fictions that aim to be compelling. The reader of an ill-designed narrative and the ego of the neurotic each resist what they feel they do not want to be and refuse to imagine themselves in that light. In the case of the reader, it is being a person who would want to violate their moral principles. In the case of the neurotic, it is being a person who would have shameful or dangerous urges. Repression keeps the ego safely in the unconsciously created narrative. For example, the manifest content of a dream is a story, however illogical, random, and disconnected it may seem, it is, according to Freud, logical and coherent. It is a story designed to disguise an unconscious desire or wish. We find it less threatening to live through a horrifying nightmare that unfolds symbolically in a dream than to admit to forbidden desires or wishes. The unconscious works like the good writer: one draws us into the manifest content of a dream, the other into a well-wrought fiction. In analysis, the analysand refuses to acknowledge the latent desire or wish expressed in the dream. As the analyst gets closer, the analysand's neurotic symptom becomes more intense. The successful analyst lures the analysand into accepting the repressed wish as psychically benign or, at least, manageable. In an artistically successful case, the author holds the reader or audience in the narrative. In the unsuccessful case, the author loses their grip on the reader, who begins to resist the imaginative engagements.

To conclude, we have seen the intricacy of Imaginative Resistance and the recalcitrance of the philosophical problem(s). I have here offered another way to look at the problem in literature, which is in the spirit of Brock's. The other philosophical analyses omit the crucial element of the author. Plato, I think, tacitly understands the problem well and casts aspersions on the author for not releasing us imaginatively. The psychoanalytic account I have sketched out here adds another dimension to our understanding of the phenomenon of Imaginative Resistance and thus casts light on this thorny philosophical puzzle.

References

Billig, Michael. *Conversation Creating the Unconscious.* Cambridge: Cambridge University Press. 1999.

Britton, Ronald. *Belief and Imagination*. 1998. Reprint. Routledge: London and New York. 2004,

Brock, Stuart. "The Puzzle of Imaginative Failure." *The Philosophical Quarterly* 62, no. 248 (2012): 443–63.

Carroll, Noël. "Art and Ethical Criticism: An Overview of Recent Directions of Research." *Ethics* 110, no. 2 (2000): 350–87.

Castoriadis, Cornelius. "Logic, Imagination, Reflection." *American Imago*, 49, no. 1 (1992): 3–33.

Danto, Arthur. "The Artworld." *Journal of Philosophy*, 61, no. 19 (1964): 571–84.

De Sousa, Ronald. "The Mind's Bermuda Triangle: Philosophy of Emotions and Empirical Science." In *The Oxford Handbook of Philosophy of Emotion*, edited by Peter Goldie, 9–117. New York: Oxford University Press, 2010.

Doggett, Tyler, and Andy Egan. "Wanting Things You Don't Want: The Case for an Imaginative Analogue of Desire." *Philosophers' Imprint* 7, no. 9 (2007): 1–17.

Freud, Sigmund. *Delusion and Dream in the Light of Psychoanalysis of Gradiva and Selected Papers on Hysteria and other Psychoneuroses*. Translated by Helen M. Downey. New York: publisher unavailable, 1921.

Gay, Peter. *The Freud Reader*. New York and London: Norton & Company. 1989.

Gendler, Tamar Szabó. "The Puzzle of Imaginative Resistance." *Journal of Philosophy*, 97, no. 2 (2000): 55–81.

Gilbert, John C. "Euripides' Hippolytus Plays: Which Came First?" *The Classical Quarterly*, 47, no. 1 (1997): 85–97.

Goldie, Peter, ed. *The Oxford Handbook of Philosophy of Emotion*. New York: Oxford University Press. 2010.

Miyazono, Kengo, and Shen-yi Liao. "The Cognitive Architecture of Imaginative Resistance." In *The Routledge Handbook of Philosophy of Imagination,* edited by Amy Kind, 233–46 London and New York: Routledge, 2016.

Madison, Peter. *Freud's Concept of Repression and Defence: Its Theoretical and Observational Language*. Oxford: University of Minnesota Press. 1961.

Michael, Michael T. "The Case for the Freud-Beuer Theory of Hysteria: A Response to Grünbaum's foundational Objection to Psychoanalysis." *The International Journal of Psychoanalysis* 100, no. 1 (2019): 32–51.

Nichols, Shaun. *The Architecture of the Imagination: New Essays on Pretence, Possibility, and Fiction*. Oxford: Oxford University Press. 2006.

Walton, Kendall. *Mimesis as Make-Believe*. Cambridge, MA: Harvard University Press. 1990.

Walton, Kendall. "On the (So-Called) Puzzle of Imaginative Resistance." In *The Architecture of the Imagination: New Essays on Pretence, Possibility, and Fiction*, edited by Shaun Nichols, 137–48. Oxford: Oxford University Press, 2006.

Weatherson, Brian. "Morality, Fiction, and Possibility." *Philosophers' Imprint* 4, no. 3 (2004): 1–27.

CHAPTER 7

Craving Sameness, Accepting Difference: Imaginative Possibilities for Solidarity and Social Justice

Chandra Kavanagh

Realist accounts typically define solidarity on the basis of an allegedly static feature of human nature. We stand in solidarity with some other person, or group of people, because we share important features. Human solidarity relies on (1) totalizing claims about human nature, such as possessing the capacity for reason, (2) the capacity to labor or (3) having a particular type of body. However, those requirements are often used to further exclude groups that are already denied entry into the community of those who stand in solidarity with one another. In other words, basing solidarity on some "vital" aspect of human nature shared by some, but not all, is often used as a tool to continue to oppress those populations who are already oppressed. In opposition to such realist accounts, Richard Rorty defines solidarity as a practical tool, within which there is always an "us," with whom we stand in solidarity, and a "them," with whom we are contrasted. These boundaries are not static but alterable, and it is insofar as the boundaries between "us" and "them" are alterable that the role of the imagination adopts fundamental significance. The constructive and critical roles of the imagination provide a capacity to think beyond the accepted boundaries that determine the community of those with whom we stand in solidarity and to possibly extend them. Given the contrast of the in-group and the out-group, upon which his definition of solidarity depends, Rorty's solidarity is prone to the critique that his definition retains the risk of exclusion faced by members of oppressed groups in the realist account. I argue that by understanding Rorty's pragmatic solidarity in terms of the relational view of solidarity offered by Alexis Shotwell, it is possible to conceptualize solidarity in a manner that allows for extending the boundaries of the community with whom we stand in solidarity. Furthermore, this pragmatic, relational version of solidarity provides normative force to the responsibility to extend those boundaries.

This chapter begins with a discussion of the realist account of solidarity and a description of the consequences of this account for various oppressed groups, such as cognitively disabled people, those who are unable to work and those

© KONINKLIJKE BRILL NV, LEIDEN, 2020 | DOI:10.1163/9789004436350_009

whose bodies do not fit the historically entrenched norm. This is followed by a number of critiques of how this conception of solidarity can be easily manipulated into continuing to exclude those who are already disenfranchised. The second section offers a description of Rorty's pragmatist account of solidarity. Three noteworthy aspects characterize solidarity for Rorty: the fact that solidarity is always solidarity with a group of "us," defined over and against a group of outsiders; the fact that solidarity functions in terms of concentric circles, wherein I feel solidarity most readily for those with whom I share relevant similarities and less readily for those who I believe are importantly different from me; and the fact that the boundaries of Rorty's solidarity are extendable. The possibility of extending solidarity reveals the centrality of the imagination in facilitating the development of a more inclusive community with whom one can stand in solidarity. Therefore, imagination is crucial in cultivating solidarity with those who have been excluded. This investigation of Rorty's solidarity is followed by a description of the consequences of this position for oppressed people. Moreover, I will also explore some critiques of this version of solidarity. Finally, the summative section addresses these critiques by demonstrating how pairing Rorty's pragmatic solidarity with Shotwell's relational solidarity provides both a way forward for opening up access to solidarity and the moral requirement that solidarity be opened up.

1   A Realist Account of Solidarity

Richard Rorty provides a working definition of solidarity in his book *Contingency, Irony and Solidarity*, when he describes the conventional philosophical definition of solidarity in terms of the claim "that there is something within each of us – our essential humanity – which resonates with the presence of this same thing in other human beings."[1] Both direct and indirect realists adopt this definition, tying it to objective facts about human nature. However, to understand the realist account of solidarity, one must understand the realist's epistemological position.

In his book *Objectivity, Relativism and Truth*, Rorty notes "those who wish to ground solidarity in objectivity – call them 'realists' – have to construe truth as correspondence to reality."[2] The central realist debate revolves around what types of statements correspond to the objective world and how precisely they

---

1   Allen Buchanan, *The Heart of Human Rights* (New York: Oxford University Press, 2013).
2   Shane Phelan, "Bodies, Passions and Citizenship," in *Feminism, Identity and Difference*, ed. Susan Hekman (London: Frank Cass, 1999), 12.

CRAVING SAMENESS, ACCEPTING DIFFERENCE

reflect it. He describes realist inquiry as focused on the question of "whether only the statements of physics can correspond to 'facts of the matter' or whether those of … ethics might also?"[3] Regarding solidarity, the realist seeks to argue that solidarity is a fellow feeling that ought to be extended amongst all human beings, based on the justification that solidarity is the expression of an objective, morally salient and universal human characteristic.

For instance, in Allen Buchanan's book *The Heart of Human Rights*, he justifies his argument that all human beings share equal basic moral status on the basis of the objective claim about human nature that we share a morally salient characteristic. He claims that equal basic status "depends on being able to show that all people possess some characteristic or capacity that confers a high moral standing."[4] For Buchanan, the characteristic that guarantees solidarity is reason. He concludes that "the most likely candidate for a feature that … makes sense of the idea that those at or above the threshold all deserve a special sort of moral standing is the capacity for responsiveness to reasons."[5] Justifying inclusion in the moral community on the basis of a shared capacity for rational accountability is a common tactic for realist theorists, for instance, Martha Nussbaum makes a similar claim.

2   Critiques of the Realist Account of Solidarity

So, in a realist account, we possess an ethical obligation to stand in solidarity with those who share the capacity for reason. Feminist philosophers, such as Eva Kittay, have long criticized such positions for placing cognitively disabled people at risk. In her article "The Personal is Philosophical is Political: A Philosopher and Mother of a Cognitively Disabled Person Sends Notes from the Battlefield," Kittay writes,

> What is it philosophers have said about cognitive disability that I found so appalling that I was ready to jettison a career of more than thirty years? Plato decreed that "defective babies" should be left to die. Locke and Kant defined those who lack reason as less than human. And most troubling of all, when I looked for contemporary discussions about this group, most of

---

3   Gayle Rubin, "Thinking Sex: Notes for a Radical Theory of the Politics of Sexuality," in *Culture, Society and Sexuality: A Reader*, eds. Peter Aggleton and Richard Parker (London and New York: Routledge, 2007), 38.

4   Buchanan, *The Heart of Human Rights*, 21.

5   Buchanan, *The Heart of Human Rights*, 22.

the references I found were in discussions of animal rights, asking pointedly whether the "severely mentally retarded" could be distinguished from non-human animals in any meaningful sense.[6]

When solidarity, and thus basic moral consideration, is intertwined with the supposed presence or absence of reason, those who are believed to lack reason are relegated to a less than human status. When a particular sub-population is viewed as such, it becomes much easier to justify actions against that population that would otherwise be considered immoral, if the group possess basic moral status.

Shane Phelan's (1999) article demonstrates how the capacity for labor serves as a desideratum that "exclude[s] 'others' from equal citizenship."[7] According to Phelan, the "citizen ideal in the USA labours in the market."[8] As a result of this requirement, the right to citizenship, and therefore to political solidarity, depends upon an idealized and inherent capacity for work that a given citizen approximates, to a greater or lesser degree. As Phelan notes, laboring in the market is not simply a matter of capacity for work but also the capacity for discipline and renouncing pleasure.[9] This requirement to renounce pleasure, alongside the fundamental associations contemporary society makes between women's nature and pleasure, excludes women from full citizenship. Here, we see how claims about inherent nature can be used to deny solidarity to those who would otherwise hold a claim to it. Here the idea that all citizens have the capacity to give up pleasure and get to work excludes women, insofar as they are inherently associated with pleasure and are unable to renounce it. Therefore, women need not be included amongst the population of those with whom we stand in political solidarity. Phelan's arguments against capacity for labor and the renunciation of pleasure being used to exclude certain groups from citizenship can also be used to dismiss other types of realist parameters for determining solidarity. As is the case when the capacity to reason is a prerequisite for standing in solidarity with a given member of the community, when solidarity relies on the capacity for labor, it is easily manipulated into continuing to exclude the already excluded.

---

6   Eva Kittay, "The Personal is Philosophical is Political: A Philosopher and Mother of a Cognitively Disabled Person Sends Notes from the Battlefield," *Metaphilosophy* 40, no.3–4 (2009): 609.

7   Shane Phelan, "Bodies, Passions and Citizenship," in *Feminism, Identity and Difference*, ed. Susan Hekman (London: Frank Cass, 1999), 57.

8   Phelan, "Bodies, Passions and Citizenship," 68.

9   Phelan, "Bodies, Passions and Citizenship," 68.

CRAVING SAMENESS, ACCEPTING DIFFERENCE

Gayle Rubin (1984) provides an argument against realist conceptions of solidarity that grounds the obligation to stand in solidarity with others on the basis of whether an individual or set of individuals possesses the characteristic of human nature that supposedly bestows upon them the right to solidarity. Rubin notes a boundary between those whose sexual practices are considered natural and socially accepted and those whose sexual practices are considered unnatural and socially rejected that is justified on the basis of essentialist claims about human nature.[10] Rubin delineates an unjust refusal to stand in social solidarity with sexual minorities that is excused by realist claims about central characteristics of human nature and the presentation of sexual minorities as lacking or perverting these characteristics. This is a problem not because we base claims to solidarity on an incorrect or overly narrow set of essential characteristics, but rather, the problem consists of our basing our sense of solidarity on claims about human nature full stop because, as Rubin demonstrates, claims about what is natural are often used to justify the exclusion of those who are different.

The fact that a realist account of solidarity is so prone to unjustly retain the status quo does not merely provide an ethical and political challenge. It also indicates an epistemological problem with a realist view of solidarity. Pragmatists, such as Richard Rorty, and feminist epistemologists, such as Margaret Urban Walker, challenge this realist position. The claim that human solidarity is justified based on the shared characteristic that all people are responsive to reason is problematic not only because it excludes cognitively disabled people, but also because it relies on unverified and, quite possibly, unverifiable claims. Feminist philosophers have historically problematized viewing the moral subject in terms that tie participation in the moral community to supposedly objective components of human nature, particularly human reason. Margaret Urban Walker illustrates this problem beautifully in her book *Moral Understandings*:

> Many moral philosophers will say that in their philosophical reflections they are not "merely" reflecting on their own moral experience (much less mirroring it), but are tapping into moral reality, or the moral realm, or the structure of practical reasoning, or the nature of the right or the good. But this assumes two things. It assumes that the moral reality, realm, nature or structure is something accessible and determinate quite

---

10   Rubin, "Thinking Sex: Notes for a Radical Theory of the Politics of Sexuality," 157.

apart from anyone's acquired experience of them, and that the moral philosopher can tell when she or he has grasped these things.[11]

Walker notes the two central assumptions that plague those who wish to justify human solidarity on the basis of any claim about objective human nature: such a nature exists apart from experience, and an inquirer could access objective human nature and represent it accurately. A position that grounds human solidarity in objective claims about human nature suffers from both the moral concern that it excludes cognitively disabled people and the epistemological concern that it does so without sufficient cause.

Rorty offers a pragmatic account of solidarity that does not fall victim to the moral and epistemological critiques to which the realist account of solidarity is susceptible. Susan Haack concludes that pragmatism such as Rorty's "is best characterized by the method expressed in the pragmatic maxim, according to which the meaning of a concept is determined by the experiential or practical consequences of its application."[12] Rather than investigating the concept of solidarity to discern whether it is a universal characteristic of human nature, the investigative focus is redirected to the manner in which solidarity functions. Rorty writes, "By dropping the [realist] account of knowledge, we pragmatists drop the appearance-reality distinction in favor of a distinction between beliefs which serve other purposes."[13] This purpose-driven inquiry into solidarity focuses on the characteristics that typically appear as solidarity functions and the variety of ways in which solidarity can be put to use. Furthermore, "The question is which social constructs to discard and which to keep, and that there is no use appealing to 'the way things really are' in the course of struggles over who gets to construct what."[14] In the case of solidarity, Rorty suggests not engaging in the vain realist pursuit of the quality or qualities of human nature that are expected to ensure human solidarity and instead investigating the characteristics that define solidarity in an effort to better understand how the idea might be usefully employed.

Using this pragmatic approach, Rorty offers an account of solidarity capable of truly including excluded groups. Rorty characterizes solidarity as

---

11 Margaret Urban Walker, *Moral Understandings: A Feminist Study in Ethics* (Oxford: Oxford Scholarship, 2008), 5.

12 Susan Haack, "Reply to Commentators," *Philosophy and Phenomenological Research* 56, no. 3 (1996): 643.

13 Richard Rorty, "Feminism, Ideology, and Deconstruction: A Pragmatist View," *Hypatia* 8, no. 2 (1993): 98.

14 Richard Rorty, *Objectivity, Relativism and Truth: Philosophical Papers* (Cambridge: Cambridge University Press, 1990), 21.

CRAVING SAMENESS, ACCEPTING DIFFERENCE 161

oppositional, communitarian and extendable. Human beings define the groups with whom they stand in solidarity, over and against those with whom they feel they have important differences. The more relevantly similar another person is to oneself, the more easily she is included within one's own community. However, it is possible to extend the community of those with whom I stand in solidarity, by redefining the similarities and differences that bound my community. This potential to promote inclusivity is facilitated by the function of the imagination. The constructive side of the imagination entrenches our beliefs about the limits of the community with whom we stand in solidarity, while the critical side of the imagination is capable of stretching or breaching these boundaries, thus allowing further construction. When Rorty applies his idea of moral progress with this picture of the characteristics of solidarity and the capacity for expansion made possible through the imagination, he establishes a clear moral requirement to extend solidarity to disabled people. In his account, standing in solidarity with excluded groups is not a process of recognizing a responsibility that was always there but of creating a responsibility that ought to be there.

3   The Pragmatic Account of Solidarity, Part One: Us versus Them

Rorty defines solidarity as a way in which human beings attempt to give their lives meaning by placing these lives within a larger context. What is particular about solidarity as a method of meaning making is that solidarity "tells the story of [my] contribution to the community."[15] The community where I develop the narrative of my contribution, and thus create the meaning of my life, can vary widely. The community where I find and cultivate solidarity, "may be the actual historical one in which [I] live, or another actual one distant in time or place or a quite imaginary one consisting perhaps of a dozen heroes and heroines selected from history or fiction or both."[16] Rorty shares what H.L.A. Hart calls the "disintegration thesis"[17] which claims that community solidarity is the very groundwork from which moral norms are developed. Rorty's communitarian definition of solidarity objects to the realist claim that extending solidarity to all of humanity is, or ought to be, the case, on the grounds of objective facts about human nature. He responds with a pragmatic point about

---

15   Rorty, *Objectivity, Relativism and Truth: Philosophical Papers*, 21.
16   Rorty, *Objectivity, Relativism and Truth: Philosophical Papers*, 21.
17   H.L.A. Hart, "Social Solidarity and the Enforcement of Morality," *University of Chicago Law Review* 35, no. 1 (1967): 1.

how solidarity functions in experience, the solidarity found in a group of "us" is almost always contrasted with a group of "them," against whom we define ourselves as a community.

4   Pragmatic Account of Solidarity, Part Two: Concentric Circles

Solidarity adopts a concentric circular structure, wherein we feel it most strongly and readily for those relevantly similar to us in our community. Our sense of solidarity is weaker for those who are minorly dissimilar to us, and weaker still for those who are deeply dissimilar to us. Furthermore, the similarities and differences that we take as relevant for inclusion in the community of those with whom we stand in solidarity are determined by linguistic, historical and cultural contexts. In Rorty's account, solidarity is not indicative of some objective characteristic of human nature that carries with it a right to basic moral consideration. Rather, solidarity is a mode of constructing meaning through the narrative that I tell of my contributions to my community. Rorty puts it this way: "Our sense of solidarity is strongest when those with whom solidarity is expressed are thought of as 'one of us' where 'us' means something smaller and more local than the human race."[18] Solidarity typically manifests as "us" defined over and against "them." Furthermore, the more relevant similarities and fewer relevant differences amongst members of a group, the more easily one stands in solidarity with that group.

5   Pragmatic Account of Solidarity, Part Three: Capacity for Expansion

The final characteristic we will explore with regards to Rorty's solidarity is what we call the capacity for expansion. Rorty argues, "solidarity is not discovered by reflection but created. It is created by increasing our sensitivity to the particular details of the pain and humiliation of other, unfamiliar sorts of people."[19] Thus, differences in our communities do not mean that it is impossible, or even difficult, to extend the boundaries that delineate the in-group. In fact, such things frequently occur. For instance, in 1993, "people with mental disabilities were given the right to vote federally."[20] With the right to vote, the

---

18   Richard Rorty, *Contingency, Irony, Solidarity* (Cambridge: Cambridge University Press, 1989), 190.

19   Rorty, *Contingency, Irony, Solidarity*, 190.

20   Michael Prince, "The Electoral Participation of Persons with Special Needs," *Elections Canada: Working Paper Series on Electoral Participation and Outreach*, 2007, 14. http://elections.ca/res/rec/part/paper/special_needs/special_needs_e.pdf.

CRAVING SAMENESS, ACCEPTING DIFFERENCE

community of the politically enfranchised in Canada was extended to stand in solidarity with cognitively disabled people. Until the legislation was officially changed, "the Canada Elections Act specifically excluded 'every person who is restrained of his liberty of movement or deprived of the management of his property by reason of mental disease.'"[21] The community of the politically enfranchised in Canada, like any community, is willing to accept some differences between members, while other differences are important enough to warrant expulsion from the in-group. Prior to 1993, differences in gender, race or sexuality were acceptable, but differences in cognitive ability were considered sufficiently important to exclude cognitively disabled people from the community of the enfranchised. After 1993, differences in cognitive ability were no longer considered an appropriate justification for excluding cognitively disabled people from the enfranchised community.[22]

It is Rorty's position that "feelings of solidarity are necessarily a matter of which similarities and dissimilarities strike us as salient, and that such salience is a function of a historically contingent final vocabulary."[23] Prior to 1993, cognitive ability was a difference that we considered sufficiently salient to determine membership in the community. Many contextual factors had contributed to this situation. For instance, in the decades before the change, despite some disagreement,[24] the concept of mental age was still a largely unquestioned measure of cognitive capacity. It was only after a flurry of academic activity in the late 1970s criticizing the reliability of mental age that a widespread questioning of that concept began to make its way to the general public.[25] Prior to 1993 – and still today – the enfranchised community excluded children on the foundation that by virtue of their mental age, they do not meet the requirement "to be informed and mature" or the requirement "to have a stake in the community."[26] Given the low mental age of some who are cognitively disabled, the enfranchised community felt justified in extending their restriction on the voting rights of children to cognitively disabled people. This is just one of many possible examples illustrating how social and historical contextual factors have influenced which differences are salient and which are not,

---

21 Prince, "The Electoral Participation of Persons with Special Needs," 14.
22 Hamlin Grange, "Lifting Voting Restrictions on the Mentally Ill," Canadian Broadcasting Corporation Digital Archives. Accessed May 5, 2017. http://www.cbc.ca/archives/entry/lifting-voting-restrictions-on-mental-patients.
23 Rorty, *Contingency, Irony, Solidarity*, 24.
24 L.L. Thurstone, "The Mental Age Concept," *Psychological Review* 33 (1926): 278.
25 Leon Kamin, *The Science and Politics of I.Q.* (London: Routledge, 1976), 27.
26 Martin Hyde, "Democracy, Education and the Canadian Voting Age." (PhD diss., University of British Columbia, 2001), 90.

making possible the exclusion of cognitively disabled people from the community of the enfranchised.

From the 1980s to 1993, a concerted effort existed to change the beliefs that made cognitive ability a salient difference when it came to belonging to the community of the enfranchised. For instance, "during the 1980s, the Canadian Disability Rights Council used the Charter to challenge"[27] their exclusion from voting in federal elections. The UN International Year for Disabled Persons was celebrated in 1981, cultivating an environment that allowed for the growth of "an unprecedented level of public and political interest in Canada regarding the rights and opportunities afforded to people with disabilities."[28] As a result of these cumulative changes in context and language, the boundary of solidarity that divided the enfranchised from the disenfranchised was redrawn so as to include cognitively disabled people. The accumulated experiences of people learning about the critiques of mental age and living through the Year for Disabled Persons, where personal narratives of disability gained exposure, allowed for the paradigmatic change in context illustrated by the 1993 decision. It is though such experiences that it is possible to re-examine the boundaries of solidarity and imagine a new path forward.

6 The Relationship between Solidarity and Imagination

It is with this third quality of solidarity, the capacity for expansion, where imagination plays a central role. In their article "Standpoint Theory, Situated Knowledge and the Situated Imagination," Marcel Stoetzler and Nira Yuval-Davis note two different functions of the imagination: "imagination *constructs* its meanings while, on the other hand, it *stretches* and *transcends* them ... a necessary *condition* as well as the *product* of the dialogical process involved in the construction of knowledge."[29] Imagination is constructive, insofar as it is through the imagination that the meanings of concepts are developed. Imagination is critical, insofar as it provides the capacity to think beyond the accepted boundaries of a particular concept and critique or augment accepted meanings. Such changes become instantiated in the meaning of the concept, which is then challenged, and so on. This hermeneutic action performed by

---

27 Grange, "Lifting Voting Restrictions on the Mentally Ill," n. pag.
28 Grange, "Lifting Voting Restrictions on the Mentally Ill," n. pag.
29 Marcel Stoetzler, and Nira Yuval-Davis, "Standpoint Theory, Situated Knowledge and the Situated Imagination," *Feminist Theory* 3, no. 3 (2002): 316.

CRAVING SAMENESS, ACCEPTING DIFFERENCE

the imagination is the method by which the capacity for expansion, which characterizes solidarity, functions.

To elaborate, through its constructive function, the imagination establishes meanings that eventually become so entrenched that they form what Hans-Georg Gadamer calls the "preunderstanding,"[30] a highly influential and active groundwork of contexts, beliefs and languages inevitably creating prejudices that can go on to determine one's understanding of a given concept. For instance, we come to solidarity, and ideas about those with whom we can stand in solidarity, with a predetermined prejudice about who ought and ought not be included. Through its critical function, the imagination is capable of investigating the boundary marked by those from whom we feel we are too different to stand in solidarity. For Gadamer, the catalyst for imaginatively expanding conceptual boundaries in this way is facilitated by experience.

Gadamer notes the role of experience in altering the foundational preunderstanding, such as the prejudices we bring to solidarity, when he claims, "it is the untiring power of *experience*, that in the process of being instructed, man (sic) is ceaselessly forming a new preunderstanding."[31] Experience offers resources that allow the imagination to perform both its constructive and critical functions. For instance, a possible suggestion for experiences that might allow for individuals to push the boundaries of the community with whom they stand in solidarity would be positive interactions with those with whom they do not stand in solidarity. What is meant by a "positive" experience here is that such an experience highlights the meaningful similarities between the two individuals, or the experience puts a critical lens on the value of the perceived differences. The action of the imagination redraws the boundaries of solidarity. It is the resources offered by such experiences that allow for the investigation and possible alteration of the boundaries of the community with whom one stands in solidarity. It is through the action of the imagination adopting the resources offered by experience that (re)construction and critique of the boundaries of solidarity is actualized.

In the case of solidarity, beliefs about who is and is not included amongst those with whom one stands in solidarity are partially determined by a preunderstanding framework of the differences amongst people that matter sufficiently to exclude them from the community and the differences that do not. Preunderstanding, such as one's critically unexamined ascertainment of those

---

30   Gadamer, Hans-Georg, *Truth and Method*, 2nd ed, trans. Joel Weinsheimer and Donald G. Marshall (New York: Sheed and Ward, 1989), 271.

31   Hans-Georg Gadamer, *Philosophical Hermeneutics*, 2nd ed, trans. David E. Linge (Berkeley: University of California Press, 1976), 38.

with whom one can or cannot stand in solidarity, can be developed absent- or present-mindedly. For instance, when developed absent-mindedly, the boundaries that divide those with whom we stand in solidarity from those with whom we do not are prone to remaining unchanged and unexamined. Without the imagination's critical attention to a given preunderstanding, the boundaries of solidarity are likely to continue functioning as impermeable membranes, reconfirming again and again the position dictated by the preunderstanding. For instance, we unreflectively believe mental age is a difference important enough to exclude the cognitively disabled from the community of the enfranchised, and thus the cognitively disabled remain excluded from this community.

However, preunderstanding need not be developed absent-mindedly. As Gadamer posits, "reflection on a given preunderstanding brings before me something that otherwise *happens behind my back*."[32] The critical reflection of the imagination on the framework that determines solidarity reveals a field of possibilities hidden when considering solidarity from within the confines of an unexamined framework. Once the imaginative attention is drawn to the differences that divided those with whom I stand in solidarity from those with whom I do not, it is possible to examine the validity of those boundaries. Such an examination is inconceivable when the existence of such criteria is unacknowledged or unexamined, but once the framework is revealed and critiqued, a new field of possible questions opens up. For instance, through reflection, one realizes that the concept of "mental age" informs one's unwillingness to stand beside cognitively disabled people in solidarity as members of the community of the enfranchised. Furthermore, the critical imagination reveals that the concept "mental age" is not as coherent as once thought and that the difference signaled by the concept of mental age is not quite as important as once thought, and perhaps not even sufficiently important to continue excluding the cognitively disabled from the community of the enfranchised.

An imaginative investigation into the differences considered sufficiently important to determine the boundaries of the community of those with whom we stand in solidarity facilitates the imaginative (re)construction of those boundaries. Van Leeuwen defines constructive imagining as the "capacity to form novel representations."[33] The 1993 decision to include the cognitively disabled in the community of the enfranchised was facilitated by individuals, groups and subsections of the community forming novel representations of

---

32   Gadamer, *Philosophical Hermeneutics*, 38.

33   Neil Van Leeuwen, "The Meanings of 'Imagine' Part I: Constructive Imagination," *Philosophy Compass* 8, no. 3 (2013): 220.

CRAVING SAMENESS, ACCEPTING DIFFERENCE 167

what it is to be a person with a cognitive disability and what parameters govern inclusion in and exclusion from community of those with whom we stand in solidarity.

Experience is the engine that drives the movement of the constructive and critical roles of the imagination. These dual roles played by the imagination perform a hermeneutic function, which can be used to allow for a productive investigation and (re)construction of concepts such as solidarity. The solidarity as kinship model, proposed below as an augmentation to Rorty's account of solidarity, is the result of this critical (re)construction. A hermeneutic investigation into the concept of solidarity and how it functions focuses "on meaning that arises from the interpretive interaction between [artefacts] and the reader."[34] The category "artefacts" refers to the places where the "hermeneutical aspects of human linguisticality"[35] function, for instance, in historically produced text or context-driven conversations. Both the artefact and interpreter "flow together into one owned and shared world, which encompasses past and present and which receives its linguistic articulation in the speaking of [sic] man with man."[36] A hermeneutic analysis of solidarity includes selecting the artefacts that will serve as the focus of the investigation. One set of artefacts being investigated here is the linguistic expressions of kinship made within a variety of communities that are put to use to engender solidarity. The use of linguistic expressions of familial relations to engender solidarity demonstrates the constructive action of the imagination and its pivotal role in extending the boundaries of the community of those with whom we stand in solidarity.

Rorty's imaginative (re)construction of solidarity from its realist definition as a universal component of human nature, "which resonates to the presence of this same thing in other human beings"[37] and ensures basic moral consideration, to a pragmatic account of solidarity as a tool that functions within an "us" and "them" paradigm but can nevertheless be expanded, offers new tactics for fighting for the inclusion of excluded groups as full members of the community. Rather than engaging in tug-of-war arguments about whether cognitively disabled people possess this or that fundamental human characteristic that bestows the right to basic moral consideration, Rorty provides a definition

---

34 Susann Laverty, "Hermeneutic Phenomenology and Phenomenology: A Comparison of Historical and Methodological Considerations," *International Journal of Qualitative Methods* 2, no. 3 (2002): 22.

35 Laverty, "Hermeneutic Phenomenology and Phenomenology," 22.

36 Gadamer, *Philosophical Hermeneutics*, 25.

37 Rorty, *Contingency, Irony, Solidarity*, 189.

of solidarity and a narrative of moral progress that demand the inclusion of cognitively disabled people. In *Contingency, Irony and Solidarity*, he writes,

> The view I am offering says that there is such thing as moral progress, and that this progress is indeed in the direction of greater human solidarity. But that solidarity is not thought of as recognition of a core self, the human essence, in all human beings. Rather it is thought of as the ability to see more and more traditional differences (of tribe, religion, race, customs, [and I would say ability]) as unimportant when compared with similarities with respect to pain and humiliation.[38]

Rorty's version of solidarity provides a major insight into the inclusion of cognitively disabled people in the moral community. In his account, solidarity is a moral feeling that begins with those who also belong to my community. My community is determined by the differences that I interpret as salient. The differences that I treat as salient are not my recognition or misrecognition of an inherent human characteristic, but merely my reaction to historically contingent community norms. It is our responsibility, he writes, to

> Stay on the lookout for marginalized people – people whom we still instinctively think of as "they" rather than "us." We should try to notice our similarities with them ... to *create* a more expansive sense of solidarity than we presently have. The wrong way to think of it is as urging us to *recognize* such a solidarity as something that exists antecedently to our recognition of it.[39]

A critique of the pragmatic account of solidarity and its inclusion of cognitively disabled people argues that positioning solidarity in terms of "us" and "them" allows for an immoral privileging of "us" over "them." This could be used to exclude anyone, including cognitively disabled people, from human solidarity, thus placing them at the same risk of dehumanization as is present when we rely on an objective characteristic of human nature to justify claims to solidarity. As Rorty frankly admits, realism has advantages that he cannot claim. For instance, he cannot claim that the inclusion of cognitively disabled people in the community of those with whom we stand in human solidarity is an objective truth with associated inalienable moral rights and responsibilities.

---

38   Rorty, *Contingency, Irony, Solidarity*, 192.

39   Rorty, *Philosophy and the Mirror of Nature*, 196.

CRAVING SAMENESS, ACCEPTING DIFFERENCE 169

Shotwell's description of aspirational solidarity provides a way forward for thinking about determining salient commonalities and differences amongst the members of various privileged and oppressed groups. Furthermore, she justifies shared access to solidarity based on shared interests, specifically moving towards something better, based on "specific and appropriate expectations for the future."[40] Rather than a shared human nature, Shotwell, like Rorty, argues that we possess the capacity to stretch the boundaries of the community with whom we stand in solidarity. Furthermore, we possess the responsibility to extend these boundaries on the basis of "a desire for something better," and this desire arises "because we have the present experience of partial connection, possibility, and lack."[41] In this case, it is shared experience of unfairness and a related desire for a better world that allow a given individual access to the community of those with whom we stand in solidarity. This conception of solidarity not only allows for the possibility of expanding the community but also requires the community to expand to include all of those who are affected by the universal unfairness present when inhabiting a flawed world that one could imagine to be less flawed.

Understanding Rorty's account of solidarity in terms of a type of kinship relation helps further mitigate the realist critique. The usefulness of kinship as a concept for understanding solidarity is demonstrated, insofar as the notion of kinship is capable of capturing the complex relationship between morality and solidarity that Rorty suggests. For instance, in a family relationship, it is accepted, and even considered moral, to have a special loyalty to, or solidarity with, one's family members. However, if a situation arises when solidarity with one's family unit begins to encroach upon the rights of others, unquestioning solidarity is no longer acceptable. This special loyalty bounded by the threshold of other communities is relevantly similar to the solidarity Rorty describes. I am in solidarity with the moral norms of my community, while at the same time being able to evaluate these norms on the basis of engendering as much intersubjective agreement as possible.

Rorty argues that instead of employing an objective moral standard by which to judge a given action across communities, or allowing each community to determine its own moral standard, independent from all other communities, a type of communitarian ethics should be implemented that is founded upon "the desire to extend the reference of "us" as far as we can."[42] This move

---

40 Alexis Shotwell, "Aspirational Solidarity as Bioethical Norm: The Case of Reproductive Justice," *International Journal of Feminist Approaches to Bioethics* 6, no. 1 (2013): 113.

41 Shotwell, "Aspirational Solidarity as Bioethical Norm," 113.

42 Rorty, *Objectivity, Relativism and Truth: Philosophical Papers*, 169.

maintains the morality of using solidarity as an organizing principle in the face of the critique raised by the realist position.

The language used by people in relationships of solidarity recommends this use of kinship relation to understand our capacity to extend our feelings of solidarity to theory. Fictive kinship terms are used in Black and gay communities as expressions of solidarity with one another. Marylin White analyzes this practice, and its role as an expression of solidarity, in her article "We are Family! Kinship and Solidarity in the Black Community."[43] Moreover, William G. Hawkeswood and Alex W. Costley explore this practice as well in their book *One of the Children: Gay Black Men in Harlem*.[44] Using terms that describe fictive kinship relations to indicate solidarity is also common in labor movements, with many locals and unions referring to members as brother/sister. This more or less reflective use of language amongst solidarity groups points to kinship as a useful concept for investigating solidarity and how it functions as an organizing principle. This same practice holds true in communities of cognitively disabled people. In my own research on autobiographies written by autistic people, or by autistic people by proxy, I found a significant trend of parent, child and sibling fictive kinship terminology being used within that community to indicate and engender solidarity.[45]

The hermeneutic action performed by the imagination facilitates the capacity for feelings of solidarity to expand to include those individuals whom I would not typically include in the community with whom I stand in solidarity. It is through the action of the imagination that the notion of solidarity as kinship is rendered functional. There are those with whom we feel kinship and those with whom we do not. Imaginatively projecting the kinship relation that I have with some onto others with whom I do not have such a relationship opens up the possibility of extending kinship to others.

Furthermore, the hermeneutic action performed by the imagination engenders the usefulness of drawing a relationship between solidarity and kinship. Our imagination engages in creation and critique from within a particular preunderstanding framework. Such a framework that includes preconceived ideas about kinship, and those with whom we are kin, and solidarity, and those with whom we stand in solidarity. It will be difficult to critique or push the boundaries of this framework without a tool to engender understanding when

---

43 Marilyn White, "We are Family! Kinship and Solidarity in the Black Community," in *Expressively Black: The Cultural Basis of Ethnic Identity*, eds. Geneva Gay and Willie L. Baber (New York: Prager, 1987), 21.

44 William Hawkeswood, *One of the Children: Gay Black Men in Harlem* (Los Angeles: University of California Press, 1992), 70.

45 Donna Williams, *Nobody Nowhere: The Extraordinary Autobiography of an Autistic* (New York: Times Books, 1992), 36.

CRAVING SAMENESS, ACCEPTING DIFFERENCE

faced with the types of experiences Rorty believes can trigger the critical function of the imagination. Investigating solidarity in terms of kinship provides the imagination with a conceptual bridge for understanding how others who are meaningfully different from us can be incorporated into the community of those with whom we stand in solidarity.

Realist accounts of solidarity attempt to justify human solidarity on the basis of one or another shared and objective feature of human nature, such as the capacity for reason, the capacity for labor or the possession of a particular type of body. Such positions pose problems when it comes to the inclusion of groups who have historically been oppressed. The exclusion of oppressed groups from solidarity is a flaw that originates from realist epistemic positions. Richard Rorty offers a pragmatic account of solidarity, which makes note of the following three central characteristics: solidarity usually manifests as "us" versus "them," solidarity is most strongly felt towards those who are relevantly similar and weakens in accordance with the proliferation of relevant differences, and finally, solidarity can be extended. The inclusion of people within the community of those with whom we stand in solidarity is facilitated by the hermeneutic function of the imagination. This capacity for extension is the primary reason why Rorty's pragmatic account of solidarity is more inclusive than the realist account. However, Rorty's solidarity is prone to the critique that his "us vs them" conception of the solidarity definition does not offer the same universality of human solidarity that the realist position offers and thus leaves oppressed groups at risk of exclusion. However, by combining Shotwell's relational solidarity with Rorty's pragmatic solidarity, stretching the boundaries of the community of those with whom we stand in solidarity becomes not a possibility but a moral requirement.

References

Buchanan, Allen. *The Heart of Human Rights*. New York: Oxford University Press. 2013.

Gadamer, Hans-Georg. *Philosophical Hermeneutics*. 2nd ed. Translated by David E. Linge. Berkeley: University of California Press, 1976.

Gadamer, Hans-Georg. *Truth and Method*. 2nd ed. Translated by Joel Weinsheimer and Donald G. Marshall. New York: Sheed and Ward, 1989.

Galer, Dustin. "Disability Rights Movement." *Historica Canada*. Accessed May 5, 2017. http://www.thecanadianencyclopedia.ca/en/article/disability-rights-movement/.

Grange, Hamlin. "Lifting Voting Restrictions on the Mentally Ill." Canadian Broadcasting Corporation Digital Archives. Accessed May 5, 2017. http://www.cbc.ca/ar chives/entry/lifting-voting-restrictions-on-mental-patients.

Haack, Susan. "Reply to Commentators." *Philosophy and Phenomenological Research* 56, no. 3 (1996): 641–56.

Harding, Sandra. "Rethinking Standpoint Epistemology: What is 'Strong Objectivity?'" *The Centennial Review* 36, no. 3 (1992): 437–70.

Hart, H.L.A. "Social Solidarity and the Enforcement of Morality." *University of Chicago Law Review* 35, no. 1 (1967): 1–13.

Hawkeswood, William G. *One of the Children: Gay Black Men in Harlem*. University of California Press, Los Angeles. 1992.

Hyde, Martin. "Democracy, Education and the Canadian Voting Age." PhD. diss., University of British Columbia, 2001.

Janack, Marianne. *Feminist Interpretations of Richard Rorty*. State College: Penn State Press. 2010.

Kamin, Leon. *The Science and Politics of I.Q.* Routledge: London. 1976.

Kittay, Eva. "The Personal is Philosophical is Political: A Philosopher and Mother of a Cognitively Disabled Person Sends Notes from the Battlefield." *Metaphilosophy* 40, no. 3–4 (2009): 606–27.

Kuipers, Ronald. *Solidarity and the Stranger: Themes in the Social Philosophy of Richard Rorty*. Toronto: Institute for Christian Studies. 1997.

Laverty, Susann. "Hermeneutic Phenomenology and Phenomenology: A Comparison of Historical and Methodological Considerations." *International Journal of Qualitative Methods* 2, no. 3 (2003): 21–35.

Nussbaum, Martha. *Creating Capabilities: The Human Development Approach*. Cambridge: Belknap Press. 2011.

Phelan, Shane. "Bodies, Passions and Citizenship." In *Feminism, Identity and Difference*, edited by Susan Hekman, 56–79. London: Frank Cass, 1999.

Prince, Michael. "The Electoral Participation of Persons with Special Needs." *Elections Canada: Working Paper Series on Electoral Participation and Outreach*, 2007.http://elections.ca/res/rec/part/paper/special_needs/special_needs_e.pdf.

Rorty, Richard. *Contingency, Irony, Solidarity*. Cambridge: Cambridge University Press. 1989.

Rorty, Richard. "Feminism, Ideology, and Deconstruction: A Pragmatist View." *Hypatia* 8, no. 2 (1993): 96–103.

Rorty, Richard. *Objectivity, Relativism and Truth: Philosophical Papers*. Cambridge: Cambridge University Press. 1990.

Rorty, Richard. *Philosophy and the Mirror of Nature*. New Jersey: Princeton University Press. 1981.

Rorty, Richard. *The Rorty Reader*. Edited by Christopher J. Voparil and Richard J. Bernstein. West Sussex: Blackwell Publishing Limited, 2010.

Rubin, Gayle. "Thinking Sex: Notes for a Radical Theory of the Politics of Sexuality." In *Culture, Society and Sexuality: A Reader*, edited by Peter Aggleton and Richard Parker, 143–78. London and New York: Routledge, 2007.

Shotwell, Alexis. "Aspirational Solidarity as Bioethical Norm: The Case of Reproductive Justice." *International Journal of Feminist Approaches to Bioethics* 6, no. 1 (2013): 103–20.

Stoetzler, Marcel, and Yuval-Davis, Nira. "Standpoint Theory, Situated Knowledge and the Situated Imagination." *Feminist Theory* 3, no. 3 (2002): 239–54.

Tammet, Daniel. *Born on a Blue Day: Inside the Extraordinary Mind of an Autistic Savant: A Memoir.* New York: Free Press. 2007.

Thurstone, L.L. "The Mental Age Concept." *Psychological Review* 33 (1926): 268–78.

Van Leeuwen, Neil. "The Meanings of 'Imagine' Part I: Constructive Imagination." *Philosophy Compass* 8 (2013): 220–30.

Walker, Margaret Urban. *Moral Understandings: A Feminist Study in Ethics.* Oxford: Oxford University Press. 2007.

Wasserman, David, Adrienne Asch, Jeffrey Blustein, and Daniel Putnam. *Stanford Encyclopedia of Philosophy.* "Cognitive Disability and Moral Status." https://plato.stanford.edu/entries/cognitive-disability/.

Williams, Donna. *Nobody Nowhere: The Extraordinary Autobiography of an Autistic.* New York: Times Books. 1992.

White, Marilyn. "We are Family! Kinship and Solidarity in the Black Community." In *Expressively Black: The Cultural Basis of Ethnic Identity,* edited by Geneva Gay and Willie L. Baber, 17–34. New York: Prager, 1987.

CHAPTER 8

The Importance of Imagination/*Phantasia* for the Moral Psychology of Virtue Ethics

*David Collins**

The last few decades have seen a growing awareness of the importance of what Aristotle calls *phantasia*—often translated as "imagination"—for his ethics,[1] despite *phantasia*'s place in the exercise of practical wisdom (*phronêsis*) and ethical virtue not being made explicit in Aristotle's ethical writings.[2] Rather, Aristotle's discussion of *phantasia* is to be found in *De Anima* and other psychological writings, which in turn do not discuss the relevance of *phantasia* for his ethics.[3] In this chapter I argue that the role of *phantasia* in Aristotle's moral psychology—and by extension the moral psychology of contemporary neo-Aristotelian virtue ethics[4]—is even more central than typically has been recognized. My focus in the first half will be on Aristotle's accounts of *phantasia*, ethical virtue, and *phronêsis*, though my aim is not to defend a

---

* Thanks to Marguerite Deslauriers, Hakan Genc, John MacKinnon, Robert Roreitner, Jordan van den Hoonaard, and Tiger Zheng for helpful comments at various stages of this chapter's development.

1 See, for example, R.J. Hankinson, "Perception and Evaluation: Aristotle on the Moral Imagination," *Dialogue* 29 (1990): 41–63; Jana Noel, "*Phronesis* and *Phantasia*: Teaching with Wisdom and Imagination," *Journal of Philosophy of Education* 33 (1999): 277–86; Deborah Achtenberg, *The Cognition of Value in Aristotle's Ethics: Promise of Enrichment, Threat of Destruction* (NY: State University of New York Press, 2002); and Jessica Moss, *Aristotle on the Apparent Good: Perception,* Phantasia, *Thought, and Desire* (Oxford: Oxford University Press, 2012).

2 *Phantasia* is mentioned in a perfunctory reference in the *Eudemian Ethics* (*EE* VII.2 1235b26-29), as well as in *Nicomachean Ethics* Book VII's discussion of *akrasia* and pleasure, though its importance within Aristotle's moral psychology is not discussed.

3 Unless otherwise noted, all references to texts by Aristotle refer to *The Complete Works of Aristotle*, revised Oxford translation, 2 volumes, edited by Jonathan Barnes (Princeton: Princeton University Press, 1984), and will be abbreviated as: *de An.=De Anima/On the Soul; de Sen.=Sense and Sensibilia; de Mem.=On Memory; de Ins.= On Dreams; de Motu=Movement of Animals; EN=Nicomachean Ethics; EE=Eudemian Ethics; Met.=Metaphysics.*

4 While my focus here will be on contemporary virtue ethics modeled on Aristotle's account of the virtues, it should be noted that not all contemporary varieties of virtue ethics are Aristotelian. For instance, Christine Swanton (2015) has examined the possibilities of Humean and Nietzschean virtue ethics, Maria Carrasco (2004) and Ryan Hanley (2009) have explored the virtue ethical aspects of Adam Smith's moral sentimentalism, and Michael Slote (1997) has offered what he calls an agent-based approach not directly based on the ethical thought of any particular figure.

© KONINKLIJKE BRILL NV, LEIDEN, 2020 | DOI:10.1163/9789004436350_010

THE IMPORTANCE OF IMAGINATION/*PHANTASIA* 175

particular reading of Aristotle against alternative readings, but to give a charitable and plausible overview of what his account seems to have been in order to consider the implications for contemporary virtue ethics and for moral psychology broadly. In other words, my concern is not so much with what Aristotle's view really is, in light of the nuances and apparent tensions in his writing, as with what his discussions of *phantasia* and ethical virtue suggest about the connections between imagination and the ethical dimensions of thought and action generally.

I begin by outlining Aristotle's account of *phantasia* along with the basic neo-Aristotelian virtue ethical framework. With these laid out, I examine the central role of *phantasia* in the moral psychology of Aristotle's ethics, and contemporary virtue ethics modeled after Aristotle, focusing especially on its importance for choice, desire, and *phronêsis*. I conclude by looking at some implications of this for contemporary virtue ethics, and for moral psychology in general.

1   Aristotle's Account of *Phantasia*

According to *De Anima*, the treatises on dreams and memory in the *Parva Naturalia*, and *De Motu Animalium*, *phantasia* is a capacity or mode of cognizing[5] possessed by all creatures that have perception and desire.[6] It is connected to both perception and thought, sharing certain features of each and necessarily accompanying both,[7] as well as being necessarily involved in phenomena ranging from purposive action to remembering and dreaming. But, we might still ask, what exactly is this capacity, and what is its relation to the other capacities or parts of the soul with which it is connected?

---

5   For Aristotle, *phantasia* would seem to be a capacity (*dunamis*) and not a distinct part (*meros*) of the soul. On this, see *de An.* III.9 432b1-3; cf. Michael Wedin, *Mind and Imagination in Aristotle* (New Haven: Yale University Press, 1988), 23. *De Anima* is not clear on this matter, but certain remarks in the *Parva Naturalia* (esp. *de Ins.* 1 459a15-23) characterize *phantasia* as belonging to the same part of the soul as perception, with the imaginative part and the perceptive part being one in number but distinct in their being, or essential nature—which I take to mean something along the lines of imagin*ing* and perceiv*ing* being different types of activities of the soul, but being activities of the same general part of the soul, viz. the part in virtue of which a being receives appearances of things. This understanding presupposes that Aristotle takes the soul to have parts and not merely capacities; while this is not uncontroversial, see Klaus Corcilius and Pavel Gregoric, "Separability vs. Difference: Parts and Capacities of the Soul in Aristotle," in *Oxford Studies in Ancient Philosophy XXXIX*, ed. Brad Inwood (Oxford: Oxford University Press, 2010): 81–119, for a defense of this view.

6   *de An.* II.2 413b22-25, III.10 433b28-29; cf. Victor Caston, "Why Aristotle Needs Imagination," *Phronesis* 51 (1996): 44.

7   *de Ins.* 1 459a16-18; *de An.* III.3 427b16-17, III.7 431a14-18.

Given that Aristotle sees it playing an important role in a wide range of phenomena, it is odd that he does not offer more of an explanation of *phantasia* itself. The closest he comes is in *De Anima* III.3, supplemented by remarks in III.9 and III.11. Here, he appears to define *phantasia* as "that in virtue of which an image [*phantasma*] arises for us," saying also that it is "a movement resulting from an actual exercise of a power of sense," and adding that "because imaginations [that is, images (*phantasmata*)] remain in the organs of sense and resemble sensations, animals in their actions are largely guided by them."[8] In a sentence that is often taken to be the core of his account of *phantasia*, he writes:

> since when one thing has been set in motion another thing may be moved by it, and [*phantasia*] is held to be a movement and to be impossible without sensation, that is, to occur in beings that are percipient and to have for its content what can be perceived, and since movement may be produced by actual sensation and that movement [that is, *phantasia*] is necessarily similar in character to the sensation itself, [it] cannot exist apart from sensation or in creatures that do not perceive, and its possessor does and undergoes many things in virtue of it, and it is true or false.[9]

A number of *phantasia*'s essential features can be seen here. For one, it requires perception, both insofar as no creature has the capacity of *phantasia* without also having the capacity for perception and insofar as all images must initially arise from a particular perception (*aisthêma*).[10] For another, an image cognized through *phantasia* is similar to the perception from which it arose, where this is both a matter of the image resembling this perception and a matter of it having similar effects—for example, causing an emotion (*pathê*) or a desire (*orexis*) to be felt toward the object of the *phantasma*, just as the perceptual experience could cause its percipient to have an emotion or a desire for its object. Thirdly, unlike perception, which for Aristotle always involves veridical cognition of its objects, at least when it is of what Aristotle calls proper

---

8   *de An.* III.3 428a1-2, III.3 429a2-6. I say "appears to define" because the phrase quoted occurs as the antecedent to a conditional, although from what he goes on to say subsequently, Aristotle does seem to take imagination to be essentially what this phrase describes.

9   *de An.* III.3 428b10-16.

10   Cf. *de An.* III.3 427b15-16.

THE IMPORTANCE OF IMAGINATION/*PHANTASIA* 177

sensibles or perceptibles,[11] *phantasia* is explicitly described as being possibly either true or false.

This last point is important since, as Victor Caston notes, Aristotle introduces *phantasia* at least partly to account for errors that *seem* perceptual, like optical illusions, hallucinations, or dreams.[12] For Aristotle to maintain that perception is veridical he must offer an account of what occurs when we seem to perceive something to be the case that is not—for example, when we see lines converging that we know are parallel. The emphasis on *phantasia's* role in seemingly perceptual errors leads Malcolm Schofield to take *phantasia* to be a capacity for "non-paradigmatic sensory experiences" of quasi-perceptual phenomena.[13] This, however, restricts the scope of *phantasia* so that it would no longer account for a number of things Aristotle employs *phantasia* to explain, such as locomotion in animals[14] and the deliberation of practical reason.[15] Deborah Modrak's characterization of *phantasia* as a capacity for "awareness of a sensory content that represents a particular object ... *under conditions which are not conducive to veridical perception*"[16] is preferable, as it retains the ties between *phantasia* and quasi-perceptual errors while allowing it to provide veridical awareness of its objects—for example, remembering past events accurately—despite characteristically being exercised in conditions when veridical perception is impossible, such as when an object is not present—for example, a past object or event, or an anticipated future experience—or when perception is interfered with, such as attempts to see through fog or hear underwater.

Though wider in scope, Modrak's characterization still does not fully account for Aristotle's claims that *phantasia* is necessarily involved in locomotion, in thinking, and in deliberation, since these often occur in conditions conducive to veridical perception. Jessica Moss has recently presented what she calls Aristotle's basic conception of *phantasia* as "essentially the capacity to have an experience very like the perception of some x but which is not directly caused by perceptual contact with any actual x (where x is a proper, common, or incidental perceptible [...])" due to being "a capacity for making

---

11   *de An.* III.3 428b18-19.
12   See Caston, "Why Aristotle Needs Imagination."
13   Malcolm Schofield, "Aristotle on the Imagination," in *Essays on Aristotle's De Anima*, ed. Martha Nussbaum and Amelia O. Rorty (Oxford: Oxford University Press, 1992): 252.
14   *de An.* III.10 433a10-31; cf. *de Motu* 701b13-35, 702a16-19.
15   *de An.* III.7 431a14-17, III.11 434a7-10.
16   Deborah Modrak, "Aristotle on *Phantasia*," in *The Routledge Handbook of Philosophy of Imagination*, ed. Amy Kind (New York: Routledge, 2016): 25, my emphasis.

present to the mind something that one has perceived before."[17] She argues that this conception can account for everything Aristotle calls on *phantasia* to explain without adding anything to what Aristotle writes. Moss bases this conception on three claims of Aristotle's, which are: (1) *phantasia* necessarily arises from, and so depends on, sensory perception; (2) it operates independently of its objects such that one can have a *phantasma* of something not present; and (3) *phantasmata* are similar to the perceptions (*aisthêmata*) from which they arise, and are able to evoke the same psychological effects.[18] Moss contends that these three claims suffice to account for the relations Aristotle takes to obtain between *phantasia* and the awareness of quasi-perceptual phenomena, locomotion, and practical and theoretical reasoning.

Because perception grounds *phantasia*, a brief explanation of Aristotle's account of perception is needed to clarify the connection between it and *phantasia*. For Aristotle, perception begins with a perceptible object (*aisthêton*) coming into mediated contact with one of the body's several sensory organs. This contact causes a movement (*aisthêma*) in the percipient's perceptual system, where the central sensory organ—for Aristotle, the heart—registers this *aisthêma* and produces a perceptual experience (*aisthêsis*) of the *aisthêton*. Additionally, sense-perception causes another movement, a *phantasma*, to arise concurrently with this activity.[19] If and when the *phantasma* reaches the heart, sometimes after a delay, it results in a quasi-perceptual experience (*phantasia*) resembling the related *aisthêma*.[20] The intentional object of this imagining is the object that caused the *aisthêma* that led to the *phantasma*, even when the *phantasma* no longer resembles the object due to physiological interference or to combination with other *phantasmata*.[21] The presence of both *aisthêma* and *phantasma* is how Aristotle explains how sensory experiences can be retained and later recalled when the causal chain of *aisthêton*—*aisthêma*—*aisthêsis* alone would not account for this. Because it allows for the re-presentation, or the retention and re-enactment, of sensory images it explains both how we can remember formerly perceived

---

17   Moss, *Aristotle on the Apparent Good*, 53.

18   Moss, *Aristotle on the Apparent Good*, 52.

19   As Dorothea Frede notes "[t]here would be an unbridgeable causal gap if the *phantasma* or image were not produced while the sense-perception was still in operation" (Frede, "The Cognitive Role of *Phantasia* in Aristotle," in *Essays on Aristotle's De Anima*, eds. Martha Nussbaum and Amelia O. Rorty (Oxford: Oxford University Press, 1992): 284).

20   On these points, see Caston, "Why Aristotle Needs Imagination," 47–48; Stephen Everson, *Aristotle on Perception* (Oxford: Oxford University Press, 1997), Ch. 4, esp. 168–69 and 175–78; and Moss, *Aristotle on the Apparent Good*, 51–52.

21   *de Ins.* 3 461a12-25; *de An.* III.6 430b2-3; cf. Caston, "Why Aristotle Needs Imagination," 49.

THE IMPORTANCE OF IMAGINATION/*PHANTASIA* 179

objects and how we can reason about the objects we perceive, by making these images available to modes of cognition other than perception. Thus, *phantasia* serves a necessary role in Aristotle's psychology, bridging what would otherwise be a gap between perception and reason.

That Aristotle takes *phantasia* to connect perception with reason in this way can be seen from several remarks about the necessity of *phantasia* for practical reasoning about particulars, and its necessity for abstract reasoning about general concepts. For Aristotle, perception itself is a mode of cognizing objects, and to feel pleasure or pain when perceiving something is to adopt an attitude towards it analogous to a judgment of it being good or bad, leading to pursuit or avoidance.[22] Moreover, he writes: "to the thinking soul images [*phantasmata*] serve as if they were contents of perception (and when it asserts or denies them to be good or bad avoids or pursues them). That is why *the soul never thinks without an image*."[23] He reasserts this in the next chapter, writing: "when the mind is actively aware of anything it is necessarily aware of it along with an image [*phantasma*]; for images are like sensuous contents [*aisthêmata*] except in that they contain no matter."[24]

The point is that abstract thought—thought about a universal object or "intelligible"—is always abstracted from mental images that stand for or exemplify features of that intelligible. For instance, thinking about the general concept "humanity" requires us to have one or more images of humans retained from perception and available for recall; we must, in other words, be able to picture some human. While each mental image of a human will be a particular one—or an "indeterminate singular"—originating from one or more perceptions of particular humans, certain of its features—for example, eye, hair, and skin colour—will be ignored in favour of others taken to exemplify humanity in general.[25] This points to *phantasia*'s role in forming the concepts with which reason operates and suggests that even if the form of our reasoning is good, its accuracy or soundness will only be as good as its contents—the concepts employed—with these only being as good as our *phantasmata* are veridical, with faulty reasoning not only being due to errors in logic but also to nonveridical *phantasmata* or to irrelevancies in our abstractions from veridical ones.[26]

---

22   Moss, *Aristotle on the Apparent Good*, 29–30; cf. *de An.* III.7 431a8-13.

23   *de An.* III.7 431a14-17, my emphasis; cf. *de Mem.* 1 449b31-450a1.

24   *de An.* III.8 432a7-9.

25   *de Mem.* 1 450a1-6.

26   Note that my use of the term "abstraction" here does not follow Aristotle's own, since he speaks of "abstraction" only with respect to mathematical entities. I thank Robert Roreitner for noting the need to clarify this.

In addition to its role in theoretical reasoning, *phantasia* also plays a significant role in practical reasoning, being involved in the practical syllogism in two respects. First, the major premise of such a syllogism will deal with a universal or general kind, and, on the interpretation outlined above, *phantasia* is necessary for the formation and cognition of abstract or universal concepts. For instance, a universal judgment that light meats are wholesome[27] requires experience of particular light meats and their effects, along with the re-presentation of these experiences via *phantasmata* standing for light meats in general and exemplifying their wholesomeness. Also, when the minor premise relates to a prospective action, *phantasia* will be necessary to "picture" the action so as to reason about it, since it will not have taken place while deliberation is underway and so cannot be perceived. This is a matter of what Aristotle calls deliberative (*bouleutikê*) *phantasia*, as distinct from, though related to, sensory (*aisthêtikê*) *phantasia*, or the general capacity for re-presenting images.[28]

While a basic form of sensory *phantasia* is shared by all animals possessing at least one sense, for example, touch, and capacities of appetite and movement,[29] only those with reason will be capable of deliberative *phantasia*.[30] Given that sensory and deliberative *phantasia* are not distinct capacities, but the same capacity exercised in different ways, in different contexts, and by beings with different parts to their souls, Aristotle's view seems to be that when sensory *phantasia* is possessed by a being that also possesses reason, the capabilities of *phantasia* are increased or the deliberative capacity of *phantasia* is activated such that the being not only can re-experience retained sensations but can recall and associate them at will.[31] The *phantasmata* can then be used in practical reasoning by imagining possible actions available in a given situation along with their potential outcomes.

R.J. Hankinson argues that the deliberative aspect of *phantasia* is due to a combination of sensory *phantasia*'s capacity for re-presenting sensory images with the rational faculties' capacities for making comparisons among different kinds of objects, since merely envisaging a possible future outcome would not

---

27 Cf. *EN* VI.7 1141b18-20.

28 *de An.* III.11 434a6-9.

29 *de An.* II.2 413b23-25, III.10 433b28-31.

30 *de An.* III.11 434a7-8.

31 *de An.* III.3 427b18-21. Cf. Aristotle's distinction between memory [*mnêmê*] and recollection [*anamnêsis*] in *de Mem.* 2 451a21-452b7, where memories typically occur automatically as a result of associations caused by outer stimuli, while recollection is a conscious, directed process initiated by the one remembering, and seems itself to require practical reason.

THE IMPORTANCE OF IMAGINATION/*PHANTASIA* 181

suffice for practical reasoning without the ability to compare multiple outcomes and make evaluative judgments among them.[32] Comparative judgments between different outcomes of various actions, and comparisons of the likelihood of certain actions leading to a particular outcome, are thus necessary for deliberation, and since such outcomes are future possibilities not yet available to perception, either *phantasia* or thought must be what makes them available for reason to compare. As Aristotle writes, "sometimes by means of the images or thoughts which are within the soul, *just as if it were seeing*, it calculates and deliberates what is to come by reference to what is present."[33] Since Aristotle takes all thinking to involve *phantasmata*, *phantasia* will still be part of such a judgment arrived at via thought, so *phantasia* is necessary for deliberation, not only for aiming at a goal or end, but for doing so from choice, that is, prohairetically.[34]

When introducing deliberative *phantasia*, Aristotle notes that deliberation not only requires images to be re-presented when their objects are not present, but that it also implies the ability "to make a unity out of several images."[35] In one respect, a capacity for combining images is necessary for *phantasia* to make multiple objects available for comparison, since the objects to be compared would need to be cognized together, with all being held in mind at the same time. In another respect, this might also refer to *phantasia*'s role in abstracting a universal or general concept—for example, humanity—from

---

32　R.J. Hankinson, "Perception and Evaluation: Aristotle on the Moral Imagination," *Dialogue* 29 (1990): 49–52.

33　*de An.* III.7 431b6-8, my emphasis.

34　Aristotle allows that animals without reason are capable of action for the sake of an end, where this requires some combination of cognition (perception, thought, or *phantasia*) and desire (*orexis*) (*de An.* III.9 432b7-433a9); lacking reason, the mode of cognition that combines with the animal's desire must be either *phantasia* or perception (*de An.* III.10 433a10-11; *de Motu* 6 700b15-701a3). Jessica Moss argues that perception alone can motivate action, since pleasure and pain motivate pursuit and avoidance, and perceptions themselves can be pleasant or painful (Moss, *Aristotle on the Apparent Good*, 22–30, 57). However, even if perceptions can themselves be pleasant or painful in addition to being *of* objects that one finds pleasant or painful, it is not clear how perception being pleasant can motivate *action* in pursuit of what is perceived, rather than motivating the perceiver to sustain the perception for as long as it remained pleasurable. Action beyond continuing the perception would seem to require an association between the present perception and a past sensation, for example, how the object tasted, or the feeling of hunger satisfied, with the desire for the remembered sensation motivating the action in pursuit of it, and with this necessarily involving sensory *phantasia* (Moss, *Aristotle on the Apparent Good*, 54–56; see esp. 56n23). On non-human animals needing sensory *phantasia* and memory in addition to perception, see *Met.* I.1 980b26.

35　*de An.* III.11 434a9.

multiple *phantasmata*—for example, many indeterminate singular images of people—since the universal concept that results will be one, and will also have an accompanying mental image or *phantasma*.[36] Moreover, the ability of *phantasia* to combine multiple images into one seems necessary for apprehending a complex or *Gestalt* object such as a situation, a context, or a state of affairs, whereas perception would seem to be limited to apprehending only the "parts" that would make up such a *Gestalt*.

This notion of *phantasia* supplying what might be called "situational awareness"—that is, an awareness of a state of affairs or series of events as a whole in which each constituent event is a part—has been explored by Dorothea Frede and Hendrik Lorenz. Lorenz focuses on *phantasia*'s role in envisaging prospective situations or courses of action,[37] with reason and deliberation being necessary for awareness of these prospects *as* prospects and so for choice between them, but Frede takes the synthesis of sensory images to be one of *phantasia*'s primary roles,[38] where this is needed for our perceptual awareness to extend from one moment to another and so to have "coherence and continuity."[39] On Frede's reading, *phantasia* is crucial for envisaging any situation at all, even our present one. "Because of [Aristotle's] emphasis on the singleness of each act of perception and on the need for the presence of its object," she writes, "it is doubtful that ... we can have something like a "panoramic" view of a whole situation, for he does not seem to include anything like a "field of vision" in his explanations" of perception. As she goes on to explain, "when I let my eyes glide over the different books on my bookshelves there is always just the piecemeal vision of this or that coloured object; the *overall impression* of all the different books (including those behind my back) would then be already a *phantasia*, a synthesis of what I perceive right now and what I have perceived a second ago and so on."[40]

This ability of *phantasia* to synthesize multiple *phantasmata* into a single object of cognition that did not originate in any one perceptual experience, when combined with *phantasia*'s freedom from veridicality, suggests that in addition to its role in deliberation *phantasia* can be employed creatively,

---

36   *de An.* III.7 431a17.

37   See Hendrik Lorenz, *The Brute Within: Appetitive Desire in Plato and Aristotle* (Oxford: Clarendon Press, 2006): 114, 179–81, 195–99.

38   Frede, "The Cognitive Role of *Phantasia* in Aristotle," 282.

39   Frede, "The Cognitive Role of *Phantasia* in Aristotle," 286.

40   Frede, "The Cognitive Role of *Phantasia* in Aristotle," 283, original emphasis.

allowing us to imagine, at will, things as being otherwise than they are—where the ability to envisage possible future situations would seem to entail this insofar as envisaging a non-actual situation involves picturing a state of affairs that is otherwise than our current one. This also allows us to combine, at will, different *phantasmata* recollected from previous experiences in order to create mental images of non-existent or not yet existing objects, for example, an author imagining a fantastical beast by combining parts of previous perceptions of animals, or an engineer imagining a bridge prior to its construction by combining mental images of beams, wires, etc. in a certain formation. Importantly, the fact that *phantasia* can be veridical, though it need not be, implies the potential to envisage future situations or outcomes accurately; an architect, for instance, needs to be able to envisage correctly how the exterior of the house she is designing will look from certain angles, what the views from inside different rooms will be, etc., in order to deliberate about how it should be designed and constructed.

In summary, for Aristotle *phantasia* is a cognitive capacity for re-presenting sensible images or *phantasmata* that are caused by sense-perceptions of objects and are similar to them in terms of both the qualitative experience of imagining them and the effects they can have on the person imagining, for example, evoking certain emotions or desires. Unlike perceptions, *phantasmata* can be experienced in the absence of their objects and need not be veridical, though they can be. Unlike objects of rational thought, which are general concepts or intelligibles, *phantasmata* are always particulars and have a significant sensible (or quasi-perceptual) aspect. Because of its similarities to perception and reason, and its ability to retain perceptual images for reason to apprehend and think about without the object being present, *phantasia* serves as a bridge linking perception and reason and thereby allows thinking to occur. In addition to making theoretical or abstract reason possible by providing the material for general concepts, and making practical reason possible by allowing us to conceive of future outcomes at which to aim in action, as well as possible actions that would realize these outcomes, *phantasia* enables us to apprehend situations or states of affairs by synthesizing perceptions of individual objects into unified wholes, letting us grasp certain events as connected parts of a coherent series of events, along with the "for the sake of" relations between possible actions and their prospective outcomes.

With Aristotle's account of what *phantasia* is, and what it does, laid out, I will now outline the basic framework of his ethics and of neo-Aristotelian varieties of contemporary virtue ethics, before going on to show the central role that *phantasia* plays in his moral psychology.

2 The Aristotelian (and Neo-Aristotelian) Virtue Ethical Framework

The central questions in Aristotle's ethics concern what it is for one to be good *qua* human, and what the good *for* a human is: what the best sort of life is to lead.[41] Aristotle notes that all our actions aim at a desired end we take to be good, and distinguishes between two sorts of "good": provisional goods that are good *for something* as means to further ends also held to be good, and the highest good, at which all provisional ends ultimately aim and which is not a means to any other end.[42] His candidate for the highest good is happiness (*eudaimonia*), understood as flourishing or "living well [*eu zen*] and doing well [*eu prattein*]."[43] Since "for the sake of living well" will always serve as a final reason for desiring any provisional good, Aristotle argues that *eudaimonia* is what we ultimately aim at in our actions.[44]

What it is for humans to live and do well is understood in terms of our characteristic activity (*ergon*).[45] For Aristotle, we are rational social animals, where the rational element of our souls distinguishes us from other animals. He defines the human *ergon* as reasoning and doing whatever else we typically do—acting, feeling, desiring—"in accordance with [a] rational principle."[46] For a human to do well, that is, to live well or flourish, is for her to reason well and act in accordance with her reasoning. Aristotle comes to define human flourishing as "activity of soul in conformity with excellence [that is, virtue],"[47] involving excellence in reasoning and deliberating as well as in desiring, feeling, and acting, with the excellence or virtue (*aretê*) of these non-rational activities being determined by what excellent reasoning deems most appropriate for a rational, embodied, social being.

Since flourishing involves possessing and exercising the virtues,[48] the main focus in Aristotle's ethical works is on the virtues, being dispositions to think,

---

41 As Kathleen Wilkes shows, these two apparently similar questions are in fact distinct, since whatever is involved in being a good X will not necessarily be the same as what is good *for* an X. See Kathleen Wilkes, "The Good Man and the Good For Man," in *Essays on Aristotle's Ethics*, ed. Amelie O. Rorty (Berkeley: University of California Press, 1980): 343–46.

42 *EN* I.1 1094a1-2, II.2 1094a18-22.

43 *EN* I.4 1095a18-20; cf. Wilkes, "The Good Man and the Good For Man," 343.

44 *EN* I.7 1097a35-b6.

45 Translating *ergon* as "function" can be misleading when applied to humans; as Wilkes notes, when a thing is "the kind of thing that cannot readily be said to have a function," its *ergon* "is its characteristic activity" (Wilkes, "The Good Man and the Good For Man," 343).

46 *EN* I.7 1097b11-1098a4.

47 *EN* I.7 1098a16-17, I.13 1102a5.

48 Note that virtues are not, on this account, "means" to be employed in order to flourish or attain happiness; rather, their exercise *constitute* such a life, where "means and ends coalesce" (Wilkes, "The Good Man and the Good For Man," 350).

THE IMPORTANCE OF IMAGINATION/*PHANTASIA*   185

feel and act *well*. Excellences of the rational and desiderative parts of the human soul[49] count as virtues since such activities are either rational or can be
done in accordance with reason. The excellences of our rational faculties—
deducing, deliberating, understanding, etc.—are counted as intellectual virtues, with ethical virtues or virtues of character being excellences of the desiring faculty,[50] including feeling and acting along with desiring insofar as action
is caused by desire.[51] Being a good human, then, is a matter of having a virtuous
character—or being disposed to feel and act well, and to be correct in one's
practical reasoning. And a virtuous action for Aristotle is not just one that
achieves a good end, but one that is done from choice (*prohairesis*) and from a
rational desire (*boulêsis*) for the good, and which either results from and expresses a stable, consistent disposition acquired through habituation,[52] or is
done in the manner of one with such a disposition.

The importance of not only *what* one does or feels, but *the way in which* one
does or feels it, comes through in Aristotle's classification of ethical virtues as
habits (*hexis*) or characteristic ways of being disposed to act and feel.[53] While
hexis is sometimes translated as "state,"[54] this should be read as a state of a
person's character—a state that one is in—and not a mental state one "has,"
such as an occurrent emotion or belief, since virtue is not a matter of having
particular emotions or beliefs, but of being disposed to feel or believe *appropriately*.[55] The notion of appropriateness, of acting "at the right times, with reference to the right objects, towards the right people, with the right aim, and in
the right way,"[56] is part of Aristotle's doctrine of the mean. As Leslie Brown
notes, ethical virtues[57] are not means because they lie at a midpoint between
two vices, but because they dispose one to act and feel in ways that are

---

49   I follow Deslauriers in taking Aristotle to hold the human soul to have four "parts": the
      nutritive, perceptive, desiderative, and rational, rather than only three as Corcilius and
      Gregoric argue; see Marguerite Deslauriers, "How to Distinguish Aristotle's Virtues," *Phro-
      nesis* 47 (2002): 101–26. Furthermore, I take each part to have potentially multiple capaci-
      ties; for example, the rational part as having capacities of practical reasoning and theo-
      retical reasoning, and the perceptive part, as argued above (see n.5), as having capacities
      for perceiving and for imagining.
50   *EN* I.3 1103a4-10.
51   *de An.* III.10 433a21, 433b10-11.
52   *EN* II.4 1105a27-35.
53   *EN* II.5 1105b25-28.
54   See, for instance, Terence Irwin's translation of Aristotle's *Nicomachean Ethics* (Indianap-
      olis: Hackett, 1999).
55   *EN* II.5 1105b29-1106a7.
56   *EN* II.6 1106b21-23.
57   N.B. the doctrine of the mean is taken only to apply to the ethical virtues and not to intel-
      lectual virtues (*EN* II.6 1106b16-18), and so intellectual virtues will have only one corre-
      sponding vice, that is, one of deficiency, rather than two.

themselves means, being neither excessive nor deficient but appropriate relative to what a given situation calls for.[58]

Although providing an account of right action was not Aristotle's main concern, many contemporary virtue ethicists aim to do so, given the importance this notion has in modern ethics. Broadly speaking, virtue ethicists understand right action as derivative of the notions of ethical virtue and the virtuous person. Rosalind Hursthouse defines right action as "what a virtuous agent would characteristically ... do in the circumstances," with a virtuous agent being one who possesses those "character trait[s that] a human being needs for *eudaimonia*, to flourish or live well."[59] This allows for people other than fully virtuous agents to perform right actions, since these are not actions that can be done only by virtuous agents, but actions of the sort that a fully virtuous agent would do; as Aristotle writes, just or temperate actions must be the sort of actions which a just or temperate person would do, but performing such acts is not sufficient for one *to be* just or temperate.[60]

While this is in keeping with Aristotle's eudaimonism, it leaves out his insistence that virtues must be acquired through experience and habituation rather than being innate or "natural" dispositions, and that right actions be prohairetic or chosen based on a rational desire. In this respect, Linda Zagzebski accounts for more of the Aristotelian understanding in her definition of a virtue as "a deep and enduring acquired excellence of a person, involving a characteristic motivation to produce a certain desired end and reliable success in bringing about that end."[61] However, neither definition makes explicit that the exercise of a virtue is *constituent of* flourishing, not a separate means to it, and neither includes any notion of a mean or a specification that the end aimed at must itself be good, that is, appropriate relative to the agent, to her situation, and to human flourishing in general. Nevertheless, Hursthouse's and Zagzebski's definitions foreground certain aspects of virtue that are underemphasized in Aristotle's formal definition of a virtue as "a state concerned with choice, lying in a mean relative to us, this being determined by reason and in the way in which the man of practical wisdom would determine it,"[62] when this is read apart from the context of his ethical thought. Thus, a synthesis might better encapsulate the Aristotelian notion of virtue, perhaps reading as follows: *an*

---

58   Leslie Brown, "Why is Aristotle's Virtue of Character a Mean?," in *The Cambridge Companion to Aristotle's Nicomachean Ethics*, ed. Ronald Polansky (Cambridge: Cambridge University Press, 2014): 64–66.

59   Rosalind Hursthouse, *On Virtue Ethics* (Oxford: Oxford University Press, 1999): 28–29.

60   *EN* II.4 1105b5-8.

61   Linda Zagzebski, *Virtues of the Mind* (Cambridge: Cambridge University Press, 1996): 137.

62   *EN* II.6 1106b36-1107a2.

ethical virtue is a deep, enduring trait of a person's character, involving choice and acquired through habituation, consisting in a disposition to aim at and reliably succeed in hitting the mean relative to that person with regard to a certain type of action or emotion, where hitting the mean involves excellence and is partly constitutive of human flourishing, and where the mean is what is appropriate for a rational, social being to do or feel in a given situation, as determined by practical wisdom.

Since what is appropriate will differ from one situation to another based on differences in the factors involved, including the agent and the context in which the situation occurs, there will be no substantive universal rules or context-independent principles telling one how to act or feel that will apply in all cases; rather, any possible rules of conduct will admit of exceptions, holding only for the most part.[63] The non-codifiability of ethics makes an agent's exercise of good judgment ineliminable in determining what is to be done. This is why ethical virtue requires *phronêsis*, which allows one to "deliberate well about what is good and expedient," to see "what sorts of thing conduce to the good life in general,"[64] and so to aim at and hit "the best for man of things attainable by action."[65]

Phronêsis or practical wisdom is not only effective deliberation, as seen from Aristotle's distinction between it and mere "cleverness," or the ability to determine the means to realize a given end. Importantly, practical wisdom is successful deliberation towards a specifically good (*agathon*) or noble (*kalon*) end, whereas cleverness can be employed to bring about a base or vicious end.[66] Hence, practical wisdom might be thought of as cleverness under the guidance of ethical virtue, where ethical virtue disposes one to aim at good or noble ends.[67] While actions are often motivated by desires for what appears pleasant (*epithumia*), because a virtuous person's desires line up with her wish or rational desire (*boulêsis*) for the good, her apprehension via practical wisdom of what is appropriate will be guided by this wish, with what she takes to be pleasant being good, and hence truly pleasant as opposed to merely apparently so. Thus, her desires, as ethically virtuous, will characteristically aim at the right target which, due to her excellence in practical deliberation, she will

---

63   *EN* I.2 1094b18-22, II.2 1104a3-9.

64   *EN* VI.5 1140a26-32. On the claim that practical wisdom allows one to "see" what is appropriate, see *EN* VI.9 1142a26-31, where Aristotle clarifies that this is not sensory perception but rather the sort by which one "grasps" a mathematical truth.

65   *EN* VI.7 1141b13.

66   *EN* VI.12 1144a24-37.

67   *EN* VI.5 1140a26-27.

characteristically succeed in hitting. As such, ethical virtue is necessary for *phronêsis*, just as *phronêsis* is necessary for ethical virtue.[68]

Now that both Aristotle's account of *phantasia* and the key elements of his ethical thought—and by extension those of neo-Aristotelian virtue ethics—have been outlined, the role that *phantasia* plays in the moral psychology inherent in Aristotle's ethics, and neo-Aristotelian virtue ethics, can be set out. In particular, the following sections will focus on the necessary role of *phantasia* in three of the most central aspects of virtue ethical moral psychology: desire, choice, and practical wisdom.

3 *Phantasia*, Desire, and Choice

The primary normative focus in virtue ethics is on an agent's character and only secondarily on actions and their consequences,[69] where these are never considered apart from their relation to character, with character involving the relation between an agent's desires and feelings on the one hand and her rational faculties on the other. As J.M. Cooper writes, "having a character at all ... consists in a settled, trained disposition of a person's capacity and tendency to experience some range of non-rational desires, or other non-rational feelings, and, partly in consequence of those desires or feelings, to act in certain characteristic ways."[70] Actions fall within the sphere of ethics insofar as they express their agent's character, where this is the case when actions are not merely voluntary, but are purposeful and deliberate, that is, when they result from decision or choice (*prohairesis*). This is because a choice to perform a certain action is made on the basis of a desire for the end aimed at in the action, and will involve practical reasoning to determine either that the action is a means to the end, or that performing the action will be partly constitutive of the end, especially when the end is *eudaimonia*. Thus, an action done as the result of a choice will express the state of the desiderative part of the agent's soul, as well as the state of her rational capacity for deliberation.

Phantasia is necessarily involved in deliberate choice, at least insofar as one can choose to perform an action only if one can imagine doing otherwise, even

---

68 Cf. *EN* VI.13 1144b31-33.

69 Since virtue ethics is often misconstrued as being unconcerned with actions or their outcomes, I should stress that these *are* morally relevant for deliberation and evaluation in virtue ethics, but are always relevant only along with a number of other factors over which outcomes do not take automatic precedence.

70 J.M. Cooper, "Some Remarks on Aristotle's Moral Psychology," *The Southern Journal of Philosophy* XXVII, Supplement (1988): 26.

THE IMPORTANCE OF IMAGINATION/*PHANTASIA*   189

when this includes imagining not acting. Even aside from *phantasia*'s involvement in choosing among possible actions, Aristotle holds *phantasia* to be a precondition for any voluntary action even if the agent, in the moment, did not conceive of other possibilities. In his discussion of purposive action or locomotion, Aristotle takes *phantasia* to be operative in envisaging the end at which an action aims when this is not yet present to perception, and specifies that a *phantasma* of the end is what triggers the desire that in turn causes the physical action. As he writes in *de Motu Animalium*, the parts of the agent's body "are suitably prepared by the affections, these again by desire, and desire by [*phantasia*, which] in its turn depends either upon thinking or upon sense-perception."[71] That is, in order for a being's body to move purposively towards an object of choice, its desires must cause a heating or chilling in its body via affections—that is, feelings of pleasure or pain—which lead muscles to expand or contract which moves the body to act, with the desire arising due to a *phantasma* that itself either arises from a contemporaneous perception, is recalled in memory, or results from creative or deliberative *phantasia*.

The *De Motu* passage reinforces the claim in *De Anima* that there is no desire without *phantasia*.[72] In adding that *phantasia* is either deliberative or sensory, and in specifying that *phantasia* comes about through either thought or perception, Aristotle can be read here as saying that even when one perceives the object at which an action aims—for example, a thirsty person seeing water—a *phantasma* will be involved in the process by which a desire for this object is formed.[73] Moreover, if having a *phantasma* of an object is necessary for desiring it, and if *phantasia*'s objects are particulars, then a desire tied to a specific *phantasma* will be shaped by the particular way the *phantasma* characterizes the object—that is, by how one imagines the object to be. Just as the details that we recollect of a past event will influence how we feel about the event, imagining the taste of water as being refreshing will lead to a different desire than would imagining it as being tasteless.

Aristotle writes that choice is found only in beings with reason,[74] which suggests that the type of desire that is operative in a chosen or prohairetic action is rational desire (*boulêsis*) rather than appetitive desire (*epithumia*) or passionate desire (*thumos*), which are shared by animals lacking in reason. The

---

71 *de Motu* 702a17-19.

72 *de An.* III.10 433b29.

73 It is plausible to take thirst itself to be a desire for liquid rather than a merely physiological state in which the body needs hydration, with *phantasia* being involved in preparing the desire via a thirsty person imagining the taste or the feeling of coolness or refreshment that would accompany drinking.

74 *EN* III.2 1111b13.

three types of desire are differentiated for Aristotle in terms of their objects,[75] with *boulêsis* being desire for the good, *epithumia* desire for the (physically or sensually) pleasant, and *thumos* desire for the honourable or proper—or, more specifically, for what *seems* to be good, pleasant or honourable, respectively. *Boulêsis* is frequently translated into English as "wish," with this referring to a rational desire for the end for the sake of which particular actions or objects are chosen.[76] However, the deliberate (*bouleutou*) desire by which Aristotle comes to define choice[77] would also seem, *qua* deliberate, to be a rational desire for the particular actions or objects that one sees as conducive to, or partly constitutive of, the end that one wishes, and which are seen as choiceworthy.[78] If this is right, then an action done from choice, that is, prohairetically, will be motivated by rational desires at two levels, one involving the end for the sake of which the choice is made—ultimately, *eudaimonia*—and one involving the object of the choice, where this rational desire can—and in the virtuous person, will—coincide with the agent's appetitive and passionate desires for this object.[79]

The way in which *phantasia* operates in preparing the desire that leads to action seems to be the same operation that Hankinson argues is involved "when we see something *as an example of something choiceworthy*."[80] The impression of an object's choiceworthiness would be distinct from a judgment of theoretical reason *that* it is choiceworthy, with the latter judgment being a further cognitive process that would itself involve a *phantasma*, but which would not necessarily accompany every impression of a thing's choiceworthiness. Such an impression goes beyond mere perception, since choiceworthiness is

---

75   See Deslauriers, "How to Distinguish Aristotle's Virtues," for an extended argument that the types of desire are distinguished from one another by the objects at which they aim, and not by belonging to different parts of the soul.

76   This sense of "wish" is most notable in *EN* III.4.

77   *EN* III.3 1113a9-11.

78   *EN* III.2 1111b25-30, III.5 1113b3-5.

79   At *EN* III.2 1111b28, Aristotle writes that "we *wish* to be healthy and *choose* the things that will give us health," with, I would argue, the things that will give us health being objects of our *boulêsis* rather than *epithumia* or *thumos*. This can be seen by considering a person who chooses to undergo a necessary amputation for the sake of his health; it will not be pleasant and is not especially honourable, so the motivating desire behind this choice would have to be *boulêsis*. The three types of desire will often overlap, and in most cases an object of choice will seem pleasant to the person choosing—although, I argue, the deliberate choice of what seems pleasant will presuppose a conception of pleasure as being good, and so the evaluation of someone's character on the basis of their choices will ultimately involve an evaluation of their rational desires. Virtues, then, will be tendencies to feel non-rational desires in line with a rational desire for what is genuinely good.

80   Hankinson, "Perception and Evaluation: Aristotle on the Moral Imagination," 50.

THE IMPORTANCE OF IMAGINATION/*PHANTASIA* 191

neither a proper, common, nor incidental sensible, but is a non-perceptible quality that an incidental sensible (that is, an object) can have.[81] Hence, *phantasia* is necessarily involved in apprehending an object as choiceworthy, where this is a matter of our desiring that object on the basis of our *phantasma* of it, that is, how it seems or appears to us, along with our conception of the good.[82]

As Deborah Achtenberg argues, *phantasia* operates here through our envisaging a particular object or action as part of a greater whole, such as a whole life, where the whole that is imagined as including this part—for example, a life that includes having done this action in a certain way, for a certain reason, on this occasion, along with the expected outcomes of doing so—stands in evaluative comparison to other possible wholes that one can imagine, for example, a life that included having done something else on this occasion, and the expected outcomes of doing that.[83] Furthermore, our evaluation of one of the possible wholes that we picture as being preferable to the others will be based on which of the wholes, as we imagine them, we find more desirable. While this might be thought to support a quasi-Humean reading of Aristotle's moral psychology in making evaluation of choiceworthiness a matter of desire rather than rational judgment,[84] if I am right that the operative desire in deliberate choice is a rational desire, the ultimate desire on the basis of which we find one envisaged possible life preferable to another will be our *wish* for a good/*eudaimon* life, with this being determined by prior reasoning—and imagining—about what kind of life will be *eudaimon*.[85]

Moreover, since our wish for the good will involve some *phantasma* or image of what we take to be good, insofar as all thinking involves *phantasmata*, our evaluation of the prospective wholes that would result from choosing one option over another—where this determines which option we find more choiceworthy—will also involve at least an implicit comparison between each of these wholes as we picture them and our picture of the good. For instance, if our conception of a good human life is a hedonistic one, we will picture a good life as involving as many pleasurable experiences as possible. When faced

---

81   There is nothing that an object's being choiceworthy *looks like* (or sounds like, or tastes like, etc.) in the way that there is something that an object's being pink, or being round, or being large (or small) in relation to other objects looks like, and so this quality cannot be apprehended through mere perception unaccompanied by *phantasia*.

82   Cf. Noel, "*Phronesis* and *Phantasia*: Teaching with Wisdom and Imagination," 281–83.

83   Achtenberg, *The Cognition of Value in Aristotle's Ethics*, 180–82.

84   Cf. Moss, *Aristotle on the Apparent Good*.

85   Hence, contra the quasi-Humean reading of Aristotle, although our desires will guide us in our ethical evaluations, these desires will themselves often have been guided by reason through prior reflection, judgment, and deliberation.

with the choice of abstaining or indulging in some pleasure, the possible future outcomes and, ultimately, overall lives that we envisage having if we abstain or indulge will be desired, and evaluated, based on their resemblance to our image of the good life. In this way, deliberation can have a role in how one conceptualizes one's ends without contradicting Aristotle's insistence that we do not deliberate about which ends to aim at but about the means to attain them,[86] since he seems to mean that we don't deliberate about whether the good should be our end, but this does not exclude deliberation about what will constitute the good, and so allows deliberation to shape our conception of this end, including how we imagine it.[87]

The deliberation involved in forming a deliberative desire, where this desire is involved in the choice of one object or action over another, need not occur immediately preceding that choice, since we do not always stop to posit each possibility and weigh one against another. Rather, this could be prior deliberation about which things are conducive to human flourishing, based on past experience and involving reflection on the outcomes of certain actions, especially when the outcomes differed from those that one imagined would follow, with one's idea of the good being refined based on this. For example, one could initially imagine a flourishing life to involve giving to those in need, and then be surprised when one's attempt to help someone backfired—for example, the person took offense at the attempted generosity because of the inadvertently patronizing way one went about it. Reflection on this experience could lead to a revision in one's conception of generosity—for example, not merely giving others in need money, but doing so tactfully with respect for their autonomy—which would modify one's deliberative desire on future occasions when one encounters another in need, with future experiences of the outcomes of *these* choices possibly further refining one's image of an overall good life.[88] Since this deliberation would require one to remember both the outcomes that one anticipated would follow from one's actions and the outcomes that actually followed, it necessarily involves *phantasia* since these things, as past, are not available to perception.

---

86   *EN* III.3 1112b12.

87   *EN* VI.5 1140a25–28; cf. David Wiggins, "Deliberation and Practical Reason," in *Essays on Aristotle's Ethics*, ed. Amelia O. Rorty (Berkeley: University of California Press, 1980): 223–27.

88   *Phantasia* is not fixed or determined by the perceptions from which certain *phantasmata* arise, but is responsive to reason insofar as what we imagine, or how we imagine things, can be affected by our thinking, with our thinking in turn being affected by the *phantasmata* we have with which to think.

THE IMPORTANCE OF IMAGINATION/*PHANTASIA*   193

Phantasia is therefore necessarily active in prohairetic action in three respects: in the formation of the desire that motivates one's choice, in *how* this desire motivates the choice—that is, in seeing particular options in the context of some greater whole they will partly constitute, with the ultimate whole being a full life—and in envisaging multiple possible actions and their likely outcomes, both in themselves and as fitting into a larger context or whole that they would partly constitute. Along with playing these roles in choice and desire, *phantasia* is necessary for practical reasoning in further respects, with the capacity or tendency to imagine veridically being necessary for one to possess *phronêsis*, that is, excellence in practical reasoning, which, as discussed above, is necessary for ethical virtue.

4   *Phantasia* and *Phronêsis*

As noted, *phronêsis* is an intellectual virtue or excellence of the rational part of the soul, specifically the capacity for practical reason or deliberation about things that can be otherwise.[89] Aristotle defines it as "a true and reasoned state of capacity to act with regard to the things that are good or bad for man," which disposes one to "calculat[e] well with respect to some good end," or effectiveness in calculating the means to a given end with this end being conducive to or partly constitutive of human flourishing.[90] Aristotle's insistence that one cannot have ethical virtue without also having *phronêsis* sets up a contrast between "natural" virtue—that is, an innate disposition to desire and feel in certain ways that accord with the good, without this disposition being acquired from experience or being prohairetic—and "full" virtue, being an acquired disposition to desire and feel, and hence to act, in certain ways because these are good. In other words, *phronêsis* is necessary for a person to be able to see or judge that a certain action would be the appropriate thing to do in a given circumstance and to choose to do this because it is appropriate, rather than acting in a way that happens to be appropriate to one's circumstances because one is "naturally" disposed to be generous, courageous, honest, etc.

In "Practical Wisdom: A Mundane Account," Hursthouse argues that attending to the differences between a practically wise person (*phronimos*) and one with natural virtue will lead to a better understanding of *phronêsis* than will contrasting the *phronimos* with those who are *akratic* or vicious.[91] One salient

---

89   *EN* VI.1 1139a6-13.
90   *EN* VI.5 1140b4-5, VI.5 1140a30, VI.12 1144a25.
91   Hursthouse, "Practical Wisdom: A Mundane Account," 283–307.

difference she notes is that while a naturally kind person will be inclined to aim at the same end as the *phronimos*, she is more likely to make a mistake in realizing this aim due to a failure to grasp what to do in order to realize this end in the given situation. For instance, a naturally kind-hearted person might be inclined to want to give spare change to someone who appears in need, but might go about doing so in a way that inadvertently offended the other's self-respect or autonomy, or might not realize that giving a small amount to one person on one occasion would not be as genuinely helpful in the long term as, say, volunteering at a food bank. In asking what allows the *phronimos* to get things right where one whose desires and feelings are naturally oriented towards the good might get things wrong, Hursthouse warns against assuming that this is propositional knowledge of what would be good, since this would make *phronêsis*, and by extension, ethical virtue, in principle codifiable and so able to be learned second-hand instead of needing to be acquired through experience.[92] Instead, she argues that *phronêsis* involves "knowledge-how" vs. "knowledge-that," being a matter of the *phronimos* having certain acquired intellectual capacities "that enable him to avoid the mistakes in action to which [others] are prone."[93]

These capacities of the *phronimos* are themselves intellectual virtues that are connected with *phronêsis*—viz. practical intelligence or insight (*nous praktikê*), understanding or comprehension (*sunesis*), discernment (*gnômê*), and good deliberation (*euboulia*)[94]—which, on Hursthouse's reading, are jointly constitutive of the rational element of *phronêsis* rather than *phronêsis* being a fully distinct intellectual disposition. The first of these, practical *nous*, is a capacity by which the *phronimos* apprehends what is appropriate to do in a given situation, with this apprehension being closer to perception than to rational inference, and is characterized by Aristotle as an eye with which one sees correctly.[95] The appropriate action in a situation is a particular, and Aristotle writes that of such particulars "there is perception but no scientific knowledge," adding "[t]his perception is not the kind with which [each of our senses apprehends] its proper object, but the kind with which we perceive that in mathematics the triangle is the ultimate figure."[96]

---

92   Hursthouse, "Practical Wisdom: A Mundane Account," 284.

93   Hursthouse, "Practical Wisdom: A Mundane Account," 285.

94   See *EN* VI.11 1143a26-28: "when we speak of judgement [*gnômê*] and understanding [*sunesis*] and practical wisdom [*phronêsis*] and comprehension [*nous*] we credit the same people with possessing judgement [*gnômê*] and comprehension [*nous*] and with having practical wisdom [*phronêsis*] and understanding [*sunesis*]."

95   *EN* VI.11 1143b13.

96   *EN* VI.8 1142a26-29, translation Martin Ostwald (New York: Bobbs-Merrill, 1962). By "ultimate figure," Aristotle likely means that it is the smallest enclosed two-dimensional

THE IMPORTANCE OF IMAGINATION/*PHANTASIA* 195

Not only is what is called "perception" here not that of proper sensibles such as colours; it does not seem to be the perception of common sensibles such as movement or shape, since we do not come to grasp that a triangle is the fewest-sided enclosed shape in the way that we perceive, say, that an object is three-dimensional or that it is moving faster than another. Instead, what the triangle example suggests is that practical *nous* involves an exercise of *phantasia*[97] in which one comes to realize that no enclosed two-dimensional shape with fewer than three sides is possible, not through an inference, but through becoming aware that this is impossible to imagine—that is, that no *phantasma* of only two lines can form a closed shape. The *phronimos*'s apprehension of the actions that are possible in a situation, and of which is the most virtuous or appropriate in the context of the situation, then, would be akin to the way a Sudoku player suddenly "sees" which number goes in a certain square, where this involves a change in how the numbers are imagined in relation to one another, but no change in any of the sensibles she perceives.[98]

As Hursthouse argues, *gnômê* and *sunesis* are necessary for one to possess practical *nous*. *Gnômê*, or discernment, is "a correct critical sense or judgment of what is fair" or equitable,[99] and so is linked to being able to sense and judge qualitative proportionality. Since the mean at which the virtuous person aims is a matter of acting and feeling proportionally—that is, neither too much nor too little relative to one's context—and since what counts as neither too much nor too little, but the right amount, can vary from one context to another, and so can admit of exceptions to general principles about what types of actions will be generous, courageous, etc., it is through *gnômê* that the *phronimos* judges each case on its own terms and discern when a general principle does not apply: that is, when a situation is an exception to the rule. This lets the *phronimos* be aware of when a normally vicious action, such as lying, usually expressing a dishonest character, is in fact appropriate—for example, when telling the truth would lead to needlessly hurt feelings. This capacity for discernment

---

shape, or as Martin Ostwald explains on 161, n.37, "that every polygonal figure in geometry can be resolved into a number of triangles, but that the triangle in turn cannot be resolved into a simpler figure."

97   This reading is supported by the claim at *de Ins.* 1 459a15-23 that *phantasia* and *aisthêsis* belong to the same part of the soul. If Aristotle held this, as he seems to have from his remarks in the *Parva Naturalia*, then in saying that practical *nous* grasps its object through perception could mean that it does so not through *aisthêsis*, but through an activity of the part of the soul that receives appearances.

98   While it is beyond the scope of this paper to explore this further, there is an interesting connection between this apprehension through practical *nous* and what J.J. Gibson, in *The Ecological Approach to Visual Perception* (Boston: Houghton Mifflin, 1979), calls apprehending a situation's affordances.

99   *EN* VI.11 1143a20-24, translation Martin Ostwald.

would develop from extensive experience in various spheres of action, and especially from encountering exceptions to general principles about what types of action are virtuous. As Hursthouse notes, attributing the discernment of what counts as the mean in a given situation to *gnômê* might seem to leave little for practical *nous* to contribute to seeing what a situation calls for.[100] However, this can be solved if one takes *nous* to be the capacity by which one apprehends that a certain virtue—for example, honesty rather than generosity—is what is called for, with *gnômê* being the capacity by which one discerns what way of acting will count as that virtue's mean in this case, with both capacities operating in tandem in any exercise of *phronêsis*.

Since both *gnômê* and *nous* involve apprehending a particular moral fact about the situation one is in, both require *sunesis* or excellence in comprehending situations correctly, or at least those aspects of a situation "concerning which doubt and deliberation are possible"[101]—for example, the possibilities it affords for action. Aristotle characterizes *sunesis* as applying to both situations one experiences first-hand and those one encounters through another's description.[102] This could be thought of as interpreting or conceptualizing the situation accurately based on correctly apprehending the particular details of the situation that one experiences, or hears described, along with how these details connect or relate to each other. Put in terms of "seeing the forest for the trees," it would be a matter of getting a correct idea of the forest based on seeing the particular trees, or hearing them described. Clearly one cannot correctly grasp what actions a situation affords or which virtues it calls for, or discern what way of acting will hit the mean of these virtues in a particular situation, without first correctly apprehending the situation itself, and so *sunesis* necessarily underlies *nous* and *gnômê*.

Phantasia is necessary for *sunesis* insofar as situations are not objects of proper, common, or incidental perception, but must be grasped through what David Wiggins calls "situational apperception,"[103] or the imaginative combination of *phantasmata* of the particular details that make up the situation—the "trees" that make up the "forest," so to speak, where the former but not the latter are perceptible. By extension, *phantasia* is also necessary for *nous* and *gnômê* insofar as these capacities themselves rest on the exercise of *sunesis*, in addition to being involved in the quasi-perceptual aspects of *nous* and *gnômê*, that is, "seeing" rather than inferring what a situation calls for. Additionally,

---

100   Hursthouse, "Practical Wisdom: A Mundane Account," 288.

101   *EN* VI.10 1143a6-7; translation Martin Ostwald.

102   *EN* VI.10 1143a13-17.

103   Wiggins, "Deliberation and Practical Reason," 232–33.

THE IMPORTANCE OF IMAGINATION/*PHANTASIA*   197

phantasia is necessary for the fourth intellectual virtue involved in *phronêsis*, excellent deliberation or *euboulia*, insofar as deliberation about what to do involves having *phantasmata* of different possible future actions and their outcomes, as discussed above. Therefore, because it is centrally involved in the exercise of the four intellectual capacities that jointly comprise *phronêsis*, *phantasia* is central for *phronêsis*. And since *phronêsis* is necessary for ethical virtue, *phantasia* is central to ethical virtue, in addition to its roles in preparing the virtuous person's rational desire for the good and in allowing for her actions to be prohairetic.

This necessary involvement of *phantasia* in choice, desire, and the various intellectual capacities that make up *phronêsis*—especially *sunesis* as it is exercised in situational apperception—reveals its central place in the moral psychology of Aristotelian and neo-Aristotelian virtue ethics, insofar as choice, desire, and *phronêsis* are the core components of this moral psychology. This entails that what, and how, agents imagine in their apprehension of a range of ethically salient factors—for example: (i) the immediate situation they are in; (ii) themselves as elements of this situation; (iii) the possibilities this situation affords for action, relative to the capacities they imagine themselves to have for acting; (iv) the outcomes of these possible actions, and their likelihood; (v) a *eudaimon* or flourishing human life; and (vi) how a given possible action and its likely outcome(s) fit into the context of a whole life—will be relevant in ethical assessments of their characters. In other words, how broadly and how veridically one characteristically imagines will matter for how good, that is, how virtuous or how close to virtue, one is. Mistakes in grasping the morally salient features of one's situation—or in discerning the appropriate things to feel and do in that situation, or in one's conception of a good life and hence of what things are good to aim at in action—will result from a failure to imagine correctly, where these failures will impede virtuous action along with the development of a fully virtuous character.

From this it follows that, along with the other dispositions mentioned by Aristotle in connection with full virtue, the virtuous person will have a disposition to imagine *well*, or veridically, where this includes both remembering past situations, feelings, etc. accurately and envisaging future possibilities and outcomes in ways that will map onto what would actually occur—for example, envisaging correctly how one would feel if one's action resulted in a certain outcome—where at least the latter, if not the former, would have to be developed through experience and habits of imagining just as *phronêsis* and ethical virtues are acquired from habituation. A further implication of the connection between *phantasia* and ethical virtue concerns a potential solution it offers to the problem of the moral education of the emotions, that is, of how one can develop a disposition to feel in certain ways, since feeling an emotion does not seem to be something that we do that is up to us, but something we undergo,[104] and since dispositions must be prohairetic in order to count as virtues. Given *phantasia*'s role in thinking, deliberation, and creative imagining in which *phantasmata* are combined to form new wholes, and its role in preparing one's desires, it would seem that one can come to be disposed to feel in certain ways. This would be through deliberately imagining certain things, for example, actions or objects, as fitting into a greater context that involved certain outcomes, where habitually imagining these things as preceding these outcomes could lead us to form a disposition to respond emotionally to these things when we think of or perceive them in a way that matches how we feel about the imagined outcomes. For example, one could prohairetically form a disposition to feel less angry at minor frustrations or interpersonal slights by habituating oneself to imagine negative consequences following these angry reactions. Of course, the same process would be involved in the *mis*-education of emotions, and so exercising *phantasia* in this way would not be sufficient for developing dispositions to feel virtuously, though it seems necessary for the development of such dispositions and explains how the emotions one comes to be disposed to feel can be prohairetic despite not being up to us at the moment they are felt.

5 Implications for Contemporary Ethics and Moral Psychology

I have argued that *phantasia*, as Aristotle characterizes it, grounds the most important concepts in Aristotle's moral psychology—specifically, choice, desire, and *phronêsis*, along with the associated intellectual virtues of *nous*, *gnômê*, and *sunesis*—and so is central to his moral psychology and his conception of ethical virtue. Implicit in my argument has been the view that, because of the centrality of *phantasia* in Aristotle's ethical thought, greater attention to the nature of *phantasia* and to its role in choice, desire, and *phronêsis* can add to our understanding of these aspects of Aristotle's moral psychology in their own right. So far I have focused on Aristotle's ethics and psychology on the assumption that what applies here will also apply, for the most part, to contemporary neo-Aristotelian virtue ethical approaches insofar as they map onto Aristotle's ethical thinking. For instance, insofar as the concept of *phronêsis* is as central in neo-Aristotelian virtue ethics as it is in Aristotle's own ethical works, the importance of *phantasia* for the development and exercise of

---

104   *EN* II.5 1106a4-6. For a detailed discussion of this problem, see Kosman 1980.

THE IMPORTANCE OF IMAGINATION/*PHANTASIA*   199

phronêsis in Aristotle's thought should also hold for neo-Aristotelian virtue ethics. However, the proposed extension of what holds for *phantasia* in Aristotle's thought to what holds for imagination in contemporary virtue ethics might be questioned on the grounds that what Aristotle meant by *phantasia* does not map cleanly onto what we mean by "imagination" today. In the remainder of this paper I address this possible worry and briefly defend the relevance of a conception of imagination that is close to Aristotle's *phantasia*, at least with respect to what it does—or, rather, to what we do in exercising it— for both contemporary virtue ethics and for moral psychology across ethical frameworks.

One worry about bringing Aristotle's *phantasia* into current philosophical discussions is that most contemporary thinkers no longer conceive of imagination as exclusively or primarily sensory, but admit of propositional imagining,[105] or "running a belief off-line," that is, supposing it to be true without believing it. It is not clear that the role Aristotle assigns to *phantasia* in the various psychological operations discussed above could be fulfilled by propositional imagining without a quasi-perceptual component, since perceiving an object or state of affairs—or quasi-perceiving it through sensory imagination— seems to stimulate our feelings and desires more fully and more effectively than merely believing that it obtains.[106] If the form of imagination that allows us to grasp possible actions and future states affectively is necessarily sensory, and if some people can only imagine propositionally, a virtue ethicist admitting this role of imagination in her moral psychology would seem to be committed to denying that such people could ever be virtuous—a conclusion that is likely to be resisted.

One response to this worry—though it is beyond the scope of this paper to develop it in any depth—would be to question the dichotomy of propositional and sensory imagination, and to argue that these are not two distinct forms of imagination but are two aspects of any act of imagining, such that imagining that P always involves some quasi-perceptual activity of "imaging" P, however low-level, and that forming a mental picture of some object always involves imagining something to be the case, even if this is a matter of imagining only

---

105   See Amy Kind, "Introduction," in *The Routledge Handbook of Philosophy of Imagination*, ed. Amy Kind (New York: Routledge, 2016): 4–6.

106   This is intuitively plausible from introspection and the observation of others; one way of reducing apprehension of something negative that one believes will occur is not to picture it occurring, and conversely those playing games of make-believe can make themselves feel afraid, as part of the game, more effectively by picturing the object of their make-believe fear, for example, a monster under the bed, rather than by simply thinking that it exists.

that it exists in some undefined imaginary space. Another response would be to question whether anyone really cannot imagine sensorily.[107] As long as everyone is capable of sensory imagining, as well as imagining propositionally, the claim for the necessity of this form of imagining for situational apperception, moral deliberation, and the formation of rational desires for the good would be less problematic.

Since contemporary virtue ethicists of a neo-Aristotelian persuasion already make use of versions of Aristotelian psychological concepts such as parts of the soul or their faculties—for instance, in maintaining a distinction between intellectual and ethical virtues—without taking these concepts or Aristotle's philosophy of mind literally, it would be no more anachronistic for them to posit a faculty of imagination to play the same role in moral psychology that *phantasia* plays in Aristotle's. Moreover, none of the functions that *phantasia* is held to perform in connection with the exercise of *phronêsis*, choice, or desire necessarily presuppose a literal understanding of Aristotle's psychological concepts, such as parts of the soul, etc., nor are they implausible as mental processes that people actually do engage in. Unless one were sceptical of *any* sensory or non-propositional imagining, which virtue ethicists are unlikely to be, there would seem to be no obvious problem with contemporary virtue ethicists taking imagination to play the role(s) in moral psychology that Aristotle attributes to *phantasia*.

What has been said in the previous sections about *phantasia*'s role and importance should, then, also extend to contemporary neo-Aristotelian virtue ethics and the place of imagination in its moral psychology. But not all contemporary forms of virtue ethics are neo-Aristotelian, so it might be thought that what has been discussed above about *phantasia* might not apply in those cases. However, there seems to be no specific reason to think that it wouldn't, as the functions that imagination is taken to perform with respect to choice, desire and deliberation do not seem to rest on anything unique to an Aristotelian framework. The virtuousness of an agent's desires and sentiments on a virtue ethical approach modeled on the moral theories of Hume or Smith, say, or on Michael Slote's agent-based virtue ethics, require the agent to imagine the object of these sentiments and desires accurately in order to feel towards it or desire it appropriately, since imagining the object inaccurately—for example,

---

107   See William James, *The Principles of Psychology, volume 2* (New York: Dover Publications, 1890): 56–66, for the suggestion made on the basis of empirical findings that those claiming not to have any sensory imagination say so because they think of sensory imagination as being strictly visual, and that they do engage in quasi-perceptual imagining, but in an auditory, or tactile, or motile mode rather than in a visual one.

misconstruing an action the results of which one desires—would affect what, and how, one felt. And the aspect of imagination that allows for situational apperception would seem to be equally required for perspectival thinking in a Nietzschean virtue ethics.

Furthermore, the capacities to apprehend the situations we occupy and the possibilities for action they afford, to foresee with a fair degree of accuracy the probable outcomes of these actions, to envisage the things we experience as capable of being otherwise, and "to explore how experience would play out under the influence of various values and commitments"[108]—and to do all these veridically—are plausibly necessary for good moral judgment on any ethical framework. To grasp and respond to elements of a situation that will be salient for care ethics, such as the emotional states and perspectives of others involved in that situation, and the ability to balance competing desires and values in order to come to a fair and equitable compromise when called for, would seem to require the exercise of imagination in its synthesizing and empathetic roles. Correctly and fully grasping a situation and envisaging the probable immediate and long-term outcomes of potential courses of action will be obviously central to any consequentialist moral reasoning aiming at maximizing value in a future state of affairs through one's actions. The ethical relevance of a utility calculation or cost-benefit analysis, for instance, requires one to have apprehended all possibilities for action and taken all morally or axiologically relevant elements of the possible outcomes of these actions into account, where this involves an exercise of the imagination. And, for Kantian ethics, the imagination seems required in addition to pure reason for judging correctly when a situation calls for the exercise of an imperfect duty, as well as for determining when the maxim one wills in one's action can be universalized without contradiction, since this involves envisaging the results of a counterfactual, for example, what would occur if everyone were to will the same.[109]

If I am right that imagination is centrally important in non-Aristotelian and non-virtue-ethical approaches to moral philosophy for much the same reasons for its importance in Aristotle's ethics and in neo-Aristotelian virtue ethics, what I have argued concerning the role of *phantasia* in Aristotle's moral psychology can be taken to point to a greater role for imagination in moral psychology in general than has typically been acknowledged, at least in recent

---

108 Mark Johnson, "Moral Imagination," in *The Routledge Handbook of Philosophy of Imagination*, ed. Amy Kind (New York: Routledge, 2016): 355–67.

109 Cf. Immanuel Kant, *Groundwork of the Metaphysics of Morals*, eds. and trans. Mary Gregor and Jens Timmermann (Cambridge: Cambridge University Press, 1785/2012), 4:420–24.

Anglo-American ethics.[110] For one thing, it suggests that a tendency towards what could be called literal-mindedness—that is, not just instrumental reasoning, but any thinking from a fixed or needlessly limited perspective or set of premises and presuppositions, without an awareness of how the things one is thinking about might be otherwise, what one would conclude if one's presuppositions were otherwise, etc.—should be seen as a serious problem insofar as such a tendency will hinder what is needed for good (whether virtuous, correct, effective, etc.) ethical thinking.[111] Moreover, it suggests grounds for worries about activities or practices that tend to promote the development of a disposition for literal-mindedness—for instance, the frequent use of technologies that operate based on pre-determined one-to-one relations of actions/inputs and results/outputs, regardless of the purposes they are used for, or an adherence to ways of thinking and understanding that involve viewing particular phenomena through fixed frameworks of general categories, with little sensitivity to contextual differences in the particulars, for example, theories that reduce agents to tokens of general social types and their actions to expressions of these types.[112] Insofar as habituation in such ways of acting and thinking would stunt our capacities to imagine beyond these one-to-one relations and fixed frameworks—to "think beyond theory," as it were—and make us less disposed to conceive of things as being possibly otherwise than they are characterized by the fixed options one is given, they should be seen as detrimental to ethical development, ethical thinking and responsiveness, and ethical

---

110   Or at least what is considered mainstream moral philosophy, since much work in aesthetics and philosophy of literature looking at the benefits of engaging with art and literature for moral education seems often to be overlooked by ethicists—though less so among virtue ethicists, interestingly enough. Some exceptions to this from within what would likely be counted as "mainstream" moral philosophy are Martha Nussbaum, *Love's Knowledge: Essays on Philosophy and Literature* (Oxford: Oxford University Press, 1990), Sophie Grace Chappell, *Knowing What To Do: Imagination, Virtue, and Platonism in Ethics* (Oxford: Oxford University Press, 2014), and Johnson, "Moral Imagination," 355–67. As Johnson notes, many who *have* given imagination a prominent role in moral psychology within Anglo-American philosophy fall within the tradition of American pragmatism—for example, Dewey, Putnam, and Rorty (see Johnson, "Moral Imagination," 359–63).

111   Cf. Hannah Arendt, "Thinking and Moral Considerations," *Social Research* 38, no. 3 (1971): 417–46 for a similar position arrived at through different, though I think compatible, considerations. See especially pp. 423–24 in connection with this chapter's discussion of imagination.

112   The worries G.E.M. Anscombe raises about Mill's failure to see "that acts of murder and theft could be otherwise described" (G.E.M. Anscombe, "Modern Moral Philosophy," *Philosophy* 33 (1958): 3), and the effects of considering under-described and decontextualized thought experiments in ethics (Anscombe, "Modern Moral Philosophy," 13), seem at least in part to be worries about literal-mindedness and a disposition to imagine poorly.

action—or, for virtue ethicists, as likely impediments to virtue and so to overall human flourishing.

References

Achtenberg, Deborah. *The Cognition of Value in Aristotle's Ethics: Promise of Enrichment, Threat of Destruction*. Albany, NY: State University of New York Press. 2002.

Anscombe, G.E.M. "Modern Moral Philosophy." *Philosophy* 33 (1958): 1–19.

Arendt, Hannah. "Thinking and Moral Considerations." *Social Research* 38, no. 3 (1971): 417–46.

Aristotle. *Nicomachean Ethics*. Translated by Martin Ostwald. New York: Bobbs-Merrill. 1962.

Aristotle. *The Complete Works of Aristotle*, Revised Oxford Translation, 2 vols. Edited by Jonathan Barnes. Princeton, NJ: Princeton University Press. 1984.

Aristotle. *Nicomachean Ethics*, 2nd edition. Translated by Terence Irwin. Indianapolis, IN: Hackett. 1999.

Brown, Leslie. "Why is Aristotle's Virtue of Character a Mean?" In *The Cambridge Companion to Aristotle's Nicomachean Ethics*, edited by Ronald Polansky, 64–80. Cambridge: Cambridge University Press, 2014.

Carrasco, Maria A. "Adam Smith's Reconstruction of Practical Reason." *Review of Metaphysics* 58 (2004): 81–116.

Caston, Victor. "Why Aristotle Needs Imagination." *Phronesis* 51 (1996): 20–55.

Caston, Victor. "Phantasia and Thought." In *A Companion to Aristotle*, edited by Georgios Anagnostopoulos, 322–34. Malden, MA: Wiley-Blackwell, 2009.

Chappell, Sophie Grace. "Three Kinds of Moral Imagination." In Sophie Grace Chappell, *Knowing What To Do: Imagination, Virtue, and Platonism in Ethics*, 29–59. Oxford: Oxford University Press, 2014.

Cooper, John M. "Some Remarks on Aristotle's Moral Psychology." *The Southern Journal of Philosophy* XXVII, Supplement (1988): 25–42.

Corcilius, Klaus and Gregoric, Pavel. "Separability vs. Difference: Parts and Capacities of the Soul in Aristotle." In *Oxford Studies in Ancient Philosophy* vol. XXXIX, edited by Brad Inwood, 81–119. Oxford: Oxford University Press, 2010.

Deslauriers, Marguerite. "How to Distinguish Aristotle's Virtues." *Phronesis* 47 (2002): 101–26.

Everson, Stephen. *Aristotle on Perception*. Oxford: Oxford University Press. 1997.

Frede, Dorothea. "The Cognitive Role of *Phantasia* in Aristotle." In *Essays on Aristotle's De Anima*, edited by Martha Nussbaum and Amelie O. Rorty, 279–98. Oxford: Oxford University Press, 1992.

Gibson, John J. *The Ecological Approach to Visual Perception*. Boston: Houghton Mifflin. 1979.

Hanley, Ryan P. *Adam Smith and the Character of Virtue*, Cambridge: Cambridge University Press. 2009.

Hankinson, R.J. "Perception and Evaluation: Aristotle on the Moral Imagination," *Dialogue* 29 (1990): 41–63.

Hursthouse, Rosalind. *On Virtue Ethics*. Oxford: Oxford University Press. 1999.

Hursthouse, Rosalind. "Practical Wisdom: A Mundane Account." *Proceedings of the Aristotelian Society* 106 (2006): 283–307.

James, William. *The Principles of Psychology*, vol. 2. New York: Dover Publications. 1890.

Johnson, Mark. "Moral Imagination." In *The Routledge Handbook of Philosophy of Imagination*, edited by Amy Kind, 355–67. New York: Routledge, 2016.

Kant, Immanuel. *Groundwork of the Metaphysics of Morals*. Translated and edited by Mary Gregor and Jens Timmermann. Cambridge: Cambridge University Press. 1785/2012.

Kind, Amy. "Introduction." In *The Routledge Handbook of Philosophy of Imagination*, edited by Amy Kind, 1–11. New York: Routledge, 2016.

Kosman, L.A. "Being Properly Affected: Virtues and Feelings in Aristotle's Ethics." In *Essays on Aristotle's Ethics*, edited by Amelie O. Rorty, 103–16. Berkeley, CA: University of California Press, 1980.

Lorenz, Hendrik. *The Brute Within: Appetitive Desire in Plato and Aristotle*, Oxford: Clarendon Press. 2006.

Modrak, D. "Aristotle on *Phantasia*." In *The Routledge Handbook of Philosophy of Imagination*, edited by Amy Kind, 15–26. New York: Routledge, 2016.

Moss, Jessica. *Aristotle on the Apparent Good: Perception, Phantasia, Thought, and Desire*. Oxford: Oxford University Press. 2012.

Moss, Jessica. "Was Aristotle a Humean? A Partisan Guide to the Debate." In *The Cambridge Companion to Aristotle's Nicomachean Ethics*, edited by Ronald Polansky, 221–41. Cambridge: Cambridge University Press, 2014.

Noel, Jana. "*Phronesis* and *Phantasia*: Teaching with Wisdom and Imagination." *Journal of Philosophy of Education* 33 (1999); 277–86.

Nussbaum, Martha C. *Love's Knowledge: Essays on Philosophy and Literature*. Oxford: Oxford University Press. 1990.

Schofield, Malcolm. "Aristotle on the Imagination." In *Essays on Aristotle's De Anima*, edited by Martha Nussbaum and Amelie O. Rorty, 249–77. Oxford: Oxford University Press. 1992.

Slote, Michael. "Agent-Based Virtue Ethics." In *Virtue Ethics*, edited by Roger Crisp and Michael Slote, 239–62. Oxford: Oxford University Press, 1997.

Swanton, Christine. *The Virtue Ethics of Hume and Nietzsche*. Malden, MA: Wiley-Blackwell. 2015.

Wedin, Michael. *Mind and Imagination in Aristotle*. New Haven: Yale University Press. 1988.

Wiggins, David. "Deliberation and Practical Reason." In *Essays on Aristotle's Ethics*, edited by Amelie O. Rorty, 221–40. Berkeley, CA: University of California Press, 1980.

Wilkes, Kathleen V. "The Good Man and the Good For Man." In *Essays on Aristotle's Ethics*, Amelie O. Rorty, 341–57. Berkeley, CA: University of California Press, 1980.

Zagzebski, Linda. *Virtues of the Mind*. Cambridge: Cambridge University Press. 1996.

CHAPTER 9

The Infanticidal Logic of Mimesis as Horizon of the Imaginable

A. Samuel Kimball

Image and *imagine* derive from the Latin *imagō*, which is cognate with *imitāre*, to imitate, and *aemulus*, emulous. The three Latin stems descend from the Indo-European *aim-*, copy, and are perhaps akin to the Hittite *himma-*, ritual substitute.[1]

Mimesis, of unattested origin, has been hypothesized to derive either from *mimo*, itself an uncertain Indo-European stem that is "perhaps imitative of rapid repetition,"[2] or, alternatively, "possibly" from the Latin *minus*, which descends from the Indo-European *mei-*, little.[3]

1 Introduction

In this discussion,[4] I propose to address a limit to what is available to human imagination by explaining why reflections on the nature of mimesis, a technique of non-biological reproduction, ought to address both the empirical event of infanticide and the more general arche-violence of the infanticidal, which compromise human sexual reproductivity. The answer I offer is that doing so discloses how mimetic representation covers up the scarcely imaginable inescapability of a violence that is constitutive of life if not of being, that imposes a non-transcendable costliness to existence, and that renders human first-person self-consciousness susceptible to self-blinding referential error. I shall develop this explanation first by examining how Aristotle programs the

---

1 Adapted from Calvert Watkins, ed., *The American Heritage Dictionary of Indo-European Roots*, 3rd ed. (Boston: Houghton Miffling Harcourt, 2011), 2. In the first edition (1985), Watkins identifies the root of mimesis as mimos, "a Greek noun of unknown origin" meaning a mime. He does not list mimesis in either his second or third editions.

2 Joseph T. Shipley, *The Origins of English Words: A Discursive Dictionary of Indo-European Roots* (Baltimore: Johns Hopkins University Press, 1984), 254.

3 Shipley, *The Origins of English Words*, 237–38.

4 I want to thank the students in my spring 2016 course on the Classical Background of Western Literature. Their high-spirited and acute questioning helped inspire this essay. My thanks, then, to Michelle Acker, Jensen Alex, Juliusz Dzierlatka, Ellen Glod, Adam Friedman, Kayla Hilliar, Lily Hohman, Carleshia Jimerson, Hayeon Park, Natalia Roldan, Jordyn Searcey, and Nichole Sellers.

© KONINKLIJKE BRILL NV, LEIDEN, 2020 | DOI:10.1163/9789004436350_011

THE INFANTICIDAL LOGIC OF MIMESIS AS HORIZON OF IMAGINABLE   207

western world's mimetic misreadings of Sophocles' tragedy, *Oedipus the King*, by refusing to recognize in Oedipus' swollen feet a father's hatred and attempted destruction of his newborn son, by ignoring Apollo's willingness to curse an infant in order to destroy the child's parents, and by failing to apprehend Sophocles' critique of Greek religious practices, a cultural critique that he puts into the mouth of Oedipus. Having established the infanticidal violence of the parents as the imaginative abyss that the western reception of Oedipus has been unable to cross, I shall then turn to the way in which, living with the excruciating awareness of the non-existence his parents intended for him, he understands life in terms of an economy of incalculable loss—indeed, of losses that are themselves necessarily lost in advance of being imagined or even imaginable—which makes of life that for which his kingdom, Sophocles' Greek society, and western philosophy subsequently have had no name and which might provisionally be called lifedeath. I shall conclude by linking Oedipus' infanticidal critique of his world to Sophocles' glimpse of an impossible futurity that, being the condition of the possibility of mimetic representation, nevertheless itself eludes all such mimesis. The result will be to indicate how the infanticidal logic of mimesis demarcates the amimetic horizon of the imaginable for a consciousness that conceives of its own operations, especially its thinking, as conceptive.[5]

2   **Aristotelian Mimesis, the Unpitied Child, and the Tragedy of Oedipus the King**

In the *Poetics*, Aristotle explains that mimesis is a defining human capability, present by nature in the newborn child and providing it with a means of its initial socialization. Thus does Aristotle observe that "imitation comes naturally to human beings from childhood"; that, long before we can speak and then during the course of acquiring language, children "learn their earliest lessons through imitation"; and that we are, in fact, born with "a strong propensity to imitation."[6] This affirmation of what is natural in the child, however, conceals the fact that Aristotle implicitly traces the origin of mimesis not to human reproduction as such but to a biological conception that results in a certain kind of birth—that of the healthy child who should be named, welcomed into a family, and cared for rather than that of a deformed child who

---

5   This chapter thus extends the argumentation I offer in *The Infanticidal Logic of Evolution and Culture* (Newark: University of Delaware, 2007), especially in Chapter 8, "The Wounded Infant and the Infanticidism of the Gods: Oedipus' Cultural Critique," 203–30.

6   Aristotle, *Poetics*, 6; 48b.

lawfully ought to be left to die. In the *Politics*, Aristotle recommends infanticide, as does Plato in his *Laws*, when the neonate is born crippled in some way: "let it be lawful," Aristotle writes, "that no cripple child be reared."[7] The child who is disabled upon his or her advent—that is, by reproductive chance—marks a limit at which mimesis loses its generativity and is cut off from its nature by the law that secures the child's right to life but only through the father's ironic right to terminate that life. This right inheres in the father as a metonymical figure of the state, that form of social organization which "belongs to a class of objects which exist in nature"; the state is the natural home of the being that "is by nature a political animal,"[8] and it confers upon the father the right—the natural right, as if law and nature were categorically congruent in their differentiation—to dispose of children whose defects are presumptively anomalous with respect to "the natural growth of things," Aristotle's explanatory first principle.[9]

What happens if, following Aristotle, we read his commentary on *Oedipus the King* by beginning with a specific "ordinance of custom," a specific cultural practice, which Aristotle affirms without analyzing—namely, the custom that "forbids the exposure of infants merely in order to reduce numbers..."?[10] If we understand this injunction to constitute an ethical imperative that is foundational for the ideal form of polity, how should we judge the ruler, Laius in Sophocles' drama, who commands that his healthy newborn be left to die of exposure; and all the more so a ruler who deliberately mutilates his son? Oedipus' name, of course, means "swell-foot,"[11] a noun phrase derived from the consequence of having had the tendons of his feet "pierced" (and likely fettered or yoked) in preparation for his abandonment, intended to be fatal.[12] The royal father maims his child, presumably to mark it as anathema and thus to warn away the stranger who might be moved at the infant's helplessness to save it from death by exposure or predation. How should we judge this father's harrowing act and the life he intends to make disappear without a trace on a "trackless mountain"?[13]

---

7   Aristotle, *Politics*, 294; Book VII, Ch. 16.

8   Aristotle, *Politics*, 28; Book I, Ch. 2.

9   Aristotle, *Politics*, 26; Book I, Ch. 2.

10   Aristotle, *Politics*, 294; Book VII, Ch. 16.

11   According to Thomas Gould, in his commentary to his translation of Sophocles' drama, *Oedipus the King by Sophocles* (Englewood Cliffs: Prentice-Hall, 1970), "The name 'Oedipus' was thought to come from *oidein* 'to swell,' and *pous*, 'foot'" (14n8).

12   Gould, *Oedipus the King by Sophocles*, 93, l. 719.

13   Gould, *Oedipus the King by Sophocles*, 123n1034.

THE INFANTICIDAL LOGIC OF MIMESIS AS HORIZON OF IMAGINABLE   209

Moreover, how should we judge Laius's infanticidal actions in relation to his motivation to avoid an oracular curse, presumably from the god Apollo, "the god who is the foremost of all gods, the Sun," the chorus confirm?[14] In Sophocles' tragedy, Jocasta reports that "It was foretold to Laius—I shall not say by Phoebus [Apollo] himself, but by his ministers—that when his fate arrived he would be killed by a son who would be born to him and me."[15] No character in the play, including the seer, recalls the crime for which Apollo condemns Laius. That crime, according to Greek myth, occurred when, having escaped an attempt on his life by his distant relations (Amphion and Zethus) before he could assume the throne of Thebes, Laius had been given refuge by King Pelops, whose hospitality his guest had repaid by abducting this king's son, Chrysippus, and sodomizing him.[16] If by Apollonian decree Oedipus unknowingly takes revenge against Laius on behalf of the boy Laius victimized, how should we judge the god who imposes the burden of such involuntary vengeance, which Oedipus undertakes in apparent ignorance of Laius's history of a cross-generational rape prior to Laius's savage assault on his own son's body? Does the father's child deserve to be thus scripted by Apollo—subject to an interpellation that leads to the maiming that haunts this son with every step he will ever take—in order to be the god's instrument for punishing his father?[17]

---

14   Gould, *Oedipus the King by Sophocles*, 87, l. 660.

15   Gould, *Oedipus the King by Sophocles*, 91–92, ll. 711–14.

16   See Pausanias, *Description of Greece*, trans. W.H.S. Jones and H.A. Omerod, Loeb Classical Library (Cambridge: Harvard University Press, 1918), 9.5.6; accessed April 29, 2019. https://www.theoi.com/%20Text/Pausanias9A.html. See also Apollodorus. *The Library*, trans. Sir James George Frazer, Loeb Classical Library, vols. 121 and 122 (Cambridge: Harvard University Press, 1921) 3.5.5; accessed April 29, 2019, https://www.theoi.com/Text/%20Apollodorus3.html.

17   In the *Nichomachean Ethics* (trans. Marton Ostwald [Indianpolis: Bobbs-Merrill/The Library of Liberal Arts, 1962]), Aristotle struggles to understand the nature of pity precisely when it comes to the threat of infanticide. The demonstration begins with how Aristotle equivocates about the relation of pity to virtue. On the one hand, Aristotle defines pity as one of the emotions or passions rather than as a dispositional capacity or characteristic: "By 'emotions' I mean appetite, anger, fear, confidence, envy, joy, affection, hatred, longing, emulation, pity, and in general anything that is followed by pleasure or pain..." (40; II.5; 1105b). As such, pity would be involuntary: "We are neither praised nor blamed for our emotions..." for "no choice is involved" when we experience that by which "we are said to be moved" (40–41; II.5; 1105b-1106a). On the other hand, our "capacity" to be "moved" by our passions is essential to the attainment of virtue, which represents the supreme consequence of voluntary action. Thus, although virtue is not a passion, the "right" judgment on which virtue depends affects one's emotional experience. Virtue, then, must be felt in relation "to the right person, to the right extent, at the right time, for the right reason, and in the right way..." (50, II.9; 1109a). In consequence, as Aristotle infers in his *Rhetoric*, the rightness of one's judgments will eventuate in indignation at the

My questions are not merely rhetorical, for in his *Rhetoric* Aristotle names the class of vulnerabilities of which the infant Oedipus might be considered to be exemplary, even though in the *Poetics* Aristotle does not think to use this category to understand the onset of Oedipus' life. "All unpleasant and painful things excite pity," Aristotle writes,

> if they tend to destroy and annihilate; and all such evils as are due to chance, if they are serious. The painful and destructive evils are: death in its various forms, bodily injuries and afflictions, old age, disease, lack of food. The evils due to chance are: friendlessness, scarcity of friends (it is a pitiful thing to be torn away from friends and companions), deformity, weakness, *mutilation*, evil *coming from a source from which good ought to have come*; and the frequent repetition of such misfortunes.[18]

If mimesis begins in childhood and is natural to humans, would not the new-born be the very figure of nascent mimesis, and would not the spectacle of

---

"unmerited good fortune" that befalls others and pity at "their unmerited distress" (*Rhetoric and Poetics*, trans. Rhys Roberts and Ingram Bywater [New York: The Modern Library, 1954], 115; II.8). In other words, pity is not simply or exclusively involuntary. To feel pity requires analysis, discrimination, and evaluation, for the undeserved nature of another's suffering is not a given but a perception that depends on the development and education of one's moral judgment. In consequence, pity foregrounds the difference between subject and object, the one who pities and the one who is pitied, for the act of pitying, which must be at least partially voluntary, is different from the person pitied, whose pitiable circumstances might, in fact, be entirely involuntary. To be virtuous, the one who pities must do so voluntarily. The one who pities voluntarily must also be able to recognize an infanticidal attitude, as Aristotle tacitly suggests when he reflects on acts that cannot easily be classified as either voluntary or involuntary but are both. Thus, "a problem arises in regard to actions that are done through fear of a greater evil or for some noble purpose, for instance, if a tyrant were to use a man's parents or children as hostages in ordering him to commit a base deed, making their survival or death depend on his compliance or refusal. Are actions of this kind voluntary or involuntary?" They would be, in fact, "of a mixed nature, although they come closer to being voluntary than to being involuntary actions ... Such actions, then, are voluntary, although in themselves they are perhaps involuntary, since nobody would choose to do any one of them for its own sake" (Aristotle, *Nichomachean Ethics*, 52–53; III.1; 1110a). In the myth of Laius, the roles of tyrant, victim, and hostage are repeatedly displaced, such that it is the guest who holds a king's son hostage, and it is this same man who years later in effect holds his own son hostage. And if Laius appears to be under threat from Apollo, then it is the god himself who holds the infant Oedipus prisoner to his will. In all these scenarios, Aristotle finds it difficult to understand "mixed actions" precisely when he imagines an infanticidal scenario and misses the opportunity to clarify its pertinence for understanding the nature of pity and its relation to moral virtue.

18   Aristotle, *Rhetoric and Poetics*, 114; Book II, Ch. 8; 1386a.

THE INFANTICIDAL LOGIC OF MIMESIS AS HORIZON OF IMAGINABLE 211

parents pitilessly mutilating their otherwise healthy infant, abandoning it in the wilderness to die of exposure or to be devoured by predators, constitute the voluntary commission of an evil by "a source," a parental source, "from which good ought to have come"? Indeed, what if the evil were perpetrated by the state's central paternal authority, the one person charged with securing the good of the entire polity, most especially the young through whom the polis (in the case at hand, the city-state of Thebes) has its future? Would not this evil be precisely the luck of the draw for the child thus detested, the mischance of having been born to hate-filled parents who seek to exterminate it before its mimesis-driven development can begin? And, further, would not the imagination and representation of this evil constitute *the* clarifying purpose, *the* purifying aim of the dramatic enactment that Aristotle defines in terms of the psycho-mimetic affect of pity? Would the parents' evil not arouse precisely the two emotions that Aristotle attributes to the particular mimetic efficacy of tragedy's cathartic power?

For Aristotle, of course, the forms of poetry, including "the composition of tragedy," are species of imitation—in fact, of mimetic affective regulation. Thus, the mimetic power of tragedy, which is "an imitation of an action that is admirable, complete and possesses magnitude," comes from "effecting through pity and fear the purification of such emotions," from the way tragic action produces a cathartic relief from the primal affect that it arouses.[19] In the *Rhetoric*, Aristotle clarifies how tragic mimesis brings about such catharsis—that is, by imagining certain disasters that excite pity, by dramatizing these catastrophes, by putting such pity-evoking evils "before our eyes," and by symbolically or metonymically linking them to other like disasters:

> it follows that those who heighten the effect of their words with suitable gestures, tones, dress, and dramatic action generally, are especially successful in exciting pity: they thus *put the disasters before our eyes*, and make them seem close to us, just coming or just past. Anything that has just happened, or is going to happen soon, is particularly piteous: so too therefore are the *tokens* and the actions of sufferers—the garments and the like of those who have already suffered; the words and the like of those actually suffering.[20]

And yet Aristotle backs away from this demonstrative conclusion precisely when the disaster is the loss of an adult son. Again, from his *Rhetoric*: "Amasis

---

19   Aristotle, *Poetics*, 10; 49b.
20   Aristotle, *Rhetoric and Poetics*, 115; Book II, Ch. 9; 1386a-b.

did not weep, they say, at the sight of his son being led to death, but did weep when he saw his friend begging; the latter sight was pitiful, the former terrible, and the terrible is different from the pitiful; it tends to cast out pity, and often helps to produce the opposite of pity."[21] What about the loss of a child being carried to its intended death? What about the torture and abandonment of an infant, its life as yet involuntary, who is borne away under orders to be disposed of? Of this prospect, dramatized in Sophocles' *Oedipus the King*, Aristotle is silent, both in his *Rhetoric* and his *Poetics*, despite the fact that Oedipus' ankles along with the "swaddling clothes" in which he explicitly imagines his abandoned infant body had been wrapped are just the kinds of "tokens" Aristotle will characterize as piteous. According to Thomas Gould, "The word *spargana*, 'baby wrappings,' 'swaddling clothes,' is used in tragedy and comedy to refer to tokens ... by which the parents (or others) can later identify an exposed child."[22] If the others include Oedipus' fellow Thebans, then is Oedipus not asking to be identified—decades later—precisely as having been pitilessly mutilated and exposed, precisely as having been an intended infanticide? And if the others also include contemporary readers two-and-a-half millennia later, then is he not asking of us a similar recognition?

Tokens imaged or named, of course, are not the same as the imaging or naming of the tokens; the disaster put before one's eyes is not the same as the act of putting them there, of making them visible, of imagining or evoking them, of bringing them close in order to feel their devastating emotional consequences. In the canonical readings of Sophocles' tragedy, the disaster at hand—infanticidal aggression—either remains invisible or is brushed aside with little or no regard for the lifelong suffering of the child who survived the assault and abandonment. Such pitiless readings turn a blind eye to—they refuse to imagine—Oedipus as infant victim and instead attend to the charges (a regicide that is also a patricide, and incest) that Oedipus appears to accept as the abominable fate or destiny to which his own courageous inquiry into the death of the former king had, nearly all commentators suppose, blindly and ironically led him. How has the terrible violence of Laius and Jocasta against the body of their infant son been missed? Why has it been largely ignored by a tradition of literary commentary that accuses Sophocles' protagonist of violent transgressions that this tradition refuses to see evinced in the horrific parental violence perpetrated against Oedipus? Where is the expression of pity, which Aristotle considers to be tragedy's very telos, toward Oedipus in the history of the reception of Sophocles' drama? How has the tradition so relentlessly

---

21 Aristotle *Rhetoric and Poetics*, 145; Book II, Ch. 8; 1386a.

22 Gould, *Oedipus the King by Sophocles*, 124n1035.

THE INFANTICIDAL LOGIC OF MIMESIS AS HORIZON OF IMAGINABLE 213

mimed the casting out of the luckless son by casting out its pity for the victimized newborn?

Canonical readings of Oedipus are not only pitiless in their attitude toward the life history of Oedipus but unseeing with respect to the multiple efforts that Oedipus makes to bring his infanticidal heritage before the uncomprehending collective gaze of his Thebans subjects. I have elsewhere analyzed how Oedipus endeavors to communicate his cultural critique in a kingdom beleaguered by a plague the blame for which his political antagonists, his brother-in-law Creon and the state's seer Teiresias, wish to lay at his feet.[23] Here, I will restrict my exposition to underscoring how Oedipus himself tacitly interprets the Theban plague as the return of a kingdom-wide repression by enacting the meaning of pity as an antidote to infanticide.

Oedipus repeatedly speaks in the name of the pity that he, the survivor of a pitiless birth, feels for the children of Thebes. As the play opens, Oedipus addresses a group of sons and daughters, "chosen" to represent all the youth of the city-state, and the priest who supplicates the king on their behalf: "My *children*, ancient Cadmus' *newest care* ... ,"[24] Oedipus says. The next time Oedipus speaks, which is after hearing the priest describe the blight that has devastated all agricultural and animal production and that has rendered women barren or made them miscarry,[25] it is to declare his pity for all the children whose care is his most basic kingly responsibility: "*Pitiable children*," he calls out to them.[26]

These references to pity contrast with the absence of this emotional orientation among the Thebans, an absence that is *the* defining feature of the plague. The chorus of elders explicitly characterize the plague's productivity and reproductivity disastrousness in terms of Thebes's collective pitilessness, a pitilessness from which they beseech Oedipus to save them: "What our glorious earth gives birth to does not grow," they bemoan. "Without a birth from cries of labor do the women rise ... And with their deaths the unnumbered the city

---

23   Although many scholars acknowledge that Laius mutilated his son and attempted to have him die, they have not seen cause to interpret Sophocles' tragedy as a critique of the infanticidal father. This is not surprising in light of the fact that the battered child syndrome was not named as such until 1962 (see David Bakan, *Slaughter of the Innocents: A Study of the Battered Child Phenomenon* [Boston: Beacon Press, 1971], 10; see also C. Henry Kempe, accessed April 29, 2019, http://www.kempe.org/about/history/), and that the first systematic investigation of and theorizing about animal infanticide as evolutionarily adaptive rather than as anomalous did not occur until 1984 (see Glenn Hausfater and Sarah Blaffer Hrdy, *Infanticide: Comparative and Evolutionary Perspectives* [New York: Alidine, 1984]).

24   Gould, *Oedipus the King by Sophocles*, 13, l. 1.

25   Gould, *Oedipus the King by Sophocles*, 16, ll. 25–27.

26   Gould, *Oedipus the King by Sophocles*, 22, l. 58.

dies. Her children lie *unpitied* on the ground, spreading death, unmourned..."[27] Unpitied, their corpses are in plain sight, exposed to the elements, in stark and dramatic contrast to the body of the son Laius had ordered be left unmourned, out of sight, and presumably undiscoverable in the aforementioned "trackless" wilderness of Mount Cithaeron.

In pursuing the source of the plague, which Creon reports on his return from Delphi is the unavenged murder of the former king,[28] Oedipus would seem to be unwittingly embarking on a path of discovery that will reveal him to be the cause of the (re)productivity calamity at hand. And yet he has a defense against the charge that he is the one who killed Laius, since the sole survivor of the attack that left Laius dead had years before declared in public that "bandits chanced on [Laius's retinue] and killed him—with the force of many hands, not one alone,"[29] whereas Oedipus confesses to have killed a small group of hostile travelers with no help from others.[30] As Oedipus explains to Jocasta about the testimony the survivor, now a herdsman, had given to all of Thebes: "You said he spoke of robbers as the ones who killed [Laius]. Now: if he continues still to speak of many, then I could not have killed him. One man and many men just do not jibe."[31] The entire plot—the Aristotelian "source and (as it were) the soul of tragedy,"[32] the pity-evoking heart of tragic drama—turns on Oedipus' intention to question the survivor about the number of assailants. Oedipus suggests that if the herdsman says that one alone assailed the former king, then "the doubt is gone. The balance tips toward me. I did it."[33] Jocasta demurs: "No! He told it as I told you. Be certain. He can't reject that and reverse himself. The city heard these things, not I alone."[34] The next 332 lines prepare for the cross-examination, and yet Oedipus never asks the herdsman the question that is his sole purpose in summoning him. Why not? The answer involves the way in which Oedipus allows a messenger from Corinth to lead the witness and thus to implicate the ruler himself, and then the way in which Oedipus forecloses his interrogation of this man before asking him the plot-driving question: Did one man or many kill the former king?

---

27   Gould, *Oedipus the King by Sophocles*, 36–37. ll. 171–82.

28   Gould, *Oedipus the King by Sophocles*, 28–29, ll. 99–107.

29   Gould, *Oedipus the King by Sophocles*, 31, ll. 122–23.

30   Gould, *Oedipus the King by Sophocles*, 100–01, ll. 798–813.

31   Gould, *Oedipus the King by Sophocles*, 105, ll. 842–45.

32   Aristotle, *Poetics*, 12; 50b.

33   Gould, *Oedipus the King by Sophocles*, 105, ll. 846–47.

34   Gould, *Oedipus the King by Sophocles*, 106, ll. 848–50.

After Oedipus sends for the herdsman, a Corinthian delegate arrives to announce the death of this city-state's king, Polybus, whom Oedipus has just said he has always believed to be his father. In an exchange that defies credulity, Oedipus, the only one to solve the riddle of the Sphinx, seems not to understand the messenger's hints that Oedipus was adopted and that he would not be at risk of the prophesied patricide were he to assume the kingship of his foster city.[35] The Corinthian then claims to recognize in Oedipus' swollen feet the aforementioned "tokens" of the infant he once rescued[36] and gave to Polybus, who raised the child as his own. When the herdsman arrives, the Corinthian further claims to recognize him as the shepherd from whom he had received the discarded son of Laius. Despite the empirical impossibility of recognizing in the facial and other features of the adult Oedipus what he would have looked like as a newborn infant, the herdsman reluctantly agrees that Oedipus is the very person not Laius, the audience might have expected, but rather Jocasta had ordered him to destroy. The herdsman says that Jocasta gave him the mutilated child who "was reported to have been [Laius's] son."[37] Oedipus asks: "What was her purpose?" The herdsman answers: "I was to kill the boy" in order to avoid the "dreaded prophecies" that he would "kill his parents."[38] (The herdsman does not mention the charge of incest that the blind seer, Tieresias, had earlier leveled against Oedipus, a charge also absent in the report Creon gives of the oracular explanation for the cause of the plague.) At the climactic moment of his cross-examination, Oedipus asks: "Then why did you give him up to this old man [the Corinthian]?" To which the herdsman responds: "In *pity*, master, so he would take him home, to another land."[39] I underscore the herdsman's eye-witness testimony: "In pity." It is his pity that motivated him to defy the royal command of Laius (or is it of Jocasta, or both?) to destroy the infant. It is through his pity that Oedipus lives. It is by the herdsman's pity, then, that the Apollonian curse comes to pass. Having elicited the recognition that the infant Laius hated survived because of the pity felt by strangers, Oedipus has put the affective solution to the riddle of what plagues Thebes in the mouth of the one who is called to bear witness to the helplessness that inspired him to disobey a king's orders and save an infant. The riddle of the plague is its unrecognized infanticidal meaning, a meaning that Thebes

---

35 See Gould, *Oedipus the King by Sophocles*, 120–22, ll. 994–1020.

36 Gould, *Oedipus the King by Sophocles*, 122–23, ll. 1025–034.

37 Gould, *Oedipus the King by Sophocles*, 134, l. 1171.

38 Gould, *Oedipus the King by Sophocles*, 134–35, ll. 1174–176.

39 Gould, *Oedipus the King by Sophocles*, 135, ll. 1177–178.

refuses, that the curse of Apollo rationalizes, and that the canonical readings of the play have not been able to imagine.

Oedipus has brought this meaning *to the lips* of the herdsman. To put this meaning *before the eyes* of his people, Oedipus blinds himself by destroying not his *cycloi* but his *arthra*, the unusual word for which Sophocles alone uses to mean eyes, and that he has earlier in the play employed to mean ankles. Laius had pierced the "ball joints" that are Oedipus' ankles, and Oedipus mimes this infanticidal aggression when he pierces the "ball-joints" that are his eyes.[40] In Aristotle's aforementioned words, Oedipus thereby puts the infanticidal disaster of his advent before the gaze of his people so that they might see not *his* ironic blindness but *their own*, might not behold *his* tragic demise when he confronts an autobiographical truth he had not anticipated but *their* collective aversion to an unimaginable truth that is inscribed in what plagues their society. Alas, to no avail. "This suffering sends terror through men's eyes, terrible beyond any suffering my eyes have touched," the chorus cry out, recoiling not in pity but in aversion: "I cannot look at you—though there's so much I would ask you, so much to hear, so much that holds my eyes—so awesome the convulsions you send through me." And yet Oedipus does not want to terrify his people but to evoke their compassion: "Ah! Ah! I am a man of misery," he cries out. "Where am I carried? *Pity* me!"[41] Referring his desire to be pitied to the circumstances of his birth, Oedipus subsequently asks, in his apostrophe to the mountain wilderness: "Alas, Cithaeron, why did you receive me? Or when you had me, not killed me instantly? I'd not have had to show my birth to mankind"[42]—not his alleged crimes but *his birth* and the mutilation of his body and attempted infanticide that followed. Or, again, as he importunes Creon: "let me live on mountains—on Cithaeron famed as mine, for my mother and my father, while they yet lived, made it my destined tomb..."[43]

Evoking the specter of his jeopardy in infancy, Oedipus beseeches Creon to care for his "two wretched and pitiable girls" in the language that is the antidote to infanticide.[44] He thereby contrasts himself to his father, as the classicist Charles Segal emphasizes: Oedipus "does not perpetuate in his own life his father's aggression against his child," Segal acknowledges.[45] In fact, "In regarding his daughters with *compassion* [in other words, *pity*] rather than with

---

40   See Gould, *Oedipus the King by Sophocles*, 46-46n261; 93n718; 123n1032; and 145n1270.

41   Gould, *Oedipus the King by Sophocles*, 147–48, ll. 1297–309.

42   Gould, *Oedipus the King by Sophocles*, 155, ll. 1391–393.

43   Gould, *Oedipus the King by Sophocles*, 161, ll. 1451–453.

44   Gould, *Oedipus the King by Sophocles*, 163, l. 1462; see also 164–66, ll. 1480–514.

45   Charles Segal, *Oedipus Tyrannus: Tragic Heroism and the Limits of Knowledge*, 2nd ed. (New York: Oxford University Press, 2001), 146.

THE INFANTICIDAL LOGIC OF MIMESIS AS HORIZON OF IMAGINABLE   217

abhorrence, violence, or rejection, and in trying to *provide for their future*, Oedipus has drastically reversed the treatment that he received from Laius and Jocasta."[46] And yet Segal cannot bring himself to integrate his glimpse of parental violence with his interpretation of the protagonist's existential transformation. Thus, although Segal can believe that "Oedipus overcomes in himself the animal brutishness of incest and parricide,"[47] he leaves unremarked the fact that Oedipus has survived the pitiless infanticidal aggression of his parents to become the pitying king of the Thebans, his symbolic "children," as he repeatedly addresses them. The eyes and ears of his community are as uncomprehending as are those of the tradition that convicts Oedipus and that then protects itself from the guilt associated with this scapegoating interpretation by extolling him as one of western literature's exemplary tragic figures.

This tradition, like Oedipus' Theban citizenry, evidently cannot countenance the implications of the literal meaning of Oedipus' name. Near the beginning of the play, when Oedipus asks why Thebes had never tracked down the murderers (plural) of Laius, Creon answers: "when Laius was killed, we had no one to help us in our troubles"—those brought on by the Sphinx's siege. Oedipus then asks: "What kind of trouble blocked you from a search [literally 'stood in the way of your feet?" Creon responds: "The subtle-singing Sphinx asked us to turn [literally "to look to"] from the obscure to what lay at our feet."[48] To turn to feet, however, is to turn to the origin of Oedipus' name—not his birth name, for he never receives a "proper" name, but the name he adopts when he emigrates from Corinth and defeats the Sphinx, his triumphant reception when he enters the city-state providing him with the immigrant's freedom to assume whatever identity he wishes. Why does Oedipus fabricate just the identity that everyone presumes is his birth name when, in fact, he was discarded before being properly named in the *amphidromia*, the walking-around-the-hearth ceremony at which the newborn *brephos*, not yet a person claimed by its father, became a *pais*, a child with the right to life by virtue of being formally named and accepted into the paternal household?[49] Because

---

46   Segal, *Oedipus Tyrannus: Tragic Heroism and the Limits of Knowledge*, 146.
47   Segal, *Oedipus Tyrannus: Tragic Heroism and the Limits of Knowledge*, 146.
48   Gould, *Oedipus the King by Sophocles*, see 31–32, ll. 126–31, and 32n131.
49   According to Cynthia Patterson, "Killing or causing the death of a newborn child (very often called a *brephos*, a term also used to refer to the fetus in the womb) in the first days of life was something quite different—legally, morally, and terminologically it seems—from killing a child [*pais*] who was a recognized and named member of a family." That recognition occurred during the *amphidromia*, also known as the *dekatê*, the tenth-day naming ceremony. The Greeks thus distinguished exposure, "a limited and specific act affecting not a recognized member of the household or *oikos* but rather a newborn

he wants us to hear not merely the literal meaning of the noun phrase that symbolically betokens his infancy but the narrative this noun phrase summarizes: "my parents hated me and wanted me dead, but I survived by the kindness of strangers who pitied me."

At the end of the tragedy, it should be no wonder that Oedipus would mourn his abandonment by the very gods themselves—not, however, for *his* crimes but for the sins *of his parents*, whose mortal abandonment of their child these gods mime: "I am the gods' most hated man," Oedipus laments;[50] he is *echthistos*, most hated, this hatred giving the last emphasis to the absence of pity from the gods. Oedipus refers specifically to Apollo, whom the Greeks worshipped at Delphi, the name of which is the plural form of *delphus*, "womb."[51] Apollo should be understood as the uterine god whose generative blessing depends not on his divine favor but on the attitude with which the newborn is greeted by mortal parents. If Oedipus is the pitiless target of Apollo, it is not because he is guilty of patricide and incest but because his parents sought to take away the life they have begotten, and because years later their kingdom has multiplied this earlier pitilessness, reproducing its infanticidal consequences. It is this pitiless infanticidal violence Oedipus would bring to light, a different kind of light, an amimetic light, than that provided by the Apollonian sun god.

3 Oedipus as Visitant from an Impossible Futurity

From Aristotle to the present, Oedipus is read as a mimetic character. He is the biological son of the Theban king and queen, Laius and Jocasta, and the adopted son of Corinth's rulers, Polybus and Merope. Doubting his parentage, he visits Apollo's oracle, where he hears of his appalling future. To avoid this destiny, he flees and on his way to Thebes is assaulted by highway robbers, whom he kills. Oedipus' history (part biography, part autobiography), however, is established only by attestation, Oedipus' or someone else's; neither the individual events of this history nor their concatenation into a teleologically determined life trajectory, to which Oedipus is ostensibly ironically blind, are ever verified outside of someone's uncorroborated testimony. Indeed, as several

---

brephos who had as yet no place within the family unit" ("'Not Worth the Rearing': The Causes of Infant Exposure in Ancient Greece," *TAPA/ Transactions and Proceedings of the American Philological Association* 115 [1985], 105). In other words, "The critical distinction is not between killing and letting die but between *pais* and *brephos*" (105n6).

50 Gould, *Oedipus the King by Sophocles*, 167, l. 1519.

51 Watkins, *The American Heritage Dictionary of Indo-European Roots*, 34.

THE INFANTICIDAL LOGIC OF MIMESIS AS HORIZON OF IMAGINABLE   219

scholars have noted, Oedipus' guilt is also never factually established.[52] In other words, in his tragedy Sophocles suspends the empirical. Why? The answer, I propose, is that such bracketing enables Oedipus to speak (while simultaneously condemning him to the role of scapegoat, the existential cost he must pay in order to attempt his infanticidal critique) as the voice of an unimaginable because impossible future, a future that cannot be named as such, a future that violates the etymological meaning of *future* as the *being* that *will be*,[53] a future that is not to be and that therefore cannot be translated in terms of an ontological predication, a future that cannot be conceived mimetically, an amimetic infanticidal future. Through the example of the infanticidal fate he has escaped, Oedipus becomes a figure of how each human life occurs within an economy of incalculable—which is to say unimaginable—loss.

The Thebans have not been able to imagine such futurity as the archive of the non-empirical deathliness that attaches to life as life's inconceivable costliness. They understand death only empirically—that is, as their personal loss and the like loss suffered by their friends and neighbors. They do not apprehend that these losses constitute only one manifestation of the general economy within which life "is" lifedeath; and that within this economy, the plague is an empirical translation (a reduction to an empirical concept) of the non-empirical deathliness that "is" the backdrop of all existence.

At the same time, however, in their emotional response to the plague, the chorus of Theban citizens are on the verge of intuiting this more general infanticidal economy, for the plague confronts them with a communal loss that overwhelms their cognitive capacity to represent in rational, arithmetic terms. Thus, the deaths of "her children" are "unnumbered"[54]—that is, unimaginable, but in two different ways. The first unimaginableness is, once again, empirical: the deathliness is so widespread and the cause so mysterious that, though the Thebans can register its devastation, they cannot take the proper measure, cannot calculate, the extent of their suffering. The second unimaginableness, however, is non-empirical: the deathliness at hand is the threatened loss of the

---

52   See Frederick Ahl, *Sophocles' "Oedipus": Evidence and Self-Conviction* (Ithaca: Cornell University Press, 1991); Sandor Goodheart, "*Λῃστὰζ Εφαχε*: Oedipus and Laius' Many Murderers." *Diacritics* 8.1 (1978); and Philip Vellacott, *Sophocles and Oedipus: A Study of Oedipus Tyrannus with a New Translation* (Ann Arbor: University of Michigan Press, 1971).

53   *Future* derives from the Latin *futūrus*, "that is to be." Although *be* derives from the Old English *bēon*, its Germanic source, **biju*, "I am, will be," like the Latin *futūrus*, descends from a common Indo-European root, *bheuə*, "to be, exist, grow" (Watkins, *The American Heritage Dictionary of Indo-European Roots*, 12).

54   Gould, *Oedipus the King by Sophocles*, 37, ll. 180–81.

city-state itself and with it the future existence of the entire people, who are able to survive the death of any individual child or even whole groups of children but not the death of itself *in toto*. Confronted with the unimaginable prospect of its self-annihilation, Thebes begins to glimpse its precarious existence this side of its near-apocalyptic disappearance—near-apocalyptic rather than absolutely apocalyptic insofar as the empirical world beyond Thebes were to survive Thebes' demise as Thebes itself has lived on despite the hitherto secret of their former king's infanticidal violence. That violence is the cost the former king calculated he must pay in order to protect himself from the curse that would destroy his kingship, a cost he wanted to conceal; it is also the cost, likewise invisible to his kingdom, that his kingdom has tacitly paid in order to have him as their king. In relation to this calculated costliness, the plague descends on Thebes not only as an empirical disaster but as another order of disastrousness altogether, one that entails the recognition of the non-empirical deathliness that attaches to and is the aforementioned backdrop of each and every person's individual existence. So Oedipus understands: the plague is a visible disaster that points to the unimaginable disaster that can never be made visible, that can never be imagined as such.

When the herdsman appears to recognize in Oedipus the mutilated child he had saved, decades earlier, out of pity, Oedipus accepts this man's testimony not because it is reliable, not because it is what happened in fact, but because it describes the condition of radical neonatal vulnerability and dependency into which all children are born, a condition all adults have survived, their survival thus translating the meaning of the man who calls himself "Oedipus." We are all like Oedipus in having been exposed, if not to the enacted violence of parents or others, nevertheless to the possibility of such violence. Surviving this possibility, we have lives that have been purchased at a cost that is necessarily beyond imagination. Why? Because the cost in question is the incalculable sum of the alternative futures (which depend on or arise from all the non-actualizable events that constitute these alternative temporal trajectories) that the life of any individual prevents from coming to pass, including the prospect of a life infanticidally extinguished shortly after its birth.

Insofar as Oedipus' people accept the report that he was victimized by his parents, insofar as Oedipus himself can imagine that his mutilated feet are not a birth defect but a deliberate assault from a father who did not want him to live, this person can stand before his world as a figure who embodies one of the many futures that his father chose against, including the specific future that this Apollo-cursed father hoped to escape. Under these (auto)biographical circumstances, Oedipus "is" or "would be"—if the ontological predicate were still pertinent—a figure of all the futures that, in being chosen against, will not

THE INFANTICIDAL LOGIC OF MIMESIS AS HORIZON OF IMAGINABLE 221

come to pass. That is why it is so important to avoid the common interpretive error of thinking that Oedipus has discovered his guiltiness as an empirical fact, for if he has, then he is merely a son who is embroiled in a family conflict in which he takes unwitting revenge and winds up the ironic victim of his incomplete knowledge. If his guilt is not empirically established, however, he becomes a figure of what his kingdom has collectively denied (namely, the pitiless destruction of the heir to the kingdom); and thus he is not only a ghost, not merely the return of *a past* that his culture has repressed, but a spectral figure of the *indeterminate futurity* that would have come to pass had the former king pitied his child. That is, he is not a real visitor from a future that will come to pass but something like a *visitant*.[55] In being an "Oedipus," someone who was to be left to die unburied in a "trackless" landscape and thus condemned to leaving no remains, Oedipus would be the dead child and its lost future; in addition, he would be the deathliness more generally of all the lost futures that any life entails and that can never be "tracked" or archived. In this respect, Oedipus is not a person but the figure of the lost futurity that is lost as lost. In other words, Oedipus hails from an unimaginable future that, if it could speak, would give voice to the lost opportunities that occur whenever humans choose and so set in motion one future and not all the other possible futures that will never be heard beckoning human ears. Oedipus personifies these futures as an "oedipus," as a "swell-foot" intended for non-existence. He "is" the particular future his parents did not want, the future they hoped would not be; and he "is" the more general futurity, the infinite futurity, that is lost (and lost as lost) whenever a person decides and thus allocates resources one way rather than another—which includes, paradigmatically, whenever a child, this child and

---

55   I mean by *visitant* a version of what Jacques Derrida calls the *arrivant*, a strange figure of and from a futurity that, on the one hand, does not happen, that does not come to pass, that does not become present, that therefore "is" impossible to designate by any ontological predicate; but that, on the other hand, "is" nevertheless the very possibility of this impossibility. Of the "absolute *arrivant*," Derrida says that he means "whatever, whoever, in arriving, does not cross a threshold separating two identifiable places, the proper and the foreign, the proper of the one and the proper of the other, as one would say that the citizen of a given identifiable country crosses the border of another as a traveler, an emigré or a political exile, a refugee ... The absolute *arrivant* does not yet have a name or an identity" and is "not someone or something that arrives, a subject, a person, an individual, or a living thing, even less one of the migrants I just mentioned" (Jacques Derrida, *Aporias*, trans. Thomas Dutoit [Stanford: Stanford University Press, 1993], 34). If revenants and ghosts, including the returning to the present of what once did come to pass, "are" figures of the *arrivant*, the visitant "would be" not that which dies but that which "is" the deathliness of life, that which delimits the impossible futurity that is the other side of the now possible future that can arrive.

not a different child, is conceived. No longer simply a mimetic character, Oedipus "is" the very amimetic non-existence of the non-existent futures that "would be" alternative to the future that will come to pass.

From out of this amimetic archive, Oedipus *emerges* onto the stage as a mimetic character who attempts to designate the non-existent futurity in question, the withdrawal of life that is the condition of the possibility of life, by refusing a proper name and instead calling himself a name that signifies the death that was meant for him.[56] The amimetic visitant from a future that will never be the future, Oedipus must be blamed, scapegoated, and exiled for his culture's mimetic *emergency*.

Such a prospect has been unimaginable to the tradition that has been unable to conceive of the infanticidal horizon of human existence. And so Oedipus is not interpreted as the personification of all those humans who have been left to die without a trace; nor, more radically, is he encountered as the strange figure (for which there is no concept) of all those who might have been but were not conceived, birthed, and cared for. He is not understood as the voice of all the losses that are themselves lost. Nor is he recognized as the impossible figuration in the present of a future that will never come to pass and thus that will never be able to be mimetically represented. Rather, he is regarded as a specific individual who is overtaken by events that are able to be mimetically figured, with the consequence that this figuration immunizes the Thebans in the play, Sophocles' Athenian audience, and subsequently Sophocles' and Aristotle's readers from seeing in their assignment of responsibility to Oedipus that they are repeating Laius and Jocasta's infanticidal aggression against their child. A recognition of Oedipus as a figure of lost opportunity would constitute a catharsis that is beyond Aristotelian catharsis; it would be an inconceivable catharsis of catharsis, which is to say a catharsis without catharsis.

4 Coda: Thinking Contra-conceptively beyond the Imaginable

Elsewhere, relying on the work of Page duBois, Robert Con Davis, and Jacques Derrida, I have examined how the western world conceives of thought as

---

56   He thus lives as one who literally embodies what Derrida calls "the gift of death." See Derrida, *The Gift of Death*, 2nd ed., trans. David Wills (Chicago: University of Chicago Press, 2007), especially his analysis of the *Akedah*, the narrative of God's call to Abraham to sacrifice his son Isaac, in Chapter three, "Whom to Give to (Knowing Not to Know)" (53–81), and his analysis of the gift of death (acronymically GOD), in Chapter four, "*Tout autre est tout autre*" (82–115).

THE INFANTICIDAL LOGIC OF MIMESIS AS HORIZON OF IMAGINABLE 223

conceptive, how it posits the essential generativity of conceptuality, how it equates thinking with being.[57] As duBois (1988) has demonstrated, Plato does so by drawing an analogy between thinking and conceiving. As duBois and Davis (1993) demonstrate, Aristotle literalizes Plato's analogy and explicitly locates the generativity of thinking in the male. Throughout his corpus, Derrida, of course, seeks to deconstruct this "ontotheological" tradition in which being is conceived not only as presence but as self-presencing—that is, self-begetting.

When Derrida subjects the experience of thinking to his radical phenomenological reduction, he is able to show how thought appears to be spontaneously self-producing, as if it were independent of any material support or mediation (linguistic or otherwise), as if its signified content had no need of any "accessory signifier," but arose entirely from out of its own immateriality. Unlike Plato and Aristotle and the philosophical inheritors of the thinking they inaugurated, however, Derrida concludes that the experience in question "is not merely one illusion among many" but the founding metaphysical illusion whereby the truth of being is precomprehended in and as "pure auto-affection," pure self-production.[58]

If so, then thought would have as its limit horizon the relation of what is to what is not, to what cannot come to pass, to the loss that is lost as lost and that is the precondition of what is not lost, to the incalculable subtraction of possible life in the reproductive advent of any individual life, and therefore to what is not conceivable or imaginable. Sophocles' Oedipus ought to be read, then, with an eye to the amimetic economy—the aneconomy—in which life "is" lifedeath. This tragic figure ought to be recalled from the cultural archive that has been so constituted as to resist registering the infanticidal shadow cast by the Apollonian sun god.[59] A character who bears the name of an unnamed victim, of the repudiated child whose parents did not want him to live, he

---

57 See A. Samuel Kimball, "Counter-Conceiving the Law of the Father," Chapter 6 in *The Infanticidal Logic of Evolution and Culture* (Newark: University of Delaware Press, 2007), 165–83.

58 Jacques Derrida, *Of Grammatology*, corrected ed., trans. Gayatry Chakravorty Spivak (Baltimore: Johns Hopkins University Press, 1997), 20.

59 In *Archive Fever*, Jacques Derrida locates in the cultural formations that make up a society's archival memory a strange deconstructive economy of preservation *and* destruction, which upsets the categorical opposition of life and death. As Derrida explains, the very logic of archivization destroys the archive as the place and repository of the memory it is designed to keep. The archivization of memory requires the mortality of those whose memories the archive keeps "alive." Unless human memory is transferrable to and storable in a non-human medium, able to be inscribed on a different kind of substrate than that of the mind or psyche, able to be archived outside of human consciousness—unless memory be detachable from the person who would remember, no archive would occur.

(See *Archive Fever: A Freudian Impression,* trans. Eric Prenowitz, [Chicago: University of Chicago Press, 1995]).

The transferability of memory is its iterability in a context other than and divorceable from the context of its production. Thus, what Derrida has written about "readability" applies to the retrievability of archival memory: "In order for my 'written communication' to retain its function as writing, i.e., its readability, it must remain readable despite the absolute disappearance of any receiver, determined in general. My communication must be repeatable—iterable—in the absolute absence of the receiver or of any empirically determinable collectivity of receivers. ... A writing that is not structurally readable—iterable—beyond the death of the addressee would not be writing" Jacques Derrida, "Signature Event Context," *Limited Inc* [Evanston: Northwestern University Press, 1977, 1988], 7.

Iterability makes possible the transferability and retrievability of memory but at the cost of destroying the "life" of memory: Thus, Derrida insists, the archive "will never be either memory or anamnesis as spontaneous, alive and internal experience. On the contrary: the archive takes place at the place of originary and structural breakdown of the said memory" (Derrida, *Archive Fever: A Freudian Impression,* 11).

The amimetic "economy" of this breakdown is evident in the lost opportunity that attends any (archived) decision, as is readily evident in any allocation of scarce resources. As has been noted, insofar as such allocation sets in motion a trajectory of possibility, it cuts off all the trajectories of possibility that different allocations of resources might have initiated. In marking the commencement of a given future, of what comes to pass and thus of what becomes subject to remembrance, the archivable event of decision destroys the aforementioned incalculable futurity—all the other futures, henceforth no longer possible, that will not come to pass and thus will not become subject to recollection; all the futurity that is lost in advance of commencing; all the loss that cannot be named as lost, that defies mimetic representation, that is lost as lost, and thus that is unimaginable as unimaginable.

Since lost opportunity destroys the archive from within the very activity of archiving any and all decision, it revalues the "economy" of the archive as amimetic—that is, as the evacuation of any reserve that could be retrieved, drawn or capitalized on, and converted to mimetic representation.

The amimetic "economy"—the "aneconomy"—of the breakdown of memory expresses a non-visible, non-presentable danger, a destructive and mute operation that Freud names the death drive. The death drive destroys the archive, "since it always operates in silence" and "never leaves any archives of its own." In fact, "It destroys in advance its own archive..." (Derrida, *Archive Fever: A Freudian Impression,* 10). And yet, as repetition compulsion, as the iterability that dispenses with life, and likewise as the incalculable loss of the being that might have been, the anarchivic violence of the death drive is necessary to the very possibility of the archive, since the archive requires the separability of memory from the life and mind in which it arises. In the archive of western literature, this anarchivic violence has left traces of its operation by way of the motif of the child's infanticidal jeopardy, on the one hand, and, on the other hand, the avoidance of naming the child's peril by the commentators whose readings conceal the traces in question. This is especially the case when the readings are offered in the name of mimesis, the paradigmatic program by which the elements of the archive of western literary representation are made to "articulate the unity of an ideal configuration," one that conceals, unimaginably so, its amimetic, anarchivic, death-driven—in short, infanticidal—economy.

ought to be regarded not just as the figure upon whom has been visited a murderousness to which western culture has been blind, but as the stranger through whom unimaginably impossible futures visit a world that cannot accept its own (infanticidal) past, let alone that (infanticidal) futurity of which it cannot conceive.

Pity beyond pity.

References

Ahl, Frederick. *Sophocles' "Oedipus": Evidence and Self-Conviction*. Ithaca: Cornell University Press, 1991.

Apollodorus. *The Library*. Trans. Sir James George Frazer. Loeb Classical Library, Volumes 121 and 122. Cambridge: Harvard University Press, 1921. https://www.theoi.com/Text/%20Apollodorus3.html. Accessed April 29, 2019.

Aristotle. *Nichomachean Ethics*. Trans. Marton Ostwald. Indianpolis: Bobbs-Merrill/The Library of Liberal Arts, 1962.

Aristotle. *Poetics*. Trans. Malcolm Heath. Penguin Books, 1996.

Aristotle. *Politics*. Trans. T.A. Sinclair. Penguin Books, 1972.

Aristotle. *Rhetoric and Poetics*. Trans. Rhys Roberts and Ingram Bywater. New York: The Modern Library, 1954.

Bakan, David. *Slaughter of the Innocents: A Study of the Battered Child Phenomenon*. Boston: Beacon Press, 1971.

Con Davis, Robert. *The Paternal Romance: Reading God-the-Father in Early Western Culture*. Urbana: University of Illinois Press, 1993.

Derrida, Jacques. *Aporias*. Trans. Thomas Dutoit. Stanford: Stanford University Press, 1993.

Derrida, Jacques. *Archive Fever: A Freudian Impression*. Trans. Eric Prenowitz. Chicago: University of Chicago Press, 1995.

Derrida, Jacques. *The Gift of Death*. 2nd ed. Trans. David Wills. Chicago: University of Chicago Press, 2007.

Derrida, Jacques. *Of Grammatology*. Corrected ed. Trans. Gayatry Chakravorty Spivak. Baltimore: Johns Hopkins University Press, 1997.

Derrida, Jacques. "Signature Event Context." *Limited Inc*. Evanston: Northwestern University Press, 1977, 1988.

duBois, Page. "The Platonic Appropriation of Reproduction" and "Conclusion: The Defective Female Body." In *Sowing the Body: Psychoanalysis and Ancient Representations of Women*, 169–83 and 184–88. Chicago: University of Chicago Press, 1988.

Goodhart, Sandor. "Λήσταζ Εφαχε: Oedipus and Laius' Many Murderers." *Diacritics* 8.1 (1978): 8–38.

Gould, Thomas. *Oedipus the King by Sophocles*. Englewood Cliffs: Prentice-Hall, 1970.

Hausfater, Glenn and Sarah Blaffer Hrdy. *Infanticide: Comparative and Evolutionary Perspectives*. New York: Alidine, 1984.

Kempe, C.H. http://www.kempe.org/about/history/. Accessed April 29, 2019.

Kimball, A. Samuel. *The Infanticidal Logic of Evolution and Culture*. Newark: University of Delaware Press, 2007.

Kimball, A. Samuel. "The Wounded Infant and the Infanticidism of the Gods: Oedipus' Cultural Critique." In *The Infanticidal Logic of Evolution and Culture*, 203–30. Newark: University of Delaware Press, 2007. 203–30.

Patterson, Cynthia. "'Not Worth the Rearing': The Causes of Infant Exposure in Ancient Greece." *TAPA/Transactions and Proceedings of the American Philological Association* 115 (1985): 103–23.

Pausanias. *Description of Greece*. Trans. W.H.S. Jones and H.A. Omerod. Loeb Classical Library Volumes. Cambridge: Harvard University Press, 1918. https://www.theoi.com/%20Text/Pausanias9A.html. Accessed April 29, 2019.

Segal, Charles. *Oedipus Tyrannus: Tragic Heroism and the Limits of Knowledge*. 2nd ed. New York: Oxford University Press, 2001.

Shipley, Joseph T. *The Origins of English Words: A Discursive Dictionary of Indo-European Roots*. Baltimore: Johns Hopkins University Press, 1984.

Vellacott, Philip. *Sophocles and Oedipus: A Study of Oedipus Tyrannus with a New Translation*. Ann Arbor: University of Michigan Press, 1971.

Watkins, Calvert, ed. *The American Heritage Dictionary of Indo-European Roots*. Boston: Houghton Mifflin Harcourt, 1985; 3rd ed., 2011.

CHAPTER 10

The Relationship between Imagination and Christian Prayer

Michel Dion

1 Introduction

Marcel Proust said that imagination is the obscure/secret receiver of images.[1] Imagination could be considered as the receiver as well as the real producer of images. However, the way images are created and safeguarded in our memory for an unpredictable duration could indeed remain obscure. We are not quite conscious of the way our imagination produces given images of past and present events and phenomena. Imagination seems interconnected to the unconscious, although we often try to use it consciously. Imagination could be under the control of human will, while being subjected to unconscious wants and desires. The phenomenon of Christian prayers could be analyzed in order to see how imagination is inextricably linked to the act of praying. Christian prayers could be analyzed through semiological, linguistic, philological, philosophical, historical, or religious/spiritual perspectives.

This chapter aims to analyze the structural relationships between imagination and Christian prayer. The analysis involves five interpretative steps. First step: a Wittgensteinian criticism of religious language could lay down the deep challenge of analyzing Christian prayer as a discourse, that is, as a text which conveys a set of assumptions, or *a priori* assertions (beliefs). It could help us to avoid ideological traps which are involved in any language about God. Second step: the analysis of imagination in the works of major novelists from the 19th–20th century. In order to see how imagination could be connected to spiritual discourse, we should better circumscribe the nature of imagination. Psychoanalysis, philosophy and theology have their own way of looking at imagination. Literature implies imagination at various levels and degrees. Writers use their imagination to create their literary works. Readers try to decipher the worldview writers unveil in their literary works. Such an interpretative quest cannot exclude the decisive role of imagination. Literary works are themselves expressing how some characters use their imagination within the plot (plays,

---

1 Marcel Proust, *Pastiches et mélanges* (Paris: Gallimard, 1970), 166.

© KONINKLIJKE BRILL NV, LEIDEN, 2020 | DOI:10.1163/9789004436350_012

short stories, and novels). So, we will see how major novelists of the 19th–20th century (Dostoyevsky, Proust, Mann, Woolf, Musil) dealt with imagination, more particularly the interconnectedness between imagination and time as well as between imagination and human relationships. Third step: a Sartrean phenomenological approach (involving perception, thinking, and imagination) could improve the extent to which observation could still be active in the act of praying. Fourth step: we will analyze the way some Christian Mystics described human imagination: imagination as inner powerlessness (Saint John of the Cross), imagination as the source of divine gifts (Saint Teresa of Lisieux), or imagination as a paradoxical power towards the Mystery (Saint Teresa of Avila). Fifth step: we will draw assumptions which constitute the conceptual basis of Christian prayer, while referring to those three notions of imagination. The object of such beliefs is either God (imagination as inner powerlessness), or the relationships between a human being and God (imagination as the source of divine gifts), or even the act of praying itself (imagination as a paradoxical power towards the Mystery).

2   A Wittgensteinian Criticism of Religious Language

What do we know about life? As Ludwig Wittgenstein[2] said, we actually know that: (1) the world exists, (2) the meaning of the world is external to the world itself, (3) life is the world: the meaning of life is the meaning of the world. Representing language is representing a given form of life, (4) the individual will fills the world, (5) human will could be right or wrong, (6) good and evil are interdependent with the meaning of the world: we cannot know the meaning of the world without defining the meaning of good/evil; we cannot define the meaning of good/evil without explaining the meaning of the world. Religious morality sets up various norms of good/evil. However, every reasonable argument that is at the real origin of such norms is quite frail. It could be replaced by reasonable counterarguments. The ultimate ground of good/evil is either unknowable, or non-existent.[3]

Those who believe in God perceive that the facts of the world cannot give an adequate response to all possible questions. They are also convinced that life has a given meaning. Believers have a feeling of total dependency towards God. Schleiermacher defined religion as the sense of the Infinite, that is, the feeling, aspiration, and respect for the Infinite. Everything that is finite is then

---

2   Ludwig Wittgenstein, *Carnets 1914–1916* (Paris: Gallimard, 2005), 139–43, 148.

3   Ludwig Wittgenstein, *Remarques mêlées* (Paris: GF-Flammarion, 2002), 29, 72.

considered as an integral part of a Wholeness. Religion implies that every finite thing or being is a representation of the Infinite. Religion should never impose its own faith and feeling of the Infinite. Schleiermacher underscored the extreme importance of religious tolerance, since the natural need to be in touch with the Infinite makes various forms of faith arise.[4] The individual will is thus fully dependent on God's Will. God becomes Fate, that is, identical to the world itself. When looking at the complexity of the world, believers do not search for causal explanations. Indeed, we cannot distinguish believers and unbelievers if we do not focus on their praxis. Wittgenstein rightly said that only praxis could give meaning to words. The way various believers talk about God (or good/evil) could be quite different from one another. But the "acid test" is their own praxis. The meaning of their words emerges as soon as it is actualized in given practices. According to Paul Ricoeur, Wittgenstein made us more aware that cultural forms will be actualized through social action. The act of interpretation focuses on events (what happens).[5] Ultimately, the concept of God will be internalized through education, and thus through life experiences.[6] But a human being also has the power to be independent from God or Fate. The world is everything that happens. The world is the totality of facts and could be broken down into facts. A fact is the existence of a given state of things. A state of things implies a given connection between objects/entities.[7] Insofar as God is the world itself, then God is the way everything happens.[8] Both attitudes (dependency vs. independence) reflect given interpretations. Interpreting is thinking, that is, elaborating hypotheses that could be true or false.[9] A human being continuously interprets his or her situation and the world he or she lives in. Interpreting requires us to accept the multiplicity of historically-based situations and of worlds people live in. Interpreting necessitates being open to radical otherness, that is, to radically different modes of thinking, feeling, speaking, and behaving. Interpreting means that the Absolute Truth is either non-existent, or ungraspable.

Wittgenstein defined faith as love. Believing that faith is an act of heart/soul implies that believers are not really concerned with the historical truth. If believers were confronted with the historical inaccuracy of the Gospel, then they would not lose their faith. Wittgenstein concluded that faith is not mediated

---

4   Friedrich Schleiermacher, *Sur la religion* (Aubier: Montaigne, 1944), 152–62.
5   Paul Ricoeur, *Anthropologie philosophique. Écrits et conférences 3* (Paris: Seuil, 2013), 288.
6   Wittgenstein, *Remarques mêlées*, 85–86.
7   Ludwig Wittgenstein, *Tractatus logico-philosophicus* (Paris: Gallimard, 2012), 33–40.
8   Wittgenstein, *Carnets 1914–1916*, 139–43, 148.
9   Ludwig Wittgenstein, *Recherches philosophiques* (Paris: Gallimard, 2014), 299.

by reason, and thus by historical criticism.[10] This is a theological short cut. As soon as we accept that doubt is an integral part of faith, we must admit that faith is mediated by reason. Doubt opens the door to historical criticism as well as to existential questioning about God's existence. Wittgenstein understood that Kierkegaard defined faith as passion, that is, as an existential decision to choose a given frame of reference. Such an existential decision implies that believers have confidence in the validity of their frame of reference.[11] However, he did not see that doubt is an integral part of faith, for Blaise Pascal as well as for Soeren Kierkegaard.

But what is the realm of existential doubt? Are we able to define its scope of application? The ultimate outcome of postmodernist philosophies is the acknowledgment that facts could be untrue. Only imagination could qualify given facts as being "real facts." Baudrillard rejected the hypothetical idea that real facts are self-evident.[12] Baudrillard defined simulation as feigning to own what we do not own. Simulation thus implies an absence. It makes the frontiers between the real and the imaginary quite blurred.[13] Simulation unveils the absence of a deep reality, so that it makes an appearance transform itself into a reality (hyperreality). The appearance claims to be more real that the real. Hyperreality provokes an implosion of contents, and thus the total neutralization of meaning. In doing so, simulation has cut off any connection to reality as such. Insofar as the real is made impossible, illusion can never arise and shake our truth claims. Simulation prevents any attempt to prove real facts.[14]

The Wittgensteinian criticism of religious language makes us better understand the limitations of any philosophical analysis of Christian prayer as discourse. It unveils the deep challenge to relativize language as the ground of meanings. Now, we will see how major novelists of the 19th–20th century looked at imagination. Their literary works were so philosophically enlightening that they could help us to grasp the various functions of imagination in human life.

---

10   Wittgenstein, *Remarques mêlées*, 32–33.
11   Wittgenstein, *Remarques mêlées*, 53, 64, 71–72.
12   Jean Baudrillard, *Fragments. Cool Memories III, 1990–1995* (London/New York: Verso, 2007), 119, 135.
13   Jean Baudrillard, *Simulacra and Simulation* (Ann Arbor: The University of Michigan Press, 1994), 3–6.
14   Baudrillard, *Simulacra and Simulation*, 19, 23, 31, 81–83.

THE RELATIONSHIP BETWEEN IMAGINATION AND CHRISTIAN PRAYER   231

3   Imagination and Literature

In 19th–20th century literature, major novelists focused on the interconnectedness between imagination and Time, as well as between imagination and human relationships. According to Ricoeur, there are novels which explore various temporal experiences in order to imagine/re-present our ordinary temporality in new way.[15] This is indeed the case for *À la recherche du temps perdu* (Marcel Proust), *Mrs. Dalloway* (Virginia Woolf), and *The Magical Mountain* (Thomas Mann). Ricoeur asserted that such imaginative variations about time mirror and confirm our existential having-to-die, that is, our being-for-death.[16] Being is being-in-time ("within-time-ness"). Within-time-ness is grounded on *Dasein's* temporality.[17] In daily life, our actions take place in-time.[18] According to Ricoeur, within-time-ness as everydayness is the basic character of being. Events happen in-time. Being-in-time is the temporal mode of being-in-the-world.[19] Only an entity that is a self (only a human being) could be in-the-world. The being of the world is correlated to the being of the self.[20] But what does being-in-time mean? Ricoeur was referring to Kant : time could be conceived as quantity (its seriality), as quality (its import), as relation (its structural order), and as modality (its global character).[21] Being-in-time presupposes that everything occurs in-time.[22] Ricoeur agreed with Heidegger[23] that within-time-ness does not coincide with the succession of nows.[24] Conventional time is an existential (ontical) reality that cannot define a human being, from an existential-ontological perspective. Being-in-time makes up an integral part of what-it-means-to-exist, as a human being in a world.

According to Roland Barthes, novels are paradoxically intertwined with time. Novelists try to destroy existential duration as the inexplicable link to human existence. Denying temporality imposes disorder. Novelists also attempt to conquer duration, that is, to elaborate a new understanding of human

---

15   Paul Ricoeur, *Temps et récit. 2. La configuration dans le récit de fiction* (Paris: Seuil, 1991), 191.

16   Paul Ricoeur, *Temps et récit. 3. Le temps raconté* (Paris: Seuil, 1985), 251.

17   Martin Heidegger, *Being and Time* (New York: Harper and Row Publishers, 1962), 381–82.

18   Paul Ricoeur, *Temps et récit. 1. L'intrigue et le récit historique* (Paris: Seuil, 1991), 120.

19   Paul Ricoeur, *La mémoire, l'histoire et l'oubli* (Paris: Seuil, 2003), 498.

20   Paul Ricoeur, *Soi-même comme un autre* (Paris: Seuil, 1996), 360.

21   Paul Ricoeur, *Parcours de la reconnaissance* (Paris: Gallimard, 2009), 92; Immanuel Kant, *The Critique of Pure Reason* (New York: St. Martin's Press, 1965), 185.

22   Paul Ricoeur, *Temps et récit. 1. L'intrigue et le récit historique* (Paris: Seuil, 1991), 159.

23   Heidegger, *Being and Time*, 473–74.

24   Ricoeur, *Temps et récit. 1.*, 124.

temporality. Any constructive temporality rebuilds an order whose foundations will eventually be shaken.[25] Imagination is a way to transcend Time. It serves the Eternal.[26] Time is a mystery. We cannot measure time. Any temporal measure is nothing but social convention (conventional trime). Our consciousness of duration could disappear. Such phenomenon could be caused by continuous monotony. We can lose temporal consciousness, because we do not have any perceptual sense that focuses on the flow of time. Although we acknowledge the existential (ontical) reality of time, we cannot find out its real duration.[27] The only function of time is to let human beings use it to favor the progress of humankind. Progress only happens in-time. In eternity, there is neither duration, nor progress. In eternity, nothing changes.[28] Eternity makes everything immutable. Time rather produces change, and thus acquires an objective reality. Thomas Mann made it quite clear that time is a basic element of all narratives, since it is a foundation of life itself. Mann distinguished two different kinds of narrative time. On one hand, narratives have their own time (listening to a symphony and reading a novel take time). On the other hand, narratives have a contents-related time, that is, the imaginary time of those narratives.[29] So, narrative time lies either in the narrative itself, or in the plot.

Imagination could be closely linked to the past in addition to regrets and rememberings. We often imagine that some accessory parts of our speeches and attitudes do not impregnate others' consciousness. Proust believed that rememberings always defeat oversights.[30] Rememberings produce much more egoistic attitudes and beliefs than pure imagination.[31] When re-creating given rememberings, we are using our imagination. The power of imagination is thus progressively decreasing. However, when rememberings spontaneously arise in our consciousness, then they open the way to pure imagination.[32] Virginia Woolf described rememberings in the following way: something (the object) was (the prior now) here (*locus*), in these circumstances (situation).[33] Woolf looked at the past as the source of our dreams, torments, and discussions. The

---

25   Roland Barthes, *Le degré zéro de l'écriture* (Paris: Seuil, 1953), 58.

26   Marcel Proust, *Jean Santeuil* (Paris: Quarto Gallimard, 2001), 465.

27   Thomas Mann, *La Montagne magique* (Paris: Le livre de poche, 2010), 77–78, 121, 164, 212, 253, 394, 619.

28   Mann, *La Montagne magique*, 280, 377, 526, 790–91.

29   Mann, *La Montagne magique*, 394, 617–20.

30   Marcel Proust, *À l'ombre des jeunes filles en fleurs* (Paris: Flammarion, 1987), 138–39.

31   Marcel Proust, *Sodome et Gomorrhe* (Paris: Flammarion, 1987), 235.

32   Marcel Proust, *Albertine disparue* (Paris: Gallimard, 1992), 125.

33   Virginia Woolf, *Mrs. Dalloway* (New York: Harcourt Brace Jovanovich, 1981), 9.

THE RELATIONSHIP BETWEEN IMAGINATION AND CHRISTIAN PRAYER   233

past is something that is over. However, it could enrich us.[34] The pastness of the past unveils the fact that some objects of thought (events, words, deeds, feelings, and phenomena) are now safeguarded by our memory. Any object of thought is present in one's consciousness. Its presencing makes it an object of thought rather than a pure external object. The presentness of the past shows that such objects of thought could still influence us in the here-and-now.

People look at the same past event in a very different way. Although people observe or experience the same event, they do not reach a common interpretation for a specific event. They share a given spatio-temporal unity. They observed (or participated in) the same event. However, they do not necessarily perceive it and interpret it in the same manner. The same event gives birth to multiple interpretations. If a human being interprets his or her situation as well as the world he or she lives in, then he or she will embrace a specific viewpoint for considering various objects of thought (events, actions, words, feelings, phenomena). Although people observe the same object and/or participate in it, they will not necessarily agree either with the nature of such objects, or with the proper way of interpreting them. As Ricoeur said, a common time does not gather people, but rather divides them. Ricoeur described the Proustian notion of lost time. It could have three different meanings: (a) the time over: a human being fights the erasing of stains, that is, oversight; (b) the cleared time: some signs are not acknowledged as signs, so that time has lost part of its substance; (c) the spreaded time: the *locus* of time is multiplied. Ricoeur believed that Mann focused on the experience of an unfathomable past as it impregnates one's present memory.[35]

Imagination could also be strictly connected to the future, and thus to expectations and hopes as well as to old age and death. Imagination always focuses on our deepest hopes. In doing so, it sets up individuals and social groups for disappointment.[36] Facing old age and death is easier for people who do not have a powerful imagination.[37] According to Klein, Damm and Giebeler, imagination makes us believe that phenomena and processes continuously exist in the outer world. It makes phenomena and concepts interconnected. Imagination realizes a conjunction between past experiences (memory) and world orientation through various conceptions of continuity (future).[38] However, as Baudrillard rightly said, memory could give deep meaning to an event that did

---

34   Woolf, *Mrs. Dalloway*, 42, 49, 58, 163, 188.

35   Ricoeur, *Temps et récit. 3.*, 234–40.

36   Marcel Proust, *Les plaisirs et les jours* (Paris: Gallimard, 1979), 220–21.

37   Marcel Proust, *Le temps retrouvé* (Paris: Gallimard, 1972), 299–300.

38   Jürgen Klein, Vera Damm, and Angelika Giebeler, "An Outline of a Theory of Imagination," *Zeitschrift für allgemeine Wissenschatstheorie* 14, no. 1 (1983): 20–21.

not have any meaning, when happening in the present.[39] Giving meaning to an object of thought does not depend on the fact that a particular object has an intrinsic meaning. It is not necessarily related to the conventional meaning given to such object. Attributing meaning to an object of thought is an exercise of freedom. If a human being is being-free, then he or she projects meaning to every reality. A projected meaning does not necessarily coincide with any conventional meaning that has been usually attributed to a given object of thought.

Imagination could mirror the way relationships to oneself and/or to others is or should be. When talking with other people, we believe that our mind is listening. From a Proustian viewpoint, this is the power of imagination.[40] Imagination has no experience at all. Every hope annihilates any life experience that was connected to the power of imagination.[41] Imagination is often controlled by a powerful desire to own what we can never own.[42] We can only imagine what is not here-and-now.[43] Imagination could make absolutely wonderful what we do not own, although the final image (in our mind) is unrealistic.[44] Being who-we-are implies to believe that we are more than who we are here-and-now. Self-transcendence needs the power of imagination. However, most of the time, people are unable to use their imagination in order to actualize such a principle in their own life.[45]

Other's suffering is an object of my own perception and interpretation. If a given idea, ideal, or utopia is the basis of our suffering, then it could be much more difficult to grasp how an idea, ideal, or utopia could make us suffer in this or that manner. Believing that others could feel pain in the name of an idea, ideal, or utopia could be more difficult than believing in their physical suffering.[46] Proust strongly believed in the power of imagination. We often imagine that others are concerned with who-we-are as well as with our words and deeds, while they do no worry about our own being, thinking, sayings, and behaviors.[47] We imagine others' feelings as though they would be direct responses to our own feelings.[48] Proust asserted that our heart evolves through the

---

39   Baudrillard, *Fragments. Cool Memories III*, 29.

40   Proust, *À l'ombre des jeunes filles en fleurs*, 295.

41   Proust, *Jean Santeuil*, 130–31.

42   Proust, *À l'ombre des jeunes filles en fleurs*, 87.

43   Proust, *Le temps retrouvé*, 229.

44   Proust, *Jean Santeuil*, 273.

45   Robert Musil, *L'homme sans qualités* (Paris: Seuil, 1956), 666–67.

46   Fedor Dostoyevsky, *Les frères Karamazov* (Paris: Gallimard, 1973), 333.

47   Proust, *Sodome et Gomorrhe*, 224.

48   Proust, *À l'ombre des jeunes filles en fleurs*, 292.

THE RELATIONSHIP BETWEEN IMAGINATION AND CHRISTIAN PRAYER 235

impulses of imagination.[49] Imagination could be so powerful that it could give birth to the feelings it has artificially created.[50] When our imagination is secretly convinced that it will not be possible to get in touch with other human beings, then it completely misinterprets their self and world.[51] We often imagine the world as if it would be unequivocal, whether or not external phenomena and inner events can be. Through the power of their imagination, some people believe that they could participate in others' suffering, or that they could suffer with them, while they are unable to do so.[52] Robert Musil maintained that the power of human imagination is quite limited, even when it is involved in attitudes of empathy and compassion.

Major novelists of the 19th–20th century make us more aware of the interconnectedness between imagination and Time, not only because their novels imply a narrative temporality, but also because they represent human within-time-ness through imagination. Such novelists also emphasized the interconnectedness between imagination and human relationships, when ideas, ideals, utopias are at stake, or when others' suffering is an object of an existential concern.

4 A Sartrean Phenomenological Approach: Perceiving, Thinking, and Imagining

Jean-Paul Sartre defined image as the relationship of consciousness to a given object or phenomenon, that is, the way consciousness is self-presenting an object or phenomenon. Sartre argued that there are three kinds of consciousness: perceiving, thinking, and imagining.[53]

> Le mot d'image ne saurait désigner que le rapport de la conscience à l'objet; autrement dit, c'est une certaine façon qu'a l'objet de paraître à la conscience, ou, si l'on préfère, une certaine façon qu'a la conscience de se donner un objet ... une image n'est rien d'autre qu'un rapport ... Percevoir, concevoir, imaginer, tels sont les trois types de consciences par lesquelles un même objet peut nous être donné.[54]

---

49 Proust, *Jean Santeuil*, 807.
50 Proust, *La Prisonnière*, 341.
51 Proust, *À l'ombre des jeunes filles en fleurs*, 265.
52 Robert Musil, *L'homme sans qualités* (Paris: Seuil, 1956a), 461–62, 1014.
53 Jean-Paul Sartre, *L'imaginaire* (Paris: Gallimard, 1988), 21–30, 118.
54 Sartre, *L'imaginaire*, 21–23

Firstly, perceiving an object or phenomenon implies that we only have access to one side of the object or the phenomenon at once.[55] Knowing the object or the phenomenon requires the adoption of various perspectives about its nature and qualities. Perceiving an object or a phenomenon will give birth to (and strengthen) the inner certainty that the object or the phenomenon exists. Embracing different viewpoints will make me learn something important about the object or the phenomenon. Through perception, we always learn something new about the object or the phenomenon. When representing the object or the phenomenon, our consciousness remains passive: it receives all information from the object or the phenomenon. The perception of any object or phenomenon has infinite dimensions. The object of perception is wider and deeper than what consciousness draws from it. Perceptions could deceive us. Perceiving an object or a phenomenon refers to the perception of facts as well as to the power of imagination. According to Dostoyevsky, we often consider some events as though they were the direct consequences of facts, while they are subproducts of our imagination.[56] When our imagination takes an improbable idea as the basis of a feasible project, it could intoxicate itself. If a passionate desire is mixed with this improbable idea, then what is believed to be a feasible project would be defined as necessity.[57] Imagination makes us believe that some ideas or projects could be easily realized. It does not take the huge weight of reality into account.[58] Imagination does not have the power to assess what is true or untrue.[59] Truth is not determined by the way imagination gives birth to possibilities, but rather by prior reality we cannot know.[60] Proust suggested that imagination always creates something that is beyond reality.[61] Our imagination is closely linked to experiences of self-transcendence.

Secondly, thinking about an object or a phenomenon suggests that we already have a concrete concept of the object or the phenomenon. Such a preliminary (pre-critical, pre-philosophical) concept could be improved by life experiences. However, the concrete concept is given. We do not have to learn anything before its conscious arising. Thinking about an object or a phenomenon could make us refer to human nature as well as to pleasures/desires and happiness. If every human being were to always be courageous in any situation,

---

55 Sartre, *L'imaginaire*, 239–41.
56 Fedor Dostoyevsky, *Crime et châtiment* (Paris: Le livre de poche classique, 1972), 479.
57 Fedor Dostoyevsky, *Le joueur* (Paris: Le livre de poche classique, 1972a), 150.
58 Proust, *Albertine disparue*, 90.
59 Proust, *À l'ombre des jeunes filles en fleurs*, 221.
60 Proust, *Jean Santeuil*, 727.
61 Proust, *Sodome et Gomorrhe*, 159.

THE RELATIONSHIP BETWEEN IMAGINATION AND CHRISTIAN PRAYER 237

then all fears would be imaginary.[62] Courage implies that fears, anxieties, and risks are already present in our historically-rooted (existential) situation. Talking about the ambiguous nature of a human being presupposes that we could imagine a better human nature.[63] Stripping our imagination of pleasures reduces such pleasures to nothingness. The way specific characteristics of happiness are gathered by the power of imagination requires that some desires have been priorly identified as the basic source of happiness. Proust did not believe that we know the essence of happiness.[64]

Thirdly, imagination expresses concrete knowledge about the object/phenomenon. The object of the image is equivalent to what our consciousness has drawn from it. The object of the image and the way we are conscious of it are made contemporaneous. The image is defined through the way we are conscious of its object. An image describes the whole object, without distinguishing its multiple aspects. An image provides a feeling of certainty. In the world of images, nothing happens. We experience what Sartre called "quasi-observation," that is, an observation that cannot give us more knowledge about the observed object/phenomenon. From the outside, we observe the object or the phenomenon. Within the object or the phenomenon, we perceive what is this object or the phenomenon. According to Sartre, the consciousness of an image could take for granted that: (a) the object does not exist (non-existence), (b) the object is absent (existing as being absent), (c) the object exists somewhere (existing without a precise *locus*), (c) any claim about the existence of the object is suspended (phenomenologically suspended existence). Each of those four positioning acts are basically constitutive of the consciousness of the image. In each case, we experience quasi-observation. In each case, the object is positioned as nothingness. However, the meaning of nothingness is different from one instance to another. In any representation of God, believers agree that God is absent from human life (nothingness as absence), or that God is existing somewhere (nothingness as existing without a precise spatial *locus*). Agnosticism implies that the individual is unable to decide whether God exists or not (nothingness as the impossibility to claim anything about the object's existence). Sometimes, we consider an image to be a perception. Such distortion happens when we strongly desire to be convinced of the object's existence. The imagining consciousness produces and safeguards the object/phenomenon through a given image. It is basically spontaneous and creative. It is always creating and re-creating the qualities of

---

62   Dostoyevsky, *Crime et châtim*ent, 32.
63   Musil, *L'homme sans qualités*, 514.
64   Proust, *À l'ombre des jeunes filles en fleurs*, 13, 180.

the object or the phenomenon. Quasi-observation implies that the object or the phenomenon is nothing more that the way we are aware of it. Nothing really exists outside consciousness. The existence of consciousness can only be the self-awareness of its own existence.[65] Objective existence of any object is not denied. Rather, we put the emphasis on the existence of things, deeds, words, events, feelings, and phenomena, as objects of thought. Only a human being experiences the meaning of his or her existence. Such experience is mediated by our consciousness. Only a human being "exists," while other species are simply "living" beings. Thus, nothing can exist outside the consciousness of the existing being. When transposed into a given image, the object is something unreal. The unreal could be present in our own life. However, we do not have any access to it, as an object. The presence of the unreal in our life will strengthen our desires and hopes.[66]

David Tracy believed that imagination should not be primarily related to perception, but rather to language.[67] Any text cannot be fully accomplished without the readers' imagination, since readers are those who could express the meaning of the literary work. A literary work is always an appeal to the readers' freedom, that is, to their basic freedom to interpret the literary work in one way or another. Literature is the work of total freedom which is aimed at total liberties. As the free product of creative activities, literature expresses the whole human condition, said Sartre.[68]

A Sartrean phenomenological approach of imagination unveils how our consciousness of the image (like God's image) is possible. God's image is the object of a quasi-observation. Believers cannot claim that through their God's image, they concretely know something about God's Essence and Life. God's image is a representation of an object we can experience, without providing any knowledge about its objective existence.

5 Imagination and Prayer: The Case of Christian Mystics

When using our imagination, we position a past event of our life as something which is done and absent. Imagination could also be used to create an imagined future, as a future for-us which is not-already-there. According to Sartre,

---

65   Jean-Paul Sartre, *L'imagination* (Paris: PUF, 2012), 104.

66   Sartre, *L'imaginaire*, 32–38, 116, 240–41, 351.

67   David Tracy, *The Analogical Imagination. Christian Tradition and the Culture of Pluralism* (New York: Crossroad, 1981), 128.

68   Jean-Paul Sartre, *Qu'est-ce que la littérature?* (Paris: Gallimard, 1969), 111, 121, 333–34.

THE RELATIONSHIP BETWEEN IMAGINATION AND CHRISTIAN PRAYER 239

imagination presents something concrete toward which the existing object or phenomenon is overcome.[69]

> ...l'objet imaginaire peut être posé comme inexistent ou comme absent ou comme existant ailleurs ou ne pas être posé comme existant. Nous constatons que le caractère commun à ces quatre thèses c'est qu'elles enveloppent toutes la catégorie de négation quoique à des degrés différents. Ainsi l'acte négatif est constitutif de l'image.[70]
>
> Lorsque l'imaginaire n'est pas posé en fait, le dépassement et la néantisation de l'existant sont enlisés dans l'existant, le dépassement et la liberté sont là mais ils ne se découvrent pas, l'homme est écrasé dans le monde, transpercé par le réel, il est le plus près de la chose. Pourtant, dès lors qu'il appréhende d'une façon ou d'une autre (la plupart du temps sans représentation) l'ensemble comme situation, il le dépasse vers ce par rapport à quoi il est un manque, un vide, etc.[71]

Imagination cannot be isolated from moral issues, and thus from the frontiers between good and evil. Events are not possible events, but rather actualized and knowledgeable events. If given events have produced morally good as well as morally wrong consequences, then they are interpreted in a way that makes goodness and evil unavoidable.[72] When our imagination focuses on change, then it cannot be shaken by any morality.[73] Morality should always be defined as imagination. When morality is fixed, then moral imagination becomes impossible. The defeat of good does not come from the victory of evil. When false good acquires more influence among individuals and social groups, then the power of Evil largely grows.[74] In Christian prayer, the frontiers between good and evil are particularly relevant. Believers perceive themselves not only as finite beings, but above all, as sinners.

Could God be imagined in an effective and existential way? Robert Musil asserted that God is always imagined as though God were not living.[75] However, this is not the way Christian Mystics looked at God as well as human imagination. Among Christian Mystics, we could identify three basic notions of imagination: imagination as inner powerlessness (Saint John of the Cross);

---

69   Sartre, *L'imaginaire*, 348–49, 358–59.

70   Sartre, *L'imaginaire*, 351.

71   Sartre, *L'imaginaire*, 359.

72   Proust, *Albertine disparue*, 240.

73   Musil, *L'homme sans qualités*, 310–11.

74   Musil, *L'homme sans qualités*, 428, 596.

75   Musil, *L'homme sans qualités*, 248.

240   DION

imagination as the source of divine gifts (Saint Teresa of Lisieux); imagination
as paradoxical power towards the mystery (Saint Teresa of Avila).

6 Imagination as Inner Powerlessness: The Awareness of the Infinite Discrepancy

Imagination as inner powerlessness makes it possible to be more aware of the
infinite discrepancy between finite beings and God. The infinite discrepancy is
felt as deficiency, lack, or gap as it is created by existential finitude. Saint John
of the Cross (1542–1591) described imagination as inner powerlessness. The
dark side of the soul implies sensitive purification (first night: the night of the
senses) as well as spiritual purification (second night: the night of the spirit).
As Plotinus[76] said, goodness is more than simple self-purification. The second
night prepares the soul for the loving union with God. It requires the practice
of virtues in daily life, at every moment.[77] Saint John of the Cross believed that
imagination is unable to develop any reliable way of reasoning. Every spiritual
effect comes from God: everything is given by God and received by our free
will. Imagination cannot give us access to God. It cannot provide us any spiritual benefit. Saint John of the Cross defined imagination as the inner powerlessness, and language as the external powerlessness. The second night gives us
free spirit insofar as our spirit is released from its subjection to imagination
and language. Imagination is thus something suspicious. It could give us the
conviction that we could be more powerful, more perfect, more spiritually focused than we are.[78] Inner powerlessness implies that we are unable to give
any form to our spiritual experiences.

7 Imagination as the Source of Divine Gifts: The Awareness of the Breakthrough

As the source of divine gifts, imagination makes us more aware of the break-
through between Eternal and human temporality. The Eternal breaks into human (temporally finite) existence by providing such divine gifts. According to
Saint Teresa of Lisieux (1873–1897), imagination is the real origin of divine
gifts. Saint Teresa of Lisieux considered that dreams could be divine gifts that

---

76   Plotinus, *The Enneads* (London: Penguin Books, 1991), 19.
77   Saint John of the Cross, *La nuit obscure* (Paris: Seuil, 1984), 123–28, 158–60.
78   Saint John of the Cross, *La nuit obscure*, 95–100, 163–79.

THE RELATIONSHIP BETWEEN IMAGINATION AND CHRISTIAN PRAYER   241

play a specific role in one's spiritual growth. God gives us dreams and thus night images that could help us to better spiritually evolve throughout time and space. There are some mysterious dreams whose meaning is not self-evident. God wants to make us continuously search for the meaning of such dreams, that is, the meaning that actually mirrors God's Will.[79] Jacques Maître dealt with the dream of the three Carmelites (May 10, 1896) as conveying the anxiety of self-annihilation, as it was experienced by Saint Teresa of Lisieux.[80] The anxiety of self-annihilation follows from the subjective certainty that we are not loved by our significant others (for instance, relatives and friends). It presupposes that love is the ultimate basis of being. Not-being-loved implies self-annihilation. Self-annihilation has two important grounds: having lost who-we-are and being unable to decide "who-we-would-like-to-be." The self is then temporarily annihilated. It cannot be annihilated in a definitive way, since it is always here-and-now. The anxiety of self-annihilation could be relative (it follows from the certainty of not-being-loved: the relative loss of self as subject to-be-loved), or absolute (through death: the total loss of self as living being). While searching for the meaning of this dream, Saint Teresa of Lisieux tried to be more strongly convinced of the existence of Heaven and of heavenly beings. Jacques Maître explained that the anxiety of relative self-annihilation could be overcome through the certainty of being loved: being loved by those people who are very significant for her (more particularly, her late mother), as well as by all supranatural (heavenly) beings. Imagination is then our capacity to feel Divine gifts in our existential condition.[81]

8   Imagination as Paradoxical Power towards the Mystery: The Awareness of the Communicational Area

Imagination opens the door to the mystery of being, and thus to the mystery of God. In doing so, it makes us more aware of the communicational realm between finite beings and the Infinite. Saint Teresa of Avila (1515–1582) believed that imagination opens the door to the mystery. According to Charles-André Bernard, imaginary representation provides a kind of immediacy and self-evidence that cannot be unveiled by any word. The mystical person uses an

---

79   Saint Teresa of Lisieux, *Manuscrits autobiographiques* (Lisieux: Carmel de Lisieux, 1957), 26–27.

80   Jacques Maître, *L'Orpheline de la Bérésina. Thérèse de Lisieux (1873–1897)* (Paris: Cerf, 1995), 299–319.

81   Maître, *L'Orpheline de la Bérésina. Thérèse de Lisieux*, 303.

imaginary representation to concretely realize the presence of the whole mystery in his/her own life. Bernard described three basic characteristics of imaginary visions that have nothing to do with hallucinations: (a) the impression of beauty implies that the mystical person gets in touch with a transcendental world; (b) the spiritual efficacy of the imaginary vision; (c) the physical effects of the vision (benefits for physical health).[82] Imagination has the power to open our mind to given mysteries and to favor our spiritual growth. Facing the mystery, imagination has a paradoxical power: it could open our mind to given mysteries, while distorting our interpretations of what we are seeing and experiencing. Imagination could help us to safeguard mysteries as mysteries. But it could also distort mysteries in substituting human will to God's Will. Saint Teresa of Avila believed that an imaginary vision must be distinguished from a spiritually-oriented vision of Christ. Unlike a spiritual vision, an imaginary vision does not have any positive effect on the soul as well as on the body.[83] Moreover, the imaginary vision cannot prove the omnipotence of God. Imagination cannot produce images which overcome what every human being could conceive. The images produced by one's imagination do not have the same effects on the soul and body as those created by the spiritual presence of Christ. Saint Teresa of Avila asserted that without-God-images have superior worth than any image of God that our soul could secretly keep. However, because we are finite beings, we need concrete images of God in order to be in His Divine Presence at every moment. Such images of God are then crystallised into the imagination.[84] Imagination makes us continuously produce new images. Imaginary vision is closely linked to one's will. Spiritual vision is not related to the power of human will. We cannot call for more visions, more images than what we experience. Imaginary vision depends on human will, while spiritual vision depends on God's Will.[85]

Christian Mystics have used three basic notions of imagination: inner powerlessness (Saint John of the Cross), source of divine gifts (Saint Teresa of Lisieux), and paradoxical power towards the mystery (Saint Teresa of Avila). In doing so, they improve our understanding of the potential role of imagination in Christian prayer. However, we need to grasp the inner structure of Christian

---

82   Charles-André Bernard, *Le Dieu des mystiques. Tome II. La conformation au Christ* (Paris: Cerf, 1998), 171–72, 239–40; Saint Teresa of Avila, *Livre de la vie* (Paris: Gallimard, 2015), 277–81.

83   Saint Teresa of Avila, *Livre de la vie*, 263–64, 285.

84   Saint Teresa of Avila, *Livre de la vie*, 277–80.

85   Saint Teresa of Avila, *Livre de la vie*, 285–86.

prayer and see how imagination is connected to the basic assumptions about praying.

9   The Assumptions behind Christian Prayers

According to Wittgenstein, we could never say what would be an illogical world. The fact that we could talk about the world in a logical way expresses that the world must be logical. Any logical consideration is rooted in the will to undertand the essence (ground) of things, that is, the essence of what is experienced.[86] What takes place in the here-and-now is "this-or-that." We can only say that it is "this-or-that." If God has put in the world some true propositions, then God has made necessary all consequences of such propositions. Wittgenstein defined the Mystical as the facticity of the world. The awareness of the facticity of the world is inherently mystical.[87]

Taking Wittgensteinian criticism of religious language into consideration requires us to analyze the structure of Christian prayers, at least the assumptions which constitute the conceptual basis of Christian prayer. Praying to God implies twenty-five assumptions about God, the act of praying, or the relationships between God and human beings. Every assumption occurs in a context of the interconnectedness between reason and faith. In each case, believers must make such assumptions reasonable, while safeguarding the contents of their faith. At every moment, believers could open the door to a philosophical criticism of religious language, given the fact that any of those assumptions is self-evident and remains quite frail. Each of those twenty-five assumptions cannot be empirically proven and follows from believers' existential situation. In each case, imagination is used to strengthen the believer's faith and to get rid of any criticism about religious language and experience.

Christian prayer implies seven basic assumptions about God. In every case, imagination remains inner powerlessness (Saint John of the Cross), since it can never claim to grasp God's Essence and Will. Those seven assumptions about God imply a powerless imagination that can never seize any aspect of Divine Life:

(1)   the assumption that God exists: imagination could create various images of God that are used, consciously or not, during prayers;

---

86   Wittgenstein, *Recherches philosophiques*, 77.

87   Wittgenstein, *Tractatus logico-philosophicus*, 41, 70, 72, 111.

(2) the assumption that God can grasp the meaning and contents of human prayers: imagination presupposes a divine mechanism to hear and decipher the meaning of one's prayers;

(3) the assumption that God can know to what extent prayers are impregnated with sincerity:[88] Martin Luther rejected the abuse of prayer as well as stupid prayers.[89] True prayers come from the depths of the human heart, that is, from the whole person.[90] Imagination could give birth to images of God's judgment, that is, Divine reactions of receptivity or repulsion toward sincere or insincere prayers;

(4) the assumption that God will hear only sincere prayers:[91] imagination gives images about God's hearing, and thus the certainty to be heard;

(5) the assumption that God is concerned with human prayers: imagination provides images of a God/Goddess who is ultimately concerned with His/Her creatures' well-being;

(6) the assumption that God can give a precise response to every human prayer: imagination could make it self-evident that God's omnipotence implies the capacity to respond to all human prayers;

(7) the assumption that God/Goddess freely responds to human prayers, so that His/Her responses do not necessarily fulfill the contents of such prayers.[92] Imagination could then create Divine motives not to fulfill one's prayer in accordance with the real contents of the prayer, and/or not to fulfill it in the expected delay. Imagination could let God be free to choose the best way to fulfill those contents. Believers could be astonished to find out God's Infinite Wisdom;

Christian prayer implies five assumptions about the relationships between a human being and God. In every case, imagination (like faith) is the source of divine gifts (Saint Teresa of Lisieux). Those five assumptions about the relationships between God and human beings imply an imagination whose powers directly come from God:

---

88 Karl Barth, *La prière* (Paris: Delachaux & Nietstlé, 1967), 16; Maurice Nédoncelle, *God's Encounter with Man. A Contemporary Approach to Prayer* (New York: Sheed and Ward, 1964), 24–28.

89 Martin Luther, "Sermons on the Catechism, 1528," in *Martin Luther. Selections from his writings*, ed. John Dillenberger (New York: Doubleday & Company, 1961), 216.

90 Olivier Clément, *Sources. Les mystiques chrétiens des origines* (Paris: Stock, 1982), 166.

91 Gabriel Marcel, *Foi et réalité* (Aubier: Éditions Montaigne, 1967), 116.

92 Paul Tillich, *Systematic Theology. Volume 1. Reason and Revelation. Being and God* (Chicago: The University of Chicago Press, 1951), 213; Maurice Nédoncelle, *God's Encounter with Man. A Contemporary Approach to Prayer* (New York: Sheed and Ward, 1964), 83–86.

(8) the assumption that there are communicational links between a human being and God: imagination makes possible communicational realms between God and humankind;

(9) the assumption that praying is being-in-dialogue with God: prayer presupposes a personal (dialogical) relationship to God.[93] If prayer is kind of dialogue, then it must imply an exchange of words and ideas. Is there any origin of the dialogue between God and human beings? According to Hans Urs von Balthasar, dialogue begins with God's initiative, that is, the Word of God as it was revealed to humankind. This is the origin of the dialogue between God and human beings. In a Christian framework, anything that has existed before the Word of God was not included in the actual dialogue between God and human beings.[94] God has already spoken through the Gospel as well as the divine Laws. Thus, prayers are human responses to God's initiative: God's first words which are addressed to humankind.[95] Otherwise, we should admit that human beings could have taken the initiative of the dialogue. However, Ricoeur dealt with the prayers of complaint. In this case, believers are deeply troubled by God's silence, while trying to recover trust and confidence in God's Providence.[96] Imagination makes it possible for believers to create a temporal and spatial unity of dialogue with their God;

(10) the assumption that sinners can never fully understand God, who is at the midst of their prayers.[97] Imagination could acknowledge its own limitations and create images of the unimaginable;

(11) the assumption that human beings have reasonable motives to believe that God will respond to their prayers.[98] However, believers do not have any certainty about God's responses. Praying is acknowledging that God remains free to respond to one's prayers.[99] Imagination could use reason to increase probabilities of Divine responses;

(12) the assumption that human beings have the capacity to grasp the way God has responded to their prayers: imagination is often used to interpret the signs of God's response.

---

93 Olivier Clément, *Sources. Les mystiques chrétiens des origines* (Paris: Stock, 1982), 165.

94 Hans Urs Von Balthasar, *La prière contemplative* (Paris: Fayard, 1972), 3–5.

95 Karl Barth, *La prière* (Paris: Delachaux & Nietstlé, 1967), 22.

96 Paul Ricoeur, "La plainte comme prière," in *Penser la Bible*, eds. André LaCocque and Paul Ricoeur (Paris: Points, 2016), 313.

97 Karl Barth, *The Epistle to the Romans* (London/Oxford: Oxford University Press, 1968), 316.

98 Barth, *La prière*, 35.

99 Marcel, *Foi et réalité*, 122.

Christian prayer implies thirteen assumptions about the act of praying. In every case, imagination is a paradoxical power towards the Mystery (Saint Teresa of Avila). In every case, imagination could help believers to be in touch with God, while safeguarding the gap between the finite and the Infinite. Although prayers are structured around words and sentences, they could reject the use of language. Ultimately, the unsaid-prayer should be preferred to the actually-said-prayer. Life could then become a prayer:

(13) the assumption that praying puts believers in face of their God: only God listens to believers' prayers.[100] Imagination creates temporal and spatial unity to meet God through prayers;

(14) the assumption that language is a meaning system through which human being can create prayers. Imagination is not used to criticize religious language and experience, but rather to give meaning to prayers. Prayers are considered as means to be-in-dialogue-with-God;

(15) the assumption that prayers could be actualized through language, thought, or life experiences, so that words are not more important than thoughts and deeds.[101] If living is living-with-God, then praying could have linguistic, conceptual and cognitive, or behavioral components.[102] Imagination is used to create an overall Divine power to hear everything that comes from creatures;

(16) the assumption that language has the inner capacity to make prayers meaningful: God has given such capacity to humankind. Prayer is a divine grace, something supranatural.[103] However, prayers are made possible through the divine Spirit who lies in the depths of the soul.[104] Without the divine Spirit, human beings would be unable to pray. Imagination could be used to be convinced that religious language is meaningful and cannot give birth to any meaningless word, demand, thanks, or complaint;

(17) the assumption that the structure, types, and contents of prayers could largely vary from an individual to another, from culture to culture, from

---

100 Romano Guardini, *Initiation à la prière* (Paris: Livre de vie, 1951), 229.

101 Rudolph Bultmann, *Theology of the New Testament. Volume I* (New York: Charles Scribner's Sons, 1951), 161.

102 Barth, *La prière*, 18, 25, 52.

103 Barth, *La prière*, 25, 37–39.

104 Paul Tillich, *Systematic Theology. Volume III. Life and the Spirit. History and the Kingdom of God* (Chicago: The University of Chicago Press, 1963), 116–17.

THE RELATIONSHIP BETWEEN IMAGINATION AND CHRISTIAN PRAYER   247

an era to another : prayers of love; prayers of petition/supplication,[105] particularly in distress and misery; prayers of repentance; prayers of thanks; prayers of mercy; prayers in times of indecisiveness; prayers of complaint; prayers of intercession.[106] A human being freely creates the forms and contents of prayers he or she would prefer to use.[107] Imagination could provide God's image that is open to all cultural and individual variations about the act of praying;

(18) the assumption that prayers usually focus on human anxieties, needs, and perils. There is a belief that God could do much more wonderful things than simply responding to human needs and distress.[108] When praying to God, we use words of our religious tradition. Even without words, we refer to the way contemplation was perceived by our own religious tradition.[109] Imagination is impregnated with those religious influences, whether prayers use words or not. Although there is cultural and religious diversity, every prayer is based on the same (existential) human predicament;

(19) the assumption that believers who pray to God acknowledge their own existential finitude (at least their needs, desires, and thus their existential inadequacy), and even the fact that they are sinners, while being united with God.[110] Imagination could help believers create mental and physical discontinuity between finite beings and the Infinite;

(20) the assumption that prayers are freely enunciated and convey something new that is addressed to the divine Spirit: this newness will make believers convinced that their prayers will be heard by the divine Spirit.[111] Praying is not always repeating the same words in the same situation. But

---

105   Tillich, *Systematic Theology. Volume I. Reason and Revelation. Being and God*, 267; Tillich, *Systematic Theology. Volume III. Life and the Spirit. History and the Kingdom of God*, 191; David Tracy, *The Analogical Imagination. Christian Theology and the Culture of Pluralism* (New York: Crossroads, 1981).

106   Tillich, *Systematic Theology. Volume I. Reason and Revelation. Being and God*, 267.

107   Romano Guardini, *Initiation à la prière* (Paris: Livre de vie, 1951), 230.

108   Martin Luther, "Sermons on the Catechism, 1528," in *Martin Luther. Selections from his writings*, ed. John Dillenberger (New York: Doubleday & Company, 1961), 227.

109   Tillich, *Systematic Theology. Volume III. Life and the Spirit. History and the Kingdom of God*, 236.

110   Karl Barth, *The Epistle to the Romans* (London/Oxford: Oxford University Press, 1968), 316; Maurice Nédoncelle, *God's Encounter with Man. A Contemporary Approach to Prayer* (New York: Sheed and Ward, 1964), 29–35; Rudolph Bultmann, *Theology of the New Testament. Volume II* (New York: Charles Scribner's Sons, 1955), 86.

111   Tillich, *Systematic Theology. Volume III. Life and the Spirit. History and the Kingdom of God*, 191.

even the same words will produce newness that will be heard by the divine Spirit. Imagination could elaborate different ways to be heard by the divine Spirit and use anthropomorphic images to mirror such interconnectedness between the self and the divine Spirit (for instance, the divine Spirit as a mother listening to her children's complaints);

(21) the assumption that prayers are oriented towards a better understanding of God's Will.[112] Imagination could provide images of existential situations in which a better understanding of God's Will could make our existence more pleasant and meaningful;

(22) the assumption that prayers use such communicational links in order to be received by God. Imagination could make us believe that God always receives all human prayers through secret and incomprehensible mechanisms;

(23) the assumption that every successful prayer reunites us with God: every successful prayer implies speaking to God as the object of the dialogue. However, said Tillich, God is not an object, except if God is simultaneously a subject.[113] Every successful prayer takes for granted that the individual who prays is subjected to the subject-object structure, while God absolutely overcomes such an existentially-based structure. Imagination could identify various paths to make one's soul reunited with God. However, the way souls could be reunited with God takes for granted that God can be reduced neither to a pure subject (Personal God), nor to a knowledgeable object (thus annihilating Divine Absoluteness). Praying is taking the risk of distorting God's Essence into an account. Praying to God should prioritize the absolute need to safeguard God's Absoluteness;

(24) the assumption that prayers should never be considered as magical rituals: Tillich acknowledged that it is not self-evident to distinguish Spirit-determined and magical praying. Genuine prayers are directed to God.[114] Imagination could be used to deceive our reasonable judgment about the contents of prayers as well as about their expected results. Imagination should never be considered as the servant of magical powers. Consciously or not, believers could favor magical outcomes to the detriment of God. In doing so, they will distort the nature of imagination as well as the nature of Christian prayer;

---

112   Barth, *The Epistle to the Romans*, 458.

113   Tillich, *Systematic Theology. Volume III. Life and the Spirit. History and the Kingdom of God*, 119–20.

114   Tillich, *Systematic Theology. Volume III. Life and the Spirit. History and the Kingdom of God*, 279–80, 289.

THE RELATIONSHIP BETWEEN IMAGINATION AND CHRISTIAN PRAYER   249

(25) the assumption that prayers are useless, when a believer's life has become
      a prayer: our own life is a prayer, so that saying this or that prayer to God
      is no longer useful.[115] Imagination creates a mental and spiritual con-
      sciousness in which everything external to the self is integrated into the
      self, as though interiority were intertwined with exteriority.

10   Conclusion

We have seen how some Christian Mystics considered the role of imagination.
It is striking to observe that imagination is perceived quite negatively as inner
powerlessness (Saint John of the Cross), or positively as the source of divine
gifts (Saint Teresa of Lisieux). However, Saint Teresa of Avila looked at imagination as a paradoxical power towards the mystery. Nowadays, her notion of
imagination could remind us that imagination has a positive as well as a negative impact on the human soul. The analysis of the twenty-five assumptions
makes us more aware that faith and imagination play a decisive role on the way
the act of praying is performed.

Future research could look at the status of prayer, when nothing is said by
believers ("unsaid prayer"), or when their whole life becomes a prayer ("life as
prayer"). Praying then becomes a quasi-text. Ricoeur said that action as quasi-
text reflects basic components of a text without really being a text.[116] Prayer
could imply words. But in some cases, prayers could be considered as a quasi-
text, since nothing is said. Rather, the action is the "quasi-text." Interiority is
then expressed as contemplation. According to Ricoeur, action could be read
in very different ways. However, there is a limited field of possible interpretations for every human action. Interpreting the quasi-text (prayer as action)
makes the agent interpret himself or herself, said Ricoeur.[117] Ricoeur referred
to Marcel Proust:[118] readers who read a book find how to read in themselves.
When we read a quasi-text, we release ourselves from the mode of reading that
the quasi-text conveyed. We respond to the mode of reading that the quasi-text
suggests to all readers. The quasi-text says something to us. As readers, we say
something to the text. Ricoeur called such action "the reflexivity of reading."[119]
George Lindbeck talked about the textualization of reality: every behavior is

---

115   Clément, *Sources. Les mystiques chrétiens des origines*, 190–91.
116   Ricoeur, *Temps et récit. 1.*, 115.
117   Ricoeur, *Soi-même comme un autre*, 211.
118   Proust, *Le temps retrouvé*, 277.
119   Ricoeur, *Temps et récit. 3.*, 302, 321.

considered to be a quasi-text.[120] A philosophical and spiritual analysis of Christian prayer could focus on the act of praying as a quasi-text. In doing so, it could enrich the various ways in which Christian prayer is deciphered, particularly when prayers do not refer to words and thoughts.

References

Barth, Karl. *La prière*. Paris: Delachaux & Nietstlé. 1967.

Barth, Karl. *The Epistle to the Romans*. London/Oxford: Oxford University Press. 1968.

Barthes, Roland. *Le degré zéro de l'écriture*. Paris: Seuil, 1953.

Baudrillard, Jean. *Fragments. Cool Memories III, 1990–1995* London/New York: Verso. 2007.

Baudrillard, Jean. *Simulacra and Simulation*. Ann Arbor: The University of Michigan Press. 1994.

Bernard, Charles-André. *Le Dieu des mystiques. Tome II. La conformation au Christ*. Paris: Cerf. 1998.

Braidotti, Rosi. "Animals, Anomalies, and Inorganic Others." *Proceedings of the Modern Language Association of America* 124, no. 2 (2009): 526–32.

Bultmann, Rudolf. *Theology of the New Testament. Volume I*. New York: Charles Scribner's Sons. 1951.

Bultmann, Rudolf. *Theology of the New Testament. Volume II*. New York: Charles Scribner's Sons. 1955.

Clément, Olivier. *Sources. Les mystiques chrétiens des origins*. Paris: Stock. 1982.

Dostoyevsky, Fedor. *Crime et châtiment*. Paris: Le livre de poche classique. 1972.

Dostoyevsky, Fedor. *Le joueur*. Paris: Le livre de poche classique. 1972.

Dostoyevsky, Fedor. *Les frères Karamazov*. Paris: Gallimard. 1973.

Guardini, Romano. *Initiation à la prière*. Paris: Livre de vie. 1951.

Heidegger, Martin. *Being and Time*. New York: Harper and Row Publishers. 1962.

Kant, Immanuel. *The Critique of Pure Reason*. New York: St. Martin's Press. 1965.

Klein, Jürgen, Vera Damm, and Angelika Giebeler. "An Outline of a Theory of Imagination." *Zeitschrift für allgemeine Wissenschatstheorie* 14, no. 1 (1983): 15–23.

Lindbeck, George A. "The Church's Mission to a Postmodern Culture: Postmodern Theology." In *Christian Faith in a Pluralist World*, edited by Frederic B. Burnham, 37–55. San Francisco: HarperCollins Publishers, 1989.

---

120 George A. Lindbeck, "The Church's Mission to a Postmodern Culture: Postmodern Theology," in *Christian Faith in a Pluralist World*, ed. Frederic B. Burnham (San Francisco: HarperCollins Publishers, 1989), 50–51.

Luther, Martin. "Sermons on the Catechism, 1528," In *Martin Luther. Selections from his writings*, edited by John Dillenberger, 207–39. New York: Doubleday & Company, 1961.

Maître, Jacques. *L'Orpheline de la Bérésina. Thérèse de Lisieux (1873–1897)*. Paris: Cerf. 1995.

Mann, Thomas. *La Montagne magique*. Paris: Le livre de poche. 2010.

Marcel, Gabriel. *Foi et réalité*. Aubier: Éditions Montaigne. 1967.

Musil, Robert. *L'homme sans qualités*. Paris: Seuil, 2 volumes (Volume 1, 1956; Volume 2, 1956).

Nédoncelle, Maurice. *God's Encounter with Man. A Contemporary Approach to Prayer*. New York: Sheed and Ward. 1964.

Plotinus. *The Enneads*. London: Penguin Books. 1991.

Proust, Marcel. *Albertine disparue*. Paris: Gallimard. 1992.

Proust, Marcel. *À l'ombre des jeunes filles en fleurs*. Paris: Flammarion, 2 volumes (Volume 1, 1987; Volume 2, 1987a).

Proust, Marcel. *Jean Santeuil*. Paris: Quarto Gallimard. 2001.

Proust, Marcel. *La Prisonnière*. Paris: Gallimard. 1989.

Proust, Marcel. *Les plaisirs et les jours*. Paris: Gallimard. 1979.

Proust, Marcel. *Le temps retrouvé*. Paris: Gallimard. 1972.

Proust, Marcel. *Pastiches et mélanges*. Paris: Gallimard. 1970.

Proust, Marcel. *Sodome et Gomorrhe*. Paris: Flammarion, 2 volumes (Volume 1, 1987b; Volume 2, 1987c).

Rahner, Karl. *Prière de notre temps*. Paris: Éditions de l'épi. 1966.

Ricoeur, Paul. *Anthropologie philosophique. Écrits et conférences 3*. Paris: Seuil. 2013.

Ricoeur, Paul. *La mémoire, l'histoire et l'oubli*. Paris: Seuil. 2003.

Ricoeur, Paul. "La plainte comme prière." In *Penser la Bible*, edited by André LaCocque and Paul Ricoeur, 287–313. Paris: Points, 2016.

Ricoeur, Paul. *Parcours de la reconnaissance*. Paris: Gallimard. 2009.

Ricoeur, Paul. *Soi-même comme un autre*. Paris: Seuil. 1996.

Ricoeur, Paul. *Temps et récit. 1. L'intrigue et le récit historique*. Paris: Seuil. 1991.

Ricoeur, Paul. *Temps et récit. 2. La configuration dans le récit de fiction*. Paris: Seuil. 1991.

Ricoeur, Paul. *Temps et récit. 3. Le temps raconté*. Paris: Seuil. 1985.

Saint John of the Cross. *La nuit obscure*. Paris: Seuil. 1984.

Saint Teresa of Avila. *Livre de la vie*. Paris: Gallimard. 2015.

Saint Teresa of Lisieux. *Manuscrits autobiographiques*. Lisieux: Carmel de Lisieux. 1957.

Sartre, Jean-Paul. *L'imaginaire*. Paris: Gallimard. 1988.

Sartre, Jean-Paul. *L'imagination*. Paris: PUF. 2012.

Sartre, Jean-Paul. *Qu'est-ce que la littérature?* Paris: Gallimard. 1969.

Schleiermacher, Friedrich. *Sur la religion*. Aubier: Montaigne. 1944.

Tillich, Paul. *Systematic Theology. Volume i. Reason and Revelation. Being and God*. Chicago: The University of Chicago Press. 1951.

Tillich, Paul. *Systematic Theology. Volume iii. Life and the Spirit. History and the Kingdom of God*. Chicago: The University of Chicago Press. 1963.

Tracy, David. *The Analogical Imagination. Christian Tradition and the Culture of Pluralism*. New York: Crossroad. 1981.

Von Balthasar, Hans Urs. *La prière contemplative*. Paris: Fayard. 1972.

Wittgenstein, Ludwig. *Carnets 1914–1916*. Paris: Gallimard. 2005.

Wittgenstein, Ludwig. *Recherches philosophiques*. Paris: Gallimard. 2014.

Wittgenstein, Ludwig. *Remarques mêlées*. Paris: GF-Flammarion. 2002.

Wittgenstein, Ludwig. *Tractatus logico-philosophicus*. Paris: Gallimard. 2012.

Woolf, Virginia. *Mrs. Dalloway*. New York: Harcourt Brace Jovanovich. 1981.

PART 4

Phenomenological and Epistemological Perspectives

∵

CHAPTER 11

The Work Texts Do: Toward a Phenomenology of Imagining Imaginatively

Charles Altieri

> The concept of an aspect is related to the concept of imagination. In other words, the concept "Now I see it as..." is related to "Now I am imagining that..." Doesn't it take imagination to hear something as a variation on a particular theme. And yet one does perceive something in so hearing it.
>
> WITTGENSTEIN, *Philosophy of Psychology—A Fragment* 254

When is the last time that you read contemporary criticism that was explicitly concerned with the activity of the imagination? Such occasions seem increasingly rare: imagination now is very rarely spoken of, like the family member whose past seems an embarrassment for an eager new generation of social climbers. I contend that this disappearance of imagination from critical discourse presents a substantial problem for literary studies. With no mode of production specific to what literary texts embody, and with no sense of the kinds of power for which they strive, one comes to see immediately the negative, side of contemporary criticism's turn to moral and political critical orientations. But my purposes here are not primarily to elaborate problems in contemporary attitudes. In my view Derek Attridge has done a fine job articulating the limitations of what he calls criticism's turn to the instrumental roles of using literature to establish objects of knowledge.[1] For Attridge, literary critics increasingly ignore the values produced by attention to the singularity of the texts in order to pursue how other disciplines like sociology and economic history might stage relations between texts and their historical contexts, or, one might add now, stage relations between texts and the neurophysiology responsible for us making them present in the first place.

Instead my job here is to develop one reason for this change in a way that may help lead us back to fascination with how particular authors pursue values that depend on the working of imagination. Devoting oneself to studying these values will probably never have the appeal of being able to test new

---

1 Derek Attridge, *The Singularity of the Literature* (Abingdon, Oxon: Taylor & Francis Group, 2004), 9 ff.

generalizations or feeling that one is constructing knowledge on which others can build. But this loss of social purpose can be compensated for by a much richer sense of what specific literary experiences can offer individual agents. And the turn to imagination is simply more accurate to the distinctive powers literary texts both engage and develop. It is rarely for purposes of knowledge that one re-reads texts or let's oneself dwell on how they handle details and shape structures. Without a powerful account of the productive forces these texts cultivate and shape as significant singular objects, we cannot see them as contributing anything distinctive to social life. They become mere instances of general conditions elaborated by the critic.

I

Of course those of us who teach such values may be the latest generation of Causabons, doomed to what is not just unfashionable but genuinely benighted. I cannot be without fear that this is the case. But my fear only intensifies my desire to try out the alternatives by diagnosing why the concept of productive imagination has lost its currency and by developing what powers a renewed secular model of its workings might afford our social practices.

Romantic poetry sought to resist the primarily discursive social focus of their predecessors by what Coleridge theorized as the "esemplastic imagination." This version of imagination could explain how imaginative writing might afford its society two fundamental tasks. First, writing, especially poetic writing, might demand what Nietzsche would call "slow reading" because it could make present the work of subjective energies in the process of establishing emotional significance for the phenomena engaged by the texts.[2] Tracking the

---

2   Friedrich Nietzsche, *Daybreak* (Cambridge: Cambridge UP, 1999), 5. In paragraph 5 of the preface he writes (tr. Hollingdale):

"A book like this, a problem like this, is in no hurry; we both, I just as much as my book, are friends of lento. It is not for nothing that I have been a philologist, perhaps I am a philologist still, that is to say, A TEACHER OF SLOW READING:- in the end I also write slowly. Nowadays it is not only my habit, it is also to my taste - a malicious taste, perhaps? - no longer to write anything which does not reduce to despair every sort of man who is 'in a hurry.' For philology is that venerable art which demands of its votaries one thing above all: to go aside, to take time, to become still, to become slow - it is a goldsmith's art and connoisseurship of the WORD which has nothing but delicate, cautious work to do and achieves nothing if it does not achieve it lento. But precisely for this reason it is more necessary than ever today, by precisely this means does it entice and enchant us the most, in the midst of an age of 'work,' that is to say, of hurry, of indecent and perspiring haste, which wants to 'get everything done' at once, including every old or new book:- this art does not so easily get anything done, it teaches to read WELL, that is to say, to read slowly, deeply, looking cautiously before and aft, with reservations, with doors left open, with delicate eyes and fingers ... My patient friends, this book desires for itself only perfect readers and philologists: LEARN to read me well!"

productive power of these subjective energies just is the means by which we come to encounter the text's power: concerns for discursive meaning or truth values simply require displacing the qualities of the productive activity traced by the slow reading.

By this focus on action, a poem like "Tintern Abbey" could criticize the passions of the poet's youth yet dialectically find those passions the source of an abiding faith in how the imagination could view the symbolic force of this fusion of nature and mind. Second, poetry could honor this sense of expanded spirit at home in nature by claiming for itself a distinctive mode of truth—not truth to the facts of nature but truth to what the spirit's enthusiasms might establish because of the specific deployment that gets exemplified in the work. These ways of focusing consciousness provide public articulations of what might be involved in our reflections on our experiences.[3]

These Romantic experiments in isolating imagination as a productive force do not have to be taken as efforts to shore up a waning body of Christian beliefs. But the enthusiastic speculation on what enthusiasm might involve did not fare well in the twentieth century, where critics and writers encountered intense demands to justify what they could contribute to a secular world shaped by the discoveries of science. Nor did the role of example promise a feasible alternative to truth since example seemed to justify attending merely to how experience seemed to emerge for particular subjects. A scientific culture demanded ways of turning such experiences into objects of study rather than indulgences in sympathetic participation. So the dominant force in American literary criticism in the middle of the twentieth century—the writing and teaching of the New Criticism—endeavored to reject most of Romantic poetry while trying to save its celebration of the imagination by transforming it into terms more appropriate for a restrained, secular set of discursive practices. I.A. Richards has to be the primary figure in this story because of how thoroughly his book on Coleridge became prelude to his utter psychologizing of reading as the activation of both positive and negative impulses in the mind. Gone entirely is Coleridge's model of expressive encounter fusing the mind with the forces driving nature.

The Christian New Critics hated Richards' versions of psychology, as they hated all scientism, but in order to combat the increasing importance of

---

3 I think these doctrines were produced because the Romantic poets recognized the power of what was involved in their freeing the imagination from the over-control of rhetoric so that it could become a heuristic and affective instrument in its own right. But when they theorized, they imposed their philosophical anxieties on the activities of imagination and tried problematically to show how they might contribute to philosophical contexts largely shaped by idealist responses to empiricism. Jonathan Culler implies the same critique I am making in his argument that literary studies has retained a very strong component of theological thinking even after the society it addresses has pretty much abandoned such concerns.

"empirical truth" in their society they had to put the claims for their beloved imagination in even more secular terms than Richards had used. They had to insist that the imagination was a vehicle for developing what they called "non-discursive truths" capable of establishing objective ways of reflecting on experience that were undeniably as real as what empiricism could show yet indemonstrable by any resource science could invoke. And, in the same spirit, they transformed Coleridge's notion of organicism: what had been evidence in the text of how the mind could fuse with nature became merely a formal condition characterizing the density and fusion of internal relations within the literary text. The New Critics purchased a kind of truth for imagination by gutting its distinctive views of expressive agency and turning all assertion into paradox and dramatic irony. They thought they could expunge manifest signs of subjectivity while projecting the need to treat texts very much as persons.

The most amusing, and perhaps the saddest aspect of my narrative, involves Paul de Man's largely successful effort to resuscitate Romantic poetry by showing how that poetry had brilliantly challenged every value that the New Critics would deploy to save the concept of a distinctive literary imagination:

> The lesson to be derived from the evolution of American formalist criticism is twofold. It reaffirms first of all the necessary presence of a totalizing principle as the guiding impulse of the critical process. In the New Criticism, this principle consisted of a purely empirical notion of the integrity of literary form, yet the mere presence of a such a principle could lead to the disclosure of distinctive structures of literary language (such as ambiguity and irony) although these structures contradict the very premises on which the New Criticism was founded.[4]

Ambiguity and irony contradict an empirical notion of literary form because these are states that cannot be the properties of objects: such states have to be interpreted as deriving from intentions.

So de Man can also argue that the New Critics could not sustain their claim for the autonomy of the art object. It depended on a notion of the "intentional fallacy" that had to treat literary form itself as a property of objects rather than a property derived from intentions:

---

4 Paul de Man, "Form and Intent in the American New Criticism," in *Blindness and Insight: Essays in the Rhetoric of Contemporary Criticism* (New York: Oxford University Press, 1971), 32.

THE WORK TEXTS DO 259

The difference between the stone and the chair distinguishes a natural object from an intentional object. The intentional object requires a reference to a specific act as constitutive of its being.[5]

The New Critics banished the role of the maker but insisted on all the powers of what could only be made rather than found:

Second, the rejection of the principle of intentionality, dismissed as fallacious, prevented the integration of these discoveries within a truly coherent theory of literary form. The ambivalence of American formalism is such that it was bound to lead to a state of paralysis.[6]

This critique seems to me exactly right. We do not find active formal principles in an object; we construct them as the activity of a subject.[7] But then de Man has his own dilemma. How can we characterize this attributed presence of a composing intelligence? By his next book, *Allegories of Reading*, he developed an elaborate theoretical position defining this subjectivity as playing the dual roles of simultaneously admitting the fictionality of what is imagined and trying to posit a quasi-objective illusory substance for that difference from actual natural objects. He learned from Sartre to treat intentionality as an ontological issue rather than a psychological one. That is, intentionality cannot be subsumed into active being. Instead it is always trying to evade the fact of the subject's difference, or non-being in the world of objects. Imagination then becomes the vehicle by which intentionality produces essentially rhetorical constructs oriented toward constituting substance for an insubstantial self. The building of fictional spaces derives from efforts at naturalizing a freedom that is fundamentally negative, as in Sartre's philosophy. And Romanticism becomes the often self-aware attempt to put theology to this constructive but also deceptive cultural task of establishing substance for human subjectivity.

We might quarrel about the details that are given short shrift in my account of the fate of imagination over two centuries. But I do not think we can quarrel about the results—that criticism has abandoned the concept and that the lack of a model for literary production has left ambitious critics no choice but to turn to other disciplines for grounding their work on what literary imaginations have produced. I am not sure any talk now about imagination will have

---

5   de Man, "Form and Intent in the American New Criticism," 24.
6   de Man, "Form and Intent in the American New Criticism," 32.
7   de Man, "Form and Intent in the American New Criticism," 25.

much impact on this situation. But as modes of reading with names like "suspicious reading," "critical reading," "surface reading," and "distant reading" compete for attention, I think one has to try virtually any strategy to return to the kinds of "slow reading" that have proved so effective in specifying how imaginations work in specific literary texts.[8]

The first step is to see that de Man could collapse imagination into intentionality because he treated consciousness as an ontological issue rather a psychological one. Imagination had one central inescapable task of concealing and partially acknowledging the illusory basis by which we construct a meaning-bearing human world different from the world we find in the objects that confront us. Even if this is true, such thinking effectively killed "imagination" as a key term for giving positive accounts of the arts. But the entire idea of an ontology of intentionality seems to me problematic. In an age of neuroscience it is hard not to think that de Man, like Sartre, offers at best an oversimplified sense of nature as objects rather than consisting also of relations and forces, among which there are the functions of mental life. So he necessarily also has an oversimplified sense of intention as only a principle compensating for this lack of objectivity by producing constant illusion and self-evasive fictions. The way out of de Man's morass is first just to examine the variety of functions imagination performs, rather than to derive these functions from what they might seem to have to perform within a given philosophical schema. Then we can shift our focus from an ontology of imagination to a psychological locus for theorizing about imagination, where multiple functions might be visible that matter for our recognizing what human powers we can exercise in secular worlds.

Therefore I will elaborate a phenomenological approach to imagination that I hope will provide an entirely secular yet highly suggestive model capable of both eliciting and justifying practices of slow reading. And if we can return to faith in slow reading, we can also return to making claims for the social significance of literary experience because of the self-reflexive modes the active imagination can afford social life. In my view this active imagination invites participation in sensibilities at work in trying to clarify the nature and possible consequences of our affective investments in various aspects of experience.

---

8 The basic essay proposing the principles of surface reading by Stephen Best and Sharon Marcus does a fine job of criticizing the orientation of suspicious reading. But in so doing it has to wobble on what the surface consists in. Surface ranges from sheerly manifest details to anything implied by the formal relations that are visibly aspects of the surface. This wobbling seems to me inevitable if we try to deal with a temporal process of multiple modes of attention to the constraints of spatial pictures. This is why I find "slow reading" much more suggestive—it allows for those multiple orientations shaped by a mode of overall attention rather than figures for what the object may or may not contain.

THE WORK TEXTS DO   261

And in a society where resentment is a terrifying logical response to deep divisions in wealth and power without any decent ideological defense for those differences, such acts of participation may make possible a competing psychological economy based largely on appreciating what can be accomplished when imagination achieves its full powers.

II

When I call upon phenomenology I refer to a form of practical analysis attempting to clarify distinctive psychological features of imagination at work within practical experience.[9] I am not qualified to engage the ontological questions inseparable from phenomenology for Husserl, Heidegger, and their heirs. And I am concerned only with what one might call a phenomenology that clarifies how we typically use expressions like "imaginatively," and "with imagination." This means that my version of phenomenology need not deal with all aspects of imaginative life, especially with hallucination. Instead the theory will have to take account only of how attributions about value can be inseparable from the functions we analyze.[10]

Fortunately I can develop this practical orientation by elaborating several categories from Edward Casey's brilliant *Imagining: A Phenomenological Study*, while also making some modifications to put this study in dialogue with contemporary concerns of artists and critics. Then I will turn to John Ashbery's early poem "The Instruction Manual" to spell out how a writer can not only deploy the imagination imaginatively but deliberately build a model, or an instruction manual, by which self-reflexively to elaborate in purely secular terms what the powers of imagination can produce and solicit.[11] Ashbery is aware

---

9   One reason for my choice of using phenomenological questioning is that we thereby gain a way of separating literary criticism from the domain of neural science, at least in most of its current operations. Neural science wants to know what parts of the brain are activated as particular agents respond to different kinds of situations. The situations are usually simple so that one can elicit measurable responses and so that one can pursue standard, publicly significant patterns of reaction. The imagination at work in neural science goes into the design of the experiment: the respondents have to be directed into common theaters. This is no way to elicit what is imaginatively interesting about the object, or what holds out appeals to be valued well beyond the time of imagining. So until neural science develops new directions of inquiry, one can say that concern for what is imaginative in the potential life a constructed object can sustain for attention will remain a distinctive concern for the humanities.

10 This last question and much of this chapter are the result of continuing lively discussion with my colleague Geoffrey O'Brien.

11 I do not claim that Ashbery cares about a phenomenology of the imagination (although this poem has affinities with the work of Raymond Roussell who did care a great deal about phenomenology).

that he is at every point in the poem undercutting a rhetoric about how imagination is a source of non-discursive truth developed by the New Critics who were Ashbery's teachers at Harvard: the poem offers a daydream and not a vision. But he is by no means content with irony. The poem deploys a manual that relocates imaginative power to emphasize control of tone and perspective and the weaving of the lyrical ego into manifestly public registers of affective life. Ashbery simply denies the poem any access to what might be called "truth." But the poem finds consolation because it can put on stage the fascinated ego's capacity to flesh out fascination with the lives and loves of other people. In effect Ashbery builds a model of secular imagination at work as it interprets an individual's pleasures in entertaining his own bonds to society. And in the process this poem offers the possibility that its way of imagining may afford a release from the kinds of anxieties that produced Romantic metaphysics: there is no need to offer elaborate reconciliations of the energies of self-consciousness and the sheer presence of the world beyond that self-consciousness because even the daydream affords a great deal of the life beyond the ego that we need to engage.

I am still not sure whether my exposition is primarily an effort at literary history—defining a post-new critical poetics in its foregrounding of an apparently thin surface and playful fascination with particulars rather than demanding the depth, compression and complexity dominant in Modernist poetics[12]—or primarily a theoretical effort to define something about imagination that has shaped and will shape a variety of literary texts within at least the span of Western literary history. Since I think the first alternative follows a familiar critical path, I will argue for the second option. Given this desire I probably should now deal with poems about place, from Vergil's *Georgics*, to Jonson's "To Penshurst," to Marvell's "Upon Appleton House," to Bryant's "The Prairie."[13] But this too seems too predictable, and not sufficiently responsive to the force of Casey's abstract analyses. So I will turn instead to a comparison between Ashbery's poem and Yeats's "Leda and the Swan" because I want to draw out how the two poems try out parallel functions, despite their quite different subject matters and imaginative orientations. This level of focus seems to me the strongest means for elaborating the possible roles of literary criticism if it boldly departs from a language of knowing and turns instead to a renewed sense of the orientations a focus on making can deploy. If despite their historical differences we find a significant self-conscious sense of shared

---

12   There is much to say about how Frank O'Hara deploys imaginative processes that closely parallel Ashbery's, in effect by treating the speaker's own daily life as a series of encounters much like those in "The Instruction Manual."

13   I thank Virginia Jackson for bringing this remarkable poem to my attention.

THE WORK TEXTS DO   263

resources in these two texts, we can have some confidence that we are pursuing vital features of imaginative activity worth guiding our readings of poems
and of other kinds of literary texts from a variety of cultural situations.

III

Casey's book is devoted to the imagination in practical life, not in literature—
so it positions us to see the many practical roles imagination can play, even as
it makes discourse about "truth" either impossible or reductive to what the
actions involve.[14] In order to elaborate the four categories I will borrow from
him, I want to develop a simple social scenario as our test case. Consider two
people planning to have lunch. Notice first that however much such actions
might seem determined in retrospect, at the moment of imagining these
agents seem free from all practical restrictions—at both poles of subject and
object. One can picture the couple with almost unlimited freedom to determine where they will go and what the menu might be, in contrast to all practical judgment. (Even if they know they cannot afford something they can imagine treating what they can afford as if it were the place they wished they could
attend.) Second, we see that this sense of freedom correlates with an infinite
set of possibilities for composing and combining the details of the situation, in

---

14   My case for the importance of keeping imaginative activity at the center of criticism
      shares a poststructuralist resistance to the authority of the conceptual order. But my case
      does not stress as its alternative to the conceptual order a domain of sheer event or singu-
      larity that extends the play of differences and calls for a idealization of the other (either
      as the other to language and to the demands of the ego). Rather it seeks to restore a sense
      of the capacities of images to carry distinctive modes of agency. I borrow Kant's definition
      of "purposiveness" in his *Critique of Judgment* (Section 10) as a condition opposed to hav-
      ing a purpose that submits an object to practical use. Purposiveness is the sense of a
      maker at work in the constant shaping of relations. Then I think I can say that the purpo-
      siveness of a text is neither in the subject nor in the object but in the awareness of their
      constant interaction. Purposiveness is only thinkable in the social space where subjects
      exist because of what they make manifest in their relation to objects. I hesitate to say that
      this space may depend on imagination to exist at all because this reveals my own involve-
      ment in Romantic views of imagination. But they do not have to wrong about everything
      for us to want to gain some distance from their ideology.
         This restoration promises to clarify what kind of identifications the texts invite, as well
      as projecting what is involved in taking on such identifications as provisional means of
      exploring the values that the text engages and elaborates. Imagination is not singular but
      common, at least as a force we can deploy. So even when it produces singular states, it
      does so within an atmosphere shaped by a purposiveness that also invites exploring what
      identification might involve. Reading for these modes of production honors the labor of
      the writing and anchors the reading process in something other than the reader's needs
      and desires, something that resists the authority of the individual consumer.

sharp contrast with the demands in typical situations where perception shapes discourse. Think here of fourteenth century Florentine and Siennese painting, so of a piece with the fantastic dimension of saint's lives.

Perception works in terms of the logic of picturing. It activates a relation to a physical world with its own deep structure, independent of the perceiver, who contributes a perspective but not a shape. In the order of perceptions there are degrees of visibility: some properties of the scene are foregrounded; some grasped only fleetingly; and some assert pressures that are not noticed at all (like a history of previous interactions). There is a history and a shape to the menu that determines how its particular aspects are to be read. But with an imagined situation there is no inherent logic and no pressure to recognize specific salient details. Saliency is determined by the imaginers, and there is (phenomenologically) no other world that imposes underlying demands. As Jeff Blevins put it in conversation, "imagination is the only guarantee for the shape taken by its contents." Our constructed menu might be fit for the gods.

Such freedom does not entail that imaginers will not choose to present their materials as if they were bound to the logic of perception. But these literary imaginings will usually have moments when authors revel in their freedom and simply select what feels right rather than what would be demanded were they to follow a historian's practice. Yet at the same time, the freedom itself can appear as insubstantial because its world is not bound to the logic of perception. Freedom within the imagination can be both illusory and purposive. Because imaginative activity seems a mere projection, we are always tempted to locate causes for it, yet it seems also capable of treating itself as shaping what emerges.

This freedom to act and freedom from latent structure have two significant consequences that complete my borrowing from Casey. The third feature stressed by a phenomenology of imagination is its capacity for staging infinitely subtle tonalities for situations—as perhaps every lover knows. Because there are no clear constraints on the subject or the ways details are related to one another, there are no categorical principles by which we can expect to draw out the relations among those details so as to conform to any prevailing notion of sense. Shem will never catch up with Shaun. The principles of relation are shaped simply by the details and our modes of apprehending them as aspects of a concretely emerging set of conjunctions. A face does not have to resemble what we think faces show; so one possibility for an imaginative representation is to reveal subtle desires and demands and fears that take strange shapes as they escape our typical routes of repression. Imaginative figuration has virtually unlimited control over the play of surfaces, fold upon fold, as details breed details, gestures breed corresponding gestures, and affective tones multiply freely—think of Picasso's portraits of women. But an observer also has to recognize that this kind of imaginative activity pays a significant price

THE WORK TEXTS DO   265

for its freedom. Because of their freedom from the logic of perception the fantasy features have no specifiable depth: viewers or readers might find the figures of imagination suggestive but they might also find them simply unintelligible.

This issue of interpretability leads us to our fourth feature. The play of surfaces often creates the very desire for in depth interpretation that it frustrates. Few events in the domain of the arts are as depressing as the effort to pin down imaginative flights of fancy in terms of psychoanalytic or moral explanations, as in Freud's reading of *La Tempesta*. Purposiveness, if it is manifest at all, need be manifest only within the arrangement of surface details and so cannot provide a discursive rationale for them, however plausible the effects achieved. I agree with Casey's claim that because of the plural surfaces imagination can develop, the only effective way to offer interpretations of imaginative activity is to grant the product the force of self-evidence. The work is replete, and so can only stand beside efforts at interpretation in partial mockery and in partial yearning for what might anchor it within the interpretive models provided by a culture.

I mean by the force of self-evidence simply a distinctive process by which we establish the significance of imaginative activity. Typically we determine meanings by the conjunction of appropriate contexts that bear on what the speaker might want to say and how that statement might be appropriate for the occasion. With imagined worlds there is a paucity of effective external contexts so that we have to rely on what see as relations among the textual units given by the action. We still build contexts that make features significant, but we have little justification for invoking these contexts beyond the way that the contexts proposed seem to emerge out of our concrete need to connect specific elements and ways of speaking within the act in question.[15]

---

15   This claim to self-evidence seems very close to the traditional aestheticist thesis that the work of art shapes its own end. And there are in fact significant similarities between what Casey observes and what the Kantian tradition believes. The Romantics were right that imagination is always concrete, even when say dreams present quite abstract material. More important, the Romantics were also right about expressions of the imagination having this power of establishing conditions of self-evidence where the practical interpretive intelligence is always a belated interloper. However the Romantics thought that these conditions of self-evidence derived from realizing deep truths about the world rendered. In contrast, when we stress phenomenology and the modeling it can encourage, we have to root our sense of organization solely in the nature of the specific noetic properties of imagination. Because it makes no claim to deeper significance, this phenomenological perspective helps elaborate how imagination can play a significant role in freeing us to see fresh possible arrangements of situations—practically and formally. These arrangements can be deployed for their own sake or as a deliberate means of looking differently at phenomena to which we have become habituated.

IV

Idealist and Romantic thinkers could not resist making too much of a good thing by interpreting imagination's claims to freedom and to modes of self-evidence as giving us access to "the one life within us and abroad." So I turn to Ashbery's "The Instruction Manual" as both an implicit critique of Romantic views of imagination and a modeling of quite different means of accessing its substantial powers that come much closer to honoring its phenomenological qualities as elemental features of practical life. I am especially interested in how Ashbery's tone suggests the capacity to release imagination from the self-congratulatory posturing of Romantic lyricism so that it might participate more fully in a new kind of social space not shaped in accord with the authority of the poet. In essence imagination in this poem develops possibilities for bringing a sense of emotional resonance to bear on the world—not by interpreting that world but by fleshing out details so that they reach out both to the possible sources of feeling in the public scene and to how an audience might be expected to internalize those feelings as elements that reveal its own capacity for shared sympathy and understanding. As model, the poem becomes an instruction manual for what can be accomplished in escaping the task of writing instruction manuals. The poem's daydream becomes a mode of self-evidence both producing and referring to how imagination can do work in the actual world. In fact Ashbery in choosing the daydream establishes a mode of lyricism where production and reference are completely interwoven.

The poem begins with the speaker's wishing he did not have to write an instruction manual and envying those he sees from his window not oppressed by that task. He engages these alternatives by reverting to his typical practice of daydreaming—in this case of Guadalajara, the city in Mexico he most wants to see for the first time. So he composes the city in his daydream. First the details seem conventional and general. How not begin with a band playing European music in the public square and the flower girls handing out flowers. It is almost

---

Emphasizing these relational traits makes Casey, and my use of Casey, even more hostile toward interpreters than was the Kantian tradition. For self-evidence is not the basis of interpretation, not a direct means of aligning with intention, but a model of how products of imagination emerge that resist all our languages of purpose, even as it toys with them and depends on them to bring out what is unexpected and cannot be aligned with the language of motives, acts, and judgments. Of course writers and painters can use the imagination in the service of such judgments. But when imagination is released to seek its own conditions of operation, it will offer only surface relations, endless surface relations in endlessly shifting configurations. And then the rhetoric of ends in themselves will seem an effort to convert sheer necessity into a mode of valuation, as if in the end we could resurrect the language of purposiveness with its governing intentions.

THE WORK TEXTS DO 267

as if the imagination followed a script already written and rewritten. But soon we realize that this speaker has a penchant for particular persons and colors, from one particular girl in rose and blue to serving girls in green offering green and yellow fruit, and eventually to a parade where attention is focused on a dapper little man in deep blue:

> ...On his head sits a white hat
> And he wears a mustache which has been trimmed for the occasion.
> His dear one, his wife, is young and pretty; her shawl is rose, pink, and white.[16]

The poetry here resides in the attention to made-up detail as a condition of a strange tone that at once acknowledges distance and self-indulgently tries to bridge that divide. Details bubble over in long lines because everything flows so easily from the conjunction of dream, conventional detail, and enthusiastic participation. Within the framework provided by these clichéd details, scenes take shape that seem impossible not to visualize. So perhaps what I am treating as stock elements are better seen as the effects of a cultural grammar into which the dream enters. The grammar offers at once a panoply of details and a sense of a shared world because the speaker's dream offers access to what proves a common space for fantasy. And the commonness miraculously has no deleterious effect on the sheer exuberance of what is permitted within the dream.

Now the way is prepared for treating the imagination as a complex actualizing of thoughts that Wittgenstein's understanding of philosophical grammar make possible. The poem moves beyond seeing to envisioning full participation in this constructed world as its texture of embedded desires also becomes visible:

> Here come the boys! They are skipping and throwing little things on the sidewalk
> Which is made of gray tile. One of them, a little older, has a toothpick in his teeth.
> He is silenter than the rest, and affects not to notice the pretty young girls in white,
> But his friends notice them, and shout their jeers at the laughing girls.[17]

---

16   John Ashbery, *Collected Poems 1956–1987* (New York: Library of America, 2008), 6.
17   Ashbery, *Collected Poems 1956–1987*, 6.

Then, for first time after setting up the dream, the narrator intrudes as "I" because he wants to hear a conversation between a particular girl and a boy that his story has produced. It is as if the collective picture of young boys and girls matters only for the particular sense of romance that it might elicit. Then, perhaps weary of this "I," our narrator takes up a voice that could be essentially a native guide, now strikingly in the first person plural:

> Let us take this opportunity to tiptoe into one of the side streets.
>   Here you may see one of those white houses with green trim
>   That are so popular here. Look—I told you!...
>   An old woman in gray sits there, fanning herself with a palm leaf fan.
>   She welcomes us to her patio, and offers us a cooling drink.
>   "My son is in Mexico City," she says. "He would welcome you too,
>   If he were here. But his job is with a bank there.
>   Look, here is a photograph of him."
>   And a dark – skinned lad with pearly teeth grins out at us from the
> worn leather frame.
>   We thank her for her hospitality, for it is getting late
>   And we must catch a view of the city, before we leave, from a good high
> place.[18]

It seems as if the more the narrator daydreams, the more he is enfolded within the details of the dream, so he becomes the only one capable of guiding us through this self-enclosing picture. Then as the role of guide takes hold, so do the pronouns "We" and "you" that make this "Here" a fully social object (capable of being balanced with "there" to recapitulate in another key the situation of the entire poem). "Here" inspires a playful but profound range of indexical references—from the space produced by the dream in which green trim is so popular, to the hypothetical that her son would welcome us if he were "here," to the mother's directing attention to the photograph. We might also note that as "here" takes over, there is no need to rely on references to "I." How could such intense participation not establish a sense that the subject shares his or her world? And how could such detail not shape intersubjective space, even producing dialogue on the diegetical and authorial levels?

The affective power of the poem depends on its correlating two aspects of imaginative life—its productive dimensions by which it escapes writing the demanded instruction manual, and the self-reflexive dimension by which the poem fleshes out and takes pleasure in its own productive powers to develop a

---

18   Ashbery, *Collected Poems 1956–1987*, 7.

different kind of instruction manual. For Ashbery the core of imaginative life is the sheer capacity to select details in a way that elicits all of its powers to inhabit and extend what the details bring to consciousness. The text becomes the presentation of a series of actions inviting an audience to participate in the transformation of scattered, insistently arbitrary details into a dense, coherent, and playful particularizing of elements that function as examples of life in Guadalajara. And the scene as it emerges fills out three worlds—an imagined picture of an intricate social scene, a rendering of practices by which the imagination itself becomes a manifest principle of activity, and a lightly held but intense social critique of a work life that requires using the imagination as a vehicle for escape.[19] As the speaker elaborates each of these worlds, he mobilizes for self-consciousness the processes by which we can come to appreciate what is involved in our capacities to give significance to fictional sequences— without forcing that significance into discursive intelligence.

Each choice in the poem is experienced as playfully uncaused. But over time the scene takes on a level of coherence that deepens our engagement, even while we know that the only evidence for the coherence is within the imaginative process itself. There is no external arbitrator for what significance can unfold. Yet Ashbery is careful to produce an increasingly dense social world, because the imagined characters find their affective lives embedded in the public details dwelt on and dwelt among by the imagination. As we develop the projected world there seems less to divide us than to unite us. And the entire phenomenon of the dream providing its own self-evidence takes on social force by offering a powerful metaphoric emblem for how this freedom of imagining can take on social weight without needing to be explained. Ultimately this playful tone affords means of reminding ourselves of our beings in common as we dwell on what begins as only an individual's escapist dream. The freedoms of imagination need not preclude putting that freedom to work in fleshing out for self-consciousness what "dwelling" might involve.

There is not much left to the poem, but what remains considerably deepens the poem's affective intensity, in part because the poem seems intent on drawing out how the imagination comes to realize its own limitations. Then it can embrace these limitations, to assert another aspect of its potential power (not addressed by Casey) more closely woven into the constraints of practical

---

19   See on this third point Jasper Bernes, "John Ashbery's Free Indirect Labor," MLQ 74, no. 2 (December 2013): 517–39. In conversation Geoffrey O'Brien also stresses the social. And in his own long poem "People on Sunday" establishes a dialogue with Ashbery's poem suggesting a much denser sense of social lives impinging on one another. See O'Brien's *People on Sunday* (New York: Wave Books, 2013), 64–74.

existence. Once the attention of "we" orients itself to the overall view of the city, there need only be a series of isolated observations based on the expression "There can be." But then we almost have to ask how there be an interesting end for a daydream that has no inherent logic? Ashbery's response to our question is to shift tonalities. The last specific detail the poem offers is the young boy and girl "now" in the heat of the day lurking "in the shadows of the bandstand." This move to the shadows then allows the poem turn to the past tense in order to offer explicit self-reflection on what the imagination has enabled, and, more strikingly, failed to enable:

> We have seen young love, married love, and a mother's love for her son,
> We have heard the music, tasted the drinks, and looked at colored houses.
> What more is there to do, except stay? And that we cannot do.
> And, as a last breeze freshens the top of the weathered old tower, I turn my gaze
> Back to the instruction manual, which has made me dream of Guadalajara.[20]

In this adventure imagination cannot conquer the pressures of time and loss. And it cannot successfully evade the loneliness (or capitalist driven isolation) that has in fact shaped the poem from the start. So at the end the poem seems to take responsibility for the fact that what seemed so casual and so free also had a drivenness to it almost successfully resisted by the imagination's capacity to dwell in the present tense. There is ultimately a pathos to the dream condition because, however enticing the engagement in the lives of other people, it is tragically provisional: we cannot stay in our fictions, which is probably why we have license to enjoy them so thoroughly. But the more the poem admits the limitations of its own imaginings, the fuller becomes it presentation of how the imagination can switch registers so that it comes to speak for the dreamers rather than for the object of the dream. One freedom the imagination has it the freedom to reflect on its escapist tendencies and to make those tendencies the focus for bonding its productions to the self-reflexive languages we typically use in characterizing tragic aspects of experience.

Pure imagination has no pathos because there is no other, no pressure of the real to impose limitation and pain. Ashbery's writing, on the other hand is drenched in pathos because he is so acutely aware that time and loss are the inescapable accompaniments of presence and pleasure. But Ashbery can still honor the freedom of imagination by treating is the necessary condition of a perpetual conflict between the urge to flee into the daydream and the

---

20   Ashbery, *Collected Poems 1956–1987*, 7.

THE WORK TEXTS DO 271

recognition that daydreams too have their existential implications. The acknowledgement of necessity in "The Instruction Manual" is charmingly and imaginatively handled—by treating necessity as the literal emergence of what Wallace Stevens called "the pressure of reality." In moving toward conclusion Ashbery deploys an extended simile of the breeze (a staple of Romantic lyricism) to suspend time for a moment and further delay the task at hand. Then, as the speaker returns to his instruction manual, we recognize in retrospect that accepting our isolation may be the necessary precondition for appreciating what we need from other people. These real world needs provide the drive to freedom in the first place, and then freedom finds itself fascinated by what might bind it to the lives of other people—in the dream and in the need to accept what dreaming cannot accomplish. Here the freedom is not the same as in most Romantic poetry because it is not the result of liberating the imagination from bondage by an epistemic process. Instead freedom plays the role of the source of imaginative activity in the first place.

v

"Leda and the Swan" obviously has a very different sensibility. Yet it utilizes essentially the same four properties of imagination that Casey emphasizes.[21] And it engages in the same struggle to align the imagination with the interpretation of human suffering, albeit in sharply different ways that cultivate contrasts rather than smooth them out into a generalized pathos.

---

21 Were I to make the historical case for a distinctive post-new critical treatment of imagination I would emphasize how in "The Instruction Manual" there is no grand drama for imagination; there is only the possibility of keeping some control over one's life by manifesting a sense of autonomy, self-consciously limited to the daydream and existentially to the making of the art work. So the question of what constitutes the values involved in choosing come to the fore, again without any trust that the authority here has any public sanction at all. In this respect I think also of Ashbery's friend Frank O'Hara's "I do this, I do that" poems. They seem just the record of interesting events in which the poet plays a part. But if we treat them as also modeling how the imagination works, the poems become a lot more than records of states of sensibility. They become celebrations of sites where there can be immediate decisions capable of engaging the imagination. The poems invite identifying with the activity of becoming interested in what the imagination finds itself wanting to inhabit:

"[I]t seems they were all cheated of some marvelous experience which is not going to go wasted on me which is why I'm telling you about it." (*The Collected Poems of Frank O'Hara*, 360; see also pp. 202 and 335).

In Ashbery's and O'Hara's poems the individual has no content aside from the qualities of the making and the generic needs that underlie this mode of serious play. The poems share the desire for an audience that also motivates confessional poetry, but without any visible deep personal need for a hearing.

Consider for example how important it is for the speakers in both poems to choose details that trouble our conceptual structures—if only in Yeats's insistence on sonnet compression. We might say that the details put the freedom of imagining to the test of whether it can be exercised imaginatively. The chosen details project a kind of gravity that gives a body to the intentions of the chooser. The imagination stresses the madeness of the details and our awareness of that madeness frees us to seek complex modes of relatedness among them. For example, Ashbery's intense refusal of any confessional impulse is as powerful a mode of calling for attention to the details of constructing speakers as any more assertively content-ridden sense of self. Reading poetry may just involve seeing into this interplay between what choices naturalize our sense of the action and which ones stress the ultimate specificity of the shaping intelligence.

Form becomes in many respects another kind of naturalizing, this time in the domain of mind pushed into awareness of its own radical selectiveness and of its historical dependencies. Attributions of form afford a second level for the details by introducing entire explicit and often subtle systems based on choice rather than contingent features of descriptions. So we are invited to treat form as the attribution of a logic to choice that is not based on practical concerns but on the possibilities of fleshing out the way imagination affords self-referring structures providing coherence for the relations among the details. As we will see, this clearly applies to how writers manipulate fixed verse forms, use syntactic figures like chiasmus, and foreground where structure extends features of what constitutes self-evidence. But it is no less present in how "The Instruction Manual" is built on discrete units focusing on various features of Guadalajara as various forms and tones of address.

Finally these productive energies become inseparable from what the poem treats as the force of the self-evidence by which it takes on a shape and even a role in the social world. The two poems diverge in many ways. Yet both poems rely for their communicative power on the reach for social significance made possible not by overt generalization but by extending and sharpening the powers of specific figures. By stressing the specificity of relational features the text can come to constitute a distinctive or singular attitude that carries exemplary force. We need not seek truth from imagination because its powers of exemplification provide an alternative way of predicating what might be possible.

VI

The efforts at intensified force and the synthetic power of images we see in Yeats's poem are almost totally foreign to the attitudes and emotions explored by Ashbery. For later Yeats, the spirit of casual playfulness would abandon the concentrative force by which the authorial ego can hope to transcend the

THE WORK TEXTS DO   273

banalities of ordinary existence. Where Ashbery wanders into the imagined
world sponsored by the idea of Guadalajara, the opening lines of "Leda and the
Swan" are devoted to theatricalizing a sense of the demands a single world-
historical event can make on consciousness—as what is represented and as
the pressure on the representing:

> A sudden blow: the great wings beating still
> Above the staggering girl, her thighs caressed

These details will not allow the readers to relax but demand complete concentration. Here any spirit of playfulness would count as turning one's eyes away
from this emerging tragedy—not a celebration of imagination but an evasion
of its purest modes of intensity.

Yet there is much to learn from Ashbery in appreciating how this poem unfolds. Notice for example how the poem from the start insists on its autonomy:
it is willing to commit to a beginning that offers no underlying rationale and
whose claims for intensity can only be justified by what further evidence the
poem can produce that this particular focus on the individual retains the immense consequences of the rape.[22] Notice too how a sense of pure event justifies a parallel to Ashbery's freedom in selecting details, combined here with a
pronounced freedom in selecting the modes of syntax that will best mobilize
the linguistic surface:

> A sudden blow: the great wings beating still
> Above the staggering girl, her thighs caressed
> By the dark webs, her nape caught in his bill,
> He holds her helpless breast upon his breast.[23]

Even the syntax challenges the authority of understanding in order to stress
the apparent arbitrariness of what happens to Leda. For there seem two possibilities of organizing this sentence—one as the processing of an absolute
construction separate from concerns for modification and the other a series of
participles that never quite connects grammatically to the "he" that is the subject of the main clause. Both remain perennially present as conditions of
feeling.

---

22   Needless to say that this opening sense of selectedness is crucial also to how novels can
      produce a sense of control by the author of the world to come. I think in particular of the
      openings of *Great Expectations* and *Mrs. Dalloway*, as if the more a major novel aims to
      develop a realistic sense of the world, the more it is likely to dwell at its inception on the
      authorial freedom to select what and how those naturalizing effects are to be deployed.
      One need look no farther than the opening of Anna Karenina.
23   W.B. Yeats, *Collected Poems* (New York: Scribner, 1996), 214.

Why do these alternatives matter? First, they are again signs of the absoluteness of an imagining that produces autonomous event qualities difficult to reconcile with our ordinary procedures for making sense. (Imagination seems to have strange affinities with rape.) Second, the absoluteness of the imagining links the poem's sense of the radicalness of making with a striking capacity to blend details that evoke the order of perception without submitting to it. There is no background here: all the details align with the focus on the present tense of the rape. Just because imagination has no obligations to the logic of the perceptual order, it can explore means of intensifying the present that might bring sufficient intensity and scope to constitute another order of being. And this order of being might be capable for the moment of providing modes of self-consciousness that are not compatible with practical life (although "there we cannot stay"). Finally, one might argue that the greatness of this poem consists largely in its unwillingness to be satisfied with achieving the level of intensity established by its beginning. Yeats wants to extend this intensity by correlating it with a radical sense of structure. It is as if the rest of the poem were an instruction manual making the freedom of self-evidence itself a domain of pure compositional intelligence that extends what we can mean by "intensity" and by "event":

> How can those terrified vague fingers push
> The feathered glory from her loosening thighs?
> And how can body, laid in that white rush,
> But feel the strange heart beating where it lies?
> A shudder in the loins engenders there
> The broken wall, the burning roof and tower
> And Agamemnon dead.
>   Being so caught up,
> So mastered by the brute blood of the air,
> Did she put on his knowledge with his power
> Before the indifferent beak could let her drop?

Perhaps only an emphasis on self-evidence has a chance of answering this final question since it boggles the practical understanding. Such a serious question may demand the fecklessness of imagination.

This poem is a sonnet, but a strange one. Most sonnets, Italian and Shakespearean, assume that the form requires elaborating fundamentally discursive strategies so that they gather and structure affective consequences. The opening quatrains pose a problem or dilemma, and the closing elements propose a redirection of the mind and feelings so that the problem proves in fact an

THE WORK TEXTS DO   275

instrument of discovery. But in Yeats's poem the thinking is charged with urgency: rather than allowing reflective distance, the details selected emphasize the immediacy of the situation, and the form is under such urgent pressures that the statement of historical consequences in line 11 is broken off, as if the details were so ominous that the poem had immediately to establish an attitude by which to confront those consequences. Then the final lines offer two very tight rhymes followed by what is virtually an off-rhyme between "up" and "drop." This final question is not something that will be easily resolved into the pressures of form. Yet the poet does not just admit defeat. There is a brilliant supplemental formal process that makes the final four syllables parallel the five syllable unit in the second part of the broken line 11. "Could let her drop" completely echoes "Being so caught up," so that there is another level of parallelism at least acknowledging the difficulties that the off rhyme poses for any sense of satisfying closure.

Yeats responds to the challenge of developing an emotional stance that can adapt itself to both the shock and the scope of the initiating situation by from the beginning stressing not just the imagination's freedom in selecting telling details but also its constructive capacity to provide distinctive frames for those details. The overall structure of the poem balances two levels of statements of fact with two questions making quite different demands on the reader ... The two statements of fact try to compare what proves incomparable for consciousness—the momentariness of the rape and the general sense that a civilization is doomed because of it. But the differences in the two questions try to address and resolve this immense gap between event and the need for comprehension. The first question is emotional, seeking empathy with Leda; the second question is philosophical, seeking to develop a stance toward knowledge that can encompass human vulnerability to being raped by what drives the course of history. The more forceful the first question, the more inevitable the need for this second effort at consoling generalization.[24]

---

24   It is interesting to me that Yeats's concern for the structure of two assertions balanced by two different kinds of questions was apparent even in the rather dreadful first version of the poem, as presented in Giorgo Melchiori's remarkable chapter on the role Leda played in Yeats's imagination:

> Now can the swooping godhead have his will
> Yet hovers, though her helpless eyes are pressed
> By the webbed toes; and all that powerful bill
> Has suddenly bowed her face upon his breast.
> How can those terrified vague fingers push
> The feathered glory from her loosening thighs?
> All the stretched body's laid in that white rush
> And feels the strange heart beating where it lies.

Both questions do not quite allow specific answers that might count as knowledge in the practical world, in part because, as Wittgenstein might say, what would pass as answers do not appear to overcome any kind of specific doubt. We can know that Leda must be feeling something, but if want any fuller sense of that feeling we must rely on the kind of attunement only imagination can provide. The second question asks not for shared feeling but for a shared knowledge—between Leda and Zeus and implicitly between Leda and the audience—that can't even be aligned directly with emotion. This "knowledge" clearly lies beyond the domain of propositions—perhaps it offers a kind of "knowing how" rather than a "knowing that." Even Leda probably cannot say whether she can put on the god's knowledge with this power, especially since the possibility of knowledge, and the pain of knowledge, turn on the phase, "Could drop." This phrase suggests that there is a power beyond Zeus, the power that undid his father and will eventually undo the Greek gods as well. What can this knowledge be?

Perhaps this knowledge can only be imagined by reflecting on the disturbing gulf between human impotence and some unidentifiable level of shaping force that makes history. Then the imagination is probably the only mental power that can dwell on this level of awareness without trying to formulate this knowledge as if it were another claim to propositional adequacy. If discursive reason is stretched to its limit simply so that it can flesh out what Leda is experiencing, it seems paradoxically far more helpless in relation to how she develops self-consciousness. So we are invited to explore the possibility that these questions do not quite ask for what typically passes for knowledge. These questions might offer a mode of affirmation, or at least of relatedness to being, precisely because of the way imagination relies on self-evidence and so can pretty much bypass the roles played by understanding. Yet there is no mysticism involved, no special world for which the imagination holds the key. Instead Yeats suggests that issues of manner must come to the fore.

Here both questions posed by the poem invite us to ignore the entire domain of indicative sentences. They function as something closer to exclamations so that the questioning itself is the measure of intensity. And then the ability to stay within the question is the poem's suggested response to its sense of

---

A shudder in the loins engenders there
The broken wall, the burning roof and Tower
And Agamemnon dead...
Being so caught up
Did nothing pass before her in the air?
Did she put on his knowledge with his power
Before the indifferent beak could let her drop? (p. 74)
See Melchiori, *The Whole Mystery of Art* (New York: Macmillan, 1961), 73–163.

THE WORK TEXTS DO 277

tragedy: the richest response to tragedy is to ram all of the intensity possible into the questioning that marks both our impotence and our imaginative capacity to correlate feeling and willing on levels that understanding cannot hope to provide. The self-evidence afforded by taking questions as exclamations gets raised to the highest plane of what is involved in becoming full witnesses to tragic conditions.

VII

Now let me refine and summarize some basic theoretical claims that try to generalize from these examples. I cannot say that all work of literary merit emphasizes imagination or exemplarity. But I think I can say that most work will rely on visibly non-rational processes of selection, resistance to practical interpretation, and some version of self-evidence, so that the relations that imagination provides establish the work's claim to be involved in practical life. 1) In most situations there will be several levels of embedded imaginative activity—and in how the author establishes a presence, in how characters emerge as something with more density and presence than they would have as elements of argumentative structures. The crucial feature is how the text calls attention to its manner as defining the significance of its matter. The "how" of imagining establishes the modality of what is imagined. What is imagined is imagined as something or in some mode of activity or as soliciting perspectives with which we may be quite unfamiliar. "Leda and the Swan" issues less from a personal speaker than a speaking position something like a collective consciousness in terror of its vulnerability. And "Instruction Manual" manages a marvelous process of treating the utterly banal with an expansive compassion and grace that changes our understanding of the dynamics of lyricism.

2) The selecting of details is how imagination produces a world in which it solicits our responding imaginative activity. In realist fiction we tend to ignore the axis of selection so we can devote our attention to the axis of represented action. But precisely because there are so many details available within how realism identifies with the perceptual order, there is an enormous freedom and a powerful need to control the sense of focus by careful selection. The realist text appears as already naturalized, but it is does not emerge that way for the author facing a blank page. If one goes back to oral narrative one sees that the dynamics of choice becomes central because the audience is familiar with the options for the narrator, yet still capable of being surprised. And I imagine the Victorian serial novel as a perfect emblem for the genre in which the profusion of sentences is dramatically and syntactically making constant modifications in the expectations and investments of its readers. One could say that Joyce's

originality in *Ulysses* and *Finnegans Wake* consists largely in emphasizing the degree to which the author's choosing is everywhere constitutive so that only the working of self-evidence will enable us to offer coherent interpretations of the several levels composed by such choosings.

3) Within aesthetics this claim to self-evidence has been asserted as a special power of imagination. Imagination produces objects that are ends in themselves while interventions in the world of givens are bound to discursive processes. Yet I think it silly to seek a single framework in which the discursive can be measured against the non-discursive. Each activity involves a power that we have to describe and delimit. The important aspect of the imaginative power we have been considering is its capacity to put details and states together that do not necessarily cohere in ways that are bound by knowledge claims. This freedom is accompanied by an obvious weakness: we need testing before we make any existential claims based on imaginative products. But at the same time the foregrounding of choice is also an obvious strength because writers can produce states in which, among other relations, interrogatives function as exclamations and therefore bypass indicatives. So we can imagine imagination affording affinities with persons and states of being, or even what we want to call knowledge, that we can only deal with in terms of how the internal relations establish self-evidence. Yeats's questions are so powerful because their only answers are in what the poems offer as conditions of experience embedding this strange "could" within history. And "The Instruction Manual" can compose an alternative version of instruction because it specifies how the imagination organizes what can be involved in dreaming of Guadalajara. Abstract commentary can indicate that this alternate world is being constructed, but the power of that world depends on our attuning to how it composes internal relations that stand on their own. In this case the details are not even metaphoric: rather they directly exemplify the power of imagination to interpret its own productions. Here Ashbery oddly provides the same process that Tolstoy does in Anna Karenina's suicide.

4) We have to ask what use is this responsiveness to modes of evidence that cannot add up to any kind of propositional knowledge. And we have to ask how this knowing can be mediated by images that refuse the logic by which picturing operates. Why care about these thin surfaces that cannot be held responsible to the levels of intricate and partially hidden depths that accompany perception? Why not relegate all imagination to phantasy and illusions about powers of mind independent of causality? I think this very line of questioning establishes the logic of a possible answer, one that I have implicitly been relying on throughout this chapter. It is quite common to be in practical situations where we do not worry about evidence or even about responsibility to the

truth latent in situations. On such occasions the important thing is not to separate imagination from reality but to preserve imagination's authority to define what kind of reality the relations among images project. Imagination is an instrument for clarifying or developing pictures rather than for applying them as knowledge bearing propositions.

Consider for example how we treat feelings and emotions when we are committed to appreciating acts of imagination. We could just name the feelings if we were worried about how to act with respect to them: beware the angry person, pursue what seems possible from gestures of friendship. But instead we have been attending to how our ways of naming make possible states of appreciation entirely focused on specific situations—as dramatic moments and as figures embodying an author's modes of attributing significance to these moments. Consequently we cannot quite say what Leda is feeling, or knowing, or what the characters so briefly glimpsed in Guadalajara are likely to do with their lives. We seek participation, even if this means dwelling in uncertainty, rather than seeking a knowledge that also recognizes its own thinness because the knowledge is limited to the confines of what makes an epistemically plausible proposition. The goal of participation perhaps requires that we be content with the intensity of our questions as the fullest measure of attunement.

I think Marx realized that the only way he could give priority to social relations was by a theory of historical determinism. Only a sense of necessity will stabilize priorities and give reasons for acting that are not limited to self-interest. Analogously, it may take a sense of the significance of pure questioning in order to free literary theory from the appeal of knowledge claims so that it can look for other, more indirect social uses for what we come to care about through individual texts. These individual texts can make assertions about truth values, just as any speech act can propose such assertions. But if we read them as assertions we are stuck with their referential value—true or false— and the manner becomes irrelevant once it is deciphered. The logic of perception seeks examples that illustrate concepts so that we get a sense of what is typical about the object. The logic of imagination, in contrast, seeks a different kind of exemplification based not on the concept but on how the particular activity might suggest analogical uses or significant differences as we sort out what particular constructions can be useful for projecting onto other scenes. This kind of exemplification makes the manner of presentation central to the reading process. Such exemplification may emphasize the particular fullness of a powerful experience. Or it can be more generic, making present on various levels what can be compared to other literary texts, as the turn to pathos dramatizes in "Instruction Manual." In such cases the labors of imagination take on worldliness because they affect our sense of how experience impinges on our values.

References

Ashbery, John. *Collected Poems 1956–1987.* New York: Library of America. 2008.

Attridge, Derek. *The Singularity of the Literature.* Abingdon, Oxon: Taylor & Francis Group. 2004.

Bernes, Jasper. "John Ashbery's Free Indirect Labor." MLQ 74, no. 4 (December 2013): 517–39.

Best, Stephen, and Sharon Marcus. "Surface Reading: An Introduction." *Representations* 108, no. 1 (2009): 1–21.

Casey, Edward. *Imagining: A Phenomenological Study.* Bloomington: Indiana University Press. 1976.

de Man, Paul. *Blindness and Insight: Essays in the Rhetoric of Contemporary Criticism.* New York: Oxford University Press. 1971.

Melchiori, Giorgio. *The Whole Mystery of Art.* New York: Macmillan. 1961.

Nietzsche, Friedrich. *Daybreak: Thoughts on the prejudices of morality.* Translated by R.J. Hollingdale. Edited by Maudemarie Clark and Briak Leiter. Cambridge: Cambridge University Press. 1999.

O'Brien, Geoffrey G. *People on Sunday.* New York: Wave Books. 2013.

O'Hara, Frank. *The Collected Poems of Frank O'Hara.* Edited by Donald Allen. Berkeley: University of California Press. 1995.

Yeats, W.B. *Collected Poems.* New York: Scribner. 1996.

CHAPTER 12

Conceiving and Imagining: Examples and Lessons

Jody Azzouni

1   Descartes' Distinction

There's a phenomenological distinction between what's imaginable and what's conceivable (but not imaginable). Descartes illustrates this distinction twice in his Meditations. His discussion of the piece of wax in Meditation Two is translated by Cress thus:

> Perhaps the wax ... never really was the sweetness of the honey, nor the fragrance of the flowers, nor the whiteness, nor the shape, nor the sound, but instead was a body that a short time ago manifested itself to me in these ways, and now does so in other ways. But just what precisely is this thing that I thus imagine? Let us focus our attention on this and see what remains after we have removed everything that does not belong to the wax: only that it is something extended, flexible, and mutable. But what is it to be flexible and mutable? Is it what my imagination shows it to be: namely, that this piece of wax can change from a round to a square shape, or from the latter to a triangular shape? Not at all: for I grasp that the wax is capable of innumerable changes of this sort, even though I am incapable of running through these innumerable changes by using my imagination. Therefore, this insight is not achieved by the faculty of imagination. ... It remains then for me to concede that I do not grasp what this wax is through the imagination; rather, I perceive it through the mind alone.[1]

At the beginning of Meditation Six, Descartes revisits his distinction, which he now describes as one between imagination and pure intellection. Cress translates what he writes thus:

> So, for example, when I imagine a triangle, I not only understand that it is a figure bounded by three lines, but at the same time I also envisage with

---

1   René Descartes, *Meditations on First Philosophy*, 3rd ed., trans. Donald A. Cress (Indianapolis: Hackett Publishing Company, Inc. 1993), 21–22.

© KONINKLIJKE BRILL NV, LEIDEN, 2020 | DOI:10.1163/9789004436350_014

the mind's eye those lines as if they were present; and this is what I call "imagining." On the other hand, if I want to think about a chiliagon, I certainly understand that it is a figure consisting of a thousand sides, just as well as I understand that a triangle is a figure consisting of three sides, yet I do not imagine those thousand sides in the same way, or envisage them as if they were present. And although in that case—because of force of habit I always imagine something whenever I think about a corporeal thing—I may perchance represent to myself some figure in a confused fashion, nevertheless this figure is not a chiliagon. For this figure is really no different from the figure I would represent to myself, were I thinking of a myriagon or any other figure with a large number of sides.[2]

Descartes tries to parlay this pure phenomenological distinction into a metaphysical one between faculties of mind: imagination isn't essential to minds, intellection is. My aims are more limited; I'll, instead, illustrate this distinction with examples from our experiences of word- and sentence-tokens, and objects. The ways that the distinction between imaginability and conceivability plays out in these experiences show experience to be strikingly layered and complex. I illustrate, in addition, how conceivability is limited by experience, and that this yields a perhaps surprising result: what's conceivable doesn't guide us to metaphysical possibility, it's not even a guide to *possible experience*.

Descartes' examples turn on the imagination being finitary in a way he denies intellection is. We can imagine a square, a pentagon, a hexagon, a heptagon ... but imagination soon falters. We can no longer successfully imagine distinct successive polygons despite easily conceiving them. Descartes' point about the wax is similar: the changes we recognize (by intellection) that a piece of wax is capable of are so "innumerable" that we can't imaginatively survey them, despite easily conceiving of them. This limitation in imagination is tightly linked to limitations in what we can perceive and what we can retain of what we perceive in working memory. It's further linked, therefore, to constraints on the diagrams mathematicians can use in reasoning: not only must such diagrams be finite, they're also limited in how large or intricate they can be.[3]

---

2   Descartes, *Meditations on First Philosophy*, 47–48.

3   *Pace*, Solomon Feferman, "And so on...: reasoning with infinite diagrams," *Synthese* 186 (2012): 371–86. I argue in Jody Azzouni, "Does Reason Evolve?" that some mathematical proofs, that of the Cantor-Bernstein theorem, for example, are referentially complex insofar as they involve diagrammatic (and linguistic) references to two kinds of abstracta, where results about

CONCEIVING AND IMAGINING 283

Descartes's distinction is important, especially in philosophy of mathematics, and especially in relation to infinity. For it can be said that we can only imagine the potential infinity that intuitionism allows us, and not the actual infinities of classical set theory—which can only be conceived. This distinction, coupled with a refusal to allow conceivability a methodological role in mathematical proof, may be *a* factor behind constructivist scruples in twentieth-century intuitionism, and perhaps even finitism. But the distinction between conception and imagination manifests itself in interesting cases not having anything obviously to do with imagination being finitary, or with mathematics and mathematical proof.

2   Imagining and Conceiving: Language Examples

My first set of examples are our experiences of the meaningfulness of language vehicles. By "language vehicles" I primarily mean word- and sentence-tokens that we see and write as well as the verbal utterances we hear and utter. Let's begin this way. Wittgenstein writes:

> Make the following experiment: *say* 'It's cold here' and *mean* 'It's warm here.' Can you do it?—And what are you doing as you do it? And is there only one way of doing it?[4]

How we *can* do this is similar to how we *can* speed up our heart rate. We can't speed up our heart rate "directly" by sheer intending, the way we can move our arms. Similarly, what we *can't do* with meaningful expression-tokens is systematically experience them, ours or others, as *saying* something different from what we experience them as saying. We can't, that is, hear or say "It's cold here," and spontaneously *understand* or *experience* it as meaning "It's warm here." The experience of hearing "It's cold here," with its (straightforward) meaning is automatic and seamless. It's misleading to describe the experience as giving an "interpretation" to an expression, as many philosophers do.

What we *are* capable of, and what we perceive ourselves as capable of, is *using* the sentence-token, despite our involuntary experience of its fixed meaning, to express instead "It's warm here"—by means of sarcasm (for example).

---

one kind of abstracta (arbitrarily-long or infinite diagrams) imply results about the other (sets or functions).

4 Ludwig Wittgenstein, *Philosophical Investigations*, trans. G.E.M. Anscombe (New York: The MacMillan Company, 1953), 140e, paragraph 510, italics in the original.

Indeed, there are *lots* of ways to satisfy Wittgenstein's request; strategies for this are quite open-ended. This is, no doubt, a point Wittgenstein intends. None of these methods, however, lead to an experience of the sentence-token with a different meaning, either by the speaker or by the hearer.

The meaning of a sentence-token—induced by our understanding sentence-tokens in contexts of utterance—is *involuntary* in the most natural sense of the word: we have no choice. Just listen to someone speaking your native language—someone you can understand—while trying to hear the words as mere noise. It's impossible. It *is* possible to screen that someone out *altogether*—to "background" the utterances, as it were. But it's *not* possible to attend to the sound of a person's speech (in a language you're native to) yet hear it as mere noise: to deliberately and successfully fail to understand the meanings of the familiar uttered sentence-tokens.

The involuntariness of language experience (for native speakers) leads to certain kinds of *meaning illusions*. Here's an example.[5] Suppose a beetle inadvertently traces the following (scripted) phrase in the sand: IT'S SO COLD HERE. Even if we know that a *beetle* is involved, that there is no secret controlling of said beetle by intelligent English-speaking fun-loving extraterrestrials—that is, even if we're absolutely sure that the resulting shape is due only to a monstrously improbable event—we nevertheless involuntarily experience the shape as meaningful words. In this respect our experience of understanding an expression is exactly like our experience of visual illusions that resist permeation by what we know: for example, the various versions of the Müller-Lyer illusion that occur even if we know the lines are the same size.[6]

It's not unreasonable to think that a scripted "IT'S SO COLD HERE" is *not* meaningful (and not composed of word-tokens) unless it's produced appropriately—unless, for example, it's produced by a language-user under normal circumstances (not because of, for example, strangely organized, but otherwise involuntary, muscle spasms). This is what motivates calling our involuntary experience of such a scripted item, even in the full knowledge that it hasn't been produced under appropriate circumstances, a meaning *illusion*.

It's striking that these meaning-illusion experiences are, if anything, even more involuntary if the right sorts of sounds are involved. Should an avalanche—equally improbably—generate the clear articulation of what

---

5   I've changed this example from Hilary Putnam, *Reason, Truth and History* (Cambridge: Cambridge University Press, 1981), 1, replacing the ant with a beetle. Beetles, I think, are large enough to leave tracks in the sand that ants are incapable of.

6   Those unfamiliar with the Müller-Lyer illusion need only type "Müller-Lyer illusion" into a search engine, and a dozen or so illustrations of it will immediately appear. This is true of all the visual illusions I mention in this chapter.

CONCEIVING AND IMAGINING

sounds like words shouted by a human voice full of concern, I'M COMING; PLEASE WATCH OUT; I'M COMING; PLEASE WATCH OUT ... even with full knowledge of the source of these sounds, it's impossible not to hear them as meaningful—and, indeed, as a warning!

These meaning illusions often (although not invariably) induce the impression that a mind *must be* behind the production of the items in question—that *someone* must have intentionally done this. This is because, typically, items of these particular shapes have a low probability of occurring by sheer accident. Were accidental occurences of them much more common, we'd still experience these meaning illusions but we wouldn't have the accompanying thought that someone did this *deliberately*.

Despite the involuntary experience of language experience for us (for native speakers), we're all aware that *it's possible* to experience the sounds "It's cold here," without involuntarily experiencing its (native) meaning as native speakers do. We know it's possible for that sequence of sounds to have no meaning at all in another language. English speakers recognize, similarly, that it's possible that English could have been different, that it could have been that the phrase "It's cold here," had as its meaning for us English speakers, "It's warm here." It's commonly known that English words have their meanings contingently.

I want to stress something, however, that arises from our *experience* of language and not (merely) from this bit of common-sense knowledge that we (happen to) have. Consider a meaningful token of a word or sentence. It's our *experience* of that token, of how we experience its meaningfulness that enables us to conceive experiencing that token *without* that meaning; this is different from our experience of its shape or spelling. The *token* itself changes if its shape/spelling changes, "dog" to "dig," say. Changing the meaning isn't experienced as changing the token.[7] Part of our experience of word- and sentence-tokens, therefore, is that a word-token's shape and color are *intrinsic* to it. We experience the token itself to change if its shape and color do; not so with its meaning.

---

7 For example, that tokens of "gift" in German, "brat" in Swedish, and "crap" in Romanian, don't mean what they mean in English. Sometimes, of course, we speak of a "word" as a perceived shape/sound *along with* its meaning. My point about meaning experience is that we can, and do, speak of a word without essentially tying it to its meaning, and that doing so corresponds to an aspect of that experience. This is true whether we're speaking of word-tokens or -types, or, as we often do, of both. For discussion of the tortured phenomenology involved with types and tokens, see Jody Azzouni, *Semantic perception: How the Illusion of a Common Language Arises and Persists* (Oxford: Oxford University Press, 2013), Section 0.1.

Nevertheless, we can't *imagine* hearing the sounds "It's cold here" and experiencing them as meaningless or as meaning "It's warm here." We *cannot*, in Descartes' phrase, "envisage ... as if [it] were present" the meaninglessness of "It's cold here," or of it having a different meaning; we can't imaginatively experience this "in real time" the way we might imagine walking down a hallway we're familiar with. Therefore: To *conceive* of an experience doesn't mean we can *imagine* that experience.

Is it right to describe this inability, vis-à-vis "It's cold here," as a limitation of "imagination"? After all, we *do* say things like: "I can imagine people being unable to understand the phrase 'It's cold here' because their language isn't English." Yes, it's true we use "imagine" this way. But this just shows that "imagine," like most (or all) ordinary words, is used in ways that needn't illuminate *perceptual experience*. I'm describing a genuine difference in the phenomenology. To the extent this genuine difference isn't captured by how we ordinarily use words like "imagine" or "conceive," to that same extent, *my* use of these words in this chapter can be seen as a refinement or an adaptation of ordinary language for philosophical purposes.

The upshot: Although we involuntarily experience meanings, we nevertheless experience meaningfulness as a *projection* onto something else that's not meaningful. We *experience*, that is, a token's shape and color, its three-dimensionality or flatness, as *intrinsic* to it. We don't similarly experience its meaning—that's experienced as something *additional* to *it*, something *projected* onto it.

Sometimes we involuntarily experience shapes as words with meanings we don't know. This is especially the case when those shapes appear in sentences and resemble in certain ways words with meanings we know, for example, "All brilligs are happy." If we experienced *every* design, more so, every *object*, as possessing meanings—some known and some unknown—we would experience *everything* as meaningful. (We'd have the experience, as it were, of living in a world entirely composed of pieces of *language*.) We don't have that experience.[8] But even if we did (so I claim) we could still experience meaning as I say we do, as not intrinsic to objects and designs. That is, our impression that meaning isn't intrinsic to tokens isn't derived from our recognition of locality (our recognition that some designs are meaningful and some aren't). Just as we experience the distance between two objects as not intrinsic to those objects, we similarly experience the meaningfulness of something as not intrinsic to it.

---

8   As far as I know, no one has that experience: The human experience of meaning is as something *local*: only some objects are experienced as meaningful.

CONCEIVING AND IMAGINING

It changes the something to change its specific properties; it doesn't change that something to render it meaningless.[9]

3 Experiencing the Functionality of Objects

Consider our experience of forks. A striking point about it, and about our experience of *many* artifacts, actually: cars, trains, tools, furniture, clothing, ..., is that we involuntarily experience them as having particular *functional properties*. We often, additionally, (involuntarily) experience them as having certain parts relevant to those functional properties. Forks have prongs and handles, cars have wheels, windshields, tailpipes, and so on.

Part of this experience (as with meanings) is that these functional properties are *projections* onto objects that have other properties intrinsically. It's our way of experiencing forks that enables us to expect that someone who has never seen forks before (or cars or pianos, and so on) *won't experience* these functional properties. We experience a fork, for example, with all its functional properties, *while experiencing it at the same time* as a mere physical object. How an experience of a fork's functionality differs from an experience of the physical properties of a fork is striking: Were we told that someone who perceived the fork nevertheless couldn't "see" its color (even when staring carefully at the fork) or couldn't "feel" its metallic hardness, even after touching it carefully, we would think something was wrong with that person—with that person's *senses*. But this isn't true if we're told that someone doesn't recognize an object is a fork. (That the person doesn't see that thing *as a fork.*)

Contrast our ability to conceive this as a possible experience with the *actual* possibility of seeing something, say, as both black and red (which can happen while reading black letters, as in synesthesia), or the possible experience of a fork with three prongs although only two of those prongs appear to emerge from the fork ("the impossible trident"). How we experience objects and colors doesn't allow us to conceive these as possible experiences—*not even after we've had these experiences* ("how on earth does something look like this?"); and so, we find it shocking when we learn that such cases *are* possible. We don't understand these cases in two ways: first, in the ordinary sense that (for some of

---

9 A warning: These observations about conceivability—induced by experience—are independent of whether, in fact, what's conceivable is *possible* to experience (although, of course, in the case of meaningful words, it *is* possible to experience them as meaningless). Nevertheless, conceivability, in general, is no indicator of *possible experience*. I discuss this a little in the next section and in Section 6.

them, and to some extent) there are disputes about their neuropsychological basis; but, second, in that our ordinary experiences don't allow a conception of these as *possible* experiences. In saying this, I'm not making a point about our conception of reality, and how *it's* violated, that an impossible trident can't be something that exists—that it's not possible for a thing (in the world) to have two colors. This is true, of course; but my point is one about *experience*. Our experience of how things are in space doesn't allow us to conceive of impossible tridents; it doesn't allow us to conceive how we can experience something being two colors (all over) at the same time. Our experience of tools and sentences, however, *does* allow for a conception of experiencing them as without function or meaning.

I used the phrase "mere physical object" earlier, and I stressed that how we experience forks allows us to distinguish that fork's *forkness* (to adopt a particularly ugly bit of nomenclature) from its physical properties (although, clearly, something wouldn't be a fork—or a *successful* fork, anyway—if it didn't have certain physical properties, its shape in particular). Notice, however, that this talk of "physical properties" or of "mere physical objects" isn't a scientific one, and isn't meant to be. There's no allusion, in particular, to the science of physics. This notion of "physical properties"—and how they're experienced as distinct from the functional properties an object can also be involuntarily experienced to have—is something that nonscientists (and *pre*scientists) are entirely aware of. No one has to be trained in a particular jargon (or, more generally, in the sciences) to understand any of this.[10]

What in *perceptual experience* allows this? Something simple. We don't experience these various properties and relations of things as *the same*: we don't experience the functional properties of a fork, a car, or a piano as the same as the other properties of those objects: we don't experience the functionality of a knight (in chess) *as* its particular shape or color or *as* it's being a particular kind of physical artifact. So too, we don't experience depth *as* color, shape, or the other properties we experience as intrinsic qualities of

---

10 This prescientific/prephilosophical notion of "physical property" is open to refinement and/or collapse. The colors of objects, for example, may be excluded for well-known reasons. I touch on this shortly, but for phenomenological purposes it doesn't matter. We *experience* colors in the sense meant. This isn't the case, necessarily, with other "sensory" qualities we experience. Items *emit* sounds or odors. But those *aren't* experienced as the properties of the items in question. It's striking (but I can't pursue this any further now) that the experience of objects and object borders involves a recognized imposition on *visually*-experienced properties, and not on the sensory properties detected by any of the other senses—except, perhaps, touch (although I doubt it).

CONCEIVING AND IMAGINING

things. Furthermore, we don't, generally, experience these properties as even linked to one another—causally or otherwise.[11]

This is what enables a conception of them as coming apart experientially, seeing a fork without experiencing its functionality. We see the fork's *forkness* as something *over and above* its mere physical properties, properties projected onto a purely physical item. (Some philosophers are tempted—perhaps in part because of this—to describe experiences of depth and functionality as inferences from what is "directly" or "actually" perceived. I'll touch on this in Section 4.)

Nevertheless, those of us brought up in fork-cultures can't *imagine* this experience. A personal confession: I don't experience chopsticks the way I experience forks; I see chopsticks only as sticks—wooden sticks, mostly—sometimes quite nicely ornamented wooden sticks. I always recognize these, after a moment, to be "chopsticks." This is especially the case when I run across chopsticks, as I occasionally do, outside a restaurant. *I* can't imagine a chopstick as those brought up with them can.[12]

Although it's a matter of one's upbringing what *particular* items are experienced as tools, and more generally, what *particular* artifacts are recognized to be the particular artifacts that they are, the capacity to *see* the functional properties of objects (to have this kind of experience) is surely species-specific: not even shared, I suspect, with those animals—certain primates, certain birds, otters—that have come upon (a few) methods of tool-making.

Some last remarks about this particular kind of cognitive experience. There is a sense in which a person could describe a fork's forkness as "subjective." To do this is to acknowledge recognition of the projective nature of this experience—in contrast to the experience of the physical/intrinsic properties of an object. It might seem we ordinarily think something similar about certain apparently physical properties as well: it doesn't take all that much work to impress philosophical beginners with the apparent "subjectivity" of colors and shapes by drawing their attention to facts about perspective (circular coins

---

11   We are, thus, experientially unaware of the role of color experience as a depth indicator.

12   At a Christmas fair in Germany in 2018, I saw what looked *exactly like* contemporary tools (pliers with bright apparently-enameled handles, screwdrivers with apparently shiny new steel shanks, etc.) that were actually entirely made of chocolate, sugar coloring, etc. I *experienced* these items as tools, and that experience *didn't* vanish upon realizing that they were (instead) edibles. I still had "the feeling" that I would be able to open and close the pliers even though I now knew this was extremely unlikely. (Making a piece of chocolate that looks exactly like something isn't the same as making a toy—with toys that expectation makes sense.) It's important to realize—despite obviously being the result of cultural permeation of a cognitive developmental process—how psychologically rigid the resulting experiences are.

that "look elliptical") or to facts about color-contrast illusions, or even less subtly, with illustrations of how colors change when lights are dimmed.

Notice, though, the contrast between how the "subjectivity" of perceived shapes or colors is established, and how the "subjectivity" of the functional properties of tools or words is instead recognized. In the former case, the result *really can be* described as a discovery—not something we *perceptually experience*. When the phenomenon in question is unfamiliar, it's surprising as color-contrast illusions still are to those who don't work with color-graphic programs—*Adobe Illustrator*, for example. Even simple phenomena need to be exhibited to remind people how colors shift under these circumstances—for example the effect on colors by dimming ambient light or changing its spectrum. The phenomena aren't naturally kept in mind otherwise because they aren't built into our *perceptual experience* of colored objects. That is, how color-appearances depend on ambient light isn't visible in (as it were) the colors we see—in contrast to how functionality not being intrinsic to a fork *is* visible in the fork. And in other cases, as with coins that (from certain angles) are supposed to look *quite* elliptical, we even have to be convinced that the coin "looks *quite* elliptical"—because (let's be honest) it really *doesn't*.

Our experience of the nonintrinsicality of functionality, by contrast, is completely obvious. Even a small child will understand if we say to her: *He doesn't know what a fork is; that's why he's backing away from it so fearfully*. There is a great experiential divide between cases where we establish the so-called subjectivity of what we see on the basis of inference (and, sometimes, on the basis of rather subtle, and often fallacious argument), and cases where we simply experience the phenomenon in action.

To summarize: All of us have a pretheoretical notion of what I'll call "the purely physical" that arises directly from our experience of objects. By "pretheoretical," I mean not only prescientific but prephilosophical. In particular, there is a well-known distinction between primary and secondary qualities that's established in the way I've been describing the "subjectivity" of colors to be established. The view takes those properties of an object that are derived from its mass—for example, impenetrability and shape—to be primary qualities that really inhere in the object in question. Color, by contrast, is taken to be a secondary quality, not a property of the object itself but at best a "power" of it. This distinction has no echo in the phenomenology of perceptual experience—in our experience of the sensory properties of objects. We experience meanings and functionality as projections onto objects even though our experience of both meanings and functionality is involuntary. We must instead, as I've indicated, make empirical experiments of various sorts to show the same thing about colors, which otherwise are experienced as intrinsic to

CONCEIVING AND IMAGINING

colored objects. Notice, finally, that the involuntary imposition of meaning on physical objects doesn't obliterate our ability to *see* the physical properties of those objects or obliterate our knowledge that our experience of understanding those physical objects (inscriptions, sounds) as meaningful is *imposed* on something that has those properties intrinsically. (Although, it must be said, it does seem to affect our ability to remember the physical qualities of an object. There are studies that show it's easier for us to remember the functional properties of objects—that something is a pen, for example—than it is to remember its physical qualities, its exact shape, say, or even its color.)

In any case, the perceptual experience of functionality nicely illustrates the distinction I'm drawing between what we can imagine and what we can only conceive of. We can easily conceive not experiencing the functionality of a fork, failing—that is—to recognize that something is a fork even though we ourselves cannot imagine it.

4 Perceptual Content? Cognitive Content? Neither?

I've been avoiding an issue that I should at least stake a position on—even if I can't now treat it in the detail it deserves. I've been avoiding the issue by largely avoiding the word "see"; instead using "experience" and "perceptual experience" to describe *everything* we experience perceptually: colors, sounds, depth, functionality, meaning, etc. (This, however, has been a mostly stylistic maneuver because "see," too, has generic uses.) There is a longstanding (although contentious) philosophical distinction between what we, as it's sometimes put, "directly" see, hear, smell and so on—what may be called *perceptual content*—and what we remember (later) about that content, or what we infer from that content. This distinction *somewhat* occurs in natural language: our use of "see" for example, seems genuinely ambiguous in line with this distinction. Although I can see the stove we're sitting next to and I can see what you're getting at, I can't "see the stove and what you're getting at."[13]

One might hope to ground many of the cases of imagination/intellection I've so far given, one way or the other, in this antecedent distinction between perceptual content and the further content that arises from perceptual content via inference. We see the physical properties of a fork; we infer (or remember having learned) its functional properties. The involuntary nature of the

---

13   This is the conjunction reduction test: it's a good tool for recognizing ambiguity and distinguishing usages that are meant literally from those that are metaphorical.

experience of functionality (or depth, for that matter) is then taken to be irrelevant to this division because some inferences are unconscious, rapid, or automatic. Or, we "directly" see both the physical properties and the functional properties, and/or both are part of perceptual content.[14]

What's experienced—what's "given" in that experience—as opposed to what's inferred or remembered *on the basis of* that experience, are also aspects of experience; they're aspects of the phenomenology. And the options I've just mentioned badly correspond to the division of experienced properties, shape, color, etc., on the one hand, and meaning and functionality, on the other. One problem is that certain experienced properties, depth for example, which *are* experienced, are genuinely troubling: they seem sensory, but not as color and shape are. On the other hand, they don't *seem* to be inferred from "sensory impressions" (e.g., colors and shapes) or remembered. We recognize (or think we do) the pedigree of what's remembered or inferred—that's part of the experience of remembering and inferring: we remember something on the basis of something else, and the same is true for inference.[15] The experience of depth isn't like this. Furthermore, the experience of depth can "flip" in strange ways that don't correspond to what happens when we recognize an inference—for example, the foregroundedness of the face of a two-dimensional depiction of a cube can experientially flip back and forth. The experience of functionality and meaning are similarly "flippy," and are similarly resistant to looking like inferences or the results of memory.[16] We experience these as we do depth: different from experiencing color or shape but different, as well, from the experience of inference or memory.

Unsurprisingly, there is a (centuries long) on-going debate about what should be included or excluded from "perceptual content." Many (contemporary) philosophers see pure perceptual content as rich, as including not only

---

14 There does seem to be a widespread assumption here that we're faced with a Procrustian bed: either inference (of some sort) or (sensory) perception are the only choices. But why? Why, that is, are we trapped at this juncture into forcing the experience of functionality and meaning into being either an ampliative inference/interpretation or instead as a sensory experience, as part of perceptual content? Why, that is, aren't they instead allowed "to be their own things"? Is it because we haven't folk concepts already in place that allow further categorization?

15 Cognitive processes have a certain phenomenology; this is something that's been recently realized by a number of philosophers—although I don't (necessarily) agree with how they think that phenomenology goes. See David Pitt, "The phenomenology of cognition, or what is it like to think that P?," *Philosophy and phenomenological research* 69 (2004): 1–36; Galen Strawson, *Mental Reality* (Cambridge, MA: MIT Press, 1994), among others.

16 See Jody Azzouni, *Semantic perception: How the Illusion of a Common Language Arises and Persists* (Oxford: Oxford University Press, 2013), e.g. Chapter 4, for details.

functional properties, but other properties that one might otherwise be prone to think the result of inference, for example, that I *see* one of two (identical) twins and not the other. That is, on some views, perceptual content is *singular*. This contrasts with earlier views that survived well into the twentieth century (e.g., Russell's) on which functional properties, as well as depth were the result of cognitive processing—of inference.

I believe, contrary to the above, that there is no principled distinction between perceptual content, on the one hand, and content that goes beyond this (content due to cognition or memory). Certainly (I claim), there is no stable distinction that can be drawn on purely phenomenological grounds—on the basis of experience. The reasons involve what I've just described, but go beyond this, and are complex; I'll only touch on this complexity in the next paragraph.

The first point is that, despite linguistic differences between "perceive," "see," and the like, and words like "infer," "imply," and the like,[17] the phenomenology, as I've indicated, supports no such distinction. One reason for this lies in our experience of inference. Included in our experience of inference (of all sorts—deductive and otherwise) are tacit elements. We *recognize* that we draw inferences, often, on a basis that we're only partially aware of—either in the sense that we're unaware of certain assumptions, or in the sense that the assumptions are bundled together in a way that we haven't distinguished.[18] We can *recognize*—this is an experience we can have—that an inference *isn't* explicit, even as we recognize (or think we do) that it's valid. This is why "unconscious inference" isn't an oxymoron. The result, however, is that the immediate and involuntary experience of the "forkness" of forks (or the meaning of words) can't be easily—nonquestionbeggingly—adjudicated as "inference," or, on the other hand, as something that's part of perceptual content. It's part of the phenomenology of *perceptual experience* that immediacy and involuntariness aren't *desiderata* of pure perceptual content. A similar argument can be run for memory. Many philosophers disagree with me, Siegel[19] for example,

---

17   For example, that we "infer" A from B, but we don't "see" A from B.

18   The best examples are mathematical, if only because in that subject-area reasoning is so focused on as the means of justification. So, for example, I can realize, by moving an imagined triangle on an imagined sphere, that its angles don't change on this basis, or that (unlike similar triangles with different areas on flat planes) scaling up triangles on a sphere *does* change their angles. This visual process—which is nevertheless inferential—buries specific assumptions (e.g., constant curvature) by which I recognize these inferences.

19   Susanna Siegal, *The Contents of Visual Experience* (Oxford: Oxford University Press, 2010).

and Descartes[20] for that matter (although they also disagree with each other on how the adjudication goes). Philosophers—these philosophers in particular—also offer "methods" that can supposedly be applied to perceptual experience to manage the needed adjudication. I don't think any such methods work, but as I mentioned, there is much more to say here that I must leave for future work.[21]

5   Experiencing the Boundaries of Objects as Projections

Things are about to get a little weird. (Literally.) What I want to next establish is the projective nature of our experience of objects and their boundaries. By "our experience of objects and their boundaries," I mean, where objects are perceived to begin and leave off. For example, we experience a chair as definitively beginning and ending in space. So too, we experience a tree as distinct in its location, and separated from, the ground it's rooted in. Similarly for rivers, their banks, and the surrounding landscape. Or tools and toys, as well as the bodies of people or animals—for example, a cat. The ways that objects move often cue (without our explicit awareness) our experiences of boundaries; but we can (and do) experience stationary items, large boulders for example, as definitively beginning and ending in space, and distinct from the landscape surrounding them. My claim, to be established in this section, is that we can conceive (but not imagine) someone not having *our* experiences of where objects begin and leave off.

What makes it harder to get a phenomenological grip on the projective nature of our experience of objects and their boundaries than it is to grasp the projective nature of functionality is that—even though perceived functionality is *itself* an important contextual factor influencing where we see objects beginning and ending—the contextual factors influencing object-experience, for the most part, aren't *experienced* as doing this.[22] Nevertheless, many

---

20   Descartes, *Meditations on First Philosophy.*

21   I'll add, however, that the widespread view I criticized in Section 1, that our experience of the meaning of a sentence is an "interpretation," is itself another version of the attempt to treat what appears to be cognitive content as not part of the perceptual content (of words and sentences).

22   Contextual factors have far-reaching causal effects on our experience of: colors, objects, sentences and word meanings, and much else besides. Even when those contextual factors are visible to us, their effect on experience is nevertheless still invisible, except by (laborious) empirical inspection (i.e., by Mill's methods). See Azzouni, *Semantic perception: How the Illusion of a Common Language Arises and Persists* specifically with respect

CONCEIVING AND IMAGINING

examples show, about the parts that we experience artifacts to have, that among the cues that induce the perception of the boundaries of objects or parts of objects are experiences of functional roles. The same is true of our own body parts: we distinguish hands functionally from arms, even though there is no obvious visual border between a hand and the rest of the arm. Similar for cheeks or the chin vis-à-vis faces, or the waist and the rest of the trunk.

The projective nature of the experience of objects and their boundaries, apart from this, is easily recognized by means of thought experiments that *everyone* can recognize (with a little thought) to be conceivable. We can *easily* conceive what it would be like to experience objects and their boundaries differently from how we do—although simultaneously we can't make ourselves *actually experience* things that way. We can't *imagine* it.

Consider the following thought experiment.[23] Imagine (this is the part you *can* imagine) you're sitting peacefully in your garden at dusk—as you often do. But *this* time, you experience something like a peculiar hallucination. (I'll indicate in a moment why it isn't *really* an hallucination). Suddenly ... *all the object boundaries you normally experience are gone*; you're not experiencing the presence of boundaries between objects anymore. (*Am I having a stroke?* you mutter *sotto voce*.) Later, when you—stutteringly—try to explain what this experience was like to someone else, you say things like: "I was experiencing everything as *One*." Or you might even say (as if you've had a mystical insight): "Everything *is* one." (You could find yourself adding, in shock: "Including *me*, by the way.") And indeed, in some circles anyway, it would be common to classify this as a kind of mystical experience of the genuine metaphysical *oneness* of everything.

We experience *objects*, for the most part; we don't experience object boundaries except on those occasions when they strike us as sharp—for example, those of chess pieces. We experience hands as things too; but we don't experience *their* boundaries: a wrist isn't an *experienced* boundary. The same is true of trees or boulders, and lots of other things, for that matter. So this experience is that of the vanishing of *objects*.

In trying to describe this experience, how you now perceptually experience everything around you, you might say: "It's sort of like everything is water now." You might also say: "Everything that I used to see as distinct objects I now only see as so many patterns in the One." Neither of these is a correct descriptions of

---

to our experience of the meaningfulness of language artifacts; the same is also easily exhibited in color-contrast illusions.

23 This and the thought experiments to follow are drawn from Jody Azzouni, *Ontology Without Borders* (Oxford: Oxford University Press, 2017), 253–89.

this possible experience because in trying to convey how your experience has changed—how everything looks to you now—you're not mentioning the important ways in which *everything continues to look exactly the same*. Because, after all, it isn't that everything *really* looks like water now; it isn't like everything you're seeing is kind of undulating now in that watery way that you've experienced in the past (patterns of dye, for example, suffusing through a liquid). The latter experience *isn't* one we have subsequent to our experience of objects having vanished; it's instead an experience of something else, where we'd (accurately) say that something only "looks like" objects—as patterns in sand sometimes "remind us of objects." The same is true of formations of clouds that occasionally "look like" camels or faces, and so on. And as I'm describing this experience we can conceive, the perception of depth is entirely untouched as well: it's not that everything has been strangely *flattened*. That's a different experience we can conceive of—but it's not what I'm describing here. Finally, it's not an experience of everything being "one." We can conceive this experience, but it involves more than the experience of objects vanishing.[24]

That's why—above—I parenthetically wrote that these experience aren't (really) hallucinations. They leave our experience of the physical aspects of objects exactly the same: they only affect the experience of objects and their boundaries. Physical distinctions—discontinuities in physical properties—are still experienced. It's just that objects are no longer experienced *as* distinguished, *as* distinct objects.

Just as we can conceive an experience of the objects all around suddenly vanishing (having no boundaries between one another) or as ceasing to be *distinct* objects, we can also conceive the experience of the objects all around suddenly having different boundaries. We experience trees as distinct from the ground those trees are growing in. Someone might experience trees as simply parts of one big "Mother Earth," and consequently experience trees as protuberances *of* the ground, rather than as *distinct* objects. Notice that it isn't the case that differences in color, or even physical discontinuities necessarily induce an experience of those discontinuities as simultaneously a border

---

24   A cartoon that would trigger an experience of distinct objects turning into an experience of one object—an experience many of us have had—is one in which the point-of-view slowly rises above a forest landscape (of trees, etc.) to reveal it's the top of someone's head. We "realize" it's someone's head. (At a certain point, the experience of object-border locations "flips.") Cartoons exploiting this aspect of our experience of objects are quite common.

CONCEIVING AND IMAGINING   297

between where an object begins and leaves off, as our experience of multi-colored objects, or snap-together toys, indicates.[25]

Here are other examples, Consider a flat plane covered in identically sized and colored polka dots, evenly spaced in infinite rows and columns. *We* (because in these cases we're object-cued to color shifts along the polka-dots' boundaries) involuntarily experience these polka-dot-shaped colors as distinct objects against a background (that we perceive as *nothing*). We nevertheless recognize (we can conceive this; we can't imagine it) an experience of exactly the same distribution of colors, and color-discontinuities, but nevertheless an object-experience of arrays of tiny pixels making up each polka-dot—*those* are the experienced objects. Or instead (more weirdly) an experience of objects as polka-dot halves—even without any color-change cues across the invisible vertical dividing each polka dot half from the other one it's joined to. Or, conceivably, any of numerous other ways of imposing objecthood onto this color-distribution pattern.

Imagine now moving polka dots. Movement cues of various sorts even more strongly impel *us* to see the shifting colors as single moving objects. But we can conceive an experience of pairs of polka-dots as single objects whose parts are moving in *lockstep*—or as single objects made up of parts in some other way entirely.

Let's consider some even more drastic conceivability thought experiments. Can an object be experienced as being located at two places at the same time? I don't mean by this: Suppose that spacetime is curved in some strange way. No—just again consider our ordinary two-dimensional plane with some polka dots on it. And I don't mean: consider the idea that some (large) object is discontinuously located in two places. I'm not speaking of a (big) object that has noncontiguous polka-dot-shaped parts—that some of the polka dots are parts of the same objects. (That's conceivable *too*; but it's not what I'm trying to describe *here*.) There is this object *O* that's an entire polka dot here *and* an entire polka dot there.

This *isn't* conceivable, some philosopher is likely to say, because it violates Leibniz's law. Leibniz's law, roughly, is that if there is a property that *A* has but *B* doesn't have, then *A* can't be identical to *B*. It seems to follow from this that the same object can't have different spatial locations; it can only have parts

---

25   Consider again the chocolate "tools" of footnote 12. Imagine they seem laid out on a platter; but we discover instead that what we're seeing is a (big) single piece of chocolate candy that includes the platter. They're still perceived as distinct items, despite knowledge otherwise, until we try to pick one up to eat, and have to instead unevenly break it off the "platter." Only then does the experience of where the object borders are "flip."

distributed in different spatial locations. This is because if A is located in one place and B is located in another place then there seems to be a property, the-location-of-A, that B doesn't have, and furthermore, a second property, the-location-of-B, that A doesn't have.

No—the suggested experience doesn't violate Leibniz's law, because the reasoning described in the last paragraph is fallacious. The *same object* is perceived to have so-and-so spatial locations *as well as* such-and-such spatial locations. The logical trick that makes this experience cogent: The "object" O—that both polka-dot A and and polka-dot B are—doesn't violate Leibniz's law because O has *two* sets of location-properties, A-relative properties and B-relative properties. Someone might say in response: "*That* amounts to the object being partially in one place and partially in another." No, that's a different experience. The experience I'm describing is the experience of an object that is the same object (entirely) there *as well as* here. Remember: What's being requested isn't that *we* experience this, or that we're enabled to imagine ourselves experiencing this. That's not possible. What's being requested is that we recognize (conceive) an experience like this where all the properties and relations are experienced just as *we* do (for example, the colors, the other physical properties, as well as the discontinuities in color, or in mass, and so on). And that the someone experiencing this could say: "No, it's not that part of the object is here, and the other part is there. That's something different, that's a description of a different object from the one I'm seeing." We're being asked to conceive a particular experience that we simultaneously can't imagine.[26]

A philosopher might stubbornly say: *Now wait just a minute.* We know objects can have relations to themselves. But the relations that objects can have to themselves are supposed to be boring and trivial—like self-identity. Objects can have interesting relations to their parts, and their parts can have interesting relations to one another. But the so-called objects that *you're* describing have interesting relations to themselves (like an object being two feet away from itself). I don't like that. *So? This is a contradiction? How?*

---

26 As often happens, the scholastics (or some of them) were onto this. Adams (Robert M. Adams, "Primitive Thisness and Primitive Identity," *Journal of Philosophy* 76, no. 1 (1979): 5–26. Reprinted in: Jaegwon Kim, Daniel Z Korman, and Ernest Sosa, *Metaphysics: An Anthology*. 2nd ed. (Maldon, MA: Wiley-Blackwell. 2011), 112, 120, note 18, page references are to the reprint) describes the violated principle as "the same thing cannot be in two places at once—that is, cannot be spatially distant from itself"—and he notes that Occam denies it's a necessary truth. Such a denial by Occam is tantamount to accepting the conceivability of the case in question. I deny, however, that this yields a result about *necessity*. See Section 6.

CONCEIVING AND IMAGINING

(There are Sci-Fi scenarios in bad movies, bad television, bad stories, and in comic books too, where people meet themselves because "universes have collided" or something dumb like that. Incoherent? Not as far as *conceivable* object experiences are concerned.)

These object experiences aren't experiences of everything as "one," as I earlier described the garden experiences. Those were cases of losing one's sense of object-boundaries altogether. Here the idea is an experience of what we ordinarily take to be two otherwise distinct objects as the same object. Imagine John and Sarah, say, who have never met—John lives in London, Sarah in Melbourne. We can conceive an object-experience of Sarah and John as the same object without, as a result, there being any further experienced connection between them.[27] If we conceive of this possible experience as one identifying every object with every "other" object, we get a different way in which someone could (suddenly) have the mystical experience that "everything is one."

One last (strange) example: An experience of all the numbers being the same object. *Oh*, we might respond (if we didn't initially understand the suggestion), *you mean that all the numbers are aspects of the One (or something like that)*? No—bringing up "aspects" is to euphemistically suggest the experience is of one thing where the various numbers are its parts. That's not the thought; it's that each number is the same object as any other number.

How is it we can conceive these object experiences? Unlike the cases of conceiving alternative meanings of sounds and inscriptions that we're familiar with, we can't entertain the suggestion that these conceptions are based on common-sense knowledge of empirical facts about the object experiences that people have had. In saying this, I'm presuming (possibly falsely) that there are no uncontentious cases of people having the experiences that I've described in the last section.

I don't care if I'm (subsequently) corrected about this, especially because it doesn't affect either the distinction between conceiving and imagining, or the examples of the distinction that I've given. I recognize that there are mystical traditions that seem to indicate that people actually have experiences similar to the ones of this section; some of those mystical traditions describe having these experiences as appropriate spiritual goals. There may also be scientific studies—ones I'm currently unfamiliar with—of methods of inducing such experiences, as there now are for inducing out-of-body experiences.[28]

---

27   Again, in terms of the "trick" I've described: the experience of *A* and *B* being the same doesn't require *A*-relative properties to be nomologically (or conceptually) connected to *B*-relative properties *in any way at all*.

28   A personal confession: I'd like to have some of these experiences—they sound like fun.

Regardless, our ability to conceive these kinds of experiences, despite our inability to imagine them, is due to our *actual* experience of object boundaries similar to our *actual* experiences of functionality and meaning. Our experience of objects and their boundaries, we recognize, *separates from* our experience of physical discontinuities. Some of the examples in this section indicate this, cheeks, wrists, and snap-together toys; generally, neither color discontinuities nor other physical discontinuities seem necessary and sufficient for the experience of an object boundaries. Part of the reason for this (I speculate) is that where we see an object as beginning and leaving off is psychologically infiltrated by our experience of that object's perceived functional properties; but functional properties, generally, cross-classify with the physical properties that operate as foundations for them. This chapter, however, isn't the place to explore this fertile thought further.

6 Some Conclusions

Philosophers regularly draw distinctions, and they usually illustrate their distinctions with examples. Often, very often, the examples illustrating the purported distinctions are more interesting than the distinctions themselves. I'd like to think, however, that I've managed both an interesting gloss on an admittedly very old distinction, as well as having managed a number of surprising (and new) examples of the distinction.

I've claimed that the distinction between what we can conceive and what we can only imagine is due to our own recognition of the ways that our experience is locked into being a certain way simultaneously with that experience being structured so that (apparently) nothing in what that experience is of *requires* our experience to be so locked in. So, in particular cases (say, when experiencing the physical contours of human beings), our perception of the boundaries of such objects seems to operate in tandem with our perception of certain physical discontinuities, although our experience of those boundaries doesn't identify them with those physical discontinuities. This is because, simply, we experience object boundaries as different from physical discontinuities.

There is, of course, an echo of a kind of a priori structure to the experience of object boundaries, as well as to our experience of meaningfulness and functionality. Indeed, Descartes' examples of the conceivable incline us to think that what's conceivable is possible. The language and object examples I've given incline us to think what's conceivable is possibly experiential. Both inferences are false and so these echoes (of a priori structure) are misleading.

CONCEIVING AND IMAGINING

Conceivability of a kind of experience is not—all by itself—a (genuine) recognition of the *possibility* of a kind of experience.[29] There are at least two reasons why. The first is that what kind of experience is possible is surely relative to the neurophysiological facts that determine experience, and it could be that what we find conceivable violates those facts. It may be, for example, that perceptual experiences of color determines (certain) experiences of depth. More dramatically, Church's[30] undecidability result—that there is no decision procedure for contradiction—prevents us from relying on the apparent intelligibility of a conceivable experience as showing there is no contradiction that rules it out. I'll spell this out slightly since it seems to me the point isn't widely appreciated. When focusing specifically on syntax, the point translates to this: apart from narrow cases that don't generalize (e.g., "A & ¬A"), any two syntactically-similarly characterized passages of formal discourse can differ insofar as one is contradictory and the other isn't.[31] This point applies to any moderately rich proposition-like notion, such as propositional content.

Conversely, as I indicated in Section 3, we have experiences that, despite *being* experiences, remain inconceivable. Conceivability is neither necessary nor sufficient either for (metaphysical/logical) possibility or for possible experience.

A question naturally arises. Despite this, do phenomenological results about the conceivability/imaginability distinction in cases of meanings and objects have *any* metaphysical implications?—either ones similar to the kinds of implications that Descartes hoped to draw, or different ones? No—they don't, for the reasons I gave in the last two paragraphs. Apart from this, however, I think it's relatively clear that meaning properties and functional properties are genuine projections. I mean by this that there is nothing in the world that they correspond to. It isn't, that is, that there are meaning properties or functional properties antecedently existing *in the world* that our experience has to correspond to in order for that experience to correctly capture the phenomena being experienced, or for that experience to be true to the world. This isn't shown by how experience is structured; it's shown by the common-sense facts about people who are not brought up among forks, or other artifacts, and by the experience of non-native speakers vis-à-vis the sentences and words of a language.

---

29 I find it tempting to slip into writing otherwise, however; and I've mistakenly done so in earlier discussions of some of this material—at least in passing.

30 Alonzo Church, "A Note on the Entscheidungsproblem," *Journal of Symbolic Logic* 1 (1936): 40–41, 101–02.

31 If this were false, we could design a decision procedure for contradiction.

I further claim (but will not show here) that the boundaries of objects—and thus objects—are similarly not to be found in the world. This is more controversial because, for contemporary philosophers, realist attitudes towards object boundaries are more widely held than corresponding realist attitudes about meaning or functionality. Relatedly, there is a long illustrious tradition dedicated to establishing the metaphysical presence—in the world—of one or another species of object boundaries (usually under the philosophical rubric of "individuation conditions"). That is, many metaphysicians—including contemporary ones—believe there are objects and their boundaries *in the world* and that our experience of object boundaries must be evaluated against this reality.

To refute realism about objects and their boundaries, it's insufficient to exploit the differences between what we can imagine and our conception of objects and their boundaries. After all, as I've noted, that we can conceive something *as* possible shouldn't be taken to imply (on those grounds alone) that it *is* possible. Perhaps the way the world is forces objects to have certain boundaries and not others, regardless of the alternatives we're capable of conceiving. What's needed at this point is a successful analysis of exactly what a metaphysically-genuine object boundary is.[32]

One possibility, of course, for establishing the metaphysical presence of objects and their boundaries is providing philosophically-convincing necessary and sufficient conditions for the boundaries of objects in terms of (say) some set of underlying physical properties and relations. Nothing I've said in *this* chapter rules out the potential success of such an analysis. I show in *Ontology Without Borders* that it can't be done, but that issue goes beyond questions of experience, possible experience, and what we can imagine, as opposed to what we can conceive. That is, it goes quite beyond the topics of this chapter.

Is the distinction between the imaginable and the conceivable philosophically useless? Yes, if we try to make it do work in metaphysics, or to enable a metaphysical understanding of our mental faculties, as Descartes attempted. But it *is* valuable if we want to understand the nature of mathematical proof and mathematical concepts, or—more generally—if we want to understand the benefits and infirmities our particular kind of mind poses for formulating concepts adequate for capturing truths about the world—more grandly, the prospects we have for understanding the true and the real.

---

32   Trouble looms because, phenomenologically, it's quite unclear what we're *seeing* when what we see distinguishes one object from another (e.g., when they're bordering on one another). Our experience of objects, that is, is a poor basis for even hints of what—metaphysically speaking—object boundaries could be.

References

Adams, Robert M. "Primitive Thisness and Primitive Identity." *Journal of Philosophy* 76, no. 1 (1979): 5–26. Reprinted in: Kim, Jaegwon, Daniel Z Korman, and Ernest Sosa. *Metaphysics: An Anthology*. 2nd ed. Maldon, MA: Wiley-Blackwell. 2011.

Azzouni, Jody. "Does Reason Evolve? (Does the Reasoning in Mathematics Evolve?)." In *Humanizing Mathematics and its Philosophy:Essays Celebrating the 90th Birthday of Reuben Hersh.*, edited by Bharath Sriraman, 253–89. Cham, Switzerland: Birkhäuser. 2017.

Azzouni, Jody. *Ontology Without Borders*. Oxford: Oxford University Press. 2017.

Azzouni, Jody. *Semantic perception: How the Illusion of a Common Language Arises and Persists*. Oxford: Oxford University Press. 2013.

Church, Alonzo. "A Note on the Entscheidungsproblem." *Journal of Symbolic Logic* 1 (1936): 40–41, 101–02.

Descartes, René. *Meditations on First Philosophy*. 3rd ed. Translated by Donald A. Cress, Indianapolis: Hackett Publishing Company, Inc. 1993.

Feferman, Solomon. "And so on...: reasoning with infinite diagrams." *Synthese* 186 (2012): 371–86.

Kim, Jaegwon, Daniel Z. Korman, and Ernest Sosa, eds. *Metaphysics: An Anthology*. 2nd ed. Maldon, MA: Wiley-Blackwell. 2011.

Pitt, David. "The phenomenology of cognition, or what is it like to think that P?" *Philosophy and phenomenological research* 69 (2004): 1–36.

Putnam, Hilary. *Reason, Truth and History*. Cambridge: Cambridge University Press. 1981.

Siegal, Susanna. *The Contents of Visual Experience*. Oxford: Oxford University Press. 2010.

Sriraman, Bharath., ed. *Humanizing Mathematics and its Philosophy: Essays Celebrating the 90th Birthday of Reuben Hersh*. Cham, Switzerland: Birkhäuser. 2017.

Strawson, Galen. *Mental Reality*. Cambridge, MA: MIT Press. 1994.

Wittgenstein, Ludwig. *Philosophical Investigations*. Translated by G.E.M. Anscombe. New York: The MacMillan Company, 1953.

CHAPTER 13

The Dance of Perception: The Rôle of the Imagination in Simone Weil's Early Epistemology

Warren Heiti

> We have within us the sparks of knowledge, as in a flint: philosophers extract them through reason, but poets force them out through the sharp blows of the imagination, so that they shine more brightly.[1]

1. For the French philosopher Simone Weil, the imagination plays an indispensable and fundamental rôle in knowing. In her dissertation at the Ecole Normale Supérieure (1929–1930) and her lectures on philosophy at the *lycée* in Roanne (1933–1934), she describes perception as an interaction—a dance—between mind and world, and the imagination is the site at which this interaction takes place. She borrows from Descartes the idea that the mind, in imagining, contemplates the image of a bodily thing. But the rôle of the imagination in her epistemology is ultimately Kantian. For Weil, the imagination is what integrates active understanding and passive sensibility; and by integrating them, it transcendentally produces experience. What is unique to her account is its physical dimension.[2] According to Weil, thinking is essentially activity, but the original action is a *re*action of the body to an external stimulus. Such reactions generalize across similar stimuli, resulting in meta-images (or general ideas) which are responsible for categorizing things and structuring perception. The imagination is Weil's answer to the question, "What are the transcendental preconditions of the possibility of my experience of the world?" The raw wash of sensations is necessary, but not sufficient, to answer this question; and similarly with the structured emptiness of concepts. The imagination is what takes the signet ring of the conceptual realm and presses it into the melting wax of sensation—and thus produces experience.

---

[1] René Descartes, "Private thoughts," in *The Philosophical Writings of Descartes*, vol. 1, trans. John Cottingham, Robert Stoothoff, and Dugald Murdoch (Cambridge: Cambridge University Press, 1985), AT X.217.

[2] Steven Burns suggests that this dimension makes her account un-Kantian and original. I do not disagree. But her general strategy is inspired by Kant, and it is that inspiration that I am trying to acknowledge.

THE DANCE OF PERCEPTION
305

In his monograph on Weil, Peter Winch argues that her thought undergoes a significant development from her dissertation "Science and Perception in Descartes" to her *Lectures on Philosophy*. According to him, her dissertation confronts a dilemma that is not solved until the lectures: "order is the product of thought, but thought can only be exercised on what already exhibits order."[3] Weil herself articulates the dilemma in her late "Essay on the Notion of Reading": "It is in this way that at every moment of our life the meanings we ourselves read in appearances take hold of us as though from outside. We can therefore argue endlessly about the reality of the external world. Because what we call the world are the meanings we read—it isn't real. But it seizes us as though from outside—so it is real."[4] "Reading" ("lecture"), for Weil, is a term of art, and to read is to perceive appearances as meaningful.[5] The legacy of positivist science and philosophy has instructed us to shuck the value and seek the underlying fact. But Weil recommends meditating on the contradiction that she identifies in the passage above. On the one hand, the fact that we read *meanings* might imply that we are projecting them onto the blank (and otherwise meaningless) world; on the other hand, the fact that we are *seized* by these meanings suggests that we are the patient in this interaction, and that the agent is something else—something that is independent of the perceiver.

Nevertheless, there remains a problem about the source of the order or structure necessary for thinking. For knowledge, my thinking does need structure, but it also needs to be answerable to something.[6] When we turn to defining that something, we face a dilemma: either it is made out of the same stuff as thought, or it isn't. In the first case, idealism swallows the world; in the second case, there is the risk of crude incommensurability (if the world is substantially different from thinking, then how could thinking be constrained by it?). Either horn is fraught with difficulties. Winch argues that Weil's response to the dilemma is "to abandon the thesis that all order is the product of thought.

---

3   Peter Winch, *Simone Weil: "The Just Balance"* (Cambridge: Cambridge University Press, 1989), 33.

4   Simone Weil, "Essay on the Notion of Reading," trans. Rebecca Fine Rose and Timothy Tessin, *Philosophical Investigations* 13, no. 4 (October 1990): 298; translation altered. Cf. Weil, "Essai sur la notion de lecture," *Les Études philosophiques,* Nouvelle Série, 1ère Année, no. 1 (Janvier/Mars 1946): 14.

5   That formulation is misleading if it is taken to imply that there is another way to perceive appearances, i.e., as otherwise than meaningful—but such a view is not Weil's. Reading, for her, is not something that we can cease doing.

6   Cf. John McDowell, *Mind and World* (Cambridge: Harvard University Press, 1996). The recognition of these two needs is one of the motivating themes of McDowell's investigation.

'When we give birth to thought, it will be born into a world that is already ordered.'[7] And it is ordered by the body.

Briefly, Weil's solution is as follows: thought is intentional (it is *about* something) and it requires order. Assuming that thought is not only its own object, we look elsewhere; but the sensations of empiricism are insufficient to supply the requisite order: "the 'material' on which thinking must work cannot be an inarticulate splurge of passive sensation."[8] However, the world is *already ordered* by the reactions of the body. At a proto-conceptual level, the body has a set of gestures—what Weil calls "congenital reactions"—that generalize across stimuli. For example, stimulated by various different foods—bread, apples, and so on—the human body salivates. This reaction serves to classify these stimuli under the general idea "food." Thus, the world's welter of multitudinous particulars is limited (it is conceptually structured), and thought can get a grip.

Winch's characterization of Weil's solution is in many ways accurate and insightful, but there are two modest but important amendments which I would like to suggest. Firstly, the solution that Winch locates in the lectures is already available in the dissertation. Secondly, the rôle of the imagination—which is consistent across the dissertation and the lectures, but which Winch does not discuss—is indispensable to the solution. For Weil, the imagination is an amphibious faculty: half mental, half physical, it mediates the relation between mind and body. In a striking image, Weil compares the imagination to an oracle:

> I will go and ask oracles about things; I will not consult mute things, nor myself who am ignorant, but I will go to this third, ambiguous being that is a composite of myself and the world acting on each other. This seems to have been what the Greeks did at Delphi; they questioned this point of intersection between matter and a mind in the person of a woman whom they probably thought they had reduced to being no more than that. Since I wish to believe only in myself, I will consult this bond of action and reaction between the world and my thought in myself alone. I will name this bond the imagination...[9]

---

7 Winch, *Simone Weil: "The Just Balance,"* 33; he seems to be quoting his own translation: "Quand nous ferons naître la pensée, elle naîtra ainsi dans un univers déjà rangé" (Weil, *Leçons de philosophie* [Paris : Union Générale d'Éditions, 1959], 24).

8 Winch, *Simone Weil: "The Just Balance,"* 18.

9 Simone Weil, "Science and Perception in Descartes," in *Formative Writings 1929–1941*, eds. and trans. Dorothy Tuck McFarland and Wilhelmina Van Ness (Amherst: The University of Massachusetts Press, 1988), 69; cf. Weil, "Science et perception dans Descartes," in *Œuvres complètes, Tome 1: Premiers écrits philosophiques*, eds. Gilbert Kahn and Rolf Kühn (Paris: Éditions

THE DANCE OF PERCEPTION 307

The imagination, so defined, is indispensable to the solution for two reasons: firstly, it is Weil's response to the interaction problem—that is, the problem, perhaps best articulated by Elisabeth of Bohemia, of explaining how mental and extended substances can interact.[10] Secondly, as I indicated earlier, it is her answer to the question, "What are the transcendental preconditions of the possibility of my experience of the world?" Roughly two millennia before Kant, Aristotle clearly articulates the problem: "Let us admit that the soul knows or perceives the elements out of which each of these composites is made up; but by what means will it know or perceive the composite whole ...? For each *is*, not merely the elements of which it is composed, but those elements combined in a determinate mode or ratio ... Nothing, therefore, will be gained by the presence of the elements in the soul, unless there be also present there the various formulae of proportion and the various compositions in accordance with them."[11] So, too, with experience: it is not merely sensations, but sensations structured by concepts; not merely raw material, but material in*formed*. Sensations and concepts, considered individually, are each insufficient to generate experience. Something further is necessary to integrate the offerings of sensibility and understanding: and that is the imagination.[12]

2. In the first part of her dissertation, Weil sketches a portrait of Descartes that is largely unfamiliar to the Anglo-American tradition. For reasons of space, I shall omit most of the details of her account (despite its interest as an alternative reading of a fundamental thinker in the history of philosophy). However, for the purpose of the present investigation, there are two features which I

Gallimard, 1988), 200. Henceforth, references to this text (and other texts by Weil) will be given in the following format: Weil, "Title," #/#, where the first number refers to the English translation, and the second number refers to the French original. Cf. Zwicky: "Primary process thought is the point at which the mind emerges from the body, 'like a mushroom out of its mycelium' as Freud puts it; and the point at which the body coalesces out of mind" (Jan Zwicky, "Dream Logic," in *Thinking and Singing*, ed. Tim Lilburn [Toronto: Cormorant Books, 2002], 143). Zwicky does not specify the source for Freud's metaphor, but it is *The Interpretation of Dreams*, trans. James Strachey (Harmondsworth: Penguin Books, 1976), §VII.A (p. 672).

10   Cf. Elisabeth's letter to Descartes, 6 May 1643, in *The Correspondence between Elisabeth of Bohemia and René Descartes*, trans. Lisa Shapiro (Chicago: The University of Chicago Press, 2007), AT III.661.

11   Aristotle, *De Anima*, trans. J.A. Smith, in *The Basic Works*, ed. Richard McKeon (New York: The Modern Library, 2001), I.4.409b30-410a9.

12   Sensations and concepts may be needed, but why is a *third* thing needed? Thanks to Steven Burns for this crucial question, which I try to address in §8. Absent some metaphysical assumptions about the separateness of sensations and concepts, a third thing may *not* be needed. And the problem may be circumvented if we conceive of imagination as a process or activity rather than a thing.

must mention: Weil's version of Descartes is a philosopher for whom the imagination is epistemically indispensable, and whose conception of geometry retains its link with the concrete earth.[13] He is not a shallow, arch-rationalist dualist; while he does associate the imagination with the body, the body is not despised. On the contrary, it is the way in which the mind makes direct contact with the world. And one paradigm of making that contact is the imagination engaged in geometry.

> "The study of mathematics," writes Descartes to Princess Elizabeth, "chiefly exercises the imagination" (3:692). Similarly, he writes in a passage from the *Rules*: "Henceforth, we will do nothing without the aid of the imagination" (10:443). It is in the imagination, he says again in the *Rules* (10:416) that the idea of everything that can be related to the body must be found. Since the mind engaged with geometry makes use of the imagination, it does not handle empty ideas. It grasps something.[14]

This conception of the imagination accords with Weil's unorthodox conception of Cartesian science: "Thus Cartesian science is far more packed with matter than is ordinarily thought. It does not disdain geometrical figures, since Descartes explicitly says that 'the ideas of all things can be fashioned' from them alone (10:450). It is so bound to the imagination, so joined to the human body, so close to the most common labors, that one may be initiated into it by studying the easiest and simplest crafts; especially those that are the most subject to order, like that of weavers, embroiderers, or lacemakers."[15] In addition to being "packed with matter," Cartesian science exhibits a characteristic method: it "avails itself of the most familiar comparisons, drawn sometimes from aspects of nature closest to us, such as eddies in rivers, but especially from trades and tools, the slingshot, the pressing of grapes. We might think that these comparisons are only methods of popularization; on the contrary, they are the very substance of Cartesian physics."[16] These comparisons ("comparaisons") are essentially imagistic analogies: for example, the motion or structure

---

13   McFarland and Van Ness suggest that the dissertation's portrait of Descartes shows the influence of Alain (McFarland and Van Ness, "Introduction," in Weil, *Formative Writings* [Amherst: The University of Massachusetts Press, 1988], 23). Sepper argues that in Descartes' early philosophy, the imagination "stood at the center of cognitional activity by virtue of the analogical relationships among all things" (Dennis L. Sepper, "Descartes and the Eclipse of the Imagination," *Journal of the History of Philosophy* 27, no. 3 [July 1989]: 380).

14   Weil, "Science and Perception in Descartes," 50/179.

15   Weil, "Science and Perception in Descartes," 51/179–180.

16   Weil, "Science and Perception in Descartes," 51/180.

THE DANCE OF PERCEPTION   309

of imperceptibly little things is compared to the motion or structure of perceptible things. Descartes declares that "comparisons are the most appropriate means of setting forth the truth about physical questions that the human mind can possess."[17]

Having unsettled an oversimplified picture of Descartes' project, Weil argues that imagination is inseparable from ordinary perception. She calls upon an image from the *Dioptrics* that will remain with her for the rest of her life: "the blind man who directly perceives the objects at the end of his stick, not the sensations that the pressure of the stick makes on his hand."[18] The image's lesson is at once counter-intuitive and intuitive. On the one hand, the man's perception is obviously mediated by the stick. On the other hand, the perception depicted in the image is familiar to all of us: think of the last time that you wrote a grocery list. It would require a special effort to transfer one's attention from the list on the paper to the pressure of the pencil in one's fingers. As Weil writes, "Right now I feel the paper at the end of my pen ... The pressure of the penholder on my hand—the only thing, it seems, I should feel—I must pay attention to in order to notice, just as I need to pay attention to see glazes of red or yellow pigment on the canvas that portrays the Gioconda, instead of seeing the skin of a woman."[19] The default focus is the whole perceived object (rather than the instrument of perception or the atomistic constituents of the object). Furthermore, in cases where an instrument is the only means of perception, then the instrument is *a condition of possibility* and *not* an intermediary. The lesson can be generalized: "for each of us the blind man's stick is simply his own body."[20] If our bodies and their sense organs can be considered instruments, then perception by means of them is not mediated: this is just what direct perception is like here.

Weil draws a further implication, and claims that Descartes constructs "a theory of sensations as signs, using the example of drawings in which we see not marks on paper but men and towns (6:113)."[21] This theory is Weil's own theory of reading, which receives its mature elaboration in her "Essay on the Notion of Reading" (to which I alluded in §1 above). Indeed, the theory of the

---

17   Descartes, letter to Morin, 12 September 1638, AT 11.368, qtd in Weil, "Science and Perception in Descartes," 52/180. For the role of comparisons in Descartes' philosophy, see Peter Galison, "Descartes's Comparisons: From the Invisible to the Visible," *Isis* 75 (1984): 311–26.

18   Weil, "Science and Perception in Descartes," 53/182. Cf. Descartes, *Dioptrics*, in *The Philosophical Writings of Descartes*, vol. 1, AT VI.84.

19   Weil, "Science and Perception in Descartes," 79/210.

20   Weil, "Science and Perception in Descartes," 79/211.

21   Weil, "Science and Perception in Descartes," 53/182.

imagination that Weil develops in the dissertation and early lectures continues in her later work under the name of "reading."[22] When we look at a drawing, we perceive not its elements (the lines of graphite on paper), but the thing that the drawing depicts; similarly, when we read a letter, we perceive meanings, not pencilled letters. With effort, we can shift our perception to the lines and letters; but for a literate perceiver, the original perception is holistic, and the perception of a whole's parts is the result of a subsequent analysis. In the lectures, Weil explicitly connects this insight with gestalt psychology:

> It is ... the things as a whole that have an affect on our bodies, and not their particular aspects.... What we are saying now has to do with something very important—the theory of forms (Gestalt theory).... the body grasps relationships, and not the particular things. When one says that it is the relationships that make an impression on us, and that it is the things as a whole that do too, these two ideas are closely related one to the other. For example, someone makes a series of raps on the table: one can repeat the series without having counted them.[23]

The connexion between the two ideas is presumably the fact that some wholes *are* patterned sets of relations. And Weil is claiming that the perception of the pattern is prior to any quantitative analysis of parts.

Again, the lesson can be generalized: we perceive not blank sensations, but meaningful states of affairs. We can abstract sensations or concepts from experience, but again that abstraction is secondary; in the default case, our experience consists in sensations that are always already conceptually structured. "And so Descartes finds in perception," Weil concludes, "a 'natural geometry' and 'an operation of thought that, although it is only a simple act of imagination, nevertheless contains a form of reasoning similar to that used by surveyors when, by standing in two different spots, they measure inaccessible places' (6:138)."[24] This theory of perception, and the rôle of geometry in it, is

---

22   Weil makes this connexion explicit: "In such cases we ordinarily talk about an effect of the imagination; but perhaps it is better to use the word 'reading'" ("Essay on the Notion of Reading," 229/15).

23   Simone Weil, *Lectures on Philosophy*, transcribed by Anne Reynaud-Guérithault and translated by Hugh Price (Cambridge: Cambridge University Press, 1978), 32 / Simone Weil, *Leçons de philosophie*, transcribed by Anne Reynaud-Guérithault (Paris: Union Générale d'Éditions, 1959), 23. While uncommon, "affect" is not a typo; it is being used here in its psychological sense; and it echoes Spinoza. Independently, Zwicky also connects Weil's notion of reading with gestalt psychology: "what Weil terms 'les significations,' Max Wertheimer calls *Gestalten*" (Zwicky, "What Is Ineffable?," *International Studies in the Philosophy of Science* 26, no. 2 [June 2012]: 200).

24   Simone Weil, "Science and Perception in Descartes," 53–54/182.

THE DANCE OF PERCEPTION 311

continuous from Weil's dissertation to her lectures: "There is already ... an elementary geometry in perception," she writes in the lectures. "Everything happens as if our bodies already knew the geometrical theorems which our mind does not yet know."[25] To claim that there is a natural or elementary geometry in perception is to claim that we perceive patterns rather that chaos.

3. Having sketched an unconventional portrait of Descartes, and having emphasized the centrality of imagination to it, Weil embarks, in the second part of her dissertation, on her own meditation. By thus imitating Descartes, Weil shows her understanding that the Cartesian meditation must be inflected in the first person singular. Let me retrace the relevant moves. As Winch observes, I begin in a state of pure *passivity*, like someone "wallowing with eyes closed in a warm bath."[26] However, like Descartes, I find that the activity of doubting is revelatory. Let me assume that all of the contents of my consciousness are illusory—for example, my perception that I am writing at a chipboard desk, looking across the rooftops of the city to the Salish Sea. Still, in this swirl of illusion, is there any indubitable residue, anything that I can say that I know? When I try to doubt the existence of the desk, or when I turn that doubt on my own existence, cannot I say, with Descartes, that the act of doubt implies the existence of a doubting subject: namely, a thinking thing? Weil's innovation is to suggest that there is something more basic than doubting, more basic than thought. But to formulate her insight in that way is already to distort it. For what I find is not the existence of a *thing*. Instead, I find that the *activity* of thinking exists.[27] And this activity is expressed, initially, in doubting. In believing, I may be passive; by appearing to me, things may elicit belief from me. Unsolicited, the desk appears to me, it seizes my consciousness, it occupies my thoughts—but I can always refuse to believe that appearance. "And through this power of thinking—which so far is revealed to me only by the power of doubting—I know that I am. I can, therefore I am [*Je puis, donc je suis*]."[28] As

---

25   Weil, *Lectures on Philosophy*, 51/49.

26   Winch, *Simone Weil: "The Just Balance,"* 8.

27   In this way, Weil deftly sidesteps Lichtenberg's criticism of Descartes' cogito argument. "We should say *it thinks*, just as we say *it lightens*. To say *cogito* is already to say too much as soon as we translate it *I think*" (Georg Christoph Lichtenberg, "Notebook K," in *The Waste Books*, trans. R.J. Hollingdale [New York: New York Review of Books, 2000], §18). Cf. Hobbes' objection to Descartes' second meditation, AT VII.172–74.

28   Weil, "Science and Perception in Descartes," 59/189 (translation altered). McFarland and Van Ness translate "*je puis*" as "I have power." But this translation is less than felicitous, as it risks substantializing what Weil characterizes as pure activity.

Winch observes, what is important is "the way the formula characterizes thought itself—as *activity*."[29]

Having established that *acting is*, Weil next asks whether she is able to do anything in addition to doubting. For example, what about daydreaming? (In Weil's later work, "imagination" becomes a pejorative term more or less synonymous with "daydreaming"—that is, thinking about what isn't there. But in the dissertation, imagination is importantly distinct from daydreaming.)[30] Do I not express my power in daydreaming about whatever I want? Weil notices that there is a difference between believing and doubting: while I always retain the power to doubt, I cannot will myself to believe. "Even though I would like to, I can never arouse in myself the same belief in the existence of things in my daydreams as that inspired in me by what I call real things. Thus I recognize that my power over my belief is only a negative one; I can doubt, but I cannot believe."[31] My belief is elicited *involuntarily* by the appearance of real things—just as my assent is elicited by truth.

This involuntary quality is a clue: it implies that I neither control nor cause these appearances. Here, Weil is following Descartes in Meditation Six. My ideas of sensible things must be produced by "a certain active faculty"; but this faculty "cannot be in me, since it clearly presupposes no act of the understanding, and these ideas are produced without my cooperation and often even against my will."[32] If this active faculty is not in me, then something other than me must exist. "It *is* true that events take me by surprise, even when they are desired; in what I perceive, even when it is pleasant, there is always something I have not desired, something that takes hold of me and imposes itself on me like an alien thing. This is what makes me almost invincibly convinced that, if my daydreams exist only for me, on the other hand this paper, this table, the

---

29   Winch, *Simone Weil: "The Just Balance,"* 9. Cf. Weil, "Science and Perception in Descartes," 73/204. There is a resonance with the pure activity of Aristotle's "thinking thinking thinking" (Aristotle, *Metaphysics*, in *The Basic Works*, edited by Richard McKeon [New York: The Modern Library, 2001], Λ.7.1072b19).

30   There are a number of other early texts, in particular "Imagination et perception" (1925) and "Sur l'imagination" (1931–1932), which would considerably enrich, but also complicate, the conception of imagination under discussion here. Weil's thinking in these texts is not fully consistent with her thinking in the dissertation and the lectures at Roanne. A study of the inconsistencies, and an attempt to explain them, is deserving of a separate paper.

31   Weil, "Science and Perception in Descartes," 60/190.

32   René Descartes, *Meditations on First Philosophy*, 3rd ed., trans. Donald A. Cress (Indianapolis: Hackett Publishing Company, 1993), AT VII.79.

THE DANCE OF PERCEPTION   313

heavens, the earth, Paris, all exist independently of me."[33] But, Weil concludes, "this conviction is not a proof" of the existence of the external world.[34]

Nevertheless, we do learn something from these reflections: doubting is different from believing and perceiving. I am always free—always able—to doubt, and when I do, I act. But believing and perceiving are mixed activities: to some extent, I am passive when they occur. With perceiving, in particular, the content is a constraint: I cannot generate it *ex nihilo*. (We might say: matter is *necessary* for the specification of form.)[35] Like Descartes, Weil then makes a fresh start, returning to the axiom: "But who am I? A thing that exercises this power that I call thinking.... So, in order to know myself, I must know the extent of this power."[36] She contrasts what we might call "power over," which is limited, with "real power," which is infinite: "A power such as I would attribute to a king, which is a relation between one thing and another (for example, between the king's words and the actions of his subjects) can be measured. But my power is not this shadow of power."[37] In principle, she enjoys real, infinite power—at least insofar as she can doubt. But insofar as she needs *content* for her thinking—that is, insofar as her thinking is *intentional*, or *about* something other than itself—her power is limited. From the fact of that limitation, she argues, in a few dense sentences, to the conclusion that external things exist:

> My sovereignty over myself, which is absolute as long as I want only to suspend my thought, disappears as soon as it is a matter of giving myself something to think about. Freedom is the only power that I possess absolutely. Therefore, something other than myself exists. Since no power is limited by itself, it is enough for me to know that my power is not absolute to know that my existence is not the only existence.[38]

Now, this conclusion requires some scrutiny. Why was the earlier argument—the one modelled on Descartes' argument from Meditation Six—not adequate to draw the conclusion that external things exist? Because the involuntariness

---

33   Weil, "Science and Perception in Descartes," 60–61/191.
34   Weil, "Science and Perception in Descartes," 61/191.
35   Cf. Aristotle, *Metaphysics*, Z.8.1034a5-8.
36   Weil, "Science and Perception in Descartes," 62/192.
37   Weil, "Science and Perception in Descartes," 62/192–93. Here, Weil is following Descartes in Meditation Four; there, Descartes argues that his "will or free choice" is like God's because "I experience that it is limited by no boundaries whatever" and "I experience [it] to be so great in me that I cannot grasp the idea of any greater faculty" (Descartes, *Meditations*, AT VII.56–57).
38   Weil, "Science and Perception in Descartes," 62/193.

of a phenomenon, while it is a clue, is not sufficient to establish the phenomenon's mind-independent existence. Weil observes that she gets angry "suddenly, often even when I want to remain calm."[39] That willing, on the one hand, and sensing or feeling, on the other, can come apart in this way is significant for two reasons: firstly, it indicates that, for all I know, I am the source of my feeling of frostbite, for example, and the cold that (putatively) caused that frostbite, even if I suffer it unwillingly. Secondly, at this point in Weil's meditation, her only clear and distinct truth is that *acting is*; insofar as she is passive in feeling frostbite, such feeling, however involuntary, cannot be the ground of anything's existence. Weil's original argument for the external world departs from Descartes. I know that I am not alone because my acting is limited. And it is limited by another power. I and the world act on each other, and we suffer each other. On this account, knowing the world, even its most "inanimate" aspects, will turn out to be an intersubjective achievement.[40] The medium through which I and the world encounter each other is the embodied imagination.

4. I have spent some time discussing the frame and opening moves of Weil's dissertation because they are important to her characterization of the imagination: firstly, according to her unorthodox portrait of Descartes, imagining is an indispensable form of philosophical and scientific thinking; and secondly, it is the point of intersection between mind and world, the point at which the active and passive aspects of the perceiver are integrated. I want now to outline some of the philosophical background for her account of the imagination.

Weil's conception of the imagination borrows from Descartes, Spinoza, and Kant (as well as Aristotle and the Stoics). She follows Descartes in associating the imagination with the body: Descartes states explicitly that when the mind

---

39   Weil, "Science and Perception in Descartes," 61/191.

40   Cf. Lorraine Code, "Taking Subjectivity into Account," in *Feminist Epistemologies*, eds. Linda Alcoff and Elizabeth Potter (New York: Routledge, 1993), 15–48. At the 2017 meeting of the Canadian Philosophical Association in Toronto, Lorraine Code asked whether Weil's epistemology is a social epistemology. The answer is *yes*, if one acknowledges that society can include more-than-human beings. In her Cartesian meditation, Weil does not encounter other humans, but she does enlarge her knowledge by interacting with other subjects who are not reducible to objects. Some of these subjects would be called "inanimate" by the Western tradition, but other traditions have treated them differently. See A. Irving Hallowell, "Ojibwa Ontology, Behavior, and World View," in *Culture in History*, ed. Stanley Diamond (New York: Columbia University Press, 1960), 19–52; and Nurit Bird-David, "'Animism' Revisited: Personhood, Environment, and Relational Epistemology," *Current Anthropology* 40, supplement (February 1999): S67–S79.

THE DANCE OF PERCEPTION   315

imagines, "it turns toward the body,"[41] and imagining is "merely the contemplating of the shape or image of a corporeal thing."[42] But what, exactly, is an image? In the Roanne lectures, Weil paraphrases and abridges one of Spinoza's discussions of the imagination,[43] and in the course of doing so, she also offers a definition of "image"; that definition, while influenced by Spinoza, is her own. Here is Spinoza's definition:

> Further, to retain the usual terminology, we will assign the word "images" to those affections of the human body the ideas of which set forth external bodies as if they were present to us, although they do not represent shapes. And when the mind regards bodies in this way, we shall say that it "imagines."[44]

Compare Weil's definition:

> (Les « images » sont les traces des choses sur le corps, traces qui sont en réalité celles des réactions du corps à l'égard des choses.)
> ("Images" are the traces which things leave in the body, traces which in fact are the reactions of the body to things.)[45]

Images are proto-conceptual and spontaneous *modifications of the body* (in response to other bodies). Images are also *intentional*: they are *of* or *about* bodies. Not all images are veridical—sometimes we have an image when no corresponding body is present. But images themselves are blameless. Spinoza makes it clear that the error is located not in the image, but in the mind's failure to have an idea that "excludes the existence" of the imagined thing.[46] So imagining is the mind's turning toward the body and contemplating its reactions to

---

41   Descartes, *Meditations*, AT VII.73.

42   Descartes, *Meditations*, AT VII.28.

43   See Benedict de Spinoza, *Ethics*, trans. Samuel Shirley (Indianapolis: Hackett Publishing Company, 1992), IIP40S1.

44   Spinoza, *Ethics*, IIP17S.

45   Weil, *Lectures on Philosophy*, 58/58. As Steven Burns has correctly observed, this conception of imagination is constrained. It does not seem to cover the full range of what we would ordinarily recognize as imagination: visual, musical, culinary, mathematical, philosophical, literary, and so on. But I think that Weil is defining "image" narrowly for a special purpose. As will become clearer in §6 below, Weil is trying to account for images in a way that does not presuppose the mental theatre.

46   Spinoza, *Ethics*, IIP17S. This error theory is not dissimilar to Descartes' theory in Meditation Four. It is not the intellect's perception that is blameworthy, but the will's premature affirmation or rejection of that perception. For Spinoza (as for Hobbes), there is no faculty

things. Those reactions, whether congenital or conditioned, are responsible for general ideas: such ideas are *meta-images*, that is, images of sets of similar images. (I shall elaborate on this point in §6 below.) Any thinking, then, which involves generalities or similarities—any thinking which is not radically particularist—depends on the imagination.

Furthermore, the duality of the imagination—its active and passive aspects—is crucial to Weil's project. The aim of this project is more or less Spinozistic (and ultimately Stoic):[47] understanding is active, and insofar as the agent understands, she becomes more free and converts passions (or reactions) into actions. As she suggests in her sketch of Spinoza's philosophy of the emotions, "One frees oneself from feelings in so far as one understands them."[48] An action just is an understood passion. Importantly, passivity is ineliminable: insofar as the world participates in my perceiving and thinking—insofar as I am part of nature, and my perceiving or thinking is *about* something other than itself—I am passive.[49] The aim is not to eliminate this content, but to understand it; and understanding consists in actively perceiving patterns. Knowledge will not free me from the causal nexus by making me immune to it. But if I *understand* my place in the nexus, then I am not merely shoved around by the world; instead, I take responsibility for what happens to me (and through me).[50]

It is through the imagination, "this knot of action and reaction that attaches me to the world that I must discover what is my portion and what it is that resists me.... The world is not outside my thought; it is above all what is not me in me."[51] Weil's characterization of the world—"what is not me in me"—is suggestive: rather than conceiving of the world as an object thrown against a subject in an oppositional relationship, we might conceive of the world as extending into the interior of the agent. Or, to phrase the thought after John McDowell, we might conceive of the conceptual sphere being *open* to reality.[52] Ideally, this relation will be complementary: "Not only do I have a grasp on the world, but my thought is, as it were, a component part of the world, just as the world, in

---

of will (cf. Spinoza, *Ethics*, IP32; Hobbes, *Leviathan*, I.VI.53); so the idea in Spinoza does the same work as the will in Descartes.

47   For Spinoza's Stoicism, see Susan James, "Spinoza the Stoic," in *The Rise of Modern Philosophy*, ed. Tom Sorrell (Oxford: Oxford University Press, 1993), 289–316.

48   Weil, *Lectures on Philosophy*, 207/268. Cf. Spinoza, *Ethics*, IIIDef2-3.

49   Cf. Spinoza, *Ethics*, IVP3.

50   Steven Burns rightly describes this position as compatibilist. Indeed, I believe that Weil's compatibilism fits Hume's account: see David Hume, "Of Liberty and Necessity," *An Enquiry Concerning Human Understanding* (Indianapolis: Hackett Publishing Company, 1993), 53–69.

51   Weil, "Science and Perception in Descartes," 70–71/201–02.

52   See McDowell, *Mind and World*, §II.2 (p. 26).

THE DANCE OF PERCEPTION   317

another way, is part of my thought."[53] For Weil, such a complementary relation
is an achievement, however, rather than the default condition.

5. In the dissertation, Weil reconstructs the world geometrically. My action is
abstractly represented by straight-line motion,[54] that motion is analysable into
a series of points, and that series is infinitely continuable.[55] Insofar as the
world exhibits geometrical structure—insofar as it consists in interrelated
polydimensional wholes—it can be understood. Furthermore, that structure is
already present in the body's proto-conceptual reactions to the world. The
body, itself a polydimensional structure, is primed to receive the images of the
world. This theory of perception is traceable through Spinoza back to Aristotle,
Plato, and Empedokles: "like is known only by like."[56] Aristotle reproaches Empedokles (and Plato in his *Timaios*) for allegedly assuming that the relevant
similarity is elemental; instead, it is, he claims, formal: "By a 'sense' is meant
what has the power of receiving into itself the sensible forms of things without
the matter."[57] In perceiving, the soul receives the form of the perceived thing
"in the way in which a piece of wax takes on the impress of a signet-ring without the iron or gold."[58] Such impressions are not formless sense data; they are
images, that is, complex structures or forms. And to perceive is to imagine: to
imitate, in one's embodied soul, the form of the perceived thing. Weil's geometrical reconstruction of the world, then, is a re-imagination of the world as
a set of interrelated forms.

My relationship with the world is redefined, in this model, as the relationship between straight-line motion and an infinitely complex combination of
straight-line motions. These motions are *co-modifying*. Weil writes, "I am

---

53   Weil, "Science and Perception in Descartes," 80/212.
54   Straight-line motion is a representation of what Spinoza, following Hobbes, calls *conatus*:
      inertial motion, or the tendency of a thing to continue in its current state unless modified
      by another thing. Cf. Spinoza, *Ethics*, IIIP7, and Hobbes, *Leviathan*, I.II.1.
55   McFarland and Van Ness offer a helpful gloss on the reconstruction: "By combining
      straight-line motions she arrives at a series of geometrical forms—the oblique line, the
      circle, the ellipse—that corresponds in its increasing complexity to the series of numbers.
      Generalizing from this, she postulates that the world is constituted by an infinitely com-
      plex combination of straight-line movements, and that this combination is at least theo-
      retically reducible to a movement comparable to the simple straight-line movement she
      has at her disposal" (McFarland and Van Ness, "Introduction," 28–29). This project might
      sound analytic and reductionist; however, the project of reconstructing the world on the
      combination of geometrical units has precedent in Plato's *Timaios*, which in turn follows
      Pythagoras. Furthermore, we must remember that geometry, in Weil's reading of Des-
      cartes, is not a disembodied theory; it is, instead, a measuring of the real earth.
56   Cf. Aristotle, *De Anima*, 1.2.404b10-20, 1.5.409b26.
57   Aristotle, *De Anima*, II.12.424a17-18.
58   Aristotle, *De Anima*, II.12.424a19-20.

always a dual being, on the one hand a passive being who is subject to the world, and on the other an active being who has a grasp on it ... I can unite [the two parts of myself] indirectly, since this and nothing else is what action consists of.... Not the appearance of action..., but real action, indirect action, action conforming to geometry, or, to give it its true name, work."[59] Insofar as I suffer the world, sensibility and understanding are confusedly mixed, and the world is an opaque and alien force shoving me around. The aim is to transform the confused intermingling into an integrity in which the rôles of the two faculties are clarified. If I wish to know the world, I must re-imagine it: not as a baffling adversarial force, "a will foreign to mine,"[60] but as an "obstacle" ("l'obstacle"). For Weil, "obstacle" is a term of art: it is that aspect of the world to which one responds with "work" ("le travail"). Simone Pétrement, in her discussion of Weil's early essay "Concerning Perception," offers a helpful definition of work: "So work is essentially *indirect* action, action applied to the *means*."[61] Work, so defined, is an act of practical wisdom (rather than an aimless burst of force). While the passive spectator suffers the brutality of the world, the worker re-imagines the world as an obstacle, something which must be approached obliquely. Winch astutely invokes Weil's image of a sailboat tacking against the wind as an analogy for work.[62] In knowing, the mind does not blindly collide with the world; it turns away from the world, and returns to it indirectly. Such indirection can take the form of reflection—the worker is the one who thinks about how best to circumvent the obstacle—but it must return to the world.

Work, for Weil, offers the promise of reintegrating the two aspects of the imagination (passive sensibility and active understanding): "Only through the intermediary of the world, the intermediary of work, do I reunite them; for if through work I do not reunite the two parts of myself, the one that undergoes and the one that acts, I at least cause the changes I undergo to be produced in me, so that what I am subject to is my own action."[63] This thought is Spinozistic (and Stoic): I am the patient of my own actions, I am the cause of the changes I undergo, insofar as I understand those changes. Whatever I do, I will be changed by the world. But when I work, turning away from the world in order to return to it more thoughtfully, I assume responsibility for the changes in myself. I also use my body as a tool to learn about other bodies. The metaphor

---

59   Weil, "Science and Perception in Descartes," 78/209.

60   Weil, "Science and Perception in Descartes," 71/202.

61   Simone Pétrement, *Simone Weil: A Life*, trans. Raymond Rosenthal (New York: Schocken Books, 1976), 61.

62   Cf. Winch, *Simone Weil: "The Just Balance,"* 56. Cf. Weil, "Science and Perception in Descartes," 76/207, 80/212.

63   Weil, "Science and Perception in Descartes," 78/209.

THE DANCE OF PERCEPTION 319

of body as tool is misleading if it is taken to imply an alienated and dualistic relation between mind and body. On the contrary, for Weil, when one uses one's own body as a tool—an ὄργανον—mind and body are most fully integrated: almost paradoxically, one's body is a medium through which the mind achieves *immediate* contact with the body of the world. (This point was discussed in §2 above.) My body is "the point of intersection" between my simple movement and the complex movement of the world: it moves and is moved.[64] The most obvious example of work is manual labour; Weil considers the particular example of a farmer using a scythe.[65] Because it affords immediate contact with the world, work is, for Weil, epistemically indispensable. Indeed, her defence of work is, in a sense, a repudiation of the Aristotelian distinction between characterological and epistemic virtues,[66] and of the glorification of contemplation.[67] Contemplation is not the highest human activity; the various ways of making contact with reality all require a bodily element.[68]

6. At the climax of the dissertation, Weil offers the following definition of perception:

> La perception, c'est la géométrie prenant possession en quelque sorte des passions mêmes, par le moyen du travail.
> Perception is geometry taking as it were possession of the passions themselves, by means of work.[69]

I have suggested that the theory of perception presented in the dissertation already anticipates the theory outlined in the lectures. The aphorism above, which defines perception in terms of geometry, is key to seeing the connexion. The lectures pursue an ascetic regime of thinking, starting with a paring back of ambitions to the barest materialism, and then attempting to find the mind in that apparently barren landscape.

The very first lecture starts, auspiciously enough, with *action*: "*Study of the ways in which thought in other people shows itself* (objective psychology). Actions: reflex (from an external point of view everything is at the level of

---

64   Weil, "Science and Perception in Descartes," 79/210.
65   Weil, "Science and Perception in Descartes," 81/212.
66   Aristotle, *Nicomachean Ethics*, trans. David Ross (Oxford: Oxford University Press, 2009), I.13.1103a4-7.
67   Aristotle, *Nicomachean Ethics*, X.8–9.
68   Thanks to Steven Burns for help with rephrasing this point.
69   Weil, "Science and Perception in Descartes," 79/210.

reflexes), custom, habit, voluntary actions."[70] One of the questions that Weil's theory is designed to address is: "What is the origin of general ideas?" Earlier I indicated that her response is broadly Spinozistic: general ideas are *meta-images*, the result of a surfeit of similar images, which in turn are the body's reactions to other bodies. (They are meta-images in the sense that they are images *of collections of images*.) The ground of general ideas is, then, the imagination; and since the imagination belongs to the body, the mind finds its roots in the material world.

Furthermore, as the original thought is an image, so the original action is a *reaction*. Weil writes, "It is, then, reflexes that the body gives us, that is to say reactions which are brought about by known stimuli."[71] She then draws a distinction between "congenital" and "acquired or conditioned" reflexes. As examples of the former, she offers "secretion of digestive juices, movement of the leg when someone strikes it."[72] These reflexes do not involve any will or effort; they are autonomic and genealogically prior to theoretical reflection (although such reflection might also be understood as a species of conditioned reflex). Later in the lectures, Weil suggests that congenital reflexes are synonymous with what she calls "spontaneous language": "it is something *animal* (and so human too). It is what conveys affections. It is natural in the sense that it is made up of natural reactions of muscles, glands and lungs."[73] Importantly, these reactions are also general:

---

70 Weil, *Lectures on Philosophy*, 27/17. As Winch observes, in her notebooks Weil meditates on a line from Goethe's *Faust* which is crucial to her own thinking here: "In the beginning was the deed" (Goethe qtd in Weil, *First and Last Notebooks*, trans. Richard Rees [London: Oxford University Press, 1970], 24). In these same notebooks, Weil also writes, "Philosophy ... is *exclusively* an affair of action and practice" (362). Goethe's revision of John points to the importance of wordlessness: the sense in which the λόγος is not a word but what Weil, referring to the beginning of the Book of John, translates as "rapport" or "médiation"— that is, a geometrical structure rather than a lexical atom (Weil, *Intuitions pré-chrétiennes* [La Colombe: Éditions du Vieux Colombier, 1951], 166; cf. Weil, *Intimations of Christianity*, trans. Elisabeth Chase Geissbuhler [London: Routledge, 1957], 197). If we wish to understand how linguistic communication is possible, we should look for what it shares with non- or extra-linguistic communication. Winch is right to see a similarity with Wittgenstein's thought: complicated language-games emerge from more "primitive" ones (where "primitive" means "primary" rather than "backward").

71 Weil, *Lectures on Philosophy*, 30/21.

72 Weil, *Lectures on Philosophy*, 30/21.

73 Weil, *Lectures on Philosophy*, 65/66. (Cf. Ludwig Wittgenstein, *On Certainty*, trans. Denis Paul and G.E.M. Anscombe [Oxford: Basil Blackwell, 1979], §475.) Analogously, Weil conceives of "language proper" as a kind of "conditioned reflex."

THE DANCE OF PERCEPTION   321

If we examine the relation between reactions and stimuli, we see that the latter are limitless in number, while the former are limited. The salivary gland, for example, always secretes saliva, whatever the food is. It is as if it were able to discern the general character of food throughout the infinite variety of foods....

So, by means of our reactions we generalise stimuli.[74]

Already, before bringing in Spinoza, and relying instead on behaviourist psychology, Weil begins to sketch her theory of general ideas. And, again, it is her ascetic or minimalist method that indicates this starting place: she is trying to see whether she can discover the mind—its conditions of possibility—while making only materialist assumptions: "It is by studying matter that we shall find mind."[75] Through its correlation with unlimited stimuli which are similar in way Σ, a single reaction P serves to sort those stimuli into kind Σ: "It is in this way that the body classifies things in the world before there is any thought.... So, from the very fact that we have a body, the world is ordered for it; it is arranged in order in relation to the body's reactions."[76] These reactions—these meta-images—do the work in Weil's epistemology that is done by the categories in Kant's: they *organize* sensations into experience. There are important differences, however: meta-images belong to us, not insofar as we are rational agents, but insofar as we are imagining bodies. Furthermore, meta-images cannot belong uniquely to humans; following Aristotle, we can say that the capacity to imagine is shared by any animal soul.[77] For an animist such as Spinoza, the capacity will be distributed even more widely. Additionally, a glance around us reveals organisms whose survival suggests that their meta-images have managed to track reality.[78]

7. The upshot of Weil's theory is that reactions are the transcendental ground of the possibility of coherent experience:

Both congenital and acquired reflexes establish a classification among things in the world....

---

74   Weil, *Lectures on Philosophy*, 30/21–22.

75   Weil, *Lectures on Philosophy*, 40/34. She also acknowledges that the rivalry among materialism, idealism, and dualism has a moral dimension (Weil, *Lectures on Philosophy*, 33/24–25).

76   Weil, *Lectures on Philosophy*, 31/22.

77   Cf. Aristotle, *De Anima*, III.11.433b29.

78   Cf. Konrad Lorenz qtd in Zwicky, *Wisdom & Metaphor*, 2nd ed. (Kentville: Gaspereau Press, 2008), R26. Cf. Zwicky, "Imagination and the Good Life," §1.5.

So, when we are on the point of giving birth to thought, it comes to birth in a world that is already ordered.[79]

We can experience the world because it is coherently structured, and to say that it is structured is to say that it consists in wholes standing in relations with each other. Alternatively, it is to say, with Weil, that there is "an elementary geometry" in perception.[80] As I suggested in §6, the recognition of that elementary geometry is the key to seeing the continuity between the dissertation and the lectures. Weil writes, "Everything happens as if our bodies already knew the geometrical theorems which our mind does not yet know.... // It is the same cause really (imagination) which enables us to perceive the most ordinary things, and do geometry..."[81] The thesis, that the same imagination is at work in ordinary perception and geometry, is straight out of the dissertation: to repeat the climax: "Now I recognize that the two kinds of imagination, which are found separately in the emotions and in geometry, are united in the things I perceive. Perception is geometry taking as it were possession of the passions themselves, by means of work."[82] Let me elaborate this thought.

In the lectures, Weil argues, in a Kantian fashion, that the imagination is responsible for our experience of spatio-temporal objects. She asks, "What is in the foreground of consciousness? Is it what is imagined or what is felt?"[83] The disjunction is somewhat artificial, since Weil has argued (in the dissertation) that sensations do not come to us independently of their meanings. In any event, she answers here that what is in the foreground is imaginatively-inflected sensation: "we have never seen a real cube. Cubic space is really the result of the gesture of grasping the object. The space which we imagine the cube to fill is essentially a relationship between sensations and myself, and consists in a disposition to act in a certain way."[84] To see something *as* a cube—that is, *to see a cube*—is to have a sensation of a rectangular face inflected with the physical trace—the meta-image—of many other cube-like things.[85] That formulation sounds cumbersome, and it fails to do justice to the ordinary phenomenology of perceiving a real cube. But it is not meant to describe that phenomenology;

---

79 Weil, *Lectures on Philosophy*, 32/23–25.
80 Weil, *Lectures on Philosophy*, 51/49.
81 Weil, *Lectures on Philosophy*, 51/49–50.
82 Weil, "Science and Perception in Descartes," 79/210.
83 Weil, *Lectures on Philosophy*, 48/45.
84 Weil, *Lectures on Philosophy*, 49/46.
85 Again, the phrase *seeing-as* is misleading here if it is taken to imply that the perceiver is interpreting a sensation for which there are alternative interpretations (i.e., alternative ways of seeing-as).

THE DANCE OF PERCEPTION   323

it is instead trying to describe what is happening backstage. The imagination, the body's archive of meta-images, is continuously working, fleshing out our flat sensations into polydimensional experiences. And the imagination's work is not fanciful or false: on the contrary, imagining is governed by laws, and to imagine is to be in contact with reality: "So, space, depth, shapes are given to us by our imagination. We must not forget, in this case, that 'imagination' should not be taken as something completely synonymous with fantasy or as something arbitrary: when we see two points we are not free to see anything except a straight line."[86] In other words, imagination does make a contribution to perception, but that contribution is not capricious; it is responsive to structure independent of itself. As such, it satisfies one of the requirements for knowledge: recall that knowledge is not possible in the absence of some kind of mind-independent constraint.

And so we reach the climax of the first set of lectures:

> C'est le rapport essentiel entre nous et l'extérieur, rapport qui consiste en une *réaction,* un *réflexe,* qui constitue pour nous la *perception* du monde extérieur. *La simple perception de la nature est une sorte de danse* ; c'est cette danse qui nous fait percevoir.[87]
>
> Our *perception* of the external world constitutes the essential relation between us and what is outside us, a relation which consists in a *reaction*, a reflex. The elementary perception of nature is a sort of dance; this dance is the source of our perceiving.[88]

But what exactly does it mean to say that perception is a dance? As Winch suggests, a dance is indeed "a *pattern* of movements,"[89] but Weil does not restrict the sense modality to vision. For a spectator, a dance might be experienced via visual images; but for a dancer, the same dance might be experienced via kinaesthetic images. Even in dances where one partner leads, each partner must be responsive to the movements of the other; and in a solitary dance, the dancer must nevertheless be responsive to the "geometry of the emotions" that music is.[90]

---

86   Weil, *Lectures on Philosophy*, 51/49.

87   Weil, *Lectures on Philosophy*, 50/50.

88   Weil trans. Winch, *Simone Weil: "The Just Balance,"* 41. Price translates the last clause thusly: "it is this dance that makes perception possible for us" (Weil, *Lectures on Philosophy*, 50).

89   Winch, *Simone Weil: "The Just Balance,"* 41.

90   The quoted phrase is from Zwicky, "Practising Bach," *Forge* (Kentville: Gaspereau Press, 2011), 26.

The key idea is that a dance is a pattern of movements—what Weil might call an "elementary geometry"—to which our body responds with patterns of its own (whether that response takes the shape of visual or kinaesthetic images). More precisely, our body perceives patterns by imitating them. Furthermore, a dance is not only physical but also *inter*active or *co*-responsive.[91] Perception is a dance because it is a pattern of movements in which both our body and the body of the world participate. The agent who perceives clearly is not merely bruised by the random force of the world. When we understand what we perceive, our imagination focusses the images given to our body by the world and discerns their interrelations—and thus transforms a passion into an action.[92]

8. We have found that the imagination, for Weil, is an amphibious faculty. It mediates (and makes possible) the relation between mind and body. This duality leads to a couple of references to two imaginations,[93] which we might interpret as imagination under the aspect of (active) understanding and imagination under the aspect of (passive) sensibility. Recall the passage (from §1) in which Weil characterizes imagination as an oracle, "this bond of action and reaction between the world and my thought in myself alone." That passage continues: "I will name this bond the imagination, as opposed to the understanding, the name of the 'I' who thinks, and the sensibility, my name insofar as I am acted upon."[94] And so Weil shows her Kantian hand. Recall the famous passage in the first *Critique* in which Kant draws the same distinction: "If the receptivity of our mind, its power of receiving representations in so far as it is

---

91 Cf. Zwicky on the collaborative experience of meaning (Zwicky, *Lyric Philosophy*, 2nd ed. [Kentville: Gaspereau Press, 2011], L250). Corbí's notion of "passive receptivity"—a notion inspired by Weil's work—is helpful here (Josep Corbí, "First Person Authority and Self-Knowledge as an Achievement," *European Journal of Philosophy* 18, no. 3 [2009]: §10.1 [pp. 345–47]). The notion of passive receptivity is meant to dissolve the dichotomy between action and passion. It is worth mentioning that Corbí also uses the metaphor of dancing to illustrate what he means. See also Abram, who describes perception as "this silent or wordless dance ... this improvised duet between my animal body and the fluid, breathing landscape that it inhabits" (David Abram, *Spell of the Sensuous* [New York: Vintage Books, 1997], 53).

92 For example, I realize that her loudness is not, as I initially surmised, an expression of brashness, but rather an attempt to compensate for incapacitating shyness, and thus my irritation dissolves into empathy; or I gradually recognize that my flash of anger is not caused, but only occasioned, by the jar that exploded on the kitchen floor, and as I turn to the work of sweeping up the glass, my attitude of blame dissipates.

93 See Weil, "Science and Perception in Descartes," 71/202, 79/210.

94 Weil, "Science and Perception in Descartes," 69/200.

THE DANCE OF PERCEPTION 325

in any wise affected, is to be entitled sensibility, then the mind's power of producing representations from itself, the spontaneity of knowledge, should be called the understanding.... Without sensibility no object would be given to us. Without understanding no object would be thought. Thoughts without content are empty, intuitions without concepts are blind."[95]

Is imagination then a third faculty, in addition to understanding and sensibility? A crucial question. I have suggested that imagination is the *integrity* of understanding and sensibility. Weil offers a couple of metaphors that go some distance toward making sense of that suggestion:

> If I were only understanding and sensibility, I would know that I see a flash of lightning or hear thunder almost in the same way I know that the words I see in silent film titles are uttered by the voice of a man or a woman.... I would be always like a spectator at a badly staged play in which the storm, riot, or battle is represented in a ludicrous way.[96]

Here understanding and sensibility are not *integrated with* but *added to* each other, in the way that words might be appended to the picture in a silent film. Analogously, I would have a sense impression of lightning, to which would be added the concept "lightning," impression and concept each retaining its independence and being merely externally related to the other. Sensibility and understanding would thus run on parallel but separate tracks. Like the spectator at the badly staged play, I would be able to label what I perceive (for example, "that performer is attempting to depict anger") without being moved by it. But this is not the way that things are:

> But this supposition is absurd, so contrary is it to reality, for the only way sense impressions reach my mind is by causing a disturbance in it, and, far from being an understanding to which senses have been added like

---

95   Immanuel Kant, *Critique of Pure Reason*, trans. Norman Kemp Smith (New York: Palgrave Macmillan, 2007), B75/A51. Kant is not the inventor of this distinction, which is traceable at least as far back as Aristotle's distinction between the passive and active intellect: see Aristotle, *De Anima*, Bk III, Ch. 5. The conclusion of this chapter is not the place to start a discussion of Kant's productive imagination. However, for some leads, see Peter Strawson, "Imagination and Perception," in *Experience & Theory*, eds. Lawrence Foster & J.W. Swanson (Amherst: The University of Massachusetts Press, 1970), 31–54; Mary Warnock, "Imagination and Perception," *Imagination* (Berkeley: University of California Press, 1976), 13–34; and Richard Kearney, "The Transcendental Imagination," *The Wake of Imagination* (London: Routledge, 2003), 155–77.

96   Weil, "Science and Perception in Descartes," 69–70/200–01.

telephone operators to a staff headquarters, I am first and foremost nothing but imagination. From the fact that thunder crashes it follows, not that I become aware of a sound, but that my thinking is disturbed at its source ... The world and my mind are so thoroughly intermingled ... The slightest disturbance of the senses hurls me into the world...[97]

I am first and foremost nothing but imagination. For Weil, as for Aristotle and Spinoza, the original form of thinking is imagination—and it will be at the root of all further thinking.[98] The contributions of understanding and sensibility can be analysed out, but it does not follow that they made their contributions atomically (any more than the possibility of analytically distinguishing skeleton from muscle shows that skeleton and muscle began separately and were then combined into an organism). The senses do not merely relay neutral information to HQ, which then interprets that information; again, Weil's metaphor is designed to illustrate a merely external relation. But in fact I have no experience of meaning-free sense data. On the contrary, to perceive the flash of lightning is to read its meaning. For example, if I am swimming in a lake, and I perceive lightning, then I perceive something bright but also threatening. On the other hand, if I am safely sheltered in a cabin, watching lightning fracture the sky over the lake, then I perceive something bright and perhaps also sublime. Afterwards, I might be able to analyse out the brightness and distinguish it from its valence—but that is not how it comes to me. In perceiving, what comes first is the complex whole of conceptually structured sensation: experience *means* something to me.

Here someone might object: "You're making some highly questionable assumptions. Can't we imagine someone else, swimming in the same lake, who perceives the lightning as a bright and thrilling risk? Sure, such a person would be reckless, but the different 'readings' of these two swimmers show that what you are calling 'meaning' is not perceived but projected. Both swimmers perceive the same meteorological phenomenon, but that phenomenon, objectively considered, is neither threatening nor thrilling—it's just 'a natural electrical discharge of short duration and high voltage.' It could kill you, but it isn't 'threatening' because it's intention-less."—Notice, however, that the objector

---

97 Weil, "Science and Perception in Descartes," 70/201. Cf. Weil, *First and Last Notebooks*, 24, qtd in Winch, *Simone Weil: "The Just Balance,"* 14.

98 Cf. Aristotle, *De Anima*, III.7.431a16 and 431b2; David Ross, *Aristotle*, 6th ed. (London: Routledge, 1995), 152; Spinoza, *Ethics*, IIP40S2; and Genevieve Lloyd, "The Power of Spinoza," *Hypatia* 15, no. 2 (Spring 2000): 53.

THE DANCE OF PERCEPTION   327

has offered a reading of his own: to claim that it's *"just* a natural electrical discharge" is to read the phenomenon through the spectacles of positivism. Heidegger's critique remains insightful: positivism, no less than the "pseudoscience" it purports to expose, is a metaphysical position.[99] The lightning *is* a natural electrical discharge—but it is not *only* that. From the possibility of reading the lightning in more than one way, it does not follow that all readings are equal.[100] Some readings are more accurate than others. Indeed, some readings are *corrections* of mistaken readings.

Weil offers an example of imagining that she repeats, over a decade later, in the "Essay on the Notion of Reading." Compare:

> Thus at times something at a bend in the road frightens me; what is it? Not a sense impression; impressions have no more access to my thought than do the strange designs formed by the letters when I am reading. What frightens me is the idea, formed by the imagination out of what I see, of a hostile and powerful will that threatens me. A few moments later my imagination forms another idea: that of some harmless being, a tree.[101]
>
> If at night, on a deserted road, instead of a tree I think I see a man lying in wait, a threatening human presence forces itself on me, and, as in the case of the letter, makes me tremble even before I know what it's all about; I draw near, and suddenly everything is different, I no longer tremble, I read a tree and not a man. There is not an appearance and an interpretation...[102]

When Weil writes that the idea of a threat is "formed by the imagination out of what I see," we must understand that act of forming as occurring transcendentally. It is not as if I first receive the sense impressions, which are subsequently processed and shaped by the imagination: "There is *not* an appearance *and* an interpretation" (my emphases). The point of the comparison with (literal) reading is again the insight from gestalt psychology: perception of wholes is prior to perception of their components. The fact that components can (sometimes) be discerned retrospectively through analysis does not establish their

---

99   See Martin Heidegger, "What Is Metaphysics?" in *Basic Writings*, ed. David Farrell Krell (New York: HarperCollins Publishers, 1993), 93–110.
100   Cf. Zwicky, *Wisdom & Metaphor*, §§97–98.
101   Weil, "Science and Perception in Descartes," 71–72/202–03.
102   Weil, "Essay on the Notion of Reading," 299/15.

epistemic or ontological priority—it does not mean that the wholes were constructed out of separate components. Weil is arguing that the imagination is always already at work in experience, and it *must* be at work if there is to be experience.

But Weil does not leave us there, at the mercy of these faculties. Weil's project, in her study of the imagination, is not only descriptive; it has a normative dimension.[103] I have hinted at the possibility of *integrating* sensibility and understanding by way of the imagination. Since imagination, for Weil, is a condition of the possibility of experience, we cannot stop imagining any more than we can stop experiencing. We can, however, aspire to understand the images that appear to us. To understand, according to this (Spinozistic-Stoic) epistemology, is not to master or control. It is instead to see clearly how any given image is interrelated with other images. That may sound like a meagre achievement, especially when measured by the yardstick of the free market, since it does not multiply our choices. But it is real freedom for the Stoics, and Descartes, and Spinoza; as Descartes writes, "In order to be free I need not be capable of being moved in each direction; on the contrary, the more I am inclined toward one direction—either because I clearly understand that there is in it an aspect of the good and the true, or because God has thus disposed the inner recesses of my thought—the more freely do I choose that direction."[104] The more clearly I perceive truth, the less I vacillate in its presence, the less I yank against the harness of necessity.[105] According to this view, understanding is not the value-free grasp of the basic facts; instead, it is appreciating *why* an image has the meaning it does. Sometimes an act of understanding situates an image in a causal sequence; sometimes it notices similarities between this image and other images. Truth is liberatory, not because it gives power over, but because it gives peace.

Acknowledgements

This chapter is inspired by Jan Zwicky's "Imagination and the Good Life," *Common Knowledge* 20, no. 1 (Winter 2014): 28–45. In that essay, she offers a list of

---

103 For the normative dimension of imagination, see Iris Murdoch, "Ethics and the Imagination," *Irish Theological Quarterly* 52, no. 1–2 (March 1986): 81–95; Jennifer Church, "Seeing Reasons," *Philosophy and Phenomenological Research* LXXX, no. 3 (May 2010): 638–70; and Zwicky, "Imagination and the Good Life."

104 Descartes, *Meditations*, AT VII.57–58.

105 Cf. the infamous Stoic metaphor of the dog tied to the cart: SVF 2.975 (A.A. Long and D.N. Sedley, *The Hellenistic Philosophers* [Cambridge: Cambridge University Press, 1987], 386).

THE DANCE OF PERCEPTION

"significant philosophical discussions of imagination." Her list includes works by Aristotle, Kant, and Blake, among others. I wish respectfully to submit that Weil's dissertation and early lectures belong on this list. A version of this chapter was presented at the 2017 meeting of the Canadian Philosophical Association in Toronto. Thanks to Kaveh Boveiri, Lorraine Code, Kay Rollans, and Sonia Sedivy for their questions and comments on that version. I would like especially to thank Steven Burns for his generous and insightful editorial advice on several drafts of this chapter, and for his philosophical engagement with Weil's work.

References

Abram, David. *The Spell of the Sensuous*. New York: Vintage Books, 1997.

Aristotle. *De Anima*. Translated by J.A. Smith. In *The Basic Works*, edited by Richard McKeon, 533–603. New York: The Modern Library, 2001.

Aristotle. *Metaphysics*. Translated by W.D. Ross. In *The Basic Works*, edited by Richard McKeon, 681–926. New York: The Modern Library, 2001.

Aristotle. *Nicomachean Ethics*. Translated by David Ross. Oxford: Oxford University Press, 2009.

Bird-David, Nurit. "'Animism' Revisited: Personhood, Environment, and Relational Epistemology." *Current Anthropology* 40, supplement (February 1999): S67–S79.

Church, Jennifer. "Seeing Reasons." *Philosophy and Phenomenological Research* LXXX, no. 3 (May 2010): 638–70.

Code, Lorraine. "Taking Subjectivity into Account." In *Feminist Epistemologies*, edited by Linda Alcoff and Elizabeth Potter, 15–48. New York: Routledge, 1993.

Corbí, Josep. "First Person Authority and Self-Knowledge as an Achievement." *European Journal of Philosophy* 18, no. 3 (2009): 325–62.

Descartes, René. *Meditations on First Philosophy*. 3rd ed., translated by Donald A. Cress. Indianapolis: Hackett Publishing Company, 1993.

Descartes, René. *Philosophical Essays and Correspondence*. Edited by Roger Ariew. Indianapolis: Hackett Publishing Company, 2000.

Descartes, René. *The Philosophical Writings of Descartes*. Volumes 1 and 2, translated by John Cottingham, Robert Stoothoff, and Dugald Murdoch. Cambridge: Cambridge University Press, 1984–1985.

Elisabeth of Bohemia. *The Correspondence between Elisabeth of Bohemia and René Descartes*. Translated by Lisa Shapiro. Chicago: The University of Chicago Press, 2007.

Freud, Sigmund. *The Interpretation of Dreams*. Translated by James Strachey. Harmondsworth: Penguin Books, 1976.

Galison, Peter. "Descartes's Comparisons: From the Invisible to the Visible." *Isis* 75 (1984): 311–26.

Hallowell, A. Irving. "Ojibwa Ontology, Behavior, and World View." In *Culture in History*, edited by Stanley Diamond, 19–52. New York: Columbia University Press, 1960.

Heidegger, Martin. "Wehat Is Metaphysics?" Translated by David Farrell Krell. In *Basic Writings*, edited by David Farrell Krell, 93–110. New York: HarperCollins Publishers, 1993.

Hobbes, Thomas. *Leviathan*. Edited by A.P. Martinich and Brian Battiste. Peterborough: Broadview Press, 2011.

Hume, David. *An Enquiry Concerning Human Understanding*. 2nd ed., edited by Eric Steinberg. Indianapolis: Hackett Publishing Company, 1993.

James, Susan. "Spinoza the Stoic." In *The Rise of Modern Philosophy*, edited by Tom Sorrell, 289–316. Oxford: Oxford University Press, 1993.

James, Susan with Genevieve Lloyd and Moira Gatens. "The Power of Spinoza: Feminist Conjunctions." *Hypatia* 15, no. 2 (Spring 2000): 40–58.

Kant, Immanuel. *Critique of Pure Reason*. Translated by Norman Kemp Smith. New York: Palgrave Macmillan, 2007.

Kearney, Richard. *The Wake of Imagination*. London: Routledge, 2003.

Lichtenberg, Georg Christoph. *The Waste Books*. Translated by R.J. Hollingdale. New York: New York Review of Books, 2000.

Long, A.A. and D.N. Sedley. *The Hellenistic Philosophers*. Volume 1: Translations of the principal sources with philosophical commentary. Cambridge: Cambridge University Press, 1987.

McDowell, John. *Mind and World*. Cambridge: Harvard University Press, 1996.

McFarland, Dorothy Tuck and Wilhelmina Van Ness. "Introduction." In Weil, Simone, *Formative Writings 1929–1941*, edited and translated by McFarland and Van Ness, 23–29. Amherst: The University of Massachusetts Press, 1988.

Murdoch, Iris. "Ethics and the Imagination." *Irish Theological Quarterly* 52, no. 1–2 (March 1986): 81–95.

Pétrement, Simone. *Simone Weil: A Life*. Translated by Raymond Rosenthal. New York: Schocken Books, 1976.

Ross, David. *Aristotle*. 6th ed. London: Routledge, 1995.

Sepper, Dennis L. "Descartes and the Eclipse of the Imagination, 1618–1630." *Journal of the History of Philosophy* 27, no. 3 (July 1989): 379–403.

Spinoza, Benedict de. *Ethics*. Translated by Samuel Shirley. Indianapolis: Hackett Publishing Company, 1992.

Strawson, Peter. "Imagination and Perception." In *Experience & Theory*, edited by Lawrence Foster & J.W. Swanson, 31–54. Amherst: The University of Massachusetts Press, 1970.

Warnock, Mary. *Imagination*. Berkeley: University of California Press, 1976.

THE DANCE OF PERCEPTION 331

Weil, Simone. "Essai sur la notion de lecture." *Les Études philosophiques*, Nouvelle Série, 1ère Année, no. 1 (Janvier/Mars 1946): 13–19.

Weil, Simone. "Essay on the Notion of Reading." Translated by Rebecca Fine Rose and Timothy Tessin. *Philosophical Investigations* 13, no. 4 (October 1990): 297–303.

Weil, Simone. *First and Last Notebooks*. Translated by Richard Rees. London: Oxford University Press, 1970.

Weil, Simone. "Imagination et perception." In *Œuvres complètes*, tome 1, 297–98.

Weil, Simone. "Sur l'imagination." Transcribed by Elisabeth Bigot-Chanel and Yvette Argaud, edited by Gilbert Kahn. *Cahiers Simone Weil* 8 (1985): 121–26.

Weil, Simone. *Intimations of Christianity among the Ancient Greeks*. Translated by Elisabeth Chase Geissbuhler. London: Routledge, 1957.

Weil, Simone. *Intuitions pré-chrétiennes*. La Colombe: Éditions du Vieux Colombier, 1951.

Weil, Simone. *Leçons de philosophie*. Transcribed by Anne Reynaud-Guérithault. Paris: Union Générale d'Éditions, 1959.

Weil, Simone. *Lectures on Philosophy*. Transcribed by Anne Reynaud-Guérithault, translated by Hugh Price. Cambridge: Cambridge University Press, 1978.

Weil, Simone. *Œuvres complètes*. Edited by André A. Devaux and Florence de Lussy. *Tome 1: Premiers écrits philosophiques*. Edited by Gilbert Kahn and Rolf Kühn. Paris: Éditions Gallimard, 1988.

Weil, Simone. "Science and Perception in Descartes." In *Formative Writings 1929–1941*, edited and translated by Dorothy Tuck McFarland and Wilhelmina Van Ness, 31–88. Amherst: The University of Massachusetts Press, 1988.

Weil, Simone. "Science et perception dans Descartes." *Œuvres complètes*, tome 1, 161–221.

Winch, Peter. *Simone Weil: "The Just Balance."* Cambridge: Cambridge University Press, 1989.

Wittgenstein, Ludwig. *On Certainty*. Translated by Denis Paul and G.E.M. Anscombe. Oxford: Basil Blackwell, 1979.

Zwicky, Jan. "Dream Logic and the Politics of Interpretation." In *Thinking and Singing*, edited by Tim Lilburn, 121–51. Toronto: Cormorant Books, 2002.

Zwicky, Jan. *Forge*. Kentville: Gaspereau Press, 2011.

Zwicky, Jan. "Imagination and the Good Life." *Common Knowledge* 20, no. 1 (Winter 2014): 28–45.

Zwicky, Jan. *Lyric Philosophy*. 2nd ed. Kentville: Gaspereau Press, 2011.

Zwicky, Jan. "What Is Ineffable?" *International Studies in the Philosophy of Science* 26, no. 2 (June 2012): 197–217.

Zwicky, Jan. *Wisdom & Metaphor*. 2nd ed. Kentville: Gaspereau Press, 2008.

CHAPTER 14

One Imagination or Many? Or None?

Rob van Gerwen

1 Introduction

The question whether we have one imagination or many, or, rather, none, ridiculous though it may seem, begins to make sense once you delve into the various candidates. In this chapter, I discuss several answers to this question, to show the wealth of the possibilities. For instance, associations often come up without a clear perceptual clue – or with a clue that seems totally unconnected; imagery pops up whilst we read a novel; and while watching a film we process the weird lapses between disparate images pasted together: sometimes we infer what happened between the events shown in the shots, at other times we fill in the emotional aspect of the events because something we expected is not shown to us. Examples such as these abound, considering the ways in which we process the various art forms. And these mental operations seem to have only one thing in common: they are not built from the data we receive directly through our senses, from the things and events that we perceive directly. Does this mean that we have different sorts of imagination defined nominally as "capacities adding to our perceptions?" Or are all these acts just acts of one imagination? But then what is this one mental power: is it a receptive or a spontaneous mode of thinking?

Might not these various operations share some core operation inducing us to refer to them with a single name, imagination? Or should we provide them with new, or old names, such as, respectively, association, reading, reasoning, intimation, and so on, distinguishing species of the genus of imagination defined nominally – much like "furniture" which denotes no particular objects – by understanding "imagination" as a genus-term that has no extension. Yet it is not as though these capacities are totally unconnected to a particular type of mental operation, but neither do they all differ from perception in one single way. I am assuming, for now, that our view of perception is clear and evident, but shall return to this assumption shortly. These questions cannot be solved through empirical scientific research – they are philosophical questions about how best to talk about imagination, and about perception.

© KONINKLIJKE BRILL NV, LEIDEN, 2020 | DOI:10.1163/9789004436350_016

2 Perception

Immanuel Kant distinguished imagination from fantasy, treating the former as a function of the senses, though critically distinct from their input. If we could take, for argument's sake, perception to consist in an assembly of data from vision, touch, hearing, smell and taste into a comprehensive bodily experience of the world surrounding us, then, assumably, perception would consist only of stuff that reaches the senses. There is, indeed, a causal chain from the things and events we are present to, to our perception. With acts of imagining that chain is intentional – or there is none, as with fantasy.

Perception is, indeed, viewed as somehow a causal process. Treating imagination against the background of this view as an *addendum* to perception is, however, I think, a figment of philosophers' tendency to divide perception in distinct sensory streams, as in John Locke's distinction between primary and secondary qualities, which are all so-defined, as sensuous impressions. One might wonder how such incommensurable streams of data – views, sounds, tastes, smells, tactile properties – can ever combine into a coherent perception of the world for us to move in.

Viewing perception as a causal process would seem to deprive us of the capacity to make sense of someone's claim to seeing that the closed door, that one is clearly seeing and feeling before one, also hides a corridor, several other rooms and a coffee vending machine – because these things one does not see or feel with one's senses nor do they cause any such sensations. We then say: "You can only imagine them, and as such they are not truth-valuational." Kant distinguishes this – what he calls: – reproductive imagination from fantasy, productive imagination. Imagination, so conceived, that is, not as fantasy, would be best characterised as putting something (a perception_t) before the mind that does not present itself to the senses. Reproductive imagination introduces elements in perception that could be or may have been perceived: perceptions temporally qualified, so to speak.[1]

There is however, an internal coherence amongst these data streams that copies the way the world is. The sounds and vistas and tactile and olfactory properties of things and events are connected with these things in just the way we perceive them to be connected. This match allows us to move and act in the world. The more varied the sensuous information is that we receive about a

---

[1] Phenomenologists have argued extensively that this is a flawed presentation of perception: we do perceive that the door has a backside, even though we do not actually (?) see it.

situation, the better we are equipped to foresee its affordances.[2] If we hear the loud noise of some event, we instantaneously fill in the lacunas left for the other senses, visualising the event, and, for instance, if it is an explosion, the smell of the dust and smoke – and we may duck according to the events' nearness. One might think that all of this is the spontaneous contribution of imagination, since we only actually hear the blast, but then one must explain this specific role in perception of this mental supplement – which lacks a physical counterpart like the eyes are for vision.[3]

Why would this strange faculty add such imaginary views, sounds and smells? It would definitely be more parsimonious if we would treat these supplements as integral to perception. They are at work in every single perception, because perception is time-based – as it is polymodal, involving all sense modalities synchronously – it is not just the sum total of the data of the various senses, nor is it merely in the now. Rather, perception retains what preceded it and envisions what is anticipated in the world as much as in our mind. These imaginary sensuous data are normally obliterated instantly once they are verified by present data from the senses. You no longer need to envision the view of the explosion, its dust, and the smell of all that once you have turned the corner and see what happened before you. That does not mean that the acts of imagination did not occur – they did, and because of them we are not surprised when, indeed we round the corner.

This is the process that turns our perceptions into meaningful wholes, in the background.[4] We don't take our clues one at a time, nor are we anxious multiple times in the process.

I have come to think, then, that perception presents a lot more to our mind than what meets the senses. When we hear a car nearing us, we are immediately ready to see the direction it is driving in, the distance it still has to cover and the speed with which it will do this, as well as its approximate form – before actually seeing the car. Turning our head to see the car only serves as a verification of what perception has already been telling us. Perception consists in this intermodal exchange between the sense modalities. And so imagination

---

2 For this term, see Gibson, J.J., *The Ecological Approach to Visual Perception* (London, Hillsdale, NJ: Lawrence Erlbaum Associates, 1986).

3 See the section on Schematism in Immanuel Kant, *Critique of Pure Reason*, eds. W.S. Pluhar and P. Kitcher (Indianapolis: Hackett Publishing Co. 1996, orig. 1787), B209–B219.

4 Possibly, this type of synthesising is what people suffering from failings in the autistic spectrum are missing. The term "synthesising" is misleading, though, as it suggests an activity, but filling out the holes in unimodal or secondary qualities, is not something perceivers do actively. Such failure of imagining is, I think, what Wittgenstein calls aspect blindness, or meaning blindness. For lack of this capacity, autistic persons often reason from details to wholes.

ONE IMAGINATION OR MANY? OR NONE?

would seem out of a job.[5] Thence, only one type of imagination would remain: fantasy. And this we may indeed define as a spontaneous mental power that makes us think and feel about things that do not present themselves to perception, where perception is characterised broadly, as the whole input of our perceptive apparatus – including sensuous data, obviously, but also meanings, and pasts and futures of what meets each of our senses.[6] And the output of a fantasy may have nothing to do with our perception at all.

Yet it may make sense to distinguish what literally – causally – presents itself to our senses and what is added to this by sheer anticipation and memory by imagination. As said above, it makes sense to think of perception as in a way caused by types of property, but this alone cannot possibly provide a view of what perception is. The person perceives and since persons live a life with a past and a future, imagination (perception_t) is integral to their perceptions.

Some elements in our experiences one might attribute to perception, others to imagination – but the distinction is artificial, much like the distinction between primary and secondary qualities. I am unsure about the spontaneous aspect of our imaginings, because they answer to some temporal processing. The mark distinguishing a perception from an imagination is, rather, verifiability. I can be said to perceive the other side of the door while it is still closed, because of a multitude of clues predicting that when I open it, that backside will show itself to my perception. This verifiability is available to current perception, even though it is an element in its near future, or from its near past. Such is the nature of the affordances we perceive in the things, persons and events present to us.

However, when I think that a character in a film has made a trip by airplane – because I saw her pack her bags, and now I see her waiving for a cab in what is clearly a different city – I should attribute that insight to imagination, in its more spontaneous aspect, because there is no way for my perception to verify her trip by watching the movie.

I am not saying there is anything in films that we can verify in real perception; what is perceived in films is mediated by the screen. But the flight I cannot possibly verify by perceiving images on the screen, exactly because these images are left out. The truth-in-the-film, as Walton calls it, is in part a product

---

5 Cf. Derek Matravers, "Why We Should Give Up on the Imagination," *Midwest Studies in Philosophy* 34 (2010), 190–99.

6 In this, I follow Richard Wollheim, "A Reply to the Contributors," in *Richard Wollheim on the Art of Painting. Art as Representation and Expression*, ed. Rob van Gerwen (Cambridge, New York: Cambridge University Press, 2001); James Gibson, *The Ecological Approach to Visual Perception* (New York: Houghton Mifflin, 1979); and Derek Matravers, *Fiction and Narrative* (Oxford: Oxford University Press, 2014).

of my imagination, and therefore, remains merely plausible. It is a truth in the fiction – that part I am not debating – but not one that we gather through perceiving the scenes on the screen.

Associations are memories of past affordances, and something similar holds for our introjected figures – the model our parents form, since earliest youth, for our engagements with people in later situations – and emotional dispositions.[7] These latter types of products of the imagination are based in part on receptivity and possible verification even though these possibilities where in the past and may or may not have been verified even then.[8] One problem with our memories is that they concern affordances which may not have been realised at the time, and which therefore, in retrospect, produce a measure of uncertainty and melancholy.

3 Art Forms' Phenomenologies

Alternatively, we might feel inclined to think along a different line about imagination, linking its various forms to examples taken from the arts. Reading a novel, our imagination processes the meanings of words and sentences by turning them into sights and sounds in our mind. Listening to a piece of music, we imagine hearing what the musician is doing with their instrument, but we, also, imagine that the sounds of the music are somehow in a space of its own – Roger Scruton refers to the acousmatic space of music, to distinguish it from the acoustics where sounds tell us about the events that cause them.[9] Jerrold Levinson thinks that listening to music we hear its expression as that of an intra-musical persona.[10] All these are distinct acts of imagination – compared with the roles imagination plays in our everyday perception of the world. When we watch a figurative painting, we may imagine the life that went on

---

7 See Richard Wollheim, *The Thread of Life* (Cambridge, New York: Cambridge University Press, 1984), and *On the Emotions* (New Haven and London: Yale University Press, 1999).

8 Although, of course, there is a clear connection with the requirement of verification of the positivist's, I am not using verification as a demarcation criterion for something to count as knowledge, but as a criterion to establish what counts as receptivity, and what as spontaneity in the area of perception. From the point of view of the philosophy of science I am a falsificationist coherentist – but not so in the area of perception. Nor do I think that something is perceived only when it is verified. But neither do I think that in everyday life people are in the business of setting up hypotheses about reality. We perceive objects, persons and situations as affording certain actions.

9 Roger Scruton, *The Aesthetics of Music* (Oxford: Clarendon Press, 1997).

10 Jerrold Levinson, "Musical Expressiveness," in *The Pleasures of Aesthetics*, ed. Jerrold Levinson (Ithaca: Cornell University Press, 1996), 90–128.

ONE IMAGINATION OR MANY? OR NONE?

before or after the depicted scene occurred – think of Gotthold Lessing's argument in *Laocoon* that pictures should present a pregnant moment in the process, not the climax of a scene, and that in doing this the spectator's imagination is mobilised into making up the temporal aspects of the situation.[11] When we watch a movie we may be said to make use of several varieties of the imagination to turn the movie into one coherent whole: we listen to the texts read out or spoken like we read a novel, allowing them to mobilise our imagination into supplying extra imagery, we interpret the music that we hear – though none of the characters in the film is aware – as prompting that the situation has a certain significance – deadly, romantic, horrifying, what have you – and we fill in details that are not shown and are intentionally left out in editing, or that the editing induces us to fill in, and so on.

We could also start from the phenomenological specifications of the various art forms. A painting somehow requires us to take in what is on the canvas in a twofold manner: by watching the configuration of the painted daubs and by seeing something in them.[12] Cinema requires that we accept sitting in the dark where only the visual as it is presented on the screen before us and the sounds that are somehow connected with that should be taken in. But a film is not a stable whole like a painting is; it is made up of shots pasted together to form scenes, and scenes pasted together to tell a story. Oftentimes the shots that together form one scene represent different view points of a single situation and we are required to view them as belonging to the visual experiences of one of the characters. The shots connecting two different scenes always involve a lapse either in time or in space, or in both, an ellipsis that needs to be filled up if the story is to develop. Some of these ellipses are filled through reasoning. Alternatively, the ellipsis may occur within a single scene, and be of a different nature from the temporal ellipsis that invites our reasoning. What gets left out is not a slice of time, but a certain perceptual input that we would normally expect to be presented to us. I am thinking of the famous shower scene in Alfred Hitchcock's *Psycho*, but also, more clearly though less known, of scenes in Robert Bresson's *L'Argent*. We perceive the scene all right, but because certain vital perceptual aspects are kept under wraps, we fill that in by imagining the event. I call this mechanism – or deviant choice of presenting sensuous

---

11   Gotthold Ephraim Lessing, *Laokoon oder die Grenzen der Malerei und Poesie* (Stuttgart: Philipp Reclam Jun., 1964, orig. 1766).

12   See Richard Wollheim, "Seeing-As, Seeing-In, and Pictorial Representation," in *Art and its Objects*, 2nd ed. (Cambridge: Cambridge University Press, 1980), 205–26, and "On Pictorial Representation," in *Richard Wollheim on the Art of Painting. Art as Representation and Expression*, ed. Rob van Gerwen (Cambridge, New York: Cambridge University Press, 2001), 13–27.

information – intimation, for suggesting things it does not show and thereby making the situation more intimate than it would have been had we seen or heard all the details of the event.

My last example is of reading a book. Lessing argued that literature is well-suited to convey processes in a situation, such as the way characters feel about things, or the development of their psychologies, but less for conveying just how things or characters look. It would be boring to read lengthy descriptions of people's outward appearances – it would take many pages – and the reading of such descriptions would seriously hinder the story's flow. But, more importantly, providing such elaborate descriptions would not be necessary at all, as we are already turning the words into images ourselves, which makes reading a novel a personal, and, again, intimate experience.[13]

4   An Ontological Fallacy

Contrary to a certain view, I do not think that imagination in the cinema theater functions as a fantastic transmogrifier of veridical perceptions of real actors in a studio into fictional characters in a non-existent fictional world. According to Greg Currie, "A fiction does not have the kinds of properties–shape, size, colour – that could be represented pictorially."[14] Consequently, he argues, we cannot possibly see fictional characters, but must, instead, be seeing actors in the studio, as these do have said properties. Therefore, according to Currie, what we think we are seeing on the screen must be due to imagination transforming actors into characters, and so on. This seems like such a truism that it should be futile to try to dismantle it. Yet, I think that the argument involves an ontological fallacy and, as a consequence, fails to describe the experience of movie spectators.

The argument is a fallacy because it starts from an assessment of the real existence of the represented to decide what it is that we see in the representation: if the things and events are real, then we are allowed to claim to be seeing them in the film; if, however, they prove to be fictional, then we must decide that we are using our imagination to act as though these fictional events really occur; "the same sort of imagining I engage in when I read a novel," Currie

---

13   Perhaps, cinematographic intimation is a literary device applied to film? (What does this claim amount to? Why should I make it?).

14   Gregory Currie, *Image and Mind* (Cambridge, New York: Cambridge University Press, 1998), 12.

ONE IMAGINATION OR MANY? OR NONE?

thinks.[15] But, we have already seen above that the acts of the imagination typical of reading are different from the imaginings that sometimes occur while watching a film. While reading, sensation has little other to do than discern the words on the page, after which imagination kicks in to built said mental visualisations. Really, what the movie spectator perceives in the cinema theater is mostly visual, and it is what the films present them with. In fact, it is much harder, when not impossible, to see what is on the screen as something happening in studios of which few, if any, details are shown to us.

It makes good sense, though, to argue as Currie does in regard to the acting in stage theatre. Here, the actors are present to the audience as the real persons that they are, inviting the audience to transform their playing into the actions of their characters. Actors and spectators are involved in a transfiguring co-operative behaviour. If spectators do not play along, the fiction will all but disappear – similar to what happens if the actors perform badly. The real situation is available both to the actors and the spectators, and they need some act of imagination to abstract from that reality and to imagine seeing fictional events.[16] It should be evident that actors and spectators co-operate in this process: spectators remain as silent as possible to not disturb this intimate interaction between all real persons present. An instructive instance of this intimacy could be an actor stepping out of his playing to address the audience when he thinks they are too noisy – to then step back in, hoping this did not destroy the delicate pact between actors and spectators.[17] There is some sort of pact, too, between a film and its spectators, but it is not a pact with the real actors, or amongst real people as in the stage theatre, but with the projection on the screen: spectators act as though what they are watching is a report of real events.[18] That is how spectators in the cinema theater co-operate in answer to film's phenomenological specifications. Other than that, the spectator is not in the business of transforming, in their imagination, everything they know is really happening – such as actors playing a scene for the umpteenth time in a

---

15   Currie, *Image and Mind*, 179.

16   See Kendall L. Walton, *Mimesis as Make-Believe. On the Foundations of the Representational Arts* (Cambridge, Massachussetts: Harvard University Press, 1990).

17   It is fruitful to look at the possible varieties of what Bertolt Brecht baptised alienation, which takes different forms on stage (Brecht), in film (Godard) or literature (Burroughs). Alienating devices disrupt the delicate co-operation between the work and the appreciation, between perception and imagination in its various forms.

18   I am thinking of the argument in Derek Matravers, "The paradox of Fiction: The Report versus the Perceptual Model," in *Emotion and the Arts*, eds. Mette Hjort and Sue Laver (Oxford: Oxford University Press, 1997), 78–94.

studio – into something happening in the world of the film, whether it is fictional or not.

Unlike the experience of reading a novel, our experience of films is primarily perceptual, and imagination only plays a role in our comprehension of the narrative, and the emotional appeal of particular scenes, and ellipses caused by editorial cuts between shots. The experience of film is not mere perception of real events that are globally transfigured by imagination: Currie, by starting from the ontology of the represented, confuses film with stage theatre and reading.

5   Imaginings Are Ours, and Come in Kinds

Perhaps, we should distinguish acts of imaging as they are ruled by the data received – such as the acts just mentioned with which we respond to the phenomenological characteristics of the various art forms – from acts of imagining that are autonomous, spontaneous, like when we fantasise that sixteen yellow elephants are flying through the air, singing an age-old anthem. We do not require our fantasy in order to appreciate a work of art, because the artist's material manipulations guide our thoughts and feelings. But one might insist that it requires imagining to see a farm in (really existing) combinations of coloured paint on a canvas. I think, however, with Richard Wollheim, that this would assume a flawed view or representational seeing, which is twofolded.[19] Appreciating a work of art is a function of perceiving it, and this would seem to include all the extra activity just mentioned. In the measure in which we would require our fantasy while appreciating works, we risk losing the connection with the work – and failing the relevant norms of correctness.[20]

Different types of imaginative aspects of perception may be due to the different phenomenologies of the art forms, but they are not just what these phenomenologies amount to, or are they? They are guided by the perception of the work.[21] While works of art are out there, imaginations are ours. Imagination makes the perceived personal, or, if you will, turns it into a subjective experience. We saw this effect clearly in intimation. Yet, the subjectivity is not exclusionary. I defend a subjective realism: we see subjective properties or values in

---

19   Richard Wollheim, "On Pictorial Representation," 13–27.

20   These norms of correctness are met in the presence of the work, by shared viewing and suitable prompting. See Richard Wollheim, "Criticism as Retrieval," in *Art and its Objects*, 2nd ed. (Cambridge, New York: Cambridge University Press, 1980), 185–204., and "On Pictorial Representation."

21   Both seeing-as and seeing-in are permeable to thought, whilst remaining types of seeing.

ONE IMAGINATION OR MANY? OR NONE? 341

the object, and these include aesthetic ones – they are not idiosyncratic and private, but are of a shareable kind – hence the possibility of suitable prompting.[22] We do not reach consent when, after a certain stretch of intelligent pointing out, one of us withdraws for simply being impatient. Agreed, impatience, and mere preferences are human-all-too-human, but that does nothing to remove conceptually the claims of aesthetic normativity, or the prospects of aesthetic consensus.[23] Subjectivism is not a relativism, it is a realism.[24]

Perhaps I should conclude by stipulating kinds of imagining, as though imaginations – plural – are distinct organs, or faculties of the mind. Thus, say, iconic imagining takes place when we read a novel and build a view in our minds of situations described, adding, also, visual details to our own liking so as to fill in any holes in the description. Secondly, rational imagining is what we do with temporal ellipses in cinema. Thirdly, emotional imagining, as with intimation:

> whereas perception suffices as a means of empathetic recognition with experiential aspects of real-life embodied events [person-to-person encounters], for the empathetic recognition of represented events an additional act of imagination is needed.[25]

In all, imagining turns some event into something personal and subjective.

6 Conclusion

In conclusion, there may be two varieties of the mental activity of putting something before the mind that is not present to the senses, to be distinguished

---

22 The thought that aesthetic experiences concern reflections that we can share amongst each other is elaborated in Immanuel Kant, *Critique of Judgment* (Indianapolis: Hackett, 1987, orig: Berlin und Libau: Lagarde und Friederich, 1790), in his notion of "the communicability of feeling." It is sported again in the notion of "suitable prompting" developed in "On Pictorial Representation" (Wollheim).

23 As Kant saw rightly. Aesthetic normativity is grounded transcendentally in the assumption of a common sense – a sensus communis – but in empirical practice all spectators will be hesitant about how they judged something aesthetically. Hence, in his terms, the judgement of taste is conditionally universally necessary. See Kant, *Critique of Judgment,* The fourth moment, Necessity.

24 See Rob van Gerwen, *Zullen we contact houden. Hoe we de geest uit ons wereldbeeld verwijderen* (Utrecht: Klement, 2018) (in Dutch; *Shall We Stay in Touch. How We Remove the Mind from Our Worldview*).

25 Rob van Gerwen, *Art and Experience.* Volume XIV of *Quaestiones Infinitae* (Utrecht: Universiteit Utrecht, 1996), 177.

on the basis of what induces them. Some of these activities are induced by meanings inhering the perceived, I call this imagination, briefly (1). The other activities are merely caused, and the nature of the causal chain need not be clear to the subject (2). This distinction is important because whereas the former allows conversation about the appropriateness of an imagination, the latter does not. Examples of the former are reading – iconic imagination – the processing of temporal or modal ellipses – a certain type of filling in events through reasoning, and, respectively, a type of supplementing feelings through an enlivened empathy – intimation. Examples of the latter are associations, dreaming, fantasy: it is not clear immediately, if ever, where the imagery comes from, but it is there and has no relation with the perceived that one knows of.

Caused imaginings are idiosyncratic. It makes no sense to ask others to share them. Others may wonder, admire, or be sceptical about them, but there are no norms of correctness, no suitable prompting to the nature of the things that caused them, no conversation, really. Psychologists, such as Freud, argue that the cause must somehow have something to do with the subject's history of experiences, so it may benefit them to try and find out as much as possible about the nature of the causes, but beyond that there is no general semantic interest in them as might be relevant to others. They are merely relevant for empirical psychology, as Kant said.

The philosophically interesting type of imaginings – short: imagination – are related to what is there to be perceived by everyone. Hence, here, there is room for conversation about their appropriateness. They form part and parcel of critical aesthetic discussions.

It seems that the only imagination that is clearly distinct from perception is fantasy.

The acts of imagination that are discussed in this chapter are called imagination because they cannot be reduced to perception *per se*. But that distinction presupposes that perception is conceived of as the processing of the causes of sensations, the primary and secondary qualities, whereas in contrast, these acts are integral to perception. It is the causal atomism of thinkers, such as the empiricists that makes us think so hard about imagination. Once we realise that perception is more than taking in primary and secondary qualities, but is the capacity that allows us to move about in the world, we can start to understand perception's richness.

Representations assume such complicated acts of perception, and the arts can be said to play with these, which in a sense adds to our thinking of them as separate acts of imagination. It is clear, for instance, that you cannot perceive what is left out from a scene. In real-life, however, these things are never "left

ONE IMAGINATION OR MANY? OR NONE?

out" – people make the whole trip in an aeroplane, and they see all the relevant aspects of a slap in the face of someone. No ellipses and intimation in real-life. In this sense, art seems to be an accessory to philosophers' attempts to analyse away into separate details what is better left whole.[26] As a consequence, the isolation of these aspects of perception into separate doings makes us think of them as processes distinct from perception, even though they are integral to how we view – as in: veridically receive – the nature and meaning of our surroundings. This segmentation inhibits our understanding of perception.

Rather than saying that first there is the input of the five senses and then some add-on operation – to be called the imagination – and having to explain what this supplemental cognitive power is assumed to be, and to be doing, I suggest that we switch to a more holistic view of perception. The senses do not perceive – nor does our brain, for that matter – the person does. Perceiving is picking up impossibilities and possibilities for actions, affordances. Picking up primary or secondary qualities does not add up to finding your way in reality. We do need these qualities, they are necessary – as is our brain and its complicated processes. But they are not sufficient. Perception is not caused – by these qualities or processes or otherwise. Perception is something we do. And our whole psychology is at stake in it, including our memories, our interests, our plans for the future. In fact, so I argued, such assumably extra-perceptual acts of imagination are integral to perception.

Through our imagination's acts we make the world a place for us to live in. Imagination forms the thread of our life, it is the core of our subjectivity. But it is merely the sticky bit of our perceptions.

It makes perfect sense to think in isolated manner about the different aspects of perception that are discussed in this chapter, but not, it seems to me, to treat hem as acts of a substantive power of imagination. "Imagination" may be just a term to refer to these operations or aspects of perception, but nothing substantial may be denoted by it. This is not true of the term "perception." It is real activity that the term refers to: the way we get to know the nature and affordances of the world out there. And we get to know these through the operations of our senses combined with the acts delineated above. But talking about a power of imagination or about distinct acts of imagination does not really help us to understand the richness with which we perceive things, meanings and events.

---

26   Which attempt resulted in said distinction between primary and secondary qualities. But the fact that we can say separate things about things or processes does not mean that these processes are just these parts that we should so identify.

References

Currie, Gregory. *Image and Mind*. Cambridge, New York: Cambridge University Press. 1998.

Gerwen, Rob van. *Art and Experience*. Volume XIV of *Quaestiones Infinitae*. Utrecht: Universiteit Utrecht. 1996.

Gerwen, Rob van. *Zullen we contact houden. Hoe we de geest uit ons wereldbeeld verwijderen*. Utrecht: Klement. 2018.

Gibson, J.J. *The Ecological Approach to Visual Perception*. London, Hillsdale, NJ: Lawrence Erlbaum Associates. 1986.

Kant, Immanuel. *Critique of Judgment*. trans. Werner S. Pluhar. Indianapolis: Hackett. 1987.

Kant, Immanuel. *Critique of Pure Reason*. eds. W.S. Pluhar and P. Kitcher. Indianapolis: Hackett Publishing Co. 1996.

Lessing, Gotthold Ephraim. *Laokoon oder die Grenzen der Malerei und Poesie*. Stuttgart: Philipp Reclam Jun., 1964.

Levinson, Jerrold. "Musical Expressiveness." In *The Pleasures of Aesthetics*, edited by Jerrold Levinson, 90–128. Ithaca: Cornell University Press, 1996.

Matravers, Derek. *Fiction and Narrative*. Oxford: Oxford University Press. 2014.

Matravers, Derek. "The paradox of Fiction: The Report versus the Perceptual Model." In *Emotion and the Arts*, edited by Mette Hjort and Sue Laver, 78–94. Oxford: Oxford University Press, 1997.

Matravers, Derek. "Why We Should Give Up on the Imagination." *Midwest Studies in Philosophy* 34 (2010): 190–99.

Scruton, Roger. *The Aesthetics of Music*. Oxford: Clarendon Press. 1997.

Walton, Kendall L. *Mimesis as Make-Believe. On the Foundations of the Representational Arts*. Cambridge, Massachusetts: Harvard University Press, 1990.

Wollheim, Richard, "A Reply to the Contributors." In *Richard Wollheim on the Art of Painting. Art as Representation and Expression*, edited by Rob van Gerwen, 241–63. Cambridge, New York: Cambridge University Press. 2001.

Wollheim, Richard. "Criticism as Retrieval." In *Art and its Objects*. 2nd ed., edited by Richard Wollheim, 185–204. Cambridge, New York: Cambridge University Press. 1980.

Wollheim, Richard. "On Pictorial Representation." In *Richard Wollheim on the Art of Painting. Art as Representation and Expression*, edited by Rob van Gerwen, 13–27. Cambridge, New York: Cambridge University Press. 2001.

Wollheim, Richard. *On the Emotions*. New Haven and London: Yale University Press. 1999.

Wollheim, Richard. "Seeing-As, Seeing-In, and Pictorial Representation." In *Art and its Objects.* 2nd ed., edited by Richard Wollheim, 205–26. Cambridge, New York: Cambridge University Press. 1980.

Wollheim, Richard. *The Thread of Life.* Cambridge, New York: Cambridge University Press. 1984.

CHAPTER 15

Nietzsche on Theatricality and Imagination

Roderick Nicholls

Dionysos, the true hero of the stage ... is not truly present but imagined as being present. The spectator, in a state of Dionysiac excitement, transferred on to a masked figure the whole image of the god and dissolved, so to speak, the reality of the figure into a ghostly unreality.[1]

This chapter explores imagination from a pragmatic perspective but its central argument regarding imagination and theatricality concentrates on Friedrich Nietzsche's distinctively aesthetic version of pragmatism.[2] I begin by clarifying the latter in historical context through a contrast with the role assigned to the imagination in Kant's epistemology and in the light of subsequent Romantic efforts to expand the scope of imaginative experience. I then highlight a critical, often overlooked linguistic dimension to Nietzsche's pragmatism which sets up the chapter's first conclusion: all conscious experience possesses an imaginative quality explicable in terms of a theatrical structure (as I will refer to it) and clearly illuminated in Nietzsche's analysis of dream construction. A second, closely related conclusion is drawn from his analysis of the deliberately designed performances of ancient Greek tragedies: the role of spectator within those overtly theatrical performances offers a fascinating and corroborating aesthetic parallel to what happens when dream consciousness heightens and intensifies the theatricality of normal waking consciousness. In sum, this chapter suggests how the unique complexity of theater aesthetics might be productively accommodated within a pragmatic account of imagination.

---

1 Friedrich Nietzsche, *The Birth of Tragedy* in *The Birth of Tragedy and Other Writings*, eds. Raymond Geuss and Ronald Speirs (Cambridge: Cambridge University Press, 1999), 45.
2 The meaning of this term is, of course, highly contested. So one job of my overall argument is to fill out the sense in which Nietzsche is a pragmatist. At the outset, however, suffice it to say that the description emerging from this chapter is rooted in John Dewey and William James (not Charles Peirce) and aligned with neo-pragmatic views now associated with Richard Rorty. I am indebted to Andrew Reynolds who encouraged me to distinguish pragmatism with generic naturalism.

© KONINKLIJKE BRILL NV, LEIDEN, 2020 | DOI:10.1163/9789004436350_017

1   Kant's Transformation of the Imagination

In his magisterial account of the emergence of the creative imagination as a concept central to European philosophy during the 150 years culminating in early 19th century Romanticism, James Engell locates "the great metamorphosis" in Kant's critical works: they "form an isthmus across which ideas passed and were transformed," says Engell, "as they migrated from the Enlightenment to Romanticism."[3] Yet this section will indicate how that the metamorphosis was shaped by a Cartesian argument which led Kant toward a philosophical dead-end. As Nietzsche puts it, Descartes' project of re-conceiving the natural world in a radically non-Aristotelian way demonstrated "a boldness worthy of reverence" but his belief that a non-material mind is the differentiating feature of human beings, prevented him from placing "our species back among the animals."[4] By contrast, Nietzsche conceived himself at the beginning of a divergent, post-Darwinian philosophical lineage that rejects Cartesian dualism and takes what is of value in the Kantian metamorphosis in a different, intriguingly positive direction.

Consider Nietzsche's root counter-assumption expressed by someone who frequently and explicitly associated himself with Nietzsche on this issue: "like all other animals" we are "causal products of natural forces";[5] and if we are "linked in a single web of causal relations to all other occupants of space time," the logical consequence is "seeing the mind too as just one more slice of a vast web of relationships."[6] If mental phenomena do not possess some intrinsic, metaphysically distinct first-person quality then, as Richard Rorty says, a familiar metaphor is highly misleading: the contents of individual minds are displayed on "the screen of our private Cartesian theatre even before we learn to talk."[7] And how, then, should we treat the epistemological problem embedded in that metaphor, namely, the problem of reconciling the subjectivity of mental life with the objectivity required for knowledge of a material world? From

---

3   James Engell, *The Creative Imagination: Enlightenment to Romanticism* (Cambridge, MA: Harvard University Press, 1981), 118.

4   Friedrich Nietzsche, *Twilight of Idols and Anti-Christ*, ed. Michael Tanner, trans. R.J. Hollingdale (Penguin, 1990), *Anti-Christ* 14. All references to Nietzsche's works will be to standardized section numbers.

5   Richard Rorty, *Contingency, Irony, and Solidarity* (New York: Cambridge University Press, 1989), 28.

6   Richard Rorty, *Truth and Progress: Philosophical Papers* (Cambridge: Cambridge University Press, 1998), 94 and 113.

7   Rorty, *Truth and Progress*, 100.

the perspective of Nietzsche's lineage, the central part of Kant's first *Critique*, the "Transcendental Analytic," is dedicated to solving a pseudo-problem and regarding the main point of this chapter, moreover, Kant claims to succeed by attributing immense power to the imagination (conceived as a faculty of a metaphysically distinct mind).

That said, Nietzsche did enthusiastically embrace two "valuable sides" of Kant's critical philosophy.[8] First, there is "the healthy bit of sensualism (*Sensualismus*) that Kant took into his theory of knowledge"[9] and articulated in famous pronouncements, for example: "our nature is so constituted that our *intuition* can never be other than sensible"; "without sensibility no object would be given to us" and "thoughts without content are empty."[10] Second, while Kant accepted the "overwhelming sensualism (*Sensualismus*) which had overflowed out of the previous century,"[11] he also addressed a major weakness in the Locke to Hartley empiricist tradition by insisting that human cognition involves an intensely constructive activity: "the senses can think nothing" and without being conceptually constructed by the understanding, our intuitions "are blind."[12]

Their combined impact, however, is undercut by Kant's unquestioned dualism. Despite his "healthy sensualism," says Nietzsche, Kant certainly does not do what is "essential: to start from the *body* and employ it as a guide."[13] Indeed, he seriously "miscalculates" by treating the "central nervous system and the senses, the 'mortal frame,'"[14] as a passive medium through which physiological sensations are somehow given to an active mind. Then the body simply disappears. Indeed, the most basic act of accepting material from bodily organs requires the postulation of a special mental faculty (the mind's "receptivity for sensory impression"). Contrary to a Lockean version of Quine's second dogma of empiricism, in other words, Kant rightly argues that sense-perception depends upon a constructive interpretation of sensory stimuli. But he immediately goes wrong by treating the activity by which "anything is possible as an

---

8   Friedrich Nietzsche, *Dawn: Thoughts on the Presumptions of Morality,* trans. Brittain Smith (Stanford: Stanford University Press, 2011), preface 3.

9   Nietzsche, *Dawn*, preface 3.

10   Immanuel Kant, *Critique of Pure Reason*, trans. N.K. Smith, 2nd ed. (Houndmills: Palgrave Macmillan, 1991), B 75.

11   Friedrich Nietzsche, *Beyond Good and Evil*, ed. Michael Tanner, trans. R.J. Hollingdale, rev. ed. (London: Penguin, 2003), 11.

12   Kant, *Critique of Pure Reason*, B 75.

13   Friedrich Nietzsche, *The Will to Power*, ed. Walter Kaufmann, trans. Walter Kaufmann and R.J. Hollingdale (New York: Vintage Books, 1968), 532.

14   Nietzsche, *Anti-Christ*, 14.

object of experience,"[15] as a purely mental process. Beyond the initial *a priori* "framing"[16] of sensible intuitions by space and time (described in the "Transcendental Aesthetic"), Kant emphasizes that if we are to become conscious of anything then "the spontaneity of our thought requires that it [a sensible manifold] be gone through ... taken up and connected" at a higher level by an act "I name *synthesis.*"[17]

There are two essential components of the requisite transcendental synthesis. One is a table of categories. Yet Nietzsche argues that Kant's "proudest discovery" forms part of an elaborate begging of the question: he "asked himself, how are synthetic judgments *a priori* possible? – And what, really, did he answer? *By means of a faculty.*"[18] Comparing Kant to the doctor in Molière's *The Imaginary Invalid*, Nietzsche is incredulous: "is that an answer? An explanation? Or is it not rather merely a repetition of the question? How does opium induce sleep? 'By means of a faculty,' namely the *virtus dormitive.*"[19] Nietzsche does not pursue the way imagination is implicated in this fallacy. Transcendental synthesis, however, is a ceaseless activity. So a second – a performative – faculty is needed to apply the categorial forms which make synthetic judgment possible: "the power of imagination, a blind but indispensable function of the soul, without which we should have no knowledge whatsoever, but of which we are scarcely ever conscious."[20] With this assignation, Kant is effectively claiming to discover extraordinary new powers possessed by a traditionally recognized faculty.

Yet how persuasive is his view of the imagination as a mysterious shape-shifting faculty to which he repeatedly turns when facing complications in solving his inherited epistemological problem? Consider, for instance, that since all intuition is sensible, Kant argues that imagination "belongs to *sensibility*"; on the other hand, however, since the spontaneous "synthesis of intuitions" conforms to the *a priori* categories, he conceives the imagination as "an action of the *understanding* on the sensibility." Explanation, therefore, amounts to simply naming imagination as the "third thing"[21] needed to relate or mediate between sensibility and the understanding. Mediating, moreover, requires "schemata" but

---

15   Immanuel Kant, *Critique of Pure Reason*, trans. N.K. Smith, 2nd ed. (Houndmills: Palgrave Macmillan, 1991), B103. Throughout this chapter, all emphases in any cited passage by any author, is in the original sources. No emphasis is ever added.
16   Kant, *Critique of Pure Reason*, B 11.
17   Kant, *Critique of Pure Reason*, B 102.
18   Nietzsche, *Beyond Good and Evil*, 11.
19   Nietzsche, *Beyond Good and Evil*, 11.
20   Kant, *Critique of Pure Reason*, B 126.
21   Kant, *Critique of Pure Reason*, B 126.

while a schema provides "a rule of synthesis of the imagination ... the schema is in itself always a product of imagination."[22] One of the imagination's powers, therefore, is the ability to relate two incommensurable things by the *sui generis* production of schematic rules governing its own activity. Nietzsche's Molière-like ridicule, then, aptly captures the fact that Kant's claims to apodictic certainty rest on circular reasoning buoyed by lofty rhetoric describing imagination as "an art concealed in the depths of the human soul, whose real modes of activity nature is hardly ever to allow us to discover, and to have open to our gaze."[23]

The range of Kantian imagination is also noteworthy. John Dewey, for example, is skeptically dismissive of the "mysterious potencies" allegedly possessed by this "special faculty" but in referring to it as single and "self-contained" Dewey underestimates the faculty's striking range.[24] Consider that it has, so to speak, two separable sub-departments: the "productive" imagination performing transcendental synthesis; and the "reproductive imagination" (or Fancy, the term used in the empiricist/associationist tradition) which "falls within the domain, not of transcendental philosophy, but of psychology" (operating according to the laws of association).[25] More importantly, all other mental faculties depend on the pervasive powers of the productive imagination. This is most evident in Kant's account of the transcendental unity of apperception, which is to say: the ultimate condition for the possibility of diverse representations "belonging together in one consciousness"[26] and hence "the ground of the possibility of all knowledge, especially of experience."[27] No experience would be "my experience," in other words, without the transcendental unity of apperception, and the latter is inseparable from the imagination. Indeed, at one point he identifies the imagination as the primordial faculty animating all powers of the understanding: *"the unity of apperception in relation to the synthesis of imagination is the understanding*; and the same unity, with reference to the *transcendental synthesis* of the imagination, the *pure understanding."*[28]

Engell uses an excellent analogy to sum up Kant's view of the imagination. It is, he says, both complete and yet very confusing because "like a full dictionary

---

22   Kant, *Critique of Pure Reason*, B 180.

23   Kant, *Critique of Pure Reason*, B181.

24   John Dewey, *Art as Experience* (New York: TarcherPerigee, 2005), 278.

25   Kant, *Critique of Pure Reason*, B 103.

26   Kant, *Critique of Pure Reason*, A 116.

27   Kant, *Critique of Pure Reason*, A 118.

28   Kant, *Critique of Pure Reason*, A 119.

entry, it is really a series of definitions and usages, some overlapping, others quite distinct, which together convey the meaning of the idea and echo the intellectual and philosophical milieu of the time."[29] Given Kant's remarkably capacious concept, Richard Rorty makes an odd statement about one post-Kantian line of succession: Romanticism held "an expansionist view of a mysterious faculty called the 'imagination' ... at the centre of the self."[30] Still, in weaving together a multitude of conceptual strains and shades of meaning inherited from his predecessors, Kant's great transformation had the unanticipated effect of creating a tempting philosophical door of opportunity for an even more ambitious expansion of the imagination. And the purpose of the next section is to show why Nietzsche shuts the door of Romanticism tightly and how he starts to integrate the "two valuable sides" of Kant's critical philosophy into his own pragmatic view of imagination.

2 Nietzsche's Version of the Productive Imagination in Historical Context

Recent interpretations of early German Romanticism (*Frühromantik*) diverge markedly, but they converge on one historical point. *Frühromantik* willingly accepted the *Transcendental Analytic*'s account of the necessary conditions for the possibility of objective empirical knowledge. To secure and protect this objectivity, however, Kant was adamant that any additional cognitive powers were strictly limited. In the third *Critique*, for example, he argued that aesthetic judgments were necessarily subjective. Art did not provide access to a different kind of knowledge. Yet *Frühromantik* just as strongly opposed Kant's restriction precisely because its members relentlessly sought the "ground of subjectivity that cannot itself lie within subjectivity."[31] They believed this transcendental ground of both knowing and Being could indeed be expressed – not discursively but aesthetically. Thus the role of the productive imagination in constructing empirical knowledge must be augmented by a creative power able to intuitively grasp "infinite Being" in finite particulars.

Samuel Coleridge, for instance, was following in the footsteps of *Frühromantik* when he famously distinguished the "primary" from "secondary"

---

29   Engell, *The Creative Imagination*, 129.

30   Rorty, *Contingency, Irony, and Solidarity*, 19.

31   Frederick C. Beiser, *The Romantic Imperative: The Concept of Early German Romanticism* (Cambridge, MA: Harvard University Press, 2006), 78. Beiser notes that there is "little disagreement about ... the central figures of this movement," sometimes referred to as Jena Romanticism, which flourished from 1797 to 1801, 7.

imagination – the latter boldly overstepping Kant's epistemological boundaries. And his advocacy of the "act of surpassing openness to reality other than the self" embodied in the artistic creations of the secondary imagination, showed Coleridge to be "far more Platonist than Kantian."[32] This makes sense, particularly in light of Frederick Beiser's claim that *Frühromantik* owed a "profound debt to the Platonic tradition."[33] Beiser often notes that the *Republic*'s notorious attitude toward artists notwithstanding, this movement took the key Platonic texts to be the *Phaedrus* and *Symposium*. In those works, an aesthetic construal of human cognition went far beyond the scope of the first *Critique*, not just the *Transcendental Analytic* (where *a priori* judgments synthesized sensory input, making empirical knowledge possible) but also the *Transcendental Dialectic* (where reason exercised a strictly defined, "regulative" extension of that knowledge). Specifically, *Frühromantik* took from Plato the idea that "aesthetic experience is not *suprarational*, still less *antirational*; rather, it is *hyperrational,* consisting in the act of intellectual intuition of reason."[34] The hyperrationality of "intuition" (perception or vision) is, however, at complete odds with Kant's third *Critique*'s position regarding the subjectivity of aesthetic judgment. So Beiser reasonably concludes that the influence of that work on *Frühromantik* is most certainly "more negative than positive."[35]

In drawing this conclusion, Beiser explicitly criticizes a central theme of Manfred Frank's interpretation of *Frühromantik*. And that is interesting because Frank's post-modernist flavored approach supports those scholars who identify Nietzsche with the movement's signature idea: namely, art is the best model for philosophy's mode of expression as well as the cognitive goal to which it aspires. Jos de Mul, for instance, says that "after Schelling we find the most pregnant expression of this aestheticization of worldview" characteristic of *Frühromantik* "in the philosophy of Nietzsche."[36] Yet such a claim is superficial at best. Nietzsche, in fact, offers Schelling as one example of those "innocent, youthful" philosophers who rejected Kant's "healthy bit of sensualism" and followed the "song and dance" of "the malicious fairy Romanticism."[37] This

---

32   J. Robert Barth, *The Symbolic Imagination: Coleridge and the Romantic Tradition* (Princeton, NJ: Princeton University Press, 1977), 113.

33   Beiser, *The Romantic Imperative*, 59.

34   Beiser, *The Romantic Imperative*, 61.

35   Beiser, *The Romantic Imperative*, 79.

36   Jos de Mul, *Romantic Desire in (Post) Modern Art and Philosophy* (Albany, NY: State University of New York Press, 1999), 75.

37   Nietzsche, *Beyond Good and Evil*, 11.

move compounded the misleading consequences of Kant's alleged discovery of the complicated mental bureaucracy which provided a solution to his epistemological problem. For the deluded *Frühromantiker* sought an even more exotic philosophical chimera: a "faculty for the 'supra-sensible'" which "Schelling baptized ... intellectual intuition."[38] And in another allusion to Molière's doctor, Nietzsche sarcastically calls their new discovery "an antidote to sensualism" or "in short – *sensus assoupire*."[39] *Frühromantik*, therefore, embraced a faculty designed to numb the senses despite the fact that "we possess knowledge today to precisely the extent that we have decided to accept the evidence of the senses – to the extent that we have learned to sharpen and arm them and to think them through to their conclusions."[40]

Judith Norman nicely sums up Nietzsche's historical break. "An essentially idealist epistemological project of representing or somehow indicating a transcendental ground," she says, "lies at the heart of Jena romanticism" while "Nietzsche, on the other hand, comes out of a different line of descent from Kant" and his resulting "conception of the self is naturalistic" through and through.[41] A major premise of this chapter's argument is that Nietzsche, inspired by a robust form of "sensualism," developed a thoroughly naturalized version of the Kantian productive imagination guided by a very non-Cartesian notion: "the body is a more astonishing idea than the old soul."[42] Above all, then, philosophers must recognize humanity's cognitive powers as an outgrowth of evolutionary development. Those powers exist not as the primary function of a metaphysically unique "organ for knowledge" but the consequence of demonstrated survival value: "we 'know' (or believe or imagine) just as much as may be useful in the interests of the species."[43] And Nietzsche tells a detailed Darwinian tale about the origin of our prized possession in a seminal early essay (unpublished in his lifetime). Once upon a time, it begins, there was "a planet on which clever animals invented cognition" and then formed "the most flattering valuation of cognition" not knowing the "intellect" originally functioned as an "art of dissimulation" which developed over millennia because it provided a significant selective advantage to creatures who lacked the "horns

---

38 Nietzsche, *Beyond Good and Evil*, 11.

39 Nietzsche, *Beyond Good and Evil*, 11.

40 Nietzsche, *Twilight of Idol*, "'Reason' in Philosophy," 3.

41 Judith Norman, "Nietzsche and Early Romanticism," *Journal of the History of Ideas* 63, no. 3 (2002): 513.

42 Nietzsche, *The Will to Power*, 689.

43 Friedrich Nietzsche, *The Gay Science*, trans. Walter Kaufmann (New York: Vintage Books, 1974), 354.

354   NICHOLLS

or the sharp fangs of the beast of prey with which to wage the struggle for existence."[44]

There is a significant thread of thematic continuity with Kant. Regarding the ceaselessly constructive activity making conscious experience possible, imagination and intellect are conceptually inseparable. But Nietzsche's jarring transformation is plain. Kant's "art concealed in the depths of the human soul" was integral to a transcendental faculty securing *a priori* knowledge whereas Nietzsche talks of an "art of dissimulation" performed by an "astonishingly" complex physiological apparatus in the service of a species' survival. The "primal power of the human imagination" refers to the activity of the brain and central nervous system creatively synthesizing the mass of sensory stimuli bombarding us, into "a hot, liquid stream" flow of "metaphors."[45] For Nietzsche, then, the conditions necessary for the possibility of consciousness are: "the stimulation of a nerve is first translated into an image: first metaphor! The image is then imitated by a sound: second metaphor."[46] He is describing an "*aesthetic*" process "by which I mean an elusive transference, a stammering translation into a quite different language" performed by "*an artistically creative subject.*"[47] And this, in a nutshell, is Nietzsche's naturalized version of the productive imagination (PI, henceforth).

The sense in which cognition is aestheticized must be clarified, though. For the weave of PI's metaphorical fabric is realized by habitual routines, conventions, and standard designations which fit or force new and unfamiliar stimuli into familiar imagistic and linguistic (hence conceptual) patterns. The strange and different is, by default, excluded. Rorty, it is worth noting, frequently uses Nietzsche inspired terminology – "inventing new metaphors"[48] – to laud novelty and creative human advances. But he, too, acknowledges that our cognitive framework was shaped by practical necessity (ultimately, the need to protect the social unit). Nietzsche has a well-known normative interest in early humanity's arbitrary, cruel, and strictly enforced measures designed to ensure behavioral conformity of all kinds. Immediately relevant, however, is that PI characterizes a process in which ruthless simplification is dominant. Nietzsche captures the cognitive dynamic in a fine formulation: "truths are metaphors which have become worn by frequent use and have lost all sensuous vigor,

---

44   "On Truth and Lying in a Non-Moral Sense in Nietzsche," *The Birth of Tragedy and Other Writings*, ed. Raymond Geuss, and Ronald Speirs (Cambridge: Cambridge University Press, 1999), 141–53.

45   Nietzsche, "On Truth and Lying," 148.

46   Nietzsche, "On Truth and Lying," 144.

47   Nietzsche, "On Truth and Lying," 148.

48   Rorty, *Contingency, Irony, and Solidarity*, 27.

coins which, having lost their stamp, are now regarded as metal and no longer as coins."[49] The tendency of cognitive frameworks, in other words, is to buffer and distance ourselves from new, enlivening experiences. Hence PI is an "art of dissimulation" whether it is viewed from the perspective of creativity or conformity.

Nevertheless, John Dewey adds an important qualification: while "all conscious experience ... has of necessity, some degree of imaginative quality," all conscious experience is not, in the narrow sense, "aesthetic experience."[50] The selective advantage of PI's cognitive activity, after all, did not originally lie in the creation of art-works (not to mention seeking truth for its own sake which is a very late cultural development.) "Our senses," Nietzsche says, are not designed to be "subtle, faithful, organs" of appreciation and hence listening to new music can be "hard and painful for the ear" or reading a novel can make "our senses hostile and reluctant."[51] Even when immersed in every-day perceptual experiences we skim, scan, and lazily overlook novelty, oddities, the beauty of the natural world, and the like. Our synthetic, imaginative contributions to conscious experience consist, ironically enough, in shaping behavior which is rote and pragmatic in the crude sense of the word. In sum, PI's aesthetic activity is integral to all cognition: "we fabricate (*Erdichten*) the greater part of our experience ... and can hardly be compelled *not* to contemplate some event, as its 'inventor' (*Erfinder*) ... one is much more of an artist than one realizes."[52] But PI tends to work against normatively esteemed aesthetic activities associated with so-called creative imagination.

Creative imagination (CI, henceforth) will be examined in this chapter's section. To conclude this section, however, I will underline a key methodological point to start putting a clearer pragmatic edge on PI's naturalism. For instance, when a pragmatist like Dewey uses the word "imagination" he is never referring to some sort of faculty. Instead, it is a non-technical, idiomatic way of talking about a circumscribed "phase of natural events" played across "the entire dramatic field of self-world interaction."[53] The same is true of "mind" which "is primarily a verb" denoting "all the ways in which we deal consciously and expressly" with the complex environment in which we live.[54] Despite his more flamboyant style Nietzsche also uses such words idiomatically. And going

---

49   Nietzsche, "On Truth and Lying," 147.

50   Dewey, *Art as Experience*, 233.

51   Nietzsche, *Beyond Good and Evil*, 192.

52   Nietzsche, *Beyond Good and Evil*, 192.

53   David Granger, "Expression, Imagination, and Organic Unity: John Dewey's Aesthetics and Romanticism," *Journal of Aesthetic Education* 37, no. 2 (2003): 53.

54   Dewey, *Art as Experience*, 274.

forward, PI and CI will always be referring to the primordially productive and ingeniously creative sides of the spectrum of imaginative activity. Both characterize complex forms of causal interaction with the world. The next section will continue to focus on PI but with the purpose of demonstrating exactly how self-conscious interaction is possible.

3   Nietzsche's "Extravagant Surmise": Linguistic Behavior and Play-Acting

In this section I will finally be able to leave behind the Cartesian epistemological scenario which (I have assumed from the outset) irremediably distorted Kantian views of the imagination. Disinterest in that scenario runs through Nietzsche's oeuvre: "the opposition of subject and object" and "the opposition of the 'thing in itself' and appearance" are distinctions "I leave to the epistemologists" who are ensnared in a pseudo-problem generated by faulty metaphysics.[55] In *Truth and Lying*, he says "the word appearance (*Erscheinung*) contains many seductions and for this reason I avoid using it as far as possible"[56] but when it is used, the reference is not to a subjective idea (i.e. an epistemological starting-point in the task of relating "appearance" to a non-subjective "reality" in a representational way). Instead, Nietzsche uses the word simply to mark the end-result of a complex causal interaction between an organism and the total environment in which it is immersed. By taking this theoretical approach, Richard Rorty claims, he belongs with figures such as Wittgenstein, Ryle, and Dennett in a lineage which "naturalizes mind ... by making all questions about [its] relation to the rest of the universe *causal* questions, as opposed to questions about the adequacy of representation or expression."[57]

Dismissing epistemology in this way can create the impression that the naturalizing process leads to an implausible reductive materialism. And sensitive to such a charge, Rorty argues, early pragmatists William James and Dewey often lost their nerve. They were left unsure "whether they wanted to just forget about epistemology or whether they wanted to devise a new improved epistemology of their own" and hence they went through phases of advocating alternate metaphysical theories (for example, "radical empiricism" or "panpsychism") designed for "closing the epistemological gap between subject and

---

55   Nietzsche, *The Gay Science*, 354.
56   Nietzsche, "On Truth and Lying," 148.
57   Rorty, *Contingency, Irony, and Solidarity*, 15.

NIETZSCHE ON THEATRICALITY AND IMAGINATION 357

object."[58] More charitably, their backsliding was likely motivated by a desire to deal with the Cartesian trump card invariably raised to support dualism: namely, the existence of a phenomenologically powerful, first-person experience of an inner-world palpably possessed by self-conscious beings. This section, then, aims to articulate Nietzsche's plausible and consistently pragmatic explanation of how self-conscious experience is possible.

His explanation of "the problem of consciousness (more precisely, of becoming conscious of something")[59] does not, needless to say, take the form of a Kant-like transcendental deduction of *a priori* mental conditions. Yet imagination continues to play a crucial role in Nietzsche's account. It is tied to the "aesthetic" activity performed by *Truth and Lying*'s "artistically creative subject" and, more specifically, to the fact that PI encompasses linguistic behavior. As we causally interact with the world, sensory stimuli are synthetically transformed into a complex metaphorical fabric composed not just of images, but sounds and signs, too. Again, Rorty adds helpful context: "the development of linguistic behavior – of social practices that use increasingly flexible vocal cords and thumbs to produce longer and more complex strings of noises and marks – is readily explicable in naturalistic, Darwinian terms."[60] The species, Nietzsche says, improvised "a way of designating things which has the same validity and force everywhere" and once an effective means of communication within populations was established by means of "valid tokens of designation – words – established conventions," chances of survival increased.[61]

The most focused and refined version of his evolutionary story is contained in a brilliant later aphorism entitled "On the 'genius of the species.'"[62] There, Nietzsche argues, enhanced comprehension of "physiology and the history of animals" shows that communication can occur within a species without participants being aware of what they are doing.[63] Indeed in principle, he says, organisms with a different line of descent, physiology, and repertoire of skills would be able to interact adaptively with their environment and engage in forms of perceiving, thinking, feeling, remembering, etc. even though "none of this would have to 'enter our consciousness' (as one says metaphorically)."[64]

---

58 Rorty, *Truth and Progress*, 297.
59 Nietzsche, *The Gay Science*, 354.
60 Rorty, *Truth and Progress*, 297.
61 Nietzsche, *Truth and Lying*, 138.
62 Nietzsche, *The Gay Science*, 354.
63 Nietzsche, *The Gay Science*, 354.
64 Nietzsche, *The Gay Science*, 354. As a contemporary aside, if an engineered central processor constructed of metal, silicon chips and plastic possessed sufficiently sophisticated

Still, every species is defined by a very specific biological and cultural genealogy cut through with massive contingency. In the case of this "most endangered animal," for instance, human beings did not live as "a solitary ... beast of prey" because we "*needed* help and protection" from other members of our "herd."[65] Communication, therefore, might be perfectly possible in biological principle without consciousness of what we were doing. But if members of the species were aware of "what distressed" them, what each other "thought" about a situation, and the like, communication could be much more effective.[66]

In short, the ability to communicate consciously was a significant selective advantage in the struggle for existence. "Consciousness," according to Nietzsche, "developed in proportion to the degree of its utility"; it is an evolved consequence of the process in which a needy species gained a selective edge when members could "communicate and understand each other quickly and subtly" within an increasingly complex "sign-world."[67] The contrast with the Cartesian narrative could not be starker. The latter begins with each individual having privileged access to a metaphysically distinct, inner world that defines one's self and then (after the core epistemological difficulties have allegedly been resolved and as a minor after-thought) the contents of that world can be communicated to others in a linguistic medium devised for this purpose. Nietzsche proposes a complete reversal. Consciousness emerges as a new form of linguistic behavior which, *ipso facto*, preceded consciousness. Nietzsche's "perhaps extravagant surmise" is that "consciousness is really a net of communication between human beings" or, more pointedly: "my idea is that consciousness does not really belong to man's individual existence but rather to his social or herd nature."[68]

The logic of Nietzsche's reasoning still needs clarification. For instance, his surmise entails that "the emergence of our sense impressions into our own consciousness and the ability, as it were, to exhibit them externally, increased proportionately with the need to communicate them *to others* by means of signs."[69] Yet Nietzsche cannot presume that an awareness of the need for more effective communication motivates development of the self-awareness which will then satisfy the relevant need. That would be an egregious begging of the question of the kind he would ridicule in others. For the surmise also entails

---

input devices and the means of responding to its environment in an equally sophisticated way, then the same could be said of a machine.

65   Nietzsche, *The Gay Science*, 354.
66   Nietzsche, *The Gay Science*, 354.
67   Nietzsche, *The Gay Science*, 354.
68   Nietzsche, *The Gay Science*, 354.
69   Nietzsche, *The Gay Science*, 354.

NIETZSCHE ON THEATRICALITY AND IMAGINATION

(the other side of the coin) that "the human being inventing signs, is at the same time the human being who becomes ever more keenly conscious of himself."[70] To fulfill its main aim, therefore, this section must still identify a mechanism to explain exactly how members of this species could become consciously aware of their previously non-conscious behavior.

Consider Nietzsche's characteristically pregnant but enigmatic comment: "consciousness is ... a form of play-acting."[71] What does this mean? In his now classic "just so story," Daniel Dennett concisely and precisely unpacks the explanatory content of the suggestion that consciousness is, in effect, a variation within existing linguistic behavior. In a philosophical style surprisingly reminiscent of Nietzsche, Dennett asks us to entertain a scenario in which proto-humans are collaboratively engaging in practical tasks, utilizing sounds and signs to exchange information with no self-awareness – until one day, all of a sudden:

> [O]ne of these hominids mistakenly asked for help when there was no helpful audience within earshot – except itself! When it heard its own request, the stimulation provoked just the sort of other-helping utterance production that the request from another would have caused. And to the creature's delight, it found that it had provoked itself into answering its own question.[72]

If this happens once, it could – and is likely to – happen again. Indeed, there is a tendency for this novel behavior to snowball and part of the snowballing effect is that an individual talking to oneself will not only become conscious of oneself as-an-Other. Almost inevitably, the speaker will start to attribute the same behavior to others. For they are all, as Nietzsche frequently claims, highly imitative "herd animals" using a common language. Others, then, start to be treated as if they were self-conscious and they, too, start to behave accordingly (i.e. play-acting) analogous to the way children are primed to pick up instantly on the unwritten rules of pretence-based games.

To sum up, linguistic behavior has the potential to trigger a "form of play-acting" within the species. Becoming a proficient performer skilled in using a pre-existing system of sounds and signs in a new way is, in other words, functionally identical to attaining consciousness of self and others. Now, insofar as they would find this tentative explanation of consciousness as a form of

---

70   Nietzsche, *The Gay Science*, 354.
71   Nietzsche, *The Will to Power*, 289.
72   Daniel C. Dennett, *Consciousness Explained* (Boston, MA: Back Bay Books, 1992), 12.

play-acting to be plausible, Rorty's argument that Nietzsche initiated a lineage shared by analytic philosophers broadly construed as pragmatists, is strengthened. Still, Nietzsche's primary interest was not in the array of follow-up problems addressed by those working in contemporary philosophy of mind and language. Rather, he focused on "the problem of consciousness" as a normative problem, believing that this new form of linguistic behaviour had a secondary effect that poses a danger to the species. The next section uses the more generic concept of theatricality to clarify this danger.

4 Theatricality as a Normative Problem

Nietzsche's first book was both a passionate defence of Dionysos, the god of theater, and an unprecedented critique of the person who allegedly destroyed theater's role in Greek culture, Plato's mentor Socrates. To claim, then, that a form of play-acting posed a normative danger for Nietzsche seems odd. For he was a declared antagonist of Plato whose notorious criticism of mimetic art was that it encouraged an attraction to copies – of actions, ideas, etc. – which were already misleading copies of what was truly real. And theater was particularly dangerous. Plato did not argue that in pretending to be a silly, intemperate, and dishonest god, for example, a well-trained actor could convince spectators that he was such a god. His argument, in other words, was not that only fools would confuse an actor with the god outside the theater but inside it, all people are liable to act like fools. Rather, he was disturbed by theater's unique blend of metaphysical and moral falsity which could sanction a skilful presentation of a transparently imaginary and morally reprehensible character as entertaining and emotionally believable.

Theater, Plato concluded, encouraged a human attraction to the corrupting effects of artifice, pretence, and surface appearance. In a word, he could not tolerate the theatricality of the theater. Platonic criticisms of theater recur in Rousseau's *Letter to M. D'Alembert*, Jane Austen's *Mansfield Park*, and elsewhere. Although they might be dismissed as an intolerant, morally prudish aesthetic lapse in figures who should know better, "theatrical" retains this pejorative sense well beyond the purview of aesthetics and independently of any commitment to Platonic metaphysics. For the word perfectly captures the jarring ring of falseness which sounds when people make a spectacle of themselves and behave primarily to impress others (deliberately or unintentionally). Marvin Carlson details how this way of identifying a kind of inauthenticity became widespread within diverse intellectual discourses: "even when it does not appear in precisely these terms," he says, we tend to forget that the habit of

NIETZSCHE ON THEATRICALITY AND IMAGINATION 361

ascribing theatricality to persons who present a façade of themselves, not the real thing, "is in significant measure a modern reworking of a very ancient criticism of theater."[73]

Given that Nietzsche explains consciousness as a form of play-acting, it is not surprising that he also reworks theatricality based not only on his rejection of a stable, metaphysically unified self[74] but, more radically, on his skepticism regarding the unequivocally positive value of human consciousness. Just consider how Nietzsche's normative attitude to this form of play-acting is conveyed in language redolent of the pejorative meaning of theatricality: "all becoming conscious," he says, "involves a great and thorough corruption, falsification, reduction to superficialities, and generalization."[75] True, self-conscious human beings are, *ex hypothesi*, performing in a manner that provides a selective advantage as the species causally interacts with the world. But this is part of a cognitive simplification process and when PI takes a self-reflexive turn, simplifying acquires a distinctively negative color. Bluntly put, to become self-conscious is to be deceived about oneself. Paradoxical as that may sound, this self-deception is a predictable side-effect of the species learning to play-act in the very public "sign world" of a "herd."[76] After all, as we started talking to others about ourselves, in a language designed for communicating with others in very practical ways, how could we not misconceive ourselves?

This consequence can be named "the so-called ego"[77] – the ego (*Ich*) with which human beings naturally identify. Yet all "the inner processes and drives" that actually motivate us rarely enter consciousness. More accurately, "we register" consciously only what we can linguistically express.[78] And since language was designed for working in a social environment, when co-opted to describe our personal states of mind it is a relatively crude instrument. For

---

73   Marvin Carlson, "The Resistance to Theatricality," *SubStance*, no. 2/3 (2002): 240.

74   It should be noted that regarding the critique of any Cartesian self, Nietzsche not only shares a line of descent with analytic philosophers. There is also a (better-known) commonality with theorists such as Derrida and Judith Butler and related poststructuralist critiques. The fact that the latter normatively affirmed a concept akin to theatricality – performativity – with which Nietzsche shows sympathy, only underlines the need to carefully qualify Nietzsche's position.

75   Nietzsche, *The Gay Science*, 354.

76   As Walter Kaufman noted long ago, Nietzsche's argument anticipates Wittgenstein's rejection of the very possibility of private languages. Nietzsche, *The Gay Science*, 297n.

77   The title of: Nietzsche, *Dawn*, 115. The "so-called ego" stands in illuminating opposition to Kant's transcendental unity of apperception. For the synthetic activity of his productive imagination is a necessary condition of the latter (see page 4, above) whereas the former is the creation of Nietzsche's naturalized PI.

78   Nietzsche, *Dawn*, 115.

instance, "wrath, hate, love, compassion, craving, knowing, joy, pain ... are all names for *extreme* states" whereas those of "the milder middle degrees" and particularly those that "elude us" are what "weave the web of our character and our destiny."[79] This ego is a "so-called" ego because "we are none of us what we appear to be solely in those states for which we have consciousness and words."[80] And if we identify with "this seemingly clearest block print of the Self ... we misread ourselves."[81]

Even as we become self-aware creatures, then, PI remains a powerful "art of dissimulation." Yet this does not pin-point the practical, normative problem with the theatricality of consciousness because physical survival or psychological health sometimes requires a "useful blindness."[82] Under certain circumstances both conscious clarity and blissful blindness can be pragmatically valuable. Identifying with the so-called ego, by contrast, is always dangerous. Consider the title of another *Dawn* aphorism – "*Pseudo-egotism*."[83] The danger is that human beings who identify with their so-called ego "virtually without exception" never care for their "genuine" selves.[84] For their self-image is shaped by a public language and its substance, moreover, it is largely constituted by what others say about us or by what we surmise they say. That creates potential for an intriguing visual twist within the so-called ego because the latter unwittingly finds itself within a crazy, phantom world of cascading mirror-effects generated by what we say to ourselves about ourselves while feeding on what we think others say about us. Within each node of the "net of communication between human beings" which constitutes consciousness, as Nietzsche puts it, "phantom egos" of people are "formed in the heads of those around them" in all-enveloping "fog."[85] "One person is always in the head of the other which, in

---

79   Nietzsche, *Dawn*, 115.
80   Nietzsche, *Dawn*, 115.
81   Nietzsche, *Dawn*, 115.
82   Nietzsche, *Gay Science*, 284. References to the uses of blindness, deception, and ignorance are common. A more ebullient expression of this value – "delight in blindness," for example (*Gay Science* 287) – is apparent in the final section's discussion of theater aesthetics.
83   Nietzsche, *Dawn*, 105. This is the conceptual source of Nietzsche's sympathy for the Buddhist critique of a substantial ego and consequent approaches to a more profound view of self-care. See: Roderick Nicholls, "Care of Self and Amor Fati as a Spiritual Ideal," in *The Philosophy of Spirituality*, eds. Heather Salazar, and Roderick Nicholls (Leiden, NL: Brill, 2018), 216–18.
84   Nietzsche, *Dawn*, 105.
85   Nietzsche, *Dawn*, 105.

turn, is in other heads,"[86] making it exceedingly difficult to distinguish who we are from the phantoms.

This visual twist requires no epistemologically unique mental vision or intuition. Rather, the ubiquitous phantoms enveloping us like a fog are the result of on-going causal processes. And becoming conscious or aware of something is akin to seeing something you did not see before. It is a sophisticated and usually silent way of talking about what we are doing, including the talking (writing, typing, etc.) about our talking fed by continuous input from other people. Such meta-communication is, quite obviously, perfect material to be exploited by the imaginative activity of the brain and central nervous system. Contemporary electronic networks of communication, therefore, magnify the inherent theatricality of consciousness and, as such, the normative danger posed by PI's creation of a virtual self – identifying with one's so-called ego (which is, to some degree or other, fictional) – is magnified. To get a more detailed sense of how exactly this happens, however, the next section examines the hyper-theatricality of dream-worlds.

5   Creating Dreams: A Model for Understanding PI

Nietzsche's analysis of dream-consciousness illuminates the theatrical nature of PI's pervasive role in conscious life very well because the complicating variable of continuous input from other people (or the external environment in general) is minimized. This analysis, of course, cannot depend on a "Cartesian theater," Daniel Dennett's favorite image for modelling the non-material metaphysical place in the brain where a unitary self or "Central Witness" views the mental contents of one's consciousness.[87] So Coleridge's well-known representations of dreams as theatrical dramas – with stage-designs, costumes, exotic characters, etc. – is a useful foil for setting up Nietzsche's position.

Very briefly, Coleridge coined a term for the metaphysical stage on which dreams were performed in his post-Kantian theater. Within a Romantic mental bureaucracy, "Somnial or Morphean Space" provides room for Coleridge's secondary imagination to operate independently of sensible intuition.[88] Contravening Kant's critical restriction on imagination, its power of intellectual

---

86   Nietzsche, *Dawn*, 105.

87   Daniel Dennett, *Intuition Pumps and Other Tools for Thinking* (New York: WW Norton & Co., 2013), 281.

88   Jennifer Ford, *Coleridge on Dreaming: Romanticism, Dreams and the Medical Imagination* (Cambridge University Press, 1998), 145.

intuition could supposedly access the objective ground of subjectivity. According to Jennifer Ford, the "esemplastic" powers of this faculty operating in Morphean Space could create an art-work representing "something external to the dreamer" (Reality, the Infinite, God, or transcendental Other).[89] Nietzsche, in sharp contrast, stays within PI's naturalistic terms of reference. Dream-worlds are hyper-theatrical, proto-typically virtual end-results of innumerable causal threads which dynamically connect the brain and central nervous system, other physiological behavior, and silent talk about the latter events, within the relatively limited environment of the sleeping organism.

In this Nietzschean context, how are we to understand a private theatrical work performed on a virtual stage-space? Start with the simple fact that the waking human organism is interactively immersed in a vast environment, largely responding to what is other-than-self. The biggest change when asleep is the minimization of an array of inputs (and corresponding patterns of response). Sleepers do not converse, for example, even if someone is in the bedroom talking in a way that we would respond to, if awake. We can still be aware of – or, in the sense noted above, "see" – all manner of things (albeit in a relatively shadowy, inchoate, and arbitrary way). For we are not in a coma and hence memory, meta-communicative activities, and indeed all PI-related activity can still operate in varying degrees. Without a unitary Cartesian self or "Central Witness," however, Nietzsche's dream-worlds must be thoroughly collaborative creations. As the final section will demonstrate, a live theatrical performance is CI's collaborative art-form *par excellence*. So claiming a parallel between the two makes sense in principle. But right now, devilishly difficult details must be addressed. Exactly how is such a performance possible without any overall direction by conscious agency? What participants engage in the requisite collaboration (and how)? How are we to conceive the audience watching the performance?

The best approach is to flesh out elements of dream-works matching those of standard theatre productions performed in physical spaces: script, director, actors, and audience. First, a standard theatrical script is typically a text-heavy set of instructions created by a playwright to animate performers' voices and bodies in ways that are partly predictable (but usually designed to be receptive to contributions from collaborators in a process that is successful insofar as the results are aesthetically not predictable). Dream performances are in that sense unscripted. Yet *Dawn* justifiably refers to a dream's "text" several times[90]

---

89   Ford, *Coleridge on Dreaming*, 145.

90   Nietzsche, *Dawn*, 119.

NIETZSCHE ON THEATRICALITY AND IMAGINATION   365

because the erratic flow of dreams depends on a wealth of potential physiological triggers for PI's improvised responses. *Twilight of the Idols* also treats the latter as script-like material which could be performatively exploited. This includes "our general feelings" when asleep and "every sort of restraint, pressure, tension, explosion, and the play encounter play of our organs, likewise and especially the condition of the nervous system."[91] Similarly, *Human, All-Too Human* refers to the activity of our digestive system, the state of our internal organs, circulation of the blood, various postural positions, feel of the bedclothes, etc.[92] In addition to memory-shreds from the previous day on which the dream analyses of empiricist philosophers had concentrated, Nietzsche noted recurring stimuli such as house noises, temperature fluctuations, and intrusions from outside the house (bells, wind, etc.)

Regarding the role of director, *Dawn's* aphorism, "experience and invention (*Erleben und Erdichten*)"[93] is enlightening. Given Ernest Behler's translation of *Erdichten*, it would not be inaccurate to identify the dream-work's director with "imagination."[94] By that logic, though, every theatrical element could be generically attributed to PI which scarcely explains difficult questions regarding collaboration. Methodologically, moreover, this would be tactical backsliding. For Nietzsche's approach to concepts like imagination, intellect, reason, and mind presupposes, like Dewey's, that noun references misleadingly imply the existence of self-contained faculties. Dewey's preference is to use "primarily verbs" which idiomatically denote patterns of activities with functional commonalities.[95] And Nietzsche uses the subtle flexibility of ordinary language rather than technically precise terminology for conveying conceptual nuances (my stipulated acronyms, PI and CI, are used purely for efficiency.) Yet his style does create difficulties for translators[96] and perhaps the best

---

91   Nietzsche, *Twilight of Idols,* "The Four Great Errors," 4.

92   Friedrich Nietzsche, *Human, All Too Human 1: A Book For Free Spirits,* trans. Gary Handwerk (Stanford, CA: Stanford University Press, 1997), 13.

93   Nietzsche, *Dawn,* 119.

94   Ernst Behler, "Nietzsche's Conception of Irony," in *Nietzsche, Philosophy, and the Arts,* eds. Salim Kemal, Ivan Gaskell, and Daniel W. Conway (New York: Cambridge University Press, 1998), 29.

95   Dewey, *Art as Experience,* 274.

96   Translations of *Erdichten* in the title of *Dawn,* 119 include "imagination" offered by Behler in *Irony,* 1998; "invention" by Hollingdale in Nietzsche, *Daybreak: Thoughts on the Prejudices of Morality* (Cambridge: Cambridge University Press, 1982), 119; and "make-believe" by Smith in Nietzsche, *Dawn,* 2011. Smith helpfully notes that *Erdichten* is formed by "adding the prefix er- to ... the customary verb for 'to write literature'" hence "to make-up" or to "fantasize' (*Dawn,* 2011, 119n41)." Things get more complicated when nouns are unavoidable. "Die dichtende Vernunft ... *sich vorstellt*" becomes: for Smith "the make-believing

noun-phrase to express the kind of imagining done by a director is the literal and (in English) less loaded: "poeticizing reason" or "reason that is writing literature."[97]

Nietzsche's earliest discussion of dreams exemplifies the conceptual/linguistic fluidity between imagining and reasoning. As a rudimentary script, he offers sensations of straps wrapped around the feet of a sleeper. With the arousal of the sleeper's whole system – "reaching even the functioning of the brain" – there is eventually a conscious effect of "snakes encircling his feet."[98] Creating this effect requires "the mind."[99] But that word refers to the cerebral activity of the dreamer performing as a theater director – offering causal suggestions to actors seeking a fitting motivation for behavior in scripted circumstances, which is to say: "*searching for and representing the causes* for ... aroused sensations."[100] This directorial role is not different in kind from the constant stream of automatic and routine judgments performed daily as a waking person fabricates the coherent perceptual weave of everyday life shaped by pragmatic demands. The difference is that make-believing inventing, fabricating reason is less constrained by those demands and so can improvise motivations to explain fantasy effects *ex post facto*, with "*very free*, very arbitrary interpretations ... of the nerve impulses."[101] *Twilight of the Idols* zeroes in on the overall theoretical point: we "become conscious of [a sensation] only when we have furnished it with a motive of some kind."[102] In constructing a dream-work, for example, "a distant cannon shot" resonates in the background of a sleeper's consciousness until it acquires "'meaning'" in the context of a "little novel" created in the interim; only then can it "step into the foreground" (i.e. into consciousness)[103] as a recognizable sound.

Before dealing with the mechanics of this process, I should dispel any impression that Nietzsche is elevating the role of director to dominant *auteur*. *Dawn*, for instance, considers why certain script variables "generally remains pretty much the same from night to night" – same bed, ambience, relatively stable physiology, etc. – and yet it "elicits such divergent commentary" in the

---

faculty of reason ... *imagines*"; for Hollingdale "the inventive reasoning faculty ... *imagines*"; and for Behler, "imagining reason." Behler's wording is in line with another Smith translation note (n62, below).

97   This is Smith's suggestion for a literal translation, *Dawn*, 119n.44.

98   Nietzsche, *Human, All Too Human*, 13.

99   Nietzsche, *Human, All Too Human*, 13.

100   Nietzsche, *Human, All Too Human*, 13.

101   Nietzsche, *Human, All Too Human*, 13.

102   Nietzsche, *Twilight of Idols*, "Four Great Errors," 4.

103   Nietzsche, *Twilight of Idols*, "Four Great Errors," 4.

NIETZSCHE ON THEATRICALITY AND IMAGINATION

performance of the resulting dream-work.[104] It is not simply that our life-experiences vary every day. More importantly, "our daily experiences toss willy-nilly to this drive or that drive." This irrational feeding of "greedily" over-nourished drives and "starving and stunting" of other ones[105] is due to the hard-wired self-ignorance of our "so-called ego" because "nothing is more incomplete than the image" of self tied to the existence of that ego. And the more we identify with it, the more the intimate, deeply felt but "unknown world of the 'subject'"[106] becomes an alien, inner, Other. This is the immediately relevant point because the divergent content and tone of dream-works has much to do with which of these drives and impulses can seize nutritional sources, grow, and exert power. Here, in short, are the so-far missing actors. In contrast to the productions of a directorial *auteur*, moreover, these are assertive actors who drive the fast-evolving script toward performative completion. Nietzsche uses the French theatrical word term to reflect their power: actors are "the prompter (*souffleur*) of this [make-believing] reason."[107]

Nevertheless, the underlying difficulties of Nietzsche's analysis now come to a head. For the process in which conative actors participate in creatively eliciting "meaning" from a rudimentary script, culminates in the production of conscious fantasy – a performance, Nietzsche says, "in which the dreamer is the chief character."[108] But if the dreamer is not the audience watching the performance of the actors as they represent the fictional characters, what exactly is the audience? Now, the final section will discuss the frequently made aesthetic point that a live theater performance (by contrast with a film playing on a screen or a play in rehearsal) is incomplete without an audience. Regarding dream-works, however, this never becomes a vague platitude. Quite the contrary, it is necessarily true because the very existence of the snake vignette or any more complex production necessarily depends upon the sleeping person's consciousness of them. In other words, Berkeley's counter-intuitive "*esse est percipi*" applies to dreams, if nothing else. For a dream offers a dizzyingly paradoxical scenario: it is the performance of a story involving fictional characters played by actors and watched by an audience which is unaware of the behind-the-scenes business making the performance possible (including an awareness that the lead character created by the dreamer, is the dreamer). Still, Nietzsche's idea is not simply that dream consciousness is an exceedingly

---

104 Nietzsche, *Dawn*, 119.
105 Nietzsche, *Dawn*, 119.
106 Nietzsche, *Dawn*, 116.
107 Nietzsche, *Dawn*, 119.
108 Nietzsche, *Twilight of Idols*, "Four Great Errors," 4.

complex kind of play-acting. So the status of the audience in his account of the construction of dreams must make also make sense when it comes to waking consciousness.

Nietzsche's later works propose a radical, multiple-self theory to explain the phenomenologically powerful sense in which a human being is an audience to the life they are undergoing (waking or sleeping), consistent with his pragmatic naturalism. Well before that, however, *Human, All-Too Human* had suggested a simple way of understanding one of the most puzzling aspects of a dream-audience. Recall, for instance, Nietzsche description of make-believing reason's collaborative function: "the cause is deduced from the effect and conceived *after* the effect."[109] The snakes are perceived as the cause of the subliminally felt (or plain unfelt) sensation although they are actually the final effect of the process originally initiated by the sensation. "All this occurs with extraordinary rapidity," Nietzsche argues, "so that judgment gets confused, just as it might in watching a magician" who can make things "appear to be simultaneous, or even to occur in reverse order"[110] What occurs is the primordial exemplification of a skilled magician's sleight-of-hand. That is certainly not a sufficient explanation. Indeed, it prompts the logical next question: namely, how can a person perform such a conjuring trick on oneself? Yet it is highly suggestive of a workable solution to this question.

Consider a parallel to the argument Michael Polanyi once made regarding "tacit knowledge." When performing a task using a tool with which I am highly skilled, the tool becomes an extension of my own body. And I can properly focus on the object of my attention (what I am using the tool on) if and only if I am unaware of the tool (its weight, feel in my hand, etc.)[111] True, a dreamer involuntarily falls into a comparable state whereas the crafter can do so only after preparation, experience, and training. The next section shows how this difference is transformed within an actual theater performance into an aesthetic achievement of CI. But Nietzsche expresses the immediate philosophical takeaway when he discusses dreams: the constant activity of make-believing inventing, fabricating reason encompassed by PI ensures that "between waking and dreaming no *essential* difference exists."[112] The net of communication (which defines consciousness) forms a continuous spectrum of theatricality with the often-mundane productions of waking consciousness at one end and the hyper-theatricality of dreams at the other.

---

109   Nietzsche, *Human, All Too Human*, 13.
110   Nietzsche, *Human, All Too Human*, 13.
111   Michael Polanyi, *The Tacit Dimension* (New York: DoubleDay & Co., 1966), 32.
112   Nietzsche, *Dawn*, 119.

To close this section, it is worth noting a remark of Graham Parkes. "All our so-called consciousness is a more or less fantastical commentary on an unknown, perhaps unknowable, yet felt text," Parkes says, is "often quoted in the secondary literature" but "it is not clear that the import" of Nietzsche's statement is ever "fully appreciated."[113] That is quite right. *Composing the Soul* is the best overall account of Nietzsche's philosophical psychology (and, specifically, his multiple-self theory). Its argument, then, adds substantial support to the previous section's claim that Nietzsche had a deep normative ambivalence to our possession of consciousness due to its self-deceiving character. Parkes tends to use a literary construal of many of the passages I have cited, whereas my argument is that a pragmatically oriented theatrical approach can explain how PI creates the fabric of consciousness. Martin Puchner, on the other hand, says that for Nietzsche "there is no stable agent behind the theatrical act, no unmasked actor behind the character; theatricality has become a primary condition of reality"[114] a statement that nicely captures my argument so far. Oddly enough however, it does so without having any direct connection to the issue of imagination as I deal with it. For Puchner's primary interest is in Nietzsche's "theatrical philosophy" (which includes his concept of history and style of writing) and, more to the point, is informed by the widespread belief that his early "fascination with theater from Greek tragedy to Richard Wagner" had little lasting philosophical significance.[115] The next section undercuts that latter belief in the process of arguing that Nietzsche's understanding of Greek theater provides the perfect model for completing this chapter's thesis regarding theatricality and imagination.

6 Creating Theater Performances: A Model for Understanding CI

Early in his superb, book-length argument regarding Nietzsche's theater aesthetics, David Kornhaber says that while historians of theater often note Nietzsche's "supposedly formative influence" on modern drama, this claim is usually vague.[116] No justification comes from classical scholars studying *The*

---

113 Graham Parkes, *Composing the Soul: Reaches of Nietzsche's Psychology* (Chicago: University of Chicago Press, 1996), 296.

114 Martin Puchner, "Kenneth Burke: Theater, Philosophy, and the Limits of Performance," in *Staging Philosophy: Intersections of Theater, Performance, and Philosophy* (Ann Arbor: University of Michigan Press, 2006), 41.

115 Puchner, "Kenneth Burke," 41.

116 David Kornhaber, *The Birth of Theater from the Spirit of Philosophy: Nietzsche and the Modern Drama* (Evanston, IL: Northwestern University Press, 2016), 12.

Birth of Tragedy and related writings on Greek culture because they typically assume that Nietzsche's philological/literary interests far outweigh any concern with theatrical performance.[117] Philosophers simply overlook the issue or dismiss his early enthusiasm for theater (and seeming antipathy to it later) as a biographical matter explained by his tumultuous personal relationship with Wagner. Kornhaber forces a change in perspective. Throughout Nietzsche's life, he insists, the theater was "never far from his thoughts"; he "loved going to it, loved talking and writing about it, and loved dabbling in it."[118] Theoretically, moreover, Nietzsche's early writings directly engaged Goethe, Schiller, and Lessing (all prominent practitioners of theater) who formed the backbone of "the great German classical tradition."[119]

This section benefits from Kornhaber's refreshing new outlook. But its main purpose is to complete an independent argument regarding imagination and a conceptually broad sense of theatricality. According to the Nietzschean proposal articulated so far: the "net of communication between human beings" is a continuum on which we make distinctions – most obviously, between dream and waking consciousness – according to degrees of theatrical intensity at network nodes (i.e. conscious individuals); and determined largely by imposed or habitually engrained practical constraints operating on, or within, the total physiological system at specific times. Going forward, I will use Nietzsche's account of ancient Greek theater as a model to display theatrical intensity on a different axis of the continuum. Which is to say I shift focus from PI to CI, under the ongoing stipulation that these acronyms denote patterns of behavior with functional commonalities (not some psychological or metaphysical faculty). There is also a new stipulation. Relative to PI, CI characterizes a range of normatively affirmed behavior. A specific type of theater, then, will act as an imaginative aesthetic ideal displaying a point of maximum theatrical intensity on the CI axis.

Let me begin, however, with a much more modest proposal by Gilbert Ryle. Like any philosopher in the Rorty and Nietzsche lineage, Ryle emphatically rejects the idea that imagination is a Kant-like "department of the Mind"; but he also sharply criticizes a common habit of identifying imagination with make-believe.[120] Nietzsche, as frequently cited, often associates PI with the

---

117   Henceforth, as the section title indicates, "theater" will normally refer to "theater performances."

118   Kornhaber, *The Birth of Theater*, 13.

119   Kornhaber, *The Birth of Theater*, 44.

120   Gilbert Ryle, *On Thinking*, ed. Konstantin Kolenda, new ed. (Oxford, UK: Blackwell Publishers, 1982), 52. Ryle, says Rorty, was an important figure in the line that "liberated us"

NIETZSCHE ON THEATRICALITY AND IMAGINATION

latter notion: for example, "to experience is to make-believe (*Erdichten*)."[121] Yet Ryle's positive proposal regarding the "imaginativeness" that we esteem, is a good segue to CI. For this quality tends to be blocked by the routine-driven mundane demands shaping PI's fabrication of everyday experience (and dreams can scarcely be aesthetically esteemed despite the charms of their fantastic, nonsensical, made-up character). "Imaginativeness," by contrast, is what "shows itself in any of those moments" when a person "innovates, when he invents, discovers, explores, essays, experiments, and so on, that is when he makes or attempts to make moves which are new in the sense of being undrilled, unrehearsed and (for him) unprecedented."[122] In my terms, all these normatively affirmed ways of acting – in areas from scholarship to athletics – fall under the purview of CI as opposed to PI. It is in this light that Nietzsche always dissociates theater from make-believe often, moreover, with comparisons to athletic contests.

The skills of actors (like those of fellow dancers in theatrical performances) are athletic, he says, and those of a playwright and/or director are analogous to "the virtue of the pentathlon athlete."[123] Like the way "Olympic Games brought the separate Greek tribes together in political and religious unity," all practitioners also collaborate in real time to create art-works in a "dramatic festival" which is "a festive reunification of [all] the Greek art-forms."[124] I will elaborate on these comparisons momentarily but note, at this point, the wrinkle Nietzsche puts on Ryle's proposal that we identify "imaginativeness" with the performance of "undrilled, unrehearsed" moves in diverse areas of life. In one sense, of course, this is true. What makes this possible, however, is some deliberately designed regimen or, in fact, "a piece of tyranny" deadly "opposed to a policy like *laisser aller*"[125] which recommends, as we say: to just act naturally. For executing striking, improvisational moves and pulling off unlikely imaginative strokes is effectively performing surprising variations on (or sometimes even breaking) well-established, highly specialized procedures and stylistic conventions which have been previously mastered through pain, effort, and discipline. Great writers and orators, for example, voluntarily submit to "protracted obedience in one direction" and internalize the means by which "every

---

       from Cartesian/Kantian "notions like 'in the mind' or 'created in the mind.'" Rorty, *Truth and Progress*, 250.

121   Nietzsche, *Dawn*, 119 (Smith translation).

122   Ryle, *On Thinking*, 61.

123   Friedrich Nietzsche, *Greek Music Drama*, ed. Jill Dr Marsden, trans. Paul Bishop (New York: Contra Mundum Press, 2013), 8.

124   Nietzsche, *Greek Music Drama*, 20.

125   Nietzsche, *Beyond Good and Evil*, 188.

language has hitherto attained strength and freedom – the metrical constraint, the tyranny of rhyme and rhythm," and so on.[126] The inventive freedom of accomplished artists (like athletes) who can respond imaginatively to fast-changing circumstances is causally dependent on the voluntary but semi-automatic operations of the "thousand-fold laws" embodied in behavior through years of training and practice (including rehearsals in the case of performing artists). "Going with the flow" – acting with a confident and seemingly "natural" air – is, in short, the effect of its opposite.

This wrinkle on Ryle permeates Nietzsche's account of ancient Greek theater which he credits with making Europeans "accustomed to unnatural stage conventions" (including the "beautiful unnaturalness" of operatic singing). He also argues that extremely competitive theater practitioners went "alarmingly far" in setting difficult constraints to test and excite their "inventiveness."[127] For example, they accepted a "limited number of actors, the use of chorus, the limited cycle of myths"[128] and various other "cruel demands."[129] A Sophocles wrote his "beautiful speeches" according to exacting stylistic specifications knowing that they would be delivered under equally unforgiving conditions – for example, a "stage as narrow as possible" which precluded "any effects by means of deep backgrounds."[130] In that space, moreover, actors had to recite and sing well over a thousand verses over many hours and endured other "entirely unnatural" restrictions that charged them with "a heroic task worthy of a marathon contestant," for example, simultaneously executing complex, choreographed steps wearing huge masks, high-heels, and heavy robes in dazzlingly bright day-time light.[131]

Surprisingly, perhaps, *Birth of Tragedy* spends even more time on the active role of the "spectator" (*Zuschauer*) looking onto the unfolding "spectacle" (*Schauspiel*). But at the beginning of this section, I pointed to Nietzsche's rationale. The normatively desired culmination of this type of performance is a collective transformation of audience members which raises the level of theatrical intensity defined by CI to its normative peak. To fully understand this phenomenon, though, the idea of audience participation must be taken very

---

126 Nietzsche, *Beyond Good and Evil*, 188.
127 Nietzsche, *Gay Science*, 80.
128 Nietzsche, *Greek Music Drama*, 12.
129 Nietzsche, *Greek Music Drama*, 22.
130 Nietzsche, *Gay Science*, 80.
131 Nietzsche, *Greek Music Drama*, 12.

NIETZSCHE ON THEATRICALITY AND IMAGINATION

seriously. At first glance, for instance, to say that Athenians had a deep love and refined appreciation for "beautiful speeches" flawlessly delivered looks like a demand placed on other participants.[132] But the reciprocal demand was on an audience having acquired its own second nature, which is to say spectators themselves must also be well-trained. They needed knowledge of, and a taste for, the performance of other participants' skills and this required specialized practice of their own. A deficiency in contemporary German audiences, therefore, explained Nietzsche's seeming philosophical about-face in a later aphorism, "Of the theater," when he judges a typical performance that he attends, as "a nauseous spectacle."[133] The problem does not lie primarily with scripts like "the Fausts and Manfreds" but in the unwillingness and culturally fostered inability of contemporary audiences to prepare themselves. Hence playwrights increasingly respond to what audiences are capable of and/or demanding: namely, an "intoxicating emotional wine" or "entertaining narcotic" for busy people who come to the theater in the evening with "blind and tired eyes" – theater "as the hashish-smoking and betel-chewing of the cultured European."[134]

Let me sharpen the point on the question, though. Exactly how was the transformative effect prepared in Greek theater? For one thing, to maximize overall cognitive sensitivity and perceptive acumen, performances took place on festive occasions. Thus spectators could enter the *theatron* (literally, a place of seeing) not as tired, bored people desiring "distraction" but in a "calm and meditation-promoting" frame of mind possessing "the fresh senses of the early morning."[135] They were additionally primed to be "stimulated" by all manner of intensively crafted sounds and signs attuned to their extraordinary "aesthetic erudition."[136] The actor, says Nietzsche, is a "Dionysian man" insofar as he "possesses the art of communication to the highest degree" and theater encompasses all the sonic and verbal nuances of overt, linguistic forms of communication: "representation, imitation, transfiguration, transmutation, every kind of mimicry and play-acting."[137] Greek actors also utilized "the language of gesture and musical tone" in highly sophisticated, stylized ways.[138] So music and dance had a powerful synergistic effect on the "tone and cadence" of the

---

132   Nietzsche, *The Gay Science*, 80.
133   Nietzsche, *The Gay Science*, 86.
134   Nietzsche, *The Gay Science*, 86.
135   Nietzsche, *Greek Music Drama*, 14.
136   Nietzsche, *Greek Music Drama*, 18.
137   Nietzsche, *Twilight of Idols*, "Skirmishes of an Untimely Man," 10.
138   "The Dionysiac World-View," in Nietzsche, *The Birth of Tragedy and Other Writings*, ed. Raymond Geuss and Ronald Speirs (Cambridge: Cambridge University Press, 1999), 134.

verse[139] integral to the "rhythm" that is the physiological origin of all poetry.[140] As the performance began to build, the increasingly excited spectator started to experience systematic synesthetic effects magnified by her progressive integration into the collective consciousness.

Gary Schapiro gives a fine analysis of the visual process. Architectural design, for instance, forms a physical framing device to facilitate a constantly refocusing of the spectator's eye. The intense activity rippling through this local communication net becomes a fascinating physical/ physiological analogue to Kantian cognitive structuring in which every "framing is also a reframing."[141] Schapiro concludes that *The Birth of Tragedy* is a "story ... about becoming visible, of the arrangement and projection of visual images whether, actual, virtual, or hallucinatory."[142] And the "drama is complete," Nietzsche claims, only when the spectator, enters an "enchanted" state of peak "intoxication" (*Rausch*) as part of a collective "epidemic" and *"sees the god."*[143] Hence clarifying the causal conditions making this culminating audience "vision" of Dionysos possible, is an essential complement to the many excellent accounts of the philosophical meaning gleaned from literary works.[144] For these accounts indirectly corroborate my claim that such a vision lies on the CI axis of the continuum of human consciousness, distinct from characteristic PI make-believe. As such, moreover, Nietzsche distances himself from much theater aesthetics by arguing that "drama does not begin when someone disguises himself and seeks to deceive other people" or specifically, as Shakespeare's Bottom puts it, entertains people by virtue of agreed upon conventions of make-believe.[145] Instead, "the original phenomenon of *drama*" (using the Greek word for "action") is the "experience of seeing oneself transformed before one's eyes and acting as if one had really entered another body, another character."[146]

Frequent references to "the Apolline dream-world" on the stage,[147] then, are apt insofar as PI and CI constitute axes on the same continuum. But this also

---

139 Nietzsche, "The Dionysiac World-View," 137.

140 Nietzsche, *The Gay Science*, 80.

141 Gary Shapiro, "Ubersehen: Nietzsche and Tragic Vision," *Research in Phenomenology* 25, no. 1 (January 1995): 30.

142 Shapiro, "Ubersehen," 37.

143 Nietzsche, *The Birth of Tragedy and Other Writings*, "Birth of Tragedy," 44.

144 To cite just one example, Dionysian wisdom represents "the most terrifying and questionable aspects of our existence in a way that incites us to affirm, rather than deny it." Bernard Reginster, "Art and Affirmation," in *Nietzsche on Art and Life*, ed. Daniel Came (Oxford: Oxford University Press, 2014), 33.

145 Nietzsche, *Greek Music Drama*, 16.

146 Nietzsche, *The Birth of Tragedy*, 43–44.

147 Nietzsche, *The Birth of Tragedy*, 46.

NIETZSCHE ON THEATRICALITY AND IMAGINATION

means that CI's intoxicated theater audience is significantly distinct from PI's dream audience. After all, a trained "spectator's gaze" understands the diverse semiotic mix exploited in the theater, for example, "wax dolls and real flowers stand along side others which are painted" and garish, gigantic masks cover the faces of real people.[148] A person enters the theater voluntarily and assimilates and processes all these communicative sights, sounds, and signs with her entire physiological system alerted and intensely ready, like an athlete entering the arena. And if anything, as Kornhaber puts it, there is a kind of "dual consciousness"[149] in that culminating, performative moment when the spectator transfers "on to that masked figure the whole image of the god ... and dissolves, so to speak, the reality of the figure into a ghostly unreality."[150]

My pragmatic account of CI ensures that Nietzsche's theater aesthetics is free of any neo-Romantic coloring. It also undercuts any attribution of his normative judgments (enthusiastic or critical) to a traumatic personal experience with Wagner. They are logical responses to different varieties of theater rooted in his understanding of CI. But I will conclude with another caution. At the turn of the twentieth century, for example, the avant-garde theater rebelled against naturalists' efforts to create an illusion of reality with which the audience could imaginatively identify. They argued that practitioners should find ways of exploiting the ineradicable tension between what is real and what *Birth of Tragedy* called "semblance" or "unreality" even though this would place tough imaginative demands on the audience (which, in turn, posed commercial risks). Their argument was that this tension distinguishes the medium.[151] Proponents of this change, moreover, rallied under a slogan calling for the "retheatricalization of theater."[152] And in a retrospective look at the lasting effects of this movement, Erika Fischer-Lichte makes significant use of Nietzsche in articulating the nature of the change being advocated. In effect, her position reflects the overall argument of this chapter regarding Nietzsche's transformation of Kant's view of the productive imagination into a rich account of the dynamic relationship between PI and CI. For the effort to retheatricalize theater, she says: tried to "bring about a radical shift of focus from" the problem of how theater can represent a supposedly given reality "to the subjective

---

148 Nietzsche, "The Dionysiac World-View," 133–35.
149 Kornhaber, *The Birth of Theater*, 33.
150 Nietzsche, *The Birth of Tragedy*, 45.
151 For a detailed discussion consistent with the argument of this chapter, see: Roderick Nicholls, "The Fictionality of Theatrical Performance," in *Fiction in Art: Explorations in Contemporary Theory*, ed. Ananta Sukla (London: Bloomsbury Academic, 2015), 263–83.
152 Mary Ann Frese Witt, *Metatheater and Modernity: Baroque and Neobaroque* (Fairleigh Dickinson, 2012), 90.

conditions underlying perception and cognition, and subsequently, to the problem of how to construct reality" in the theater.[153]

References

Barth, J. Robert. *The Symbolic Imagination: Coleridge and the Romantic Tradition*. Princeton, NJ: Princeton University Press, 1977.

Behler, Ernst. "Nietzsche's Conception of Irony." In *Nietzsche, Philosophy, and the Arts.* Edited by Salim Kemal, Ivan Gaskell, and Daniel W. Conway. New York: Cambridge University Press, 1998.

Beiser, Frederick C. *The Romantic Imperative: The Concept of Early German Romanticism*. Cambridge, MA: Harvard University Press, 2006.

Carlson, Marvin. "The Resistance to Theatricality." *SubStance*, no. 2/3 (2002): 238–50.

Dennett, Daniel C. *Consciousness Explained*. Boston, MA: Back Bay Books, 1992.

Dennett, Daniel, D.C. *Intuition Pumps and Other Tools for Thinking*. New York: W.W. Norton & Co, 2013.

Dewey, John. *Art as Experience*. New York: TarcherPerigee, 2005.

Engell, James. *The Creative Imagination: Enlightenment to Romanticism*. Cambridge, MA: Harvard University Press, 1981.

Fischer-Lichte, Erika. "From Theatre to Theatricality: How to Construct Reality." *Theatre Research International* 20, no. 2 (Summer 1995): 97–105.

Ford, Jennifer. *Coleridge on Dreaming: Romanticism, Dreams and the Medical Imagination*. Cambridge: Cambridge University Press, 1998.

Granger, David. "Expression, Imagination, and Organic Unity: John Dewey's Aesthetics and Romanticism." *Journal of Aesthetic Education* 37, no. 2 (2003): 46–60.

Kant, Immanuel. *Critique of Pure Reason*. Translated by N.K. Smith. 2nd edition. Houndmills: Palgrave Macmillan, 1991.

Kornhaber, David. *The Birth of Theater from the Spirit of Philosophy: Nietzsche and the Modern Drama*. Evanston, IL: Northwestern University Press, 2016.

Mul, Jos de. *Romantic Desire in (Post) Modern Art and Philosophy*. Albany, NY: State University of New York Press, 1999.

Nicholls, Roderick. "Care of Self and Amor Fati as a Spiritual Ideal." In *The Philosophy of Spirituality*. Edited by Heather Salazar and Roderick Nicholls, 214–49 Leiden, NL: Brill, 2018.

---

153   Erika Fischer-Lichte, "From Theatre to Theatricality – How to Construct Reality," *Theatre Research International* 20, no. 2 (Summer 1995): 104.

Nicholls, Roderick. "The Fictionality of Theatrical Performance." In *Fiction in Art: Explorations in Contemporary Theory*. Edited by Ananta Sukla, 263–83. London: Bloomsbury Academic, 2015.

Nietzsche. *Daybreak: Thoughts on the Prejudices of Morality by Nietzsche*. Translated by R.J. Hollingdale Cambridge: Cambridge University Press, 1982.

Nietzsche, Friedrich. *Beyond Good and Evil*. Edited by Michael Tanner. Translated by R.J. Hollingdale. London: Penguin, 2003.

Nietzsche, Friedrich. *Dawn: Thoughts on the Presumptions of Morality*. Translated by Brittain Smith. Stanford, CA: Stanford University Press, 2011.

Nietzsche, Friedrich. *Greek Music Drama*. Edited by Jill Dr Marsden. Translated by Paul Bishop. New York: Contra Mundum Press, 2013.

Nietzsche, Friedrich. *Human, All Too Human 1 / A Book For Free Spirits*. Translated by Gary Handwerk. Stanford, CA: Stanford University Press, 1997.

Nietzsche, Friedrich, "On Truth and Lying in a Non-Moral Sense" in *The Birth of Tragedy and Other Writings*. Edited by Raymond Geuss, and Ronald Speirs, 141–53. Cambridge: Cambridge University Press, 1999.

Nietzsche, Friedrich. *The Birth of Tragedy and Other Writings*. Edited by Raymond Geuss and Ronald Speirs. Cambridge: Cambridge University Press, 1999.

Nietzsche, Friedrich. The Dionysiac World View in *The Birth of Tragedy and Other Writings*. Edited by Raymond Geuss, and Ronald Speirs, 141–53. Cambridge: Cambridge University Press, 1999.

Nietzsche, Friedrich. *The Gay Science*. Translated by Walter Kaufmann. New York: Vintage Books, 1974.

Nietzsche, Friedrich. *The Will to Power*. Edited by Walter Kaufmann. Translated by Walter Kaufmann, and R.J. Hollingdale. New York: Vintage Books, 1968.

Nietzsche, Friedrich. *Twilight of Idols and Anti-Christ*. Edited by Michael Tanner. Translated by R.J. Hollingdale. London: Penguin, 1990.

Norman, Judith. "Nietzsche and Early Romanticism." *Journal of the History of Ideas* 63, no. 3 (2002): 501–19.

Parkes, Graham. *Composing the Soul: Reaches of Nietzsche's Psychology*. Chicago: University of Chicago Press, 1996.

Polanyi, Michael. *The Tacit Dimension*. New York: DoubleDay & Co., 1966.

Puchner, Martin. "Kenneth Burke: Theater, Philosophy, and the Limits of Performance." In *Staging Philosophy: Intersections of Theater, Performance, and Philosophy*. Edited by David Krasner, and David Z. Saltz, 41–56. Ann Arbor, MI: University of Michigan Press, 2006.

Reginster, Bernard. "Art and Affirmation." In *Nietzsche on Art and Life*. Edited by Daniel Came. Oxford: Oxford University Press, 2014.

Rorty, Richard. *Contingency, Irony, and Solidarity*. Cambridge: Cambridge University Press, 1989.

Rorty, Richard. *Truth and Progress: Philosophical Papers.* Cambridge: Cambridge University Press, 1998.

Ryle, Gilbert. *On Thinking.* Edited by Konstantin Kolenda. New edition. Oxford: Blackwell Publishers, 1982.

Shapiro, Gary. "Ubersehen: Nietzsche and Tragic Vision." *Research in Phenomenology* 25, no. 1 (January 1995): 27–44.

Witt, Mary Ann Frese. *Metatheater and Modernity: Baroque and Neobaroque.* Vancouver, CA: Fairleigh Dickinson, 2012.

PART 5

Postmodern Perspectives

∴

CHAPTER 16

Simulacral Imagination and the Nexus of Power in a Post-Marxist Universe

Keith Moser

At the end of the 1960s, Jean Baudrillard and Michel Serres astutely observed that controlling the means of disseminating information to the masses was on the verge of becoming more important than regulating the production of primary materials in the capitalist paradigm. These unconventional and highly original thinkers predicted that this trajectory, which ultimately culminated in the advent of the era of information, would soon become even more pronounced in Western civilization. In spite of the evident fundamental differences that exist between Baudrillard and Serres, they both realized that this decisive change would forever alter the very nature of power itself in the modern world. In comparison to their more widely read Marxist colleagues from the aforementioned time period who continued to propose outdated theories about a society revolving almost exclusively around the production of material goods, Baudrillard and Serres attempted to generate a fresh new perspective about power and how it is now wielded. Specifically, both philosophers posit that semiosis is the basis of social control in the contemporary landscape epitomized and dominated by omnipresent technology that has permeated every facet of our quotidian existence. Baudrillard and Serres's post-Marxist vision, which reflects a new human condition, implores us to think harder about the veritable origins of power in consumer republics.[1] They insist that "the products of imagination"[2] endlessly devoured by consumer citizens represent a different kind of authority that derives its force from "well-controlled and prescribed images"[3] connected to "the tension between appearances and reality."[4]

---

1   The historian Lizabeth Cohen originally coined the expression "consumer republic." See Lizabeth Cohen, *A Consumers' Republic: The Politics of Consumption in Postwar America* (New York: Vintage Books, 2003).
2   Nick Wiltsher and Aaron Meskin, "Art and Imagination," in *The Routledge Handbook of Philosophy of Imagination*, ed. Amy Kind (London: Routledge, 2016), 182.
3   Ivana Markova, "From Imagination to Well-Controlled Images," in *Handbook of Imagination and Culture*, eds. Tania Zittoun and Vlad Glaveanu (Oxford: Oxford University Press, 2017), 338.
4   Dennis Sansom, "Can Irony Enrich the Aesthetic Imagination?: Why Søren Kierkegaard's Explanation of Irony Is Better Than Richard Rorty's," *The Journal of Aesthetic Education* 51, no. 2 (2017): 17.

Although Baudrillard and Serres both assert that consumerist signs concretize the nexus of power, they reach strikingly dissimilar conclusions about the inception of the digital age in their late philosophy. Whereas the increasing sophistication and proliferation of virtual technology convince Baudrillard that resistance to the new social order predicated upon commercial simulacra is futile, Serres envisions that the birth of the digital era could decentralize power like never before and lead to an unprecedented democratization of knowledge. Given the apparent disdain that the philosopher expresses for those that use (mis-)information as a hegemonic tool to expand their sphere of influence or to maintain their privileged social position in numerous works, the Serres scholar William Paulson notes this "surprising turn" in recent works such as *Petite Poucette*.[5] As the end of this essay will explore, Serres makes a critical distinction between various types of electronic mediums that justifies his cautious optimism and eliminates this theoretical ambivalence. The philosopher's detractors like Julien Gautier have heavily criticized his humanistic aspirations for the creation of a more sustainable, peaceful, democratic, and just world linked to the Internet, but the final section of this chapter will highlight that Serres's rather positive outlook is grounded in sound interdisciplinary logic.[6] The fact that Baudrillard and Serres develop equally compelling, discordant frameworks for understanding how the digital revolution has modified the essence of power demonstrates the complex nuances of this subject. Moreover, their late philosophy also underscores the uncertainty of the changing world in which the modern subject now lives.

1   The Crisis of Late Capitalism and the Birth of a New Social Order through Signs

Even though Baudrillard and Serres adopt radically different positions about the importance of the Internet in the context of this discussion, they both identify the "crisis of late capitalism" as the historical origin of this profound social transformation. According to theorists and researchers like Fredric Jameson, Paul Mattick, Vartan Messier, Andrew Koch, and Rick Elmore,[7] the capitalist

---

5   William Paulson, "Writing that Matters," *SubStance* 83 (1997): 35.

6   Julien Gautier, "La douteuse fable de Michel Serres." *Revue Skhole.fr*, June 25 2013. http://skhole.fr/petite-poucette-la-douteuse-fable-de-michel-serres.

7   See Fredric Jameson, *Late Marxism: Adorno, or, The Persistence of the Dialectic* (New York: Verso, 1990); Paul Mattick, *Economic Crisis and Crisis Theory* (New York: Routledge, 1981); Vartan Messier, "Consumerism After Theory: Globalization and the End of Transnational Discourse in Néstor García Canclini's Cultural Empiricism," *ATENEA* 28, no. 1 (2007): 21–40; and

model suddenly found itself in a dire predicament around World War II. In a society in which "all of the basic needs of the masses have been satisfied," the limits of production had been reached.[8] Since the capitalist paradigm relies upon constant growth and expansion in order to sustain itself, it needed to evolve drastically if it was to survive. In comparison to the finite nature of production itself, the imagination knows no bounds. For this reason, marketers would begin to promote the unbridled consumption of utopian images "laden with purely symbolic meaning" denoting a chimerical, consumerist paradise that has never existed anywhere with the exception of a digital screen.[9] In this vein, the post-Marxist view of power contends that nearly every purchase is a misguided attempt to procure metonymical pieces of an exploitative dream conceived for the sole purpose of generating revenue for a corporation. Instead of disappearing in the midst of a crisis, the capitalist system found a way to reinvent and reinforce itself by selling prepackaged fantasies with no basis in reality. Far from being innocent forms of idealistic reverie or escapism, the ubiquitous simulations of the good(s) life[10] that bombard the modern subject from all sides in the hyper-real space serve a hegemonic function that is vital to the continued survival of the capitalist model.

In their analysis of late capitalism and Baudrillard's philosophy, Emil André Røyrvik and Marianne Blom Brodersen explain, "In the postmodern society of simulation and hyperreality, Baudrillard contends that capitalism is organized around sign-values. The modern logic of production has ended, the referent as well as depth, essence and any 'outside' have all disappeared and societies are organized around the play of images, signs, codes and models."[11] Offering a similar interpretation of Baudrillard's reworking of the concept of symbolic power in global society as Røyrvik and Brodersen, Douglas Kellner declares, "we live in 'hyperreality' of simulations in which images, spectacles and the play of signs (or simulacra) replace the logic of production and class conflict as key constituents of contemporary societies."[12] Røyrvik, Brodersen, and Kellner highlight Baudrillard's deep conviction that production itself is no longer the

---

Andrew Koch and Rick Elmore, "Simulation and Symbolic Exchange: Jean Baudrillard's Augmentation of Marx's Theory of Value," *Politics & Policy* 34, no. 3 (2006): 556–75.

8   Messier, "Consumerism After Theory," 25.

9   Koch and Elmore, "Simulation and Symbolic Exchange," 565.

10   I originally created this term in my monograph *J.M.G. Le Clézio: A Concerned Citizen of the Global Village* (2012).

11   Emil Royrvik and Marianne Brodersen, "Real Virtuality: Power and Simulation in the Age of Neoliberal Crisis," *Culture Unbound* 4 (2013): 639.

12   Douglas Kellner, "Baudrillard, Semiurgy and Death," *Theory, Culture & Society* 4, vol. 1 (1987): 129.

most salient feature of the capitalist system. Evidently, Baudrillard does not theorize that production no longer occurs at all in Western society. Baudrillard maintains that the production of primary materials is of secondary importance compared to what commercial goods and services *represent* in a carefully manufactured, imaginary symbolic realm. After peeling back the thick layers of semiosis that conceal the banality of the images that we consume on a daily basis, Baudrillard argues that the actual use-value of the myriad of gadgets that we endlessly acquire to keep the monetary wheels spinning is quite limited. In essence, brainwashed clients constantly obey the summons to devour hyper-real simulacra, thereby submitting themselves to the new invisible social order without realizing it.

In reference to this calculated onslaught of commercial signs that has obliterated any meaningful distinction between public and private space, as Kelly Maddox notes in her Baudrillardian exploration of the nefarious effects of mass media saturation,[13] Baudrillard reveals, "Neo-functionalism will be in the image of neo-capitalism, that is to say, an intensification of the play of signifiers, a mathematization and cybernetization by the code ... The era of the signified and its function is over, it's the era of the signifier and of the code that has begun."[14] In this passage from Baudrillard's early essay *Pour une critique de l'économie politique du signe*, the philosopher hypothesizes that the pervasiveness of the hyper-real code has ushered in a new historical era in which (mis-) information itself is synonymous with power. By distancing himself from outmoded Marxist theories related to class conflicts, Baudrillard tries to uncover the true source of power that lurks beneath the surface of the seductive image. In *Pour une critique de l'économie politique du signe* and throughout his entire *œuvre*, the philosopher exposes "the hegemony of a code" that billions of customers around the globe instinctively internalize in the absence of critical reflection.[15] Due to the colossal gap between these signs and actual concrete reality, Baudrillard explains that most clients are merely pledging their allegiance to empty, contrived simulations when they purchase a given item in a store or online. For Baudrillard, the skillful imposition of image-based reality is the latest and most repressive form of subjugation ever conceived. In simple terms, the *simulacral*

---

13   Kelly Maddox, "Au-delà des frontières: Société de consommation et écriture migrante dans Un Petit pas pour l'homme de Stéphane Dompierre," *Voix Plurielles* 2 (2008): 91. The complicity of the mainstream media in the creation and transmission of hyper-real fantasies will be explored in the following section of the essay.

14   Jean Baudrillard, *Pour une critique de l'économie politique du signe* (Paris: Gallimard,1972), 248. All English translations are my own unless otherwise indicated.

15   Baudrillard, *Pour une critique de l'économie politique du signe*, 250.

imagination is "an instrumental apparatus for social control and domination by political authorities and other powerful institutions."[16]

Similar to Baudrillard, theories related to the crisis of late capitalism and the reconstitution of power through hyper-real codes have been at the forefront of Serres's thought for nearly half a century. Starting with the first volume of the *Hermès* series published in 1968, Serres boldly hypothesizes that communication has already begun to take precedence over production. As Roy Boyne asserts, "his five books, with the collective title *Hermès: la communication*, were based on the idea that communication in contemporary Western societies had become more important than production."[17] Despite being initially ostracized by his more famous Marxist colleagues and excluded from trendy philosophical circles[18] because of his post-Marxist observations and reflections, as Alexis Feertchak underscores, Serres would continue to refine his novel ideas about communication and symbolic power.[19] In his seminal work *Le Parasite,* the philosopher concludes, "Assessment, in the beginning was production ... I would like to know what that even means to produce ... Production without a doubt is rare"[20] Like Baudrillard, Serres contends that production is no longer the main driving force of late capitalism. As the philosopher posits in *Le Parasite,* the capitalist paradigm was forced to adapt to a new situation.

In a revealing conversation with Raoul Mortley, Serres affirms, "I myself thought ... that production was not important in our society, or that it was becoming much less so, but what was important was communication, and that we were reaching a culture, or society, in which communication would hold precedence over production."[21] Later in this same exchange, he further reiterates, "The group of technologies which have now passed into everyday life, which range from telephone communications, for example, to data processing and computers. That technology has in my view meant far more in the modern world than the production of primary materials." In this interview, Serres

---

16   Majid Yar, *The Cultural Imaginary of the Internet: Virtual Utopias and Dystopias* (Basingstoke, UK: Palgrave Macmillan, 2014), 51.

17   Roy Boyne, "Angels in the Archive: Lines Into the Future in the Work of Jacques Derrida and Michel Serres," *Cultural Values* 2, no. 2–3 (1998): 208.

18   In this regard, it should be noted that Serres was forced to teach in history departments for much of his academic career. In the dedication of his essay *Rome,* Serres recounts the inner turmoil induced by this marginalization.

19   Alexis Feertchak, "Michel Serres ou le joyeux Pantope," *Iphilo,* April 26, 2014, https://iphilo.fr/2014/04/26/michel-serres-ou-le-joyeux-pantope/.

20   Michel Serres, *Le Parasite* (Paris: Grasset, 1980), 10–11.

21   Raoul Mortley, "Chapter III: Michel Serres," in *French Philosophers in Conversation: Levinas, Schneider, Serres, Irigaray, Le Doeuff, Derrida,* ed. Raoul Mortley (New York: Routledge, 1991), 51.

encourages mainstream philosophers to transcend the limitations of Marxist thought in an attempt to comprehend the complexity and paradoxes that are emblematic of the power struggles of the twenty-first century more fully. In another discussion with David Webb in the context of Serres's "relatively new concept of communication," the philosopher offers the following synopsis of the philosophical and professional journey that led him to focus on the unending exchange of signs mediated through technology instead of the traditional emphasis on the regulation of primary materials in most academic arenas:

> It was then that I parted ways, breaking with the vulgate shared by most philosophers of the time, which was broadly speaking a Marxist one (especially with Althusser at the Ecole Normale), and which sought to foreground problems of production. I said no, the society of tomorrow will be a society of communication and not a society of production. The problems of production are virtually resolved in the West, and it is the problems of communication that will now take center stage.[22]

Given that the modern subject is fully immersed in a technologized world from birth that only vaguely resembles the one described by Karl Marx, Serres maintains that this new historical and social development requires different paradigms for understanding the nexus from which power emanates. From 1968 to the present, Serres's philosophy has attempted to address all of the most pertinent issues that confront modern humans whose quotidian experiences are vastly different from their not-so-distant predecessors.[23]

In his lengthy essay *Hominescence* in which he most clearly articulates his vision of the appearance of this new type of humanity inextricably linked to the age of information, it is apparent that Serres possesses a rich historical and philosophical perspective of the phenomenon of exploitation through semiosis. In *Hominescence*, the philosopher reminds the reader that ancient civilizations like the Carthaginians exercised social control through the symbolic realm of spectacle.[24] Thus, Serres insists that this form of symbolic power is not entirely a new philosophical problem. As Ivana Markova reveals, "It has

---

22 David Webb, "The Science of Relations: An Interview," *Angelaki* 8, no. 2 (2003): 230.

23 Since we now appear to share very little in common with our human ancestors for various reasons linked to the rise of technology and the birth of modern medicine, Serres argues that it is time for contemporary philosophers to start discussing a new human condition. For a more comprehensive explanation of Serres's theories about this new type of humanity, see Chapter three from my latest book *The Encyclopedic Philosophy of Michel Serres: Writing the Modern World and Anticipating the Future* (2016).

24 Michel Serres, *Hominescence* (Paris: Editions Le Pommier, 2001), 193.

been well known since the origins of humankind that all kinds of social groups, political and religious regimes, institutions, and the media manipulate, transform, and channel images through the enforced routes by persuasion and influence."[25] Nonetheless, he also adamantly argues that modern *Homo sapiens* have created powerful exo-Darwinian[26] tools that allow us to harness the seductive force of semiosis like never before. The omnipresent influence of the technological devices through which the vast majority of our experiences are now filtered has taken this phenomenon to unparalleled heights. Serres explains that simulations have never spellbound the masses to this alarming extent. As an encyclopedic epistemologist with deep humanistic affinities, Serres has always devoted a considerable amount of attention to trying to understand the nature of hegemonic power and how to engage in peaceful resistance to it. Serres's tireless efforts to comprehend this new social order characterized by a constant barrage of meaningless, commercial simulacra made him perfectly suited from the very beginning to be "the first ... philosopher of information."[27]

2 The Passive Medium of Television and the Pervasive Influence of the Corporate Establishment Media

In addition to outlining a similar assessment of the post-Marxist conditions that forced the capitalist paradigm to shift its focus, Baudrillard and Serres blame the same hegemonic entities for their complicity in the transmission of the hyper-real fictions impulsively consumed by the archetypical "citizen consumer."[28] In particular, both philosophers deconstruct the pervasive notion of the corporate establishment media as a benevolent fourth estate that protects public interests. As opposed to being a "watchdog," Baudrillard and Serres illustrate that the transnational corporations that own the means of releasing (mis-)information to the masses have a vested interest in ensuring that a system from which they derive unheralded profits is never questioned. In this regard, it is noteworthy that six multinational companies (Disney, Viacom, Time Warner, General Electric, CBS, and News-Corp) control ninety percent of

---

25 Markova, "From Imagination to Well-Controlled Images," 338–39.

26 For a more comprehensive explanation of Serres's concept of exo-Darwinian evolution that transcends the pragmatic limitations of this essay, see pages 217–18 from *Récits d'humanisme* in addition to *Hominescence* and *L'Incandescent*.

27 Fanie De Beer, "Methodology and Noology: Amazing Prospects for Library and Information Science," *SA Jnl Libs & Info Sci* 77, no. 1 (2011): 87.

28 Jean Baudrillard, *Le Système des objets* (Paris: Gallimard, 1968), 218.

the American media.[29] Highlighting that it is not by accident that the world's most influential and lucrative corporations have taken over media outlets all around the world, the media researcher Andrew Kennis explains, "Today's corporate conglomerate-driven commercial media … was constructed as a result of a concerted effort of business interests."[30] By determining how information is filtered and packaged for the immediate consumption of acritical, purchaser citizens, who are constantly inundated with commercial propaganda that lauds the alleged virtues of consumerism, the corporate titans who own the media are easily able to "manufacture consent" to the new social order from a Chomskyian perspective. Baudrillard and Serres demonstrate that the establishment media could be accurately described as a hegemonic weapon of the integrated political and social elite designed for the purpose of keeping the "bewildered herd" in line.[31] From the onset, the goal of handing over the reins of the media to transnational entities was the creation of a docile, submissive citizenry that would blindly support the status quo.

Owing to this total domination, Baudrillard claims that it is no longer possible to "think against the current hegemony"[32] in an era in which "the dialectical stage, the critical stage is empty."[33] In essence, Baudrillard affirms that "all 'critical distance' … has vanished into the play of signs."[34] In response to theorists like Mel Alexenberg who advocate for the development of a critical visual literacy[35] in order to minimize the effects of virtual immersion linked to a corporate agenda, Baudrillard argues that no one can "maintain a 'critical' position in the face of dramatic global transformations which seem to absorb all opposition."[36] In an article entitled "'Self-Immolation by Technology': Jean

---

29   Ashley Lutz, "These 6 Corporations Control 90% of the Media in America," *Business Insider*, June 2012. https://www.businessinsider.com/these-6-corporations-control-90-of-the-media-in-america-2012-6.

30   Andrew Kennis, "Theorizing and Historicizing the Media Dependence Model." (Presentation, Annual Meeting of the International Communication Association, Chicago, May 21, 2009), 4.

31   Noam Chomsky, *Media Control: The Spectacular Achievements of Propaganda* (New York: Open Media Series, 2002), 27.

32   Anthony King, "Baudrillard's Nihilism and the End of Theory," *Telos* 2 (1998): 89.

33   Jean Baudrillard, *Simulacra and Simulation*, trans. Sheila Glaser (Ann Arbor: University of Michigan, 1994), 161.

34   Richard Smith. "Baudrillard's Nonrepresentational Theory: Burn the Signs and Journey Without Maps," *Environment and Planning D: Society and Space* 21, no. 1 (2003): 79.

35   See Mel Alexenberg, *Educating Artists for the Future: Learning at the Intersections of Art, Science, Technology, and Culture* (Chicago: University of Chicago Press, 2008).

36   King, "Baudrillard's Nihilism and the End of Theory," 89.

SIMULACRAL IMAGINATION AND THE NEXUS OF POWER

Baudrillard and the Posthuman in Film and Television,"[37] Jon Baldwin probes the concept of "digital reduction" that is closely tied to Baudrillard's notion of the "murder of the real." Providing an operational definition of this term and summarizing Baudrillard's stance, Baldwin reveals, "In digital reduction we witness the supersession, in Baudrillard's terms, of the symbolic, alterity and singularity of the human by the semiotic, simulation and technological."[38] For Baudrillard, we are immersed in a symbolic world of floating signifiers conceived by the aforementioned political and social elite through digital technology that now concretizes the totality of the social imaginary in which consumer citizens dwell.

In *Pour une critique de l'économie politique du signe*, Baudrillard explains that the evident mission of the corporate media apparatus is to ensure that a meaningful dialogue about real issues related to social injustice and inequality never transpires. Positing that no genuine communication is taking place at all when purchaser citizens internalize exploitative codes that are utterly divorced from reality, Baudrillard declares, "What characterizes the mass media is that they are anti-mediators, intransitive, they create non-communication if one accepts the definition of communication as an exchange."[39] In this passage, Baudrillard asserts that any kind of authentic exchange between an artificial, banal sign merely conjured for the sake of unloading a surplus of goods in a post-Marxist climate is impossible. The relationship between commercial simulacra and the clients that are expected to consume them frivolously is one-dimensional. Furthermore, in this section of the essay, the philosopher contends that the properties of the dominant medium itself (i.e. the television) through which these hegemonic messages are broadcasted to the masses hinder communication to the point of preventing it from occurring at all.

According to Baudrillard, the problem is that the television viewer has a passive, one-sided relationship with the object through which he or she devours simulations for countless hours each day. As the late Baudrillard scholar Gerry Coulter underscores, "Television is the ideal medium of a hyper-real world because it is image-based and between reality and the image exchange is impossible."[40] Clearly articulating his philosophical position about the

---

37   Jon Baldwin, "'Self-Immolation by Technology': Jean Baudrillard and the Posthuman in Film and Television," in *The Palgrave Handbook of Posthumanism in Film and Television*, eds. Michael Hauskeller, Thomas Philbeck, and Curtis Carbonell (New York: Palgrave Macmillan, 2015), 19–27.

38   Baldwin, "Self-Immolation by Technology," 19.

39   Baudrillard, *Pour une critique de l'économie politique du signe*, 208.

40   Gerry Coulter, *Jean Baudrillard: From the Ocean to the Desert, or the Poetics of Radicality* (New York: Intertheory, 2012), 28.

deleterious effects of television, Baudrillard affirms, "There is no *response* to this functional object ... The television by its mere presence represents social control at home ... it is the certainty that people no longer speak to each other, that they are definitively isolated from each other facing words for which there is no response."[41] First, Baudrillard outlines how the invention of the television fundamentally changed the dynamics of human relationships. In many households, the television set is constantly illuminated, and everyone who is present silently watches the images that flicker across the screen. Even people who live under the same roof often barely speak to each other at all because their eyes are glued to the television at nearly all times. Instead of paying attention to issues that impact the quality of their lives and those around them, the television viewer invests all of his or her emotions in contrived distractions.

Isolated from any real human interaction, Baudrillard theorizes that our symbolic defenses are weak. Quickly recognizing the comatose-like mental state actuated by this medium, journalists and marketers seized the opportunity to flood these clients with idealistic simulacra representing an enticing, utopian realm linked to the social act of consumption. Baudrillard's theories about the passive nature of this particular electronic medium offer an intriguing lens for explaining the inability of the modern subject to challenge the fantasy-based, imaginary structure of simulations that are so far-fetched and ludicrous that they should be automatically dismissed. There is often a disconcerting lack of scrutiny regarding commercial signs, because we are used to spending most of our time in a hyper-real space in which we are unable to respond at all. Additionally, Baudrillard maintains that the television is the perfect vehicle for the corporate mainstream media to promulgate their prefabricated version of events. In a space that facilitates non-communication, acceptance, and compliance, the validity of the information being reported by journalists who are presented "with a script, a screenplay, that has to be followed unswervingly" in advance is rarely questioned.[42] The fact that many television reporters repeat the same exact lines verbatim when discussing current events, a disquieting phenomenon that is often satirized on programs like *The Daily Show*, gives credence to Baudrillard's notion that journalists are not allowed by their corporate bosses to deviate from the official master narrative whatsoever. As opposed to trying to represent reality from the most objective standpoint possible, Baudrillard suggests that most mainstream reporters mindlessly disseminate signs of the real. The philosopher describes journalists as marionettes who have to answer to the transnational puppeteers who are pulling the strings behind the

---

41   Baudrillard, *Pour une critique de l'économie politique du signe*, 211.

42   Jean Baudrillard, *The Intelligence of Evil*, trans. Chris Turner (New York: Berg, 2005), 124.

SIMULACRAL IMAGINATION AND THE NEXUS OF POWER 391

stage of these media (pseudo-) spectacles.[43] For Baudrillard, mainstream news coverage creates its own (hyper-) reality that substitutes itself for the real thing in the collective imagination of the viewer that consumes it as an image. In this manner, Baudrillard steadfastly asserts that the establishment media does not serve the role of keeping politicians honest or protecting us from illegitimate manifestations of authority, but rather it is a deep-seated form of oppression connected to a larger framework of exploitation.

Numerous researchers like Steven Connor, Gaspare Polizzi, Trina Marmarelli, and William Paulson[44] highlight that Serres also expresses the same derision for both the mainstream media and television. Similar to Baudrillard, Serres implies that the modern subject has been "taken over by the media and advertising."[45] In several works, Serres decries "the essence of a public seduced into consumption and advertising."[46] Like Baudrillard, Serres laments that television viewers are unreflective automatons who passively internalize consumerist simulacra without any regard for their verisimilitude. In two separate conversations with Michel Polacco and Darius Rochebin, which will be further analyzed in the final section of this chapter, the philosopher describes the television viewer as an obedient zombie that is unable to engage in critical reflection about the commercial images he or she consumes on a regular basis.

In his essay *Atlas*, Serres also makes a similar philosophical claim as Baudrillard concerning the imposition of a hyper-real realm of (mis-)information deliberately propagated by the corporate establishment media. Clearly dismissing the notion of the media as a fourth estate, the philosopher maintains, "information creates reality, far from representing it, it influences public opinion, it often substitutes itself for judicial power ... defines truth ... in order to ensure its dominance in the world at large ... Power belongs to those who own these channels."[47] In reference to the "white power of the virtual," Serres further elucidates in *Hominescence*, "what roles do these media networks play in today's societies? ... Due to their internal structure itself, these networks create another reality, another society, a new ideology, another type of education,

---

43   For a discussion of Baudrillard's theories related to media pseudo-events, see William Merrin, "Implosion, Simulation and the Pseudo-Event: A Critique of McLuhan," *Economy and Society* 31, no. 3 (2002): 369–90.

44   See Steven Connor, "Thinking Things," *Textual Practice* 24, no. 1 (2010): 1–20; Gaspare Polizzi, and Trina Marmarelli, "Hermetism, Messages, and Angels," *Configurations* 8, no. 2 (2000): 245–70; and William Paulson, "Writing that Matters," 22–36.

45   Steven Connor, "Michel Serres's Les Cinq sens," in *Mapping Michel Serres*, ed. Niran Abbas (Ann Arbor, MI: University of Michigan Press, 2005), 166.

46   Polizzi and Marmarelli, "Hermetism, Messages, and Angels," 261.

47   Michel Serres, *Atlas* (Paris: Editions Julliard, 1994), 179, 179.

another kind of politics and so on, another way of being and another type of truth ... Leaving the role of representing a reality that is already there behind, they play the role of creating their own."[48] According to Baudrillard and Serres, the extremely redundant information[49] endlessly transmitted to us by news outlets is not indicative of a sincere effort to frame reality for the benefit of the public at large, but rather this steady stream of simulacra creates its own alternative (hyper-)reality that reflects the core of a new social order. In these passages from *Atlas* and *Hominescence*, Serres explains that transnational entities hijacked the media because they realized that a new form of power was possible through the omnipresent exchange of signs in informational vectors. Positing that this dream of controlling the populace through ubiquitous representations has succeeded beyond the wildest imagination of the simulators of (hyper-)reality, Serres concludes, "Are we ignoring today the omnipotence of the media and its sounds and images, for which there is no counter-power?"[50] Given that the corporate media apparatus now controls much of the information superhighway, Serres argues that there are very few obstacles that stand in the way of the goal of creating subservient, acritical, and indoctrinated citizens who are incapable of questioning the semiotic, hegemonic forces that enslave them.

Leaving little room for doubt that he considers the corporate mainstream media to be one of the most tyrannical and debasing manifestations of covert power ever conceived, Serres provocatively compares the multinational companies that own the dominant informational channels to the Taliban. As the philosopher contends, "We are thus condemned to choose between multinationals and the Taliban."[51] Serres further explains, "a powerful financial group can control access to posters, announcements, and noises in order to monopolize any definition of culture. Due to repetition in all places at all times, it transforms this into dollars."[52] Although the comparison between the corporate establishment media and terrorist groups like the Taliban might seem to be exaggerated, Serres's intentions are rather clear. In *L'Incandescent,* the philosopher tries to shock the reader out of his or her complacency by revealing dubious, hidden forms of power that operate through exploitative codes. Serres

---

48   Michel Serres, *Hominescence* (Paris: Editions Le Pommier, 2001), 212.

49   In this regard, Serres affirms in *Les cinq sens*, "The media propagates a few hundred words and takes advantage of flaws or vulgarity ... to sell more (products)." (Paris: Editions Grasset et Fasquelle, 1985), 377.

50   Michel Serres, *Rameaux* (Paris: Editions Le Pommier. 2004), 145.

51   Michel Serres, *L'Incandescent* (Paris: Editions Le Pommier. 2003), 137.

52   Serres, *L'Incandescent*, 137.

SIMULACRAL IMAGINATION AND THE NEXUS OF POWER 393

attempts to stimulate a fruitful dialogue about the oppressive nature of the signs that we often consume without a passing thought.

Baudrillard and Serres articulate the same apprehension about the pivotal role of the mainstream media in the inception of hyper-reality and in the appearance of a new social order. Nevertheless, Serres's theories about the establishment media are even more complex and multifaceted than those of Baudrillard. Specifically, Serres posits that the media serves a dual purpose in contemporary global society. In addition to promoting the hollow virtues of consumerism, the philosopher asserts that the overwhelmingly macabre content of news reports is a vestige of what René Girard calls the "sacred." In the Girardian view of violence, sacred remedies are sacrificial substitutes designed to reduce or minimize bloody mimetic conflicts that could easily spiral out of control. According to Girard, whose understanding of violence has profoundly influenced Serres by his own admission, sacred solutions for curtailing aggression would gradually enter into the symbolic realm in Western civilization. In this vein, the act of consuming symbolic representations of death and carnage on the screen allows the subject to satisfy his or her cathartic fix, thereby preventing real conflicts from tearing apart the social fabric at its seams.

Theorizing that devouring grotesque simulations is indeed a hidden remnant of the sacred, Serres declares, "Put yourself in front of the television and watch the news from the morning, to the afternoon, to the evening; take out your pencil and just count the word that is repeated the most often ... Well, it's the word 'death'; or the word 'cadaver' or the image of a dead body or the word 'victim.'"[53] The philosopher's content analysis of the most frequent words and images that bombard us when we watch the news underscores that simulated violence has another objective that far transcends its entertainment value.[54] Later in this same televised exchange with Michel Polacco, Serres summarizes his ideas about the sacred function of the media. As the philosopher himself explains, "I have begun to think of the media as an immense Church,[55] a Church that harks back to human sacrifice, to polytheistic violence, to funerary rituals of death ... that are always present. The media plays the role of a fundamentalist Church that is always talking about death ... How could the West not be melancholic? From *hors-d'oeuvres* to dessert, we only consume

---

53   Michel Polacco, *Michel Serres: Petites chroniques du dimanche soir* (Paris: Editions Le Pommier, 2006), 207–08.

54   The undeniable popularity of the "Faces of Death" series, banned in several countries, demonstrates that simulations of death and extreme violence are both "entertaining" and lucrative. See Michael Patrick Welch's article entitled "Lifting the Mask from 'Faces of Death.'"

55   This word is capitalized in the original French multiple times in this passage.

death."[56] Even though outlets for venting frustration in a more appropriate and less destructive fashion than resorting to actual violence are theoretically devised to prevent even greater atrocities from transpiring, Serres highlights the adverse consequences of these signs. The philosopher hypothesizes that it is difficult to have a positive outlook on life when one is constantly surrounded by such morose simulations. Moreover, these simulacra also protect the system from the indignation of those at the bottom of the ladder who are not reaping any benefits from the current socioeconomic paradigm. Instead of voicing their outrage in a subversive manner that could undermine the privileges of the integrated political and social elite, purchaser citizens are trained to release their aggression in an imaginary, symbolic space that is disconnected from the true source of their anger. This purging of negative emotions through the consumption of signs quells any semblance of genuine revolt that could prove to be detrimental to the establishment. The endless assault of morbid simulacra including depictions of extreme violence is yet another hegemonic strategy related to the redistribution of power and wealth in the modern world.

3 The Deleterious Effects of Proliferation and the Destruction of Reality

In their voracious zeal to eliminate dissent and to manufacture consent to the new world order, Baudrillard and Serres affirm that the simulators of hyperreality have eroded the real in the process. Baudrillard's key concept of proliferation, which is also a recurring theme in Serres's philosophy as well, explains how this disquieting phenomenon has occurred. Offering an operational definition for the notion of proliferation and what it encompasses in his thought, Baudrillard opines, "by giving you a little too much one takes away everything ... the more immersed one becomes in the accumulation of signs, and the more enclosed one becomes in the endless over-signification of a real that no longer exists."[57] Baudrillard's concept of proliferation asserts that simulations have become so ubiquitous that "there is nothing outside of their operational logics."[58] As Douglas Kellner underscores, "*Radical semiurgy*, the production and proliferation of signs, has created a society of simulations governed by

---

56 Polacco, *Michel Serres: Petites chroniques du dimanche soir*, 208–10.

57 Jean Baudrillard, *Seduction*, trans. Brian Singer (New York: St. Martin's Press, 1990), 30–33.

58 Ross Abbinnett, "The Spectre and the Simulacrum," *Theory, Culture & Society* 25, no. 6 (2008): 69–70.

hyperreality ... As simulations proliferate, they come to refer only to themselves: a carnival of mirrors reflecting images projected from other mirrors onto the omnipresent television screen ... *No exit.* Caught up in the universe of simulations."[59] Baudrillard describes the modern subject as a mindless consumer robot that is drowning in a sea of enticing, insignificant signs at all times. The philosopher's concept of proliferation highlights that the self-referential network of commercial simulacra through which we experience the world has become so extensive that it encompasses all facets of our existence.

According to Baudrillard, the far-reaching effects of proliferation have led to an "acute crisis of simulation."[60] We no longer have any meaningful frame of reference to anything that exists outside of the logic of the code. The philosopher contends that our tenuous grasp of reality has been withered away by the signs that have replaced the real for all intents and purposes. The extreme proliferation of consumerist simulacra explains how we have lost the ability to distinguish between concrete reality and its omnipresent symbolic representation on our plethora of screens. Highlighting our increasing incapacity to discern between reality and its simulation, Andrew Root muses, "What is real? In our media-filled world, have we mistaken the image for the real thing."[61] Root further reiterates, "an image-based digital world makes it more difficult to construct meaning, seeing how it is that our screens may hollow out our experience of reality."[62] Probing the dire social ramifications of the destruction of the real through the phenomenon of proliferation, Kaye Cederman concludes, "There is no longer the ability for us to confront how 'reality' itself has been altered ... what Baudrillard calls the hyperreal world of simulation ... proliferates in a myriad of regurgitating forms denoting the search for happiness, fulfillment, and comfort."[63] For Baudrillard, burying all traces of the real underneath an avalanche of commercial signs is a deliberate hegemonic strategy related to the forceful imposition of a new post-Marxist, social order revolving around signs.

Additionally, as Cederman notes, these all-encompassing simulations that have taken on a life of their own through proliferation may be void of any real substance, but they have a strong ideological foundation reflecting the empty values of consumerism. Prospective clients are constantly being told that the quality of their life will radically improve if they decide to purchase a given

---

59   Kellner, "Baudrillard, Semiurgy and Death," 128.

60   Baudrillard, *Seduction*, 48.

61   Andrew Root, "A Screen-Based World: Finding the Real in the Hyper-Real," *Word & World* 32, no. 3 (2012): 237.

62   Root, "A Screen-Based World: Finding the Real in the Hyper-Real," 238.

63   Kaye Cederman, "Education: A Renewable Course," *Yearbook of the Irish Philosophical Society* (Jan. 2009): 17, 20.

product. In this regard, the media theorist Robert Crawford persuasively argues that the content of every single advertisement is the same. In order to peddle their latest "must-have" object, marketers create a fantasy world in which "consumption is depicted as the shortcut to happiness and well being."[64] Baudrillard contends that the act of purchasing is quite literally an attempt to acquire signs of happiness and to breathe life into chimerical dreams that are grounded in hyper-reality.

After indicating that "profusion is evidently the most striking aspect" of modern life, Baudrillard outlines his theories about the systematic exploitation of the timeless pursuit of happiness in *La Société de Consommation*.[65] The philosopher theorizes that encouraging the masses to seek happiness in utopian simulacra is an effective ideological tool for compelling purchaser citizens to comply with the demand to consume incessantly and extravagantly. As Baudrillard proclaims, "We are here at the heart of consumption as total organization of everyday life, total homogenization, where everything is taken over and superseded in the ease and translucidity of an abstract 'happiness' ... Does not the mass of consumers experience plenty as an effect of nature, surrounded as they are by the fantasies of the Land of Cockaigne?"[66] Baudrillard maintains that the problem with the grandiose vision of abstract happiness that undergirds the summons to consume is that it has no connection to genuine feelings of contentment and ontological purpose which cannot be bought in a department store. After the ephemeral ecstasy of the purchase itself quickly fades, unsatisfied and disenchanted customers are confronted with "the void of their own mental screen" that is emblematic of the banality of the image that motivated them to spend money frivolously.[67] In *La Société de Consommation*, Baudrillard illustrates that the exploitation of the pursuit of happiness is one of the most powerful instruments of oppression in the arsenal of the simulators of hyper-reality who endlessly strive to solidify their control by imploding the real through the *simulacral imagination*.

It is perhaps in his experimental text *La Légende des anges* in which Serres most clearly expresses his palpable anxiety concerning the disappearance of reality due to the proliferation of images in the modern world. The Serres scholar Roy Boyne explains that this unclassifiable essay "is an extended conversation

---

64   Robert Crawford, "Selling Modernity: Advertising and the Construction of the Culture of Consumption in Australia," *Antipodean Modern* (ACH) 25 (2006): 115.

65   Jean Baudrillard, *La Société de Consommation* (Paris: Editions Denoël. 1970), 19.

66   Jean Baudrillard, *The Consumer Society*, trans. George Ritzer. (London: Sage. 1998), 29, 32.

67   Jean Baudrillard, *The Transparency of Evil: Essays on Extreme Phenomena,* trans. James Benedict (New York: Verso. 1993), 14.

SIMULACRAL IMAGINATION AND THE NEXUS OF POWER   397

between Pia and Pantope."[68] In this work, Serres attaches himself to a long-standing French tradition that takes advantage of literary characters to engage in philosophical inquiry about complex subjects. Similar to his predecessors like Montaigne, Rabelais, and Voltaire, Serres seamlessly blends literature and philosophy to create a vivid portrait "of a cosmos utterly saturated with communication."[69] The rather dystopian vision of modernity generated by Serres in *La Légende des anges* reveals a similar conception of power as the one outlined by Baudrillard in numerous essays. Delving into the etymology of the word "angels," Serres demonstrates that commercial simulacra accost the modern subject everywhere he or she goes in contemporary consumer republics. In the original sense of the term, "angels" are messengers that are charged with the task of delivering various bits of information. The philosopher reminds us that angelic entities can be either benevolent or maleficent in the Judeo-Christian tradition.

In *La Légende des anges*, Serres suggests that malevolent angels are now on the brink of effacing the real entirely because of the proliferation of simulated hyper-reality. Serres's observations related to "Villeneuve" represent a microcosmic reflection of these fears. In this archetypical urban space, the philosopher posits that nothing exists outside of the simulations consumed by the citizens of this metropolis. As the narrator reveals, "Villeneuve has no outside. It is organized around a single band upon which the outside is conflated with the inside ... Contemporary communication removes all obstacles: we know how to link very different things together, dots to words, spaces to speeches or things to signs."[70] In this passage, Serres asserts that the sophistication of modern technology has allowed a self-referential network of signs to proliferate itself like never before. In this space in which everything is carefully manufactured for the consumption of the inhabitants of Villeneuve, the traditional philosophical distinction between "inside" and "outside" has no meaning. The philosopher decries the plight of the modern subject engulfed in commercial simulacra.

Describing Villeneuve as an all-embracing, omnipresent informational apparatus from which there truly is "no escape" from a Baudrillardian standpoint, the narrator affirms, "Villeneuve industrializes signs, it makes things with information."[71] The key word in this revealing characterization of Villeneuve is the verb "to industrialize." For Serres, it is the unending industrial production

---

68   Boyne, "Angels in the Archive," 208.
69   Boyne, "Angels in the Archive," 208.
70   Michel Serres, *La Légende des anges* (Paris: Flammarion, 1999), 57.
71   Serres, *La Légende des anges*, 59.

of signs by the system that separates late capitalism from earlier capitalist paradigms. In economic terms, the reproduction of symbolic images has replaced production itself as both the engine of prosperity and the nexus of power. Reiterating that there is not even a fleeting reprieve from the proliferation of commercial simulacra, the narrator explains, "The inhabitants of Villeneuve no longer go to work anymore, not to the factory, not to the office, like one thinks, but they go to school, starting in the morning, and this instruction never ends, not at noon, not during the night, the television, the radio, the media and telecommunications ... never stop making noise."[72] In this section of the narrative, Serres asserts that it is becoming increasingly more difficult to find a space that has not been tainted by this parasitic noise or supportive propaganda upon which late capitalism relies to sustain itself.

Several critics including Philipp Schweighauser, Marjorie Perloff, William Paulson, and Marcel Hénaff have also noted that "Villeneuve" is an elaborate metaphor that Serres employs to discuss his well-founded apprehension about excessive urbanization. In addition to the evident ecological concerns raised by ever-expanding megalopolises in an interconnected and interdependent biosphere, Serres "denounces the city as the hegemonic space of signs, of relations, and representations."[73] With billboards, flashing neon lights, and other forms of advertisements on nearly every street corner, Serres argues that the very properties that define urban spaces are conducive to the transmission of hyper-real codes. Given that much of the world's global population now lives in a major city, as the concept of the "rural exodus"[74] illustrates, the philosopher envisions that it will soon be even harder to escape the all-encompassing confines of "Villeneuve." In his controversial essay *Amérique*, Baudrillard also links urbanization to the proliferation of screen-based reality. In reference to the historical realities of the rural exodus, Baudrillard declares, "Later cities would be extensive ... Everything would become infrastructure cradled in light and artificial energy."[75] In this section of *Amérique*, Baudrillard underscores that large metropolitan areas provide the perfect institutional infrastructure for attacking the sensibilities of purchaser citizens with a litany of signs that reflect a larger social imaginary. In *La Légende des*

---

72   Serres, *La Légende des anges*, 60.

73   Marcel Hénaff, "Of Stones, Angels, and Humans: Michel Serres and the Global City," in *Mapping Michel Serres*, ed. Niran Abbas (Ann Arbor, MI: University of Michigan Press, 2005), 172.

74   Serres often discusses how the rural exodus has profoundly altered the essence of human civilization in numerous works and epitexts. For instance, see *L'Incandescent* and *Hominescence*.

75   Jean Baudrillard, *Amérique* (Paris: Editions Grasset & Fasquelle, 1986), 26.

anges, Serres appears to convey the same message about the perils of the urban space that facilitates favorable conditions for the proliferation of exploitative, commercial simulacra.

4   The Marginalization of Subversion and the Manufacturing of Consent through Prefabricated Models

In addition to proposing strikingly similar theories for explaining how the force of proliferation mediated through technology serves the hegemonic purpose of preventing the bewildered herd from dismantling the new social order, Baudrillard and Serres posit that prefabricated models effectively marginalize subversion in consumer republics. Both thinkers assert that the system creates artificial, sanctioned models of revolt that paradoxically reinforce the capitalist paradigm. Baudrillard and Serres affirm that purchaser citizens are no longer able to differentiate between actual rebellion and insignificant signs of subversion. When many misguided dissidents try to destabilize the establishment and liberate themselves from tyranny, they are merely pledging their allegiance to a mass-produced image of revolt. In spite of their admirable intentions, many discontents are drinking "the nectar of simulation" in a society in which hyper-real codes are deeply entrenched.[76]

Several researchers including Mark Poster, Trevor Norris, Alex Cline, and Douglas Kellner[77] have explored Baudrillard's theories related to how subversion has been relegated to the status of non-existence through the transmission of prepackaged simulacra. Summarizing Baudrillard's rather pessimistic perspective about the possibility of fighting back against the informational warfare that concretizes modern forms of subjugation, Trevor Norris asserts, "Any form of resistance is readily incorporated and assimilated back into the code."[78] In *La Société de Consommation,* Baudrillard demystifies the "industrial

---

76   Alex Cline, "Statues of Commodus-Death and Simulation in the Work of Jean Baudrillard," *International Journal of Baudrillard Studies* 8, no. 2 (2011): n.p. https://baudrillardstudies.ubishops.ca/statues-of-commodus-death-and-simulation-in-the-work-of-jean-baudrillard/.

77   In addition to Kellner and Cline's previously cited articles, see Mark Poster, "Consumption and Digital Commodities in the Everyday," *Cultural Studies* 18, no. 2–3 (2004): 409–23, and Trevor Norris, "Consuming Signs, Consuming the Polis: Hannah Arendt and Jean Baudrillard on Consumer Society and the Eclipse of the Real," *International Journal of Baudrillard Studies* 2, no. 2 (2005): n.p. https://baudrillardstudies.ubishops.ca/consuming-signs-consuming-the-polis-hannah-arendt-and-jean-baudrillard-on-consumer-society-and-the-eclipse-of-the-real/.

78   Norris, "Consuming Signs, Consuming the Polis," n. pag.

production of differences" that has become a lucrative niche in the market.[79] The philosopher explains that the system endlessly creates prefabricated models that supposedly allow clients to express their individuality and freedom. Given that there are no choices that exist outside of these paradigms, Baudrillard proclaims, "the freedom and sovereignty of the consumer are mystification pure and simple."[80] Deconstructing the appealing notion of the sovereign spender that exercises a certain amount of control over the system through the "power of the purse strings," Baudrillard reveals that all of the options for displaying one's individuality through the act of consumption are predetermined. As Mark Poster underscores, "The purchase itself is no mere acquisition but a submission to the publicity departments of untold corporations of one's preferences."[81] In *La Société de Consommation*, Baudrillard maintains that this same logic applies to the consumer items proudly worn by subversive subcultures as well.

Theorizing that all models for personalizing the act of unbridled consumption are the same, Baudrillard declares, "As a result, to differentiate oneself is precisely to affiliate to a model, to label oneself by reference to an abstract model ... In this way, the whole process of consumption is governed by the production of artificially diversified models."[82] Further clarifying that these supposed differences from one model to the next are extremely marginal in nature, the philosopher argues, "so personalization consists in a daily realignment to the smallest marginal difference (SMD)."[83] For Baudrillard, all consumer robots who consume prefabricated images resemble each other. Furthermore, every client who tries to conform to these prepackaged models strengthens the economic system by procuring metonymical parts of these paradigms. In *La Société de Consommation*, Baudrillard offers the concrete example of hippies to illustrate how trendy signs of subversion are often quite disconnected from actual resistance. Articulating his deep skepticism that the hippie movement ever truly represented a credible threat to the hegemonic forces that govern the modern world, "The question would seem rather to be the following: do the hippies and their community represent a real alternative to the processes of growth and consumption? Are they not merely the inverted and complementary image of those processes?"[84] According to Baudrillard, subversive counter-cultures who buy the same exact clothes and accessories to

---

79   Baudrillard, *The Consumer Society*, 125.

80   Baudrillard, *The Consumer Society*, 72.

81   Poster, "Consumption and Digital Commodities in the Everyday," 409.

82   Baudrillard, *The Consumer Society*, 88–89.

83   Baudrillard, *The Consumer Society*, 89–90.

84   Baudrillard, *The Consumer Society*, 181.

SIMULACRAL IMAGINATION AND THE NEXUS OF POWER 401

voice their displeasure with the establishment are reinforcing their own servitude. He contends that the "systematic repetition of images produces conformity because it transforms images into social [hyper-]reality and establishes them as truth."[85] As I highlight in my recent article "The Ubiquity of the Simulated Object That Has Consumed the Modern Subject: The Problematic Search for Happiness and Identity in a Globalized, Hyper-real World,"[86] Baudrillard's critique of sanctioned types of revolt in *La Société de Consommation* is timeless. Do Goths, Punks, and Hipsters really know the difference between genuine subversion and contrived representations of it?

Serres's framework for understanding how prepackaged, insignificant models including images of subversion are such an effective hegemonic device for controlling human behavior draws inspiration from Girard's theories about the origins of mimetic violence. As Maria Assad notes, Serres builds upon Girard's ideas regarding the critical role of mimesis "in the domain of human relations."[87] It is evident that Girard's theories related to mimetic conflicts are at the heart of Serres's reflections about the "ordering of the human collective."[88] Serres claims that mimesis, or imitation, represents the very basis of our collective identity. From an evolutionary standpoint, Serres contends that *Homo sapiens* have a heightened biological penchant for emulating the actions of those around them in comparison to other species. As the philosopher underscores, "We are animals that like to imitate, who willingly repeat a gesture or a word. You tell me something, I repeat it, and a hundred other people that I tell it to repeat it in turn, as if mimesis, as if imitation is the core of the social link *par excellence*. This is how to explain fashion ... we are the most imitative animals, even more imitative than monkeys."[89] In this exchange with Michel Polacco, Serres theorizes that our inherent need to be accepted by other people as social animals predisposes us to follow others and to repeat their behavior. As the philosopher's example of the fashion industry illustrates, this unfortunate genetic trait explains why prefabricated models have been so successful in disguising the true nature of the act of consumption. Fashion is constantly evolving through

---

85   Markova, "From Imagination to Well-Controlled Images," 330.

86   Keith Moser, "The Ubiquity of the Simulated Object That Has Consumed the Modern Subject: The Problematic Search for Happiness and Identity in a Globalized, Hyper-real World," *The International Journal of Baudrillard Studies* 11, no. 1 (2014): n. pag.

87   Maria Assad, *Reading with Michel Serres: An Encounter with Time* (State University of New York Press, 1999), 19.

88   Edwin Sayes, "From the Sacred to the Sacred Object: Girard, Serres, and Latour on the Ordering of the Human Collective," *Techné: Research in Philosophy and Technology* 16, no. 2 (2012): 105.

89   Polacco, *Michel Serres: Petites chroniques du dimanche soir*, 58.

the creation of new seductive images, because it is part of an economic system that necessitates unfettered growth.

In *Récits d'humanisme*, Serres outlines how advertisers have tapped into the evolutionary flaw of mimesis to sell a surplus of products and to manufacture consent to powerful market forces. As the philosopher maintains,

> Our desires stem from mimicking ... We imitate, we reproduce, we repeat ... all of our great revolutionary discoveries-from the Stone Age to the Paleolithic, writing in Antiquity, the printing press during the Renaissance ... and new technologies more recently ... These replicators, whose similarity to us stimulates and reproduces our mimetic desires, seem to imitate themselves the process of living DNA. This is the major danger that confronts our children: we plunge them into a universe of replicated codes, we could crush them with redundancy ... Sports, the media, advertisement, and business repeat ... Imitate me, become automatic vehicles for the repetition of our brand names, so that our repeated gestures multiply and repeat our commercial success.[90]

In this passage, Serres explains that our natural tendency to mimic the actions of those around us has been the source of many monumental human achievements throughout history. However, mimesis is also a dangerous force when it is placed in the hands of unscrupulous individuals attempting to control the population. In the modern world, omnipresent, hyper-real codes encourage purchaser citizens to imitate the images projected on their screens. To be more precise, consumer republics create mimetic models that short-circuit rational thought appealing to the most primitive of our evolutionary traits. Although Serres's argument is more biological in nature than Baudrillard's aforementioned theories, both philosophers pinpoint prefabricated models as one of the most important hegemonic tools for minimizing subversion, or even eliminating it entirely.

5 The New Essence of Power and Forms of Resistance in the Digital Age

Baudrillard and Serres clearly identify many of the same strategies employed by the political and social elite to marginalize dissent. Nevertheless, in their reflections concerning how the digital age has fundamentally altered the

---

90   Michel Serres, *Récits d'humanisme* (Paris: Editions Le Pommier. 2006), 193–94.

essence of power in their late philosophy, they appear to be on opposite ends of the philosophical spectrum regarding this issue. In recent works such as *The Transparency of Evil, The Intelligence of Evil*, and *The Gulf War Did Not Take Place*, Baudrillard theorizes that the birth of the digital era has ushered in "the final stage of simulation" that he terms "Integral Reality."[91] According to Baudrillard, the pervasiveness of virtual technology has created "a world of images that have lost their referents" entirely.[92] Consequently, "agency, autonomy, and freedom are non-existent."[93] The philosopher adopts the pessimistic position that the destruction of meaning and the implosion of the real are complete and irreversible in the modern world. In semiotic terms, Baudrillard declares that the signifier has become completely "unhinged from the signified."[94]

In *The Intelligence of Evil*, Baudrillard explains that the force of virtual technology has allowed the hegemonic powers that control consumer republics to proliferate commercial images on an even wider scale. Prophetically announcing the death of the "reality principle," Baudrillard hypothesizes, "What we see now, behind the eclipse of the 'objective' real, is the rise of Integral Reality, of a Virtual Reality that rests on the deregulation of the very reality principle ... Reality continues to exist; it is its principle that is dead. Now, reality without its principle is no longer the same at all. If, for many different reasons, the principle of representation, which alone gives it a meaning, falters, then the whole of the real falters."[95] In this troubling section of *The Intelligence of Evil*, Baudrillard asserts that the modern subject is no longer capable of formulating mental models to speculate about the reality of the external world. Additionally, in Freudian thought, the "reality principle" is associated with a maturation process that enables us to avoid impulsive behavior.[96] Constantly immersed in virtual images on our television, computer, smartphone, and tablet screens, our capacity for rational thought has been decimated in the digital era. In the wake of the disappearance of the "reality principle," Baudrillard argues that resistance to the new social order is no longer possible at all. As Paul Moran and Alex Kendall highlight, "Baudrillard's theory is thus predicated on the idea

---

91   Lee Barron, "Living with the Virtual: Baudrillard, Integral Reality, and Second Life," *Cultural Politics* 7, no. 3 (2011): 394.

92   Lisa Penaloza, and Linda Price, "Consumer Resistance: A Conceptual Overview," *Advances in Consumer Research* 20 (1993): 127.

93   Yar, *The Cultural Imaginary of the Internet*, 55.

94   Root, "A Screen-Based World: Finding the Real in the Hyper-Real," 24.

95   Baudrillard, *The Intelligence of Evil*, 17–18.

96   Kendra Cherry, "What is the Reality Principle? Weighing the Costs and Benefits of Behavior?," *Verywell*, May 6, 2016, https://www.verywellmind.com/what-is-the-reality-principle-2795801.

that there is no hope for future change and that no one is really committed to change in the first place."[97] In his monograph *Jean Baudrillard: From the Ocean to the Desert, or the Poetics of Radicality*, Gerry Coulter notes that the only form of optimism provided by Baudrillard is that "all systems create the conditions of their own demise."[98] For those who are discontent with the current situation, the philosopher implies that the only appropriate course of action is to wait until the system destroys itself from the inside due to its own excesses. Baudrillard adamantly affirms that the crisis of simulation has reached a point of no return in the digital age. Reminding the reader that all great civilizations eventually disappear, the philosopher asserts that the present era will one day come to an end as well.

In stark contrast to Baudrillard, Serres has been accused of being too optimistic about how virtual technology has modified power relations in contemporary Western society. In recent works like *Hominescence*, *Rameaux*, and *Petite Poucette*, Serres is undeniably positive, even euphoric, when he discusses the repercussions of the inception of the digital era. Given the philosopher's aforementioned derision for the simulators of hyper-reality who take advantage of ubiquitous codes to subdue the masses, Serres's humanistic aspirations related to virtual devices are initially befuddling. However, the philosopher's explanation of the vital difference between active and passive mediums sheds light on this progression in Serres's thought. In revealing conversations with Michel Polacco and Darius Rochebin, Serres contends that the television is a very different kind of medium compared to the Internet. In both of these exchanges, Serres uses an automobile metaphor to underscore what he considers to be a crucial distinction between various sorts of electronic mediums.

Theorizing that the act of surfing the web, sending tweets, or updating one's Facebook page is a much more interactive experience than passively internalizing commercial simulacra in front of a television screen, Serres muses,

> But, especially now, the latest cultural revolution is that of computers. The person speaking on television is lecturing, with no interactivity. This approach is a little old-fashioned, whereas computers offer this kind of interactivity. The latest cultural revolution concerns the body. As you know, the body is never wrong. In front of a computer, we lean forward in an active position like a car driver. On the other hand, in front of the

---

97   Paul Moran and Alex Kendall, "Baudrillard and the End of Education," *International Journal of Research & Method in Education* 32, no. 3 (2009): 329.

98   Coulter, *Jean Baudrillard: From the Ocean to the Desert*, 1.

television, the situation is reversed as we are in the passive position of the passenger.[99]

For a sensorial philosopher[100] like Michel Serres, the fact that our body is more active when we are interacting with a computer screen as opposed to watching a television program reverses the situation entirely. In a medium in which our sensorial faculties are being stimulated, Serres maintains that we are less prone to be passive receptacles of consumerist signs. As the philosopher's metaphor also illustrates, the Internet user possesses more freedom regarding the specific path that he or she ultimately decides to pursue. Whereas all of the content that the television viewer consumes is prepackaged and predetermined, the journey of the Internet surfer cannot be entirely predicted or scripted from the outset. Cyberspace is replete with an infinite number of informational passageways that bifurcate in all different directions.

In addition to being more difficult for authorities to control, the Internet is different from the television because more voices are being heard. As an earlier section of the essay explores, it is impossible to respond to the consumerist messages emanating from the television screen. Explaining that the unique properties of the Internet have already begun to change the distribution of power in the digital era, Serres reveals, "In politics, media, instruction, justice ... the former world only had a few of them (voices) ... The new one, as part of a network, is comprised of as many senders as receivers ... we are all stars and planets, emitters, receivers. Through networked communications, each and every one of us possesses all of the power imaginable. What are we going to do with it tomorrow?"[101] According to Serres, the invention of the Internet has placed more power in the hands of common people than any other form of human ingenuity. In this passage from *Yeux*, Serres implores the reader to take advantage of this decentralization of power and knowledge in order to imagine a more egalitarian and just society. The philosopher argues that the World Wide Web has the potential to be the most significant counter-hegemonic tool ever conceived. Although Serres still scoffs at the notion that the corporate establishment media represents a fourth estate, he foresees that the Internet could play the role of a legitimate "fifth estate" depending on how this powerful tool is utilized and who controls access to it in the future.[102] Serres realizes

---

99   Polacco, *Michel Serres: Petites chroniques du dimanche soir*, 245.

100 For a more comprehensive explanation of Serres's theories about human corporality and our five senses, see the philosopher's aptly named essay *Les cinq sens* in addition to Nicholas Chare's article "Pressing the Flesh."

101 Michel Serres, *Yeux* (Paris: Editions Le Pommier, 2014), 139.

102 Michel Serres, *Le Mal propre* (Paris: Editions Le Pommier, 2008), 30.

that many obstacles currently stand in the way of transforming his humanistic dream into a reality,[103] but the positive characteristics of the Internet have given him hope for the first time that a better world is within our reach.

As noted by Joshua Goldstein, Adrian Karatnycky, and Olena Prytula,[104] the role of social media in organizing resistance to oppressive regimes, as evidenced by the Orange Revolution in the Ukraine, cannot be overstated. Moreover, in a testament to how the dawning of the digital era has radically transformed society to its core, Serres maintains in his essay *Temps des crises* that the younger generation is faced with the daunting task of rebuilding antiquated institutional structures from scratch. After highlighting that all of our outmoded institutions are in a state of crisis because they are disconnected from the quotidian lived experiences of the modern subject, Serres reminds us that every "crise" represents a golden opportunity to reconstruct everything in a better fashion this time around. Even the very nature of authority itself must be reconstituted in the coming years due to the sweeping social changes actuated by virtual technology. Serres posits that global society has arrived at a pivotal crossroads. In this changing landscape, the philosopher argues that we have the ability to reshape power and to prevent ourselves from endlessly falling prey to it. For Serres, the essence of power is now to be determined.

6   Conclusion

In conclusion, Jean Baudrillard and Michel Serres are two of the most important French philosophers whose invaluable contributions to the reworking of the concept of symbolic power are often overlooked. Even though they are overshadowed by canonical figures like Karl Marx, Michel Foucault, Louis Althusser, and Antonio Gramsci, Baudrillard and Serres develop highly original and cogent theoretical frameworks for understanding the nexus of power in the modern world. Specifically, both philosophers compellingly assert that it is

---

103   For instance, Serres is astutely aware of the many forms of online predation that provide a dangerous safe haven for illicit activities such as prostitution, gambling, human trafficking, and terrorism. See pages 173–78 of my book *The Encyclopedic Philosophy of Michel Serres: Writing the Modern World and Anticipating the Future* (2016).

104   See Joshua Goldstein, "The Role of Digital Networked Technologies in the Ukrainian Orange Revolution," *Internet & Democracy Case Study Series* (Berkman Center Research Publication. Cambridge, MA: Harvard University, 2007); Adrian Karatnycky, "Ukraine's Orange Revolution," *Foreign Affairs* 84, vol. 2 (2005): 35–52; and Olena Prytula, "The Ukrainian Media Rebellion," in *Revolution in Orange*, eds. Anders Aslund, and Michael McFaul (Washington, DC: Carnegie Endowment for International Peace, 2006), 103–24.

SIMULACRAL IMAGINATION AND THE NEXUS OF POWER

impossible to comprehend the hegemonic origins of power without first exploring the advent of the post-Marxist era. A close examination of Baudrillard and Serres's interdisciplinary philosophy reveals the inherent limitations of any theories related to power that focus exclusively on production. Baudrillard and Serres demonstrate that (mis-) information is now the opiate of the masses used to manufacture consent to a new social order and to suppress dissension. Both philosophers also indict the corporate establishment media for their complicity in the incessant dissemination of commercial simulacra. Baudrillard and Serres also identify many of the same hegemonic tools employed by the integrated political and social elite to subjugate the population in the current era of information. In spite of these important similarities, their respective post-Marxist visions of power abruptly diverge in their late philosophy. For Baudrillard, the digital revolution represents the final proverbial "nail in the coffin"[105] for the modern subject for whom resistance is no longer a viable option. Conversely, Serres envisions that the Internet could one day be the greatest democratic and liberating force that the world has ever known. Only time will tell which imaginative portrait of late capitalism and the digital age is the most accurate, but it is certain that the future of humanity lies in the answer to this question.

References

Abbas, Niran, ed. *Mapping Michel Serres*. Ann Arbor, MI: University of Michigan Press. 2005.

Abbinnett, Ross. "The Spectre and the Simulacrum." *Theory, Culture & Society* 25, no. 6 (2008): 69–87.

Alexenberg, Mel. *Educating Artists for the Future: Learning at the Intersections of Art, Science, Technology, and Culture*. Chicago: University of Chicago Press. 2008.

Assad, Maria. *Reading with Michel Serres: An Encounter with Time*. State University of New York Press. 1999.

Baldwin, Jon. "'Self-Immolation by Technology': Jean Baudrillard and the Posthuman in Film and Television." In *The Palgrave Handbook of Posthumanism in Film and Television*, edited by Michael Hauskeller, Thomas Philbeck, and Curtis Carbonell, 19–27. New York: Palgrave Macmillan. 2015.

Barron, Lee. "Living with the Virtual: Baudrillard, Integral Reality, and Second Life." *Cultural Politics* 7, no. 3 (2011): 391–408.

Baudrillard, Jean. *Amérique*. Paris: Editions Grasset & Fasquelle. 1986.

---

105   Yar, *The Cultural Imaginary of the Internet*, 64.

Baudrillard, Jean. *The Consumer Society*. Translated by George Ritzer. London: Sage. 1998.

Baudrillard, Jean. *Pour une critique de l'économie politique du signe*. Paris: Gallimard. 1972.

Baudrillard, Jean. *Seduction*. Translated by Brian Singer. New York: St. Martin's Press. 1990.

Baudrillard, Jean. *Simulacra and Simulation*. Translated by Sheila Glaser. Ann Arbor: University of Michigan. 1994.

Baudrillard, Jean. *The Gulf War Did Not Take Place*. Translated by Paul Patton. Bloomington, IN: Indiana University Press. 1995.

Baudrillard, Jean. *The Intelligence of Evil*. Translated by Chris Turner. New York: Berg. 2005.

Baudrillard, Jean. *La Société de Consommation*. Paris: Editions Denoël. 1970.

Baudrillard, Jean. *Le Système des objets*. Paris: Gallimard. 1968.

Baudrillard, Jean. *The Transparency of Evil: Essays on Extreme Phenomena*. Translated by James Benedict. New York: Verso. 1993.

Boyne, Roy. "Angels in the Archive: Lines Into the Future in the Work of Jacques Derrida and Michel Serres." *Cultural Values* 2, no. 2–3 (1998): 206–22.

Cederman, Kaye. "Education: A Renewable Course." *Yearbook of the Irish Philosophical Society* (Jan. 2009): 15–24.

Chare, Nicholas. "Pressing the Flesh." *Parallax* 18, no. 2 (2012): 95–99.

Cherry, Kendra. "What is the Reality Principle? Weighing the Costs and Benefits of Behavior?," *Verywell*, May 6, 2016, https://www.verywellmind.com/what-is-the-reality-principle-2795801.

Chomsky, Noam. *Media Control: The Spectacular Achievements of Propaganda*. New York: Open Media Series. 2002.

Cline, Alex. "Statues of Commodus-Death and Simulation in the Work of Jean Baudrillard." *International Journal of Baudrillard Studies* 8, no. 2 (2011): n.p. https://baudrillardstudies.ubishops.ca/statues-of-commodus-death-and-simulation-in-the-work-of-jean-baudrillard/.

Cohen, Lizabeth. *A Consumers' Republic: The Politics of Consumption in Postwar America*. New York: Vintage Books. 2003.

Connor, Steven. "Michel Serres's Les Cinq sens." In *Mapping Michel Serres*, edited by Niran Abbas, 153–69. Ann Arbor, MI: University of Michigan Press. 2005.

Connor, Steven. "Thinking Things." *Textual Practice* 24, no. 1 (2010): 1–20.

Coulter, Gerry. *Jean Baudrillard: From the Ocean to the Desert, or the Poetics of Radicality*. New York: Intertheory. 2012.

Crawford, Robert. "Selling Modernity: Advertising and the Construction of the Culture of Consumption in Australia." *Antipodean Modern* (ACH) 25 (2006): 114–43.

De Beer, Fanie. "Methodology and Noology: Amazing Prospects for Library and Information Science." *SA Jnl Libs & Info Sci* 77, no. 1 (2011): 85–94.

Feertchak, Alexis. "Michel Serres ou le joyeux Pantope," *Iphilo*, April 26, 2014, https://iphilo.fr/2014/04/26/michel-serres-ou-le-joyeux-pantope/.

Gautier, Julien. "La douteuse fable de Michel Serres," *Revue Skhole.fr*, June 25 2013, http://skhole.fr/petite-poucette-la-douteuse-fable-de-michel-serres.

Goldstein, Joshua. "The Role of Digital Networked Technologies in the Ukrainian Orange Revolution." *Internet & Democracy Case Study Series*. Berkman Center Research Publication. Cambridge, MA: Harvard University, 2007. https://papers.ssrn.com/sol3/papers.cfm?abstract_id=1077686.

Hénaff, Marcel. "Of Stones, Angels, and Humans: Michel Serres and the Global City." In *Mapping Michel Serres*, edited by Niran Abbas, 170–89. Ann Arbor, MI: University of Michigan Press, 2005.

Jameson, Fredric. *Late Marxism: Adorno, or, The Persistence of the Dialectic*. New York: Verso. 1990.

Karatnycky, Adrian. "Ukraine's Orange Revolution." *Foreign Affairs* 84, vol. 2 (2005): 35–52.

Kellner, Douglas. "Baudrillard, Semiurgy and Death." *Theory, Culture & Society* 4, vol. 1 (1987): 125–46.

Kennis, Andrew. "Theorizing and Historicizing the Media Dependence Model." Presentation at the Annual Meeting of the International Communication Association, Chicago, May 21, 2009.

King, Anthony. "Baudrillard's Nihilism and the End of Theory." *Telos* 2 (1998): 89–106.

Koch, Andrew & Rick Elmore. "Simulation and Symbolic Exchange: Jean Baudrillard's Augmentation of Marx's Theory of Value." *Politics & Policy* 34, no. 3 (2006): 556–75.

Lutz, Ashley. "These 6 Corporations Control 90% of the Media in America," *Business Insider*, June 2012, https://www.businessinsider.com/these-6-corporations-control-90-of-the-media-in-america-2012-6.

Maddox, Kelly. "Au-delà des frontières: Société de consommation et écriture migrante dans Un Petit pas pour l'homme de Stéphane Dompierre." *Voix Plurielles* 2 (2008): 90–98.

Markova, Ivana. "From Imagination to Well-Controlled Images." In *Handbook of Imagination and Culture*, edited by Tania Zittoun and Vlad Glaveanu, 319–44. Oxford: Oxford University Press, 2017.

Mattick, Paul. *Economic Crisis and Crisis Theory*. New York: Routledge. 1981.

Merrin, William. "Implosion, Simulation and the Pseudo-Event: A Critique of McLuhan." *Economy and Society* 31, no. 3 (2002): 369–90.

Messier, Vartan. "Consumerism After Theory: Globalization and the End of Transnational Discourse in Néstor García Canclini's Cultural Empiricism." *ATENEA* 28, no. 1 (2007): 21–40.

Moran, Paul & Alex Kendall. "Baudrillard and the End of Education." *International Journal of Research & Method in Education* 32, no. 3 (2009): 327–35.

Mortley, Raoul. "Chapter III: Michel Serres." In *French Philosophers in Conversation: Levinas, Schneider, Serres, Irigaray, Le Doeuff, Derrida*, edited by Raoul Mortley, 46–60. New York: Routledge, 1991.

Moser, Keith. *J.M.G. Le Clézio: A Concerned Citizen of the Global Village*. Lanham, Boulder, New York, Toronto, Plymouth, UK: Lexington Books. 2012.

Moser, Keith. *The Encyclopedic Philosophy of Michel Serres: Writing the Modern World and Anticipating the Future*. Augusta, GA: Anaphora Literary Press. 2016.

Moser, Keith. "The Ubiquity of the Simulated Object That Has Consumed the Modern Subject: The Problematic Search for Happiness and Identity in a Globalized, Hyper-real World." *The International Journal of Baudrillard Studies* 11, no. 1 (2014): n.p. https://baudrillardstudies.ubishops.ca/the-ubiquity-of-the-simulated-object-and-the-search-for-happiness-and-identity-in-a-globalized-hyper-real-world/.

Norris, Trevor. "Consuming Signs, Consuming the Polis: Hannah Arendt and Jean Baudrillard on Consumer Society and the Eclipse of the Real." *International Journal of Baudrillard Studies* 2, no. 2 (2005): n.p. https://baudrillardstudies.ubishops.ca/consuming-signs-consuming-the-polis-hannah-arendt-and-jean-baudrillard-on-consumer-society-and-the-eclipse-of-the-real/.

Paulson, William. "Writing that Matters." *SubStance* 83 (1997): 22–36.

Penaloza, Lisa and Linda Price. "Consumer Resistance: A Conceptual Overview." *Advances in Consumer Research* 20 (1993): 123–28.

Perloff, Marjorie. "'Multiple Pleats': Some Applications of Michel Serres's Poetics." *Configurations* 8, no. 2 (2000): 187–200.

Polacco, Michel. *Michel Serres: Petites chroniques du dimanche soir*. Paris: Editions Le Pommier. 2006.

Polizzi, Gaspare, and Trina Marmarelli. "Hermetism, Messages, and Angels." *Configurations* 8, no. 2 (2000): 245–70.

Poster, Mark. "Consumption and Digital Commodities in the Everyday." *Cultural Studies* 18, no. 2–3 (2004): 409–23.

Prytula, Olena. "The Ukrainian Media Rebellion." In *Revolution in Orange*, edited by Anders Aslund and Michael McFaul, 103–24. Washington, DC: Carnegie Endowment for International Peace, 2006.

Rochebin, Darius. "Pardonnez-moi: L'Interview de Michel Serres," *Radio Télévision Suisse*, October 21, 2014, https://www.youtube.com/watch?v=ocnG21PdUMc.

Root, Andrew. "A Screen-Based World: Finding the Real in the Hyper-Real." *Word & World* 32, no. 3 (2012): 237–44.

Royrvik, Emil, and Marianne Brodersen. "Real Virtuality: Power and Simulation in the Age of Neoliberal Crisis." *Culture Unbound* 4 (2013): 637–59.

Sansom, Dennis. "Can Irony Enrich the Aesthetic Imagination?: Why Søren Kierkegaard's Explanation of Irony Is Better Than Richard Rorty's." *The Journal of Aesthetic Education* 51, no. 2 (2017): 17–32.

Sayes, Edwin. "From the Sacred to the Sacred Object: Girard, Serres, and Latour on the Ordering of the Human Collective." *Techné: Research in Philosophy and Technology* 16, no. 2 (2012): 105–22.

Schweighauser, Philipp. "The Desire for Unity and Its Failure: Reading Henry Adams Through Michel Serres." In *Mapping Michel Serres.* edited by Niran Abbas, 136–52. Ann Arbor, MI: University of Michigan Press, 2005.

Serres, Michel. *Atlas.* Paris: Editions Julliard. 1994.

Serres, Michel. *Les Cinq Sens.* Paris: Editions Grasset et Fasquelle. 1985.

Serres, Michel. *Hominescence.* Paris: Editions Le Pommier. 2001.

Serres, Michel. *L'Incandescent.* Paris: Editions Le Pommier. 2003.

Serres, Michel. *La Légende des anges.* Paris: Flammarion. 1999.

Serres, Michel. *Le Mal propre.* Paris: Editions Le Pommier. 2008.

Serres, Michel. *Le Parasite.* Paris: Grasset. 1980.

Serres, Michel. *Rameaux.* Paris: Editions Le Pommier. 2004.

Serres, Michel. *Récits d'humanisme.* Paris: Editions Le Pommier. 2006.

Serres, Michel. *Rome.* Paris: Grasset. 1983.

Serres, Michel. *Temps des crises.* Paris: Editions Le Pommier. 2009.

Serres, Michel. *Yeux.* Paris: Editions Le Pommier. 2014.

Smith, Richard. "Baudrillard's Nonrepresentational Theory: Burn the Signs and Journey Without Maps." *Environment and Planning D: Society and Space* 21, no. 1 (2003): 67–84.

Webb, David. "The Science of Relations: An Interview." *Angelaki* 8, no. 2 (2003): 227–38.

Welch, Michael Patrick. "Lifting the Mask from 'Faces of Death,'" *St. Petersburg Times*, October 26, 2000, https://www.tampabay.com/.

Wiltsher, Nick, and Aaron Meskin. "Art and Imagination." In *The Routledge Handbook of Philosophy of Imagination*, edited by Amy Kind, 179–91. London: Routledge, 2016.

Yar, Majid. *The Cultural Imaginary of the Internet: Virtual Utopias and Dystopias.* Basingstoke, UK: Palgrave Macmillan. 2014.

CHAPTER 17

Jean-François Lyotard, the Radical Imagination, and the Aesthetic of the Differend

Victor E. Taylor

A work can become modern only if it is first postmodern. Postmodernism thus understood is not modernism at its end but in the nascent state, and this state is constant.

JEAN-FRANÇOIS LYOTARD, *The Postmodern Condition: A Report on Knowledge*

While Jean-François Lyotard (1924–1998) wrote widely in philosophy as well as in a variety of other humanities related disciplines, he mostly is associated with the critical term "postmodernism" and its influence in and deployment across the arts, humanities, and social sciences from the late 1970s through the early 2000s. Postmodernism, generically conceived as an *after*-modernist artistic style from the mid twentieth century onward, ubiquitously was identified with pastiche, bricolage, eclecticism, and an overarching cultural nihilism.[1]

---

1   In a 1987 *Chicago Review* essay entitled "Postmodern and Late Modern: The Essential Definitions," Charles Jencks summarizes postmodernism's reception in arts by way of American art critic Clement Greenberg:
    Clement Greenberg, long acknowledged as the theorist of American Modernism, defined Postmodernism in 1979 as the antithesis of all he loved: that is as the lowering of aesthetic standards caused by "the democratization of culture under industrialism." Like our "Decadence" columnist, he saw the danger as a lack of hierarchy in artistic judgment although he did not go so far as the Frenchman in calling it simply "nihilism." Another art critic, Walter Darby Bannard, writing in the same prestigious magazine five years later, continued Greenberg's crusade against the heathens and restated the same (non-) definitions, except with more brutal elaboration: "Postmodernism is aimless, anarchic, amorphous, self-indulgent, inclusive, horizontally structured, and aims for the popular." Why does he leave out "ruthless kitsch" or the standard comparison with Nazi populism that the architectural critic Ken Frampton always adds to the list of horrors? Ever since Clement Greenberg made his famous opposition ("Avant Garde and Kitsch") in a 1939 article, certain puritanical intellectuals have been arguing that it has to be one thing or the other, and it is clear where they classify Postmodernism, although of course if it is really "horizontally structured" and "democratic," it cannot be at the same time neo-Nazi and authoritarian. But consistency has never been a virtue of those out to malign a movement. See Charles Jencks, "Postmodern and Late Modern: The Essential Definitions," *Chicago Review* 35, no. 4 (1987): 31–32.

© KONINKLIJKE BRILL NV, LEIDEN, 2020 | DOI:10.1163/9789004436350_019

Lyotard's definition and use of the term, however, was more specific and philosophically nuanced than what the popular conception of the term offered. As the epigraph indicates, postmodernism is not simply the time after modernism; nor is it something with a temporal end. Primarily, Lyotard's work on postmodernism drew from his early and late analysis of Kantian aesthetics and was further informed by his reading of *Wittgensteinian* language philosophy, more precisely the concept of "language games." In Lyotard's writings, especially his book *The Postmodern Condition: A Report on Knowledge*, postmodernism not only included a "war on totality" or totalizing discourses in general—a rejection of an ethico-politics of exhaustion—it also initiated a new aesthetics emerging from a conflict between feeling and reason in a post-Kantian context. From this point of departure, a Lyotardian aesthetic begins with a radicalization of the Kantian sublime and the insufficiency of reason to capture or take hold of the art-imagination through a sufficient or exhausting linguistic capacity for understanding. In this sense, for Lyotard, a radical epistemic uncertainty links to aesthetic possibility and the creation of new "worlds."

When postmodernism dwells on the comprehensive failure of totalizing epistemological and metaphysical regimes, it at the same time highlights the work of the human imagination. To create new artistic, political, and ethical worlds or the conditions for those realities, for instance, the imagination must play a central role in forming these *new* possibilities. For Lyotard, the postmodern largely was seen as an ineluctable intervention of imaginative powers, with rule discovery as the critical creative activity suspending what was or is for what can be. In this sense, the imagination is not responsible for filling-in the space of inquiry or aesthetic, ethical, or political suspension. Its responsibility or duty is to a perennial state of openness and ongoing experimentation. To simply identify the postmodern or postmodernism with a time or style or dictum, as I discuss below, is to miss the point—the postmodern involves radical, imaginative disruption, without speculative resolution, which, in effect, would be the closing of the imagination.

Before examining Lyotard's conceptualization and use of postmodernism or postmodernism(s), it is important to briefly review historically how the term was understood and utilized by artists, architects, and critics prior to and during the development of his later aesthetics in the 1980s and 1990s. Postmodernism is historically and philosophically complex but its reductive association with eclecticism and pastiche (more generous than Greenberg's definition) in art and architecture, primarily, were made highly visible by such public examples as Charles Moore's The Piazza d'Italia (1978) and Michael Graves' Portland Building or the Portland Municipal Services Building (1982). Lyotard's intellectual predicament at the time was acute. While postmodernism and its subsequent aesthetic possibilities were incredibly influential in the arts and humanities over a near twenty-year period, the postmodern also was incredibly misunderstood and seriously vulgarized in the academy and in popular culture—intellectually discounted and equated sometimes with the logic of late capitalism, vapid pluralism, expressivism, and the generic newest new. Lyotard attempted to recontextualize or, even, rehabilitate the term in order to reassert its radical capacity vis-à-vis a revised analytics of the Kantian sublime. Inevitably, the popular understanding of the postmodern culturally prevailed (as it does today) and Lyotard in his later work de-emphasized this salvaging project and focused his attention on pressing the underlying philosophical significance of postmodernism through concepts such as, the "differend," which he developed in *The Differend: Phrases in Dispute* (1988), "paganism," "event," and the "figural."

The late Bill Readings' *Introducing Lyotard: Art and Politics* (1991)[2] was the second[3] major English language book-length study of Lyotard's work, especially as it related to aesthetics, ethics, and politics. Readings' choice of title (emphasizing the act of "introducing") was a way to draw attention to the many misperceptions (representations) not only of Lyotard's work, but also, as previously mentioned, of postmodernism as a critical term. The proposed title of the monograph, in fact, was initially *Introducing Lyotard: Here He Is* but Routledge rejected it—ostensibly for reasons of marketing and bookshelf categorizing.[4] The "here he is," nevertheless, is preserved in the introduction as a subsection. As a subtitle, however, it would have underscored an intention to situate Lyotard in the context of poststructuralism and its controversial place in the academy during the "theory era." The following lengthy passage from the preface reads like a shorten prospectus for the book and illustrates the problem at the time of rendering Lyotard's thought and place in the theory conversation:

> Ironically, this book sets out to show that Lyotard's interest in the post-modern is not a matter of trend-spotting, though it is certainly an historical accident that he has become best known in the USA for having participated in this particular national obsession in cultural punditry. More

---

2 Bill Readings, *Introducing Lyotard: Art and Politics* (New York: Routledge, 1991).

3 The first major book-length study of Lyotard was Bennington's *Lyotard: Writing the Event*. See Geoffrey Bennington, *Lyotard: Writing the* Event (Manchester: Manchester University Press, 1988).

4 As a graduate student at Syracuse University, I worked with Bill Readings on an extensive Lyotard independent study during the time he was writing *Introducing Lyotard*. The detail regarding the "here he is" subtitle was from my conversations with him in the spring of 1988.

significantly, taking on the term "postmodernity" has led Lyotard's writing to be taken up across a number of disciplines: literature, philosophy, legal studies, political science, art history, intellectual history and cultural studies are some. Indeed, the name of Lyotard is one of the more cross-disciplinary sites of theoretical discussion in the American academy today (in a manner interestingly distinct from that of Derrida, who tends to be asked what "deconstruction" can do for various fields). Lyotard's willingness to engage with the Frankfurt school, for example, has made his writing more urgent for American philosophy and political science departments than that of Derrida (for whom the British Left constructed a peculiarly post-Althusserian genealogy which had little purchase). The effect of this in publishing has been a flow of translations, and the recent appearance of *The Differend*, along with the forthcoming *Discours, figure* should stimulate further interest, not least as they correct the understanding of Lyotard as primarily a theorist of the postmodern. Special issues of *Diacritics* and *SubStance* indicate the extent to which Lyotard has become, on the basis of the relatively small amount of material available in translation, a dominant figure on the theory circuit. And this in spite of the fact that he spends much of his time attacking the hegemony of theoretical metalanguages.[5]

The act of introducing, for Readings, meant critically differentiating Lyotard from the other better known philosophers/theorists of the day, namely Jacques Derrida and Gilles Deleuze. Perhaps with the exception of Derrida, Lyotard's writings intersect the widest range of disciplines among his contemporaries, as noted by Readings. The subtext of the above passage, however, is more pointed, especially considering the reference to the Frankfurt school. The main criticism of postmodernism (and poststructuralism) by scholars at the time was that it was "apolitical" or, worse, in league with late capitalism—this was the political point of Frederic Jameson's forward to the English translation of *The Postmodern Condition: A Report on Knowledge*. Similar criticisms were made of Derrida, which prompted him to write *Specters of Marx: The State of the Debt, the Work of Mourning and the New International* in 1993 and *Marx and Sons* in 2002, which were (belated) direct and thorough deconstructions of the metaphysical assumptions underpinning Marxism ... in its many forms. Lyotard, however, pursued a different path in his refutation of the charges of quietism and callous collusion—postmodernism was against all forms of hegemony and master narratives, with Marxism being just one example. Therefore, as the

---

5   Readings, *Introducing Lyotard: Art and Politics*, xii.

Readings passage points out, Lyotard was intellectually waging war on two fronts—art and politics. Postmodernism in Lyotardian terms, then, was neither an artistic style, as described earlier, nor was it a program of acquiescence or conspiracy with the ends of late capitalism. Postmodernism, if it could be defined at all, was an activity of thinking aligned with the radical powers of imaginative disruption ... across discursive fields.

Introducing Lyotard, firstly as an act of or performing an introduction by Readings, means an attempt to "present" Lyotard and distinguish him from his poststructuralist contemporaries and outline his conceptualization of postmodernism as something different from the common sense or received understanding of the term. Introducing Lyotard, secondly as Lyotard as an "introducer" of radical discourses, refocuses Readings study on the ways in which Lyotard introduced into aesthetics and politics, primarily, a radical disruption—one deriving from his reading of the Kantian sublime. According to Readings, there are three forms of disruption introduced by Lyotard, and these entail attending to the dominance of the figural vis-à-vis knowledge, narrative history, and the aesthetic object:

> Lyotard adopts the postmodern as an evocation of the figural force of the event in the thought of historical time. The thought of time disrupts historical assurance with regard to the conditions of knowledge, the writing of history, and the status of the aesthetic object. In *The Postmodern Condition* and *Le Postmoderne expliqué aux enfants*, this disruption takes three exemplary forms:
>
> (i)   Narrative introduces a temporality to knowledge in excess of that permitted by the "history of ideas";
> (ii) Deconstruction insists that the possibility of writing history depends upon the effacement of the event of inscription;
> (iii) The aesthetic object is detached from the temporality of original creation and repetition so as to no longer be a commodity circulating between artist and critic.[6]

There are three faux continuities or linearities corresponding to the "force of the figural" (that which refuses to be captured in discourse/language/reason). First, knowledge, as it is defined in early modern to post-Enlightenment philosophy, generally, presumes a continuity (isomorphism) between mind and world through a series of narrative linkages called the "history of ideas." Here,

---

6   Readings, *Introducing Lyotard: Art and Politics*, 42.

THE RADICAL IMAGINATION, AND THE AESTHETIC OF THE DIFFEREND   417

knowledge is posited as "sufficient," i.e., sufficient reason. For Lyotard, following Kant, reason is disrupted by feeling, in particular the feeling associated
with the sublime and, therefore, its (reason's) legislative primacy over experience faces a major failure. Second, since there is something, a feeling, that is in
excess of the power of reason or confines of knowledge, events and/or acts
taken to be in history are not representable in discourse/language, e.g. "Aus-
chwitz." And, third, the aesthetic object, analogous to the historical event, too,
is not containable within discourse/language/reason and, therefore, is in excess of the strictures of continuity. Rather than marketing a postmodern alternative style or endlessly refuting the idea of postmodernism as a particular
style or as a companion/accomplice to late capitalism, Lyotard introduces the
notion of postmodernism as a non-temporal radical disruption in our conceptualization of and dependency on the sufficiency of continuity in knowledge,
history, and aesthetics (politics).

What does this mean for a postmodern aesthetics? To answer the question
today, the focus of this essay needs to shift to the next generation of Lyotard
scholarship. However, before moving on to that topic it is important to note a
major contribution made by Readings in his introductory work—seeing clearly Lyotard's deconstruction of representationalism and his incredulity toward
unquestioned linkages, which are the bases for grand narratives. Readings
makes the following critical observation early in *Introducing Lyotard* and then
consistently returns to it in the context of art (aesthetics), politics, and ethics.
"Language and the world," he writes, "do not share a nature: there is a supplementary violence to the operation that makes words into things, a violence
that makes things into words, produces discontinuities, disruptions and im-
motivations in the world."[7] This is a statement about ontology, about the
world's resistance to being circumscribed, fully explained, and ontologically
limited. He adds to this the idea that, "[i]f expression is a figure for signification, violence is a figure for expression. To put it another way, the figural is not
the coming to consciousness of the sensible, but the subterranean distortion
and violence of the unconscious. It finds the sensible (motivated) in the abstract (unmotivated) and the abstract in the sensible."[8] In this sense, "figural
distortion," as a violence, saves the world from completion and sufficiency—
art, politics, ethics ... thinking ... are always open activities, always drifting and
forming necessary unnecessary linkages. There is at least one important qualification; the violence propelling these necessary unnecessary linkages is indifferent to a *telos*, which means that the heterogeneity of phrases resists every,

---

7 Readings, *Introducing Lyotard: Art and Politics*, 23.
8 Readings, *Introducing Lyotard: Art and Politics*, 23.

"good" or "bad," intellectual and imaginative closure demanded by phrases or narratives of determination.

In 1985, Lyotard, with Thierry Chaput (1949–1990), curated an exhibition entitled *Les Immatériaux* at the Centre Georges Pompidou. John Rajchman describes this philosophical-artistic endeavor as having "...the distinction not simply of intersecting with philosophical questions, but actually of being the work of a philosopher, arguably even a work of philosophy, even if it was not recognized as such at the time."[9] *Les Immatériaux* attempted to draw attention to, not "materialize," several aesthetic and critical problems relating to the issue of (re)presentation and the state of communication technology. From Lyotard's perspective, modernism sought to make the unpresentable representable in art and understanding. His radical re-writing of this modernist edict as a postmodern aesthetic changed the trajectory of the task ... postmodernism sought to leave the unpresentable unrepresentable. *Les Immatériaux*, as the title suggests, offers an extended meditation on that which does not enter into sufficient materiality, especially in the techno-scientific context of reducing everything (absolutely everything) to data points. In this way, Lyotard's project resonates with Derrida's later *Archive Fever*, a work drawing out the spectral elements of memory, cataloging, and representing.[10]

Peter W. Milne in his essay "Lyotard's 'Critical' 'Aesthetics'" discusses the conflict-correlation between art and critical discourse. If art exists to be revealed by criticism, it falls short of finding its potential; and, if criticism is only that which parasitically attaches itself to art, it, too, falls short of finding its potential. In this instance, the "potential" is not a hidden meaning but an activity that resists aesthetic or linguistic sufficiency or closure. Milne writes:

> I want to claim, for the work that this "now" requires, the labour of finding words, idioms, adequate to its singular situation, of responding to its always unique demands. This is a liberation from the repetitions of the system and its existing categories, its forms of thought – a liberation from the categorizing that reduces what is new to the already known. It is a liberation that allows something new to take place. In order to be freed of such hope, one must, in Lyotard's view, be freed from discourses of emancipation. The work of art has this "critical function" – it can interrupt discourse,

---

9   John Rajchman, Tate Papers, "*Les Immatériaux* or How to Construct the History of Exhibitions," 2009, 2, https://www.tate.org.uk/research/publications/tate-papers/12/leimmateriaux-or-how-to-construct-the-history-of-exhibitions.

10   See Antony Hudek, "The Affective Economy of the Lyotardian Archive," in *Rereading Jean-François Lyotard: Essays on His Later Work,* eds. Heidi Bickis and Rob Shields (New York: Routledge), 16.

THE RADICAL IMAGINATION, AND THE AESTHETIC OF THE DIFFEREND   419

defy it and reveal its limitations, refuse its strictures and demand that it adapt to what it does not yet recognize.

As Milne emphasizes, the "work," which can be the work of art or work criticism, situates itself in relation to a "demand." The "work" suffers under the barrage of known phrases but, at the same time, it refuses the sufficiency of those phrases. It also resists those pre-set linkages in favor of the possibility of something new, a phrasing that has yet to be phrased and one that is not yet circumscribed or limited by the "what is known." *Les Immatériaux*, to restate Milne's observation, was an attempt at a "liberation from the repetitions of systems and existing categories." The exhibition had an aesthetic and critical function, although the line separating the two activities was difficult to discern, intentionally. The operating theme of the exhibition could be described as: the work of art *does* something ... the work of art *is* not something. The *doing* in this instance is doing the work of disruption, as I mention previously. *Les Immatériaux* called attention to and challenged the sense-making domains of available aesthetic, political, and techno-cognitive idioms. As Lyotard described in the exhibition catalog: "The insecurity, the loss of identity, the crisis is not expressed only in economy and the social, but also in the domains of sensibility, of the knowledge and the power of man (futility, life, death), the modes of life (in relation to work, habits, to food ... etc)."[11] For Lyotard, *Les Immatériaux* offers a series of instances in which the "domains of sensibility" are disrupted and opened ... brought to crisis. This disruption/openness/crisis is not merely limited to the level of a *techno-cyber-comm* life; it is also pertinent to life as a "modality" across a universe of human instances and experiences.[12]

---

11   Yuk Hui, and Andreas Broeckmann, "Introduction," in *30 Years: Les Immatériaux: Art, Science, Theory*, eds. Yuk Hui and Andreas Broeckmann (Lüneburg: Meson Press, 2015), 9.

12   In *"The Immaterials* of Lyotard (1985): A Figural Program," *Appareil* (2012): 5, Jean-Louis Déotte writes: "Despite accents that could have been attributed to Baudrillard, especially on the status of messages without real references, concerning signs referring only to other signs, the definition of the matter that ceases to be given can no longer, at best, be the origin of a trace, so that we can testify, therefore always lost, fallen into the fore-blow of a temporality with two strokes (the aftermath Freudian), in spite of that, there is undoubtedly in this phenomenologist who has always been Lyotard at bottom, a fascination for the new sensitive and human reality, from side to side technological. It was not an exhibition of denunciation, there was even this kind of jubilation, which supposes a passion. Lyotard is not Jean Clair or Georges Steiner. In a way, and it's more his ground, by summoning all the artistic modernity of Moholy Nagy to Duchamp, Kossuth to Monory, Sonia Delaunay to Dan Graham, Peter Eisenman, etc., there can be no doubt about the general purpose of the exhibition. Neither technophile nor technophobe, the exhibition *The Immaterials* put in scene a new situation posing a challenge for the thought."

Is *Les Immatériaux* a "postmodern" exhibition? An exhibition of postmodernism? Both? Answering these questions brings us closer to the radical aesthetic Lyotard was proposing. Planning for *Les Immatériaux* occurred after Lyotard completed *The Differend: Phrases in Dispute* (1983), which is significant given his focus on phrase incommensurability. The exhibition also was partly in response to Simon Nora and Alain Minc's concept of the "computerized society," a concept that played an important role in creating the framework for the French *Minitel* system.[13] *The Differend* and "computerized society" form the initial two initiation points for the exhibition, which is easy to see considering that language, message, and modalities of communication were the key thematic points common to Lyotard's philosophical writings in and around the time of the exhibition.

Les Immatériaux was constructed with five categories in mind, with all relating to a system of telecommunication: medium, receiver, emitter, referent, and code.[14] The *plan de l'exposition* below shows the sixty sites[15] and the non-linear pathways plus partitions challenging the visitor movement within the space:

The discontinuous and disrupted space of the exhibition depicted in the plan broke the visitor's culturally received expectation of communicative smoothness. Unlike a conventional exhibition space, sites were disarticulated and the "narration" that was broadcasted to the headsets exacerbated the separation of site and sense. The exhibition became a domain of disruption/openness/crisis. If we are to understand *Les Immatériaux* to have been either/both

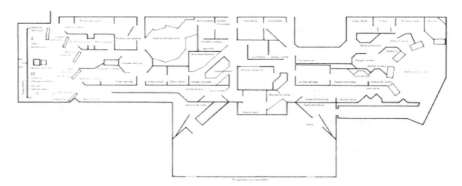

FIGURE 17.1   Plan de l'exposition. The exhibition floor plan is reproduced in Jean-Louis Déotte, "*Les Immateriaux* de Lyotard (1985): un programme figural," *Appareil* (2012): 10.

---

13   Hui and Broeckmann, "Introduction," 9.
14   Hui and Broeckmann, "Introduction," 11.
15   See Déotte, "*The Immaterials* of Lyotard (1985): A Figural Program."

THE RADICAL IMAGINATION, AND THE AESTHETIC OF THE DIFFEREND 421

a postmodern exhibition or/and an exhibition of postmodernism (or neither), the problem of communication[16] needs to be addressed in terms of the five categories. In addition, along with these categories, what I will call the "aesthetic of the differend" needs to be a primary concern in the discussion.

What is the differend and how does it critically shape an aesthetics? Bill Readings defines the differend as, "[a] point of difference where the sides speak radically different or heterogeneous languages, where the dispute cannot be phrased in either language without, by its very phrasing, prejudging the issue for that side, being unjust. Between two language games, two little narratives, two phrases, there is always a differend which must be encountered."[17] *Les Immatériaux* was a staging of the differend. Sites were dispersed throughout the space with little to no organizational continuity. One site did not explain or contextualize another site—each occupied the space singularly, without a meta or master framework (with the exception of the larger problem of communication). If communication technology was to be the solution to addressor/addressee misunderstandings or word-thing confusions, as the postmodern condition seemed to indicate, then *Les Immatériaux* demonstrated that as a technology it failed. Where one was supposed to find communicative smoothness, transparency, and speed, there was instead disruption, blockages, and hesitation. Equipment, for instance, did not work or work as designed (the headsets conked out as visitors toured the sites) and the exhibition plan, as mentioned, was more of a labyrinth than an orderly curated grid.

Rather than "walking through" *Les Immatériaux*, post event, I would like to remain focused on the "aesthetic of the differend." Readings definition is merely a first clarification and it does not follow what could be the implications of the term/concept beyond its initial communicative disruptions or, at least he does not do this in the glossary definition. However, Readings does point to one key element making the differend a critical force of thought: that the "differend marks a point where existing representational frameworks are unable

---

16   Jean-Louis Déotte (*"The Immaterials* of Lyotard (1985): A Figural Program,*"* 2) explains this in the following terms: "The framework of intelligibility used by Lyotard has hitherto been that of Jakobson: the schema of communication, which implies that each message is inseparable from a pole configuration: the addressee, the addressee, the referent, the code, the support. But, unlike strict structuralism, for Lyotard, the poles do not really exist before the message: the sentence is a whole that each time redefines the poles of communication. Each sentence regime is a new world: a (denotative) phrase of knowledge is not a performative or a command phrase, etc. Each sentence is like a blow in a game between speakers, each sentence can be defined in a game of language that is a game with rules."

17   Readings, *Introducing Lyotard: Art and Politics*, xxx.

to deal with difference without repressing or reducing it."[18] It is here that one finds, I'll argue, the beginning of the "aesthetic of the differend" and the radicality of the postmodern imagination.

If we set aside the too easy notion that postmodernism and postmodern art and thought merely celebrate the eclectic and the plural, then the underlying and perhaps unarticulated heterogeneity of these terms comes into better view. In this sense, *Les Immatériaux* is both a postmodern exhibition and an exhibition on postmodernism. The sites manifest juxtaposition, paralogy, and misalignment, which fit under the generic observations regarding a postmodern style. Beside that family resemblance-at-first-glance feature, however, the "organization" or "disorganization" of the exhibition plan calls out the more radical and under recognized aspects of a postmodern aesthetic—the refusal of a sufficient totality in all things. In the absence of a meta or master discourse unifying the exhibition, one finds a proliferation of the differend. The singular instance of a differend or the non-nexus of differends exist as a resistance to an aesthetic that reconciles feeling to reason and object to thought/language.

Feeling and reason are two different and irreconcilable language games; moreover, neither has jurisdiction over the other. It is this point of incommensurability and dispute that is at the center of the "aesthetic of the differend" and *Les Immatériaux*. In his essay entitled "After Six Months of Work ... (1984)," Lyotard provides an overview of the exhibition, explaining his intentions from concept to installation. He saw challenging the "project of domination" or the "project of modernity," which is a modernist project best represented by Descartes' philosophy, as "probably" the "most important thing" the exhibition was interested in examining:

> And above all, I would say that what this exhibition is interested in—probably the most important thing—is that we know very well that there was a metaphysics corresponding to the technoscience of domination. Which was the metaphysics of the subject, the metaphysics of Descartes and of all thinking of the subject up to and including the twentieth century.[19]

Les Immatériaux confounds techno-science's "project of domination," a project built upon a Cartesian reduction of the world to the knowing subject. In

---

18   Readings, *Introducing Lyotard: Art and Politics*, xxx.

19   Jean-François Lyotard, "After Six Months of Work ... (1984)," in *30 Years: Les Immatériaux: Art, Science, Theory*, eds. Yuk Hui and Andreas Broeckmann (Lüneburg: Meson Press, 2015), 33.

this sense, techno-science, along with any technology proffering master explications, is susceptible to the force of the differend—the force of an incommensurability that pre-empts totality, Cartesian, Kantian, or other. An embrace of this force is a critical element of the "aesthetic of the differend." Throughout "After Six Months of Work ... (1984)," Lyotard discusses the philosophical considerations behind the exhibition and its installations in the context of politics as well as the history of philosophy and technology. In the final section, which begins ironically with the line "I should like to add a few disordered remarks," he focuses his attention on the spatial layout of the exhibition and its disruptive anti-structure. As if by extension, Lyotard treats the exhibition's physical space as the space of language games, a phrase universe— discontinuous and non-hegemonic in "nature." He compares the installation zones as transmission spaces—similar to the transitions in radio reception as one drives from the "Mexican border to Santa Barbara."[20] The act "re-tuning" marks a space of difference, a difference between what is being sent and what is or can be received. The metaphor is significant in light of Lyotard's references to "archipelagos"—the discrete entities artificially constelled and unified under a geographic name.

In the final sentences of Lyotard's reflection, "re-tuning," domains or zones of "domination," and disrupted structures of communication, flow into a meditation on "many possible worlds."[21] Lyotard writes, "...I also want to say ... that the multiplicity of routes through the exhibition—above all if we manage to resolve the technical question of being able to record them at will at the exit— allows it to transpire that, fundamentally, the exhibition contains many possible worlds."[22] These worlds exist in a non-totalized space and the "visitor" or human subject had and has in the world the option of many routes—each fundamentally free from the hegemony of a master space. Just as there are many possible routes there are many exhibitions—not only in 1985 but today as the exhibition continues in another time-world, which makes the choice of verb tense tricky. The many routes, the many imaginative pathways, the many exhibitions, the many zones of transmittal and reception are resistant to the injustice of uniformity/unification under a single phrase or realm of phrases. This is where one finds the "aesthetic of the differend." Passage through the exhibition offers these many worlds through "feeling," a feeling that explanatory discourses are proliferating and/or insufficient. Techno-science, as well as any other totalizing discourse, yields to the postmodern imaginative pre-space,

---

20   Lyotard, "After Six Months of Work," 65.
21   Lyotard, "After Six Months of Work," 65.
22   Lyotard, "After Six Months of Work," 65.

the "before" of possibilities that the rule of modernism, in particular, forgets. *Les Immatériaux* becomes the work of spectral remembering ... the remembering of a feeling that another world is waiting just one more actual and figurative step away.

References

Bennington, Geoffrey. *Lyotard: Writing the Event.* Manchester: Manchester University Press. 1988.

Déotte, Jean-Louis. "*The Immaterials* of Lyotard (1985): A Figural Program." *Appareil* (2012): 1–15.

Hudek, Antony. "The Affective Economy of the Lyotardian Archive." In *Rereading Jean-François Lyotard: Essays on His Later Work*, edited by Heidi Bickis and Rob Shields, 11–24. New York: Routledge, 2017.

Hui, Yuk, and Andreas Broeckmann. "Introduction." In *30 Years: Les Immatériaux: Art, Science, Theory*, edited by Yuk Hui and Andreas Broeckmann, 9–24. Lüneburg: Meson Press, 2015.

Jencks, Charles. "Postmodern and Late Modern: The Essential Definitions." *Chicago Review* 35, no. 4 (1987): 31–58.

Lyotard, Jean-François. "After Six Months of Work ... (1984)." In *30 Years: Les Immatériaux: Art, Science, Theory*, edited by Yuk Hui and Andreas Broeckmann, 29–66. Lüneburg: Meson Press, 2015.

Lyotard, Jean-François. *The Postmodern Condition: A Report on Knowledge.* Translated by Geoff Bennington and Brian Massumi. Minneapolis: University of Minnesota Press. 1984.

Milne, Peter W. "Lyotard's 'Critical' 'Aesthetics.'" In *Rereading Jean- François Lyotard: Essays on His Later Works*, edited by Heidi Bickis and Rob Shields, 189–208. New York: Routledge, 2016.

Rajchman, John. Tate Papers. "*Les Immatériaux* or How to Construct the History of Exhibitions." 2009, 1–7, https://www.tate.org.uk/research/publications/tate-papers/12/les-immateriaux-or-how-to-construct-the-history-of-exhibitions.

Readings, Bill. *Introducing Lyotard: Art and Politics.* New York: Routledge. 1991.

CHAPTER 18

The Possibility of a Productive Imagination in the Work of Deleuze and Guattari

Erik Bormanis

1 Introduction

The goal of this chapter is to interrogate the concept of the "imagination" as it plays out in the tradition of postmodernism. If, however, what we generally call "postmodernism" has taught us anything at all, then it has taught us that our methods and categories of organization—such as the very term "postmodernism"—should be regarded with a critical eye. Foucault, at the beginning of *The Order of Things,* recounts a fictional taxonomy given in Borges' essay "The Analytical Language of John Wilkins," which includes the following 14 categories of classification:

> ...(a) belonging to the Emperor, (b) embalmed, (c) tame, (d) sucking pigs, (e) sirens, (f) fabulous, (g) stray dogs, (h) included in the present classification, (i) frenzied, (j) innumerable, (k) drawn with a very fine camelhair brush, (l) *et cetera,* (m) having just broken the water pitcher, (n) that from a long way look like flies.[1]

By elaborating such an exotic and bizarre system of organization, Foucault argues, Borges presents us with a challenge to the ready-made systems of thought with which we in the west organize our encounters with the world. This happens not through the conceivability of strange and wondrous creatures (the *imagination,* Foucault claims, is kept within its proper boundaries), but rather insofar as our thought encounters its limit, insofar as it runs up against the table, surface, or common medium upon which these various categories could be inscribed. It is not, in short, the imaginative ideas of a "fabulous" creature or "sirens" which challenges our thought, but rather the internal consistency of the list itself, a list which fails to cohere in a way that immediately makes sense.

This passage forces Foucault to ask: "On what 'table,' according to what grid of identities, similitudes, analogies, have we become accustomed to sort out so

---

1 Michel Foucault, *The Order of Things* (USA: Random House, Inc., 1970), xv.

© KONINKLIJKE BRILL NV, LEIDEN, 2020 | DOI:10.1163/9789004436350_020

many different and similar things?"[2] Foucault suggests that the process of ordering, which purports to arise from the things themselves, that is to say "objectively," is only ever possible due to the imposition of a grid, where the "powers of contagion"[3] inherent to each category are neatly contained. Such a grid is not itself given in our experience of the world, rather, it is arbitrarily imposed as a necessary condition for such ordering. This is because categorization not only requires a spacing or boundary-drawing exercise, but also a surface upon which these boundaries are articulated; Descartes' epistemic criteria of "distinctness," we might say, implies a surface upon which things are distinguished. Any semblance of order therefore always involves an arbitrary *grid* within which we situate the things we encounter. By drawing our attention to this grid, Foucault, like most thinkers of the "postmodern" tradition, wants to point out how such gridding is essentially arbitrary, even though it is sometimes unavoidable.

Upon what surface, and according to what kind of a grid, then, could we interrogate "the imagination" in such a tradition, a tradition which would seem to undermine the very tools with which we are accustomed to classifying diverse series of thinkers—and the divergent thoughts of even a single thinker—and then declare *this* or *that* to be an accurate account of the subject? Strangely enough, it is on precisely this point, of the insufficiency of our modes of categorization, that most "postmodern" thinkers might be said to agree. Therefore, an account of the imagination that were to somehow take this insufficiency of categorization into account, or indeed, which would show it to be essential, would therefore seem to be one we might properly designate as "postmodern."

My focus here will be on a problem internal to the collaborative thought of Gilles Deleuze and Félix Guattari, specifically, on how their account of a "productive desire," leads them to often speak disparagingly of the imagination as "merely" representational, or what amounts to saying the same thing, the products of the imagination as "merely imaginary." I will argue that there is reason to believe that the imagination, like desire, should be understood as a productive faculty in the work of Deleuze and Guattari themselves. Indeed, I will argue further that this notion of a productive imagination is essential to the "postmodern" project.

To pursue this line of thought, I plan to elaborate several key moments in Deleuze and Guattari's thought, as well as a brief account of Aristotle and Kant's treatment of the imagination. First, we will consider Deleuze's concept of the dogmatic "Image of Thought," discussed in *Difference and Repetition*,

---

2 Foucault, *The Order of Things*, xix.
3 Foucault, *The Order of Things*, xv.

THE POSSIBILITY OF A PRODUCTIVE IMAGINATION 427

where he suggests a non-representational model of thought and a corresponding non-representational faculty of the imagination. Despite this promising suggestion for the imagination, however, in *Anti-Oedipus*, Deleuze and Guattari consistently bemoan the merely "imaginary" consequences of desire understood as *lack*, which implies that they still take the imagination to be a merely representational faculty. It is here, however, we will also need to briefly discuss Aristotle's account of desire in the *De Anima*, which in many ways lies at the root of our misconceptions (according to Deleuze and Guattari) about human faculties. As we will see, Aristotle lays out the way we still think about the various faculties of our soul (including both desire and the imagination), but also presents us with a way around thinking of the imagination as merely representational; namely, he presents us with an account of the imagination as introducing a difference or a clearing into an image which no longer corresponds objectively to a state of given affairs.

I will then read this insight into Deleuze and Guattari's treatment of art as a "monument" from *What is Philosophy*, and Deleuze's treatment of cliché in *Francis Bacon: The Logic of Sensation*. As we will see, once we abandon the representational image of thought, as Deleuze urges us to do, then the imagination itself can be meaningfully rehabilitated as a capacity to clear away images and allow for the space to generate something new. Imagination, understood as in this precise sense as productive imagination is an essential component of the postmodern tradition's general emphasis on the forms of thought, discourse, and being, which modernity could not take seriously.

2   Representation and the *Image of Thought*

We began by considering the postmodern tendency to eschew any ready-made categories or methods of sense-making, and here it would be pertinent to begin with Deleuze's own critique of such approaches. The critique runs through his entire career, but, for reasons that will become clear, I will focus on the 1968 text *Difference and Repetition*, specifically the chapter on the "Image of Thought."

In an attempt to rigorously arrive at the truth, what we know as philosophy generally purports to begin without presuppositions, to achieve its status as "science," as Hegel would say, by forming a self-enclosed system with no foundation external to itself. However, as Deleuze points out, throughout the history of philosophy and across vastly different philosophical approaches, there lies a commitment to a particular *way* of articulating what it means to think at all. Deleuze describes our commitment to this as follows: "the supposition that thought is the natural exercise of a faculty, of the presupposition that there is a natural capacity for thought endowed with a talent for truth or an affinity with the true, under the double aspect of a *good will on the part of the thinker* and an *upright nature on the part of thought*."[4] The presupposition that Deleuze locates here is not a specific factual claim, but rather a criterion for what establishes a philosophical claim *as* "philosophical" at all; a considered belief that thought, at least, has a specific character. Such an account of thought treats it as a faculty we each *individually* possess and which happily accords with the "truth." If this is the case, then when we think, we reveal or recognize something that everybody in principle should know, or which they could not deny inasmuch as they too possess this common faculty of thought. Anyone who doesn't *recognize* what "everybody knows" or that which "no one can deny"[5] would therefore be a person who knows in principle, but has a "bad will," who lacks the wherewithal, in terms of moral fiber or character, to see what we all take to be the case. This is a fundamental presupposition, according to Deleuze, that underlies all philosophical endeavor.

Inherent to this way of understanding thought includes understanding it in terms of "representation." As Deleuze writes, "*everybody knows, no one can deny*, is the form of representation and the discourse of the representative."[6] It would be too difficult, here, to elaborate convincingly on why this is the case. However, we can note that representation is tied to *recognition*, insofar as recognition presupposes some prior knowledge. For example, in order to recognize someone, I must have met them somewhere before (or take them to be someone I know — though I may misrecognize them), and I must be capable of *representing* their image in my mind in order to compare the present person before me with the person I know. Recognition therefore relies upon a correspondence between our present state of mind and some previously established state of affairs. As Deleuze writes, however, "the form of recognition has never sanctioned anything but the recognizable and the recognized; form will never inspire anything but conformities."[7] Thus, the image of thought is no harmless presupposition: it prejudges any given situation, dictating what can and cannot make an appearance before thought. Thought, in other words, becomes limited to a *re*-presentation of some prior reservoir of knowledge.

---

4 Gilles Deleuze, *Difference and Repetition*, trans. Paul Patton (New York: Columbia University Press, 1994), 131.

5 Deleuze, *Difference and Repetition*, 130.

6 Deleuze, *Difference and Repetition*, 130.

7 Deleuze, *Difference and Repetition*, 134.

THE POSSIBILITY OF A PRODUCTIVE IMAGINATION   429

Thus, the image of thought circumscribes the possibilities available to thought, limits what *can* be thought to that which is already articulated. Nevertheless, we might object that we do in fact recognize many things in daily life, and that these acts of recognition are crucial to our existence as human beings. Despite my earlier attempts at complication, for example, I still need to recognize certain thinkers as the ones we call "postmodernists" in order to write this chapter. As Deleuze notes, however, it would be difficult and dangerous to claim that in these acts of recognition "the destiny of thought is at stake."[8] As if only the mundane realities of what "everybody knows" should be called thinking. If we allow recognition to dominate our accounts of thinking in this way then nothing new could ever arise, and in that precise sense we can say that thought would lack a "destiny," and would be consigned to the fate of an eternal recognition, never moving beyond itself as a static and lifeless totality. Thought, if we subscribe to this dogmatic image, is necessarily *representational*, in the sense that it consists only in dredging up something past, bringing to mind once more some idea, thought, or image.

Deleuze, more than most thinkers in the postmodern tradition, aims to replace the models he critiques with new ones, and here, he suggests that we replace the dogmatic image of thought with an understanding of *the encounter*. He writes:

> Thought is primarily trespass and violence, the enemy, and nothing presupposes philosophy: everything begins with misosophy. Do not count upon thought to ensure the relative necessity of what it thinks. Rather, count upon the contingency of an encounter with that which forces thought to raise up and educate the absolute necessity of an act of thought or a passion to think. The conditions of a true critique and a true creation are the same: the destruction of an image of thought which presupposes itself and the genesis of the act of thinking in thought itself.[9]

The encounter is not an encounter at the level of thought as we understand it, of encountering some precise image or idea. Rather, the encounter begins at the level of sense. "Sense," however, should not be understood solely in its typical English meanings, for the French word *sens* includes the connotation of a sign and direction in addition to the connotations of something understood, something meaningful, etc. Therefore, If we encounter something, we are sent in a new direction, we are on the way to something of which *we must now make*

---

8   Deleuze, *Difference and Repetition*, 135.
9   Deleuze, *Difference and Repetition*, 139.

sense. This object we encounter cannot be an object which we recognize, because for Deleuze, recognition creates nothing new, it only recreates, represents what we already know; thus, when we speak of the "encounter" we must characterize the object encountered as fundamentally unrecognizable, something "imperceptible"[10] (*insensible*).[11] Thinking begins where recognition fails, where we cannot *represent*, we must rather start anew, generate new concepts for this object or experience which we cannot recognize. In thinking we are called to *make sense*; and this thinking begins precisely where the image of thought breaks down, finds its accumulated resources too poor for the task. It begins at the level of a fundamental encounter with a world or reality which exceeds it.

There is no better example of the encounter, to my mind, than Foucault's own encounter with Borges' "Chinese Encyclopaedia," with which I began this chapter. Foucault begins *The Order of Things* with this example, and it forms the affective impetus, on Foucault's account, of the origin of the book. He writes:

> This book first arose out of a passage in Borges, out of the laughter that shattered, as I read the passage, all the familiar landmarks of my thought – *our* thought, the thought that bears the stamp of our age and our geography – breaking up all the ordered surfaces and all the planes with which we are accustomed to tame the wild profusion of existing things, and continuing long afterwards to disturb and threaten with collapse our age-old distinction between the Same and the Other.[12]

One imagines what this insight must have been like, to realize, as if in a flash, the arbitrariness of our systematic organization of the world. Foucault makes sense of his affective experience (soliciting laughter, whether mirthful, cruel, or whatever), as resulting from butting up against[13] a limit of our thinking. He is not recognizing some age-old truth that has been revealed to him, but rather,

---

10 Deleuze, *Difference and Repetition,* 140.
11 See Ranciere's critique of Deleuze's project of "imperceptibility," in "Is there a Deleuzian Aesthetics?," Trans. Radmila Djordjevic. *Qui Parle?* 14, no. 2 (2004): 1–14, and Katharine Wolfe's rebuttal in "From Aesthetics to Politics: Rancière, Kant and Deleuze," *Contemporary Aesthetics* 4 (January 1, 2006): n. pag. https://www.contempaesthetics.org/newvolume/pages/article.php?articleID=382.
12 Foucault, *The Order of Things,* xv.
13 One might think here of Jean-Luc Nancy's use of "*à même,*" meaning roughly, "right-at" or "right-up-against" throughout his work, as indicating an encounter or proximity to something that would not involve the contemplative distance we usually associate with forms of thought.

THE POSSIBILITY OF A PRODUCTIVE IMAGINATION 431

he is feeling thought facing its own limit, something "impossible to think."[14] From this impossibility, Foucault can then begin to ask "what kind of impossibility are we faced with here?"[15] I take it that this is precisely the logic of the encounter: we encounter something unthinkable, something for which we lack the appropriate concepts or methods. It is *here* that thought is solicited, and I believe this is precisely what Deleuze has in mind when he suggests the "image of thought" be replaced with "the encounter."

As I mentioned above, in the chapter on the image of thought Deleuze deals specifically with the faculty of the imagination as it has been understood in relation to the image of thought. The image of thought delineates the imagination as one of the faculties we possess which we can then exercise as part of a "common sense" which contains and unifies our various faculties in a central point or "subject." This common sense, Deleuze wants to argue, essentially presupposes that all faculties can communicate with one another homogeneously, that they work together in pursuits of various projects or ends which serve as their unifying principle. Imagine, for example, that I am trying to think of a considerate gift for a friend's birthday; in pursuit of this, presumably, I would try to remember conversations we've had where they might have mentioned something they needed, what I know they enjoy, and I might even entertain various possibilities before I then come to a decision. In short, I marshal my faculties in pursuit of my practical aims. The imagination, in this example, is simply one faculty among others, organized by a common sense. It is in this organizational scheme of common sense that we can speak of an imagination "the aim of which is to rediscover or re-create."[16] It is within this schema of common sense that the imagination becomes subordinated to a reproductive, representational function.

The encounter, however, dis-organizes common sense, this happy cooperation of the faculties, allowing each faculty to have its own "disjointed, superior or transcendent exercise."[17] To be sure, in the chapter on the Image of thought, Deleuze is explicitly concerned with thinking and sense, rather than the imagination, and we have already discussed the "encounter" in sensation as involving an object, affect, or percept, which is essentially imperceptible, meaning that we do not have a ready-made way of recognizing the thing we are encountering. In thought, "the problem is not to direct or methodically apply a thought which pre-exists in principle and in nature, but to bring into being that which

---

14 Foucault, *The Order of Things*, xv.
15 Foucault, *The Order of Things*, xv.
16 Deleuze, *Difference and Repetition*, 138.
17 Deleuze, *Difference and Repetition*, 143.

does not yet exist (there is no other work, all the rest is arbitrary, mere decoration)."[18] When we are *really* thinking, when we are *forced* to think, the work of thought is to create, to bring something new into existence. True thought would only happen when we encounter something (like Borges' list) which frustrates our habitual interpretive frameworks, and which demands a *new* concept adequate to the task. This need not even be something so grand as the generation of an entirely new concept in a historical sense (though these would be most important), but indeed, would characterize even our learning concepts that are culturally familiar. When a child first learns to say, "that's unfair!," we can imagine the *force* of this realization: "my share is less than it ought to be!" and the subsequent thought "How do I make sense of this? Oh, this is unfair!" It is when the use of the concept of fairness becomes rote that we are no longer really thinking: "Oh yes, the world is unfair, but what can we do about it?"

Similarly, then, the imagination, if it were to be unmoored from common sense, should have its own creative capacities. Like thought and sense, however, the imagination would have to be solicited to imagine, or called to imagine precisely by something we *cannot* imagine, something to which the imagination cannot adequately and immediately respond. Hence Deleuze's open-ended question: "is there an *imaginandum*, a *phantasteon,* which would also be the limit, that which is impossible to imagine?"[19] Unfortunately, to my knowledge, Deleuze never pursues this specific line of thought farther, but I would like to note here that Deleuze at least acknowledges the possibility for an imagination which, like thought, would not be subordinated to the image of thought, to generating only images which are already imaginable. Imagination, then would acquire its own "destiny," rather than being consigned, as thought, to the "fate" of an eternal repetition of the same.

We see then that Deleuze enjoins us to struggle against the dogmatic image of thought, the prevailing paradigm of thinking which prejudges everything, which insinuates itself everywhere, allowing only for the propagation and recognition of its own image. We must reject this in favor of opening ourselves up to "encounters" that would call to thought from across an unstable or ungiven *gap* to generate new concepts, and I would like to suggest here, also call the imagination to generate new images that are not results of some previous iterations, clichés or mere representations.

---

18   Deleuze, *Difference and Repetition,* 147.

19   Deleuze, *Difference and Repetition,* 143.

THE POSSIBILITY OF A PRODUCTIVE IMAGINATION

3   Productive Desire and "Mere" Imagination

Despite Deleuze's hopeful suggestion that the faculty of the imagination can become transcendental, freed from its subjugation to a common sense and an upright moral standard, in his work with Guattari in *Anti-Oedipus* he seems to be less hopeful for such rehabilitation. Throughout the *Anti-Oedipus*, Deleuze and Guattari generally describe the imagination in only negative terms: as precisely reproductive, representational, generative only of mere fantasy or phantasy. Nevertheless, as I will show, their account of "productive desire" (which they oppose to desire as lack and it's "merely imaginary" products) should lead us to reconsider the imagination and the representational role to which Deleuze and Guattari seem to consign it.

Deleuze and Guattari famously, in *Anti-Oedipus*, set themselves the task of opposing two dogmatic characterizations of desire to which philosophers and psychoanalysts more or less subscribe; ideas of desire as orbiting a central point and the notion of desire as a *lack,* both of which are involved in Freud's oedipal account of sexuality. For Deleuze and Guattari, the traditional logic of desire, inherited from Plato's famous account in the *Symposium,* wherein he defines desire as a lack, misleads us insofar as it commits us to a dichotomy between production and acquisition. That is, desire for Plato is seen as the desire for an object we would like to acquire, rather than an object we want to produce. We can understand this fairly clearly in relation to what Deleuze and Guattari claim, alongside Spinoza, to be the central question of political philosophy: "'Why do men fight *for* their servitude as stubbornly as though it were their salvation?'"[20] It is not that we lack an object, here—a servitude to which we are not yet subject—but we fight precisely to maintain this servitude, to *produce it.* It is, moreover, quite revealing that Deleuze and Guattari claim that Wilhelm Reich, taking up this claim from Spinoza, is not content to attribute such self-negating pursuits to mere ignorance or illusion (which would involve the imagination classically understood, involving a lack of contact with the real), but rather, posits "an explanation formulated in terms of desire: no, the masses were not innocent dupes; at a certain point, under a certain set of conditions, they *wanted* fascism, and it is this perversion of the desire of the masses that needs to be accounted for."[21] Desire is an explanation of political reality precisely to the extent and insofar as it involves *making something happen.* In

---

20   Gilles Deleuze and Félix Guattari, *Anti Oedipus,* trans. Robert Hurley, Mark Seem, and Helen R. Lane (Minneapolis: University of Minnesota Press, 1983), 29.

21   Deleuze and Guattari, *Anti Oedipus,* 29.

other words, desire must be in contact with the real, it must produce, and does produce, specific political actions and structures.[22]

For Deleuze and Guattari, then, desire is not a lack; it does not search for some longed-after or absent object it seeks to acquire. Feeding into this idea of lack, however, is the further determination and specification of *what object* is lacking (we see how this is precisely opposed to the encounter). In *Anti-Oedipus,* we see a thoroughgoing critique of one object in particular that serves, in psychoanalysis, as the organizing principle of desire: Daddy-Mommy. Given what we have already noted at the outset, it should be clear that the postmodern approach to such an organizational principle, one which tames desire's powers of contagion or production, must be interrogated carefully and critically. Though Deleuze and Guattari acknowledge their debt to Melanie Klein for her theory of partial objects, her insistence upon an oedipal framework[23] nevertheless forms a central example of the tyranny of Oedipus. In the example cited by Deleuze and Guattari, Melanie Klein is meeting with a young child named Dick, and presents him with two trains, one smaller, and one larger, which she names Dick-train and Daddy-train, respectively. When Dick then picks up the Dick-train, he rolls it through the station, which Klein then refers to as "Mummy," asserting that Dick is going inside Mummy. There remains more, but the point is clear: "Say that it's Oedipus, or you'll get a slap in the face. The psychoanalyst no longer says to the patient: 'tell me a bit about your desiring-machines won't you?' Instead he screams: 'Answer daddy-and-mommy when I speak to you!'"[24] This railroading of our experience as desiring creatures into a prefabricated model to which desire must then conform in analysis is indicative of a certain *taming*, a certain delimitation of *what counts* as legitimate desire, a dogmatic commitment to what must always already be the organizational structure of desire. Recognition, in other words, only recognizes itself. As Deleuze and Guattari point out, however: "A child never confines himself to playing house, to playing only at being daddy-and-mommy. He also plays at being a magician, a cowboy, a cop or a robber, a train, a little car."[25] Once more, desire *produces*, it establishes connections, it invests things with a surplus value; not because they *resemble* or *represent* mommy-daddy, but

---

22   For further explanation of this point, see Eugene Holland's *Deleuze and Guattari's Anti-Oedipus: Introduction to Schizoanalysis* (London: Routledge, 1999).

23   Deleuze and Guattari attribute this to Klein's possible desire to "avoid any sort of contretemps with the International Psycho-Analytic Association that bears about its door the inscription 'let no one enter here who does not believe in Oedipus.'" (Deleuze and Guattari, *Anti Oedipus,* 45).

24   Deleuze and Guattari, *Anti Oedipus,* 45.

25   Deleuze and Guattari, *Anti Oedipus,* 46.

THE POSSIBILITY OF A PRODUCTIVE IMAGINATION   435

rather because and only to the extent that they are desired, integrated into the desiring-machines of the child. As Deleuze and Guattari suggestively write, "the unconscious is an orphan."[26]

Desire produces, then, and it is furthermore not organized around some central point which serves as a foundational principle preconditioning or pre-configuring the productions of desire. We might then ask what this has to do with the imagination. Readers of *Anti-Oedipus*, indeed, might even note that Deleuze and Guattari often refer to the imagination in a rather disparaging way, claiming, for example, that in psychoanalysis: "Desiring-production is per-sonalized, or rather personologized (*personnologisée*), imaginarized (*imagi-narisée*), structuralized ... production is reduced to mere fantasy production, production of expression."[27] Psychoanalysis, on Deleuze and Guattari's read-ing, *makes something* of us; instead of a multiplicitous and expansive desire, we are made to become "subjects," we are structured, and our desires therefore become merely representational. Imagination, they would seem to think, is the merely representational faculty in which desire produces not the real, but mere images of the real—in which the "classical theater, the classical order of representation"[28] becomes the structure of the unconscious. The imagination is complicit in this project, insofar as it has a place in the schema as producing these images, drawing from a familiar cast of characters, from "mommy," and "daddy."

This, interestingly enough, is consonant with Deleuze and Guattari's cri-tique of Kant, wherein they claim that despite Kant's efforts to elaborate a more productive form of desire, he nevertheless uses examples which are mere fancy or imagination. They write: "as Kant would have it, we are well aware that the real object can be produced only by an external causality and external mechanisms; nonetheless this knowledge does not prevent us from believing in the intrinsic power of desire to create its own object—if only in an unreal, hallucinatory, or delirious form."[29] Kant fails, on Deleuze and Guattari's ac-count, to follow through with his account of desire because he relegates it to generating a mere "psychic reality."[30] In this way, then, Deleuze and Guattari's discussion of productive desire places the imagination in the service of desire-as-lack, where imagination becomes the faculty we use to represent to ourselves, psychically, the object we lack. We desire the images of "mommy" or

---

26   Deleuze and Guattari, *Anti Oedipus,* 49.
27   Deleuze and Guattari, *Anti Oedipus,* 55.
28   Deleuze and Guattari, *Anti Oedipus,* 55.
29   Deleuze and Guattari, *Anti Oedipus,* 25.
30   Deleuze and Guattari, *Anti Oedipus,* 25.

"daddy," and the imagination has its role in conjuring these ghostly phantasms. As long as desire is understood in terms of desire-as-lack, the imagination will also be reduced to imagining only absent presences, or perhaps presences which were never present, never anything truly real.[31]

4 Aristotle on Desire and Imagination

My goal is to understand how we might come to an understanding of the imagination freed from the image of thought and productive desire. At this point, however, it would be helpful to consider briefly two figures from the history of philosophy who Deleuze and Guattari consistently oppose: Aristotle and Kant. Indeed, for both of these figures, desire and imagination are understood to be intimately connected, and understanding this connection will helpfully bridge the gap between Deleuze and Guattari's accounts of desire and the imagination.

Here, however, it would be productive to attend to the way Aristotle begins his analysis of imagination by distinguishing it from thought and perception. Defining imagination, Aristotle writes: "...it is clear that imagination is not the same activity as conceiving that something is so, for the former experience is available to us whenever we want it ... but to form an opinion is not up to us, since it has to be either true or false."[32] When we conceive something, we form an opinion which we must at least understand it be either true or false (though we can clearly be mistaken in our opinions), and this therefore requires that there be some state of affairs which we take to be either true or false. The imagination, however, need not correspond to some external state of affairs; it simply presents an image to us, and this image need not be true or false.[33] A distinguishing characteristic of the imagination, therefore, is precisely its connection with desire, its capacity to be exercised whenever we want it. We should keep this in mind, as Deleuze and Guattari's concept of desiring-production as opposed to a centralized account (common sense, or the subject), or an account of desire-as-lack, will have significant consequences for how we then understand imagination.

---

31 Such, for example, would be Jean Baudrillard's focus on simulacra, from *Simulacra and Simulation*; or the focus on the "immemorial" throughout the tradition of psychoanalysis and continental philosophy more generally such as in the work of Henri Bergson and Luce Irigaray.

32 Arisotle, *De Anima*, trans. Joe Sachs (Santa Fe: Green Lion Press, 2004), 427b15–427b22.

33 See Aristotle's definition at 428a.

THE POSSIBILITY OF A PRODUCTIVE IMAGINATION 437

This line of thought, however, is best pursued through Aristotle's own analysis of the imagination. For Aristotle, a further distinguishing characteristic of imagination is something that we might call its remoteness. Elaborating on the above-cited passage, he writes: "when we have the opinion that something is terrifying or frightening we immediately feel the corresponding feeling, and similarly if we think it is something that inspires confidence, but with the imagination we are in the same condition as if we were beholding terrifying or confidence-inspiring things in a painting."[34] Imagination, Aristotle observes, is marked precisely by its distance from direct experience; a painting of a tiger, for example, does not inspire us with fear in the same way that an encounter with a real tiger would. We should note well, however, that Aristotle not only refers here to *affect*, which imagination does not immediately inspire, and uses a representational metaphor (the painting) to describe the way imagination holds things at a distance. Though Aristotle would certainly claim that the imagination, as an activity of the soul, is real, and even a prerequisite for thought, it occupies for Aristotle an ambivalent space, a space we might describe as both representational and distancing. On this later point, despite the fundamental role that the imagination plays in Aristotle's account, we should note that it also opens up a space of indetermination, a space within which we can fall into error. Imagination is understood, for Aristotle, always in relation to its capacity for falsehood: "...perceptions are always true, but most imaginings turn out to be false."[35] That something can be false suggests that it is not part of what counts as fully "real" or "present." The imagination, for Aristotle, is the imagination precisely and to the extent that it is dislocated from objective states of affairs, though it is nevertheless drawn from our sense-perception insofar as imagination is precisely "a motion [change] coming about as a result of the being-at-work of sense perception, and corresponding to it."[36] Imagination for Aristotle would therefore seem to be subordinated to sense perception, which furnishes it with a "material" for subsequent re-presentations. When I think of a fabulous creature, say a Siren (corresponding to Borges' list), I piece it together out of material (perceptions) which I have previously perceived. Nevertheless, Aristotle almost seems to be claiming that the imagination is not necessarily subject to the givens of our experience, insofar as it can be false, it seems to create something *other* than a mere representation, even if Arisostle would only understand that as a failed attempt at an accurate representation.

---

34   Arisotle, *De Anima*, 427b22–427b29.

35   Arisotle, *De Anima*, 428a13.

36   Arisotle, *De Anima*, 429a1-3.

I would like here to pursue a thought: that it is precisely because our *desire* brings an image to mind that we are not affected by it in the same way; insofar as we are "in control," the image does not inspire an immediate affect. It is because I *myself* generate the image, that it becomes in some sense relative. I will use this as a clue for how to approach the imagination in a properly "postmodern" way, namely, by suggesting that because the desire and imagination are intimately connected, if we conceive of desire as productive, so too must the imagination be productive. We should remind ourselves here, moreover, that Deleuze characterizes the image of thought as "lack[ing] the claws of absolute necessity – in other words, of an original violence inflicted upon thought; the claws of a strangeness or an enmity which alone would awaken thought from its natural stupor or eternal possibility."[37] I mention this because I understand Deleuze's project, in general, to be a way of undermining a representational paradigm which pre-judges, pre-articulates everything that it claims to interrogate; and here, we see that the essential thing for Deleuze is to always be *gripped* by an alternative, a difference, which then opens up a space of further exploration, an empty space or clearing to which thought would then have to respond. It is precisely this capacity that the imagination seems to lack in Aristotle, although he suggests that the imagination is not constrained to simply represent faithfully the givens of our everyday experience.

Imagination then, unlike thought, is not something that necessitates us in any way; it does not operate in the realm of real production, which is the task of thought (though thought, to be sure, requires the imagination to supply it with its material—we always think with images, according to Aristotle). Insofar as Deleuze and Guattari understand imagination to involve a retreat from the real, then they are in agreement with Aristotle on this point. I want to argue here, however, that given their emphasis on desiring-production, as opposed to desire-as-lack, we can and should suggest an account of the imagination that is itself productive, that itself serves as a font of creativity—but one which is decidedly *real*.

As we mentioned, earlier, Deleuze and Guattari locate a revolutionary philosophical moment in Kant. They claim that Kant "must be credited with effecting a critical revolution as regards the theory of desire, by attributing to it 'the faculty of being, through its representations, the cause of the reality of the objects of these representations.'"[38] While it might indeed sound like an outlandish claim to say that desire *causes a reality*, I believe the strangeness of this claim is precisely a strangeness that Deleuze and Guattari push us to consider.

---

37   Deleuze, *Difference and Repetition,* 139.
38   Deleuze and Guattari, *Anti Oedipus,* 25.

THE POSSIBILITY OF A PRODUCTIVE IMAGINATION   439

We might make sense of Kant's claim, here, as suggesting that insofar as desire desires an object, it is the cause of the representation of that object *as* the object of desire. Desire introduces a "surplus value" into a representation, making it not only a representation of the object as it is in truth, but as the object as it is *and* as the object desired. There is a difference, for example, between imagining a glass of water that I'm using as an example in my writing, and a glass of water that I desire.[39] The "desired water," then, would be caused *by* my desire. As we mentioned previously, however, this leads only to a mental image, one which fails to attain the status of something real and productive. On this point, I believe Kant and Aristotle are in agreement: the imagination represents merely imaginary images.

Desire, however, structures reality, and it does so directly, without any appeal to mediating representations. If this is the case, however, then we should entertain the notion that if desire is directly productive, so too would the imagination be productive. But this leaves it up to us to ask what the imagination might produce if it can be freed from the shackles of our dogmatic image of thought, its common sense, and its representational paradigm. There is no better place to turn, here, than Deleuze's and Guattari's later work in *What is Philosophy*, where they specifically pose the question of what constitutes a work of art.

5   Productive Imagination in the Work of Art

Given our conclusions regarding the possibilities that Deleuze's philosophy opens up for an account of a productive imagination, it now remains to be seen what, exactly, such imagination might produce. In *What Is Philosophy*, Deleuze and Guattari famously claim that philosophy is the "art of forming, inventing, and fabricating concepts."[40] That is, philosophy creates concepts to construct provisional structures for an experience that would be nothing but chaos without these structures, even if such concepts must always be reinvented. Similarly, they conceive of art as fundamentally a response to this same

---

39   Tamar Schapiro argues that for Kant we must necessarily *act* on a desire, which would situate Kant much closer to Deleuze and Guattari on the subject of desire. Eric Wilson, however, argues against this reading of Kant. See Tamar Schapiro, "Foregrounding Desire: A Defense of Kant's Incorporation Thesis," *Journal of Ethics: An International Philosophical Review* 15, no. 3 (2011), 147–67., and Eric Entrican Wilson, "Habitual Desire: On Kant's Concept of Inclination," *Kantian Review* 21, no. 2 (2016): 211–35.

40   Gilles Deleuze and Félix Guattari, *What Is Philosophy?*, trans. Hugh Tomlinson and Graham Burchell (New York: Columbia University Press, 1994), 2.

chaos, a response which structures this swirling, ever-changing mix of affections and perceptions in such a way that they can *endure*.

We should clarify that for Deleuze and Guattari, art is not a matter of conveying some kind of content, some perception or affection which once belonged to me and that I then transmit to you. On the contrary, art *is* a bloc of sensation; it is affection itself, it is a "power of contagion," to use a phrase common in the postmodern vocabulary. Despite this, art, strangely enough, is itself an organization, a structuring. When it comes to art we are concerned with a specific organization of affect or sensation such that it becomes autonomous or independent. Art makes us *feel* something, and for Deleuze and Guattari it does this through constructing what they call "monuments."

Above all, Deleuze and Guattari suggest, art always "preserves, and it is the only thing in the world that is preserved."[41] By this, they do not mean to suggest that art is *archival,* preserving in the same way as a database of our tax returns would preserve; or, similarly, it is not commemorative in the same way that public statues or photograph of our first birthday would be commemorative. On the contrary, art is always an event – it does not refer to something other than itself – but is itself a "bloc of sensations, that is to say, a compound of percepts and affects."[42] A work of art "preserves" only insofar as it embodies in itself, in its very material existence, a sensation. The work of J.M.W. Turner, in this respect, can be instructive. *The Fighting Téméraire tugged to her last berth to be broken up, 1838* might very well be interestingly and importantly related to the actual event of the *Téméraire* (apparently, referred to by her crew as "Saucy" Téméraire,[43] which already indicates a deviation from a merely archival function) being tugged away, this relation to a past event is not what makes the painting art. On the contrary, it is the sensation evoked by the color, the texture, the brushstrokes of the painting. In this way, what makes a work of art "art," is precisely its material and how that material is articulated, rather than its indexical reference to something other than itself. The artist, for Deleuze and Guattari, must always strive to make her work "stand up on its own,"[44] that is, to make the material itself embody sensation, such that the sensation persists as long and to the extent that the material of the artwork itself persists.

Art is material; here, before us, is a novel, a poem, a painting, a sculpture, etc., and the bloc of sensations lasts for as long as the material lasts. It remains

---

41   Deleuze and Guattari, *What Is Philosophy?*, 163.

42   Deleuze and Guattari, *What Is Philosophy?*, 164.

43   Nigel Reynolds, "Turner's Fighting Temeraire Sinks the Competition," *The Telegraph*, September 6, 2005, http://www.telegraph.co.uk/news/uknews/1497703/Turners-Fighting-Temeraire-sinks-the-opposition.html.

44   Deleuze and Guattari, *What Is Philosophy?*, 164.

THE POSSIBILITY OF A PRODUCTIVE IMAGINATION 441

to be seen, however, of what this "bloc of sensations" really consists. We have already seen that Deleuze and Guattari refer to these blocs of sensation as "compound[s] of percepts and affects,"[45] but percept and affect mean something quite specific in this context. Above all, the language of percept and affect are intended to deter us from thinking in terms of a human subject who perceives and is affected. They write: "Sensations, percepts, and affects are *beings* whose validity lies in themselves and exceeds any lived. They could be said to exist in the absence of man because man, as he is caught in stone, on the canvas, or by words, is himself a compound of percepts and affects."[46] It would lead us too far astray, here, to give a full account of Deleuze and Guattari's ontology, which would support the claim that any individual *thing* is itself a compound of un-personalized, un-individualized affects or percepts.[47] The world, for Deleuze and Guattari is fundamentally *chaos,* a swarming of dislocated sensations and percepts, and human beings are themselves only tentative and precarious *compounds* of such sensations. Art, then, is made of the same *stuff* as human beings, and as such the validity of art is not dependent upon either the artist or the audience investing it with a meaning, situating it within a narrative (as if one could "get" a Turner painting by detailing the event it represents, or could "get" Van Gogh's *Sunflowers* by correctly identifying them as sunflowers). As Deleuze and Guattari write: "percepts are no longer perceptions; they are independent of a state of those who experience them. Affects are no longer feelings are affections; they go beyond the strength of those who undergo them."[48] Perceptions dislocated from a perceiver, affects dislocated from a feeling individual — these are what can be embodied in, become a "monument" in the work of art.

How is this "imagination?" Recall Deleuze's claim in *Difference and Repetition* that the imagination should detach itself from common sense and achieve its own autonomous existence, and his suggestion that the imagination can do this by being solicited by an object which is itself unimaginable. This means, I take it, that one must imagine what has not yet been imagined, must imagine what is so-far *impossible to imagine,* but in so doing, to make such imagining possible, if only because it has now become a real being of sensation. This may seem like a bizarre claim to make, but it is essentially the claim that in order to really free the imagination, we must break with what we have previously

---

45   Deleuze and Guattari, *What Is Philosophy?*, 164.

46   Deleuze and Guattari, *What Is Philosophy?*, 164.

47   For a fuller account of this claim, see Elizabeth Grosz, *Chaos, Territory, Art* (New York: Columbia University Press, 2008).

48   Deleuze and Guattari, *What Is Philosophy?*, 164.

442 BORMANIS

imagined, or in other words, we must free ourselves from the *clichés* which the imagination merely represents in order to imagine something new; and it is only on this condition that we can really be said to be "imaginative" at all.

Indeed, I believe this very point can be helpfully located in Deleuze's discussion of "the cliché" in *The Logic of Sensation,* his book-length discussion of the work of Francis Bacon. He writes that "...it would be a mistake to think that the painter works on a white and virgin surface. The entire surface is already invested virtually with all kinds of clichés, which the painter will have to break with."[49] The painter, claims Deleuze, does not paint upon an empty surface, upon which she would inscribe whatever fanciful figure or idea pops into her mind. Rather, the painter – the original painter – is the one who knows that the white space of the canvas is already besieged by clichés, temptations to an automatic response which would re-create or re-present typical or acceptable images. Indeed, as Deleuze notes, modernity has become especially enmeshed in this problem of the cliché: "Clichés, clichés! ... Not only has there been a multiplication of images of every kind, around us and in our heads, but even the reactions against clichés are creating clichés. Even abstract painting has not been the last to produce its own clichés..."[50] Thus, there is a difference between painting *like* Cézanne, Monet, Van Gogh, etc., and *being* such an artist. Each of these painters contributed, briefly and provisionally perhaps, towards the project of breaking with clichés, freeing us from dogmatic or constrained approaches to painting. After such a decisive change, however, the temptation arises to *repeat* the style that such artists created, to take it up as itself up *as* a cliché. This, I think, is a phenomenon we all recognize, and which can be accounted for by the concept of the imagination as producing something which cannot be imagined, but which then contributes to furthering the repertoire of available clichés.

The decisive action in painting, and perhaps in most art, then, remains the gesture of clearing: "the painter does not have to cover a blank surface but rather would have to empty it out, clear it, clean it."[51] Perhaps, then, we can say that the imagination, if it is to be productive, would produce precisely this emptiness, this clearing. Certainly, such an account of the imagination would fit Deleuze's characterization of "transcendental imagination" as imagining without an image. Is this not precisely what breaking with a cliché, as described by Deleuze, involves? We must clear away every other image, we must

---

49   Gilles Deleuze, *Francis Bacon: The Logic of Sensation*, trans. Daniel W. Smith (Minneapolis: University of Minnesota Press, 2003), 12.

50   Deleuze, *Francis Bacon: The Logic of Sensation*, 73.

51   Deleuze, *Francis Bacon: The Logic of Sensation*, 71.

THE POSSIBILITY OF A PRODUCTIVE IMAGINATION 443

introduce a *difference*, something *new* to the canvas, and such a task can be said to be accomplished by the imagination. But this imagination is not subordinated to its role of representing already given images, but rather, as truly productive, as designating our capacity to clear away such images. We see, then, how the imagination is still related to sense-perception, it generates blocs of sensation, but when it is exercised most effectively, it can escape from cliché, if only for a moment, to create a new bloc of sensation.

There are two further reasons to support this understanding of the imagination. The first is that it corresponds to our everyday usage of the term. When we call someone "imaginative," it denotes their capacity to create or do something new or surprising, whether this would involve an unorthodox solution to a practical task, a surprising turn of phrase, or a novel approach to a scientific problem. Second, it seems to correspond to artists' account of their own work. In *Brutality of Fact: Interviews with Francis Bacon,* David Sylvester asks why Bacon painted Velasquez' *Pope Innocent x*, and Bacon responds: "I became obsessed by it. I buy book after book with this illustration in it of the Velasquez *Pope* because it just haunts me, and it opens up all sorts of feelings and areas of — I was going to say — imagination, even, in me."[52]

Here is an account of the imagination that is both similar to the Aristotelian account of imagination and a critical response to it. Essentially, the imagination would certainly treat things "as if they're in a painting," creating a kind of *spacing*, only this time not between the viewer and the painting, but rather as a precondition of the painting itself; the imaginative spacing needed to generate something new. We see already how it is a precondition for painting: the imagination is needed to clear away clichés from the canvas and from the mind of the artist. Deleuze and Guattari suggest, however, that blocs of sensation, which constitute all art, "need pockets of air and emptiness because even the void is sensation ... A canvas may be completely full to the point that even the air no longer gets through, but it is only a work of art if, as the Chinese painter [Huang Pin-hung] says, it nonetheless saves enough empty space for the horses to prance in."[53] Deleuze and Guattari's point, here, would seem to be that a painting must be able to "breathe"; it is not solely about the creative act of the artist who places something new onto a canvas they have managed to truly clear, but also the necessity for the sensation to still *live* in the painting. There is therefore a way the imagination would have to live on in the painting itself, providing it with a dynamic rhythm, openings for further pathways of sensation.

---

52   Deleuze, *Francis Bacon: The Logic of Sensation,* 71.
53   Deleuze and Guattari, *What Is Philosophy?,* 166.

This brings us to a word of warning; we should hesitate before understanding this productive imagination as either individualistic or heroic. To be sure, we have already mentioned how the goal of the artist is not to depict their own perceptions or affections, but rather to construct blocs of sensation out of percept and affect, dislocated from any individual perceiving or affective being. Similarly, in the chapter on the image of thought, to really think, and just as much to really imagine, was to be seized by the "absolute necessity" of an "involuntary thought,"[54] or for the imagination perhaps, an involuntary image. To be sure, the painter would have an idea of this or that thing which she would want to paint, and all possibilities are not equal, even once the artist has cleared away the persistent clichés. As Bacon claims, again in the interviews with Sylvester, "in my case all painting — and the older I get the more it becomes so — is an accident. So I foresee it in my mind. I foresee it, and yet I hardly ever carry it out as I foresee it. It transforms itself by the actual paint."[55] There is indeed some original intention, if only in the sense of a vague probability, but the success of the painting is not dependent upon whether or how effectively Bacon can realize this intention. On the contrary, the painting is only a painting insofar as it is a material which subsists in its own right, contributing itself to the various pathways of sensation.

Lastly, we should not be misled to attribute Deleuze with an especially "heroic" image of the painter, as if the painter were some creative genius who is able to clear away all clichés for themselves and for us. "The greatest transformation of the cliché," writes Deleuze, "will not be an act of painting, it will not produce the slightest pictorial deformation. It would be much better to abandon oneself to clichés, to accumulate them, multiply them, as so many prepictorial givens: 'the will to lose the will' comes first."[56] In the interviews with Sylvester, Bacon describes this 'will to lose the will' as ultimately being "…despair. Because it really comes out of an absolute feeling of its impossible to do these things, so I might as well just do anything. And out of this anything, one sees what happens."[57] The attempt to escape cliché, it seems, is doomed to fail, or at least is doomed to always be provisional, insofar as every escape itself becomes a new cliché; the imagination, as always, opens up a space for the new to appear, but is constantly pulled back into drawing upon ready-made images. This, it seems to me, is one of the key aspects of the process of production in the imagination.

---

54   Deleuze, *Difference and Repetition,* 139.

55   David Sylvester, *The Brutality of Fact: Interviews with Francis Bacon* (London: Thames and Hudson, 2016), 16.

56   Deleuze, *Francis Bacon: The Logic of Sensation,* 76.

57   Sylvester, *The Brutality of Fact: Interviews with Francis Bacon,* 13.

THE POSSIBILITY OF A PRODUCTIVE IMAGINATION   445

6   Conclusions: Productive Imagination and Its Limits

We see, then, following Deleuze and Guattari, that the imagination can be rehabilitated from its role as merely representational if we conceive of it as the
productive imagination, and moreover, that this productive imagination can
be described as the faculty of clearing away clichés, of opening up spaces for
new images to appear. [Admittedly, I have given a very specific account here,
not only of the postmodern tradition, of which Deleuze and Guattari are idiosyncratic examples (but who would be a "pure" representative?), but also of
the history of art, taking Bacon's approach and testimony as a central anchor of
my analysis. Nevertheless, I take this to be appropriate given the subject matter, given what we might call the iconoclastic tendencies of the "postmodern"
tradition.] There may, however remain a notable dogmatism, a new kind of
cliché that arises out of Deleuze and Guattari's analysis of art as the creation
monuments or blocs of sensation. The work of both Allan Kaprow and Carolee
Schneemann for example, focuses on evoking real time, and would therefore
seem to be interestingly opposed to Deleuze and Guattari's preservational sensibility of art as monument.

Nevertheless, I believe this understanding of the imagination as being genuinely productive, like desire, is an insight that is fundamental to the postmodern tradition. This might describe the shared emphasis in the tradition on various dimensions of human life which we previously took to be mere
"representations" of some original, present, thing. This would be the case for at
least Foucault, Derrida and Baudrillard. Foucault, famously, emphasizes the
importance of discourse, or how power relations are embedded in our language and our practices; throughout Derrida's career, and in *Of Grammatology*
specifically, Derrida elaborates a thoroughgoing critique of the metaphysics of
presence which subordinate writing (which is necessarily separate from its author) to an original speech; and in *Simulacra and Simulation,* Baudrillard
makes a related claim that in contemporary society there are no longer real
things or even copies of such originals, but only *simulacra,* that is, copies of
copies. No doubt, however, each thinker presents their own unique challenges:
for example, Deleuze and Guattari claim that desire is real and productive, and
so, the products of desire would need to be interrogated seriously ("the masses"
would not be merely deceived by ideology, but are in fact invested in the current state of affairs); whereas Baudrillard claims that there is no longer a real at
all, because everything has become mediatized. These are all different angles
into, approaches on, and points of egress from a similar problem, attempts to
break with similar iterations of *doxa.* Nevertheless, for each of these authors,
we see that aspects or dimensions of human life that used to be subordinated
to something "more real" or something which grounded them, must be

liberated from such subordination. In each case, we see the imagination at work in an attempt to break with tradition, *doxa,* and cliché, and in the case of Deleuze and Guattari in particular, we ought to be willing to follow their own insights about thought and desire into the open spaces of the imagination and beyond the representational paradigm to which they so often consign it.

References

Arisotle, *De Anima.* Translated by Joe Sachs. Santa Fe: Green Lion Press. 2004.

Baudrillard, Jean. *Simulacra and Simulation.* Translated by Sheila Faria Glaser. Ann Arbor: University of Michigan Press. 1994.

Bergson, Henri. *Matter and Memory.* Translated by Nancy Margaret Paul and W. Scott Palmer. Brooklyn: Urzone Inc. 1988.

Deleuze, Gilles. *Difference and Repetition.* Translated by Paul Patton. New York: Columbia University Press. 1994.

Deleuze, Gilles. *Francis Bacon: The Logic of Sensation.* Translated by Daniel W. Smith. Minneapolis: University of Minnesota Press. 2003.

Deleuze, Gilles, and Félix Guattari. *Anti Oedipus.* Translated by Robert Hurley, Mark Seem, and Helen R. Lane. Minneapolis: University of Minnesota Press. 1983.

Deleuze, Gilles, and Félix Guattari. *What Is Philosophy?* Translated by Hugh Tomlinson and Graham Burchell. New York: Columbia University Press. 1994.

Foucault, Michel. *The Order of Things.* USA: Random House. 1970.

Grosz, Elizabeth. *Chaos, Territory, Art.* New York: Columbia University Press. 2008.

Holland, Eugene. *Deleuze and Guattari's Anti-Oedipus: Introduction to Schizoanalysis.* London: Routledge. 1999.

Irigaray, Luce. *An Ethics of Sexual Difference.* Translated by Carolyn Burke and Gillian C. Gill. Ithaca: Cornell University Press. 1984.

Kant, Immanuel. *Critique of Judgment.* Translated by James Creed Meredith. New York: Oxford University Press. 2007.

Rancière, Jacques. "Is there a Deleuzian Aesthetics?" Translated by Radmila Djordjevic. *Qui Parle?* 14, no. 2 (2004): 1–14.

Reynolds, Nigel. "Turner's Fighting Temeraire Sinks the Competition." *The Telegraph,* September 6, 2005. http://www.telegraph.co.uk/news/uknews/1497703/Turners-Fighting-Temeraire-sinks-the-opposition.html.

Schapiro, Tamar. "Foregrounding Desire: A Defense of Kant's Incorporation Thesis." *Journal of Ethics: An International Philosophical Review* 15, no. 3 (2011): 147–67.

Sylvester, David. *The Brutality of Fact: Interviews with Francis Bacon.* London: Thames and Hudson. 2016.

Wilson, Eric. "Habitual Desire: On Kant's Concept of Inclination." *Kantian Review* 21, no. 2 (2016): 211–35.

Wolfe, Katherine. "From Aesthetics to Politics: Rancière, Kant and Deleuze." *Contemporary Aesthetics* 4 (January 1, 2006); n.p., https://www.contempaesthetics.org/newvolume/pages/article.php?articleID=382.

PART 6

Imagination in Scientific Modeling and Biosemiotics

∵

CHAPTER 19

Of Predators and Prey: Imagination in Scientific Modeling

Fiora Salis

1 Introduction

Imagine you have two populations, one predator and one prey (for example, foxes and rabbits, herbivores and plants, or parasites and hosts), interacting in a homogeneous environment that never changes. The prey population has limitless supplies of food and it will grow exponentially when the predator population is absent. Predators have infinite appetite, they feed exclusively on the prey population and they will starve when this is absent. With these assumptions in place, you can now use the following differential equations to predict the growth rates of the two populations interacting with each other:

1. $dx / dt = Ax - Bxy$,
2. $dy / dt = -Cy + Dxy$,

where x stands in for the size of the prey population, y for the size of the predator population, t for time, A for the growth rate of the prey population, B for the predation rate coefficient, C for the mortality rate of the predator population, and D for the growth rate of the predator population feeding on the prey population. These equations are known as the Lotka-Volterra model of predator-prey interaction. The model predicts that the dynamic interaction between the two populations will show a cyclical relationship in their numbers and that the increase and decrease rates of the predator population generally track those of the prey population. When the size of the predator population (y) increases, so does the rate at which predators consume prey (Dxy). This leads to a further increase in the size of the predator population and a consequent decrease in the size of the prey population (x). When the size of the prey population decreases, the size of the predator population (y) and the rate at which predators consume prey (Dxy) decrease too. As a consequence, the number of prey (x) increases again, and this leads to an increase in the number of predators (y) starting again the cycle.

© KONINKLIJKE BRILL NV, LEIDEN, 2020 | DOI:10.1163/9789004436350_021

In reality, biological populations interact in environments that are inhomogeneous and that change through time. Prey populations don't have limitless supplies of food and they may not grow exponentially in the absence of predators. Predators don't have infinite appetite, don't feed exclusively on just one prey population, and do not starve when one prey population is absent. The linguistic assumptions and mathematical equations describe an imaginary system constituted by two imaginary populations interacting under imaginary conditions. This, in turn, affords the generation of certain hypotheses and the assessment of their truth-likeness. The model predicts that the dynamic interaction between the imaginary populations will show a cyclical relationship in their numbers. Transferring the model outcomes onto reality requires exiting the imagination to export these results onto reality. Imagination is therefore vital to the construction of the model and to the generation of model outcomes that can be transferred onto reality.

The Lotka-Volterra model exemplifies what Godfrey-Smith[1] identifies as the characteristic strategy of model-based science. In modeling, scientists present a description of an imaginary system as the object of study. The description is called model description and the imaginary system is called a model system. They study the model system to discover new information and then translate what they have learned about the imaginary system into knowledge of reality based on a relation of resemblance. According to this view, modelers "gain understanding of a complex real-world system *via* an understanding of simpler, hypothetical system that resembles it in relevant respects.[2]" The model system is further interpreted as a representation of reality. Model-based science, hence, involves a strategy of indirect representation.[3]

The imaginary systems described in modeling do not exist in the real world. They are what Thomson-Jones[4] calls missing systems. When modeling certain aspects of reality, scientists present model descriptions involving the attribution of properties that only concrete objects could have. However, there are no objects instantiating these properties and scientists are aware of this. This aspect of the modeling practice poses a serious question about the nature of models and the way in which they enable knowledge of reality. What are models

---

1 Peter Godfrey-Smith, "The Strategy of Model-Based Science," *Biology and Philosophy* 21 (2006): 725–40.

2 Godfrey-Smith, "The Strategy of Model-Based Science," 726, italics in original.

3 See Michael Weisberg, "Who is a Modeler?," *The British Journal for the Philosophy of Science* 58, no. 2 (2007): 207–33, for a similar idea.

4 Martin Thomson-Jones, "Missing Systems and the Face Value Practice," *Synthese* 172, no. 2 (2010): 283–99.

OF PREDATORS AND PREY 453

and how do they contribute to a scientific understanding of reality? Call the first the ontological problem and the second the epistemic problem.

In recent years, several accounts of the ontology of models have been put forward on the basis of a fruitful analogy between missing systems and the objects described in literary works of fiction. Godfrey-Smith originally presented the analogy in an explicit way:

> I take at face value the fact that modelers often *take* themselves to be describing imaginary biological populations, imaginary neural networks, or imaginary economies ... Although these imagined entities are puzzling, I suggest that at least much of the time they might be treated as similar to something that we are all familiar with, the imagined objects of literary fiction. Here I have in mind entities like Sherlock Holmes' London, and Tolkien's Middle Earth.[5]

Godfrey-Smith recognizes that fictional entities are puzzling and that they are beset with ontological controversies.[6] To avoid such controversies, proponents of the fiction view of models have looked at the literature in aesthetics and found a working explanation in Walton's[7] theory of fiction as a game of make-believe.[8] Walton's theory dispenses with fictional entities by explaining our thoughts and discourse about fictional characters in terms of the imaginative activities involved in games of make-believe. Analogously, the fiction view of

---

5   Godfrey-Smith, "The Strategy of Model-Based Science," 735, italics in original.
6   For a review of these controversies see Fiora Salis, "Fictional Entities," *Online Companion to Problems in Analytic Philosophy* (2013), http://hdl.handle.net/10451/10860.
7   Kendall Walton, *Mimesis as Make-Believe* (Cambridge, MA: Harvard University Press, 1990).
8   See Anouk Barberousse and Pascal Ludwig, "Models as fictions," in *Fictions in Science: Philosophical Essays in Modeling and Idealizations*, ed. Mauricio Suárez (New York: Routledge, 2009), 56–73; Roman Frigg, "Models and Fiction," *Synthese* 172, no. 2 (2010): 251–68; Roman Frigg and James Nguyen, "The Fiction View of Models Reloaded," *The Monist* 99, no. 3 (2016): 225–42; Roman Frigg and James Nguyen, "Models and Representation," in *Springer Handbook of Model-Based Science*, eds. Lorenzo Magnani and Tommaso Bertolotti (Berlin: Springer, 2017): 73–126; Arnon Levy, "Modeling Without Models," *Philosophical Studies* 172, no. 3 (2015): 781–98; Adam Toon, *Models as Make-Believe: Imagination, Fiction, and Scientific Representation* (Basingstoke, UK: Palgrave Macmillan, 2012); Fiora Salis, "Scientific Discovery through Fictionally Modelling Reality," in *Scientific Discovery and Inferences*, eds. Emiliano Ippoliti and Tom Nickles (Netherlands: Springer, 2018), 1–12., https://doi.org/10.1007/s11245-018-9582-0; Fiora Salis, "The New Fiction View of Models," *The British Journal for the Philosophy of Science* (2019): 1–39, https://doi.org/10.1093/bjps/axz015. For a critical discussion of these views see Frigg and Nguyen (2017).

models explains the face value practice of modeling in terms of the imaginative activities of scientists as participants in games of make-believe.

These theories put imagination at the center of the modeling practice and, as a consequence, present us with the further issue of explaining how imagination enables knowledge of reality. Pre-theoretically, imagination is often thought of as completely free and unconstrained. In this vein, many think of imagination as a means to escape reality, as when we engage in daydreams and fantasies that provide diversion and create new things that depart from reality. Pessimists about our ability to gain knowledge through imagination emphasize the freedom of imagination.[9] There is, however, another pre-theoretical notion of imagination as a means to learn about reality, as when we engage in problem solving, mindreading, counterfactual reasoning, and thought experiments. The key to this second notion is in the idea that imagination can be constrained in ways that effectively enable knowledge of reality.[10] As I will argue, make-believe fits well with the constrained uses of imagination in modeling.

In this chapter, I will put forward my favorite account of theoretical modeling that, coherently with the original insight of the fiction view, recognizes the essential role of imagination in modeling. The approach is both pragmatic and practice oriented. It is pragmatic to the extent that it construes models as objects of sort that are created by an agent and can be endowed with different functions in different contexts. Thus, the Lotka-Volterra model can be used as an example of mathematical modeling in the biology classroom, or it can be used to make predictions about the dynamic interaction between foxes and rabbits. The approach is also practice oriented in that it puts the modeling practice at the center of the account and it aims to explain its main features coherently with the way in which modelers think and talk about models.

In Section 2, I will present six criteria that can be used to assess any account of models. In Section 3, I will briefly outline Walton's theory of make-believe. In Section 4, I will advance an account of the ontology of models in terms of the analogy between models and literary works of fiction as human-made artifacts created through the imaginative activities of scientists. In Section 5, I will discuss the notion of imagination involved in modeling as constrained in ways

---

9   René Descartes, *Meditations on First Philosophy*, ed. and trans. John Cottingham (Cambridge: Cambridge University Press, 1985); Shannon Spaulding, "Imagination through Knowledge," in *Knowledge through Imagination*, eds. Amy Kind and Peter Kung (Oxford: Oxford University Press, 2016), 207–26; John Norton, "Thought Experiments in Einstein's Work," in *Thought Experiments in Science and Philosophy*, eds. T. Horowitz and G.J. Massey (Savage, MD: Rowman & Littlefield Publishers, 1991), 129–48.

10   Amy Kind and Peter Kung, "Introduction," in *Knowledge through Imagination*, eds. Amy Kind and Peter Kung (Oxford: Oxford University Press, 2016), 2–38.

OF PREDATORS AND PREY

that enable knowledge of reality. In Section 6 I will conclude by addressing recent criticisms against the fiction view and the relevance of scientific imagination in modeling.

2   What Account of Models?

Before addressing the two key questions of this chapter, we should identify the criteria by which we want to evaluate a theory of models. The most important criteria are the theoretical requirement of naturalism and five explanatory conditions, model building, truth in the model, attribution of properties, learning about the model, and learning about reality.

Frigg originally formulated naturalism as a theoretical principle according to which any account of modeling "should be able to make sense of scientific practice."[11] A theory of models should explain the modeling practice coherently with the way in which modelers think and talk about models. As Godfrey-Smith points out in the above quote, modelers "often *take* themselves to be describing imaginary biological populations, imaginary neural networks, or imaginary economies.[12]" Coherently with this initial observation, Thomson-Jones[13] articulates the following picture of the face-value practice of modeling. Modelers present model descriptions that specify model systems as the objects of study. Model descriptions involve the attribution of properties that only concrete objects could have, yet there are no objects instantiating these properties. Modelers are aware of this, yet they think and talk *as if* there were such systems. The face-value practice is a claim about the social practice of modeling that involves both psychological and social components. Hence, the focus of an account of models should be on the ways in which scientists think and talk about models as members of specific scientific communities. This account needs to meet the five explanatory conditions introduced above.

First, there's the problem of how scientists build models. Model building involves the deliberate stipulation of certain false assumptions. For example, the Lotka-Volterra model falsely assumes that prey have limitless supplies of food and that the environment never changes. Modelers, however, are not engaged in an act of deception (not even unwittingly). They are not presenting a false description of some system of interest as true, and they do not expect

---

11   Frigg, "Models and Fiction," 113.
12   Godfrey-Smith, "The Strategy of Model-Based Science," 735.
13   Martin Thomson-Jones, "Missing Systems and the Face Value Practice," *Synthese* 172, no. 2 (2010): 283–99.

others to believe the content of the false description. So, what are they doing, exactly?

Second, discourse about models involves claims that can be assessed for truth and falsity in the model. It is true in the Lotka-Volterra model that when the size of the prey population decreases the size of the predator population decreases too. It is false in the model that when the size of the predator population increases the size of the prey population also increases. But how can we distinguish between these two types of claims?

Third, when building a model and when assessing discourse about the model, scientists attribute properties that only concrete objects can have. In the Lotka-Volterra model, the predator population feeds on the prey population and it has a size that increases and decreases through time. How can an imaginary object have any of these properties?

Fourth, models are objects of enquiry that are studied and developed to elicit certain truths that go beyond the original truths stipulated by model descriptions. For example, in the Lotka-Volterra model we find out that the population size of the predator population tracks that of the prey population. How are these further truths in the model generated?

Fifth, models are tools for the investigation of reality. The Lotka-Volterra model enables certain predictions about real biological populations. Standard accounts explain learning about reality in terms of a relation of similarity between model systems and targets, where similarity is usually construed as the sharing of properties in certain respects and to certain degrees.[14] Model systems, however, cannot have any of the properties that they are supposed to share with targets. So, how can they be similar?

3 Make-Believe

What sort of imagination is involved in modeling? In the philosophical literature on models, imagination is often construed as mental imagery, which is an ability to form a sensory-like representation of something real or non-existent in any sensory modality (imagining seeing, imagining hearing, imagining tasting, and so on). Specifically, the variety of imagery that is usually assumed is that of visual imagery. Harré interprets the "imagining of models" as providing

---

14   Ronald N. Giere, *Explaining Science: A Cognitive Approach* (Chicago: The University of Chicago Press, 1988).

OF PREDATORS AND PREY   457

scientists with a "picture of mechanisms of nature."[15] Levy claims that "[i]magining typically involves having a visual or other sensory-like mental state – a 'seeing in the mind's eye.'"[16] And Weisberg attributes to Godfrey-Smith the view that scientists form a "mental picture" of the "model system."[17]

In recent work, Salis and Frigg[18] have challenged this ordinary understanding of imagination as neither necessary nor sufficient in scientific modeling. The Lotka-Volterra model requires imagining that two biological populations having unrealistic features interact in an environment that never changes. These imaginings can but need not be accompanied by any mental images. They require grasping theoretical concepts and relations (growth rate of a biological population, predation rate coefficient, mortality rate) within the fictional scenario described by the model. Inspired by Walton's notion of make-believe, Salis and Frigg submit that modeling only requires propositional imagination of the make-believe variety, where propositional imagination (imagining that p, where p is a proposition) is an ability to entertain alternative states of affairs and situations, with or without any mental images. Scientists imagine *that* the predator population has infinite appetite, *that* the prey population has unlimited supplies of food, *that* the two populations interact in an environment that never changes. Obviously, these imaginings do not require forming any mental image of any particular biological population or any particular environment.

In fact, Walton's (1990) theory of fiction as a game of make-believe is particularly well suited to develop an account of models that satisfies our six criteria. Walton advances a notion of make-believe as a social imaginative activity that is constrained by the use of props and principles of generation. Props are concrete, ordinary objects that prescribe to imagine certain things. Principles of generation are conditional rules that determine what is to be imagined in the presence of a prop. Toy trucks, dolls, teddy bears and hobbyhorses are paradigmatic examples of props in children's games of make-believe that are constrained by principles of generation. A hobbyhorse prescribes to imagine that there is a horse in the room in virtue of the principle of generation that if there is a hobbyhorse in the room then one is encouraged to imagine that there is a horse in the room. Individuals who are encouraged to imagine in the presence

---

15   Rom Harré, "Where Models and Analogies Really Count," *International Studies in the Philosophy of Science* 2 (1988): 34–35.

16   Levy, "Modeling Without Models," 785.

17   Weisberg, *Simulation and Similarity: Using Models to Understand the World* (New York: Oxford University Press, 2013), 51.

18   Fiora Salis and Roman Frigg, "Capturing the Scientific Imagination," in *The Scientific Imagination*, edited by Peter Godfrey-Smith and Arnon Levy (Oxford: Oxford University Press, 2020).

of the prop engage in pretense, where "pretense" refers to one's participation in a game of make-believe and has nothing to do with deception. Together, props and principles of generation determine, enable and constrain the imaginings of participants in a game of make-believe, independently of whether one does or does not imagine accordingly. The proposition that the horse has reins attached to its mouth is among the imaginings prescribed in the game if there is a hobbyhorse with reins attached to its mouth, independently of whether a participant in the game imagines it (one may not notice the reins on the hobbyhorse).

Hobbyhorses, toy trucks, dolls and teddy bears are designed to function as props in children's games of make-believe. For example, hobbyhorses are intended to count as horses and dolls are intended to count as babies. Other objects that were not designed to function as props can become props because of the stipulation of *ad hoc* principles of generation. In one of Walton's preferred examples, children play a game where they stipulate that stumps are bears so that if there is a stump in the woods it is to be imagined that there is a bear in the woods. The distinction between these two types of props determines an important distinction between two different types of games, authorized and unofficial. A game of make-believe is authorized when it involves objects that were designed to function as props; it is unofficial when it involves objects that become props in virtue of *ad hoc* principles of generation.

Walton extends the notion of a prop to representational works of art, including literary works of fiction. He proposes to construe objects that were originally designed to work as props in games of make-believe as representations. Waltonian representations are props in authorized games of make-believe. The concrete texts of fictional stories (such as marks on paper or on a computer screen and utterances in an episode of storytelling) are props that have been designed by their authors to prescribe imagining certain things. For example, the text of Raspe's *Baron Munchausen* prescribes to imagine that Munchausen rides on a cannon ball. They are concrete objects that prescribe to imagine certain things, independently of whether these things exist or not. Imaginings do not have any ontological import and do not commit us to postulate any fictional entities. Imagining a talking donkey does not commit one to the existence of any talking donkey. Indeed, imaginings can be about nothing at all! In this sense, Walton's notion of representation is distinct from the traditional notion of representation discussed in philosophy of science, where representation is construed as representation *of* something. This distinction will be useful to understand an important ambiguity in the notion of representation in the literature on models that I will discuss in the next section.

OF PREDATORS AND PREY   459

Some imaginings are appropriate in certain contexts, while others are not. This distinction is captured by the notion of fictional truth – or fictionality. The imaginings that conform to the principles of generation are fictional, or fictionally true, and fictionally false if they don't. Hence, fictional truth is not a variety of truth but a property of the propositions that conform to the prescriptions to imagine of a game of make-believe. It is fictional in Raspe's tale that Munchausen rides on a cannon ball; it is not fictional that he rides on an atomic bomb. Furthermore, fictional truths divide between primary fictional truths and implied fictional truths. Primary fictional truths are generated from the prop's prescriptions to imagine. Implied fictional truths are generated indirectly from the primary truths via further principles of generation that work as rules of inference in the game. Inspired by Lewis,[19] Walton identifies two main principles of generation, the reality principle and the mutual belief principle. The reality principle keeps the world of the game as close as possible to the real world. The mutual-belief principle imports the mutual beliefs of the members of the community in which the game originated. (More on these two principles in Section 5).

4   Models as Artifacts

Upholders of the fiction view of models build their proposals on Walton's theory of fiction as a game of make-believe. They divide between upholders of the indirect fiction view[20] and upholders of the direct fiction view.[21] Upholders of the indirect fiction view propose a theory of models that fits well with naturalism and is coherent with the strategy of indirect representation that Godfrey-Smith (2006) identifies as typical of model-based science. They distinguish between model descriptions and the imaginary systems they specify and construe the latter as the vehicles of representation of targets. On this view, model descriptions are props in authorized games of make-believe, which specify imaginary systems interpreted as akin to the imaginary objects of fiction. This idea is usually paired with an antirealist ontology of fictional entities that generates certain well-known problems. Most importantly, it has been argued that

---

19   David K. Lewis, "Truth in Fiction." *American Philosophical Quarterly* 15, no. 1 (1978): 37–46.
20   Frigg, "Models and Fiction"; Roman Frigg, "Fiction and scientific representation," in *Beyond Mimesis and Convention: Representation in Art and Science*, eds. Roman Frigg and Matthew C. Hunter (Netherlands: Springer. 2010), 98–138; Frigg and Nguyen, "The Fiction View of Models Reloaded"; Frigg and Nguyen, "Models and Representation."
21   Levy, "Modeling Without Models"; Toon, *Models as Make-Believe.*

if model systems are the vehicles of representation of targets and there are no model systems, then they cannot stand in a representation relation with targets.[22]

To avoid this problem, upholders of the direct fiction view of models reject model systems and propose to identify the vehicles of representation of targets with model descriptions. On this view, model descriptions are props in games of make-believe that prescribe to imagine that real world targets have features that they do not really have. The main problem with this proposal is that it does not fit well with the face value practice of modeling and hence fails to satisfy naturalism. In fact, the direct fiction view cannot account for the indirect strategy of model-based science and for the surrogative reasoning typically afforded by models.[23]

To avoid the problems faced by these standard approaches, I address the ontological problem of what models are in terms of a distinct analogy with literary works of fiction. The idea is not new and in fact has been anticipated by Cartwright's (2010) construal of models as fables and by Salis' (2019) interpretation of models as literary works of fiction. Here, however, I will develop the same idea in a more robust way, by combining the Waltonian framework with the recognition that models, just like fictional stories, are human-made artefacts created by an agent and endowed with a particular function in a context.[24] In this section, I will develop an account of models as artifacts while in the next section I will focus on their specific epistemic function.

---

22   Toon, *Models as Make-Believe.*

23   Frigg and Nguyen, "The Fiction View of Models Reloaded"; Tarja Knuuttila, "Imagination Extended and Embedded: Artifactual Versus Fictional Accounts of Models," *Special Issue of Synthese on Modeling and Representation* (2017): 1–21, https://doi.org/10.1007.

24   The idea that models are human-made artifacts created by an agent in a context has been originally advanced and developed by upholders of the artifactual view of models. See Marcel Boumans, "Mathematics as Quasi-Matter to Build Models as Instruments," in *Probabilities, Laws, and Structures*, eds. Dennis Dieks, Weceslao J. Gonzalez, Stephan Hartmann, Michael Stöltzner, and Marcel Weber (Netherlands: Springer, 2012), 307–18; Adrian Currie, "From Models-as-Fictions to Models-as-Tools," *Ergo* 4, no. 27 (2017): 759–81; Tarja Knuuttila, "Representation, Idealization, and Fiction in Economics: From the Assumptions Issue to the Epistemology of Modelling," in *Fictions in Science: Philosophical Essays on Modeling and Idealization*, ed. Mauricio Suárez (New York: Routledge, 2009), 205–31; Tarja Knuuttila, "Modelling and Representing: An Artefactual Approach to Model-Based Representation," *Studies in History and Philosophy of Science Part A*, 42, no. 2 (2011): 262–71; Knuuttila, "Imagination Extended and Embedded"; Tarja Knuuttila, and Atro Voutilainen, "A Parser as an Epistemic Artefact: A material view on models," *Philosophy of Science* 70 (2003): 1484–495. However, upholders of this view do not recognize any essential role for imagination in modeling.

Literary works of fiction are syntactic-semantic entities created by their authors in certain cultural contexts and endowed with certain functions. Their syntactic component is constituted by concrete symbols functioning as props in authorized games of make-believe. Their semantic component is constituted by the propositions that are among the fictional truths generated by the props and the principles of generation in force in the game. Together, the primary and implied fictional truths of the story constitute the work's content. Ursula Le Guin's novel *The Left Hand of Darkness* prescribes readers to imagine that there is a society of individuals who are ambisexual (they change sex at different times in their lives). Of course, there is no such a society (nobody can change sex). Yet, the story prescribes to imagine in this way to explore certain cultural and societal consequences of sex and gender.

Analogously, models are constituted by model description and model content. A model description is constituted by concrete linguistic and mathematical symbols (such as marks on paper or on a computer screen) functioning as props in authorized games of make-believe. They are originally designed to prescribe imagining certain propositions. These propositions are the primary fictional truths from which further implied fictional truths can be inferred via the principles of generation. Together, the primary and implied fictional truths constitute the model's content. On this proposal, a model M is constituted by model description D and model content C, so that $M = [D, C]$. Model descriptions are essential components of models that enable and constrain the model content together with the principles of generation. Since both model description and model content exist, the entire model exists.

The proposed analogy fits well with the face-value practice of modeling, it is coherent with the indirect strategy of model-based science and it incorporates the original insight of the fiction view of models. Modelers select and manipulate model descriptions that are designed to prescribe imaginings that certain systems are so and so. Like the texts of literary works of fiction, model descriptions involve the attribution of properties that only concrete objects could have, yet there are no objects instantiating these properties. For example, the differential equations of the Lotka-Volterra model *per se* are objects composed of certain mathematical symbols together with an interpretation. A mathematician could study them independently of any empirical or theoretical enquiry. A modeler, however, can write these equations as a model of predator-prey interaction when she stipulates certain linguistic assumptions and endows the equations with a particular interpretation for a particular end. The linguistic assumptions specify the objects and features of a stylized system that can be mathematically described by the two equations. This system does not exist in the real world. It's an imaginary system that is akin to the fictional characters of literary fictions. Coherently with Walton's antirealism, I assume that there are no fictional entities and therefore no model systems.

The analogy avoids the main problem faced by the indirect fiction view of models. Frigg[25] originally distinguished between two different notions of representation involved in the Waltonian interpretation of models as fictions, p-representation and t-representation. P-representations are props in authorized games of make-believe. They are concrete objects designed to prescribe imagining certain things without any ontological commitment to the existence of such things. In this sense, they correspond to a non-relational notion of representation. T-representations, however, do stand in a representational relation to some target. If they fail to represent something then they are not representations at all. This distinction maps neatly onto that between model descriptions and models. Model descriptions are props in authorized games of make-believe that prescribe to imagine something without any ontological commitment. They are non-relational (Waltonian) representations. Models, however, are distinct objects that can be endowed with a relational representational function by an agent. Since models exist they can be the vehicles of representation of targets.

Now we can address the first problem posed by the modeling practice. How do scientists build models? As stated above, modelers deliberately stipulate certain false assumptions that specify a non-existent system. Yet, they don't do this with any deceptive intention. The analogy with literary works of fiction indicates a plausible explanation. The author of fiction creates a new story and the characters involved therein through the activity of storytelling. The text of a fictional story does not describe any real facts. The author knows that the story is false and she does not intend to deceive her audience. She tells a story created through her own imagination and she presents it to an audience that is expected to imaginatively engage with it. In other words, the story is the product of the author's imagination and the object of an audience's imaginative response. It is a human-made artifact created by an agent's imagination through the deployment and manipulation of certain linguistic symbols. Analogously, a modeler builds a model through her own imagination and presents it in a way that encourages the right kind of attitude as one of imagination. In fact, modelers often introduce models via the use of locutions that directly appeal to imagination. Maxwell investigates "the motion of an imaginary fluid" conceived as "merely a collection of imaginary properties."[26] Maynard Smith

---

25   Frigg, "Fiction and Scientific Representation."
26   William D. Niven, *The Scientific Papers of James Clerk Maxwell* (New York: Dover Publications, 1965), 159–60.

invites his readers to "imagine a population of replicating RNA molecules."[27] And when studying the nature of the embryo Turing posits that "the matter of the organism is imagined as continuously distributed."[28]

Second, how can we distinguish between claims that are true in the model and claims that are not? Answering this question requires that we distinguish between truth and falsity in the model from truth and falsity in reality. The model description is composed of claims that are false in reality. However, the same claims are true in the model. It is true in the Lotka-Volterra model that the prey population has infinite supplies of food. It is false that the prey population has infinite food in, say, the Adriatic Sea. Walton's notion of fictional truth satisfies this criterion by contributing an explanation of truth in the model as distinct from genuine truth. Fictional truth is spelled out in terms of conformity with the prescriptions to imagine in force in a game of make-believe. It is fictional that the prey population has infinite supplies of food. Genuine truth has nothing to do with conformity with any prescriptions to imagine. In fact, it is simply false that the prey population has infinite food, say in the Adriatic Sea.

Third, discourse about models involves the attribution of properties to model systems that only concrete objects could have. But how can the imaginary systems specified in modeling have any such properties? The answer is straightforward. They can't! Model systems are usually construed as abstract objects[29] or as non-existent objects.[30] It has been already pointed out that neither abstract objects nor non-existent objects can have any concrete properties.[31] So, what are scientists really doing when they seem to attribute such properties to model systems? The analogy with fiction contributes a natural

---

27   Quoted in Jay Odenbaugh, "Semblance or similarity? Reflections on Simulation and Similarity," *Biology and Philosophy* 30 (2015): 284.

28   Quoted in Levy, "Modeling Without Models," 782.

29   Gabriele Contessa, "Scientific Representation, Interpretation, and Surrogative Reasoning," *Philosophy of Science* 74 (2007): 48–68; Giere, *Explaining Science: A Cognitive Approach*; Ronald N. Giere, "Why Scientific Models Should not be Regarded as Works of Fiction," in *Fictions in Science: Philosophical Essays on Modeling and Idealization*, ed. Mauricio Suárez (New York: Routledge, 2009), 248–58.

30   Frigg, "Models and Fiction"; Frigg, "Fiction and Scientific Representation"; Frigg and Nguyen, "The Fiction View of Model Reloaded"; Fiora Salis, "Scientific Discovery through Fictionally Modelling Reality," in *Scientific Discovery and Inferences*, eds. Emiliano Ippoliti and Tom Nickles (Netherlands: Springer, 2018), 1–12, https://doi.org/10.1007/s11245-018-9582-0; Fiora Salis, "The New Fiction View of Models," *The British Journal for the Philosophy of Science* (2019): 1–39, https://doi.org/10.1093/bjps/axz015.

31   R.I.G. Hughes, "Models and Representation," *Philosophy of Science* (*Proceedings*) 64 (1997): 325–36; Fiora Salis, "The Nature of Model-World Comparisons," *The Monist* 99, no. 3 (2016): 243–59.

explanation of this aspect of the modeling practice. Discourse about fiction involves a similar attribution of properties that only concrete individuals, objects and places can have. Explaining this feature of our discourse about fictions requires the recognition of the essential role of imagination. We merely imagine that Munchausen rides on a cannon ball. Similarly, scientists merely imagine that the predator population feeds exclusively on one prey population in an environment that never changes.

The analogy between models and fictions builds on the recognition of the essential role of imagination in modeling. This recognition, however, poses also the problem of how imagination can provide an effective tool for the investigation of reality. In the next section I will address the epistemic problem of how we learn with models and address the last two explanatory conditions, learning about models and learning about reality. As I will argue, the key to an understanding of models as epistemic artifacts is in the notion of constrained imagination that is afforded by the Waltonian notion of make-believe.

5 Learning through Imagination

Scientific models and literary works of fiction are human-made artefacts created and endowed with a function by an agent in a context. The functions that literary fictions and scientific models can have are usually very different. Walton[32] emphasizes that literary fictions have a special cognitive function in providing us with a special insight into ourselves. Other functions are possible, including ethic and civic education,[33] and of course pure entertainment and engagement in fantasy. Scientific models have certain functions that differentiate them sharply from literary works of fiction. In particular, models have a distinctive epistemic function. That is, they are objects of enquiry and tools for the investigation of reality.

As objects of enquiry, models are studied for the purpose of eliciting certain truths that are not among the original truths stipulated by model descriptions. In the Lotka-Volterra model, we find out that the size of the predator population tracks that of the prey population. The Waltonian framework contributes an explanation of how we learn about models in terms of the derivation of certain implied fictional truths from the primary fictional truths of the model via the principles of generation in force in a game of make-believe. Thus,

---

32 Walton, *Mimesis as Make-Believe*, Sections 1.4 and 7.5.

33 Martha Nussbaum, "Exactly and Responsibly: A Defense of Ethical Criticism," *Philosophy and Literature* 22, no. 2 (1998): 343–65.

learning about a model consists in exploring the model content through the principles of generation. There is, however, no clear understanding of what principles of generation are at work in modeling. Here I propose an overarching taxonomy of types of constraints on imagination in modeling based on the current literature in cognitive science and philosophy, architectural, context-specific, and epistemic.

Architectural constraints are so called because they pertain to the cognitive architecture of the mind and operate on all uses of imagination across contexts. Two of these constraints emerge from the contemporary literature in cognitive science, mirroring and quarantining. Mirroring is displayed when imaginings carry inferential commitments that are similar to those carried by beliefs having the same propositional content.[34] If I believe that the sky is blue today, I also believe that today is a sunny day. Similarly, if I imagine that the sky is blue today then I also imagine that today is a sunny day. Typically, the inferences we make depend on background assumptions and on the particular interests that direct our reasoning. The inferences we make in modeling, for example, depend upon the primary truths of the model (the model's assumptions) and the particular aim of the investigation (the goal of the enquiry). Since our theoretical or practical interests vary from context to context, mirroring operates together with context-specific constraints to determine the inferences that are allowed in particular cases.

Quarantining constrains the inferences that we make to a particular episode of imagination so as not to directly affect our belief system and our processes of decision-making.[35] Imaginings do not entail beliefs and do not guide action in the real world. If I believe that today is a sunny day I may take my sunglasses when leaving the house. However, imagining that today is a sunny day will not motivate me to do the same thing when leaving the house. When considering the imaginary populations of the Lotka-Volterra model, imagining that the dynamic interaction between the two imaginary populations will show a cyclical relationship in their numbers does not automatically entail a belief in the same proposition. While imaginings cannot directly affect our beliefs and lead to actions in the real world (at least not in a normal and healthy individual), they can indirectly affect our beliefs and processes of decision-making. This,

---

34 Alan Leslie, "Pretense and Representation: The Origins of 'Theory of Mind,'" *Psychological Review* 94, no. 4 (1987): 412–26; Shaun Nichols, "Imagining and Believing: The Promise of a Single Code," *Journal of Aesthetics and Art Criticism* 62 (2004): 129–39; Shaun Nichols and Stephen Stich, *Mindreading. An Integrated Account of Pretence, Self-Awareness, and Understanding Other Minds* (New York: Oxford University Press, 2003).

35 Leslie, "Pretense and Representation"; Nichols and Stich, *Mindreading*.

however, requires exporting what one has learned in imagination outside of it in a way that I will qualify at the end of the section.

Context-specific constraints are so called because they depend upon the interpretative conventions and aims of an episode of imagination and hence do not apply to all uses of imagination across contexts but only to those that pertain to particular modeling practices. The original assumptions of a game of make-believe determined by props and principles of generation initially limit and define a particular episode of imagination. But what principles of generation contribute the further constraints that are needed to develop the model content and thereby learn about the model? As stated above, Walton (1990) appeals to reality orientation and mutual belief orientation. We can now briefly explore these principles in the context of modeling.

Mutual belief orientation is at work when features of an imagined episode are imported into a game of make-believe from the mutual beliefs of the community where the game originated. One can only draw certain relevant inferences in the geocentric model of the solar system if one assumes the mutual beliefs about the cosmos of ancient civilizations such as those of Aristotle and Ptolemy. Among these, for example, are the beliefs that the Sun and the Moon revolve around the Earth, and that the stars are fixed on a celestial sphere that rotates around it.

Reality orientation is at work when features of an imagined episode are imported into the game from reality itself. Given that the sort of imagination involved in models is supposed to enable knowledge of reality, one may think that imagination in models must be constrained in a reality oriented way. However, Salis and Frigg[36] emphasize that reality orientation is not privileged in models. For example, the Lotka-Volterra model does not import any facts from reality to constrain the sort of inferences made within it. This does not mean that some different specification of reality orientation may not be at work in some other models. Thus, Bechtel and Abrahamsen[37] consider computational models in chronobiology and cognitive science and argue that computational models of circadian rhythms are grounded in empirical discoveries, while computational models in neuroscience typically do not involve direct empirical evidence but generate indirect evidence that a certain mechanism may adequately produce particular behavioral data. This implies that some types of models (in chronobiology) are constrained by reality and therefore are

---

36   Salis and Frigg, "Capturing the Scientific Imagination."

37   William Bechtel and Adele Abrahamsen, "Dynamic mechanistic explanation: Computational Modeling of Circadian Rhythms as an Exemplar for Cognitive Science," *Studies in History and Philosophy of Science* 41 (2010): 321–33.

OF PREDATORS AND PREY 467

more realistic, while some other models (in computational neuroscience) are less constrained by reality and therefore are less realistic. The divide between realistic and un-realistic models presents a fruitful opportunity to study the limits of reality-orientation.

More context-specific constraints in modeling are possible and new empirical research in this area may contribute a better understanding of what they are. Among them are theoretical constraints determined by the particular theoretical framework wherein a model is developed, mathematical constraints provided by the particular formulas used in a model, experts' opinion, data analysis, and possibly more.

Not all constrained uses of imagination are aimed at gaining knowledge. This requires the recognition of a further type of constraints on imagination, namely epistemic. Epistemic constraints are determined by the particular epistemic purposes (the sort of knowledge we want to acquire) of an episode of imagination. The traditional analysis of knowledge has three main conditions, truth, belief, and justification. While the traditional notion usually applies to knowledge claims that we make about reality, a different notion involving distinct specifications of these constraints applies to knowledge claims about the imaginary scenarios associated with models. To briefly explore these differences, I identify two main types of knowledge claims that are generated through imagination in modeling, knowledge claims about the imaginary system specified by the model and knowledge claims about reality.

Knowledge claims of the first sort are about models as objects of enquiry. They are made within an authorized game of make-believe, such as "the prey population has infinite supplies of food" (in the Lotka-Volterra model). These claims are not true but merely fictionally true and the relevant attitude toward their content is not belief but imagination. Justification poses a number of issues. The role of justification in the traditional theory of knowledge is that of ensuring that "a true belief isn't true merely by accident."[38] Thus, one is justified in believing a certain proposition p if and only if one has some grounds that properly increase the probability that her belief that p is true. What types of grounds probabilify knowledge claims about imaginary systems? Just as different context-specific constraints operate on particular uses of imagination in distinct scientific practices, different types of grounds apply to imaginings used according to the epistemic purposes of particular practices. Empirical evidence may play a crucial justificatory role in models in chronobiology, while it may play a more limited role in neuroscientific models. Empirical

---

38 Matthias Steup, "Epistemology," in *The Stanford Encyclopedia of Philosophy*, ed. Edward N. Zalta, 2018, https://plato.stanford.edu/archives/sum2018/entries/epistemology.

observations may play a justificatory role in Newton's model of the solar system, while they may play a very limited role in macro-economic models. Theoretical justification may play an important role in macro-economic models and a more limited role in biological models. And more fine-grained distinctions about the specific constraints at work in these modeling practices and even in specific cases could be made through novel empirical research through case studies.

Models as tools for the investigation of reality enable knowledge claims about reality. These claims derive from two main theoretical hypotheses generated through modeling, model-world comparisons and direct attributions. Those generated from model-world comparisons can only be assessed within unofficial games of make-believe and therefore involve similar epistemic constraints as knowledge claims about imaginary systems. They can only be assessed within a game of make-believe (even if unofficial), and hence are fictionally true, and the attitude one has towards them is imagination. One caveat is in order though. The truth-conditions of these claims are only partially constrained by the prescriptions to imagine of a certain game (those concerning features of the imaginary system). Imaginings about reality, however, are constrained by reality itself and therefore their justification comes from empirical evidence. For example, to compare the ways in which the imaginary populations interact with the ways in which real biological populations interact, one must assess the claim with respect to the imaginary scenario of the model and with respect to reality. If real populations do not behave in similar ways, then the comparative claim will be false.[39]

Finally, knowledge claims generated from direct attributions export what one has learned about the model system into reality through the mediation of comparative claims. For example, one may formulate the prediction that the dynamic interaction of real fox and rabbit populations will be cyclical via the assumption of a relevant type of similarity between imaginary populations and real populations. Direct attributions are exclusively about reality and can be assessed for truth. Furthermore, the attitude one has towards them is belief and they are justified by empirical evidence.

6   Conclusions

From the literature on scientific models emerge three main objections against the idea that models crucially rely on imagination, the objection from

---

39   See Salis, "The Nature of Model-World Comparisons" for an extensive discussion of model-world comparisons in the contemporary debate on models.

OF PREDATORS AND PREY 469

inter-scientists variation, the objection from intersubjective access, and the objection from variations in the face value practice.

Weisberg presents the problem of inter-scientists variation by claiming that "[i]nsofar as models are fictions, there may be considerable differences in the way these are conceived by different scientists."[40] The problem concerns cross-scientist agreement about the properties of a model, including those determined by the model's primary truths and by the model's implied truths. For example, real biological populations are located in space. The Lotka-Volterra model does not say anything about the spatial location of the imaginary populations described in the model. Weisberg suggests that if the imaginary systems specified in a model are objects that would be concrete if they were real then they must have a spatial location. That is, if one assumes that the reality principle is privileged in modeling. Theorists have to fill in this gap in the model description by imagining that the model populations have a spatial location, and "[t]heorists will imagine the spatial arrangement of predators and prey in different ways."[41] So, how can different scientists engaging with the same model imagine the same fictional system?

The answer is that in fact the framework of make-believe does not commit to the reality principle. Some questions that may be answerable in the real world are left indeterminate and are even irrelevant in the world of the fiction. How many hairs does Sherlock Holmes have? Surely, if he were a real individual, he would have a definite number of hairs! This question, however, is unanswerable in the context of the fiction and it would be completely irrelevant in discourse about Sherlock Holmes. Similarly, asking what is the spatial location of the imaginary predator and prey populations is unanswerable and irrelevant in the Lotka-Volterra model. In fact, it is doubtful that any scientist properly engaging with the model would imagine that particular property. This is because, as stated in the previous section, the principles of generation at work in a game of make-believe depend upon disciplinary practices and interpretative conventions and, as Weisberg emphasizes, the reality principle is not privileged in modeling.[42]

Knuuttila[43] presents the objection from intersubjective access to model systems under the assumption that imaginings are private and idiosyncratic mental states that vary across individuals. If the assumption is correct, then how can different scientists engaging with the same model imagine the same fictional system? The answer to this objection starts by rejecting Knuuttila's assumption.

---

40   Weisberg, *Simulation and Similarity*, 57.

41   Weisberg, *Simulation and Similarity*, 61.

42   Weisberg, *Simulation and Similarity*, 59.

43   Knuuttila, "Imagination Extended and Embedded."

The sort of imagination at work in games of make-believe is not private but rather socially enabled and constrained by ordinary objects – the props – and publicly shared rules of interpretation – the principles of generation. As human-made artifacts that are constructed and deployed within the modeling practice, models have a material constitution provided by model descriptions that scientists can perceive and that they can interpret on the basis of certain shared conventions and stipulations. Scientists are participants in games of make-believe where their imaginings are not private, ineffable and inaccessible but rather social, expressible and accessible cognitive states that depend upon the use of props and principles of generation. The imaginings of any individual model may be subjective and idiosyncratic. Yet, they are enabled and constrained by the use of props and by the principles of generation in force in the game. Modelers are participants in games of make-believe involving concrete objects that they can perceive and interpret according to the principles of generation of the game. Thus, whenever two modelers disagree on the content of a particular model, they can solve their dispute on the basis of the objective and intersubjectively available symbols together with their interpretation.

Finally, Weisberg presents the objection from variations in the face value practice by arguing that some models are particularly abstract and do not seem to involve reference to any concrete imaginary systems. According to him, "for all the examples that can be given where theorists seem to invoke a fictional scenario, there are also many where they do not involve a fictional scenario, or at least don't do so in a straightforward way."[44] He discusses particular examples such as Karlin and Feldman's[45] model of unsymmetric equilibria in cases of loose-linkage equilibrium. The model involves extremely abstract properties of infinite populations such as the frequency of certain chromosomes and the recursion relations relating these frequencies to subsequent generations. Weisberg claims that "these properties might be said to abstract over all real and imagined populations, but no reference is made to these populations."[46]

Granted, the authors do not explicitly use the expressions "imaginary populations" or "imaginary properties," and the linguistic and mathematical descriptions they present do not involve reference to any specific populations. It is not clear, however, that this model's ontological commitments differ from

---

44 Weisberg, *Simulation and Similarity*, 66.
45 Samuel Karlin and Marcus Feldman, "Linkage and Selection: New Equilibrium Properties of the Two-Locus Symmetric Viability Model," *Proceedings of the National Academy of Sciences of the United States of America* 62, no. 1 (1969): 70–74.
46 Weisberg, *Simulation and Similarity*, 66.

OF PREDATORS AND PREY

471

those classically discussed by upholders of the fiction view of models, which involve explicit reference to imaginary systems. The model description may not include the word "imaginary," but it does refer to entities that do not exist and that would be concrete if they were real. The model refers to "the chromosomes AB, Ab, aB, and ab" and the interpretation of the mathematical description (the model equation) involves reference to frequencies in "the next generation."[47] Similarly, the Lotka-Volterra model does not refer to any particular populations of predator and prey but only to predator and prey populations. If it is clear that the Lotka-Volterra model specifies an imaginary system of interest, it is also clear that Karlin and Feldman's model specifies an imaginary system involving infinite populations, chromosomes and generations. The model is very abstract, but it does require some interpretation of its linguistic and mathematical symbols. Since it is clearly not intended to involve reference to real entities, and scientists are aware of this, it requires an appeal to make-believe for a correct interpretation.

In conclusion, explaining the modeling practice requires appealing to constrained uses of imagination. Models are human-made artefacts created through a scientist's imagination in particular practices of modeling. These practices are akin to games of make-believe in that they are imaginative activities constrained by the use of props and by principles of generation. The concrete linguistic and mathematical model descriptions are the props that enable the imaginings of scientists together with principles of generation that can vary across contexts. In this way, models are intersubjectively available objects of enquiry and tools for the scientific investigation of reality that can be shared by theorists whose imaginings are socially constrained and determined.

References

Barberousse, Anouk, and Pascal Ludwig. "Models as fictions." In *Fictions in Science: Philosophical Essays in Modeling and Idealizations*, edited by Mauricio Suárez, 56–73. New York: Routledge. 2009.

Bechtel, William, and Adele Abrahamsen. "Dynamic mechanistic explanation: Computational Modeling of Circadian Rhythms as an Exemplar for Cognitive Science." *Studies in History and Philosophy of Science* 41 (2010): 321–33.

Boumans, Marcel. "Mathematics as Quasi-Matter to Build Models as Instruments." In *Probabilities, Laws, and Structures*, edited by Dennis Dieks, Wenceslao J. Gonzalez,

---

47   Quoted in Weisberg, *Simulation and Similarity*, 66.

Stephan Hartmann, Michael Stöltzner, and Marcel Weber, 307–18. Netherlands: Springer. 2012.

Cartwright, Nancy. "Models: Parables v Fables." In *Beyond Mimesis and Convention. Representation in Art and Science*, edited by Roman Frigg and Michael C. Hunter, 19–32, Berlin and New York: Springer. 2010.

Contessa, Gabriele. "Scientific Representation, Interpretation, and Surrogative Reasoning." *Philosophy of Science* 74 (2007): 48–68.

Currie, Adrian. "From Models-as-Fictions to Models-as-Tools." *Ergo* 4, no. 27 (2017): 759–81.

Descartes, René. *Meditations on First Philosophy*. Edited and translated by John Cottingham. Cambridge: Cambridge University Press. 1985.

Frigg, Roman. "Fiction and Scientific Representation." In *Beyond Mimesis and Convention: Representation in Art and Science*, edited by Roman Frigg and Matthew C. Hunter. Netherlands: Springer. 2010.

Frigg, Roman. "Models and Fiction." *Synthese* 172, no. 2 (2010): 251–68.

Frigg, Roman, and James Nguyen. "Models and Representation." In *Springer Handbook of Model-Based Science*, edited by Lorenzo Magnani and Tommaso Bertolotti, 73–126. Berlin: Springer. 2017.

Frigg, Roman, and James Nguyen. "The Fiction View of Models Reloaded." *The Monist* 99, no. 3 (2016): 225–42.

Giere, Ronald N. *Explaining Science: A Cognitive Approach*. Chicago: The University of Chicago Press. 1988.

Giere, Ronald N. "Why Scientific Models Should not be Regarded as Works of Fiction." In *Fictions in Science: Philosophical Essays on Modeling and Idealization*, edited by Mauricio Suárez, 248–58. New York: Routledge. 2009.

Godfrey-Smith, Peter. "The Strategy of Model-Based Science." *Biology and Philosophy* 21 (2006): 725–40.

Harré, Rom. "Where Models and Analogies Really Count." *International Studies in the Philosophy of Science* 2 (1988): 118–33.

Hughes, R.I.G. "Models and Representation." *Philosophy of Science (Proceedings)* 64 (1997): 325–36.

Karlin, Samuel, and Marcus Feldman. "Linkage and Selection: New Equilibrium Properties of the Two-Locus Symmetric Viability Model." *Proceedings of the National Academy of Sciences of the United States of America* 62, no. 1 (1969): 70–74.

Kind, Amy, and Peter Kung. "Introduction." In *Knowledge through Imagination*, edited by Amy Kind and Peter Kung, 2–38. Oxford: Oxford University Press. 2016.

Knuuttila, Tarja. "Representation, Idealization, and Fiction in Economics: From the Assumptions Issue to the Epistemology of Modelling." In *Fictions in Science: Philosophical Essays on Modeling and Idealization*, edited by Mauricio Suárez, 205–31. New York: Routledge. 2009.

Knuuttila, Tarja. "Imagination Extended and Embedded: Artifactual Versus Fictional Accounts of Models." *Special Issue of Synthese on Modeling and Representation* (2017): 1–21, https://doi.org/10.1007.

Knuuttila, Tarja. "Modelling and Representing: An Artefactual Approach to Model-Based Representation." *Studies in History and Philosophy of Science Part A*, 42, no. 2 (2011): 262–71.

Knuuttila, Tarja, and Andrea Loettgers. "Basic Science Through Engineering: Synthetic Modeling and the Idea of Biology-Inspired Engineering." *Studies in History and Philosophy of Biological and Biomedical Sciences* 44 (2013): 158–69.

Knuuttila, Tarja, and Atro Voutilainen. "A Parser as an Epistemic Artefact: A Material View on Models." *Philosophy of Science* 70 (2003): 1484–495.

Leslie, Alan. "Pretense and Representation: The Origins of 'Theory of Mind.'" *Psychological Review* 94, no. 4 (1987): 412–26.

Levy, Arnon. "Modeling Without Models." *Philosophical Studies* 172, no. 3 (2015): 781–98.

Lewis, David K. "Truth in Fiction." *American Philosophical Quarterly* 15, no. 1 (1978): 37–46.

Nichols, Shaun. "Imagining and Believing: The Promise of a Single Code." *Journal of Aesthetics and Art Criticism* 62 (2004): 129–39.

Nichols, Shaun, and Stephen Stich *Mindreading. An Integrated Account of Pretence, Self-Awareness, and Understanding Other Minds*. New York: Oxford University Press. 2003.

Niven, William D. *The Scientific Papers of James Clerk Maxwell*. New York: Dover Publications. 1965.

Norton, John. "Thought Experiments in Einstein's Work." In *Thought Experiments in Science and Philosophy*, edited by T. Horowitz and G.J. Massey, 129–48. Savage, MD: Rowman & Littlefield Publishers. 1991.

Nussbaum, Martha. "Exactly and Responsibly: A Defense of Ethical Criticism." *Philosophy and Literature* 22, no. 2 (1998): 343–65.

Odenbaugh, Jay. "Semblance or Similarity? Reflections on Simulation and Similarity." *Biology and Philosophy* 30 (2015): 277–91.

Salis, Fiora. "Fictional Names and the Problem of Intersubjective Identification." *Dialectica*, 67, no. 3 (2013): 283–301.

Salis, Fiora. "Scientific Discovery through Fictionally Modelling Reality." In *Scientific Discovery and Inferences*, Topoi, edited by Emiliano Ippoliti and Tom Nickles, 1–11. Netherlands: Springer 2018, https://doi.org/10.1007/s11245-018-9582-0 (online first).

Salis, Fiora. "The Nature of Model-World Comparisons." *The Monist* 99, no. 3 (2016): 243–59.

Salis, Fiora. "The New Fiction View of Models." *The British Journal for the Philosophy of Science* (2019): 1–39, https://doi.org/10.1093/bjps/axz015.

Salis, Fiora, and Roman Frigg. "Capturing the Scientific Imagination." In *The Scientific Imagination*, edited by Peter Godfrey-Smith and Arnon Levy. Oxford: Oxford University Press, 2020.

Spaulding, Shannon. "Imagination through Knowledge." In *Knowledge through Imagination*, edited by Amy Kind and Peter Kung, 207–26. Oxford: Oxford University Press. 2016.

Steup, Matthias. "Epistemology." In *The Stanford Encyclopedia of Philosophy*, edited by Edward N. Zalta, 2018, https://plato.stanford.edu/archives/sum2018/entries/epistemology.

Thomson-Jones, Martin. "Missing Systems and the Face Value Practice." *Synthese* 172, no. 2 (2010): 283–99.

Toon, Adam. *Models as Make-Believe: Imagination, Fiction, and Scientific Representation*. Basingstoke, UK: Palgrave Macmillan. 2012.

Walton, Kendall. *Mimesis as Make-Believe*. Cambridge, MA: Harvard University Press. 1990.

Weisberg, Michael. *Simulation and Similarity: Using Models to Understand the World*. New York: Oxford University Press. 2013.

CHAPTER 20

Geometry and the Imagination

Justin Humphreys

Geometry seems to depend on the formation and manipulation of figures in the imagination. This dependence could be investigated as a problem of empirical psychology, art history, or even pure mathematics.[1] But our questions are philosophical: what is the imagination, and how could it help to explain our geometrical knowledge? The first three sections consider the problem of geometrical cognition as it emerges within a tradition, outlining how Aristotle, Proclus, and Kant understand imagination to be necessary for geometrical cognition. The last section discusses two challenges for such theories: the rise of non-Euclidean geometry, and the reduction of mathematics to logic. In light of these challenges, we ask whether a philosophically elaborated conception of imagination might still be explanatory of geometrical knowledge.

I Aristotle

Ancient sources preserve a remarkable myth attesting to the privileged status accorded to mathematics by the Platonists. An oracle reveals that a plague raging in Delos can be cured only by doubling the local god's altar in size. When none of their architects can discover how to duplicate the cube, the Delians send an envoy to ask Plato for a solution. The philosopher grasps that the god is not jealous at the size of the altar but means to admonish the Hellenes for their neglect of mathematics.[2] Plato's view that mathematics purifies the psyche,

---

1 Eva Brann, "Mental Imagery," *The St. John's Review* (Summer 1985), 71–79 offers a philosophically informed discussion of the psychological problem of mental imagery. Pierre Descargues, *Perspective: History, Evolution, Techniques* (New York: Van Nostrand Reinhold, 1982) tracks the history of perspective in art, while Erwin Panofsky, *Perspective as Symbolic Form* (New York: Zone Books, 1991) provides a theoretical analysis of this development. David Hilbert, and Stephan Cohn-Vossen, *Geometry and the Imagination* (New York: Chelsea Publishing Company, 1952) takes an intuitive approach to geometry, developing the reader's capacity for actively visualizing figures. However, the choice of this English title as a translation of *Anschauungliche Geometrie* suggests a Kantian identification of an intuitive procedure in geometry with the exercise of imagination.
2 Theon of Smyrna, *On Mathematics Useful for the Understanding of Plato* 2.3–12 and Eutocius, *Commentary on Archimedes Sphere and Cylinder* 8.4–90.13. These are translated, with other

---

© KONINKLIJKE BRILL NV, LEIDEN, 2020 | DOI:10.1163/9789004436350_022

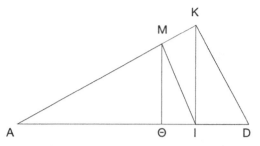

FIGURE 20.1   The problem of mean proportionals. Given A, M, and D, find K and I such that AM:AI::AI:AK::AK:AD

turning it from mere sensation to the contemplation of purely intelligible being, finds a dramatic illustration in the Delian problem of cube duplication.[3]

Though the myth anachronistically presents the problem as arising in Plato's time, a first step towards its solution comes with Hippocrates of Chios' earlier observation that if two lines could be found in continued proportion between two given lines, of which the greater was double the lesser, the cube would be doubled.[4] Thus, cube duplication is equivalent to the problem of finding mean proportionals: Given two intersecting, straight lines AM, AD, it is required to find the lines AI, AK, between them in continued proportion.[5]

Archytas, the Italian geometer contemporary to Plato, constructs a solution by carving out the unknown points from solids. Archytas begins with a semicircle with a diameter of the given length AD' and with a chord of the shorter given length AB. He draws an equal semicircle, so that as AD' pivots on A, it traces the surface of a torus. He then erects a right semi-cylinder on the base ABD,' which will meet the torus on a certain curve. Next, he rotates the given semicircle about its axis AD,' generating the surface of a cone, which intersects the torus at K. Finally, he draws a triangle AKD, such that AM=AB, while KI and

---

texts relating to the cube duplication problem, in Ivor Bulmer-Thomas, *Selections Illustrating the History of Greek Mathematics*, Vol.1 (Cambridge, MA: Harvard University Press, 1956), 257–61.

3   Plato, *Republic* 526e-527b.
4   Eutocius, *Commentary on Archimedes' Sphere and Cylinder* iii.88.4–90.13 in Bulmer-Thomas, *Selections Illustrating the History of Greek Mathematics*, 257–58. Bulmer-Thomas verifies this inference algebraically: if x and y are mean proportionals between given lines a and b, then n $\frac{a}{x} = \frac{x}{y} = \frac{y}{b}$. Thus, $y = \frac{x^2}{a} = \frac{ab}{x}$. Eliminating y, $x^3 = a^2 b$, so that $\frac{a^3}{x^3} = \frac{a}{b}$.
5   Wilbur Knorr, *The Ancient Tradition of Geometric Problems* (New York: Dover, 1986), 39–41 connects this "reduction" of the cube duplication to the problem of mean proportionals to Hippocrates' systematization of geometry, in which clever reductions of problems make them susceptible to geometrical analysis.

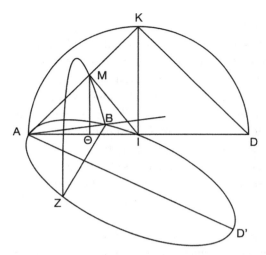

FIGURE 20.2   Archytas' constructed solution to the problem of mean proportionals. Since KI is perpendicular to AD, AM=AB. Since MΘ is perpendicular to AD, AMI is a right angle. Thus, AMI, AIK, and AKD are similar angles, so AM:AI::AI:AK::AK:AD

MΘ are both perpendicular to AD. This stereometric construction allows one to compare planar angles necessary for a verbal proof that $AM:AI::AI:AK::AK:AD$.[6]

Archytas' construction is kinematic, meaning that any description of his procedure requires words like "pivoting," "erecting," and so forth, that ascribe motions to geometrical objects like triangles and semicircles. In the *Republic*, Plato insists that such ascriptions are "absurd" but nevertheless necessary components of the geometrical procedure.[7] The diagrams used by geometers, as well as the language of kinematic construction are mere images of unchanging geometrical objects.[8] This metaphysical separation of sensible material things from ideal mathematical objects supports Plato's pedagogical program, according to which learning geometry consists in "bringing up knowledge from oneself" in recollection.[9] Far from teaching the truth of things, for Plato diagrams merely occasion geometrical cognition, the objects of which originate in the psyche of the geometer.

---

6   Here I follow the reconstruction of Knorr, *The Ancient Tradition of Geometric Problems*, 50–55. A detailed critical discussion of Archytas' kinematic procedure is available in Bartel Leendert van der Waerden, *Science Awakening* (Oxford: Oxford University Press, 1961), 149–53.
7   Plato, *Republic* 527a1-b1.
8   Plato, *Euthydemus* 290b-c. *Republic* 510d-e explicitly classifies geometrical diagrams as images, as does the possibly pseudo-Platonic *Rival Lovers* 132a-b.
9   Plato, *Meno* 85D.

The question of the meaning of kinematic construction motivates several mathematicians and philosophers to distinguish construction problems from discursive proofs.[10] It is Plato's student, Aristotle, who appeals to the imagination in attempting to reconcile two plausible but potentially conflicting doctrines. Aristotle endorses Plato's view that mathematical things are unchanging, and thus that geometrical motions cannot be real.[11] But he denies the Platonic view that diagrams refer to entities that are really separate from material bodies.[12] Indeed, Aristotle takes the objects of geometry to be quantitative parts or properties of sensible, material things.[13] Aristotle's challenge is to walk a via media between an empiricism that reduces mathematical knowledge to sensory perception and a Platonism that posits a separate realm of ideal, mathematical objects.

Aristotle's middle path stems from his observation that one gains special access to the objects of geometry through the use of diagrams. But a diagram exists in the changing, sensible world, and is slightly different from every other material particular. How can it disclose unchanging, universal truths? Aristotle holds that this is possible because in using a diagram the geometer abstracts away from its incidental properties, focusing only on its quantitative features. Thus, perceptible features like the medium in which it a figure is drawn or the real lengths of its parts are systematically ignored by the geometer.[14] Aristotle

---

10   The geometer Menaechmus conceived of all geometrical propositions as "problems" requiring kinematic construction. Plato's successor as head of the Academy, Speusippus, argued to the contrary that genesis in geometry is merely metaphorical, and suggested calling all geometrical propositions "theorems." See Prolcus, *in primum Euclidis Elementorum librum commentarii* 77–78.

11   As Aristotle puts it in *De Caelo* 280a4, in the physical world "there must be a genesis involving separation in time" but in geometry "nothing is separated in time." David Lachterman, *The Ethics of Geometry* (New York: Routledge, 1989), 61–63 shows how this passage from *De Caelo* expresses Aristotle's commitment to the Platonic denial of motion in geometry. Though construction takes time to perform, the geometrical relations revealed by the construction are timeless. Thus, the procedure of kinematic construction casts no doubt on the unchanging nature of geometrical objects like lines and circles or on the permanence of mathematical knowledge.

12   Aristotle, *Metaphysics* 1090a29-30, 1093b27-28.

13   Aristotle, *Metaphysics* 1059b12-14. Emily Katz, "Geometrical Objects as Properties of Sensibles: Aristotle's Philosophy of Geometry," *Phronesis* 64 (2019): 465–513, argues for a development of this "properties interpretation" of Aristotle's philosophy of geometry.

14   I discuss this point in Justin Humphreys, "Abstraction and Diagrammatic Reasoning in Aristotle's Philosophy of Geometry," *Apeiron* 50, no. 2 (2017): 197–224. For more on the use of diagrams in ancient geometry, see Kenneth Manders, "The Euclidean Diagram," Chapter 4 in Paolo Mancosu [Ed.] *The Philosophy of Mathematical Practice*, Oxford: Oxford University Press, 2008, 80–133 and Riviel Netz, *The Shaping of Deduction in Greek Mathematics*, Cambridge: Cambridge University Press, 1999.

holds that this sort of abstraction is possible due to the imagination, the cognitive foundation of the abstractionist theory.

Aristotle defines the imagination (φαντασία) as a motion produced by active sensation.[15] A material particular such as a diagram is thus necessary and sufficient to cause the motion of imagination, though the awareness produced need not be of that material particular. In such a case, the diagram acts to initiate an episode of the imagination, in which its productive and presentational functions give it an autonomous role in geometrical cognition. Aristotle indicates that the imagination is productive insofar as it is an image-maker. It is presentational in the sense that the images it produces are placed "before our eyes," so that imagining is something like looking at a picture.[16] To imagine something is, then, both to produce a representation and to be aware of the object represented. This representational conception of imagination underwrites Aristotle's view that the images produced by the imagination are like objects of perception for the thinking psyche, so that there is no thinking without accompanying images (φαντάσματα).[17] One thinks intelligible forms in images, which allow non-perceptible, discursive concepts to be presented in particulars.[18] Objects may at once be grasped as intelligible definitions and as affections (πάθη) of physical things, in cognitions in which the products of imagination "are like (ὥσπέρ) sense-objects, except without matter." The image is not the object thought but the representation that makes one aware of that object.[19]

In the geometrical case, this conception of cognition requires that thinking and drawing are similar insofar as both depend on the imagination. In drawing diagrams,

---

15   Aristotle, *De Anima* 428b30-429a4. Some commentators regard this definition as showing that Aristotle conceives of the imagination as reproductive or parasitic on the perceptual episode that brings it about, attributing to Aristotle a conception of imagination similar to that of the British Empiricists. In Justin Humphreys, "Aristotelian Imagination and Decaying Sense," *Social Imaginaries* 5, no. 1 (2019), 37–55, I argue that the definition does not commit Aristotle to this purely reproductive conception of imagination. Rather, he is committed only to the weaker view that imagination cannot be active on its own, but requires an active perception to trigger it.

16   Aristotle, *De Anima* 427b18-24.

17   Aristotle, *De Anima* 431a14-18, 432a4-14.

18   Aristotle, *De Anima* 431b2.

19   Erick Jiménez, *Aristotle's Concept of Mind* (Oxford: Oxford University Press, 2017), 63–67 argues that the object of thought is not the form of the phantasm. Rather, the phantasm is merely associated with the thought, so that even a false image could "symbolize" veridically. Indeed, geometrical reasoning depends on an image that has particular features and thus does not perfectly correspond to the universal grasped by the intellect.

Though we do not make any use of the fact that the size of the triangle is determinate, we none the less draw it with a determinate size. And similarly, someone who is thinking, even if he is not thinking of something with a size, places something with a size before his eyes, but thinks of it not as having a size. If its nature is that of things which have a size, but not a determinate one, he places before his eyes something with a determinate size, but thinks of it simply as having size.[20]

How can a diagram add to one's geometrical knowledge? In simply perceiving it, one grasps the particular as particular, adding nothing universal. Reasoning discursively from definitions makes no reference to an object with a determinate quantity, as required in geometry. For example, from the definition a triangle as a closed, three-sided figure alone, no comparison of angles is possible. However, when the imagination takes away the irrelevant features of the diagram, one can treat the remaining, particular figure as standing in for the universal definition. This enables one to "see" the universal concept in a particular, licensing general inferences about triangles.

I have been arguing that abstraction neutralizes or eliminates some aspects of perception, allowing the geometer to observe a diagram in an "as if" attitude. Though this is not explicated in Aristotle's psychological works, it is suggested in a passage from the *Poetics*, which explains how one can enjoy images of fearful and horrible things, such as corpses and wild beasts. Aristotle explains that one enjoys such images because

> To learn is pleasurable not only for philosophers, but also for others, though they share in this only a little. For it is on account of this that we enjoy seeing images (εἰκόνες), so that in contemplating there is a coincidence of learning and inferring what each thing is, for instance, "that this is that."[21]

An external image gives pleasure when one observes it in a contemplative attitude, learning and inferring what each thing in the image is. The resultant recognitional capacity – one's ability to make identifications – is pleasurable insofar as it draws one into "theorizing" or thinking reflectively about what is depicted in the image.

---

20   Aristotle, *De Memoria* 449b30-450a5, Trans. Richard Sorabji, *Aristotle on Memory*, Second Edition (Chicago: The University of Chicago Press, 2004), 48–49.

21   Aristotle, *Poetics* 1448b12-18.

GEOMETRY AND THE IMAGINATION   481

Aristotle's theory of geometrical cognition is analogous to his conception of aesthetic experience. Just as one views an artful representation in an "as if" attitude, the geometer views a figure as representing a discursive concept. The presentational capacity of imagination enables one to estrange some particular features of interest from a diagram, while the productive capacity of imagination allows one to manipulate the estranged properties or parts, to put into imaginary motion that which is properly unchanging. Aristotle's conception of imagination thus allows him to endorse Archytas' procedure of kinematic construction, while insisting that it involves no real change. Instead, Aristotle may maintain that the motions that produce the completed figure and present it to the geometer are psychological changes, episodes of the imagination in which one grasps truths that are unchanging but inseparable from the world disclosed in perceptual experience. Seven centuries later, Proclus formulates a Platonic response that makes extensive use of this psychological framework in order to undermine Aristotle's own abstractionism.

II   Proclus

Though for Aristotle the imagination offers an alternative to Plato's view that mathematical objects are separate from material particulars, the Neoplatonists employ the imagination to vindicate the Platonic view that mathematical beings constitute an order of existence that is separate both from material bodies and from immaterial forms.[22] Thus, in the two parts of the Prologue to his *Commentary on the First Book of Euclid's Elements*, Proclus turns Aristotle's sophisticated descriptive psychology on its head in arguing for a Platonic, ontological conception of mathematical objects.

Proclus' first *Prologue* offers his programmatic philosophy of mathematics. The second argues that specifically geometrical reasoning requires the imagination. According to Proclus, mathematical being (ἡ μαθηματικὴ οὐσία) is intermediate between pure being grasped by first philosophy and material being grasped by the senses.[23] Between the simple, indivisible forms grasped by intellect, and the changing world of particulars grasped by the senses, lies a region of diverse beings grasped discursively by reason (διάνοια).[24] Thus, there

---

22   See Syrianus, *Commentary on Aristotle's Metaphysics M & N,* 93, 20–94, 19.

23   Proclus, *Procli Diadochi in primum Euclidis Elementorum librum commentarii,* edited by Gottfried Friedlein (Leipzig: Teubner, 1873), 3.

24   In order to gain knowledge of this intermediate domain, reason has a double function, both "unfolding" the simple objects of intellect in discursive, conceptual definitions, and gathering together and referring back to intellect the knowledge it gains from them. See Proclus, *in primum Euclidis Elementorum* 4.

482   HUMPHREYS

is not just one kind of substance but an "ordered procession" of beings that require intermediate faculties, between intellect and sensation.[25] According to this Platonic conception, mathematical beings are images of their intellectual counterparts, just as reflections in water and shiny surfaces are images of sensible objects.[26]

Though Proclus presents this ontology of mathematical objects as a straightforward interpretation of Plato,[27] it amounts to a polemic against the Aristotelian conception of abstraction. Proclus objects that the selection of certain features of interest via abstraction amounts to an arbitrary choice. Moreover, abstraction attributes the necessity, exactness, and certainty of geometry to perceptible particulars. But since perceptible particulars are confused and constantly changing, they have no property that is pure and free from its opposite.[28] In contrast, mathematical beings must be separate from matter and change but also possess the diversity required for the discursive, syllogistic assertions of mathematics. Thus, mathematical beings cannot be grasped from the sensible world but instead are generated by the psyche:

> We must therefore posit the psyche as the generatrix of mathematical forms and ideas (ψυχὴν ἄρα τὴν γεννητικὴν ὑποθετέον τῶν μαθηματικῶν εἰδῶν τε καὶ λόγων). And if we say that the psyche produces them by having their patterns in her own essence and that these offspring are the projections (αἱ προβολαὶ) of forms previously existing with her, we shall be in agreement with Plato and shall have found the truth with regard to mathematical being.[29]

Because the imagination projects patterns contained in the psyche into diversity and plurality, the psyche must be thought of as giving birth to mathematical being. In this view, pure concepts in the psyche are "seeds" that give rise to

---

25   Proclus, *in primum Euclidis Elementorum* 5, 12.

26   Proclus, *in primum Euclidis Elementorum* 10.

27   Proclus uses the divided line of Plato's *Republic* (509e–511e) as the model for his division of the powers of the psyche. Indeed, Plato explicitly identifies reason (διάνοια) as the cognitive state of the geometer and claims that such geometrical thinking is not about visible figures but about the intelligible beings imitated by those visible figures. Proclus attributes this doctrine of intermediates to Plato, who divided the powers of the psyche according to a hierarchical conception of being. See Dmitri Nikulin, *Matter, Imagination and Geometry* (Burlington, VT: Ashgate, 2002), 128–32 for more discussion of intermediacy in Proclus' theory.

28   Proclus, *in primum Euclidis Elementorum* 12.

29   Proclus, *in primum Euclidis Elementorum* 13.

GEOMETRY AND THE IMAGINATION

the objects discussed by geometers. Indeed, it is only in this "projected" state that pure ideas can be presented to discursive reasoning.[30]

The latter *Prologue* presents Proclus' argument that geometrical thinking occurs with the aid of imagination. Geometrical beings are ideal and unchanging, but the actual procedure of geometrical demonstration makes use of combinations and divisions of figures.[31] It is to explain how this multiplicity and motion are possible that Proclus introduces the imagination, which enables one to reason discursively about geometrical objects. As Nikulin puts it, for Proclus the imagination is "a thinking capable of producing images in and through which it tends to know intelligible objects."[32] The imagination is non-discursive and passive, receiving definitions from discursive reason. As a receptacle, the imagination is associated with materiality, since it both serves as a vehicle of thinking but can also potentially misrepresent its target.[33]

Drawing on Aristotle's notion of intelligible matter, Proclus identifies the imagination as passive intellect:

> For imagination, both by virtue of its formative activity and because it has existence with and in the body, always produces individual pictures that have divisible extension and shape, and everything that it knows has this kind of existence. For this reason, a certain person has ventured to call it passive intellect.[34]

---

30   This conception of the intermediacy of mathematical existence, combined with Proclus' Neoplatonic view that the intellect is separate from the psyche, gives rise to a puzzle. If the psyche produces them as mere images of intellectual forms, the intellect does not seem to be required to generate and grasp mathematical beings. However, if mathematical beings derive from intellect rather than from the psyche, in grasping mathematical truths, the psyche would not be self-moving but would be determined by something external, namely the intellect. Proclus avoids this dilemma by arguing that the psyche draws the principles of mathematical objects both from herself *and* from intellect. The psyche is consequently both receptive of the pure ideas of intellect, and productive in presenting those ideas to herself discursively. Proclus' ontology of mathematical objects thus commits him to the view that mathematical knowledge requires a descent of pure, simple, and indivisible intellectual forms to a state of plurality and division. See Proclus, *in primum Euclidis Elementorum* 15.16–16.16.

31   Proclus, *in primum Euclidis Elementorum* 50.

32   Nikulin, *Matter, Imagination and Geometry*, 180, cf. 51.17–20.

33   Nikulin, *Matter, Imagination and Geometry*, 83, 142 notes that intelligible matter allows for diversity in a "quasi-material" receptacle that makes entities divisible and extended, while still maintaining that qua intelligible, mathematical things are "immaterial." Nikulin suggests that Proclus may have adopted this view under the influence of Plotnius and Porphyry.

34   Proclus, *in primum Euclidis Elementorum*, 51.20–52.4, Morrow Trans, modified.

By identifying imagination with the passive intellect, Proclus makes it the material substrate in which intelligible forms are grasped, since it is only when it is informed by productive intellect that one thinks.[35]

Proclus' attribution to Aristotle of this identification of imagination and passive intellect is clearly not accurate, but it is philosophically fruitful.[36] For Aristotle, the dependence of geometrical reasoning on the imagination threatens to make geometry merely empirical, and thus requires the peculiar theory of abstraction, in which sensible objects are "purified" of their incidental attributes. Proclus bypasses this problem by placing the contents of imagination in the intellect. Instead of having to specify how sensible contents can stand in intelligible relations, Proclus' project becomes one of spelling out how purely intelligible ideas can be thought in multiplicity.

Nikulin points out that Proclus' theory rests on his conception of matter as that which allows unified concepts to be reasoned about in multiplicity. Pure definitions (λόγοι καθαροί) without parts, expressed in geometrical matter, become diverse, infinitely divisible, and extended.[37] This process of diversification via imagination gives rise to the realization of a mere concept of geometry in intelligible matter, a compound which is open to inspection by discursive reason in ways that pure definitions are not. Indeed, though the definition of a circle has no shape, when it is drawn out in intelligible (or "geometrical") matter, a circle really becomes circular.[38] Rabouin argues that for Proclus, the imagination may even represent properties that are in principle unavailable to reason, so that it has an "opacity" that allows for a productive divergence of geometrical definitions from geometrical figures.[39] The intelligible substrate of imagination thus exceeds the content of discursive

---

35   Nikulin, *Matter, Imagination and Geometry*, 184; cf. Proclus, *in primum Euclidis Elementorum* 52.3, 56.17–18.

36   Recall that Aristotle conceives of the imagination as a motion triggered by active sensation. This determination by sensation is sufficient to distinguish imagination from passive intellect in Aristotle's division of the psyche. For Aristotle, but not for Proclus, the imagination could function without any contribution from intellect, such as in one's experience of illusions and dreams.

37   "Pure definitions" are mentioned by Proclus, *in primum Euclidis Elementorum*, 49.25. For a more comprehensive discussion, see Dmitri Nikulin, "Imagination and Matter in Proclus," *Ancient Philosophy* 28 (2008): 161.

38   Proclus, *in primum Euclidis Elementorum* 53–54.

39   David Rabouin, "Proclus' Conception of Geometric Space and Its Actuality" in *Mathematizing space*, 105–42, edited by Vincenzo De Risi. Berlin: Birkhäuser, 2015, 124 argues that Proclean geometry is opaque in the sense that it can represent properties that are in principle inconceivable by discursive reason, canonically in reductio proofs. Admitting that reductio proofs exploit this non-correspondence, I do not see that Proclus countenances false images in geometry. On the contrary, it is the verbal part of a reductio proof that is

GEOMETRY AND THE IMAGINATION

definitions, making geometry something more than the logical derivation of a conclusion from premises. Whereas for Aristotle, the imagination served as a way to deny the Platonic separation of the mathematical objects from sensible substances, for Proclus it allows for a plausible defense of recollection, in which one comes to know what one already possesses by expressing and displaying it in the matter of the imagination.[40]

For Proclus, definitions are "wrapped up" in discursive reason but unfolded and exposed in imagination, which acts as their receptacle.[41] In constructive proofs but not in proofs by contradiction, the imagination starts "from what is partless within it and proceeds to project each knowable object."[42] Thus, the imagination serves to explain the projection of the partless concept into intelligible matter. Proclus' doctrine of the imagination allows him to reconcile Platonism, according to which mathematical definitions are pure and completely separate from matter, with the apparently constructive procedure of Euclidean geometry.

> We invoke the imagination and the intervals that it furnishes, since the form itself is unmoving, ungenerated, indivisible, and free from all underlying matter. But the elements hidden in the form are produced distinctly and individually on the screen of the imagination. What projects the images is reason; the source of what is projected is the form within reason (τὸ μὲν προβάλλον ἡ διάνοια, τὸ δὲ ἀφ᾽ οὗ προβάλλεται τὸ δινοητὸν εἶδος); and what they are projected in is this so-called passive intellect that unfolds in revolution about the partlessness of genuine intellect, setting a distance between itself and that indivisible source of pure thought, shaping itself after the unshaped forms, and becoming all the things that constitute the reason and the unitary ideas in us.[43]

---

    shown to contain an absurdity, an absurdity that emerges only in comparison to a pure figure in the imagination.

40   Nikulin, "Imagination and Matter in Proclus," 162.

41   Proclus, *in primum Euclidis Elementorum* 54.27–55.6. Nikulin points out that the reason-imagination relation is not one between form and matter. Rather, it is one between a principle (λόγος), which is already discursive and has multiplicity, and what is generated by the principle. The final, completed figure that is presented all at once in unity requires that discursive reason and imagination together play an active role in constituting the geometer's object. As Nikulin, *Matter, Imagination and Geometry*, 236 puts it, "both dianoia and phantasia have their shared in the constitution of geometrical entities."

42   Proclus, *in primum Euclidis Elementorum* 95.10–14.

43   Proclus, *in primum Euclidis Elementorum* 56, Morrow Trans, modified.

Proclus' discursive reason at once employs conceptions that are inherent in itself and comprehends that which is "outside of itself."[44] Insofar as it involves reason looking outside itself, geometrical cognition cannot be the mere grasp of discursive definitions. Thus, Proclus' conception of geometrical cognition rests on his description of the imagination as a power to project unified concepts into multiplicity.[45] In such cases, reason at once employs conceptions that are inherent in itself and is "looking at things outside of itself."[46] Without this capacity to externalize as images the concepts immanent within reason, reason's power to think discursively would never be activated.

Proclus countenances kinematic constructions about unchanging, partless objects, as illustrated in his interpretation of Euclid's First Proposition: to construct an equilateral triangle on a given line segment AB. The construction proceeds first by drawing a circle through B with center A, then by drawing a circle through A with center B, and finally by connecting A and B with straight lines to the point at which the circles meet, C.

The construction uses two postulates, rules that correspond to the motions required for producing figures. Euclid's third postulate, "to describe a circle with any center and distance" is invoked in drawing the circles about A and B. Euclid's first postulate, to "draw a straight line from any point to any point," is invoked in connecting the lines to C to form the triangle.

Since Euclidean postulates codify the geometrical "motions" necessary for kinematic construction, Proclus can entertain an objection to the geometer's procedure. If geometrical objects are motionless and without parts, how can there be motion and diversity in such objects, as required by the construction? Proclus responds that, as in the Prologue, such motions are located in the "unwritten tablet" of passive intellect or imagination, rather than in the definitions of reason. One might yet object that because it is intelligible, passive intellect could not be affected by bodily motion. Proclus holds that this motion is not bodily but imaginary. Because it is partless, intellect "is moved, but not spatially; and imagination has its own kind of motion corresponding to its own partlessness."[47] For Proclus, the motions attributed to geometrical figures in construction problems are imaginary, since they are not contained in the geometrical definitions but are the effects of unwrapping those definitions in

---

44   Proclus, *in primum Euclidis Elementorum* 55.

45   Thus, Plato's views are vindicated because "Although the causes of the geometrical forms in accordance with which the understanding projects its demonstrations about them exist previously in the understanding, the several figures that are divided and compounded are projections in the imagination." Proclus, *in primum Euclidis Elementorum* 57, Morrow Trans.

46   Proclus, *in primum Euclidis Elementorum* 55, Morrow Trans.

47   Proclus, *in primum Euclidis Elementorum* 185–86, Morrow Trans., cf. 56.14–22.

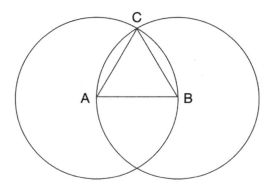

FIGURE 20.3   Euclid I.1. The radius AB=AC and the radius BC=BA. But AB=BA. Therefore, AB=AC=BC, so the constructed triangle is equilateral

the imagination.[48] Likewise, in unwrapping definitions, the motion of intellect is imaginary, which is consistent with the doctrine that the intellect and its objects are completely immaterial and disembodied.

Proclus and Aristotle both relegate the motions necessary for kinematic construction to the imagination. But while Aristotle maintains that geometry does not investigate causes, Proclus holds that constructive proofs (as opposed to proofs by contradiction) tell one *why* the proved proposition is true.[49] Moreover, Proclus rejects Aristotle's abstractionism, arguing that geometrical facts are about a separate region of ideal objects. These ideal objects bear a relation of resemblance to the sensible figures that represent them, but they are not properties of those figures.[50]

If Proclus' conception of the imagination allows him to conceive of geometrical diagrams as imitations of mathematical beings, this Platonic thought is carried through to its logical conclusion in considering how those beings are images of first principles. In Proclus' view, merely developing a capacity to reason by diagrams reminds one of mathematical beings, which themselves remind one of the forms. One can thus discover a symbolic meaning concerning how the intellect produces the cosmos in Euclid's propositions. In Euclid's First Proposition, the construction of the equilateral triangle symbolizes the psyche, while the circles symbolize the active and passive intellect, which together generate the psyche.[51] In other words, the construction illustrated in Figure 20.3 is an allegory showing how in establishing the various orders of reality,

---

48   Nikulin, *Matter, Imagination and Geometry*, 248–49 notes how Proclus identifies the construction with the unfolding of "secret" properties held within the definition. See Proclus, *in primum Euclidis Elementorum* 186.9–14, 51.17–20.
49   Proclus, *in primum Euclidis Elementorum* 202.
50   Proclus, *in primum Euclidis Elementorum* 207.
51   Proclus, *in primum Euclidis Elementorum* 213–14.

intellect leaves geometrical propositions as traces of its constituting activity. Given this ascription of religious meaning to geometry, one might expect, that modern philosophers would reject Proclus' theory as mystical. It is remarkable then, that in the course of attempting to put metaphysics on a sound scientific basis, the chief of modern philosophers, Immanuel Kant, would reach the conclusion that imagination is required for geometrical knowledge.

III   Kant

Kant's critical philosophy examines reason's limits in order to enumerate the kinds of judgment in principle available to finite, rational beings.[52] The Preface to the first edition of the *Critique of Pure Reason* suggests that a central purpose of this project is to recover metaphysics from a state of degradation. Once the queen of the sciences, metaphysics is now scorned and abandoned, mourning like Hecuba, the ruler of the vanquished Trojans.[53] Kant's philosophical project is one of rapprochement, a return to metaphysics akin to the reconciliation of quarreling lovers. Returning the philosopher to his original mistress, critical philosophy restores its queen in her proper role at the head of the kingdom of knowledge.[54] Kant demonstrates the possibility of metaphysical judgments that are in principle reducible neither to judgments of mathematics nor to the judgments of physical science. But since Kant supposes that geometrical judgments can have the status of knowledge, one may inquire: how are geometrical judgments possible?

Kant's understanding of geometry depends on a distinction among three possible forms of judgment, expressed by three types of predication.[55] Suppose that A is the subject and B the predicate of an affirmative sentence. If what is expressed by "A is B" could not be otherwise, the judgment is necessary and universal or "a priori"; if not, it is "empirical."[56] While empirical judgments require observation for their validation, Kant cites mathematical propositions as canonical cases of a priori judgment. If B is contained in the concept of A, then the judgment is analytic or "explicative." Just by understanding the definition

---

52   Kant, *Kritik der Reinen Vernunft*, B. xx–xxii.

53   Kant, *Kritik der Reinen Vernunft*, A.viii–ix.

54   Kant, *Kritik der Reinen Vernunft*, A.850/B.878 argues that this return is necessary because metaphysics is the science concerned with the essential ends of reason, so that reason's fulfillment as reason depends on the possibility of a critical metaphysics.

55   Kant dismisses the possibility of empirical, analytic judgments as "absurd" (B11) but see Saul Kripke, *Naming and Necessity* (Cambridge, MA: Harvard University Press, 1972).

56   Kant, *Kritik der Reinen Vernunft*, B.3–5.

GEOMETRY AND THE IMAGINATION

(the "concept") of the subject term, one could make a correct analytic judgment.[57] Synthetic judgments, in contrast, involve supplementation of the concept of A, in virtue of which they are called "ampliative."[58] Thus, the question, "how are geometrical judgments possible?" turns out to be a special case of the question, "how a priori synthetic judgments are possible?"

Kant's answer to this more general formulation of the question is twofold. First, he argues that all synthetic judgments require a representation in space and time, the pure forms of intuition. The faculty of intuition thus provides the grounds of all synthetic judgment. Second, he makes the case that there are a priori forms of intuition, and thus that synthetic judgments can have non-empirical grounds. Hence, although space and time are required to represent the object of both mathematical and empirical judgments, mathematics consists of necessary propositions that could never be determined empirically. As a result of its peculiar synthetic a priori status, mathematics must "exhibit all its concepts in intuition," that is, "it must construct them."[59] The synthetic structure of mathematical judgment thus requires a construction in intuition. This construction depends on the faculty of the imagination.

Kant defines the imagination (*Einbildungskraft*) as the faculty of representing in intuition an object that is not present.[60] When one imagines an object, one synthesizes its parts into a whole and takes that synthesis as one's intentional object. Though this synthesized representation has sometimes been understood as the object of non-empirical inspection, Tinguely has argued that this visual metaphor is misleading. A Kantian representation is better understood through tactile metaphors, since it is actively "arranged" and "set out" by imagination and "grasped" in intuition.[61] When the imagination is productive, it constructs a concept synthetically, generating an immediate awareness in a subject of the object constructed.[62] This direct awareness is what Kant calls

---

57   Kant, *Kritik der Reinen Vernunft*, A.718/B.746.

58   Kant, *Kritik der Reinen Vernunft*, A.6–7/B.10–11. Kant's characterization of analytic judgments in terms of the containment of the predicate in the concept of the subject has been criticized as unclear or metaphorical (W.V.O. Quine, *From A Logical Point of View* (Cambridge, MA: Harvard University Press, 1980), 20–21). As we shall see, Kant's view that mathematical judgments depend on a construction carried out by imagination offers powerful basis for the interpretation of this conception of containment.

59   Kant *Prolegomena* 4:283, cf. Kant, *Kritik der Reinen Vernunft*, B. xiv, A.10.

60   Kant, *Kritik der Reinen Vernunft*, B.151.

61   Joseph Tinguely, *Kant and the Reorientation of Aesthetics* (New York: Routledge, 2018), 45–47.

62   Kant, *Kritik der Reinen Vernunft*, A.78/B.103.

the displaying of a concept in intuition, where "intuition" indicates the immediate relation between a mode of knowledge and an object.[63]

The role of imagination in producing geometrical knowledge is parallel to its role in producing empirical knowledge. In the empirical case, intuition is an awareness of an object of sensation, which is a product of sensibility, the faculty of receiving representations. The intuition is not yet a conceptual grasp of the object, which requires an additional determination by the understanding. The move from physiological inputs to conceptual judgments involves a two-fold synthesis by the imagination, first from subconscious stimuli to conscious appearances, and then from non-conceptual appearances to conceptual judgments.[64] To use Horstmann's illustrative example, suppose Peter falls into a swimming pool filled with cold and dirty water. The first synthesis moves from changes in Peter's bodily state into unified appearances, for example, the taste of brackish water and a feeling of coldness on the skin. The second synthesis moves from these non-conceptual appearances to Peter's judgment, "I am in a dirty pool."[65]

The empirical intuition produced by the imagination is an immediate awareness of a pre-conceptual appearance. In contrast, in mathematics, the synthetic function of the imagination is determined *by a concept* one already possesses. Consequently, while an appearance is the object of an empirical intuition, Kant identifies the object of a pure intuition as a schema, a representation that is both particular ("sensible") and necessary ("intellectual").[66] The schema is neither a concrete representation in time and space, nor a discursive concept lacking spatiotemporal form.[67] The schema of a geometrical concept, for example, is not a sensible image, but a rule for generating such images: "the schema of the triangle can exist nowhere but in thought. It is a rule of synthesis

---

63   Kant, *Kritik der Reinen Vernunft*, A.19.

64   Rolf-Peter Horstmann, *Kant's Power of Imagination* (Cambridge: Cambridge University Press, 2018), 11 has clarified several "stages" in Kant's account of the genesis of a perceptual judgment. Unprocessed sensations have no space or time determinations before being unified in a non-conceptual intuition. The appearances rendered in these intuitions are then unified in representations that enter into the conceptual predicative complexes of empirical judgment.

65   See Horstmann, *Kant's Power of Imagination*, 36–45 for an argument that the imagination is active at both stages.

66   Kant, *Kritik der Reinen Vernunft*, A.138/B.177 – A.140/B.179. Kant's terminology here is potentially misleading, since the way in which a schema is "sensible" does not entail that it is derived from sensations. Rather, the schema merely restricts the concept it represents to the conditions of sensibility.

67   Kant, *Kritik der Reinen Vernunft*, B181. The schema of a geometrical concept, for example, is not an image on paper, but a rule for generating such images.

GEOMETRY AND THE IMAGINATION

in the imagination, in respect to pure figures in space."[68] The sensible aspect of a schema is its capacity to represent a universal concept by picking out a particular; its intellectual aspect is its capacity to determine synthetic activity. Schemata are products of the imagination that act as rules constraining further exercises of the imagination.

This synthetic function of the imagination in geometry comes sharply into focus in Kant's Transcendental Doctrine of Method, specifically in the chapter on "The Discipline of Pure Reason." There, Kant argues that while metaphysics must be restricted to making negative judgments on the use of reason, mathematics advances synthetically, through the construction of concepts.[69] In other words, mathematical knowledge depends on grasping the universal in the particular, so that the single model one considers serves as the schema of its general concept. The schema representing the concept is a construction in the aforementioned, tactile sense that it sets out the salient features of the general concept in a way that can be grasped in intuition. Kant describes the construction of a concept as an act of imagination:

> To construct a concept (*Einen Begriff konstruieren*) means to exhibit (*darstellen*) a priori the intuition which corresponds to the concept. For the construction of a concept we therefore need a non-empirical intuition. The latter must, as intuition, be a single object, and yet none the less, as the construction of a concept (a universal representation), it must in its representation express universal validity for all possible intuitions which fall under the same concept. Thus I construct a triangle by representing the object which corresponds to this concept either by imagination alone, in pure intuition, or in accordance therewith also on paper, in empirical intuition - in both cases completely a priori, without having borrowed the pattern (*das Muster*) from any experience.[70]

Geometrical cognition consists both of a constructive synthesis of material corresponding to but not contained in a geometrical definition (a "concept") and a non-empirical, immediate receptive relation ("intuition") to the construction. The completed construction can be understood as a non-empirical representation or "rule" governing inferences as well as the production of any

---

68   Kant, *Kritik der Reinen Vernunft*, A141, Kemp Smith Trans.

69   Kant, *Kritik der Reinen Vernunft*, A.711/B.739.

70   Kant, *Kritik der Reinen Vernunft*, A.713/B.741, Kemp Smith Trans.

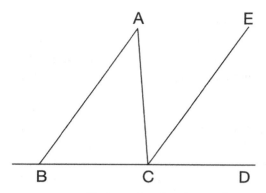

FIGURE 20.4   The internal angles of a triangle are equal to two right angles.

possible empirical representation. The role of the imagination is to perform the synthesis of this rule and to display it in intuition.[71]

To understand the work done by Kant's theory, it is helpful to consider a concrete example, as illustrated in Figure 20.4. Kant imagines one trying to discover the relation of the angles of the triangle to the right angle. From the mere concept of triangle, that of a plane figure enclosed by three straight lines, one is unable to make any progress.[72] The crucial steps of drawing lines to D and E are what allows one to make the inference, which depends on a comparison of interior and exterior angles. The geometer's procedure is synthetic in the sense that it introduces relations (equality between angles ABC and ECD, and between BAC and ACE) that are not contained in the concept triangle, into one's stock of relevant propositions.[73] The analytically given predicates

---

71   To construct a concept is to display it in intuition, a display seems to be the crucial function of imagination in geometrical cognition: "It is the concept of quantities only that allows of being constructed, that is, exhibited a priori in intuition; whereas qualities cannot be presented in any intuition that is not empirical." (Kant, *Kritik der Reinen Vernunft*, A.714–5/B.742–3, Kemp-Smith Trans) This is akin to Proclus' view that the definition could be "unwrapped" and displayed in the imagination.

72   Kant, *Kritik der Reinen Vernunft*, A.716/B.744.

73   Michael Friedman, *Kant and the Exact Sciences*, Cambridge, MA: Harvard University Press, 57–59 claims that that an idealized version of the figure is necessary for geometrical proof because Kant's logic in monadic. In this view, geometrical imagination in Kant plays the role that would be taken by polyadic quantification in modern proofs. In Friedman's "Kant on geometry and spatial intuition," *Synthese* 181, No.1, 233–35, he contrasts this reading with an interpretation on Kantian pure intuition that is conceived as a way of reading off invariant properties from an empirically given diagram. But whether Kant understands pure intuition primarily as offering an inference license in the context of proof or as licensing reading offers certain properties from diagrams, the essential point

GEOMETRY AND THE IMAGINATION   493

formed by combinations of points A, B, and C are alone insufficient to justify
any relevant inference. The required, additional premises are available within
the geometer's procedure that are unavailable in analytic judgments concerning the triangle: "I must not restrict my attention to what I am actually thinking
in my concept of a triangle (this is nothing more than the mere definition); I
must pass beyond it to properties which are not contained (*liegen*) in the concept, but yet belong (*gehören*) to it."[74] Kant designates the necessary properties
revealed by drawing along the side as "belonging" to but not being "contained"
in the concept of the triangle.[75]

Insofar as the imagination represents an *absent* object in intuition, it has the
capacity to expand the stock of premises available to the geometer. Since the
geometer's intuition is a priori, the object of the expanded intuition is not an
empirical object but a schema, a rule of inference that is added to the content
of the concept "triangle." Kant agrees with Aristotle and Proclus that geometrical knowledge rests on information that is not directly contained in discursive
definitions but only in the "expanded" representations of those definitions.
However, as opposed to both ancient philosophers, Kant is primarily concerned with showing that mathematical judgments have a distinctive a priori
and synthetic logical form. Indeed, this logical status is explanatory of the constructive procedure of geometry.[76] The geometer must construct, according to
Kant, because it is precisely through the ampliative exercise of the imagination
upon concepts that mathematical objects are displayed in intuition, and thereby made the objects of synthetic, a priori judgment.

Because the method of geometry is constructive, the geometer must always look beyond the predicates contained in any definition to identify new
predicates. Thus, Kant takes it that the mathematician's procedure could
never be purely discursive but must be "intuitive" insofar as it expands inferential resources by adopting new rules necessary for but not derived from the
concept. The decision to use the new rule must be justified in intuition, by

---

      for us is that he takes the imagination to add content to geometrical propositions that is
      not exhausted by any collection of geometrical concepts.

74   Kant, *Kritik der Reinen Vernunft,* A.718/B.746, Kemp Smith Trans.

75   Kant, *Kritik der Reinen Vernunft,* A.719 therefore distinguishes between two uses of reason:
      the *discursive* employment of reason is in accordance with concepts, while the *intuitive*
      employment occurs by means of the construction of concepts. Again, it is by means of the
      immediate awareness of construction that the geometer intuitively enriches the concep-
      tual content of the definitions of geometry, without which his procedure would be limit-
      ed to the merely discursive methods of the philosopher.

76   The method of construction is the one "by means of which I combine in a pure intuition
      (just as I do in empirical intuition) the manifold which belongs to the schema of a trian-
      gle in general, and therefore its concept." (Kant, *Kritik der Reinen Vernunft,* 718).

reconstructing the schema from which the rule is derived.[77] But is there really a sharp distinction to be made between what a concept contains, and that which merely of belongs to it? Supposing that Kant correctly describes the geometer's practice of imaginatively expanding a concept, is this procedure justified?

Though Kant's theory of geometrical judgment is confined to his *Critique of Pure Reason*, a parallel point in his aesthetic theory in the *Critique of Judgment* can help address this question. In an aesthetic judgment, the imagination compares the form of an intuition to concepts, without assigning the representation of that form any objective value. In such a comparison, if the representation is undesignedly in agreement with the concepts of the understanding, a feeling of pleasure is produced in the reflecting subject.[78] This does not amount to an empirical judgment, since the representation is not subsumed under a concept.[79] Rather, the pleasure arises due to the free play of imagination, in which representations of the imagination are referred to but not reduced to concepts.[80]

I suggest that Kant understands the role of imagination in geometry in a way that is analogous to its aesthetic function. In aesthetic judgment, the imagination produces representations and relates them to a concept without those representations being subsumed under the concept. Just so, in geometry the imagination produces representations that are in accordance with but not determined by geometrical concepts. The geometer's free use of the imagination thus corresponds to the production of ever new constructions, and hence to his discovery of geometrical properties not given in the predicates of the definitions with which he begins. Though the geometer's ultimate object is to extend knowledge

---

77   Synthetic a priori judgments are thus both necessary and, after their concepts are synthesized, can be employed in further inferences, allowing for a cumulative progression of geometry. But due to their intuitive origin, these rules can also always be "reactivated" in intuition, so that the body of a priori synthetic propositions is open to potentially infinite amplification. Thus, Kant might respond to Quine's objection that the concept of the "containment" of a predicate in the definition is unclear by arguing that the procedure of geometry could never be one of pure deduction from concepts, since any collection of concepts could never provide the resources for producing novel constructions.

78   Kant, *Kritik der Urteilskraft*, Sect. 7, p. 26 Bernard.

79   Horstmann, *Kant's Power of Imagination*, 62–63 notes that Kant speaks of an aesthetic comprehension as comprehension into an intuition in the imagination (in *Kritik der Urteilskraft*, Sect. 26). Thus, for Horstmann, imagination in the third critique is conceived as a power that functions independently of the understanding in establishing an intuition. The representation formed by the imagination thus counts as the potential material for cognitive judgment *or* for aesthetic judgment.

80   Kant, *Kritik der Urteilskraft*, Sect. 57, p. 189 Bernard.

GEOMETRY AND THE IMAGINATION

rather than to experience reflective pleasures, both geometrical discovery and aesthetic experience emerge from the free exercise of thought. The gradual enlightenment of finite, rational beings thus depends at once upon the constraining power of the concept, and upon the exercise of a freedom that pushes beyond the concept through the autonomous exercise of the imagination.

IV   The Prospects of Imagination

I have described three classic theories of geometrical imagination in this chapter. But what are the prospects not of just one or another theory, but of the concept of geometrical imagination in general? There seem to be two primary objections to the inclusion of imagination in a theory of geometrical cognition: the existence of alternative geometries, and the possibility of reducing geometrical judgments to logical derivations.

The first objection to the theories emerges from the development non-Euclidean geometry.[81] According to this objection, the existence of alternative geometries, which have consequences that seem to contradict our intuitions, is evidence against imagination-based theories of geometrical cognition. Non-Euclidean geometry shows that geometrical objects might be quite different from how we imagine them, when we drop some of Euclid's postulates. For example, hyperbolic geometry drops the assumption of Euclid's Fifth Postulate, that if a straight line meets two other straight lines, such that it makes the two interior angles on one side of it together less than two right angles, the other straight lines will meet if produced on that side on which the angles are less than two right angles. This postulate is "intuitive" in the sense that it corresponds to our "ordinary" notion of space. But, Coxeter points out, there is no physical evidence that space is actually this way.[82] Indeed, it is equally coherent to assume that parallel lines meet "at infinity," just as when one looks at parallel train tracks, they seem to converge to a single point in the distance. The existence of an alternative, coherent geometry appears to throw a stumbling block before the theories of geometrical cognition outlined in this chapter.[83]

---

81   For a discussion of the history of this development, see Jeremy Gray, *János Bolyai, Non-Euclidean Geometry, and the Nature of Space* (Cambridge, MA: The Brundy Library, 2004).

82   H.S.M. Coxeter, *Non-Euclidean Geometry*, 4th ed. (Toronto: University of Toronto Press, 1962).

83   Kant's implicit assumption that the postulate is required as a condition of our sensibility, that is, the view that our intuition must conform to the postulate, amounts to an arbitrary decision. Likewise, consider Proclus' Principle that if a line intersects one of two parallel

The relevance of imagination-based theories of geometrical cognition can be better understood by considering a concrete example of how geometers visualize spaces that are not Euclidean. Consider the Poincaré disk, a model of the hyperbolic plane of constant negative curvature. In this disk, a line is represented as the arc of a circle, with ends that are perpendicular to the disk's boundary. For example, parallel lines are represented as arcs that do not touch one another, while perpendicular lines are represented as arcs that meet orthogonally.

The possibility of hyperbolic space itself rests on a completely analytic fact, namely that Euclid's fifth postulate is not entailed by the others. In the hyperbolic plane, all the results of Euclidean geometry that make no essential use of the fifth postulate are true [Fig. 20.5]. The Poincaré disk model offers a way to visualize this space that is unavailable within Euclidean plane geometry. Indeed, this model has been useful even outside of geometry, in the work of the artist M.C. Escher, who used it to generate tessellations [Fig. 20.6].[84]

Does the existence of alternative, coherent geometries speak against the necessity of the imagination in geometrical cognition? I do not see that it does. One can imagine a visual presentation as representing certain geometrical properties, while rejecting the fifth postulate. Indeed, that is precisely what one does in employing the Poincaré disk model. So non-Euclidean spaces can be represented intuitively, even though the objects in them do not conform to Euclidean assumptions about the structure of space. But this does not disqualify the imagination from playing a constitutive role in geometrical cognition. Indeed, a neo-Aristotelian view would be that our ability to read off the negative curvature of the plane from the model depends on isolating the perceptible

---

lines, it also intersects the other. Proclus, *in primum Euclidis Elementorum* 58–59 argues that the assertion that parallel lines meet is a "perverse" use of geometrical principles, which could be concluded only from an "ungeometrical" hypothesis. But this does not give any independent reason to believe that the correct geometry is that of Euclid. Insofar as Aristotle was pre-Euclidean, it seems that he should have the least to say about the parallel postulate. Nevertheless, it has been argued that Plato and Aristotle were aware of the possibility of non-Euclidean geometry, but accepted the parallel postulate on metaphysical grounds. Again, the choice of this metaphysics seems arbitrary. For discussion, see Vittorio Hössle, "Plato's Foundation of the Euclidean Character of Geometry," in *The Other Plato*, ed. Dmitri Nikulin (Albany, NY: State University of New York Press, 2012), 161–82.

84 Escher drew his tessellations from the disk, using a straightedge and compass. Thus, Escher's method was "Euclidean" in the sense that he generated images by placing the disk in the Euclidean plane and drawing straight lines through its center. See Douglas Dunham, "Creating Hyperbolic Patterns – Old and New," *Notices of the American Mathematical Society* 50, no. 4 (April 2003): 452–55.

GEOMETRY AND THE IMAGINATION

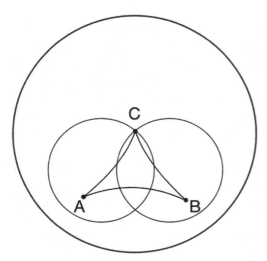

FIGURE 20.5   The Poincaré disk model of hyperbolic geometry. Consider the construction of an equilateral triangle given a segment AB in this model. As in the Euclidean proof illustrated in Figure 20.3, one constructs circles around A and B, with the shared radius AB. The same proof holds, according to which the lines drawn to C are equal to the radius. The model shows that this result is independent of Euclid's fifth postulate.

FIGURE 20.6   M.C. Escher's *Circle Limit IV* (*Heaven and Hell*). As one moves from the center of the circle outward, the tessellated demons and angels become progressively smaller.

features of the lines meeting and abstracting their perceived topology from the metrical features of the physical model. A neo-Proclean view would take the imagination to draw out the consequences of definition while suspending or denying the parallel postulate. A neo-Kantian might take the Poincaré disk to be a monogram of the pure imagination, a representation of the hyperbolic plane that could never be simply given in outer intuition. Thus, the mere existence of non-Euclidean geometries casts no doubt on theories that attribute geometrical cognition to the imagination.

This brings us to the other objection, that of logicism. If all true geometrical propositions can be deduced logically from premises, those truths are analytic. However, while it is possible to formalize elementary geometry in second-order logic, such a formalization does not immediately do away with the need for imagination. For this amounts to the use of set theory as a foundation of elementary geometry, which requires the use of expansive logical notions that may be no less mysterious than the non-discursive or imaginative element of geometry they are meant to replace. In any such theory, the question of whether intuition and imagination are required for geometry is reproduced at a higher level of abstraction. Given a second-order formalization of geometry, one might ask whether intuition, and the imaginative activity that makes it possible, is required for grasping the object of set theory. The question of the cognitive status of geometrical objects is thereby replaced with an altogether more difficult problem.

To dispense with the imagination, one needs a formalization that makes no use of the notions of set theory. Such an approach is available in Tarski's Elementary Geometry, in which, all the propositions of geometry are formalized as sentences of first-order logic. The individuals over which these sentences quantify are points.[85] Consequently, in Elementary Geometry, no set-theoretic interpretations of geometrical objects are required: higher-level objects like triangles and spheres are simply collections of individuals to which the sentences of first-order logic refer. The logician's grasp of first-order sentences is unmistakably analytic, since the predicates of each sentence are those listed in the axioms of that geometry. Logicism may thus be defined as the view that all the important results of geometry can be presented and proved in Tarski's logical system.[86]

---

85   Tarski's formalization of geometry relies on two primitive (non-logical) relations: "betweenness" and "equidistance," in addition to first-order logic. The key to this first-order formalization is that variables range over points. Thus, second order logic (set theory) is not required for the formalization.

86   Certain results in projective geometry cannot be formalized in Tarski's system. These remaining results, which fall outside of Tarski's conception of "elementary" geometry, could

GEOMETRY AND THE IMAGINATION   499

This reduction of geometry to logic casts doubt on the theories discussed in this chapter. Aristotle, Proclus, and Kant all take the role played by the imagination to be distinct from the discursive understanding one gains while deducing a conclusion from premises. Logicism about geometry is of interest precisely because it denies the necessity of any such contribution to cognition by a non-conceptual faculty. Though imagining or intuiting certain figures might be psychologically helpful for grasping some geometrical truths, they are dispensable to a complete geometry. A consequence of this view is that the intuitive content of geometry can be understood as a model of the logical system. Since geometries are taken to be structures that satisfy some system of axioms, the idea that there is one true nature of space grasped by the geometer must be abandoned.[87]

Despite these dire signs, logicism seems perfectly consistent with the view that the diagrammatic, kinematic, and intuitive reasoning envisaged by our philosophers is *cognitively* necessary for geometrical understanding. In order to really do away with the role of the imagination in geometrical reasoning, a theory on the side of cognition is needed, one that shows that all the logical operations of Tarski's system can be carried out without the aid of the imagination. The philosophy of mind presents us with one such theory. According to computationalism, any cognition that can be described in our ordinary language can be fruitfully modeled by programming a digital computer.[88] In elementary cases, this thesis certainly holds: it is trivial to show, for example, that the cognitive activity we call "adding" can be modeled on a Truing Machine. The non-trivial idea is that no cognitive activity escapes such modeling.

If computationalism is true, all our cognitions, including those we have when we are doing geometry, are instances of our following logical rules. Logicism and computationalism combined leave no room for the imagination in explanations of what we are doing, when we are doing geometry. If logicism about mathematics and computationalism in the philosophy of mind are both true, every mathematical cognition consists in executions of the rules of logic. Without a paradigm shift, to use Kuhn's old phrase, in our conception of mind

---

      be captured through enriching the assumption of Tarski's logical system.

87   Since all the axioms can be combined to make a single sentence S, whichever interpretations satisfy (i.e. make true) S are its models. Thus, the logic of geometry could have multiple models, that is, interpretations that make the sentences of the geometry true.

88   Of course, a lot of weight is being put on the word "fruitful" here. But we may follow Alan Turing, "Computing Machinery and Intelligence," *Mind* 49 (1950): 433–60, in taking this to mean just the cognition could be spelled out in explicit logical rules.

or mathematics, imaginative construction seems to be just one among potentially infinite means of carrying out a computation.

v Conclusion

This chapter has outlined several ways that the imagination has been invoked to explain features of geometrical cognition. For Aristotle, it helps to describe how particular figures can be of use in attaining universal results, and to explain why the geometer is entitled to ascribe motions to unchanging, mathematical objects. For Proclus, the imagination allows one to grasp mathematical beings that are beneath first principles, but above changing, sensible things. For Kant, the imagination has the crucial synthetic and discriminative functions necessary for extending geometrical knowledge beyond mere definitions. For all these philosophers, imagination offers something non-discursive to geometrical thinking, without reducing that thinking to perceptual receptivity. Nevertheless, the imagination has largely dropped out of our contemporary philosophy of geometry.

Why should this be the case? Non-Euclidean geometry is no less "imaginative" than Euclidean geometry, since while they make different assumptions, both require the same sort of spatial reasoning. The reduction of geometry to logic casts doubt on our theories, since in principle, the result of a richly intuitive and imaginative geometrical investigation could be replaced by deduction of first-order sentences. But the existence of such a logic is insufficient for dispensing with imagination, which could nevertheless be cognitively necessary for grasping certain geometrical facts. Instead, the dismissal of imagination could take root only with a new conception of mind, according to which thinking is fundamentally computational. When combined with computationalism, logicism suggests that geometry is calculation all the way down, leaving no room for non-discursive activity on the part of the geometer.

In conclusion, there is reason to be pessimistic about the prospects of imagination in explanations of geometry, at least if cognition is to be understood as a kind of calculation. Nevertheless, it is possible that aesthetic experience and mathematical thought are more closely linked than current theories of mind admit. If that is so, it might be worth revisiting the possibility that imagination could contribute something that defies computation to our thinking.[89]

---

89 I thank Tarwin Baker, Erick Jiménez, and John Roman for valuable comments on an earlier version of this chapter. I thank Maria Cuellar for producing the diagrams, as well as for showing me the demonstration illustrated in Figure 5.

References

Brann, Eva. "Mental Imagery." *The St. John's Review* (Summer 1985): 71–79.

Bulmer-Thomas, Ivor. *Selections Illustrating the History of Greek Mathematics*. Volume 1. Cambridge, MA: Harvard University Press. 1957.

Coxeter, Harold Scott MacDonald. *Non-Euclidean Geometry*. Toronto: University of Toronto Press. 1961.

Descargues, Pierre. *Perspective: History, Evolution, Techniques*. New York: Van Nostrand. 1982.

Dunham, Douglas. "Creating Hyperbolic Patterns – Old and New." *Notices of the American Mathematical Society* 50, no. 4 (2003): 452–55.

Friedman, Michael. *Kant and the Exact Sciences*. Cambridge, MA: Harvard University Press. 1998.

Friedman, Michael. "Kant on geometry and spatial intuition." *Synthese* 181, no. 1 (2012): 233–35.

Gray, Jeremy. *János Bolyai, Non-Euclidean Geometry, and the Nature of Space*. Cambridge, MA: The Brundy Library. 2004.

Hilbert, David, and Stephan Cohn-Vossen. *Geometry and the Imagination*. New York: Chelsea Publishing Company. 1952.

Hössle, Vittorio. "Plato's Foundation of the Euclidean Character of Geometry." In *The Other Plato*, ed. Dmitri Nikulin, 161–82. Albany, NY: State University of New York Press. 2012.

Horstmann, Rolf-Peter. *Kant's Power of Imagination*. Cambridge: Cambridge University Press. 2018.

Humphreys, Justin. "Abstraction and Diagrammatic Reasoning in Aristotle's Philosophy of Geometry." *Apeiron* 50, no. 2 (2017): 197–224.

Humphreys, Justin. "Aristotelian Imagination and Decaying Sense." *Social Imaginaries* 5, no. 1 (2019): 37–55.

Jiménez, Erick Raphael. *Aristotle's Concept of Mind*. Oxford: Oxford University Press. 2017.

Kant, Immanuel. *Kritik der reinen Vernunft*. Hamburg: Felix Meiner Verlag, 1998. Translated by Norman Kemp Smith, *Immanuel Kant's Critique of Pure Reason*. New York: St. Martin's Press. 1965.

Kant, Immanuel. *Critique of the power of judgment*. Translated by Paul Guyer and Eric Matthews. Cambridge: Cambridge University Press. 2000.

Kant, Immanuel. *Prolegomena to Any future Metaphysics*. Translated and Edited by Gary Hatfield. Cambridge: Cambridge University Press. 2004.

Katz, Emily. "Geometrical Objects as Properties of Sensibles: Aristotle's Philosophy of Geometry." *Phronesis* 64 (2019): 465–513.

Knorr, Wilbur Richard. *The Ancient Tradition of Geometric Problems*. New York: Dover. 1993.

Kripke, Saul A. *Naming and Necessity*. Cambridge, MA: Harvard University Press. 1980.

Lachterman, David. *The Ethics of Geometry*. New York: Routledge. 1989.

Manders, Kenneth. "The Euclidean Diagram." In *Philosophy of Mathematical Practice*, edited by Paolo Mancuso, 80–133. Oxford: Oxford University Press, 1995.

Netz, Riviel. *The Shaping of Deduction in Greek Mathematics*. Cambridge: Cambridge University Press. 1999.

Nikulin, Dmitri. "Imagination and Matter in Proclus." *Ancient Philosophy* 28 (2008): 153–72.

Nikulin, Dmitri. *Matter, Imagination and Geometry*. Burlington, VT: Ashgate. 2002.

Panofsky, Erwin. *Perspective as Symbolic Form*. New York: Zone Books, 1991.

Proclus. *A Commentary on the First Book of Euclid's Elements*. Translated by G.R. Morrow. Princeton University Press. 1970.

Proclus. *Procli Diadochi in primum Euclidis Elementorum librum commentarii*. Edited by Gottfried Friedlein. Leipzig: Teubner, 1873.

Quine, Willard Van Orman. *From A Logical Point of View*. Cambridge, MA: Harvard University Press. 1980.

Rabouin, David. "Proclus' Conception of Geometric Space." In *Mathematizing Space*, edited by Vincenzo De Risi, 105–42. Berlin: Birkhäuser, 2015.

Sorabji, R. *Aristotle on Memory*. Chicago: The University of Chicago Press. 2004.

Syrianus. *On Aristotle's Metaphysics 13–14*. Translated by John Dillon, and Dominic O'Meara. Ithaca: Cornell University Press. 2006.

Tarski, Alfred. "What is Elementary Geometry?" In *The Axiomatic Method with Special Reference to Geometry and Physics*, edited by Léon Henkin, Patrick Suppes, and Alfred Tarski, 16–29. Studies in Logic and the Foundations of Mathematics. Amsterdam: North-Holland Publishing Company, 1959.

Tarski, Alfred, and Steven Givant. "Tarski's System of Geometry." *The Bulletin of Symbolic Logic* 5, no. 2 (1999): 175–214.

Turing, Alan. "Computing Machinery and Intelligence." *Mind* 49 (1950): 433–60.

Van der Waerden, Bartel Leendert. *Science Awakening*. Oxford: Oxford University Press. 1961.

CHAPTER 21

Art and Imagination: The Evolution of Meanings

Wendy Wheeler

If your theory is found to be against the second law of thermodynamics I can give you no hope; there is nothing for it but to collapse in deepest humiliation.

ARTHUR EDDINGTON, astrophysicist, 1915

1   Selves and Imaginations: Sign Systems within Sign Systems

Here is a possibly surprising idea. Imagination is a sign. More accurately, and according to the semiotic doctrine of the great American semiotician and scientist Charles Sanders Peirce (1839–1914), whose philosophy underpins much biosemiotic endeavor, we should speak not of "the sign," but rather of "semeiotic" (Peirce's spelling of the range of semiotic phenomena) as consisting always of *sign relations*. The imagination, thus, is a sign relation, and one which produces further sign relations. Art (as well as philosophy, science, and culture more generally) is a whole world of sign relations that are the fruit of the sign relations we call "imagination."

Going deeper into the layers of living being, and thinking about the many varied organisms that populate the Earth, the self is also, perhaps equally surprisingly, a sign relation. This claim applies to all living organisms, not just humans. Semiosis runs throughout nature and culture and joins them in an evolutionary continuum. Selves are the result of beings that *must* be receptive (though not necessarily self-consciously so) to the world around them. This is what evolutionary adaptability means. Selves, also then, are constituted by sign relations, and these produce (to different evolutionary extents and degrees of "semiotic freedom"[1]) imaginations that give expression (as functional behaviors, or meanings, of and for the organism) to the organism's being and telos.[2]

---

1   See Jesper Hoffmeyer, *Biosemiotics: An Examination into the Signs of Life and the Life of Signs*, trans. Jesper Hoffmeyer, and Donald Favareau, ed. Donald Favareau (Scranton, PA and London: University of Scranton Press, 2008).

2   Telos in the Aristotelian sense of Final Cause. An organism's telos is, at the very least, fullest possible flourishing, self-repair and reproduction.

© KONINKLIJKE BRILL NV, LEIDEN, 2020 | DOI:10.1163/9789004436350_023

When biosemioticians talk of the basis of self as grounded in sign relations, they mean that the organismic self consists of a relation between the three aspects of the sign that Peirce called the Object, the Representamen and the Interpretant. This will be explained in more detail below. For the moment, we can say that the basis of self consists in (the relation between) 1. the Object as the sensing, internally and externally communicative body (i.e. body *plus* communicative relation to environment, although the latter aspect is so natural to the living organism in terms of food, poison, predators and potential mates etc. that the relation is, with the exception of *Homo sapiens*, usually largely unreflective); 2. The Representamen: the body as experienced by the organism, i.e. often nonconsciously, always partially,[3] and generally in ignorance of absolutely all and every one of the internal and external semiotic relations belonging to the object it represents (or points towards); 3. The Interpretant: all the effects in the world of that Representamen (including, of course, the Representamen-Object relation). Bearing in mind that the interpretant can, itself, become a new object (or objects), with developed Representamen and Interpretants, it should be clear that this sign relation is dynamic and can grow into "a more developed sign."[4] Thus, adaptability and the growth of knowledge (or semiotic freedom) is possible over time. However, it's important to remember that, from a broader biosemiotic point of view, and recasting how we think about cognition, both knowledge growth and evolution are structurally similar features of complex living systems. As Gregory Bateson wrote in a letter in the *London Review of Books* in 1980 in response to a hostile review of his *Mind and Nature: A Necessary Unity* from Nick Humphreys,[5] "evolution and thinking are formally similar processes."[6]

A sense of self begins with primitive awareness (again, not *self*-conscious, of course) of a difference between self and not-self, and evolves and extends as an

---

3 As should become clear later, Jakob von Uexküll's term "umwelt," although the usual translation in German of the English word "environment," specifically refers to the species *semiotic* environment, i. e. those signs are detected by the senses of any particular species, but not necessarily others. For example, some birds and insects perceive in the ultraviolet range of the spectrum, whereas humans do not. Similarly, dogs experience and are informed by many more olfactory signs than *Homo sapiens*.

4 Charles Sanders Peirce, *Collected Papers of Charles Sanders Peirce, Volumes I and II: Principles of Philosophy and Elements of Logic* (Cambridge, MA: Harvard University Press, 1932), vol. 2, par. 228; Justus Buchler, ed., "Logic as Semiotic: The Theory of Signs," *Philosophical Writings of Peirce* (Mineola, NY: Dover Publications, 195), 99.

5 Nick Humphreys, "New Ideas, Old Ideas: Review of Gregory Bateson's *Mind and Nature A Necessary Unity*," *London Review of Books*, December 6, 1979, 6.

6 Gregory Bateson, "Syllogisms in Grass," *London Review of Books* (Letters), January 24, 1980.

ART AND IMAGINATION 505

embodied system of semiotic relations within larger such systems.[7] In the beginning, imagination is a small thing, but it can, and it does, grow. Every living thing is immersed in a world of biosemiosis, a constant series of "conversations" that flow around and through it, and to which it contributes and also makes changes, in self and in others. The word we have given to these flows of information in which all living things participate, changing the evolutionary drift of the conversation as they do so, is cybernetics. These are information and thermodynamic feedback systems characterized by both positive (inflaming) and negative (calming) feedback.[8] Both are necessary to the generation of new imaginings, functions and meanings. We might also say that these self-generating sign systems linking bodies, environments and meanings are what we call mind.[9] I will return both to this, and to Bateson's claim, noted above, about thinking and evolution being formally similar processes, later.

Further implications of a biosemiotic understanding that semiosis runs through all life from the beginning, are that it is possible to describe its linkages and its growth, and that we can learn about our own human forms of semiosis (both linguistic and non-linguistic: gestural, anthropological, psychological and so on) through tracing the modes and history of semiosis as it is expressed within the bodies and evolutionary history of other organisms and their natural and cultural ecological systems. In 1982, Juri Lotman suggested

---

7 This is, to put it mildly, a simplification. This is because this question of the emergence of a sense of self is quite intimately tied to the emergence of life itself. Here, we have only theories, of course, and this is not the place to go into these in detail. However, Terry Deacon's work on the role of linked catalytic sets capable of resisting the force of entropy seems probably the most productive. What this argument suggests is that the ontology of living being is relational, informational – that is to say biosemiotic – from the start. See, for an example of this argument, Terrence W. Deacon, Alok Srivastava, and Joshua Augustus Bacigalupi, "The transition from constraint to regulation at the origin of life," *Frontiers in Bioscience* 19 (2014): 945–57.

8 The common understanding of positive (good) and negative (bad) feedback has things more or less exactly the wrong way round. Generally speaking, too much positive feedback (in the cybernetic sense) is disruptive to communication systems because it encourages system runaway. Control of the system is best achieved, generally speaking and again in the cybernetic usage, by use of negative feedback. The example of system runaway reference is to Kurt Lewin's misunderstanding of the meaning of feedback at an early Macy Conference. See also Margaret Mead's example of system runaway due to positive feedback. Mead cites building more roads as an answer to traffic blockage problems. More roads increase road usage and encourage vehicle production, leading to even worse traffic blockage. See Stewart Brand, "In conversation with Gregory Bateson and Margaret Mead," *CoEvolutionary Quarterly* 10, no. 21 (1976): 32–44.

9 Jesper Hoffmeyer, "Semiotics of Nature," in *The Routledge Companion to Semiotics*, ed. Paul Cobley (London and New York: Routledge, 2010), 29–42; Gregory Bateson, *Steps to an Ecology of Mind* (Chicago, IL: University of Chicago Press, 1972).

that the semiosphere is the relational biosphere.[10] This has been widely accepted amongst biosemioticians. It is important to note also that this is an *ecological systems* biocybernetic view.[11] As Gregory Bateson never tired of pointing out, "the unit of survival is the *organism* plus *environment*."[12] Drawing upon the same sorts of insights upon which biosemiotics has drawn regarding evolutionary development (via repetition with difference) of patterns, Bateson also noted, as suggested above, that this "organism-environment" system is identical with mind:

> If, now, we correct the Darwinian unit of survival to include the environment and the interaction between organism and environment, a very strange and surprising identity emerges: *the unit of evolutionary survival turns out to be identical with the unit of mind.*[13]

This patterning, and its means of metaphoric growth via iconic signs (i.e. similarity with difference, the basis of metaphoric substitution),[14] should give us some clues about the nature of human imagination and its expression in the patterns of art. But before going on to discuss this further, it's necessary first to be clearer about Peirce's theory of semiotics as that underpins biosemiotic thinking.

11   The Biosphere Is Identical to the Semiosphere

In 1908, Peirce wrote to his regular correspondent Lady Victoria Welby, inventor of significs (another semiotic theory of meaning), that he despaired of making people understand the full extent of his conception of semiosis:

---

10   Kaie Kotov, and Kalevi Kull, "Semiosphere is the Relational Biosphere," in *Towards a Semiotic Biology: Life is the Action of Signs*, eds. Claus Emmeche and Kalevi Kull (London: Imperial College Press, 2011), 179–94; Peter Harries-Jones, *Upside-Down Gods: Gregory Bateson's World of Difference* (New York: Fordham University Press, 2016), 2.

11   Søren Brier, *Cybersemiotics: Why Information Is Not Enough!* (Toronto: University of Toronto Press, 2008).

12   Gregory Bateson, *Steps to an Ecology of Mind* (Chicago, IL: University of Chicago Press, 1972), 491.

13   Bateson, *Steps to an Ecology of Mind*, 491.

14   N.B. Metaphor here does not mean "not real." It means evolutionary development of an organismic body or an idea on the basis of similarity and difference. Hence the human use of metaphor as a primary mode of thinking using signs that are icons derives, itself in evolutionary fashion, from the metaphoric nature of biological evolution. See Wendy Wheeler, *Expecting the Earth: Life/Culture/Biosemiotics* (London: Lawrence & Wishart, 2016).

ART AND IMAGINATION   507

> I define a Sign as anything which is so determined by something else, called its Object, and so determines an effect upon a person, which effect I call its Interpretant, that the latter is thereby mediately determined by the former. My insertion of "upon a person" is a sop to Cerberus, because I despair of making my own broader conception understood.[15]

However, it is clear from this quote, as from the one which follows, that Peirce's understanding of semiosis was universalist and biosemiotic in nature:

> It seems a strange thing, when one comes to ponder over it, that a sign should leave its interpreter to supply a part of its meaning; but the explanation of the phenomenon lies in the fact that the entire universe, – not merely the universe of existents, but all that wider universe, embracing the universe of existents as part, the universe which we are accustomed to refer to as "the truth," – that all this universe is perfused with signs, if it is not composed exclusively of signs.[16]

The above quotation provides something more for our picture of sign relations, however, and that is the potential variability of meaning interpretation (what Peirce called the interpretant, see below). This is, of course, especially the case where we move into great abstraction, as with human language in anthroposemiosis. It is possibly for this reason that evolution has produced a countervailing force in the establishment of law-like habits of mimicry of opinion. In nonhuman organisms, this conserves energy and also prevents potentially life-threatening and destructive innovation. In *Homo sapiens*, it does the same (think about humans' preferences for well-beaten tracks through woods, for example) and it also feels, and is, challenging to go against the tenets and belief structures (the conceptual tracks) of the tribe or congregation.

Charles Peirce gave several accounts of the sign relation in general – all recognizably similar.[17] According to Peirce, this relation (always "live" and capable of growing) is tripartite and consists of what he called the object, the representamen and the interpretant:

---

15   "Sign," in *The Commens Dictionary: Peirce's Terms in His Own Words*, eds. M. Bergman and S. Paavola, new edition, accessed 3 June 2019, http://www.commens.org/dictionary/entry/quote-letters-lady-welby-43.

16   Charles Sanders Peirce, *The Essential Peirce: Selected Philosophical Writings. Vol. 2, 1893–1913,* ed. The Peirce Edition Project (Bloomington, IN and Indianapolis, IN: Indiana University Press, 1998), 394.

17   Peirce's various definitions can be found under "Sign" at the *Commens Digital Companion to Peirce*: http://www.commens.org/dictionary/term/sign.

> A sign, or representamen, is something which stands to somebody for something in some respect or capacity. It addresses somebody, that is, creates in the mind of that person an equivalent sign, or perhaps a more developed sign. That sign which it creates I call the interpretant of the first sign. The sign stands for something, its object. It stands for that object, not in all respects, but in reference to a sort of idea, which I have sometimes called the ground of the representamen.[18]

The object (whether an existent thing, *ens reale*, or an idea, *ens rationis*) is the thing not ever fully known.[19] Although it is the task of science to explore this (especially in regard to *ens reale*), no object is ever fully, wholly and certainly known. For example, we may not know its atomic or molecular structure, its behavior under various conditions, how it is perceived and interpreted by other animals (including human ones), or, most certainly, its relation to everything else in the universe. The representamen is the object as represented for organisms in the species umwelt.[20] Sometimes described as the "sign proper," the representamen must "point" in some way or other to the object. If it doesn't do this, it is not functioning as a sign at all. The interpretant is the effect (or difference) that the representamen-object relation makes in the real world of experience. This is why Peirce is the inventor of American Pragmatism. His understanding of meaning is that it can be summed up in the way an idea or understanding (or representamen-interpretant relation) actually works in the world: what *difference* it makes, the sum total of all its effects in the world, how it *functions*. Gregory Bateson read Peirce, and here we can see the effect of a

---

18 Charles Sanders Peirce, *Collected Papers of Charles Sanders Peirce, vol. 2, par. 228;* Buchler, "Logic as Semiotic: The Theory of Signs," 99.

19 Philosopher of semiotics and history John Deely has pointed out that the sign relations of *ens reale* (mind independent objects) and *ens rationis* (mind dependent objects) both function in sign relations in exactly the same fashion. See John Deely, *Purely Objective Reality* (New York and Berlin: Mouton de Gruyter. 2009).

20 This is a realism, but not a crude one. Although all species apprehend (imperfectly and with evolutionarily derived limitations) the same world, they do so according to scale, speed of life and other sensory constraints imposed by evolutionary needs (See Jakob von Uexküll, "A Stroll through the Worlds of Animals and Men: A Picture Book of Invisible Worlds," in *Instinctive Behavior: The Development of a Modern Concept*, ed. and trans. C.H. Schiller (New York: International Universities Press, 1957), 320–91). Thus, some birds and insects see in the ultraviolet end of the light spectrum whereas other species, including humans, do not. Similarly, a molehill may work as a sign for humans, insects and worms, but the kind of sign it works as – what it signifies and what interpretants it produces – will be quite different for each species. For a bat or a butterfly, it may well not work as a sign at all.

ART AND IMAGINATION 509

Peircean understanding on Bateson's work on information: "Information is a difference which makes a difference."[21]

But if I say that imagination is a sign relation, what, in its barest outline, does this sign relation consist of? As suggested above, it is the activity of a self consisting in: the semiotic relation between a perceiving being, i.e. an organism with senses of any kind, "a sense of aboutness" in Jesper Hoffmeyer's words, and not confined to organisms with brains or nervous systems,[22]; an environment (a semiotic environment, henceforth referred to as an umwelt in the sense used by Jakob von Uexküll meaning specifically a species sign-world),[23]; a representation (model) of that self (plus environment), and (normally ongoing) interpretants. In nonhuman organisms, these latter seem relatively fixed and dominated by habit. *Homo sapiens* has evolved considerably more semiotic freedom, and its production of interpretants (including interpretations) generally seem quite frequent and, although also dominated by habit, the source, too, of habit breaking creativity. In both nonhuman and human animals, the sources of new sign relations, and thus, in material terms, an evolution of species selves (including human individuals), are likely to be changes in the umwelt. In humans, of course, new sign relations include ideas and abstractions. These essentially chance stressors (change of climate, loss of habitat, and so on, and, for humans, rapid and significant cultural change also) are likely to generate a reorganization of the sign relations of organismic selves. Very obviously, were it not for organisms' *biosemiotic* receptivity (a flexibility unknown to any kind of machine), no such evolutionary adaptation would be possible. As Ilya Prigogine wrote in his exploration of thermodynamic feedback systems and the end of the idea of determinism,

---

21 Bateson, *Steps to an Ecology of Mind*, 459.

22 For examples of plant cognition, see Anthony Trewavas, "Intelligence, Cognition and Language of Green Plants," *Frontiers in Psychology* 7 (2016): 1–9; Jesper Hoffmeyer, "Semiotic Individuation and Ernst Cassirer's Challenge," *Progress in Biophysics and Molecular Biology* 119, no. 3 (2015): 607–15. As Hoffmeyer explains, "Brains, of course, lend tremendously increased power to the cognitive regime of a species, but the brain in itself is just a tool for the semiotic body, not an independent organ of semiosis. There is no semiosis without a body, but plenty of semiosis without brains" Hoffmeyer, "Semiotic Individuation," 611.

23 Jakob von Uexküll, "A Stroll through the Worlds of Animals and Men," 320–91. The normal translation of the German *Umwelt* is environment. In von Uexküll's usage umwelt refers specifically to the fact that species environments are semiotic environments. An umwelt in von Uexküll's sense is the organism species' phenomenal world. Not all organisms perceive identical worlds. In von Uexküll's most famous example, the world of the ticks he studied contains only three signs: the smell of butyric acid given off by mammalian sweat, the blood temperature of 37°C of mammals, and mammalian hairiness.

If the world were formed by stable dynamic systems, it would be radically different from the one we observe around us. It would be a static, predictable world, but we would not be here to make the predictions. In our world, we discover fluctuations, bifurcations, and instabilities at all levels. Stable systems leading to certitudes correspond only to idealizations, or approximations. Curiously, this insight was anticipated by Poincaré.[24]

In discussing the laws of thermodynamics he wrote,

These laws can only have one significance, which is that there is a property common to all possibilities; but in the deterministic hypothesis there is only a single possibility, and the laws no longer have any meaning. In the indeterministic hypothesis, on the other hand, they would have meaning, even if they were taken in an absolute sense; they would appear [merely] as a limitation imposed on freedom.[25]

Prigogine goes on to point out that in our indeterministic universe, nature is necessarily characterized by unity (i.e. repetition of habits and patterns) and teeming diversity (i.e. difference).[26] Thus, any deterministic plan to order selves, societies and imagination is finally doomed to fail because it flies in the face of nature and the laws of thermodynamics by disallowing the conditions of creative adaptation. Such a world – in which habits, meanings and genuine diversity were destroyed – would be subject to the forces of semiocide. It would imitate the conditions of absolute lifelessness.

On the biosemiotic account, the self (material, physical and with observable behaviors – whether our own self or those of other organisms-in-an-environment) is the (incompletely known) object. The representamen is the self (or those selves) as we represent them (in art or in science, or simply to ourselves). The interpretant consists of all the meanings (including functions) which result from the representamen. It should be clear that these sign relations are precisely the "tools" of the imagination also. The further we move from the earthed animal, and the animistic human animal alone, the more we move into the realm of abstracted imagination (and thus perhaps further into a realm less tested by the bonds that finally bind us to the Earth). The work of art, we can say at this stage, is made of those sign relations *that play with* the

---

24   Ilya Prigogine, *The End of Certainty: Time, Chaos, and the New Laws of Nature* (New York and London: The Free Press, 1997), 55–56.
25   Prigogine, *The End of Certainty*, 55–56.
26   Prigogine, *The End of Certainty*, 56.

relations of the sign and its history, that look for patterns (source of aesthetic pleasure for artist and observer alike), and seek new patterns, thus meanings, within old ones. The general purpose is to know more about the object (through science) and more about representamen, interpretation, or interpretants (in the arts and humanities most obviously, but also in the social sciences), as these appear pragmatically in the world themselves.

The simplest definition of a sign is the representation of something else not present or not fully known. This is one of the widely accepted definitions of imagination: "The act or power of forming a mental image[27] of something not present to the senses or never before wholly perceived in reality."[28] There is also the iconic sign association of "image" (L. imago: likeness, representation, portrait) and the fantasmatic and abstracted aspect of imagining. The *Oxford English Dictionary* gives:

> The power or capacity to form internal images or ideas of objects and situations not actually present to the senses, including remembered objects and situations, and those constructed by mentally combining or projecting images of previously experienced qualities, objects, and situations. Also (esp. in modern philosophy): the power or capacity by which the mind integrates sensory data in the process of perception.[29]

The modern word usage dates from the 12th and 13th centuries and is derived from a mixture of Latin and Old French. The Latin *imaginatio* means originally mentally picturing, and, in post-classical Latin, in the 8th–9th centuries A.D., the act of scheming or plotting. The word comes into something similar to its modern sense in the Romance languages and in English during the 13th and 14th centuries.

It is importantly worth noting at this point that this essentially modern usage coincides with a philosophical, that is to say *theological*, development in the late 13th and early 14th centuries. This concerns the recognition, by John Duns Scotus (1266–1308), that sign relations, far from being minted by God as straightforward truth in the books of nature and of scripture, are somewhat trickier than this. Where *interpretation* enters in, the meaning of signs is never entirely determined. Thus, the drive behind the Reformation was intended to

---

27 "Image," in *Merriam-Webster Dictionary* (Merriam-Webster Incorporated, 2019), https://www.merriam-webster.com/dictionary/image.

28 "Imagination," in *Merriam-Webster Dictionary* (Merriam-Webster Incorporated, 2019), https://www.merriam-webster.com/dictionary/imagination.

29 Oxford English Dictionary, s.v. "Imagination," accessed June 3, 2019, https://www.oed.com/.

fix meanings, and also to do away with the Roman Catholic Church's subtlety of interpretation, doctrine and liturgical practice by presenting Biblical scripture in the blunt, fundamentalist vernacular.[30] Similarly, the Scientific Revolution which followed in the seventeenth century was also intended to do away with doubt and ambiguity, and to present, instead, a deterministic universe ruled by God's laws.[31] While earthed in the physical umwelt, sign relations are at least more grounded (although imperfectly – natural mimicry can be deceptive), but Scotus's appalled recognition was to see that sign relations raised to abstractions in the human mind are extended imaginings, and as such (and like all signs) are indifferent to the truth or falsity of the terms they abstractively bring together beyond mere immediate sensation. Signs in sensation keep us (or bring us back to) our captivation by the Earthly umwelt. But this "forgetting" that sign relations begin in bodily sensations and experience before they raise to abstract thinking, opens to way to the nominalist thought that all products of the human mind may be fictions. It also feeds off a history of both classical and monotheistic dualisms in which mind and body (*res cogitans* and *res extensa* in Descartes) can be thought of as separate things.

In fact, as Hoffmeyer notes:

> As John Deely has often observed, what comes first in experience is neither what the medievals called *ens reale* (mind-independent being, "reality") nor what they called *ens rationis* (what is not independent of my mind). The partition of our experience into two such domains occurs only after the fact, after the process wherein sensation has become sense

---

30   As James Simpson *Burning to Read: English Fundamentalism and Its Reformation Opponents* (Cambridge, MA and London: Belknap Press of Harvard University Press, 2007) argues, the Reformers singularly failed in this ideal (as of course they must). Readers must both read the text for salvation and also hate it. For that salvation cannot be effected through anything the reader actually does, and is doomed to fail because of the abject condition of human nature. The Calvinist Protestant doctrine of predestination means that you are *already* elect (saved) or doomed (irredeemable) even as you search for signs of meaning. Under the paradox of a "semiotic field" in which one must search for signs of redemption (Simpson, *Burning to Read*, 6) that are always uncertain, a second paradox is revealed: "evangelical reading repudiates ambiguity in its affirmation of scriptural clarity; but evangelical reading practice derives in the first place from, and only from, the recognition of verbal ambiguity" (Simpson, *Burning to Read*, 5). One can quite see why all articles of interpretation – statues, stained glass windows, frescoes and decorated walls and rood screens in churches – should be forbidden in fundamentalist Puritan theologies.

31   For an account of the theological roots of radical doubt and Cartesian radical skepticism as a means for overcoming doubt by furnishing firm philosophical foundations, see Wheeler, *Expecting the Earth*, especially Chapter 2.

ART AND IMAGINATION 513

perception and understanding.[32] Thus, in the words of Bains: there is a "prederivative" sense of being, and this "sense" of being, whatever it be, is prior to being in either of the derived senses; and it is this prior being – the being proper to experience – that semiotics takes as its province.[33]

Nominalism, which holds that only particulars (substances) are real and causally efficacious, and that generals (or universals) such as color, beauty and all relations in general have no ontological reality and are just fictions of the human mind, was an important strand of thought in the Protestant Reformation and in the Scientific Revolution of the seventeenth century that the Reformation made possible. Martin Luther was himself a nominalist, as were Francis Bacon and all the early scientists. It was not until Charles Peirce in the nineteenth and very early twentieth centuries that semiotics, and effectively an implied biosemiotics, was extensively theoretically developed.[34] We can take it from this that, whatever theological thought on the matter, art remains a privileged space of creativity, of iconicity and indexicality, and of imagining both what has been and what has never been, and of combination in the recognition of hitherto unnoticed similarities and differences. It should not surprise us, though, that artistic realism grows in strength during the same period in a Protestant country, the Netherlands in the early Fifteenth Century.

III   Information Technology and Biosemiotics: Information versus Meaning

Use of the term "information biology," and daily talk about codes, messages and communication, is very common in the contemporary biological sciences. But in order to understand why the current sense of information is inadequate, and why we would do better to understand biology in general, and whole living organisms in particular, in biosemiotic terms, we need to turn to a sharper focus on the question of signs systems and relations, interpretations and meanings. Certainly, where imagination and art are concerned, it is the question of

---

32   John N. Deely, *Intentionality and Semiotics* (Scranton, PA: University of Scranton Press, 2007), 7.

33   Paul Bains, *The Primacy of Semiosis: An Ontology of Relations* (Toronto and London: University of Toronto Press, 2006), 68; Jesper Hoffmeyer, "Semiotic Scaffolding: A Unitary Principle Gluing Life and Culture Together," in "Biosemiotics and Culture," eds. Wendy Wheeler and Louise Westling, special issue, *Green Letters: Studies in Ecocriticism* 19, no. 3 (2015): 243–44.

34   Wheeler, *Expecting the Earth*, 21–22.

interpretation and *meaning* that we must make central. The latter are, and certainly must be, governed by habit – a sort of law; but, as suggested above, they are *not* determining. Indeed, if they were, there could be no such thing as natural (or cultural) evolution. As with an earlier and related psychology of meanings, the "cognitive revolution" beginning in the 1950s, in which technological developments fractionated a developing field and sent it in unhelpful directions,[35] so too Claude Shannon's brilliant technological work on communication (including his coinage of the term BIT – Binary Information Digit – which Shannon, himself, attributed to John W. Tukey) had a similar distorting effect on our understanding of information.[36]

Shannon began his groundbreaking 1948 essay "A Mathematical Theory of Communication" by stating that he was not interested in meanings. He was interested in the technical problem of signal maintenance through a communication channel. Rather unhelpfully, what counts as "information" in this account is the unexpected, that is to say signals that are lost or distorted, and thus hard to understand or process. As a result, the technological idea of information that has dominated information theory and AI, has tended to distract western cultural understandings.[37] Information engineers describe "information" as "the unexpected," or communicative "noise," which is experienced as disruptive positive feedback. The expected they describe as "redundancy." But as Gregory Bateson has pointed out, for living organisms it is redundancy – i.e. pattern, repetition and habit, i.e. the stuff of memory and time – that makes and conserves meanings and cultures: "The essence and *raison d'être* of communication is the creation of redundancy, meaning, pattern, predictability, information, and/or the reduction of the random by restraint."[38] The continuation of life, we might say, lies, as Peirce suggested, in the interplay of pattern or habit (or repetition) and the unexpected or chance occurrence.[39] It is no coincidence that any group or regime wishing to disrupt and conquer another

---

35   Jerome Bruner, *Acts of Meaning* (Cambridge, MA and London: Harvard University Press, 1990), 4–13.

36   See Claude E. Shannon's "A Mathematical Theory of Communication" (Parts one and two) from *The Bell System Technical Journal* 27 (1948): 379–423; 623–56.

37   For further accounts of this, see Phillip Guddemi, "Two Roads which Diverged," in "Ranulph Glanville and How to Live the Cybernetics of Unknowing," special issue, *Cybernetics and Human Knowing* 22, no. 2–3 (2015): 183–87; Harries-Jones, *Upside-Down Gods*, 135–41; and Andrew Pickering, *The Cybernetic Brain: Sketches of Another Future* (Chicago and London: Chicago University Press, 2010).

38   Bateson, *Steps to an Ecology of Mind*, 131–32.

39   Charles Sanders Peirce, *The Essential Peirce: Philosophical Writings. Vo1. 1 (1867–1893)*, eds. Nathan Houser and Christian Kloesel (Bloomington, IN and Indianapolis, IN: Indiana University Press, 1992), 215–24.

ART AND IMAGINATION   515

will take aim at that culture's habitual life: the habits, languages, rituals, mores that are bearers of its signs of meaning. George Orwell grasped this entirely of course:

> "You don't grasp the beauty of the destruction of words. Do you know that Newspeak is the only language in the world whose vocabulary gets smaller every year?" … "Don't you see that the whole aim of Newspeak is to narrow the range of thought? In the end we shall make thoughtcrime literally impossible because there will be no words in which to express it."[40]

The term which the Estonian semiotician Ivar Puura has given to this process of killing meanings is semiocide. This will be discussed further at the conclusion of this chapter.

Of course, and perhaps for polemical reasons, *Nineteen Eighty-Four* imagines a world in which language is deterministic and where other forms of semiosis are negligible. As all known totalitarian regimes have demonstrated, a culture (like any other lifeform) prevented from *creative* free adaptation via self-maintenance and self-reproduction in the presence of stressors cannot survive in the long run since it has no chance of the self-regeneration required to escape from the second law of thermodynamics (closely related to the behavior of information) and the relentless force of entropy.

Evolutionary processes require diversity and freedom. Uniformity and control is death. In an unpredictable world, where chance events and changes (for example, in the environment) may happen, it is crucial that the organism can respond creatively. The work of Denis and Ray Noble indicates that far from evolutionary change being random, the cell (and organism) under pressure (from the environment – either endosemiotic or exosemiotic, both natural and cultural[41]) sends messages to the DNA (which is not itself active, but is an inert molecule to be read by the cell, more like a library) asking for a similar alternative to that part of the DNA string responsible for the failing function (or biological "meaning"). The DNA offers a number of substitutes based on similarity, one of which is selected by the cell.[42] This similarity cannot only take over the failing informational/semiotically encoded function, but also necessarily

---

40   George Orwell, *Nineteen Eighty-Four* (London: Penguin, 1989), 60.

41   In truth, the distinction between nature and culture is a false one. Culture is natural and evolutionary. As the existence of natural metaphors evolving into cultural metaphors demonstrates, many patterns are repeated in both nature and culture. See Wheeler, *Expecting the Earth*, 2016.

42   Ray Noble, and Denis Noble, "Was the Watchmaker Blind? Or Was She One-Eyed?," *Biology* 6, no. 4 (2017): 1–19.

introduces a difference. This difference can become also the site of new possibilities. In other words, the substitution via similarity, and the happenstance introduction of potentially creative differences, works exactly as metaphor in human language works. This "natural metaphor," as Bateson also notes, is the basis of all evolutionary development:

> It becomes evident that metaphor is not just pretty poetry, it is not either good or bad logic, but is in fact the logic upon which the biological world has been built, the main characteristic and organizing glue of this world of mental process that I have been trying to sketch for you.[43]

Chance introduces, alongside repetition, the need – if life is to continue via evolution – for the creative, innovative "difference which makes a difference."[44]

Pattern, repetition, habit and memory are all central aspects of the kind of usually negative feedback which makes self-sustained purposiveness, self-organized in response to a telos (Aristotle's Final Cause), possible.[45] They are, essentially and usually, corrective because, under normal conditions of social sanity, they remind us of significant patterns, of past meanings, and of what has and hasn't worked well before. In the absence of pattern, habit and law (i.e. agreements and rules for meanings), no communication (including articulate human language) would be possible at all. These are the link between a remembered past (whether by cell or organism) and the Darwinian "striving" for a remembered future. We cannot, like Humpty-Dumpty thinks he can, make words mean just what we want them to mean. In other words, pattern, repetition and similarity all make meanings. Meanings, themselves, are not wholly deterministic (as we all know). They are semiotic relations between senders and receivers, and they can go wrong (i.e. are not determined) because they rest on context and on the interpretation of signs. Thus, as I shall go on to discuss with reference to the work of Jerome Bruner, the meaning of something is a matter of collective agreement. It is communal, and not simply a matter of individual subjective reaction.

Molecular biochemist and biosemiotician Jesper Hoffmeyer has, similarly, pointed out that information theory, thought of technologically as deterministic, cannot help us out when it comes to the crucial aspect of living organisms. This crucial aspect of organisms, and of their parts, consists of their

---

43 Gregory Bateson and Mary Catherine Bateson. *Angels Fear: Towards and Epistemology of the Sacred* (New York: Bantam Books, 1988), 28.

44 Bateson, *Steps to an Ecology of Mind*, 459.

45 Arturo Rosenblueth, Norbert Wiener, and Julian Bigelow. "Behavior, Purpose and Teleology," *Philosophy of Science* 10, no. 1 (1943): 18–24.

ART AND IMAGINATION

interpretive capacities. This is true not only of whole organisms in their exosemiotic engagement with their semiotic environments (umwelten), but also of the endosemiotic life within. Here, biological memory and interpretation really matter – as they do also to individual organisms and their adaptive learning, and to human culture. Pointing out that "natural selection simply presupposes an intentionality – a 'striving' to use Darwin's own term – that is not accounted for" in the conventional deterministic biological framework,[46] Hoffmeyer comments on the problems for the latter view both in terms of a conventional ignoring of the semiotic language used (with all its equally ignored implications) within the contemporary biological framework itself, but also in terms of recent discoveries:

> It will not help either to answer the objection by reference to information theory. For many kinds of processes, such as DNA methylation or RNA editing, are now known to interfere with the supposed deterministic control exerted by the "information" carried in the DNA. But more than anything else, the recent finding, that small nucleic acid sequences of 20–24 nucleotides, so-called microRNAs, play a key role in gene regulation, has signalled a major shift away from the classical view of the gene. Approximately 500 different microRNAs have now been identified in human cells, and it is believed that as much as a third or more of all our genes are prone to regulation by microRNA. Genetic information therefore does not "determine" anything in the strict sense of this word, rather it "specifies." But a specification is no innocent thing when seen in the light of normal scientific ontology, for the meaning of a specification depends on a process of interpretation ...Natural selection therefore depends – as Darwin well knew – upon the interpretive activity of organisms, and strictly speaking it is not, of course, nature in all abstractness that selects. The selective agency must instead be exerted by some definite entity, and this entity is the lineage. It is the lineage – seen as a historical and transgenerational subject – that acts as the selective agent via its overall reproductive patterns. By virtue of the genetic specifications carried forward from generation to generation by individual organisms, the lineage maintains – and continually updates – a selective memory (the memory pool of genomes) of its past that in most cases will be a suitable tool for producing individuals capable of dealing with the future. This agential aspect of natural selection, however, is never admitted in the standard account of this process...[47]

---

46   Hoffmeyer, "Semiotics of Nature," 32.
47   Hoffmeyer, "Semiotics of Nature," 32–33.

Readers will do well to remember the collective core of memory and meaning found in biosemiotic systems when I come on, shortly, to discuss possible reasons – here those mentioned by Jerome Bruner in relation to the making of meanings – for contemporary failures of imagination, where "imagination" is turned into merely a conventional and closed doctrine. As demonstrated in the genetic and epigenetic systems, and echoed in the lives of social animals such as human beings, meanings are collective and intergeneration affairs – but they are ones which must always remain open to chance, to difficulty, to adaptations, and to more developed sign relations and meanings.

IV   Where Are We Going Wrong? Failures of Imagination and Failures of Meaning

Following the invention of the mass printing moveable type printing press by Johannes Gutenberg in 1439, a religious, social and eventually political revolution was visited upon Europe. In 1517, and within 80 years of its invention, Martin Luther, Professor of Moral Theology at the University of Wittenberg, had sent his 95 theses, condemning the sale of indulgences by the Church, to the Archbishop of Mainz, and also almost certainly, as the stories have it, pinned them on the door of All Saints Church in Wittenberg in conformity with university practice. The revolutionary effects were considerable. The disruption and wars unleashed lasted on and off until the Peace of Westphalia in 1648.

Since we generally understand religions as systems for managing human spiritual and social needs, a revolution – in this case the Protestant Reformation – indicated the presence of a major disruption in human self-understandings. That the Reformation made use of, indeed would have been impossible without, this new communications technology makes sense. The technology was much faster than the old method of inscription of books by hand, and its effects were to disrupt the hold of the traditional (and of course somewhat corrupted) authorities in the form of the Roman Catholic Church. Thus, the need for a new dispensation, doctrine and authority was widely felt. Luther, and then Jean Calvin, along with other Protestant reformers in Europe, provided that.

Our own technological communications revolution remains in its relatively early stages. The first digital computers were in use only 70 to 80 or so years ago. The vast spread of such technology on handheld devices such as tablets and smart phones appears to have brought us to our own Reformation revolution point. This is not the place to go into a fully detailed account of this (which would require a book in itself at least), but we can see some of the outlines of the new religion. It should be unsurprising that these often manifest in

ART AND IMAGINATION 519

movements which are recognizably religious or quasi-religious and which alter, as did the Protestant Reformation itself, our sense of what it means to speak of having a self-identity.

The self-identity that was disturbed by the Protestant Reformation of sixteenth-century Europe was essentially a collective (Christian and Catholic) identity based on the shared doctrines of the Church in Latin which were mediated by priests. In internalizing the "voice" and words of God by removing priestly mediation, and rewriting Scripture in the familiar vernacular, the Reformation revolution threw self-responsibility firmly upon the individual. Here a new experience of individual internal conceptual space was opened in the unmediated conversation with the Divinity. This, in turn, paved the way for the development of liberal individualism, and, in more or less direct proportion to the ending of religious belief and observance, has, in our time much aided by digital communications technology, both intensified a narcissistic self-focus (infamously instantiated in the ubiquitous "selfie") and has also lifted human beings even further into an even more intense focus upon the ungrounded world of virtual reality where sign relations are often not at all subject to the grounding experience of enworlded embodiment. Needless to say, religion doesn't go away; like almost all evolutionary phenomena, it just takes different forms. We can see these disruptive influences arising elsewhere, as in Jerome Bruner's description of information technology's fractionating influence in the cognitive revolution from the 1950s onward:

> It would make an absorbing essay in the intellectual history of the last quarter-century to trace what happened to the originating impulse of the cognitive revolution, how it became fractionated and technicalized ... All we need note now are a few signposts along the way, just enough of them to give a sense of the intellectual terrain on which we were all marching. Very early on, for example, emphasis began shifting from "meaning" to "information," from the *construction* of meaning to the *processing* of information. These are profoundly different matters. The key factor in the shift was the introduction of computation as the ruling metaphor and of computability as a necessary criterion of a good theoretical model.[48]

Interestingly, one can see, in Bruner's account of the effects of this phenomenon in Chapter 1 of *Acts of Meaning*, the old backwards drag that essentially religious doctrines always seem to have as a part of their vaunted discovery of the new heaven. The new "reductionist" metaphor, Bruner says, was surprisingly

---

48 Bruner, *Acts of Meaning*, 4.

able to accommodate the old reductionism and mechanism of stimulus-response models which got rid of meaning, agency and free will, as well as teleological purpose and other uncomfortable matters:

> ...even the old S-R learning theorist and associationist student of memory could come right back into the fold so long as they wrapped their old concepts in the new terms of information processing. One did not have to truck with "mental processes" or with meaning at all. In place of stimuli and responses, there was input and output, with reinforcement laundered of its affective taint by being converted into a control element that fed information about the outcome of an operation back into the system. So long as there was a computable programme, there was "mind."[49]

The same gestures of strange rehabilitation of old religious doctrines are currently enacted in the scientifically and philosophically incoherent claims of some contemporary identity politics. In these, a supposed "essence" (a "sense" of being a man or a woman or, less frequently, a different race, age or species) is claimed, against the evidence of biological fact and evolution, as simply the experience of a "feeling." This is a contemporary, supposedly secular, version of a "soul." Just as with Ray Kurzweil's idea that identity is a computable program which will, one day and come "The Singularity," be up-loadable onto a computer, thus ensuring immortality, so with the idea that identity is an immaterial essence – a soul – separable from an enworlded biological body. Kurzweil offers us an example of an influential individual who thinks that bodies are essentially advanced machines and that human minds are programs run on human brains which are computers.[50]

This entirely subjective claim may be made, and also of course doubted. Certainly any science-based society would require evidence and collective

---

49   Bruner, *Acts of Meaning*, 7.
50   It's worth looking at Ray Kurzweil's predictions, say for 2019, at https://en.wikipedia.org/wiki/Predictions_made_by_Ray_Kurzweil#2019. Worth noting, in particular, are the specific ways and areas that those predictions that are wrong actually go wrong. They all seem to lie in human psychology, i.e. in what sorts of things actually motivate human beings (regarding virtual sex, for example, or the pleasures of driving) beyond a utilitarian account. As Charles Dickens recognized in his anti-Benthamist novel of 1854, *Hard Times*, the utilitarian view takes insufficient account of human meaning-making and its embeddedness in place and history. See John Stuart Mill's two essays on Jeremy Bentham (1838) and on Samuel Taylor Coleridge (1840) in J.S. Mill, *Utilitarianism and Other Essays* (London: Penguin, 1987). Kurzweil, one might say, remains caught in a "super-rational" technological fantasy. It's not truly rational because it allows no *reasoning* in regard to the sorts of things humans really value.

ART AND IMAGINATION

agreement. Importantly, Bruner reminds us that meaning is, indeed, both collective and also handed on. Cultures are made of meanings – very often narratives of some sort, sign systems which hang together – which can be transformed over time and often adapted to meet new context and needs. Meaning-making is, of course, not a computation made with BITS, but an act of imagination. Its growth is largely based on the recognition of similarities within differences, and these similarities – although in original form easily recognizable iconic signs – may well take obscure forms of patterning that require a lively and/or specialized mind to perceive.

Asking how, against the mistakes of the fractionated cognitive revolution, we can "construct a mental science around the concept of meaning and the processes by which meanings are created and negotiated within a community," Bruner writes:

> Begin with the concept of culture itself – particularly its constitutive role. What was obvious from the start was perhaps too obvious to be fully appreciated, at least by us psychologists who by habit and by tradition think in rather individualistic terms. The symbolic systems that individuals used in constructing meaning were systems that were already in place, already "there," deeply entrenched in culture and language. They constituted a very special kind of communal tool kit whose tools, once used, made the user a reflection of the community .... human beings do not terminate at their own skins; they are expressions of a culture. To treat the world as an indifferent flow of information to be processed by individuals each on his or her own terms is to lose sight of how individuals are formed and how they function. Or to quote Geertz again, "there is no such thing as human nature independent of culture"... By virtue of participation in culture, meaning is rendered *public* and *shared.* Our culturally adapted way of life depends upon shared meanings and shared concepts and depends as well upon shared modes of discourse for negotiating differences in meaning and interpretation.[51]

This is true, and no biosemiotician would ever make the mistake of thinking that the semiotic relational ontology s/he was concerned to understand and describe could possibly be anything other than a matter of an ecology of meanings tied to embodied experience and the species umwelten.[52] In the latter, not all meanings are shared because sign recognition is specific to the evolutionary

---

51   Bruner, *Acts of Meaning*, 11–13.
52   von Uexküll "A Stroll Through the Woods of Animals and Men."

specificities of the bodies involved. Nonetheless, all normally equipped members of species share sign systems and there is also often overlap of objects (though, as said earlier, very often with different representamen and interpretants) between species.

Equally, the cognitive psychologists' approach noted by Bruner, in which meaning is computationally processed information without nuance, and accessible to individuals regardless of history and place (context or umwelt), is already a deracinated one. A fully intentional understanding of meaning must be rooted in sense since the latter is our first and last guarantee of self, communication and evolutionary survival. Imagination, rather than ungrounded fantasy (the two are not the same at all), thus must follow an embodied line going back to its historical source. The latter (origin of life) may well not be easily knowable, but we can at least honor its figure in recognizing the semiotic and embodied nature of our own histories of communicative life in both nature and culture. As Jesper Hoffmeyer has noted, identity is closely tied to an account of what constitutes life in the first place, and, according to Hoffmeyer, that must include the sign action, repeated through every subsequent evolution of life and being, of a relation, via internalization, between a relevant semiotic environment (umwelt) and organism. Hoffmeyer calls this "an 'inside exterior.'"[53] Clearly, this semiosis depends upon a *model* of the umwelt. This world-modelling is thus, we might say, *the* primal act of imagination. More detail will be helpful, so here I provide this four-stage accomplishment as Hoffmeyer describes it:

> *first*, the formation through membrane building of an asymmetry between an inside and an outside in an autocatalytically closed system, a protocell; *second*, an exchange of chemical substances (a proto-communication) between individual units in swarms of such protocells; *third*, creation of a self-referential mechanism: a redescription of important constituents (proteins) in a digital code such as RNA or DNA; and, *fourth*, the transformation of the outer membrane to become an interface linking the interior and the exterior. In modern cells millions of glycoprotein receptors at the surface of the cell membrane take care of this function, exerting a selective channelling of signs across the cell membrane. Through an elaborate "signal transduction" system inside the cell events from the outside are connected to appropriate targets inside the cell and nucleus ... Only through the completion of this fourth step has the protocell reached the stage of a living unit, a genuine cell:

---

53   Hoffmeyer, "Semiotics of Nature," 36.

ART AND IMAGINATION

Only then does the system's understanding of its environment matter to the system, and this is how the logic of the Möbius strip becomes realized *in actu*: relevant parts of the environment become internalized as an "inside exterior," a phenomenal world or perceptual model, the Umwelt.[54]

This, then, is the decisive step in the evolutionary process of attaining true semiotic competence, i.e. the competence to make meaningful distinctions in space-time where formerly there were only differences. The semiotic looping of organism and environment into each other through the activity at their interface, the closed membrane, lies at the root of the strange future-directedness or "intentionality" of life, its Darwinian 'striving' towards growth and multiplication.[55]

"Meaningful distinctions in space-time" are of course crucial. What gets "inside'" from "outside," via the creation of a model of the latter, or imagination at its most primal founding level, gets there because it *matters* to, has *significant meaning* for, the organism. This tells us something important about imagination and art. As the biologist James A. Shapiro has remarked, life is much more like a poem than a machine.[56] But the poem, painting, music, or narrative etc. must be finally grounded in the earth and matter, must matter to the artist and to her or his audience. It does this through the play of patterns and the making of new ones from and within old ones which constitute not information but meaning. Notwithstanding the great creative power of human imagining, in the end some link must remain to that great 3.8 billion years old chain of "endless forms most beautiful" which links imagination and art to experience of being in the world.[57]

It is doubtless for this reason that G.K. Chesterton affirmed the material nature of Heavenly things. Unlike Hell, which is without meaning or hope, Heaven produces structure, constraint and meaning. It was dwelling on the constraints of embodied structure that informed Chesterton's conviction that

---

54 Hoffmeyer, "Semiotics of Nature," 40.

55 Hoffmeyer, "Semiotics of Nature," 36–37.

56 James A. Shapiro, "DNA as Poetry: Multiple Messages in a Single Sequence," *Huffington Post*, January 24, 2012, http://huffingtonpost.com/james-a-shapiro/dna-as-poetrymultiple-me_b_1229190.html.

57 Charles Darwin, (1859). *On the Origin of Species by Natural Selection*, London: John Murray. The closing sentence of the final chapter "Conclusion" (Chapter XIV, page 490) reads as follows: "There is grandeur in this view of life, with its several powers, having originally been breathed into a few forms or one; and that, whilst this planet has gone cycling on according to the fixed law of gravity, from so simple a beginning endless forms most beautiful and most wonderful have been, and are being, evolved."

religion and poetry keep us grounded in the things of the Earth, whereas an excess of abstract imagination can lead us astray. In youth, Chesterton had suffered a serious mental breakdown which he accounted for as the result of unconstrained imagination. This led him to believe that the God-created things of the Earth were of themselves intrinsically good. In distinction, abstraction is the door by which the devil enters in. Thus "the work of heaven alone is material – the making of a material world. The work of hell is entirely spiritual."[58]

Gregory Bateson took a similar view. Citing William Blake as someone "who knew that the Poetic Imagination was the only reality,"[59] Bateson reminded us that poets have always had this truth to say, that language and meaning reverberate first in the body and the Earth. Imagination and meaning, as Chesterton saw, lived first in the flesh of the world before taking flight into articulate abstraction:

> But there are bridges between the one sort of thought and the other, and it seems to me that artists and poets are specifically concerned with these bridges. It is not that art is the expression of the unconscious, but rather that it is concerned with the relation *between* the levels of mental process ... mind is immanent not only in those pathways of information which are located inside the body but also in external pathways ... The ideas which seemed to be me can also become immanent in you.[60]

In a sort of revisiting of Chesterton, Bateson was saying similarly that biosemiotic structures ground us by anchoring us on the Earth and across the gap that can open up between our abductive animal umwelt and our human-animal imagination. Oddly enough, *because* nature is more like poetry than machinery, the poetic structuring has *more reality*. Answering the question "what is poetry?," Simon Leys writes "It is not merely a literary form made of rhythmic and rhyming lines – though Chesterton also wrote (and wrote memorably) a lot of these. Poetry is something much more essential. Poetry is grasping reality, making an inventory of the visible world, giving names to all creatures, naming what *is*."[61]

---

58   Simon Leys, "Chesterton. The Poet who Dances with a Hundred Legs," in *The Hall of Uselessness. Collected Essays*, ed. Simon Leys (New York: New York Review Books, 2011), 101.

59   Bateson, *Steps to an Ecology of Mind,* 469.

60   Bateson, *Steps to an Ecology of Mind,* 469–71.

61   Leys, "Chesterton," 100.

ART AND IMAGINATION 525

Having given some of the outlines of a biosemiotic understanding, it's time to conclude with a summary of the biosemiotic understanding of imagination I am offering here. Taking a cue from other organisms (with whom, of course, we share vast eons of our evolutionary history), we can infer and reiterate that imagination in its primitive forms is a sort of non-conscious (and in *Homo sapiens* initially prelinguistic) modelling of the world that each species inhabits. In the relations of the sign, and made specifically manifest in the interpretant, a sort of model, map or *image* comes into being. The image, or world model, is what will tend to govern behavior. I think we must also imagine that this semiotic linkage between the world of the object, the world of the representamen, and the world of interpretant-derived behaviors will also be governed by *feeling* that is eventually regulated by *habit*. Thus, for every nonhuman self, and for human selves throughout almost all of their history, reality (evolutionary success and failure) constrains the actual organization of semiosis. It is for this reason that one of the pioneers of modern semiotics, Thomas A. Sebeok, described semiotics as "the study of the difference between illusion and reality."[62] We can also add that this feeling for the Earth and its creatures must be in the first place a feeling for form and function. This is precisely what governs the primary iconic sign mode of being and its evolutionary transformation via similarity and difference – i.e. what humans (often misconceiving its living reality) call metaphor.[63]

Before finally going on to Ivar Puura's conception of semiocide, one last element needs noticing, and that concerns Peirce's three "universes" of Firstness, Secondness and Thirdness. Peirce's universes are associated with modes of inference: Firstness with abduction (iconic signs, similarity), Secondness with induction (indexical signs, natural relations, contiguity), Thirdness with deduction (symbolic signs, logical necessity and law). The First universe of primary iconic signs, metaphor and abduction is what concerns us most in this instance. Abduction is the form of inference based on seeming chance and informed guessing. It is a sort of following your nose and, Peirce says, something close to animal knowing.[64] Imagination and art that takes its hand from the Earth and reality, and slips too readily into abstraction and ideological belief only, has already crossed the Styx into the Hell of unconstrained spirituality.

---

62   Paul Cobley, Introduction to *The Routledge Companion to Semiotics*, ed. Paul Cobley (London and New York: Routledge, 2010), 3–4.

63   Paul Ricoeur, *The Rule of Metaphor: The Creation of Meaning in Language*, trans. R. Czerny, K. McLaughlin, and J. Costello (London: Routledge, 2003).

64   Peirce, *The Essential Peirce*, 217–18; Wheeler, "Meaning," 131.

v   The Obliteration of Meaningful Distinctions in Space and Time: Ivar Puura and Semiocide

When we speak of habit, we are talking of the preservation of meaningful distinctions in space (the environment) and time (history). These distinctions are an accumulated knowledge evolved over time. As John Stuart Mill noted of Coleridge in his essay of 1840, the latter's strength as a thinker (as well as a poet and philosopher) lay in his understanding that, if something had endured, it was generally because it had some value:

> The influence of Coleridge, like that of Bentham, extended far beyond those who share in the peculiarities of his religious or philosophical creed. He has been the great awakener in this country of the spirit of philosophy, within the bounds of traditional opinions. He has been, almost as truly as Bentham, "the great questioner of things established," for a questioner needs not necessarily be an enemy. By Bentham, beyond all others, men have been led to ask themselves, in regard to any ancient or received opinion, Is it true? And by Coleridge, What is the meaning of it? ...The long duration of a belief, he thought, is at least proof of an adaptation in it to some portion or other of the human mind[65]

We can frame this within the insight, already referred to, that meanings are evolutionary. For *Homo sapiens* in particular, where culture makes the evolution of meanings much quicker, they endure, albeit it often in adapted forms, because they answer to enduring human needs. But we should also remember, with Duns Scotus, that freed from their lived relation with Earth, human abstractions can produce monsters.

Meditating on the part that memory and place play in a specifically human semiosis, Puura notes that these natural and cultural markers of a group's collective life are sustained by the history of semiosis both within us and, in culture and language, without. The separation of this "inside exterior" is a vast philosophical and biological error. Our memory of attending to place, and then, as humans, to past and future, is rich and vast:

> The diversity of nature is overwhelming. Every living creature, being part of a greater whole, carries in itself memories of billions of years of evolution and embodies its own long and largely still unknown story of origin. By wholesale replacement of primeval nature with artificial environments,

---

65   Mill, *Utilitarianism and Other Essays*, 187: 177–78.

ART AND IMAGINATION

it is not only nature in the biological sense that is lost. At the hands of humans, millions of stories with billions of relations and variations perish. The rich signscape of nature is replaced by something much poorer. It is not an exaggeration to call this process semiocide.[66]

We recognize the destructive colonizing or contemptuous intent in the move to obliterate a people's customary habits and meanings. Understanding semiocide to be "a situation in which signs and stories that are significant for someone are destroyed because of someone else's malevolence or carelessness, thereby stealing a part of the former's identity," Puura is also concerned with its cultural manifestations:

> When semiocide is targeted at some nation or group of people, it can manifest itself as ideological pressure or as sacrilege that often goes together with physical violence or occupation. A form of semiocide – linguacide, i.e. suppression of national languages – is something we remember from our own recent past[67] and can see everywhere in the world today. Semiocide has also been the destruction of totems of indigenous people and the banishing of people from their home signscape – from the native land of their forefathers, taking away from them everything which all together means home[68] ... If we took time to get to know ourselves better, we would discover nature in ourselves. Deep in our memory our sensations are related to the signs of nature that we see, smell and hear even when we have not yet become aware of this. Nature that is intimately familiar to us embodies the signscape that carries traditions going back through centuries, helps culture to persist and helps human beings to stay human[69]

Part of the place of imagination and art, it seems to me, is to recover those bridges within and their links without – that "inside exterior" upon which our humanity and selfhood rests. This involves a close attentiveness to nature within and without, and the patterns, the bridges, which join nature to culture

---

66 Ivar Puura, "Nature in Our Memory," *Sign Systems Studies* 41, no. 1 (2013): 152.

67 Until the fall of the Berlin Wall in 1989, and the subsequent ending of the Soviet Union, the official language in Puura's home country of Estonia was Russian. The Estonian language was suppressed.

68 Puura, "Nature in our Memory," 152.

69 Puura, "Nature in our Memory," 152. Originally published as Ivar Puura, "Loodus meie mälus," *Eesti Loodus* 11 (2002): 24–25. All quotations from Estonian are translated by Elin Sütiste and Timo Maran.

in a seamless way of the enfleshed mind. Interviewing Olafur Eliasson for *Art-Review* in December 2014, Martin Herbert writes:

> That is, moving art, in a manner so often concerned with light, colour and landscape, into the outside world and the outside world into the purview of art, establishing porosity between inside and outside, art and science, art and social project or education or architecture – as see everything from the aforementioned works to the *Green River* series (1998), in which he poured uranin, a bright green luminous dye used to test plumbing leaks, into rivers; *The Weather Project* (2003), his misted artificial sun for Tate Modern's Turbine Hall; and the four manmade waterfalls he set up in New York, *New York City Waterfalls* (2008). Eliasson agrees to some degree … But to him, evidently … borders aren't that interesting in themselves. What matters is the real-world pragmatics of what happens when they're dissolved.[70]

Icelandic-Danish artist Olafur Eliasson's work does seem to embody the practice of relatedness, of a concern for people in and as nature, and with the "inside exterior" linkages, models and maps I am identifying as part of a biosemiotically aware and pragmatic imagination at work in art. Famous for his *The Weather Project* exhibited (and experienced) at Tate Modern in London in 2003[71] in which the Turbine Hall was illuminated by a giant yellow/orange sun in the vast mist filled space, Eliasson also showed a retrospective – *In Real Life* – at Tate Modern between July 2019 and January 2020. *The Weather Project* effortlessly engaged its viewers who, without prompting, arranged themselves in collective patterns, often moving in unison, on the Turbine Hall floor where they could see these patterns played out in the large mirrored ceiling above. Yellow is the most effective color for human vision. The sodium which produces it is volatile and requires neon to stabilize it. The effect – good for night vision, hence its use for street lamps and road tunnels – is to render everything clearer, but in monochrome. Yet from the proto-fog created by monochrome light and wet mist pumped into the exhibition space, gallery visitors were able to create patterns of themselves which made something clearer. Perhaps it was

---

70   Martin Herbert, "Interview with Olafur Eliasson," *ArtReview*, December 2014, https://art-review.com/features/december_2014_feature_olafur_eliasson/.

71   See Olafur Eliasson, "The Weather Project," video, 2:07, January 6, 2012, https://youtu.be/IsT9vEpfNq4.

ART AND IMAGINATION

our group participation in making the weather. Eliasson has said that he is very interested in interaction between people and the world around us.[72]

Eliasson's preoccupations with time, space and relationship between people and world are played out in his work repeatedly. For him "art is about dialogue" and "turning thought into physical action."[73] This pragmaticist view, evident in Charles Peirce's account of the Interpretant, informs all Eliasson's practice. This includes the *Little Sun* project that brings together art and pragmaticism in providing solar-powered replacement lights for people without electricity who have been dependent on using kerosene lamps, which are bad for people's health, in their Ethiopian villages.[74] In the BBC1 film on Eliasson mentioned above, and affirming the biosemiotic understanding of the evolutionary continuum that is nature-culture that quite evidently permeates Eliasson's imagination, art thinking and practice, the Head of Studio Research in Eliasson's Berlin studio describes the studio itself as "an agile organism."[75]

Imagination requires distinctions. Its primal movement is with iconic signs, and thus with similarity and difference. No human infant could acquire human language without this primal semiotic act. No organism could survive in its absence. The attempted erasure of distinctions, and the judgements they carry, is perhaps our greatest contemporary threat. It is tantamount to the attempted erasure of life itself. Semiocide – of nature-culture similarities and differences – is a puritanical war not only on representation and art, familiar from the Protestant Reformation 400 years ago and lingering on in newer political forms still, it is a silencing war on past, present and future, on what links them, and the great gift of life: its entropy-defying, self-imagining, self-conserving and self-making anew with each generation.

References

Bains, Paul. *The Primacy of Semiosis: An Ontology of Relations*. Toronto and London: University of Toronto Press. 2006.

Bateson, Gregory. *Steps to an Ecology of Mind*. Chicago, IL: University of Chicago Press. 1972.

---

72 Olafur Eliasson, "Miracles of Rare Device," video, 62:00, July 28, 2019, https://www.bbc.co.uk/iplayer/episode/m00077pm/imagine-2019-6-olafur-eliasson-miracles-of-rare-device.

73 Eliasson, "Miracles of Rare Device," 2019.

74 See the *Little Sun* project description at https://olafureliasson.net/archive/artwork/WEK107424/little-sun.

75 Eliasson, "Miracles of Rare Device," 2019.

Bateson, Gregory. "Syllogisms in Grass." *London Review of Books* (Letters), January 24, 1980.

Bateson, Gregory, and Mary Catherine Bateson. *Angels Fear: Towards and Epistemology of the Sacred*. New York: Bantam Books. 1988.

Brand, Stewart. "In conversation with Gregory Bateson and Margaret Mead." *CoEvolutionary Quarterly* 10, no. 21 (1976): 32–44.

Brier, Søren. *Cybersemiotics: Why Information Is Not Enough!* Toronto: University of Toronto Press. 2008.

Bruner, Jerome. *Acts of Meaning*. Cambridge, MA and London: Harvard University Press. 1990.

Buchler, Justus, ed. "Logic as Semiotic: The Theory of Signs." *Philosophical Writings of Peirce*. Mineola, NY: Dover Publications. 1955.

Cobley, Paul. Introduction to *The Routledge Companion to Semiotics*, edited by Paul Cobley, 3–12. London and New York: Routledge. 2010.

Darwin, Charles. *On the Origin of Species by Natural Selection*. London: John Murray. 1859.

Deacon, Terrence W., Alok Srivastava, and Joshua Augustus Bacigalupi. "The Transition from Constraint to Regulation at the Origin of Life." *Frontiers in Bioscience* 19 (2014): 945–57.

Deely, John N. *Intentionality and Semiotics*. Scranton, PA: University of Scranton Press. 2007.

Deely, John N. *Purely Objective Reality*. New York and Berlin: Mouton de Gruyter. 2009.

Eliasson, Olafur. "Miracles of Rare Device." video, 62:00, July 28, 2019, https://www.bbc.co.uk/iplayer/episode/m00077pm/imagine-2019-6-olafur-eliasson-miracles-of-rare-device.

Eliasson, Olafur. "The Weather Project." video, 2:07. January 6, 2012. https://youtu.be/IsT9vEpfNq4.

Guddemi, Phillip. "Two Roads which Diverged," In "Ranulph Glanville and How to Live the Cybernetics of Unknowing," special issue, *Cybernetics and Human Knowing* 22, no. 2–3 (2015): 183–87.

Harries-Jones, Peter. *Upside-Down Gods: Gregory Bateson's World of Difference*. New York: Fordham University Press. 2016.

Herbert, Martin. "Interview with Olafur Eliasson." *ArtReview*, December 2014, https://artreview.com/features/december_2014_feature_olafur_eliasson/.

Hoffmeyer, Jesper. "Surfaces Within Surfaces. On the Origin of Agency and Life." *Cybernetics and Human Knowing* 5 (1998): 33–42.

Hoffmeyer, Jesper. *Biosemiotics: An Examination into the Signs of Life and the Life of Signs*, translated by Jesper Hoffmeyer, and Donald Favareau, edited by Donald Favareau. Scranton, PA and London: University of Scranton Press. 2008.

Hoffmeyer, Jesper. "Semiotics of Nature." In *The Routledge Companion to Semiotics*, edited by Paul Cobley, 29–42. London and New York: Routledge, 2010.

ART AND IMAGINATION

Hoffmeyer, Jesper. "Semiotic Individuation and Ernst Cassirer's Challenge." *Progress in Biophysics and Molecular Biology* 119, no. 3 (2015): 607–15.

Hoffmeyer, Jesper. "Semiotic Scaffolding: A Unitary Principle Gluing Life and Culture Together." In "Biosemiotics and Culture," edited by Wendy Wheeler, and Louise Westling. Special issue, *Green Letters: Studies in Ecocriticism* 19, no. 3 (2015): 243–54.

Humphreys, Nick. "New Ideas, Old Ideas: Review of Gregory Bateson's *Mind and Nature: A Necessary Unity*." *London Review of Books*, December 6, 1979.

"Image." In *Merriam-Webster Dictionary*. Merriam-Webster Incorporated, 2019. https://www.merriam-webster.com/dictionary/image.

"Imagination." In *Merriam-Webster Dictionary*. Merriam-Webster Incorporated, 2019. https://www.merriam-webster.com/dictionary/imagination.

Kotov, Kaie, and Kalevi Kull "Semiosphere is the Relational Biosphere." In *Towards a Semiotic Biology: Life is the Action of Signs*, edited by Claus Emmeche, and Kalevi Kull, 179–94. London: Imperial College Press, 2011.

Leys, Simon. "Chesterton. The Poet who Dances with a Hundred Legs." In *The Hall of Uselessness. Collected Essays*, edited by Simon Leys, 100–13. New York: New York Review Books, 2011.

Mill, John Stuart. *Utilitarianism and Other Essays*. London: Penguin. 1987.

Noble, Ray, and Denis Noble, "Was the Watchmaker Blind? Or Was She One-Eyed?" *Biology* 6, no. 4 (2017): 1–19.

Orwell, George. *Nineteen Eighty-Four*. London: Penguin. 1989.

Peirce, Charles Sanders. *Collected Papers of Charles Sanders Peirce, Volumes I and II: Principles of Philosophy and Elements of Logic*. Cambridge, MA: Harvard University Press. 1932.

Peirce, Charles Sanders. *The Essential Peirce: Philosophical Writings. Vol. 1 (1867–1893)*, edited by Nathan Houser, and Christian Kloesel. Bloomington, IN and Indianapolis, IN: Indiana University Press. 1992.

Peirce, Charles Sanders. *The Essential Peirce: Selected Philosophical Writings. Vol. 2, 1893–1913*, edited by The Peirce Edition Project. Bloomington, IN and Indianapolis, IN: Indiana University Press. 1998.

Pickering, Andrew. *The Cybernetic Brain: Sketches of Another Future*. Chicago and London: Chicago University Press. 2010.

Prigogine, Ilya. *The End of Certainty: Time, Chaos, and the New Laws of Nature*. New York and London: The Free Press. 1997.

Puura, Ivar. "Nature in Our Memory." *Sign Systems Studies* 41, no. 1 (2013): 150–53.

Ricoeur, Paul. *The Rule of Metaphor: The Creation of Meaning in Language*. Translated by R. Czerny, K. McLaughlin, and J. Costello. London: Routledge. 2003.

Rosenblueth, Arturo, Norbert Wiener, and Julian Bigelow. "Behavior, Purpose and Teleology." *Philosophy of Science* 10, no. 1 (1943): 18–24.

Shannon, Claude E. "A Mathematical Theory of Communication: Part One." *The Bell System Technical Journal* 27 (1948): 379–423.

Shannon, Claude E. "A Mathematical Theory of Communication: Part Two." *The Bell System Technical Journal* 27 (1948): 623–56.

Shapiro, James A. "DNA as Poetry: Multiple Messages in a Single Sequence." *Huffington Post*, January 24, 2012, http://huffingtonpost.com/james-a-shapiro/dna-as-poetry-multiple-me_b_1229190.html.

"Sign." In *The Commens Dictionary: Peirce's Terms in His Own Words*, edited by M. Bergman, and S. Paavola, new edition. Accessed June 3, 2019, http://www.commens.org/dictionary/entry/quote-letters-lady-welby-43.

Simpson, James. *Burning to Read: English Fundamentalism and Its Reformation Opponents*. Cambridge, MA and London: Belknap Press of Harvard University Press. 2007.

Trewavas, Anthony. "Intelligence, Cognition and Language of Green Plants." *Frontiers in Psychology* 7 (2016): 1–9.

Uexküll, Jakob von. "A Stroll through the Worlds of Animals and Men: A Picture Book of Invisible Worlds." In *Instinctive Behavior: The Development of a Modern Concept*, edited and translated by C.H. Schiller, 320–91. New York: International Universities Press. 1957.

Wheeler, Wendy. *Expecting the Earth: Life/Culture/Biosemiotics*. London: Lawrence & Wishart. 2016.

Wheeler, Wendy. "Meaning." In *The Edinburgh Companion to Animal Studies*, edited by Lynn Turner, Undine Sellbach, and Ron Broglio, 337–53. Edinburgh: Edinburgh University Press. 2018.

PART 7

Aesthetic Perspectives

∴

CHAPTER 22

Image, Image-Making, and Imagination

Dominic Gregory

1 Introduction

Despite the importance and ubiquity of visual imagery as a means of representation, philosophers have tended instead to concentrate upon language, because of its standing as the natural vehicle for voicing conceptual thoughts and discursive reasoning. The relative philosophical neglect of images has been coupled with a parallel neglect of those mental states to which visual images seem to be most closely linked. Recent philosophers, at least, have covered reams of paper with reflections about beliefs and other mental states whose instances typically revolve around linguistically articulable information, but they have spent far less time investigating the imagination, for instance, or dreams.[1]

One feature of visual imagery that acts as both an enticement to investigation, and as a potential obstacle to its progress, is its sheer diversity. Visual images may be realized using radically different media, for instance: thus mental visual imagery exploits neurological resources, while frescos employ pigments and plaster. And the range of styles that visual images manifest might make one wonder whether the category of "visual images" really possesses the unity that surely characterizes the phenomenon of human linguistic representation, and which makes it natural to see all human languages as different branches of a single tree. The pictures produced by small children in the West seem to be very different to those produced during Ancient Egypt's Middle Kingdom, for instance, and those last are very different again to Hokusai's drawings.[2]

---

1 The imagination plays an important part in the philosophical ideas of many philosophers before the twentieth century, however: it features prominently in Hume's Empiricist system, for example, and in Kant's Transcendental Idealism. See David Hume, *A Treatise of Human Nature*. 2nd ed. Eds. L.A. Selby-Bigge and P.H. Nidditch (Oxford: Clarendon Press, 1978), and Immanuel Kant, *Critique of Pure Reason*, trans. and eds. Paul Guyer and Allen Wood (Cambridge: Cambridge University Press. 1999). There are encouraging recent signs of a growing philosophical interest in the imagination: for instance, see Amy Kind, ed., *The Routledge Handbook of Philosophy of Imagination* (London: Routledge, 2016).

2 A wish to understand better the remarkable variety of pictorial styles has been a driving force within art history, for example: Wölfflin provides a famous early attempt to theorize in a

---

© KONINKLIJKE BRILL NV, LEIDEN, 2020 | DOI:10.1163/9789004436350_024

The striking differences between different modes of image-making are also relevant here, as they can seem to put additional pressure on the idea that there is any interesting unity to the class of visual images at all. Are medical imaging techniques that cleverly use standardized causal pathways to generate handily pictorial records of bodily facts—X-rays, say—really to be assimilated to the production of pictures by artists, with their creative and deliberate use of pictures as a means of communication and aesthetic expression? Are astronomical images that translate into visible form data relating to invisible radio waves really engaged in the same business as standard photographs, which just record visible facts? And where do mental visual images fit into things?

The power of the imagination is, for many of us at least, intimately connected to visual imagery. Our most vivid imaginings commonly revolve around mental visual imagery, and there is a great deal of toing-and-froing between our imaginations and nonmental visual imagery. Pictures can shape our imaginings: I can employ mental visual imagery to imagine Muddy Waters shaking hands with Beethoven, for example, despite only ever having seen pictures of both men. Pictures can, conversely, capture what we imagine: skilled artists may be able to translate mental visual images into concrete form; and one can easily conceive of pictures that just happen to correspond to mental visual images that one has produced.

The imaginative exploitation of imagistic resources therefore allows us to translate core aspects of what we imagine into material form, while the concrete objects thereby produced often play a central part by, in turn, extending our imaginative powers. Our imaginative capacities shape the making of images, while the making of images has the ability to shape our imaginative capacities. What are the connections between vision, mental visual images, and indeed nonmental visual images that allow for this traffic between the contents of our minds and images located in the outside world? And how are image-makers able to exploit the distinctive powers of imagery, to extend the modes of representation that are available to us, and hence also to extend the resources upon which our imaginations can draw?

The current essay will investigate various aspects of the issues just broached. It will start by exploring "visual imagery" as a general category: it will argue, in particular, that deep semantic differences exist between visual images of different sorts; and it will initially identify one very striking range of cases that encompasses both suitable mental and nonmental visual images. It

---

systematic way about stylistic variations. See Heinrich Wölfflin, *Principles of Art History. The Problem of the Development of Style in Later Art*, 7th edition. Trans. MD Hottinger (Mineola, NY: Dover Publications, 1932).

will proceed to develop a philosophical account of what is distinctive about the range of visual images thus identified. Subsequent sections then use the resulting ideas to investigate some of the ways in which various strategies for creating visual images exploit in remarkably inventive ways possibilities that are latent within the general phenomenon of imagistic representation.[3]

2 Visual Images in General

The domain of visual images may be carved up into lots of different categories: there are the visual images which existed before 1900, and then there are the rest; there are the visual images that show cute small dogs, and then there are the rest; and so on. But one particularly significant way of dividing up visual images, at least for our purposes, is to distinguish between those images that are *representations* and those which are not. This way of differentiating between visual images is complicated, however, by the fact that many visual images function, in representational terms, on multiple levels.

While visual images often help to shape the contents of our imaginings, for instance, the contents of our imaginings often outrun what those images display. Use visual imagery to imagine a cow. Now imagine that the cow is fifty years old. The visual image that you produced serves to represent a fifty-year-old cow in your imagination, but there is nothing inherent within the meaning of the image itself that determines that the imagined cow is fifty years old. The fact that the image displays a fifty-year-old cow is, rather, a supplementary addition to the image's content, an addition owed to something like a *supposition* that the cow shown in the image is fifty years old.[4] You could have used an indiscernible image in imagining a thirty-year-old cow, for instance, or a tenyear-old one.

Visual images may also communicate relatively abstract ideas, by exploiting previously understood connections between visible items and general concepts. Few adults would miss the nod to mortality contained within Guercino's initiation within painting of the *Et in Arcadia ego* theme, for instance, with the picture's portrayal of two young men gazing at a skull. And visual images may

---

3 Parts of the following discussion will employ some ideas that are developed in more detail, in a more general context, in Dominic Gregory, *Showing, Sensing, and Seeming: Distinctively Sensory Representations and Their Contents* (Oxford: Oxford University Press, 2013).

4 Peacocke notes the way in which supposition-like elements of imaginings may add to the contents of visual images. See Christopher Peacocke, "Imagination, Experience, and Possibility" in *Essays on Berkeley*, eds. John Foster and Howard Robinson (Oxford: Clarendon Press, 1985), 19–35.

perhaps also communicate abstract ideas in other ways: Barnett Newman's painting *Anna's Light*—which presents the viewer with a large expanse of relatively uniform redness—is about as stereotypically "non-representational" as pictures get, yet maybe it does indeed express "the flood of life made possible by [the 'break of origin']."[5] We can sidestep some of these complexities, however, if we focus upon just some of the representational layers involved in visual imagery.

One capacious category of representational visual images encompasses those that represent things by showing what they look like. The visual images that feature in our imaginings do this: your earlier mental visual image of a cow displayed a cow by showing things as looking a certain way, for instance. Similarly, Guercino's painting represents a skull by showing things as looking a certain way. By contrast, Newman's *Anna's Light* does not seem to show what anything looks like, any more than an arbitrary patch of brickwork does, even if the picture does engage in representational work at another level.

The category of visual images that show what things look like evidently cuts across radically different media. Your previous mental visual image of a cow characterized a cow in very broadly the same sort of way as many pictures of cows do, in that it represented a cow by showing something that possessed a suitable kind of visual appearance. There are, of course, huge differences of other sorts between genuine pictures of cows and your mental visual image, just as there are huge differences between silent "inner speech" and real outer speech. But those additional differences ought not to blind us to the fact that there are also, at a very high level, similarities in the ways that the representations work: they have the same kinds of meanings, at a very basic level.

While some visual images show what things look like, then, not all of them do. It is worth emphasizing that paradigmatically "non-representational" pictures, like the Newman painting mentioned above, are not the only examples of visual images that do not show what things look like. The outer regions of the category of visual images—where it starts to be questionable whether we are dealing with "images" at all—contain many items that do not perform that function; consider, for example, topographical maps, or flow-charts. More interestingly, though, many more central cases of representational visual images seem also not to be engaged in the business of showing what things look like.

Cubist pictures often represent things by merely incorporating allusions to ways of representing items by showing what they look like, for instance, without themselves capturing visual appearances: Picasso and Braque produced numerous paintings which depict items like guitars, drinking glasses, and

---

5   Yve-Alain Bois, *Painting as Model* (Cambridge, MA: MIT Press, 1993), 213.

pipes, using graphical echoes of bits of pictured guitars, glasses, and pipes. Similarly, pictures by young children often represent items without showing what they look like, relying instead upon relatively abstract diagrammatic forms of representation. It is, for instance, surely perverse to assume that, when three-year-old children represent their parents using blobs with faces, whose arms and legs are displayed using lines coming straight out of the blobs, they are purporting faithfully to capture the visual appearances of familiar people.[6]

The contents of visual images that show things as looking certain ways are bound to vision in a way that the contents of pictures like, say, many Cubist still-life paintings are not. One who understands Magritte's famous painting of a pipe (the one captioned "Ceci n'est pas une pipe") thereby has an appreciation of what it is like to see a pipe of a certain kind, for instance, whereas one who understands some of Picasso's pictures of pipes does not, just as a result of understanding the pictures, come to appreciate what the depicted pipes look like. In this respect, the Picasso pictures are similar to many verbal representations that make reference to pipes: you understand the sentence "A man smoked a pipe," but your mere understanding of that sentence does not lead you to an appreciation of just what the relevant pipe is meant to look like.

The domain of visual images—understood as incorporating both mental and nonmental cases—is thus *semantically heterogeneous*: it encompasses representations whose most basic meanings differ quite starkly in kind. On the one hand, there are those visual images that show things as looking certain ways, a class that encompasses many pictures and which also contains the mental visual images that feature in our imaginings. And, on the other hand, there are the rest. (It may be that the category of "the rest" is itself semantically heterogeneous.) This hardly implies that there is no point in investigating visual images *per se*, of course. But it does mean that we may, in good conscience, focus on just some visual images, to the exclusion of others.

Indeed, the previous remarks suggests a potential "divide and conquer" strategy which one might follow in philosophical investigations of visual imagery. One might distinguish between images that belong to different fundamental semantic categories—that is, which possess elementary meanings of distinct sorts—and one might investigate the nature of the images that belong within each of those categories. One might, too, explore the interactions that

---

6   For an interesting discussion of the representational characteristics of children's pictorial art, with a helpful survey of prior literature, see Part v from John Willats, *Art and Representation: New Principles in the Analysis of Pictures* (Princeton, NJ: Princeton University Press, 1997).

exist between the ways in which images of the relevant sorts may be produced and the sorts of meanings that they thereby come to possess.

What follows makes a modest start on some of that work. In particular, it will concentrate upon those visual images that show things as looking certain ways. As we will see in the next section, those cases form a nicely unified range of instances, one that is amenable to a coherent theoretical investigation, and their theoretical unity will enable us to shed clearer light upon some very important features of many, if not all visual images.

3   Distinctively Visual Representations in Particular

Use mental visual imagery to imagine a bicycle. Your mental visual image shows things as looking a certain way, and it thereby represents a bicycle. Similar remarks apply to lots of pictures of bikes, although it is conceivable that a picture of a bike might depict a bike without showing things as looking a certain way, just as some Cubist paintings depict pipes without showing what they look like. Your visual mental image of a bike is therefore a "distinctively visual" image of a bike.

More generally, let's say that a visual image is a *distinctively visual* image precisely if it shows things as looking certain ways. The category of distinctively visual images supplies us with many paradigmatic examples of visual images. Mental visual images seem always to be distinctively visual, for instance, and huge numbers of pictures, from many cultures and times, are also distinctively visual images. The famous Paleolithic cave paintings at Lascaux contain images that depict horses by showing things as looking certain ways, for instance, just as pictures of horses on Ancient Greek vases do, and just as George Stubbs's pictures of horses do too.

Distinctively visual images have contents, or meanings, of a special sort: the nature of what one grasps when one looks comprehendingly at, say, a distinctively visual picture of a pipe is different in type to the nature of what one grasps when one comprehendingly views some Cubist paintings that depict pipes, for instance, or when one understands an utterance of the sentence "A woman smoked a pipe." To give those contents a label, let's say that distinctively visual images have *distinctively visual* contents.

While the focus of the current chapter is on visual images, it is worth noting that the category of distinctively visual images falls within a much wider family of representations that are not inherently linked to vision. Our imaginings often feature mental *nonvisual* imagery, for example: one can imagine someone's voice; one can imagine a foul smell; and one can imagine something hot

IMAGE, IMAGE-MAKING, AND IMAGINATION 541

pressing against one's skin. But mental auditory images and many playbacks of audio recordings are alike in showing things as sounding certain ways, while mental olfactory images show things as smelling certain ways; and mental tactual images may capture what things feel like against the skin.

Distinctively visual images thus belong to a very broad family of "distinctively sensory" representations that serve to represent what they represent in ways that are intimately linked to corresponding varieties of sensory experience. The purely mental members of this family—mental visual images, mental auditory images, and the rest—play a very prominent role within our imaginative lives.[7] And note how natural it is to think of the representations within this much broader category as being imagistic: a playback of an audio recording may present us with an "auditory image" of certain events, for instance.

It should also be emphasized that the "distinctively visual" nature of distinctively visual images derives simply from the nature of their *contents*—that is, from the nature of the information that we grasp when we understand them—rather than from any facts about what the representations themselves *look like*. Many people have been attracted to the idea that pictures of, say, bicycles must somehow "look like" bikes but there are no reasons for thinking that, in general, distinctively visual images of bikes must look like bikes.[8] The mental visual image of a bike that you used in imagining a bike was presumably some sort of complex neurological state, for instance, and it seems unlikely that the relevant state will itself look like a bicycle in any significant way.

What is especially visual about the distinctively visual contents of distinctively visual images? Well, for one thing, the "ways that they show things as looking" amount to types of visual experiences. Produce again a mental visual image of a bike. Your visual mental image represents a bike by showing things as looking a certain way. Imagine that things were to look that way to you in the course of a visual experience. Then it would look to you, in the course of that visual experience, as if a bike were really to be present in front of your eyes; that is, you would have a visual experience of a certain type, one that involves the apparent presence of a bike.

More generally, consider a distinctively visual image that explicitly shows something of a certain kind, because it shows things as looking a certain way. Anyone to whom things looked that way would seem to see an item of the

---

7   For a treatment of visual images within the broader context sketched in the text, see Dominic Gregory, *Showing, Sensing, and Seeming: Distinctively Sensory Representations and Their Contents* (Oxford: Oxford University Press, 2013).

8   The accounts of pictorial depiction developed in Budd (1993) and Hopkins (1998) provide sophisticated developments of the idea that pictures of things should "look like" what they depict, for instance.

relevant sort. Distinctively visual images explicitly show things like bicycles and the rest, that is, because their contents feature ways for things to look involving appropriate sorts of items. Some of the most basic representational properties of distinctively visual images are thus owed to the fact that their contents involve types of visual experiences.[9]

Distinctively visual images are not just connected to vision by virtue of the fact that their contents involve ways for things to look, however. Consider the following sentence: "The way that things look to Clint Eastwood right now is different to the way that they looked to him a moment ago." That sentence makes reference to two ways for things to look, and the sentence's meaning consequently involves those ways for things to look. But the sentence's meaning is not linked to vision in the way that, say, the content of your earlier mental visual image of a bicycle was. Distinctively visual contents thus somehow involve ways for things to look in a special fashion.

To isolate what is crucial here, compare your earlier visual mental image of a bike with Figure 22.1.

Like your mental visual image of a bike, Figure 22.1 shows a bike because it shows things as looking a certain way. And, when you view and comprehend Figure 22.1, you come to be aware of the way that the picture shows things as looking. But note that your awareness of that way for things to look takes a striking form: you appreciate *what it would be like* for things to look to someone the way that Figure 22.1 shows things as looking. (You can, in the wake of viewing Figure 22.1, imagine "from the inside" seeing the scene shown in the image, for instance.)

Your comprehending viewing of Figure 22.1 thus involves a crucially "subjective" ingredient. And this ingredient was missing from, say, your earlier encounter with the sentence "The way that things look to Clint Eastwood right now is different to the way that they looked to him a moment ago." For in that last case, your understanding of the sentence provided you with no awareness at all of what it would be like for things to look to you either of the ways mentioned. But the same subjective feature is present in other, distinctively visual, cases. When you entertained your earlier mental visual image of a bike, for example, you thereby appreciated what it would be like for things to look to someone the way that your mental visual image showed things as looking.

---

9   It is worth noting that it is not being claimed here that distinctively visual images must always themselves *represent* visual experiences; it is not being claimed that, for instance, a mental visual image of a chair inevitably represents the chair as being seen by someone. See fn.11 for a little more on this point.

FIGURE 22.1 A bicycle
PHOTOGRAPH BY DOMINIC GREGORY

More generally, the distinctively visual contents of distinctively visual images do indeed involve ways for things to look in a special manner. For they characterize ways for things to look simply in terms of what it would be like for us, in subjective terms, if we were to enjoy visual experiences in which things looked those ways to us.

We have therefore managed to identify another, very important, respect in which distinctively visual images are linked to vision itself. And this particular facet of their nature is manifested in fairly striking phenomena. It means that we can learn what things look like from pictures, for example, because our encounters with pictures lead us to an awareness of what it would be like to see the depicted items. Similarly, our ability to use mental visual imagery to imagine an item of a certain kind reflects our awareness of what those sorts of items look like.

Here is a summary of what we have so far. Many visual images—but not all—show things as looking certain ways. Mental visual images perform this representational function, for instance, as do many pictures. These "distinctively visual" images have contents of a kind that are linked to vision itself in certain notable respects. In particular, the ways that distinctively visual images show things as looking amount to types of visual experiences. And distinctively visual contents pick out these types of visual experiences—the ways that they show things as looking—in terms of what it would be like for us if things were to look those ways to us. Furthermore, by showing things as looking certain ways, distinctively visual images are able to display scenes of various sorts. Figure 22.1 shows a bike, for example, because the way that it shows things as looking involves the presence of a bicycle. The next section explores an important aspect of distinctively visual images that we have so far ignored.

4   Issues of Perspective

Look around yourself for a moment. All of the things that you just seemed to see, you seemed to see from a particular viewpoint. More generally, vision is spatially *perspectival*: the scenes that we encounter, in the course of visual experiences, are always organized for us around a central perspective, with the items that we see being located in various directions, and at various distances, from that place. And this feature of vision is reflected in the nature of the distinctively visual images that we have encountered previously.

Figure 22.1 shows a bike in a perspectival fashion, for instance. Likewise, if you use mental visual imagery to imagine a house, the mental visual image will show a house from a certain perspective. By contrast, Barnett Newman's abstract painting *Anna's Light* does not show us "the flood of life" from some particular spatial viewpoint, any more than the sentence "The flood of life can be rather overwhelming" does. Note that the perspectives involved in the contents of distinctively visual images need not be the viewpoints occupied by *us* while we encounter the images: you can use mental visual imagery to imagine what things look like from somewhere on the moon even while safely at home on Earth, for instance.

How does the spatially perspectival nature of distinctively visual images relate to the perspectival nature of vision itself? Reconsider Figure 22.1. That image shows a bike, and it does so because it shows things as looking a certain way. More specifically, the picture shows a bike because it shows things as looking a certain way *from a particular viewpoint*, a viewpoint that is located fairly near to and in front of the relevant bicycle.[10] Figure 22.1 consequently shows the bike from that place.

---

10   A distinctively visual image may show things as looking a certain way from a particular perspective without characterizing that perspective as being *occupied*: CCTV footage often shows what things looked like from unoccupied perspectives, for example. Distinctively visual images are thus able to display scenes, by showing things as looking certain

IMAGE, IMAGE-MAKING, AND IMAGINATION

The spatially perspectival nature of Figure 22.1's representation of a bike thus results from the fact that the picture show things as looking a certain way from a particular viewpoint.[11] Analogous points apply to other distinctively visual images. If you visualize a peacock, for instance, your visual image will show the peacock in a spatially perspectival fashion, because it will show things as looking a certain way from a particular viewpoint. More generally, any image which displays a scene, by showing things as looking a certain way, will have to show things as looking a certain way *from somewhere*. But the image will therefore display the scene in a spatially perspectival manner.

That feature of distinctively visual images reflects a significant property of vision itself. For when, in the course of real visual experiences, things look certain ways to us, we ourselves occupy particular viewpoints. And the natures of the viewpoints that we occupy are reflected in the visual experiences themselves: when things look to us to be a certain way, they look to us to be a certain way from somewhere. By contrast, the assumed representation of the flood of life in Newman's painting *Anna's Light* is not owed to the fact that the image shows things as looking a certain way from somewhere. The image's representation of the flood of life consequently lacks the spatial perspectivalness that is present in distinctively visual imagery and in vision itself.

The spatially perspectival nature of distinctively visual images prevents them from realizing certain representational possibilities. In particular, they cannot perform, merely using their most basic representational features alone, any representational functions that require a complete lack of spatial perspectivalness. One could not, for example, use unsupplemented mental visual imagery to imagine that the square root of every prime number is irrational. But there are nonetheless many representational possibilities that remain open to distinctively visual images, in principle at least.

Nothing up to this point implies that each distinctively visual image may only show things as looking *one* way, for instance. For an image is distinctively visual, we have said, if it shows things as looking a certain way. But this leaves

---

ways, without representing the relevant scenes as being seen. For more on this point and for more on the general idea of a visual "perspective," see Gregory, *Showing, Sensing, and Seeing: Distinctively Sensory Representations and Their Contents*, and Dominic Gregory, "Imagery, the Imagination and Experience," *Philosophical Quarterly* 60, no. 241 (2010): 735–53.

11 A picture may show things as looking a certain way from "a particular viewpoint," even though there is no really existing viewpoint from which the picture displays its scene: such pictures do not single out a specific real place as being the one from which things look like *that*. The idea of a "specific viewpoint" that is being used to thus needs fairly careful philosophical handling; see Chapter three from Gregory, *Showing, Sensing, and Seeing: Distinctively Sensory Representations and Their Contents*.

open the possibility that some distinctively visual images show things as looking a multiplicity of ways. Equally, any way that a distinctively visual image shows things as looking must be a way that the image shows things as looking from some perspective. But nothing up to this point implies that each distinctively visual image may only show things as looking a certain way from *one* perspective. Maybe some distinctively visual images show things as looking just one way from many distinct perspectives, for example; and maybe some show things as looking many ways from many perspectives.

Are any of those theoretical possibilities actually realized? The next few sections will look at how different ways of producing distinctively visual images systematically yield representations that do indeed realize some of the many perspectival possibilities that the general idea of distinctively visual imagery makes available.

5   Projective Systems

Compare Figures 22.2 and 22.3. Both of those pictures are distinctively visual images: Figure 22.2 captures the look of some train tracks running into the distance, for instance, and Figure 22.3 captures the look of some people on a street. But, despite being alike in that way, the images are also evidently very different. In particular, the images seem to be very different with regards to their depictions of space.

Just intuitively, for instance, Figure 22.2 is pinned to a particular location at one time: it shows what things look like from one place in the depicted scene. And mental visual images are similar: while temporally extended passages of evolving mental visual imagery can show things from numerous viewpoints over a period of time, individual mental visual images that show what things look like at a unique time—"snapshot-like" ones, for short—capture what things look like from just one place.

Figure 22.3, by contrast, has a striking "mobility." Hockney remarks that images like Figure 22.3, which exploit certain techniques sometimes found in computer games, but also in Indian, Oriental, and Persian art, involve "not ... a single fixed or momentary viewpoint but ... many viewpoints," and that the process of viewing such pictures reflects "our physical experience of moving through the world" and visually regarding its contents.[12]

The putative differences just noted, and which will be explored in more detail in the next section, amount to differences in the *contents* of the relevant

---

12   David Hockney, *Secret Knowledge (New and Expanded Edition): Rediscovering the Lost Techniques of the Old Masters* (London: Thames and Hudson, 2006), 204.

IMAGE, IMAGE-MAKING, AND IMAGINATION 547

FIGURE 22.2 William H. Rau (American, 1855–1920), *New Main Line at Duncannon*, about 1890–1900, Gelatin silver print 44 × 54.6 cm (17 5/16 × 21 1/2 in.), The J. Paul Getty Museum, Los Angeles
DIGITAL IMAGE COURTESY OF THE GETTY'S OPEN CONTENT PROGRAM

images; they reflect differences in the meanings that we grasp when we look comprehendingly at the images. But they seem to correspond to other important differences between the images. In particular, there are striking contrasts between Figures 22.2 and 22.3 that relate to their particular modes of production as *pictures*.

Pictures may be made by exploiting actual and possible projections of actual and possible scenes, using any one of a variety of distinct "projective systems." Willats provides a nice summary of the relevant notion of a projective system: "A standard text on engineering drawing ... defines projection as 'the formal means adopted for representing the three-dimensional attributes of objects or arrangements on one of more planes of projection.' The projection lines or rays are imagined as coming from objects in the scene, and these rays intersect a two-dimensional plane known as the plane of projection or picture plane. The geometry of these intersections forms the geometry of the picture."[13]

---

13   Willats, *Art and Representation: New Principles in the Analysis of Pictures*, 8.

FIGURE 22.3   Screenshot from *Paperboy* (Atari Games, 1984)
THIS SCREENSHOT FALLS UNDER THE "FAIR USE" PROVISION OF SECTION 107 OF TITLE 17 OF THE UNITED STATES CODE

Different projective systems provide different ways of capturing three-dimensional arrangements of edges on a two-dimensional surface. They may involve distinct treatments of the lines of projection and of the angles at which the lines of projection pass through the picture plane.

In some projective systems, for example, the lines of projection are parallel. "Orthogonal projection"—as commonly used in, say, architectural drawings—is a system in which the lines of projection are parallel and perpendicular to the flat picture plane. "Oblique projection" is a system in which the lines of projection are parallel but in which they are not perpendicular to the flat picture plane. One standard mark of uses of oblique projection is displayed by Figure 22.3; notice how that picture employs diagonal parallel lines to display receding parallel lines within the depicted scene.

By contrast, in "perspectival" projective systems the lines of projection are not parallel, but rather meet at a single point placed in front of both the projected scene and the flat picture plane. Receding parallel lines, within scenes that are projected using perspectival systems, trace lines on the picture plane that tend towards convergence at a single point on the plane: this feature is

IMAGE, IMAGE-MAKING, AND IMAGINATION 549

displayed by the lines which depict train tracks in Figure 22.2, for example. Western art since the Renaissance is chock-full of pictures that use "linear perspective"—the system in which the "picture plane" is a genuine plane rather than, say, a curved surface—more or less strictly, and the use of ordinary cameras has generated untold millions of pictures in very strict linear perspective.

Given a projective system, a scene to be projected, and a suitably situated picture plane, the lines of projection that issue from the scene may be viewed as tracing outlines on the picture plane. Those outlines correspond to potential pictures of the scene, pictures featuring outlines that are congruent to those traced on the relevant picture plane. Reversing all that, patterns of outlines within pictures may be viewed as corresponding to potential picture planes resulting from projections of potential scenes, using a given projective system.[14]

The different projective systems just outlined are capable of producing distinctively visual images featuring certain characteristic stylistic traits, ones that arise from interactions between the visual properties of the images themselves and the nature of what they represent. As noted previously, for instance, pictures in linear projection use converging lines to represent parallel edges that recede in the depicted scene, while pictures in oblique projection use parallel diagonal lines for the same purpose. But the different ways in which the pictures are produced also mean that they amount to imagistic explorations of radically different modes of spatially perspectival representation, as we will now see.

6 Space

Strict uses of linear perspective result in pictures that, in line with snapshot-like mental visual images, show what things look like from a single location.

---

14 Kulvicki uses this correspondence to develop an account of the fundamental contents of pictures in linear perspective that is rather different to the more general view of visual images being developed here: he identifies their contents with the class of all of those possible scenes whose projections to a point, going via a picture plane, would trace on the plane the outlines involved in the relevant picture. This implies, to my mind problematically, that the most basic meaning that belongs to, say, Figure 22.2 does not determine that the photo represents a scene that recedes in space rather than a wholly flat surface; because, for any three-dimensional scene that would produce a given picture plane using linear perspective, some two-dimensional scene would also produce the same picture plane using linear perspective. See Chapter three from John Kulvicki, *On Images: Their Structure and Content* (Oxford: Oxford University Press, 2006).

For one of the characteristic features of linear perspective is that the lines that are traced on the picture plane, by the relevant lines of projection, are all orientated towards a single point. The resulting image consequently provides an encapsulation of an arrangement of edges that are visible from a single location that looks out onto the depicted scene. And this is something that we tend to appreciate when we view those pictures, and which leads us to regard them as possessing a spatial "fixedness."

But now consider images that have been created using projective systems in which the lines of projection are parallel to each other and hence do not converge at a single point—Figure 22.3, for example. In these cases, the figures traced on the picture plane by parallel lines of projection that are relatively close to each other will approximate the figures that would have been traced on the picture plane by lines of projection that converged at a suitably situated location. More generally, relatively circumscribed portions of the resulting image are naturally interpreted as showing how things look from one place. While suitably small portions of images like Figure 22.3 are naturally interpreted in that fashion, though, the images as a whole are not naturally interpreted as showing how things look from just one perspective.

Imagine a possible situation that Figure 22.3 might be used to capture, through an employment of oblique projection. Consider the parallel lines of projection that lead out from the nearby edges of items corresponding to what is shown on the far left of Figure 22.3. Contrast them with analogous lines of projection leading out from nearby edges corresponding to what is shown on Figure 22.3's far right.

The figures traced on the picture plane by those pairs of contrasting lines of projection do not approximate the figures that would have been traced on the plane by a bunch of lines of projection converging on a single point looking onto the depicted scene. Rather, the lines leading out from the items shown on the far right of Figure 22.3 approximate those that converge upon a *different* place to the ones leading out from the items shown on the image's far left. And those different places are at a constant distance from, and are similarly orientated towards, those different assemblages of items. Spatially disparate portions of visual images like Figure 22.3 are thus naturally interpreted as showing how things look from different places that bear regular spatial relationships to the items displayed in the images.

Uses of linear perspective lead, then, to visual images that are pinned to one spot, and which are thus similar in certain important respects to the mental visual images that commonly feature in our imaginings. By contrast, uses of orthogonal and oblique projection generate visual images that have the metaphorical mobility noted by Hockney, and which is a phenomenon that does not seem to have a counterpart within the mental realm of snapshot-like

IMAGE, IMAGE-MAKING, AND IMAGINATION   551

mental visual images. For, as our eyes roam over the surfaces of images like Figure 22.3—a process which exploits the status of those visual images as external objects of sight—we are treated to views of the depicted items from a changing series of spatially distinct viewpoints, ones whose spatial relationships mirror aspects of the spatial relationships being traced by our gazes.

Uses of different projective systems may thus yield distinctively visual images whose contents are of strikingly different sorts. In particular, they may result in visual images whose contents explore different sorts of spatially perspectival possibilities. Pictures using strict linear perspective, that are pinned to a single location, are somewhat akin to momentary visual experiences, and to snapshot-like mental visual images. But pictures generated using, say, oblique projection show things as looking numerous different ways from numerous different places, which puts them at a distance from momentary visual experiences and from snapshot-like mental visual images, but which places them nearer to—although, as we will see in the next section, not right alongside—our mobile visual explorations of the world.

7   Time

We saw in the previous section that different methods for producing distinctively visual images may yield distinctively visual images whose contents explore different perspectival possibilities with respect to space. But where does that leave another important perspectival aspect of distinctively visual images—namely, their connections to time?

Reconsider Figure 22.2. We naturally construe that picture as showing how things look from a single place at a single point in time. And this makes sense, given that the image employs linear perspective fairly strictly: the lines in the picture roughly correspond to the figures that would be traced on a picture plane by the lines of projection leading out from points on the edges of the items that are visible within a single scene at a single place and time.

Figure 22.3 is somewhat similar: it displays a single situation at one time. While the items depicted on, say, the far-right of the picture are shown from spatially distinct perspectives to those from which the items depicted on the far-left are shown, those perspectives are nonetheless simultaneous. The "mobility" of Figure 22.3 is consequently rather different to ordinary motion. For the changes in the spatial locations of the perspectives from which we are shown the items in Figure 22.3, and which we uncover over time as we move our eyes across the image occur outside of the time-frame that contains the scene shown in the image itself; it is as if we are able to move around freely in a world that has otherwise stopped.

FIGURE 22.4   Kanō Tsunenobu, *Scenes from the Tale of Genji* (1677) (Isabella Stewart Gardner Museum, Boston)
THIS IMAGE IS LICENSED UNDER A CREATIVE COMMONS ATTRIBUTION BY THE ISABELLA STEWART GARDNER MUSEUM, BOSTON (HTTPS://WWW.GARDNERMUSEUM.ORG/ORGANIZATION/RIGHTS-REPRODUCTIONS)

Figure 22.4 which also uses oblique projection, is a trickier case.

One might be tempted to interpret Figure 22.4 along the pattern established by Figure 22.3; as showing a single scene that is frozen in time, from a series of spatially distinct perspectives. Yet that interpretation of Figure 22.4 is wrong.

Figure 22.4 shows a host of scenes from Murasaki Shikubu's 11th Century novel *The Tale of Genji*, scenes that did not occur at the same time within the novel's narrative. Appropriate spatial shifts in the perspectives from which Figure 22.4 shows the various scenes that it displays consequently also correspond to shifts in the temporal locations of those perspectives. Moreover, the spatial shifts in pictorial viewpoint that result when we focus upon distinct portions of Figure 22.4 that are separated by significant amounts of cloud do not tidily track the required spatial shifts in the focus of our gaze. The scene shown by the far-right portion of Figure 22.4, for instance, is not displayed by the picture from a perspective that is to the right of the one from which Figure 22.4 shows the scene depicted on its far-left. (The bodies of cloud separating the different bits of Figure 22.4 in fact function like the frames that surround individual pictures within a comic strip.)

Different types of still pictures are thus able to realize very different sorts of possibilities for the temporally perspectival aspects of distinctively visual imagery. And, of course, distinctively visual images that evolve over time are capable of realizing further possibilities, by exploiting more or less close relationships between their own temporal properties and the temporal properties that they show things as having.

Passages of film, and of mental visual imagery, may show what things look like from a series of spatially and temporally distinct perspectives, for example.

IMAGE, IMAGE-MAKING, AND IMAGINATION

And, very often, the time occupied by our encounters with the relevant passages of visual imagery corresponds to the temporal period occupied by the scenes that the imagery displays. If I now use some mental visual imagery to imagine a duck waddling along, for instance, the time taken up by the duck's waddling in my imagination corresponds to the actual length of the passage of visual imagery.

But the ways in which visual images are produced can break that correspondence, by feeding into temporal characteristics of the meanings that the images possess. The use of slow-motion in film, for example, produces passages of visual imagery which shows what things look like from a series of temporally-evolving perspectives that occupy a much shorter period than the playback of the film itself occupies. It seems that mental visual images can perform similar tricks, too. I can, on the one hand, use mental visual imagery to imagine a duck waddling along very slowly; but I can also, by employing appropriate intentions alongside my production of mental visual images, use mental visual imagery to imagine a duck waddling at a normal pace, but in slow motion.

8   Subjectivity

Compare Figure 22.2 with Figure 22.5. Like Figure 22.2, Figure 22.5 is a distinctively visual image, although they are stylistically quite different. And those stylistic differences—the sketchy nature of Figure 22.5 versus the detailed, more "realistic" nature of Figure 22.2—line up with differences in the contents of the images.

The way that Figure 22.5 shows as looking is much less specific than the way that Figure 22.2 shows things as looking: parts of Figure 22.5 merely provide us with information concerning aspects of the visible contours belonging to what it depicts, whereas Figure 22.2 supplies us with much more thoroughgoing information about contours, tonal values, and more besides. These sorts of discrepancies are commonly systematically associated with different ways of producing visual images. The ways that high-resolution color digital cameras tend to show things as looking are, in the sorts of respects just indicated, considerably more specific than the ways that linocuts tend to show things as looking, for instance.

We can better understand the precise nature of these differences in imagistic content using some of this essay's earlier ideas. According to the view sketched in Section 3, the ways that distinctively visual images show things as looking amount to types of visual experiences. But one type of visual experiences may be more specific than another, in that the first type permits far less overall variation in its instances than does the second type. Correspondingly,

FIGURE 22.5 *Old man (perhaps Tobit) reading to a seated woman* (17th century)
COPY AFTER REMBRANDT VAN RIJN, © VICTORIA AND ALBERT MUSEUM, LONDON. I ORIGINALLY REPRODUCED THIS IMAGE IN *SHOWING, SENSING, AND SEEMING: DISTINCTIVELY SENSORY REPRESENTATIONS AND THEIR CONTENTS* (2013)

we may understand the differences in specificity between the ways that Figures 22.2 and 22.5 show things as looking in terms of differences in the specificity of appropriate types of visual experiences.

The fact that things look to someone the way that Figure 22.5 shows things as looking tells us nothing about how dark the cat (depicted towards the bottom right) is which she apparently sees, for instance. By contrast, the fact that things look to someone the way that Figure 22.5 shows things as looking tells us a lot more about the tonal contrasts present among the things that he can see. Figure 22.5 is consequently neutral with regards to many tonal facts about the things that it displays, whereas Figure 22.2 is considerably more committal with regard to tonal matters.

These sorts of differences are also present within mental visual imagery. One mental visual image can be much less detailed than another with regards to, say, color information. I can use mental visual imagery to imagine the inside of my office at work, for example, yet the resulting mental visual images provide me with no very detailed information about the color of the carpet there, which I am unable to recall. The images' relative neutrality with regards to the carpet's color reflects the fact that the way that the image shows things as

IMAGE, IMAGE-MAKING, AND IMAGINATION

looking does not settle the precise color of the carpet, in that visual experiences in which things look that way may differ with regards to the color of the carpet that is then apparently visible, at least within certain limits; my office's carpet certainly is not neon green, for instance.

At this point, another idea introduced earlier becomes relevant. We saw in Section 3 that distinctively visual images do not just single out ways for things to look in any old manner. Rather, they identify them in terms of *what is like* to have visual experiences in which things look the relevant ways. (Your understanding of Figure 22.1—the photo of a bike—led to you appreciate what it would be like to encounter that bike in the course of a visual experience of a certain sort, for example.) But this idea allows us to link up the differences in specificity that were just noted with a particularly important "subjective" dimension along which the informativeness of visual images may vary.

Your understanding of Figure 22.5 involves a grasp of the way that the picture shows things as looking, mediated by your appreciation of what it is like for things to look that way to someone. But the way that the picture shows things as looking is pretty unspecific. Your understanding of the picture consequently leads you to appreciate what it would be like to see a scene that has an assemblage of various relatively lightly specified visible features. You are aware that the apparently seen people would have a certain overall look, for example, but there is nothing in your appreciation of what the visual experiences would be like that forces them to involve an encounter with, say, a man whose gown is dark in tone rather than light.

And this contrasts with the outcome of your understanding of Figure 22.2. For, in that case, your awareness of the way that the picture shows things as looking takes you to an appreciation of what it would be like to see a scene featuring a much richer assemblage of more fully specified visible features. You are aware that, if you were to have a visual experience in which things looked as Figure 22.2 shows them as looking, significant areas of the visible scene would feature dark colors, whereas other areas of the scene—the distant buildings on the hillside, say, and the expanses of water on either side—would be much lighter in tone. Your understanding of Figure 22.2 thus carries you to a much more vivid appreciation of what it would be like to have visual experiences in which things look the way that the picture shows them as looking; it is, in this subjective sense, more informative about the ways that it shows things as looking than is Figure 22.5.[15]

---

15   The sorts of differences being considered here are particularly easy to illustrate using contrasts between, for example, very bare prints and drawings—so consider many of Matisse's drawings and prints, for instance, which provide almost no coloristic or tonal information—and images that provide a great deal of coloristic and tonal information, like many modern photographs. Various practical constraints arising from publication in

Different ways of producing distinctively visual images are often engineered to affect these levels of subjective informativeness. The amounts of detail provided by many photographic technologies often provide us with a relatively specific appreciation of what it would be like to have visual experiences in which things look certain ways, for instance—although there the focus is commonly upon aspects of vision that are independent of binocular depth perception, such as color and texture, and which can be captured using flat pictures. Holograms and other methods for producing apparently three-dimensional distinctively visual images, by contrast, supply much more information about those subjective features of ways for things to look that result from the binocular perception of depth.

How do distinctively visual images provide us with an awareness of what it would be like to have visual experiences in which things look the ways that the images show things as looking? There is not obviously a single answer to this question that applies across all possible media—the range of potential strategies that may be employed looks set to mirror the diverse nature of distinctively visual imagery itself.

In some cases, mimicry is surely the key: Figure 22.2 makes us aware of aspects of what it would be like to see a scene that features certain shapes by featuring portions that are themselves suitable shapes. We are then able to move from our consciousness of what the image looks like to an awareness of, say, what the shape of various depicted telegraph poles would be like. Yet distinctively visual images cannot always do their work using mimesis. Our production of mental visual images also features an appreciation of what it is like for things to look certain ways, for example. But it is hard to believe that the jumble of neurons answering to my mental visual image of a rainbow must itself be correspondingly multicolored.

9 Conclusion

Visual images play a central role in our imaginative lives. Many of our imaginings revolve around mental visual images, for example, and different sorts of pictures have the power to lead us to different forms of imaginings. Those who are suitably skilled have the ability to capture visual imaginings in pictorial form, and, by imaginatively exploiting the representational capacities of pictures, they are also able to produce images that significantly shape both what we imagine and how we imagine it as being. This chapter has investigated various general aspects of visual imagery, with a view of arriving at a clear

---

print mean, though, that in the text I have restricted the discussion to the consideration of differences with regards to tonal values.

IMAGE, IMAGE-MAKING, AND IMAGINATION

understanding of its nature and of the ways in which image-makers are able to exploit its distinctive character.

The total field of visual images is bewilderingly diverse and the array of methods for producing them is similarly various. But we can impose a certain amount of order on things by focusing our attentions on some, but not all, visual images. The previous discussion concentrated upon the semantically unified category of distinctively visual images—those images that show things as looking certain ways—a category that encompasses very many pictures, for instance, but also the mental visual images that are so prominent within our imaginative lives. This chapter then investigated some of the ways in which methods for producing distinctively visual images may interact with their distinctively visual meanings.

We have seen that a wide range of possibilities that are latent within the concept of distinctively visual imagery are in fact realized in imagistic form. Distinctively visual images may show things as looking numerous ways from many places, for example, both at one time and at many different times; and they may provide us with more or less information about what it would be like to see the sorts of items that they display. Furthermore, these differences in the natures of the most elementary meanings that the images possess correspond systematically to differences in the ways that the images are produced: our intentions can affect the contents of mental visual images, for instance, and there can be sophisticated interactions between the visible properties of pictures and our most basic interpretations of them.

More generally, one important strand in the development of visual imagery is the creative exploration of diverse semantic possibilities. These developments crucially shape the ways in which visual images are used, and they shape their aesthetic and expressive qualities. The imaginative acts which pictures like Figure 22.2—those that are in strict linear perspective—tend to encourage are somewhat different to the ones that pictures like Figure 22.3—which uses oblique projection—are apt to stimulate, for instance. To investigate these differences further, however, we must develop appropriate tools for studying the fundamental layers of meanings possessed by visual images, just as linguists, logicians, philosophers and others have developed tools for studying the basic semantic properties of language. And this will surely be worthwhile: the crafting of such tools will bring us to a firmer appreciation of the special nature of a singularly valuable means of representation.

References

Abell, Catharine. "Canny Resemblance." *Philosophical Review* 118, no. 2 (2009): 183–223.

Bois, Yve-Alain. *Painting as Model*. Cambridge, MA: MIT Press. 1993.

Budd, Malcolm. "How Pictures Look." In *Virtue and Taste: Essays on Politics, Ethics and Aesthetics*, edited by Dudley Knowles, John Skorupski, and Flint Schier, 154–75. Oxford: Basil Blackwell, 1993.

Gregory, Dominic. "Imagery, the Imagination and Experience." *Philosophical Quarterly* 60, no. 241 (2010): 735–53.

Gregory, Dominic. *Showing, Sensing, and Seeming: Distinctively Sensory Representations and Their Contents*. Oxford: Oxford University Press. 2013.

Hecht, Heiko, Robert Schwartz, and Margaret Atherton, eds. *Looking into Pictures*. Cambridge, MA: MIT Press, 2003.

Hockney, David. *Secret Knowledge (New and Expanded Edition): Rediscovering the Lost Techniques of the Old Masters*. London: Thames and Hudson. 2006.

Hopkins, Robert. *Picture, Image and Experience*. Cambridge: Cambridge University Press. 1998.

Hume, David. *A Treatise of Human Nature*. 2nd ed. Edited by L.A. Selby-Bigge and P.H. Nidditch. Oxford: Clarendon Press, 1978.

Hyman, John. *The Objective Eye: Color, Form and Reality in the Theory of Art*. Chicago: University of Chicago Press. 2006.

Kant, Immanuel. *Critique of Pure Reason*. Translated and edited by Paul Guyer and Allen Wood. Cambridge: Cambridge University Press. 1999.

Kind, Amy, ed. *The Routledge Handbook of Philosophy of Imagination*. London: Routledge 2016.

Knowles, Dudley, John Skorupski, and Flint Schier, eds. *Virtue and Taste: Essays on Politics, Ethics and Aesthetics*. Oxford: Basil Blackwell, 1993.

Kulvicki, John. *On Images: Their Structure and Content*. Oxford: Oxford University Press. 2006.

Lopes, Dominic. *Understanding Pictures*. Oxford: Oxford University Press. 1996.

Peacocke, Christopher. "Imagination, Experience, and Possibility." In *Essays on Berkeley*, edited by John Foster and Howard Robinson, 19–35. Oxford: Clarendon Press, 1985.

Peacocke, Christopher. "Depiction." *Philosophical Review* 96, no. 3 (1987): 383–410.

Willats, John. *Art and Representation: New Principles in the Analysis of Pictures*. Princeton, NJ: Princeton University Press. 1997.

Wöllflin, Heinrich. *Principles of Art History. The Problem of the Development of Style in Later Art*. 7th ed. Translated by MD Hottinger. Mineola, NY: Dover Publications, 1932.

Wollheim, Richard. "In Defense of Seeing-in." In *Looking into Pictures*, edited by Heiko Hecht, Robert Schwartz, and Margaret Atherton, 3–16. Cambridge, MA: MIT Press, 2003.

CHAPTER 23

Depiction, Imagination, and Photography

Jiri Benovsky

§1. Imagination plays an important role in depiction. In this chapter,[1] I discuss the role imagination (as well as inference and knowledge/belief) plays in depiction with a focus on photographic depiction. I partly embrace a broadly Waltonian view, but not always, and not always for Walton's own reasons. I start by emphasizing an important general feature of the relation of depiction, namely the fact that it is a ternary relation which always involves "something external." I then turn my attention to Walton's view, where this third relatum of the relation of depiction is largely analyzed in terms of the role imagination plays in depiction. I consider the objection to his view that not all cases of depiction involve imagination – for instance, documentary photographs. From this discussion, two points will emerge: first, we will see that it is an unnecessary mistake to insist too heavily on the fact that photographs are produced in a mechanical way (as opposed to, say, paintings), and second, we will see that the notion of "imagining-seeing," as it is articulated by Walton, is perhaps too strong and does not entirely do justice to the external character of the role imagination plays here. Focusing mainly on photographs, I then illustrate the view for which I want to advocate by a series of different cases, where the nature of the role that imagination, knowledge/belief, and inference play in depiction will become apparent.

§2. Let us start with some general remarks about depiction. *Prima facie*, depiction seems to be a relation between a picture and what the picture depicts; Dalí's *Temptation Of Saint Anthony*, for instance, depicts four elephants, a horse, and Saint Anthony. But depiction is a ternary relation, not a binary one between a picture and its depictum. Thus, instead of

(i)   P depicts E

we have

(ii)   P depicts E for S

where "P" stands for "Picture" (such as a painting, or a photograph), "E" stands for "Entity" (a macroscopic object, or perhaps a state of affairs, or anything that can plausibly be depicted), and "S" stands for "Subject" (that is, the conscious

---

1   This article is an updated version of Jiri Benovksy, "Depiction and imagination," *Northern European Journal of Philosophy* 17, no. 1 (2016): 61–80.

being who looks at P). One could also speak here about pictorial representation, instead of depiction. Unless one wants to treat these terms as synonyms, I take it that the notion of representation is a larger one than the notion of depiction, and I will discuss this issue in the concluding section of this article; for the time being, I will stick to depiction (as we shall see, the frontier between depiction and a larger notion of representation is a fuzzy and delicate one).

Take Wollheim's account of depiction, where the ternary nature of this relation is obviously apparent: roughly, pictures depict because we see things in them. Thus, in Wollheim's view, the general schema above becomes

(iii)   S sees E in P

Wollheim's notion of depiction is crucially linked to his notion of twofoldness. As he puts it, "What is distinctive of seeing-in, and thus of my theory of representation, is the phenomenology of the experiences in which it manifests itself. Looking at a suitably marked surface, we are visually aware at once of the marked surface and of something in front of or behind something else. I call this feature of the phenomenology 'twofoldness' ... I understand it in terms of a single experience with two aspects, which I call configurational and recognitional."[2] Central in his view is the idea that to understand depiction we need to look at the experience a subject has of a picture. In his view, this experience is to be understood in terms of a union of a perception of the surface of a picture and of what we see in it – the depicted object(s) – thus giving rise to a new form of perception, namely, seeing-in.

I shall come back to this, when I discuss Walton's view, which is in many ways similar to Wollheim's, but for now I only wish to insist on the ternary nature of the relation of depiction. This nature manifests itself, perhaps in a less explicit way, in other accounts of depiction as well. According to the resemblance account of depiction, one could naïvely think that depiction is an intrinsic property of pictures and that pictures depict because they resemble their depicta – in short, P depicts E, because P resembles E. Nobody really defends such a naïve view, and for a good reason: in this binary way of conceiving of the resemblance account, something important is left out, namely the fact that resemblance is a context-dependent matter. This is true in general, and not only when it comes to depiction. Take for instance the resemblance relations between

(A)   a red round object
(B)   a red square object
(C)   a blue square object

---

2   Richard Wollheim, "On Pictorial Representation," *The Journal of Aesthetics and Art Criticism* 56, no. 3 (1998): 221.

DEPICTION, IMAGINATION, AND PHOTOGRAPHY

Does A resemble B more than C? Which pair of objects in the list is the most resembling one? Well, it depends on the context, that is, in what respect one wants to consider the resemblance relations. B resembles more A than C with respect to its color, while it resembles C more than A with respect to its shape. In general, when it comes to resemblance, there is always a context, provided by the evaluator, on which the resemblance relation depends. In the case of depiction, the context is provided by S (in "P depicts E for S"), but it can also be suggested to S by the creator of P, or by the context in which P is being shown. The third relatum of the relation of depiction can thus be enriched in various ways, but the main point I want to emphasize here is that it has to be there – no S, no resemblance, and so, no depiction. This is apparent in Hopkins' resemblance theory of depiction: "The notion of resemblance can yield a characterization of our experience of depiction if we suppose that a depiction of something *is seen as* resembling it. The central problem this immediately poses is to say *in what respect* we see pictures as resembling what they depict."[3]

Other theories of depiction, like for instance Goodman's "symbolic account," also exhibit the ternary nature of the relation of depiction. In Goodman's view, pictures depict in very much the same way words do – they are symbols in representational systems, where representation is a matter of convention.[4] If this is so, the third relatum of the relation of depiction fixes the relevant conventions, in a purely arbitrary way. Thus, here again, S (the convention fixer) is a necessary element in the understanding of the notion of depiction.

One way or another, there is always something "external" in depiction. Depiction is not an intrinsic property of pictures, it is not a relation between a picture and its depicta, it is not a mind-independent affair, and it always essentially involves a subject as a third relatum. The various accounts of depiction available then differ in the analysis they provide of the role S plays.

Kendall Walton insists on the *imaginative* faculties of S. According to his view, pictures depict by being props in games of make-believe. He illustrates this idea by comparison with games children play: in the game, an object, say, a shampoo bottle, can represent another object, say, a pirate ship, when being used in a game in the bathtub. In the fictional world of the game, the bottle represents a ship, not so much because it resembles a ship,[5] but because it was

---

3   Robert Hopkins, "Explaining Depiction," *The Philosophical Review* 104, no. 3 (1995): 439–40, italics added.

4   See Nelson Goodman, *Languages of Art: An Approach to a Theory of Symbols* (Indianapolis: Hackett Publishing, 1968).

5   Although, as Walton rightly remarks, some objects are better props than others. An empty shampoo bottle floats and has a vaguely adequate shape, for instance, and so is a better prop in a game about a pirate ship than, say, a paper envelope. The object's intrinsic properties, and some type of resemblance between it and what it is a prop for, are then not to

decided, in a controlled and imaginary way, that it does represent it. Speaking of depiction in the case of pictures, Walton adopts a notion similar to Wollheim's notion of seeing-in, and he also argues that it gives rise to a single new type of experience made of two elements: perception and imagination, mixed together in a phenomenologically complex whole.[6] An important thing to note here is that Walton considers this to be a perceptual affair. Imagination, in his view, permeates the perception of the picture, and this is how we *see* Dali's painting (the marked surface) *and* at the same time we *see in* the painting four elephants, a horse, and Saint Anthony. Thus, the two actions – to perceive and to imagine – become part of a single experience of "imagining-seeing." Paintings, thus, play the role of props that prescribe specific imaginings.[7] Consequently, these specific imagining-seeings give rise to fictional truths, not in the sense of a new type of truth, but in the simple sense that it is fictional that, in such-and-such a game of make-believe, it is part of the game that we see four elephants with long spindly legs.[8]

Noël Carroll,[9] Jerrold Levinson,[10] as well as others, raised an objection to Walton's view on the grounds that it appeals to imagination too much, and too often. The general concern is that Walton claims that, in all cases of depiction, we play games of make-believe, by appealing to our imagination, thus effectively making every such case part of a fiction. This seems then to imply that there are no non-fictional visual representations. Carroll objects by raising the counter-example of documentary photographs, such as, for instance, aerial photographs used in cartography: there is nothing fictional here, no games of make-believe, and no imagination needed for such pictures to depict what they do.

Earlier in "On the Nature of Photographic Realism," Walton claims that "there is a sharp break, a difference of kind, between painting and photography,"[11] and perhaps this could be the key to answer the objection. Indeed, contrary to paintings, in Walton's view, photographs are

---

    be ignored (Kendall Walton, *Mimesis as Make-Believe: On the Foundations of the Representational Arts* (Cambridge, MA: Harvard University Press, 1990): 302).

6   See Walton, *Mimesis as Make-Believe*, 295.

7   See Walton, *Mimesis as Make-Believe*, 21–23; 38.

8   Walton, *Mimesis as Make-Believe*, 41–42.

9   Noël. Carroll, "Critical study: Mimesis as make-believe," *The Philosophical Quarterly* 45, no. 178 (1995): 97–98.

10   *Jerrold Levinson*, "Wollheim on Pictorial Representation," *The Journal of Aesthetics and Art Criticism* 56, no. 3 (1998): 277.

11   Kendall Walton, "On the Nature of Photographic Realism," *Critical Inquiry* 11, no. 2 (1984): 246–77.

DEPICTION, IMAGINATION, AND PHOTOGRAPHY

> (MEC) produced in a mechanic way
> and
> (TRANS) transparent

What Walton means here is that photographs are produced in a purely mechanical way and that because of this they are like aids to vision – prosthetic devices, akin to surveillance cameras, televisions, mirrors, or telescopes – that help us to *see*, literally, through them.[12] As he sums it up: "Putting things together, we get this: part of what it is to see something is to have visual experiences which are caused by it in a purely mechanical manner. Objects cause their photographs and the visual experiences of viewers mechanically; so we see the objects through the photographs. By contrast, objects cause paintings not mechanically but in a more "human" way, a way involving the artist; so we don't see through paintings."[13] Thus, in Walton's view, (TRANS) *because* (MEC). In order to secure (TRANS), Walton then goes quite far when he articulates (MEC): he claims that photographs are produced in a *purely* mechanical manner, apparently setting aside, in this place, the role the photographer plays in the creation of photographs. I shall come back to this below; let us first see if this could be used to answer the objection above. What Walton claims is that photographs are transparent (this accounts for the difference between photographs and paintings, and so this could help to challenge Carroll's counterexample), but that they *also* are depictions that give rise to imagining seeing (this allows him to keep his general theory of depiction).[14] When looking at a photograph of a long deceased member of a family, we can thus both literally

---

12   For a detailed exposition and discussion, see Costello and Phillips (2009).

13   Walton, "On the Nature of Photographic Realism," 261. See also page 254 from this same article in which Walton affirms, "Painting and drawing are techniques for producing pictures. So is photography. But the special nature of photography will remain obscure unless we think of it in another way as well-as a contribution to the enterprise of seeing. The invention of the camera gave us not just a new method of making pictures and not just pictures of a new kind: it gave us a new way of seeing ... Mirrors are aids to vision, allowing us to see things in circumstances in which we would not otherwise be able to; with their help we can see around corners. Telescopes and microscopes extend our visual powers in other ways, enabling us to see things that are too far away or too small to be seen with the naked eye. Photography is an aid to vision also, and an especially versatile one. With the assistance of the camera, we can see not only around corners and what is distant or small; we can also see into the past ... Photographs are transparent. We see the world through them." Moreover, see page 252 from this same text in which Walton maintains, "My claim is that we see, quite literally, our dead relatives themselves when we look at photographs of them."

14   See Kendall Walton, "On Pictures and Photographs: Objections Answered," in *Film Theory and Philosophy*, eds. Richard Allen and Murray Smith (Oxford: Clarendon Press, 1997), 68.

see her (this is (TRANS)), *and* at the same time *imagine seeing* her (directly, without a prosthetic device, namely, the photograph). Photography is thus special in the sense that it involves these two aspects, while paintings are not transparent (since they are not produced in a mechanical way).

Unfortunately, such a Walton-inspired reply to the objection would not work. The objection was not concerned with whether photographs and paintings are pictures of the same kind or not, and the objector can happily agree that they aren't. Rather, the objection raised the worry that in all cases of depiction, imagination is in Walton's view essentially involved, which makes it impossible for there to be non-fictional visual representations – and this is where documentary photographs can be used as counter-examples, not because they are photographs, but because they are documentary, and, according to the objector, because their depictive capacities do not depend on any type of imagination or game of make-believe. Walton's view then actually seems to embrace the spirit of the objection, since Walton explicitly claims, and insists on, that photographs, including documentary photographs, *are* depictions and *do* serve as props in games of make-believe, exactly as paintings do – it's just that, in addition to their depictive capacities, they are transparent. Thus, instead of a sharp break and a difference of kind, what we have here is a situation where paintings and photographs are both essentially depictions and depict in the same manner, it's just that photographs have a further capacity (transparency) that paintings do not possess.

§3. In my view, Walton got many things right. He is right to insist on the role imagination plays in depiction, and he is right to say that photographs are transparent while paintings are not. In what follows I will defend a broadly Waltonian view, but not really for Walton's own reasons, and I will depart from some of his claims, which in my view are not correct and not needed.

Before I spend some time on the relationship between depiction and imagination, let me more quickly address the issue of (TRANS) and (MEC). I agree that photographs are transparent, but not that they are produced in a purely mechanical way. This latter claim is too strong, as we shall see shortly, *and* it is not necessary to establish the fact that they are transparent. We can accept that since photographs are produced in a *partly* mechanical way, they can play the role of "aids to vision" or "prosthetic devices" that allow us to see, literally, the objects they are photographs of. One way to see the relevant difference between photographs and paintings is to acknowledge that a photograph is always a photograph of *something existing* (however blurred or distorted it can appear to be), while this is not so in the case of paintings. *This* metaphysical claim is what transparency is about, and this is due to the *partly* mechanical way photographs are produced. Nothing stronger is needed.

The process of production of photographs is, granted, partly mechanical, but it also *necessarily* involves a photographer's decisions (as we shall see, this will be important when it comes to understand the role of imagination in photographic depiction, so the point here is not only a point about transparency). Taking a photograph is like playing a musical instrument. When a pianist plays the piano, the resulting music is partly mechanically produced by the instrument, but crucially and essentially it is the product of how the pianist used this instrument – no musician, no music. In the case of photography, things are similar. At various stages of the process of production of photographs, the photographer *has* to intervene and *has* to take decisions. For instance, it is simply *impossible* to take a photograph without a decision about aperture and shutter speed – the two most basic settings on any photographic camera. This decision will have a profound effect on what the resulting photograph will look like, as for instance Photo 1 and Photo 2 in §5 below illustrate. Consider a claim such as Scruton's: "...with an ideal photograph, it is *neither necessary nor even possible* that the photographer's intention should enter as a serious factor in determining how the picture is seen ... The causal process of which the photographer is a victim puts almost every detail *outside of his control*."[15] Scruton's claim is about *ideal* photographs. It is not entirely clear how "ideal" is helpful here, but what is clear is that such a claim about any *normal* photograph is unnecessarily strong and strictly speaking false.[16] It is right to insist on the partly causal and mechanical nature of the process of production of photographs, but very strong claims like Scruton's do not do justice to the *necessity* of the involvement of a conscious being in this process. No aperture setting, no photograph. No shutter speed setting, no photograph. (This also rings true for other stages of the process of production of photographs where decisions have to be made about, for instance, focal length or exposure.) Granted, one can use an automated photographic camera, where one does not make such decisions oneself before every shot, but that does not mean that the decision was not taken, it only means that it was taken by somebody else (perhaps, the engineers who programmed the automated camera). Documentary photographs such as aerial photographs used in cartography – an example Carroll had in mind – are good examples of this: in such cases these decisions *are* automated, but since they are very important, the decisions about aperture, shutter speed, exposure, and focal length are very carefully made and the programming carefully done, before the shooting.

---

15   Roger Scruton, "Photography and Representation," *Critical Inquiry* 7, no. 3 (1981): 588, 593; italics added.

16   For a detailed critical discussion of Scruton's view, see Phillips (2009).

Furthermore, in most cases of contemporary photography, *digital manipulation* is also an essential and necessary feature of the process of production of digital photographs – very much in the same sense in which chemical manipulation is essential and necessary to traditional film photography. Rejecting these claims would lead one to an implausibly strong conception of photography, where virtually nothing would count as a photograph. Scruton seems to make such a strong claim when he says that "actual photography is the result of the attempt to pollute the ideal of [the photographer's] craft with the aims and methods of painting."[17] As far as I understand his claim, Scruton means to say that we have a notion of what an ideal photograph would/should be (namely, an image created in a purely mechanical and causally closed manner, where no chemical or digital or other human manipulation would play any part), but that actual photography does not fit this standard. Consequently, actual photographs are not really photographs. Perhaps it is a terminological issue to decide whether actual photographs can be properly called photographs or not, but perhaps it is an issue concerning the very plausibility and relevance of Scruton's claim – indeed, when talking about "ideal" photographs, he just seems to be talking about something entirely different than what most of us take to be photographs. For myself, I have to say I am interested in actual photographs, and not in some non-existent (in fact, impossible, as we shall now see) ideal type of images. Photographs as we know them are definitely not "ideal" in Scruton's sense (on *this* point, of course, Scruton is right). Let us focus on the case of digital photography. First, light goes through a lens and hits a sensor; this gives rise to a RAW file which is a recording of the way photons hit the photodetectors constituting the sensor's surface. The RAW file is not yet a photograph – it needs to be interpreted/converted in order to become an image, that is, an image we can see anything on (or in). In the case of an automatic point-and-shoot digital camera, this step is usually done by a piece of software built-in the camera which has been programmed in a certain way in order to convert the RAW file into an image file that can then be printed or viewed on a computer monitor. In the case of more sophisticated cameras (typically, DSLRs), this automatic treatment of RAW files can be deactivated and can be postponed – one can copy the RAW file on a computer and only then manually convert the RAW file into an image file. Once we keep in mind the way digital photographs are produced, it then becomes simply obvious that digital manipulation is an unavoidable, necessary, and essential step in their process of production. Without digital manipulation, there would simply

---

17   Scruton, "Photography and Representation," 578.

be no photographs. Photons hitting the camera's sensor produce electrical inputs, which have to be "tampered with" in order to produce any picture at all. An important point to note here is that these digital manipulation steps are not purely mechanical and purely causal conversions of electrical inputs into image files; rather, they are steps *where decisions have to be taken* – at the very least, these include decisions about exposure, brightness, contrast, and white balance. As we have seen, these decisions can either be taken by the photographer who manually works on her RAW files, or they can be automatized, which means that they are taken not by the photographer herself but by the team of engineers who programmed the camera's built-in software. But one way or another, we easily see here that the steps that lead to a creation of a digital photograph include, as a matter of necessity, digital manipulation where decisions have to be taken. This is of course not the end of the story, but at least a rough version of the claim I want to take on board is established: in principle, not only digitally manipulated pictures count as photographs, but digital manipulation is in fact a necessary step in the process of production of digital photographs.

This situation is entirely similar to the case of traditional film photography, where some of the steps in the process of production include necessary chemical and other manipulation (when using a developer, a stop bath, a fixer, and an enlarger), and where human intervention is as essential as it is in the case of digital photography (decisions are taken about exposure, brightness, contrast, color, and other things in a way which is technologically different from digital photography but in principle very similar).

In summary, the process of production of a photograph involves (in all normal cases) one mechanical part and two parts where the photographer's decisions are crucial. First, the photographer plays a crucial role in creating the conditions in which a mechanical process can then take place. The photographer decides when and where the photographs shall be taken, and she makes decisions about settings such as aperture or shutter speed. Then, a purely mechanical causal chain takes place, in which – granted – the photographer plays no significant role (apart from the fact that, often but not necessarily, she is holding the camera). But this is not yet the end of the process of the creation of a photograph. After this stage, there merely exists an exposed film or a RAW file, but not yet a photograph. For a photograph to come into existence, the film must be developed, or the RAW file must be converted into an image file, etc. At this stage, again, the photographer's decisions matter, and are necessary ingredients of the whole process. Only after this third stage has taken place does a photograph exist (Thus, if a camera falls on the floor and accidentally "takes a picture," this is not enough for a photograph to come into existence – the film (or file) needs to be developed in order to create a photograph, so at least this part of the process will not be accidental and will involve decisions).

In short, without the first and the third steps, where the photographer's involvement is essential, no photograph would come into being (in normal cases). Furthermore, these two steps are *what makes photography interesting*. The purely mechanical part of the process is of interest only to engineers and hardware geeks, but the first and third stages are what matters to artists, or even amateur photographers (remember the comparison with the pianist). The decisions involved in the first and third stages are not only necessary – again, there is no way to take a photograph without setting up an aperture, a shutter speed, or a focal length – but they also are expressive tools that the artist photographer can use to achieve such and such an effect on the resulting picture. This is how the photographer can, similarly to the musician, play her instrument. And relevantly, this is how she can trigger the spectator's imaginative capacities. So, let us turn now our attention to how exactly imagination plays a role in photographic depiction.

§4. In Walton's view, imagining-seeing is a single perceptual act, where the seeing part and the imagining part are united together in a single phenomenological whole: "One does not first perceive Hobbema's picture and then, in a separate act, imagine that perception to be of a mill. The phenomenal character of the perception is inseparable from the imagining which takes it as an object ... Imaginings also, like thoughts of other kinds, enter into visual experiences. And the imaginings called for when one looks at a picture inform the experience of looking at it. The seeing and the imagining are inseparably bound together, integrated into a single complex phenomenological whole."[18]

I believe that Walton is on the right track here, but parts of what he says are unnecessarily strong – namely that "the seeing and the imagining are *inseparably* bound together." The first thing to remember from Wollheim, which is something Walton himself agrees on, is that we have the capacity of going back and forth between the experience of a picture as a picture, and the experience of seeing in the picture what we see in it. But if this is true, and it is, it then means that we are capable, at least partly, to switch on and off the imaginative capacities that allow us to see in the picture in addition to merely see it. Most often, imagining and seeing are indeed found in our experience bound together, but not inseparably. It is possible, both phenomenologically and

---

18   Walton, *Mimesis as Make-Believe,* 295. This echoes Kant's claim that "imagination is a necessary ingredient of perception" (*Critique of Pure Reason,* Trans. Paul Guyer and Allen Wood (Cambridge and New York: Cambridge University Press, 1997), A120.

conceptually, to isolate the element of imagination. According to Walton himself, imagination plays the role it plays in games of make-believe where pictures are used as props in a controlled way where the props often prescribe specific, controlled, imaginings. If this is so, then the idea that imagination is separable, phenomenologically and conceptually, actually turns out to be quite naturally integrated into Walton's view.

Remember that depiction is a ternary relation. S, the third relatum, appeals abundantly to her imagination in order to imagine-seeing something in the pictures that she sees. We can isolate the element of imagination, and try to better understand it, while acknowledging that it is often bound with perception. In what follows, I want to isolate imagination, as well as inference and knowledge/belief, from "mere perception," and discuss, on the basis of some examples, the role it plays in depiction, focusing on photographic depiction.

§5. One could think that photographs fail to depict color when they are black and white, that they misrepresent shape when they are distorted, that they fail to depict what lies in the background when the depth of field is shallow, or that they fail to depict features beyond the frame. In what follows, we will see some examples that will enable us to see that, given the essential role the photographer's intentions play in the creation of photographs, given the tools photographers have at their disposal, and given the central role of imagination, knowledge/belief, and inference in the viewing of a photograph, photographs can depict much more than what one might initially think. Indeed, as we shall see, photographs are essentially narrative imagination-triggering media. As I already mentioned several times above, when speaking about imagination, one should also have in mind other faculties of the spectator of a photograph such as her inferential capacities, as well as her knowledge or beliefs. This is how photographs can get narrative powers. To see this, let us start by having a close look at these two photographs of a woman in a street:

These are two photographs of the same reality, but they tell an entirely different story. Of course, the "reality" is not *exactly* the same, since they were taken shortly one after the other, and the people in the background moved, the bus moved, and the woman moved a bit as well (although she was posing, since these photographs are staged). But these factors are irrelevant to the idea I want to convey here. In short, the idea is that the reality a photograph is a photograph of is one thing, and the story it tells is another – very different – one. Photo 1 tells a story about the woman: she is the center of interest, her vaguely sad/worried look is among the core elements of the content of the photograph, and the fact that the other people shown in this photograph are blurred, while she is not, makes her both special and somewhat lonely and detached from the other people around her. Photo 2, taken just a very short

FIGURE 23.1 A woman in the street I
PHOTOGRAPH BY JIRI BENOVKSY

FIGURE 23.2 A woman in the street II
PHOTOGRAPH BY JIRI BENOVKSY

time after Photo 1, of the same street and the same woman at the same place, and with the same framing, tells an entirely different story. The woman is unrecognizable, her expression is impossible to see. The other people and the bus play the crucial role, their movements are depicted[19] by showing their trajectories, and the story this photograph tells is perhaps one of a busy city and its continuous movements, where people do not stand out but are rather somewhat anonymously part of a crowd (of course, *your* imagination might provide a different story, you might also perhaps want to focus on the sitting woman who is not moving in Photo 2, etc.).

To understand how these stories are told, and how imagination is triggered here, we can now introduce the notion of *attention management*, which is easy to grasp by raising the question: "Where will the spectator of the photograph look first when she sees it?" In the case of Photo 1, there is no doubt that the spectator of the image will first look at the woman, while in the case of Photo 2 it will perhaps not be her but rather in quick succession all the moving people and the bus. This is at least part of the reason why the woman will be perceived as the most important element in Photo 1, while in Photo 2 it is the behavior/ movement of all the elements in the picture that will be perceived as being its main content.

As Carroll[20] shows, when it comes to *cinematographic* narration, the motion picture maker uses attention management techniques to guide and control the spectator's attention, by exploiting her natural perceptual capacities and tendencies, in order to "force" her to perceive the reality that a movie depicts in a way the director wants her to see it. As Carroll rightly says, the motion picture maker has several tools at her disposal to achieve this aim: typically, she decides the *order* in which one sees things, she decides for how long one sees this-and-this element of the movie, she decides at what relative size (scale) one sees the various elements, etc. When it comes to photographs, the basic idea is roughly the same, while the techniques are of course different. In the case of Photo 1, the photographer guides and controls the attention of the spectator of the image very easily and precisely: again, there is no doubt that anyone who looks at this photograph will first notice the woman as being its central element, and only then examine the remaining elements of the reality being shown in the photograph, immediately understanding that the photographer wanted to show them as being secondary. Here, the photographer exploits our

---

19   On depiction of movement in this way, see Jiri Benovksy, "Photographic Representation and Depiction of Temporal Extension," *Inquiry* 55, no. 2 (2012): 194–213.

20   See Chapter five from Noël Carroll, *The Philosophy of Motion Pictures* (Malden, MA: Blackwell Publishing, 2008).

natural perceptual tendency to first visually focus on what is sharp and only then pay attention to what is blurred (probably simply because what is sharp is bearing more information than what is blurred – in evolutionary terms, one might think that paying attention to what is sharp provides more information and thus more tools useful to survival than what is blurred/dark/etc.). The picture maker – as well as the motion picture maker – can here actually *force* the attention of the spectator of the image to focus on the woman: it would in fact be impossible, for any normal spectator in normal conditions, *not* to notice the woman and take her to be the central element of the picture (our natural perceptual tendencies are not easy to overcome!). The photographic techniques used here are the most standard ones: indeed, the only difference between how these two photographs were made is that Photo 1 has been taken using a wide aperture and a short shutter speed, while Photo 2 was taken using a small aperture and long shutter speed (framing, exposition, and all other settings were the same). As is clearly apparent here, making a decision about what aperture and what shutter speed one uses when taking a photograph results then in an entirely different picture – and, an entirely different story – *and*, an entirely different content.

Indeed, by using attention management techniques, to tell us what is important and what is secondary, the photographer can tell a story and trigger the imagination of the spectator of a photograph in different ways. In the example of Photo 1, we have seen a typical case of a photograph with a shallow depth of field (due to the wide aperture used) to illustrate how attention management works, but of course there are many other tools the photographer has at her disposal. The choice of a long exposure time, for instance, in the case of Photo 2, makes salient the movement of the moving elements in the picture, forcing thus the attention of the spectator of the image to attend to their movements in a way she would not, were the photograph taken with a short exposure time. The choice of exposure of the main subject relative to its environment or to the other elements in the picture – making the main subject lighter or darker than the secondary elements – can also play a similar role, as can of course the choice of size/scale/magnification of the main subject relative to its surroundings. These (and other) photographic techniques can thus make some of the depicted elements more salient or more perceptually important than others, and the photographer can in this way guide the attention of the spectator of the image to them (or their behavior – say, movement), thus being able to tell a story, using here the imaginative faculties of the spectator. Indeed, imagination plays a crucial role in the viewing of photographs like Photo 1 and Photo 2. We saw above how the photographer can control and guide the attention of the spectator of her photograph, and quite obviously, while doing so, she also appeals to the spectator's imaginative faculties. S, the third element of the

DEPICTION, IMAGINATION, AND PHOTOGRAPHY

ternary relation of depiction, is thus to be understood as a being whose imagination is triggered by the photograph – and the photographer's intentions.

Long exposure photographs, like Photo 2, are a good example of how this works, not only when it comes to imagination. In the making of Photo 2, a long exposure time was used in order to show the trajectories of some of the people and the bus. These trajectories are shown on the photograph, but a bit of imagination, inference, as well as knowledge and previous experience with long exposure photographs, are needed to get the idea of people moving. Typical examples of long exposure photographs, perhaps even more telling, include photographs of a moving car at night: what can be seen on the resulting photograph is only a line of light, due to the car's headlights, but not the car itself at all. The photograph clearly shows a trace, a light line, a trajectory of light. But to understand such a photograph as being a photograph of, say, a car going dangerously fast in the night on a mountain road, one needs of course to appeal to imagination, but also to inference and knowledge: previous knowledge (or inferred knowledge) of this type of pictures and this kind of effect of long exposure time seems required, and someone with poor imagination and no such knowledge might entirely misunderstand the story such a photograph tells. The photographer's job is to guide the attention of her spectators to what she wants to show them, and then to appeal to their imaginative and inferential faculties in such a way that the photograph will be understood.

Multiple exposure techniques also illustrate well how this works. For instance, this multiple exposure photograph depicts five non-contiguous temporal parts of the skier, which creates an appeal to the spectator's imagination to "fill in the gaps" and imagine the movement of the skier, with all its intermediate parts (and, perhaps, the future parts as well):

Such techniques can also be used to create photographs with almost a cinematographic effect where a more-or-less complex story can be almost explicitly told, leaving it then to imagination to fill in the details of the story, such as on this photograph:

Of course, both Photo 3 and Photo 4 have been retouched and the multiple-exposure technique used here is one realized in post-production. But this does not make these pictures to be non-photographic – they are photographs as much as Photo 1 and Photo 2. Indeed, *all* photographs have to be in *some* ways retouched, whether in the camera in a transparent manner where the camera was programmed to do some retouching (colors, white balance, contrast, sharpening, ...) in a way inconspicuous to the user, or outside the camera's body in the darkroom when developing negatives, or in Photoshop when developing RAW files. Whether such techniques are built-in the camera's body (where they can be both automated and/or manually controlled), or whether they are done (again, automatically or manually) outside the body, they are

FIGURE 23.3   Multiple-exposure photograph
PHOTOGRAPH BY JIRI BENOVKSY

FIGURE 23.4   Multiple-exposure photograph
PHOTOGRAPH BY JIRI BENOVSKY

necessary steps in the creation of any photograph: a photograph only ever exists at the very end of this process of production, which necessarily includes such techniques. Furthermore, deciding *which* post-production techniques count as being part of a normal process of creation of photographs and which are "too much" is a matter of degree, a vague matter best resolved by accepting that most post-production techniques are indeed perfectly "normal."[21]

§6. Imagination, knowledge, and inference also play an important role in the depiction of color by black and white photographs. Let us consider this example:

Suppose one asks: "What color is the phone booth? What color is the bus?" The answer is not difficult to give, and it is more than likely that almost everyone will say that they are red. An easy answer, but a process involving not only imagination, but also knowledge, belief, and inference (thus, the notion of imagination involved here can both be propositional imagination, i.e. imagination-that, and perceptual imagination, i.e. imagination penetrating the very perception of, say, the phone booth which can almost look red to the spectator of this black and white image). The spectator of the photograph has to appeal to some pieces of knowledge and make a simple inference. She has to recognize that the place is London (perhaps by noticing the Elizabeth Tower), she has to know that buses and phone booths in London are red, and she has to infer from that the color of the phone booth and the bus. The photographer can (and often does) count on and exploit such knowledge the typical spectator of such photographs will have (of course, she might not, if she's never seen a London bus). Here is a place where depiction works better in the case of photography than in the case of painting. Indeed, spectators of photographs know that these are pictures of a special kind – as we have seen above, they are always pictures *of something existing*. Granted, photographs do not typically depict reality *as it is* (they only depict things from one side, they can involve distortions, blurred background, etc.), but they always at least partly depict something *that was there*, even if they perhaps misdepict it – this is the basis for (TRANS). This then triggers imagination of the spectators of photographs in a particular way: it suggests the viewer to bring into her mind what the reality is probably like, comparing the photograph to her own knowledge of the world. This *can* also be the case in the case of a painting, and it often is, but not always and not in the same way as in the case of photographs. In the case of photographs viewers have, so to say, a piece of knowledge (i.e. "There was something

---

21   For a more comprehensive discussion related to this point, see especially Section four from Jiri Benovsky, "The limits of photography," *International Journal of Philosophical Studies* 22, no. 5 (2014): 716–33.

FIGURE 23.5   Representation of color by a black and white photograph
THIS IMAGE FIRST APPEARED IN BENOVKSY, "DEPICTION AND IMAGINATION"

there, in the world, at the time this photograph was taken") which they do not have – at least not in principle – in the case of paintings, and this piece of knowledge makes them interact with photographs in a special way, namely by mentally comparing the picture with what they know the world looks like. Again, imagination, knowledge, and inference work together, and can be appealed to, triggered, and exploited by the photographer.

§7. As a final case, let us now see how photographs can depict things located beyond the frame. Of course, a photograph of a mirror or of a television set, for instance, can show us something which lies beyond the frame, but since the mirror or the television set are part of what is included in the frame, this is not really a case of depiction of something that genuinely lies beyond. An illustrative example of genuine depiction of something that lies beyond the frame is this photograph of a juggler:

The photograph depicts three clubs, manipulated by the juggler, and a very tiny part of what can only be a fourth club – this interpretation of what the little white square-shaped region on the top of the photograph is, is also confirmed by the juggler's look, directed towards it. The photograph thus depicts a little white square-shaped bit of a club, but it easily also depicts the whole

FIGURE 23.6 The juggler
THIS IMAGE FIRST APPEARED IN BENOVKSY, "DEPICTION AND IMAGINATION"

club – and, perhaps, more clubs as well. (In fact, there were five.) This is depiction of an object *via* depiction of one of its parts, and it is commonplace in many, if not almost all, photographs. Again, the spectator's imaginative and inferential capacities "fill in" the missing parts. Perhaps less common, and less obvious, but still a clear case of depiction of what lies beyond the frame would be a case where the framing of the photograph would cut out even the little part of the club – so, no part of it would be depicted at all, but the juggler's look would probably be enough to trigger the imagination of the spectators of the photograph in such a way that they would understand that there are more than three clubs.

The piece of knowledge, special to photography, that "there was something in the world when the picture was taken" plays a crucial role again here in the triggering of our imagination when we look at this photograph: because it makes us think not only about the picture but also about the world there was when the picture was taken, it makes our imagination run. The role imagination plays here is similar to the role it plays in ordinary perception of non-visible parts of objects we ordinarily see – an idea found in Husserl (1907), and recently expressed in Nanay: "When we see an object, we also represent those parts of it that are not visible ... We represent the occluded parts of perceived objects by means of mental imagery ... The exercise of mental imagery is necessary for amodal perception: for the representation of those parts of the perceived objects that are not visible."[22]

§8. One can multiply examples such as those I have discussed above at will (including, for instance, cases of hardly depicted objects in a very blurred background, where context can help to understand ("guess") what they are). These cases are not exceptional and there is nothing special about them: they exhibit typical, standard, and normal cases of photographs produced by normal photographic means. They show us that narrative powers lie at the core of the nature of photography and photographic depiction, and that imagination (as well as knowledge, belief, and inference) is essential in the viewing of photographs. What is clearly apparent here is that (MEC) is unnecessarily strong. The photographers' intentions play a *central* and *necessary* role in the making of photographs and in what they depict. Think again of Photo 1 and Photo 2 of the woman in the street. The photographer chooses either to use a wide aperture and short exposure time, or a small aperture and long exposure time, and the result is profoundly different – what the resulting photographs depict is entirely different. Not only are these decisions that the photographer makes part of any normal process of creating a photograph, but as we have seen they are steps the photographer *has* to take in order to be able to take any photograph (deciding to use an automated system is also an important decision). Unless someone makes a decision about aperture and shutter speed, there simply is no photograph at all in the first place. And, more often than not, photographers – especially artists – carefully take such decisions themselves, work on the narrative powers of their photographs in many ways, and exploit not only natural perceptual tendencies of the spectators of their photographs, as we have seen above, but also, and crucially, they appeal to their imagination, knowledge, and inferential capacities. To continue the comparison with music, we can see here that thinking of photography – especially art photography – as a purely mechanical affair, where human intervention plays little or no part is a bit like saying that music produced by a piano is purely mechanically produced. Yes, of course, a key was hit, and a hammer then hit a string, and this

---

22   Bence Nanay, "Perception and Imagination: Amodal Perception as Mental Imagery," *Philosophical Studies* 150, no. 2 (2010): 239–40.

DEPICTION, IMAGINATION, AND PHOTOGRAPHY

produced a sound in a purely mechanical way, and yes, the pianist plays no part in this mechanical process, but *what's interesting* in the music, even when produced by such a mechanical instrument, essentially involves the pianist's beliefs, intentions, and interpretation. Likewise, the photographer – especially the artist – "plays the camera" in a very similar way: the camera is her – mechanical – instrument that she can use in order to produce images according to her intentions and the way she wants to show us the world.

§9. In the preceding sections, I set aside on purpose a possible distinction between depiction and representation. Of course, as mentioned in §2, one can use "depiction" and "pictorial representation" as synonyms, and in this case, there is no distinction to be made. But it is useful to make one, as for instance Peacocke and Hopkins both show:

> We can draw a distinction between what a picture depicts and what it represents. There is a Saul Steinberg cartoon depicting persons wearing numerical labels. The viewer is intended to appreciate that these persons represent the streets and avenues of Manhattan: one person, labelled "Bway," is roughly dressed and knocks some of the more staid individuals sideways as he rushes diagonally to City Hall. This cartoon depicts people dressed in various ways, and the people in turn represent particular streets in Manhattan; but the cartoon does not depict streets and avenues.[23]

How do pictures represent? No doubt they do so in many ways. If a painting shows a seated woman, if she symbolizes Despair, and if the work expresses melancholy, we should not assume that the representational relations here are all the same. Nonetheless, perhaps one form of representation is especially pictorial. Perhaps, in other words, there is a form of representation that is distinctively exhibited by pictures and that it is distinctive of pictures to exhibit. It seems more likely that our painting exhibits this distinctive form in representing a seated woman than in representing Despair.[24]

If one has in mind a resemblance-style account of depiction, it is then more than natural to make a distinction about what a picture strictly speaking depicts and what it represents, where it can clearly represent much more than what it depicts. For Hopkins, for instance, the distinction makes perfect sense, and in his view depiction is a genuinely pictorial affair, while representation is

---

23   Christopher Peacocke, "Depiction," *Philosophical Review* 96, no. 3 (1987): 383.

24   Robert Hopkins, "Explaining Depiction," *The Philosophical Review* 104, no. 3 (1995): 425.

a larger notion that pictures can share with other representative means (like linguistic descriptions, for instance).

But if one embraces an account according to which depiction is to be understood in terms of imagination, the frontier between depiction and representation gets much less clear-cut – and perhaps it even fades away. Take Hopkins' example from the quote above. Under a Walton-style account of depiction, the question about what it depicts – the seated woman, Despair, or melancholy – is a question about how much (and how) imagination is used. Imagination can get us much further than resemblance, and if imagination is the crux of depiction, then pictures can depict much more here than under a resemblance account of depiction. In the preceding sections, I argued for and illustrated the claim that depiction is rooted in imagination, and in some of these cases I have gone quite far in the claims about what the photographs used in my examples depict. Thus, in my view, there is a vague distinction to be made between depiction and representation, but it is only a matter of degree, not of a kind. We can talk about representation to signify that *a lot* of imagination was used in experiencing a picture, and talk about depiction when we want to stick to a "first level experience" – for instance, to say that Photo 1 depicts a woman in the street, or to say that Photo 6 depicts *three* clubs. Our imagination, however, is able to take us further than this, and we can have a much richer experience of these photographs, which will make them depict more and more things the further we go. I have nothing against the idea of using the term "representation," instead of "depiction," after a – vague – limit has been reached, if we keep in mind that both of these terms refer to a notion of the same kind, that is, a notion of depiction or representation based on how we experience pictures by using our imagination, knowledge, beliefs, and inferential capacities.

References

Benovksy, Jiri. "Photographic Representation and Depiction of Temporal Extension." *Inquiry* 55, no. 2 (2012): 194–213.

Benovsky, Jiri. "The limits of photography." *International Journal of Philosophical Studies* 22, no. 5 (2014): 716–33.

Carroll, Noël. "Critical study: Mimesis as make-believe." *The Philosophical Quarterly* 45, no. 178 (1995): 93–99.

Carroll, Noël. *The Philosophy of Motion Pictures*. Malden, MA: Blackwell Publishing. 2008.

Costello, Diarmuid, and Dawn M. Phillips. "Automatism, Causality and Realism: Foundational Problems in the Philosophy of Photography." *Philosophy Compass* 4, no. 1 (2009): 1–21.

Goodman, Nelson. *Languages of Art: An Approach to a Theory of Symbols*. Indianapolis: Hackett Publishing. 1968.

Hopkins, Robert. "Explaining Depiction." *The Philosophical Review* 104, no. 3 (1995): 425–55.

Hopkins, Robert. "Factive Pictorial Experience: What's special about photographs?" *Noûs* 46, no. 4 (2012): 709–31.

Husserl, Edmund. *Ding Und Raum: Vorlesungen*. Hague: Martinus Nijhoff. 1907.

Kant, Immanuel. *Critique of Pure Reason*. Translated by Paul Guyer and Allen Wood. Cambridge and New York: Cambridge University Press. 1997.

Levinson, Jerrold. "Wollheim on Pictorial Representation." *The Journal of Aesthetics and Art Criticism* 56, no. 3 (1998): 227–33.

Nanay, Bence. "Perception and Imagination: Amodal Perception as Mental Imagery." *Philosophical Studies* 150, no. 2 (2010): 239–54.

Peacocke, Christopher. "Depiction." *Philosophical Review* 96, no. 3 (1987): 383–410.

Phillips, Dawn. "Photography and Causation: Responding to Scruton's Scepticism." *British Journal of Aesthetics* 49, no. 4 (2009): 327–40.

Scruton, Roger. "Photography and Representation." *Critical Inquiry* 7, no. 3 (1981): 577–603.

Walton, Kendall. *Mimesis as Make-Believe: On the Foundations of the Representational Arts*. Cambridge, MA: Harvard University Press. 1990.

Walton, Kendall. "On Pictures and Photographs: Objections Answered." In *Film Theory and Philosophy*, edited by Richard Allen and Murray Smith, 60–75. Oxford: Clarendon Press, 1997.

Walton, Kendall. "On the Nature of Photographic Realism." *Critical Inquiry* 11, no. 2 (1984): 246–77.

Wollheim, Richard. "On Pictorial Representation." *The Journal of Aesthetics and Art Criticism* 56, no. 3 (1998): 217–26.

Wollheim, Richard. *Painting as an Art*. Andrew M. Mellon Lectures in Fine Arts. National Gallery of Art. Washington, DC, Cambridge, MA: Harvard University Press. 1987.

CHAPTER 24

Imagination and Identification in Photography and Film

David Fenner

Films and Photographs have much in common. They are similar in respect of features such as lighting, framing, composition, staging, mise en scene, focus/depth of focus, they both readily lend themselves to interpretation and to evaluation, and likely many other things. They are different in important ways, too. While a photograph may be compared to a single translucent frame of a film, an average film contains about 173,000 frames (two hours at 24 FPS). And there is normally no sound accompanying photographs while nowadays it is exceptional when a film without accompanying sound is released. Clearly films contain a great deal more sensory stimulation – or what we might simply call information – than do photographs. It is common when museum-goers view two-dimensional works of art for them to spend about ten to twenty seconds in consideration of a single piece. This might seem almost silly in terms of building any sort of aesthetic experience, but compared with how much time we are permitted to view an individual film frame – again, 24 frames per second has been the canonical number for some time – ten to twenty seconds is an eternity. That comparison may strike some as odd; while there are some films – Kurosawa's *Rashomon* and Bergman's *Fanny and Alexander* come to mind first – that reward aesthetic consideration of a single frame, it seems reasonable to expect that most filmmakers believe that the aesthetic experiences for which they are attempting to provide artistic vehicles are about the length of the runtime of the film. Perhaps slightly longer if the film makes a big enough impact to keep audience members in their seats after the theatre lights come back on.

In many respects films are aesthetically "easier" than photographs. They are easier in pragmatic ways – you sit rather than wander a gallery; there is the potential of popcorn and soda pop – but more to the point they are easier in aesthetic ways. Since they provide so much information, the viewer has much less "work" to do when she attends to them. By work I mean imaginative work. Roger Scruton writes:

> When I summon the image of a horse in the absence of a real horse, or
> invent the description of a battle which I have heard about from no other

© KONINKLIJKE BRILL NV, LEIDEN, 2020 | DOI:10.1163/9789004436350_026

IMAGINATION AND IDENTIFICATION IN PHOTOGRAPHY AND FILM 583

source, my image and thought go beyond what is given to me, and lie within the province of my will. Such inventive acts are paradigm cases of imagination.[1]

When one looks at a photograph – a photograph that is a work of art, to be clear – the world that is textually presented is bounded in space (framed) and in time in stark ways. The viewer knows that the world of the photograph extends beyond the frame just as she knows that the photo's world extends in time before and after the moment of the shot. But none of this is given. It may be hinted at – when the representational aspects of the photo are strong, its world is certainly hinted at – but filling in that world, both spatially and temporally, is the work of the viewer.

As an imaginative viewer, I can fill in what lies beyond the visual frame with whatever I wish. Perhaps one of the most famous photographs is the 1945 V-J Day Times Square Kiss – taken by Alfred Eisenstaedt and published on the cover of *Life* magazine – in which a sailor passionately kisses a nurse. The title tells me the temporal context – I know what day in history the photo was taken – and the representative content in the photo (even if I didn't have a title) tells me this is Times Square in New York. It strikes me – as I imagine it strikes most – as an expression of exuberation and joy, of celebration and abandon. But what is not given in the picture is mine to contribute, and so while the visual clues lead me in certain directions, suggesting what might lie beyond the frame – others engaged in exuberant celebration of V-J Day, the reality being captured actually in color – I can imagine anything I wish. I can imagine that there may be planes flying overhead, folks throwing confetti from windows, or cars swerving to miss the two. But I can also imagine King Kong just out of frame, the spaceship from *The Day the Earth Stood Still* flying overhead, or the alien invaders from *War of the Worlds* coming up Broadway.

While this is obviously the case with (still) photographs, it is clearly too the case with film. No matter how sweeping an epic it may be, a film offers a slice of time, yet the world in which the film is situated is over thirteen billion years old. The desert in David Lean's *Lawrence of Arabia* is such an important part of the film that a pan-and-scanned version is, arguably, not the same film as the one Lean created (echoes of the arguments against colorizing films may be heard at this point). Something similar is true with Stanley Kubrick's *2001: A Space Odyssey*. The camera does not move in many scenes, and this arguably enhances the depth of at least some of those scenes. This is lost in a pan-and-scan version. In both of these examples, the director seems to be encouraging us to think of the

---

1   Roger Scruton, "Imagination," in *A Companion to Aesthetics*, ed. David Cooper (Oxford: Blackwell Publishers 1995), 214.

spatial context as extending forever, or at least for a very long and very grand way. We are encouraged, then, to think about what lies beyond the spatial dimensions of the screen on which we view these films. While Lean and Kubrick offer strong hints at what they would like for us to imagine, the fact of the matter is that it is up to us to provide, through the exercise of imagination, the world beyond the screen.

There may be those who would argue that, especially in the case of photographs, the object meant for our consideration (aesthetic, cognitive, etc.) is simply and exclusively what is given. To add more is, at the very least, to potentially injure the appreciative experience of whatever formal virtues are present in the composition. I concede that this is the case for some works of art, but photographs and films have special places in the art world; as art forms they were born out of the capture of (at first, anyhow, visual) reality. While there are certainly abstract photos and even abstract films of which the claims of formalists – that is, narrow formalists who seek to discount the representational aspects of works as illegitimate for consideration (and I quickly admit there are very few of these folks around anymore) – may be warranted, these cases are surely the exceptions and not instances of the rule.

As most photographs and most films continue to breed rich aesthetic experiences when viewed as the capture of a slice of reality, the work of the audience-member's imagination is not only important, it is absolutely necessary. The value of the experience of consideration of the work depends on it.

Alan Goldman, in his 1995 book *Aesthetic Value*, offers a theory of the value of aesthetic objects and experiences that could be described as escapist. This is my word; I do not recall that he or others have ever used that work to describe his views. The core of the theory may lend itself to this interpretation. This is it:

> The value of such works lies first in the challenge and richness of the perceptual, affective, and cognitive experience they afford. Symbolic and expressive density combines here with sensuous feel. From the subjective side, all one's perceptual, cognitive, and affective capacities can be engaged in apprehending these relations, even if one's grasp of them is imperfect or only implicit. These different facets of appreciation are not only engaged simultaneously but are also often indissolubly united, as when formal relations among musical tones or painted shapes are experienced as felt tensions and resolutions and perhaps as higher-order or more ordinary emotions as well.[2]

---

2 Alan H. Goldman, *Aesthetic Value* (Boulder, CO: Westview Press, 1995), 150.

IMAGINATION AND IDENTIFICATION IN PHOTOGRAPHY AND FILM   585

His account is this:

> When we are so fully and satisfyingly involved in appreciating an art-
> work, we can be said to lose our ordinary, practically oriented selves in a
> world of the work ... [It] can engage us so fully as to constitute another
> world for us, at least temporarily.[3]

Goldman's theory places the locus of aesthetic value in the aesthetic experience.
It describes a synergy or dynamic that occurs between the object and the subject, both necessarily contributing to the resulting aesthetic experience, both
offering some part, doing some work, that leads to the experience of the sort
he describes. The theory is not about the experience having a single nature –
cognitive or affective or fixed on the appreciation of sensory stimuli – rather
the experience is about all of these things. But more than that, the contemplative experience is not the final end. The ultimate result is that one takes the
experience to constitute another world. I would extend this slightly by saying
the experience transports us to appreciation of the world that the aesthetic object, through our consideration and attention, constitutes. This last addition,
in honesty more mine than his, is what allows me to think of this theory as an
escapist one.

That escape, if I can use that word, is predicated and dependent on the exercise of the viewer's imagination to fill in those parts of the artwork's world
which are not given formally (again, "narrowly formally"). Perhaps one of the
best examples of this exercise is the phenomenon of "identifying" with some
aspect that is presented in a photo and a film.

For a subject to identify with an aesthetic object or some part of an aesthetic
object – such as a human character – is for a subject to find some basis upon
which she can see aspects of herself in or through an aesthetic object. This is
decidedly a psychological phenomenon, and to talk about it philosophically is
to take as an empirical occurrence. There is a very wide range of ways in which
a subject may identify with an aesthetic object or a part of an aesthetic object.
- Identification with a person portrayed to some degree or in some way in the
  object
- Identification with some state that this "aesthetic person," this fictional
  character, is in – states of trouble, fear, excitement, love, happiness, pain,
  longing, unfulfillment, guilt, shame, joy, resoluteness, righteousness

---

3   Goldman, *Aesthetic Value*, 151.

- Identification with some character trait this person possesses – a virtue, a vice, a physical characteristic, a temperament, a mental habit, a behavioral habit
- Identification with some aspect of the history or "narrative" of this person – upbringing, struggle, challenge, limitation, grounding
- Identification with sexual or gender aspects of the object
- Identification with the racial or ethnic aspects of the object
- Identification with religious or spiritual aspects of the object
- Identification with aspects of the object having to do with class or socioeconomic status
- Identification with national or political aspects of the object
- Identification with a time period or aspects related to a particular time period
- Identification with moral themes portrayed in some way in the object

And I am sure there are many more ways that identification can happen. If in fact identification is a natural occurrence, at least for whose psychologically disposed to it, then it may seem odd to talk about its merits. That is, we do not debate whether to breathe or not, whether to eat or not, whether to sleep or not. Yet if one can offer a case for the enhancement of aesthetic value where manipulation of identification is possible, then the matter turns from being a simple psychological one to being of some philosophical interest. Where does the psychological phenomenon of identification have merit? Where it can be seen, when employed, to raise the level of quality of an aesthetic (or art) object. If we are proceeding along the lines of the modified Goldmanian view I mentioned above, then where identification leads to an enhancement of the content of an aesthetic experience constituting for the subject another world, there identification should be encouraged.

How does identification – of any sort mentioned above – contribute to the constitution of another world? In a range of ways. First, identification allows for personal exploration. Through identifying with, say, a character in literature or in film, I am able to explore aspects of myself that a focus on the amalgam between me and the fictional character reveals. The film theorist André Bazin wrote that "Tarzan is only possible on the screen."[4] I take this to mean that personal identification with a fictional character in only possible when that character is what he called a "tracing" or a "mold." A stage actor does not present this. An actor on stage is a real person, and though he plays a role, we do not as a matter of course lose sight of the fact that, as an actor playing a role,

---

4 André Bazin, "Theatre and Cinema," 1920, reprinted in *Film Theory and Criticism*, eds. Leo Braudy and Marshall Cohen (New York: Oxford University Press, 1999), 410.

he is in fact a real and complete human being. But a fictional character on the screen we take to be only that: a fictional character, an "aesthetic person." There is space left into which we can pour ourselves. If we take the character on the screen only as a character, that character is never fully given to us. For an aesthetic object to constitute a full world is impossible, and it is equally impossible for a film character to constitute a full person, regardless of how much biographical detail the film offers us. What space is left between the screen character and a full person we may at will fill in with the detail of our choice. When faced with an heroic character, one may well fill in the blanks with aspects of herself, thereby subjectively creating out of the objective character and her own subjective contribution a new person, a person who is partly the subject herself. Hence personal identification. This can work with all sorts of character identification – one can fill in the blanks of an antagonist with elements of himself to form an amalgamated person that serves as a platform to explore one's weaknesses or darker side, for instance – and this sort of exploration is something available to the subject only when attention on aspects of oneself are brought into focus by seeing in another oneself. Or, in the case of "aesthetic persons," actually creating a person from the amalgam of fictional character and oneself. Is there any doubt that such an exercise is valuable?

Personal identification, as I describe it above, not only is born of the exercise of imagination but also allows for enhanced imaginative engagement, both with the particular object under consideration but also more broadly, as a means of honing one's imaginative skills and proclivities, to form a greater basis upon which to reap reward when future opportunities for imaginative engagement present themselves. Pouring oneself into the mold of a fictional character, to go back to Bazin, takes an effort of will. In some cases this is easy – as when the fictional character is already fairly similar to oneself, or when a great deal of biographical detail is offered in the object, or when there is a great investment in the character due to the subject's heightened sympathies or the shear length of the film or book – but in some cases the act of will that personal identification requires is substantial. Practice in pouring oneself in the mold allows for more deft pouring, more frequent pouring, more success in pouring oneself in the mold, even when the identification takes this greater act of will.

Perhaps most basically for our purposes, given the theory of aesthetic value I mean to be employing, personal identification is valuable because the degree to which I am an occupant of the world the aesthetic object constitutes for me, the richer, more indelible, more present, more effective will be that constitution. This is in largest measure why I slip in describing Goldman's theory from talking about appreciation of another world to transport to it. To live in a world is a richer experience by far than merely appreciating it from a distance, and when one is a citizen of a world, where all distance is erased, one has the greatest chance of having the most rewarding experience. Part of the evidence set for this lies in the plans so many of us have for our retirements. We do not wish to look at pictures of, read books about, study films of, Scotland, Italy, China, France, New Zealand, Tibet. We want to actually go there. Epcot is insufficient. We need to stand on the soil, breathe the air, and smell the smells. This is the richness of experience of which other worlds may be constituted, and so it stands to reason that this is the level of aesthetic experience that we want to pursue and to which we want to aspire. Immersion, not visitation. Citizenship – if only temporary – not tourism.

Identification of all the sorts listed above is one set of means through which one can achieve the soul of what Goldman describes as valuable about aesthetic objects. This makes identification philosophically interesting – not merely in terms of its study as a psychological phenomenon but in terms of how it can be manipulated specifically to enhance aesthetic experience. High quality personal identification – to continue to focus on personal identification as our exemplar of imaginative consideration of photographs and films – is found along a variety of paths.

- The easy path: the fictional character is similar in relevant respects to the subject, and filling in the remaining holes imaginatively with aspects of oneself is relatively easy. I think there is no reason to shun the easy way; it may be that less effort expended here will allow for a greater investment elsewhere, as it may be that a good means of high-powered focus on one aspect of personal exploration happens when the identification is easily achieved.
- Tough path number one: an amalgam between the subject and the fictional character is tough because the fictional character is so different from the subject. Should the subject wish to make the investment, it is possible that the return on that investment will be rich. If the fictional character is so different, the creation of the amalgam may present an opportunity for reflection that is unique or extraordinary. Such reflection may be personally rewarding but it may also be aesthetically rewarding given the novelty and unusualness of the experience. One may find the constituted aesthetic world more different than expected given the level of unusualness that identification with a particular fictional character may occasion.
- Tough path number two: an amalgam between the subject and the fictional character is tough because the fictional character is so slightly formed. The investment here is one of self – the subject must inform the fictional character with much more of herself. The imaginative exercise here may be a

valuable one, but, on the other hand, if the amalgam ends up being too much oneself, there is little of the "otherness" that we hope informs the aesthetic world newly constituted for us. That is, it would seem an axiom that the more engaging and interesting the newly constituted aesthetic world, the richer the aesthetic experience. If the world created is too much like the one of the subject, if the transportation from the subject's world to the new one is like a drive to the corner convenience store, the chances for a rich aesthetic experience would seem to diminish. This path is more likely in the case of photographs than film, of course.

– Tough path number three: an amalgam between the subject and the fictional character is tough because the resulting amalgam would occasion some particular personal reflection with which the subject does not wish to engage. Uncovering painful memories used to be the purview of clinical psychotherapists. Perhaps there are theories that connect the effects of psychotherapy with aesthetic value, but those theories are not at play here. A negative association or painful memory may drive one right out of an aesthetic frame of mind, a frame of mind open to the creation of a new aesthetic world. This would be contrary to the enhancement of aesthetic value, and without strong reason to the contrary, the investment of the identity amalgam here probably should not be encouraged.

– Tough path number four: an amalgam between the subject and the fictional character is tough because the fictional character is evil, and the resulting amalgam will only cast light on negative aspects of the subject. But I may be overstating here. Identification with evil characters can not only be illuminating, it can be fun. My younger son loves Darth Vader, and he gets much greater joy in identifying with Darth Vader than with any of the other characters, as pleasant or good as they may be. Surely there are more textual works created with a focus on Satan rather than on God.

As it was with the earlier list, this one is not comprehensive. The point, however, is that there are a plurality of investment paths when it comes to the imaginative activity of personal identification, and we ought not lose sight of that fact.

The goal, given the aesthetic value theory employed here, is a subject having an aesthetic experience that is characterized by the constitution of a new world, one presented – or perhaps better said, suggested, given the necessary imaginative investment – through the aesthetic object (or event, of course) under consideration. So we should ask: is one of the paths listed above better than another in pursuit of this goal?

– Easy path – the problem here is the proximity one. If it is right to take as an axiom that the greater remove from the subject's actual world to that suggested by the aesthetic object will result in greater imaginative engagement and richer aesthetic experiences (supposing they are repeated and so plural), then the easy path may suffer from a contemptuous familiarity. We need to be careful here, because on occasion the close world can be a very powerful one, and the too-fantastical world can seem too alien. But there can be no laws governing these dynamics; while there may be some stability possible in standards of judgment, aesthetic experiences per se are incorrigible.

– Tough path number one (an amalgam between the subject and the fictional character is tough because the fictional character is so different from the subject): in these cases the imagination must be stretched – imaginative "exercise" is the correct expression in a couple different senses. Given the work that needs to be done by the viewer, the reward is potentially all the greater. The investment of a high level of imaginative activity can, as mentioned earlier, set up the viewer for more and deeper success in the future; novel insights and illuminations about one's personality and psychology could result more easily than would be available in simpler identifications; and it might well be expected that aesthetic experiences will be richer and more lasting. The last of these might be expected because of the commonality of the occasions when artworks that require the greatest investment of attention and consideration render deep and repeatably deep experiences. Kubrick's *2001* is a very long film; the dialogue is scant; the transitions – while editorially wonderful – are sometimes extreme; much that seems very important goes unexplained; and the last nine minutes are, for many, challenging, to say the least. And yet, *2001* is a great film. "Great" on the measures of the test of time, on how many times viewers are drawn to return to it, on how it rewards interpretive exploration time after time, and on how often critics and writers on aesthetics (the present being a case in point) talk about it. Aesthetic investments do not always pay off. Kevin Reynold's *Waterworld*, Ridley Scott's *Prometheus*, David Lynch's *Dune*, and Kubrick's *Eyes Wide Shut* are all films that require substantial aesthetic engagements of time and attention, but, if the primary trajectory of critical comments on these films is to be believed, they do not always pay off in rich experiences. Yet, to return to Goldman's theory as a base, those films – and photographs, despite the fact that my examples are tending toward film – that constitute new worlds for us are likely to require large imaginative investments if indeed the world to be constituted is new and fresh.

– Tough path number two (an amalgam between the subject and the fictional character is tough because the fictional character is so slightly formed): In this case, the devil is in the details as regards the value of experiences resulting from imaginative investments here. One could argue that in the classic Times Square photograph mentioned above, the characters are slightly formed. We do not know if the two figures know one another, for example. But we do know – or can respectably guess – that the man is indeed a sailor (and so young, probably recently involved in combat, and so very happy to be home and safe) and the woman a nurse (and so probably having seen over the last years her share of malady and pain). What if they were not wearing uniforms? Perhaps the photograph would still have merit, but it likely would not have made the cover of *Life* nor been so iconic that I can discuss it with reasonable assurance that readers will know the photo I mean. And part of the reason for me saying this is that the characters would not have been sketched out with as much detail. Could this mean more imaginative investment were required? Certainly, and it might be that the ambiguities that come with a sketchier sketch might have increased the critical reception of the photograph in line with a decrease in its popular appeal. This is why I say the devil is in the details. Slightly formed characters may be useless when it comes to seeking rewards for identifications, but they might also provide opportunities for the greatest reward as they require greater imaginative investments.

– Tough path number three (an amalgam between the subject and the fictional character is tough because the resulting amalgam would occasion some particular personal reflection with which the subject does not wish to engage): while aesthetic analyses of photographs and films may find agreement across a range of judges, and perhaps even occasion theorists to advance views on what accounts for the stability of standards, aesthetic experiences are messy things. They rely for their being on elements that particular subjects bring with them to the experiences: how much knowledge about the history of art, the artist, this work, or its provenance are they bringing with them? How deeply do they understand contextual aspects relevant to the work or its representational features? How much patience do they have in considering the work? How much time do they have? Have they – and I'm thinking here again of those last nine minutes of *2001* – contextualized their own personal experiences through employment of psychogenetic substances? These sort of matters fuel the vigor of the formalist and the attraction of her approach, but while the formalist may win when it comes to aesthetic analysis, it is difficult to escape the Deweyan insight that aesthetic experiences are first and foremost events experienced – and valued – by individual subjects. The more discussed photographs of Robert Mapplethorpe may be inaccessible to those for whom the representational contents are shocking, as may well be the case with the photographs by Sally Mann, Jock Sturges, or Rene Serrano. The photographs by these artists may elicit such reactions from many, and each one of those occasions may be an instance where imagination cannot be engaged and identification – with anyone portrayed – cannot be achieved. Given the messiness of aesthetic experience, though, this kind of occasion may happen much more frequently than merely with such large examples as Mapplethorpe et al. Representational contents of photographs and films are sure to connect with other sorts of experiences of individuals – and this is more often than not a good thing – but sometimes the connection can be a negative one. In those cases, the opportunity for identification will be lost, as will of course any hope of positive return on imagination investment.

– Tough path number four (an amalgam between the subject and the fictional character is tough because the fictional character is evil, and the resulting amalgam will only cast light on negative aspects of the subject): There have been over the last decade some exciting contributions to the literature of the relationship between ethics and aesthetics, from people like Jerrold Levinson, Noel Carroll, Berys Gaut, and Marcia Eaton. Questions about the potential ethical value of aesthetic objects where the objects themselves portray evil (of some stripe or some degree, intentional or not) have been considered. For present purposes review of these conversations is not necessary. Yet it is interesting still to think about whether there is value in the personal identification of oneself with a character in a film or a photograph who is or does evil. As I said in my example above, my younger son got quite a kick out of pretending to be Darth Vader. I'm unsure about the depth of that identification – James Earle Jones' voice, the height, the black cape and mask, the light saber – what's there not for a kid to love? Deeper personal identifications, however, are made all the time with characters that are less than savory. They can illuminate parts of ourselves that lie hidden, dormant, or latent. They can offer us the opportunity for safe exploration. They can teach us lessons about ourselves and about the nature of good and evil. They can enliven our appreciation of the wide range of human experience captured – for our purposes – in photographs and films. Are these sorts of identification ancillary to aesthetic experiences or integral to them? I would argue the latter; it is the fostering of the wealth of an aesthetic experience for a viewer to call upon the active use of her imagination in the creation of an identification with a character. To parse up such experiences is merely to tacitly adopt a formalist approach.

Imagination provides us the vehicles by which we can travel to other worlds, the suggestions of which are offered by the contents – usually representational contents – of aesthetic objects, in our case photographic and filmic artworks. Such travel is a sign of the value of the experiences we have with these objects.

Identification with a character depicted in a photograph or film is but one of the seats on the experiential vehicle, but I wager it is the seat most often and most readily sat in when one's artistic imagination is switched on. In the review above, it seems clear that while the quality of the depiction of the character portrayed will influence the value of our imaginative experience, as will negative triggers (we simply concentrated on psychological ones), the overall quality of the aesthetic experience we achieve in attention to photos and films depends very much on the depth to which one's imagination is switched on.

References

André Bazin, "Theatre and Cinema," 1920. Reprinted in *Film Theory and Criticism*, edited by Leo Braudy and Marshall Cohen, 408–18. New York: Oxford University Press, 1999.

Goldman, Alan H. *Aesthetic Value.* Boulder, CO: Westview Press. 1995.

Scruton, Roger. "Imagination." In *A Companion to Aesthetics*, edited by David Cooper, 212–17. Oxford: Blackwell Publishers, 1995.

CHAPTER 25

Imagination in Musical Composition, Performance, and Listening: John Cage's Blurring of Boundaries in Music and Life in *4′33″*

Deborah Fillerup Weagel

> An imaginative mind is essential to the creation of art in any medium, but it is even more essential in music precisely because music provides the broadest possible vista for the imagination since it is the freest, the most abstract, the least fettered of all the arts.
>
> AARON COPLAND, *Music and Imagination* 17

I recently visited the J. Paul Getty Museum in Los Angeles for the first time. My experience began by taking a tram from the parking area up a hill to the museum. As I made the ascent, plush green vegetation surrounded me, both on the hill and in the distance. Once I disembarked from the tram, I walked up stairs and admired some outdoor sculptures, including Aristide Maillol's 1938 reclining female nude entitled *L'Air.*[1] I entered the building, obtained a map and guide to the exhibits, and started my tour. I was somewhat frustrated at first, because after observing art works in one upstairs area of the museum, I needed to descend, go out of the building, and walk to a different area to see additional pieces. Eventually, I understood that this was how the museum was purposefully situated: as a visitor I did not enter a single building and stay inside for the tour, secluded from the outside. On the contrary, a fundamental part of the experience was to go inside and outside buildings, and stroll through walkways, patios, and balconies. I was to observe not only art pieces on display, but also to participate in nature, to see views of nearby cityscapes, to take note of homes embedded in green hillsides, and to find aesthetic beauty in the constant stream of automobiles on the serpentine freeway in the valley below.[2]

---

1 Aristide Maillol, *L'Air*, Sculpture (Los Angeles, J. Paul Getty Museum, 1938).
2 The J. Paul Getty Museum is housed at two centers: the Getty Center in Los Angeles and the Getty Villa in Malibu (which specializes in the art and cultures of Greece, Rome, and Etruria). The villa comprises multiple buildings, gardens, and walkways, as well as views of the Pacific Ocean. It is possible to visit both the Getty Center and the Getty Villa in one day, but the latter requires the acquisition of tickets in advance.

© KONINKLIJKE BRILL NV, LEIDEN, 2020 | DOI:10.1163/9789004436350_027

IMAGINATION IN MUSICAL COMPOSITION, PERFORMANCE, & LISTENING   595

From a musical perspective, John Cage's seminal composition *4'33"* also takes the performer and audience into realms that extend beyond a designated space, the concert hall. Often called his "silent" piece, Karl Katschthaler suggests that Cage's "intention with *4'33"* was not to show us the absence of music as the presence of silence, but rather to make us hear a whole world of sounds, which are absent when we listen to the presence of music."[3] In creating this particular musical composition, Cage not only drew upon his own imagination and creativity, but he also challenged the performer(s) and audience/listeners to step out of traditional boundaries that existed in a concert hall. Similar to my experience at the Getty Museum (where art extended to views of the gardens, surrounding hillsides, nearby cityscapes, and even the stream of cars on the freeway), the sounds of everyday life (the quiet hum of air conditioning, the rustling of paper, a siren in the distance, a squeaking chair, even someone breathing), became part of the musical experience. In fact, in this particular work, these sounds were the music. In this essay, I propose that Cage's piece *4'33"* involved not only imagination in its composition, but it also expected a certain degree of imagination on the part of the performer(s) and audience as well.

John Milton Cage Jr. (1912–1992) was born in Los Angeles and was exposed to imaginative thinking from boyhood. His father, John Milton Cage Sr., was an inventor who succeeded in finding "solutions for problems" in a variety of fields, such as "electrical engineering, medicine, submarine travel, seeing through fog, and travel in space without the use of fuel."[4] He told his son John that when a person insists that something cannot be done, "that shows you what to do."[5] So his father taught him to question tradition, to not rely completely on the experience or authority of others, and to find his own solutions for challenges of various kinds in life.

Later when the younger Cage became the student of renowned composer and music theorist Arnold Schoenberg, he did not hesitate to continue with his musical aspirations despite his teacher's advice to find a different field of endeavor. Cage relates the following exchange:

> When I asked Schoenberg to teach me, he said, "You probably can't afford my price." I said, "Don't mention it; I don't have any money." He said, "Will you devote your life to music?" This time I said "Yes." He said he would

---

3   Karl Katschthaler, "Absence, Presence and Potentiality: John Cage's *4'33"* Revisited," in *Silence and Absence in Literature and Music*. Word and Music Studies 15, eds. Werner Wolf and Walter Bernhart (Leiden: Brill-Rodopi, 2016), 177.

4   The John Cage Trust, "John Cage: An Autobiographical Statement," *John Cage: Official Website*. Accessed June 20, 2019. https://johncage.org/autobiographical_statement.html.

5   The John Cage Trust, "John Cage: An Autobiographical Statement," n. pag.

teach me free of charge. I gave up painting and concentrated on music. After two years it became clear to both of us that I had no feeling for harmony. For Schoenberg, harmony was not just coloristic: it was structural. It was the means one used to distinguish one part of a composition from another. Therefore he said I'd never be able to write music. "Why not?" "You'll come to a wall and won't be able to get through." "Then I'll spend my life knocking my head against that wall."[6]

Cage succeeded in finding his own approaches to composition by going against some of the well-meaning counsel of Schoenberg, a powerhouse in the musical world, and by discovering his own unique talents and abilities in that field. He eventually became known for his avant-garde compositions, and he made genuine contributions to the way people viewed music in the twentieth century and beyond.

It is important to note, however, that Schoenberg may have had a stronger influence on Cage than at first realized. In his article "John Cage, Arnold Schoenberg, and the Musical Idea," David W. Bernstein acknowledges that "in many ways, Cage turned his back on the past, rejecting compositional choice through his use of chance operations, seeking instead a musical continuity that avoided relationships between sounds."[7] Bernstein points out that Schoenberg, on the other hand, was trained in "nineteenth-century traditions, expressing a quintessential organicism articulated by 'relationships between tones.'"[8] Although he can understand why various scholars do not see a strong influence of Schoenberg on Cage, due to the differences in style, he argues that the former actually had a profound impact on the latter. Cage not only studied with Schoenberg privately, but he also attended his music courses at the University of Southern California (USC) and the University of California, Los Angeles (UCLA). Cage said in an interview that Schoenberg "was a magnificent teacher, who always gave the impression that he was putting us in touch with the musical principles"[9] Bernstein points out that Cage was influenced by Schoenberg's explorations with the "emancipation of the dissonance" (such as in his twelve-tone compositions), his teachings on repetition and variation,

---

6 The John Cage Trust, "John Cage: An Autobiographical Statement," n. pag.

7 David W. Bernstein, "John Cage, Arnold Schoenberg, and the Musical Idea," in *John Cage: Music, Philosophy, and Intention, 1933–1950*, ed. David W. Patterson (New York: Routledge, 2002), 15–16.

8 Bernstein, "John Cage, Arnold Schoenberg, and the Musical Idea," 16.

9 Bernstein, "John Cage, Arnold Schoenberg, and the Musical Idea," 23.

and his writings about the musical idea (which included a concern for the wholeness of a musical work).[10]

With an inventor as a father and one of the twentieth century's most important music theorists and composers as a mentor (and one that was notably creative in his own way with his twelve-tone music), Cage established a strong foundation for a career as an imaginative musician and composer. He exhibited a certain tenacity, audacity, and creativity in his work and eventually became an important figure in the post-war avant-garde movement. He was known for his experiments with indeterminacy and electroacoustic music. He also enjoyed using musical instruments in unique and nontraditional ways, such as with his prepared piano pieces (in which a piano was "prepared" by placing various objects on or between the strings, thereby altering the sound). Perhaps his most important work, however, one which brought him much acclaim, was his "silent" piece *4'33"*.

Peter Gena writes of three significant milestones in the history of western music: the development of music notation prior to 1000 CE, the emergence of sound recording, and perhaps John Cage's *4'33"*.[11] The piece is so named because the first performance by pianist David Tudor, which took place at the Maverick Concert Hall near Woodstock, New York, on August 29, 1952, lasted four minutes and thirty-three seconds. In his book *No Such Thing as Silence: John Cage's 4'33"*, Kyle Gann describes the scene:

> Pianist David Tudor sat down at the piano on the small raised wooden stage, closed the keyboard lid over the keys, and looked at a stopwatch. Twice in the next four minutes he raised the lid up and lowered it again, careful to make no audible sound, although at the same time he was turning pages of the music, which were devoid of notes. After four minutes and thirty-three seconds had passed, Tudor rose to receive applause— and thus was premiered one of the most controversial, inspiring, surprising, infamous, perplexing, and influential musical works since Igor Stravinsky's *Le sacre du printemps*.[12]

---

10   See, for example, Jack Boss' *Schoenberg's Twelve-Tone Music: Symmetry and the Musical Idea*. See also Arnold Schoenberg's two books, *Fundamentals of Musical Composition* and *The Musical Idea and the Logic, Technique, and Art of Its Presentation*.

11   Peter Gena, "John Cage the Composer," in *A John Cage Reader in Celebration of His 70th Birthday*, eds. Peter Gena and Jonathan Brent (New York: C.F. Peters, 1982), 2.

12   Kyle Gann, *No Such Thing as Silence: John Cage's 4'33"* (New Haven, CT: Yale University Press, 2010), 2–3.

In discussing this first performance, John Cage acknowledged that there was not complete silence, but there were miscellaneous sounds, and it was his intent that the audience listen carefully to them.[13]

One version of *4'33"* that was published by Henmar Press in 1961 (even though the score indicates publication in 1960) comprises one page. The work is in three movements, as can be seen by the following:

I

TACET

II

TACET

III

TACET

The term "tacet" in music indicates that a voice or instrument should be silent. So the instructions call for three movements of silence. Although at the premiere the piece lasted four minutes and thirty-three seconds, on this score it explains that it "may be performed by any instrumentalist or combination of instrumentalists and last any length of time."[14] In the case of the premiere, each movement began with the closing of the keyboard lid.

The sounds of everyday life became very important to Cage; they were music to him. In a conversation with Joan Retallack, he suggested "that music takes place wherever we are and is expressed by the sounds that we hear and call simply ambient sound; or, we call them silence!"[15] Cage described the "ambient" sounds he heard during the premiere of *4'33"*: "You could hear the wind stirring outside during the first movement. During the second, raindrops began pattering the roof, and during the third the people themselves made all kinds of interesting sounds as they talked or walked out."[16] Just as my experience at the Getty Museum enlarged the boundaries of a traditional museum space, where the repetition and variation of plants in an outdoor cactus garden exemplified art as much a painting on a wall, Cage broadened the space at the Maverick Concert Hall to include non-vocal and non-instrumental sounds, including wind, the pattering of raindrops, and even the sounds of people talking and leaving the venue.

---

13 Gann, *No Such Thing as Silence: John Cage's 4'33"*, 4.

14 John Cage, *4'33"* (New York: Henmar Press, 1960), n. pag.

15 John Cage, *Musicage: Cage Muses on Words, Art, Music*, ed. Joan Retallack (Middletown, CT: Wesleyan University Press, 1996), 190.

16 Gann, *No Such Thing as Silence: John Cage's 4'33"*, 4.

By means of *4'33"* Cage exhibited a strong sense of both imagination and creativity, something his father encouraged (to seek to do what others said could not be done), and his music teachers, including Schoenberg, helped ignite, through their own expertise, example, and courage. In the article "Explaining musical imaginations: Creativity, performance, and perception," David J. Hargreaves, Raymond MacDonald, and Dorothy Miell make a distinction between imagination and creativity. They point out that "imagination is essentially *perceptual*" and involves "internal mental processes," whereas "creativity ... involves *production*," in which "imagination is very likely to have been involved."[17] Igor Stravinsky, in *Poetics of Music*, seems to concur with this concept when he writes, "What we imagine does not necessarily take on concrete form and may remain in a state of virtuality."[18] Although what we imagine may not result in actual output or production, a concept or idea often precedes some type of concrete product, so there is a process which can take place. There is often a period of time in which a composer conceives a new work prior to its actual realization. As Robert Jourdain explains, "Composers are thinkers in sound, and their stock in trade is auditory imagery. They manipulate tones in their mind's ear as accurately as writers manipulate words."[19] Their imagination and auditory imagery can be based on experience, training, interaction with other musicians and artists, general knowledge, exposure to the work of other composers, past production, and interaction with other fields, stimuli, and experts.

In the article "The Process of Composition from Detection to Confection," composer Robert Saxton writes, "I am frequently asked three questions by listeners: Where does your inspiration come from? When starting a piece, what do you think of first? Would I understand your music? In the space of five seconds I have been confronted with the fundamental issues of creative work, both at a philosophical and practical level."[20] He explains that a musical composition may come initially into his mind as a whole, and in some cases with

---

17 David J. Hargreaves, Raymond MacDonald, and Dorothy Miell, "Explaining musical imaginations: Creativity, performance and perception," in *Musical Imaginations: Multidisciplinary perspectives on creativity, performance, and perception*, eds. David J. Hargreaves, Dorothy E. Miell, and Raymond A.R. MacDonald (Oxford: Oxford University Press, 2012), 3.

18 Igor Stravinsky, *Poetics of Music in the Form of Six Lessons*, trans. Arthur Knodel and Ingolf Dahl (Cambridge, MA: Harvard University Press, 1970), 53.

19 Robert Jourdain, *Music, the Brain, and Ecstasy: How Music Captures our Imagination* (New York: William Morrow, 1997), 161.

20 Robert Saxton, "The Process of Composition from Detection to Confection," in *Composition, Performance, Reception: Studies in the Creative Process in Music*, ed. Wyndham Thomas (Aldershot, UK: Ashgate, 1998), 1.

explicit details. He also describes how he might begin a work: "I am hearing sounds and colours in my mind's ear. I sense the shape, the progress of the piece as a whole, and I hear and see the rise and fall of the lines. I also have an overall sense of what is possibly best described as the music's harmonic orbit— its internal tensions, internal rate of change and its inner energy."[21] The conception period is initiated with the desire or idea to compose the piece and goes up to the "aural detection stage,"[22] a process which may take a short period of time, such as a day, or even a year or more. Saxton explains that it is "not temporally an ordered hearing of the music's progress," but it may possibly be a time for "overall planning, for creating a framework ... flexible enough to allow real invention."[23]

Next Saxton takes that musical idea, something initially perceived in his imagination and which might include some general planning, and begins to write the notes. He presents some of the more complicated concerns involved in this process:

> I can hear the beginning of the music in my mind's ear and begin to write it down. But does what I notate scan correctly when considered in relation to the whole? The situation is now becoming complex because I have not been able to construct a plan in any detailed sense, for the simple reason that it is impossible to précis what does not yet exist. In reality, what happens is that either I know that what I have composed in 'in scale,' or I am aware that the proportions of the piece will not be exactly as I had planned because of the nature of the harmonic rhythm, phrase-lengths, texture, register and perceived rate of succession of my initial musical sounds. Do I alter this or is it an 'idée fixe'? For all my planning, surely I owe it to the musical material to develop and transform its hidden secrets. Do I do this by developing its internal structures or by imposing external methods? The answer is, of course, that I do both.[24]

So in the act of realizing his piece, he relies on some initial concepts and general plans, but also remains open to variation and change as he moves forward. He is keenly aware of the need to be flexible, to allow previously unimagined and unconceived material to enter into the written score.

---

21 Saxton, "The Process of Composition from Detection to Confection," 3.
22 Saxton, "The Process of Composition from Detection to Confection," 4.
23 Saxton, "The Process of Composition from Detection to Confection," 4.
24 Saxton, "The Process of Composition from Detection to Confection," 5–6.

IMAGINATION IN MUSICAL COMPOSITION, PERFORMANCE, & LISTENING   601

Saxton also draws upon an array of experience, training, and knowledge in the course of creating and composing. He has "a repertoire of technical possibilities stored" in his "memory bank"[25] that provides a "tool box" from which to work. He reflects upon the work of the great masters, such as Beethoven, and considers critical work by authors like Charles Rosen in his book *The Classical Style*. He thinks about a poem called "The World" by Welch poet Henry Vaughan, that he once set to music, and remembers an article entitled "The First Four Notes of *Lulu*" by George Perle. He contemplates ideas presented in *An Introduction to Mathematics* by Alfred North Whitehead and another composition he wrote called "The Circles of Light," which was inspired by Dante's *Divine Comedy*. He reviews the ending of the novel *The Wandering Jew* by Stefan Heym in which Christ and the Wandering Jew are united. He pays homage to Albert Einstein who, at the celebration of Max Planck's sixtieth birthday, spoke of the "daily effort" that "comes from no deliberate intention or programme, but straight from the heart."[26] Saxton elaborates further, "When I discuss composing music I have to cover the wide field that I have covered ... It is only at the level which is at once the most simple and the most complex that the whole process begins and to which, in the end, perception and reception can be related."[27] In the end, he explains, "I mix and compound—not to confound, but to share my excitement and the thrill of inventing and thinking."[28] So from the point of first conceiving a project, to perceiving some of its possibilities, and to actually writing a piece, a composer can participate in the act of imagination and creation, drawing upon many experiences and influences.

Based on this narrative of the compositional process by Robert Saxton, how might John Cage be considered both imaginative and creative in writing the piece *4′33″*? The latter composer also had a "repertoire of technical possibilities stored" in his "memory bank." In the article "Music I: to the late 1940s," David W. Bernstein writes of Cage's development as a composer from his earliest piano lessons at the age of eight from his aunt, Phoebe James, to his *Sonatas and Interludes* (1946–48).[29] As a young piano student, he was exposed to late nineteenth-century repertoire for the most part, but when he was in Paris

---

25   Saxton, "The Process of Composition from Detection to Confection," 6.
26   Saxton, "The Process of Composition from Detection to Confection," 15.
27   Saxton, "The Process of Composition from Detection to Confection," 15.
28   Saxton, "The Process of Composition from Detection to Confection," 15.
29   In a 1987 interview with Peter Dickinson, John Cage spoke of the musicians on his mother's side of the family. He explained, "My Aunt Phoebe was a singer, pianist, and piano teacher. Aunt Marge had a contralto voice. She sang in a Protestant church. I used to go and sit on the front row. Her voice was so beautiful it would bring tears to my eyes" (Peter Dickinson, "John Cage: Interview with Peter Dickinson, BBC studios, New York City, June

in 1930 he heard some works by Stravinsky and Scriabin. This experience aroused his interest in modern music. When he returned to Los Angeles, he set some texts by Gertrude Stein to music in his Three Songs (1933), which includes "a curious combination of triadic figures and dissonant part writing."[30] Cage's first composition teacher was Richard Buhlig, who encouraged him to compose music based on Schoenberg's twelve-tone method, which Cage explored in the second movement of his Sonata for Clarinet (1933) and in other works, such as *Composition for Three Voices* (1934).

Then Cage worked with other teachers as well. He studied, for example, with Henry Cowell, who likely taught him "dissonant counterpoint," which sets up "dissonance, rather than consonance" as the "norm," so that "consonance is resolved by dissonance."[31] During this time, Cage also worked with more traditional contrapuntal techniques. Eventually Cowell suggested that Cage study with Adolph Weiss, who was an expert in Schoenberg's approaches and techniques. So Cage worked with Weiss in 1934 and also attended classes by Cowell at the New School for Social Research in New York. Towards the end of 1934, Cage returned to Los Angeles where he began studying directly with Arnold Schoenberg. From this great master, he learned about both repetition and variation, but since Schoenberg said they are really equivalent, Cage decided to focus more on repetition:

> In all my pieces coming between 1935 and 1940, I had Schoenberg's lessons in mind; since he had taught me that a variation was in fact a repetition, I hardly saw the usefulness of variation, and I accumulated repetitions. All of my early works for percussion, and also my compositions for piano, contain systematically repeated groups of sounds or durations.[32]

Eventually, Cage's focus became percussion music, which included the concept that noise could be perceived as music. He also learned from Schoenberg that dividing a composition into parts helped to establish its musical structure. Some of these concepts and ideas became important to Cage's *4'33"*.

Cage began experimenting in innovative ways not only with percussion music, but with electronic music and prepared piano. He wanted to found a

---

        29, 1987," in *Cage Talk: Dialogues with and about John Cage*, ed. Peter Dickinson (Rochester, NY: University of Rochester Press, 2006), 26).

30   David W. Bernstein, "Music I: to the late 1940s," in *The Cambridge Companion to John Cage*, ed. David Nicholls (Cambridge: Cambridge University Press, 2002), 63.

31   Bernstein, "Music I: to the late 1940s," 65.

32   Bernstein, "Music I: to the late 1940s," 67.

IMAGINATION IN MUSICAL COMPOSITION, PERFORMANCE, & LISTENING 603

Center of Experimental Music in the 1940s, and he envisioned composers working together with sound engineers. This particular project was somewhat of a failure, but during this time period he explored sound effects in a variety of ways. For example, in his *Imaginary Landscape No. 2*, composed in 1942, there were "parts for an electronic buzzer and a radio aerial coil connected to a phonograph pick-up amplified through a loud speaker."[33] In *Imaginary Landscape No. 3*, he included the "instruments" mentioned above, plus "an audio frequency oscillator, variable-speed turntables ... which play frequency records and a recording of a generator whine, and an amplified marimbula."[34] He then explored prepared piano, where he inserted a variety of different objects (screws, bolts, wood, cloth, rubber, plastic, bamboo, etc.) to create unique sounds to the piano. Many of these prepared piano pieces were composed to accompany modern dancers, such as his *Totem Ancestor* (1942), originally a solo for Merce Cunningham. Bernstein points out that during the 1940s, silence became more and more important to Cage, and this is evident in his prepared piano piece *The Perilous Night*, a concert work, where some measures were left empty.[35]

In addition to his composition studies and his many musical explorations, Cage pursued additional interests. For example, he was a writer as well as a composer, and his book *Silence*, first published in 1961, contains his lectures and writings that cover about a twenty-year period.[36] In one of the early lectures included in the book, "Future of Music: Credo," which was presented in Seattle at a meeting for an arts society, Cage spoke of the importance of "noise":

> Wherever we are, what we hear is mostly noise. When we ignore it, it disturbs us. When we listen to it, we find it fascinating. The sound of a truck at fifty miles per hour. Static between the stations. Rain. We want to capture and control these sounds, to use them not as sound effects but as musical instruments. Every film studio has a library of "sound effects" recorded on film. With a film phonograph it is now possible to control the

---

33   Bernstein, "Music I: to the late 1940s," 75.

34   Bernstein, "Music I: to the late 1940s," 76.

35   Bernstein, "Music I: to the late 1940s," 79–80.

36   Certain writers, such as Samuel Beckett, have also included silence in their work. See, for example, my article "Silence in John Cage and Samuel Beckett: *4'33"* and *Waiting for Godot.*" Film directors, such as Krzysztof Kieslowski, have also explored silence and ambient sound in their movies. See my article "Silence in Krzysztof Kieslowski's *The Decalogue:* A Cagian Perspective." Various writers have integrated musical themes and structures in their writing, and some musicians have incorporated texts and words in their music. See my book *Words and Music: Camus, Beckett, Cage, Gould.*

amplitude and frequency of any one of these sounds and to give to it rhythms within or beyond the reach of the imagination. Given four film phonographs, we can compose and perform a quartet for explosive motor, wind, heartbeat, and landslide.[37]

So here, more than a decade prior to the premiere of *4'33"*, Cage verbally acknowledged the value of extraneous sound in addition to experimenting with the use of silence in some of his compositions.[38]

Cage also became interested in Eastern philosophy and influences, such as Zen Buddhism. In his book on Cage, Rob Haskins explains that in Zen, "the sorts of things apprehended with the senses," such as "emotions, intellectual ideas, physiological urges, even a sense of individual self—are only momentary phenomena that have no overall importance."[39] Various activities that are part of daily life are acknowledged but not extraordinary, because "they simply are what you do."[40] This attitude towards everyday experiences influenced Cage's perception of music. He realized that the ordinary sounds of daily life should be recognized even if they are not extraordinary, and they can be considered music. In addition, Cage studied the I Ching or *Book of Changes*, an ancient text that deals with sixty-four states of being. As Haskins writes, each state of being is "represented by a hexagram in which each of the six lines is either solid or divided in the middle—the 64 states are in constant flux."[41] He explains further that any particular hexagram "offers a 'snapshot' of the momentary state of the universe, which is constantly changing to another. The commentaries are designed to advise those who would consult the book as an oracular tool."[42] Cage incorporated the I Ching into some of his compositions, including *Music of Changes* (1951). He provided a variety of charts for this piece, and they dealt with various aspects of the music, such as pitches, rhythms, articulation, dynamics, and even superimposed musical layers. The I Ching was

---

37   John Cage, *Silence: Lectures and Writings* (Middletown, CT: Wesleyan University Press, 1961), 3.

38   As Edward Lippman explains, "Cage's central belief is that music will not continue to be constituted almost entirely of tones but will be made up of sound in general, including environmental sound. Thus, noise and electronically produced sound will play a part in music, which will then consist of organized sound, or really of sound and silence, whether this material is selected and arranged consciously in every respect or distributed entirely or partially by chance" (Edward Lippman, *A History of Western Musical Aesthetics* (Lincoln, NE: University of Nebraska Press, 1992), 434).

39   Rob Haskins, *John Cage* (London: Reaktion Books, 2012), 61.

40   Haskins, *John Cage*, 61.

41   Haskins, *John Cage*, 62.

42   Haskins, *John Cage*, 62.

IMAGINATION IN MUSICAL COMPOSITION, PERFORMANCE, & LISTENING 605

FIGURE 25.1   Sixty-four hexagrams from the King Wen sequence of the I Ching.
FILE: WIKIMEDIA COMMONS, HTTPS://COMMONS.WIKIMEDIA.ORG/WIKI/
FILE:KING_WEN_(I_CHING).PNG

used to see how these aspects in the charts were to interact with each other, in what was part of his "aleatory" or "chance" music. As Haskins indicates, Cage was somewhat "unfulfilled" by the result and felt more like a "clerical worker dutifully accomplishing his appointed tasks."[43] It was only shortly after the creation of this composition, that Cage presented the sounds of everyday life in 4′33″, a piece that did not require this more tedious and intricate work.

As with composer Robert Saxton, Cage's musical compositions were influenced by his musical training and experience as well as by other nonmusical input. The importance of influences outside a person's artistic focus should not be underestimated. In her book *The Creative Habit: Learn It and Use It for Life*, dancer and choreographer Twyla Tharp writes that for her, "the first steps of a creative act are like groping in the dark: random and chaotic, feverish and fearful, a lot of busy-ness with no apparent or definable end in sight."[44] She claims that she needs an idea, that she cannot just walk into the dance studio and expect some type of inspiration. She explains, "You can't just dance or paint or write or sculpt. Those are just verbs. You need a tangible idea to get you going."[45] She goes through a process she calls "scratching," where she

---

43 Haskins, *John Cage*, 65.
44 Twyla Tharp, *The Creative Habit: Learn It and Use It for Life* (New York: Simon and Schuster Paperbacks, 2003), 94.
45 Tharp, *The Creative Habit: Learn It and Use It for Life*, 94.

digs "through everything to find something."[46] Tharp provides various ways a person can "scratch" for ideas and inspiration: reading, everyday conversation, other people's handiwork (such that can be found in a museum, theater, exhibition, etc.), mentors/heroes, nature, and the environment. She acknowledges that "scratching can look like borrowing or appropriating, but it's an essential part of creativity. It's primal, and very private."[47] For Tharp, an award-winning choreographer who created dances for ballet companies all over the world, scratching is a necessary step in the creative process. In some ways, scratching can be associated with the imaginative/perceptual experience that precedes the actual act of creation.

John Cage immersed himself in all kinds of stimuli and interacted with some of the most important musicians, dancers, artists, and writers of his day (and also had other hobbies and interests, including his fascination with mushrooms). One specific influence, however, for his silent piece *4'33"* included Robert Rauschenberg's white paintings. These were canvases created in the summer of 1951 at Black Mountain that Rauschenberg simply painted white. Some critics found them of little value, such as Hubert Crehan, who said they were nothing but "dada shenanigans."[48] However, Cage applauded them and was inspired by them. Kyle Gann points out, "For Cage, the whiteness wasn't a divine presence but an absence that refused to dominate the viewer, in a way analogous to the 'silent' piece he'd been contemplating."[49] Cage himself acknowledged the influence of the white paintings when he explained, "Actually what pushed me into [writing *4'33"*] was not guts but the example of Robert Rauschenberg. His white paintings ... When I saw those, I said, 'Oh yes, I must; otherwise I'm lagging, otherwise music is lagging.'"[50] In an epigraph for a lecture Cage gave on Rauschenberg, he wrote:

> To Whom It May Concern:
> The white paintings came
> first; my silent piece
> came later.[51]

---

46   Tharp, *The Creative Habit: Learn It and Use It for Life*, 95.

47   Tharp, *The Creative Habit: Learn It and Use It for Life*, 95.

48   Gann, *No Such Thing as Silence: John Cage's 4'33"*, 158.

49   Gann, *No Such Thing as Silence: John Cage's 4'33"*, 158.

50   Gann, *No Such Thing as Silence: John Cage's 4'33"*, 160.

51   Gann, *No Such Thing as Silence: John Cage's 4'33"*, 160.

IMAGINATION IN MUSICAL COMPOSITION, PERFORMANCE, & LISTENING   607

Clearly inspired by these white works, Cage found beauty in the potential shadows, dust, or particles that might fall on them, and he reasoned that "a cough or a baby crying" would "not ruin a good piece of modern music."[52]

So Cage did not create his silent piece in a vacuum; he composed it after having studied music with a few of the finest teachers available and after having interacted with some of the most creative people of his era. He started with an imaginative idea and proceeded to make that possibility a reality. Aaron Copland, in his book *Music and Imagination*, suggests that a "composer is a kind of magician; out of the recesses of his thought he produces, or finds himself in possession of, the generative idea."[53] He goes on to explain:

> Although I say "the recesses of his thought," in actuality the source of the germinal idea is the one phase in creation that resists rational explanation. All we know is that the moment of possession is the moment of inspiration; or to use Coleridge's phrase, the moment when the creator is in "a more than usual state of emotion." Whence it comes, or in what manner it comes, or how long its duration one can never foretell... The inspired moment may sometimes be described as a kind of hallucinatory state of mind: one half of the personality emotes and dictates while the other half listens and notates.[54]

Copland acknowledges that a composer experiences inspiration in a variety of ways. In order to create each day, however, often times one must engage the "critical faculty"[55] to bring a work to completion. So Cage, drawing upon both inspiration and reason, produced *4'33"*, one of the most inventive and creative compositions of the twentieth century.

Although imagination is an important component of the creative process for a composer, it is also imperative for the performer. Stravinsky writes about the importance of performing, of sharing a musical work with an audience. He explains that in this capacity the musician is an "intermediary" between the composer and the listener, and therefore has a genuine "moral responsibility."[56] Copland also describes the performer as an "intermediary,"

---

52   Gann, *No Such Thing as Silence: John Cage's 4'33"*, 159.
53   Aaron Copland, *Music and Imagination: The Charles Eliot Norton Lectures, 1951–1952* (New York: Mentor Books-New American Library, 1959), 52.
54   Copland, *Music and Imagination*, 52–53.
55   Copland, *Music and Imagination*, 53.
56   Igor Stravinsky, *Poetics of Music in the Form of Six Lessons*, trans. Arthur Knodel and Ingolf Dahl (Cambridge, MA: Harvard University Press, 1970), 132.

a person who "brings the composer's work to life—a kind of midwife to the composition."[57] He continues to explain that the performer

> partakes of the same dedication of purpose, the same sense of self-discovery through each performance, the same conviction that something unique is lost, possibly, when his own understanding of a work of art is lost. He even partakes of the involuntary nature of creation, for we know that he cannot at will turn on the wellsprings of his creativity so that each performance may be of equal value. Quite the contrary, each time he steps out upon the concert platform we wish him luck, for he shares something of the creator's uncertain powers of projection. Thus we see that interpretation, even though it may rightfully be thought of as an auxiliary art, does share some elements of creativity with the mind that forms the work of art.[58]

Sometimes such a musician can bring an interpretation to a piece that is beyond what the composer has ever imagined. This can be an illuminating experience for the composer, the performer, and the audience.

In the article "How do people communicate using music?," David J. Hargreaves, Raymond MacDonald, and Dorothy Miell write that "music is a fundamental channel of communication: it provides a means by which people can share emotions, intentions, and meanings."[59] They explain that music "can exert powerful physical and behavioural effects, can produce deep and profound emotions within us, and can be used to generate infinitely subtle variations of expressiveness by skilled composers and performers, such that highly complex informational structures and contents can be communicated extremely rapidly between people."[60] Performers play a major role in this means of communication. It is their responsibility to interpret the score, which often includes notes, rests, dynamics, musical symbols, tempo markings, some type of text, and other instructions. The performers respond to what is usually on a written page and make it come alive, as it were, to provide their unique interpretation of the score, within its parameters. Their contribution can and should involve a certain degree of imagination and engagement to be successful.

In performance, it is usually most desirable to use a score that reflects the composer's original intentions, not one that includes additional or altered

---

57   Copland, *Music and Imagination*, 52.
58   Copland, *Music and Imagination*, 52.
59   Hargreaves, MacDonald, and Miell, "How do People Communicate Using Music?," 1.
60   Hargreaves, MacDonald, and Miell, "How do People Communicate Using Music?," 1.

IMAGINATION IN MUSICAL COMPOSITION, PERFORMANCE, & LISTENING

instructions and markings by an editor. In the article "A Performer's Responsibility," Susan Bradshaw emphasizes the importance of avoiding scores that have been "confusingly overlaid with editorial encumbrances, however well intentioned."[61] She explains that "in its pristine state," the score becomes a type of "custodian of some original truth, however elusory," and it becomes the "single unadulterated starting point for interpretation."[62] While she acknowledges that most scores do not provide instructions for every detail of the performance, when the musicians begin to take too much creative license, without continued reference to the specifications of the composer, the result can be "inarticulate half-truths deprived of any real perspective."[63] She suggests that in a performance there is an "ever-fragile balance between background and foreground (between melody and harmony, rhythm and meter), that has continually to be renewed if the trust assumed to exist between composer, performer and listener is not to be betrayed."[64] So for the performer, ideally it is important to start with a "pristine" and "unadulterated" score, to make every effort to follow the instructions (through notation, symbols, words, etc.) as carefully as possible, and to avoid taking grand liberties that might result in presentation of "half-truths."

Yet, where is the imagination and creativity in performance if the musician has such restrictions? Aaron Copland writes that in reality "the written page is only an approximation."[65] While a musician should be aware of how a piece should be performed stylistically, considering the time period in which it was composed and the individual personality and traits of the composer, there is no one way of interpreting it. Copland emphasizes, however, that "each different reading must in itself be convincing, musically and psychologically—it must be within the limits of one of the possible ways of interpreting the work."[66] He comments that as a composer himself, he would like to believe that each of his pieces could be presented and interpreted "in several ways."[67] Martin Lotze, Gabriela Scheler, and Niels Birbaumer agree that performing music well requires certain skills, including "an innate, but also highly trained, ability to imagine a musical piece in relation to the expressive, emotional, and,

---

61   Susan Bradshaw, "A Performer's Responsibility," in *Composition, Performance, Reception: Studies in the Creative Process in Music*, ed. Wyndham Thomas (Aldershot, UK: Ashgate, 1998), 53.

62   Bradshaw, "A Performer's Responsibility," 53.

63   Bradshaw, "A Performer's Responsibility," 54.

64   Bradshaw, "A Performer's Responsibility," 54.

65   Copland, *Music and Imagination*, 59.

66   Copland, *Music and Imagination*, 58.

67   Copland, *Music and Imagination*, 58.

of course technical details."[68] A performer should also be able to choose a particular interpretation and "transpose the image into the reality," and this involves "creative processes" that are "grounded on both musical experience and emotional associations."[69] These particular abilities involve a certain "auditory imagination" that enables the creative performer to convey emotional, structural, technical, and stylistic aspects of the music to the audience.[70]

So now we will consider how these ideas about performance relate to Cage's *4'33"*. First, he provided not one, but several versions of the score. The first was the 1952 version used by David Tudor in the premiere, which has since been lost. This score was dedicated to Tudor, who later attempted to recreate it from memory. In his 1989 reconstruction, there is a more conventional notation for keyboard, with staff lines, treble clef, bass clef, bar lines, and time signature (4/4), but no notes. All the measures are blank. Then Cage made another version of the score for Irwin Kremen for his twenty-eighth birthday, on June 5, 1953. On this manuscript, which is sparser than the first version, there are vertical lines on blank pages that indicate the different movements. There is also a note on the first page indicating that the piece can be performed by any one instrument or any combination of instruments. Another significant version is a typewritten score indicating three movements with Roman numerals, and "TACET" written under each numeral (as presented and discussed earlier in this essay). So what started out as a piano piece with a set duration (for which David Tudor used a stop watch), had evolved into a work that could be presented by any number of performers for any length of time. A performer would need to begin by deciding which version of those available to use.

Then the musician would interpret the score and act as an intermediary between the composer and listener. The performer would need to analyze which parts of the composition should be adhered to rather faithfully, and determine how imagination and creativity could also be expressed. In the case of *4'33"*, there are aspects of the score (any of the available versions) that suggest a stricter reading, while in other ways a performer is also given tremendous leeway. For example, while there is variance among the different written versions, one constant is the division of the piece into three movements. Kyle Gann explains, "The specific three-movement division used for *4'33"* ... has its roots in this need for structure as the socially agreed-upon aspect of music.

---

68 Martin Lotze, Gabriela Scheler, and Niels Birbaumer, "From Music Perception to Creative Performance: Mapping Cerebral Differences Between Professional and Amateur Musicians," in *Musical Creativity: Multidisciplinary Research in Theory and Practice*, eds. Irène Deliège and Geraint A. Wiggins (Andover: Psychology Press, 2006), 275.

69 Lotze, Scheler, and Birbaumer, "From Music Perception to Creative Performance," 275.

70 Lotze, Scheler, and Birbaumer, "From Music Perception to Creative Performance," 275.

An unarticulated stretch of silence would presumably have seemed too amorphous."[71] Carmen Pardo concurs that the piece includes "a structure that barely contains any indications beyond its division in three parts. Yet, even in these structures time is not free, it remains bound to an organization."[72] Although when performing from the score, this three-part structure should be observed, Cage does not indicate how to do this, so it needs to be determined by the performer. Richard Kostelanetz suggests that Cage's "scores are designed to encourage a greater variety of interpretations than usual. There is no 'right way' to do them, though there are wrong ways, especially if a performer violates the instructions that are not left to chance."[73] In the case of the premiere, David Tudor closed the keyboard lid of the piano to signal the beginning of a new movement. This is an area where the performer can follow the three-part structure, yet still draw upon his or her own imagination and creativity.

Although there can be a certain pressure put on musicians to stand out and be unique in the concert hall, the focus should really be on presenting the sincerest interpretation possible. In the article, "Creativity in performance," Eric F. Clarke points out that "the overwhelming majority of concerts, recordings, and broadcasts deal with a more or less static musical repertory," so "the primary way to attract an audience, or sell recordings, is to focus on the personal identity and creative attributes of the performer."[74] He continues to explain: "The emphasis on creativity in performance is strongly bound up with the institution of the public concert, which emerged in Europe around the middle of the 18th century, and with Romantic and post-Romantic musical traditions that still play a central role in the dominant culture."[75] In response to this phenomenon

---

71 Gann, *No Such Thing as Silence: John Cage's 4'33"*, 54–55.

72 Carmen Pardo, "On the Time Suspended," in *John Cage: Paisajes imaginarios, Conciertos & Musicircus/Imaginary Landscapes, Concerts & Musicircus*, curated by Joan Cerveró (Espai d'art contemporani de Castelló, 2009), 328.

73 Richard Kostelanetz, "John Cage's Anarchism," in *John Cage: Paisajes imaginarios, Conciertos & Musicircus/Imaginary Landscapes, Concerts & Musicircus*, curated by Joan Cerveró (Espai d'art contemporani de Castelló, 2009), 335.

74 Eric F. Clarke, "Creativity in Performance," in *Musical Imaginations: Multidisciplinary Perspectives on Creativity, Performance, and Perception*, eds. David J. Hargreaves, Dorothy E. Miell, and Raymond A.R. MacDonald (Oxford: Oxford University Press, 2012), 18.

75 Clarke, "Creativity in Performance," 18. In his book *Musical Elaborations*, Edward W. Said describes a musical performance as an "extreme occasion" (Edward W. Said, *Musical Elaborations* (New York: Columbia University Press, 1991), 17). He writes that what most performers attempt to accomplish on stage, due to training and experience, is something many people in the audience cannot replicate. The sense of awe that many listeners experience at a concert is also often not just dependent on the performers, but also on managers, concert associations, ticket sellers, electronic media, jet travel, etc. There is frequently

in *4′33″*, Cage disrupts the more traditional focus on the performer and encourages astute listening on behalf of the audience.

Cage not only blurred the boundaries of the definition of music, but he also upset the division between performer and listener. In 1982, he told William Duckworth in reference to *4′33″*,

> Well, I use it constantly in my life experience. No day goes by without my making use of that piece in my life and in my work. I listen to it every day ... I don't sit down to do it; I turn my attention to it. I realize that it's going on continuously. So, more and more, my attention, as now, is on it. More than anything else, it's the source of my enjoyment of life.[76]

By this means Cage leads the performer and listener out from the concert hall and onto the streets, into nature, in the home environment, anywhere, and invites them to really listen to the sounds, noises, screeches, traffic, birds, creaks, hums, horns, and voices of daily life. The performer can opt not to follow the score of *4′33″* in a stricter sense and follow, rather, the "spirit" of the piece. The result will be similar to what musician Emil Gilels experiences with his own performances of one particular work: "It is different each time I play."[77]

Finally, there are expectations required of a music listener in general, including imagination. Copland wrote that "it is the freely imaginative mind that is at the core of all vital music making and music listening."[78] Those audience members who attended the premiere of *4′33″* with an imaginative and open mind most likely appreciated it more than those who thought it was simply a prank. As Kyle Gann writes,

> John Cage's *4′33″* is one of the most misunderstood pieces of music ever written and yet, at times, one of the avant-garde's best understood as well. Many presume that the piece's purpose was deliberate provocation, an attempt to insult, or get a reaction from, the audience. For others, though, it was a logical turning point to which other musical developments had inevitably led, and from which new ones would spring.[79]

---

a network of non-musician professionals involved in bringing the performance to the stage.

76 Gann, *No Such Thing as Silence: John Cage's 4′33″*, 186.
77 Clarke, "Creativity in performance," 17.
78 Copland, *Music and Imagination*, 17.
79 Gann, *No Such Thing as Silence: John Cage's 4′33″*, 10–11.

IMAGINATION IN MUSICAL COMPOSITION, PERFORMANCE, & LISTENING   613

It is understandable that initially some listeners had difficulty understanding the piece. Stravinsky provides some explanation for those who may not have responded well to the composition at first hearing. He suggests that the listener's experience can be quite "harrowing," because the person "has no point of reference and possesses no basis for comparison."[80] Nonetheless, there are ways that a person can develop greater imagination in listening.

In the *The Mind's Ear: Exercises for Improving the Musical Imagination for Performers, Composers, and Listeners*, Bruce Adolphe provides exercises for developing greater musical imagination. He suggests that one of the biggest reasons some people do not engage in new music, or nontraditional music, is due to their own "lack of imagination."[81] His book focuses on helping performers, composers, and listeners expand their skills beyond traditional methods and approaches, and some of his exercises could be helpful in better appreciating and participating in Cage's *4′33″*. For example, there is an exercise in two parts, entitled "Hearing Ordinary Sounds in Your Mind." In the first part, a person attempts to hear various sounds in his or her mind, as if these sounds had actually been recorded. Such sounds include breaking glass, a siren, footsteps coming up marble stairs, footsteps walking on mud, a pencil writing on paper, an eraser rubbing out some words on paper, and hammering a nail into a wall.[82] Then in Part two of the exercise, certain musical elements are added to the basic everyday sounds listed in Part one. Some of the suggestions include the following: "Hear breaking glass in a steady pulsing rhythm with accents every few beats," "hear a siren, starting very softly in the distance (*pp*); it gets louder as it approaches (crescendo; it is loud and very near (*ff*); it disappears into the distance (diminuendo to silence)," and "hear a pencil writing on paper in very fast, light strokes with sudden silences interrupting every so often."[83] Someone who desires to acquire more astute listening skills, especially for nontraditional music, could certainly participate in such exercises and develop a keener musical imagination.

---

80   Igor Stravinsky, *Poetics of Music in the Form of Six Lessons*, 133. Many listeners struggled to accept Arnold Schoenberg's twelve-tone music. In *The Language of Modern Music*, Donald Mitchell writes, "There were many who thought Schoenberg had stepped right outside the bounds of musical sanity. It speaks for the composer's courage that he never faltered in his belief in his inspiration, though only too well aware of how his exploration of new territories would be received" (Donald Mitchell, *The Language of Modern Music* (Philadelphia: University of Pennsylvania Press, 1993), 29).

81   Bruce Adolphe, *The Mind's Ear: Exercises for Improving the Musical Imagination for Performers, Composers, and Listeners*, 2nd ed. (Oxford: Oxford University Press, 2013), 8.

82   Adolphe, *The Mind's Ear*, 25.

83   Adolphe, *The Mind's Ear*, 25.

Copland writes that "listening is a talent, and like any other talent or gift, we possess it in varying degrees."[84] He views a listener as the interpreter of the interpreter, and this is not easy to do because "the listener … is expected to know in advance what the performance *ought* to sound like before he hears what it *does* sound like."[85] An informed listener is aware of the historical period of a particular composition, the biography and works of the composer, the point in the composer's history when the piece was written, etc., and in this way a listener can make a more sophisticated appraisal. Copland stresses the importance of engaged listening: "The dream of every musician who loves his art is to involve gifted listeners everywhere as an active force in the musical community. The attitude of each individual listener, especially the gifted listener, is the principle resource we have in bringing to fruition the immense musical potentialities of our own time."[86]

In addition, the listener comes to the concert hall with a certain degree of experience, both musical and nonmusical, which can also inform the interpretation of the musical performance. In the article "Expectation and Interpretation in the Reception of New Music: A Case Study," Adrian Beaumont claims that "any listener's initial response to a piece of music must be conditioned by previous listening, and in some cases also reading and performing, experiences."[87] The overall response can also be affected by other influences that may not even pertain to music. Listeners "actively process and evaluate" various musical compositions and performances based on "their personal, musical and cultural networks of association, which also have a historical dimension."[88] Although some people may view the listener as a "passive recipient" to the active role of the performer, Hargreaves, MacDonald, and Miell acknowledge that a listener may "play an active role in shaping the content and meaning of the message."[89]

A distinction can be made between "hearing" and "listening." Robert Jourdain suggests that "when we experience music in the background, we passively *hear* and do not actively *listen*."[90] He goes on to discuss the topic of "attending

---

84   Copland, *Music and Imagination*, 18.

85   Copland, *Music and Imagination*, 60.

86   Copland, *Music and* Imagination, 29–30.

87   Adrian Beaumont, "Expectation and Interpretation in the Reception of New Music: A Case Study," in *Composition, Performance, Reception: Studies in the Creative Process in Music*, ed. Wyndham Thomas (Aldershot, UK: Ashgate, 1998), 93.

88   David J. Hargreaves, Jonathan James Hargreaves, and Adrian C. North, "Imagination and creativity in music listening," in *Musical Imaginations: Multidisciplinary perspectives on creativity, performance, and perception*, eds. David J. Hargreaves, Dorothy E. Miell, and Raymond A.R. MacDonald (Oxford: Oxford University Press, 2012), 169.

89   Hargreaves, MacDonald, and Miell, "How do People Communicate Using Music?," 4.

90   Jourdain, *Music, the Brain, and Ecstasy: How Music Captures our Imagination*, 245.

to music," which involves our attention, "a nervous system's exposure to sensation."[91] He writes that attention is "complicated in a multilevel mammalian mind, and terribly complex in the symbol-clogged minds of human beings."[92] He explains further:

> Much of a human brain's experience is of activities of other parts of the brain. This is particularly true at the highest levels of information processing, levels that we call analytical. These can be turned upon internal imagery so intently that we become momentarily blind to experience right before our eyes ... At the highest level of cognition, we always view the world through a narrow telescope, always labor under a kind of tunnel vision. Even when our eyes are focused wide, we're able to consider only a few aspects of the scene before us at any moment.[93]

Jourdain claims that this also happens to us as human beings when we listen to music, that "we incessantly shift focus between its many aspects, always on the lookout for more crucial features."[94] He writes that usually when the "average listener" is asked to respond to a musical performance, that person is often only able to recall "the most prominent features."[95]

In simple terms, listeners as interpreters can have an active or passive role in listening to music, and even when effort is made to listen attentively, there is a constant shift of focus. When John Cage brought noise into the concert hall and asked listeners to view it as music, he was, in a sense, asking them to go beyond just "hearing" the sounds in the background. He attempted to bring this noise to their attention, to view it as something valuable, artistic, and perhaps even aesthetically pleasing. Even with focused concentration, they might shift attention from the sirens outside to the quiet whispers of another listener, to the rustle of paper, or to the hum of the air conditioner, yet Cage sought to bring these sounds from the background to the foreground. In his analysis of *4'33"*, Herbert Henck wrote: "Ainsi la musique dépasse le cadre de l'exécution, du concert. Elle devient discipline, école de concentration, d'observation, de regard et d'écoute, de recueillement des sens et d'attention illimitée, indivise, qui ne connaît plus le vouloir, le désir, l'attente" [Thus the music goes beyond the performance space in a concert. It brings about discipline, a sense of

---

91   Jourdain, *Music, the Brain, and Ecstasy: How Music Captures our Imagination*, 249.
92   Jourdain, *Music, the Brain, and Ecstasy: How Music Captures our Imagination*, 249–50.
93   Jourdain, *Music, the Brain, and Ecstasy: How Music Captures our Imagination*, 250.
94   Jourdain, *Music, the Brain, and Ecstasy: How Music Captures our Imagination*, 250.
95   Jourdain, *Music, the Brain, and Ecstasy: How Music Captures our Imagination*, 250.

concentration, observation, watching and listening, awareness of the senses, of unlimited and undivided attention that does not know want, desire, or expectation.][96]

In his seminal book *Noise: The Political Economy of Music*, Jacques Attali writes, "When Cage opens the door to the concert hall to let the noise of the street in, he is regenerating all of music: he is taking it to its culmination. He is blaspheming, criticizing the code and the network."[97] He points out:

> When he sits motionless at the piano for four minutes and thirty-three seconds, letting the audience grow impatient and make noises, he is giving back the right to speak to people who do not want to have it. He is announcing the disappearance of the commercial site of music: music is to be produced not in a temple, not in a hall, not at home, but everywhere; it is to be produced everywhere possible it is possible to produce it, in whatever way it is wished, by anyone who wants to enjoy it.[98]

It is this very sentiment, this particular approach to his piece, that eventually led Cage out of the concert hall with it. Ultimately his silent composition did not need a traditional venue, performer, or audience to be enjoyed and appreciated.

Although some people may have initially rejected Cage's silent masterpiece, with the passage of time more and more listeners have come to accept and appreciate it. Their own musical imagination has expanded, and what seemed perhaps appalling or even ridiculous at first, is now greater understood and in some cases admired. More than twenty years after the premiere, Cage acknowledged that there were no longer such "battles" in distinguishing "musical sounds" from "noises."[99] He announced, "We no longer discriminate against noises."[100] Writing about it now, over sixty years after the premiere, it has become more apparent that *4'33"* was one of the great musical compositions of the twentieth century. It helped both performers and listeners develop greater musical imagination as it upset the boundaries between traditional musical performance and life.

---

96 Herbert Henck, "Le son du silence: *4'33"* du John Cage," *Revue d'esthétique* 13–15 (1987–1988): 239; my translation.

97 Jacques Attali, *Noise: The Political Economy of Music*, Theory and History of Literature 16, trans. Brian Massumi (Minneapolis, MN: University of Minnesota Press, 1985), 136.

98 Attali, *Noise: The Political Economy of Music*, 136.

99 John Cage, *Empty Words: Writings '73–'78* (Middletown, CT: Wesleyan University Press, 1979), 177.

100 Cage, *Empty Words*, 177.

IMAGINATION IN MUSICAL COMPOSITION, PERFORMANCE, & LISTENING   617

In conclusion, John Cage stirred up the musical world with his silent piece *4′33″*. Through his imagination and creativity, he disrupted the boundaries of music and life, and this also required an imaginative interpretation of his work by performers. In turn, listeners needed imagination in order to better appreciate the performer's interpretation. To take this a step further, the piece could be performed and listened to by a single individual outside a concert hall, anywhere and anytime. As Kyle Gann suggests, "Ultimately, we are left with the conundrum that *4′33″* has expanded into an infinite river of a piece into which any of us can dip any time we please. Someone can frame it, in performance or on recording, to draw attention to it. But for those who have an affinity for Cage's appreciation for the physicality of sound, even that is no longer necessary."[101]

Furthermore, his silent piece did not solely affect the way we perform and perceive music. While at the Getty Museum, it was the influence of John Cage (a fellow Los Angeles native) and his *4′33″* that helped me look beyond bronze statues, framed paintings on a wall, or intricate Oriental porcelain vases to find visual art. Through the model of his silent piece, it occurred to me that I could include the natural landscape both at and beyond the museum, the distant cityscapes, and the flow of cars on the freeway as part of my aesthetic experience. Currently, it is also Cage's example that helps me recognize that I do not even need a museum to appreciate visual art. I can engage with it every day in my surroundings where I live in New Mexico. I can observe the pinkish-red hues of the setting sun as I relax on my back patio. When I drive to Santa Fe, I can admire pungent green sage growing naturally in the high desert and the massive blue sky that dominates much of the landscape. I can also simply walk out the front door of my home in Albuquerque and appreciate the asymmetrical cactus garden intermingled with drought-tolerant plants, such as Russian sage, catnip, baby's breath, and red yucca.[102] Cage not only helped to blur the boundaries involving music composition, performance, and listening, but also the general lines between all forms of art and life.

---

101   Gann, *No Such Thing as Silence*, 187.

102   In his book *Silencing the Sounded Self: John Cage and the American Experimental Tradition*, Christopher Shultis discusses some of the similarities of essayist, philosopher, and naturalist Henry David Thoreau and John Cage: "And for Cage and Thoreau, observation is central to the role of the artist" (Christopher Shultis, *Silencing the Sounded Self: John Cage and the American Experimental Tradition* (Boston: Northeastern University Press, 1998), 53). Wherever we are, we can carefully listen to the sounds and observe the sights of nature and of our environment in order to find the "art" that is naturally there.

References

Adolphe, Bruce. *The Mind's Ear: Exercises for Improving the Musical Imagination for Performers, Composers, and Listeners.* 2nd ed. Oxford: Oxford University Press. 2013.

Attali, Jacques. *Noise: The Political Economy of Music.* Theory and History of Literature 16. Translated by Brian Massumi. Minneapolis, MN: University of Minnesota Press. 1985.

Beaumont, Adrian. "Expectation and Interpretation in the Reception of New Music: A Case Study." In *Composition, Performance, Reception: Studies in the Creative Process in Music*, edited by Wyndham Thomas, 93–104. Aldershot, UK: Ashgate, 1998.

Bernstein, David W. "John Cage, Arnold Schoenberg, and the Musical Idea." In *John Cage: Music, Philosophy, and Intention, 1933–1950*, edited by David W. Patterson, 15–45. New York: Routledge, 2002.

Bernstein, David W. "Music I: to the Late 1940s." In *The Cambridge Companion to John Cage*, edited by David Nicholls, 63–84. Cambridge: Cambridge University Press, 2002.

Boss, Jack. *Schoenberg's Twelve-Tone Music: Symmetry and the Musical Idea (Music since 1900).* Cambridge: Cambridge University Press. 2016.

Bradshaw, Susan. "A Performer's Responsibility." In *Composition, Performance, Reception: Studies in the Creative Process in Music*, edited by Wyndham Thomas, 53–65. Aldershot, UK: Ashgate, 1998.

Cage, John. *4'33".* New York: Henmar Press. 1960.

Cage, John. *Empty Words: Writings '73–'78.* Middletown, CT: Wesleyan University Press. 1979.

Cage, John. *Musicage: Cage Muses on Words, Art, Music.* Edited by Joan Retallack. Middletown, CT: Wesleyan University Press, 1996.

Cage, John. *Silence: Lectures and Writings.* Middletown, CT: Wesleyan University Press. 1961.

Clarke, Eric F. "Creativity in Performance." In *Musical Imaginations: Multidisciplinary perspectives on creativity, performance, and perception*, edited by David J. Hargreaves, Dorothy E. Miell, and Raymond A.R. MacDonald, 17–30. Oxford: Oxford University Press, 2012.

Copland, Aaron. *Music and Imagination: The Charles Eliot Norton Lectures, 1951–1952.* New York: Mentor Books-New American Library. 1959.

Dickinson, Peter. "John Cage: Interview with Peter Dickinson, BBC studios, New York City, June 29, 1987." In *Cage Talk: Dialogues with and about John Cage*, edited by Peter Dickinson, 25–51. Rochester, NY: University of Rochester Press, 2006.

"File: King Wen (I Ching).png." *Wikimedia Commons.* Accessed June 21, 2019. https://commons.wikimedia.org/wiki/File:King_Wen_(I_Ching).png.

Gann, Kyle. *No Such Thing as Silence: John Cage's 4'33".* New Haven, CT: Yale University Press. 2010.

IMAGINATION IN MUSICAL COMPOSITION, PERFORMANCE, & LISTENING 619

Gena, Peter. "John Cage the Composer." In *A John Cage Reader in Celebration of His 70th Birthday*, edited by Peter Gena and Jonathan Brent, 1–3. New York: C.F. Peters, 1982.

Hargreaves, David J., Jonathan James Hargreaves, and Adrian C. North. "Imagination and Creativity in Music Listening." In *Musical Imaginations: Multidisciplinary perspectives on creativity, performance, and perception*, edited by David J. Hargreaves, Dorothy E. Miell, and Raymond A.R. MacDonald, 156–72. Oxford: Oxford University Press, 2012.

Hargreaves, David J., Raymond MacDonald, and Dorothy Miell. "Explaining Musical Imaginations: Creativity, Performance and Perception." In *Musical Imaginations: Multidisciplinary perspectives on creativity, performance, and perception*, edited by David J. Hargreaves, Dorothy E. Miell, and Raymond A.R. MacDonald, 1–14. Oxford: Oxford University Press, 2012.

Hargreaves, David J., Raymond MacDonald, and Dorothy Miell. "How do People Communicate Using Music?" In *Musical Communication*, edited by Dorothy Miell, Raymond MacDonald, and David J. Hargreaves, 1–25. Oxford: Oxford University Press, 2005.

Haskins, Rob. *John Cage*. London: Reaktion Books, 2012.

Henck, Herbert. "Le son du silence: *4'33"* du John Cage." *Revue d'esthétique* 13–15 (1987–1988): 237–39.

Jourdain, Robert. *Music, the Brain, and Ecstasy: How Music Captures our Imagination*. New York: William Morrow. 1997.

Katschthaler, Karl. "Absence, Presence and Potentiality: John Cage's *4'33"* Revisited." In *Silence and Absence in Literature and Music*. Word and Music Studies 15, edited by Werner Wolf and Walter Bernhart, 166–79. Leiden: Brill-Rodopi, 2016.

Kostelanetz, Richard. "John Cage's Anarchism." In *John Cage: Paisajes imaginarios, Conciertos & Musicircus/Imaginary Landscapes, Concerts & Musicircus*, curated by Joan Cerveró, 335–39. Espai d'art contemporani de Castelló, 2009.

Lippman, Edward. *A History of Western Musical Aesthetics*. Lincoln, NE: University of Nebraska Press. 1992.

Lotze, Martin, Gabriela Scheler, and Niels Birbaumer. "From Music Perception to Creative Performance: Mapping Cerebral Differences Between Professional and Amateur Musicians." In *Musical Creativity: Multidisciplinary Research in Theory and Practice*, edited by Irène Deliège and Geraint A. Wiggins, 275–89. Andover: Psychology Press, 2006.

Maillol, Aristide. *L'Air*. Sculpture. Los Angeles, J. Paul Getty Museum, 1938.

Mitchell, Donald. *The Language of Modern Music*. Philadelphia: University of Pennsylvania Press. 1993.

Pardo, Carmen. "On the Time Suspended." In *John Cage: Paisajes imaginarios, Conciertos & Musicircus/Imaginary Landscapes, Concerts & Musicircus*, curated by Joan Cerveró, 327–33. Espai d'art contemporani de Castelló, 2009.

Said, Edward W. *Musical Elaborations*. New York: Columbia University Press. 1991.

Saxton, Robert. "The Process of Composition from Detection to Confection." In *Composition, Performance, Reception: Studies in the Creative Process in Music*, edited by Wyndham Thomas, 1–16. Aldershot, UK: Ashgate, 1998.

Schoenberg, Arnold. *Fundamentals of Musical Composition*. Rev. ed. London: Faber and Faber, 1999.

Schoenberg, Arnold. *The Musical Idea and the Logic, Technique, and Art of Its Presentation*. Edited by Severine Neff. Bloomington, IN: Indiana University Press, 2006.

Shultis, Christopher. *Silencing the Sounded Self: John Cage and the American Experimental Tradition*. Boston: Northeastern University Press. 1998.

Stravinksy, Igor. *Poetics of Music in the Form of Six Lessons*. Translated by Arthur Knodel and Ingolf Dahl. Cambridge, MA: Harvard University Press. 1970.

Tharp, Twyla. *The Creative Habit: Learn It and Use It for Life*. New York: Simon and Schuster Paperbacks. 2003.

The John Cage Trust. "John Cage: An Autobiographical Statement." *John Cage: Official Website*. Accessed June 20, 2019. https://johncage.org/autobiographical_statement .html.

Weagel, Deborah. "Silence in John Cage and Samuel Beckett: *4'33"* and *Waiting for Godot*." In *Pastiches, Parodies & Other Imitations/Pastiches, Parodies & Autres Imitations*. Samuel Beckett Today/Aujourd'hui 12, edited by Marius Buning, Matthijs Engelberts, and Sjef Houppermans, 249–62. Leiden: Rodopi, 2002.

Weagel, Deborah. "Silence in Krzysztof Kieslowski's The Decalogue: A Cagian Perspective." *Journal of Comparative Literature and Aesthetics*, vol. 34, nos. 1–2 (2011): 1–12.

Weagel, Deborah. *Words and Music: Camus, Beckett, Cage, Gould*. New York: Peter Lang. 2010.

CHAPTER 26

Kinesthetic Imagining and Dance Appreciation

Renee M. Conroy

1 How to Look at Dance

Dance critic and theorist Walter Terry concludes his 1982 guide *How to Look at Dance* with a series of remarks about the role of what he calls "kinesthetics" in dance art appreciation.[1] Of the spiritual "Fix Me, Jesus" from Alvin Ailey's landmark *Revelations* (1960), Terry writes:

> Ailey conceived a duet of supplication for a man and a woman. It is reverent yet quietly ecstatic, and the key gesture is a reach toward the invisible Jesus. The culmination of this motif of reaching is achieved at the final moment, when the woman steps on her partner's thigh and with her entire body – not merely her hand and arm – reaches heavenward. Dance moments such as these demand, or at least invite, a kinesthetic response from the viewer.[2]

Terry also suggests that "Kinesthetics in the individual can be developed ... to minimal or maximum degrees," and proposes that dance-related appreciative activities are understood usefully "as a sort of game of recognition."[3] He concludes his primer with this final piece of advice for audiences of dance art:

> So ... do not refrain from participating in the dance movements you watch in the theater or on television. Reach out with all your kinesthetic powers at the ready toward the dance in all its forms, and you will discover that you have cause to rejoice.[4]

---

1 Walter Terry defines "kinesthetics" as follows: "it means that you not only *look* at dance but you respond to it with your own body." He continues, "If the eye can retain an image of something seen and the ear capture and recall a melody, so can the viewer of a dance event receive in his or her own muscles echoes of action." See Walter Terry, *How to Look at Dance* (New York: William Morrow and Co., Inc., 1982), 173. All italics used for emphasis are in original.
2 Terry, *How to Look at Dance*, 173.
3 Terry, *How to Look at Dance*, 174, 177.
4 Terry, *How to Look at Dance*, 178–79.

© KONINKLIJKE BRILL NV, LEIDEN, 2020 | DOI:10.1163/9789004436350_028

In one way, Terry's recommendations are unremarkable. It is customary for dance critics, theorists, teachers, choreographers, professional dancers, and dance lovers to regard so-called "kinesthetic empathy" as a key element in dance art appreciation.[5] Hence, it is not surprising that Terry assumes that there is some important relation between experiencing a dance performance bodily and attaining fulsome engagement with the work performed. Nor is it exceptional that he advocates "watching" dance corporeally by attending to the physical responses we have to movement sequences we observe on stage. His directives echo philosopher Sibyl S. Cohen's more strident expression of the prevailing danceworld perspective: "The viewer would be totally unable to experience dance aesthetically if his or her experience of it was limited to 'merely seeing.' To achieve any aesthetic value – any aesthetic satisfaction – the dance must be perceived through the lived body."[6]

In another way, however, Terry's guidance is unusual. Particularly striking is the language he selects to reaffirm the danceworld adage that a crucial part of dance appreciation is what I describe as "dancing along," which I regard as:

> ...sensations of doing what the dancers are doing or feeling what (one imagines) the dancers feel as they whirl, leap, and spin on stage. (They may also include the feeling of being muscularly inspired to get up out of your seat and dance.) 'Dancing along' is, roughly put, the experience of physically 'being moved' by the dance one watches in whatever form this might happen to manifest itself.[7]

Of interest in this chapter is the fact that Terry's talk of appreciative demands, audience participation, and game-playing is reminiscent of Kendall Walton's

---

5 The canonical expression of this idea comes from the writings of the first New York Times dance critic John Martin, who championed a form of muscular sympathy he called "metaki-nesis" as a central component of dance art appreciation. For a detailed treatment of his position, see John Martin, *The Modern Dance* (New York: A.S. Barnes and Company, 1933).

6 Sibyl S. Cohen, "Ingarden's Aesthetics and Dance" in *Illuminating Dance: Philosophical Explorations*, ed. Maxine Sheets-Johnstone (New Jersey: Associated University Presses, Inc., 1984), 152.

7 Renee M. Conroy, "Body Matters: The Aesthetic Relevance of 'Dancing Along'" in *Feminist Aesthetics and the Philosophy of Art: Critical Visions, Creative Engagements*, ed. L. Ryan Musgrave (Springer, 2020), Chapter 10. Emphasizing the qualitative aspect of kinesthetic responses to dance performances does not commit me to a phenomenological framework, although many dance academics embrace the writings of Maurice Merleau-Ponty or Jacques Derrida as their theoretical foundations. Instead, I mean the phrase "dancing along" to be intellectually impartial between phenomenological or existential approaches to dance theory and those utilized by aestheticians who work in broadly analytic traditions.

account in *Mimesis as Make-Believe: On the Foundations of the Representational Arts*, a philosophical classic published eight years after *How to Look at Dance*. Thus, Terry's distinctive way of advocating kinesthetics as an appreciative tool suggests an intriguing enterprise for those who work at the intersection of analytic philosophy and artistic practice: applying the theoretical framework defended famously by Walton to the arts of dance, and, more specifically, investigating its potential to inform current debates about the relationship between dancing along and the appreciation of danceworks.

There are several reasons for which this project merits philosophical attention. First, although Walton intends his theory of make-believe to apply to most traditional artistic genres, his monograph focuses extensively on literary works and paintings. He does add conceptual nuance to his analysis by discussing important differences between these artforms and sculpture, photography, decorative arts, and music without lyrics. He also addresses dramatic plays, but does not give the performing arts any sustained attention in *Mimesis as Make-Believe*.

Indeed, Walton never mentions dance in his well-known treatise. At best, it is implicated in asides such as the following: "There is enormous diversity among even the initial examples [on my list of canonical representational arts]. I note now that they include both literary works and works of the visual arts, as well as hybrids such as theater, film, and opera."[8] While Walton does not refer explicitly to dance, he presumably counts it among the hybrid artforms.[9] This assumption is especially plausible if one associates dance art with traditional romantic and classical ballets that make use of a written libretto to supplement performances or with contemporary works – such as Mark Morris' *Socrates* (2010) – in which choreographic structures are accompanied by live singing while the lyrics are translated on a screen above the stage to facilitate audience members' apprehension of crucial connections between the movement and the music.

The fact that Walton does not refer specifically to the arts of movement need not be regarded by dance aficionados or philosophers as troubling given that his theory can cover many canonical danceworks by extension. Nor should

---

8   Kendall Walton, *Mimesis as Make-Believe: On the Foundations of the Representational Arts* (Cambridge: Harvard University Press, 1990), 4. The words "dance," "ballet," and "movement" do not appear in Walton's index for *Mimesis as Make-Believe*, nor do any of their cognates. In addition, no choreographers or professional dancers are named in the index.

9   Although I do not share it, this is not an unusual view for philosophers of art to hold. See, for example, Stephen Davies' discussion of hybrid artforms in his essay "Ontology of Art," in *The Oxford Handbook of Aesthetics*, ed. Jerrold Levinson (London: Oxford University Press, 2003), 177–78.

Walton's choice not to address dance-related examples be regarded as a barrier to the current project insofar as there is, at least, superficial continuity between Walton's theory and Terry's appreciative advice. We can, in fact, sharpen Terry's counsel by appealing to Walton's familiar thesis that artworks function as props in games of make-believe and, thereby, prescribe imaginings. Terry writes, "Dance moments such as these demand ... a kinesthetic response from the viewer ... [and] if [natural] empathy is developed aesthetically [in a dance context], it becomes kinesthetic."[10] Given that imaginative activity is generally regarded as a necessary component of empathetic response, we can reasonably reconstruct the belief that underlies Terry's counsel as follows: danceworks (at least sometimes) prescribe kinesthetic imaginings.

We have, then, a *prima facie* reason to think the project I propose is conceptually viable. Is it theoretically desirable? In the past three decades, much ink has been spilled over the details of Walton's view, and his intricate system has been challenged on a variety of fronts. Still it has not been tested for exhaustiveness by considering how it does – or does not – fit the case of dance art. So, one reason to explore potential applications of Walton's conceptual framework to dance is that we might learn something new about the strengths and liabilities of mimesis as make-believe by regarding Terry's locutions as unwitting anticipations of Walton's account.

A second reason to pursue this project is practical: such an enterprise might render mainstream issues that occupy aestheticians with a special interest in dance almost exclusively. Although the philosophy of dance literature is more robust than is suggested by the introductory paragraphs typical of essays in this domain – which often bemoan the fact that "philosophy neglects the dance"[11] – this subfield of aesthetics does have an isolationist tenor.[12] Thus,

---

10   Terry, *How to Look at Dance*, 173.

11   Several articles by Francis Sparshott – including "Why Philosophy Neglects the Dance," in *What is Dance? Readings in Theory and Criticism*, ed. Roger Copeland and Marshall Cohen (London: Oxford University Press, 1983), 94–102 – have popularized this view. But it is important to note that, in recent years, there has been a substantial amount of new philosophical literature that discusses dance-related issues. If one considers the replete bibliography that accompanies Aili Bresnahan's entry "The Philosophy of Dance" in *The Stanford Encyclopedia of Philosophy* (Winter 2019 Edition), ed. Edward N. Zalta, https://plato. stanford.edu/archives/win2019/entries/dance/, it is evident that we need no longer fear that philosophy neglects the arts of dance, though there is still much work to be done to render this subfield of aesthetics continuous with discussions in other more firmly established philosophical domains. (One recent book that aims to forge such connections is Graham McFee, *Dance and the Philosophy of Action: A Framework for the Aesthetics of Dance* (Hampshire: Dance Books Ltd., 2018).)

12   I argue that there are at least two primary reasons for this. First, disagreements within the philosophy of dance often fail to exhibit the argumentative structure typical of those in other philosophical arenas. (See Renee M. Conroy, "The *Beat* Goes On: Reconsidering

KINESTHETIC IMAGINING AND DANCE APPRECIATION

considering how Walton's famous framework might be brought to bear on current disputes in the philosophy of dance holds forth the possibility of greater integration between dance-related concerns and those central to contemporary dialogues in the philosophy of art.

With the promise of these outcomes in mind, I begin to explore in three stages the role kinesthetic imaginings might play in dance art appreciation. First, I review two recent debates between philosophers of dance about the relevance – or lack thereof – of audience members' bodily reactions to live dance performance. Second, I consider how Walton's much-discussed thesis that artworks are props in games of make-believe could be applied to the case of dance art and, in particular, to Terry's proposal that danceworks (or the performances of them) prescribe a distinctive mode of imaginative engagement. Third, I introduce several philosophical challenges that emerge from a preliminary application of Waltonian theses to Terry's injunction that "In order to see and savor all that is present in a [dance art] performance, we must bring something [physical] of ourselves to the occasion."[13]

My investigation is motivated by the following questions. Should danceworks be regarded as artistic entities that enjoin us normatively to undertake kinesthetic imaginings? What kind(s) of imaginings might they mandate? What is the strength of their appreciative directives? What is a kinesthetic imagining as opposed to a more familiar form of imaginative engagement with an artwork or a mere bodily reaction to one? What non-question-begging reasons are there to think that a work of dance art is especially well-poised to command its audiences to regard it bodily, as well as visually, aurally, and cognitively? And, finally, how plausible is it that dance art performances not only authorize, but potentially require, a special brand of imagining that exceeds what is appropriate to achieving full absorption in other performing artforms?

A complete treatment of Terry's provocative proposals *vis-à-vis* Walton's account of make-believe would attempt to answer all these queries. In this brief

---

Dancework Identity," in *Thinking Through Dance: The Philosophy of Dance Performances and Practices*, eds. Jenny Bunker, Anna Pakes, and Bonnie Rowell (Hampshire: Dance Books Ltd., 2013), 103–04 for more on this point; see also McFee, *Dance and the Philosophy of Action* for attempts to rectify this concern.) This leaves those new to this area of aesthetic theory without a concrete sense of what the pressing issues are and where the lines of theoretical demarcation lie. Second, anecdotal evidence reveals hesitance on the part of philosophers of art who do not have an insider background in theater dance performance to engage in substantive discussion about the artform for fear of not knowing what might be appropriate to say given the complex history and practices of the art(s) of dance.

13   Terry, *How to Look at Dance*, 165.

chapter, I sketch only the beginning of such an analysis by taking conceptual liberties of various kinds. I refrain, for example, from defining the devilishly slippery phrase "kinesthetic imaginings," though I take it, at a minimum, to imply mental acts that have movement experiences as their objects or that give rise to physical sensations of moving. I also set aside several important complications about numerical identity, imaginative capabilities, and conceptual possibility, and do not offer an account of what is required to be (regarded imaginatively as) the same person across worlds. Although this approach can be only partially satisfying, it is enough to reveal several challenges that lie in wait for the aesthetician who aims to defend the importance of bodily responses to the appreciation of dance art. It also indicates why philosophers cannot simply adopt as an unanalyzed assumption dance insiders' repeated claim that mobilizing what Terry calls "kinesthetics" is a requisite for responsible aesthetic engagement with dance art performances.

Several additional caveats are appropriate. First, I confine my considerations to danceworks created within Western European theatrical traditions and to performances that reflect their norms. Second, my intellectual conceit is broadly analytic. Although many substantial theoretical treatments of dance are based on phenomenological or existentialist frameworks, I attend only to recent discussions that do not appeal to these philosophical systems. These two constraints are reasonable because they align with Walton's approach in *Mimesis as Make-Believe*.

Third, by dancing along I mean something broader than is implied by the common, but contentious, phrase "kinesthetic empathy." Dancing along sometimes manifests itself as the physical sensation of executing the movements one observes on stage; it can, thus, be a mode of putatively sharing the dancers' experiences. However, our kinesthetic responses to live dance performance need not take this form; in my experience they often do not. For example, my felt bodily response to viewing a company of sylphs traverse the stage in an undulating serpentine pattern might resonate with me as a wave-like visceral sensation, though no corps member experiences her calculated walking as having a surging or swelling character. Whereas the locution "kinesthetic empathy" naturally invites the thought of being in a somatic state qualitatively similar to that of a particular dancer (or the character she represents), my preferred term of art does not have this implication. Although one's experiences of dancing along might track the movement performances of individuals, they can also be elicited by attending to the choreography as a whole or to the perceived relationships between the movement, the music, the lighting, the sets, and the costumes. This is important because, although I focus in this chapter on cases of kinesthetic imagining that take as their objects the contributions of

KINESTHETIC IMAGINING AND DANCE APPRECIATION 627

individual dancers, I leave open the possibility that a full treatment of Walton's influential theory will consider imaginings that attend to – or are precipitated by – broader movement phenomena.

Finally, what I offer is not a fine-grained analysis of Walton's expansive conceptual system. It is a broad strokes application of a handful of his basic principles to a bit of uncharted artworld territory. I pay special attention to the foundational concepts imaginings, props, and games of make-believe, but do not address the complex treatment Walton gives to the differences (and relationships) between what he labels representations, depictions, and narrations. Hence, the possibility that dance art might be explored productively by appeal to additional Waltonian tools remains open.

2   Dancing Along: Two Philosophical Debates

Terry's primer and Walton's tome were penned more than thirty years ago. To illustrate how older ideas can find new life in contemporary debates, I begin with a brief overview of a on-going dispute aesthetician David Davies frames usefully in terms of three positions: moderate optimism, moderate pessimism, and extreme pessimism.[14]

What are the philosophers Davies describes optimistic or pessimistic about? The core issue is whether the suggestive results of behavioral and neuroscientific studies conducted on dancers have legitimate bearing on aesthetic theories about the nature of dance art appreciation. Moderate optimists, as construed by Davies, are sanguine about the potential significance of laboratory experiments to developments in the philosophy of dance; pessimists are, to varying degrees, not. While this theoretical disagreement was precipitated by scrutiny of scientific tests involving dancers – and so found its home naturally in the philosophy of dance – it is not a discussion about dance art, as such. Instead, the quarrel turns on the degree to which one should take experimental research to be relevant to philosophical theory, in general, and to aesthetic theory, in particular. I call this the methodological debate.

Another dispute waits in the wings. Although conceptually distinct from on-going dialog about the relevance of scientific experimentation to philosophical aesthetics, this disagreement can also be described in terms of optimists and pessimists. What I refer to as the appreciative debate turns on the

---

14   See David Davies, "Dancing Around the Issues: Prospects for an Empirically Grounded Philosophy of Dance," *Journal of Aesthetics and Art Criticism* 71, no. 2 (Spring 2013): 195–202.

question of whether an audience member's bodily reactions to a dance art performance are capable of enhancing her appreciation of the work performed or improving her understanding of its artistic properties. As one might expect, optimists argue that kinesthetic responses to live performances can increase understanding and/or appreciation of works of dance art; pessimists demur. The central conflict is over whether experiences of dancing along have the requisite properties to ground accurate perceptions of a dancework's objective features, or whether – being bodily – such reactions are too subjective or idiosyncratic to constitute a mode of perception capable of distinguishing reliably between the essential features of a dancework, the contingent features of a particular performance, and the immediate physical condition of the individual viewer.

Barbara Montero, an appreciative optimist, argues that "proprioceiving" a dancer's movements might enable audience members to recognize some objective aesthetic qualities of a dancework, such as its gracefulness.[15] Noël Carroll and Margaret Moore, also appreciative optimists, recommend that viewers' attention to bodily responses can clarify their perception of objective features of the music and its relationship to the choreography, both of which are partially constitutive of some works of dance art.[16] I suggest, more cautiously but in the spirit of optimism, that episodes of dancing along can help us come to see and value what is at stake in dance generally, and can enhance our interest in particular works to productive ends.[17]

By contrast, Graham McFee embraces the theoretical pessimism of David Best.[18] He acknowledges that kinesthetic responses to live dance performance occur and are often relished by audience members, but argues that our understanding of dance art must be grounded in the projective sense modalities of sight and hearing if viewers' judgments about danceworks are to be assessed

---

15 See Barbara Montero, "Proprioception as an Aesthetic Sense," *Journal of Aesthetics and Art Criticism* 64, no. 2 (Spring 2006): 231–42; "Practice Makes Perfect: The Effect of Dance Training on the Aesthetic Judge," *Phenomenology and the Cognitive Sciences* 11, no. 1 (Winter 2012): 59–68; and "The Artist as Critic: Dance Training, Neuroscience, and Aesthetic Evaluation," *Journal of Aesthetics and Art Criticism* 71, no. 2 (Spring 2013): 169–75. Montero's position is developed most fully in *Thought in Action: Expertise and the Conscious Mind* (London: Oxford University Press, 2016).

16 See Noël Carroll and Margaret Moore, "Moving in Concert: Dance and Music," in *The Aesthetic Mind: Philosophy and Psychology*, eds. Elizabeth Schellekens and Peter Goldie (London: Oxford University Press, 2011), 333–45.

17 See Renee M. Conroy, "Responding Bodily," *Journal of Aesthetics and Art Criticism* 71, no. 2 (Spring 2013): 203–10.

18 See David Best, *Expression and Movement in the Arts: A Philosophical Inquiry* (London: Lepus Books, 1974), 141–52.

for correctness or appropriateness.[19] McFee also maintains that our kinesthetic responses to the movement we observe – including overt behavior such as toe-tapping or sitting up straighter in our seats – are, at best, indications that we already comprehend what is happening on stage. As a result, he claims that bodily responses to live dance performance cannot be the mechanism by which we acquire understanding, though they might be evidence of apt visual-cum-aural apprehension of the work's properties.

There is, as it happens, a strong correlation between being a methodological pessimist (or optimist) and being an appreciative pessimist (or optimist). It should be noted, however, that this is merely a contingent feature of the two philosophical disputes about dancing along as they stand currently: a commitment to pessimism in one domain does not entail a commitment to pessimism in the other. I, for instance, am moderately pessimistic about the relevance of current scientific experimentation to aesthetic theory, but am openly optimistic about the potential for our bodily responses to enhance our appreciation of live dance art performances in ways that are open to public evaluation.

My hopefulness is, in part, a product of the fact that I regard understanding an artwork and appreciating it as discrete activities and distinct achievements. In my view, understanding is the cognitive condition of having true or otherwise appropriate beliefs about a work and its properties, while appreciation involves having a positive conative disposition toward an artistic object (or a presentation of it). As philosopher Robert Stecker points out, the ideal to which most art-lovers aspire is "appreciative understanding" since this cognitive-conative pairing renders multiple interactions with challenging artistic creations most gratifying. But understanding and appreciation need not – and often do not – go hand-in-hand.[20]

How do the two come apart, and what is the role of each in the ideal of appreciative coalescence many art buffs seek? Stecker mentions one case in which a person is intrigued by an artwork prior to knowing much about it, only to find the piece dull when significant insight is achieved. A useful dance example might be some people's experience of Trisha Brown's early postmodern tour de force *Accumulation* (1971) which, in virtue of the title, suggests a methodical accretion of movement over time. Upon seeing the dancework for the

---

19 See Graham McFee, *Understanding Dance* (London: Routledge, 1992), 264–73; *The Philosophical Aesthetics of Dance: Identity, Performance, and Understanding* (Hampshire: Dance Books Ltd., 2011), 185–205; "Defusing Dualism: John Martin on Dance Appreciation," *Journal of Aesthetics and Art Criticism* 71, no. 2 (Spring 2013): 187–94; and *Dance and the Philosophy of Action*, 206–62.

20 Robert Stecker, *Interpretation and Construction: Art, Speech, and Law* (Malden: Blackwell Publishing Ltd., 2003), 75–76.

first time, audience members are often enraptured by the structural puzzle it poses given that it is not obvious how the seemingly random step acquisition proceeds. But once it is revealed that the movement repertoire develops by following a specific rule, the allure of the work can dissipate quickly. What was captivating – because baffling – becomes for many no more interesting than the monotonous developmental exercises of a class warmup.

There are also cases in which understanding is easy to come by but inadequate to produce interest. For instance, it is not difficult to grasp the point Steve Paxton aimed to make in *Satisfyin' Lover* (1967), a choreographic work intended to democratize dance and undermine expectations about the importance of specialized movement techniques in dance art performance by showcasing ordinary walking. Nonetheless, people find it challenging to be disposed to watch this non-technical work repeatedly, though these same dance lovers are emotionally compelled to get tickets to *Don Quixote* (Marius Petipa, 1869) whenever it comes to town and to purchase annual memberships to Sadler's Wells. Hence, having artistic understanding is insufficient for achieving the conative state characteristic of artistic appreciation. It is also, in some cases, not necessary for developing an appreciative affection for an artwork given that the interpretive enigmas posed by many artistic creations are precisely what incline viewers to savor them numerous times in the stimulating attempt to unravel their mysteries.

The goal, of course, is to have one's dispositions to investigate an art object buttressed by one's knowledge about it. As aesthetician Ronald Moore reminds us, artworks are special because they can be almost infinitely replete. The good ones truly do reward attention by "repaying repeated viewings" in spades.[21] Moore's sentiments capture precisely why many art-lovers embrace the ideal to which Stecker refers when he speaks of appreciative understanding. For instance, the more I learn about William Forsythe's choreographically complex *One Flat Thing, reproduced* (2000) the more I want to watch it: my initial interest is continually reignited by my newly gotten insight. I thereby recognize that this dancework is virtually inexhaustible and am gratified to know that there is still more to discover in it, even as I relish – to what seems like the fullest extent possible – what it has to offer me today.

Why is dancing along an important part of coming to appreciative understanding of dance art? One reason might be that at least some danceworks have properties that are understood fully only if audiences attend to how the movement performances they witness resonate with them physically. I have

---

21   These points are drawn from Ronald Moore's lectures on aesthetics given at the University of Washington, Seattle, WA between 2002 and 2009.

KINESTHETIC IMAGINING AND DANCE APPRECIATION 631

suggested elsewhere that Laura Dean's postmodern masterpiece *Skylight* (1982) might be such a work given that it is designed to produce physical exhaustion in both dancers and audience members.[22] To somewhat different ends, Doug Elkin's Bessie Award-winning creation *Center of My Heart* (1996) and the last section of Mark Morris' *Grand Duo* (1993) invite similar responses on the part of audience members in virtue of their repetitive rhythmic nature coupled with the transcendent kinetics of movement sequences that are performed repeatedly at various speeds, slowly building audience members' tension level to the breaking point until the dancers finally reach the ecstatic release of a breakneck pace.[23] To fail to have the experience of being worn out by watching these works is, in a significant way, to fail to grasp both their objective movement qualities and their artistic objectives.

Since, however, to offer the above as justification for the claim that dancing along can contribute to appreciative understanding is merely to assert what McFee denies, a more philosophically productive tactic might be to attend to the nature of the art form rather than the identity-constitutive properties of works created in it. Two points are worth emphasizing. First, a fundamental goal of dance art is to draw attention to our collective condition as embodied animal-agents. We are all movers with wills limited by physical laws who consciously express our agency – and unconsciously reveal our psychological complexity – through constrained, but near constant, movement. The arts of dance are, thus, an exaggeration of what comes naturally to every human. As such, they are a lens through which we can see clearly aspects of ourselves that are often overlooked because, as the medium through which we experience the world and manifest our attitudes toward it, our bodies become partially invisible to us. To the extent that the underlying aim of all danceforms is help us recognize anew that which we otherwise look through, appreciative understanding of a dance art performance is enhanced by reflecting actively on our own embodied condition, including attending to when and how the dancers' whirlings and twirlings engender kinesthetic responses in us.

---

22   Conroy, "Responding Bodily," 208–09.

23   Martha Graham's study in grief *Lamentation* (1930) might also be appealed to in defense of the claim that full understanding of the features of some danceworks is achieved only when attention is given to the way (good) performances of them resonate physically with audience members. In this case, the basic expressive character of Graham's solo can be divined easily by observing the contorted movements of the dancer bound in a fabric sheath, but the desperateness the work obviously expresses becomes poignant only when one notes how physically uncomfortable many of the movements make us feel as we watch them.

Second, choreographers report with startling consistency that they design their works explicitly to inspire bodily reactions in viewers in order to facilitate reflection on the universal condition of being an embodied-thinker. As freelance dance writer and critic Graham Watts writes of Angelin Preljoçaj's visceral re-envisioning of the twelve biblical apostles, *MC 14/22* (*Ceci est mon corps*) (2000):

> Back in 2001, when an early iteration was performed by Ballet Preljoçaj at the Festival D'Avignon, the choreographer described *MC14* during a pre-performance presentation as "...a work giving emphasis to the male body; the stage is punctuated by six tables in a space where questions are asked and recurrent intensity is put before a world where galloping virtuality is overtaking physical experience." These comments remain pertinent today, continuing to resonate in a work that combines the strong physicality and sensuality for which the often provocative choreography of Preljoçaj is especially noted.[24]

Thus, when we follow Walter Terry's appreciative counsel and "reach out with all [our] kinesthetic powers at the ready toward the dance" we are recognizing the invitation offered by the dancemaker, which is a key part of playing the game of partaking in dance art rather than watching gymnastics or competitive flag twirling. While active attention to our own kinesthetic responses might (or might not) improve our ability to perceive specific properties of individual danceworks, it can uncontroversially contribute to our appreciative understanding of a guiding intention of most dance art creations by anchoring our experiences of them in an artistic practice in which corporeal participation is a central value.

Although these reflections might be persuasive from the perspective of the studio, the appreciative optimist's philosophical position would be strengthened if it could be argued that danceworks, qua props in games of dancerly make-believe, prescribe kinesthetic imaginings. If this were so, then the pessimist could not deny that there is a normative injunction of some kind to attend to dance performances in way that acknowledges kinesthetic responses, even if this mode of engagement falls short of reliably generating accurate beliefs about the features of the works performed. As a qualified appreciative optimist, I find this prospect attractive. Furthermore, Walton's suggestion that artworks, in general, mandate certain imaginative activities in virtue of being

---

24   Graham Watts, "Resurrecting the Last Supper," Playbill for Scottish Ballet's performance at Sadler's Wells Theatre, London, June 2017, 10.

KINESTHETIC IMAGINING AND DANCE APPRECIATION 633

complex props in artworld games seems well-suited to provide a preliminary framework from which to develop the idea that the arts of dance require a special brand of imaginative participation that can, if suitably fostered, give rise to bodily experiences that are qualitatively similar across diverse audience members.

3 Waltonian Basics: Imaginative Games and Kinesthetic Imaginings

Every student of introductory aesthetics is familiar with Kendall Walton's influential thesis that works of art are props in games of make-believe. That is, they are objects or events that issue imaginative imperatives, prescribing certain acts of imagining on the part of perceivers while proscribing others. In this way, according to Walton, artworks generate the fictional truths that we might intuitively (but imprecisely) describe as collectively constituting a particular fictional world or (more accurately, on his view) as demarcating and populating the world of the work.

Walton's account is highly nuanced, and its details need not detain us here. He does, however, offer a useful summary in the opening paragraph of his influential monograph *Mimesis as Make-Believe*:

> In order to understand paintings, plays, films, and novels, we must look first at dolls, hobbyhorses, toy trucks, and teddy bears. The activities in which representational works of art are embedded are best seen as continuous with children's games of make-believe. Indeed, I advocate regarding these activities as games of make-believe themselves, and I shall argue that representational works function as props in such games, as dolls and teddy bears serve as props in games of make-believe.[25]

Given that my application of these suggestive ideas treats Walton's multilayered intellectual framework in only the broadest strokes, several preliminary clarifications are needed to defuse *prima facie* worries about the applicability of Walton's famous theory to the optimist's defense of dancing along.

First, the subtitle of Walton's monograph is *On the Foundations of the Representational Arts*. Hence, the book offers an analysis of so-called representational artworks, which Walton takes to be tantamount to a theoretical treatment of fictions. But it is crucial to remember that he gives both familiar words – "representation" and "fiction" – broader referential scope than is

---

25 Walton, *Mimesis as Make-Believe*, 11.

traditional. For Walton, these are qualified terms of art that illuminate central features of our interactions with works of art.

Acknowledging the breadth of representational artworks for Walton is important because one might worry that his theory, if it pertained to dance at all, would apply to only an undesirably narrow range of danceworks, viz., those with narrative content (such as traditional story ballets) and those in which the dancers take on some kind of non-dancerly role or character (for instance, that of a dying swan, a grieving woman, or Vestris). Works of so-called "pure dance" might appear to be ruled out *ab initio*.

There are two important points to make in response to what I call the scope concern. First, even if it were the case that by "representation" Walton meant something akin to narrative or depictive or character-based, the vast majority of danceworks created before the 1950's – and many choreographed since – would be ripe for analysis using his theoretical account of props and games. Consider the rich choreographic and aesthetic variety reflected in the following iconic dance art creations: the tragic romantic ballet by Filippo Taglioni *La Sylphide* (1832), the comic classical ballet by Arthur Saint-Léon *Coppelia* (1870), Valslav Nijinsky's ground-breaking modern ballet *L'Apres Midi D'un Faune* (1912), Mary Wigman's masterpiece of German expression dance *Hexentanz* (1913), Isadora Duncan's poignant solo etude *Mother* (c. 1923), George Balanchine's neo-classical balletic gem *Apollo* (1928), Doris Humphrey's religious reflection *The Shakers* (1930), Kurt Jooss' theatrical magnum opus *The Green Table* (1932), Martha Graham's retelling of Medea in *Cave of the Heart* (1946), Daniel Nagrin's psychological study of gangsters *Strange Hero* (1948), Paul Taylor's mysterious but playful *3 Epitaphs* (1956), Pina Bausch's homage to Nijinsky *The Rite of Spring* (1975), Twyla Tharp's parody of classical ballet *Push Comes to Shove* (1976), Mark Morris's multi-media tribute *Socrates* (2010), and *The Second City* and Hubbard Street Dance Chicago's collaborative romp *The Art of Falling* (2014).

Second, the scope concern arises only if one does not take seriously – or regards as seriously flawed – Walton's arguments that creations such as abstract paintings (for example, classic Malevich or Kandinsky compositions) and works of "music alone" (such as Handel's *Water Music* or Vivaldi's *Four Seasons*) are representations in his special sense. On his telling, even the most abstract works enjoin a set of more-or-less specific imaginings on the part of audience members while ruling out others. Modernist paintings, for example, call upon us to imagine that the two-dimensional canvas is a three-dimensional space in which figures can overlap such that some sit in front of others, while some music without lyrics prescribes that we hear mere strings of tones in time as expressive of human emotions. The imaginative games authorized by works like these are importantly different from those typical of our engagement with

KINESTHETIC IMAGINING AND DANCE APPRECIATION 635

novels, plays, or realist paintings; but insofar as these nonfigurative, non-depictive, or non-narrative artworks command certain imaginative acts, they count as representations for Walton. So, too, would danceworks that are self-consciously abstract or seem to be predominantly about movement itself, such as George Balanchine's *Concerto Barocco* (1941), Trisha Brown's *Trio A* (*The Mind is a Muscle*) (1966), and William Forsythe's *In the Middle Somewhat Elevated* (1987). As a result, we can set aside any initial worries about the scope of Walton's theory as it might apply to the arts of dance.

One thought-provoking, and very useful, element of *Mimesis as Make-Believe* is Walton's sensitive treatment of various kinds of imagining. I consider several of the instructive distinctions he draws below. First, however, I address another preliminary worry about the applicability of Walton's theory to dance art, to which I refer as the adequacy concern.

Walton discusses literature and realist paintings at great length. Thus, his primary preoccupation is with imaginings of a particular kind, namely, propositional imaginings or those in which it is imagined that something is the case (for example, that a war is fought over how to break eggs or that Carabosse put a spindly curse on Sleeping Beauty). If, however, there is a special kind of activity described aptly as "kinesthetic imagining," it seems not to take this form. Whatever else it might be, kinesthetic imagining is regarded typically as a mental mode in which we envision what it's like to have a particular motional experience rather than imagining that something is the case or that some proposition is true. Consider Geraldine Silk's kinetically replete description from "Dance, the Imagination, and Three-Dimensional Learning":

> My earliest memory of experiencing a ballet probably occurred at the age of four, watching Balanchine's New York City Ballet. I can still see the passionate red costume that Maria Tallchief wore in the "Firebird," or the pale blue tunic that Allegra Kent wore in Debussy's "Afternoon of a Faun." When I saw their rippling muscles, I felt every nuance of movement: the triple *fouetées* (turns), the *arabesque penchée* (high leg extension), the leaps through space, being caught on her partner's shoulder, I identified with the movement. Even though I had not yet danced these steps or danced *en pointe*, my kinesthetic awareness was so acute as to imagine and feel the dancer flying through the air, landing on her partner's shoulder, raising her leg in a stylish *attitude*, even though my legs were not as long or as highly trained as hers, nor did I then have the same technical skill. To this day, I am still able to *feel* the dance.[26]

---

26 Geraldine Silk, "Dance, the Imagination, and Three-Dimensional Learning," in *Ways of Knowing: Literature and the Intellectual Life of Children*, ed. Kay Vandergrift (Lanham: Scarecrow Press, 1996), 4.

Silk recounts eloquently the phenomenon to which Terry refers when he advises appreciative attention to kinesthetics, and she gestures at a crucial relation between her imaginative activities and her felt experience of certain movements that constituted her sense of dancing along with Tallchief and Kent. If, however, Walton's account is dedicated to exploring props that prescribe propositional imaginings, and kinesthetic imagining is a different species of imaginative activity, then Walton's framework might be ill-suited to illuminate Terry's recommendation and Silk's report.

I do not think the adequacy concern poses an insurmountable problem, though I suspect it will take some fancy theoretical footwork to dance around it fully. Fortunately, there are two compatible ways to allay this worry. First, Walton acknowledges that many art-based games prescribe appreciatively vital imaginings that are nonpropositional in character. Hence, although these imaginative acts are not his primary focus, Walton's account makes room explicitly for imaginings of being, doing, or experiencing something – as opposed to imagining that some state of affairs obtains – as an element of our participation with art objects. As Walton writes, "Props prescribe nonpropositional imaginings as well as propositional ones. They do not thereby generate fictional truths, but the mandated nonpropositional imaginings are a distinctive and important part of our games of make-believe."[27]

Furthermore, according to Walton, our participation in art-based games can render us reflexive props. In some cases, by imagining as a work prescribes we also generate fictional truths about ourselves; and "it is in a first-person manner that appreciators are to, and do, imagine about themselves; they imagine, from the inside, doing things and undergoing experiences."[28] Walton's much discussed example of this phenomenon is that of Charles' apparently trepidatious responses to the oozing, green slime he sees on the cinema screen.[29] He argues that when Charles claims to be genuinely terrified of the slime even though the boy does not flee the theater or warn others of imminent danger, his statement expresses a fictional truth in virtue of the fact that Charles' own bodily responses – such as his increased heart rate, sweaty palms, and shrinking in the seat – count as emotions in the world of the game he plays with the two dimensional, pixelated image. So, just as it is fictionally true in the work-world of the movie that a green slime exists and is bearing down on unsuspecting villagers, so it is fictionally true of Charles the moviegoer that he fears the slime because his

---

27 Walton, *Mimesis as Make-Believe*, 43.

28 Walton, *Mimesis as Make-Believe*, 213–14.

29 The original discussion of this famous case is in Kendall Walton, "Fearing Fictions," *Journal of Philosophy* 75, no. 1 (Winter 1978): 5–27.

KINESTHETIC IMAGINING AND DANCE APPRECIATION

"quasi-emotions" (Walton's technical term for phenomenological sensations typical of emotional episodes) are props that prescribe him to imagine of himself that he is afraid in the world of his movie-watching game. To apply: Walton's theoretical framework leaves open the possibility that Silk's participation in Tallchief's performance of George Balanchine's *The Firebird* (1949) involves her in various kinds of imagining simultaneously. She might be imagining that Tallchief is a magical bird, which is prescribed by the ballet/ballerina qua prop, but also be imagining of herself that she is moving in the manner of Tallchief-qua-fictional-avian as she flies through the air. The latter could involve something like "quasi-kinetics" that mandate Silk to imagine that she is actually feeling the lead dancer's movements as part of her dance-watching game.

A second way to ameliorate the adequacy concern is to consider the possibility that, although it is natural to think of the imaginative activities described by Silk as more akin to experiences of moving than to thoughts or beliefs about movements, it is unduly hasty to assume that this mode of imagining is wholly nonpropositional. On closer inspection, we might ascertain that while the phenomenology of kinesthetic imaginings looms large in our memories, as it does for Silk, there is nonetheless a propositional component involved in imagining what it's like to perform a series of *fouettes* or how it feels to perch in a grand lift on a partner's shoulder. Perhaps, for instance, these imaginative episodes rely implicitly on nonoccurrent propositional beliefs about what is required physically to execute these particular dance steps. Hence, there are at least two plausible strategies available to neutralize the adequacy concern, though developing them is beyond the scope of this chapter.

Having set *prima facie* objections about scope and adequacy aside, I review briefly Walton's analysis of imagining in general as it is presented in the first chapter of *Mimesis as Make-Believe*. While the distinctions Walton draws initially are not specific to art-based imaginings, they are nonetheless instructive insofar as they reveal a matrix of possibilities for the form a kinesthetic imagining might take. They also remind us of the wide variety of imaginative acts typical of our participation in games of dance art.

As Walton emphasizes, there are many kinds of imagining which can serve a host of purposes and be elicited in numerous ways. First, imaginings can be of a proposition (imagining that there is a firebird), of a thing (imagining a firebird), or of doing something (imagining seeing a firebird). Second, as already noted, imaginings can be propositional (I imagine that I am a dancer in Eliot Feld's company or that the dancer playing the role of Juliet is in love with the dancer in the Romeo-part) or nonpropositional (I imagine the sensation of the stage lights on my skin or the feeling of landing on a partner's shoulder in a grand lift). Third, imaginings can be from the inside about myself or others, or they can take a third-person perspective on myself or others. Fourth, some imaginings involve mental imagery (actively visualizing a scenario with the "mind's eye"), while others do not (for example, simply holding in mind the delightful, but implausible, thought that I am able to execute thirty-two consecutive *fouette* turns *en pointe*).

Fifth, imaginings can be deliberate (as when a dancer rehearses choreography in her head as a remedy for sleeplessness), or they can be spontaneous (as when a movement motif from Mark Morris' *Grand Duo* (1993) in which the dancers crouch holding their index fingers together to create negative space induces me to see them as surveyors on a tollroad). Sixth, imaginings can be occurrent (actively engaged) or nonoccurrent (functioning in the background as necessary support for whatever is being imagined or might reasonably be imagined next). For instance, I might occurrently imagine of the *Grand Duo* dancers that they are surveyors, while nonoccurrently imagining that the law of gravity holds, which explains the dancer-surveyors' ability to remain low to the ground in the world of the work. And seventh, imaginings can be solitary (like a private daydream) or social (like our collective experiences in the theater when we all imagine of the prima ballerina in *Coppelia* that she is a young girl who is pretending to be a doll).

Thus, Walton's taxonomy reveals a matrix of possibilities for so-called kinesthetic imaginings: to begin, they might take a first-person or a third-person point of view. They can also be spontaneous or deliberate, occurrent or nonoccurrent, solitary or social, among other things. In what follows, I articulate eight forms of imaginative activity that seem most promising as candidates for the kind of imagining that Silk and Terry describe by appealing to kinesthetics. For purposes of clarity, I consider each as a potential mode of engagement with one specific choreographic pattern, a repeated movement motif from the last solo Mark Morris created for himself *Italian Concerto* (2007). The gesture involves alternating vertical motions of the arms in front of the torso and is referred to by Morris and his company members as "the milking phrase." The importance of this example is that the solo was designed to reflect both Morris' life-long artistic style and his idiosyncratic abilities as an aging dancer. The movement themes are also frustratingly enigmatic from the perspective of the untutored audience member but have very specific somatic resonance and expressive connotations for Morris and his dancers.[30]

---

30   This description was reported by Stephanie Jordan in September 2016 in her presentation "On Writing About Mark Morris: Knowing Too Much?" at the *Engagement: Philosophy and Dance* conference hosted by Texas State University. As part of her research for *Mark*

So, to start I might spontaneously or deliberately imagine myself as myself doing the milking phrase from Morris' *Italian Concerto* from the first-person perspective, as though performing the work. Alternatively, I might spontaneously or deliberately imagine myself as myself doing the milking phrase from the third-person perspective, as though watching myself in a studio mirror or on a video. These forms of imagining would involve envisioning what it would feel like from the inside, or look like from the outside, for me – with all my physical limitations and technical foibles – to perform Morris' signature choreography.

Perhaps, however, this perspective is too limiting. Given that the solo was created explicitly by Morris to reflect his physical quirks and private preoccupations, I might regard it as preferable to put myself imaginatively in his shoes. In fact, I might find it difficult to resist doing this inasmuch as the movements I observe strike me as inconsistent with what I know of my own physical abilities or as contrary to my deeply engrained movement style. Hence, I might deliberately or spontaneously imagine myself as Mark Morris doing the milking phrase from *Italian Concerto* from either the first-person perspective (as though I were he performing the solo) or the third-person perspective (as though I were he observing the performance).

All eight kinds of possible imaginings will, presumably, be guided by shared beliefs and communal norms and will be, in that sense, social in nature. In my imaginative activities I do not intend to indulge in private fantasies about *Italian Concerto* or engage in flights of fancy about having a career as a dancer instead of a philosopher. My aim is to participate in a performance of the dance-work in a manner consistent with playing an in principle public game of dancerly make-believe in which Morris, qua performer, functions as a prop. I assume, in addition, that all these imaginings are occurrent and that I am aware of this to some degree. There will likely be additional nonoccurrent imaginings in play as I watch the work unfold on stage, but the preliminary combinations canvassed above capture the underlying form of various imaginative acts I could execute from my seat in an attempt to take up Terry's injunction that I should reach out with all my kinesthetic powers toward the dance.

Having sketched only a few potential ways an episode of kinesthetic imagining could be structured, the value of appealing to Walton's framework is

---

Morris: Musician-Choreographer (Hampshire: Dance Books Ltd., 2015), Jordan learned this solo and perfected it with Morris' company members. She demonstrated the milking phrase in her keynote address, in which she reflected on the degree to which acquiring insider information about the images the dancers utilize when performing Morris' works can stymie appreciation as a viewer.

immediately evident. It affords theorists a wide range of rudimentary alternatives that call for detailed analysis if we are to give the suggestion that dance-works prescribe kinesthetic imaginings a place in any full-fledged theory of dance art appreciation. To this extent, Walton's conceptual tools highlight the radical inadequacy of dancers' frequent appeals to kinesthetics without further explanation or defense. This modest outline also exposes an assortment of difficulties the appreciative optimist must address to get the idea that there is a normative injunction to imagine kinesthetically in dance art contexts off the ground. In the last section of this chapter, I summarize the two I regard as most interesting because they are the most daunting.

4   Next Steps: Confronting Challenges

Setting aside the issue of precisely what a kinesthetic imagining is, there is still the question of whether the imaginative stances I have recommended as candidates for this kind of mental engagement could be fit for purpose. If the goal is to claim *à la* Walton that works of dance art prescribe cognitive acts of the aforementioned varieties, then audience members must be capable of taking up the imaginative invitation offered in dance performances. It is unclear, however, that it is possible to imagine myself to be another person (such as Mark Morris) in a way that is robust enough to generate the somatically rich appreciative engagement Terry extols. I call this the conceptualizability challenge.

As Walton points out, it is clearly metaphysically impossible that I should be a numerically distinct individual. He argues that while this is a barrier to my believing that I am Morris, it need not preclude my imagining that I am the person who choreographed *Italian Concerto* for myself as a reflection on my long career as a certain kind of dancer.[31] So, while I cannot believe that I am a numerically different person, Walton proposes that I can imagine being Mark Morris by imagining that a set of Morris-distinctive descriptors apply to me.

This suggestion, in an undeveloped form, is philosophically contentious. It can be successful only if I can imagine that it is metaphysically possible that I – rather than a counterpart of me – am the one and only person who choreographed *Italian Concerto* for myself. It is, of course, absurd to claim that every property-ascription that is in fact true of me must have been true of me, that is, to urge that all counterfactual claims about me are false. Surely, I could have been taller, had hair of different hue, worn a different wedding dress, or elected

---

31   Walton, *Mimesis as Make-Believe*, 32–25.

KINESTHETIC IMAGINING AND DANCE APPRECIATION 641

not to attend my senior prom. But could I have been a fundamentally different kind of person psychologically, with a much more auspicious professional career and an unrecognizable panoply of talents? Perhaps, but this claim requires defense of a kind Walton does not offer. Without any reason to think that I could exist as a male choreographer with a history and physical skill set drastically divergent from my own, it might yet be a metaphysical impossibility that I could have had the distinctive property of choreographing *Italian Concerto* for myself.

The rub is that imagining myself under this description as I watch Morris (or one of his acolytes) perform this solo appears to be the very kind of activity in which I would need to engage in order to have movement sequences that are notoriously puzzling from an observer's perspective provoke a robust and appropriate kinesthetic reaction in me qua inexpert viewer. To achieve Terry's goals, it seems that I must imagine both that Morris's choreography has a specific set of expressive meaning(s) to him and that it has a certain full-body feel when he dances it. This is accomplished most readily by imagining (from the first-person point of view) that I, Morris, am performing the movements I, Renee, observe on stage; but if this is the case, then dance appreciators confront a serious difficulty. After all, it is not obvious that we are able to imagine that which is ontically impossible, although some philosophers defend the view that we are able to do so. More to the present point, given the basic principle that "ought implies can," props in games of dancerly make-believe can normatively require audience members to imagine being the dancers they watch on stage only if such imaginings are possible for us to undertake. But this remains an open, and highly complex, metaphysical issue.

In addition, it is a genuine psychological challenge to explain how I, qua audience member, could be motivated to attempt to imagine in a manner I am not confident is possible. Walton skirts this problem by positing two different imaginings that "though distinct, are significantly linked."[32] In one I imagine myself (from the first-person perspective) doing the milking phrase, and in the other I imagine Morris performing this same movement sequence. He offers the tantalizing suggestion that the second imagining is accomplished "by means of" the first, creating a causal chain of mental states that implicate collectively both Morris and me but that does not require me to imagine a relation of identity between us.[33] Nor, presumably, does it require me to imagine of myself that I lack any of my essential properties, whatever those might be.

---

32 Walton, *Mimesis as Make-Believe*, 34.
33 Walton, *Mimesis as Make-Believe*, 34.

Perhaps this sketchy suggestion could be made into a feasible solution, but two issues persist. First, Walton does not tell us enough about it to ascertain how the imaginative by-means-of relation functions so as to avoid the apparent metaphysical-conceptual conundrum, a weakness in *Mimesis as Make-Believe* born of the fact that he pays little attention to cases in which we might be enjoined by artistic practices to imagine being someone else. Second, whatever the details of the relation might be, this re-description of what is going on is a far cry qualitatively from the direct imaginative engagement Silk describes so powerfully. This could indicate that Walton's treatment of the imagination is, in general, too cognitive to capture the character of the immediate bodily phenomena to which dance insiders refer regularly when they appeal to kinesthetics, kinesthetic awareness, or kinesthetic empathy.[34] I leave the complications that arise under the auspices of the conceptualizability challenge unresolved to present another putative problem that makes direct contact with extant debates in philosophical aesthetics.

Suppose that, in virtue of the difficulties associated with imagining myself to be another person, we reject the last four potential forms of kinesthetic imagining articulated in the preceding section. We are still left with the possibilities of spontaneously or deliberately imagining myself as myself doing the milking phrase from the first-person perspective or from a third-person point of view. But now we encounter the specter of so-called imaginative resistance because there are legitimate reasons for which an audience member might not want to imagine herself as herself doing the movements she observes on stage. I refer to this as the complicity challenge.

Consider, for example, a pacifist watching a performance in which two females partner one another in ways that appear violent or a person with puritanical sensibilities giving audience to a male soloist performing erotic gyrations. Here we might confront the danceworld analog of the oft-discussed problem with artworks that are regarded as morally deviant in virtue of the supposedly immoral attitudes they invite audiences to adopt or the ethical propositions they incite us to accept as true in the world of the work. Even if it is possible to take up such perspectives, many appreciators will refuse to do so – even in imagination – on the grounds that these outlooks inspire cognitive or conative dissonance and/or have the potential to entrench bad moral habits feared to have real world consequences.[35]

---

34   Thanks to Anna Pakes for making this point.

35   For a helpful overview of the various puzzles and debates associated with imaginative resistance, as well as treatment of the origin of some of them in Kendall Walton's work, see Shen-yi Liao and Tamar Szabó Gendler, "The Problem of Imaginative Resistance," in

KINESTHETIC IMAGINING AND DANCE APPRECIATION 643

Furthermore, professional dancers can have artistic, rather than moral, reasons to resist imagining themselves as those who perform the choreography they watch on stage. If, for example, I have spent my entire life training in a tradition in which pointed feet and (hyper) extended knees are cardinal virtues, then I might be tremendously uncomfortable imagining myself flopping about the stage with relaxed joints and turned-in feet, though I would not be similarly distressed to imagine myself as someone else performing movements that violate all the canons of the danceform with which I am personally and physically aligned. In short, the standard problem of imaginative resistance may take on a new flavor when we consider the case of practicing dancers who enjoy their artform from the darkness of a theater seat precisely because dance includes a multiplicity of physically inconsistent artistic genres.

To close: the complicity and conceptualizability challenges indicate that it will not be as easy to defend dancing along as dance insiders, and some appreciative optimists in the aesthetics community, anticipate. Thus, bringing Waltonian insights to bear on the case of dance art enriches current discussions that implicate kinesthetic imagining, while also suggesting additional directions they might take. The approach introduced in this chapter also demonstrates how scrutinizing the relevance of dancing along through the lens of Walton's theory can inspire new questions about artworld games of make-believe, especially those that require players to imagine of themselves that they are someone else. I hope it, thereby, sets the stage for dance to emerge from the theoretical wings and share the spotlight in contemporary philosophy of art.

References

Best, David. *Expression and Movement in the Arts: A Philosophical Inquiry.* London: Lepus Books. 1974.

Bresnahan, Aili. "The Philosophy of Dance." In *The Stanford Encyclopedia of Philosophy*, edited by Edward N. Zalta, Winter 2019 Edition. https://plato.stanford.edu/archives/win2019/entries/dance/.

Carroll, Noël and Margaret Moore. "Moving in Concert: Music and Dance." In *The Aesthetic Mind: Philosophy and Psychology*, edited by Elizabeth Schellekens and Peter Goldie, 333–45. London: Oxford University Press, 2011.

The Routledge Companion to the Philosophy of Literature, eds. John Gibson and Noël Carroll (New York: Routledge, 2015), Chapter 35.

Cohen, Sibyl S. "Ingarden's Aesthetics and Dance." In *Illuminating Dance: Philosophical Explorations,* edited by Maxine Sheets-Johnstone, 146–66. New Jersey: Associated University Presses, Inc., 1984.

Conroy, Renee M. "Body Matters: The Aesthetic Relevance of 'Dancing Along.'" In *Feminist Aesthetics and the Philosophy of Art: Critical Visions, Creative Engagements,* edited by L. Ryan Musgrave, forthcoming. New York: Springer Press, 2020.

Conroy, Renee M. "Responding Bodily." *Journal of Aesthetics and Art Criticism* 71, no. 2 (Spring 2013): 203–10.

Conroy, Renee M. "The *Beat* Goes On: Reconsidering Dancework Identity." In *Thinking Through Dance: The Philosophy of Dance Performances and Practices,* edited by Jenny Bunker, Anna Pakes, and Bonnie Rowell, 102–26. Hampshire: Dance Books, Ltd., 2013.

Davies, David. "Dancing Around the Issues: Prospects for an Empirically Grounded Philosophy of Dance." *Journal of Aesthetics and Art Criticism* 71, no. 2 (Spring 2013): 195–202.

Davies, Stephen. "Ontology of Art." In *The Oxford Handbook of Aesthetics,* edited by Jerrold Levinson, 155–80. London: Oxford University Press, 2003.

Jordan, Stephanie. *Mark Morris: Musician-Choreographer.* Hampshire: Dance Books Ltd., 2015.

Shen-yi Liao, and Tamar Szabó Gendler. "The Problem of Imaginative Resistance." In *The Routledge Companion to the Philosophy of Literature,* edited by John Gibson and Noël Carroll, 405–18. New York: Routledge, 2015.

Martin, John. *The Modern Dance.* New York: A.S. Barnes and Company. 1933.

McFee, Graham. *Understanding Dance.* London: Routledge. 1992.

McFee, Graham. *The Philosophical Aesthetics of Dance: Identity, Performance and Understanding.* Hampshire: Dance Books, Ltd. 2011.

McFee, Graham. "Defusing Dualism: John Martin on Dance Appreciation." *Journal of Aesthetics and Art Criticism* 71, no. 2 (Spring 2013): 187–94.

McFee, Graham. *Dance and the Philosophy of Action: A Framework for the Aesthetics of Dance.* Hampshire: Dance Books Ltd., 2018.

Montero, Barbara. "Proprioception as an Aesthetic Sense." *Journal of Aesthetics and Art Criticism* 64, no. 2 (Spring 2006): 231–42.

Montero, Barbara. "Practice Makes Perfect: The Effect of Dance Training on the Aesthetic Judge." *Phenomenology and the Cognitive Sciences* 11, no. 1 (Winter 2012): 59–68.

Montero, Barbara. "The Artist as Critic: Dance Training, Neuroscience, and Aesthetic Evaluation." *Journal of Aesthetics and Art Criticism* 71, no. 2 (Spring 2013): 169–75.

Montero, Barbara. *Thought in Action: Expertise and the Conscious Mind.* London: Oxford University Press, 2016.

KINESTHETIC IMAGINING AND DANCE APPRECIATION   645

Silk, Geraldine. "Dance, the Imagination, and Three-Dimensional Learning." In *Ways of Knowing: Literature and the Intellectual Life of Children*, edited by Kay Vandergrift, 1–28. Landam: Scarecrow Press, 1996.

Sparshott, Francis. "Why Philosophy Neglects the Dance." In *What is Dance? Readings in Theory and Criticism*, edited by Roger Copeland and Marshall Cohen, 94–102. London: Oxford University Press, 1983.

Stecker, Robert. *Interpretation and Construction: Art, Speech, and the Law*. Malden, MA: Blackwell Publishing Ltd. 2003.

Terry, Walter. *How to Look at Dance*. New York: William Morrow and Co., Inc. 1982.

Walton, Kendall. "Fearing Fictions." *Journal of Philosophy* 75, no. 1 (Winter 1978): 5–27.

Walton, Kendall. *Mimesis as Make-Believe: On the Foundations of the Representational Arts*. Cambridge, Massachusetts: Harvard University Press. 1990.

Watts, Graham. "Resurrecting the Last Supper." Playbill for Scottish Ballet's performance at Sadler's Wells Theatre, London, June 2017, 10–14.

CHAPTER 27

Imagination in Games: Formulation, Re-actualization and Gaining a World

Ton Kruse

1 Imagination: Belief and Experience

Imagination is commonly understood as the cognitive faculty of forming ideas, images or concepts of external or internal objects, situations or states, which are not necessarily accessible through the senses. Jérôme Dokic and Margherita Arcangeli propose in their essay *The heterogeneity of experiential imagination*[1] that imagination is the re-creation of conscious experiences. Their proposed theoretical framework adds two meaningful notions to the concept of imagination: re-creation and experience.

Dokic and Arcangeli point out that theorists have said that what can be imagined is "only what can be experienced."[2] From this follows that what can be imagined has to be, at least partly, based upon what we have, at least once, experienced, first of all sensorially. This is why imagination can be seen as a re-creation, as opposed to an original creation: "Imagination is the general capacity to produce sui generis occurrent mental states, which we call imaginings ... What type of mental state the subject is in depends on the non-imaginative conscious state that is re-created."[3]

The imagination of ideas and concepts, cognitive imagination, is understood as belief-like by Dokic and Arcangeli. It is distinguishable from sensory imagination that they understand as perception-like. Dokic and Arcangeli argue that cognitive imagination "can be construed as experiential (experience-like – TK), provided that at least some of our occurrent beliefs are conscious."[4] Their argument follows from the assumption that a belief or a notion can be perceived as an experience to the consciousness: "There is something it is like to have an occurrent belief, which is reducible to neither sensory nor affective

---

1 Jérôme Dokic and Margherita Arcangeli, "The Heterogeneity of Experiential Imagination," in *Open MIND II*, eds. Thomas Metzinger and Jennifer Windt (Cambridge, MIT Press, 2016), 1.
2 Dokic and Arcangeli, "The Heterogeneity of Experiential Imagination," 1.
3 Dokic and Arcangeli, "The Heterogeneity of Experiential Imagination," 3.
4 Dokic and Arcangeli, "The Heterogeneity of Experiential Imagination," 11.

© KONINKLIJKE BRILL NV, LEIDEN, 2020 | DOI:10.1163/9789004436350_029

phenomenology."[5] Having a belief "does something" to the way we are in the world, we might say. It is something that is neither sensory nor has anything to do with emotions; it alters something cognitively by which our understanding and perception of the world and of our being in the world changes.

Dokic and Arcangeli also propose a distinction between objective imagination (imaginings about the world, external perspective) and subjective imagination (imaginings about yourself, internal perspective) in their essay.[6] But more importantly, they propose that both imagination and experiences are ways of gaining information about the world and oneself (and here I would like to add: about oneself in the world):

> Many external experiences are ways of gaining information about the world, and many internal experiences are ways of gaining information about oneself. Now one might claim that belief, unlike perceptual or introspective experience, is not individuated in terms of ways of gaining information. Of course some of our beliefs result from various ways of gaining information about the world and ourselves, but it is logically possible to have a belief that is not the result of any source of information ... If belief is an experience, it is clearly an external experience: one can believe all sorts of states of affairs that do not involve or concern oneself. It follows that cognitive imagination, as the recreation of an external doxastic experience, is better seen as a sub-species of objective imagination, along with sensory imagination.[7]

In this chapter, we will accept the notion that imagination is experiential (experience-like), and that experiences, including "occurrent" beliefs (seen as experiential, objective, cognitive (belief-like) imaginations, as Dokic and Arcangeli point out), can be viewed as ways of "gaining information" about the world and about oneself.

I will approach this notion of gaining information as the acquisition of knowledge: not just as the mere accumulation of data and facts obtained by investigation, study and instruction, but also as the theoretical and practical understanding[8] of a subject or a case. Understanding may be subsumed under belief when belief is seen as: that which is (perhaps tentatively) accepted or

---

5 Dokic and Arcangeli, "The Heterogeneity of Experiential Imagination," 12.

6 Dokic and Arcangeli, "The Heterogeneity of Experiential Imagination," 10.

7 Dokic and Arcangeli, "The Heterogeneity of Experiential Imagination," 12.

8 As defined by the online version of the Merriam-Webster dictionary, "understanding" is (a). the power of comprehending, especially: the capacity to apprehend general relations of particulars; and (b). the power to make experience intelligible by applying concepts and

considered (or understood) to be true and real, especially (but not necessarily, as Dokic and Arcangeli point out) when based on the examination of evidence.

We will also accept in this chapter that when a belief is formed, it usually finds its origins in various pieces of acquired information – which again I understand as both data and understanding obtained by experience or research and by study. These pieces of information are arranged in such a way so that they form a more or less coherent idea or concept: a proposition that can be seen as the formulation of the belief (as a cognitive imagination).

Since formulation and forming are verbs and thus refer to the action of creating, of making or forming, the term re-creation does not appear to describe the entire spectrum of imagination as a cognitive faculty. Therefore, I propose that the term creation is perhaps more fitting, since something new is formed (not a pre-existent or previously held belief or mental state). This usually occurs (but not necessarily) from pieces of information that were already acquired, including non-imaginative conscious states that are re-created, or were previously formulated.[9] In this chapter, I propose that imagination can be seen as an act of formulation. I also propose that imagination is not just experience-like, but really is a true experience itself – that can function (in itself) as a way to gain information about the world and about oneself (in the world). Just like sensory experiences are used to gain information empirically. I will base my theory on the work of Hans-Georg Gadamer and Paul Ricoeur, wherein the act of formulation is understood as an occurrence of language-use, in which what is said (formulated and proposed) becomes present as a dialectic of meaning and reference.

The role imagination plays in understanding now comes in sight. But before investigating the notion of imagination and its function in understanding further, we will first look at the relation between language and the understanding

---

categories. According to this entry, "understanding" also entails both "explanation" and "interpretation."

9   As Dorothy and Jerome Singer explain, "The imaginative process is broader than simply imaging a concrete stimulus. Imagination may involve elaborated verbal sequences conducted privately in consciousness, or it may take on story-like forms such as a reminiscence or wished-for future sequence of events. For individuals in particular vocational, scholarly, scientific, or artistic fields, imagination may involve elaborate potential activity ... Mozart described how whole sequences of music appeared in his 'mind's ear' and then were translated mentally into musical bars and note sequences. He often wrote out pages of musical notation, which could then be printed with relatively few corrections or changes and distributed to musicians for performance." Dorothy G. Singer and Jerome L. Singer, *Imagination and Play in the Electronic Age* (London: Harvard University Press, 2007), 16.

IMAGINATION IN GAMES 649

of experiences. We will do that in the context of a human activity where imagination by definition is a creator of new experiences: games and play.

2 Games: Experience and Language

An essential part of games is the engagement in the game. Taking part in a game, or attending a game, must be seen as both an experience and as an occurrence. But before one can enter a game as a player or as an attendant, one has to understand the game: its narrative, its rules and goals. But more importantly, the game is distinguishable from other realities by the formulation of these aspects (its narrative, rules and goals). These formulations take place and shape in language: it is a (hi)story that is told, an order that is set and explained, and is about strivings that are adopted, shared or opposed.

Johan Huizinga, the well-known Dutch scholar from the beginning of the twentieth century, said in his study of games and play *Homo Ludens*: "While playing, the language-forming spirit repeatedly jumps over from the physical to the thought."[10] Additionally, he posits, "Through the inflow of the spirit, which removes the absolute determination (of a, by forces, determined being in a likewise determined world – TK),[11] the presence of the game becomes possible, conceivable, understandable."[12] By language, by naming, distinguishing and formulating, the game is understood as a demarcated part of reality, as an imagined world within the world – with its own history, order and goals. The relationship between the experience of the game and its understanding is not best understood by seeing language as a mere medium for understanding (understanding by or through language), because understanding takes place in language (by formulation). The relationship between understanding and experience is mirrored in the "relationship between thinking and speaking, of which the enigmatic, intimate entanglement precisely causes the concealment of language in thought," as Hans-Georg Gadamer says in his seminal work *Truth and Method*.[13] He specifies the relationship between thought and language as follows:

10　Johan Huizinga, *Homo ludens. Proeve eener bepaling van het spel-element der cultuur* (Haarlem, Netherlands: L. Brummel et al., 1950), 32. All translations are my own unless otherwise indicated.

11　I am using the term "determination" in the same sense as Huizinga all throughout this chapter.

12　Johan Huizinga, *Homo ludens. Proeve eener bepaling van het spel-element der cultuur*, 31.

13　Hans-Georg Gadamer, *Waarheid en methode* (Nijmegen, Netherlands: Uitgeverij Vantilt, 2014), 370.

The linguistic word is not a sign that one makes or gives to another, not an existing thing that one picks up and charges with the ideality of meaning, to thereby make another being visible ... It has always been meaning. But that does not mean, on the other hand, that the word precedes every experience of being and is externally added to an experience that has already been gained, because it submits the experience to itself ... It is rather part of the experience itself that she searches for and finds the words that express her. People are looking for the right word, the word that really belongs to the case, so that it comes to speak in it itself.[14]

Language is not a mere image of the case, nor a mere sign of the case, the case itself is present in language. As Gadamer reiterates, "The thought state of affairs (the species) and the word ... are closely related. Their unity is so close that the word does not take second place in the spirit alongside the species, but is that in which knowledge finds its completion, that is, in which the species is fully thought."[15]

The mysterious entanglement of language and understanding is the origin of the establishment of the world of the game. This world within the world is formed (formulated, told) and understood in language simultaneously. Gadamer further clarifies this entanglement:

Language is not just one of the capabilities with which man, who is in the world, is equipped, but on it is based and in it appears that people somehow have a "world." For humans, the world exists in a way that it does not exist for any other living entity that exists in the world. This being-there of the world is linguistically constituted ... Not only is the world only world insofar as it is said – the very existence of language is solely based in the world showing itself in it (sich darstellt). The original human nature of language thus means at the same time the original linguistic nature of the human way of being-in-the-world ... To have a world means to relate to the world. However, being able to relate to the world requires that one keeps enough freedom to what one finds in the world to imagine it as it is. Being capable of this is to have-world and have-language at once.[16]

---

14   Gadamer, *Waarheid en methode*, 397.
15   Gadamer, *Waarheid en methode*, 406.
16   Gadamer, *Waarheid en methode*, 421.

IMAGINATION IN GAMES   651

Or, as Paul Ricoeur clarifies, "Language use ... is always about something: it refers to a world that it says it describes, expresses or represents. The occurrence is ... the establishment of a world in language."[17]

Let's now look a little closer at the relationship between language and being in the world. As Gadamer points out: obviously not only humans exist in the world. Animals also exist and experience, the human animal is no different there. What makes human experience different from the experience of animals is having language. Paul Ricoeur states that:

> The experience ... is a blind experience, trapped within the fence of emotion ... It is precisely the emotional ground that forces objectification in an explanation: ... a bringing out of that emotion, which without that expression would remain enclosed within man as an impression ... The language is the light of emotion.[18]

By telling the experience, by giving words to the experience, the experience achieves a new status to the consciousness. It no longer is an experienced occurrence that occurs or has passed: in telling what happened (or even: what happens) and what was (is) experienced, both the occurrence and the experience achieve a (first) degree of objectification. This means that man is no longer determined by what happens to him. When words are being given to the occurrence and the experience of that event, it is no longer a mere situation, but it transforms into a narrative. It becomes a story that is part of a larger story which can be understood.

The occurrence and its experience take on an initial, more or less set shape in language that is not only experienced, but that can also be understood, looked at from a certain degree of distance. Ricoeur adds:

> The dialectic of "sense" and reference adds ... a new dimension to the dialectic of events and meaning. But the dialectic of meaning and reference is so original that it can serve as an independent guideline. Only this dialectic says anything about the relationship between language and the ontological condition of being in the world. Language is not a world in itself. It is not a world at all. But because we are in the world, because we are influenced by situations and because we use our understanding to orient

---

17   Paul *Ricœur, Tekst en betekenis. Opstellen over de interpretatie van literatuur* (Baarn, Netherlands: Ambo, 1991), 50.
18   Paul *Ricœur, Symbolen van het kwaad 1* (Rotterdam: Lemniscaat, 1970), 10.

ourselves in those situations, we can also say something, we can put experiences into words.[19]

Gadamer adds to this the insight that transcending the contingent environment and situation that define you in language, thus means an "elevation to the world."[20]

The formulation of the experience in language is an occurrence and an experience in itself. In the formulation, the experience is imagined (experienced again) and understood (there is something it is like to have a belief).[21] This is an active action and an occurrence at the same time in which what is experienced and done is understood, or where one begins to understand. As Ricoeur theorizes, "Something happens when someone speaks."[22] And it is important to realize here that one speaks to oneself when one thinks (often or not literally). Ricoeur refers to linguists Ferdinand de Saussure and Louis Hjemslev, but also to Emile Benviniste, when he says this, pointing out the difference between language as a semiotic system or scheme and language as in use (saying something that has a worldly sense and meaning). The first is virtual and timeless and the latter has a place and a time, and more importantly a "subject": someone is saying. The semiotic system has no subject, it is self-referential, but "the occurrence is that someone speaks, that someone expresses himself by speaking out."[23] For Ricoeur, perhaps the greatest "eventness" of language-use (formulation) is "the establishment of a world in language."[24] Lastly, we need to take the assumption of an "other" into account, says Ricoeur, when we think about language use as an occurrence and as an experience: "language-use assumes an other." Not only is someone speaking, but someone is also being addressed – whether or not that someone is oneself, I would add. It is noteworthy here that Ricoeur sees three dimensions of the occurrence of formulation, language-use: one is saying something (one makes a proposition); one does something while saying it (how one gives what one says context, motivation and force); and one does something by saying it (the effect of what one says).[25] The event-like nature of formulation as language-use now becomes clear in all the aforementioned aspects. With this "eventness" of formulation, it becomes

---

19   Ricœur, *Tekst en betekenis. Opstellen over de interpretatie van literatuur*, 83.

20   Gadamer, *Waarheid en methode*, 422.

21   See footnote 5 – having a belief is experiential.

22   Ricœur, *Tekst en betekenis. Opstellen over de interpretatie van literatuur*, 49.

23   Ricœur, *Tekst en betekenis. Opstellen over de interpretatie van literatuur*, 50.

24   See footnote 16.

25   The effect of what one says can be both external and internal. The latter must not be overlooked in my view.

IMAGINATION IN GAMES

clear that formulation is experiential in the same sense that Dokic and Arcangeli view (both sensory and cognitive) imagination as experiential.

It is relevant to point out here that this process of formulation has an open finitude. No word can precisely express what we mean or intend. Gadamer says that this is not because of a deficiency of words, but because our intellect, our mind, is not entirely "present to itself": "it knows not really what it knows."[26] The mind does not know itself in its entirety, but is searching and researching itself. Perhaps a more positive lens from which to analyze this quality would be the notion that the mind itself has an infinite quality to it. I am alluding to the manner in which we cannot grasp a case in its entirety at once in thought. This is why we are continually trying to adjust our formulations that describe and explain a case and looking for new ways to say things. We constantly endeavor to find different aspects and dimensions of a case, thereby leading to a greater understanding. Sometimes we will be more successful in finding better functioning formulations than at other times. In simple terms, things usually are not just *this or that*, but rather *this and that*. And the latter in many divergent ways as well. According to Gadamer:

> Speaking is ... never merely sharing the singular under general terms. In the use of words the visual given is not made available as a separate case of something general, but it has become present in the saying itself ... How the importance of the things that we encounter in understanding, is played out, is itself a linguistic process, so to speak: a game with words that spell out the intended meaning ... This is not about a game with language or with what appeals to us in the experience ... but about the game of language itself, which appeals to us, makes proposals and withdrawals, asks and finds its fulfillment in the answer itself.[27]

We may conclude here that the formulation of imaginings in which we both re-create[28] and create[29] experiences can be seen as a "game of language" (Gadamer), as language-use (Ricoeur). This game of language, the act of formulation, is the faculty of imagination, really of thought itself, and can be understood as an experience and an occurrence itself. This applies both to imagined sensory experiences and to cognitive imagination (Like Dokic and Arcangeli

---

26 Gadamer, *Waarheid en methode*, 405.

27 Gadamer, *Waarheid en methode*, 464.

28 We re-actualize pre-existant, previously gained, experiences and information.

29 We make new formations of information which suggest a non pre-existent understanding: a new, belief-like formulation.

stated, there is something it is like having an occurrent belief).[30] In this process, act, experience and occurrence, we gain a world in the sense that we free ourselves from being determined by our situation where our experiences remain "blind" impressions (Ricoeur), and come to understand ourselves (our situations and experiences) as part of a larger whole that stretches both back into the past, as well as forward into the future, thus connecting us to the larger narrative of human history and understanding.

In the context of this game of language, we can now return to our engagement in game and to what Huizinga hypothesizes about games: "The game lies outside the distinction wisdom – foolishness, it is equally outside that of truth – untruth. It is also outside of good and bad. In the game itself, although it is an activity of the mind, there is no moral function, neither virtue nor sin."[31] Huizinga states that the game is excepted from all of the categorical oppositions: "We maintain that in the game we are dealing with a function of living creatures, which cannot be determined completely biologically as well as logically or ethically."[32] Hence, the question becomes clear: what is the point of game, its reason for existence – our reasons for our engagement in it, if we cannot find a clearly distinguishable, instrumental and practical purpose for it?

3   Games: Experiential Imagination and Understanding

Huizinga rightfully sees that the game is an abundance, for it serves no practical purpose and thus is entirely free.[33] When we are playing a game, we are engaging in it "just for fun." Yet, at the same time, we take it very seriously. Since there is no fun in doing a game unless you take it seriously, the person "who doesn't take the game seriously, is a game spoiler."[34] Though played in all earnesty, the game is at the same time unreasonable, says Huizinga, since it transcends all practical reason. Thus, he concludes: "We are more than just reasonable creatures, because the game is unreasonable."[35] We can understand game and play as transcending our determination: we let ourselves not be determined, be defined by our situation – by what is necessary, needed or available – or

---

30   Dokic and Arcangeli, "The Heterogeneity of Experiential Imagination," 12.

31   Huizinga, *Homo ludens. Proeve eener bepaling van het spel-element der cultuur*, 34.

32   Huizinga, *Homo ludens. Proeve eener bepaling van het spel-element der cultuur*, 34.

33   Huizinga, *Homo ludens. Proeve eener bepaling van het spel-element der cultuur*, 35, and Gadamer, *Waarheid en method*, 107.

34   Gadamer, *Waarheid en methode*, 107.

35   Huizinga, *Homo ludens. Proeve eener bepaling van het spel-element der cultuur*, 31.

IMAGINATION IN GAMES   655

even: by what is considered real, present or believed to be possible. Instead, we want to have a world, not a situation. Evidently, games serve such a purpose, a purpose which cannot be understood very well in practical terms. The game is "set aside," says Huizinga, and is distinguished from "ordinary life."[36] "In the imperfect (real – TK) world and the confused life it achieves a temporary, limited perfection. The order that the game imposes is absolute. The slightest deviation from it spoils the game, deprives it of its character and makes it worthless."[37] One last characteristic of game Huizinga mentions is something that lies in the heart of what this book wants to investigate: imagination.[38] Imagination that is experienced, and thus becomes, is made "real" in a particular sense. By formulating the role or part one takes on in playing a game, the role becomes "real" in a specific sense. It is the "as if" and "make believe" that becomes real in the demarcated reality of the world of a game. From the perspective of ordinary life and practical reason, the role or situation of the game is feigned, pretended – but from the perspective of the imagination, the game is real. By formulating the case, the case itself is "fully thought"[39] and understood, and in this "game of language" the case presents itself (even when played out).

Let's now look a little closer at this status of "reality" of the game from an ontological perspective. What is game, what is its nature, and how does that relate to those who engage themselves in it by either making it up, taking part in it or attending it?

Gadamer starts his analysis of the ontology of the game with the etymology of the word itself, as it is used in a variety of divergent ways, such as: the play of light, the game of waves, the interplay of factors, the game of words. The role of language in thought, imagination and understanding becomes apparent in a particular sense here, since the noun "Spiel" and the verb "spielen" in the German language (in Dutch, "spel" and "spelen") are split into two different words in the English language: "game" and "play." In English, the verb play can also be a noun, whereas *a* play is "Schauspiel" in German and "toneelstuk" in Dutch. For the expression children's play, the word remains "Spiel" and "spel." The semantic nuances of game and play in German and Dutch differ from the English words. The same is true for the usage of the words which translate into "game" and "play" in English. It is important to address this issue, because it

---

36   Huizinga, *Homo ludens. Proeve eener bepaling van het spel-element der cultuur*, 37.
37   Huizinga, *Homo ludens. Proeve eener bepaling van het spel-element der cultuur*, 38.
38   Huizinga, *Homo ludens. Proeve eener bepaling van het spel-element der cultuur*, 41.
39   Gadamer, *Waarheid en methode*, 406.

demonstrates how our native language in which we originally learned to name and formulate constitutes our understanding of the case we name or formulate.

Returning to Gadamer's etymology of the word "Spiel," which translates into both "game" and especially into "play," a semantic grounding is found in the movement of going back and forward, as the term finds its etymological origins in the word "dance" (the same holds true for the English term "play"). Gadamer points out that this movement has no particular goal, but is done for joy: as having meaning in itself.[40] But more importantly, he says that play refers to the performance of the movement itself, "regardless of who or what performs the movement."[41] The ontological nature of the game or the play is thus not dependent on any subject other than itself. In essence, the game constitutes itself. In German, we can say "etwas spielt" in reference to something that is "going on" with someone, or in a given situation. In Dutch, we say "er speelt iets." This always refers to something that is doing something to those involved, rather than to someone who is doing something. Gadamer speaks of "the primacy of the game over the consciousness of the player":[42] He implies that the game "does" itself. It has its own nature to which the player is submitted, as opposed to obeying whatever the player feels or wants. The game plays itself, it "goes" automatically. When we engage ourselves in it, it happens by itself, of its own accord. In a fundamental sense, Gadamer points out that "all playing is a being-played." As he further clarifies, "It is the game that captivates the player, entangles him, plays with him."[43] The game "prescribes and arranges" everything that those who are engaged in it do and may do. It is the game that determines the scope of freedom.[44]

The next step Gadamer takes is to point out that each game thus gives the player an order. It commands the player to do something, to be something even. Additionally, it demands that the player submits himself to what the play (the game) asks of him. After the player accepts these demands, and succeeds in successfully executing them, the command of the game is "portrayed," "depicted," or "represented." Given that the game serves no other (practical or sensible) goal, Gadamer concludes that the ontological way of being of the game is: "Selbstdarstellung," self-(re)presentation.[45] A game may set certain goals for

---

40   Gadamer, *Waarheid en methode*, 109.

41   Gadamer, *Waarheid en methode*, 109.

42   Gadamer, *Waarheid en methode*, 109.

43   Gadamer, *Waarheid en methode*, 111.

44   Gadamer, *Waarheid en methode*, 112.

45   Gadamer, *Waarheid en methode*, 112. Given that Gadamer studied with Martin Heidegger, it is logical to frame his usage of the term "Darstellung" not in the common sense perspective of re-presentation, but in the sense of presentation. It is a manner of demonstrating

IMAGINATION IN GAMES

the players in and of itself. Nonetheless, the point of the game itself is not synonymous with the realization of these goals. It is really about the engagement
in playing that particular game. Gadamer refers to this engagement and dedication to playing the game as a playing-out of oneself – a self-(re)presentation.
As he argues, "In this way, the self-depiction of the game ensures that the player, by playing – that is to say, by representing – as it were, comes to his own
self-depiction."[46] The self-depiction of the player thus must be understood as a
self-(re)presentation. The player is presenting a way of being to and of himself,
but also to other players or someone attending the game, and watching it.

The possibility of attending a game while not being a player oneself is where
Gadamer sees the game taking a fundamental turn to becoming art-like, toward becoming an artistic play. The contemplator of the play "sees" (in a double
sense, both literally and metaphorically) it as it is intended. In the contemplator the game is "elevated to its ideality."[47] The game, or the play, is experienced
by the contemplator as something that needs to be contemplated, imagined,
and understood, rather than as something that is merely "done."[48] Through this
mental movement the game can be considered as an autonomous work, that
does not ontologically depend on either the player or the contemplator / attendant. Gadamer shows that this can be found in the possibility of repeat with
different players and contemplators.[49] In the repeat (performance), the game
remains itself and can be identified as that very same game. In this regard, he
underscores what Martin Heidegger terms "the keeping of the work," explained
by the philosopher himself as: "Only when the work is preserved does the work
show itself in its "being-created" as the true, and that means: present as (a-TK)
work."[50] Gadamer posits that "Everyone just asks what that would be: what the
'intention' is. The players no longer exist, but only what they play."[51] The game
achieves an autonomy towards those who play it or make it up, as to those who
attend it and contemplate it. It exists separately from all the aforementioned:
it is "kept," and it remains even when it is not being played. It commands all

---

the ontological way of being of a case, or the revelation of being in something: Sein ist
Sichdarstellen.

46 Gadamer, *Waarheid en methode*, 113.
47 Gadamer, *Waarheid en methode*, 115.
48 Gadamer, *Waarheid en methode*, 115.
49 Gadamer, *Waarheid en methode*, 116.
50 Martin Heidegger, *De Oorsprong van het kunstwerk* (Amsterdam: Boom, 2009), 82.
51 Gadamer, *Waarheid en methode*, 117.

those who engage themselves in it – instead of "being told" what to do or be. It demands to be understood as intended.[52]

The demarcated world of the game, or the play, transcends ordinary reality. It no longer matters if any of what is played happened in reality or exists in reality, "because it tells a truth that is elevated from that."[53] All, players and attendants are looking for what the game (the play), which is almost like an autonomous, living entity, intends and means. It is here where the game as an art-like work (as a composition or a formulation) obtains its full meaning: "the joy that one derives from the offered spectacle is ... the joy of knowledge."[54] It is also here where we see the same movement as in the "game of language." As we have seen, the formulation of a belief-like imagination is an occurrence (of language-use) and experience in itself. All mental movements, which revolve around the imagination (objective imagination: cognitive and sensory imagination[55]), are ultimately aimed at gaining knowledge about the world, and about oneself in the world.

4 Games: Re-actualization and Comprehension

The game realizes a state of autonomy in relation to its maker, player, performer, or contemplator, after it adopts a degree of formal fixation (once it is identifiable as that particular game by its form). It achieves an art-like quality, the quality of a "work." This autonomy has both formal and semantic features. In a formal sense, the game or work is identifiable as that particular game or work, regardless of where or when it is performed, or by whom. From a semantic standpoint, it no longer depends on its maker or performer to be meaningful. The meaning is constituted by its particular formulation, not by who (once) formulated it, nor by whom is performing it now. In his analysis of this phenomenon, Ricoeur asserts:

> The separation between the verbal (and performative-TK) meaning ... and the mental intention of the author gives the concept of inscription (= formal fixation-TK) a decisive importance that goes beyond the mere recording of prior oral (and performative-TK) language-use. The

---

52   "The semantic autonomy (...) that is now emerging is still dominated by the dialectic of events and meaning." Paul *Ricœur, Tekst en betekenis. Opstellen over de interpretatie van literatuur*, 87.

53   Gadamer, *Waarheid en methode*, 117.

54   Gadamer, *Waarheid en methode*, 117.

55   See Dokic and Arcangeli.

IMAGINATION IN GAMES 659

inscription separates the author's intention from the verbal (and performative-TK) meaning ... and thus seals the semantic autonomy.[56]

Having established the semantic autonomy of the game or work, which is constituted by its (fixated or inscribed) formulation, we now need to examine the possibility of its understanding more closely. This understanding is what is commonly called the working of a game or a play, or any work of art. Let us now return to the dialectic of meaning and reference. The heart of all understanding is, as Ricoeur maintains, "that all expressions are inevitably about something."[57] Ricoeur explains that this something must ultimately be understood as the "world," "in the sense that we all understand when we say of a newborn child that it came into the world."[58] He then defines a world as "the whole of references that are opened by" all products of humanity, of the human mind, that he has ever read, seen and understood.[59] In her seminal work *The Human Condition*, Hannah Arendt refers to all of these intellectual products as "work" in opposition to the products of "labour." The products of work constitute a durable world, whereas the products of labor merely maintain the processes of living (producing and consuming). In this fundamental distinction between work and labor, we uncover yet again the purpose of the transcending of determination (and gaining a world) through human imagination, as is done in game and play, which we have outlined earlier.

At first glance, a game or work is perceived as being strange. Owing to the act of engagement, the initial distance is removed by "placing it in a new proximity ... that integrates what's other into what's own."[60] Understanding starts with the appropriation of the formulation, as it shows itself to us, as a dialectic of meaning and reference. The form is approached under the assumption that it makes sense, even if that sense is not yet entirely clear to us. Ricoeur rightfully points out that this "making sense" out of a game or a work by the contemplator must not be understood in the way that the natural scientist explains a phenomenon.[61] The game or work is not just explained, but it is understood as well. It is important to reflect upon this distinction a little further. A formalist approach is not sufficient to understand a work. It is merely a step on the way to understanding. Understanding is "the realization, the activation

---

56   Ricœur, *Tekst en betekenis. Opstellen over de interpretatie van literatuur*, 91.

57   Ricœur, *Tekst en betekenis. Opstellen over de interpretatie van literatuur*, 98.

58   Ricœur, *Tekst en betekenis. Opstellen over de interpretatie van literatuur*, 99.

59   Ricœur, *Tekst en betekenis. Opstellen over de interpretatie van literatuur*, 99 – I stretch Ricoeur's view on texts here to all intellectual creations of humanity, not limited to texts.

60   Ricœur, *Tekst en betekenis. Opstellen over de interpretatie van literatuur*, 105.

61   Ricœur, *Tekst en betekenis. Opstellen over de interpretatie van literatuur*, 112.

of the semantic possibilities"[62] of a formulation, such as a game or a work of art. The term "activation" designates something being done and something happening in the present tense. It is the same occurrence as any language-use in which things are not only named and mentioned, but also presented to understanding: "that in which knowledge finds its completion, that is, in which the species (the case) is fully thought."[63] It is an occurrence that is experienced, even if you yourself are the one doing it. In the case of understanding a game or work, understanding is a re-actualization of the (fixed) formulation in the here and now of the contemplator. It is yet again "situated in an environment and a hearing, and resumes its referring function to a world and to individuals that was interrupted and disabled"[64] while it was being "kept."[65]

The understanding or interpretation of a work is often seen as being strictly subjective and personal: as if it were mere opinion. Nevertheless, the appropriation of a work loses its arbitrary and strictly subjective nature insofar as it is a resumption of the work itself.[66] It is precisely because understanding "stays" with what it wants to understand – that which is actually there, the actual form of what presents itself to the contemplator: the exact formulation – that which it comes to understand, is in fact knowledge of what is understood. In the case of a game or a work, the person who engages himself in it first has to imagine all the particulars that he sees as part of a whole that intends to mean something. Then, the player or attendee must subsume all particulars as part of a complete formulation, in which all particular parts are shown in relation to each other. These relations are not arbitrary, they are meaningful as a dialectic of meaning and reference (one has to assume that the internal relations are about something, and are not just accidental). They bring forth meaning: the relations that are shown give the particulars in the formulation a meaningful internal context. Likewise, each particular of the game or work, as does the whole, also refers to what is outside the game or work. In the same manner, these external relations are not arbitrary, but rather they are meaningful and defined by specific qualities and references that can be described and argued.

While this idea may sound very abstract in theory, it is easy to see in practice. For instance, I remember someone trying to understand the painting by René Magritte "The son of man" (1964). Since what is presented to the contemplator

---

62   Ricœur, *Tekst en betekenis. Opstellen over de interpretatie van literatuur*, 124.

63   Gadamer, *Waarheid en methode*, 406.

64   Ricœur, *Tekst en betekenis. Opstellen over de interpretatie van literatuur*, 124.

65   See footnote 49.

66   Ricœur, *Tekst en betekenis. Opstellen over de interpretatie van literatuur*, 130.

IMAGINATION IN GAMES

in this work is, at least partly, "figurative" (in contrast to "abstract"), one would perhaps expect that understanding is done by a straightforward telling of what one sees. In this work, however, it is not sufficient to reach an understanding (in any good work it never is), because what is presented to us simply cannot entirely "be" in ordinary life or reality. Behind the man in a trench coat and bowler hat with an apple "floating" in front of his face, there is a low, brick wall behind which we can see a calm sea under a dark, cloudy sky. The painting is done realistically, but in a fairly unnatural and clumsy looking manner. The person trying to understand the painting described the picture, although not in a very detailed and accurate manner. Instead of starting to probe the relations between that which was presented in the composition in a dialectic of meaning and reference, she started to fantasize about what would be behind that wall: if there would be a beach, and if so, what would be on it. In this instance, the contemplator did not "stay" with what was presented to her, but she added things that actually were not there (we cannot see behind that low brick wall on the painting, so there really is nothing there to consider). Whatever she thus found was arbitrary and did not add to anyone's understanding of the painting at all, including her own.

Ricoeur argues that the mental movement that is made in understanding can be separated into three phases: "In the first phase, understanding is an open-minded guessing of the meaning of (the work) as a whole. In the second phase, understanding is a perfected type of conception, supported by explanatory procedures." Ricoeur labels the last phase "comprehension" in which understanding gets appropriated and where the work is fully re-actualized.[67] As he suggests, "Understanding is not simply repeating the language event in an event that is similar: it is the creation of a new occurrence ... of which the original occurrence has become the object."[68] The event of language-use is an occurrence that is experienced. Now what is experienced asks to be understood. Imagination may well be the cognitive faculty by which all three phases of understanding are done. What is experienced is re-created – imagined – before the "minds eye" and thus experienced again. Moreover, Gadamer insists that:

> The actual experience is always a negative one. If we gain an experience based on an object, it means that we have not seen things right so far and now know better how things are. It is not simply a mistake that is understood and ... corrected, but an insight that is obtained, with far-reaching consequences. Therefore, it cannot be a randomly picked up

---

67   Ricœur, *Tekst en betekenis. Opstellen over de interpretatie van literatuur*, 134.

68   Ricœur, *Tekst en betekenis. Opstellen over de interpretatie van literatuur*, 135.

object to which one gains an experience, but it must be so that one can gain a better understanding on the basis of this, not only about this object, but about what one thought they knew before.[69]

In the act of imagination, the (presently and previously) gained parts of information are pieced together. They are re-imagined, so they can form a provisional understanding of what is experienced. Not only is a provisional understanding of an experience achieved through imagination, but the provisional understanding is also being tested and researched by what is presented to it through imagination. Consequently, an understanding that can rightfully be named "comprehension" is achieved through the application of the faculty of imagination.

When it comes to the question of the status of such re-actualizations or re-activations, Ricoeur posits:

> Testing procedures, however, also include rebuttal procedures, similar to the criteria of verifiability that Karl Popper proposes in his 'Logic of scientific discovery.' The role of falsification is fulfilled here by the conflict between competing interpretations. An interpretation must not only be possible, but must also be more likely than another interpretation. To resolve this conflict, criteria of relative superiority can easily be derived from the logic of subjective probability.[70]

Confronted with and tested on what is presented, one interpretation or understanding will function better than another. Evidently, Ricoeur avers that this is not the same as empiric verification, because testing understanding is an argumentative discipline.[71] Like Gadamer,[72] he points to the juridical interpretation of laws in comparison: "it is a logic of uncertainty and qualitative probability."[73] In the original reason for its formulation and in its various applications and evolution, a law has historical dimensions. But the law must now be applied to a specific, present case: what does that law, with its historical dimensions, mean for us now, in this specific context? It is in this manner in which a game, or rather a work, is understood. Along with its precise formulation by which it is presented to us, its origins and historical dimensions are taken into account.

69　Gadamer, *Waarheid en methode*, 337.

70　Ricœur, *Tekst en betekenis. Opstellen over de interpretatie van literatuur*, 139.

71　Ricœur, *Tekst en betekenis. Opstellen over de interpretatie van literatuur*, 164.

72　Gadamer, *Waarheid en methode*, 309. See Gadamer's remarks on "the exemplary meaning of legal hermeneutics."

73　Ricœur, *Tekst en betekenis. Opstellen over de interpretatie van literatuur*, 164.

IMAGINATION IN GAMES 663

All of this occurs in a present context in which its working is re-activated and for which it becomes relevant.

In order to develop the will or desire to engage oneself in a game or a work, there has to be some motivation found in what presently is of interest to us. After all, there is no practical need for us to want to engage ourselves in game or art. As Gadamer points out:

> It seems that the case only becomes interesting to us in the light of someone who is able to describe it well. We therefore are interested in the case itself, but it only comes to life by the aspect under which it is shown to us.[74]

This phenomenon can be seen in practice when one takes school children (or even adults) to a museum – or when one presents a new game to them. Unless you are able to show them something about it that is of interest to them presently, it can be really hard to make them do that game, or to make them study a painting or sculpture and learn something worthwhile.

5 Resuming: Autonomy and Gaining Knowledge

We started this exploration from the vantage point of the semantic and formal autonomy of the game or work. We have observed that the fixation or inscription of the form of the game or work (its formulation) makes its working autonomous in relation to the intentions of its maker. Likewise the act of formulation endows the game or work also with an autonomous nature towards anyone else who engages himself in it – whether this is a player or an attendant / contemplator. The game or work defines what the player plays and the contemplator understands: the autonomous form defines what is part of the game or work, and what is not. Adding to a game or work what is not actually there, to what the actual shape gives, "spoils" the game or any learning capacity that a work has.

It is worth highlighting that this formal autonomy is directly fixed to the semantic autonomy: the working of the game or work. The form is not merely shape, but rather it shapes the semantics, it defines all meaning. What there is to be experienced defines that which can be understood. In simple terms, what is not there cannot be understood. This formal and semantic autonomy starts with the first act of the maker(s): after the first act (of making, of formulating),

---

74   Gadamer, *Waarheid en methode*, 272.

there is already something there to be understood. What is there will contribute to what follows: the maker(s) will have to deal with what they have already done, and thus is already there in the process of making. This is the reason why we say that a work (or a game) "arises," or "comes into being." Its "making" comes not just forth from any intentions a maker or makers might have had, but also happens "of its own accord." For this reason, Ricoeur contends:

> That the author is represented by the text, that he resides in the space of meaning defined and set by the writing. The text is the place where the author appears. But does he appear as any other than as the first reader? The distance that separates the author from his own text already occurs in the first reading that contains all problems of explanation and interpretation.[75]

This is of course true for any formulation, regardless of whether it is a text, a work in another medium, a game, or – really – any formulated thought and imagined experience. Once the form is set in an act of formulation, it can be "viewed" and contemplated. It can be understood and has a (space of) meaning that is defined by its shape. Thus, the duality of form and meaning can never be broken down into two distinct entities (i.e. body and mind, body and spirit) that might "exist" separately.

From the formal and semantic autonomy of game and art, we looked at how understanding of such an autonomy is possible, and what the nature of such understanding could be. We have seen that understanding is a dialectic of meaning and reference: all expressions are inevitably about something. In a game or work, relations are defined internally and externally. What is in the game or work also refers to what is outside of the game or work: to what came before and to what is around. The game or work ultimately says something about the world and about being in the world. It is noteworthy here that the world is something other than the mere situation someone is in. It really is about the totality of references that are opened up by all intellectual creations of humanity. "Situation" refers to what is necessary, or needed, and to what is available then and there, as determined by natural and impersonal forces. A world refers to what transcends the need and that which is available. Both the game and the work transcend the determination of the human condition as "situation."

As Hannah Arendt claims, "in a world that is strictly oriented towards utility and usability, all purposes will inevitably only function for a short time and will

---

75   Ricœur, *Tekst en betekenis. Opstellen over de interpretatie van literatuur*, 112.

IMAGINATION IN GAMES

be transformed into means for more distant purposes."[76] Arendt differentiates use from sense, so a game or work may be of no use but does "make sense" from a literal perspective. Building upon this insight, she adds that "the meaning (sense – TK) of something must be permanent and not lose any of its character, whether it is realized or, put more accurately: pervades man, or escapes him."[77] She concludes:

> It is this sustainability that gives the things of the world their relative independence from the people that made them ... gives them their "objectivity," whereby they ... resist, "stand against," the insatiable demands and needs of their living creators and users ... In other words, the subjectivity of the people is opposed by the objectivity of the world made by man, rather than the sublime indifference of an unmoved nature, whose overwhelming elemental power, on the contrary, propels them relentlessly in their own biological cycle, which is so fully involved in the all-embracing cycle of nature's household.[78]

The value of game and art is found in their unusability that separates those who are engaged in them from being determined by the forces of cause and effect, and of indifferent biological needs and processes. But more importantly, game and art create a durable world that evades such temporality and subjectivity. This realm should be understood in different terms than those used to describe indifferent cycles and processes. In game and art we gain a human world that deals not just with the question of "what," but also sheds light on the questions of "who" and "why." The "why" question is not broached from the standpoint of an explanation of forces, but it is inextricably linked to meaning.

Furthermore, we have seen that the formulation of a game or work is re-activated and re-actualized through engagement. The game or work is re-imagined in a present environment and for a present hearing, and thus resumes its referring function. Like the original formulation, this re-actualization is an occurrence and an experience in which knowledge of the world is gained in addition to knowledge of oneself as being in the world. Again: this is not about gaining insight in the earth as a natural cosmos of forces, nor about the earth as a means for instrumental thought, but about its "destination ... to be a home for people during their stay on earth," as Hannah Arendt said.[79] The referring

---

76   Hannah Arendt, *De menselijke conditie* (Amsterdam: Boom, 2009), 139.

77   Arendt, *De menselijke conditie*, 140.

78   Arendt, *De menselijke conditie*, 125.

79   Arendt, *De menselijke conditie*, 158.

activity of the game or work has an open nature. It could be described as a network or a web of relations that are defined and are possible (while others are impossible, or less likely or fitting). In descriptive and argumentative reasoning, what is understood as true is found, tested and verified. We found that the functioning of juridical interpretation can function as an adequate model for the process of understanding. Which is a process of re-activation (with and within its historical dimensions) of the original formulation, of application, and ultimately comprehension. The contemplator or player experiences something through which he or she learns something about the world and about being in the world, through his or her engagement in the game or the work. The game or work asks to be understood as an experience through which the participants gain a better understanding about what they thought they knew before (about the world, about being in the world, as a place of which we ask: can it be a "home" for me and others during our time on earth?).

6 Imagination in Games: Re-actualization and Gaining a World

Let's now return to the faculty of imagination. One might say that one can involuntary imagine some sensation, maybe even a belief. One might even be involuntarily caught up in a game, or a work of art, almost like a reflex. Where I have indicated earlier that the game plays itself, that it "goes" automatically, and where Gadamer has stated that all playing is a being played, it seems justifiable to point to any involuntary nature in the application of imagination. Nonetheless, here is exactly where we encounter the mysterious entanglement of language and thought that Gadamer underscores. Occurrences can evidently be experienced but never be understood. Yet, when it comes to the experience of any formulation of thought, such as a game or a work, we cannot separate language and experience anymore. Because what is experienced is thought, is idea. As Arendt affirms, "the work of art finds its origin in the human mind,"[80] "works of art are things of thought."[81] This means that to be able to experience a game or a work, to be able to engage in it, one has to have grasped some of its demarcations and definitions: its narrative, rules and objectives. Because thought and language are so typical of human existence, of human consciousness and the ability to comprehend, I believe we usually are not entirely aware of what we think and understand. As Gadamer declared:

---

80 Arendt, *De menselijke conditie*, 152.
81 Arendt, *De menselijke conditie*, 153.

IMAGINATION IN GAMES

our mind is not entirely present to itself, it knows not really what it knows. Can there be anything "known" or "understood" if it is not named and described? As Ricoeur asserted: the experience is blind, trapped within the fence of emotion as a mere impression, unless it is given "light" by giving words to it (language-use).

What does the faculty of imagination do other than forming (imagining) images, ideas, and concepts of external or internal objects, situations or states? And is that formation anything other than a formulation? Can a human being experience something without trying to understand that experience? Can an occurrence, which has been sensed, but which does not change your understanding in any way, be truly named an experience? Would experiences that are not "illuminated" by language, or adequately described to oneself (perhaps because the experience was traumatizing, or because one's vocabulary is insufficient to describe it fully), not remain mere impressions that are immediately forgotten? Or, remain as impressions that might return as (perhaps troubling) memories that ask to be understood still? Is the illumination of experiences by language anything else than understanding them as meaningful?

My key assumption is that if game, like art, has no purpose or instrumental value, as Huizinga maintained, that they are both an "abundance," their engagement is no other than understanding. And what then is it that asks to be understood in them? Where everyone asks: what would that be? What does it mean? As Ricoeur revealed: language use is always about something. It refers to a world that it describes, expresses and represents. It is the establishment of "a world" in language. Imagination is the cognitive faculty whereby a world is established, and wherein man becomes part of a world. It is where he transcends his "absolute determination," his being determined by all the consecutive situations that make up his biological life. Situations that merely pass, disappear and are forgotten. Imagination establishes earth as a home for our earthly existence, it creates a more or less durable world, through all intellectual creations of people, in which meaning achieves a lasting status that outlasts the ephemeral nature of the practical and biological needs, states, and all passing situations of its inhabitants. Similar to all other products of human thought, we imagine ourselves as being in a world when we engage in game and art.

Consequently, when one questions the utility of the humanities, one really questions the usefulness of humanity. It is human nature to want to understand, to search for ways to make the earth into our home. And how can earth become a home if not by imagining it really is a world that we live in?

Through the act of imagination, it truly is.

References

Arendt, Hannah. *De menselijke conditie*. Amsterdam: Boom. 2009.

Dokic, Jérôme, and Margherita Arcangeli. "The Heterogeneity of Experiential Imagination." In *Open MIND 11*, edited by Thomas Metzinger and Jennifer Windt, 1–20. Cambridge: MIT Press. 2016.

Gadamer, Hans-Georg. *Waarheid en methode*. Nijmegen, Netherlands: Uitgeverij Vantilt. 2014.

Heidegger, Martin. *De Oorsprong van het kunstwerk*. Amsterdam: Boom. 2009.

Huizinga, Johan. *Homo ludens. Proeve eener bepaling van het spel-element der cultuur*. Haarlem, Netherlands: L. Brummel et al. 1950.

Ricœur, Paul. *Symbolen van het kwaad 1*. Rotterdam, Lemniscaat. 1970.

Ricœur, Paul. *Tekst en betekenis. Opstellen over de interpretatie van literatuur*. Baarn, Netherlands: Ambo. 1991.

Singer, Dorothy G., and Jerome L. Singer. *Imagination and Play in the Electronic Age*. London: Harvard University Press. 2007.

CHAPTER 28

"'I AM not mad, most noble Festus.' No. But I Have Been": Possible Worlds Theory and the Complex, Imaginative Worlds of Sarban's *The Sound of his Horn*

Riyukta Raghunath

1 Introduction

What if Hitler had won the war? What if Hitler's totalitarian government and its racial ideologies were realized in some possible world? This is the premise that Sarban's *The Sound of his Horn*[1] explores. Written as a *mise en abyme, The Sound of his Horn* is a time travel story that presents "historical multiplication" where "a new branch of history is created,"[2] thereby creating a new world that exists as a parallel world or in this case as a counterfactual world to the pre-existing world of the text. *The Sound of his Horn* is classified as a counterfactual historical fiction, a genre that comprises fictional worlds whose histories run contrary to the history of the actual world.

The text opens with the frame story – written in first person and narrated by the protagonist Alan Querdillon's friend – in which readers find out about Alan's capture and subsequent imprisonment as a prisoner of war in the Battle of Crete. Readers also learn about Alan's escape from the camp after being held captive for two years, including the journey that ensues after. After tunnelling his way out of the camp, Alan decides to make his way to the coast. He sleeps during the day and walks at night to avoid capture. While travelling through a forest one night, he passes a barrier of what he calls "Bohlen rays," a mysterious fence of rays that create a temporal anomaly that transports Alan into the future. Here, it is year 102. Through Alan, readers learn about this future to which Alan has travelled. This part of the text forms the embedded story, narrated by Alan. As Alan unpacks the world around him, he discovers that this world is

---

1 Sarban, *The Sound of his Horn* (Leyburn: Tartarus Press, 2011) Kindle edition.
2 Hilary P. Dannenberg, *Coincidence and counterfactuality: Plotting time and space in narrative fiction* (Lincoln, NE: University of Nebraska Press, 2008), 128.

© KONINKLIJKE BRILL NV, LEIDEN, 2020 | DOI:10.1163/9789004436350_030

wildly different from his world, in fact it is counterfactual to the world he originates from. For example, it has been more than a hundred years since the Nazis won the Second World War. While Alan does not mention anything about the wider counterfactual world because the whole story takes place on an estate that he lands in, readers do learn that the Second World War has been renamed the war of the German rights and the world is presently controlled by the Nazis. The new world that is depicted is largely dystopian: non-Aryans are genetically mutilated and bred as slaves; hunting is a sport where women are dressed to resemble hunting birds and predatory cats; feudalism prevails, and feudal lords rule the land.

Possible Worlds Theory[3] is mainly concerned with the relationship between the actual world, that is the world we inhabit, and possible worlds, that are worlds created through imagination. The basis for the theory can be traced back to its philosophical origins where it was developed by analytical philosophers[4] to interrogate reference and modality. Before offering an overview of Possible Worlds Theory within narratology, it is necessary to define the concept of "world" more generally in order to be clear about how it is used within the theory. The term "world" is frequently used in narratology, but there is no single definition of the term and as such it has been used variously between disciplines. As Ronen points out, philosophers such as Kripke use the term "world" "within the context of a general semantic model"[5] to solve logical problems posed by propositions that express modality as opposed to the literary uses of the term where "world" is used "in order to systematize the structure of the work of art from within,"[6] that is it is used to describe the internal structure of texts. It is not uncommon to refer to fictional texts using world as a metaphor. As Ronen states, "talking about 'the world of Milton,' 'the world of Romance,' 'the world of *War and Peace*' and 'the impossible world of Marques' is commonly accepted in discourse on literature, although presumably in each case we mean something different."[7] According to Ronen, there are two main

---

3   See Marie-Laure Ryan, *Possible worlds, artificial intelligence, and narrative theory* (Bloomington, IN: Indiana University Press, 1991); Alice Bell, *The possible worlds of hypertext fiction* (Basingstoke, UK: Palgrave Macmillan, 2010).

4   See Saul Kripke, "Semantical Analysis of Modal Logic 1 Normal Modal Propositional Calculi," *Mathematical Logic Quarterly* 9, no. 5–6 (1963): 67–96; Saul Kripke, "Semantical Considerations on Modal Logic," in *Readings in Semantics*, (Urbana: University of Illinois Press, 1974), 803–14; David Lewis, *On the Plurality of Worlds* (Cambridge: Cambridge University Press, 1983).

5   Ruth Ronen, *Possible Worlds in Literary Theory* (Cambridge: Cambridge university Press, 1994), 102.

6   Ronen, *Possible Worlds in Literary Theory*, 103.

7   Ronen, *Possible Worlds in Literary Theory*, 97.

interpretations for the term "world"- one being the "structural definition of the term world"[8] and the other "proceeding from an ontological definition of world."[9] The structural definition presupposes that when a reader reads a text (fiction or nonfiction) they construct in their imagination a world – a systematic structure that consists of objects, individuals, and situations. The ontological definition, which is "imposed by a philosophical framework on our understanding of the worlds of literary texts" is used to theorize how readers think about the world of literary texts relative to other domains.

Based on the ontological and structural definitions of world as outlined above, Possible Worlds narratologists maintain that a world created by fiction is a specific type of possible world. This is because as Doležel[10] points out a fictional world is a possible word but emphasizes that it is a *special* kind of possible world in that it is rich and complex compared to the possible worlds of logic. According to him, possible worlds in the form of hopes, wishes, and fears differ crucially from possible worlds created by fictional texts, because although these are worlds created through imagination, they are stored and preserved in the form of a text unlike the former that is created through the process of some temporary mental activity. Ronen further underlines the significance of fictional worlds as autonomous structures having the potential to project a modal universe that is similar to that of our actual world. She suggests that fictional worlds are in a way "parallel" to the actual world when she states that "fictional worlds, unlike possible worlds, manifest a world model based on the notion of parallelism rather than ramification."[11] This is because just like our system of reality that has an actual world and its set of possible worlds, a fictional world too has an actual world and its many alternate possible worlds. Possible Worlds Narratologists have embraced and adopted this concept of autonomous fictional worlds to establish a modal structure of the fictional universe that comprises at its center a textual actual world with its corresponding inhabitants and situations, surrounded by infinite possible worlds in the form of hopes, wishes, dreams, and stories known as textual possible worlds.

The Sound of his Horn establishes very interesting ontological mechanics because not only does it present two textual actual worlds within its textual universe, but it also presents one world that seems like an epistemological

---

8   Ronen, *Possible Worlds in Literary Theory*, 97.

9   Ronen, *Possible Worlds in Literary Theory*, 97.

10   Lubomír Doležel, *Heterocosmica: Fiction and Possible Worlds* (Baltimore: Johns Hopkins University Press, 1998), 16.

11   Ronen, *Possible Worlds in Literary Theory*, 8.

extension of our actual word and another which is counterfactual and far removed from a reader's experience of the actual world. Furthermore, the text does not provide any explanation to the reader in terms of how Adolf Hitler won the Second World War or how the world changed so drastically. Instead, readers are presented with a dystopian counterfactual world that they are expected to make certain inferences about and piece together. The text plays with the reader further by presenting the protagonist as a potentially unreliable narrator, thereby pushing the reader to question the existence of this world. In this chapter, using Possible Worlds Theory I show how readers make sense of two textual actual worlds established in the text. Additionally, through a Possible Worlds examination of unreliable narration, I also show how the theory can be used to describe the manner in which readers process complex and seemingly interdependent ontologies that are presented in *The Sound of his Horn*.

2 The Textual Universe of *The Sound of his Horn*

As evidenced through the brief plot summary above, two textual actual worlds are presented to the reader. One, from which Alan originates and the other future counterfactual world that Alan travels to. I'm calling this textual actual world one (TAW1) and textual actual world two (TAW2) respectively. Ryan[12] states that, when reading any kind of fiction, readers construct the textual actual world as being similar to the actual world and only make adjustments when dictated by the text. She calls this the principle of minimal departure. As per this principle, while constructing TAW1 readers will conceive this world as being an epistemological extension of the actual world because the text does not dictate any adjustments. TAW1 includes Alan and his friend who narrates his experience of the counterfactual future to which he travels. In TAW1 we learn that the Second World War ends in 1945, with Hitler and the Axis Powers losing to the Allies. Conversely, in TAW2 Hitler has won the Second World War and the Nazi regime is still in power 102 years after the war. There are many instances in the text when the counterfactual nature of TAW2 is revealed to the reader. To pick an illustrative example: as a result of passing through the Bohlen rays, Alan is being treated on the Count's estate. Curious about the Count, Alan questions the nurse who tells him that the Count is the Reich Master Forester:

---

12   Marie-Laure Ryan, *Possible worlds, artificial intelligence, and narrative theory*, 1991.

"'I AM NOT MAD, MOST NOBLE FESTUS.' NO. BUT I HAVE BEEN"

> "The Count?" I asked. "Who is the Count?" She came and looked down at me, so that I could just make out her features in the grey light from the window. She murmured something in German, then explained in English "Count Johann von Hackelnberg." "And who is he?" I persisted, being determined to make the most of this opportunity when she seemed to have been startled into treating me as a sane person. But she paused and considered me before replying, as if my ignorance had reminded her that I was not normal after all: still, she did answer "Well, he is the Reich Master Forester." "Is he?" I said. "I thought Marshal G[ö]ring was that." I might have mentioned the name of our ship's cat for all the recognition she showed.[13]

This conversation between Alan and the nurse takes place at night after Alan hears noises, which the nurse confirms is the Count returning home after hunting. Here, when the nurse tells Alan that the Reich Master Forester is Count Johann von Hackelnberg, Alan does not recognize the name. Moreover, he is surprised because where Alan comes from Marshall Göring is the Reich Master Forester, a name that the nurse does not recognize. Here, the counterfactual fabric of the textual universe is made explicit to the reader. Readers also get some insight into the feudal hunting system that is in place in TAW2:

> The grille was raised with a jerk and a clang, and there bounded into the pit some twenty large animals. Cheetahs, I thought them for a second, springing forward with such eagerness they seemed to run upon their hind legs ... In repose they would have been models for a sculptor of ideal feminine beauty, but as they bounded into that arena, circling it with a fluid speed of movement almost too quick for the eye to follow, they were utterly unhuman: women transformed by a demonic skill in breeding and training into great, supple, swift and dangerous cats.
>
> Their heads and necks were covered by a close-fitting helmet of spotted skin which bore the neat, rounded ears of a leopard, but the oval of the face was exposed, and each face as I saw it upturned to the lights was contorted in a grin, with red lips drawn back from strong white teeth, and in each pair of eyes a pale glitter of pure madness ... I remembered the Doctor's remark about the dumb slaves and guessed that the surgeons had operated on these women too.[14]

---

13   Sarban, *The Sound of his Horn*, Kindle edition, 539–55.

14   Sarban, *The Sound of his Horn*, 1085.

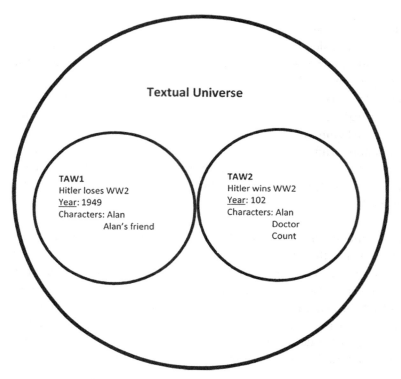

FIGURE 28.1   The textual universe of *The Sound of his Horn*

As evidenced in this excerpt, in TAW2, women are bred as slaves. They are genetically mutilated by surgeons to resemble cats. These cat-women are forced to hunt on their prey – genetically altered bird-women, which the Count and his guests enjoy as a sport. Furthermore, in an encounter with the doctor, when Alan suggests that he be handed over to the police because he was a prisoner of war who had escaped the camp, the doctor appears confused: "'The police?' he repeated thoughtfully. 'It is not necessary. The Master Forester has jurisdiction in the Reich forest,'"[15] suggesting that the Count is some kind of feudal lord. Evidently, the text presents a world that is continuously at odds with the reader's actual world in that it is not only counterfactual to the actual world, but it is also dystopian and as such, far removed from the reader's experience of the actual world. The ontological landscape of *The Sound of his Horn* can be visualised as depicted in Figure 28.1. It shows the textual universe with its two textual actual worlds as established so far. We know that two textual actual

15   Sarban, *The Sound of his Horn*, 598.

worlds exist in the textual universe because not only does Alan escape the camp and travel into TAW2, he also manages to arrive in TAW2, by tunnelling his way across the fence of Bohlen rays. Past the fence, Alan reappears in September 1943 in TAW1. With the war still in progress, Alan is captured and thrown into another prisoner of war camp. When the War ends in 1945, Alan is released by the Russian army. TAW1 includes Alan and his friend among others, it is 1949 and Hitler is defeated in the Second World War. Events from 1942 when Alan is captured, and 1943 when he reappears across the fence are also included in this world. TAW2 on the other hand, comprises Alan, the cat/bird-women, the Count, the doctor and the nurse treating Alan. In constructing TAW2, as Ryan's principle of minimal departure states, readers will begin by assuming that TAW2 is similar to the actual world, but as the text challenges these assumptions, the readers will be expected to make more departures from the actual world in order to effectively construct TAW2. The text further complicates and exploits conceptualisation of TAW2 by presenting Alan as a seemingly unreliable narrator thereby making readers further question the plausibility of TAW2.

3　Alan as an Unreliable Narrator

The text is composed of eight parts. Parts I and VIII narrated by Alan's friend in the form of a first-person narration forms the frame story of the text. At the end of the novel, the text returns to the frame story set in 1949, again narrated by Alan's friend. Parts II to VII, in the form of a flashback comprises the story that Alan narrates. As such, all the nightmarish events contained in Alan's story that make up TAW2 is established only through a first-person narration, with Alan as the narrator. While narrating his experiences, from escaping the prisoner of war camp to traveling to TAW2, Alan alerts the reader to his potential unreliability several times explicitly. For example, before Alan begins narrating his story to his friend, he warns:

> 'I AM not mad, most noble Festus.' No. But I have been. Not just unbalanced, or queer, but beautifully barmy; certifiable beyond the shadow of a doubt. I'm all right again now. Really all right, I believe. Only, having slipped into the other gear very suddenly once, I know how easily and swiftly it can happen ... It's not unknown, of course, for a man in a prisoner-of-war camp to go round the bend.[16]

16　Sarban, *The Sound of his Horn*, 239.

This passage captures Alan's direct speech and appears at the beginning of Part II. Here, Alan declares that he is not presently mad but specifies that he was mad sometime in the past. He uses the metaphor of a gear to show how he slipped in and out of being mad. He also states that it is not out of the ordinary for men in prisoner of war camps to lose their mind. This is the first instance in the text where Alan explicitly refers to his unreliability. As he explicitly reveals later,

> I am sure, in my own case at least, that I was twice as active in mind, twice as sensitive to what was going on while I was round the bend as I was after I came into the straight again and was back in the cage once more. I was glad it was a different cage they put me back in. None of the fellows there knew that I had been off my head, and the psychiatrists passed me as perfectly normal when we all got out. Of course, I didn't tell 'em what I'm telling you.

Here, again Alan uses the idea of moving in and out of being mad stating that while he was mad, he was very aware of what was going on around him. After coming back, his fellow prisoners or the psychiatrists at the camp did not notice anything wrong with him, consequently subverting his unreliability. However, Alan highlights that it could be because he did not tell any of them the story of what actually happened to him, the one that he is about to tell his friend now. This gives readers the chance to judge Alan's story and subsequently his unreliability, for themselves.

Alan begins to recount the experience of his escape. While on the run, he comes across a vast expanse of land. He explains:

> Had that narrow track led me to a farm, I think I would have leant with my head upon the door and begged for the peasants' pity; but it led to no human habitation ...I have often wondered how much of that scene I really saw that night. I can say what I later knew to be there—or thought I knew. I know exactly how it looked to the eyes I had on the other side—if you understand me—but I'd give anything to be able to recollect precisely what I saw with my real vision—the vision I'm using now. The trouble is, I suppose, that I had been going gradually round the bend all that night. The fatigue and anxiety had found out my flaw and were extending it all the time, until, just about when I reached that open ridge the fissure in my mind was complete.[17]

---

17   Sarban, The *Sound of his Horn*, 364.

Here, Alan contrasts the phrase "eyes I had on the other side" with the phrase "my real vision – the vision I'm using now." This suggests that he has two types of eyes, the one he has now which he claims is his "real" vision and the one he had while he was in TAW2. The juxtaposition of the two phrases may be inferred by readers to mean that there is some sort of discrepancy between his two types of eyes. Alan attributes this discrepancy to fatigue and anxiety that has resulted in him going crazy while he was on the run. Alan's admission that he is crazy may be interpreted by readers as compromising his credibility. It also further implies that TAW2 could be a figment of his imagination or some kind of hallucination that Alan was experiencing as a result of being delirious from exhaustion and dehydration. Alan further describes:

> There was one other thing I saw, and, again, I'd give so much to know which eyes I saw it with; for in my heart I'm still not convinced that the shock I received was real. But all I know is that I did notice something there, between me and those inviting woods, something at odds with experience; a phenomenon that would have been unremarkable enough in a dream and which might yet be not impossible in reality.[18]

In this passage, Alan is referring to the fence of "Bohlen rays." Here again, Alan draws on his concept of having two sets of vision to underline the illogicality of what he witnesses. He claims that what he saw is incompatible with his experience of TAW1, but states that it is within the realm of possibilities. By further stating that the fence of rays was too ordinary to be in a dream, Alan suggests that he may not have imagined TAW2; he may have in fact travelled to another textual actual world.

While on the one hand Alan's evaluation of TAW2 seems uncertain, he also admits that he has spent so much time questioning his reliability but has found nothing that would help him know for sure whether or not TAW2 actually existed out there. He confides in his friend:

> Ah well! You'd not believe the times I've been over the evidence for my sanity during these two years, and the care with which I've sifted it to find the little flaw, the sign of hidden weakness, and I never can find it. I ought to; I ought to be able to find out why I went out of my mind for a period, because, don't you see, that would be the best proof of sanity—not my own sanity alone, but the sanity of all this order that we believe in, the proper sequence of time, the laws of space and matter, the truth of all our

---

18   Sarban, The *Sound of his Horn*, 381.

physics; because you see, if I wasn't mad there must be a madness in the scheme of things too wide and wild for any man's courage to face.[19]

Alan here explains to his friend that for the two years that he has been back from TAW2, for the sake of his sanity, he has been scrutinizing every single detail pertaining to TAW2, but in vain. Finding a weakness or flaw that confirms he was mad would mean that TAW2 does not exist outside the realm of his imagination, as such reassuring him and restoring his faith in the natural order of space and time.

As I have demonstrated, Alan both questions and confirms his credibility, and it is through instances such as these that Alan's unreliability is gradually revealed to the reader thereby making him what is called in narratology an "unreliable narrator." The term "unreliable narrator" was coined by Booth in his "Rhetoric of Fiction."[20] According to Booth, a narrator is "reliable when he speaks for or acts in accordance with the norms of the work (which is to say the implied author's norms), unreliable when he does not."[21] Here, Booth proposes that a narrator be classified as unreliable if they are in disagreement with the implied author or the narrative in general. This definition of an unreliable narrator has been developed further by theorists who have reviewed the concept from a reader's point of view.[22] For example, Chatman proposes that:

> In "unreliable narration" the narrator's account is at odds with the ... reader's surmises about the story's real intentions. The story undermines the discourse. We conclude, by "reading out" between the lines, that the events and existents could not have been "like that" and so we hold the narrator suspect.[23]

Chatman here explains how readers of fiction make judgements about a story's plausibility based on any inconsistencies there may be in the textual universe. As discussed, Alan gives readers reasons to be suspicious of his sincerity throughout and as such they are not confident that Alan is saying the truth about TAW2. This makes Alan an unreliable narrator. However, a reader can

---

19   Sarban, *The Sound of his Horn*, 265.

20   Wayne Clayson Booth, *The Rhetoric of Fiction* (Chicago: University of Chicago Press, 1983).

21   Booth, *The Rhetoric of Fiction*, 159.

22   See Seymour Benjamin Chatman, *Story and discourse: Narrative structure in fiction and film* (Ithaca, NY: Cornell University Press, 1980); David Herman, *Basic Elements of Narrative* (New York: John Wiley & Sons, 2011); Shlomith Rimmon-Kenan, *The Concept of Ambiguity--the Example of James* (Chicago: University of Chicago Press, 1977).

23   Chatman, *Story and Discourse*, 233.

"'I AM NOT MAD, MOST NOBLE FESTUS.' NO. BUT I HAVE BEEN"

never be completely sure if Alan is reliable or not. This is because just as much as there is evidence in the text for Alan's unreliability, there is also some evidence that suggests that Alan has been speaking the truth all along. Furthermore, Alan's honesty in telling us that he is unsure could also mean that we are more likely to believe him.

3.1   *Possible Worlds Theory and Unreliability*
In Ryan's discussion of the authenticity of textual actual worlds, she maintains that:

> in impersonal narration ... the speaker has absolute authority, and his or her discourse yields directly to what is to be taken as the [textual] actual world. But a personal narrator is a mind interposed between facts and the reader, and the discourse reflects the contents of his or her mind.[24]

Here, Ryan explains the difference between third-person and first-person narratives. According to Ryan, the statements made by a third-person narrator represent the textual actual world because this type of narrator has "absolute authority."[25] In contrast, in first-person narration, the narrator's statements are their personal or subjective representation of the textual actual world. As such, readers do not perceive the textual actual world directly, but only through the mental world of a first-person narrator. According to Ryan, "the existence of unreliable narrators in fiction demonstrates a possible gap between the world projected by the narrator's declarations (what would be called the narratorial actual world, or NAW), and the facts of the TAW [textual actual world]."[26] What Ryan states here is that a textual actual world narrated by an unreliable narrator is essentially a narratorial actual world or a textual actual world according to a narrator. This is because, as Ryan points out, when the text presents an unreliable narrator the narratorial actual world does not match the textual actual world because the "[textual] actual facts potentially conflict with the narrator's declarations."[27] That is: NAW ≠ TAW when there is an unreliable narrator.

Given this scenario, Ryan proposes that readers "must sort out, among the narrator's assertions, those which yield objective facts and those which yield only the narrator's beliefs."[28] Applying this to an example from *One Flew over*

---

24   Ryan, *Possible Worlds, Artificial Intelligence, and Narrative Theory*, 113.
25   Ryan, *Possible Worlds, Artificial Intelligence, and Narrative Theory*, 113.
26   Ryan, *Possible Worlds, Artificial Intelligence, and Narrative Theory*, 113.
27   Ryan, *Possible Worlds, Artificial Intelligence, and Narrative Theory*, 113.
28   Ryan, *Possible Worlds, Artificial Intelligence, and Narrative Theory*, 113.

the Cuckoo's Nest that comprises a single textual actual world that is created by an unreliable narrator, Ryan explains how readers are able to regard Chief Bromden's belief that "the mental hospital where he is a patient have sensitive equipment to detect his fear"[29] as constituting his hallucination "[b]ut [readers] accept as fact the statement that orderlies are mopping the floor in the hallway."[30] Here Ryan's suggestions about decoding what is fact and what is not is similar to Chatman's suggestion as seen above, where he states that readers must "read out aloud"[31] and decide that the textual actual world "could not have been like that."[32]

According to Ryan, the textual actual world and narratorial actual world are conflicting worlds because readers are able to read between the lines and infer that they each describe a different version of the textual actual world. That is, while the narratorial actual world here comprises the sensitive equipment, the textual actual world does not. According to the definition, a narratorial actual world is a *mental world* that is created by a homediegetic narrator. Consequently, in texts such as this where, as Ryan claims, there is enough textual evidence to confirm that the narrator is unreliable, it is easy to infer what is the narratorial actual world (or the mental world) and what is the textual actual world.

By invoking Vogt's classification of the different types of unreliable narration, the narrative unreliability in texts such as *One Flew over the Cuckoo's Nest* can be categorized under "ironic-unreliable narration or ironic-unreliable focalization."[33] This is because in such narratives "unreliabilty can be understood as a trait of a homodiegetic narrator,"[34] as is in the case of Chief Bromden whose narration is unreliable because he suffers from schizophrenia. In ironic-unreliable narratives, as Vogt claims, "readers detect a discrepancy between the narrative world and the account or interpretation that the narrator or focalizer offers, and they naturalize these inconsistencies by resorting to the narrator's or focalizer's mind."[35] Here, Vogt explains the manner in which readers

---

29   Ryan, *Possible Worlds, Artificial Intelligence, and Narrative Theory*, 113.

30   Ryan, *Possible Worlds, Artificial Intelligence, and Narrative Theory*, 113.

31   Chatman, *Story and Discourse*, 233.

32   Ryan, *Possible Worlds, Artificial Intelligence, and Narrative Theory*, 113.

33   Robert Vogt, "Combining Possible-worlds Theory and Cognitive Theory: Towards an Explanatory Model for Ironic-Unreliable Narration, Ironic-Unreliable Focalization, Ambiguous-Unreliable and Alterated-Unreliable Narration in Literary Fiction," in *Unreliable Narration and Trustworthiness: Intermedial and Interdisciplinary Perspectives*, ed. Vera Nünning (Berlin: De Gruyter, 2015), 132.

34   Vogt, "Combining Possible-worlds Theory," 131.

35   Vogt, "Combining Possible-worlds Theory," 131–32.

are able to distinguish between what Ryan calls the narratorial actual world and the textual actual world. The inconsistencies that are caused by Chief Bromden's assertions in the text can be evaluated and resolved. As Vogt explains, this resolution is a result of the reader detecting world conflicts and believing one world "to be more adequate in relation to the [textual universe] than the narrator's."[36] Vogt calls this process of choosing one world over another "hierarchization of worlds"[37] through which a "reader reconstructs an alternative course of facts and events" in the textual universe.

In contrast, deciding whether or not Alan is unreliable is not straightforward because as in the case of *The Sound of his Horn* "a homodiegetic narrator questions his account or evaluation of the facts and events"[38] and the process of arranging the conflicting worlds within the text is challenging because the reader is unable "to decide what is the case in TAW [textual actual world]."[39] Vogt terms this type of narrative unreliability as "ambiguous-unreliable narration."[40] As a solution to the process of deciding what happens in the textual actual world, Herman echoes Chatman and Ryan, when he states that an unreliable narrator "cannot be taken by his or her word compelling the AUDIENCE to 'read between the lines'— in other words, to scan the text for clues about how the STORYWORLD really is, as opposed to how the NARRATOR says it is."[41] Subsequently, while reading *The Sound of his Horn*, the reader is suspicious of Alan's experiences in TAW2. This is because Alan continuously reminds the reader that before he stumbled into the counterfactual TAW2, he was tired and delirious from having not eaten and asserts that he could have easily been out of his mind. Alan even confides in his friend that his memories of TAW2 are garbled. Furthermore, Alan's uncertainty coupled with the questionable nature of events in TAW2 makes it hard for the reader to believe him. This is because the events from TAW2 as narrated by Alan seem unlikely especially when readers compare it to TAW1 that is narrated by Alan's friend. This is because, as Chatman proposes above, most readers would assume that "it could not have been like that"[42] because while the Second World War was still in progress in TAW1, it could not have been that there was a world out there where it was hundred and two years after the Second World War. This seems physically impossible in relation to TAW1 and in relation to the actual world.

---

36   Vogt, "Combining Possible-worlds Theory," 141.
37   Vogt, "Combining Possible-worlds Theory," 141.
38   Vogt, "Combining Possible-worlds Theory," 139.
39   Vogt, "Combining Possible-worlds Theory," 141.
40   Vogt, "Combining Possible-worlds Theory," 133.
41   Herman, *Basic Elements of Narrative,* 194.
42   Chatman, *Story and Discourse,* 233.

682 RAGHUNATH

However, as I discuss below, Possible Worlds Theory's accessibility relations can be used as a way of determining Alan's (un)reliability and ultimately determining how the textual actual world really is.

3.2 Accessibility Relations and the Textual Universe of The Sound of his Horn

In first-person unreliable narration, as Ryan questions, "the text constitutes the reader's sole source of information about the represented state of affairs. How then can [they] test the accuracy of the narrator's declarations?"[43] According to Ryan, in unreliable narration, there is no way of verifying the narrator's claims about the textual actual world because the narrator is the reader's only access to truth. As a possible solution to this problem, theorists such as Chatman and Herman have suggested that when a reader is suspicious about a narrator's reliability they can "read out aloud"[44] or "read between the lines ... and scan the text for clues"[45] in order to decide what the truth is in the textual actual world. In this case, while constructing the textual universe of *The Sound of his Horn*, the principle of minimal departure can be used to explain how readers will begin by using their knowledge about physical laws, general truths, people, places and entities in the actual world until the text indicates a difference between the textual actual world and the actual world. While constructing TAW1, the reader will assume that TAW1 is an epistemological extension of the actual world owing to what Ryan calls the "accessibility relations" between them. To explain, Ryan[46] identifies nine types of accessibility relations between the actual world and the textual actual world to determine the similarity between the two domains. They are: Identity of properties (A): "objects common to TAW and AW have common properties"; Identity of Inventory (B): "TAW and AW are furnished with the same objects"; Compatibility of inventory (C): "TAW's inventory includes all members of the AW as well as some native members"; Chronological compatibility (D): "TAW is not older than the AW"; Physical compatibility (E): "they share natural laws"; Taxonomic compatibility (F): "both worlds contain the same species"; Logical compatibility (G): "both worlds respect the principle of noncontradiction and excluded middle"; Analytical compatibility (H): "they share analytical truths"; and Linguistic compatibility (I): "language in which TAW is described can be understood in AW."[47]

---

43   Marie-Laure Ryan, "The Pragmatics of Personal and Impersonal Fiction," *Poetics* 10, no. 6 (1981): 530.
44   Chatman, *Story and Discourse*, 233.
45   Herman, *Basic Elements of Narrative*, 194.
46   Ryan, *Possible Worlds, Artificial Intelligence, and Narrative Theory*, 32–33.
47   Ryan, *Possible Worlds, Artificial Intelligence, and Narrative Theory*, 32–33.

FIGURE 28.2   Accessibility relations between TAW1 and the actual world

	A	B	C	D	E	F	G	H	I
TAW1	+	+	+	+	+	+	+	+	+

Figure 28.2 shows the accessibility relations that can be perceived for TAW1. As evidenced, all accessibility relations are upheld between the two domains, denoted using (+) in the table: in TAW1 readers learn that England was dive-bombed in 1943 after which Alan was captured and sent to a prisoner of war camp. When the war ended in 1945, Alan was released by the Russians. As such, the text does not dictate any changes and as the principle of minimal departure proposes, the reader will perceive a similarity between TAW1 and the actual world. In contrast, while constructing TAW2, readers will be able to detect a discrepancy between TAW1 and their actual world and also between TAW1 and TAW2. This is because, as Ryan claims, for a textual actual world to be similar to the actual world, certain accessibility relations must apply between the two domains.[48]

The accessibility relations between TAW2 and the actual world, would therefore appear to be as shown in Figure 28.3. The table shows the perceived accessibility relations between TAW2 and the actual world, with (+) being used to denote the relations that are upheld and using (-) to denote those that are not. According to Ryan, a textual actual world is chronologically compatible with the actual world if "the TAW [textual actual world] is not older than the AW [actual world]."[49] In this case, TAW2 is not accessible to the actual world or TAW1 because it is set in the future and as such, it is older than both the actual world and TAW1. She asserts that a textual actual world is analytically compatible if "it shares analytic truths."[50] In TAW2, Adolf Hitler wins the Second World War, feudal lords and the feudal system are in place, but in the actual world and in TAW1 Adolf Hitler is defeated in the Second World War and a feudal system similar to the one depicted in TAW2 does not exist. In addition, Ryan states that a textual actual world is taxonomically compatible if "it contains the same species, and the species are characterized by the same properties."[51] In TAW2, Non-Aryans are genetically mutilated to resemble animals and they are bred as slaves whereas in the actual world and in TAW1 no forms of genetically modified slaves exist. As such, readers will perceive these

---

48   Ryan, "Accessibility Relations," 558–59.
49   Ryan, "Accessibility Relations," 559.
50   Ryan, "Accessibility Relations," 559.
51   Ryan, "Accessibility Relations," 559.

FIGURE 28.3   Accessibility relations between TAW2 and the actual world

	A	B	C	D	E	F	G	H	I
TAW2	-	-	-	-	-	-	+	-	+

differences between TAW2 and the actual world as indicative that TAW2 is not an epistemological extension of the actual world. The only accessibility relations that can be conceived are that of logical and linguistic compatibility between TAW2 and the actual world.

Despite these anomalies, owing to the nature of counterfactual historical fiction, readers expect to be presented with a counterfactual world that diverges from the events of the actual world. Furthermore, a reader with enough knowledge of the actual world may recognize that the dystopian TAW2 depicted in the text is an exaggeration of Hitler's totalitarian government and racial ideologies in the actual world. As Yoke confirms, "to appreciate the impact of Sarban's fabricated world, we must examine the real world of Hitler's Reich."[52] Yoke draws on Waite's[53] detailed psychohistorical study on Adolf Hitler that documents his behaviour, his likes, dislikes, fetishes and so on to show how the evil and dystopian textual actual world accurately reflects Hitler's psychopathic ideologies. According to Yoke, "at the heart of Sarban's world is the Nazi philosophy of leadership."[54] As an example, Yoke explains that Hitler wished to transform German society into one that was based on race and this can be seen in TAW2 where non-Aryan people are not only bred as slaves, but they are also genetically transformed into and treated as animals. To clarify further, while reading *The Sound of his Horn*, the actual world in which Hitler correlated slaves to animals may be invoked in the mind of a reader with sufficient knowledge. For in the words of Adolf Hitler:

> Only after subjugated races were employed as slaves was a similar fate allotted to animals, and not vice versa, as some people would have us believe. At first it was the conquered enemy who had to draw the plough and only afterwards did the ox and horse take his place.[55]

It is this thinking that is realized in TAW2. Similarly, another example which illustrates the inhuman manner in which the Count's slaves are treated is when Kit North, a bird woman who befriends Alan in TAW2, describes the officers:

---

52   Carl Yoke, "'A Dance of Apes': Sarban's The Sound of His Horn," in *Just the Other Day: Essays On the Suture of the Future,* eds. Edgar Chapman and Car Yoke (Lewiston, NY: Edwin Mellen Press, 2003), 54.

53   Robert Waite, *The Psychopathic God: Adolph Hitler* (New York: Da Capo Press, 1993).

54   Yoke, "Dance of Apes," 61.

55   Adolf Hitler, *Mein kampf* (London: Hurst And Blackett Ltd, 1939), 200.

FIGURE 28.4 Rethinking the accessibility relations between TAW2 and the actual world

	A	B	C	D	E	F	G	H	I
TAW2	~	~	~	-	~	~	+	~	+

> "These forester officers are monomaniacs, and the most inhuman thing about them is the way they fail completely to see that you are a human being: they'll fuss and fiddle about with you for hours to get you exactly dressed for your part in one of their shows, and yet you feel that they understand nothing at all about girls, or human beings of any sort." She had a fine steel chain bearing a numbered tag round her neck. I turned it over; there was no name-just a group of letters and a number.[56]

The above passage exemplifies the manner in which subjected identities within TAW2 are dehumanized by the Count's officers. In addition to being dressed as animals and birds, they were also given number tags, entirely stripping them of any personal identity. A reader with enough knowledge may recognize that this alludes to how the Jewish prisoners were treated in the concentration camps. After they were captured and thrown into concentration camps, their heads were shaved, they were given uniforms, and they were branded with a number tattooed on their forearm.[57] In order to understand the epistemological significance of TAW2 to the actual world, the text draws and relies heavily on a specific set of knowledge that is gained from knowing about Hitler's personality and Hitler's Reich during the Second World War.

In reviewing the accessibility relations between TAW2 and the actual world from the point of view of a reader who possesses the required background knowledge, some degree of accessibility relations (denoted using ~) can be established between the two domains. This is depicted in Figure 28.4.

As the analysis has shown, while the actual world and TAW2 are compatible in terms of the language used and the adherence to the laws of contradiction, some correlation can also be drawn between the two domains' properties and inventories. Additionally, counterparts of actual world historical individuals also exist in TAW2. For example, a counterpart of Hermann Göring, called Count von Hackelnberg who is the Reich Master Forester (like Göring in the actual world) is presented in TAW2. If readers are able to make the epistemological

---

56   Sarban, *The Sound of His Horn*, 1445.

57   See Marilyn Harran, *The Holocaust Chronicle* (Illinois: Publications International, Ltd., 2000); Michael Berenbaum, *The World Must Know: The History of the Holocaust as Told in the United States Holocaust Memorial Museum* (Baltimore: Johns Hopkins University Press, 2005).

connection between the Count in TAW2 and Hermann Göring in the actual world, they may be able to further see how TAW2 is accessible from the actual world. TAW2 can also be said to be physically, taxonomically, and analytically compatible to some extent – the two domains share some truths in that TAW2 is an exaggerated retrogression of the actual world presented as a future dystopia. Therefore, in *The Sound of his Horn,* while it is possible to interpret TAW2 as too horrific to be real and consequently consider there to be almost no accessibility relations between TAW2 and the actual world, as I have shown, for a reader with sufficient knowledge of the actual world there is some evidence, albeit implicit to support its plausibility. Therefore, a revised understanding of the accessibility relations between TAW2 and the actual world potentially influences readers' perception of whether or not the narrator is reliable.

4 The Possible Worlds of *The Sound of his Horn*

As the analysis so far has evidenced, two accessible textual actual worlds are created in the text, with TAW2 being a world potentially created through unreliable narration and as such being a mental world, or as Ryan terms it a narratorial actual world. One of the issues that readers face while reading unreliable narratives is the problem of hierarchizing worlds, that is, deciding which is a textual actual world and which is the narratorial actual world. Vogt suggests that in ambiguous-unreliable narration readers construct two separate textual universes for the same text depending on whether they trust the narrator or not. He explains:

> Even after having finished the narrative, the conflicting worlds remain unresolved for the reader. For this reason, the reader can construct separate fictional universes on the basis of the same text—one in which the narrator is ironic-unreliable and another in which he is to be trusted.[58]

Here, Vogt explains the manner in which readers resolve conflicting worlds within a text by isolating each possibility into a separate textual universe. In applying Vogt's conjectures to *The Sound of his Horn,* two possible textual universes can be imagined. As I have hitherto discussed, readers with enough knowledge of the actual world are more likely to believe Alan and his description of TAW2. For this type of reader, Alan is most likely a reliable narrator. The

---

58   Vogt, "Combining Possible-worlds Theory," 141–42.

"'I AM NOT MAD, MOST NOBLE FESTUS.' NO. BUT I HAVE BEEN"

ontological landscape of the textual universe to this type of reader resembles Figure 28.1 depicted above. Conversely, to a reader without this knowledge, no accessibility relations are perceived between the two domains and as such Alan may be perceived as an unreliable narrator. Consequently, for this type of reader only one textual actual world exists within the textual universe with TAW2 being one of the many textual possible worlds constructed by Alan.

While Ryan uses the term narratorial actual world to describe worlds created by unreliable narrators, I argue that this is problematic when applied to *The Sound of his Horn* because while we are unsure whether or not TAW2 really exists within the textual universe, we are also unsure about the individual events that have taken place in TAW2. For example, it may be that a counterfactual world truly exists within the textual universe but some of the events that Alan has narrated about that world may be fallacious. Therefore, readers have no way of distinguishing between Alan's description of mental worlds or narratorial actual world and his description of TAW2. In addition, Alan is not *necessarily* an unreliable narrator; he is only *possibly* an unreliable narrator. This is because while the text gives us enough reasons to question Alan's reliability, it does not give us enough to confirm or validate it. Besides, given the nature of counterfactual historical fiction texts, readers expect to be presented with a counterfactual world. In such a case, I suggest using a different approach that involves categorising TAW2 as a specific type of textual possible world, that is a F-universe, which as I show below is more comprehensive.

4.1 F-universe

According to Ryan, an F-universe is created when "dreams, hallucinations, fantasies, and fictional stories [are] told to or composed by characters."[59] For readers who perceive Alan as an unreliable narrator, TAW2 can be conceived as a fantasy or a world of make-believe that Alan constructs. By invoking Ryan's[60] terminology explicitly, TAW2 can be rightly identified as a F-universe or fantasy universe that is created through elaborate mental processes such as dreams and storytelling. F-universe is a more suitable method of describing the counterfactual world that Alan creates through storytelling because it more closely resembles the internal configurations of actual and textual universes. That is, it projects a complete universe with its own actual world at the center and possible worlds around it. For example, in *The Sound of his Horn*, the F-universe created by Alan has its own actual world – I call this F-TAW or fantasy textual actual world in keeping with Ryan's conventions – with its own

---

59   Ryan, *Possible Worlds, Artificial Intelligence, and Narrative Theory*, 119.
60   Ryan, *Possible Worlds, Artificial Intelligence, and Narrative Theory*, 119.

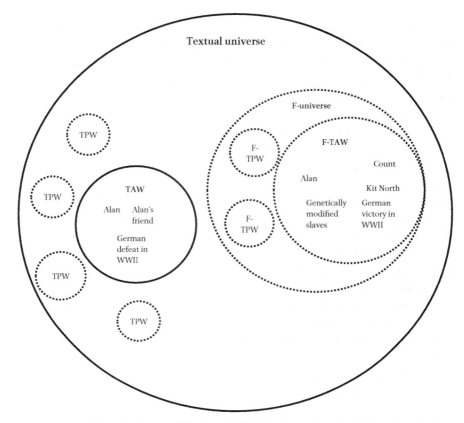

FIGURE 28.5 Textual universe of *The Sound of his Horn* from the point of view of readers for whom Alan is an unreliable narrator

inhabitants and events such as genetically mutilated slaves, the Count, Axis victory in World War II, and the feudal system. Therefore, if the reader perceives Alan as an unreliable narrator, then the ontological configuration of the textual universe of *The Sound of his Horn* can be diagrammatically represented as shown in Figure 28.5. This figure shows the internal ontological configuration of the textual universe which includes a textual actual world and a fantasy universe. In the textual actual world, Germany is defeated in the Second World War and Alan is at home having been released from the prisoner of war camp at the end of the war. In the textual actual world, Alan narrates a story to his friend. The textual actual world is surrounded by textual possible worlds and these are worlds created by characters in the textual actual world through mental processes such as wishes and hopes. For example, there are instances in the text when Alan wishes he could escape from the prisoner of war camp or he imagines that he was never captured. Figure 28.5 also shows the F-universe within the textual universe, one that Alan creates through the story that he

"'I AM NOT MAD, MOST NOBLE FESTUS.' NO. BUT I HAVE BEEN"

narrates to his friend, that is more elaborate than propositions that make up textual possible worlds. The F-universe includes an F-TAW (fantasy textual actual world) in which Nazi Germany wins the Second World War. In this world, Alan lives on the Count's estate where he meets genetically modified slaves and befriends Kit North. The F-TAW is surrounded by F-TPWs or fantasy textual possible worlds. As Ryan states, "the members of F-worlds have at their disposal the entire array of world-creating activities: the characters in the dream may dream, the heroes of fictional fictions may write fiction."[61] This can be seen in the F-TAW in the form of wishes and hopes when for example Kit North and Alan hope to escape the estate someday.

5 Conclusion

Within Possible Worlds Theory, a narratorial actual world is used to label and describe a textual actual world that is created through unreliable narration. As Ryan puts it, "in fiction told by [an] unreliable narrator ~ (NAW=TAW),"[62] that is, the narratorial actual world is more or less similar to the textual actual world. This is mainly because a narratorial actual world is the narrator's personal and somewhat inaccurate view of the textual actual world that is presented to the reader. However, as I argue here, this is a concept that can be used only when it is possible to differentiate between the narratorial actual world and the textual actual world. In *The Sound of his Horn,* while it is impossible to decide whether or not the narrator is unreliable, it is also impossible to discern which among the narrator's statements are a true representation of the textual universe and which are not. This is mainly owing to the genre that the text falls under – counterfactual historical fiction – that presupposes that devices such as time-travel and alternative historical timelines will be introduced. By introducing degrees of accessibility in Ryan's typology of accessibility relations, I have shown how TAW2 although distant from readers' experience of the actual world can be conceived as an accessible textual actual world. Furthermore, I proposed that readers who have enough background knowledge to make the epistemological link between the actual world and TAW2 are more likely to believe the narrator's claims about a TAW2, and as such they will perceive the textual universe as comprising two textual actual worlds. Alternatively, readers who disbelieve the narrator's claims about the existence of TAW2 will consider it as part of Alan's mental world. Opposed to simply classifying this world as a textual possible world because it is a mental construct or a narratorial actual

---

61 Ryan, *Possible Worlds, Artificial Intelligence, and Narrative Theory,* 119.
62 Ryan, *Possible Worlds, Artificial Intelligence, and Narrative Theory,* VII.

world because it is a world created through unreliable narration, I have theorised that whole worlds created by unreliable narrators can be conceived as a F-universe or fantasy universe. Presuming also that some readers may believe Alan travelled to TAW2, but only question specific events relating to this world, I show how associated terminology such as F-TPW can be used to describe these events, thereby demarcating an F-TPW from an F-TAW, facilitating a more nuanced dissection of the F-universe.

Possible Worlds Theory as a method of analysis has sometimes been accused of oversimplifying the text "by reducing the content" and as a result of which the text appears to "have no more contact with real situations than an algebraic formula ."[63] While this approach may seem minimalistic, the vocabulary and analytical tools that Possible Worlds Theory offers to dissect and describe texts such as *The Sound of his Horn* that present complex ontologies are too sound to ignore. Such an approach is useful to explain the internal configuration of texts, which is sometimes necessary to understand the context of such texts more generally. While this chapter focused on a single text that plays with ontology, further applications of the theory to texts that complicate reader comprehension either through ambiguous-unreliable narration or implicit accessibility relations are needed to expound upon the theory's analytical and interpretive capabilities even further.

References

Bell, Alice. *The Possible Worlds of Hypertext Fiction*. Basingstoke, UK: Palgrave Macmillan. 2010.

Berenbaum, Michael. *The World Must Know: The History of the Holocaust as Told in the United States Holocaust Memorial Museum*. Baltimore: Johns Hopkins University Press. 2005.

Booth, Wayne Clayson. *The Rhetoric of Fiction*. Chicago: University of Chicago Press. 1983.

Chatman, Seymour B. *Story and Discourse: Narrative Structure in Fiction and Film*. Ithaca, NY: Cornell University Press. 1980.

David, Lewis. *On the Plurality of Worlds*. Cambridge, England: Cambridge University Press. 1986.

Dannenberg, Hilary P. *Coincidence and Counterfactuality: Plotting Time and Space in Narrative Fiction*. Lincoln, NE: University of Nebraska Press. 2008.

---

63   Paul Werth, *Text worlds: Representing conceptual space in discourse* (Singapore: Prentice Hall, 1999), 80.

Doležel, Lubomír. *Heterocosmica: Fiction and Possible Worlds*. Baltimore: Johns Hopkins University Press. 1998.

Herman, David. *Basic Elements of Narrative*. New York: John Wiley & Sons. 2011.

Harran, Marilyn. *The Holocaust Chronicle*. Illinois: Publications International, Ltd. 2000.

Hitler, Adolf. *Mein Kampf*. London: Hurst And Blackett Ltd. 1939.

Kripke, Saul. "Semantical Considerations on Modal Logic." In *Readings in Semantics*, edited by Zabeeh F. Farhang, E.D. Kleme, and A. Jacobson, 803–14. Urbana: University of Illinois Press, 1974.

Kripke, Saul. "Semantical Analysis of Modal Logic I Normal Modal Propositional Calculi." *Mathematical Logic Quarterly* 9, no. 5–6 (1963): 67–96.

Rimmon-Kenan, Shlomith. *The Concept of Ambiguity – the Example of James*. Chicago: University of Chicago Press. 1977.

Ronen, Ruth. *Possible Worlds in Literary Theory*. Cambridge: Cambridge University Press. 1994.

Ryan, Marie-Laure. "Possible Worlds and Accessibility Relations: A Semantic Typology of Fiction." *Poetics today* 12, no. 3 (1991): 553–76.

Ryan, Marie-Laure. *Possible Worlds, Artificial Intelligence, and Narrative Theory*. Bloomington, IN: Indiana University Press. 1991.

Ryan, Marie-Laure. "The Pragmatics of Personal and Impersonal Fiction." *Poetics* 10, no. 6 (1981): 517–39.

Sarban. *The Sound of his Horn*. Leyburn: Tartarus Press. 2011. Kindle edition.

Vogt, Robert. "Combining Possible-worlds Theory and Cognitive Theory: Towards an Explanatory Model for Ironic-Unreliable Narration, Ironic-Unreliable Focalization, Ambiguous-Unreliable and Alterated-Unreliable Narration in Literary Fiction." In *Unreliable Narration and Trustworthiness: Intermedial and Interdisciplinary Perspectives*, edited by Vera Nünning, 131–54. Berlin: De Gruyter, 2015.

Waite, Robert. *The Psychopathic God: Adolph Hitler*. New York: Da Capo Press, 1993.

Werth, Paul. *Text Worlds: Representing Conceptual Space in Discourse*. Prentice Hall, 1999.

Yoke, Carl. "'A Dance of Apes': Sarban's The Sound of His Horn." In *Classic and Iconoclastic Alternative History Science Fiction*, edited by Edgar Chapman and Car Yoke, 49–70. Lewiston, NY: Edwin Mellen Press, 2003.

PART 8

Non-Western Perspectives

∴

CHAPTER 29

The Deep Frivolity of Life: An Indian Aesthetic Phenomenology of *Fun*

Arindam Chakrabarti

1 Introduction

What makes something—a thought, a poem, a musical idea, a feeling—*deep*? This chapter demonstrates why light-hearted fun or festive frivolity and frolic insofar as it springs from the spirit of play, of non-competitive sport, need not be "shallow." I begin with a wild act of imagination which both structures the analysis of "fun" that follows and, in the process, illuminates the very nature of imagination. What if Socrates tried to analyze the 21st century concept of "fun?" Taking advantage of classical Indian aesthetics of humor and other modern Indian poetics of laughter, I wish to arrive at a demonstration of the possibility of showing the profundity of the sense of lightness and fun of— even a predominantly painful—human life. Philosophy, thus, turns out to be itself an imaginative activity, namely, an art of combining depth and frivolity through an aesthetic phenomenology of fun.

1. Imagine Socrates, reincarnated in 2006, gate-crashing into a night-club or a dance-party in Boston or Bangalore. Picture him striking up a conversation with a slightly bored and recently jilted rich youth, handsome and fashionably dressed with affected inattention to his own attire, sitting in a dark corner, nursing a tall glass of beer. As they both watch the boisterous floating crowd on the dance-floor, Socrates, with his famous fondness for young boys and dialectical conversation, asks our fidgety young man:

> Now, clearly you are not happy my friend! You look more like the man whom both your sage Buddha[1] and I myself[2] compare to the itching and scratching fellow whose itch increases the more he scratches until it begins to hurt! Why do you come and spend time and money in this place? What do you think those slightly inebriated boys and girls are doing over

---

[1] See *Māgandiya Sutta,* and *Majjhima Nikāya,* 75.17.
[2] Plato, *Gorgias* 494, 4c.

696   CHAKRABARTI

there in the middle of this deafening music which is about to give me a heart-attack?

The courteous and natural response, I guess, would be: "I have no idea Grandpa what you mean by 'happy' and why you bring up this disgusting analogy of a skin-disease, but we are here to have FUN; those kids over there are trying to have a good time. Do you have a problem with that? And you have no business prying into whether or not, personally, I am having a good time." The stereotypical image of Socrates requires him, at this point, to latch on to the word "good" and the word "time" and go off into all sorts of metaphysical tangents about whether time could be good or bad, or only people, and whether goodness of times could be purchased at a price and so on. In the pages that follow, I will not be further developing my thought experiment along those lines. Instead, for the purposes of this chapter, I shall imagine Socrates to be more intrigued by the first and natural typically 21st century remark: "We are here to have fun" and ask his irritatingly basic question: "What is this *fun*?"

2. Owing to the nearly irresistible Americanization of the earth, or at least of the affluent youth culture in both the East and West, in addition to the role of television and the internet with which we have nearly *amused ourselves to death* (in the words of Neil Postman),[3] a new set of values or even life-goals has come to take the place of the old ones. Knowledge, *Eudaimonia* (being deservedly happy because of being ethically virtuous), fairness, honor—even freedom or long life—have become much less important for a very large segment of younger people than having fun, if possible, all the time. Just as the new aesthetic value of the "cool" has taken over the place of the old-fashioned beautiful, the category of the *awesome-amazing* has replaced the older category of the sublime. This new intrinsic value "fun" seems to have taken over the place of old-fashioned piety, power or pleasure: *dharma, artha, kāma.* I say "intrinsic value" because money, relationships, jobs, cars, houses, travels—all these things are said to be coveted for they lead to a fun life or fun times, but one is not supposed to ask: "What purpose does *fun* serve?" It is supposed to be an end-in-itself. Lee Siegel, who wrote a seminal study on humor in Sanskrit Literature and more recently a best-selling novel *Love in a Dead Language*,[4] contends that this omni-presence of fun as the single most important secular value can be traced back to early childhood indoctrination. He claims that

---

3   See Neil Postman, *Amusing Ourselves to Death: Public Discourse in the Age of Show Business* (London: Penguin Books, 2005).

4   See Lee Siegel, *Laughing Matters: Comic Tradition in India* (Chicago: University of Chicago Press, 1987); Lee Siegel, *Love in a Dead Language* (Chicago: University of Chicago Press, 2000).

THE DEEP FRIVOLITY OF LIFE   697

several generations of American children starting from the early nineteen fifties have been brought up on these illustrated first-books which reinforce the paramount importance of "fun" with family, with toys, with pets, at work, and with friends. Thus, the personal, domestic, environmental and social life of a child has been subconsciously shaped to seek fun in everything.

This phenomenon is reflected in two rather serious matters of considerable importance to modern, that is—Westernized, life. One is education and the other is business management. A humorless teacher has much less chance of success, now, in the field of higher education especially in the Humanities and Social Sciences than a humorous one. A joke or two is routinely planned even by a popular science lecturer. Even a physics teacher hopes to reach her brighter students more easily if she starts a lecture by asking how many quantum physicists it takes to change a light-bulb. The expected answer that it takes two physicists and a cat, one to screw in the bulb, the other to observe the first doing it, while the cat is dead and/or alive, actually jogs the memory and imagination of the students in a way mere dry theories cannot. The ubiquity of jokes and the avalanche of funny remarks in mass media has spilled over to the atmosphere of the classroom. Education has to be fun.[5] Similarly, big companies urge their managers to take "structured fun" courses.[6] For more than a decade now, professional stand-up comedians are regularly hired by big offices to entertain and train their personnel, to relax them and to teach them how to relax and befriend clients. Fun is a marketing mantra. Hence more and more advertisements such as the AMUL cheese hoardings in Kolkata try to make people laugh with current affairs jokes or simple puns like "kyaa cheeze hai!" Vernacular equivalents of the word such as "mazaa" or "masti" are regularly used in local product-promotion in India.

3. This gives us the first clue into the nature of fun: Perhaps, at the heart of fun lies humor or laughter, since to be funny is to be laughter-evoking or humorous. Now, laughter, of course, can be of many kinds. And it is not clear at all that all of them are constitutive of fun. Bharata in his *Nāṭyaśāstra* distinguishes between six kinds of laughter and each of them can be either originating in oneself or caught by a natural contagion (*saṃkramaṇa*) from another person, since even when the reason is not fully understood, laughter can spread from

---

5 For a more comprehensive discussion of the pivotal role of humor in academia, see Stephen Paul Halula, "What Role Does Humor in the Higher Education Classroom Play in Student-Perceived Instructor Effectiveness?" (PhD diss., Marquette University, 2009).

6 See Robert C. Ford, Frank McLaughlin, and John W. Newstrom, "Questions and Answers about Fun at Work," *Human Resource Planning* 26, no. 4 (2003): 18–33.

one person to another. Hence, Abhinvagupta says that there can be twelve kinds of laughter. The basic six kinds are:

i. *smita* (slight smile of somewhat introspective pleasure, which does not reveal the teeth)

ii. *hasita* (with a little glimpse of the teeth, a flash of a merry grin)

iii. *vihasita* (with creases around the eyes and on the cheek, a sweet sonorous giggle)

iv. *upahasita* (with slightly inflated nostrils, a peal of laughter with some shaking of the head)

v. *apahasita* (inappropriate cheeky loud belly laugh which brings tears in one's eyes)

vi. *atihasita* (an unstoppable hysteric conceited guffaw which makes one roar)[7]

A chart of pictures used by Charles Darwin in his *Expression of Emotions in Man and Animals*[8] illustrates at least the first three kinds. Now I doubt that the first and the last kind, *smita* and *atihasita* or *aṭṭa-hāsya* can be called fun. The latter is commonly enacted by villains in village theatre or even Hindi films when they are enraged and are showing utter disdain for their adversaries which is not fun for either them or the victims. Such thunderous laughs can be scary rather than funny. The bashful face of girl in love may on the other hand break into the first kind of touch of a smile, when there is pleasure but no fun.

In this regard, Rabindranath in his late nineteenth century masterly collection of conversation-essays called "The Five Elements" clearly distinguishes between pleasure and mirth, comparing pleasure with *light* and mirth with *lightning*, and trying to give reasons why we smile for pleasure but laugh in mirth. His word for mirth is *kautuk-hasya* whereas his word for fun is *aamod*. The reason why mirth or fun that makes us laugh cannot be identified with pleasure or happiness is clearly stated by Tagore: "Amusement and mirth are not exactly happiness: rather they are mild degrees of pain or sadness. We may feel some pleasure when sadness impinges on our consciousness in small measure."[9] He takes the example of a funny poem about Krishna appearing in front of Radha's door on a winter night with his hookah asking for a light or some tobacco. This incongruity strikes a mild blow stimulating our sensibilities in addition to yielding the unique kind of pleasure which we call mirth.

---

7 See Chapter six from Bharata, *The Natyashastra*.

8 Charles Darwin, *The Expression of the Emotions in Man and Animals*, 3rd ed. (London: Harper Collins, 1998).

9 Rabindranath Tagore, *Selected Writings on Literature and Language*, eds. Sukanta Chaudhuri and Shankha Ghosh (New Delhi: Oxford University Press, 2001), 81.

THE DEEP FRIVOLITY OF LIFE   699

But surely Rabindranath Tagore's theory of the comical as a mild self-inflic-
tion of pain has nothing to do with any masochistic practice of taking pleasure
in pain. That is why the next essay picks up the topic of the limits or measure
of mirth. If these limits are crossed, teasing laughter turns into painful torture.
The central idea is that humor and jollity comes out of excitement, any stimulation of our dull sensibility. Those who find the risk and panic of very dangerous roller-coaster rides or fast merry-go-rounds too much to take do not derive
any fun from them. But those whose threshold of "tolerable fear/pain" is higher
enjoy such risks as fun. The oddity or jolt such as a man slipping or dropping
his pants awkwardly but nor hurting or humiliating himself can stimulate or
titillate us. In a minimal sense, any excitement is fun.

4. Now, humor is a vast subject. Divided somewhat crudely into *Wit, Humor*
and *Satire*, literary humor is just the tip of this life-pervading ice-berg. Philosophers as diverse as Abhinavagupta and Henri Bergson have very interesting
and controversial things to say about different forms and causes of humor. But
it may not be a necessary or sufficient condition of fun. Some fun activities
such as rock-climbing or going for a vacation in Egypt and seeing the tomb of
Tutenkhamen, for those who enjoy those sorts of things, may not involve a
single laugh and there may be nothing funny (humorous) at all about some
forms of fun such as a game of chess. On the other hand, an avalanche of very
humorous (hilarious) jokes can get on someone's nerves–as many Groucho
Marx movies or Robin Williams' torrentially goofy garrulity may do–such that
it yields no fun at all in spite of being so uniformly funny.

Rabindranath himself helps us here by supplying another clue to the essence of fun. Not just any slight pain is adequate for mirth, he says, but one
that is due to a playful breaking of a rule or routine. In the second essay on
Mirth he remarks: "Fun cannot be experienced without the slight distress
caused by breaking rules. Fun is not subject to normal everyday rules: it is oc-
casional and intermittent, and requires effort. The excitement generated by
friction between the distress and the effort is the main ingredient of fun."[10] In
these self-consciously inconclusive dialogues, Tagore expresses a considerable
sense of mystery around the concepts of amusement and fun: "Mirth is a
somewhat mysterious thing. Beasts, too feel joy and sorrow, but not mirth. Perhaps one finds some trace of this *rasa* (of humor) in the nature of the ape, but

---

10   Rabindranath Tagore, *The Complete Works of Rabindranath Tagore*, http://www.tagore-
        web.in/. An English translation of "Panchabhuut-Kautuk-haasya" and "Kautuk haasyer
        Maatraa" is available in the chapters "Mirth" and "The Measure of Mirth" in Tagore, *Se-
        lected Writings on Literature and Language*.

apes resemble humans in many other respects as well."[11] When does this entertaining amusing degree of incongruity and pain exceed the limit and become cruelty or suffering? Rabindranath comes up with a puzzling example: "Curiosity is often cruel: there is cruelty in humour too. It is reported that Siraj-ud-Daulah used to tie two men together by their beards and put snuff up their nostrils; when they both started to sneeze, he would feel amused."[12] Farces and circus-jokers often walk a fine line between laughable misadventures and pitiable suffering. Tagore ends his essay on measures of mirth with a very unexpected twist which makes it as a philosophical essay itself a lot of fun simply because he forces us to imagine a mockery of the greatest human suffering by a cruel devil of a cosmic satirist. This entire concluding passage is worth quoting:

> When people die in hordes during a famine, no one finds it a farcical matter of joke. But we can easily imagine that this might be a highly comic scene for a humour-loving devil: he may glance laughingly at all those emaciated beings possessed of immortal souls and say: "See, your six systems of philosophy, your poetry of Kalidasa, your 330 million gods are all around you: you lack nothing but two lowly fistfuls of rice, and simply because of that your immortal souls, your world-conquering humanity are fluttering at your throats, waiting to fly out of your mouths."[13]

This is of course an extreme scenario of fun at humanity's expense. But verging on the absurd or bizarre, it shows how Tagore takes the idea of the co-existence of suffering and humor to its logical culmination.

5. Can we then say that humor and rule-breaking together or disjunctively capture the essence of fun? In so far as an escape from the drudgery of daily rituals seems to be a big element in the notion of fun that seems plausible. But very soon, if we observe fun behavior, we realize that fun has its own rules and rituals. With its cousin *games* (as in "fun and games") though fun is engaged in for distraction, most parties, festivities, dances, dinners, even watching funny talk-shows on television, to come to think of it, have pretty rigid rules of their own. Just as games cannot be played whimsically by making up "private arbitrary rules," the participatory social aspect of fun such as playing that singing game called "antyakshari" or the intelligent game called "20 questions," or such non-game like festivities such as the color festival—Holi or Diwali are rituals

---

11   Tagore, *The Complete Works of Rabindranath Tagore*, n. pag.
12   Tagore, *The Complete Works of Rabindranath Tagore*, n. pag.
13   Tagore, *The Complete Works of Rabindranath Tagore*, n. pag.

THE DEEP FRIVOLITY OF LIFE 701

of different sorts and come with their own rules. Consequently, fun cannot be a total release from rules. Perhaps also, one has to keep following some rules just in order to give public notice of which rules one is occasionally flouting. That is why the clown actually masters trapeze and other difficult gymnastics in which he periodically bungles and fails in a crafty and calculated manner.

6. There seems to be another very important element in fun which neither humor nor rule-transgression can quite cover. Fun is the opposite of work. It is closely tied to the not all that clear notion of *leisure*, which consists in taking a break from work. Abhinavagupta's most favorite phrase while discussing the aesthetic attitude of marveling at a charming work of art is "*camatkāra*," a certain stirring or quickening (*druti*) of the melted heart. However, he also uses the phrase: "repose of the heart" (*hṛdaya-viśrānti*).[14] Fun, like charm, is enjoyed when the heart finds rest in a sort of "this is it" feeling. Nonetheless, the search for fun makes people restless: well there is only one way a restless heart can find fulfilment, by resting. Hence the importance of the notion of leisure as against work.

But many creative kinds of hard work such as cooking, painting, gardening, sculpture, even fairly labor-intensive forms of physical exercise such as weight-lifting (let us remember Shasthicharan from Sukumar Ray's *Abol Tabol* translated into English as *Rhymes without Reason* who used to throw up and juggle with elephants just for fun[15]) can be great fun. Not all fun is the opposite of work in the sense of energy-burning movement of muscle. Indeed, fun is almost always exhausting. In fact, simple lying about and a lack of exercise is seldom fun. It is an effect and cause of boredom, the real enemy of fun. Fun is more a function of *sattva* and *rajas* among the Sāṃkhya *guṇa*-s, rather than of *tamas*. The renowned theorist of idleness Jerome K. Jerome makes this wise observation: "It is no fun doing nothing when you have nothing to do."[16]

7. Perhaps, then, the secret of fun lies, not in worklessness or leisure but in the notion of flippancy, unseriousness, shallowness and frivolity. This also explains its crucial distinction from pleasure which often comes with the claim of depth and seriousness. After a very thickly pleasurable or erotic evening with a serious lover or wife or husband, if one utters "that was fun," then that

---

14   Arindam Chakrabarti, "The Heart of Repose, The Repose of the Heart: A Phenomenological Analysis of the Concept of Viśrānti," in *Sāmarasya: Studies in Indian Arts Philosophy and Interreligious Dialogue*, eds. Sadananda Das and Ernst Furlinger (New Delhi: DK Printworld, 2005), 27–36.

15   See Sukumar Ray, *The Select Nonsense of Sukumar Ray*, trans. Sukanta Chaudhuri (New Delhi: Oxford University Press, 1987).

16   Jerome K. Jerome, "Idle Thoughts of an Idle Fellow," (Project Gutenberg, 1997), par. 3, https://www.gutenberg.org/files/849/849-h/849-h.htm#link2H_4_0003.

may be taken as an insult. One is then rightly suspected of having flirted rather than loved. Well, what then is flippancy? Some readers may object to my choice of topic on the grounds that fun is such a frivolous idea that it does not deserve to be the basis of a philosophical reflection. In my defense, I have already illustrated that the concept of frivolity is not easy to unpack. It is by no means an unimportant concept. Just as the idea of error occupies a very major part of the Advaita Vedānta theory of knowledge, serious philosophy of reality (and its value) is at its deepest when it tries to understand the notion of fiction and flippancy.

The mystery of such insubstantial things as rainbows, mirages, shadows and reflections on mirrors constitute the central concerns of substantial philosophy. For instance, we all know that there is no semi-circular substance with a seven-hued surface out there on the sky when we all unmistakably "see" the rainbow. Such shallowness of a public illusion merits the profoundest philosophical meditations. Thus, laughter and mirth, the rituals of mildly risky collective rule- breaking, those pleasurable packets of weak pain, those exhausting respites from work, and the celebration of self-mockery, make excellent topics of moral psychology.

8. With a touch of confessed trickery and make-believe, do our funs also have an element, not only of release from the pressure of rules and work but a sort of taking leave of morality? There is a strong element of amoralism in the cult of fun: Everything is fair not only in love and war but most notoriously in fun and festivity. Mikhail Bakhtin in his study of Rabelais has dealt at great length on this dissident, ethics-rupturing norm-flouting nature of a carnival and all the frolic that goes along with it[17] (e.g. *Mardi Gras*). This is also the reason why solemn moralists cannot stand the valorization of fun. Certain forms of Protestant Christianity, rigid Islam and Brahmo Dharma have historically frowned upon fun as vulgar and devilish. It is a bit hard for a practicing traditional Hindu not to value fun as a good thing since the two major gods in her pantheon are puckishly or crazily addicted to fun. Krishna or Vishnu is called "*Raṅga-nātha*" the lord of play or amusement, and Shiva is called "*Nāṭa-rāja*" the king of Actors/ Dancers. Pretending and make believe and God's playing magic tricks on his audience seem to lie at the heart of Hindu theology and metaphysics! Nevertheless, recent nationalistic misappropriation of neo-Hinduism has slipped into a sort of funless teeth-clenching seriousness which is always angry (and envious). It feels self-important enough to want to protect

---

17   See Mikhail Bakhtin, *Rabelais and His World* (Bloomington, IN: Indiana University Press, 2009) in addition to Renate Lachmann, Raoul Eshelman, and Marc Davis, "Bakhtin and Carnival: Culture as Counter-Culture," *Cultural Critique* 11 (1988–1989): 115–52.

THE DEEP FRIVOLITY OF LIFE   703

its own endangered Dharma than to feel relaxed and safe being protected by it. If these Hindutva zealots ever dance, that is no dance of fun but a communal death-dance of cruel carnage which Rabindranath would never have condoned as "kautuk" or "aamod," but would have perhaps lashed out against as sheer bestiality in the name of patriotic or religious seriousness. This is the kind of seriousness that we need to *make fun of* rather than treat as fun.

9. This use of "making fun of" reveals a different angle related to the notion of fun. Often fun is a collective activity consisting of teasing another group or individual who form the butt or target of fun. Such fun is not revelry but raillery, more mockery than mirth. Satire or *prahasanam* is a literary form which derives from this aspect of fun at the expense of someone or some community. Our ethnic or racist jokes, our political humor, Bankim Chandra's incomparable *Kamalakanta*[18] sketches are examples of this kind of pungent fun. Moreover, sometimes such ridicule is directed to oneself as when Tagore writes the poem with the theme: "In my next birth, I shall have to become my own sharpest critic,"[19] or when Sri Ramakrishna Paramhamsa anticipates about he and his wife appearing together in public eliciting the public criticism: "Look, the Hamsa (swan) and Hamsi (she-swan) have come!"[20] Making fun of oneself then becomes a wonderful antidote to egotism and pride. This is what Bankim Chandra was so good at when he wrote *The Life of Muchiram Gur*.[21]

2   Derision and Hedonic Error, Mixed Pain-Pleasure, Self-Ignorance

In *Philebus*, Plato has a very clear conviction that derisive fun is pleasure at the expense of the pain of another.[22] On a deeper level, he seems to suggest that the apparent titillation at the spectacle of another person suffering is at its core a mixed state of empathic suffering at the sight of a fellow-human, blended with a pleasure at one's own claimed superiority in so far as one is not the butt of the joke. However, Plato exposes an emotional error behind such mixed pleasures. It is only to the extent that one does not know what one is feeling at the time, that one experiences fun because of such satire or ridicule.

---

18   Bankim Chandra, *Kamalakanta: A Collection of Satirical Essays and Reflections* (Kolkata, India: Rupa & Company, 1992).

19   Tagore, *The Complete Works of Rabindranath Tagore*, n. pag.

20   Ramakrishna Paramahansa, *The Great Master, The Internet Archive*, https://archive.org/details/SriRamakrishnaTheGreatMaster.

21   For the latest Bengali edition, see Bankim Chandra, *Muchiram Gurer Jivancharita* (Scotts Valley, CA: CreateSpace, 2018).

22   Plato, *Philebus* 48C-50B.

One covers up the painful nature of this confused state by the convulsive laughter which verges on tears. This theory of comedy as based on foolish self-deceptive painful pleasure, though not entirely accepted by Aristotle, had a profound impact on his theory of comedy as well (in so far as we can reconstruct his theory of comedy, that is).

Death and the Illogical—two paradigmatic targets of humor come together in the amazing example that Bergson takes from Mark Twain towards the end of his famous work on laughter.[23] Specifically, Bergson presents this exchange between Twain and a reporter:

> QUESTION. Isn't that a brother of yours?
>
> ANSWER. Oh! Yes, yes, yes! Now you remind me of it, that WAS a brother of mine. That's William- - BILL we called him. Poor old Bill!
>
> Q. Why? Is he dead, then?
>
> A. Ah! Well, I suppose so. We never could tell. There was a great mystery about it.
>
> Q. That is sad, very sad. He disappeared, then?
>
> A. Well, yes, in a sort of general way. We buried him.
>
> Q. BURIED him! BURIED him, without knowing whether he was dead or not?
>
> A. Oh no! Not that. He was dead enough.
>
> Q. Well, I confess that I can't understand this. If you buried him, and you knew he was dead—
>
> A. No! No! We only thought he was.
>
> Q. Oh, I see! He came to life again?
>
> A. I bet he didn't.
>
> Q. Well, I never heard anything like this. SOMEBODY was dead. SOMEBODY was buried. Now, where was the mystery?
>
> A. Ah! That's just it! That's it exactly. You see, we were twins,—defunct and I,—and we got mixed in the bath-tub when we were only two weeks old, and one of us was drowned. But we didn't know which. Some think it was Bill. Some think it was me.
>
> Q. Well, that is remarkable. What do YOU think?
>
> A. Goodness knows! I would give whole worlds to know. This solemn, this awful tragedy has cast a gloom over my whole life. But I will tell you a secret now, which I have never revealed to any creature before. One of us had a peculiar mark,—a large mole on the back of his left hand: that

---

23   Mark Twain, *Mark Twain Laughing: Humorous Anecdotes by and about Samuel L. Clemens*, ed. Paul M. Zall (Knoxville, TN: University of Tennessee Press, 1987).

THE DEEP FRIVOLITY OF LIFE 705

was ME. THAT CHILD WAS THE ONE THAT WAS DROWNED! ... etc., etc.[24]

Bergson concludes, "A close examination will show us that the absurdity of this dialogue is by no means an absurdity of an ordinary type. It would disappear were not the speaker himself one of the twins in the story. It results entirely from the fact that Mark Twain asserts he is one of these twins, whilst all the time he talks as though he were a third person who tells the tale. In many of our dreams we adopt exactly the same method."[25]

10. Since fun is a search for a liberation from drudgery or tedium, there is also an element of yearning for novelty and a tendency to get bored easily in the pursuit of fun. "O! Whatever!!," an interjection made popular by Bollywood movies and FM or MTV culture, shows what has been called a certain *blasé* or "who cares" attitude which may well be a direct fall-out of the amoral, shallow, frenetic search for variety and novelty or even gimmicks just for change's sake.

11. A balanced view of the concept of fun thus needs to pay attention to this family-resemblance character of that concept which cannot be precisely defined. But it seems to have all the aforementioned features: humor, rule-breaking, leisure, frivolity/ shallowness, amorality, ridicule (including self-ridicule), and novelty. But is it still worth counting as an ultimate value, or is its prevalence to be lamented as a tragic decline of our "weighty Indian values" as a consequence of Western influence?

12. At this point of our discussion, we should turn to Rabindranath Tagore's own philosophical corner-stone: the idea of surplus, extra or left-over. To quote from his essay "The Religion of an Artist," which first appeared in 1936: "Life is perpetually creative because it contains in itself that surplus which ever overflows the boundaries of the immediate time and space, restlessly pursuing its adventure of expression in the varied forms of self-realisation ... Self-forgetting, and in a higher degree, self-sacrifice is our acknowledgment of this our experience of the infinite."[26]

Analyzed from this angle, our love of fun has the same source as our love of useless knowledge or unself-interested creative activities, and indeed of all such acts of sacrifice which leave a surplus as the sacred left-over, the "*huta-śeṣa*" which we call "*prasāda*"!

---

24 Henri Bergson, *Laughter: An Essay on the Meaning of the Comic*, trans. Cloudesley Brereton and Fred Rothwell (New York: The Macmillan Company, 1914), 58b–59a.
25 Bergson, *Laughter: An Essay on the Meaning of the Comic*, 59a.
26 Rabindranath Tagore, *The English Writings of Rabindranath Tagore: A miscellany*, ed. Sisir Kumar Das (New Delhi: Sahitya Akademi, 1994), 580.

Tagore insists that the religion of man originates from the craving for "more," the yearning for something beyond the pragmatic practical needful measured scientific truth. It consists in the limit-crossing exuberance that he rightly sees celebrated in the Upanishads. It is too bad that Tagore did not get exposed to Abhinavagupta. Finding an unending source of self-marveling in the exuberance of creative energy right here in the sensuous life of the body is something that Abhinavagupta talks about in the *Parātriṃśikāvivaraṇam*. Life becomes a constant celebration when one realizes that the self is an actor on the stage of an insubstantial shadow world where the sense organs are one's own spectators. A deeper spiritual sense of fun then emerges, which pours itself out in such songs as *bodro dhoom legechhe hridi-komol-e/ mojaa dekhichhe aamaar mon-paagole//* in all its musical ecstasy:

> O What a carnival has started today in my heart-lotus
> My mad mind is having a lot of *fun* witnessing this!
> Seeing all this, the sense-organs and all the inner distracting enemies
> Are speechless in awe.
> Taking this chance, the doors of wisdom have opened up.[27]

One then realizes what precisely our imaginary youth, whom Socrates found to be unhappy and restless, are really thirsting for. This is the fun to which Sri Ramakrishna refers in his assertion that "the world may have to be rejected as a snare of illusion to the mere possessor of knowledge (jnani). But to those who possess higher wisdom (vijnani), the world is a great 'fun-place.'"[28]

This world is a fun-factory—here, we eat, share, and lap up as much fun as possible (e shongshaar mojar kuti, khaai daai aar moja luti!), with minimal—nearly non-existent—expectations out of it. One can then laugh at the fact that people laugh at such unfunny things and seek pleasure in such pathetic possessions as cars and bungalows, jobs and careers when death makes a joke out of all that. With the taste of that genuine fun of what Tagore calls "the Exuberant Extra," the world's laughter appears to be only a mimicry or semblance of laughter and hence gives rise to a sense of cosmic absurdity which promises to be fun at its infinite best.

---

27   "Bodro Dhoom Legechhe Hridi Komole," YouTube Video, 13:48, August 30, 2018, https://www.youtube.com/watch?v=LtFRhaKpeRo. My translation of this well-known and often-sung song in Bengali.

28   *The Gospel of Sri Ramakrishna*, trans. Swami Nikhilananda (New York: Ramakrishna-Vivekananda Center, 1942), 139.

References

Bergson, Henri. *Laughter: An Essay on the Meaning of the Comic*. Translated by Cloudesley Brereton and Fred Rothwell. New York: The Macmillan Company. 1914.

"Bodro Dhoom Legechhe Hridi Komole." YouTube Video, 13:48. August 30, 2018. https://www.youtube.com/watch?v=LtFRhaKpeRo.

Chakrabarti, Arindam. "The Heart of Repose, The Repose of the Heart: A Phenomenological Analysis of the Concept of Viśrānti." In *Sāmarasya: Studies in Indian Arts Philosophy and Interreligious Dialogue*, edited by Sadananda Das and Ernst Furlinger, 27–36. New Delhi: DK Printworld, 2005.

Chandra, Bankim. *Kamalakanta: A Collection of Satirical Essays and Reflections*. Kolkata, India: Rupa & Company. 1992.

Chandra, Bankim. *Muchiram Gurer Jivancharita*. Scotts Valley, CA: CreateSpace. 2018.

Darwin, Charles. *The Expression of the Emotions in Man and Animals*. 3rd ed. London: Harper Collins. 1998.

Ford, Robert C., Frank McLaughlin, and John W. Newstrom. "Questions and Answers about Fun at Work." *Human Resource Planning* 26, no. 4 (2003): 18–33.

Halula, Stephen Paul. "What Role Does Humor in the Higher Education Classroom Play in Student-Perceived Instructor Effectiveness?" PhD diss., Marquette University, 2009.

Jerome, Jerome K. "Idle Thoughts of an Idle Fellow." Project Gutenberg, 1997. https://www.gutenberg.org/files/849/849-h/849-h.htm#link2H_4_0003.

Lachmann, Renate, Raoul Eshelman, and Marc Davis. "Bakhtin and Carnival: Culture as Counter-Culture." *Cultural Critique* 11 (1988–1989): 115–52.

Postman, Neil. *Amusing Ourselves to Death: Public Discourse in the Age of Show Business*. London: Penguin Books. 2005.

Ray, Sukumar. *The Select Nonsense of Sukumar Ray*. Translated by Sukanta Chaudhuri. New Delhi: Oxford University Press. 1987.

Siegel, Lee. *Laughing Matters: Comic Tradition in India*. Chicago: University of Chicago Press. 1987.

Siegel, Lee. *Love in a Dead Language*. Chicago: University of Chicago Press. 2000.

Tagore, Rabindranath. *Selected Writings on Literature and Language*. Edited by Sukanta Chaudhuri and Shankha Ghosh. New Delhi: Oxford University Press. 2001.

Tagore, Rabindranath. *The Complete Works of Rabindranath Tagore*. http://www.tagoreweb.in/.

Tagore, Rabindranath. *The English Writings of Rabindranath Tagore: A miscellany*. Edited by Sisir Kumar Das. New Delhi: Sahitya Akademi. 1994.

The Gospel of Sri Ramakrishna. Translated by Swami Nikhilananda. New York: Ramakrishna-Vivekananda Center, 1942.

Twain, Mark. *Mark Twain Laughing: Humorous Anecdotes by and about Samuel L. Clemens*. Edited by Paul M. Zall. Knoxville, TN: University of Tennessee Press. 1987.

CHAPTER 30

The Symbolic Force of Rocks in the Chinese Imagination

Yanping Gao

The theory of the five Elements (i.e. water, fire, earth, wood and metal) as a deep understanding of natural law and of human cultivation through interaction with nature is deeply woven into the fabric of Chinese culture including traditional medicine and the Chinese zodiac. The rocks and stones in question in this chapter, which are regarded as "the bone of the earth," share the same intellectual sophistication as Chinese thought related to matter in general. As early as the Han dynasty, *Shen Nong Ben Cao Jing* (Pharmacopoeia of the Heavenly Husbandman) identified different kinds of minerals as remedies, some of them being from rocks. *Shi Yao Er Ya* (Synonymic Dictionary of Minerals and Drugs) from the Tang dynasty, an import treatise on minerals by Mei Biao, was actually a book for alchemists exploring possible transformations between different types of matter under certain conditions. Nevertheless, during the Song dynasty, owing to the proliferation of scientific monographs devoted to specialized subjects, a whole series of books emerged that focused on stones and minerals, such as rock catalogues. As I will reveal in this chapter, the starting point of these studies was aesthetic rather than medical.[1] Meanwhile, Chinese literati contributed to the aesthetics of rocks through a delicate appreciation and image-making connected to the forms and materiality of rocks. Indeed, aesthetics has always played a pivotal role in rock culture that far transcends medicine and mystery.

In one of his poems about rocks from "An Account on Lake Tai Rock" (太湖石记), the Chinese poet from the Tang dynasty Bai Juyi posits, "Unlike poetry, music, and wine, the rocks have no patterns or sound or smell or taste."[2] Nonetheless, Bai Juyi is undoubtedly one of the most famous connoisseurs of rocks throughout Chinese history. In fact, few civilizations have revered stones and rocks as much as the Chinese. Petrophilia, or the adoration of rock, has a

---

1   For more detailed information about the history of mineral studies in China, see Joseph Needham, *Science and Civilisation in China*, vol. 3 (Cambridge: Cambridge University Press, 1959), 643–46.

2   Bai Juyi, *Bai Juyi Ji* 白居易集, Band 4, ed. Gu Xuejie 顾学颉 (Beijing: Zhonghua Book Company, 1999), 1543.

© KONINKLIJKE BRILL NV, LEIDEN, 2020 | DOI:10.1163/9789004436350_032

THE SYMBOLIC FORCE OF ROCKS IN THE CHINESE IMAGINATION 709

remarkable tradition in Chinese culture that could even go back as far as two thousand years. Rocks were initially arranged in the emperor's parks, as a prerogative of the imperial family. Later, this enthusiasm spread to the *literati* and common people, as the symbolism associated with rocks during the Tang dynasty became even more pronounced on multiple levels. This vogue of rock appreciation became even more popular during the Song dynasty when rock catalogues ("石谱") from various authors appeared. It is especially noteworthy that the rocks or stones in question here certainly do not include crystals or jewels that are treasured in many civilizations. Instead, this chapter focuses on what are often referred to as "common rocks" that are identified with special characters and endowed with profound symbolism by Chinese *literati* and intellectuals.

In the Chinese imagination, rocks are not merely the object of fetishism, given that they carry their own subjectivity and spirit. This chapter first explores how Chinese *literati* integrate rocks and images of them laden with symbolic meaning into their own lives. Moreover, I also underscore how their tastes related to the "ideal" rock (especially Lake Tai Rock) inform their aesthetic sensibilities overall. From an interdisciplinary angle, I also probe the metaphysical and spiritual origins of this petrophilia that are inextricably linked to Chinese Daoist philosophy. As an object of projection or contemplation, rocks play an important role in both the collective and personal imagination of Chinese people. As I underscore unique Chinese sensibilities, I will also return to the Western tradition as a counterpart from time to time when necessary.

I　Petrophilia: Stone as a Companion Species

The interaction between human beings and the natural world, in addition to the ecological interdependency that these quotidian encounters entail, is a deeply rooted concept in traditional Chinese culture initially connected to the birth of agriculture. In the case of rocks, stone worship related to various pantheistic divinities existed from the very beginning. In the Han rhapsodic Fu, vivid descriptions of rocks became very common in "poetry on objects" (yong-wushi 咏物诗). Nevertheless, as Xiaoshan Yang points out, "In this genre, the poetic rock lacks specificity as a physical object and functions instead as an emblem whose meaning can be easily decoded. The poet evidences little material relationship with the rocks he describes."[3] In other words, the rock in this

---

3　For a more comprehensive discussion about the importance of poetry dedicated to objects, see Xiaoshan Yang, *Metamorphosis of the Private Sphere: Gardens and Objects in Tang-Song Poetry* (Cambridge, MA: Harvard University Press, 2003), 94–98.

context is a concept that is deprived of its own materiality.[4] It is essentially a fixed item attached to a socially constructed symbolism. Thus, its materiality does not affect the spectator physically.

From a historical perspective, it is later including the ninth century that the physical interactions between stones and humans come into play. Stones would become a "companion species" for their owner. As Xiaoshan Yang reveals, "These new orientations are illustrated in the poetic representation of the Lake Tai rock from the mid-Tang to the Northern Song."[5] From this point on, stones were deeply appreciated and endowed with a sort of subjectivity, thereby playing the role of a companion species in the daily life of the *literati*. While serving as an administrator in Suzhou, a city near Lake Tai (Tai Hu), Bai Juyi was overwhelmed by the bizarre and grotesque features of a couple of Lake Tai rocks. He took them back home immediately and "domesticated" them. Bai derived much inspiration and satisfaction from being with these stones. In the poem "A pair of Rocks"(Shuangshi 双石), Bai addresses these rocks as close friends: "Turning my head around, I ask the pair of rocks: Can you keep company with an old man like me? Although the rocks cannot speak, they promise that we will be three friends."[6] His friend Niu Senru, the prime minister at the time, was so obsessed with stone collection that he made painstaking efforts to classify them appropriately. According to Bai, he "treats them [the rocks] as noble friends, respects them as great philosophers, treasures them as jewelries, and loves them as his own descendants."[7] Or, as Niu himself claims, he admires and loves rocks as much as one would an older brother: "As if facing a brother ten years my senior."[8] In the Song dynasty, Sushi's contemporary, the poet Mi Fu, is widely considered by historians to be the ultimate connoisseur of rocks among Chinese *literati*. As he was traveling to assume the responsibilities of a magistrate in Wuwei county in Anhui, a region that is famous for its stone, he suddenly saw a stone with a grotesque shape standing upright in the municipal garden. In a state of shock, he immediately bowed to it in a sign of respect and admiration before addressing it as "Elder Brother Rock."[9] Through the act of submission and obedience, Mi Fu gives up his own

---

4   Xiaoshan Yang, "Petrophilia and Its Anxiety, The Lake Tai Rock in Tang-Song Poetry," *Landscape and Garden* (风景园林) 10 (2019): 81.

5   Yang, "Petrophilia and Its Anxiety," 81.

6   English translation courtesy of Yang, *Metamorphosis of the Private Sphere: Gardens and Objects in Tang-Song Poetry*, 100–01.

7   Bai Juyi, *Bai Juyi Ji* 白居易集, Band 4, 1544.

8   English translation courtesy of Yang, *Metamorphosis of the Private Sphere: Gardens and Objects in Tang-Song Poetry*, 107.

9   See Jing Xuezhi 金学智, *Chinese Garden Culture* 中国园林文化 (Beijing: China Architecture and Building Press, 2005), 359.

THE SYMBOLIC FORCE OF ROCKS IN THE CHINESE IMAGINATION   711

subjectivity surrendering himself completely to the rock. During these poignant instants, the rock becomes the dominant object, as opposed to playing a passive role, in terms of fetishism. All of these aforementioned figures treat the rock not merely as a pet, but rather as what is called a companion species nowadays: an object which possesses equivalent subjectivity.

Chinese petrophilia could be described as a thought system epitomized by a deep connection between nature and human beings that attempts to break "an oppositional and merely human-centered view."[10] Although some stones are certainly cherished in Western culture, this type of petrophilia only exists in Asia. Even Michelangelo never created a sculpture glorifying the stone *per se*, although he explicitly confessed that "I love sleep, but I love the stone more" ("Caro m'è'l sonno, e più l'esser di sasso)[11] in addition to using unpolished stones to represent human beings. Until recently, a similar esteem for natural stones is evident in the thought of Goethe, Emerson and Thoreau. However, stones are in a special category of their own for Chinese *literati* in comparison to Goethe's petrophilia, for instance, as I will later clarify.

II   The Materiality and Emergence of the Chinese Rock

Limestone, especially Lake Tai Rock, was deemed to be the "ideal rock" for rock enthusiasts. For this reason, rock connoisseurs share many of the same aesthetic judgments. They also tend to use Lake Tai Rock as a basis of comparison for appreciating all other stones. Lake Tai Rock was formed from limestone deposits nearly three-hundred million years ago in this area of China. These ancient formations assumed extravagant shapes when the area was covered by sea. To be more precise, the deposits were sculpted by hard pebbles in the lake during heavy storms. In "A Pair of Rocks," Bai Juyi offers one of the earliest descriptions of the aesthetic attributes of Lake Tai Rock. As the poet writes, "Dark sallow, two slates of rocks. Their appearance is grotesque and ugly" (苍然两片石, 厥状怪且丑).[12] His friend Niu Senru holds a similar attitude. For him as well, a good stone should be (tong 通), perforated (tou 透), ugly, and dark. This petrophilia continued on an upward trajectory until the Song dynasty. The previously mentioned artist Mi Fu enumerated the physical features of an ideal

---

10   Wolfgang Welsch, "Art Transcending the Human Pale-Toward a Transhuman Stance," *International Aesthetics* (外国美学 Beijing), 21 (2013): 329.

11   Quoted in Welsch, "Art Transcending the Human Pale-Toward a Transhuman Stance," 329.

12   English translation courtesy of Yang, *Metamorphosis of the Private Sphere: Gardens and Objects in Tang-Song Poetry*, 100.

rock that is "lean" (thou 瘦), "wrinkled" (zhou 皱), "leaked" (lou 漏) and "perforated" (tou 透). This ideal corresponds to Bai Juyi's formulation of "grotesque and ugly."

Thus, in characterizing rocks as "lean, wrinkled, leaked, and perforated," Mi Fu follows in Bai's footsteps by setting the basic aesthetic parameters of what constitutes Chinese rock. The writer Li Yu (1611–1680) from the Qing dynasty borrows this basic idea. In his own appreciation of stones in general, he affirms, "The beauty of rocks, lies in the perforated (tou), leaked (lou), lean (shou)" (言山石之美者，俱在透、漏、瘦三字。).[13] A more prosaic description of Lake Tai rocks is found in Du Wan's 杜绾 *Yunlin Stone Catalogue*, which describes more than one hundred kinds of stones that appeal to the Chinese imagination. Identifying Lake Tai Rock as one of the most ideal rocks, he explains, "They are naturally hard and glossy, with contours of 'hollow concaves'(qiankong 嵌空), 'pierced holes'(chuanyan 穿眼), 'intertwining twists'(wanzhuan 宛转), 'strange precipices' (xianguai 险怪)... They have a net of raised patterns all over. Their surfaces are covered with small cavities, worn by the wind and waves."[14] This passage also pinpoints several criteria for good rocks, including "hollow concaves" and pierced holes characterized by "perforated," "leaked," and "intertwining twists" (wanzhuan 宛转) that make the contours wrinkled. Most of these rocks are grotesque stones. In addition to Lake Tai Rock, there is a rock called Jianghua rock that "is very strange ... The four sides are penetrated, and [it] looks extremely dangerous and terrible."[15] This stone has a "perforated and grotesque appearance ... with deep holes inside."[16]

A brief explanation of the various connotations of the words "shou," "tou," "lou," and "zhou" is probably necessary here, in spite of the fact that all four terms are somewhat ambivalent even in Chinese. "Shou" in Chinese means thin and leak, demonstrating that rocks should be without any kind of "fat" or lumps. "Zhou" means wrinkled and not smooth when the surface of the stone is textured or cracked, or full of grooves, perforations, and indentations. "Lou" means leaked with holes in the surface that make the stone in question far from smooth or complete. The term "Tou," which literally means "go through," refers to a perforated structure. As Li Yu elucidates, "there are passages from

---

13   Li Yu 李渔, *Xian Qing Ou Ji* 闲情偶记 (Changsha: Yuelu Press, 2016), 171. All English translations are my own unless otherwise indicated.

14   Yang, *Metamorphosis of the Private Sphere: Gardens and Objects in Tang-Song Poetry*, 99–100.

15   Du Wan 杜绾, *Yunlin Stone Catalogue* 云林石谱, eds. Wang Yuan, Zhu Xuebo, and Liao Lianting (Shanghai: Shanghai Bookstore Publishing House, 2019), 5.

16   Du Wan, *Yunlin Stone Catalogue*, 4.

THE SYMBOLIC FORCE OF ROCKS IN THE CHINESE IMAGINATION 713

one place to another place."[17] In essence, there is a fluid space from one hole to another that results in an interplay of void and form.

In the Chinese imagination, rock aesthetics have also deeply influenced artistic creation. The scholar-public statesman from the Song dynasty Shu Shi 苏轼 (1037–1101) describes the rocks in Wen Tong's painting 文同 (1018–79) as "ugly but refined" (wen 文).[18] In this specific context of the ideal rock, "refined" is synonymous with "wrinkled." Most importantly, rock aesthetics has always been a major part of traditional Chinese gardening even to the present day. In his well-known manual for garden design *Yuan Yan* 园冶, the architect Ji Cheng (1582–1642) from the Ming dynasty identifies the features of "shou," "tou," "lou," and "zhou" as the golden standard for gardening. He suggests that the best rock is Lake Tai Rock with its "deep hollows," "eyeholes," "twists" and "strange grooves" (qiankong 嵌空、chuanyan 穿眼、wanzhuan 婉转、xianguaishi 险怪势).[19] Lake Tai rocks are widely utilized as a "scholarly stone" (gong shi 供石), or they are arranged in the shape of a mountain in gardens. When the originally chosen rocks do not meet the ideal standard, they are intentionally tossed back into the lake until they erode enough to assume the ideal "shou, tou, lou, zhou" shape.

During his trips to China, this cultural practice surprised the French traveler Jean-François Gerbillon (1654–1707). In reference to the extraordinary rocks Gerbillon saw displayed in the emperor's apartment, Bianca Maria Rinaldi notes,

> "the rich people among them go to any expense for this sort of bagatelle: they will pay for more for some old rock which has something grotesque or extraordinary, as, for example, if it has several cavities, or if it is pierced through to the other side," he had a very good eye to appreciate what he saw as the attributes as "grotesque or extraordinary," "cavities," or "pierced through to the other side," but then he compared what he saw in his home, and realized that, the Chinese rather have these grotesque rocks, "than they would for a block of jasper or some beautiful statue in marble, but if they do not use marble at all in their buildings, it is not because they do not have it; the mountains near Peking are full of very beautiful white marble, that they use only to adorn their graves."[20]

---

17   Li Yu, *Xian Ting Ou Ji*, 171.
18   In Chinese, "wen" also means "texture" or "pattern."
19   Ji Chen 计成, *Yuan Yan* 园冶 (Beijing: China Architecture and Building Press, 2018), 374.
20   Bianca Maria Rinaldi, ed. *Ideas of Chinese Gardens: Western Accounts, 1300–1860* (Philadelphia, University of Pennsylvania Press, 2016), 70.

Gerbillon astutely recognized the deep reverence for rocks in Chinese culture. Specifically, he noted that the Chinese did not use marble to adorn their houses like the Europeans. He realized that the Chinese preference for limestone rather than marble or granite was a matter of rock aesthetics that was part of a larger cultural imaginary.

There are different understandings related to the materiality of stone between European and Chinese culture. Rocks are also fundamental images in Western poetic thinking. Owing to his passion for granite and primitive rock, Goethe asserts that "rocks teach us the language of hardness."[21] In *Henri d'Ofeteringen*, Novalis calls primitive rock "nature's first born."[22] Based on his studies of these innumerable traces of rock aesthetics in world literature, the French philosopher Gaston Bachelard, who devoted much of his attention to the poetics of matter in his essay *Earth and Reveries of Will: An Essay on the Imagination of Matter*, concludes, "It defies penetration, resists scratching, and stands up to wear."[23] In this seminal work, which illustrates the importance of rocks in the collective imagination of a given society, Bachelard suggests that Western poets prefer granite and marble instead of limestone. In their *material* imagination, the rocks that they venerate are solid, unaffected, impenetrable, and complete. Bachelard's conclusion is in keeping with the attitude from German philosophers like Hegel who maintain that granite constitutes the "mountain core,"[24] or a principle of solidity *par excellence*. As Heidegger explains more clearly, "This block of granite, for example, is a mere thing. It is hard, heavy, extended, bulky, shapeless, rough, colored, partly dull, partly shiny. We can take note of all these features in the stone. Thus we acknowledge its characteristics."[25]

Compared to granite or marble, limestone has a more grotesque and malleable appearance, whose shape comes from being eroded by wind, rain, water, etc. In stark contrast to the qualities of smoothness, completeness, and solidity, limestone such as Lake Tai Rock possesses different qualities that are never seen in a positive light in Western culture. Whereas the ideal Western stone described by Bachelard is solid, hard, impenetrable, massive, heavy, and complete, the ideal Chinese rock is penetrable, fragile, wrinkled, thin, gleaming, and perforated. For Western *literati* like Goethe and Heidegger, the ideal stone

---

21   Gaston Bachelard, *Earth and Reveries of Will: An Essay on the Imagination of Matter*, trans. Kenneth Haltman (Dallas: Dallas Institute of Humanities & Culture, 2002), 158.

22   Bachelard, *Earth and Reveries of Will: An Essay on the Imagination of Matter*, 143.

23   Bachelard, *Earth and Reveries of Will: An Essay on the Imagination of Matter*, 157.

24   Bachelard, *Earth and Reveries of Will: An Essay on the Imagination of Matter*, 157.

25   Martin Heidegger, "The Origin of the Work of Art," in *Poetry, Language, Thought*, trans. Albert Hofstadter (New York: Harper and Row, 1971), 22.

is granite. For Chinese intellectuals, limestone is the aesthetic ideal to be emulated. Due to these apparent cultural differences in taste, the grotesque rock never seems to be introduced into European gardens in a proper way. Based on the travel narratives composed by European Jesuits, journalists, and architects, we know that Chinese gardens heavily influenced the design of English gardens, as evidenced by *jardin anglo-chinois* style of gardening. The *jardin anglo-chinois* borrows the landscape, overall structure, and design from the traditional Chinese garden, but this model eliminates the grotesque rocks and artificial mountains. The only time the English art historian Hugh Honour saw an artificial mountain in a European garden was in a photograph from the sinologist Osvald Siren's book, which is an imitation of an authentic artificial mountain from a European painting. Not only does Honour contend that this is the only example of an artificial mountain in a European garden, but he also argues that it looks more like a ruined grotto.[26] This point of view demonstrates that Europeans have a difficult time recognizing the beauty of "grotesque" rocks, even when they derive a great deal of inspiration from Chinese gardens.

III   The Depth of the Rock

When dealing with imaginings triggered by forms of matter, Bachelard insightfully argues that our imagination could be divided into two distinct types (i.e. the formal imagination and material imagination). In Bachelard's framework for understanding the imagination, the formal imagination relates to superficial images, which "play on the surface of an element without giving the imagination time to work upon its matter."[27] Conversely, the material imagination "deserts depth, volume and the inner recesses of substance."[28] Both kinds of imagination are present in the case of Chinese rocks. With indefinite forms, there is a kind of formal association, imagining the rocks as anthropomorphic or animal-like. This sort of imagination is more closely related to apparent structures and shapes, but it cannot accurately represent the essence or depth of rocks as a form of matter. What Bachelard terms the material imagination is comparable to the rich symbolism of the rocks that the Chinese adore.

---

26   In *China and Gardens of Europe of The Eighteenth Century*, Osvald Siren mentions a photo of a false mountain in a European garden. According to Hugh Honour, this is the only false mountain in Europe as a whole. See Hugh Honour, *Chinoiserie: The Vision of Cathay,* trans. Liu Aiying and Qin Hong (Beijing: Beijing University Press, 1961), 299.

27   Gaston Bachelard, *Water and Dreams: An Essay on Imagination of Matter,* trans. Edith R. Farrell, ed. (Dallas: Dallas Institute of Humanities and Culture Publications, 1999), 10–11.

28   Bachelard, *Water and Dreams: An Essay on Imagination of Matter,* 2.

The formal imagination associated with rocks is often triggered at first sight. Moreover, it induces a state of pleasure through instantaneous imaginings and the accompanying sense of recognition (rocks as an animal, a plant, etc.). Bai Juyi lauds the stones collected by Niu Senru, owing to their malleable and irregular shapes. For Bai, these stones arouse the imaginations of celestial mountains, light clouds, immortals, or wine pots, swords, dragons, ghosts, even animals, etc.[29] A wanderer in a Chinese garden with fine specimens of the Lake Tai rocks in hand would delightfully find they "look like frozen billows of ocean spume, or enormous stone fungi burgeoning into the air, or extravagant coral formations poised in an invisible ocean."[30] The abstract or irregular quality of the rock gives the garden a more imaginative atmosphere.[31] It is possible that Victor Hugo's encounter with sandstone has the same effect. Despite his affinity for granite, when generating a distorted vision, he had a marked preference for sandstone. As the author muses, "Sandstone is the most interesting and most strangely composed stone in existence ... In the great drama of the landscape, sandstone plays a fantastic part. Sometimes it is grand and severe, sometimes buffoon-like; it bends like a wrestler, or rolls like a clown; it is a sponge, a pudding, a tent, a cottage, the stump of a tree."[32] Both irregular limestone and sandstone create dramatic landscapes.

However, it is the concept of material imagination that fully reveals the complexity and richness of rock aesthetics in the Chinese tradition. Compared to the formal imagination, the material imagination emanates directly from matter itself, rather than from incidental forms that arouse our playful fancy. Consequently, it is only through the lens of the material imagination linked to grotesque rocks that we can understand the deeper value and symbolism of *petrophilic* aesthetics in Chinese culture from a metaphysical and cosmological standpoint. It is only after contemplating the inherent features of stones themselves that we can shed light on the continued adoration of Chinese people for ugly and grotesque rocks among *literati*. In this section, I will

---

29   Bai Juyi, *Bai Juyi Ji*, Band 4, 1544.

30   François Berthier, *Reading Zen in the Rocks: The Japanese Dry Landscape Garden,* trans. Graham Parkes (Chicago: University of Chicago Press, 2005), 98.

31   C.C.L. Hirschfeld, the German garden theorist from the 18th century, through his appreciation of the *jardin anglo-chinois*, was evidently influenced by Chinese techniques when he discusses the aesthetic function of irregular stone in a garden. As he explains on pages 176–77, "those that are irregular or unusual, that life the imagination from its accustomed sphere to a realm of new images, that let it enter the world of fairies, a place of magical enchantment." See C.C.L. Hirschfeld, *Theory of Garden Art,* ed. and trans. Linda B. Parshall (Philadephia: University of Pennsylvania Press, 2011).

32   Bachelard, *Earth and Reveries of Will: An Essay on the Imagination of Matter,* 144.

THE SYMBOLIC FORCE OF ROCKS IN THE CHINESE IMAGINATION   717

delve into the depth of these rocks, of which Lake Tai Rock is a metonymical reflection.

According to the ancient Chinese worldview, all natural phenomena, including humans and rocks, are animated by the psychophysical energy known as *qi* 气.[33] Rock, as part of the earth, is regarded as a concentration of earth's "essential energy." The Chinese also believe that "The essential energy of earth forms rock ... Rocks are kernels of energy."[34] *Yunlin Stone Catalogue* from the Song dynasty reiterates that the rock represents and assembles the energy and beauty from heaven and earth as well. Specifically, this narrative recounts, "The purest energy of heaven-earth coalescing into rock. It emerges, bearing the soil ... With the size of a fist can be assembled the beauty of a thousand cliffs."[35] Given that mists always emanate from the collision of water with rock, as the vapors gather around mountain peaks enshrining the tops of cliffs and ridges, the rock is considered to be the "root of the cloud." Consequently, although the stone is from the earth, it shares *qi* from the heaven-earth reflecting the grandeur and fragility of the cosmos.

Instead, energy flows incessantly between heaven and earth according to the material imagination in traditional Chinese thought. The holes piercing the surface of the rocks are conceived of as a passageway for the flow of energy both within and outside of the stone. With the holes, the space on the rock becomes fluid physically and transformed into a more significant being. The hole, the aperture, or in some sense, the emptiness, has an ontological status in Chinese philosophy. The Daoist philosopher Laozi maintains that existence and non-existence give birth one to (the idea of) the other. Moreover, Laozi contends that emptiness is the origin of this movement. As he theorizes, "May not the space between heaven and earth be compared to a bellows? 'Tis emptied, yet it loses not its power;' Tis moved again, and sends forth air the more."[36] (天地之间，其有犹橐籥乎？虚而不屈，动而愈出"). Likewise, another Daoist philosopher Zhuangzi also emphasizes the relevance of

---

33   A cosmogonic myth from ancient China depicts the sky as a vast cave and maintains that fragments which came loose from the vault of heaven ended up on earth. The huge fragments of stone became charged with vast amounts of cosmic energy, or qi(ch'i), while falling through the air before embedding themselves in the earth. See François Berthier, *Reading Zen in the Rocks: The Japanese Dry Landscape Garden,* 89.

34   Quoted in Zhu Liangzhi 朱良志，*The Romantic Spirits of the Stone* 顽石的风流 (Beijing: Zhonghua Book Company, 2016), 98.

35   English translation courtesy of Berthier, *Reading Zen in the Rocks: The Japanese Dry Landscape Garden*, 92.

36   Lao Tse, *Tao Te Ching Or The Tao And Its Characteristics*, trans. James Legge (Auckland, New Zealand: The Floating Press, 2008), 16.

emptiness in this radical way: "all the apertures are empty (and still)" "众窍为虚," "The spirit is free from all pre-occupation and so waits for (the appearance of) things" 唯道集虚.[37] The philosophical text *The Writings of the Huai Nan Zi* 淮南子 from the Xihan dynasty offers an even more persuasive argument: "The holes and apertures are the gate and window of the spirit." ("夫孔窍者，精神之户牖也"[38]). Thus, the hole is like an organ for connecting the cosmos to the human spirit and imagination. In his appreciation of *Linglong shi*, another sort of lime stone, Zhu Changwen (1039–1098) writes, "chaos in nature is broken by holes"[39] ("凿开混沌窍"). According to Heidegger, natural stone is part of chaos. As the philosopher asserts, "A stone is wordless,"[40] for stone does not participate in the realization of a "world," which is limited to human consciousness. Nonetheless, the holes or emptiness reflected on the stone break chaos and endow the stone with subjectivity. Admiring this paradoxically significant emptiness, the poet Qing Lue 秦略 from the twelfth century declares, "It is like the heart of the saint, the hole and aperture are empty and leads to the illumination" (又如圣人心，孔窍虚明通). Due to its "leaked" (lou 漏) and perforated (tou 透) qualities, the rock is endowed with *qi* that connects it to the world, thereby establishing its own cosmology. The grotesque rock undoubtedly represents the philosophical and spiritual ideal of fusion, or the idea of dissolving oneself into the cosmos for Chinese *literati*.

When discussing the ideal Chinese rock, the very texture of "shou tou lou zhou" possesses figurative depth. Either the wrinkle or hole is a trace of human interactions with the natural world that demonstrates a meaningful response from the subject. In the context of the recorded "struggles" with nature going back thousands of years in Chinese culture, stone has a paradoxically refined but ugly appearance. As Bai Juyi describes the emergence of Lake Tai Rock, "they are shaped through millions of years, either sinking in the corner of the seas, or the bottom of the lakes."[41] The stone is the image of time or timelessness. The rock visualizes the shape of time through its texture that fosters an admiration for ancient civilizations. By gazing at the rock, we understand the ephemeral nature of our existence in addition to learning to respect the permanence of time represented in stone. Owing to their variable appearance,

---

37 English translation courtesy of "Chinese Text Project," accessed April 29, 2019, https://ctext.org.

38 Liu Kangde 刘康德, *The Interpretation of Huainanzi* 淮南子直解 (Shanghai: Fudan University Press, 2001), 306.

39 *The Complete Works of Song Poetry* 全宋诗, ed. Ancient Literature Research Institute of Beijing University (Beijing: Beijing University Press), Band 15, 9789.

40 Heidegger, "The Origin of the Work of Art," 43.

41 Bai Juyi, *Bai Juyi Ji*, Band 4, 1544.

THE SYMBOLIC FORCE OF ROCKS IN THE CHINESE IMAGINATION 719

limestone rocks exhibited in a Chinese study room or garden are considered to be a symbolic self-portrait of the *literati* owner of these rocks. In terms of symbolism, these stones could represent sensitive and difficult periods of one's life, such as political persecution. For instance, the "sophisticated" appearance of a given rock in question could be a mirror to the sophisticated soul of a poet. According to classical symbolism, "thin" rocks express a poet's feelings of loneliness. In this regard, borrowing the image of a stone to lament his own aging, the writer Yuan Hongdao from the Ming dynasty poses the following question: "how can the thin stone compare to my aged face?"[42] In these concrete examples, stones are weaved into the lives of Chinese people in a private and emotional way reflecting the singular materiality of rocks themselves.

In conclusion, we project our emotions onto rocks that are transformed through the processes described throughout this chapter. On the other hand, the rock maintains its own unchanged essence, since its presence relies on our contemplation through which the world beneath it emerges before us. A meaningful world is either conjured up through what Bachelard refers to as the material imagination, or through "signs" laden with symbolic meaning corresponding to an established cultural system. As for the latter possibility of meaning, Confucianism reveres jade as the symbol of a refined noble person. Conversely, Daoism expresses a marked preference for natural rocks that many people find to be unsightly and grotesque. Inverting the grotesque-sublime dichotomy, Daoism reveals that "ugly" stones are sublime because of their deeply rooted connection to hidden forms of cosmology and metaphysics in Chinese culture.

References

Bachelard, Gaston. *Earth and Reveries of Will: An Essay on the Imagination of Matter.* Translated by Kenneth Haltman. Dallas: Dallas Institute of Humanities & Culture. 2002.

Bachelard, Gaston. *Water and Dreams: An Essay on Imagination of Matter.* Translated by Edith R. Farrell. Dallas: Dallas Institute of Humanities and Culture Publications. 1999.

Bai, Juyi. 白居易 *Bai Juyi Ji* 白居易集. Band 4, Edited by Gu Xuejie 顾学颉. Beijing: Zhonghua Book Company, 1999.

Berthier, François. *Reading Zen in the Rocks: The Japanese Dry Landscape Garden.* Translated by Graham Parkes. Chicago: University of Chicago Press. 2005.

---

42   Quoted in Zhu Liangzhi, *The Romantic Spirits of the Stone*, 31.

"Chinese Text Project." Accessed April 29, 2019. https://ctext.org.

Du, Wan. 杜绾 *Yunlin Stone Catalogue* 云林石谱. Edited by Wang Yuan, Zhu Xuebo, and Liao Lianting. Shanghai: Shanghai Bookstore Publishing House. 2019.

Hay, John. *Kernels of Energy, Bones of Earth: The Rock in Chinese Art.* New York: China Institute in America. 1985.

Heidegger, Martin. "The origin of the work of Art." In *Poetry, Language, Thought.* Translated by Albert Hofstadter, 15–86. New York: Harper and Row. 1971.

Hirschfeld, Christian. *Theory of Garden Art.* Edited and Translated by Linda B. Parshall. Philadephia: University of Pennsylvania Press. 2011.

Honour, Hugh. *Chinoiserie: The Vision of Cathay.* Translated by Liu Aiying and Qin Hong. Beijing: Beijing University Press. 1961.

Ji, Chen. 计成 *Yuan Yan* 园冶. Beijing: China Architecture and Building Press. 2018.

Jing, Xuezhi. 金学智 *Chinese Garden Culture* 中国园林文化. Beijing: China Architecture and Building Press, 2005.

Lao Tse. *Tao Te Ching Or the Tao and Its Characteristics.* Translated by James Legge. Auckland, New Zealand: The Floating Press. 2008.

Li, Yu. 李渔 *Xian Qing Ou Ji* 闲情偶记. Changsha: Yuelu Press. 2016.

Liu, An. *The Huainanzi: A Guide to the Theory and Practice of Government in Early Han China.* Translated and Edited by John S. Major. New York: Columbia University Press. 2010.

Liu, Kangde. 刘康德 *The Interpretation of Huai Nan Zi* 淮南子直解. Shanghai: Fudan. University Press. 2001.

Needham, Joseph. *Science and Civilisation in China.* Vol. 3. Cambridge: Cambridge University Press. 1959.

Rinaldi, Bianca Maria, ed. *Ideas of Chinese Gardens: Western Accounts, 1300–1860.* Philadelphia: University of Pennsylvania Press. 2016.

Schafer, Edward H. *Tu Wan's Stone Catalogue of Cloudy Forest: A Commentary and Synopsis.* Berkeley, CA: University of California Press. 1961.

The Complete Works of Song Poetry 全宋诗. Edited by Ancient Literature Research Institute of Beijing University. Beijing: Beijing University Press, Band 15.

Welsch, Wolfgang. "Art Transcending the human Pale-Toward a Transhuman Stance." *International Aesthetics* 外国美学 (Beijing), 21 (2013): 315–36.

Yang, Xiaoshan. *Metamorphosis of the Private Sphere: Gardens and Objects in Tang-Song Poetry.* Cambridge, MA: Harvard University Press. 2003.

Yang, Xiaoshan. "Petrophilia and Its Anxiety, The Lake Tai Rock in Tang-Song Poetry." *Landscape and Garden* 风景园林 10 (2019): 81–89.

Zeitlin, Judith T. "The Petrified Heart: Obsession in Chinese Literature, Art, and Medicine." *Late Imperial China* 12 (1992): 1–26.

Zhu, Liangzhi. 朱良志 *The Romantic Spirits of the Stone* 顽石的风流. Beijing: Zhonghua Book Company. 2016.

CHAPTER 31

Magic from the Repressed: Imagination and Memories in Contemporary Japanese Literary Narratives

Amy Lee

Contemporary Japanese popular culture has an interesting multifaceted mix. On the one hand, the Japanese imagination manifests itself in its ACG culture (Animation, Comics and Games), which is loved and embraced by younger generations, considered to be more real than the physical world. This ACG culture is well-known for its renditions of impressive imaginary features of the future world, including the future of mankind, and the meticulousness with which these components are crafted. To many overseas fans, this imaginary, animated world is the signature Japanese soft power. At the same time, however, the realistically rendered futuristic, post-human imaginary world is but one aspect of Japanese popular culture. Underlying this imaginary of the future, there is a strong and deep foundation of traditional thoughts and beliefs, a hybrid creation from a transformation of ancient Chinese culture built upon a foundation of native Japanese Shintoism. The classic cyberpunk film *Ghost in the Shell* (1995) is a shining example of the cultural blending of Japan's historical and futuristic imaginary within the same "body." The post-human world that is rendered in the film is the setting for the discussion of one of mankind's oldest questions: our identity.

The film *Ghost in the Shell* follows the 1989 serialized manga of the same title and tells the story of how the public security agency Section 9 hunted for a mysterious hacker known as the Puppet Master. Major Motoko, the team leader responsible for the tracking, was a female human being living in a shell of a body that was built for high-grade combat. In the course of her investigation, she encountered not only unexpectedly complex political conflicts and calculations but was also drawn into a personal struggle regarding her very own identity and authenticity. While the technologically advanced world allows human beings to survive in a manufactured and thus replaceable body, the price mortal beings must pay is the ambiguous existence which is not quite fully human, not fully gendered, and not fully authentic. The journey of tracking down the Puppet Master, which existed as a "consciousness" only in the

© KONINKLIJKE BRILL NV, LEIDEN, 2020 | DOI:10.1163/9789004436350_033

digital world, overwhelmed Major Motoko with doubts about her own self, and challenged her sense of what qualified as an authentic existence.

Nonetheless, the critically acclaimed *Ghost in the Shell* is not merely a successful animated film with an interesting idea. The production of the film is well-known for its meticulousness. In this regard, both the characters and the setting are realistically rendered. Although the film is set in 2029 in an unnamed city, the basis of the image was actually Hong Kong, the city where I was born and have lived all my life. Sketches of street scenes of Hong Kong were so well-made that it was impossible for anyone not to recognize the unique mixture of the old and the new, the traditional street signs side by side with the highly commodified modern space, and the specific pace of the never-resting Asian cosmopolitan landscape. The combination of the theme music composed by Kenji Kawai[1] that recalls ancient Japanese religious language juxtaposed to the futuristic ideas and the realistically rendered cityscape of Hong Kong culminates in the dramatic and highly reflective end of the film. Major Motoko was so badly destroyed in the combat with Puppet Master in the end that a new body, that of a young girl, had to be found to replace her original shell. This regenerated Motoko embraced the new shell and the new identity housed inside this shell, as she remarked on the limitless possibilities in the information highway. Through reflections about one's self-identity, a recognition of the practicalities of the real world, and a hopeful anticipation concerning the future, the oldest and newest elements of Japanese culture merge powerfully in the end of this animated classic of popular culture.

A self-conscious questioning of deep-rooted traditions in the face of ultracontemporaneity is an underlying thread that runs through many Japanese cultural and artistic works today. *Ghost in the Shell* (both the manga series and the cyberpunk film) is one of many quintessential examples of Japanese culture's dialogue with itself in this respect. In the following, I argue that Japanese culture's self-reflection about its identity is conducted through the artistic imagination sweeping across binaries of history, gender, and reality. Referring to selected writings of three contemporary Japanese writers working in different genres, this chapter will demonstrate how imagination becomes the tool contemporary literary art uses to conduct a reflective dialogue with itself concerning identity. Imagination is creatively used by the following writers to transgress boundaries of time, place, and socially constructed restrictions such as gender and class in their artistic reflections. This literary imagination fosters

---

1 Kenji Kawai (1957-) is a famous Japanese composer who has composed scores for films, anime movies, and video games, both in the Asian region and internationally. His work on *Ghost in the Shell* is among one of his most famous.

MAGIC FROM THE REPRESSED

the release of the magic from the repressed, or the insights that have been buried in the cultural unconscious.

The following discussion will refer to Yumemakura Baku's (1951-) *Onmyoji* short-story series, Mukoda Kuniko's (1929–1981) prose fiction, and Nashiki Kaho's (1959-) novels of magical realism. In the works of each of these three writers, imagination is employed for the same kind of reflection of identity amidst the tension of binaries such as the traditional and the futuristic found in *Ghost in the Shell*. In the highly entertaining adventure stories of the historical onmyoji Abe no Seimei and his courtier friend Minamoto no Hiromasa, the repressed "self" is released through Yumemakura Baku's historical re-imagination of Heian Japan. In the down-to-earth reminiscences of TV screenwriter Mukoda Kuniko, the forgotten past re-emerges in the creative space to complete the present "self." Finally, Nashiki Kaho's novels, which reside in the space between the fantastic and the real, unearth the primal origin of the present "self" buried in the historical unconscious. Through the reading of these Japanese works epitomizing various kinds of imagination, the repressed truth of the self comes out in these magical fictions.

Yumemakura's popular fiction series entitled *Onmyoji* is a collection of mainly short-stories (there are a few novel-length narratives in the series too) set in the world of Heian Japan (794–1185) with the historical figures Abe no Seimei and Minamoto no Hiromasa as the main characters. Abe no Seimei (921–1005) was a court onmyoji, whose job was to make the calendar, and generally to advise the emperor on matters of spirituality and to predict astrological events. Probably because of his long life, there are a lot of stories about his legendary power. Moreover, he is also featured in quite a few folktales. Minamoto no Hiromasa (918–980) was a nobleman of the Heian court who was distantly related to the emperor of the time. Given that he was known to be a good musician, Yumemakura's stories often refer to his musical talent. These two historical figures have been re-created to be good friends and partners who investigate mysterious matters, similar to a Holmes-Watson partnership. What is special about this detective duo is the Heian setting and Seimei's professional status, allowing magic and the supernatural to be an acceptable part of the narratives. However, Yumemakura is careful to make this ancient setting relevant to contemporary readers by a quasi-psychoanalytic interpretation of the problems depicted in the stories. "A Biwa called Genjou was Stolen by an Oni" serves as an excellent example to illustrate these aforementioned features linked to the imagination. In the story, Hiromasa heard a strangely beautiful music around the palace grounds which he recognized to be coming from the famous *biwa* that was reportedly stolen from the palace. After hearing it for two consecutive nights, he sought Seimei's help convinced that someone who could play such music was not human. Along with a monk who was also a famous musician, Seimei and Hiromasa decided to find this mysterious *biwa* player one night. The player turned out to be an Indian ghost Kandata who used to be an instrument maker in his previous life. In his wanderings, he saw the *biwa* (his very own creation from his last life) in the palace and a maid servant who looked like his past wife. He stole the *biwa* and asked Seimei to capture the palace maid for him to exchange for the *biwa*. Seimei agreed, but he brought both the maid and her brother on the night of the exchange. A fight broke out, Kandata killed the maid and tried to capture Seimei but failed. Instead, Seimei successfully captured Kandata and coaxed his soul to live in the *biwa*. At the end of the narrative, everyone seemed to be happy because the stolen *biwa* was restored, Kandata's musical soul found a home in the *biwa*, and there was no more strange music at night.

The structure of the story follows a well-tried detective fiction formula: a problem arises, a detective is summoned, an investigation occurs, and the crisis is resolved. In other words, the lost item is recovered, order is restored, and everything seems to go back to normal. But Seimei and Hiromasa's adventures are more than a return to the norm, for Seimei is not a regular detective, but someone who is on the threshold between human and beyond. Right at the beginning of the series, readers are told of the rumor that Seimei's mother was a fox, thus making him not entirely human, and endowed with super-human powers. Throughout his adventures, Seimei transgressed not only the physical world and supernatural world, but also the biological and psychological realms of human life. The way he overpowered Kandata demonstrates his ability to penetrate beneath the literal reality. When Kandata asked him his name, Seimei gave him a false one. As a result, his spirit remained beyond the power of Kandata's verbal control. By using Kandata's real name, Seimei could vanquish the ghost by way of the invisible connection between the name and the being itself. As Seimei maintained, the shortest curse in the world was the name – a direct link between the essence of an object and the sound of its pronunciation – and he was a master of pulling these invisible threads between the different realms.

In another short story "The Lady of Kuchinashi," the link between the spiritual world and the physical realm features even more prominently. Hiromasa told Seimei a story about a young monk who had been visited by a mouthless lady every night for some time. This visit troubled the monk so much that he became sick. Seimei went to investigate and finally discovered that the mouthless lady was a personification of a written word. As the young monk was copying Buddhist sutras, he became carelessly distracted by erotic thoughts about a

MAGIC FROM THE REPRESSED

certain lady. Consequently, he left out one part of the word which was written as a "mouth." The visit of the mouthless lady was actually an objectification of the young monk's unconscious. He felt guilty about his erotic thoughts, and the damaged word in the sutra "haunted" him by her nightly visit. Yumemakura borrows magic from history to expose the profound depths of the human psyche. Imagination is the link between this ancient setting and the contemporary human mind.

The adventures of Seimei and Hiromasa take them from the physical world to the spiritual world and back, and reveal to them the inner worlds of the human heart from the turmoil exhibited on the surface. Yumemakura's depiction of historical characters in historical settings, with its reference to ancient Japanese literary classics, beliefs, and practices, is in fact an imaginative borrowing of ancient culture to depict contemporary issues. The unfulfilled desires return as ghosts demanding satisfaction, one's vulnerability of wanting to be loved emerges as a submission to other's (sweet or hostile) verbal command, and finally one's repressed desires never go away. They seek a pathway to reemerge in the most unexpected way catching our attention. The magic in the fictional Heian adventures is the magic that helps us with the issues that have troubled and occupied the human mind. Why are we not content? What do we desire? How do we negotiate a reasonable life when we have to live side by side with our unreasonable desires every day? What is the substance of our human self? The *Onmyoji* series is a collection of psychological drama for laymen dressed up in an imaginative historical garb.

Mukoda Kuniko (1929–1981) was a famous Japanese TV screenwriter whose prose collections are full of down-to-earth personal memories of her professional life as well as her personal life. She started writing for TV and radio in 1960 after working at a film-publicity company for a number of years, and acquired quite a reputation as a screenwriter. She had published a number of short-story and memoire-styled collections, and a few of her short stories won the Naoki Prize in 1980. Her works are noted for their accurate and detailed depictions of the practices of daily life, but which manage to convey not only the superficial realities of life and relationships, but also the poignancy of remembering through temporal transitions and the changes brought about by experience and life. Mukoda had a childhood marked by change and adaptation because her father used to work for an insurance company and had been stationed in different cities. Her works reflect this rich recollection of different life practices and attempts to adapt to new environments and to build new relationships constantly. Her memories of life with her father in her early childhood, and later her observations of the life of a single woman making her own living are particularly celebrated. She died an accidental death in 1981, when her plane (Far Eastern Air Transport Flight 103) crashed in Taiwan while she was on a research trip for her writing.

As a well-acclaimed TV screenwriter (specializing in light-hearted family drama), Mukoda had made a few interesting observations about writing and authenticity. She maintained that for the sake of being convincing, family drama on TV should always take place in a small and shabby looking sitting room, otherwise "no matter whether it is tears or laughter, it appears to be exaggerated and fake."[2] Yet, it is this same concern about authenticity that led her to write many "lies" into her screenplay. She compared family drama to "a course in the family dinner,"[3] it comes and goes, and a different dish will appear in the next meal to be enjoyed. What is most important seems to be that it always exists for enjoyment, whether every sentence uttered or every action performed by the characters conforms to the general behavior is not the core quality to be evaluated. Thus, interestingly, even a "realistic" narrative genre such as TV family drama has its unique imaginative aspects. It has to be convincing in its setting and character development, but the actions and dialogues should be creatively "convincing" because of its identity of being a course in a meal to be consumed and enjoyed. The imagination of banal and realistic daily life is designed for the audience's enjoyment.

Onna no Hitosashiyubi (1982) [A Woman's Index Finger] is a collection of free-styled reminiscences showing snapshots of the life of a single woman who earned her own living in an urban city. This collection is replete with references to quotidian practices, little problems that a single woman faced when going about her daily professional life, and some moments from her private life. The constant references to food and eating are especially noteworthy. One of the most memorable scenes is a discussion that the narrator (in the name of the writer) had with some friends about the absence of proper and decent restaurants for single women: "How come the type of delicious, reasonably-priced, and clean Japanese-styled eateries for a lone woman to patronize doesn't exist?"[4] The conclusion was "open one yourself," and was thus followed by a recollection of how the narrator started from scratch, looking for a suitable venue, planned the menu, purchased ingredients and cutleries, all the way up to the final moment of opening her restaurant called "Rice House" on a great rainy night.

---

2 Kuniko Mukoda, *A Woman's Index Finger*. Trans. Ziqian Liu (Taipei: Rye Field Publications, 2014), 116.

3 Mukoda, *A Woman's Index Finger*, 114.

4 Mukoda, *A Woman's Index Finger*, 163.

MAGIC FROM THE REPRESSED

This chapter seems to be a simple, straightforward record of an event that had happened. In this regard, the narrator even concluded with five key points that she had learned from this restaurant opening experience.[5] At the end of the chapter, the narrator confessed, "[a]lthough I was only helping with the trivial matters, once I put myself in the position of saying 'welcome' to the customers, I could not help but reflect, that for the past 25 years, as a customer of this kind of restaurant, how unmindful I had been."[6] Having gone through the experience of opening and running a restaurant, she finally realized some important truths about customers. Those who were careful to give as little trouble to the waiters as possible, those willing to take the most unfavorable seats, those who ordered the simplest and least time-consuming dishes during peak hours, and those who saved waiters the trouble to clear the table when it was busy, were indeed considerate customers who thought about the restaurant owner. Without the restaurant-opening experience, she would never have appreciated these actions from another identity position. Putting oneself in the position of another requires imagination, and she shared her experience with her readers to acknowledge the power of imagination to bring us across the boundaries of different life positions.

In her reminiscences about her father and her childhood, the narratives present a vivid description of practical life side by side with a deep reflection of the substance and meaning of life, showing the strong reflective imagination that works to transform one to another. *Chichi no wabi jo* (1978) [Father's Letter of Apology] is a collection of the narrator's childhood memories, in particular those related to her father. Although the eponymous story seems to suggest that the father wrote a letter of apology, we realize that the so-called apology was far subtler given that the sense of "feeling sorry" was merely the narrator's own interpretation. The occasion in question occurred when the father entertained some colleagues at home, and the entire family including the mother and the children had to help with the serving of food and cleaning up afterwards. After a night of drinking in the middle of winter, a few guests had vomited on the wooden floor. As her father was standing there watching without speaking a word, the young girl was on her hands and knees trying to remove the dried vomit from the cracks of the wooden boards. A week after the narrator left home and returned to her school in Tokyo, she received her father's usual letter of caution and encouragement ending with the words "you

---

5 Mukoda, *A Woman's Index Finger*, 170–72.
6 Mukoda, *A Woman's Index Finger*, 172.

were very industrious a few days ago,"[7] indirectly referring to the messy and dirty work she had undertaken. Her remembrances of the past, presented in the form of creative literature, elevated past facts to a meaningful reflection about the father-daughter relationship in modern Japan. Times have changed, and the meaning of such a basic relationship has also acquired an added critical dimension in the narrative of the now professional female writer.

Another story in the collection entitled "My lost items: A collection" records a series of things the narrator had lost throughout her life in addition to the strange encounters she had in attempting to recover or replace these same items. When she was working for a film magazine, one day she was called to help with the screening of applicants for the new position of editor. After the applicants had gone, a glove was left behind, and she was thrilled to see that it was identical to the one she had lost on a tram a few days ago. She quickly took it to the lost and found section and begged to be informed if no one claimed it. She even ran errands for the officers to curry favor in order to get the glove. Finally, "hard work was repaid, and that glove was given to me,"[8] but when she happily ran home, she discovered that both gloves were the left one of the pair. Each of these lost items described comes with a memory of her relationship to it, and her personal feelings about their role in her life. The literary imagination inspired by her personal history with these lost items becomes ponderings of a female professional working at a transformative point in time.

Tonari no Onna (1981) [The Woman Next Door] is a collection of short stories focusing on women characters, their thoughts and emotions as they embark on their own life journeys. The titular story is about an ordinary housewife Sachiko who always leaned against the wall to listen to the movements and actions next door where a trendy woman who worked in a nightclub lived. She came to know her own eroticism by listening to the erotic exchanges between the woman and her different male visitors. This form of voyeurism became the highlight of her boring and monotonous housewife's life. Through a dramatic turn of events, Sachiko played a part in interrupting the colorful erotic life next door, and the woman next door had to be vacated. One day on a bus, Sachiko looked out of the window and saw the woman next door on a motorcycle with another man: "Sachiko felt as if she had just met a fondly remembered person. She very much wanted to greet her, to say something, but the traffic light turned green, the distance between the two vehicles lengthened."[9]

---

7   Mukoda, *Father's Letter of Apology*. Trans. Qiuming Zhang (Taipei: Rye Field Publications. 2013), 22.

8   Mukoda, *Father's Letter of Apology*, 204.

9   Kuniko Mukoda, *The Woman Next Door*. Trans. Qiuming Zhang (Taipei: Rye Field Publications, 2014), 60.

MAGIC FROM THE REPRESSED

The last scene of the story has nothing dramatic in terms of action. Sachiko saw an old acquaintance, but before she had a chance to call out the vehicle moved away. But this "fondly remembered person" was instrumental to her erotic self-discovery, and they had a strangely intimate-yet-distant relationship with one another. Both women's lives had been turned upside down because of this encounter, and yet this change appeared to be so minute, so subtle, and so unremarkable that it did not seem worthy of mentioning at all. The weight of the encounter is brilliantly symbolized in the final scenes of the story. The distance between the two vehicles lengthens in a natural and inevitable manner. This is very typical of Mukoda's work that often leaves the important unsaid but hinted at symbolically - a glimpse of a different life, one that comes at the price of respect and decency, the substance of which is left to the imagination of the readers.

Omoide Trump (1980) [Memory, Poker Cards] is comprised of thirteen stories including three prize winners, such as "The Otter" which depicts the story of an elderly husband reflecting on the subtly unnerving quality of his seemingly cheerful wife Atsuko. When she was a young woman, Atsuko's singsong voice and the light-hearted manner she made up lies to deal with difficult situations and people was very attractive. In his old age and convalescence after a stroke, the husband felt uncomfortable about the darkness underneath this whimsical surface, and started to ponder the nature of these lies and what they revealed about the woman. Past events came back to his mind, and some inevitably took on heavier meaning when scrutinized including the death of their only daughter due to the unfortunate late arrival of the doctor. Atsuko claimed that she sought help from the hospital immediately when something was wrong, although the doctor in charge was late in attending to their daughter, thus delaying treatment. Years later, the husband ran into the nurse, and was told that his wife did not actually seek help from the hospital until it was too late. Was it one of her habitual "harmless" lies? Were all the lies she told really so harmless? Was she just a liar by nature? The convalescent husband did not confront Atsuko with any of these questions, but he started to reexamine Atsuko in a darker light, and her once cheerful smiles turned sinister. The story ends with the husband quietly observing his cheerful wife, her harmless lies, and her ready smiles. The unsaid of the true human condition reverberates loudly in the air.

From these collections of personal memoirs and short stories, we can see a specific type of imagination at work in the realistic and accurate depiction of daily life and its many faces. As a TV screenwriter, Mukoda was used to details and convincing generalizations. What is interesting about these realistic and accurate depictions of the most ordinary daily life and relationships is their power to convey the physical reality of Japanese life from a certain period. The narrator's personal reflections and musings in the midst of these realities and seemingly trivial events and items is also of considerable interest. The memories aroused by the events and objects reflect the long-gone dreams and desires of a submissive girl who had grown up to be an independent woman making her own way in a predominantly patriarchal society. This strong female voice is also using the literary imagination to reflect on these past events to make sense of her identity, through a critical evaluation of the past and its role in her present life. Mukoda's works represent a very specific kind of imagination which stems from a meticulous accuracy, an attention to reality which is found in many Japanese cultural texts.

Contemporary prose writer Nashiki Kaho is well-known for her special way of incorporating magic into her realistic novels. Her characters and stories are set in contemporary Japanese society, and the social and cultural environments are all described in detail. Nonetheless, even in this carefully described reality, the repressed is always lurking beneath the surface biding its time to come out and interfere with the course of events. Nashiki's novels are magical narratives of these repressed forces bursting out of their hidden realms into the objective world, pushing the relevant characters to embark on the inevitable journey to search for their own roots. This other world of the repressed resides in the depths of the human mind, or is buried somewhere in the cultural unconscious. Her characters always manage to discover not the future, but rather the past and what really matters about their identity, their core concerns, and their deepest desires in life.

Numachi no aru mori wo nukete (2003) [Through the Swampy Woods] tells the story of a young woman who inherited her family's "heirloom" from her aunt. The heirloom was not a valuable piece of jewelry, but a traditional Japanese container for making pickled vegetables. The device needs stirring and attention every day, or else the ingredients will be spoilt and emit a foul odor. What started as a cumbersome duty handed down to her through her maternal lineage became a magical journey of returning to the roots of the family generations ago. The heirloom proved to be the key to the reconstruction of her family history which originated in a remote island far from human activities. The strange occurrences related to the heirloom took the narrator away from her practical daily life to follow stories and signs guiding her to the island where her ancestors originally resided. At the end of her journey of investigation, she discovered the origins of her family seat where for generations they reproduced asexually.

The fate of the tribe underwent a tumultuous transformation when one of the girls fell in love with a man from another tribe, thus leaving the family seat to live in the outside world. This critical event completely destroyed the tribe's

MAGIC FROM THE REPRESSED 731

way of life, and slowly killed the motherland which was the swampy woods. The narrator's return was an answer to the eradication of the dying motherland and an attempt to find a way to continue life in a new form. The magical primal world of the swampy woods existed side by side with the accurately depicted contemporary society that was the world of the narrator at the beginning of the novel. In fact, it exerted its presence in the way things have meaning in the contemporary world. Nashiki's writing is a trajectory between the practical daily world and the symbolically significant "spiritual world" that lies beneath the objective reality. Through this narrative of investigation, meaning-making and discovery, the novel presents to the readers deep-seated spiritual yearnings to understand one's own identity through imaginative communication with a cultural legacy. I argue that in Japanese society there is an anxiety about the loss and obliteration of such identity markers. The novel compensates for this fear by the narrator's success in uncovering a coherent history of the tribe. It is actually a symbolic encouragement and confirmation of the unconscious that underlies Japanese popular culture today.

Rika-san (1999) [The Patterned Puppet] is a novel of how four young women from different backgrounds came together in an old house to pursue their dreams of studying the ancient female craft of thread making, fabric dyeing, and cloth weaving. The narrator inherited an old house and an old puppet called Miss Rika (Rika-san from the title) from her aunt when she died. To make the best use of the old house, she gathered a group of young women who shared a passion to learn about and practise the ancient female craft of fabrics. In the course of their interaction, the inanimate puppet Rika-san exerted an influence that drove them not only to discover the knowledge of fabrics, but also the knowledge of the female heart which had been repressed and forced to be silent throughout the patriarchal history of Japan. At the end of the novel, all four young women completed their own rite of passage, thereby coming into their own selves since they have acquired the unwritten, personal stories of their ancestors.

The end of their journey of self-actualization, which led to a new beginning in their lives, was marked by a fire in the old house. In order to let a dying father see the artistic accomplishments of his daughter, the four young women arranged a "private" exhibition at the house in which their work was showcased. A carelessly dropped lighter started a fire, and everything inside of the wooden house was entirely consumed including the puppet Miss Rika. On the surface, it was a great loss because all their work for the past year was destroyed. Yet, the fire was a symbolic moment of rebirth in many ways. As the narrator explained, "Looking at the fire, the sensation of melting deep inside the body was indeed ecstatic. Although it was destructive, at the same time there was an ambiguity coming from being touched by a sublimely clean presence."[10] The fire was a center which allowed the repressed past to surface into the present, to be recognized and cleansed, so that confusion could be removed, thus enabling clarity and purpose to lead the way for a new life. In the very last sentence of the novel, the young American lady Margaret, who had just given birth, woke up from a dream in which Miss Rika smiled at her. As the journeys complete, the past is restored to its rightful position. The future is also ready to unfold, given that the individuals in question have gained a new sense of identity and purpose.

In these two novels, as well as the highly-acclaimed *Burrows of Botanical Gardens* which depicts a miraculous journey back to one's childhood in an effort to reestablish a core identity supporting one's life and future, characters go through a life-transforming journey to a magical world beyond commonplace reality. This journey reveals repressed, forgotten, and buried stories from previous generations. These repressed stories not only construct a link between the contemporary world and the more traditional one left behind, but they also establish a basis for which the present world has meaning. It is a reminder to contemporary readers that beneath the boring reality, there is a strong foundation of values and beliefs which should never be forgotten. This rich and dramatic inner world, which contemporary characters are too busy or afraid to face, serves as a reminder of the importance to return to one's core in order to summon up the necessary courage to confront our destiny.

Yumemakura Baku, Mukoda Kuniko, and Nashiki Kaho are three highly popular contemporary Japanese writers each acclaimed for their special styles in their chosen genre of work. Yumemakura's *Onmyoji* series is well-received for its successful combination of historical characters, settings, and the modern detective fiction formula, resulting in entertaining stories which deeply resonate with contemporary Japanese (and Southeast Asian) readers. The various disturbances caused by the intrusion of the spiritual world into the physical world can be seen as an imaginative representation of the underlying problems modern Japanese people are facing in terms of their identities and sense of belonging. When the modern world has changed so much, is the preservation of ancient cultures and beliefs still valuable? Are the current social problems merely a reflection of the external environment? Or, are they actually a manifestation of repressed anxieties and buried emotions? Abe no Seimei's

---

10   Kaho Nashiki, *The Patterned Puppet*. Trans. Meihui Li (Taipei: Muses Publishing House, 2011), 354.

diagnosis of the various problems and the way he solved them by going back to the roots may very well be the theoretical framework we should adopt when reflecting upon various social issues. Mukoda Kuniko's depiction of ordinary life in her TV screenplay and her prose/fiction offers contemporary readers a realistic setting for understanding quotidian reality that compels us to observe the details and textures of the life we are leading. Memories of childhood, a bygone era, relationships with our parents, and the common objects we gain and lose in our personal journey all represent opportunities for us to uncover the inner layers of our self. In her nuanced fiction, ordinary housewives come to the realization that they are sexual beings in addition to understanding the hegemonic devices of patriarchal oppression. Furthermore, the little girl who witnessed the distribution of work in her family finally recognizes the disquieting realities of gender relations during this period in Japanese society. The magic of ordinary daily life is instrumental in the revelation of the underlying values and ideologies from this era in Japanese society. In Nashiki Kaho's fantasies, what has been unearthed is the forgotten pain, or the repressed fear of the past. The characters in her novels are brought face to face with what they have unconsciously buried or what has been collectively hidden by the community. Liberating themselves from these fears and anxieties, they demonstrate their readiness to start a new page. The magic of repression bursts open in the works of these three writers highlighting fundamental concerns and the reality of Japanese culture today. Whether it be the past and the present, the old and the new, or the magical and the psychological, the link is the narratives conceived by these writers in their imagination.

References

Mamoru, Oshii, dir. *Ghost in the Shell.* 1995; Tokyo: Kodansha Limited, Bandai Visual Co. Limited, and Manga Entertainment, 1995. DVD.

Mukoda, Kuniko. *Father's Letter of Apology.* Translated by Qiuming Zhang. Taipei: Rye Field Publications. 2013.

Mukoda, Kuniko. *A Woman's Index Finger.* Translated by Ziqian Liu. Taipei: Rye Field Publications. 2014.

Mukoda, Kuniko. *Memory, Poker Cards.* Translated by Qiuming Zhang. Taipei: Rye Field Publications. 2014.

Mukoda, Kuniko. *The Woman Next Door.* Translated by Qiuming Zhang. Taipei: Rye Field Publications. 2014.

Nashiki, Kaho. *Burrows of Botanical Gardens.* Translated by Qiuming Zhang. Taipei: Muses Publishing House. 2011.

Nashiki, Kaho. *The Patterned Puppet*. Translated by Meihui Li. Taipei: Muses Publishing House. 2011.

Nashiki, Kaho. *Through the Swampy Woods*. Translated by Ruizhu Peng. Taipei: Muses Publishing House. 2010.

Yumemakura, Baku. *Yin Yang Master*. Translated by Miya Moro. Taipei: Muses Publishing House. 2003.

CHAPTER 32

The Metaphysics of Creativity: Imagination in Sufism, from the Qur'ān into Ibn al-ʿArabī

Ali Hussain

> And not an ordinary Arab, someone who is a poet ... is needed to understand that writing [of Ibn al-ʿArabī].
>
> SHAYKH HISHĀM QABBĀNĪ[1]

1 Introduction

In his survey of Islamic theology, *Theologie Und Gesellschaft*, Joseph Van Ess offers the following remarks on the condition of the Muslim community after the passing of the prophet Muḥammad: "One had to realize that the prophetic event had ended; of the Word, only the writing remains."[2] Indeed, the ensuing chapters in that work – and countless others – that highlight the myriad of theological schools and sects with dissenting differences that emerged within the Muslim community, after this "prophetic event," appear to support the proposition that only the "writing remains" of the Word that had been revealed to the Prophet.

And yet, for all the tremendous dissonance in dogma and pragma that had overwhelmed this nascent community of faith, the various groups who considered themselves "Muslims" still managed to find within the contours of the Word that had been revealed to the Prophet traces of that divine spark beyond the writing. Sometimes, this resurrection of the original prophetic state appeared as a common bond that united members of a sect, while other times it was used to marginalize entire peoples outside the fold of Islam.

Either way, the assessment offered in *Theologie Und Gesellschaft* seems to reflect only a partial reality of a religion that continues to survive fourteen centuries after its birth. A more recent survey on Islamic thought and practice,

---

1 Hisham Kabbani, "Invoking the Beloved," Lecture, Yale University, February 24, 2013, https://sufilive.com/Invoking-the-Beloved-4872-EN-print.html.

2 Joseph Van Ess, *Theologie Und Gesellschaft im 2. und 3. Jahrhundert Hidschra: Eine Geschichte des religiösen Denkens im frühen Islam*, vol. I (Berlin: Walter de Gruyter, 1991), 1, 3.

© KONINKLIJKE BRILL NV, LEIDEN, 2020 | DOI:10.1163/9789004436350_034

Shahab Ahmed's *What is Islam? The Importance of Being Islamic* – which might be considered a much-needed reformulation of the antiquated opinions voiced by Van Ess and others – focuses on this perplexing force that seems to tie the lives of countless Muslims together despite their differences in language, culture and contentious understandings of their faith.

Ahmed's solution is to focus less on the difference in beliefs and practices and more on the shared principles that sustain them in the collective imagination of the community. The author presents the *Pre-Text*, *Text* and *Con-Text* as key operators that account for the diversity of Muslims living in the "Balkans to Bengal complex."[3] Ahmed describes the first of these concepts, the *Pre-Text*, as that which is "ontologically and alethically prior to the Text and is that upon which the Truth of the Text is contingent."[4] Simply put, the *Pre-Text* is the "Unseen" spiritual realm, while the *Text*, at least in this excerpt, seems to refer solely to the Qur'ān as the scripture recited and experienced by Muslims.

However, such a limited designation of the *Text* quickly dissipates as one reads Ahmed's entire magnum opus. Muslim philosophers, for instance, do not perceive the Qur'ān as a necessary medium with which intelligent seekers need to engage in order to interact with the *Pre-Text*. Rather, the latter should simply refer to the writings of philosophers for this knowledge.[5] On the other hand, for Sufis, the Qur'ān is but one of many texts that can channel the *Pre-Text* into the sphere of belief and social practice. Perhaps the most poignant example of this is the celebrated compendium of poetry, the *Mathnawī*, by Jalāl al-Dīn Rūmī (d. 1273), which was – and still is – regarded by many Sufi devotees as the "Qur'ān in Persian."[6] In this regard, it is the *Con-Text*, or "the body of meaning that is the product and outcome of previous hermeneutical engagement with Revelation,"[7] which decides which texts predominate as channels to access the *Pre-Text* in a given society or culture.

These three constructs together allow Ahmed to present Islam not as a static object of analysis, but as the very idiom or language through which "people express themselves so as to communicate meaningfully."[8] More than that, the author posits that Islam is "the reality of the experience itself," not only the "means by which an experience is given meaning."[9] This creative rendering of

---

3 Shahab Ahmed, *What is Islam? The Importance of Being Islamic* (Princeton: Princeton University Press, 2016), 32.
4 Ahmed, *What is Islam?*, 347.
5 Ahmed, *What is Islam?*, 348.
6 Ahmed, *What is Islam?*, 307.
7 Ahmed, *What is Islam?*, 356.
8 Ahmed, *What is Islam?*, 323.
9 Ahmed, *What is Islam?*, 323.

THE METAPHYSICS OF CREATIVITY 737

Islam as a movement to produce meaning, and meaning itself, pays homage to the name of the religion, which means – among many things – "to submit" and, thus, affirms an inward journey towards God, who is the ultimate meaning for believers.

In "Imaging Islam: Intellect and Imagination in Islamic Philosophy, Poetry and Painting," James Morris highlights how Muslim philosophers and mystics have performed Ahmed's rendition of Islam precisely through novel engagements with scripture (*Text*), in order to channel the *Pre-Text* into their *Con-Text*, using unique cultural and historical constructs. One of these figures, the celebrated *Shaykh al-Akbar* (Greatest Master) Muḥyī al-Dīn Ibn al-ʿArabī (d. 1240), Morris tells us, left us with a heritage that is "so profoundly rooted in both the letter and the deepest spirit of the Qurʾān."[10] Beyond this, it is also Ibn al-ʿArabī's ability to communicate this "deepest spirit of the Qurʾān" not only to religious scholars, but also "secular interpreters, poets, teachers, and translators,"[11] some eight centuries after his passing that makes him truly unique. This is corroborated by the quote in the epigraph, attributed to the contemporary Sufi guide, Shaykh Hisham Kabbani, who emphasizes the poetic spirit needed to understand the Greatest Master's writings.

A preliminary reading of Ibn al-ʿArabī's works does not help explain this unique dissemination among a diverse audience. On the contrary, his magnum opus, *al-Futūḥāt al-Makkiyya* (Meccan Openings) and second most-important work, *Fuṣūṣ al-Ḥikam* (Bezels of Wisdom), both contain as many – if not more – convoluted discourses on dialectical theology and metaphysics as can be found in many classical tomes of Islamic thought. If readers are not deterred by this specialized terminology, then they might very well be dissuaded by the countless controversial excerpts wherein he contravenes normative Islamic orthodoxy and scholarly consensus.[12]

In order to partially explain this attraction to Ibn al-ʿArabī and his writings by scholars and artists alike,[13] I suggest we return to Ahmed's definition of

---

10 James J. Morris, "Imaging Islam: Intellect and Imagination in Islamic Philosophy, Poetry, and Painting," *Religion and the Arts* 12 (2008): 306.

11 Morris, "Imaging Islam," 306.

12 Muḥammad Ibn al-ʿArabī, *Al-Futūḥāt al-Makkiyya* (Beirut: Dār al-Kutub al-ʿIlmiyya, 1999), VII, 339, and Muḥammad Ibn al-ʿArabī, *Fuṣūṣ al-Ḥikam* (Beirut: Dār al-Kitāb al-ʿArabī, 2002), 201 respectively.

13 A prominent example of a poet who has incorporated Ibn al-ʿArabī's Weltanschauung into his work is Abdelwahab Meddeb's *Tombeau of Ibn ʿArabī and White Traverses*. Oludamini Ogunnaike has also shown the presence of Akbarian motifs in the film *Inception*, see Oludamini Ogunnaike, "Inception and Ibn ʿArabī," *Journal of Religion & Film* 17, no. 2 (2013): 1–52.

Islam, as the "means through which an experience is given meaning." It is the very language and rhetorical style which the Greatest Master uses to express his own journey that, I posit, continues to attract readers today, in addition to the novel ideas in his works. In this regard, Ibn al-ʿArabī brilliantly conveys a subtle trait prevalent in many Sufi writings: the mystical experience is inseparable from the very language used to describe it.

In the ensuing paragraphs, we will attempt to decipher this creative rhetorical style by analyzing selections from the *Meccan Openings* and *Bezels of Wisdom*. Our focus will be on those discussions pertaining to *khayāl* (imagination) and how the author travels, semantically and spiritually, back and forth from language to meaning, and from body to spirit. Our journey will begin with the prophet Muḥammad and then delve into the significance of ʿĪsā b. Maryam (Jesus son of Mary), as an archetype of divine creativity and imagination. Thenceforth, we will conclude by synthesizing Ibn al-ʿArabī's portrayals of Muḥammad, Jesus and *khayāl* (imagination), with some final remarks on the significance of this discourse on our understanding of human creativity and art.

As will become evident, for Ibn al-ʿArabī, *ʿālam al-khayāl* (the realm of imagination) is one where dense bodies are spiritualized and subtle spirits are embodied. Alternatively, it is a realm that resides at the *barzakh* (interstice), between the physical residence of bodies and spiritual abode of spirits. In this sense, imagination for Ibn al-ʿArabī is what connects Ahmed's *Pre-Text* to both the *Text* and *Con-Text*. It is the very process of rendering what is ineffable and beyond language in the various mediums of human expression.

It is from this perspective also that art emerges in Ibn al-ʿArabī's thought as any attempt by humans – and perhaps any other created being – to reside in the imaginal realm and travel back and forth between the *Pre-Text* of creative divine inspiration and the *Con-Text* of art in all its forms. More importantly, from this perspective, scripture emerges not entirely separate from human art, but rather the ideal archetype for eloquence and sacred creativity. Simply, the Word in Ibn al-ʿArabī's thought is a blueprint for all human artistry.

2   Akbarian Muḥammadology

If there is such a body of knowledge in Christianity known as Christology, or "the part of theology, concerned with the body and work of Jesus,"[14] then a

---

14   Matt Stephon, and Hans Hillerbrand, *Encyclopaedia Britannica*, 8th ed. s.v. "Christology," 2016.

THE METAPHYSICS OF CREATIVITY

similar designation of "Muhammadology" should also be used to describe the overarching narrative of Ibn al-'Arabī's metaphysics, and many other Sufi mystics for that matter.[15]

One cannot overemphasize the centrality of the prophet Muhammad to the entire structure of Ibn al-'Arabī's thought. Consider what he says in the *Meccan Openings* regarding the Prophet's cosmological primacy: "What honor is greater than that of Muhammad, for he was the beginning of this circle [of existence], he is connected to its end and its completion is through him. In this way, through him things began and through him they are perfected."[16]

A similar sentiment can also be found in the *Bezels of Wisdom*, wherein the author references the title of the chapter devoted to Muhammad, "The Bezel of a Singular Wisdom in a Muhammadan Word": "His wisdom is singular because he is the most perfect being in this human species. This is why the affair began with him and, as such, it is also sealed."[17]

The cornerstone of this superiority, which Ibn al-'Arabī alludes to in these excerpts, is that the Prophet is both the first creation and spring for the rest of creation. Here, the Andalusian mystic is relying upon a well-known *hadīth* (prophetic narration) where the Prophet is asked by one of his companions about God's first creative act, to which the former responds: "The first thing that God created is the light of your Prophet."[18] From this perspective, it is the spirit or essence of Muhammad that is perceived as the first creation, not his physical body.

And it is this essence-beyond-form of the Prophet that became known as *al-haqīqa al-muhammadiyya* (Muhammadan Reality) among Muslim mystics, most notably Ibn al-'Arabī.[19] Returning to the reference to Christology, one might say that the Muhammadan Reality plays a similar – central – role in Muhammadology as the Logos does in Christian theology.

---

15   The superiority of the Prophet Muhammad's rank has been the focus of numerous Muslim authors, going back to the first generation of Muslims. As Michael Sells shows in "Early Sufi Qur'ān Interpretation," the sixth-generation descendent of the Prophet, Imām Ja'far al-Sādiq (d. 765) was already expounding upon *al-nūr al-muhammadī* (Muhammadan Light) a mere century after the former's passing.

16   Muhammad Ibn al-'Arabī, *al-Futūhāt al-Makkiyya*, 369.

17   Muhammad Ibn al-'Arabī, *Fusūs al-Hikam*, 214.

18   Ahmad Al-Qastalānī, *Al-Mawāhib al-Ladunniyya bi-l-Minah al-Muhammadiyya*, vol. I (Beirut: Al-Maktab al-Islāmī, 2004), 71. It should be known that while many religious scholars doubt the authenticity of this *hadīth*, it is still considered foundational for Sufi mystics like Ibn al-'Arabī.

19   Muhammad Ibn al-'Arabī, *al-Futūhāt al-Makkiyya* I, 276. On page 247, in the same volume, the author also describes *al-haqīqa al-muhammadiyya* as *haqīqat al-haqā'iq* (the reality of realities).

As Ibn al-ʿArabī proposes in the excerpts above, the cosmogenic importance of the Prophet is not simply a matter of sequence, but that his essence and spirit are also the very fabric of creation. In this grand cosmic theater of sacred history, Muḥammad is simultaneously the stage, actors, props and audience. He fulfills and unfolds the direction and production of the creative divine will.

And truly, it would not be a farfetched analogy to portray the mystic's perception of creation in its entirety as theater; a fortunate happenstance considering the focus of this volume on "art and imagination." For alongside the *ḥadīth* of the original creation, there is another narration, also central to Sufi thought, known as the *"ḥadīth* of the hidden treasure." In this instance, the prophet Muḥammad is not the speaker, but God himself who explains the original spark of life in the universe: "I was a hidden treasure, and I loved to be known. Therefore, I created creation so that I may be known by them."[20]

These two narrations harmonize with one another in the Sufi cosmology to which Ibn al-ʿArabī adheres. In combination with Aḥmed's definition of Islam as the "means to experience meaning," we can deduce that if the initial divine motivation for creating is love, then the light of the Prophet, *al-ḥaqīqa al-muḥammadiyya*, is not only that original object of love, but divine amour itself. Likewise, if the consequence of God acting upon his love is that his creation will come to know him, then the Muḥammadan Reality is not only knowledge of God, but the very process of knowing him as well.

As stated previously, this primary role granted to the spiritual reality of the Prophet Muḥammad in Ibn al-ʿArabī's Sufi metaphysics presents *al-ḥaqīqa al-muḥammadiyya* in a similar light as the Logos in Christology. As the "divine reason implicit in the cosmos, ordering it and giving it form and meaning,"[21] the Sufi Logos is perceived as being identical with the Prophet's essence, at least in Ibn al-ʿArabī's thought. The latter explicitly states in the *Meccan Openings* that *al-ḥaqīqa al-muḥammadiyya* is the "[divine] creative object ... and the First Intellect for others. It is also the Higher Pen which God created from nothing."[22]

This allows us to transition to another aspect of Sufi Muḥammadology, pertaining to the intimate relationship between the Prophet and the Qurʾān. This is a necessary step in order to venture into Christ's metaphysical significance in Ibn al-ʿArabī's thought, as a symbol of divine creativity and imagination. If identifying the Prophet's essence with the Logos presents his spiritual reality

---

20   Ibn al-ʿArabī himself mentions this ḥadīth approximately ten times in the *Meccan Openings*.

21   *Encyclopaedia Britannica,* 8th ed., s.v. "Logos." Chicago: Encyclopaedia Britannica, 2009.

22   Muḥammad Ibn al-ʿArabī, *al-Futūḥāt al-Makkiyya* I, 276.

THE METAPHYSICS OF CREATIVITY 741

as the creative force that animates the entire cosmos, then establishing a connection between him and the Qur'ān will situate him as the particular archetypal spring for all prophetic figures, including Jesus.

For Ibn al-'Arabī, the quintessential narration that establishes this connection is one attributed to the Prophet's wife 'Ā'isha, who was asked about his character after his passing. According to varying narrations, she is reported to have either said that "his character was the Qur'ān" or "he was a walking Qur'ān." This allows the Andalusian mystic to deduce that:

> She said this because he is most singular among all creation. Such a unique creation must encompass the best of manners. Moreover, God has described this character with "greatness." He also described the Qur'ān as "great." This is why the Qur'ān is his character.
>
> Thus, whoever wanted to see the Messenger from among his community who did not live during his time, then let them look at the Qur'ān. There is no difference between looking at it and gazing at the Messenger of God. It is as if the Qur'ān has been molded into a human form named Muḥammad.
>
> Moreover, the Qur'ān is divine speech and God's attribute. In turn, Muḥammad is the attribute of the Real (God), in his entirety.[23]

The Andalusian mystic extends the identification found in this narration, of the recited Qur'ān with the physical – or historical – persona of the Prophet, to the transcendent and timeless divine speech (Logos), in turn presenting the provocative image of the Prophet as a divine attribute.[24]

The key to deciphering the connection between the Prophet and the Qur'ān, on the one hand, and between him and other prophetic figures, on the other hand, resides in Ibn al-'Arabī's second most important work, the *Bezels of Wisdom*. Specifically, it is the organization of this monograph that provides a glimpse into the author's vision of *nubuwwa* (prophethood). In contrast to the *Meccan Openings*, an encyclopedic work with a rather enigmatic structure,[25] the *Bezels* is neatly categorized according to names of divine prophets and messengers.

---

23 Muḥammad Ibn al-'Arabī, *al-Futūḥāt al-Makkiyya* I, 109.

24 Nevertheless, it is not clear whether the author intends here that the name "Muḥammad" is a divine attribute (i.e. "Muḥammad" is one of the names of God), the Prophet himself is a divine attribute or both.

25 Although, Michel Chodkiewecz has hypothesized in *Ocean Without Shore* that the *Meccan Openings* does indeed have a thoroughly Qur'ānic organization and structure.

742 HUSSAIN

The 27 chapters in this book follow, rather loosely, the order of prophets found in Islamic sacred history, with the first focusing on Adam and last on Muḥammad. With that in mind, Ibn al-ʿArabī creatively departs from this historical sequence in order to augment the nuances of his mystical vision. For instance, although Jesus immediately precedes Muḥammad in Islamic prophetology, that is not the case in the *Bezels*. On the contrary, the author has chosen an enigmatic figure named Khālid as the placeholder for this penultimate phase, prior to the coming of the prophet of Islam.

Despite these differences, we can still surmise the contours of the vision that motivates the entire work. We begin with imagery that undergirds the title of the book itself, *Bezels of Wisdom*. Ibn al-ʿArabī's mastery of the Arabic language and his ability to decipher connections between homophones (similar sounding words), using his own creative etymology, appears clearly in this instance. For it is the relationship between *al-khātam* (ring) and *khātim* (seal) that animates the entire spirit of the *Bezels*: just as the Prophet Muḥammad is *khātim al-anbiyāʾ* (seal of prophets), he is also the *khātam* (ring) on the hand of God, who encompasses the prophetic bezels of all different shapes and sizes, from Adam to Jesus.[26]

This should not be surprising, considering that the Andalusian mystic also regards the spiritual reality of the Prophet, *al-ḥaqīqa al-muḥammadiyya*, to be the Logos, the original created being and means through which the cosmos continues to unfold, which includes other prophets and messengers. However, what Ibn al-ʿArabī is implicitly presenting in the *Bezels* is a much deeper and more significant idea, that just as the recited Qurʾān was revealed in stages (23 years), so was the walking Qurʾān, Prophet Muḥammad, also "revealed" in phases, according to the gradual historical appearance of those prophets and messengers mentioned in the *Bezels*.

What supports this hypothesis are the individual chapter titles in this work that focus on a single theme (e.g. prophethood, spirituality, light), whereas the culminating section, focusing on Muḥammad, designates "singularity" as the unique attribute fit solely for the prophet of Islam.[27] This presents us with a truly remarkable reworking of Islamic prophetology. From this perspective,

---

26 It is highly probable also that Ibn al-ʿArabī took into consideration the *ḥadīth*: "The black stone is the right hand of God, whoever kisses it has kissed his hand." Although this narration is considered weak according to the science of *ḥadīth*, this would not deter the author of the *Bezels* from relying upon it in his writings. Consider what he says about referencing weak *ḥadīths* that are, nevertheless, authenticated by the mystical visions of saints. See Muḥammad Ibn al-ʿArabī, *al-Futūḥāt al-Makkiyya* I, 524.

27 The previously quoted excerpt from this chapter also corroborates this singular encompassing rank granted only to the prophet Muḥammad.

THE METAPHYSICS OF CREATIVITY 743

the appearance of prophets are not discrete events, but rather the gradual emergence of a single being, the Prophet Muḥammad, also known in Sufism as *al-insān al-kāmil* (perfect human),[28] in stages.

And so, the appearance of the first prophet, Adam, whom Ibn al-ʿArabī associates with the perfection of the human form, can also be described as the manifestation of the prophet Muḥammad's own bodily perfection. Inversely, one can say that the human form of the Prophet is simply called "Adam." Likewise, the appearance of Jesus, whose unique physiology and birth is the author's main concern, can be viewed as the manifestation of the Prophet as Logos, as the *ḥaqīqa muḥammadiyya* in its entirety.

Indeed, it is for this very reason that ʿĪsā b. Maryam (Jesus son of Mary) may be considered the most quintessential – penultimate – stage in the revelation of the walking Qurʾān, Muḥammad. This is because the former contains all those aspects that appeared before him, through previous prophets, with the addition of this last and most necessary dimension: the embodiment of the Word.

3   Akbarian Christology, Creativity and Imagination

There are several concepts pertaining to Christ's image in Ibn al-ʿArabī's writings which we must first consider prior to venturing into the presence of creativity and imagination in his thought, eventually returning to the Muḥammadan Reality as the metaphysical thread that ties this entire apparatus together.

As expected, the Andalusian mystic's foundation in exploring the figure of Jesus is thoroughly Qurʾānic. He focuses on the three scriptural descriptions of Christ as: "Messenger of God, His Word that He cast to Mary and a spirit form Him."[29] Our concern in the ensuing paragraphs will be the son of Mary's status as *kalimatu Allāh* (Word of God) and a *rūḥun minh* (spirit from Him).

We begin with an excerpt from the *Meccan Openings* where the author discusses Jesus as the *kalima* (Word of God). His focus here is to situate this single Word within God's other – countless – Words, *kalimātu Allāh* (plural form):

> And He said regarding Jesus peace be upon him that he is: "His Word which He sent to Mary" and He also said about her: "she believed in the

---

28   To find out more about this concept, refer to William Chittick's *Sufi Path of Knowledge* and *Self-Disclosure of God*.

29   Qurʾān 4:171.

kalimāt (Words) of her lord" and they [these Words] are nothing other than Jesus. He made him as Words [plural] for her because he is abundant from the perspective of his outward and inward composition. Thus, every part of him is a Word ... It is like a human being when he utters the various letters that form one word that is intended by the speaker who seeks to create these words; so that he might express through them what is in his soul.[30]

The Andalusian mystic creatively extends what begins as a conversation on grammar to a profound reimagining of both Jesus and God as divine language and divine speaker, respectively. What emerges from all of this is the son of Mary not only as a single Word, but actually multiple divine expressions.

In turn, the entire universe appears as God's stream of consciousness and a constantly unfolding story. Per our discussion above, we can say that this tale began with the *ḥadīth* of the "hidden treasure." Since God loved to be known in the mirror of his creation, he has been incessantly "speaking" this creation into existence. In this case, the reality of the prophet Muḥammad is not only this uttered cosmos, but the very act of divine speech as well.

However, Ibn al-'Arabī is not satisfied to stop at this meta-cosmic perspective but returns to the human being's ability to speak as an imitation of divine speech. For just as God utters the universe into existence, we also speak micro-universes into being through our words and conversations. We ponder here two open-ended questions that arise from this creative portrayal and to which we will return later on. First, since human beings are capable of speaking in different registers (i.e. prose or poetry), and since Jesus and the rest of creation are God's uttered Words, is the son of Mary an instance of divine prose or poetry? Second, what kind of microcosms are we bringing into existence through our words and conversations?

In two *mi'rāj* (ascension) narratives found in the *Meccan Openings*, where Ibn al-'Arabī recounts his mythic celestial travels to the divine presence, retracing the Prophet Muḥammad's own journey, the former continues to explore the connection between Jesus and divine language. In the first of these accounts, Ibn al-'Arabī describes the journey in the third person, covering the tracts of a *tābi' muhammadī* (Muhammadan follower), or Sufi mystic, and his companion the *ṣāḥib al-fikr* (rational philosopher). While the "Muḥammadan follower" receives a ceremonious welcome from the angels and prophets guarding each of the seven heavens, the philosopher-companion is forced to

---

30   Ibn al-'Arabī, *al-Futūḥāt al-Makkiyya* V, 418.

THE METAPHYSICS OF CREATIVITY   745

speak with the planets orbiting these spheres, reflecting the lower rank of the latter's knowledge.

Upon reaching the second heaven, Ibn al-'Arabī tells the reader that the "Muḥammadan follower" is greeted by the cousins, Jesus and John the Baptist. He also provides important details on the specific knowledge imparted by these two prophets to their visitor:

> They reveal to him the authenticity of the message of the teacher, God's messenger [Muḥammad] prayers and blessings be upon him, through the miraculous nature of the Qurʾān. This is because this presence is that of *al-khiṭāba* [oration], *al-awzān* [poetic meters], *ḥusn mawāqiʿ al-kalām* [the beauty of appropriate speech], *imtizāj al-umūr* [the mixture of affairs] and *ẓuhūr al-maʿnā al-wāḥid fī-l-ṣuwar al-kathīra* [the appearance of one meaning in a multiplicity of forms]. He also receives the *furqān* [clear criterion for understanding] and the understanding of *kharq al-ʿawāʾid* [breaking of habits].
>
> He also comes to know from this presence the *ʿilm al-sīmiyāʾ*, which pertains to working with letters and names as opposed to vapors, blood and other things [i.e. as in *ʿilm al-kīmiyāʾ* (Alchemy)]. He also come to know the honor of words, *jawāmiʿ al-kalim* [the most encompassing of speech] and reality of *kun* [Be!] and its designation as *kalimat al-amr* [the word of command], not the past, future or *ḥāl* [state that is bound time].
>
> [From this heaven also, one comes to know] the appearance of the two letters from this word, even though it is composed of three. [He also understands] why that third *barzakhiyya* [liminal] "word," between the letter *kāf* and *nūn*, which is the spiritual *wāw*, was removed. This is the letter which gives [the realm] of *mulk* [dominion] the power to exercise influence upon the formation of created things. One also comes to know, from this presence, the secret of *takwīn* [formation].[31]

This single excerpt brings together all the various concepts discussed so far in this essay and furnishes all the necessary components needed for us to march towards the conclusion. First, Ibn al-'Arabī establishes the connection between Christ's description as *kalimatu Allāh* (Word of God) and the recited Qurʾān, as God's eternal *kalām* (speech).

Second, the Andalusian mystic tethers Jesus, and John the Baptist, to the Prophet Muḥammad, who is the walking Qurʾān and whose spiritual reality – we had described – is the Sufi Logos. This connection with the Messenger of

---

31   Ibn al-'Arabī, *al-Futūḥāt al-Makkiyya* V, 412..

Islam is reiterated in the second paragraph, albeit indirectly. The *jawāmiʿ al-kalim* (all-encompassing words) which the Muḥammadan follower is given to appreciate in this heaven is a reference to a well-known *ḥadīth* where the Prophet Muḥammad says according to the narrator: "I have been given *jawāmiʿ al-kalim*."[32] In another section in the *Meccan Openings*, Ibn al-ʿArabī provides a fascinating – and rather provocative – explanation of this unique rank given to the Prophet:

> God said: "And His Word which He cast to Mary,"[33] and He said: "She [Mary] believed in the Words of her Lord and in His Book."[34] It is also said that the "prince cut the hand of the thief" or "the prince beat the thief." In this way, whoever fulfills the command of the one who orders them, it is they [the deputy] who performed it.
>
> Know, then, that the one who cast [the Word] is Muḥammad. He cast, on behalf of God, the Words of the entire universe without exception. Some of these he cast by his own self, such as the spirits of angels and much of the higher realm, while other things he cast through causes. An example of the latter is the harvested grain that reaches your body as a spirit that glorifies and praises God. This only happens after many cycles and fluctuations. All of this comes from the one who has been given *jawāmiʿ al-kalim*.[35]

And so, the intimate relationship between Jesus and Muḥammad unfolds in the most profound and creative fashion possible. Ibn al-ʿArabī is not satisfied to simply describe Christ, the Word of God, as a manifestation of the Muḥammadan Reality. Instead, the author explains in detail how the Prophet Muḥammad is the Logos: as the sole proprietor in charge of *jawāmiʿ al-kalim*, he alone has the power and authority to cast divine words into their designated forms, including Jesus. In other words, if Muḥammad is the Logos, then *jawāmiʿ al-kalim* explains how he fulfills this role.

There are still more insights to be deciphered from the *miʿrāj* excerpt mentioned above. Alongside the connections between Jesus, the Qurʾān and the Prophet Muḥammad, Ibn al-ʿArabī establishes a third association, between Jesus and the notion of *barzakhiyya* (liminality). This key term will allow us to

---

32 This *ḥadīth* can be found in the second-most authentic compendium of prophetic narrations, *Ṣaḥīḥ Muslim*. See Muslim Al-Nīsābūrī, *Ṣaḥīḥ Muslim* (Beirut: Dār al-Kutub al-ʿIlmiya, 1991).

33 Qurʾān 4:171.

34 Qurʾān 66:12.

35 Muḥammad Ibn al-ʿArabī, *al-Futūḥāt al-Makkiyya* I, 261.

THE METAPHYSICS OF CREATIVITY 747

directly venture into Ibn al-ʿArabī's understanding of *khayāl* (imagination). Only once we have taken this excursion, can we return one last time to this excerpt to appreciate the other descriptions of the second heaven that Ibn al-ʿArabī provides here.

In this instance, Ibn al-ʿArabī is relying upon an oft-quoted verse found in Chapter 55 of the Qurʾān, *al-Raḥmān* (The Most-Merciful): "He merged the two seas, they meet. Between them is a *barzakh* [isthmus], they do not transgress."[36] As expected, he undertakes the following creative discourse on ontology using this verse:

> Know that known things are three kinds without a fourth. These are *al-wujūd al-muṭlaq* (absolute being) which is never limited, and that is the being of God, who is the necessary existent. The second is the *al-ʿadam al-muṭlaq* (absolute non-existence), which is non-existent in itself, cannot be limited and is what we call the impossible.
>
> Thenceforth, there cannot be two opposites facing one another save that there be a barrier between them ... This barrier between the absolute existent and non-existent is *al-barzakh al-aʿlā* [loftiest isthmus] or *barzakh al-barāzikh* [the isthmus of isthmuses]. It has a direction towards being and another towards non-existence.
>
> Within it [the *barzakh*] also are all the possible things, which never end. Each of these things has an immutable essence in this isthmus whereupon the absolute being [God] gazes. It is from this aspect that the things are named, and if He chooses to bring them into being, He says to it: "*Kun!*" [Be!] and it will be.
>
> Moreover, every human who has a *khayāl* [imagination] and imagines something, then their contemplation is extending into this isthmus, even though they do not know they are imagining their object from this presence.[37]

Ibn al-ʿArabī delivers us, finally, to the shore of imagination through the door of the *barzakh* and the entire backdrop of the foundation which we have discussed thus far in this chapter. In reference to the Qurʾānic verse, Ibn al-ʿArabī most probably perceives the meeting between the fresh and salty waters to correspond to the absolute existence and non-existence, respectively.

---

36   Qurʾān 55:11–12.
37   Muḥammad Ibn al-ʿArabī, *al-Futūḥāt al-Makkiyya* v, 87.

However, that is by far the most trivial conclusion from the above excerpt. Much more important is the fact that the Andalusian mystic is – essentially – equating this *barzakh al-barāzikh* (greatest isthmus) with the Muḥammadan Reality, as the container wherein all possibly existent things reside. Just as the Prophet's dominion over *jawāmiʿ al-kalim* explains his status as Logos, here also it highlights – possibly – the emergence of the contingent beings from nothingness into existence via his agency.

In turn, Ibn al-ʿArabī is informing us that the Prophet Muḥammad's reality is also cosmic imagination. This is not an abstract metaphysical concept. Rather, it is the tangible realm where human beings access and create their own contemplations and reflections. However, the underlying premise in both this last excerpt and the previous, pertaining to the *miʿrāj*, is that the property of *barzakhiyya* (liminality) is also attributed to the second heaven where Jesus and John the Baptist reside.

Earlier in our discussion, we described Ibn al-ʿArabī's vision of the prophets and messengers who appeared – historically – prior to Muḥammad as various dimensions or aspects of the Prophet of Islam. Now, we can also describe the Christic aspect of the Prophet's reality as this *barzakhiyya* and imagination. More than that, this dimension pertains to bringing things into being and casting the Words of God into their respective forms, whence they transition from nothingness into contingent existence.

The last piece of information that Ibn al-ʿArabī gives us in the *miʿrāj* narrative is the quintessential connection between this metaphysical discourse and art as a tangible human experience. By situating *khiṭāba* (oration), *awzān* (poetic meters) and *ḥusn mawāqiʿ al-kalām* (beautiful arrangement of speech) in this same heaven of Jesus and John the Baptist, the author is rooting human creativity within the cosmic divine epitomized by ingenuity, imagination and the Muḥammadan Reality.

There is an intricate network of analogies operating in this conversation that renders Ibn al-ʿArabī's sophisticated metaphysics a tangible panorama of physical performances. First, by comparing *kalimātu Allāh* (God's Words) to human speech and situating oration and poetry in the second heaven of Jesus, where *takwīn* (formation and bringing into being) is also located, the Andalusian mystic is definitively rooting these forms of human creativity in divine speech. They are not only the result of divine inspiration but are actual imitations of God's process of creating through breathing Words into forms.

In turn, Ibn al-ʿArabī is answering our first open-ended question, whether Jesus might be considered an instance of divine prose or poetry. Given that "poetic meters" flow forth from the same heaven where Jesus resides, it is possible that the Andalusian mystic perceives the former as an instance of God's poetry. Beyond this, however, Ibn al-ʿArabī is also endowing human poetry, and

THE METAPHYSICS OF CREATIVITY 749

speech generally, with the ability of *takwīn*, to bring created things into being. What those created beings exactly are is not clear from this passage. However, given that the author situates *barzakhiyya* (liminality), and by extension *khayāl* (imagination), in the same heaven of Christ, it is safe to assume that human speech also brings a micro-universe into being, each with its own *barzakh* and imagination.

This last inference leads us to the second phase in this network of analogies, pertaining to the presence of Christ in these excerpts. Jesus embodies, more vividly than other created beings, the way God creates through breathing. This unique embodiment manifests in Christ's ability to reenact his own creation and that of the universe through his own miraculous breath. In turn, whatever the son of Mary brings to life or resurrects through his breath is itself a Christic being.

Merging the analogies of human and divine speech with that of Christ's miraculous breaths and the divine *nafas al-raḥmān* (breath of the most-merciful), we arrive at the conclusion that human speech itself is a Christic process, in two ways. First, the very act of breathing, in order to speak, imitates both God's bringing Christ into being through the divine breath and the latter's performance of miracles through breathing. Second, those things humans bring into being through breathing and speaking are Christic instances that imitate God's Words and those things which Christ himself brought to life or resurrected.

Lest this seems like a convoluted set of comparisons, Ibn al-ʿArabī provides a fascinating description in the *Meccan Openings* of the life that he believes human language has. The following makes clear that the Andalusian mystic perceives the power of poetry, and human speech at large, to be intimately related to the inherent life found in the sacred spirit of language and *ḥurūf* (letters):

> Know, may God grant you and us facilitation, that letters are a nation from those who are spoken to by God and commanded to follow His commands. They also have messengers from among them and names through which they are known. Only the people of spiritual unveiling from our path know this. The world of letters is also the most eloquent of realms in tongue and clearest in proclamation.[38]
>
> "When I mold him and breathe in him from my spirit." This is in reference to the appearance of accents upon the letters after their creation. Then, they emerge as another creation, known as a word, just as each of us is known as a human being. In this way, the world of words and expressions

---

38   Muḥammad Ibn al-ʿArabī, *al-Futūḥāt al-Makkiyya* V, 214.

is created from the realm of letters. This is because letters are the materials for words, just as water, dust, fire and air are the matter from which our bodies are molded. Then, the commanded spirit flows forth and we are called human.[39]

Ibn al-'Arabī confirms our earlier conjecture by giving a fascinating portrayal of letters and words as a self-subsisting universe. In this vision, every time a person speaks, regardless of the content of their speech, they are imitating and reenacting the genesis of the universe. Essentially, they are unfolding their own "hidden treasure."

We conclude this section of the essay with one final conceptual sojourn, at the above-mentioned notion of *nafas al-raḥmān* (breath of the most-merciful). Ibn al-'Arabī mentions this term numerous times in the *Meccan Openings*. In one example, he associates it with the origination of the cosmos: "The world appeared through *nafas al-raḥmān*. This is because God has *naffasa* (alleviated) through it the pressure felt by the [divine] names, due to the absence of their effects [in the universe]."[40] The author's creative etymology emerges again as he relies upon the connection between *nafas* (breath) and *tanfīs* (alleviation) to explain the role of *nafas al-raḥmān* in bringing the world into being.

In other places, the Andalusian mystic extends this etymological network to embrace yet another key term and also include the son of Mary as a corroborating example:

> Every *nafs* [soul] is afraid of non-existence ... Meanwhile, the divine spirit is *nafas al-raḥmān*. This is why he associated it with breathing, due to the harmony between the spirit and breaths when He said: "I breathed in him from my spirit." In this manner, also, He commanded Jesus to breathe in a mold of clay bird. Thus, spirits only appear through breaths.[41]
>
> And so, words appear from letters, and letters from air, and air from *nafas al-raḥmān*. Through the divine names also appear the traces in the universes, and at this halts *al-'ilm al-'īsawī* [the Christic knowledge].[42]

By rendering the *nafas* (breath) as Christic and tethering it to *tanfīs* (alleviation) and *nafs* (soul), Ibn al-'Arabī is also positing the latter two notions as

---

39   Muḥammad Ibn al-'Arabī, *al-Futūḥāt al-Makkiyya* V, 259–60.

40   Muḥammad Ibn al-'Arabī, *al-Futūḥāt al-Makkiyya* V, 218.

41   Muḥammad Ibn al-'Arabī, *al-Futūḥāt al-Makkiyya* V, 621.

42   Muḥammad Ibn al-'Arabī, *al-Futūḥāt al-Makkiyya* V, 416.

THE METAPHYSICS OF CREATIVITY   751

artifacts that follow the archetype of Jesus. It is clear now that, for the Andalusian mystic, the words and letters we speak are universes that we give life to through our breaths, very much in the same way that God continuously brings into being. Not only that, but the source of the *nafas* (breath), which is the *nafs* (soul), and the remedy of breathing, which is *tanfīs* (alleviation), and the things it creates, which are the letters and words, are all Christic.

In this way, Jesus son of Mary emerges in Ibn al-'Arabī's Weltanschauung as the meeting point between divine and human speech, imagination and creativity. The Andalusian mystic says much more in his writings about all the concepts we have discussed so far, including imagination. However, due to the limited scope of this chapter, we restrict ourselves to the excerpts and analyses in the preceding paragraphs. In the following final section, we try to synthesize the various analytical threads presented here and also offer some final remarks on the significance of Ibn al-'Arabī's metaphysics to our understanding of human creativity and imagination.

4   Conclusion

In "Representation in Painting and Drama: Arguments from Indian Aesthetics," Ananta Sukla states that "the theater is superior to painting not because it creates the illusion of reality better, but because, for the peculiarity of its medium, it is capable of representing the indeterminate in its determinate form."[43] It is from this perspective, of "representing the indeterminate in its determinate form," that our previous exploration of the unfolding of the "hidden treasure," through the writings of Ibn al-'Arabī, has been nothing but a sojourn amidst the divine drama of creation.

In the case of the Andalusian mystic and his theosophy, the "indeterminate" is the transcendent divine essence, the "hidden treasure" *par excellence*, while the "determinate forms" are the endless and incessantly unfolding theophanies that manifest this ineffable divine essence. As we mentioned previously, paying homage to Sukla's mention of theater, in this divine drama of the "hidden treasure" the stage, play, characters and audience are all but mirrors of *al-ḥaqīqa al-muḥammadiyya* (Muḥammadan Reality), which is at once God's original creation and the very process of creation. The Prophet is at once the original object of divine love and the act of loving itself.

---

43   Ananta Sukla, "Representation in Painting and Drama: Arguments from Indian Aesthetics," in *Art and Representation*, ed. Ananta Sukla (Westport, CT: Praeger Publishers, 2001), 240.

However, if theater, painting and the arts are central components of human culture, then what Sukla informs us in "Oriya Culture: Legitimacy and Identity" is also relevant to the discussion in this chapter, in so far as "language and religion have been the central instrument in the emergence and identity of a culture."[44] The central objective in the preceding paragraphs has been to show that, for Ibn al-ʿArabī, the social and worldly dimensions of imagination, art and creativity are very much rooted in metaphysics and divinity.

However, the Andalusian mystic is not interested in the least to subject human imagination and artistic expressions to the dogmatic prescriptions of legal strictures, but rather to decipher the infinitude of potentialities inherent in divine creativity through the variety of worldly forms and manifestations. His Weltanschauung is one where the physical is enchanted and sacralized towards the metaphysical, not vice versa. Equally important also is Ibn al-ʿArabī's positioning of art forms like poetry and imagination squarely within Sufi theology. In other words, the creative dimensions of Akbarian Christology and Muḥammadology are not auxiliary to the "art" of knowing God but are central and indispensable components to that end.

Our objective in this concluding section is twofold. First, we will summarize and synthesize Ibn al-ʿArabī's vision of Christ and his creative dimensions in Sufi metaphysics. Here, we will focus specifically on bringing together the discussions of the Muḥammadan Reality and Sufi Jesus in order to better appreciate the larger narrative of Logos and imagination in the Andalusian mystic's thought. Second, we will attempt to extend Ibn al-ʿArabī's vision of poetry and language to other forms of art. Our central concern will be to gauge whether the Sufi mystic would give painting and music specifically and other forms of creative expression generally the same station which he granted poetry.

We can summarize the two analytical threads in this chapter as Sufi Muḥammadology and Christology, both through the Akbarian prism. In the first, we saw that Ibn al-ʿArabī presents the spiritual reality of the Prophet Muḥammad as simultaneously the first entity created by God and the matter from which the entire universe, and all that it contains, is created. The Andalusian mystic also makes sure that the Prophet does not appear as a passive agent in this narrative, but as the one with authority and power to cast the divine words into their respective forms, stemming from his sole proprietorship over *jawāmiʿ al-kalim* (the all-encompassing divine Words). This ontological and historical primacy of the Prophet enabled us to describe him as the Islamic equivalent of the Logos in Sufi metaphysics.

---

44   Ananta Sukla, "Oriya Culture: Legitimacy and Identity," *Journal of Comparative Literature and Aesthetics* 30, no. 1–2 (2007): 5.

THE METAPHYSICS OF CREATIVITY

Transitioning to Ibn al-'Arabī's Christology, we saw that the son of Mary facilitates an intricate network of analogies between God and human beings in the former's thought. On the one hand, the Andalusian mystic perceives Jesus' existence, as a divine Word(s), to be similar to human speech that contains letters, sentences and expressions. In order to fully appreciate this comparison, we also saw that Ibn al-'Arabī regards those letters and words that we speak and write as living nations that are "spoken to by God." In turn, all human speech, once uttered, exists in a microcosm of imagination. In this way, we re-enact the original drama of creation by unfolding the "hidden treasure" within us outwardly.

Bringing these two threads together yields a few key points. First, as mentioned previously, Christ represents an aspect or dimension of the Muḥammadan Reality, specifically the *barzakhiyya* (liminality), imaginality and the narrative of the Logos. Alternatively, we can equate this Christic facet with *jawāmiʿ al-kalim* (all-encompassing words) of the Prophet's essence. In other words, Jesus represents the Prophet's sole proprietorship over casting divine words into their respective forms.

What the Andalusian mystic does in his writings is to extend the sphere of these divine words and their receptacles to also include art and creativity. The second heaven of Jesus (i.e. the second heaven of the Muḥammadan Reality), where imagination and liminality reside, is also where oration and poetic meters can be found. As we have seen, the letters and words that give life to poetry are a nation that are spoken to by God. In turn, they are also a cosmos of forms waiting to receive the divine breath and spirit to bring them to life. It is at this crucial juncture that the Muḥammadan Reality emerges in Ibn al-'Arabī's thought as *barzakh al-barāzikh* (greatest isthmus) and imagination itself.

What this means is that the Prophet Muḥammad's essence is not only the original divine artwork, but also divine creativity in movement and the spiritual space from which human creativity springs and wherein it takes places. Of course, that is yet another way of describing the Christic aspect of the Muḥammadan Reality, since Jesus embodies and reenacts the divine creative power through breathing. In a similar fashion, artists also receive a "breath" of creative inspiration from the realm of *khayāl/barzakh* (imagination/isthmus) and reciprocate that process by breathing their "indeterminate" inspiration outwardly into a "determinate form" of art (i.e. poetry, painting, film etc.)

And so, we come to the issue of the usefulness of Ibn al-'Arabī's Muḥammadology, Christology and imagination for discussing the metaphysics of art forms other than poetry, such as painting or music. In the case of painting, and all forms of imagery, Ibn al-'Arabī provides a fascinating interpretation of the Islamic prohibition against statues and portraits, in the specific context of the

Christian idolization of Jesus. The excerpt begins with a mention of a special rank of Muslim saints known as *al-ʿīsawiyyūn al-thawānī* (the dualist Christic saints):

> They are those whose way is that of *tawḥīd al-tajrīd min ṭarīq al-mithāl* (abstract monotheism through the path of form). This is because the existence of Jesus did not come through a male human, but rather through a spirit that appeared in a human form. For this reason, the majority of the community of Jesus son of Mary, more so than other nations, have advocated for the use of images, as exists in their churches. They worship God by directing themselves to these images.
>
> As for us, [the Prophet] has sanctioned for us to worship God as though we see Him, whence he admitted Him into *khayāl* [imagination]. This is the meaning of *al-taṣwīr* [forming or putting into form]. But he forbade us from visualizing Him in the world of the senses.[45]

As expected, Ibn al-ʿArabī creatively roots the Christian – read Catholic – practice of idolizing Jesus, Mary and saints through imagery within the very notion of *tawḥīd*, or monotheism and acknowledging the oneness of God, an association that would certainly seem heretical to many Muslim scholars who hold that imagery is a transgression against *tawḥīd* and who insist on iconoclasm.

The Andalusian mystic also expands the relevance of this discussion by simultaneously rooting the Islamic and Muḥammadan command to "see God" within *khayāl* (imagination) and *taṣwīr* (molding into form), or as Ananta Sukla would describe, "to put the indeterminate into determinate forms." However, by emphasizing the departure of God in Islam from statues to imagination, Ibn al-ʿArabī is not actually restricting the permissible forms of visualizing God in the physical world.

On the contrary, the Sufi mystic is at once liberating the human perception of God from restricted sensual forms (e.g. statues) and transferring it instead to a higher spiritual realm (i.e. imagination), whereby it can become the "indeterminate" essence for the myriad of human creative expressions. In other words, for Ibn al-ʿArabī, it is not only statues or images of Jesus, saints and prophets that represent God, but the entire gamut of human expressions that necessarily communicate an aspect of the divine, through the means of the Muḥammadan Reality.

---

45   Muḥammad Ibn al-ʿArabī, *al-Futūḥāt al-Makkiyya* I, 521.

THE METAPHYSICS OF CREATIVITY 755

As for the Akbarian perspective on music, this is the subject of future research that will soon be completed. For now, it suffices to say that Ibn al-ʿArabī discusses music and melodies approximately twenty-seven times in the *Meccan Openings*. Throughout these discourses, he emphasizes the need for listeners to transcend a "natural" or purely emotional enjoyment of sound, and instead to attempt and derive *maʿrifa* (gnosis) from the power of the notes and cadences. Here again, Ibn al-ʿArabī is formulating a type of auditory *taṣwīr* in *khayāl* (imagination), whereby the basic units of music are no longer the end of the experience but a means and spring for more sophisticated listening acts.[46]

Between poetry and music, language and sound, Ibn al-ʿArabī presents us with a truly remarkable understanding of human creativity and imagination. As is the case in all other areas of his thought, the Andalusian mystic is thoroughly fixed on divinity as the source of human creative expressions. From that singular transcendent essence, through the Muḥammadan Reality and its myriad of prophetic mirrors, the infinitude of aesthetic artifacts in our world emerge as mere refractions of that one source. This is a hierarchy that he beautifully portrays in an image of a *ṣūr* (horn), which he – unsurprisingly – etymologically tethers to *ṣuwar* (forms).[47]

The findings of this essay should encourage us to undertake a deeper exploration of the relationship between Sufi metaphysics and the importance of art and creativity in pre-modern and contemporary times. In "Ibn al-ʿArabī and Joseph Campbell: Akbarian Mythology and the Metaphysics of Contemporary Art," I do this by comparing and contrasting the Andalusian mystic's thought with Campbell's groundbreaking exposition on the enchantment of modern art, *The Power of Myth*. I show that Ibn al-ʿArabī would find metaphysical relevance in many of the creative expressions of our time, including – but not limited to – video games and even films that glorify the zombie apocalypse.[48]

It is indeed a fortunate happenstance that this essay on Ibn al-ʿArabī's metaphysics of imagination and creativity should find a place in a groundbreaking volume such as this one, on art and imagination in the humanities. As Shaykh Hisham Kabbani states in the epigraph at the beginning of this paper, the sophisticated mystical writings of a Sufi mystic like Ibn al-ʿArabī require the finesse of a poet in order to be understood. What Shaykh Kabbani is also telling

---

46   Muḥammad Ibn al-ʿArabī, *al-Futūḥāt al-Makkiyya* I, 496.

47   Muḥammad Ibn al-ʿArabī, *al-Futūḥāt al-Makkiyya* I, 680–86.

48   See Ali Hussain, "Ibn al-ʿArabī and Joseph Campbell: Akbarian Mythology and the Metaphysics of Contemporary Art," *Journal of the Muhyiddin Ibn ʿArabī Society* 63 (2018): 71–86.

us, indirectly, is that art and creativity have always been married to the world's great religious traditions throughout history. From Andalusia to the Vatican, beautiful arrangements of colors, shapes and sounds immortalize the ineffable and fleeting moments of the mystical experience.

References

Ahmed, Shahab. *What is Islam? The Importance of Being Islamic*. Princeton: Princeton University Press. 2016.

Al-Nīsābūrī, Muslim. *Ṣaḥīḥ Muslim*. Beirut: Dār al-Kutub al-ʿIlmiya. 1991.

Al-Qasṭalānī, Aḥmad. *Al-Mawāhib al-Ladunniyya bi-l-Minaḥ al-Muḥammadiyya*. Vol. I. Beirut: Al-Maktab al-Islāmī, 2004.

Chittick, William. *Self-Disclosure of God: Principles of Ibn al-ʿArabī's Cosmology*. New York: State University of New York Press. 1998.

Chittick, William. *Sufi Path of Knowledge: Ibn al-ʿArabī's Metaphysics of Imagination*. New York: State University of New York Press. 1989.

Chodkiewicz, Michel. *An Ocean Without Shore: Ibn ʿArabī, The Book, and the Law*. Albany: State University of New York Press. 1993.

Encyclopaedia Britannica, 8th ed., s.v. "Logos." Chicago: Encyclopaedia Britannica, 2009.

Hussain, Ali. "Ibn al-ʿArabī and Joseph Campbell: Akbarian Mythology and the Metaphysics of Contemporary Art" *Journal of the Muhyiddin Ibn ʿArabī Society* 63 (2018): 71–86.

Ibn al-ʿArabī, Muḥammad. *Al-Futūḥāt al-Makkiyya*. Beirut: Dār al-Kutub al-ʿIlmiyya, 1999.

Ibn al-ʿArabī, Muḥammad. *Fuṣūṣ al-Ḥikam*. Beirut: Dār al-Kitāb al-ʿArabī. 2002.

Kabbani, Hisham. "Invoking the Beloved." Lecture. Yale University, February 24, 2013, https://sufilive.com/Invoking-the-Beloved-4872-EN-print.html.

Meddeb, Abdelwahab. *Tombeau of Ibn ʿArabī and White Traverses*. United States: Fordham University Press. 2010.

Morris, James. "Imaging Islam: Intellect and Imagination in Islamic Philosophy, Poetry, and Painting." *Religion and the Arts* 12 (2008): 294–318.

Ogunnaike, Oludamini. "Inception and Ibn ʿArabī." *Journal of Religion & Film* 17, no. 2 (2013): 1–52.

Sells, Michael. "Early Sufi Qurʾānic Interpretation." In *Early Islamic Mysticism: Sufi, Qurʾān, Miʿrāj, Poetic and Theological Writings*, edited by Michael Sells, 75–96. New Jersey: Paulist Press, 1996.

Stefon, Matt, and Hans Hillerbrand. *Encyclopaedia Britannica*, 8th ed., s.v. "Christology." Chicago: Encyclopaedia Britannica, 2009.

Sukla, Ananta. "Oriya Culture: Legitimacy and Identity." *Journal of Comparative Literature and Aesthetics* 30, no. 1–2 (2007): 9–19.

Sukla, Ananta. "Representation in Painting and Drama: Arguments from Indian Aesthetics." In *Art and Representation*, edited by Ananta Sukla, 221–42. Westport, CT: Praeger Publishers, 2001.

Van Ess, Joseph. *Theologie Und Gesellschaft im 2. und 3. Jahrhundert Hidschra: Eine Geschichte des religiösen Denkens im frühen Islam.* Vol. 1. Berlin: Walter de Gruyter. 1991.

PART 9

Artists Reflect on Imagination: An Imaginative Epilogue

∵

CHAPTER 33

Free Thinking about Imagination: How Is It to Imagine What Imagination Is?

Marion Renauld

Let us take our time, and relax.

Let us do what Calvino advises to his reader in the very first sentences of his novel *If on a Winter's Night a Traveler*, when he writes "Relax. Concentrate. Dispel every other thought. Let the world around you fade," for "you are about to begin reading" this book you're holding in your hands (or hand, or not holding at all thanks to a table, yours or not).

So please, let us now imagine what imagination is.

One question is "Is it even possible?" Another is "Isn't that what I was just doing, imagining that I am comfortable and starting Calvino's book (with or without pleasure)?"

One point: imagination is evidently even less clear than one thought, than what one suspected, or even imagined.

One comparative exercise: does it change anything to imagine, or know, or think that this reflection is now a computer copy of an original typewritten version (thanks to an Underwood 319) of 6 pages, just a bit modified.

As you are comfortable somewhere reading, we may try to describe what exactly happened when you were imagining the Italian book, the Italian guy, or possibly what it is like to write with a typewriter now, or whenever Calvino did it. What happens doesn't need to happen with closed eyes, even if imagination has been described as a vision of a missing thing. Things like an elephant are missing here where I am, even when carefully looking around. So what happens is that you are thinking about something that is missing, i.e. an elephant, Calvino, typewriting, and then you are supposed to see it somehow, not to say to feel it somewhere inside your body.

One question: how can we speak of something that is internal, or that is at least neither a straightforward belief nor a state of mind, not even purely notational? For imagination seems to be feelings without feelers, meanings without referents.

One issue: do I gain epistemic rewards by imagining, or is it a form of (useless) psychic delirium?

© KONINKLIJKE BRILL NV, LEIDEN, 2020 | DOI:10.1163/9789004436350_035

Well, you might think this question goes too far. You might prefer neuroscientific descriptions of what the brain is knitting, in terms of cells and kinds of electrical inputs. Obviously, the brain is here. We could claim that although the things themselves might be missing, brains can still work, imagining castles in Spain or phantom body-pains.

So the question is: how do we judge the rightness of an explanatory description of the brain and its operations?

A neuronal approach shows the mechanism, but doesn't say anything about why castles in Spain or why such and such beliefs seem to be free-runners. In order to explain the content of a belief, we change the brain into a mind. The neuronal approach explains the wood and the fire, but nothing about the about-thoughts I have when looking at it. We must do semantics. For when things are missing and the brain's burning, there is still at least one kind of thing: a sign.

Brains are like meanings in that they are not directly visible and measurable (we must know what we are looking for), but unlike signs, which are directly present and sharable. Look at the lines of Calvino's book. Listen to the sounds I make with my mouth and which evoke (awake in you the memory of) a door. Taste the promises of a hidden rose.

Is imagining opening a fake door or pretending to open a door, or is it prescribing that it is fictionally true that the door is open outside your mind? Then I remember Goodman: "never mind mind" (which goes with "essence is not essential" and "matter doesn't matter").

You did read the word "relax" and are now full of pictures of Italy. Maybe you have read Calvino himself and so on, and all these little signs are now imprinting themselves on you, inside you (where? how?). Same process as for anything: perception, belief, desire, knowledge, action. So one way to describe what has already happened is to compare it with perceptions, beliefs, memories, desires, feelings, actions and so on, and then look at differences and relations.

Let us note that there is more freedom in the laws of imagination than in anything else: you don't need a real state of affairs, you don't need facts or verification, you don't have to be sincere, you can be absurd (a pink elephant) and you can also do it with true stuff, for some say that you can even make-believe something you really believe (that elephants are big).

Well, I am not sure about this last possibility. There also seems to be less freedom than some argue for: as crazy as the things or signs that your mind can explore, finally you still cannot imagine anything you want (neither who you really are, nor what exactly Calvino was feeling when he was writing "relax").

FREE THINKING ABOUT IMAGINATION

One inquiry: What is it like to be unable to imagine? What is it like to meet a sign you refuse to imagine, think of, picture inside, and act outside as if it were true?

The problem of imaginative resistance is an intriguing one, although very confusing because of the multiple phenomena at stake, which are very different.

As many have already claimed, it is different to refuse to imagine something you dislike or disagree with, and to be unable to imagine it because of some misunderstanding, lack of clarity, or opacity of the content (imagine three). The problem of imaginative resistance shows the limits of the will as well as of the belief-process. At least, it wasn't so difficult to respond to the request to imagine Calvino's book, even if we must of course at least speak English, know what a book is and recognize Calvino as a proper name. More than that: we must actually know what imagining is, or how to do such a "thing," for if not we might instead conceive it, suppose it, stipulate it, or engage in a lot of other kinds of propositional attitudes.

One epistemic question: does the impossibility to conceive go with the impossibility to imagine? We could imagine what we clearly conceive (a one thousand angles figure), but what about what is conceptually confused (a five-fingered round leaf)?

One psychological question: what kind of (mental) attitudes does the will refuse to engage in?

For the main propositional attitude that is needed in order to possibly imagine x is the will (the desire that x or of x), unlike supposition, which is more constrained by certain antecedent signs. If you don't want to imagine, if you somehow don't want to represent for yourself the pink elephant or that you are indeed relaxed, nothing can happen. Imagining is less about beliefs, or make-beliefs, than about wanting something for free and for fun.

From such a radical perspective, a lot of things we call "imagining" are reducible to inferences, such as when I see a "pink elephant" and infer this sort of elephant must have four legs.

Although it is possible to want something which already exists or is in front of you, it is not easy to imagine that something that is the case is in fact the case. What would it mean? But you can of course imagine the case. This is why imagination supposes a false belief, but can deal with a true (a real) thing. So when Currie says, for example, that make-believe and belief can go together, he must add a false belief (a counterfactual one) or we go too far: what do we do when we imagine that London is the capital of England? Here, I imagine sea landscapes, streets and maps. I even imagine the words "London is the capital of England" written somewhere. To purely imagine this, would it be to smell the English air, or to spell a word?

So let us get slowly back to our business.

What is it like to imagine what imagination is? It is difficult to imagine a mental state like that, actually anything mental, but we can form a picture of someone lost in his thoughts, thinking of himself, or telling a story full of projections and credibility, hypothesizing the future, or we can see ourselves running after concepts and psychic sanity.

Imagination is something you don't really believe but which you somehow want to for a while (or only the sign of it). Imagination is something which is not the case but somehow resonates in you, for you want it (or only the sign-effect). Imagining has no direct effect (unlike being a witness, confessing or inferring), except when it starts to model your authentic thoughts and somehow make your body move (a belief being a disposition to act) or be moved (a feeling being a disposition to react).

So imagination seems to be epistemically fallible, but emotionally terribly efficient. Unlike beliefs, which are epistemically okay but sometimes very boring. Unlike suppositions, imagination is the power of the will and (so?) the dawn of knowledge.

An impossibility to imagine might be the symptom of what we call "aboulia," the Aristotelian lack of the will.

Generally speaking, and once again, it is good to remember that a lot of things we call "imagination" should be kept distinct, as we should also avoid any reification of mental operations or actions. Otherwise there is no difference anymore between what we do when we imagine, suppose, induce, remember, feel – not to mention when we write, read, draw, sing, whisper, knock or turn left. We might be imagining while doing all those things, but we have to add our will every time. The will of letting something missing appear. Or they could be hallucinations, illusions of the senses and magic tricks, against or for which nothing can be done. Everything we say about the imaginative experience of watching a movie is above all a perceptual experience. One question: would it be clearer to distinguish mental phenomena by looking at their props? If so, one thing to do: describe the effects of reading, watching, listening, drawing, schematizing.

By the way, Walton is right about the selfishness of the psycho-phenomenological experience of imagining (for everything about the content of a "mental experience" implies questions about the Self), but wrong about the core of the representation (he thinks it to be simulation). Goodman is speechless about brains and minds and right about the core of the representation (he thinks it to be denotation), because he emphasizes the trust we can have regarding our

FREE THINKING ABOUT IMAGINATION

emotions (affects also denote, i.e. do), because of the sharable dimension of signs (psychology is logic).

Imagined things are the products of affective (free) will.

Approaching the imagination through doxastic structures, with modal logics of possible worlds, describes what there is without values given to a p or a q. One question: does the (affective, agentive) value need to be given to an element or a relation?

A doxastic structure full of desires could be one picture of what happened when you were reading the first page. Someone had written something, you got the word, you were at least not refusing to think about it and you let go yourself relax.

Question: what does it change to imagine? For example, to imagine that you are totally relaxed while you are actually having a panic attack? What does it change to imagine what someone is feeling while you absolutely know that you cannot do that, you cannot even imagine what it is like to have my nails? You can smash together all your beliefs and even desires to have them, and even follow some rules of relations, infer some conclusions, and you might feel something similar. If you please. But as you can't have my words, you are only caught in the logic of inferences.

Let us finally note three needs of such an inquiry about imagination:

- *Epistemic.* How can we trust delirium, i.e. our free-running desires-thoughts, the act of letting appear what is missing?
- *Psychological.* What do I really want and really refuse?
- *Practical.* What do I do with what I want, refuse, and picture to do?

Addendum to *Free Thinking about Imagination*

1. I can't extract from my head (stop believing) a sort of contemporary fact that we are in a time where imagination is the (cognitive) queen in more than one kingdom: first in entertainment, second in sciences, third in day-to-day life – from personal dreams to shared advertising, from politics to love. Well, the thing is that we are living in a time in which our feet are leaving the ground, in many ways as well, and this movement doesn't seem to be reversing its course: the movement of further abstraction and the move from the (supposedly ordered) world to the (supposedly disordered) Self.

Imagination is the highest level of both, for you can think about whatever you want in any kind of way (right now, a bath and a good talk with a frog, or Billy the Squared Stone, you should know him). The more constraints you add (logical, physical, temporal, moral, aesthetic...), the farther you are from imagination: it becomes inferences and hierarchy between beliefs, degrees of interest of such and such interpretation of signs.

At this very moment in history, we want, so it seems, less true beliefs or clear signs, more freedom to interpret however one likes or feels, and to share. Imagination's reign is first for the self, above all for the world as representations and desires. Why not? Why not in the sciences and politics, why not in art, why not everywhere in day-to-day life, for we have become skeptical up to the point of the very reality of reality. Fire still burns, but signs of fire let us dream.

Concerning the inquiries about things (something day-to-day, as easy as technical, or something like a scientific experimentation), I'd copy Tolkien's words: "When I was a kid, I had no 'desire to believe.' I wanted to know." And that is why he created fairies. What was it like to imagine them? We can imagine that it consists of imagining us, here, of observing, feeling, learning vocabulary, reading, listening and then producing signs and interpretations of signs. The experience is illusory (like anything which is missing and about which we act like it is here) and (so?) unique (as nobody is experiencing my mind-body adventure). The signs are sharable and the rules of inferences are multiple.

At this very moment, we seem then to "desire to believe" a lot, or even to be forced to desire to believe what is presented to us. A dream you are the hero of. A project you are a loser in. A citizen you are, and imagining the contrary would mean desiring a false belief, but a true feeling.

2. When we ask about imagination in the philosophy of mathematics, we look for the epistemic gain we can extract from picturing, naming or manipulating 3D objects, as from knots.

When we ask about imagination in the philosophy of art, or more specifically of fiction, we look for the (epistemically valuable, true) beliefs we can extract from make-believing. Make-believing is often, in this case, picturing yourself inside the picture (you see in the film, or try to picture from the words you read).

When we ask about imagination in the philosophy of mind, we may even speak about mental pictures, instead of capacities, actions and feelings.

So imagining what imagination is could be anything. Describing imagination is like picturing pictures coming from a shared or sharable will, even randomly (I am picturing a picture of an ant carved in wood by a dolphin).

One question: how do we deal with random pictures, and how do we do it verbally? Well, it depends on what we want to get.

In the philosophy of mathematics, pictures are less randomly made than rationally. Diagrams (or figures, representations, signs) are submitted to the text, but finally above all to the rules of this game, which consists of: getting the best tools to obtain the most valuable knowledge.

FREE THINKING ABOUT IMAGINATION

I leave here the question of whether the arts are of the same kind as mathematics or sciences or know-how activities. My intuition is rather yes, thanks to Goodman, as symbolic constructions, even if we should specify how they work.

The least we can do to conceive what it is like to imagine is to leave the door open (which door?!) to such an act: picturing pictures which are allowed, when only thought, to free themselves from any kind of rules, games, or shareability. This might turn out to be insane craziness or valuable intuitions, and which is probably always affectively moving.

3. Let us finally try to clarify these three questions about imagination:
- *Epistemic.* How can we trust delirium, i.e. free-running desire-thoughts committed to the *illusionary* act of letting appear what is missing?
- *Psychological.* What do I *personally* really want and refuse?
- *Practical.* What do I do with what I *affectively, emotionally* want, refuse, and picture to do?

If we want to glean some epistemic insights, we should consider acts of imagining, within a scientific inquiry, as sharable intuitions related to shared signs and rules of interpretation. No illusion: we take the sign as a sign above all. The question is then about intuitions.

If we want to arrive at a cognitive explanation, we should consider acts of imagining, within an interaction, as shared emotions related to sharable desires, although selfish. Imaginative resistance is not about interpretative difficulties with signs, but personal affective will. The question is then about free will.

If we want to acquire some practical tools, we should consider the act of imagining as a source of action, or precisely the contrary, a source of non-action. Being emotionally affected makes you stop moving, as you can't move when moved. As a source of action, imagination can become rational mapping sticking to a goal. As a source of non-action, imagination is static free-running. A possibility is given with imagination to not do anything, even if you believe, think, feel, and want at the same time. Pure imagining is a disappearance of yourself.

Relax. Nothing will happen. Keep dreaming.

(In Guise of a) Bibliography

The philosophical background of this reflection is inextricably linked to the analytic philosophy of fiction including theorists like Gregory Currie, Peter Lamarque, Kendall Walton or John Searle (1975), in addition to the literature about imaginative resistance. I have also derived inspiration from the literary theories of people like Thomas Pavel and Gérard Genette.

On a global level, there are many novelists from all around the world (and of course the world itself). To be more precise, Goodman's works are a good toolbox for understanding philosophical delirium. There is also an article written by Tolkien in 1948 in which he insightfully reveals: "If I don't let you imagine street lamps in my Fairyland, it actually means that I don't want us to have such street lamps in our Commonland."[1]

On an academic level, you can find useful bibliographies in the few articles or books I have written including: *Philosophie de la fiction: Vers une approche pragmatiste du roman*.[2] Then all can be developed, clarified, and refined, we thus become humble footnote thinkers, forced to sign the sources of any argument.

But when your goal is to imagine what imagination is, even between epistemology and psychology, you might break any constraints about fact-checking. You're imagining! The bibliography of one act of imagining can be anything.

---

1 J.R.R. Tolkien, "J.R.R. Tolkien, On Fairy Stories," The Heritage Podcast: A Complete Liberal Arts Education, accessed June 1, 2019, http://heritagepodcast.com/wp-content/uploads/Tolkien-On-Fairy-Stories-subcreation.pdf.

2 See Marion Renauld, *Philosophie de la fiction: Vers une approche pragmatiste du roman* (Rennes: PUR, 2014).

CHAPTER 34

The Nativity of Images

Ton Kruse

A nation of images. An imagined origin of species.

It is not situated in, next to or above everything else. It is a notion of where we are. It interconnects all and everything.

A nation of image-formers. Not of makers.

The images are not constructed, but formed, formulated. They take shape, arise from what is named. They occur. Come into being.

Being born.

Without this nation of images all falls back on its own.

No origin. No relations. No meaning.

Barren.

Do you see?

A woman and a child.

She holds her child to her chest. She presses his face to her cheek. She gives it a kiss.

The child's eyes twinkle. He puts his hand on her face.

They both laugh.

A man and a dog.

He picks up a stick. The dog barks and jumps around him.

The man bends through his knees and looks at the dog, who stops jumping and dives down through its front legs.

"Fetch," says the man. He throws the stick. It spins through the air.

The dog runs after it. Following the stick with her eyes.

An image is not one thing. It is not static. And even when it is, it is still moving.

It changes the spatial dimensions in which things are. It gives all and everything its exact measurements: The case, those engaged in it, and those watching, attending.

It can't be pointed to and said of: there you see it, there it is.
But it can be pointed out, so that one might see.

It is said that someone once said: *Panta rhei.*

And it really does. But what is flowing, moving, streaming is not next to nothing. Indeed, it is relative. But not in the sense of: arbitrary, easily changeable. Because it originates in what is there. And it is moving so that it can touch us and all and everything else, that is like we are. It moves in between and around us, and it lifts us up from merely being towards being-there. It interconnects us to what and who is here, and was. And to what will.

The mother breastfeeds her child.
It will become a man. Who fathers a child with his wife.
Her grandchild.

The man takes the stick back from his dog. He rubs and strokes the dog with both hands. "Good dog," he says time and again. The dog tries to lick his face, twisting its tail with excitement. Will they do that game again? Yes! Tomorrow we will go to the beach, thinks the man. He imagines the dog fetching the stick from the breaking waves. How it will shake her skin after it lays the stick at his feet. Seawater on his face.

Don't you see?

THE NATIVITY OF IMAGES

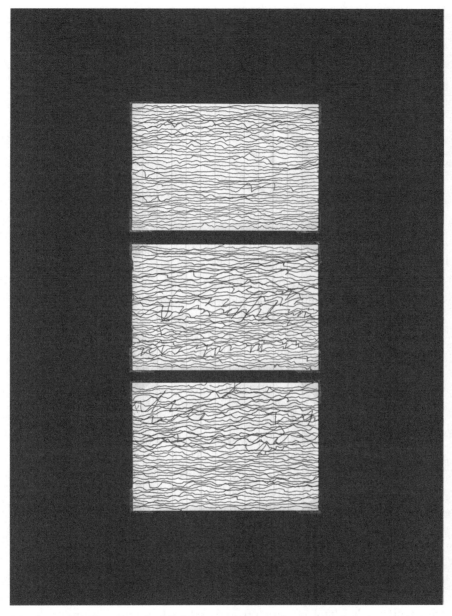

FIGURE 34.1 Ton Kruse, "9-7-2017"; ball-point on three note-book pages, three times A7; 2017

CHAPTER 35

Signal: Poetry and Imagination

Jesse Graves

Introduction

Imagination must move through a poem like blood through a body, the animating force unseen from the outside. Any part it fails to reach withers and the whole poem suffers with it. If imagination is blood, inspiration is breath to a poem, equally essential, also unseen, also elusive of definition. No poet since William Butler Yeats has made a fuller study of the imagination than Kathleen Raine. She considers it as a lost form of knowledge that once played a more central role in human understanding. The mystery of our lives has been increasingly, if unsatisfyingly, explained away through scientific and technological approaches. Raine believed that learning was essential to nurturing imagination, suggesting that poems are made from other poems and that poets must take part in a tradition of perennial evaluation and rendering.

All artists surely ask themselves the question at some point: where does this come from? Why does it (a poem, a painting, a shape, a color, a line of melody, a single image...) present itself on certain days and then elude completely on other days? I was puzzling this over one evening and wrote a draft of the following poem, considering why a few short weeks before I had composed several poems that engaged me, yet now seemed locked out of the house of poetry, and wasn't even able to find the road that leads to the house. Once inside the door, of course, the house of poetry felt like a palace with so many floors and rooms I could never explore it all—what ensues is blissful wandering, and the hope of recording any aspects of the atmosphere.

Poetry itself began to feel like my own personal "Kubla Khan"— perhaps I had only encountered it in a dream, and once disturbed I would only be able to recall it as an essence. I tried to compose this feeling into the following poem, titled "Signal." My first draft was called "The Difficulty of the Poem," which ultimately felt too explanatory, and excluded the joy of finding one's way to the "unseen fruits" of poetry. This poem is part of a manuscript in progress called *Across the River of Waking Dreams,* in which several poems merge the more narrative style of my earlier books with a speculative lyricism. Memory is a story we recreate from images. Imagination regenerates the past and enlivens

© KONINKLIJKE BRILL NV, LEIDEN, 2020 | DOI:10.1163/9789004436350_037

SIGNAL: POETRY AND IMAGINATION

the language we use to express what happened, and why, and how it felt. I hope
"Signal" catches some of the duality of writing poetry, both the searching for
the material of the poem and the awaiting of the signal that the poem is ready
to be seen. I wish I could find a less ineffable way to describe this, something
not so ethereal, yet what I have is my experience.

Signal

Before I presumed to press my face
to the window of the veiled palace,
forlorn cathedral sunken in the sea
with its halo of salt-spray mist and fog,
the poem minded its own knitted
furrow of air, tending unseen fruits.
Did I miss the invitation to enter?
Years ago, I received the first signal,
flickering in the haze between
stars, way up in the night oblivion,
infinite flecks of dust between us,
beckoning as I blinked, bewildered.

CHAPTER 36

The Echo of Voices

Umar Timol

I hear, in me, the echo of all these voices, which are perhaps only one and only voice, voices that resonate within me, voices that espouse life's wanderings, voices that are prayers for an absent deity, silent voices, interrupted time, melancholic voices, fragments of light, voices that are incantations of passion, passion for words, books, language, voices that interrogate death. "Writing is the last frontier between life and death," voices of a rebellious wound, plural voices of a half-monster, half-angel country, voices which say that poetry is not from this place, that it is consciousness of the infinite, enchanting voices, through the force of charisma, voices that talk about the nostalgia of mourning, voices of revolt, to be done with privileges, voices that talk about the ritual of writing, an almost carnal work, voices that talk about the derision of the real, impatient voices, we cannot quite flee the destiny of its anger, voices of those who have nothing, another light haunting their eyes, so many voices that resonate within me, I thought I could capture the souls of others, but these souls, their echoes, now dwell within me, a one and only voice perhaps, that of the human, so many voices, so many miracles in the wrecks of my imagination.

Translated by Keith Moser

© KONINKLIJKE BRILL NV, LEIDEN, 2020 | DOI:10.1163/9789004436350_038

CHAPTER 37

Poem, Liberty

Louise Dupré

1. The blue of a stained-glass window,[1] a wing opened in the stone, shadows blazing on the altar, and all at once time turns back to the wisdom of books. For a moment, we are without anger, without fear, so alone we forget even our father's soul. We see ourselves, body riddled with birds, able to carry the mountains and oceans, forgiveness, mercy of a journey from which we only return when the evening is finally calm and cleansed of its blood. A city shines in our eyes, a city we never took the trouble to visit.

2. This place where we cannot speak intimately, sheltered, witnessing a greatness we could not claim, except perhaps for a moment, meeting the impassive smile of the archangels. This is death, the gentle death of the liturgy, when it slides the body toward its first resting place. We don't hold back. We strip off our jewels in order to offer our hands, grave, intact. Paired, indistinct, for a moment joined together in a love without desire, without future. Speaking no longer seems to us to be anything but a worn-out word.

3. The candles' humble fire is lighting up the kneeling women, dark stains before the altar. They sigh and we sense that they are making some appeal, for the house, or the harvest, for their children's children. Prayers crushed under the weight of worry, flush with words, prayers without fervor or mystery. But no presence is revealed, their murmurings curl around themselves like ribbons. We would like to hear a song, we would like to hear voices not bound to their fate. For a moment, we think about grace with the nostalgia of the unbeliever.

4. We scarcely notice the bouquets of iris arching up from their vases like the vulvas of girls already in full ardor. We scarcely see the chubby cherubs letting loose their arrows to seduce us. Travelers, we are high on the grasses freshly fallen under the reapers' scythes, grasses they spread, in the evening, at the dying man's feet. For we are not alone in despairing of the gestures we accomplish without understanding, and this thought

---

1 "Poem, Liberty" was originally published in French in Louise Dupré, *Tout près* (Montréal: Éditions du Noroît, 1998).

consoles us, we are not alone in repeating the circles in which we are entangled.

5. Writing, this war-weary garden where we sign our steps. We have so despaired of the sirens' song that we have turned our backs on the ocean once and for all. There is fortunately always a cloister to take us in, with plants with Latin names like psalms, slow provocation hurled in the face of the conquerors when, in their exuberance, they shout their repentance too loudly, so loudly that darkness separates from light. And we no longer see our soul dozing off on the other side of the dark.

6. Perhaps it concerns a dove who has lost her way, perhaps an annunciation, wide-spread wings ruffling the veils of silence in which the penitents have wrapped themselves. But we are still able to stand up, still able to walk without waiting to be forgiven, we know of a fountain where the body is absolved of its crippling insomnia. The pattern of the water on the rocks, the rumblings of the distant city calmed, hold life for an instant in a nearly tranquil flow. Astonishing crystal of the ear.

7. This powdering of sun that's dressing up the tabernacles with a hint of mockery as if to remind us that a perfectly naked body does not hold back desire. Sun, molten light humbling the humans that we are. We will soon count on our fingers the summers that remain to us, and our heavy hand will perhaps grow tired before reaching its number, and will fall with a clatter of bracelets dropping on the paving stones. And we will let ourselves be distracted for a moment, for gems and bangles sometimes chase away anguish better than prayer does.

8. For a moment, we wish to leave everything, take off for deserts more distant than their names, carry our eyes away with us in huge trunks, with prayer books and porcelain virgins, and our childhoods so often kneeling on knot-filled parquet floors. So many times have we seen our souls burning outside of us, while we were desperately waiting for them to return. We have awakened so often feeling that cold that widens the holes in our vertebrae. Poem, yes, it is too late for sainthood.

9. The unknown, we imagine it very high, up there where stars pile upon stars, and where the rarefied air makes fervor possible. We imagine it up there where eyes can no longer distinguish one thing from another, in a gravity without weight, without absence, there where the heart arrives at what it was hoping for, where the word is relieved of its cacophony. But the sky soon collapses and sends us back among our fellow creatures, into a common suffering, into this useless striving that brings sweat to our brows. Out of breath, we struggle. We aren't made for the long haul.

POEM, LIBERTY 777

10. Not much, in fact, a long dying nailed to two crossed tree limbs, not much to remind us that we are not innocent. And yet, we will never know what we are guilty of. We carry our sin on our left side, there next to our ribs, without being able to name it except through the suffering that consumes us, bright fire of a hell into which we wake on certain nights, astonished that we have, for so many centuries, survived the threat of our punishment.

11. These incandescent shapes in the glow of the tall candle, quills of fire or perhaps burning tongues beating the infinite measure of the silence. Once again we believe that speaking may be healed, we believe in the sweet contentment of a speech capable of silencing our age-old din of words. But the rumblings quickly bring us back to the heart of the inhabited world, with its urine-stained streets, and we again put on our true face, the one which looks us square in the eye showing us the extent of our melancholy.

12. We know that the city gives no wheat, no leather, no courage hanging on the belt. Only little dreams reflected in the eyes and trees we persist in planting by our houses in order to learn to make out the shapes that are squawking in the leaves. We say turtledove, starling, chaffinch, point them out, wish that the slightest cry might become azure and song, wish for shutters on our windows, the beating of wings that carry us far, very far, into the blue of an inexhaustible sky.

13. A voice, a single voice weeping, right up close, and we are reminded of the world's distress, thrown back along the body like naked fingers, unable to hide our eyes, to wipe our cheek. Immensity of a night hurled onto our shoulders, we the unbelievers who even so learned long ago to answer the call. And we bring along our fragility and some psalms, so there may again be laughter on our lips and our daughters sturdier than crosses. We open our arms, yes, poem, liberty, minuscule consolation.

Translated by Karen McPherson
American poet, translator, and author

CHAPTER 38

Why to Wish for the Witch

Lisa Fay Coutley

When I was five, a witch lived under my twin bed, one of her gray arms longer than the other, so to stay beyond the reach of her tree-branch hand I had to lie on my left side, balanced at my bed's edge, staring always at the light coming through the purple shag carpet growing toward the bottom of my closed door, listening to hear if tonight would be one of Dad's angry nights, which meant I'd have to stand on my bed and leap to the door to escape the witch's grasp on the other side in order to run down the hall to the kitchen to stop Dad from beating Mom because I was the only one who could.

When I was twenty-two and living not with a man (for the first time in my life), with my two sons under five asleep in the room next to mine, I'd lie awake, focused on every noise a house can make, wondering if the man who'd surely stab my children to death was breaking in through the sliding glass patio doors or a basement window, and there was no witch under my bed anymore, though it seemed they were roaming about, free to enter as they pleased, and I would freeze in place, playing out various scenarios of imminent danger, unable to bring my legs to the bed's edge to rise and fight.

Maybe I told my mom about the witch. Maybe she said it was just my imagination, not to worry, not to be scared. How does a child say, *I'm afraid because he punches you in your face and you say you were careless opening a cupboard door, so I will stay awake waiting for you to go safely to sleep*, when what she knows is that a witch waits beneath sleep. She doesn't know she should feel safe in bed. Under the burden of love, her mind conjures a witch whose anatomy suits her duty, serving her nightly mission and giving her a better object for her fear, so during the waking hours of her day she can go on loving her parents.

To imagine is to picture to oneself for the purpose of seeing different, new. As a child I pictured to myself as a means of survival, my mind protecting me and subjecting me simultaneously, though always for what could be, what might. As a young mother I pictured to myself as a slave to memory, my mind and body loyal to my past. Trauma felt inevitable. I couldn't stray from that truth, couldn't imagine it was possible to be safe in our home. That reality caged my imagination until nothing could grow there into a shape of its own making to show me a new way to see the world or myself.

© KONINKLIJKE BRILL NV, LEIDEN, 2020 | DOI:10.1163/9789004436350_040

It took years for me to fall asleep without fearing every noise. It took years for me to stray from reality in my life and my writing. Maybe in a structured society our imaginations get leashed so we'll focus on a designated goal without hoping for something more. Maybe imagining feels like betraying what's been. Art depends on our ability to see the world/the self/experience from a distance to gain perspective, yet to separate the body of work from the body of memory and image means to let go, to repurpose, to trust others to hold the emotion behind what's happened and to know that's hope.

When I come to a standstill in a poem rooted in autobiography, I know it's time to lie. I am frozen in my bed, recording the sound of a Pabst can slamming hard against the countertop, describing my call to duty in a violent place, though the witch's ashen skin, her tangled hands, her uneven reach, my need to sleep at the bed's edge gets closer to the root of the fear blooming inside my small girl. Art begs us to follow emotion into rooms we've never known for the sake of discovering truths in lived experiences, and there we can see it's possible for us and for the world to otherwise take shape.

Index

Abstraction 179, 310, 478–98, 507–12, 524–26, 765
Action 10, 39, 52–58, 68–79
Aesthetic object 105, 114–23, 177–201, 235–39, 261, 263, 286–302, 322, 337–41, 401, 416–17, 431–45, 458, 560–64, 584–92, 629–37, 709–12, 733
ʿālam al-khayāl (realm of imagination) 738
Amazons (the) 11, 83–110
Animal imagination (the) 175–84, 189, 294, 320–24, 353–59, 508–10, 524–25, 651, 698
Anthropopoiesis 56–57
Antiope 85–108
Apollo 41, 86–88, 207–25
Appearance (*Erscheinung*) 17, 43, 160, 175, 195, 230, 305, 311–12, 327, 338, 356, 360, 381–411, 490, 538–39
A priori knowledge 117, 122, 202, 227, 300, 349, 357, 488–94
Arendt, Hannah 659, 664–67
Aristotle 38–39, 174–205, 312–29, 414, 426–27, 436–39, 466, 475, 478–500, 516, 704
Athena 59–63, 90
Automatic writing (technique of) 111–20, 125–34
Avant-garde theater (imagination in) 17–18, 375, 597
Ayesha 104, 108

Bachelard, Gaston 8, 24, 714–19
Bacon, Francis 427, 442–45, 513
Barbarians (concept of) 100
Bateson, Gregory 504–16, 524–28
Baudrillard, Jean 5, 19, 21, 230, 233–34, 381–411, 419, 436, 445
Beckett, Samuel 17–18, 603
Beliefs vs. imaginings 147–51, 160–61, 165, 185, 199, 227–32, 247, 257, 312, 428, 459, 465–68, 507, 519, 525–26
Biosemiotics 503–34
Breton, André 113, 117–26

Cage, John 18–19, 594–620
Carroll, Noël 562–65, 571, 592, 628

Cato 68–80
Chiomara 97–99, 108
Choice 20, 121, 148, 175, 181–200, 209, 272, 277, 292–313, 328, 337, 572, 587
Chomsky, Noam 388
Christianity (imagination in) 25, 52, 64, 75–76, 227–54, 320, 397, 519, 702, 738–39, 754
Cicero 35, 39–43
Cliché 427, 432, 442–46
Communication 9–10, 14–16, 25, 54–56, 64, 85, 91, 117, 241–48, 357–58, 362–74, 381–411, 418–23, 503–34, 535, 559, 569, 578–80, 608, 629, 632, 637–39, 646–66, 721, 725, 731–36, 761, 762–66
Communicative smoothness 420–21
Conceiving vs. imagining 8–9, 42, 223, 281–303
conceptual archipelagos 423
Consciousness 15, 113–15, 125, 140, 149–51, 556, 646–66, 698, 718, 721, 774
Copland, Aaron 594, 607–18
Constrained imagination 13, 42–43, 315, 438, 454, 457, 464, 467–71, 524
Counterfactuals 6, 201, 669–94, 640, 763
Creative imagination 443–44, 515–16, 523, 599, 605–17, 701, 705–06
Cultural memory 50–66
Currie, Gregory 338–40, 763, 767

Dance (philosophy of) 621–45
Dante 68, 71–79, 601
Daoism (imagination in) 24, 709, 717–19
Davies, David 627
Deconstruction 160, 415–17
Deleuze, Gilles 4, 115, 133, 425–50
de Man, Paul 258–60, 280
Depiction 292, 541, 546, 559–82
Derrida, Jacques 4–5, 8, 11–12, 15–16, 23–24, 221–24, 622
Descartes, René 142, 147–53, 169, 175–76, 183–201, 227, 234–38, 256, 262–71, 281–86, 294–302, 304–28, 347, 361, 385, 402, 415, 418, 422, 426–50, 454, 512, 559

782 INDEX

Desire 83, 111–22, 127–35, 600, 616, 663, 725, 730, 762–67
Dewey, John 202, 346, 591
Digital photography (imagination in) 17, 20, 389, 395, 553, 566–67
Dinesen, Isak 77–78
Dionysian 373–74
Disability (views about) 4, 155–73
Discipline 112, 158, 371, 615, 662
Dostoyevsky, Fedor 228, 236–37
Dreams 638, 671, 677, 687–88, 705, 730–32, 765–67

Ecofeminism 8, 37–38, 44–46, 111, 120–24, 123, 127, 132–34, 772
Ecolinguistics 3
Ego 150–53, 262–72, 361–67
Epicurus 43–45
Epistemology (imagination in) 9–10, 45, 58–61, 140, 156, 159–60, 304–31, 346–63, 426, 460, 464–68, 516, 671–72, 682–89, 761–68
Erechtheus 58–61
Euclidian imagination 14, 475–502
Eudaimonia (happiness) 150, 184–97

Fantasy 36–40, 132, 267, 323, 333, 433–35, 464, 520–22, 687–89
Fictional truth 459–62, 633–36
Film (imagination in) 535–83
Foucault, Michel 63–64, 112, 118–20, 406, 425–31, 445
Freud, Sigmund 265, 307, 342, 403, 419, 433
Frühromantik (Early Romanticism) 351–53
Fu Hao 105–08
Fun (concept of) 695–707
Futurity 207, 218–25

Gadamer, Hans-Georg 165–67, 648–67
Games (imagination in) 646–68, 700, 7212–22, 755, 767
Gendered imagination 83–111
Geometrical imagination 14, 195, 308–11, 317–24, 475–502
Gestalt 182, 310, 327
Goethe 370, 711, 714
Goodman, Nelson 561, 762–68
Göring, Hermann 673, 685–86

Great Divide (the) 50, 53–65
Greek mythology 11, 50–66, 83–110
Greek tragedy 38, 55–65, 92, 207–19, 369–76
Greene, Maxine 6–7, 26
Guattari, Félix 4, 115, 133, 425–50

Heidegger, Martin 231, 261, 327, 656–57, 714, 718
Hegel, Georg Wilhelm Friedrich 55, 67, 427, 714
Herodotus 35, 91–94, 104–08
Heterotopia 112, 118–19
Historical agency 11, 50–51, 116, 132
Historical judgment 67–82
Hitler, Adolf 669, 672, 675, 683–85
Hobbes, Thomas 68, 72–78, 311, 315
Hoffmeyer, Jesper 503, 505, 509, 512–17, 522–23
Hopkins, Robert 541, 561, 579–80
Hume, David 9–10, 140–74, 191, 200, 316, 535
Hursthouse, Rosalinde 186, 193–96
Hyperreality (theory of) 5, 20–21, 230, 383, 394–95

Ibn al-ʿArabī 735–60
Identification 148, 263, 475, 480, 485, 583–93, 741
Illusion 46, 118, 152, 177, 223, 230, 260, 278, 284–95, 311, 375, 433, 484, 525, 702, 706, 764
Imaginative resistance 64, 139–54, 243, 763, 767–68
Improvisation 324, 364–71
incommensurability 305, 333, 350, 420–23
Infanticide 141–47, 206–26
Integral reality (theory of) 5, 19, 403
Integrity 68, 78–79, 150–52, 318, 325
Irigaray, Luce 436

Janyl Myrza 104, 108

Kant, Immanuel 14, 67, 157, 201, 231, 263–66, 304–29, 334, 341–42, 346–75, 413–17, 426
Khawlah 103–04, 108
Kilani, Mondher 56, 62, 64
Kind, Amy 3, 7, 9–10, 13–14, 42, 45, 141, 177, 199, 201, 381, 454, 472, 535

INDEX 783

Kinesthetic empathy 622, 626, 642
Kinesthetic imaginings 622–45

Language games 320, 413, 421–23
Levinson, Jerrold 336, 562, 592, 623
Linear perspective 549–51, 557
Linguistic behavior 356–60
Lucan 68–77
Lucian 35–47
Lucretius 43–44
Lyotard, Jean-François 4, 412–24

Make-believe 122, 129, 199, 339, 365, 370–74,
    453–73, 561–64, 568–69, 623–27,
    632–44, 687, 702, 762–63
Material imagination 714–19
Matravers, Derek 335, 339
McFee, Graham 624–25, 628–31
Mental images 179, 182–83, 439, 456–57,
    475–511, 540–42, 578, 638
Mill, John Stuart 520, 526
Mimesis 17, 38–39, 206–26, 401–02, 556,
    623–26, 633–26, 633–44
Mindy-body dualism 23, 629, 766
Moral psychology 174–205
Moran, Richard 140
Morin, Edgar 2, 9, 20, 23, 25
Moss, Jessica 174, 177–81, 191
Muḥammadology 738–40, 752–53
Musical imagination 594–620
Musical performance 62, 611, 614–16
Muslim imagination 25, 112, 114–16, 735–60

Naturalism 37, 355, 368, 455, 459–60
Necroresistance 111, 125
Nietzsche, Friedrich 201, 256, 346–80
Non-Euclidean geometry 475, 495–500
Novel (the genre) 13, 17, 36, 46–47, 148,
    228–35, 273, 277, 332, 336–40, 355, 552,
    633, 635, 723, 730–31

Oedipus the King 207–25

Painting (imagination in) 264, 335–37, 437,
    440–44, 537–40, 545–57, 559, 562–66,
    575–79, 606, 633–35, 660–63, 713, 737,
    751–53
Parsipur, Shahrnush 111–38

Perception 264–65, 274–80, 296, 300,
    304–31, 333–43, 348, 361, 376, 436–44,
    478–80, 511–13, 556–80, 599–604, 628,
    646–47, 762
Performativity 361–64
Perspectivalness 201, 544–52
Petrophilia 708–20
Phantasia 8, 36–37, 43–48, 174–205, 485
Phantasma 43, 176–203
Phantasmata 43, 176–203
Photography (imagination in) 19–20,
    535–83
Phronesis 174–75, 185–203
Pictorial content 337, 340–43, 560–62,
    579–80
Pictorial representation 337, 340–43,
    560–62, 579–80
Pierce, Charles Sanders 14, 503–08
Plato 38, 83–84, 182, 202, 208, 223, 317, 352,
    360, 433, 467, 475–500
Play-acting 356–61, 368, 373
Plutarch 46, 73, 91, 97, 99
Poincaré 496–98, 510
Possible worlds (theory of) 423, 669–94
Postmodernism 3–5, 17, 230, 381–450,
    629–31
Pretence 141, 359–60
Prisoners of war 83–110
Proclus 14, 475, 481–500
Productive desire 426, 433–36
Productive imagination 8, 14, 256, 325, 333,
    425–50
Projective systems 546–51
Propositional imagination 457, 575,
    635–37
Proust, Marcel 227–28, 231–39, 249
Psychoanalysis (imagination in) 111,
    139–154, 227, 434–36

Quintilian 40

Rancière, Jacques 430
Religious productive imagination 14–15
Representational content 339–43, 356, 417,
    421, 426, 431, 435–46, 458, 462, 479, 538,
    542–45
Repression (theory of) 2, 39, 148–53
Reproductive imagination 8, 333, 350

Rhetoric 36–39, 57–60, 62, 209–12, 257–66, 350, 678, 738
Richardson, Samuel 46
Ricœur, Paul 52, 66, 229–33, 245, 249, 525, 648, 651–67, 583–84, 591–93, 623, 633–34
Ritual 53–57, 61–65, 125, 248, 515, 700–02
Rorty, Richard 6–7, 16, 17, 26, 155–71, 346–57, 360, 370–71, 381
Ryan, Marie-Laure 670, 682
Rhythm 56–57, 133

Said, Edward 5–6
Sahlins, Marshall 50–52, 56, 64
Saint John of the Cross 228, 239–42, 249
Saint Teresa of Avila 249
Saint Teresa of Lisieux 249
Sarban 669–94
Sartre, Jean-Paul 2228, 235–39, 259–60
Schoenberg, Arnold 595–99, 602, 613
Scholem, Gershom 67
Scientific modelling (imagination in) 13, 451–74
Scientific representation (imagination in) 13, 451–74
Scruton, Roger 336, 565–66, 582–83
Serres, Michel 2, 10, 12–13, 16, 18, 21–23, 381–411
Silence (treatment of) 17–18, 594–620
Simulacral imagination 5, 19–21, 381–411
Solidarity 59, 120, 123, 135, 155–73, 347, 351
Somatic imagination 22–23, 621–45
Sophocles 143, 207–25, 372
Spectator (role of the) 144, 148, 318, 323–25, 337–41, 346, 360, 372–76
Spinoza, Benedict de 310, 314–21, 326–28, 433
Stravinsky, Igor 597, 599, 602, 607, 613
Sufism 25, 735–56
Sukla, Ananta 25, 751–54
Surrealism (imagination in) 111–35
Synesius 46–47

Synthesis 182, 186, 334, 349–50, 490–92
Synthetic imagination 8, 182, 186, 334, 349–50, 490–92

Theater (imagination in) 360–76, 435, 623, 625, 638, 643, 740, 751–52
Tillich, Paul 244, 246–48, 252
Tirgatao 94–96, 108
Toon, Adam 1, 13, 453, 459–60
Transcendental imagination 8, 325, 442
Transparency 421, 564–65

Unimaginable (the) 146, 216, 219–25, 245, 441
Unreliable narrator 672, 675, 678–90

Video games (imagination in) 21, 555, 646–68
Virtue 72–75, 131, 174–203, 209–10, 240, 319, 371, 412, 580, 584, 643, 651
Visual images 37–38, 56, 195, 200, 267, 284, 288, 293, 323–25, 334–43, 374, 456–57, 475, 489, 535–57, 560–80, 583–84, 638, 754
Visualization 14, 36, 38, 475–500

Walton, Kendall 140–41, 335, 453–66, 559–80, 622–43, 764, 767
Weil, Simone 9–10, 304–31
Wittgenstein, Ludwig 227–30, 243, 255, 267, 276, 283–84, 320, 334, 356, 361, 413
Wollheim, Richard 335–37, 340–41, 560–62, 568
Women warriors 83–109
Woolf, Virginia 228, 231–33

Yeats, W.B. 262, 272–78, 772

Zen Buddhism (imagination in) 362, 604, 724
Zenobia 102–08